Webster's
Spanish
Dictionary

Spanish • English
English • Spanish
español • inglés
inglés • español

Edited by
Donald F. Solá
Cornell University

Revised by
David L. Gold
Doctor in Romance Philology
University of Barcelona

RANDOM HOUSE
REFERENCE

Originally published as *Random House Webster's Pocket Spanish Dictionary, Third Edition*

Copyright © 2000, 1995 by Random House, Inc.

Printed in 2008 in the United States of America

ISBN-13: 978-0-307-29072-4
ISBN-10: 0-307-29072-7

10 9 8 7 6 5 4 3

Guía de Pronunciación del inglés

Símbolos del AFI	Ejemplos
/æ/	*ingl.* h**a**t; como la **a** de *esp.* paro, pero más cerrada
/ei/	*ingl.* st**ay**; *esp.* r**ei**na
/ɛə/ [followed by /r/]	*ingl.* h**air**; *esp.* v**e**r
/ɑ/	*ingl.* f**a**ther; similar a las **a**s de *esp.* c**a**sa, pero más larga
/ɛ/	*ingl.* b**e**t; *esp.* **e**ntre
/i/	*ingl.* b**ee**; como la **i** de *esp.* v**i**da, pero más larga
/ɪə/ [followed by /r/]	*ingl.* h**ear**; como la **i** de *esp.* ven**i**r, pero menos cerrada
/ɪ/	*ingl.* s**i**t; como la **i** de *esp.* Ch**i**le, pero menos cerrada
/ai/	*ingl.* tr**y**; *esp.* h**ay**
/ɒ/	*ingl.* h**o**t; *esp.* p**o**ner
/ou/	*ingl.* b**oa**t; similar a la **o** de *esp.* sac**o**, pero más cerrada
/ɔ/	*ingl.* s**aw**; similar a la **o** de *esp.* c**o**rte, pero más cerrada
/ɔi/	*ingl.* t**oy**; *esp.* h**oy**
/ʊ/	*ingl.* b**oo**k; como la **u** de *esp.* ins**u**lto, pero menos cerrada
/u/	*ingl.* t**oo**; como la **u** de *esp.* l**u**na, pero más larga
/au/	*ingl.* c**ow**; *esp.* p**au**sa
/ʌ/	*ingl.* **u**p; entre la **o** de *esp.* b**o**rde y la **a** de *esp.* b**a**rro
/ɜ/ [followed by /r/]	*ingl.* b**ur**n; *fr.* fl**eu**r
/ə/	*ingl.* **a**lone; *fr.* d**e**main
/ᵊ/	*ingl.* f**ir**e (fiᵊr); *fr.* bastill**e**
/b/	*ingl.* **b**oy; como la **b** de *esp.* **b**oca, pero más aspirada
/tʃ/	*ingl.* **ch**ild; *esp.* mu**ch**o
/d/	*ingl.* **d**ad; *esp.* **d**ar
/f/	*ingl.* **f**or; *esp.* **f**echa
/g/	*ingl.* **g**ive; *esp.* **g**ato

Spanish Stress

In a number of words, spoken stress is marked by an accent (´): *nación, país, médico, día.*

Words which are not so marked are, generally speaking, stressed on the next-to-the-last syllable if they end in a vowel, *n,* or *s;* and on the last syllable if they end in a consonant other than *n* or *s.*

Note: An accent is placed over some words to distinguish them from others having the same spelling and pronunciation but differing in meaning.

Spanish Alphabetization

In Spanish, *ch* and *ll* are no longer considered to be separate letters of the alphabet. They are now alphabetized as they would be in English. However, words with *ñ* are alphabetized after *n.*

IPA Symbols	Key Words	Approximate Equivalents
n	nada, nuevo, mano, bien	not, enter
ɲ	ñapa, año	canyon, companion
ŋ	angosto, aunque	ring, anchor
p	peso, guapo	pill, applaud
r	real, faro, deber	like rice, but with single flap of tongue on roof of mouth
rr	perro, sierra	like rice, but with trill, or vibration of tongue, against upper teeth
s	sala, espejo, mas; (in Latin America) cena, hacer, vez	say, clasp
θ	(in Spain) cena, hacer, cierto, cine, zarzuela, lazo, vez	thin, myth
t	tocar, estado, cenit	table, attract
y	ya, ayer; (in Latin America) llama, calle	you, voyage
tʃ	chica, mucho	chill, batch

Diphthongs

ai	baile, hay	high, rye
au	audacia, laudable	out, round
ei	veinte, seis, rey	ray
ie	miel, tambien	fiesta
oi	estoico, hoy	coin, loyal
ua	cuanto	quantity
ue	buena, suerte	sway, quaint

Pronunciation Key for Spanish

IPA Symbols	Key Words	Approximate Equivalents
a	alba, banco, cera	father, depart
e	esto, del, parte, mesa	bet; like rain when e ends syllable and is not followed by r, rr, or t
i	ir, fino, adiós, muy	like beet, but shorter
o	oler, flor, grano	like vote, but shorter
u	un, luna, cuento, vergüenza, guarda	fool, group
b	bajo, ambiguo, vaca	by, abet
β	hablar, escribir, lavar	like vehicle, but with lips almost touching
d	dar, desde, andamio, dueña	deal, adept
ð	pedir, edredón, verdad	that, gather
f	fecha, afectar, golf	fan, after
g	gato, grave, gusto, largo, guerra	garden, ugly
h	gemelo, giro, junta, bajo	horse
k	cacao, claro, cura, cuenta, que, quinto	kind, actor
l	lado, lente, habla, papel	lot, altar
ʎ	(in Spain) llama, calle, olla	like million, but with tongue behind teeth
m	mal, amor	more, commit

Símbolos del AFI	Ejemplos
/h/	*ingl.* **h**appy; como la **j** de *esp.* **j**abón, pero más aspirada y menos aspera
/dʒ/	*ingl.* **j**ust; *it.* **g**iorno
/k/	*ingl.* **k**ick; similar a la **k** de *esp.* **k**ilogramo, pero más aspirada
/l/	*ingl.* **l**ove; *esp.* **l**ibro
/m/	*ingl.* **m**other; *esp.* li**m**bo
/n/	*ingl.* **n**ow; *esp.* **n**oche
/ŋ/	*ingl.* si**ng**; *esp.* bla**n**co
/p/	*ingl.* **p**ot; como las **p**s de *esp.* **p**a**p**a, pero más aspirada
/r/	*ingl.* **r**ead; como la **r** de *esp.* pa**r**a, pero con la lengua elevada hacia el paladar, sin tocarlo
/s/	*ingl.* **s**ee; *esp.* ha**s**ta
/ʃ/	*ingl.* **sh**op; *fr.* **ch**er**ch**er
/t/	*ingl.* **t**en; similar a la **t** de *esp.* **t**omar, pero más aspirada
/θ/	*ingl.* **th**ing; *esp.* (en España) **c**erdo, **z**apato
/ð/	*ingl.* fa**th**er; *esp.* co**d**o
/v/	*ingl.* **v**ictory; como la **b** de *esp.* ha**b**a, pero es labiodental en vez de bilabial
/w/	*ingl.* **w**itch; como la **u** de *esp.* p**u**esto, pero con labios más cerrados
/y/	*ingl.* **y**es; *esp.* **y**acer
/z/	*ingl.* **z**ipper; fr. **z**éro
/ʒ/	*ingl.* plea**s**ure; *fr.* **j**eune

Las consonantes /l̩/, /m̩/, y /n̩/ son similar a las **l**, **m**, y **n** del español, pero alargada y resonante.

English Abbreviations/
Abreviaturas inglesas

a.	adjective	*Govt.*	government
abbr.	abbreviation	*Gram.*	grammar
adv.	adverb	*interj.*	interjection
Aero.	aeronautics	*interrog.*	interrogative
Agr.	agriculture	*Leg.*	legal
Anat.	anatomy	*m.*	masculine
art.	article	*Mech.*	mechanics
Auto.	automotive	*Mex.*	Mexico
Biol.	biology	*Mil.*	military
Bot.	botany	*Mus.*	music
Carib.	Caribbean	*n.*	noun
Chem.	chemistry	*Naut.*	nautical
Colloq.	colloquial	*Phot.*	photography
Com.	commerce	*pl.*	plural
conj.	conjunction	*Pol.*	politics
dem.	demonstrative	*prep.*	preposition
Econ.	economics	*pron.*	pronoun
Elec.	electrical	*Punct.*	punctuation
esp.	especially	*rel.*	relative
f.	feminine	*Relig.*	religion
Fig.	figurative	*S.A.*	Spanish America
Fin.	finance		
Geog.	geography	*Theat.*	theater
		v.	verb

Note: If a main entry term is repeated in a boldface subentry in exactly the same form, it is abbreviated. Example: **comedor** *n.m.* dining room. **coche c.,** dining car.

A

a /a/ *prep.* to; at.
abacería /aβaθe'ria; aβase'ria/ *n. f.* grocery store.
abacero /aβa'θero; aβa'sero/ *n. m.* grocer.
ábaco /'aβako/ *n. m.* abacus.
abad /a'βað/ *n. m.* abbot.
abadía /aβa'ðia/ *n. f.* abbey.
abajar /aβa'har/ *v.* lower; go down.
abajo /a'βaho/ *adv.* down; downstairs.
abandonar /aβando'nar/ *v.* abandon.
abandono /aβan'dono/ *n. m.* abandonment.
abanico /aβa'niko/ *n. m.* fan. —**abanicar,** *v.*
abaratar /aβara'tar/ *v.* cheapen.
abarcar /aβar'kar/ *v.* comprise; clasp.
abastecer /aβaste'θer; aβaste'ser/ *v.* supply, provide.
abatido /aβa'tiðo/ *a.* dejected, despondent.
abatir /aβa'tir/ *v.* knock down; dismantle; depress, dishearten.
abdicación /aβðika'θion; aβðika'sion/ *n. f.* abdication.
abdicar /aβði'kar/ *v.* abdicate.
abdomen /aβ'ðomen/ *n. m.* abdomen.
abdominal /aβðomi'nal/ *a.* **1.** abdominal. —*n.* **2.** *m.* sit-up.
abecé /aβe'θe; aβe'se/ *n. m.* ABCs, rudiments.
abecedario /aβeθe'ðario; aβese'ðario/ *n. m.* alphabet; reading book.
abeja /a'βeha/ *n. f.* bee.
abejarrón /aβeha'rron/ *n. m.* bumblebee.
aberración /aβerra'θion; aβerra'sion/ *n. f.* aberration.
abertura /aβer'tura/ *n. f.* opening, aperture, slit.
abeto /a'βeto/ *n. m.* fir.
abierto /a'βierto/ *a.* open; overt.
abismal /aβis'mal/ *a.* abysmal.
abismo /a'βismo/ *n. m.* abyss, chasm.
ablandar /aβlan'dar/ *v.* soften.
abnegación /aβnega'θion; aβnega'sion/ *n. f.* abnegation.
abochornar /aβotʃor'nar/ *v.* overheat; embarrass.

abogado /aβo'gaðo/ **-da** *n.* lawyer, attorney.
abolengo /aβo'leŋgo/ *n. m.* ancestry.
abolición /aβoli'θion; aβoli'sion/ *n. f.* abolition.
abolladura /aβoʎa'ðura; aβoya'ðura/ *n. f.* dent. —**abollar,** *v.*
abominable /aβomi'naβle/ *a.* abominable.
abominar /aβomi'nar/ *v.* abhor.
abonado /aβo'naðo/ **-da** *n. m. & f.* subscriber.
abonar /aβo'nar/ *v.* pay; fertilize.
abonarse /aβo'narse/ *v.* subscribe.
abono /a'βono/ *n. m.* fertilizer; subscription; season ticket.
aborigen /aβor'ihen/ *a. & n.* aboriginal.
aborrecer /aβorre'θer; aβorre'ser/ *v.* hate, loathe, abhor.
abortar /aβor'tar/ *v.* abort, miscarry.
aborto /a'βorto/ *n. m.* abortion.
abovedar /aβoβe'ðar/ *v.* vault.
abrasar /aβra'sar/ *v.* burn.
abrazar /aβra'θar; aβra'sar/ *v.* embrace; clasp.
abrazo /a'βraθo; a'βraso/ *n. m.* embrace.
abrelatas /aβre'latas/ *n. m.* can opener.
abreviar /aβre'βiar/ *v.* abbreviate, abridge, shorten.
abreviatura /aβreβia'tura/ *n. f.* abbreviation.
abrigar /aβri'gar/ *v.* harbor, shelter.
abrigarse /aβri'garse/ *v.* bundle up.
abrigo /a'βrigo/ *n. m.* overcoat; shelter; (*pl.*) wraps.
abril /a'βril/ *n. m.* April.
abrir /a'βrir/ *v.* open; *Med.* lance.
abrochar /aβro'tʃar/ *v.* clasp.
abrogación /aβroga'θion; aβroga'sion/ *n. f.* abrogation, repeal.
abrogar /aβro'gar/ *v.* abrogate.
abrojo /a'βroho/ *n. m.* thorn.
abrumar /aβru'mar/ *v.* overwhelm, crush, swamp.
absceso /aβ'sθeso; aβ'sseso/ *n. m.* abscess.
absolución /aβsolu'θion; aβsolu'sion/ *n. f.* absolution; acquittal.

absoluto /aβso'luto/ *a.* absolute; downright.

absolver /aβsol'βer/ *v.* absolve, pardon.

absorbente /aβsor'βente/ *a.* absorbent.

absorber /aβsor'βer/ *v.* absorb.

absorción /aβsor'θion; aβsor'sion/ *n. f.* absorption.

abstemio /aβs'temio/ *a.* abstemious.

abstenerse /aβste'nerse/ *v.* abstain; refrain.

abstinencia /aβsti'nenθia; aβsti'nensia/ *n. f.* abstinence.

abstracción /aβstrak'θion; aβstrak'sion/ *n. f.* abstraction.

abstracto /aβ'strakto/ *a.* abstract.

abstraer /aβstra'er/ *v.* abstract.

absurdo /aβ'surðo/ *a.* **1.** absurd. —*n.* **2.** *m.* absurdity.

abuchear /aβutʃe'ar/ *v.* boo.

abuela /a'βuela/ *n. f.* grandmother.

abuelo /a'βuelo/ *n. m.* grandfather; (*pl.*) grandparents.

abultado /aβul'taðo/ *a.* bulky.

abultamiento /aβulta'miento/ *n. m.* bulge. —**abultar,** *v.*

abundancia /aβun'danθia; aβun'dansia/ *n. f.* abundance, plenty.

abundante /aβun'dante/ *a.* abundant, plentiful.

abundar /aβun'dar/ *v.* abound.

aburrido /aβu'rriðo/ *a.* boring, tedious.

aburrimiento /aβurri'miento/ *n. m.* boredom.

aburrir /aβu'rrir/ *v.* bore.

abusar /aβu'sar/ *v.* abuse, misuse.

abusivo /aβu'siβo/ *a.* abusive.

abuso /a'βuso/ *n. m.* abuse.

abyecto /aβ'yekto/ *a.* abject, low.

a.C., *abbr.* (**antes de Cristo**) BC.

acá /a'ka/ *adv.* here.

acabar /aka'βar/ *v.* finish. **a. de...,** to have just....

acacia /a'kaθia; a'kasia/ *n. f.* acacia.

academia /aka'ðemia/ *n. f.* academy.

académico /aka'ðemiko/ *a.* academic.

acaecer /akae'θer; akae'ser/ *v.* happen.

acanalar /akana'lar/ *v.* groove.

acaparar /akapa'rar/ *v.* hoard; monopolize.

acariciar /akari'θiar; akari'siar/ *v.* caress, stroke.

acarrear /akarre'ar/ *v.* cart, transport; occasion, entail.

acaso /a'kaso/ *n. m.* chance. **por si a.,** just in case.

acceder /akθe'ðer; akse'ðer/ *v.* accede.

accesible /akθe'siβle; akse'siβle/ *a.* accessible.

acceso /ak'θeso; ak'seso/ *n. m.* access, approach.

accesorio /akθe'sorio; akse'sorio/ *a.* accessory.

accidentado /akθiðen'taðo; aksiðen'taðo/ *a.* hilly.

accidental /akθiðen'tal; aksiðen'tal/ *a.* accidental.

accidente /akθi'ðente; aksi'ðente/ *n. m.* accident, wreck.

acción /ak'θion; ak'sion/ *n. f.* action, act; *Com.* share of stock.

accionista /akθio'nista; aksio'nista/ *n. m. & f.* shareholder.

acechar /aθe'tʃar; ase'tʃar/ *v.* ambush, spy on.

acedia /a'θeðia; a'seðia/ *n. f.* heartburn.

aceite /a'θeite; a'seite/ *n. m.* oil.

aceite de hígado de bacalao /a'θeite de i'gaðo de baka'lao; a'seite/ cod-liver oil.

aceitoso /aθei'toso; asei'toso/ *a.* oily.

aceituna /aθei'tuna; asei'tuna/ *n. f.* olive.

aceleración /aθelera'θion; aselera'sion/ *n. f.* acceleration.

acelerar /aθele'rar; asele'rar/ *v.* accelerate, speed up.

acento /a'θento; a'sento/ *n. m.* accent.

acentuar /aθen'tuar; asen'tuar/ *v.* accent, accentuate, stress.

acepillar /aθepi'ʎar; asepi'yar/ *v.* brush; plane (wood).

aceptable /aθep'taβle; asep'taβle/ *a.* acceptable.

aceptación /aθepta'θion; asepta'sion/ *n. f.* acceptance.

aceptar /aθep'tar; asep'tar/ *v.* accept.

acequía /aθe'kia; ase'kia/ *n. f.* ditch.

acera /a'θera; a'sera/ *n. f.* sidewalk.

acerca de /a'θerka de; a'serka de/ *prep.* about, concerning.

acercar /aθer'kar; aser'kar/ *v.* bring near.

acercarse /aθer'karse; aser'karse/ v. approach, come near, go near.

acero /a'θero; a'sero/ n. m. steel.

acero inoxidable /a'θero inoksi-'ðaβle; a'sero inoksi'ðaβle/ stainless steel.

acertar /aθer'tar; aser'tar/ v. guess right. **a. en,** hit (a mark).

acertijo /aθer'tiho; aser'tiho/ n. m. puzzle, riddle.

achicar /atʃi'kar/ v. diminish, dwarf; humble.

acidez /aθi'ðeθ; asi'ðes/ n. f. acidity.

ácido /'aθiðo; 'asiðo/ a. 1. sour. —n. 2. m. acid.

aclamación /aklama'θion; aklama'sion/ n. f. acclamation.

aclamar /akla'mar/ v. acclaim.

aclarar /akla'rar/ v. brighten; clarify, clear up.

acoger /ako'her/ v. welcome, receive.

acogida /ako'hiða/ n. f. welcome, reception.

acometer /akome'ter/ v. attack.

acomodador /akomoða'ðor/ n. m. usher.

acomodar /akomo'ðar/ v. accommodate, fix up.

acompañamiento /akompaɲa'miento/ n. m. accompaniment; following.

acompañar /akompa'ɲar/ v. accompany.

acondicionar /akondiθio'nar; akondisio'nar/ v. condition.

aconsejable /akonse'haβle/ a. advisable.

aconsejar /akonse'har/ v. advise.

acontecer /akonte'θer; akonte'ser/ v. happen.

acontecimiento /akonteθi'miento; akontesi'miento/ n. m. event, happening.

acorazado /akora'θaðo; akora'saðo/ n. 1. m. battleship. —a. 2. armor-plated, ironclad.

acordarse /akor'ðarse/ v. remember, recollect.

acordeón /akorðe'on/ n. m. accordion.

acordonar /akorðo'nar/ v. cordon off.

acortar /akor'tar/ v. shorten.

acosar /ako'sar/ v. beset, harry.

acostar /ako'star/ v. lay down; put to bed.

acostarse /akos'tarse/ v. lie down; go to bed.

acostumbrado /akostum'braðo/ a. accustomed; customary.

acostumbrar /akostum'brar/ v. accustom.

acrecentar /akreθen'tar; akresen'tar/ v. increase.

acreditar /akreði'tar/ v. accredit.

acreedor /akree'ðor/ -ra n. creditor.

acróbata /a'kroβata/ n. m. & f. acrobat.

acrobático /akro'βatiko/ a. acrobatic.

actitud /akti'tuð/ n. f. attitude.

actividad /aktiβi'ðað/ n. f. activity.

activista /akti'βista/ a. & n. activist.

activo /ak'tiβo/ a. active.

acto /'akto/ n. m. act.

actor /ak'tor/ n. m. actor.

actriz /ak'triθ; ak'tris/ n. f. actress.

actual /ak'tual/ a. present; present day.

actualidades /aktuali'ðaðes/ n. f.pl. current events.

actualmente /aktual'mente/ adv. at present; nowadays.

actuar /ak'tuar/ v. act.

acuarela /akua'rela/ n. f. watercolor.

acuario /a'kuario/ n. m. aquarium.

acuático /a'kuatiko/ a. aquatic.

acuchillar /akutʃi'ʎar; akutʃi'yar/ v. slash, knife.

acudir /aku'ðir/ v. rally; hasten; be present.

acuerdo /a'kuerðo/ n. m. accord, agreement; settlement. **de a.,** in agreement, agreed.

acumulación /akumula'θion; akumula'sion/ n. f. accumulation.

acumular /akumu'lar/ v. accumulate.

acuñar /aku'ɲar/ v. coin, mint.

acupuntura /akupun'tura/ n. f. acupuncture.

acusación /akusa'θion; akusa'sion/ n. f. accusation, charge.

acusado /aku'saðo/ -da a. & n. accused; defendant.

acusador /akusa'ðor/ -ra n. accuser.

acusar /aku'sar/ v. accuse; acknowledge.

acústica /a'kustika/ n. f. acoustics.

adaptación /aðapta'θion; aðapta'sion/ *n. f.* adaptation.

adaptador /aðapta'ðor/ *n. m.* adapter.

adaptar /aðap'tar/ *v.* adapt.

adecuado /aðe'kuaðo/ *a.* adequate.

adelantado /aðelan'taðo/ *a.* advanced; fast (clock).

adelantamiento /aðelanta-'miento/ *n. m.* advancement, promotion.

adelantar /aðelan'tar/ *v.* advance.

adelante /aðe'lante/ *adv.* ahead, forward, onward, on.

adelanto /aðe'lanto/ *n. m.* advancement, progress, improvement.

adelgazar /aðelga'θar; aðelga'sar/ *v.* make thin.

ademán /aðe'man/ *n. m.* attitude; gesture.

además /aðe'mas/ *adv.* in addition, besides, also.

adentro /a'ðentro/ *adv.* in, inside.

adepto /a'ðepto/ *a.* adept.

aderezar /aðere'θar; aðere'sar/ *v.* prepare; trim.

adherirse /aðe'rirse/ *v.* adhere, stick.

adhesivo /aðe'siβo/ *a.* adhesive.

adicción /aðik'θion; aðik'sion/ *n. f.* adiction.

adición /aði'θion; aði'sion/ *n. f.* addition.

adicional /aðiθio'nal; aðisio'nal/ *a.* additional, extra.

adicto /a'ðikto/ **-ta** *a. & n.* addicted; addict.

adinerado /aðine'raðo/ **-a** *a.* wealthy.

adiós /aðios/ *n. m. & interj.* goodbye, farewell.

adivinar /aðiβi'nar/ *v.* guess.

adjetivo /aðhe'tiβo/ *n. m.* adjective.

adjunto /að'hunto/ *a.* enclosed.

administración /aðministra'θion; aðministra'sion/ *n. f.* administration.

administrador /aðministra'ðor/ **-ra** *n.* administrator.

administrar /aðminis'trar/ *v.* administer; manage.

administrativo /aðministra'tiβo/ *a.* administrative.

admirable /aðmi'raβle/ *a.* admirable.

admiración. /aðmira'θion; að-mira'sion/ *n. f.* admiration; wonder.

admirar /aðmi'rar/ *v.* admire.

admisión /aðmi'sion/ *n. f.* admission.

admitir /aðmi'tir/ *v.* admit, acknowledge.

ADN, *abbr.* **(ácido deoxirribonucleico)** DNA (deoxyribonucleic acid).

adobar /ado'βar/ *v.* marinate.

adolescencia /aðoles'θenθia; aðoles'sensia/ *n. f.* adolescence, youth.

adolescente /aðoles'θente; aðoles'sente/ *a. & n.* adolescent.

adónde /a'ðonde/ *adv.* where.

adondequiera /aˌðonde'kiera/ *conj.* wherever.

adopción /aðop'θion; aðop'sion/ *n. f.* adoption.

adoptar /aðop'tar/ *v.* adopt.

adoración /aðora'θion; aðora'sion/ *n. f.* worship, love, adoration. **—adorar,** *v.*

adormecer /aðorme'θer; aðorme'ser/ *v.* drowse.

adornar /aðor'nar/ *v.* adorn; decorate.

adorno /a'ðorno/ *n. m.* adornment, trimming.

adquirir /aðki'rir/ *v.* acquire, obtain.

adquisición /aðkisi'θion; aðkisi'sion/ *n. f.* acquisition, attainment.

aduana /a'ðuana/ *n. f.* custom house, customs.

adujada /aðu'haða/ *n. f. Naut.* coil of rope.

adulación /aðula'θion; aðula'sion/ *n. f.* flattery.

adular /aðu'lar/ *v.* flatter.

adulterar /aðulte'rar/ *v.* adulterate.

adulterio /aðul'terio/ *n. m.* adultery.

adulto /a'ðulto/ **-ta** *a. & n.* adult.

adusto /a'ðusto/ *a.* gloomy; austere.

adverbio /að'βerβio/ *n. m.* adverb.

adversario /aðβer'sario/ *n. m.* adversary.

adversidad /aðβersi'ðað/ *n. f.* adversity.

adverso /að'βerso/ *a.* adverse.

advertencia /aðβer'tenθia; aðβer'tensia/ *n. f.* warning.

advertir /aðβer'tir/ v. warn; notice.

adyacente /aðya'θente; aðya'sente/ a. adjacent.

aéreo /'aereo/ a. aerial; air.

aerodeslizador /aeroðesliθa'ðor; aeroðeslisa'ðor/ n. m. hovercraft.

aeromoza /aero'moθa; aero'mosa/ n. f. stewardess, flight attendant.

aeroplano /aero'plano/ n. m. light plane.

aeropuerto /aero'puerto/ n. m. airport.

aerosol /aero'sol/ n. m. aerosol, spray.

afable /a'faβle/ a. affable, pleasant.

afanarse /afa'narse/ v. toil.

afear /afe'ar/ v. deface, mar, deform.

afectación /afekta'θion; afekta'sion/ n. f. affectation.

afectar /afek'tar/ v. affect.

afecto /a'fekto/ n. m. affection, attachment.

afeitada /afei'taða/ n. f. shave. **—afeitarse,** v.

afeminado /afemi'naðo/ a. effeminate.

afición /afi'θion; afi'sion/ n. f. fondness, liking; hobby.

aficionado /afiθio'naðo; afisio'naðo/ a. fond.

aficionado -da n. fan, devotee; amateur.

aficionarse a /afiθio'narse a; afisio'narse a/ v. become fond of.

afilado /afi'laðo/ a. sharp.

afilar /afi'lar/ v. sharpen.

afiliación /afilia'θion; afilia'sion/ n. f. affiliation.

afiliado /afi'liaðo/ **-da** n. affiliate. **—afiliar,** v.

afinar /afi'nar/ v. polish; tune up.

afinidad /afini'ðað/ n. f. relationship, affinity.

afirmación /afirma'θion; afirma'sion/ n. f. affirmation, statement.

afirmar /afir'mar/ v. affirm, assert.

afirmativa /afirma'tiβa/ n. f. affirmative. **—afirmativo,** a.

aflicción /aflik'θion; aflik'sion/ n. f. affliction; sorrow, grief.

afligido /afli'hiðo/ a. sorrowful, grieved.

afligir /afli'hir/ v. grieve, distress.

aflojar /aflo'har/ v. loosen.

afluencia /a'fluenθia; a'fluensia/ n. f. influx.

afortunado /afortu'naðo/ a. fortunate, successful, lucky.

afrenta /a'frenta/ n. f. insult, outrage, affront. **—afrentar,** v.

afrentoso /afren'toso/ a. shameful.

africano /afri'kano/ **-na** a. & n. African.

afuera /a'fuera/ adv. out, outside.

afueras /a'fueras/ n. f.pl. suburbs.

agacharse /aga'tʃarse/ v. squat, crouch; cower.

agarrar /aga'rrar/ v. seize, grasp, clutch.

agarro /a'garro/ n. m. clutch, grasp.

agencia /a'henθia; a'hensia/ n. f. agency.

agencia de colocaciones /a'henθia de koloka'θiones; a'hensia de koloka'siones/ employment agency.

agencia de viajes /a'henθia de 'biahes; a'hensia de 'biahes/ travel agency.

agente /a'hente/ n. m. & f. agent, representative.

agente de aduana /a'hente de a'ðuana/ mf. customs officer.

agente inmobiliario /a'hente imoβi'liario/ **-ria** n. real-estate agent.

ágil /'ahil/ a. agile, spry.

agitación /ahita'θion; ahita'sion/ n. f. agitation, ferment.

agitado /ahi'taðo/ a. agitated; excited.

agitador /ahita'ðor/ n. m. agitator.

agitar /ahi'tar/ v. shake, agitate, excite.

agobiar /ago'βiar/ v. oppress, burden.

agosto /a'gosto/ n. m. August.

agotamiento /a,gota'miento/ n. m. exhaustion.

agotar /ago'tar/ v. exhaust, use up, sap.

agradable /agra'ðaβle/ a. agreeable, pleasant.

agradar /agra'ðar/ v. please.

agradecer /agraðe'θer; agraðe'ser/ v. thank; appreciate, be grateful for.

agradecido /agraðe'θiðo; agraðe'siðo/ a. grateful, thankful.

agradecimiento /agraðeθi'miento; agraðesi'miento/ n. m. gratitude, thanks.

agravar /agra'βar/ v. aggravate, make worse.

agravio /a'graβio/ n. m. wrong. —**agraviar,** v.

agregado /agre'gaðo/ a. & n. aggregate; Pol. attaché.

agregar /agre'gar/ v. add; gather.

agresión /agre'sion/ n. f. aggression; Leg. battery.

agresivo /agre'siβo/ a. aggressive.

agresor /agre'sor/ **-ra** n. aggressor.

agrícola /a'grikola/ a. agricultural.

agricultor /agrikul'tor/ n. m. farmer.

agricultura /agrikul'tura/ n. f. agriculture, farming.

agrio /'agrio/ a. sour.

agrupar /agru'par/ v. group.

agua /'agua/ n. f. water. —**aguar,** v.

aguacate /agua'kate/ n. m. avocado, alligator pear.

aguafuerte /ˌagua'fuerte/ n. f. etching.

agua mineral /'agua mine'ral/ mineral water.

aguantar /aguan'tar/ v. endure, stand, put up with.

aguardar /aguar'ðar/ v. await; expect.

aguardiente /aguar'ðiente/ n. m. brandy.

aguas abajo /'aguas a'βaho/ adv. downriver, downstream.

aguas arriba /'aguas a'rriβa/ adv. upriver, upstream.

agudo /a'guðo/ a. sharp, keen, shrill, acute.

agüero /a'guero/ n. m. omen.

águila /'agila/ n. f. eagle.

aguja /a'guha/ n. f. needle.

agujero /agu'hero/ n. m. hole.

aguzar /agu'θar; agu'sar/ v. sharpen.

ahí /a'i/ adv. there.

ahogar /ao'gar/ v. drown; choke; suffocate.

ahondar /aon'dar/ v. deepen.

ahora /a'ora/ adv. now.

ahorcar /aor'kar/ v. hang (execute).

ahorrar /ao'rrar/ v. save, save up; spare.

ahorros /a'orros/ n. m.pl. savings.

ahumar /au'mar/ v. smoke.

airado /ai'raðo/ a. angry, indignant.

aire /'aire/ n. m. air. —**airear,** v.

aire acondicionado /'aire akondi-θio'naðo; 'aire akondisio'naðo/ air conditioning.

aislamiento /aisla'miento/ n. m. isolation.

aislar /ais'lar/ v. isolate.

ajedrez /ahe'ðreθ; ahe'ðres/ n. m. chess.

ajeno /a'heno/ a. alien; someone else's.

ajetreo /ahe'treo/ n. m. hustle and bustle.

ají /'ahi/ n. m. chili.

ajo /'aho/ n. m. garlic.

ajustado /ahus'taðo/ a. adjusted; trim; exact.

ajustar /ahus'tar/ v. adjust.

ajuste /a'huste/ n. m. adjustment, settlement.

al /al/ contr. of **a + el.**

ala /'ala/ n. f. wing; brim (of hat).

alabanza /ala'βanθa; ala'βansa/ n. f. praise. —**alabar,** v.

alabear /alaβe'ar/ v. warp.

ala delta /'ala 'delta/ hang glider.

alambique /alam'bike/ n. m. still.

alambre /a'lambre/ n. m. wire. **a. de púas,** barbed wire.

alarde /a'larðe/ n. m. boasting, ostentation.

alargar /alar'gar/ v. lengthen; stretch out.

alarma /a'larma/ n. f. alarm. —**alarmar,** v.

alba /'alβa/ n. f. daybreak, dawn.

albanega /alβa'nega/ n. f. hair net.

albañil /alβa'ɲil/ n. m. bricklayer; mason.

albaricoque /alβari'koke/ n. m. apricot.

alberca /al'βerka/ n. f. swimming pool.

albergue /al'βerge/ n. m. shelter. —**albergar,** v.

alborotar /alβoro'tar/ v. disturb, make noise, brawl, riot.

alboroto /alβo'roto/ n. m. brawl, disturbance, din, tumult.

álbum /'alβum/ n. m. album.

álbum de recortes /'alβum de rre'kortes/ scrapbook.

alcachofa /alka'tʃofa/ n. f. artichoke.

alcalde /al'kalde/ n. m. mayor.

alcance /al'kanθe; al'kanse/ n. m. reach; range, scope.

alcanfor /alkan'for/ n. m. camphor.

alcanzar /alkan'θar; alkan'sar/ v. reach, overtake, catch.

alcayata /alka'yata/ *n. f.* spike.
alce /'alθe; 'alse/ *n. m.* elk.
alcoba /al'koβa/ *n. f.* bedroom; alcove.
alcoba de huéspedes /al'koβa de 'uespeðes/ guest room.
alcoba de respeto /al'koβa de rres'peto/ guest room.
alcohol /al'kool/ *n. m.* alcohol.
alcohólico /alko'oliko/ **-ca** *a. & n.* alcoholic.
aldaba /al'daβa/ *n. f.* latch.
aldea /al'dea/ *n. f.* village.
alegación /alega'θion; alega'sion/ *n. f.* allegation.
alegar /ale'gar/ *v.* allege.
alegrar /ale'grar/ *v.* make happy, brighten.
alegrarse /ale'grarse/ *v.* be glad.
alegre /a'legre/ *a.* glad, cheerful, merry.
alegría /ale'gria/ *n. f.* gaiety, cheer.
alejarse /ale'harse/ *v.* move away, off.
alemán /ale'man/ **-ana** *a. & n.* German.
Alemania /ale'mania/ *n. f.* Germany.
alentar /alen'tar/ *v.* cheer up, encourage.
alergia /aler'hia/ *n. f.* allergy.
alerta /a'lerta/ *adv.* on the alert.
aleve /a'leβe/ **alevoso** *a.* treacherous.
alfabeto /alfa'βeto/ *n. m.* alphabet.
alfalfa /al'falfa/ *n. f.* alfalfa.
alfarería /alfare'ria/ *n. f.* pottery.
alférez /al'fereθ; al'feres/ *n. m.* (naval) ensign.
alfil /al'fil/ *n. m.* (chess) bishop.
alfiler /alfi'ler/ *n. m.* pin.
alfombra /al'fombra/ *n. f.* carpet, rug.
alforja /al'forha/ *n. f.* knapsack; saddlebag.
alga /'alga/ *n. f.* seaweed.
alga marina /'alga ma'rina/ seaweed.
algarabía /algara'βia/ *n. f.* jargon; din.
álgebra /'alheβra/ *n. f.* algebra.
algo /'algo/ *pron. & adv.* something, somewhat; anything.
algodón /algo'ðon/ *n. m.* cotton.
algodón hidrófilo /algo'ðon i'ðrofilo/ absorbent cotton.
alguien /'algien/ *pron.* somebody, someone; anybody, anyone.

algún /al'gun/ **-no -na** *a. & pron.* some; any.
alhaja /al'aha/ *n. f.* jewel.
aliado /a'liaðo/ **-da** *a. & n.* allied; ally. —**aliar,** *v.*
alianza /a'lianθa; a'liansa/ *n. f.* alliance.
alicates /ali'kates/ *n. m.pl.* pliers.
aliento /a'liento/ *n. m.* breath. **dar a.,** encourage.
aligerar /alihe'rar/ *v.* lighten.
alimentar /alimen'tar/ *v.* feed, nourish.
alimento /ali'mento/ *n. m.* nourishment, food.
alinear /aline'ar/ *v.* line up; *Pol.* align.
aliñar /ali'ɲar/ *v.* dress (a salad).
aliño /a'liɲo/ *n. m.* salad dressing.
alisar /ali'sar/ *v.* smooth.
alistamiento /alista'miento/ *n. m.* enlistment.
alistar /alis'tar/ *v.* make ready, prime.
alistarse /alis'tarse/ *v.* get ready; *Mil.* enlist.
aliviar /ali'βiar/ *v.* alleviate, relieve, ease.
alivio /a'liβio/ *n. m.* relief.
allá /a'ʎa; a'ya/ *adv.* there. **más a.,** beyond, farther on.
allanar /aʎa'nar; aya'nar/ *v.* flatten, smooth, plane.
allí /a'ʎi; a'yi/ *adv.* there. **por a.,** that way.
alma /'alma/ *n. f.* soul.
almacén /alma'θen; alma'sen/ *n. m.* department store; storehouse, warehouse.
almacenaje /almaθe'nahe; almase'nahe/ *n. m.* storage.
almacenar /almaθe'nar; almase'nar/ *v.* store.
almanaque /alma'nake/ *n. m.* almanac.
almeja /al'meha/ *n. f.* clam.
almendra /al'mendra/ *n. f.* almond.
almíbar /al'miβar/ *n. m.* syrup.
almidón /almi'ðon/ *n. m.* starch. —**almidonar,** *v.*
almirante /almi'rante/ *n. m.* admiral.
almohada /almo'aða/ *n. f.* pillow.
almuerzo /al'muerθo; al'muerso/ *n. m.* lunch. —**almorzar,** *v.*
alojamiento /aloha'miento/ *n. m.* lodging, accommodations.
alojar /alo'har/ *v.* lodge, house.
alojarse /alo'harse/ *v.* stay, room.

alquiler /alki'ler/ *n. m.* rent.
—**alquilar,** *v.*
alrededor /alreðe'ðor/ *adv.* around.
alrededores /alreðe'ðores/ *n. m.pl.* environs.
altanero /alta'nero/ *a.* haughty.
altar /al'tar/ *n. m.* altar.
altavoz /ˌalta'βoθ; ˌalta'βos/ *n. m.* loudspeaker.
alteración /altera'θion; altera-'sion/ *n. f.* alteration.
alterar /alte'rar/ *v.* alter.
alternativa /alterna'tiβa/ *n. f.* alternative. —**alternativo,** *a.*
alterno /al'terno/ *a.* alternate.
—**alternar,** *v.*
alteza /al'teθa; al'tesa/ *n. f.* highness.
altivo /al'tiβo/ *a.* proud, haughty; lofty.
alto /'alto/ *a.* **1.** high, tall; loud.
—*n.* **2.** *m.* height, story (house).
altura /al'tura/ *n. f.* height, altitude.
alud /a'luð/ *n. m.* avalanche.
aludir /alu'ðir/ *v.* allude.
alumbrado /alum'braðo/ *n. m.* lighting.
alumbrar /alum'brar/ *v.* light.
aluminio /alu'minio/ *n. m.* aluminum.
alumno /a'lumno/ **-na** *n.* student, pupil.
alusión /alu'sion/ *n. f.* allusion.
alza /'alθa; 'alsa/ *n. f.* rise; boost.
alzar /al'θar; al'sar/ *v.* raise, lift.
ama /'ama/ *n. f.* housewife, mistress (of house). **a. de llaves,** housekeeper.
amable /a'maβle/ *a.* kind; pleasant, sweet.
amalgamar /amalga'mar/ *v.* amalgamate.
amamantar /amaman'tar/ *v.* suckle, nurse.
amanecer /amane'θer; amane'ser/ *n.* **1.** *m.* dawn, daybreak. —*v.* **2.** dawn; awaken.
amante /a'mante/ *n. m. & f.* lover.
amapola /ama'pola/ *n. f.* poppy.
amar /a'mar/ *v.* love.
amargo /a'margo/ *a.* bitter.
amargón /amar'gon/ *n. m.* dandelion.
amargura /amar'gura/ *n. f.* bitterness.
amarillo /ama'riʎo; ama'riyo/ *a.* yellow.

amarradero /amarra'ðero/ *n. m.* mooring.
amarrar /ama'rrar/ *v.* hitch, moor, tie up.
amartillar /amarti'ʎar; amarti'yar/ *v.* hammer; cock (a gun).
amasar /ama'sar/ *v.* knead, mold.
ámbar /'ambar/ *n. m.* amber.
ambarino /amba'rino/ *a.* amber.
ambición /ambi'θion; ambi'sion/ *n. f.* ambition.
ambicionar /ambiθio'nar; ambisio'nar/ *v.* aspire to.
ambicioso /ambi'θioso; ambi-'sioso/ *a.* ambitious.
ambientalista /ambienta'lista/ *n. m. & f.* environmentalist.
ambiente /am'biente/ *n. m.* environment, atmosphere.
ambigüedad /ambigue'ðað/ *n. f.* ambiguity.
ambiguo /am'biguo/ *a.* ambiguous.
ambos /'ambos/ *a. & pron.* both.
ambulancia /ambu'lanθia; ambu'lansia/ *n. f.* ambulance.
amenaza /ame'naθa; ame'nasa/ *n. f.* threat, menace.
amenazar /amena'θar; amena'sar/ *v.* threaten, menace.
ameno /a'meno/ *a.* pleasant.
americana /ameri'kana/ *n. f.* suit coat.
americano /ameri'kano/ **-na** *a. & n.* American.
ametralladora /ametraʎa'ðora; ametraya'ðora/ *n. f.* machine gun.
amigable /ami'gaβle/ *a.* amicable, friendly.
amígdala /a'migðala/ *n. f.* tonsil.
amigo /a'migo/ **-ga** *n.* friend.
aminorar /amino'rar/ *v.* lessen, reduce.
amistad /amis'tað/ *n. f.* friendship.
amistoso /amis'toso/ *a.* friendly.
amniocéntesis /amnioθen'tesis; amniosen'tesis/ *n. m.* amniocentesis.
amo /'amo/ *n. m.* master.
amonestaciones /amonesta-'θiones; amonesta'siones/ *n. f.pl.* banns.
amonestar /amones'tar/ *v.* admonish.
amoníaco /amo'niako/ *n. m.* ammonia.
amontonar /amonto'nar/ *v.* amass, pile up.

amor /a'mor/ *n. m.* love. **a. propio,** self-esteem.
amorío /amo'rio/ *n. m.* romance, love affair.
amoroso /amo'roso/ *a.* amorous; loving.
amortecer /amorte'θer; amorte-'ser/ *v.* deaden.
amparar /ampa'rar/ *v.* aid, befriend; protect, shield.
amparo /am'paro/ *n. m.* protection.
ampliar /amp'liar/ *v.* enlarge; elaborate.
amplificar /amplifi'kar/ *v.* amplify.
amplio /'amplio/ *a.* ample, roomy.
ampolla /am'poʎa; am'poya/ *n. f.* bubble; bulb; blister.
amputar /ampu'tar/ *v.* amputate.
amueblar /amue'βlar/ *v.* furnish.
analfabeto /analfa'βeto/ **-ta** *a.* & *n.* illiterate.
analgésico /anal'hesiko/ *n. m.* pain killer.
análisis /a'nalisis/ *n. m.* analysis.
analizar /anali'θar; anali'sar/ *v.* analyze.
analogía /analo'hia/ *n. f.* analogy.
análogo /a'nalogo/ *a.* similar, analogous.
anarquía /anar'kia/ *n. f.* anarchy.
anatomía /anato'mia/ *n. f.* anatomy.
ancho /'antʃo/ *a.* wide, broad.
anchoa /an'tʃoa/ *n. f.* anchovy.
anchura /an'tʃura/ *n. f.* width, breadth.
anciano /an'θiano; an'siano/ **-na** *a.* & *n.* old, aged (person).
ancla /'ankla/ *n. f.* anchor.
—anclar, *v.*
anclaje /an'klahe/ *n. m.* anchorage.
andamio /an'damio/ *n. m.* scaffold.
andar /an'dar/ *v.* walk; move, go.
andén /an'den/ *n. m.* (railroad) platform.
andrajoso /andra'hoso/ *a.* ragged, uneven.
anécdota /a'nekðota/ *n. f.* anecdote.
anegar /ane'gar/ *v.* flood, drown.
anestesia /anes'tesia/ *n. f.* anesthetic.
anexar /anek'sar/ *v.* annex.
anexión /anek'sion/ *n. f.* annexation.
anfitrión /anfitri'on/ **-na** *n.* host.

ángel /'anhel/ *n. m.* angel.
angosto /aŋ'gosto/ *a.* narrow.
anguila /aŋ'gila/ *n. f.* eel.
angular /aŋgu'lar/ *a.* angular.
ángulo /'aŋgulo/ *n. m.* angle.
angustia /aŋ'gustia/ *n. f.* anguish, agony.
angustiar /aŋgus'tiar/ *v.* distress.
anhelar /ane'lar/ *v.* long for.
anidar /ani'ðar/ *v.* nest, nestle.
anillo /a'niʎo; a'niyo/ *n. m.* ring; circle.
animación /anima'θion; anima-'sion/ *n. f.* animation; bustle.
animado /ani'maðo/ *a.* animated, lively; animate.
animal /ani'mal/ *a.* & *n.* animal.
ánimo /'animo/ *n. m.* state of mind, spirits; courage.
aniquilar /aniki'lar/ *v.* annihilate, destroy.
aniversario /aniβer'sario/ *n. m.* anniversary.
anoche /a'notʃe/ *adv.* last night.
anochecer /anotʃe'θer; anotʃe'ser/ *n.* 1. *m.* twilight, nightfall. —*v.* 2. get dark.
anónimo /a'nonimo/ *a.* anonymous.
anorexia /ano'reksia/ *n. f.* anorexia.
anormal /anor'mal/ *a.* abnormal.
anotación /anota'θion; anota'sion/ *n. f.* annotation.
anotar /ano'tar/ *v.* annotate.
ansia /'ansia/ **ansiedad** *n. f.* anxiety.
ansioso /an'sioso/ *a.* anxious.
antagonismo /antago'nismo/ *n. m.* antagonism.
antagonista /antago'nista/ *n. m.* & *f.* antagonist, opponent.
anteayer /antea'yer/ *adv.* day before yesterday.
antebrazo /ante'βraθo; ante-'βraso/ *n. m.* forearm.
antecedente /anteθe'ðente; antese'ðente/ *a.* & *m.* antecedent.
anteceder /anteθe'ðer; antese'ðer/ *v.* precede.
antecesor /anteθe'sor; antese'sor/ *n. m.* ancestor.
antemano /ante'mano/ *de a.,* in advance.
antena /an'tena/ *n. f.* antenna.
antena parabólica /an'tena para'βolika/ satellite dish.
anteojos /ante'ohos/ *n. m.pl.* eyeglasses.

antepasado /antepa'saðo/ *n. m.* ancestor.

antepenúltimo /antepe'nultimo/ *a.* antepenulimate.

anterior /ante'rior/ *a.* previous, former.

antes /'antes/ *adv.* before; formerly.

antibala /anti'bala/ *a.* bulletproof.

anticipación /antiθipa'θion; antisipa'sion/ *n. f.* anticipation.

anticipar /antiθi'par; antisi'par/ *v.* anticipate; advance.

anticonceptivo /antikonθep'tiβo; antikonsep'tiβo/ *a. & n.* contraceptive.

anticongelante /antikoŋge'lante/ *n. m.* antifreeze.

anticuado /anti'kuaðo/ *a.* antiquated, obsolete.

antídoto /an'tiðoto/ *n. m.* antidote.

antigüedad /antigue'ðað/ *n. f.* antiquity; antique.

antiguo /an'tiguo/ *a.* former; old; antique.

antihistamínico /antiista'miniko/ *n. m.* antihistamine.

antílope /an'tilope/ *n. m.* antelope.

antinuclear /antinukle'ar/ *a.* antinuclear.

antipatía /antipa'tia/ *n. f.* antipathy.

antipático /anti'patiko/ *a.* disagreeable, nasty.

antiséptico /anti'septiko/ *a. & m.* antiseptic.

antojarse /anto'harse/ *v.* **se me antoja...** etc., I desire..., take a fancy to..., etc.

antojo /an'toho/ *n. m.* whim, fancy.

antorcha /an'tortʃa/ *n. f.* torch.

antracita /antra'θita; antra'sita/ *n. f.* anthracite.

anual /a'nual/ *a.* annual, yearly.

anudar /anu'ðar/ *v.* knot; tie.

anular /anu'lar/ *v.* annul, void.

anunciar /anun'θiar; anun'siar/ *v.* announce; proclaim, advertise.

anuncio /a'nunθio; a'nunsio/ *n. m.* announcement; advertisement.

añadir /aɲa'ðir/ *v.* add.

añil /a'ɲil/ *n. m.* bluing; indigo.

año /'aɲo/ *n. m.* year.

apacible /apa'θiβle; apa'siβle/ *a.* peaceful, peaceable.

apaciguamiento /a,paθigua'miento; a,pasigua'miento/ *n. m.* appeasement.

apaciguar /apaθi'guar; apasi'guar/ *v.* appease; placate.

apagado /apa'gaðo/ *a.* dull.

apagar /apa'gar/ *v.* extinguish, quench, put out.

apagón /apa'gn/ *n. m.* blackout.

aparador /apara'ðor/ *n. m.* buffet, cupboard.

aparato /apa'rato/ *n. m.* apparatus; machine; appliance, set.

aparcamiento /aparka'miento/ *n. m.* parking lot; parking space.

aparecer /apare'θer; apare'ser/ *v.* appear, show up.

aparejo /apa'reho/ *n. m.* rig. —**aparejar,** *v.*

aparentar /aparen'tar/ *v.* pretend; profess.

aparente /apa'rente/ *a.* apparent.

apariencia /apa'rienθia; apa'riensia/ **aparición** *n. f.* appearance.

apartado /apar'taðo/ *a.* **1.** aloof; separate. —*n.* **2.** *m.* post-office box.

apartamento /aparta'mento/ *n. m.* apartment. **a. en propiedad,** condominium.

apartar /apar'tar/ *v.* separate; remove.

aparte /a'parte/ *adv.* apart; aside.

apartheid /apar'teið/ *n. m.* apartheid.

apasionado /apasio'naðo/ *a.* passionate.

apatía /apa'tia/ *n. f.* apathy.

apearse /ape'arse/ *v.* get off, alight.

apedrear /apeðre'ar/ *v.* stone.

apelación /apela'θion; apela'sion/ *n. f.* appeal. —**apelar,** *v.*

apellido /ape'ʎiðo; ape'yiðo/ *n. m.* family name.

apellido materno /ape'ʎiðo ma'terno; ape'yiðo ma'terno/ mother's family name.

apellido paterno /ape'ʎiðo pa'terno; ape'yiðo pa'terno/ father's family name.

apenas /a'penas/ *adv.* scarcely, hardly.

apéndice /a'pendiθe; a'pendise/ *n. m.* appendix.

apercibir /aperθi'βir; apersi'βir/ *v.* prepare, warn.

aperitivo /aperi'tiβo/ *n. m.* appetizer.

aperos /a'peros/ *n. m.pl.* implements.

apestar /apes'tar/ v. infect; stink.

apetecer /apete'θer; apete'ser/ v. desire, have appetite for.

apetito /ape'tito/ n. m. appetite.

ápice /'apiθe; 'apise/ n. m. apex.

apilar /api'lar/ v. stack.

apio /'apio/ n. m. celery.

aplacar /apla'kar/ v. appease; placate.

aplastar /aplas'tar/ v. crush, flatten.

aplaudir /aplau'ðir/ v. applaud, cheer.

aplauso /a'plauso/ n. m. applause.

aplazar /apla'θar; apla'sar/ v. postpone, put off.

aplicable /apli'kaβle/ a. applicable.

aplicado /apli'kaðo/ a. industrious, diligent.

aplicar /apli'kar/ v. apply.

aplomo /a'plomo/ n. m. aplomb, poise.

apoderado /apoðe'raðo/ **-da** n. attorney.

apoderarse de /apoðe'rarse de/ v. get hold of, seize.

apodo /a'poðo/ n. m. nickname. **—apodar,** v.

apologético /apolo'hetiko/ a. apologetic.

apoplejía /apople'hia/ n. f. apoplexy.

aposento /apo'sento/ n. m. room, flat.

apostar /apos'tar/ v. bet, wager.

apóstol /a'postol/ n. m. apostle.

apoyar /apo'yar/ v. support, prop; lean.

apoyo /a'poyo/ n. m. support; prop; aid; approval.

apreciable /apreθia'βle; apresia'βle/ a. appreciable.

apreciar /apre'θiar; apre'siar/ v. appreciate, prize.

aprecio /a'preθio; a'presio/ n. m. appreciation, regard.

apremio /a'premio/ n. m. pressure, compulsion.

aprender /apren'der/ v. learn.

aprendiz /apren'diθ; apren'dis/ n. m. apprentice.

aprendizaje /aprendi'θahe; aprendi'sahe/ n. m. apprenticeship.

aprensión /apren'sion/ n. f. apprehension.

aprensivo /apren'siβo/ a. apprehensive.

apresurado /apresu'raðo/ a. hasty, fast.

apresurar /apresu'rar/ v. hurry, speed up.

apretado /apre'taðo/ a. tight.

apretar /apre'tar/ v. squeeze, press; tighten.

apretón /apre'ton/ n. m. squeeze.

aprieto /a'prieto/ n. m. plight, predicament.

aprobación /aproβa'θion; aproβa'sion/ n. f. approbation, approval.

aprobar /apro'βar/ v. approve.

apropiación /apropia'θion; apropia'sion/ n. f. appropriation.

apropiado /apro'piaðo/ a. appropriate. **—apropiar,** v.

aprovechar /aproβe'tʃar/ v. profit by.

aprovecharse /aproβe'tʃarse/ v. take advantage.

aproximado /aproksi'maðo/ a. approximate.

aproximarse a /aproksi'marse a/ v. approach.

aptitud /apti'tuð/ n. f. aptitude.

apto /'apto/ a. apt.

apuesta /a'puesta/ n. f. bet, wager, stake.

apuntar /apun'tar/ v. point, aim; prompt; write down.

apunte /a'punte/ n. m. annotation, note; promptings, cue.

apuñalar /apuɲa'lar/ v. stab.

apurar /apu'rar/ v. hurry; worry.

apuro /a'puro/ n. m. predicament, scrape, trouble.

aquel /a'kel/ **aquella** dem. a. that.

aquél /a'kel/ **aquélla** dem. pron. that (one); the former.

aquello /a'keʎo; a'keyo/ dem. pron. that.

aquí /a'ki/ adv. here. **por a.,** this way.

aquietar /akie'tar/ v. allay; lull, pacify.

ara /'ara/ n. f. altar.

árabe /'araβe/ a. & n. Arab, Arabic.

arado /a'raðo/ n. m. plow. **—arar,** v.

arándano /a'randano/ n. m. cranberry.

araña /a'raɲa/ n. f. spider. **a. de luces,** chandelier.

arbitración /arβitra'θion; arβitra'sion/ n. f. arbitration.

arbitrador /arβitra'ðor/ **-ra** *n.* arbitrator.

arbitraje /arβi'trahe/ *n. m.* arbitration.

arbitrar /arβi'trar/ *v.* arbitrate.

arbitrario /arβi'trario/ *a.* arbitrary.

árbitro /'arβitro/ *n. m.* arbiter, umpire, referee.

árbol /'arβol/ *n. m.* tree; mast.

árbol genealógico /'arβol henea'lohiko/ family tree.

arbusto /ar'βusto/ *n. m.* bush, shrub.

arca /'arka/ *n. f.* chest; ark.

arcada /ar'kaða/ *n. f.* arcade.

arcaico /ar'kaiko/ *a.* archaic.

arce /'arθe; 'arse/ *n. m.* maple.

archipiélago /artʃi'pielago/ *n. m.* archipelago.

archivador /artʃiβa'ðor/ *n. m.* file cabinet.

archivo /ar'tʃiβo/ *n. m.* archive; file. —**archivar,** *v.*

arcilla /ar'θiʎa; ar'siya/ *n. f.* clay.

arco /'arko/ *n. m.* arc; arch; (archer's) bow. **a. iris,** rainbow.

arder /ar'ðer/ *v.* burn.

ardid /ar'ðið/ *n. m.* stratagem, cunning.

ardiente /ar'ðiente/ *a.* ardent, burning, fiery.

ardilla /ar'ðiʎa; ar'ðiya/ *n. f.* squirrel.

ardor /ar'ðor/ *n. m.* ardor, fervor.

ardor de estómago /ar'ðor de es'tomago/ heartburn.

arduo /'arðuo/ *a.* arduous.

área /'area/ *n. f.* area.

arena /a'rena/ *n. f.* sand; arena.

arenoso /are'noso/ *a.* sandy.

arenque /a'renke/ *n. m.* herring.

arete /a'rete/ *n.* earring.

argentino /arhen'tino/ **-na** *a. & n.* Argentine.

argüir /ar'guir/ *v.* dispute, argue.

árido /'ariðo/ *a.* arid.

aristocracia /aristo'kraθia; aristo'krasia/ *n. f.* aristocracy.

aristócrata /aris'tokrata/ *n. f.* aristocrat.

aristocrático /aristo'kratiko/ *a.* aristocratic.

aritmética /arit'metika/ *n. f.* arithmetic.

arma /'arma/ *n. f.* weapon, arm.

armadura /arma'ðura/ *n. f.* armor; reinforcement; framework.

armamento /arma'mento/ *n. m.* armament.

armar /ar'mar/ *v.* arm.

armario /ar'mario/ *n. m.* cabinet, bureau, wardrobe.

armazón /arma'θon; arma'son/ *n. m.* framework, frame.

armería /arme'ria/ *n. f.* armory.

armisticio /armis'tiθio; armis'tisio/ *n. m.* armistice.

armonía /armo'nia/ *n. f.* harmony.

armonioso /armo'nioso/ *a.* harmonious.

armonizar /armoni'θar; armoni'sar/ *v.* harmonize.

arnés /ar'nes/ *n. m.* harness.

aroma /a'roma/ *n. f.* aroma, fragrance.

aromático /aro'matiko/ *a.* aromatic.

arpa /'arpa/ *n. f.* harp.

arquear /arke'ar/ *v.* arch.

arquitecto /arki'tekto/ *n. m.* architect.

arquitectura /arkitek'tura/ *n. f.* architecture.

arquitectural /arkitektu'ral/ *a.* architectural.

arrabal /arra'βal/ *n. m.* suburb.

arraigar /arrai'gar/ *v.* take root, settle.

arrancar /arran'kar/ *v.* pull out, tear out; start up.

arranque /a'rranke/ *n. m.* dash, sudden start; fit of anger.

arrastrar /arras'trar/ *v.* drag.

arrebatar /arreβa'tar/ *v.* snatch, grab.

arrebato /arre'βato/ *n. m.* sudden attack, fit of anger.

arrecife /arre'θife; arre'sife/ *n. m.* reef.

arreglar /arre'glar/ *v.* arrange; repair, fix; adjust, settle.

arreglárselas /arre'glarselas/ *v.* manage, shift for oneself.

arreglo /a'rreglo/ *n. m.* arrangement, settlement.

arremangarse /arremaŋ'garse/ *v.* roll up one's sleeves; roll up one's pants.

arremeter /arreme'ter/ *v.* attack.

arrendar /arren'dar/ *v.* rent.

arrepentimiento /arrepenti'miento/ *n. m.* repentance.

arrepentirse /arrepen'tirse/ *v.* repent.

arrestar /arres'tar/ *v.* arrest.

arriba /a'rriβa/ *adv.* up; upstairs.

arriendo /a'rriendo/ *n. m.* lease.

arriero /a'rriero/ *n. m.* muleteer.

arriesgar /arries'gar/ *v.* risk.

arrimarse /arri'marse/ *v.* lean.

arrodillarse /arroði'ʎarse; arroði-'yarse/ v. kneel.

arrogancia /arro'ganθia; arro-'gansia/ n. f. arrogance.

arrogante /arro'gante/ a. arrogant.

arrojar /arro'har/ v. throw, hurl; shed.

arrollar /arro'ʎar; arro'yar/ v. roll, coil.

arroyo /a'rroyo/ n. m. brook; gully; gutter.

arroz /a'rroθ; a'rros/ n. m. rice.

arruga /a'rruga/ n. f. ridge; wrinkle.

arrugar /arru'gar/ v. wrinkle, crumple.

arruinar /arrui'nar/ v. ruin, destroy, wreck.

arsenal /arse'nal/ n. m. arsenal; armory.

arsénico /ar'seniko/ n. m. arsenic.

arte /'arte/ n. m. (f. in pl.) art, craft; wiliness.

arteria /ar'teria/ n. f. artery.

artesa /ar'tesa/ n. f. trough.

artesano /arte'sano/ -na n. artisan, craftsman.

ártico /'artiko/ a. arctic.

articulación /artikula'θion; artikula'sion/ n. f. articulation; joint.

articular /artiku'lar/ v. articulate.

artículo /ar'tikulo/ n. m. article.

artífice /ar'tifiθe; ar'tifise/ n. m. & f. artisan.

artificial /artifi'θial; artifi'sial/ a. artificial.

artificio /arti'fiθio; arti'fisio/ n. m. artifice, device.

artificioso /artifi'θioso; artifi-'sioso/ a. affected.

artillería /artiʎe'ria; artiye'ria/ n. f. artillery.

artista /ar'tista/ n. m. & f. artist.

artístico /ar'tistiko/ a. artistic.

artritis /ar'tritis/ n. f. arthritis.

arzobispo /arθo'βispo; arso'βispo/ n. m. archbishop.

as /as/ n. m. ace.

asado /a'saðo/ a. & n. roast.

asaltador /asalta'ðor/ -ra n. assailant.

asaltante /asal'tante/ n. m. & f. mugger.

asaltar /asal'tar/ v. assail, attack.

asalto /a'salto/ n. m. assault. —asaltar, v.

asamblea /asam'βlea/ n. f. assembly.

asar /a'sar/ v. roast; broil, cook (meat).

asaz /a'saθ; a'sas/ adv. enough; quite.

ascender /asθen'der; assen'der/ v. ascend, go up; amount.

ascenso /as'θenso; as'senso/ n. m. ascent.

ascensor /asθen'sor; assen'sor/ n. m. elevator.

ascensorista /asθenso'rista; assenso'rista/ n. m. & f. (elevator) operator.

asco /'asko/ n. m. nausea; disgusting thing. **qué a.,** how disgusting.

aseado /ase'aðo/ a. tidy. —asear, v.

asediar /ase'ðiar/ v. besiege.

asedio /a'seðio/ n. m. siege.

asegurar /asegu'rar/ v. assure; secure.

asegurarse /asegu'rarse/ v. make sure.

asemejarse a /aseme'harse a/ v. resemble.

asentar /asen'tar/ v. settle; seat.

asentimiento /asenti'miento/ n. m. assent. —asentir, v.

aseo /a'seo/ n. m. neatness, tidiness.

aseos /a'seos/ n. m.pl. restroom.

asequible /ase'kiβle/ a. attainable; affordable.

aserción /aser'θion; aser'sion/ n. f. assertion.

aserrar /ase'rrar/ v. saw.

asesinar /asesi'nar/ v. assassinate; murder, slay.

asesinato /asesi'nato/ n. m. assassination, murder.

asesino /ase'sino/ -na n. murderer, assassin.

aseveración /aseβera'θion; aseβera'sion/ n. f. assertion.

aseverar /aseβe'rar/ v. assert.

asfalto /as'falto/ n. m. asphalt.

así /a'si/ adv. so, thus, this way, that way. **a. como,** as well as. **a. que,** as soon as.

asiático /a'siatiko/ -ca a. & n. Asiatic.

asiduo /a'siðuo/ a. assiduous.

asiento /a'siento/ n. m. seat; chair; site.

asiento delantero /a'siento delan'tero/ front seat.

asiento trasero /a'siento tra'sero/ back seat.

asignar /asig'nar/ v. assign; allot.

asilo /a'silo/ *n. m.* asylum, sanctuary.

asimilar /asimi'lar/ *v.* assimilate.

asir /a'sir/ *v.* grasp.

asistencia /asis'tenθia; asistensia/ *n. f.* attendance, presence.

asistir /asis'tir/ *v.* be present, attend.

asno /'asno/ *n. m.* donkey.

asociación /asoθia'θion; asosia-'sion/ *n. f.* association.

asociado /aso'θiaðo; aso'siaðo/ *n. m.* associate, partner.

asociar /aso'θiar; aso'siar/ *v.* associate.

asolar /aso'lar/ *v.* desolate; burn, parch.

asoleado /asole'aðo/ *a.* sunny.

asomar /aso'mar/ *v.* appear, loom up, show up.

asombrar /asom'βrar/ *v.* astonish, amaze.

asombro /a'sombro/ *n. m.* amazement, astonishment.

aspa /'aspa/ *n. f.* reel. —**aspar,** *v.*

aspecto /as'pekto/ *n. m.* aspect.

aspereza /aspe're θa; aspe'resa/ *n. f.* harshness.

áspero /'aspero/ *a.* rough, harsh.

aspiración /aspira'θion; aspira-'sion/ *n. f.* aspiration.

aspirador /aspira'ðor/ *n. m.* vacuum cleaner.

aspirar /aspi'rar/ *v.* aspire.

aspirina /aspi'rina/ *n. f.* aspirin.

asqueroso /aske'roso/ *a.* dirty, nasty, filthy.

asta /'asta/ *n. f.* shaft.

asterisco /aste'risko/ *n. m.* asterisk.

astilla /as'tiʎa; as'tiya/ *n. f.* splinter, chip. —**astillar,** *v.*

astillero /asti'ʎero; asti'yero/ *n. m.* dry dock.

astro /'astro/ *n. m.* star.

astronauta /astro'nauta/ *n. m. & f.* astronaut.

astronave /astro'naβe/ *n. f.* spaceship.

astronomía /astrono'mia/ *n. f.* astronomy.

astucia /as'tuθia; as'tusia/ *n. f.* cunning.

astuto /as'tuto/ *a.* astute, sly, shrewd.

asumir /asu'mir/ *v.* assume.

asunto /a'sunto/ *n. m.* matter, affair, business; subject.

asustar /asus'tar/ *v.* frighten, scare, startle.

atacar /ata'kar/ *v.* attack, charge.

atajo /a'taho/ *n. m.* shortcut.

ataque /a'take/ *n. m.* attack, charge; spell, stroke.

ataque cardíaco /a'take kar'ðiako/ heart attack.

atar /a'tar/ *v.* tie, bind, fasten.

atareado /atare'aðo/ *a.* busy.

atascar /atas'kar/ *v.* stall, stop, obstruct.

atasco /a'tasko/ *n. m.* traffic jam.

ataúd /ata'uð/ *n. m.* casket, coffin.

atavío /ata'βio/ *n. m.* dress; gear, equipment.

atemorizar /atemori'θar; atemori'sar/ *v.* frighten.

atención /aten'θion; aten'sion/ *n. f.* attention.

atender /aten'der/ *v.* heed; attend to, wait on.

atenerse a /ate'nerse a/ *v.* count on, depend on.

atentado /aten'taðo/ *n. m.* crime, offense.

atento /a'tento/ *a.* attentive, courteous.

ateo /a'teo/ *n. m.* atheist.

aterrizaje /aterri'θahe; aterri'sahe/ *n. m.* landing (of aircraft).

aterrizaje forzoso /aterri'θahe for'θoso; aterri'sahe for'soso/ emergency landing, forced landing.

aterrizar /aterri'θar; aterri'sar/ *v.* land.

atesorar /ateso'rar/ *v.* hoard.

atestar /ates'tar/ *v.* witness.

atestiguar /atesti'guar/ *v.* attest, testify.

atinar /ati'nar/ *v.* hit upon.

atisbar /atis'βar/ *v.* scrutinize, pry.

Atlántico /at'lantiko/ *n. m.* Atlantic.

atlántico *a.* Atlantic.

atlas /'atlas/ *n. m.* atlas.

atleta /at'leta/ *n. m. & f.* athlete.

atlético /at'letiko/ *a.* athletic.

atletismo /atle'tismo/ *n. m.* athletics.

atmósfera /at'mosfera/ *n. f.* atmosphere.

atmosférico /atmos'feriko/ *a.* atmospheric.

atolladero /atoʎa'ðero; atoya'ðero/ *n. m.* dead end, impasse.

atómico /a'tomiko/ *a.* atomic.

átomo /'atomo/ *n. m.* atom.

atormentar /atormen'tar/ v. torment, plague.

atornillar /atorni'ʎar; atorni'yar/ v. screw.

atracción /atrak'θion; atrak'sion/ n. f. attraction.

atractivo /atrak'tiβo/ a. 1. attractive. —n. 2. m. attraction.

atraer /atra'er/ v. attract; lure.

atrapar /atra'par/ v. trap, catch.

atrás /a'tras/ adv. back; behind.

atrasado /atra'saðo/ a. belated; backward; slow (clock).

atrasar /atra'sar/ v. delay, retard; be slow.

atraso /a'traso/ n. m. delay; backwardness; (pl.) arrears.

atravesar /atraβe'sar/ v. cross.

atreverse /atre'βerse/ v. dare.

atrevido /atre'βiðo/ a. daring, bold.

atrevimiento /atreβi'miento/ n. m. boldness.

atribuir /atri'βuir/ v. attribute, ascribe.

atributo /atri'βuto/ n. m. attribute.

atrincherar /atrintʃe'rar/ v. entrench.

atrocidad /atroθi'ðað; atrosi'ðað/ n. f. atrocity, outrage.

atronar /atro'nar/ v. deafen.

atropellar /atrope'ʎar; atrope'yar/ v. trample; fell.

atroz /a'troθ; a'ntros/ a. atrocious.

atún /a'tun/ n. m. tuna.

aturdir /atur'ðir/ v. daze, stun, bewilder.

audacia /au'ðaθia; au'ðasia/ n. f. audacity.

audaz /au'ðaθ; au'ðas/ a. audacious, bold.

audible /au'ðiβle/ a. audible.

audífono /au'ðifono/ n. m. hearing aid.

audiovisual /auðioβi'sual/ a. audiovisual.

auditorio /auði'torio/ n. m. audience.

aula /'aula/ n. f. classroom, hall.

aullar /au'ʎar; au'yar/ v. howl, bay.

aullido /au'ʎiðo; au'yiðo/ n. m. howl.

aumentar /aumen'tar/ v. augment; increase, swell.

aun /a'un/ **aún** adv. still; even. **a. cuando,** even though, even if.

aunque /'aunke/ conj. although, though.

áureo /'aureo/ a. golden.

aureola /aure'ola/ n. f. halo.

auriculares /auriku'lares/ n. m.pl. headphones.

aurora /au'rora/ n. f. dawn.

ausencia /au'senθia; au'sensia/ n. f. absence.

ausentarse /ausen'tarse/ v. stay away.

ausente /au'sente/ a. absent.

auspicio /aus'piθio; aus'pisio/ n. m. auspice.

austeridad /austeri'ðað/ n. f. austerity.

austero /aus'tero/ a. austere.

austriaco /aus'triako/ **-ca** a. & n. Austrian.

auténtico /au'tentiko/ a. authentic.

auto /'auto/ **automóvil** n. m. auto, automobile.

autobús /auto'βus/ n. m. bus.

autocine /auto'θine; auto'sine/ **autocinema** n. m. drive-in (movie theater).

automático /auto'matiko/ a. automatic.

autonomía /autono'mia/ n. f. autonomy.

autopista /auto'pista/ n. f. expressway.

autor /au'tor/ n. m. author.

autoridad /autori'ðað/ n. f. authority.

autoritario /autori'tario/ a. authoritarian; authoritative.

autorizar /autori'θar; autori'sar/ v. authorize.

autostop /auto'stop/ n. m. hitchhiking. **hacer a.,** to hitchhike.

auxiliar /auksi'liar/ a. 1. auxiliary. —v. 2. assist, aid.

auxilio /auk'silio/ n. m. aid, assistance.

avaluar /aβa'luar/ v. evaluate, appraise.

avance /a'βanθe; a'βanse/ n. m. advance. —**avanzar,** v.

avaricia /aβa'riθia; aβa'risia/ n. f. avarice.

avariento /aβa'riento/ a. miserly, greedy.

avaro /a'βaro/ **-ra** a. & m. miser; miserly.

ave /'aβe/ n. f. bird.

avellana /aβe'ʎana; aβe'yana/ n. f. hazelnut.

Ave María /aβema'ria/ *n. m.* Hail Mary.

avena /a'βena/ *n. f.* oat.

avenida /aβe'niða/ *n. f.* avenue; flood.

avenirse /aβe'nirse/ *v.* compromise; agree.

aventajar /aβenta'har/ *v.* surpass, get ahead of.

aventar /aβen'tar/ *v.* fan; scatter.

aventura /aβen'tura/ *n. f.* adventure.

aventurar /aβentu'rar/ *v.* venture, risk, gamble.

aventurero /aβentu'rero/ **-ra** *a.* & *n.* adventurous; adventurer.

avergonzado /aβergon'θaðo; aβergon'saðo/ *a.* ashamed, abashed.

avergonzar /aβergon'θar; aβergon'sar/ *v.* shame, abash.

avería /aβe'ria/ *n. f.* damage.
—**averiar,** *v.*

averiguar /aβeri'guar/ *v.* ascertain, find out.

aversión /aβer'sion/ *n. f.* aversion.

avestruz /aβes'truθ; aβes'trus/ *n. m.* ostrich.

aviación /aβia'θion; aβia'sion/ *n. f.* aviation.

aviador /aβia'ðor/ **-ra** *n.* aviator.

ávido /'aβiðo/ *a.* avid; eager.

avión /a'βion/ *n. m.* airplane.

avisar /aβi'sar/ *v.* notify, let know; warn, advise.

aviso /a'βiso/ *n. m.* notice, announcement; advertisement; warning.

avispa /a'βispa/ *n. f.* wasp.

avivar /aβi'βar/ *v.* enliven, revive.

axila /ak'sila/ *n. f.* armpit.

aya /'aya/ *n. f.* governess.

ayatolá /aya'tola/ *n. m.* ayatollah.

ayer /a'yer/ *adv.* yesterday.

ayuda /a'yuða/ *n. f.* help, aid.
—**ayudar,** *v.*

ayudante /ayu'ðante/ *a.* assistant, helper; adjutant.

ayuno /a'yuno/ *n. m.* fast.
—**ayunar,** *v.*

ayuntamiento /ayunta'miento/ *n. m.* city hall.

azada /a'θaða; a'saða/ *n. f.*, **azadón,** *m.* hoe.

azafata /aθa'fata; asa'fata/ *n. f.* stewardess, flight attendant.

azar /a'θar; a'sar/ *n. m.* hazard, chance. **al a.,** at random.

azotar /aθo'tar; aso'tar/ *v.* whip, flog; belabor.

azote /a'θote; a'sote/ *n. m.* scourge, lash.

azúcar /a'θukar; a'sukar/ *n. m.* sugar.

azucarero /aθuka'rero; asuka'rero/ *n. m.* sugar bowl.

azúcar moreno /a'θukar mo'reno; a'sukar mo'reno/ brown sugar.

azul /a'θul; a'sul/ *a.* blue.

azulado /aθu'laðo; asu'laðo/ *a.* blue, bluish.

azulejo /aθu'leho; asu'leho/ *n. m.* tile; bluebird.

azul marino /a'θul ma'rino; a'sul ma'rino/ navy blue.

B

baba /'baβa/ *n. f.* drivel.
—**babear,** *v.*

babador /baβa'ðor, ba'βero/ *n. m.* bib.

babucha /ba'βutʃa/ *n. f.* slipper.

bacalao /baka'lao/ *n. m.* codfish.

bachiller /batʃi'ʎer; batʃi'yer/ **-ra** *n.* bachelor (degree).

bacía /ba'θia; ba'sia/ *n. f.* washbasin.

bacterias /bak'terias/ *n. f.pl.* bacteria.

bacteriología /bakteriolo'hia/ *n. f.* bacteriology.

bahía /ba'ia/ *n. f.* bay.

bailador /baila'ðor/ **-ra** *n.* dancer.

bailar /bai'lar/ *v.* dance.

bailarín /baila'rin/ **-ina** *n.* dancer.

baile /'baile/ *n. m.* dance.

baja /'baha/ *n. f.* fall (in price); *Mil.* casualty.

bajar /ba'har/ *v.* lower; descend.

bajeza /ba'heθa; ba'hesa/ *n. f.* baseness.

bajo /'baho/ *prep.* **1.** under, below. —*a.* **2.** low; short; base.

bala /'bala/ *n. f.* bullet; ball; bale.

balada /ba'laða/ *n. f.* ballad.

balancear /balanθe'ar; balanse'ar/ *v.* balance; roll, swing, sway.

balanza /ba'lanθa; ba'lansa/ *n. f.* balance; scales.

balbuceo /balβu'θeo; balβu'seo/ *n. m.* stammer; babble.
—**balbucear,** *v.*

Balcanes /bal'kanes/ *n. m.pl.* Balkans.

balcón /bal'kon/ *n. m.* balcony.

balde /'balde/ *n. m.* bucket, pail. **de b.,** gratis. **en b.,** in vain.

balística /ba'listika/ *n. f.* ballistics.

ballena /ba'ʎena; ba'yena/ *n. f.* whale.

balneario /balne'ario/ *n. m.* bathing resort; spa.

balompié /balom'pie/ *n. m.* football.

balón /ba'lon/ *n. m.* football; *Auto.* balloon tire.

baloncesto /balon'θesto; balon'sesto/ *n. m.* basketball.

balota /ba'lota/ *n. f.* ballot, vote. **—balotar,** *v.*

balsa /'balsa/ *n. f.* raft.

bálsamo /'balsamo/ *n. m.* balm.

baluarte /ba'luarte/ *n. m.* bulwark.

bambolearse /bambole'arse/ *v.* sway.

bambú /bam'βu/ *n.* bamboo.

banal /ba'nal/ *a.* banal, trite.

banana /ba'nana/ *n. f.* banana.

banano /ba'nano/ *n. m.* banana tree.

bancarrota /banka'rrota/ *n. f.* bankruptcy.

banco /'banko/ *n. m.* bank; bench; school of fish.

banco cooperativo /'banko koopera'tiβo/ credit union.

banda /'banda/ *n. f.* band.

bandada /ban'daða/ *n. f.* covey; flock.

banda sonora /'banda so'nora/ *n. f.* soundtrack.

bandeja /ban'deha/ *n. f.* tray.

bandera /ban'dera/ *n. f.* flag; banner; ensign.

bandido /ban'diðo/ **-da** *n.* bandit.

bando /'bando/ *n. m.* faction.

bandolero /bando'lero/ **-ra** *n.* bandit, robber.

banquero /ban'kero/ **-ra** *n.* banker.

banqueta /ban'keta/ *n. f.* stool; (Mex.) sidewalk.

banquete /ban'kete/ *n. m.* feast, banquet.

banquillo /ban'kiʎo; ban'kiyo/ *n. m.* stool.

bañar /ba'ɲar/ *v.* bathe.

bañera /ba'ɲera/ *n. f.* bathtub.

baño /'baɲo/ *n. m.* bath; bathroom.

bar /bar/ *n. m.* bar, pub.

baraja /ba'raha/ *n. f.* pack of cards; game of cards.

baranda /ba'randa/ *n. f.* railing, banister.

barato /ba'rato/ *a.* cheap.

barba /'barβa/ *n. f.* beard; chin.

barbacoa /barβa'koa/ *n. f.* barbecue; stretcher.

barbaridad /barβari'ðað/ *n. f.* barbarity; *Colloq.* excess (in anything).

bárbaro /'barβaro/ *a.* barbarous; crude.

barbería /barβe'ria/ *n. f.* barbershop.

barbero /bar'βero/ *n. m.* barber.

barca /'barka/ *n. f.* (small) boat.

barcaza /bar'kaθa; bar'kasa/ *n. f.* barge.

barco /'barko/ *n. m.* ship, boat.

barniz /bar'niθ; bar'nis/ *n. m.* varnish. **—barnizar,** *v.*

barómetro /ba'rometro/ *n. m.* barometer.

barón /ba'ron/ *n. m.* baron.

barquilla /bar'kiʎa; bar'kiya/ *n. f.* *Naut.* log.

barra /'barra/ *n. f.* bar.

barraca /ba'rraka/ *n. f.* hut, shed.

barrear /barre'ar/ *v.* bar, barricade.

barreno /ba'rreno/ *n. m.* blast, blasting. **—barrenar,** *v.*

barrer /ba'rrer/ *v.* sweep.

barrera /ba'rrera/ *n. f.* barrier.

barricada /barri'kaða/ *n. f.* barricade.

barriga /ba'rriga/ *n. f.* belly.

barril /ba'rril/ *n. m.* barrel; cask.

barrio /'barrio/ *n. m.* district, ward, quarter.

barro /'barro/ *n. m.* clay, mud.

base /'base/ *n. f.* base; basis. **—basar,** *v.*

base de datos /'base de 'datos/ database.

bastante /bas'tante/ *a.* **1.** enough, plenty of. **—adv. 2.** enough; rather, quite.

bastar /bas'tar/ *v.* suffice, be enough.

bastardo /bas'tarðo/ **-a** *a.* & *n.* bastard.

bastear /baste'ar/ *v.* baste.

bastidor /basti'ðor/ *n. m.* wing (in theater).

bastón /bas'ton/ *n. m.* (walking) cane.

bastos /'bastos/ *n. m.pl.* clubs (cards).

basura /ba'sura/ *n. f.* refuse, dirt; garbage; junk.
basurero /basu'rero/ **-ra** *n.* scavenger.
batalla /ba'taʎa; ba'taya/ *n. f.* battle. —**batallar,** *v.*
batallón /bata'ʎon; bata'yon/ *n. m.* batallion.
batata /ba'tata/ *n. f.* sweet potato.
bate /'bate/ *n. m.* bat. —**batear,** *v.*
batería /bate'ria/ *n. f.* battery.
batido /ba'tiðo/ *n. m.* (cooking) batter; milkshake.
batidora /bati'ðora/ *n. f.* mixer (for food).
batir /ba'tir/ *v.* beat; demolish; conquer.
baúl /ba'ul/ *n. m.* trunk.
bautismo /bau'tismo/ *n. m.* baptism.
bautista /bau'tista/ *n. m. & f.* Baptist.
bautizar /bauti'θar; bauti'sar/ *v.* christen, baptize.
bautizo /bau'tiθo; bau'tiso/ *n. m.* baptism.
baya /'baia/ *n. f.* berry.
bayoneta /bayo'neta/ *n. f.* bayonet.
beato /be'ato/ *a.* blessed.
bebé /be'βe/ *n. m.* baby.
beber /be'βer/ *v.* drink.
bebible /be'βiβle/ *a.* drinkable.
bebida /be'βiða/ *n. f.* drink, beverage.
beca /'beka/ *n. f.* grant, scholarship.
becado /be'kaðo/ **-da** *n.* scholar.
becerro /be'θerro; be'serro/ *n. m.* calf; calfskin.
beldad /bel'dað/ *n. f.* beauty.
belga /'belga/ *a. & n.* Belgian.
Bélgica /'belhika/ *f.* Belgium.
belicoso /beli'koso/ *a.* warlike.
beligerante /belihe'rante/ *a. & n.* belligerent.
bellaco /be'ʎako; be'yako/ *a.* **1.** sly, roguish. —*n.* **2.** *m.* rogue.
bellas artes /'beʎas 'artes; 'beyas 'artes/ *n. f.pl.* fine arts.
belleza /be'ʎeθa; be'yesa/ *n. f.* beauty.
bello /'beʎo; 'beyo/ *a.* beautiful.
bellota /be'ʎota; be'yota/ *n. f.* acorn.
bendecir /bende'θir; bende'sir/ *v.* bless.

bendición /bendi'θion; bendi'sion/ *n. f.* blessing, benediction.
bendito /ben'dito/ *a.* blessed.
beneficio /bene'fiθio; bene'fisio/ *n. m.* benefit. —**beneficiar,** *v.*
beneficioso /benefi'θioso; benefi'sioso/ *a.* beneficial.
benevolencia /beneβo'lenθia; beneβo'lensia/ *n. f.* benevolence.
benévolo /be'neβolo/ *a.* benevolent.
benigno /be'nigno/ *a.* benign.
beodo /be'oðo/ **-da** *a. & n.* drunk.
berenjena /beren'hena/ *n. f.* eggplant.
beso /'beso/ *n. m.* kiss. —**besar,** *v.*
bestia /'bestia/ *n. f.* beast, brute.
betabel /beta'βel/ *n. m.* beet.
Biblia /'biβlia/ *n. f.* Bible.
bíblico /'biβliko/ *a.* Biblical.
biblioteca /biβlio'teka/ *n. f.* library.
bicarbonato /bikarβo'nato/ *n. m.* bicarbonate.
bicicleta /biθi'kleta; bisi'kleta/ *n. f.* bicycle.
bien /bien/ *adv.* **1.** well. —*n.* **2.** good; (*pl.*) possessions.
bienes inmuebles /'bienes i'mueβles/ *n. m.pl.* real estate.
bienestar /bienes'tar/ *n. m.* well-being, welfare.
bienhechor /biene'tʃor/ **-ra** *n.* benefactor.
bienvenida /biembe'niða/ *n. f.* welcome.
bienvenido /biembe'niðo/ *a.* welcome.
biftec /bif'tek/ *n. m.* steak.
bifurcación /bifurka'θion; bifurka'sion/ *n. f.* fork. —**bifurcar,** *v.*
bigamia /bi'gamia/ *n. f.* bigamy.
bígamo /'bigamo/ **-a** *n.* bigamist.
bigotes /bi'gotes/ *n. m.pl.* mustache.
bikini /bi'kini/ *n. m.* bikini.
bilingüe /bi'lingue/ *a.* bilingual.
bilingüismo /biliŋ'guismo/ *n. m.* bilingualism.
bilis /'bilis/ *n. f.* bile.
billar /bi'ʎar; bi'yar/ *n. m.* billiards.
billete /bi'ʎete; bi'yete/ *n. m.* ticket; bank note, bill.
billete de banco /bi'ʎete de 'banko; bi'yete de 'banko/ bank note.

billón /bi'ʎon; bi'yon/ *n. m.* billion.

bingo /'biŋgo/ *n. m.* bingo.

biodegradable /bioðegra'ðaβle/ *a.* biodegradable.

biografía /biogra'fia/ *n. f.* biography.

biología /biolo'hia/ *n. f.* biology.

biombo /'biombo/ *n. m.* folding screen.

bisabuela /bisa'βuela/ *n. f.* great-grandmother.

bisabuelo /bisa'βuelo/ *n. m.* great-grandfather.

bisel /bi'sel/ *n. m.* bevel. —**biselar,** *v.*

bisonte /bi'sonte/ *n. m.* bison.

bisté /bis'te/ **bistec** *n. m.* steak.

bisutería /bisute'ria/ *n. f.* costume jewelry.

bizarro /bi'θarro; bi'sarro/ *a.* brave; generous; smart.

bizco /'biθko/ **-ca** *n.* **1.** cross-eyed person. —*a.* **2.** cross-eyed, squinting.

bizcocho /biθ'kotʃo; bis'kotʃo/ *n. m.* biscuit, cake.

blanco /'blanko/ *a.* **1.** white; blank. —*n.* **2.** *m.* white; target.

blandir /blan'dir/ *v.* brandish, flourish.

blando /'blando/ *a.* soft.

blanquear /blanke'ar/ *v.* whiten; bleach.

blasfemar /blasfe'mar/ *v.* blaspheme, curse.

blasfemia /blas'femia/ *n. f.* blasphemy.

blindado /blin'daðo/ *a.* armored.

blindaje /blin'dahe/ *n. m.* armor.

bloque /'bloke/ *n. m.* block. —**bloquear,** *v.*

bloqueo /blo'keo/ *n. m.* blockade. —**bloquear,** *v.*

blusa /'blusa/ *n. f.* blouse.

bobada /bo'βaða/ *n. f.* stupid, silly thing.

bobo /'boβo/ **-ba** *a. & n.* fool; foolish.

boca /'boka/ *n. f.* mouth.

bocado /bo'kaðo/ *n. m.* bit; bite, mouthful.

bocanada /boka'naða/ *n. f.* puff (of smoke); mouthful (of liquor).

bocazas /bo'kaθas/ *n. m. & f. Colloq.* bigmouth.

bochorno /bo'tʃorno/ *n. m.* sultry weather; embarrassment.

bocina /bo'θina; bo'sina/ *n. f.* horn.

boda /'boða/ *n. f.* wedding.

bodega /bo'ðega/ *n. f.* wine cellar; *Naut.* hold; (Carib.) grocery store.

bofetada /bofe'taða/ *n. f.* **bofetón,** *m.* slap.

boga /'boga/ *n. f.* vogue; fad.

bogar /bo'gar/ *v.* row (a boat).

bohemio /bo'emio/ **-a** *a. & n.* Bohemian.

boicoteo /boiko'teo/ *n. m.* boycott. —**boicotear,** *v.*

boina /'boina/ *n. f.* beret.

bola /'bola/ *n. f.* ball.

bola de nieve /'bola de 'nieβe/ snowball.

bolas de billar /'bolas de bi'ʎar; 'bolas de bi'yar/ billiard balls.

bolera /bo'lera/ *n. f.* bowling alley.

boletín /bole'tin/ *n. m.* bulletin.

boletín informativo /bole'tin informa'tiβo/ news bulletin.

boleto /bo'leto/ *n. m.* ticket. **b. de embarque,** boarding pass.

boliche /bo'litʃe/ *n. m.* bowling alley.

bolígrafo /bo'ligrafo/ *n. m.* ballpoint pen.

boliviano /boli'βiano/ **-a** *a. & n.* Bolivian.

bollo /'boʎo; 'boyo/ *n. m.* bun, loaf.

bolos /'bolos/ *n. m.pl.* bowling.

bolsa /'bolsa/ *n. f.* purse; stock exchange.

bolsa de agua caliente /'bolsa de 'agua ka'liente/ hot-water bottle.

bolsillo /bol'siʎo; bol'siyo/ *n. m.* pocket.

bomba /'bomba/ *n. f.* pump; bomb; gas station.

bombardear /bombarðe'ar/ *v.* bomb; bombard, shell.

bombear /bombe'ar/ *v.* pump.

bombero /bom'βero/ *n. m.* fireman.

bombilla /bom'βiʎa; bom'βiya/ *n. f.* (light) bulb.

bonanza /bo'nanθa; bo'nansa/ *n. f.* prosperity; fair weather.

bondad /bon'dað/ *n. f.* kindness; goodness.

bondadoso /bonda'ðoso/ *a.* kind, kindly.

bongó /boŋ'go/ *n. m.* bongo drum.

bonito /bo'nito/ *a.* pretty.

bono /'bono/ *n. m.* bonus; *Fin.* bond.

boqueada /boke'aða/ *n. f.* gasp; gape. —**boquear,** *v.*

boquilla /bo'kiʎa; bo'kiya/ *n. f.* cigarette holder.

bordado /bor'ðaðo/ *n. m.,* **bordadura,** *f.* embroidery.

bordar /bor'ðar/ *v.* embroider.

borde /'borðe/ *n. m.* border, rim, edge, brink, ledge.

borde de la carretera /'borðe de la karre'tera/ roadside.

borla /'borla/ *n. f.* tassel.

borracho /bo'rratʃo/ **-a** *a. & n.* drunk.

borrachón /borra'tʃon/ **-na** *n.* drunkard.

borrador /borra'ðor/ *n. m.* eraser.

borradura /borra'ðura/ *n. f.* erasure.

borrar /bo'rrar/ *v.* erase, rub out.

borrasca /bo'rraska/ *n. f.* squall, storm.

borrico /bo'rriko/ *n. m.* donkey.

bosque /'boske/ *n. m.* forest, wood.

bosquejo /bos'keho/ *n. m.* sketch, draft. —**bosquejar,** *v.*

bostezo /bos'teθo; bos'teso/ *n. m.* yawn. —**bostezar,** *v.*

bota /'bota/ *n. f.* boot.

botalón /bota'lon/ *n. m. Naut.* boom.

botánica /bo'tanika/ *n. f.* botany.

botar /bo'tar/ *v.* throw out, throw away.

bote /'bote/ *n. m.* boat; can, box.

bote salvavidas /'bote salβa-'βiðas/ lifeboat.

botica /bo'tika/ *n. f.* pharmacy, drugstore.

boticario /boti'kario/ *n. m.* pharmacist, druggist.

botín /bo'tin/ *n. m.* booty, plunder, spoils.

botiquín /boti'kin/ *n. m.* medicine chest.

boto /'boto/ *a.* dull, stupid.

botón /bo'ton/ *n. m.* button.

botones /bo'tones/ *n. m.* bellboy (in a hotel).

bóveda /b'oβeða/ *n. f.* vault.

boxeador /boksea'ðor/ *n. m.* boxer.

boxeo /bok'seo/ *n. m.* boxing. —**boxear,** *v.*

boya /'boya/ *n. f.* buoy.

boyante /bo'yante/ *a.* buoyant.

bozal /bo'θal; bo'sal/ *n. m.* muzzle.

bragas /'bragas/ *n. f.pl.* panties.

bramido /bra'miðo/ *n. m.* roar, bellow. —**bramar,** *v.*

brasa /'brasa/ *n. f.* embers, grill. —**brasear,** *v.*

brasileño /brasi'leɲo/ **-ña** *a. & n.* Brazilian.

bravata /bra'βata/ *n. f.* bravado.

bravear /braβe'ar/ *v.* bully.

braza /'braθa; 'brasa/ *n. f.* fathom.

brazada /bra'θaða; bra'saða/ *n. f.* (swimming) stroke.

brazalete /braθa'lete; brasa'lete/ *n. m.* bracelet.

brazo /'braθo; 'braso/ *n. m.* arm.

brea /'brea/ *n. f.* tar, pitch.

brecha /'bretʃa/ *n. f.* gap, breach.

brécol /'brekol/ *n. m.* broccoli.

bregar /bre'gar/ *v.* scramble.

breña /'breɲa/ *n. f.* rough country with brambly shrubs.

Bretaña /bre'taɲa/ *n. f.* Britain.

breve /'breβe/ *a.* brief, short. **en b.,** shortly, soon.

brevedad /breβe'ðað/ *n. f.* brevity.

bribón /bri'βon/ **-na** *n.* rogue, rascal.

brida /'briða/ *n. f.* bridle.

brigada /bri'gaða/ *n. f.* brigade.

brillante /bri'ʎante; bri'yante/ *a.* **1.** brilliant, shiny. —*n.* **2.** *m.* diamond.

brillo /'briʎo; 'briyo/ *n. m.* shine, glitter. —**brillar,** *v.*

brinco /'brinko/ *n. m.* jump; bounce, skip. —**brincar,** *v.*

brindis /'brindis/ *n. m.* toast. —**brindar,** *v.*

brío /'brio/ *n. m.* vigor.

brioso /'brioso/ *a.* vigorous, spirited.

brisa /'brisa/ *n. f.* breeze.

brisa marina /'brisa ma'rina/ sea breeze.

británico /bri'taniko/ *a.* British.

brocado /bro'kaðo/ **-da** *a. & n.* brocade.

brocha /'brotʃa/ *n. f.* brush.

broche /'brotʃe/ *n. m.* brooch, clasp, pin.

broma /'broma/ *n. f.* joke. —**bromear,** *v.*

bronca /'bronka/ *n. f. Colloq.* quarrel, row, fight.

bronce /'bronθe; 'bronse/ *n. m.* bronze; brass.

bronceador /bronθea'ðor; bronsea'ðor/ *n. m.* suntan lotion, suntan oil.

bronquitis /bron'kitis/ *n. f.* bronchitis.

brotar /bro'tar/ *v.* gush; sprout; bud.

brote /'brote/ *n. m.* bud, shoot.

bruja /'bruha/ *n. f.* witch.

brújula /'bruhula/ *n. f.* compass.

bruma /'bruma/ *n. f.* mist.

brumoso /bru'moso/ *a.* misty.

brusco /'brusko/ *a.* brusque; abrupt, curt.

brutal /bru'tal/ *a.* savage, brutal.

brutalidad /brutali'ðað/ *n. f.* brutality.

bruto /'bruto/ **-ta** *a.* **1.** brutish; ignorant. —*n.* **2.** blockhead.

bucear /buθe'ar; buse'ar/ *v.* dive.

bueno /'bueno/ *a.* good, fair; well (in health).

buey /buei/ *n. m.* ox, steer.

búfalo /'bufalo/ *n. m.* buffalo.

bufanda /bu'fanda/ *n. f.* scarf.

bufón /bu'fon/ **-ona** *a. & n.* fool, buffoon, clown.

búho /'buo/ *n. m.* owl.

buhonero /buo'nero/ *n. m.* peddler, vendor.

bujía /bu'hia/ *n. f.* spark plug.

bulevar /bule'βar/ *n. m.* boulevard.

bulimia /bu'limia/ *n. f.* bulimia.

bullicio /bu'ʎiθio; bu'yisio/ *n. m.* bustle, noise.

bullicioso /buʎi'θioso; buyi'sioso/ *a.* boisterous, noisy.

bulto /'bulto/ *n. m.* bundle; lump.

buñuelo /bu'ɲuelo/ *n. m.* bun.

buque /'buke/ *n. m.* ship.

buque de guerra /'buke de 'gerra/ warship.

buque de pasajeros /'buke de pasa'heros/ passenger ship.

burdo /'burðo/ *a.* coarse.

burgués /bur'ges/ **-esa** *a. & n.* bourgeois.

burla /'burla/ *n. f.* mockery; fun.

burlador /burla'ðor/ **-ra** *n.* trickster, jokester.

burlar /bur'lar/ *v.* mock, deride.

burlarse de /bur'larse de/ *v.* scoff at; make fun of.

burro /'burro/ *n. m.* donkey.

busca /'buska/ *n. f.* search, pursuit, quest.

buscar /bus'kar/ *v.* seek, look for; look up.

busto /'busto/ *n. m.* bust.

butaca /bu'taka/ *n. f.* armchair; *Theat.* orchestra seat.

buzo /'buθo; 'buso/ *n. m.* diver.

buzón /bu'θon; bu'son/ *n. m.* mailbox.

C

cabal /ka'βal/ *a.* exact; thorough.

cabalgar /kaβal'gar/ *v.* ride horseback.

caballeresco /kaβaʎe'resko; kaβaye'resko/ *a.* gentlemanly, chivalrous.

caballería /kaβaʎe'ria; kaβaye'ria/ *n. f.* cavalry; chivalry.

caballeriza /kaβaʎe'riθa; kaβaye'risa/ *n. f.* stable.

caballero /kaβa'ʎero; kaβa'yero/ *n. m.* gentleman; knight.

caballete /kaβa'ʎete; kaβa'yete/ *n. m.* sawhorse; easel; ridge (of roof).

caballo /ka'βaʎo; ka'βayo/ *n. m.* horse.

cabaña /ka'βaɲa/ *n. f.* cabin; booth.

cabaré /kaβa're/ *n. m.* nightclub.

cabaretero /kaβare'tero/ **-a** *n. m. & f.* nightclub owner.

cabecear /kaβeθe'ar; kaβese'ar/ *v.* pitch (as a ship).

cabecera /kaβe'θera; kaβe'sera/ *n. f.* head (of bed, table).

cabello /ka'βeʎo; ka'βeyo/ *n. m.* hair.

caber /ka'βer/ *v.* fit into, be contained in. **no cabe duda,** there is no doubt.

cabeza /ka'βeθa; ka'βesa/ *n. f.* head; warhead.

cabildo /ka'βildo/ *n. m.* city hall.

cabildo abierto /ka'βildo a'βierto/ town meeting.

cabizbajo /kaβiθ'βaho; kaβis'βaho/ *a.* downcast.

cablegrama /kaβle'grama/ *n. m.* cablegram.

cabo /'kaβo/ *n. m.* end; *Geog.* cape; *Mil.* corporal. **llevar a c.,** carry out, accomplish.

cabra /'kaβra/ *n. f.* goat.

cacahuete /kaka'uete/ *n. m.* peanut.

cacao /ka'kao/ *n. m.* cocoa; chocolate.

cacerola /kaθe'rola; kase'rola/ *n. f.* pan, casserole.

cachondeo /katʃon'deo/ *n. m.* fun, hilarity.

cachondo /ka'tʃondo/ *a.* funny; *Colloq.* horny.

cachorro /ka'tʃorro/ *n. m.* cub; puppy.

cada /'kaða/ *a.* each, every.

cadáver /ka'ðaβer/ *n. m.* corpse.

cadena /ka'ðena/ *n. f.* chain.

cadera /ka'ðera/ *n. f.* hip.

cadete /ka'ðete/ *n. m.* cadet.

caer /ka'er/ *v.* fall.

café /ka'fe/ *n. m.* coffee; café.

café exprés /ka'fe eks'pres/ espresso.

café soluble /ka'fe so'luβle/ instant coffee.

cafetal /kafe'tal/ *n. m.* coffee plantation.

cafetera /kafe'tera/ *n. f.* coffee pot.

caída /ka'iða/ *n. f.* fall, drop; collapse.

caimán /kai'man/ *n. m.* alligator.

caja /'kaha/ *n. f.* box, case; checkout counter.

caja de ahorros /'kaha de a'orros/ savings bank.

caja de cerillos /'kaha de θe-'riʎos; 'kaha de se'riyos/ matchbox.

caja de fósforos /'kaha de 'fosforos/ matchbox.

caja torácica /'kaha to'raθika; 'kaha to'rasika/ rib cage.

cajero /ka'hero/ **-ra** *n.* cashier.

cajón /ka'hon/ *n. m.* drawer.

cal /kal/ *n. f.* lime.

calabaza /kala'βaθa; kala'βasa/ *n. f.* calabash, pumpkin.

calabozo /kala'βoθo; kala'βoso/ *m.* jail, cell.

calambre /ka'lambre/ *n. m.* cramp.

calamidad /kalami'ðað/ *n. f.* calamity, disaster.

calcetín /kalθe'tin; kalse'tin/ *n. m.* sock.

calcio /'kalθio; 'kalsio/ *n. m.* calcium.

calcular /kalku'lar/ *v.* calculate, figure.

cálculo /'kalkulo/ *n. m.* calculation, estimate.

caldera /kal'dera/ *n. f.* kettle, caldron; boiler.

caldo /'kaldo/ *n. m.* broth.

calefacción /kalefak'θion; kalefak'sion/ *n. f.* heat, heating.

calendario /kalen'dario/ *n. m.* calendar.

calentar /kalen'tar/ *v.* heat, warm.

calidad /kali'ðað/ *n. f.* quality, grade.

caliente /ka'liente/ *a.* hot, warm.

calificar /kalifi'kar/ *v.* qualify.

callado /ka'ʎaðo; ka'yaðo/ *a.* silent, quiet.

callarse /ka'ʎarse; ka'yarse/ *v.* quiet down; keep still; stop talking.

calle /'kaʎe; 'kaye/ *n. f.* street.

callejón /kaʎe'hon; kaye'hon/ *n. m.* alley.

calle sin salida /'kaʎe sin sa'liða; 'kaye sin sa'liða/ dead end.

callo /'kaʎo; 'kayo/ *n. m.* callus, corn.

calma /'kalma/ *n. f.* calm, quiet.

calmado /kal'maðo/ *a.* calm.

calmante /kal'mante/ *a.* soothing, calming.

calmar /kal'mar/ *v.* calm, quiet, lull, soothe.

calor /ka'lor/ *n.* heat, warmth. **tener c.,** to be hot, warm; feel hot, warm. **hacer c.,** to be hot, warm (weather).

calorífero /kalo'rifero/ *a.* **1.** heat-producing. —*n.* **2.** *m.* radiator.

calumnia /ka'lumnia/ *n. f.* slander. —**calumniar,** *v.*

caluroso /kalu'roso/ *a.* warm, hot.

calvario /kal'βario/ *n. m.* Calvary.

calvo /'kalβo/ *a.* bald.

calzado /kal'θaðo; kal'saðo/ *n. m.* footwear.

calzar /kal'θar; kal'sar/ *v.* wear (as shoes).

calzoncillos /kalθon'θiʎos; kalson'siyos/ *n. m.pl.* shorts.

calzones /kal'θones; kal'sones/ *n. m.pl.* trousers.

cama /'kama/ *n. f.* bed.

cámara /'kamara/ *n. f.* chamber; camera.

camarada /kama'raða/ *n. m. & f.* comrade.

camarera /kama'rera/ *n. f.* chambermaid; waitress.

camarero /kama'rero/ *n. m.* steward; waiter.

camarón /kama'ron/ *n. m.* shrimp.

camarote /kama'rote/ *n. m.* stateroom, berth.

cambiar /kam'βiar/ v. exchange, change, trade; cash.

cambio /'kambio/ n. m. change, exchange. **en c.,** on the other hand.

cambista /kam'βista/ n. m. & f. money changer; banker, broker.

cambur /kam'βur/ n. m. banana.

camello /ka'meʎo; ka'meyo/ n. m. camel.

camilla /ka'miʎa; ka'miya/ n. f. stretcher.

caminar /kami'nar/ v. walk.

caminata /kami'nata/ n. f. tramp, hike.

camino /ka'mino/ n. m. road; way.

camión /ka'mion/ n. m. truck.

camisa /ka'misa/ n. f. shirt.

camisería /kamise'ria/ n. f. haberdashery.

camiseta /kami'seta/ n. f. undershirt; T-shirt.

campamento /kampa'mento/ n. m. camp.

campana /kam'pana/ n. f. bell.

campanario /kampa'nario/ n. m. bell tower, steeple.

campaneo /kampa'neo/ n. m. chime.

campaña /kam'paɲa/ n. f. campaign.

campeón /kampe'on/ -na n. champion.

campeonato /kampeo'nato/ n. m. championship.

campesino /kampe'sino/ -na n. peasant.

campestre /kam'pestre/ a. country, rural.

campo /'kampo/ n. m. field; (the) country.

campo de concentración /'kampo de konθentra'θion; 'kampo de konsentra'sion/ concentration camp.

campo de golf /'kampo de 'golf/ golf course.

Canadá /kana'ða/ n. m. Canada.

canadiense /kana'ðiense/ a. & n. Canadian.

canal /ka'nal/ n. m. canal; channel.

Canal de la Mancha /ka'nal de la 'mantʃa/ n. m. English Channel.

canalla /ka'naʎa; ka'naya/ n. f. rabble.

canario /ka'nario/ n. m. canary.

canasta /ka'nasta/ n. f. basket.

cáncer /'kanθer; 'kanser/ n. m. cancer.

cancha de tenis /'kantʃa de 'tenis/ n. f. tennis court.

canciller /kanθi'ʎer; kansi'yer/ n. m. chancellor.

canción /kan'θion; kan'sion/ n. f. song.

candado /kan'daðo/ n. m. padlock.

candela /kan'dela/ n. f. fire; light; candle.

candelero /kande'lero/ n. m. candlestick.

candidato /kandi'ðato/ -ta n. candidate; applicant.

candidatura /kandiða'tura/ n. f. candidacy.

canela /ka'nela/ n. f. cinnamon.

cangrejo /kaŋ'greho/ n. m. crab.

caníbal /ka'niβal/ n. m. cannibal.

caniche /ka'nitʃe/ n. m. poodle.

canje /'kanhe/ n. m. exchange, trade. **—canjear,** v.

cano /'kano/ a. gray.

canoa /ka'noa/ n. f. canoe.

cansado /kan'saðo/ a. tired, weary.

cansancio /kan'sanθio; kan'sansio/ n. m. fatigue.

cansar /kan'sar/ v. tire, fatigue, wear out.

cantante /kan'tante/ n. m. & f. singer.

cantar /kan'tar/ **1.** m. song. —v. **2.** sing.

cántaro /'kantaro/ n. m. pitcher.

cantera /kan'tera/ n. f. (stone) quarry.

cantidad /kanti'ðað/ n. f. quantity, amount.

cantina /kan'tina/ n. f. bar, tavern; restaurant.

canto /'kanto/ n. m. chant, song, singing; edge.

caña /'kaɲa/ n. f. cane, reed; sugar cane; small glass of beer.

cañón /ka'ɲon/ n. m. canyon; cannon; gun barrel.

caoba /ka'oβa/ n. f. mahogany.

caos /'kaos/ n. m. chaos.

caótico /ka'otiko/ a. chaotic.

capa /'kapa/ n. f. cape, cloak; coat (of paint).

capacidad /kapaθi'ðað; kapasi'ðað/ n. f. capacity; capability.

capacitar /kapaθi'tar; kapasi'tar/ v. enable.

capataz /kapa'taθ; kapa'tas/ n. m. foreman.

capaz /ka'paθ; ka'pas/ *a.* capable, able.

capellán /kape'ʎan; kape'yan/ *n. m.* chaplain.

caperuza /kape'ruθa; kape'rusa/ *n. f.* hood.

capilla /ka'piʎa; ka'piya/ *n. f.* chapel.

capital /kapi'tal/ *n.* **1.** *m.* capital. **2.** *f.* capital (city).

capitalista /kapita'lista/ *a. & n.* capitalist.

capitán /kapi'tan/ *n. m.* captain.

capitular /kapitu'lar/ *v.* yield.

capítulo /ka'pitulo/ *n. m.* chapter.

capota /ka'pota/ *n. f.* hood.

capricho /ka'pritʃo/ *n. m.* caprice; fancy, whim.

caprichoso /kapri'tʃoso/ *a.* capricious.

cápsula /'kapsula/ *n. f.* capsule.

capturar /kaptu'rar/ *v.* capture.

capucha /ka'putʃa/ *n. f.* hood.

capullo /ka'puʎo; ka'puyo/ *n. m.* cocoon.

cara /'kara/ *n. f.* face.

caracol /kara'kol/ *n. m.* snail.

carácter /ka'rakter/ *n. m.* character.

característica /karakte'ristika/ *n. f.* characteristic.

característico /karakte'ristiko/ *a.* characteristic.

caramba /ka'ramba/ mild exclamation.

caramelo /kara'melo/ *n. m.* caramel; candy.

carátula /ka'ratula/ *n. f.* dial.

caravana /kara'βana/ *n. f.* caravan.

carbón /kar'βon/ *n. m.* carbon; coal.

carbonizar /karβoni'θar; karβoni-'sar/ *v.* char.

carburador /karβura'ðor/ *n. m.* carburetor.

carcajada /karka'haða/ *n. f.* burst of laughter.

cárcel /'karθel; 'karsel/ *n. f.* prison, jail.

carcelero /karθe'lero; karse'lero/ *n. m.* jailer.

carcinogénico /karθino'heniko; karsino'heniko/ *a.* carcinogenic.

cardenal /karðe'nal/ *n. m.* cardinal.

cardiólogo /kar'ðiologo/ **-a** *m & f.* cardiologist.

carecer /kare'θer; kare'ser/ *v.* lack.

carestía /kares'tia/ *n. f.* scarcity; famine.

carga /'karga/ *n. f.* cargo; load, burden; freight.

cargar /kar'gar/ *v.* carry; load; charge.

cargo /'kargo/ *n. m.* load; charge, office.

caricatura /karika'tura/ *n. f.* caricature; cartoon.

caricaturista /karikatu'rista/ *n. m. & f.* caricaturist; cartoonist.

caricia /ka'riθia; ka'risia/ *n. f.* caress.

caridad /kari'ðað/ *n. f.* charity.

cariño /ka'riɲo/ *n. m.* affection, fondness.

cariñoso /kari'ɲoso/ *a.* affectionate, fond.

carisma /ka'risma/ *n. m.* charisma.

caritativo /karita'tiβo/ *a.* charitable.

carmesí /karme'si/ *a. & m.* crimson.

carnaval /karna'βal/ *n. m.* carnival.

carne /'karne/ *n. f.* meat, flesh; pulp.

carne acecinada /'karne aθe-θi'naða; 'karne asesi'naða/ *n. f.* corned beef.

carnero /kar'nero/ *n. m.* ram; mutton.

carnicería /karniθe'ria; karnise'ria/ *n. f.* meat market; massacre.

carnicero /karni'θero; karni'sero/ **-ra** *n.* butcher.

carnívoro /kar'niβoro/ *a.* carnivorous.

caro /'karo/ *a.* dear, costly, expensive.

carpa /'karpa/ *n. f.* tent.

carpeta /kar'peta/ *n. f.* folder; briefcase.

carpintero /karpin'tero/ *n. m.* carpenter.

carrera /ka'rrera/ *n. f.* race; career.

carrera de caballos /ka'rrera de ka'βaʎos; ka'rrera de ka'βayos/ horse race.

carreta /ka'rreta/ *n. f.* wagon, cart.

carrete /ka'rrete/ *n. m.* reel, spool.

carretera /karre'tera/ *n. f.* road, highway.

carril /ka'rril/ *n. m.* rail.

carrillo /ka'rriʎo; ka'rriyo/ *n. m.* cart (for baggage or shopping).
carro /'karro/ *n. m.* car, automobile; cart.
carroza /ka'rroθa; ka'rrosa/ *n. f.* chariot.
carruaje /ka'rruahe/ *n. m.* carriage.
carta /'karta/ *n. f.* letter; (*pl.*) cards.
cartel /kar'tel/ *n. m.* placard, poster; cartel.
cartelera /karte'lera/ *n. f.* billboard.
cartera /kar'tera/ *n. f.* pocketbook, handbag, wallet; portfolio.
cartero /kar'tero/ **(-ra)** *n.* mail carrier.
cartón /kar'ton/ *n. m.* cardboard.
cartón piedra /kar'ton 'pieðra/ *n. m.* papier-mâché.
cartucho /kar'tutʃo/ *n. m.* cartridge; cassette.
casa /'kasa/ *n. f.* house, dwelling; home.
casaca /ka'saka/ *n. f.* dress coat.
casa de pisos /'kasa de 'pisos/ apartment house.
casado /ka'saðo/ *a.* married.
casamiento /kasa'miento/ *n. m.* marriage.
casar /ka'sar/ *v.* marry, marry off.
casarse /ka'sarse/ *v.* get married. **c. con,** marry.
cascabel /kaska'βel/ *n. m.* jingle bell.
cascada /kas'kaða/ *n. f.* waterfall, cascade.
cascajo /kas'kaho/ *n. m.* gravel.
cascanueces /kaska'nueθes; kaska'nueses/ *n. m.* nutcracker.
cascar /kas'kar/ *v.* crack, break, burst.
cáscara /'kaskara/ *n. f.* shell, rind, husk.
casco /'kasko/ *n. m.* helmet; hull.
casera /ka'sera/ *n. f.* landlady; housekeeper.
caserío /kase'rio/ *n. m.* settlement.
casero /ka'sero/ *a.* **1.** homemade. —*n.* **2.** *m.* landlord, superintendent.
caseta /ka'seta/ *n. f.* cottage, hut.
casi /'kasi/ *adv.* almost, nearly.
casilla /ka'siʎa; ka'siya/ *n. f.* booth; ticket office; pigeonhole.
casimir /kasi'mir/ *n. m.* cashmere.
casino /ka'sino/ *n. m.* club; clubhouse.

caso /'kaso/ *n. m.* case. **hacer c. a,** pay attention to.
casorio /ka'sorio/ *n. m.* informal wedding.
caspa /'kaspa/ *n. f.* dandruff.
casta /'kasta/ *n. f.* caste.
castaña /kas'taɲa/ *n. f.* chestnut.
castaño /kas'taɲo/ *a.* **1.** brown. —*n.* **2.** *m.* chestnut tree.
castañuela /kasta'ɲuela/ *n. f.* castanet.
castellano /kaste'ʎano; kaste'yano/ **-na** *a.* & *n.* Castilian.
castidad /kasti'ðað/ *n. f.* chastity.
castigar /kasti'gar/ *v.* punish, castigate.
castigo /kas'tigo/ *n. m.* punishment.
castillo /kas'tiʎo; kas'tiyo/ *n. m.* castle.
castizo /kas'tiθo; kas'tiso/ *a.* pure, genuine; noble.
casto /'kasto/ *a.* chaste.
castor /kas'tor/ *n. m.* beaver.
casual /ka'sual/ *adj.* accidental, coincidental.
casualidad /kasuali'ðað/ *n. f.* coincidence. **por c.,** by chance.
casuca /ka'suka/ *n. f.* hut, shanty, hovel.
cataclismo /kata'klismo/ *n. m.* cataclysm.
catacumba /kata'kumba/ *n. f.* catacomb.
catadura /kata'ðura/ *n. f.* act of tasting; appearance.
catalán /kata'lan/ **-na** *a.* & *n.* Catalonian.
catálogo /ka'talogo/ *n. m.* catalogue. —**catalogar,** *v.*
cataputta /kata'putta/ *n. f.* catapult.
catar /ka'tar/ *v.* taste; examine, try; bear in mind.
catarata /kata'rata/ *n. f.* cataract, waterfall.
catarro /ka'tarro/ *n. m.* head cold, catarrh.
catástrofe /ka'tastrofe/ *n. f.* catastrophe.
catecismo /kate'θismo; kate'sismo/ *n. m.* catechism.
cátedra /'kateðra/ *n. f.* professorship.
catedral /kate'ðral/ *n. f.* cathedral.
catedrático /kate'ðratiko/ **-ca** *n.* professor.
categoría /katego'ria/ *n. f.* category.

categórico /kate'goriko/ a. categorical.

catequismo /kate'kismo/ n. m. catechism.

catequizar /kateki'θar; kateki'sar/ v. catechize.

cátodo /'katoðo/ n. m. cathode.

catolicismo /katoli'θismo; katoli'sismo/ n. m. Catholicism.

católico /ka'toliko/ **-ca** a. & n. Catholic.

catorce /ka'torθe; ka'torse/ a. & pron. fourteen.

catre /'katre/ n. m. cot.

cauce /'kauθe; 'kause/ n. m. riverbed; ditch.

cauchal /kau'tʃal/ n. m. rubber plantation.

caucho /'kautʃo/ n. m. rubber.

caución /kau'θion; kau'sion/ n. f. precaution; security, guarantee.

caudal /kau'ðal/ n. m. means, fortune; (pl.) holdings.

caudaloso /kauða'loso/ a. prosperous, rich.

caudillaje /kauði'ʎahe; kauði'yahe/ n. m. leadership; tyranny.

caudillo /kau'ðiʎo; kau'ðiyo/ n. m. leader, chief.

causa /'kausa/ n. f. cause.
—**causar,** v.

cautela /kau'tela/ n. f. caution.

cauteloso /kaute'loso/ n. m. cautious.

cautivar /kauti'βar/ v. captivate.

cautiverio /kauti'βerio/ n. m. captivity.

cautividad /kautiβi'ðað/ n. f. captivity.

cautivo /kau'tiβo/ **-va** a. & n. captive.

cauto /'kauto/ a. cautious.

cavar /ka'βar/ v. dig.

caverna /ka'βerna/ n. f. cavern, cave.

cavernoso /kaβer'noso/ a. cavernous.

cavidad /kaβi'ðað/ n. f. cavity, hollow.

cavilar /kaβi'lar/ v. criticize, cavil.

cayado /ka'yaðo/ n. m. shepherd's staff.

cayo /'kayo/ n. m. small rocky islet, key.

caza /'kaθa; 'kasa/ n. f. hunting, pursuit, game.

cazador /kaθa'ðor; kasa'ðor/ n. m. hunter.

cazar /ka'θar; ka'sar/ v. hunt.

cazatorpedero /kaθatorpe'ðero; kasatorpe'ðero/ n. m. torpedo-boat, destroyer.

cazo /'kaθo; 'kaso/ n. m. ladle, dipper; pot.

cazuela /ka'θuela; ka'suela/ n. f. crock.

cebada /θe'βaða; se'βaða/ n. f. barley.

cebiche /θe'bitʃe/ n. m. dish of marinated raw fish.

cebo /'θeβo; 'seβo/ n. m. bait.
—**cebar,** v.

cebolla /θe'βoʎa; se'βoya/ n. f. onion.

cebolleta /θeβo'ʎeta; seβo'yeta/ n. f. spring onion.

ceceo /θe'θeo; se'seo/ n. m. lisp.
—**cecear,** v.

cecina /θe'θina; se'sina/ n. f. dried beef.

cedazo /θe'ðaθo; se'ðaso/ n. m. sieve, sifter.

ceder /θe'ðer; se'ðer/ v. cede; transfer; yield.

cedro /'θeðro; 'seðro/ n. m. cedar.

cédula /'θeðula; 'seðula/ n. f. decree. **c. personal,** identification card.

céfiro /'θefiro; 'sefiro/ n. m. zephyr.

cegar /θe'gar; se'gar/ v. blind.

ceguedad /θege'ðað, θe'gera; sege'ðað, se'gera/ **ceguera** n. f. blindness.

ceja /'θeha; 'seha/ n. f. eyebrow.

cejar /θe'har; se'har/ v. go backwards; yield, retreat.

celada /θe'laða; se'laða/ n. f. trap; ambush.

celaje /θe'lahe; se'lahe/ n. m. appearance of the sky.

celar /θe'lar; se'lar/ v. watch carefully, guard.

celda /'θelda; 'selda/ n. f. cell.

celebración /θeleβra'θion; seleβra'sion/ n. f. celebration.

celebrante /θele'βrante; sele'βrante/ n. m. officiating priest.

celebrar /θele'βrar; sele'βrar/ v. celebrate, observe.

célebre /'θeleβre; 'seleβre/ a. celebrated, noted, famous.

celebridad /θeleβri'ðað; seleβri'ðað/ n. f. fame; celebrity; pageant.

celeridad /θeleri'ðað; seleri'ðað/ n. f. speed, rapidity.

celeste /θe'leste; se'leste/ a. celestial.

celestial /θeles'tial; seles'tial/ *a.* heavenly.

celibato /θeli'βato; seli'βato/ *n. m.* celibacy.

célibe /'θeliβe; 'seliβe/ *a.* **1.** unmarried. —*n.* **2.** *m. & f.* unmarried person.

celista /θe'lista; se'lista/ *n. m. & f.* cellist.

cellisca /θe'ʎiska; se'yiska/ *n. f.* sleet. —**cellisquear,** *v.*

celo /'θelo; 'selo/ *n. m.* zeal; (*pl.*) jealousy.

celofán /θelo'fan; selo'fan/ *n. m.* cellophane.

celosía /θelo'sia; selo'sia/ *n. f.* Venetian blind.

celoso /θe'loso; se'loso/ *a.* jealous; zealous.

céltico /'θeltiko; 'seltiko/ *a.* Celtic.

célula /'θelula; 'selula/ *n. f. Biol.* cell.

celuloide /θelu'loiðe; selu'loiðe/ *n. m.* celluloid.

cementar /θemen'tar; semen'tar/ *v.* cement.

cementerio /θemen'terio; semen'terio/ *n. m.* cemetery.

cemento /θe'mento; se'mento/ *n. m.* cement.

cena /'θena; 'sena/ *n. f.* supper.

cenagal /θena'gal; sena'gal/ *n. m.* swamp, marsh.

cenagoso /θena'goso; sena'goso/ *a.* swampy, marshy, muddy.

cenar /θe'nar; se'nar/ *v.* dine, eat.

cencerro /θen'θerro; sen'serro/ *n. m.* cowbell.

cendal /θen'dal; sen'dal/ *n. m.* thin, light cloth; gauze.

cenicero /θeni'θero; seni'sero/ *n. m.* ashtray.

ceniciento /θeni'θiento; seni'siento/ *a.* ashen.

cenit /'θenit; 'senit/ *n. m.* zenith.

ceniza /θe'niθa; se'nisa/ *n. f.* ash, ashes.

censo /'θenso; 'senso/ *n. m.* census.

censor /θen'sor; sen'sor/ *n. m.* censor.

censura /θen'sura; sen'sura/ *n. f.* reproof, censure; censorship.

censurable /θensu'raβle; sensu'raβle/ *a.* objectionable.

censurar /θensu'rar; sensu'rar/ *v.* censure, criticize.

centavo /θen'taβo; sen'taβo/ *n. m.* cent.

centella /θen'teʎa; sen'teya/ *n. f.* thunderbolt, lightning.

centellear /θenteʎe'ar; senteye'ar/ *v.* twinkle, sparkle.

centelleo /θente'ʎeo; sente'yeo/ *n. m.* sparkle.

centenar /θente'nar; sente'nar/ *n. m.* (a) hundred.

centenario /θente'nario; sente'nario/ *n. m.* centennial, centenary.

centeno /θen'teno; sen'teno/ *n. m.* rye.

centígrado /θen'tigraðo; sen'tigraðo/ *a.* centigrade.

centímetro /θenti'metro; senti'metro/ *n. m.* centimeter.

céntimo /'θentimo; 'sentimo/ *n. m.* cent.

centinela /θenti'nela; senti'nela/ *n. m.* sentry, guard.

central /θen'tral; sen'tral/ *a.* central.

centralita /θentra'lita; sentra'lita/ *n. f.* switchboard.

centralizar /θentrali'θar; sentrali'sar/ *v.* centralize.

centrar /θen'trar; sen'trar/ *v.* center.

céntrico /'θentriko; 'sentriko/ *a.* central.

centro /'θentro; 'sentro/ *n. m.* center.

centroamericano /θentroameri'kano; sentroameri'kano/ -**na** *a. & n.* Central American.

centro de mesa /'θentro de 'mesa; 'sentro de 'mesa/ centerpiece.

ceñidor /θeɲi'ðor; seɲi'ðor/ *n. m.* belt, sash; girdle.

ceñir /θe'ɲir; se'ɲir/ *v.* gird.

ceño /'θeɲo; 'seɲo/ *n. m.* frown.

ceñudo /θe'ɲuðo; se'ɲuðo/ *a.* frowning, grim.

cepa /'θepa; 'sepa/ *n. f.* stump.

cepillo /θe'piʎo; se'piyo/ *n. m.* brush; plane. —**cepillar,** *v.*

cera /'θera; 'sera/ *n. f.* wax.

cerámica /θe'ramika; se'ramika/ *n. m.* ceramics.

cerámico /θe'ramiko; se'ramiko/ *a.* ceramic.

cerca /'θerka; 'serka/ *adv.* **1.** near. —*n.* **2.** *f.* fence, hedge.

cercado /θer'kaðo; ser'kaðo/ *n. m.* enclosure; garden.

cercamiento /θerka'miento; serka'miento/ *n. m.* enclosure.

cercanía /θerka'nia; serka'nia/ *n. f.* proximity.

cercano /θer'kano; ser'kano/ *a.* near, nearby.

cercar /θer'kar; ser'kar/ *v.* surround.

cercenar /θerθe'nar; serse'nar/ *v.* clip; lessen, reduce.

cerciorar /θerθio'rar; sersio'rar/ *v.* make sure; affirm.

cerco /'θerko; 'serko/ *n. m.* hoop; siege.

cerda /'θerða; 'serða/ *n. f.* bristle.

cerdo /'θerðo; 'serðo/ **-da** *n.* hog.

cerdoso /θer'ðoso; ser'ðoso/ *a.* bristly.

cereal /θere'al; sere'al/ *a. & m.* cereal.

cerebro /θe'reβro; se'reβro/ *n. m.* brain.

ceremonia /θere'monia; sere'monia/ *n. f.* ceremony.

ceremonial /θeremo'nial; seremo'nial/ *a. & m.* ceremonial, ritual.

ceremonioso /θeremo'nioso; seremo'nioso/ *a.* ceremonious.

cereza /θe'reθa; se'resa/ *n. f.* cherry.

cerilla /θe'riʎa; se'riya/ *n. f.*, **cerillo,** *m.* match.

cerner /θer'ner; ser'ner/ *v.* sift.

cero /'θero; 'sero/ *n. m.* zero.

cerrado /θe'rraðo; se'rraðo/ *a.* closed; cloudy; obscure; taciturn.

cerradura /θerra'ðura; serra'ðura/ *n. f.* lock.

cerrajero /θerra'hero; serra'hero/ *n. m.* locksmith.

cerrar /θe'rrar; se'rrar/ *v.* close, shut.

cerro /'θerro; 'serro/ *n. m.* hill.

cerrojo /θe'rroho; se'rroho/ *n. m.* latch, bolt.

certamen /θer'tamen; ser'tamen/ *n. m.* contest; competition.

certero /θer'tero; ser'tero/ *a.* accurate, exact; certain, sure.

certeza /θer'teθa; ser'tesa/ *n. f.* certainty.

certidumbre /θerti'ðumbre; serti'ðumbre/ *n. f.* certainty.

certificado /θertifi'kaðo; sertifi'kaðo/ *n. m.* certificate.

certificado de compra /θertifi'kaðo de 'kompra; sertifi'kaðo de 'kompra/ proof of purchase.

certificar /θertifi'kar; sertifi'kar/ *v.* certify; register (a letter).

cerúleo /θe'ruleo; se'ruleo/ *a.* cerulean, sky-blue.

cervecería /θerβeθe'ria; serβese'ria/ *n. f.* brewery; beer saloon.

cervecero /θerβe'θero; serβe'sero/ *n. m.* brewer.

cerveza /θer'βeθa; ser'βesa/ *n. f.* beer.

cesante /θe'sante; se'sante/ *a.* unemployed.

cesar /θe'sar; se'sar/ *v.* cease.

césped /'θespeð; 'sespeð/ *n. m.* sod, lawn.

cesta /'θesta; 'sesta/ *n. f.*, **cesto,** *m.* basket.

cetrino /θe'trino; se'trino/ *a.* yellow, lemon-colored.

cetro /'θetro; 'setro/ *n. m.* scepter.

chabacano /tʃaβa'kano/ *a.* vulgar.

chacal /tʃa'kal/ *n. m.* jackal.

chacó /'tʃako/ *n. m.* shako.

chacona /tʃa'kona/ *n. f.* chaconne.

chacota /tʃa'kota/ *n. f.* fun, mirth.

chacotear /tʃakote'ar/ *v.* joke.

chacra /'tʃakra/ *n. f.* small farm.

chafallar /tʃafa'ʎar; tʃafa'yar/ *v.* mend badly.

chagra /'tʃagra/ *n. m.* rustic; rural person.

chal /tʃal/ *n. m.* shawl.

chalán /tʃa'lan/ *n. m.* horse trader.

chaleco /tʃa'leko/ *n. m.* vest.

chaleco salvavidas /tʃa'leko salβa'βiðas/ life jacket.

chalet /tʃa'le; tʃa'let/ *n. m.* chalet.

challí /tʃa'ʎi; tʃa'yi/ *n. m.* challis.

chamada /tʃa'maða/ *n. f.* brushwood.

chamarillero /tʃamari'ʎero; tʃamari'yero/ *n. m.* gambler.

chamarra /tʃa'marra/ *n. f.* coarse linen jacket.

chambelán /tʃambe'lan/ *n. m.* chamberlain.

champaña /tʃam'paɲa/ *n. m.* champagne.

champú /tʃam'pu/ *n. m.* shampoo.

chamuscar /tʃamus'kar/ *v.* scorch.

chancaco /tʃan'kako/ *a.* brown.

chance /'tʃanθe/ *n. m. & f.* opportunity, break.

chancear /tʃanθe'ar; tʃanse'ar/ *v.* jest, joke.

chanciller /tʃanθi'ʎer; tʃansi'yer/ *n. m.* chancellor.

chancillería /tʃanθiʎe'ria; tʃansi-ye'ria/ *n. f.* chancery.

chancla /'tʃankla/ *n. f.* old shoe.

chancleta /tʃan'kleta/ *n. f.* slipper.

chanclos /'tʃanklos/ *n. m.pl.* galoshes.

chancro /'tʃankro/ *n. m.* chancre.

changador /tʃaŋga'ðor/ *n. m.* porter; handyman.

chantaje /tʃan'tahe/ *n. m.* blackmail.

chantajista /tʃanta'hista/ *n. m. & f.* blackmailer.

chantejear /tʃantehe'ar/ *v.* blackmail.

chanto /'tʃanto/ *n. m.* flagstone.

chantre /'tʃantre/ *n. m.* precentor.

chanza /'tʃanθa; 'tʃansa/ *n. f.* joke, jest. —**chancear,** *v.*

chanzoneta /tʃanθo'neta; tʃanso'neta/ *n. f.* chansonette.

chapa /'tʃapa/ *n. f.* (metal) sheet, plate; lock.

chapado en oro /tʃa'paðo en 'oro/ *a.* gold-plated.

chapado en plata /tʃa'paðo en 'plata/ *a.* silver-plated.

chaparrada /tʃapa'rraða/ *n. f.* downpour.

chaparral /tʃapa'rral/ *n. m.* chaparral.

chaparreras /tʃapa'rreras/ *n. f.pl.* chaps.

chaparrón /tʃapa'rron/ *n. m.* downpour.

chapear /tʃape'ar/ *v.* veneer.

chapeo /tʃa'peo/ *n. m.* hat.

chapero /tʃa'pero/ *n. m. Colloq.* male homosexual prostitute.

chapitel /tʃapi'tel/ *n. m.* spire, steeple; (architecture) capital.

chapodar /tʃapo'ðar/ *v.* lop.

chapón /tʃa'pon/ *n. m.* inkblot.

chapotear /tʃapote'ar/ *v.* paddle or splash in the water.

chapoteo /tʃapo'teo/ *n. m.* splash.

chapucear /tʃapuθe'ar; tʃapuse'ar/ *v.* fumble, bungle.

chapucero /tʃapu'θero; tʃapu'sero/ *a.* sloppy, bungling.

chapurrear /tʃapurre'ar/ *v.* speak (a language) brokenly.

chapuz /tʃa'puθ; tʃa'pus/ *n. m.* dive; ducking.

chapuzar /tʃapu'θar; tʃapu'sar/ *v.* dive; duck.

chaqueta /tʃa'keta/ *n. f.* jacket, coat.

chaqueta deportiva /tʃa'keta de-por'tiβa/ sport jacket.

charada /tʃa'raða/ *n. f.* charade.

charamusca /tʃara'muska/ *n. f.* twisted candy stick.

charanga /tʃa'raŋga/ *n. f.* military band.

charanguero /tʃaraŋ'guero/ *n. m.* peddler.

charca /'tʃarka/ *n. f.* pool, pond.

charco /'tʃarko/ *n. m.* pool, puddle.

charla /'tʃarla/ *n. f.* chat; chatter, prattle. —**charlar,** *v.*

charladuría /tʃarlaðu'ria/ *n. f.* chatter.

charlatán /tʃarla'tan/ -**ana** *n.* charlatan.

charlatanismo /tʃarlata'nismo/ *n. m.* charlatanism.

charol /tʃa'rol/ *n. m.* varnish.

charolar /tʃaro'lar/ *v.* varnish; polish.

charquear /tʃarke'ar/ *v.* jerk (beef).

charquí /tʃar'ki/ *n. m.* jerked beef.

charrán /tʃa'rran/ *a.* roguish.

chascarillo /tʃaska'riʎo; tʃaska'riyo/ *n. m.* risqué story.

chasco /'tʃasko/ *n. m.* disappointment, blow; practical joke.

chasis /'tʃasis/ *n. m.* chassis.

chasquear /tʃaske'ar/ *v.* fool, trick; disappoint; crack (a whip).

chasquido /tʃas'kiðo/ *n. m.* crack (sound).

chata /'tʃata/ *n. f.* bedpan.

chatear /tʃate'ar/ *v.* chat (on the Internet).

chato /'tʃato/ *a.* flat-nosed, pugnosed.

chauvinismo /tʃauβi'nismo/ *n. m.* chauvinism.

chauvinista /tʃauβi'nista/ *n. & a.* chauvinist.

chelín /tʃe'lin/ *n. m.* shilling.

cheque /'tʃeke/ *n. m.* (bank) check.

chica /'tʃika/ *n. f.* girl.

chicana /tʃi'kana/ *n. f.* chicanery.

chicha /'tʃitʃa/ *n. f.* an alcoholic drink.

chícharo /'tʃitʃaro/ *n. f.* pea.

chicharra /tʃi'tʃarra/ *n. f.* cicada; talkative person.

chicharrón /tʃitʃa'rron/ *n. m.* crisp fried scrap of meat.

chichear /tʃitʃe'ar/ v. hiss in disapproval.

chichón /tʃi'tʃon/ n. m. bump, bruise, lump.

chicle /'tʃikle/ n. m. chewing gum.

chico /'tʃiko/ a. **1.** little. —n. **2.** m. boy.

chicote /tʃi'kote/ n. m. cigar; cigar butt.

chicotear /tʃikote'ar/ v. whip, flog.

chifladura /tʃifla'ðura/ n. f. mania; whim; jest.

chiflar /tʃi'flar/ v. whistle; become insane.

chiflido /tʃi'fliðo/ n. m. shrill whistle.

chile /'tʃile/ n. m. chili.

chileno /tʃi'leno/ **-na** a. & n. Chilean.

chillido /tʃi'ʎiðo; tʃi'yiðo/ n. m. shriek, scream, screech. —**chillar,** v.

chillón /tʃi'ʎon; tʃi'yon/ a. shrill.

chimenea /tʃime'nea/ n. f. chimney, smokestack; fireplace.

china /'tʃina/ n. f. pebble; maid; Chinese woman.

chinarro /tʃi'narro/ n. m. large pebble, stone.

chinche /'tʃintʃe/ n. f. bedbug; thumbtack.

chincheta /tʃin'tʃeta/ n. f. thumbtack.

chinchilla /tʃin'tʃiʎa; tʃin'tʃiya/ n. f. chinchilla.

chinchorro /tʃin'tʃorro/ n. m. fishing net.

chinela /tʃi'nela/ n. f. slipper.

chinero /tʃi'nero/ n. m. china closet.

chino /'tʃino/ **-na** a. & n. Chinese.

chipirón /tʃipi'ron/ n. m. baby squid.

chiquero /tʃi'kero/ n. m. pen for pigs, goats, etc.

chiquito /tʃi'kito/ **-ta** a. **1.** small, tiny. —n. **2.** m. & f. small child.

chiribitil /tʃiriβi'til/ n. m. small room, den.

chirimía /tʃiri'mia/ n. f. flageolet.

chiripa /tʃi'ripa/ n. f. stroke of good luck.

chirla /'tʃirla/ n. f. mussel.

chirle /'tʃirle/ a. insipid.

chirona /tʃi'rona/ n. f. prison, jail.

chirrido /tʃi'rriðo/ n. m. squeak, chirp. —**chirriar,** v.

chis /tʃis/ interj. hush!

chisgarabís /tʃisgara'βis/ n. meddler; unimportant person.

chisguete /tʃis'gete/ n. m. squirt, splash.

chisme /'tʃisme/ n. m. gossip. —**chismear,** v.

chismero /tʃis'mero/ **-ra** n. gossiper.

chismoso /tʃis'moso/ adj. gossiping.

chispa /'tʃispa/ n. f. spark.

chispeante /tʃispe'ante/ a. sparkling.

chispear /tʃispe'ar/ v. sparkle.

chisporrotear /tʃisporrote'ar/ v. emit sparks.

chistar /tʃis'tar/ v. speak.

chiste /'tʃiste/ n. m. joke, gag; witty saying.

chistera /tʃis'tera/ n. f. fish basket; top hat.

chistoso /tʃis'toso/ a. funny, comic, amusing.

chito /'tʃito/ interj. hush!

chiva /'tʃiβa/ n. f. female goat.

chivato /tʃi'βato/ n. m. kid, young goat.

chivo /'tʃiβo/ n. m. male goat.

chocante /tʃo'kante/ a. striking; shocking; unpleasant.

chocar /tʃo'kar/ v. collide, clash, crash; shock.

chocarrear /tʃokarre'ar/ v. joke, jest.

chochear /tʃotʃe'ar/ v. be in one's dotage.

chochera /tʃo'tʃera/ n. f. dotage, senility.

choclo /'tʃoklo/ n. m. clog; overshoe; ear of corn.

chocolate /tʃoko'late/ n. m. chocolate.

chocolate con leche /tʃoko'late kon 'letʃe/ milk chocolate.

chocolatería /tʃokolate'ria/ n. f. chocolate shop.

chofer /'tʃofer/ **chófer** n. m. chauffeur, driver.

chofeta /tʃo'feta/ n. f. chafing dish.

cholo /'tʃolo/ n. m. half-breed.

chopo /'tʃopo/ n. m. black poplar.

choque /'tʃoke/ n. m. collision, clash, crash; shock.

chorizo /tʃo'riθo; tʃo'riso/ n. m. sausage.

chorrear /tʃorre'ar/ v. spout; drip.

chorro /'tʃorro/ n. m. spout; spurt, jet. **llover a chorros,** to pour (rain).

choto /'tʃoto/ *n. m.* calf, kid.
choza /'tʃoθa; 'tʃosa/ *n. f.* hut, cabin.
chozno /'tʃoθno; 'tʃosno/ **-na** *n.* great-great-great-grandchild.
chubasco /tʃu'βasko/ *n. m.* shower, squall.
chubascoso /tʃuβas'koso/ *a.* squally.
chuchería /tʃutʃe'ria/ *n. f.* trinket, knickknack.
chucho /'tʃutʃo/ *n. m. Colloq.* mutt.
chulería /tʃule'ria/ *n. f.* pleasant manner.
chuleta /tʃu'leta/ *n. f.* chop, cutlet.
chulo /'tʃulo/ *n. m.* rascal, rogue; joker.
chupa /'tʃupa/ *n. f.* jacket.
chupada /tʃu'paða/ *n. f.* suck, sip.
chupado /tʃu'paðo/ *a.* very thin.
chupaflor /tʃupa'flor/ *n. m.* hummingbird.
chupar /tʃu'par/ *v.* suck.
churrasco /tʃu'rrasko/ *n. m.* roasted meat.
churros /'tʃuros/ *n. m.pl.* long, slender fritters.
chuscada /tʃus'kaða/ *n. f.* joke, jest.
chusco /'tʃusko/ *a.* funny, humorous.
chusma /'tʃusma/ *n. f.* mob, rabble.
chuzo /'tʃuθo; 'tʃuso/ *n. m.* pike.
CI, *abbr.* **(coeficiente intelectual)** IQ (intelligence quotient).
ciberespacio /θiβeres'paθio/ *n. m.* cyberspace.
cibernauta /θiβer'nauta/ *n. m. & f.* cybernaut.
cicatero /θika'tero; sika'tero/ *a.* stingy.
cicatriz /θika'triθ; sika'tris/ *n. f.* scar.
cicatrizar /θikatri'θar; sikatri'sar/ *v.* heal.
ciclamato /θi'klamato; si'klamato/ *n. m.* cyclamate.
ciclista /θi'klista; si'klista/ *m & f.* cyclist.
ciclo /'θiklo; 'siklo/ *n. m.* cycle.
ciclón /θi'klon; si'klon/ *n. m.* cyclone.
ciego /'θiego; 'siego/ **-ga** *a.* **1.** blind. —*n.* **2.** blind person.
cielo /'θielo; 'sielo/ *n. m.* heaven; sky, heavens; ceiling.

ciempiés /θiem'pies; siem'pies/ *n. m.* centipede.
cien /θien; sien/ **ciento** *a. & pron.* hundred. **por c.,** per cent.
ciénaga /'θienaga; 'sienaga/ *n. f.* swamp, marsh.
ciencia /'θienθia; 'siensia/ *n. f.* science.
cieno /'θieno; 'sieno/ *n. m.* mud.
científico /θien'tifiko; sien'tifiko/ **-ca** *a.* **1.** scientific. —*n.* **2.** scientist.
cierre /'θierre; 'sierre/ *n. m.* fastener, snap, clasp.
cierto /'θierto; 'sierto/ *a.* certain, sure, true.
ciervo /'θierβo; 'sierβo/ *n. m.* deer.
cierzo /'θierθo; 'sierso/ *n. m.* northerly wind.
cifra /'θifra; 'sifra/ *n. f.* cipher, number. —**cifrar,** *v.*
cigarra /θi'garra; si'garra/ *n. f.* locust.
cigarrera /θiga'rrera; siga'rrera/ **cigarrillera** *f.* cigarette case.
cigarrillo /θiga'rriʎo; siga'rriyo/ *n. m.* cigarette.
cigarro /θi'garro; si'garro/ *n. m.* cigar; cigarette.
cigüeña /θi'gueɲa; si'gueɲa/ *n. f.* stork.
cilíndrico /θi'lindriko; si'lindriko/ *a.* cylindrical.
cilindro /θi'lindro; si'lindro/ *n. m.* cylinder.
cima /'θima; 'sima/ *n. f.* summit, peak.
cimarrón /θima'rron; sima'rron/ *a.* **1.** wild, untamed. —*n.* **2.** *m.* runaway slave.
címbalo /'θimbalo; 'simbalo/ *n. m.* cymbal.
cimbrar /θim'βrar, θimbre'ar; sim-'βrar, simbre'ar/ *v.* shake, brandish.
cimientos /θi'mientos; si'mientos/ *n. m.pl.* foundation.
cinc /θink; sink/ *n. m.* zinc.
cincel /θin'θel; sin'sel/ *n. m.* chisel. —**cincelar,** *v.*
cincha /'θintʃa; 'sintʃa/ *n. f.* (harness) cinch. —**cinchar,** *v.*
cinco /'θinko; 'sinko/ *a. & pron.* five.
cincuenta /θin'kuenta; sin'kuenta/ *a. & pron.* fifty.
cine /'θine; 'sine/ *n. m.* movies; movie theater.

cíngulo /'θiŋgulo; 'siŋgulo/ *n. m.* cingulum.

cínico /'θiniko; 'siniko/ **-ca** *a.* & *n.* cynical; cynic.

cinismo /θi'nismo; si'nismo/ *n. m.* cynicism.

cinta /'θinta; 'sinta/ *n. f.* ribbon, tape; (movie) film.

cintilar /θinti'lar; sinti'lar/ *v.* glitter, sparkle.

cinto /'θinto; 'sinto/ *n. m.* belt; girdle.

cintura /θin'tura; sin'tura/ *n. f.* waist.

cinturón /θintu'ron; sintu'ron/ *n. m.* belt.

cinturón de seguridad /θintu'ron de seguri'ðað; sintu'ron de seguri'ðað/ safety belt.

ciprés /θi'pres; si'pres/ *n. m.* cypress.

circo /'θirko; 'sirko/ *n. m.* circus.

circuito /θir'kuito; sir'kuito/ *n. m.* circuit.

circulación /θirkula'θion; sirkula'sion/ *n. f.* circulation.

circular /θirku'lar; sirku'lar/ *a.* & *m.* **1.** circular. —*v.* **2.** circulate.

círculo /'θirkulo; 'sirkulo/ *n. m.* circle, club.

circundante /θirkun'dante; sirkun'dante/ *a.* surrounding.

circundar /θirkun'dar; sirkun'dar/ *v.* encircle, surround.

circunferencia /θirkunfe'renθia; sirkunfe'rensia/ *n. f.* circumference.

circunlocución /θirkunloku'θion; sirkunloku'sion/ *n.* circumlocution.

circunscribir /θirkunskri'βir; sirkunskri'βir/ *v.* circumscribe.

circunspección /θirkunspek'θion; sirkunspek'sion/ *n.* decorum, propriety.

circunspecto /θirkuns'pekto; sirkuns'pekto/ *a.* circumspect.

circunstancia /θirkuns'tanθia; sirkuns'tansia/ *n. f.* circumstance.

circunstante /θirkuns'tante; sirkuns'tante/ *n. m.* bystander.

circunvecino /θirkumbe'θino; sirkumbe'sino/ *a.* neighboring, adjacent.

cirio /'θirio; 'sirio/ *n. m.* candle.

cirrosis /θi'rrosis; si'rrosis/ *n. f.* cirrhosis.

ciruela /θi'ruela; si'ruela/ *n. f.* plum; prune.

cirugía /θiru'hia; siru'hia/ *n. f.* surgery.

cirujano /θiru'hano; siru'hano/ *n. m.* surgeon.

cisne /'θisne; 'sisne/ *n. m.* swan.

cisterna /θis'terna; sis'terna/ *n. f.* cistern.

cita /'θita; 'sita/ *n. f.* citation; appointment, date.

citación /θita'θion; sita'sion/ *n. f.* citation; (legal) summons.

citar /θi'tar; si'tar/ *v.* cite, quote; summon; make an appointment with.

cítrico /'θitriko; 'sitriko/ *a.* citric.

ciudad /θiu'ðað; siu'ðað/ *n. f.* city.

ciudadanía /θiuðaða'nia; siuðaða'nia/ *n. f.* citizenship.

ciudadano /θiuða'ðano; siuða'ðano/ **-na** *n.* citizen.

ciudadela /θiuða'ðela; siuða'ðela/ *n. f.* fortress, citadel.

cívico /'θiβiko; 'siβiko/ *a.* civic.

civil /θi'βil; si'βil/ *a.* & *n.* civil; civilian.

civilidad /θiβili'ðað; siβili'ðað/ *n. f.* politeness, civility.

civilización /θiβiliθa'θion; siβilisa'sion/ *n. f.* civilization.

civilizador /θiβiliθa'ðor; siβilisa'ðor/ *a.* civilizing.

civilizar /θiβili'θar; siβili'sar/ *v.* civilize.

cizallas /θi'θaʎas; si'sayas/ *n. f.pl.* shears. —**cizallar,** *v.*

cizaña /θi'θaɲa; si'saɲa/ *n. f.* weed; vice.

clamar /kla'mar/ *v.* clamor.

clamor /kla'mor/ *n. m.* clamor.

clamoreo /klamo'reo/ *n. m.* persistent clamor.

clamoroso /klamo'roso/ *a.* clamorous.

clandestino /klandes'tino/ *a.* secret, clandestine.

clara /'klara/ *n. f.* white (of egg).

claraboya /klara'βoya/ *n. m.* skylight; bull's-eye.

clara de huevo /'klara de 'ueβo/ egg white.

clarear /klare'ar/ *v.* clarify; become light, dawn.

clarete /kla'rete/ *n. m.* claret.

claridad /klari'ðað/ *n. f.* clarity.

clarificar /klarifi'kar/ *v.* clarify.

clarín /kla'rin/ *n. m.* bugle, trumpet.

clarinete /klari'nete/ *n. m.* clarinet.

clarividencia /klariβi'ðenθia; klariβi'ðensia/ *n. f.* clairvoyance.

clarividente /klariβi'ðente/ *a.* clairvoyant.

claro /'klaro/ *a.* clear; bright; light (in color); of course.

clase /'klase/ *n. f.* class; classroom; kind, sort.

clase nocturna /'klase nok'turna/ evening class.

clásico /'klasiko/ *a.* classic, classical.

clasificar /klasifi'kar/ *v.* classify, rank.

claustro /'klaustro/ *n. m.* cloister.

claustrofobia /klaustro'foβia/ *n. f.* claustrophobia.

cláusula /'klausula/ *n. f.* clause.

clausura /klau'sura/ *n. f.* cloister; inner sanctum; closing.

clavado /kla'βaðo/ *a.* **1.** nailed. —*n.* **2.** *m. & f.* dive.

clavar /kla'βar/ *v.* nail, peg, pin.

clave /'klaβe/ *n. f.* code; *Mus.* key.

clavel /kla'βel/ *n. m.* carnation.

clavetear /klaβete'ar/ *v.* nail.

clavícula /kla'βikula/ *n. f.* collarbone.

clavija /kla'βiha/ *n. f.* pin, peg.

clavo /'klaβo/ *n. m.* nail, spike; clove.

clemencia /kle'menθia; kle'mensia/ *n. f.* clemency.

clemente /kle'mente/ *a.* merciful.

clementina /klemen'tina/ *n. f.* tangerine.

clerecía /klere'θia; klere'sia/ *n. f.* clergy.

clerical /kleri'kal/ *a.* clerical.

clérigo /'klerigo/ *n. m.* clergyman.

clero /'klero/ *n. m.* clergy.

cliente /'kliente/ *n. m. & f.* customer, client.

clientela /klien'tela/ *n. f.* clientele, practice.

clima /'klima/ *n. m.* climate.

clímax /'klimaks/ *n. m.* climax.

clínca de reposo /'klinka de rre'poso/ convalescent home.

clínica /'klinika/ *n. f.* clinic.

clínico /'kliniko/ *a.* clinical.

clíper /'kliper/ *n. m.* clipper ship.

cloaca /klo'aka/ *n. f.* sewer.

cloquear /kloke'ar/ *v.* cluck, cackle.

cloqueo /klo'keo/ *n. m.* cluck.

cloro /'kloro/ *n. m.* chlorine.

club /kluβ/ *n. m.* club, association.

club juvenil /kluβ huβe'nil/ youth club.

clueca /'klueka/ *n. f.* brooding hen.

coacción /koak'θion; koak'sion/ *n.* compulsion.

coagular /koagu'lar/ *v.* coagulate, clot.

coágulo /ko'agulo/ *n. m.* clot.

coalición /koali'θion; koali'sion/ *n. f.* coalition.

coartada /koar'taða/ *n. f.* alibi.

coartar /koar'tar/ *v.* limit.

cobarde /ko'βarðe/ *a. & n.* cowardly; coward.

cobardía /koβar'ðia/ *n. f.* cowardice.

cobayo /ko'βayo/ *n. m.* guinea pig.

cobertizo /koβer'tiθo; koβer'tiso/ *n. m.* shed.

cobertor /koβer'tor/ *n. m.,* **cobija,** *f.* blanket.

cobertura /koβer'tura/ *n. f.* cover, wrapping.

cobijar /koβi'har/ *v.* cover; protect.

cobrador /koβra'ðor/ *n. m.* collector.

cobranza /ko'βranθa; ko'βransa/ *n. f.* collection or recovery of money.

cobrar /ko'βrar/ *v.* collect; charge; cash.

cobre /'koβre/ *n. m.* copper.

cobrizo /ko'βriθo; ko'βriso/ *a.* coppery.

cobro /'koβro/ *n. m.* collection or recovery of money.

coca /'koka/ *n. f.* coca leaves.

cocaína /koka'ina/ *n. f.* cocaine.

cocal /ko'kal/ *n. m.* coconut plantation.

cocear /koθe'ar; kose'ar/ *v.* kick; resist.

cocer /ko'θer; ko'ser/ *v.* cook, boil, bake.

coche /'kotʃe/ *n. m.* coach; car, automobile.

cochecito de niño /kotʃe'θito de 'niɲo; kotʃe'sito de 'niɲo/ baby carriage.

coche de choque /'kotʃe de 'tʃoke/ dodgem.

cochera /ko'tʃera/ *n. f.* garage.

cochero /ko'tʃero/ *n. m.* coachman; cab driver.

cochinada /kotʃi'naða/ *n. f.* filth; herd of swine.

cochino /ko'tʃino/ *n. m.* pig, swine.

cocido /ko'θiðo; ko'siðo/ *n. m.* stew.

cociente /ko'θiente; ko'siente/ *n. m.* quotient.

cocimiento /koθi'miento; kosi'miento/ *n. m.* cooking.

cocina /ko'θina; ko'sina/ *n. f.* kitchen.

cocinar /koθi'nar; kosi'nar/ *v.* cook.

cocinero /koθi'nero; kosi'nero/ **-ra** *n.* cook.

coco /'koko/ *n. m.* coconut; coconut tree.

cocodrilo /koko'ðrilo/ *n. m.* crocodile.

cóctel /kok'tel/ *n. m.* cocktail.

codazo /ko'ðaθo; ko'ðaso/ *n. m.* nudge with the elbow.

codicia /ko'ðiθia; ko'ðisia/ *n. f.* avarice, greed; lust.

codiciar /koðiθi'ar; koðisi'ar/ *v.* covet.

codicioso /koðiθi'oso; koðisi'oso/ *a.* covetous; greedy.

código /'koðigo/ *n. m.* (law) code.

codo /'koðo/ *n. m.* elbow.

codorniz /koðor'niθ; koðor'nis/ *f.* quail.

coeficiente /koefi'θiente; koefi'siente/ *n. m.* quotient.

coeficiente intelectual /koefi'θiente intelek'tual; koefi'siente intelek'tual/ intelligence quotient.

coetáneo /koe'taneo/ *a.* contemporary.

coexistir /koeksis'tir/ *v.* coexist.

cofrade /ko'fraðe/ *n. m.* fellow member of a club, etc.

cofre /'kofre/ *n. m.* coffer; chest; trunk.

coger /ko'her/ *v.* catch; pick; take.

cogote /ko'gote/ *n. m.* nape.

cohecho /ko'etʃo/ *n. m.* bribe. —**cohechar,** *v.*

coheredero /koere'ðero/ **-ra** *n.* coheir.

coherente /koe'rente/ *a.* coherent.

cohesión /koe'sion/ *n. f.* cohesion.

cohete /ko'ete/ *n. m.* firecracker; rocket.

cohibición /koiβi'θion; koiβi'sion/ *n.* restraint; repression.

cohibir /koi'βir/ *v.* restrain; repress.

coincidencia /koinθi'ðenθia; koinsi'ðensia/ *n. f.* coincidence.

coincidir /koinθi'ðir; koinsi'ðir/ *v.* coincide.

cojear /kohe'ar/ *v.* limp.

cojera /ko'hera/ *n. m.* limp.

cojín /ko'hin/ *n. m.* cushion.

cojinete /kohi'nete/ *n. m.* small cushion, pad.

cojo /'koho/ **-a** *a.* **1.** lame. —*n.* **2.** lame person.

col /kol/ *n. f.* cabbage.

cola /'kola/ *n. f.* tail; glue; line, queue. **hacer c.,** stand in line.

colaboración /kolaβora'θion; kolaβora'sion/ *n. f.* collaboration.

colaborar /kolaβo'rar/ *v.* collaborate.

cola de caballo /'kola de ka'βaʎo; 'kola de ka'βayo/ ponytail.

coladera /kola'ðera/ *n. f.* strainer.

colador /kola'ðor/ *n. m.* colander, strainer.

colapso /ko'lapso/ *n. m.* collapse, prostration.

colar /ko'lar/ *v.* strain; drain.

colateral /kolate'ral/ *a.* collateral.

colcha /'koltʃa/ *n. f.* bedspread, quilt.

colchón /kol'tʃon/ *n. m.* mattress.

colear /kole'ar/ *v.* wag the tail.

colección /kolek'θion; kolek'sion/ *n. f.* collection, set.

coleccionar /kolekθio'nar; koleksio'nar/ *v.* collect.

colecta /ko'lekta/ *n. f.* collection; collect (a prayer).

colectivo /kolek'tiβo/ *a.* collective.

colector /kolek'tor/ *n. m.* collector.

colega /ko'lega/ *n. m. & f.* colleague.

colegial /kole'hial/ *n. m.* college student.

colegiatura /kolehia'tura/ *n. f.* scholarship; tuition.

colegio /ko'lehio/ *n. m.* (private) school, college.

colegir /kole'hir/ *v.* infer, deduce.

cólera /'kolera/ *n.* **1.** *f.* rage, wrath. **2.** *m.* cholera.

colérico /ko'leriko/ *adj.* angry, irritated.

colesterol /koleste'rol/ *n. m.* cholesterol.

coleta /ko'leta/ *n. f.* pigtail; postscript.

coleto /ko'leto/ *n. m.* leather jacket.

colgado /kol'gaðo/ **-da** n. **1.**
crazy person. —a. **2.** hanging,
pending.
colgador /kolga'ðor/ n. m. rack,
hanger.
colgaduras /kolga'ðuras/ n. f.pl.
drapery.
colgante /kol'gante/ a. hanging.
colgar /kol'gar/ v. hang up, suspend.
colibrí /koli'βri/ n. m. hummingbird.
coliflor /koli'flor/ n. f. cauliflower.
coligarse /koli'garse/ v. band together, unite.
colilla /ko'liʎa; ko'liya/ n. f. butt
of a cigar or cigarette.
colina /ko'lina/ n. f. hill, hillock.
colinabo /koli'naβo/ n. m. turnip.
colindante /kolin'dante/ a. neighboring, adjacent.
colindar /kolin'dar/ v. neighbor,
abut.
coliseo /koli'seo/ n. m. theater;
coliseum.
colisión /koli'sion/ n. f. collision.
collado /ko'ʎaðo; ko'yaðo/ n. m.
hillock.
collar /ko'ʎar; ko'yar/ n. m. necklace; collar.
colmar /kol'mar/ v. heap up, fill
liberally.
colmena /kol'mena/ n. f. hive.
colmillo /kol'miʎo; kol'miyo/ n.
m. eyetooth; tusk; fang.
colmo /'kolmo/ n. m. height,
peak, extreme.
colocación /koloka'θion; koloka-
'sion/ n. f. place, position; employment, job; arrangement.
colocar /kolo'kar/ v. place, locate,
put, set.
colombiano /kolom'biano/ **-na** a.
& n. Colombian.
colon /'kolon/ n. m. colon (of
intestines).
colonia /ko'lonia/ n. f. colony;
eau de Cologne.
Colonia n. f. Cologne.
colonial /kolo'nial/ a. colonial.
colonización /koloniθa'θion;
kolonisa'sion/ n. f. colonization.
colonizador /koloniθa'ðor; kolonisa'ðor/ **-ra** n. colonizer.
colonizar /koloni'θar; koloni'sar/
v. colonize.
colono /ko'lono/ n. m. colonist;
tenant farmer.
coloquio /ko'lokio/ n. m. conversation, talk.

color /ko'lor/ n. m. color.
—**colorar,** v.
coloración /kolora'θion; kolora-
'sion/ n. f. coloring.
colorado /kolo'raðo/ a. red,
ruddy.
colorar /kolo'rar/ v. color, paint;
dye.
colorete /kolo'rete/ n. m. rouge.
colorformo /kolor'formo/ n. m.
chloroform.
colorido /kolo'riðo/ n. m. color,
coloring. —**colorir,** v.
colosal /kolo'sal/ a. colossal.
columbrar /kolum'brar/ v. discern.
columna /ko'lumna/ n. f. column,
pillar, shaft.
columpiar /kolum'piar/ v. swing.
columpio /ko'lumpio/ n. m.
swing.
coma /'koma/ n. f. coma; comma.
comadre /ko'maðre/ n. f. midwife; gossip; close friend.
comadreja /koma'ðreha/ n. f.
weasel.
comadrona /koma'ðrona/ n. f.
midwife.
comandancia /koman'danθia; ko-
man'dansia/ n. m. command;
command post.
comandante /koman'dante/ n. m.
commandant; commander; major.
comandar /koman'dar/ v. command.
comandita /koman'dita/ n. f. silent partnership.
comanditario /komandi'tario/ **-ra**
n. silent partner.
comando /ko'mando/ n. m. command.
comarca /ko'marka/ n. f. region;
border, boundary.
comba /'komba/ n. f. bulge.
combar /kom'bar/ v. bend; bulge.
combate /kom'bate/ n. m. combat. —**combatir,** v.
combatiente /komba'tiente/ a. &
m. combatant.
combinación /kombina'θion; kom-
bina'sion/ n. f. combination; slip
(garment).
combinar /kombi'nar/ v. combine.
combustible /kombus'tiβle/ a. **1.**
combustible. —n. **2.** m. fuel.
combustión /kombus'tion/ n. f.
combustion.
comedero /kome'ðero/ n. m.
trough.

comedia /ko'meðia/ *n. f.* comedy; play.

comediante /kome'ðiante/ *n. m.* actor; comedian.

comedido /kome'ðiðo/ *a.* polite, courteous; obliging.

comedirse /kome'ðirse/ *v.* to be polite or obliging.

comedor /kome'ðor/ *n. m.* dining room. **coche c.**, dining car.

comendador /komenda'ðor/ *n. m.* commander.

comensal /komen'sal/ *n. m.* table companion.

comentador /komenta'ðor/ **-ra** *n.* commentator.

comentario /komen'tario/ *n. m.* commentary.

comento /ko'mento/ *n. m.* comment. —**comentar,** *v.*

comenzar /komen'θar; komen'sar/ *v.* begin, start, commence.

comer /ko'mer/ *v.* eat, dine.

comercial /komer'θial; komer'sial/ *a.* commercial.

comercializar /komerθiali'θar; komersiali'sar/ *v.* market.

comerciante /komer'θiante; komer'siante/ **-ta** *n.* merchant, trader, businessperson.

comerciar /komer'θiar; komer'siar/ *v.* trade, deal, do business.

comercio /ko'merθio; ko'mersio/ *n. m.* commerce, trade, business; store.

comestible /komes'tiβle/ *a.* **1.** edible. —*n.* **2.** *m. (pl.)* groceries, provisions.

cometa /ko'meta/ *n.* **1.** *m.* comet. **2.** *f.* kite.

cometer /kome'ter/ *v.* commit.

cometido /kome'tiðo/ *n. m.* commission; duty; task.

comezón /kome'θon; kome'son/ *n. f.* itch.

comicios /ko'miθios; ko'misios/ *n. m.pl.* primary elections.

cómico /'komiko/ **-ca** *a. & n.* comic, comical; comedian.

comida /ko'miða/ *n. f.* food; dinner; meal.

comidilla /komi'ðiʎa; komi'ðiya/ *n. f.* light meal; gossip.

comienzo /ko'mienθo; ko'mienso/ *n. m.* beginning.

comilitona /komili'tona/ *n. f.* spread, feast.

comillas /ko'miʎas; ko'miyas/ *n. f.pl.* quotation marks.

comilón /komi'lon/ **-na** *n.* glutton; heavy eater.

comisario /komi'sario/ *n. m.* commissary.

comisión /komi'sion/ *n. f.* commission. —**comisionar,** *v.*

comisionado /komisio'naðo/ **-da** *n.* agent, commissioner.

comisionar /komisio'nar/ *v.* commission.

comiso /ko'miso/ *n. m.* (law) confiscation of illegal goods.

comistrajo /komis'traho/ *n. m.* mess, hodgepodge.

comité /komi'te/ *n. m.* committee.

comitiva /komi'tiβa/ *n. f.* retinue.

como /'komo/ *conj. & adv.* like, as.

cómo *adv.* how.

cómoda /'komoða/ *n. f.* bureau, chest (of drawers).

cómodamente /komoða'mente/ *adv.* conveniently.

comodidad /komoði'ðað/ *n. f.* convenience, comfort; commodity.

comodín /komo'ðin/ *n. m.* joker (playing card).

cómodo /'komoðo/ *a.* comfortable; convenient.

comodoro /komo'ðoro/ *n. m.* commodore.

compacto /kom'pakto/ *a.* compact.

compadecer /kompaðe'θer; kompaðe'ser/ *v.* be sorry for, pity.

compadraje /kompa'ðrahe/ *n. m.* clique.

compadre /kom'paðre/ *n. m.* close friend.

compaginar /kompahi'nar/ *v.* put in order; arrange.

compañerismo /kompaɲe'rismo/ *n. m.* companionship.

compañero /kompa'ɲero/ **-ra** *n.* companion, partner.

compañía /kompa'ɲia/ *n. f.* company.

comparable /kompa'raβle/ *a.* comparable.

comparación /kompara'θion; kompara'sion/ *n. f.* comparison.

comparar /kompa'rar/ *v.* compare.

comparativamente /komparatiβa'mente/ *adv.* comparatively.

comparativo /kompara'tiβo/ *a.* comparative.

comparecer /kompare'θer; kompare'ser/ *v.* appear.

comparendo /kompa'rendo/ *n. m.* summons.

comparsa /kom'parsa/ *n. f.* carnival masquerade; retinue.

compartimiento /komparti'miento/ *n. m.* compartment.

compartir /kompar'tir/ *v.* share.

compás /kom'pas/ *n. m.* compass; beat, rhythm.

compasar /kompa'sar/ *v.* measure exactly.

compasión /kompa'sion/ *n. f.* compassion.

compasivo /kompa'siβo/ *a.* compassionate.

compatibilidad /kompatiβili'ðað/ *n. f.* compatibility.

compatible /kompa'tiβle/ *a.* compatible.

compatriota /kompa'triota/ *n. m. & f.* compatriot.

compeler /kompe'ler/ *v.* compel.

compendiar /kompen'diar/ *v.* summarize; abridge.

compendiariamente /kompendiaria'mente/ *adv.* briefly.

compendio /kom'pendio/ *n. m.* summary; abridgment.

compendiosamente /kompendiosa'mente/ *adv.* briefly.

compensación /kompensa'θion; kompensa'sion/ *n. f.* compensation.

compensar /kompen'sar/ *v.* compensate.

competencia /kompe'tenθia; kompe'tensia/ *n. f.* competence; competition.

competente /kompe'tente/ *a.* competent.

competentemente /kompetente'mente/ *adv.* competently.

competición /kompeti'θion; kompeti'sion/ *n. f.* competition.

competidor /kompeti'ðor/ **-ra** *a. & n.* competitive; competitor.

competir /kompe'tir/ *v.* compete.

compilación /kompila'θion; kompila'sion/ *n. f.* compilation.

compilar /kompi'lar/ *v.* compile.

compinche /kom'pintʃe/ *n. m.* pal.

complacencia /kompla'θenθia; kompla'sensia/ *n. f.* complacency.

complacer /kompla'θer; kompla'ser/ *v.* please, oblige, humor.

complaciente /kompla'θiente; kompla'siente/ *a.* pleasing, obliging.

complejidad /komplehi'ðað/ *n. f.* complexity.

complejo /kom'pleho/ **-ja** *a. & n.* complex.

complemento /komple'mento/ *n. m.* complement; *Gram.* object.

completamente /kompleta'mente/ *adv.* completely.

completamiento /kompleta'miento/ *n. m.* completion, finish.

completar /komple'tar/ *v.* complete.

completo /kom'pleto/ *a.* complete, full, perfect.

complexión /komplek'sion/ *n. f.* nature, temperament.

complicación /komplika'θion; komplika'sion/ *n. f.* complication.

complicado /kompli'kaðo/ *a.* complicated.

complicar /kompli'kar/ *v.* complicate.

cómplice /'kompliθe; 'komplise/ *n. m. & f.* accomplice, accessory.

complicidad /kompliθi'ðað; komplisi'ðað/ *n. f.* complicity.

complot /kom'plot/ *n. m.* conspiracy.

componedor /kompone'ðor/ **-ra** *n.* typesetter.

componenda /kompo'nenda/ *n. f.* compromise; settlement.

componente /kompo'nente/ *a. & m.* component.

componer /kompo'ner/ *v.* compose; fix, repair.

componible /kompo'niβle/ *a.* reparable.

comportable /kompor'taβle/ *a.* endurable.

comportamiento /komporta'miento/ *n. m.* behavior.

comportarse /kompor'tarse/ *v.* behave.

comporte /kom'porte/ *n. m.* behavior.

composición /komposi'θion; komposi'sion/ *n. f.* composition.

compositivo /komposi'tiβo/ *a.* synthetic; composite.

compositor /komposi'tor/ **-ra** *n.* composer.

compost /kom'post/ *n. m.* compost.

compostura /kompos'tura/ *n. f.* composure; repair; neatness.

compota /kom'pota/ *n. f.* (fruit) sauce.

compra /'kompra/ *n. f.* purchase.
ir de compras, to go shopping.

comprador /kompraˈðor/ **-ra** n.
buyer, purchaser.

comprar /komˈprar/ v. buy, purchase.

comprender /komprenˈder/ v.
comprehend, understand; include,
comprise.

comprensibilidad /komprensiβiliˈðað/ n. f. comprehensibility.

comprensible /komprenˈsiβle/ a.
understandable.

comprensión /komprenˈsion/ n. f.
comprehension, understanding.

comprensivo /komprenˈsiβo/ n.
m. comprehensive.

compresa /komˈpresa/ n. f. medical compress.

compresión /kompreˈsion/ n. f.
compression.

comprimir /kompriˈmir/ v. compress; restrain, control.

comprobación /komproβaˈθion;
komproβaˈsion/ n. f. proof.

comprobante /komproˈβante/ a.
1. proving. —n. **2.** m. proof.

comprobar /komproˈβar/ v. prove;
verify, check.

comprometer /kompromeˈter/ v.
compromise.

comprometerse /komprometerˈse/ v. become engaged.

compromiso /komproˈmiso/ n. m.
compromise; engagement.

compuerta /komˈpuerta/ n. f.
floodgate.

compuesto /komˈpuesto/ n. m.
composition; compound.

compulsión /kompulˈsion/ n. f.
compulsion.

compulsivo /kompulˈsiβo/ a. compulsive.

compunción /kompunˈθion; kompunˈsion/ n. f. compunction.

compungirse /kompunˈɟirse/ v.
regret, feel remorse.

computación /komputaˈθion;
komputaˈsion/ n. f. computation.

computador /komputaˈðor/ n. m.
computer.

computadora de sobremesa
/komputaˈðora de soβreˈmesa/ n.
f. desktop computer.

computadora doméstica /komputaˈðora doˈmestika/ n. f. home
computer.

computar /komputar/ v. compute.

cómputo /ˈkomputo/ n. m. computation.

comulgar /komulˈgar/ v. take
communion.

comulgatorio /komulgaˈtorio/ n.
m. communion altar.

común /koˈmun/ a. common,
usual.

comunal /komuˈnal/ a. communal.

comunero /komuˈnero/ n. m.
commoner.

comunicable /komuniˈkaβle/ a.
communicable.

comunicación /komunikaˈθion;
komunikaˈsion/ n. f. communication.

comunicante /komuniˈkante/ n.
m. & f. communicant.

comunicar /komuniˈkar/ v. communicate; convey.

comunicativo /komunikaˈtiβo/ a.
communicative.

comunidad /komuniˈðað/ n. f.
community.

comunión /komuˈnion/ n. f. communion.

comunismo /komuˈnismo/ n. m.
communism.

comunista /komuˈnista/ a. & n.
communistic; communist.

comúnmente /komuˈmente/ adv.
commonly; usually; often.

con /kon/ prep. with.

concavidad /konkaβiˈðað/ n. f.
concavity.

cóncavo /ˈkonkaβo/ a. **1.** concave.
—n. **2.** m. concavity.

concebible /konθeˈβiβle; konseˈβiβle/ a. conceivable.

concebir /konθeˈβir; konseˈβir/ v.
conceive.

conceder /konθeˈðer; konseˈðer/
v. concede.

concejal /konθeˈhal; konseˈhal/ n.
m. councilman.

concejo /konˈθeho; konˈseho/ n.
m. city council.

concento /konˈθento; konˈsento/
n. m. harmony (of singing
voices).

concentración /konθentraˈθion;
konsentraˈsion/ n. f. concentration.

concentrar /konθenˈtrar; konsenˈtrar/ v. concentrate.

concepción /konθepˈθion; konsepˈsion/ n. f. conception.

conceptible /konθepˈtiβle; konsepˈtiβle/ a. conceivable.

concepto /konˈθepto; konˈsepto/
n. m. concept; opinion.

concerniente /konθer'niente; konser'niente/ *a.* concerning.

concernir /konθer'nir; konser'nir/ *v.* concern.

concertar /konθer'tar; konser'tar/ *v.* arrange.

concertina /konθer'tina; konser'tina/ *n. f.* concertina.

concesión /konθe'sion; konse'sion/ *n. f.* concession.

concha /'kontʃa/ *n. f. S.A.* shell.

conciencia /kon'θienθia; kon'siensia/ *n. f.* conscience; consciousness; conscientiousness.

concienzudo /konθien'θuðo; konsien'suðo/ *a.* conscientious.

concierto /kon'θierto; kon'sierto/ *n. m.* concert.

conciliación /konθilia'θion; konsilia'sion/ *n. f.* conciliation.

conciliador /konθilia'ðor; konsilia'ðor/ **-ra** *n.* conciliator.

conciliar /konθi'liar; konsi'liar/ *v.* conciliate.

concilio /kon'θilio; kon'silio/ *n. m.* council.

concisión /konθi'sion; konsi'sion/ *n. f.* conciseness.

conciso /kon'θiso; kon'siso/ *a.* concise.

concitar /konθi'tar; konsi'tar/ *v.* instigate, stir up.

conciudadano /konθiuða'ðano; konsiuða'ðano/ **-na** *n.* fellow citizen.

concluir /kon'kluir/ *v.* conclude.

conclusión /konklu'sion/ *n. f.* conclusion.

conclusivo /konklu'siβo/ *a.* conclusive.

concluso /kon'kluso/ *a.* concluded; closed.

concluyentemente /konkluyente'mente/ *adv.* conclusively.

concomitante /konkomi'tante/ *a.* concomitant, attendant.

concordador /konkorða'ðor/ **-ra** *n.* moderator; conciliator.

concordancia /konkor'ðanθia; konkor'ðansia/ *n. f.* agreement, concord.

concordar /konkor'ðar/ *v.* agree; put or be in accord.

concordia /kon'korðia/ *n. f.* concord, agreement.

concretamente /konkreta'mente/ *adv.* concretely.

concretar /konkre'tar/ *v.* summarize; make concrete.

concretarse /konkre'tarse/ *v.* limit oneself to.

concreto /kon'kreto/ *a. & m.* concrete.

concubina /konku'βina/ *n. f.* concubine, mistress.

concupiscente /konkupis'θente; konkupis'sente/ *a.* lustful.

concurrencia /konku'rrenθia; konku'rrensia/ *n. f.* assembly; attendance; competition.

concurrente /konku'rrente/ *a.* concurrent.

concurrido /konku'rriðo/ *a.* heavily attended or patronized.

concurrir /konku'rrir/ *v.* concur; attend.

concurso /kon'kurso/ *n. m.* contest, competition; meeting.

conde /'konde/ *n. m.* (title) count.

condecente /konde'θente; konde'sente/ *a.* appropriate, proper.

condecoración /kondekora'θion; kondekora'sion/ *n. f.* decoration; medal; badge.

condecorar /kondeko'rar/ *v.* decorate with a medal.

condena /kon'dena/ *n. f.* prison sentence.

condenación /kondena'θion; kondena'sion/ *n. f.* condemnation.

condenar /konde'nar/ *v.* condemn; damn; sentence.

condensación /kondensa'θion; kondensa'sion/ *n. f.* condensation.

condensar /konden'sar/ *v.* condense.

condesa /kon'desa/ *n. f.* countess.

condescendencia /kondesθen'denθia; kondessen'densia/ *n. f.* condescension.

condescender /kondesθen'der; kondessen'der/ *v.* condescend, deign.

condescendiente /kondesθen'diente; kondessen'diente/ *a.* condescending.

condición /kondi'θion; kondi'sion/ *n. f.* condition.

condicional /kondiθio'nal; kondisio'nal/ *a.* conditional.

condicionalmente /kondiθional'mente; kondisional'mente/ *adv.* conditionally.

condimentar /kondimen'tar/ *v.* season, flavor.

condimento /kondi'mento/ *n. m.* condiment, seasoning, dressing.

condiscípulo /kondis'θipulo; kondis'sipulo/ **-la** n. schoolmate.

condolencia /kondo'lenθia; kondo'lensia/ n. f. condolence, sympathy.

condolerse de /kondo'lerse de/ v. sympathize with.

condominio /kondo'minio/ n. m. condominium.

condómino /kon'domino/ n. m. co-owner.

condonar /kondo'nar/ v. condone.

cóndor /'kondor/ n. m. condor (bird).

conducción /konduk'θion; konduk'sion/ n. f. conveyance.

conducente /kondu'θente; kondu'sente/ a. conducive.

conducir /kondu'θir; kondu'sir/ v. conduct, escort, lead; drive.

conducta /kon'dukta/ n. f. conduct, behavior.

conducto /kon'dukto/ n. m. pipe, conduit; sewer.

conductor /konduk'tor/ **-ra** n. driver; conductor.

conectar /konek'tar/ v. connect.

conejera /kone'hera/ n. f. rabbit warren; place of ill repute.

conejillo de Indias /kone'hiʎo de 'indias; kone'hiyo de 'indias/ guinea pig.

conejo /ko'neho/ **-ja** n. rabbit.

conexión /konek'sion/ n. f. connection; coupling.

conexivo /konek'siβo/ a. connective.

conexo /ko'nekso/ a. connected, united.

confalón /konfa'lon/ n. m. ensign, standard.

confección /konfek'θion; konfek'sion/ n. f. workmanship; ready-made article; concoction.

confeccionar /konfekθio'nar; konfeksio'nar/ v. concoct.

confederación /konfeðera'θion; konfeðera'sion/ n. f. confederation.

confederado /konfeðe'raðo/ **-da** a. & n. confederate.

confederar /konfeðe'rar/ v. confederate, unite, ally.

conferencia /konfe'renθia; konfe'rensia/ n. f. lecture; conference. **c. interurbana,** long-distance call.

conferenciante /konferen'θiante; konferen'siante/ n. m. & f. lecturer, speaker.

conferenciar /konferen'θiar; konferen'siar/ v. confer.

conferencista /konferen'θista; konferen'sista/ n. m. & f. lecturer, speaker.

conferir /konfe'rir/ v. confer.

confesar /konfe'sar/ v. confess.

confesión /konfe'sion/ n. f. confession.

confesionario /konfesio'nario, konfeso'nario/ n. m. confessional.

confesor /konfe'sor/ **-ra** n. confessor.

confeti /kon'feti/ n. m.pl. confetti.

confiable /kon'fiaβle/ a. dependable.

confiado /kon'fiaðo/ a. confident; trusting.

confianza /kon'fianθa; kon'fiansa/ n. f. confidence, trust, faith.

confiar /kon'fiar/ v. entrust; trust, rely.

confidencia /konfi'ðenθia; konfi'ðensia/ n. f. confidence, secret.

confidencial /konfiðen'θial; konfiðen'sial/ a. confidential.

confidente /konfi'ðente/ n. m. & f. confidant.

confidentemente /konfiðente'mente/ adv. confidently.

confín /kon'fin/ n. m. confine.

confinamiento /konfina'miento/ n. m. confinement.

confinar /konfi'nar/ v. confine, imprison; border on.

confirmación /konfirma'θion; konfirma'sion/ n. f. confirmation.

confirmar /konfir'mar/ v. confirm.

confiscación /konfiska'θion; konfiska'sion/ n. f. confiscation.

confiscar /konfis'kar/ v. confiscate.

confitar /konfi'tar/ v. sweeten; make into candy or jam.

confite /kon'fite/ n. m. candy.

confitería /konfite'ria/ n. f. confectionery; candy store.

confitura /konfi'tura/ n. f. confection.

conflagración /konflagra'θion; konflagra'sion/ n. f. conflagration.

conflicto /kon'flikto/ n. m. conflict.

confluencia /kon'fluenθia; kon'fluensia/ n. f. confluence, junction.

confluir /kon'fluir/ v. flow into each other.

conformación /konforma'θion;

konforma'sion/ *n. f.* conformation.

conformar /konfor'mar/ *v.* conform.

conforme /kon'forme/ *a.* **1.** acceptable, right, as agreed; in accordance, in agreement. —*conj.* **2.** according, as.

conformidad /konformi'ðað/ *n. f.* conformity; agreement.

conformismo /konfor'mismo/ *n. m.* conformism.

conformista /konfor'mista/ *n. m. & f.* conformist.

confortar /konfor'tar/ *v.* comfort.

confraternidad /konfraterni'ðað/ *n. f.* brotherhood, fraternity.

confricar /konfri'kar/ *v.* rub vigorously.

confrontación /konfronta'θion; konfronta'sion/ *n. f.* confrontation.

confrontar /konfron'tar/ *v.* confront.

confucianismo /konfuθia'nismo; konfusia'nismo/ *n. m.* Confucianism.

confundir /konfun'dir/ *v.* confuse; puzzle, mix up.

confusamente /konfusa'mente/ *adv.* confusedly.

confusión /konfu'sion/ *n. f.* confusion, mix-up; clutter.

confuso /kon'fuso/ *a.* confused; confusing.

confutación /konfuta'θion; konfuta'sion/ *n. f.* disproof.

confutar /konfu'tar/ *v.* refute, disprove.

congelable /konge'laβle/ *a.* congealable.

congelación /konhela'θion; konhela'sion/ *n. f.* congealment; deep freeze.

congelado /konge'laðo/ *a.* frozen, congealed.

congelar /konhe'lar/ *v.* congeal, freeze.

congenial /konge'nial/ *a.* congenial; analogous.

congeniar /konhe'niar/ *v.* be congenial.

congestión /konhes'tion/ *n. f.* congestion.

conglomeración /konglomera-'θion; konglomera'sion/ *n. f.* conglomeration.

congoja /kon'goha/ *n. f.* grief, anguish.

congraciamiento /kongraθia-'miento; kongrasia'miento/ *n. m.* flattery; ingratiation.

congraciar /kongra'θiar; kongra-'siar/ *v.* flatter; ingratiate oneself.

congratulación /kongratula'θion; kongratula'sion/ *n. f.* congratulation.

congratular /kongratu'lar/ *v.* congratulate.

congregación /kongrega'θion; kongrega'sion/ *n. f.* congregation.

congregar /kongre'gar/ *v.* congregate.

congresista /kongre'sista/ *n. m. & f.* congressional representative.

congreso /kon'greso/ *n. m.* congress; conference.

conjetura /konhe'tura/ *n. f.* conjecture. —**conjeturar,** *v.*

conjetural /konhetu'ral/ *a.* conjectural.

conjugación /konhuga'θion; konhuga'sion/ *n. f.* conjugation.

conjugar /konhu'gar/ *v.* conjugate.

conjunción /konhun'θion; konhun'sion/ *n. f.* union; conjunction.

conjuntamente /konhunta'mente/ *adv.* together, jointly.

conjunto. /kon'hunto/ *a.* **1.** joint, unified. —*n.* **2.** *m.* whole.

conjuración /konhura'θion; konhura'sion/ *n. f.* conspiracy, plot.

conjurado /konhu'raðo/ **-da** *n.* conspirator, plotter.

conjurar /konhu'rar/ *v.* conjure.

conjuro /kon'huro/ *n. m.* exorcism; spell; plea.

conllevador /konʎeβa'ðor; konyeβa'ðor/ *n. m.* helper, aide.

conmemoración /komemora'θion; komemora'sion/ *n. f.* commemoration; remembrance.

conmemorar /komemo'rar/ *v.* commemorate.

conmemorativo /komemora'tiβo/ *a.* commemorative, memorial.

conmensal /komen'sal/ *n. m.* messmate.

conmigo /ko'migo/ *adv.* with me.

conmilitón /komili'ton/ *n. m.* fellow soldier.

conminación /komina'θion; komina'sion/ *n. f.* threat, warning.

conminar /komi'nar/ *v.* threaten.

conminatorio /komina'torio/ *a.* threatening, warning.

conmiseración /komisera'θion; komisera'sion/ n. f. sympathy.

conmoción /komo'θion; komo-'sion/ n. f. commotion, stir.

conmovedor /komoβe'ðor/ a. moving, touching.

conmover /komo'βer/ v. move, affect, touch.

conmutación /komuta'θion; komuta'sion/ n. f. commutation.

conmutador /komuta'ðor/ n. m. electric switch.

conmutar /komu'tar/ v. exchange.

connatural /konnatu'ral/ a. innate, inherent.

connotación /konnota'θion; konnota'sion/ n. f. connotation.

connotar /konno'tar/ v. connote.

connubial /konnu'βial/ a. connubial.

connubio /ko'nnuβio/ n. m. matrimony.

cono /'kono/ n. m. cone.

conocedor /konoθe'ðor; konose'ðor/ -ra n. expert, connoisseur.

conocer /kono'θer; kono'ser/ v. know, be acquainted with; meet, make the acquaintance of.

conocible /kono'θiβle; kono'siβle/ a. knowable.

conocido /kono'θiðo; kono'siðo/ -da a. **1.** familiar, well-known. —n. **2.** acquaintance, person known.

conocimiento /konoθi'miento; konosi'miento/ n. m. knowledge, acquaintance; consciousness.

conque /'konke/ conj. so then; and so.

conquista /kon'kista/ n. f. conquest.

conquistador /konkista'ðor/ -ra n. conqueror.

conquistar /konkis'tar/ v. conquer.

consabido /konsa'βiðo/ a. aforesaid.

consagración /konsagra'θion; konsagra'sion/ n. f. consecration.

consagrado /konsa'graðo/ a. consecrated.

consagrar /konsa'grar/ v. consecrate, dedicate, devote.

consanguinidad /konsaŋguini-'ðað/ n. f. consanguinity.

consciente /kons'θiente; kons-'siente/ a. conscious, aware.

conscientemente /konsθiente-'mente; konssiente'mente/ adv. consciously.

conscripción /konskrip'θion; konskrip'sion/ n. f. conscription for military service.

consecución /konseku'θion; konseku'sion/ n. f. attainment.

consecuencia /konse'kuenθia; konse'kuensia/ n. f. consequence.

consecuente /konse'kuente/ a. consequent; consistent.

consecuentemente /konsekuente'mente/ adv. consequently.

consecutivamente /konsekutiβa'mente/ adv. consecutively.

consecutivo /konseku'tiβo/ a. consecutive.

conseguir /konse'gir/ v. obtain, get, secure; succeed in, manage to.

conseja /kon'seha/ n. f. fable.

consejero /konse'hero/ -ra n. adviser, counselor.

consejo /kon'seho/ n. m. council; counsel; (piece of) advice. **c. de redacción,** editorial board.

consenso /kon'senso/ n. m. consensus.

consentido /konsen'tiðo/ a. spoiled, bratty.

consentimiento /konsenti'miento/ n. m. consent.

consentir /konsen'tir/ v. allow, permit.

conserje /kon'serhe/ n. m. superintendent, keeper.

conserva /kon'serβa/ n. f. conserve, preserve.

conservación /konserβa'θion; konserβa'sion/ n. f. conservation.

conservador /konserβa'ðor/ -ra a. & n. conservative.

conservar /konser'βar/ v. conserve.

conservativo /konserβa'tiβo/ a. conservative, preservative.

conservatorio /konserβa'torio/ n. m. conservatory.

considerable /konsiðe'raβle/ a. considerable, substantial.

considerablemente /konsiðeraβle'mente/ adv. considerably.

consideración /konsiðera'θion; konsiðera'sion/ n. f. consideration.

consideradamente /konsiðeraða'mente/ adv. considerably.

considerado /konsiðe'raðo/ a. considerate; considered.

considerando /konsiðe'rando/ *conj.* whereas.

considerar /konsiðe'rar/ *v.* consider.

consigna /kon'signa/ *n. f.* watchword.

consignación /konsigna'θion; konsigna'sion/ *n. f.* consignment.

consignar /konsig'nar/ *v.* consign.

consignatorio /konsigna'torio/ **-ria** *n.* consignee; trustee.

consigo /kon'sigo/ *adv.* with herself, with himself, with oneself, with themselves, with yourself, with yourselves.

consiguiente /konsi'giente/ *a.* **1.** consequent. —*n.* **2.** *m.* consequence.

consiguientemente /konsigiente'mente/ *adv.* consequently.

consistencia /konsis'tenθia; konsis'tensia/ *n. f.* consistency.

consistente /konsis'tente/ *a.* consistent.

consistir /konsis'tir/ *v.* consist.

consistorio /konsis'torio/ *n. m.* consistory.

consocio /kon'soθio; kon'sosio/ *n. m.* associate; partner; comrade.

consola /kon'sola/ *n. f.* console.

consolación /konsola'θion; konsola'sion/ *n. f.* consolation.

consolar /konso'lar/ *v.* console.

consolativo /konsola'tiβo/ *a.* consolatory.

consolidación /konsoliða'θion; konsoliða'sion/ *n.* consolidation.

consolidado /konsoli'ðaðo/ *a.* consolidated.

consolidar /konsoli'ðar/ *v.* consolidate.

consonancia /konso'nanθianb; konso'nansia/ *n. f.* agreement, accord, harmony.

consonante /konso'nante/ *a. & f.* consonant.

consonar /konso'nar/ *v.* rhyme.

consorte /kon'sorte/ *n. m. & f.* consort, mate.

conspicuo /kons'pikuo/ *a.* conspicuous.

conspiración /konspira'θion; konspira'sion/ *n. f.* conspiracy, plot.

conspirador /konspira'ðor/ **-ra** *n.* conspirator.

conspirar /konspi'rar/ *v.* conspire, plot.

constancia /kons'tanθia; kons'tansia/ *n. f.* perseverance; record.

constante /kons'tante/ *a.* constant.

constantemente /konstante'mente/ *adv.* constantly.

constar /kons'tar/ *v.* consist; be clear, be on record.

constelación /konstela'θion; konstela'sion/ *n. f.* constellation.

consternación /konsterna'θion; konsterna'sion/ *n. f.* consternation.

consternar /konster'nar/ *v.* dismay.

constipación /konstipa'θion; konstipa'sion/ *n. f.* head cold.

constipado /konsti'paðo/ *a.* **1.** having a head cold. —*n.* **2.** *m.* head cold.

constitución /konstitu'θion; konstitu'sion/ *n. f.* constitution.

constitucional /konstituθio'nal; konstitusio'nal/ *a.* constitutional.

constitucionalidad /konstituθionali'ðað; konstitusionali'ðað/ *n. f.* constitutionality.

constituir /konsti'tuir/ *v.* constitute.

constitutivo /konstitu'tiβo/ *n. m.* constituent.

constituyente /konstitu'yente; konstitu'tiβo/ *a.* constituent.

constreñidamente /konstreɲiða'mente/ *adv.* compulsively; with constraint.

constreñimiento /konstreɲi'miento/ *n. m.* compulsion; constraint.

constreñir /konstre'ɲir/ *v.* constrain.

constricción /konstrik'θion; konstrik'sion/ *n. f.* constriction.

construcción /konstruk'θion; konstruk'sion/ *n. f.* construction.

constructivo /konstruk'tiβo/ *a.* constructive.

constructor /konstruk'tor/ **-ra** *n.* builder.

construir /kons'truir/ *v.* construct, build.

consuelo /kon'suelo/ *n. m.* consolation.

cónsul /'konsul/ *n. m.* consul.

consulado /konsu'laðo/ *n. m.* consulate.

consular /konsu'lar/ *a.* consular.

consulta /kon'sulta/ *n. f.* consultation.

consultación /konsulta'θion; konsulta'sion/ *n. f.* consultation.

consultante /konsul'tante/ *n. m. & f.* consultant.

consultar /konsul'tar/ *v.* consult.

consultivo /konsul'tiβo/ *a.* consultative.

consultor /konsul'tor/ **-ra** *n.* adviser.

consumación /konsuma'θion; konsuma'sion/ *n. f.* consummation; end.

consumado /konsu'maðo/ *a.* consummate, downright.

consumar /konsu'mar/ *v.* consummate.

consumidor /konsumi'ðor/ **-ra** *n.* consumer.

consumir /konsu'mir/ *v.* consume.

consumo /kon'sumo/ *n. m.* consumption.

consunción /konsun'θion; konsun'sion/ *n. m.* consumption, tuberculosis.

contabilidad /kontaβili'ðað/ *n. f.* accounting, bookkeeping.

contabilista /kontaβi'lista/ **contable** *n. m. & f.* accountant.

contacto /kon'takto/ *n. m.* contact.

contado /kon'taðo/ *n. m.* **al c.,** (for) cash.

contador /konta'ðor/ **-ra** *n.* accountant, bookkeeper; meter.

contagiar /konta'hiar/ *v.* infect.

contagio /kon'tahio/ *n. m.* contagion.

contagioso /konta'hioso/ *a.* contagious.

contaminación /kontamina'θion; kontamina'sion/ *n. f.* contamination, pollution. **c. del aire, c. atmosférica,** air pollution.

contaminar /kontami'nar/ *v.* contaminate, pollute.

contar /kon'tar/ *v.* count; relate, recount, tell. **c. con,** count on.

contemperar /kontempe'rar/ *v.* moderate.

contemplación /kontempla'θion; kontempla'sion/ *n. f.* contemplation.

contemplador /kontempla'ðor/ **-ra** *n.* thinker.

contemplar /kontem'plar/ *v.* contemplate.

contemplativamente /kontemplatiβa'mente/ *adv.* thoughtfully.

contemplativo /kontempla'tiβo/ *a.* contemplative.

contemporáneo /kontempo'raneo/ **-nea** *a. & n.* contemporary.

contención /konten'θion; konten'sion/ *n. f.* contention.

contencioso /konten'θioso; konten'sioso/ *a.* quarrelsome; argumentative.

contender /konten'der/ *v.* cope, contend; conflict.

contendiente /konten'diente/ *n. m. & f.* contender.

contenedor /kontene'ðor/ *n. m.* container.

contener /konte'ner/ *v.* contain; curb, control.

contenido /konte'niðo/ *n. m.* contents.

contenta /kon'tenta/ *n. f.* endorsement.

contentamiento /kontenta'miento/ *n. m.* contentment.

contentar /konten'tar/ *v.* content, satisfy.

contentible /konten'tiβle/ *a.* contemptible.

contento /kon'tento/ *a.* **1.** contented, happy. —*n.* **2.** *m.* contentment, satisfaction, pleasure.

contérmino /kon'termino/ *a.* adjacent, abutting.

contestable /kontes'taβle/ *a.* disputable.

contestación /kontesta'θion; kontesta'sion/ *n. f.* answer. —**contestar,** *v.*

contestador automático /kontesta'ðor auto'matiko/ *n. m.* answering machine.

contextura /konteks'tura/ *n. f.* texture.

contienda /kon'tienda/ *n. f.* combat; match; strife.

contigo /kon'tigo/ *adv.* with you.

contiguamente /kontigua'mente/ *adv.* contiguously.

contiguo /kon'tiguo/ *a.* adjoining, next.

continencia /konti'nenθia; konti'nensia/ *n. f.* continence, moderation.

continental /konti'nental/ *a.* continental.

continente /konti'nente/ *n. m.* continent; mainland.

continentemente /kontinente'mente/ *adv.* in moderation.

contingencia /kontin'henθia; kontin'hensia/ *n. f.* contingency.

contingente /kontin'hente/ *a.* contingent; incidental.

continuación /kontinua'θion; kontinua'sion/ *n. f.* continuation. **a c.,** thereupon, hereupon.

continuamente /kontinua'mente/ *adv.* continuously.

continuar /konti'nuar/ *v.* continue, keep on.

continuidad /kontinui'ðað/ *n. f.* continuity.

continuo /kon'tinuo/ *a.* continual; continuous.

contorcerse /kontor'θerse; kontor'serse/ *v.* writhe, twist.

contorción /kontor'θion; kontor'sion/ *n. f.* contortion.

contorno /kon'torno/ *n. m.* contour; profile, outline; neighborhood.

contra /'kontra/ *prep.* against.

contraalmirante /kontraalmi'rante/ *n. m.* rear admiral.

contraataque /kontraa'take/ *n. m.* counterattack.

contrabajo /kontra'βaho/ *n. m.* double bass.

contrabalancear /kontraβalanθe'ar; kontraβalanse'ar/ *v.* counterbalance.

contrabandear /kontraβande'ar/ *v.* smuggle.

contrabandista /kontraβan'dista/ *n. m. & f.* smuggler.

contrabando /kontra'βando/ *n. m.* contraband, smuggling.

contracción /kontrak'θion; kontrak'sion/ *n. f.* contraction.

contracepción /kontraθep'θion; kontrasep'sion/ *n. f.* contraception, birth control.

contractual /kontrak'tual/ *a.* contractual.

contradecir /kontraðe'θir; kontraðe'sir/ *v.* contradict.

contradicción /kontraðik'θion; kontraðik'sion/ *n. f.* contradiction.

contradictorio /kontraðik'torio/ *adj.* contradictory.

contraer /kontra'er/ *v.* contract; shrink.

contrahacedor /kontraaθe'ðor; kontraase'ðor/ **-ra** *n.* imitator.

contrahacer /kontraa'θer; kontraa'ser/ *v.* forge.

contralor /kontra'lor/ *n. m.* comptroller.

contramandar /kontraman'dar/ *v.* countermand.

contraorden /kontra'orðen/ *n. f.* countermand.

contraparte /kontra'parte/ *n. f.* counterpart.

contrapesar /kontrape'sar/ *v.* counterbalance; offset.

contrapeso /kontra'peso/ *n. m.* counterweight.

contraproducente /kontraproðu'θente; kontraproðu'sente/ *a.* counterproductive.

contrapunto /kontra'punto/ *n. m.* counterpoint.

contrariamente /kontraria'mente/ *adv.* contrarily.

contrariar /kontra'riar/ *v.* contradict; vex; antagonize; counteract.

contrariedad /kontrarie'ðað/ *n. f.* contrariness; opposition; contradiction; disappointment; trouble.

contrario /kon'trario/ *a. & m.* contrary, opposite.

contrarrestar /kontrarres'tar/ *v.* resist; counteract.

contrasol /kontra'sol/ *n. m.* sunshade.

contraste /kon'traste/ *n. m.* contrast. **—contrastar,** *v.*

contratar /kontra'tar/ *v.* engage, contract.

contratiempo /kontra'tiempo/ *n. m.* accident; misfortune.

contratista /kontra'tista/ *n. m. & f.* contractor.

contrato /kon'trato/ *n. m.* contract.

contribución /kontriβu'θion; kontriβu'sion/ *n. f.* contribution; tax.

contribuir /kontri'βuir/ *v.* contribute.

contribuyente /kontriβu'yente/ *n. m. & f.* contributor; taxpayer.

contrición /kontri'θion; kontri'sion/ *n. f.* contrition.

contristar /kontris'tar/ *v.* afflict.

contrito /kon'trito/ *a.* contrite, remorseful.

control /kon'trol/ *n. m.* control. **—controlar,** *v.*

controlador aéreo /kontrola'ðor a'ereo/ *n. m.* air traffic controller.

controversia /kontro'βersia/ *n. f.* controversy.

controversista /kontroβer'sista/ *n. m. & f.* controversialist.

controvertir /kontroβer'tir/ *v.* dispute.

contumacia /kontu'maθia; kontu'masia/ *n. f.* stubbornness.

contumaz /kontu'maθ; kontu'mas/ *adj.* stubborn.

contumelia /kontu'melia/ *n. f.*
contumely; abuse.

conturbar /kontur'βar/ *v.* trouble,
disturb.

contusión /kontu'sion/ *n. f.* contusion; bruise.

convalecencia /kombale'θenθia;
kombale'sensia/ *n. f.* convalescence.

convalecer /kombale'θer; kombale'ser/ *v.* convalesce.

convaleciente /kombale'θiente;
kombale'siente/ *a.* convalescent.

convecino /kombe'θino; kombe'sino/ **-na** *a.* **1.** near, close.
—*n.* **2.** neighbor.

convencedor /kombenθe'ðor;
kombense'ðor/ *adj.* convincing.

convencer /komben'θer; komben'ser/ *v.* convince.

convencimiento /kombenθi'miento; kombensi'miento/ *n. m.*
conviction, firm belief.

convención /komben'θion; komben'sion/ *n. f.* convention.

convencional /kombenθio'nal;
kombensio'nal/ *a.* conventional.

conveniencia /kombe'nienθia;
kombe'niensia/ *n. f.* suitability;
advantage, interest.

conveniente /kombe'niente/ *a.*
suitable; advantageous, opportune.

convenio /kom'benio/ *n. m.* pact,
treaty; agreement.

convenir /kombe'nir/ *v.* assent,
agree, concur; be suitable, fitting,
convenient.

convento /kom'bento/ *n. m.* convent.

convergencia /komber'henθia;
komber'hensia/ *n. f.* convergence.

convergir /komber'hir/ *v.* converge.

conversación /kombersa'θion;
kombersa'sion/ *n. f.* conversation.

conversar /komber'sar/ *v.* converse.

conversión /komber'sion/ *n. f.*
conversion.

convertible /komber'tiβle/ *a.* convertible.

convertir /komber'tir/ *v.* convert.

convexidad /kombeksi'ðað/ *n. f.*
convexity.

convexo /kom'bekso/ *a.* convex.

convicción /kombik'θion; kombik'sion/ *n. f.* conviction.

convicto /kom'bikto/ *a.* found
guilty.

convidado /kombi'ðaðo/ **-da** *n.*
guest.

convidar /kombi'ðar/ *v.* invite.

convincente /kombin'θente; kombin'sente/ *a.* convincing.

convite /kom'bite/ *n. m.* invitation, treat.

convocación /komboka'θion;
komboka'sion/ *n. f.* convocation.

convocar /kombo'kar/ *v.* convoke,
assemble.

convoy /kom'boi/ *n. m.* convoy,
escort.

convoyar /kombo'yar/ *v.* convey;
escort.

convulsión /kombul'sion/ *n. f.*
convulsion.

convulsivo /kombul'siβo/ *a.* convulsive.

conyugal /konyu'gal/ *a.* conjugal.

cónyuge /'konyuhe/ *n. m. & f.*
spouse, mate.

coñac /ko'ɲak/ *n. m.* cognac,
brandy.

cooperación /koopera'θion; koopera'sion/ *n. f.* cooperation.

cooperador /koopera'ðor/ *a.* cooperative.

cooperar /koope'rar/ *v.* cooperate.

cooperativa /koopera'tiβa/ *n. f.*
(food, etc.) cooperative, co-op.

cooperativo /koopera'tiβo/ *a.* cooperative.

coordinación /koorðina'θion;
koorðina'sion/ *n. f.* coordination.

coordinar /koorði'nar/ *v.* coordinate.

copa /'kopa/ *n. f.* goblet.

copartícipe /kopar'tiθipe; kopar'tisipe/ *m & f.* partner.

copete /ko'pete/ *n. m.* tuft; toupee.

copia /'kopia/ *n. f.* copy.
—**copiar,** *v.*

copiadora /kopia'ðora/ *n. f.* copier.

copioso /ko'pioso/ *a.* copious.

copista /ko'pista/ *n. m. & f.* copyist.

copla /'kopla/ *n. f.* popular song.

coplero /kop'lero/ *n. m.* poetaster.

cópula /'kopula/ *n. f.* connection.

coqueta /ko'keta/ *n. f.* flirt.
—**coquetear,** *v.*

coraje /ko'rahe/ *n. m.* courage,
bravery; anger.

coral /ko'ral/ *a.* **1.** choral. —*n.* **2.**
m. coral.

coralino /kora'lino/ *a.* coral.

Corán /ko'ran/ *n. m.* Koran.

corazón /kora'θon; kora'son/ *n. m.* heart.

corazonada /koraθo'naða; koraso'naða/ *n. f.* foreboding.

corbata /kor'βata/ *n. f.* necktie.

corbeta /kor'βeta/ *n. f.* corvette.

corcho /'kortʃo/ *n. m.* cork.

corcova /kor'koβa/ *n. f.* hump, hunchback.

corcovado /korko'βaðo/ **-da** *a.* & *n.* hunchback.

cordaje /kor'ðahe/ *n. m.* rigging.

cordel /kor'ðel/ *n. m.* string, cord.

cordero /kor'ðero/ *n. m.* lamb.

cordial /kor'ðial/ *a.* cordial; hearty.

cordialidad /korðiali'ðað/ *n. f.* cordiality.

cordillera /korði'ʎera; korði'yera/ *n. f.* mountain range.

cordón /kor'ðon/ *n. m.* cord; (shoe) lace.

cordura /kor'ðura/ *n. f.* sanity.

Corea /ko'rea/ *n. f.* Korea.

coreano /kore'ano/ **-a** *a.* & *n.* Korean.

coreografía /koreogra'fia/ *n. f.* choreography.

corista /ko'rista/ *n. f.* chorus girl.

corneja /kor'neha/ *n. f.* crow.

córneo /'korneo/ *a.* horny.

corneta /kor'neta/ *n. f.* bugle, horn, cornet.

corniforme /korni'forme/ *a.* horn-shaped.

cornisa /kor'nisa/ *n. f.* cornice.

cornucopia /kornu'kopia/ *n. f.* cornucopia.

coro /'koro/ *n. m.* chorus; choir.

corola /ko'rola/ *n. f.* corolla.

corolario /koro'lario/ *n. m.* corollary.

corona /ko'rona/ *n. f.* crown; halo; wreath.

coronación /korona'θion; korona'sion/ *n. f.* coronation.

coronamiento /korona'miento/ *n. m.* completion of a task.

coronar /koro'nar/ *v.* crown.

coronel /koro'nel/ *n. m.* colonel.

coronilla /koro'niʎa; koro'niya/ *n. f.* crown, top of the head.

corporación /korpora'θion; korpora'sion/ *n. f.* corporation.

corporal /korpo'ral/ *adj.* corporeal, bodily.

corpóreo /kor'poreo/ *a.* corporeal.

corpulencia /korpu'lenθia; korpu'lensia/ *n. f.* corpulence.

corpulento /korpu'lento/ *a.* corpulent, stout.

corpuscular /korpusku'lar/ *a.* corpuscular.

corpúsculo /kor'puskulo/ *n. m.* corpuscle.

corral /ko'rral/ *n. m.* corral, pen, yard.

correa /ko'rrea/ *n. f.* belt, strap.

correa transportadora /korrea transporta'ðora/ conveyor belt.

corrección /korrek'θion; korrek'sion/ *n. f.* correction.

correcto /ko'rrekto/ *a.* correct, proper, right.

corrector /korrek'tor/ **-ra** *n.* corrector, proofreader.

corredera /korre'ðera/ *n. f.* race course.

corredizo /korre'ðiθo; korre'ðiso/ *a.* easily untied.

corredor /korre'ðor/ *n. m.* corridor; runner.

corregible /korre'hiβle/ *a.* corrigible.

corregidor /korrehi'ðor/ *n. m.* corrector; magistrate, mayor.

corregir /korre'hir/ *v.* correct.

correlación /korrela'θion; korrela'sion/ *n. f.* correlation.

correlacionar /korrelaθio'nar; korrelasio'nar/ *v.* correlate.

correlativo /korrela'tiβo/ *a.* correlative.

correo /ko'rreo/ *n. m.* mail.

correoso /korre'oso/ *a.* leathery.

correr /ko'rrer/ *v.* run.

correría /korre'ria/ *n. f.* raid; escapade.

correspondencia /korrespon'denθia; korrespon'densia/ *n. f.* correspondence.

corresponder /korrespon'der/ *v.* correspond.

correspondiente /korrespon'diente/ *a.* & *m.* corresponding; correspondent.

corresponsal /korrespon'sal/ *n. m.* correspondent.

corretaje /korre'tahe/ *n. m.* brokerage.

correvedile /korreβe'ðile/ *n. m.* tale bearer; gossip.

corrida /ko'rriða/ *n. f.* race. **c. (de toros)**, bullfight.

corrido /ko'rriðo/ *a.* abashed; expert.

corriente /ko'rriente/ *a.* **1.** current, standard. —*n.* **2.** *f.* current, stream. **3.** *m.* **al c.**, informed, up to date. **contra la c.,** against the current; upriver, upstream.

corroboración /korroβora'θion; korroβora'sion/ *n. f.* corroboration.

corroborar /korroβo'rar/ *v.* corroborate.

corroer /korro'er/ *v.* corrode.

corromper /korrom'per/ *v.* corrupt.

corrompido /korrom'piðo/ *a.* corrupt.

corrupción /korrup'θion; korrup-'sion/ *n. f.* corruption.

corruptela /korrup'tela/ *n. f.* corruption; vice.

corruptibilidad /korruptiβili'ðað/ *n. f.* corruptibility.

corruptor /korrup'tor/ **-ra** *n.* corrupter.

corsario /kor'sario/ *n. m.* corsair.

corsé /kor'se/ *n. m.* corset.

corso /'korso/ *n. m.* piracy.

cortacésped /korta'θespeð; korta-'sespeð/ *n. m.* lawnmower.

cortadillo /korta'ðiʎo; korta'ðiyo/ *n. m.* small glass.

cortado /kor'taðo/ *a.* cut.

cortadura /korta'ðura/ *n. f.* cut.

cortante /kor'tante/ *a.* cutting, sharp, keen.

cortapisa /korta'pisa/ *n. f.* obstacle.

cortaplumas /korta'plumas/ *n. m.* penknife.

cortar /kor'tar/ *v.* cut, cut off, cut out.

corte /'korte/ *n. f.* court, *m.* cut.

cortedad /korte'ðað/ *n. f.* smallness; shyness.

cortejar /korte'har/ *v.* pay court to, woo.

cortejo /kor'teho/ *n. m.* court; courtship; sweetheart.

cortés /kor'tes/ *a.* civil, courteous, polite.

cortesana /korte'sana/ *n. f.* courtesan.

cortesano. 1. /korte'sano/ *a.* **1.** courtly, courteous. —*n.* **2.** *m.* courtier.

cortesía /korte'sia/ *n. f.* courtesy.

corteza /kor'teθa; kor'tesa/ *n. f.* bark; rind; crust.

cortijo /kor'tiho/ *n. m.* farmhouse.

cortina /kor'tina/ *n. f.* curtain.

corto /'korto/ *a.* short.

corva /'korβa/ *n. f.* back of the knee.

cosa /'kosa/ *n. f.* thing. **c. de,** a matter of, roughly.

cosecha /ko'setʃa/ *n. f.* crop, harvest. —**cosechar,** *v.*

coser /ko'ser/ *v.* sew, stitch.

cosmético /kos'metiko/ *a. & m.* cosmetic.

cósmico /'kosmiko/ *a.* cosmic.

cosmonauta /kosmo'nauta/ *n. m. & f.* cosmonaut.

cosmopolita /kosmopo'lita/ *a. & n.* cosmopolitan.

cosmos /'kosmos/ *n. m.* cosmos.

coso /'koso/ *n. m.* arena for bull fights.

cosquilla /kos'kiʎa; kos'kiya/ *n. f.* tickle. —**cosquillar,** *v.*

cosquilloso /koski'ʎoso; koski-'yoso/ *a.* ticklish.

costa /'kosta/ *n. f.* coast; cost, expense.

costado /kos'taðo/ *n. m.* side.

costal /kos'tal/ *n. m.* sack, bag.

costanero /kosta'nero/ *a.* coastal.

costar /kos'tar/ *v.* cost.

costarricense /kostarri'θense; kostarri'sense/ *a. & n.* Costa Rican.

coste /'koste/ *n. m.* cost, price.

costear /koste'ar/ *v.* defray, sponsor; sail along the coast of.

costilla /kos'tiʎa; kos'tiya/ *n. f.* rib; chop.

costo /'kosto/ *n. m.* cost, price.

costoso /kos'toso/ *a.* costly.

costra /'kostra/ *n. f.* crust.

costumbre /kos'tumbre/ *n. f.* custom, practice, habit.

costura /kos'tura/ *n. f.* sewing; seam.

costurera /kostu'rera/ *n. f.* seamstress, dressmaker.

costurero /kostu'rero/ *n. m.* sewing basket.

cota de malla /'kota de 'maʎa; 'kota de 'maya/ coat of mail.

cotejar /kote'har/ *v.* compare.

cotidiano /koti'ðiano/ *a.* daily; everyday.

cotillón /koti'ʎon; koti'yon/ *n. m.* cotillion.

cotización /kotiθa'θion; kotisa'sion/ *n. f.* quotation.

cotizar /koti'θar; koti'sar/ *v.* quote (a price).

coto /'koto/ *n. m.* enclosure; boundary.

cotón /ko'ton/ *n. m.* printed cotton cloth.

cotufa /ko'tufa/ *n. f.* Jerusalem artichoke.

coturno /ko'turno/ *n. m.* buskin.
covacha /ko'βatʃa/ *n. f.* small cave.
coxal /kok'sal/ *a.* of the hip.
coy /koi/ *n. m.* hammock.
coyote /ko'yote/ *n. m.* coyote.
coyuntura /koyun'tura/ *n. f.* joint; juncture.
coz /koθ; kos/ *n. f.* kick.
crac /krak/ *n. m.* failure.
cráneo /'kraneo/ *n. m.* skull.
craniano /kra'niano/ *a.* cranial.
crapuloso /krapu'loso/ *a.* drunken.
crasiento /kra'siento/ *a.* greasy, oily.
craso /'kraso/ *a.* fat; gross.
cráter /'krater/ *n. m.* crater.
craza /'kraθa; 'krasa/ *n. f.* crucible.
creación /krea'θion; krea'sion/ *n. f.* creation.
creador /krea'ðor/ **-ra** *a. & n.* creative; creator.
crear /kre'ar/ *v.* create.
creativo /krea'tiβo/ *a.* creative.
crébol /'kreβol/ *n. m.* holly tree.
crecer /kre'θer; kre'ser/ *v.* grow, grow up; increase.
creces /'kreθes; 'kreses/ *n. f.pl.* increase, addition.
crecidamente /kreθiða'mente; kresiða'mente/ *adv.* abundantly.
crecido /kre'θiðo; kre'siðo/ *a.* increased, enlarged; swollen.
creciente /kre'θiente; kre'siente/ *a.* **1.** growing. —*n.* **2.** *m.* crescent.
crecimiento /kreθi'miento; kresi'miento/ *n. m.* growth.
credenciales /kreðen'θiales; kreðen'siales/ *f.pl.* credentials.
credibilidad /kreðiβili'ðað/ *n. f.* credibility.
crédito /'kreðito/ *n. m.* credit.
credo /'kreðo/ *n. m.* creed, belief.
crédulamente /kreðula'mente/ *adv.* credulously, gullibly.
credulidad /kreðuli'ðað/ *n. f.* credulity.
crédulo /'kreðulo/ *a.* credulous.
creedero /kree'ðero/ *a.* credible.
creedor /kree'ðor/ *a.* credulous, believing.
creencia /kre'enθia; kre'ensia/ *n. f.* belief.
creer /kre'er/ *v.* believe; think.
creíble /kre'iβle/ *a.* credible, believable.
crema /'krema/ *n. f.* cream.

cremación /krema'θion; krema'sion/ *n. f.* cremation.
crema dentífrica /'krema den'tifrika/ toothpaste.
cremallera /krema'ʎera; krema'yera/ *n. f.* zipper.
crémor tártaro /'kremor 'tartaro/ *n. m.* cream of tartar.
cremoso /kre'moso/ *a.* creamy.
creosota /kreo'sota/ *n. f.* creosote.
crepitar /krepi'tar/ *v.* crackle.
crepuscular /krepusku'lar/ *a.* of or like the dawn or dusk; crepuscular.
crepúsculo /kre'puskulo/ *n. m.* dusk, twilight.
crescendo /kres'θendo; kres'sendo/ *n. m.* crescendo.
crespo /'krespo/ *a.* curly.
crespón /kres'pon/ *n. m.* crepe.
cresta /'kresta/ *n. f.* crest; heraldic crest.
crestado /kres'taðo/ *a.* crested.
creta /'kreta/ *n. f.* chalk.
cretáceo /kre'taθeo; kre'taseo/ *a.* chalky.
cretinismo /kreti'nismo/ *n. m.* cretinism.
cretino /kre'tino/ **-na** *n. & a.* cretin.
cretona /kre'tona/ *n. f.* cretonne.
creyente /kre'yente/ *a.* **1.** believing. —*n.* **2.** believer.
creyón /kre'yon/ *n. m.* crayon.
cría /'kria/ *n. f.* (stock) breeding; young (of an animal), litter.
criada /kri'aða/ *n. f.* maid.
criadero /kria'ðero/ *n. m. Agr.* nursery.
criado /kri'aðo/ **-da** *n.* servant.
criador /kria'ðor/ *a.* fruitful, prolific.
crianza /kri'anθa; kri'ansa/ *n. f.* breeding; upbringing.
criar /kri'ar/ *v.* raise, rear; breed.
criatura /kria'tura/ *n. f.* creature; infant.
criba /'kriβa/ *n. f.* sieve.
cribado /kri'βaðo/ *a.* sifted.
cribar /kri'βar/ *v.* sift.
crimen /'krimen/ *n. m.* crime.
criminal /krimi'nal/ *a. & n.* criminal.
criminalidad /kriminali'ðað/ *n. f.* criminality.
criminalmente /kriminal'mente/ *adv.* criminally.
criminología /kriminolo'hia/ *n. f.* criminology.

criminoso /krimi'noso/ *a.* criminal.

crines /'krines/ *n. f.pl.* mane of a horse.

crinolina /krino'lina/ *n. f.* crinoline.

criocirugía /krioθiru'hia; kriosiru-'hia/ *n. f.* cryosurgery.

criollo /'krioʎo; 'krioyo/ **-lla** *a.* & *n.* native; Creole.

cripta /'kripta/ *n. f.* crypt.

criptografía /kriptogra'fia/ *n. f.* cryptography.

crisantemo /krisan'temo/ *n. m.* chrysanthemum.

crisis /'krisis/ *n. f.* crisis.

crisis nerviosa /'krisis ner'βiosa/ nervous breakdown.

crisma /'krisma/ *n. m.* chrism.

crisol /kri'sol/ *n. m.* crucible.

crispamiento /krispa'miento/ *n. m.* twitch, contraction.

crispar /kris'par/ *v.* contract (the muscles); twitch.

cristal /kri'stal/ *n. m.* glass; crystal; lens.

cristalería /kristale'ria/ *n. f.* glassware.

cristalino /krista'lino/ *a.* crystalline.

cristalización /kristaliθa'θion; kristalisa'sion/ *n. f.* crystallization.

cristalizar /kristali'θar; kristali'sar/ *v.* crystallize.

cristianar /kristia'nar/ *v.* baptize.

cristiandad /kristian'daδ/ *n. f.* Christendom.

cristianismo /kristia'nismo/ *n. m.* Christianity.

cristiano /kris'tiano/ **-na** *a.* & *n.* Christian.

Cristo /'kristo/ *n. m.* Christ.

criterio /kri'terio/ *n. m.* criterion; judgment.

crítica /'kritika/ *n. f.* criticism; critique.

criticable /kriti'kaβle/ *a.* blameworthy.

criticador /kritika'δor/ *a.* critical.

criticar /kriti'kar/ *v.* criticize.

crítico /'kritiko/ **-ca** *a.* & *n.* critical; critic.

croar /kro'ar/ *v.* croak.

crocante /kro'kante/ *n. m.* almond brittle.

crocitar /kroθi'tar; krosi'tar/ *v.* crow.

cromático /kro'matiko/ *a.* chromatic.

cromo /'kromo/ *n. m.* chromium.

cromosoma /kromo'soma/ *n. m.* chromosome.

cromotipia /kromo'tipia/ *n. f.* color printing.

crónica /'kronika/ *n. f.* chronicle.

crónico /'kroniko/ *a.* chronic.

cronicón /kroni'kon/ *n. m.* concise chronicle.

cronista /kro'nista/ *n. m.* & *f.* chronicler.

cronología /kronolo'hia/ *n. f.* chronology.

cronológicamente /kronolo-hika'mente/ *adv.* chronologically.

cronológico /krono'lohiko/ *a.* chronologic.

cronometrar /kronome'trar/ *v.* time.

cronómetro /kro'nometro/ *n. m.* stopwatch; chronometer.

croqueta /kro'keta/ *n. f.* croquette.

croquis /'krokis/ *n. m.* sketch; rough outline.

crótalo /'krotalo/ *n. m.* rattlesnake; castanet.

cruce /'kruθe; 'kruse/ *n. m.* crossing, crossroads, junction.

crucero /kru'θero; kru'sero/ *n. m.* cruiser.

crucífero /kru'θifero; kru'sifero/ *a.* cross-shaped.

crucificado /kruθifi'kaδo; krusi-fi'kaδo/ *a.* crucified.

crucificar /kruθifi'kar; krusifi'kar/ *v.* crucify.

crucifijo /kruθi'fiho; krusi'fiho/ *n. m.* crucifix.

crucifixión /kruθifik'sion; krusi-fik'sion/ *n. f.* crucifixion.

crucigrama /kruθi'grama; krusi-'grama/ *n. m.* crossword puzzle.

crudamente /kruδa'mente/ *adv.* crudely.

crudeza /kru'δeθa; kru'δesa/ *n. f.* crudeness.

crudo /'kruδo/ *a.* crude, raw.

cruel /kruel/ *a.* cruel.

crueldad /kruel'daδ/ *n. f.* cruelty.

cruelmente /kruel'mente/ *adv.* cruelly.

cruentamente /kruenta'mente/ *adv.* bloodily.

cruento /'kruento/ *a.* bloody.

crujía /kru'hia/ *n. f.* corridor.

crujido /kru'hiδo/ *n. m.* creak.

crujir /kru'hir/ *v.* crackle; creak; rustle.

cruórico /'kruoriko/ *a.* bloody.

crup /krup/ *n. m.* croup.
crupié /kru'pie/ *n. m. & f.* croupier.
crustáceo /krus'taθeo; krus'taseo/ *n. & a.* crustacean.
cruz /kruθ; krus/ *n. f.* cross.
cruzada /kru'θaða; kru'saða/ *n. f.* crusade.
cruzado /kru'θaðo; kru'saðo/ **-da** *n.* crusader.
cruzamiento /kruθa'miento; krusa'miento/ *n. m.* crossing.
cruzar /kru'θar; kru'sar/ *v.* cross.
cruzarse con /kru'θarse kon; kru'sarse kon/ *v.* to (meet and) pass.
cuaderno /kua'ðerno/ *n. m.* notebook.
cuadra /'kuaðra/ *n. f.* block; (hospital) ward.
cuadradamente /kuaðraða'mente/ *adv.* exactly, precisely; completely, in full.
cuadradillo /kuaðra'ðiʎo; kuaðra-'ðiyo/ *n. m.* lump of sugar.
cuadrado /kua'ðraðo/ **-da** *a. & n.* square.
cuadrafónico /kuaðra'foniko/ *a.* quadraphonic.
Cuadragésima /kuaðra'hesima/ *n. f.* Lent.
cuadragesimal /kuaðrahesi'mal/ *a.* Lenten.
cuadrángulo /kua'ðraŋgulo/ *n. m.* quadrangle.
cuadrante /kua'ðrante/ *n. m.* quadrant; dial.
cuadrar /kua'ðrar/ *v.* square; suit.
cuadricular /kuaðriku'lar/ *a.* in squares.
cuadrilátero /kuaðri'latero/ *a.* quadrilateral.
cuadrilla /kua'ðriʎa; kua'ðriya/ *n. f.* band, troop, gang.
cuadro /'kuaðro/ *n. m.* picture; painting; frame. **a cuadros,** checked, plaid.
cuadro de servicio /'kuaðro de ser'βiθio; 'kuaðro de ser'βisio/ timetable.
cuadrupedal /kuaðrupe'ðal/ *a.* quadruped.
cuádruplo /'kuaðruplo/ *a.* fourfold.
cuajada /kua'haða/ *n. f.* curd.
cuajamiento /kuaha'miento/ *n. m.* coagulation.
cuajar /kua'har/ *v.* coagulate; overdecorate.

cuajo /'kuaho/ *n. m.* rennet; coagulation.
cual /kual/ *rel. pron.* which.
cuál *a. & pron.* what, which.
cualidad /kuali'ðað/ *n. f.* quality.
cualitativo /kualita'tiβo/ *a.* qualitative.
cualquiera /kual'kiera/ *a. & pron.* whatever, any; anyone.
cuando /'kuando/ *conj.* when.
cuando *adv.* when. **de cuando en cuando,** from time to time.
cuantía /kuan'tia/ *n. f.* quantity; amount.
cuantiar /kuan'tiar/ *v.* estimate.
cuantiosamente /kuantio-sa'mente/ *adv.* abundantly.
cuantioso /kuan'tioso/ *a.* abundant.
cuantitativo /kuantita'tiβo/ *a.* quantitative.
cuanto /'kuanto/ *a., adv. & pron.* as much as, as many as; all that which. **en c.,** as soon as. **en c. a,** as for. **c. antes,** as soon as possible. **c. más... tanto más,** the more... the more. **unos cuantos,** a few.
cuánto *a. & adv.* how much, how many.
cuaquerismo /kuake'rismo/ *n. m.* Quakerism.
cuáquero /'kuakero/ **-ra** *n. & a.* Quaker.
cuarenta /kua'renta/ *a. & pron.* forty.
cuarentena /kuaren'tena/ *n. f.* quarantine.
cuaresma /kua'resma/ *n. f.* Lent.
cuaresmal /kuares'mal/ *a.* Lenten.
cuarta /'kuarta/ *n. f.* quarter; quadrant; quart.
cuartear /kuarte'ar/ *v.* divide into quarters.
cuartel /kuar'tel/ *n. m. Mil.* quarters; barracks; *Naut.* hatch. **c. general,** headquarters. **sin c.,** giving no quarter.
cuartelada /kuarte'laða/ *n. f.* military uprising.
cuarterón /kuarte'ron/ *n. & a.* quadroon.
cuarteto /kuar'teto/ *n. m.* quartet.
cuartillo /kuar'tiʎo; kuar'tiyo/ *n. m.* pint.
cuarto /'kuarto/ *a.* **1.** fourth. —*n.* **2.** *m.* quarter; room.
cuarto de baño /'kuarto de 'baɲo/ bathroom.

cuarto de dormir /'kuarto de dor'mir/ bedroom.

cuarto para invitados /'kuarto para imbi'taðos/ guest room.

cuarzo /'kuarθo; 'kuarso/ n. m. quartz.

cuasi /'kuasi/ adv. almost, nearly.

cuate /'kuate/ a. & n. twin.

cuatrero /kua'trero/ n. m. cattle rustler.

cuatrillón /kuatri'ʎon; kuatri'yon/ n. m. quadrillion.

cuatro /'kuatro/ a. & pron. four.

cuatrocientos /kuatro'θientos; kuatro'sientos/ a. & pron. four hundred.

cuba /'kuβa/ n. f. cask, tub, vat.

cubano /ku'βano/ -na a. & n. Cuban.

cubero /ku'βero/ n. m. cooper.

cubeta /ku'βeta/ n. f. small barrel, keg.

cúbico /'kuβiko/ a. cubic.

cubículo /ku'βikulo/ n. m. cubicle.

cubierta /ku'βierta/ n. f. cover; envelope; wrapping; tread (of a tire); deck.

cubiertamente /kuβierta'mente/ adv. secretly, stealthily.

cubierto /ku'βierto/ n. m. place (at table).

cubil /ku'βil/ n. m. lair.

cubismo /ku'βismo/ n. m. cubism.

cubito de hielo /ku'βito de 'ielo/ n. m. ice cube.

cubo /'kuβo/ n. m. cube; bucket.

cubo de la basura /'kuβo de la ba'sura/ trash can.

cubrecama /kuβre'kama/ n. f. bedspread.

cubrir /ku'βrir/ v. cover.

cubrirse /ku'βrirse/ v. put on one's hat.

cucaracha /kuka'ratʃa/ n. f. cockroach.

cuchara /ku'tʃara/ n. f. spoon, tablespoon.

cucharada /kutʃa'raða/ n. f. spoonful.

cucharita /kutʃa'rita/ **cucharilla** n. f. teaspoon.

cucharón /kutʃa'ron/ n. m. dipper, ladle.

cuchicheo /kutʃi'tʃeo/ n. m. whisper. —**cuchichear**, v.

cuchilla /ku'tʃiʎa; ku'tʃiya/ n. f. cleaver.

cuchillada /kutʃi'ʎaða; kutʃi'yaða/ n. f. slash.

cuchillería /kutʃiʎe'ria; kutʃiye'ria/ n. f. cutlery.

cuchillo /ku'tʃiʎo; ku'tʃiyo/ n. m. knife.

cucho /'kutʃo/ n. m. fertilizer.

cuchufleta /kutʃu'fleta/ n. f. jest.

cuclillo /ku'kliʎo; ku'kliyo/ n. m. cuckoo.

cuco /'kuko/ a. sly.

cuculla /ku'kuʎa; ku'kuya/ n. f. hood, cowl.

cuelga /'kuelga/ n. f. cluster, bunch.

cuelgacapas /kuelga'kapas/ n. m. coat rack.

cuello /'kueʎo; 'kueyo/ n. m. neck; collar.

cuenca /'kuenka/ n. f. socket; (river) basin; wooden bowl.

cuenco /'kuenko/ n. m. earthen bowl.

cuenta /'kuenta/ n. f. account; bill. **darse c.,** to realize. **tener en c.,** to keep in mind.

cuenta bancaria /'kuenta ban-'karia/ bank account.

cuenta de ahorros /'kuenta de a'orros/ savings account.

cuentagotas /kuenta'gotas/ n. m. dropper (for medicine).

cuentista /kuen'tista/ n. m. & f. storyteller; informer.

cuento /'kuento/ n. m. story, tale.

cuerda /'kuerða/ n. f. cord; chord; rope; string; spring (of clock). **dar c. a,** to wind (clock).

cuerdamente /kuerða'mente/ adv. sanely; prudently.

cuerdo /'kuerðo/ a. sane; prudent.

cuerno /'kuerno/ n. m. horn.

cuero /'kuero/ n. m. leather; hide.

cuerpo /'kuerpo/ n. m. body; corps.

cuervo /'kuerβo/ n. m. crow, raven.

cuesco /'kuesko/ n. m. pit, stone (of fruit).

cuesta /'kuesta/ n. f. hill, slope. **llevar a cuestas,** to carry on one's back.

cuestación /kuesta'θion; kuesta-'sion/ n. f. solicitation for charity.

cuestión /kues'tion/ n. f. question; affair; argument.

cuestionable /kuestio'naβle/ a. questionable.

cuestionar /kuestio'nar/ v. question; discuss; argue.

cuestionario /kuestio'nario/ n. m. questionnaire.

cuete /'kuete/ *n. m.* firecracker.
cueva /'kueβa/ *n. f.* cave; cellar.
cuguar /ku'guar/ *n. m.* cougar.
cugujada /kugu'haða/ *n. f.* lark.
cuidado /kui'ðaðo/ *n. m.* care, caution, worry. **tener c.,** to be careful.
cuidadosamente /kuiðaðosa-'mente/ *adv.* carefully.
cuidadoso /kuiða'ðoso/ *a.* careful, painstaking.
cuidante /kui'ðante/ *n.* caretaker, custodian.
cuidar /kui'ðar/ *v.* take care of.
cuita /'kuita/ *n. f.* trouble, care; grief.
cuitado /kui'taðo/ *a.* unfortunate; shy, timid.
cuitamiento /kuita'miento/ *n. m.* timidity.
culata /ku'lata/ *n. f.* haunch, buttock; butt of a gun.
culatada /kula'taða/ *n. f.* recoil.
culatazo /kula'taθo; kula'taso/ *n. m.* blow with the butt of a gun; recoil.
culebra /ku'leβra/ *n. f.* snake.
culero /ku'lero/ *a.* lazy, indolent.
culinario /kuli'nario/ *a.* culinary.
culminación /kulmina'θion; kulmina'sion/ *n. f.* culmination.
culminar /kulmi'nar/ *v.* culminate.
culpa /'kulpa/ *n. f.* fault, guilt, blame. **tener la c.,** to be at fault. **echar la culpa a,** to blame.
culpabilidad /kulpaβili'ðað/ *n. f.* guilt, fault, blame.
culpable /kul'paβle/ *a.* at fault, guilty, to blame, culpable.
culpar /kul'par/ *v.* blame, accuse.
cultamente /kulta'mente/ *adv.* politely, elegantly.
cultivable /kulti'βaβle/ *a.* arable.
cultivación /kultiβa'θion; kultiβa-'sion/ *n. f.* cultivation.
cultivador /kultiβa'ðor/ **-ra** *n.* cultivator.
cultivar /kulti'βar/ *v.* cultivate.
cultivo /kul'tiβo/ *n. m.* cultivation; (growing) crop.
culto /'kulto/ *a.* **1.** cultured, cultivated. —*n.* **2.** *m.* cult; worship.
cultura /kul'tura/ *n. f.* culture; refinement.
cultural /kultu'ral/ *a.* cultural.
culturar /kultu'rar/ *v.* cultivate.
culturismo /kultu'rismo/ *n. m.* body building.
culturista /kultu'rista/ *n. m. & f.* body builder.

cumbre /'kumbre/ *n. m.* summit, peak.
cumpleaños /kumple'aɲos/ *n. m.pl.* birthday.
cumplidamente /kumpliða'mente/ *adv.* courteously, correctly.
cumplido /kum'pliðo/ *a.* polite, polished.
cumplimentar /kumplimen'tar/ *v.* compliment.
cumplimiento /kumpli'miento/ *n. m.* fulfillment; compliment.
cumplir /kum'plir/ *v.* comply; carry out, fulfill; reach (years of age).
cumulativo /kumula'tiβo/ *a.* cumulative.
cúmulo /'kumulo/ *n. m.* heap, pile.
cuna /'kuna/ *n. f.* cradle.
cundir /kun'dir/ *v.* spread; expand; propagate.
cuneiforme /kunei'forme/ *a.* cuneiform, wedge-shaped.
cuneo /ku'neo/ *n. m.* rocking.
cuña /'kuɲa/ *n. f.* wedge.
cuñada /ku'ɲaða/ *n. f.* sister-in-law.
cuñado /ku'ɲaðo/ *n. m.* brother-in-law.
cuñete /ku'ɲete/ *n. m.* keg.
cuota /'kuota/ *n. f.* quota; dues.
cuotidiano /kuoti'ðiano/ *a.* daily.
cupé /ku'pe/ *n. m.* coupé.
Cupido /ku'piðo/ *n. m.* Cupid.
cupo /'kupo/ *n. m.* share; assigned quota.
cupón /ku'pon/ *n. m.* coupon.
cúpula /'kupula/ *n. f.* dome.
cura /'kura/ *n. m.* priest; *f.* treatment, (medical) care. **c. de urgencia,** first aid.
curable /ku'raβle/ *a.* curable.
curación /kura'θion; kura'sion/ *n. f.* healing; cure; (surgical) dressing.
curado /ku'raðo/ *a.* cured, healed.
curador /kura'ðor/ **-ra** *n.* healer.
curandero /kuran'dero/ **-ra** *n.* healer, medicine man.
curar /ku'rar/ *v.* cure, heal, treat.
curativo /kura'tiβo/ *a.* curative, healing.
curia /'kuria/ *n. f.* ecclesiastical court.
curiosear /kuriose'ar/ *v.* snoop, pry, meddle.
curiosidad /kuriosi'ðað/ *n. f.* curiosity.
curioso /ku'rioso/ *a.* curious.

curro /'kurro/ *a.* showy, loud, flashy.
cursante /kur'sante/ *n.* student.
cursar /kur'sar/ *v.* frequent; attend.
cursi /'kursi/ *a.* vulgar, shoddy, in bad taste.
curso /'kurso/ *n. m.* course.
curso por correspondencia /'kurso por korrespon'denθia; 'kurso por korrespon'densia/ *n. m.* correspondence course.
cursor /kur'sor/ *n. m.* cursor.
curtidor /kurti'ðor/ *n. m.* tanner.
curtir /kur'tir/ *v.* tan.

curva /'kurβa/ *n. f.* curve; bend.
curvatura /kurβa'tura, kurβi'ðað/ *n. f.* curvature.
cúspide /'kuspiðe/ *n. f.* top, peak.
custodia /kus'toðia/ *n. f.* custody.
custodiar /kusto'ðiar/ *v.* guard, watch.
custodio /kus'toðio/ *n. m.* custodian.
cutáneo /ku'taneo/ *a.* cutaneous.
cutícula /ku'tikula/ *n. f.* cuticle.
cutis /'kutis/ *n. m. or f.* skin, complexion.
cutre /'kutre/ *a.* shoddy.
cuyo /'kuyo/ *a.* whose.

D

dable /'daβle/ *a.* possible.
dactilógrafo /dakti'lografo/ **-fa** *n.* typist.
dádiva /'daðiβa/ *n. f.* gift.
dadivosamente /daðiβosa'mente/ *adv.* generously.
dadivoso /daði'βoso/ *a.* generous, bountiful.
dado /'daðo/ *n. m.* die.
dador /da'ðor/ **-ra** *n.* giver.
dados /'daðos/ *n. m.pl.* dice.
daga /'daga/ *n. f.* dagger.
dalia /'dalia/ *n. f.* dahlia.
dallador /daʎa'ðor; daya'ðor/ *n. m.* lawn mower.
dallar /da'ʎar; da'yar/ *v.* mow.
daltonismo /dalto'nismo/ *n. m.* color blindness.
dama /'dama/ *n. f.* lady.
damasco /da'masko/ *n. m.* apricot; damask.
damisela /dami'sela/ *n. f.* young lady, girl.
danés /da'nes/ **-esa** *a. & n.* Danish, Dane.
danza /'danθa; 'dansa/ *n. f.* (the) dance. **—danzar,** *v.*
danzante /dan'θante; dan'sante/ **-ta** *n.* dancer.
dañable /da'ɲaβle/ *a.* condemnable.
dañar /da'ɲar/ *v.* hurt, harm; damage.
dañino /da'ɲino/ *a.* harmful.
daño /'daɲo/ *n. m.* damage; harm.
dañoso /da'ɲoso/ *a.* harmful.
dar /dar/ *v.* give; strike (clock). **d. a,** face, open on. **d. con,** find, locate. **¡Dalo por hecho!** Consider it done!
dardo /'darðo/ *n. m.* dart.

dársena /'darsena/ *n. f.* dock.
datar /'datar/ *v.* date.
dátil /'datil/ *n. m.* date (fruit).
dativo /da'tiβo/ *n. m. & a.* dative.
datos /'datos/ *n. m.pl.* data.
de /de/ *prep.* of; from; than.
debajo /de'βaho/ *adv.* underneath. **d. de,** under.
debate /de'βate/ *n. m.* debate.
debatir /deβa'tir/ *v.* debate, argue.
debe /'deβe/ *n. m.* debit.
debelación /deβela'θion; deβela-'sion/ *n. f.* conquest.
debelar /deβe'lar/ *v.* conquer.
deber /de'βer/ *v.* **1.** owe; must; be to, be supposed to. **—n. 2.** *m.* obligation.
deberes /de'βeres/ *n. m.pl.* homework.
debido /de'βiðo/ *a.* due.
débil /'deβil/ *a.* weak, faint.
debilidad /deβili'ðað/ *n. f.* weakness.
debilitación /deβilita'θion; deβilitasion/ *n. f.* weakness.
debilitar /deβili'tar/ *v.* weaken.
débito /'deβito/ *n. m.* debit.
debutar /deβu'tar/ *v.* make a debut.
década /'dekaða/ *n. f.* decade.
decadencia /deka'ðenθia; dekaðensia/ *n. f.* decadence, decline, decay.
decadente /deka'ðente/ *a.* decadent, declining, decaying.
decaer /deka'er/ *v.* decay, decline.
decalitro /deka'litro/ *n. m.* decaliter.
decálogo /de'kalogo/ *n. m. m.* decalogue.

decámetro /de'kametro/ n. m. decameter.

decano /de'kano/ n. m. dean.

decantado /dekan'taðo/ a. much discussed; overexalted.

decapitación /dekapita'θion; dekapitasion/ n. f. beheading.

decapitar /dekapi'tar/ v. behead.

decencia /de'θenθia; de'sensia/ n. f. decency.

decenio /de'θenio; de'senio/ n. m. decade.

decente /de'θente; de'sente/ a. decent.

decentemente /deθente'mente; desente'mente/ adv. decently.

decepción /deθep'θion; desep'sion/ n. f. disappointment, letdown; delusion.

decepcionar /deθepθio'nar; desepsio'nar/ v. disappoint, disillusion.

dechado /de'tʃaðo/ n. m. model; sample; pattern; example.

decibelio /deθi'βelio; desi'βelio/ n. m. decibel.

decididamente /deθiðiða'mente; desiðiða'mente/ adv. decidedly.

decidir /deθi'ðir; desi'ðir/ v. decide.

decigramo /deθi'gramo; desi'gramo/ n. m. decigram.

decilitro /deθi'litro; desi'litro/ n. m. deciliter.

décima /'deθima; 'desima/ n. f. ten-line stanza.

decimal /deθi'mal; desi'mal/ a. decimal.

décimo /'deθimo; 'desimo/ a. tenth.

decir /de'θir; de'sir/ v. tell, say. **es d.,** that is (to say).

decisión /deθi'sion; desi'sion/ n. f. decision.

decisivamente /deθisiβa'mente; desisiβa'mente/ adv. decisively.

decisivo /deθi'siβo; desi'siβo/ a. decisive.

declamación /deklama'θion; deklama'sion/ n. f. declamation, speech.

declamar /dekla'mar/ v. declaim.

declaración /deklara'θion; deklara'sion/ n. f. declaration; statement; plea.

declaración de la renta /deklara'θion de la 'rrenta; deklara'sion de la 'rrenta/ tax return.

declarar /dekla'rar/ v. declare, state.

declarativo /deklara'tiβo, deklara'torio/ a. declarative.

declinación /deklina'θion; deklina'sion/ n. f. descent; decay; decline; declension.

declinar /dekli'nar/ v. decline.

declive /de'kliβe,/ n. m. declivity, slope.

decocción /dekok'θion; dekok'sion/ n. f. decoction.

decomiso /deko'miso/ n. m. seizure, confiscation.

decoración /dekora'θion; dekora'sion/ n. f. decoration, trimming.

decorado /deko'raðo/ n. m. Theat. scenery, set.

decorar /deko'rar/ v. decorate, trim.

decorativo /dekora'tiβo/ a. decorative, ornamental.

decoro /de'koro/ n. m. decorum; decency.

decoroso /deko'roso/ a. decorous.

decrecer /dekre'θer; dekre'ser/ v. decrease.

decrépito /de'krepito/ a. decrepit.

decreto /de'kreto/ n. m. decree. —**decretar,** v.

dedal /de'ðal/ n. m. thimble.

dédalo /'deðalo/ n. m. labyrinth.

dedicación /deðika'θion; deðika'sion/ n. f. dedication.

dedicar /deði'kar/ v. devote; dedicate.

dedicatoria /deðika'toria/ n. f. dedication, inscription.

dedo /'deðo/ n. m. finger, toe.

dedo anular /'deðo anu'lar/ ring finger.

dedo corazón /'deðo kora'θon; 'deðo kora'son/ middle finger.

dedo índice /'deðo 'indiθe; 'deðo 'indise/ index finger.

dedo meñique /'deðo me'ɲike/ little finger, pinky.

dedo pulgar /'deðo pul'gar/ thumb.

deducción /deðuk'θion; deðuk'sion/ n. f. deduction.

deducir /deðu'θir; deðu'sir/ v. deduce; subtract.

defectivo /defek'tiβo/ a. defective.

defecto /de'fekto/ n. m. defect, flaw.

defectuoso /defek'tuoso/ a. defective, faulty.

defender /defen'der/ v. defend.

defensa /de'fensa/ n. f. defense.

defensivo /defen'siβo/ *a.* defensive.

defensor /defen'sor/ **-ra** *n.* defender.

deferencia /defe'renθia; deferen'sia/ *n. f.* deference.

deferir /defe'rir/ *v.* defer.

deficiente /defi'θiente; defi'siente/ *a.* deficient.

déficit /'defiθit; 'defisit/ *n. m.* deficit.

definición /defini'θion; defini'sion/ *n. f.* definition.

definido /defi'niðo/ *a.* definite.

definir /defi'nir/ *v.* define; establish.

definitivamente /definitiβa'mente/ *adv.* definitely.

definitivo /defini'tiβo/ *a.* definitive.

deformación /deforma'θion; deforma'sion/ *n. f.* deformation.

deformar /defor'mar/ *v.* deform.

deforme /de'forme/ *a.* deformed; ugly.

deformidad /deformi'ðað/ *n. f.* deformity.

defraudar /defrau'ðar/ *v.* defraud.

defunción /defun'θion; defun'sion/ *n. f.* death.

degeneración /dehenera'θion; dehenera'sion/ *n. f.* degeneration.

degenerado /dehene'raðo/ *a.* degenerate. **—degenerar,** *v.*

deglutir /deglu'tir/ *v.* swallow.

degollar /dego'ʎar; dego'yar/ *v.* behead.

degradación /degraða'θion; degraða'sion/ *n. f.* degradation.

degradar /degra'ðar/ *v.* degrade, debase.

deidad /dei'ðað/ *n. f.* deity.

deificación /deifika'θion; deifika'sion/ *n. f.* deification.

deificar /deifi'kar/ *v.* deify.

deífico /de'ifiko/ *a.* divine, deific.

deísmo /de'ismo/ *n. m.* deism.

dejadez /deha'ðeθ; deha'ðes/ *n. f.* neglect, untidiness; laziness.

dejado /de'haðo/ *a.* untidy; lazy.

dejar /de'har/ *v.* let, allow; leave. **d. de,** stop, leave off. **no d. de,** not fail to.

dejo /'deho/ *n. m.* abandonment; negligence; aftertaste; accent.

del /del/ *contr. of* **de** + **el.**

delantal /delan'tal/ *n. m.* apron; pinafore. **delantal de niña,** pinafore.

delante /de'lante/ *adv.* ahead, forward; in front.

delantero /delan'tero/ *a.* forward, front, first.

delator /dela'tor/ *n. m.* informer; accuser.

delegación /delega'θion; delega'sion/ *n. f.* delegation.

delegado /dele'gaðo/ **-da** *n.* delegate. **—delegar,** *v.*

deleite /de'leite/ *n. m.* delight. **—deleitar,** *v.*

deleitoso /delei'toso/ *a.* delightful.

deletrear /deletre'ar/ *v.* spell; decipher.

delfín /del'fin/ *n. m.* dolphin; dauphin.

delgadez /delga'ðeθ; delgaðes/ *n. f.* thinness, slenderness.

delgado /del'gaðo/ *a.* thin, slender, slim, slight.

deliberación /deliβera'θion; deliβera'sion/ *n. f.* deliberation.

deliberadamente /deliβeraða'mente/ *adv.* deliberately.

deliberar /deliβe'rar/ *v.* deliberate.

deliberativo /deliβera'tiβo/ *a.* deliberative.

delicadamente /delikaða'mente/ *adv.* delicately.

delicadeza /delika'ðeθa; delika'ðesa/ *n. f.* delicacy.

delicado /deli'kaðo/ *a.* delicate, dainty.

delicia /deli'θia; deli'sia/ *n. f.* delight; deliciousness.

delicioso /deli'θioso; deli'sioso/ *a.* delicious.

delincuencia /delin'kuenθia; delin'kuensia/ *n. f.* delinquency.

delincuencia de menores /delin'kuenθia de me'nores; delin'kuensia de me'nores/ **delincuencia juvenil** juvenile delinquency.

delincuente /delin'kuente/ *a. & n.* delinquent; culprit, offender.

delineación /delinea'θion; delinea'sion/ *n. f.* delineation, sketch.

delinear /deline'ar/ *v.* delineate, sketch.

delirante /deli'rante/ *a.* delirious.

delirar /deli'rar/ *v.* rave, be delirious.

delirio /de'lirio/ *n. m.* delirium; rapture, bliss.

delito /de'lito/ *n. m.* crime, offense.

delta /'delta/ n. m. delta (of river); hang glider.

demacrado /dema'kraðo/ a. emaciated.

demagogia /dema'gohia/ n. f. demagogy.

demagogo /dema'gogo/ n. m. demagogue.

demanda /de'manda/ n. f. demand, claim.

demandador /demanda'ðor/ -ra n. plaintiff.

demandar /deman'dar/ v. sue; demand.

demarcación /demarka'θion; demarka'sion/ n. f. demarcation.

demarcar /demar'kar/ v. demarcate, limit.

demás /de'mas/ a. & n. other; (the) rest (of). **por d.,** too much.

demasía /dema'sia/ n. f. excess; audacity; iniquity.

demasiado /dema'siaðo/ a. & adv. too; too much; too many.

demencia /de'menθia; de'mensia/ n. f. dementia; insanity.

demente /de'mente/ a. demented.

democracia /demo'kraθia; demo-'krasia/ n. f. democracy.

demócrata /de'mokrata/ n. m. & f. democrat.

democrático /demo'kratiko/ a. democratic.

demoler /demo'ler/ v. demolish, tear down.

demolición /demoli'θion; demoli-'sion/ n. f. demolition.

demonio /de'monio/ n. m. demon, devil.

demontre /de'montre/ n. m. devil.

demora /de'mora/ n. f. delay, —**demorar,** v.

demostración /demostra'θion; demostra'sion/ n. f. demonstration.

demostrador /demostra'ðor/ -ra n. demonstrator.

demostrar /demos'trar/ v. demonstrate, show.

demostrativo /demostra'tiβo/ a. demonstrative.

demudar /demu'ðar/ v. change; disguise, conceal.

denegación /denega'θion; denega'sion/ n. f. denial; refusal.

denegar /dene'gar/ v. deny; refuse.

dengue /'deŋgue/ n. m. prudishness; dengue.

denigración /denigra'θion; deni-

gra'sion/ n. f. defamation, disgrace.

denigrar /deni'grar/ v. defame, disgrace.

denodado /deno'ðaðo/ a. brave, dauntless.

denominación /denomina'θion; denomina'sion/ n. f. denomination.

denominar /denomi'nar/ v. name, call.

denotación /denota'θion; denota-'sion/ n. f. denotation.

denotar /deno'tar/ v. denote, betoken, express.

densidad /densi'ðað/ n. f. density.

denso /'denso/ a. dense.

dentado /den'taðo/ a. toothed; serrated; cogged.

dentadura /denta'ðura/ n. f. set of teeth.

dentadura postiza /denta'ðura pos'tiθa; denta'ðura pos'tisa/ false teeth, dentures.

dental /den'tal/ a. dental.

dentífrico /den'tifriko/ n. m. dentifrice, toothpaste.

dentista /den'tista/ n. m. & f. dentist.

dentistería /dentiste'ria/ n. f. dentistry.

dentro /'dentro/ adv. within, inside. **d. de poco,** in a short while.

dentudo /den'tuðo/ a. toothy (person).

denuedo /de'nueðo/ n. m. bravery, courage.

denuesto /de'nuesto/ n. m. insult, offense.

denuncia /de'nunθia; de'nunsia/ n. f. denunciation; declaration; complaint.

denunciación /denunθia'θion; denunsia'sion/ n. f. denunciation.

denunciar /denun'θiar; denun'siar/ v. denounce.

deparar /depa'rar/ v. offer; grant.

departamento /departa'mento/ n. m. department, section.

departir /depar'tir/ v. talk, chat.

dependencia /depen'denθia; depen'densia/ n. f. dependence; branch office.

depender /depen'der/ v. depend.

dependiente /depen'diente/ a. & m. dependent; clerk.

depilar /depi'lar/ v. depilate, pluck.

depilatorio /depila'torio/ a. & n. depilatory.

depistar v. mislead, put off the track.

deplorable /deplo'raβle/ a. deplorable, wretched.

deplorablemente /deploraβle-'mente/ adv. deplorably.

deplorar /deplo'rar/ v. deplore.

deponer /depo'ner/ v. depose.

deportación /deporta'θion; deporta'sion/ n. f. deportation; exile.

deportar /depor'tar/ v. deport.

deporte /de'porte/ n. m. sport. —**deportivo,** a.

deposición /deposi'θion; deposi'sion/ n. f. assertion, deposition; removal; movement.

depositante /deposi'tante/ n. m. & f. depositor.

depósito /de'posito/ n. m. deposit. —**depositar,** v.

depravación /depraβa'θion; depraβa'sion/ n. f. depravation; depravity.

depravado /depra'βaðo/ a. depraved, wicked.

depravar /depra'βar/ v. deprave, corrupt, pervert.

depreciación /depreθia'θion; depresia'sion/ n. f. depreciation.

depreciar /depre'θiar; depre'siar/ v. depreciate.

depredación /depreða'θion; depreða'sion/ n. f. depredation.

depredar /depre'ðar/ v. pillage, depredate.

depresión /depre'sion/ n. f. depression.

depresivo /depre'siβo/ a. depressive.

deprimir /depri'mir/ v. depress.

depurar /depu'rar/ v. purify.

derecha /de'retʃa/ n. f. right (hand, side).

derechera /dere'tʃera/ n. f. shortcut.

derecho /de'retʃo/ a. **1.** right; straight. —n. **2.** m. right; (the) law. **derechos,** Com. duty.

derechos civiles /de'retʃos θi'βiles; de'retʃos si'βiles/ n. m.pl. civil rights.

derechos de aduana /de'retʃos de a'ðuana/ n. m.pl. customs duty.

derechura /dere'tʃura/ n. f. straightness.

derelicto /dere'likto/ a. abandoned, derelict.

deriva /de'riβa/ n. f. Naut. drift.

derivación /deriβa'θion; deriβa-'sion/ n. f. derivation.

derivar /deri'βar/ v. derive.

dermatólogo /derma'tologo/ -a n. dermatologist, skin doctor.

derogar /dero'gar/ v. derogate; repeal, abrogate.

derramamiento /derrama'miento/ n. m. overflow.

derramar /derra'mar/ v. spill, pour, scatter.

derrame /de'rrame/ n. m. overflow; discharge.

derretir /derre'tir/ v. melt, dissolve.

derribar /derri'βar/ v. demolish, knock down; bowl over, floor, fell.

derrocamiento /derroka'miento/ n. m. overthrow.

derrocar /derro'kar/ v. overthrow; oust; demolish.

derrochar /derro'tʃar/ v. waste.

derroche /de'rrotʃe/ n. m. waste.

derrota /de'rrota/ n. f. rout, defeat. —**derrotar,** v.

derrotismo /derro'tismo/ n. m. defeatism.

derrumbamiento /derrumba-'miento/ **derrumbe** m. collapse; landslide.

derrumbarse /derrum'βarse/ v. collapse, tumble.

derviche /der'βitʃe/ n. m. dervish.

desabotonar /desaβoto'nar/ v. unbutton.

desabrido /desa'βriðo/ a. insipid, tasteless.

desabrigar /desaβri'gar/ v. uncover.

desabrochar /desaβro'tʃar/ v. unbutton, unclasp.

desacato /desa'kato/ n. m. disrespect, lack of respect.

desacierto /desa'θierto; desa-'sierto/ n. m. error.

desacobardar /desakoβar'ðar/ v. remove fear; embolden.

desacomodadamente /desako-moðaða'mente/ adv. inconveniently.

desacomodado /desakomo'ðaðo/ a. unemployed.

desacomodar /desakomo'ðar/ v. molest; inconvenience; dismiss.

desacomodo /desako'moðo/ n. m. loss of employment.

desaconsejar /desakonse'har/ v. dissuade (someone); advise against (something).

desacordadamente /desakorðaða'mente/ adv. unadvisedly.

desacordar /desakor'ðar/ v. differ, disagree; be forgetful.

desacorde /desa'korðe/ a. discordant.

desacostumbradamente /desakostumbraða'mente/ adv. unusually.

desacostumbrado /desakostum'braðo/ a. unusual, unaccustomed.

desacostumbrar /desakostum'brar/ v. give up a habit or custom.

desacreditar /desakreði'tar/ v. discredit.

desacuerdo /desa'kuerðo/ n. m. disagreement.

desadeudar /desaðeu'ðar/ v. pay one's debts.

desadormecer /desaðorme'θer; desaðorme'ser/ v. waken, rouse.

desadornar /desaðor'nar/ v. divest of ornament.

desadvertidamente /desaðβertiða'mente/ adv. inadvertently.

desadvertido /desaðβer'tiðo/ a. imprudent.

desadvertimiento /desaðβerti'miento/ n. m. imprudence, rashness.

desadvertir /desaðβer'tir/ v. act imprudently.

desafección /desafek'θion; desafek'sion/ n. f. disaffection.

desafecto /desa'fekto/ a. disaffected.

desafiar /desa'fiar/ v. defy; challenge.

desafinar /desafi'nar/ v. be out of tune.

desafío /desa'fio/ n. m. defiance; challenge.

desaforar /desafo'rar/ v. infringe one's rights; be outrageous.

desafortunado /desafortu'naðo/ a. unfortunate.

desafuero /desa'fuero/ n. m. violation of the law; outrage.

desagraciado /desagra'θiaðo; desagra'siaðo/ a. graceless.

desagradable /desagra'ðaβle/ a. disagreeable, unpleasant.

desagradablemente /desagraðaβle'mente/ adv. disagreeably.

desagradecido /desagraðe'θiðo; desagraðe'siðo/ a. ungrateful.

desagradecimiento /desagraðeθi'miento; desagraðesimiento/ n. m. ingratitude.

desagrado /desa'graðo/ n. m. displeasure.

desagraviar /desagra'βiar/ v. make amends.

desagregar /desagre'gar/ v. separate, disintegrate.

desagriar /desa'griar/ v. mollify, appease.

desaguadero /desagua'ðero/ n. m. drain, outlet; cesspool; sink.

desaguador /desagua'ðor/ n. m. water pipe.

desaguar /desa'guar/ v. drain.

desaguisado /desagi'saðo/ n. m. offense; injury.

desahogadamente /desaogaða'mente/ adv. impudently; brazenly.

desahogado /desao'gaðo/ a. impudent, brazen; cheeky.

desahogar /desao'gar/ v. relieve.

desahogo /desa'ogo/ n. m. relief; nerve, cheek.

desahuciar /desau'θiar; desau'siar/ v. give up hope for; despair of.

desairado /desai'raðo/ a. graceless.

desaire /des'aire/ n. m. slight; scorn. —**desairar,** v.

desajustar /desahus'tar/ v. mismatch, misfit; make unfit.

desalar /desa'lar/ v. hurry, hasten.

desalentar /desalen'tar/ v. make out of breath; discourage.

desaliento /desa'liento/ n. m. discouragement.

desaliñar /desali'ɲar/ v. disarrange; make untidy.

desaliño /desa'liɲo/ n. m. slovenliness, untidiness.

desalivar /desali'βar/ v. remove saliva from.

desalmadamente /desalmaða'mente/ adv. mercilessly.

desalmado /desal'maðo/ a. merciless.

desalojamiento /desaloha'miento/ n. m. displacement; dislodging.

desalojar /desalo'har/ v. dislodge.

desalquilado /desalki'laðo/ a. vacant, unrented.

desamar /desa'mar/ v. cease loving.

desamasado /desama'saðo/ *a.*
dissolved, disunited, undone.

desamistarse /desamis'tarse/ *v.*
quarrel, disagree.

desamor /desa'mor/ *n. m.* disaffection, dislike; hatred.

desamorado /desamo'raðo/ *a.*
cruel; harsh; rude.

desamparador /desampara'ðor/ *n.
m.* deserter.

desamparar /desampa'rar/ *v.* desert, abandon.

desamparo /desam'paro/ *n. m.*
desertion, abandonment.

desamueblado /desamue'βlaðo/
a. unfurnished.

desamueblar /desamue'βlar/ *v.*
remove furniture from.

desandrajado /desandra'haðo/ *a.*
shabby, ragged.

desanimadamente /desanima-
ða'mente/ *adv.* in a discouraged
manner; spiritlessly.

desanimar /desani'mar/ *v.* dishearten, discourage.

desánimo /des'animo/ *n. m.* discouragement.

desanudar /desanu'ðar/ *v.* untie;
loosen; disentangle.

desapacible /desapa'θiβle; desa-
pa'siβle/ *a.* rough, harsh; unpleasant.

desaparecer /desapare'θer; desa-
pare'ser/ *v.* disappear.

desaparición /desapari'θion; desa-
pari'sion/ *n. f.* disappearance.

desapasionadamente /desapa-
sionaða'mente/ *adv.* dispassionately.

desapasionado /desapasio'naðo/
a. dispassionate.

desapego /desa'pego/ *n. m.* impartiality.

desapercibido /desaperθi'βiðo;
desapersi'βiðo/ *a.* unnoticed; unprepared.

desapiadado /desapia'ðaðo/ *a.*
merciless, cruel.

desaplicación /desaplika'θion; de-
saplika'sion/ *n. f.* indolence, laziness; negligence.

desaplicado /desapli'kaðo/ *a.* indolent, lazy; negligent.

desaposesionar /desaposesio'nar/
v. dispossess.

desapreciar /desapre'θiar; desa-
pre'siar/ *v.* depreciate.

desapretador /desapreta'ðor/ *n.
m.* screwdriver.

desapretar /desapre'tar/ *v.*
loosen; relieve, ease.

desaprisionar /desaprisio'nar/ *v.*
set free, release.

desaprobación /desaproβa'θion;
desaproβa'sion/ *n. f.* disapproval.

desaprobar /desapro'βar/ *v.* disapprove.

desaprovechado /desaproβe-
'tʃaðo/ *a.* useless, profitless;
backward.

desaprovechar /desaproβe'tʃar/ *v.*
waste; be backward.

desarbolar /desarβo'lar/ *v.* unmast.

desarmado /desar'maðo/ *a.* disarmed, defenseless.

desarmar /desar'mar/ *v.* disarm.

desarme /de'sarme/ *n. m.* disarmament.

desarraigado /desarrai'gaðo/ *a.*
rootless.

desarraigar /desarrai'gar/ *v.* uproot; eradicate; expel.

desarreglar /desarre'glar/ *v.* disarrange, mess up.

desarrollar /desarro'ʎar; desarro-
'yar/ *v.* develop.

desarrollo /desa'rroʎo; des-
'arroyo/ *n. m.* development.

desarropar /desarro'par/ *v.* undress; uncover.

desarrugar /desarru'gar/ *v.* remove wrinkles from.

desaseado /desase'aðo/ *a.* dirty;
disorderly.

desasear /desase'ar/ *v.* make dirty
or disorderly.

desaseo /desa'seo/ *n. m.* dirtiness; disorder.

desasir /desa'sir/ *v.* loosen; disengage.

desasociable /desaso'θiaβle; desaso'siaβle/ *a.* unsociable.

desasosegar /desasose'gar/ *v.* disturb.

desasosiego /desaso'siego/ *n. m.*
uneasiness.

desastrado /desas'traðo/ *a.*
ragged, wretched.

desastre /de'sastre/ *n. m.* disaster.

desastroso /desas'troso/ *a.* disastrous.

desatar /desa'tar/ *v.* untie, undo.

desatención /desaten'θion; desa-
ten'sion/ *n. f.* inattention; disrespect; rudeness.

desatender /desaten'der/ *v.* ignore; disregard.

desatentado /desaten'taðo/ a. inconsiderate; imprudent.

desatinado /desati'naðo/ a. foolish; insane, wild.

desatino /desa'tino/ n. m. blunder. **—desatinar,** v.

desatornillar /desatorni'ʎar; desatorni'yar/ v. unscrew.

desautorizado /desautori'θaðo; desautori'saðo/ a. unauthorized.

desautorizar /desautori'θar; desautori'sar/ v. deprive of authority.

desavenencia /desaβe'nenθia; desaβe'nensia/ n. f. disagreement, discord.

desaventajado /desaβenta'haðo/ a. disadvantageous.

desayuno /desa'yuno/ n. m. breakfast. **—desayunar,** v.

desazón /desa'θon; desa'son/ n. f. insipidity; uneasiness.

desazonado /desaθo'naðo; desaso'naðo/ a. insipid; uneasy.

desbandada /desβan'daða/ n. f. disbanding.

desbandarse /desβan'darse/ v. disband.

desbarajuste /desβara'huste/ n. m. disorder, confusion.

desbaratar /desβara'tar/ v. destroy.

desbastar /desβas'tar/ v. plane, smoothen.

desbocado /desβo'kaðo/ a. foulspoken, indecent.

desbocarse /desβo'karse/ v. use obscene language.

desbordamiento /desβorða'miento/ n. m. overflow; flood.

desbordar /desβor'ðar/ v. overflow.

desbrozar /desβro'θar; desβro'sar/ v. clear away rubbish.

descabal /deska'βal/ a. incomplete.

descabalar /deskaβa'lar/ v. render incomplete; impair.

descabellado /deskaβe'ʎaðo; deskaβe'yaðo/ a. absurd, preposterous.

descabezar /deskaβe'θar; deskaβe'sar/ v. behead.

descaecimiento /deskaeθi'miento; deskaesi'miento/ n. m. weakness; dejection.

descafeinado /deskafei'naðo/ a. decaffeinated.

descalabrar /deskala'βrar/ v. injure, wound (esp. the head).

descalabro /deska'laβro/ n. m. accident, misfortune.

descalzarse /deskal'θarse; deskal'sarse/ v. take off one's shoes.

descalzo /des'kalθo; des'kalso/ a. shoeless; barefoot.

descaminado /deskami'naðo/ a. wrong, misguided.

descaminar /deskami'nar/ v. mislead; lead into error.

descamisado /deskami'saðo/ a. shirtless; shabby.

descansillo /deskan'siʎo; deskan'siyo/ n. m. landing (of stairs).

descanso /des'kanso/ n. m. rest. **—descansar,** v.

descarado /deska'raðo/ a. saucy, fresh.

descarga /des'karga/ n. f. discharge.

descargar /deskar'gar/ v. discharge, unload, dump.

descargo /des'kargo/ n. m. unloading; acquittal.

descarnar /deskar'nar/ v. skin.

descaro /des'karo/ n. m. gall, effrontery.

descarriar /deska'rriar/ v. lead or go astray.

descarrilamiento /deskarrila'miento/ n. m. derailment.

descarrilar /deskarri'lar/ v. derail.

descartar /deskar'tar/ v. discard.

descascarar /deskaska'rar/ v. peel; boast, brag.

descendencia /desθen'denθia; dessen'densia/ n. f. descent, origin; progeny.

descender /desθen'der; dessen'der/ v. descend.

descendiente /desθen'diente; dessen'diente/ n. m. & f. descendant.

descendimiento /desθendi'miento; dessendi'miento/ n. m. descent.

descenso /des'θenso; des'senso/ n. m. descent.

descifrar /desθi'frar; dessi'frar/ v. decipher, puzzle out.

descoco /des'koko/ n. m. boldness, brazenness.

descolgar /deskol'gar/ v. take down.

descollar /desko'ʎar; desko'yar/ v. stand out; excel.

descolorar /deskolo'rar/ v. discolor.

descolorido /deskolo'riðo/ a. pale, faded.

descomedido /deskome'ðiðo/ a. disproportionate; rude.

descomedirse /deskome'ðirse/ v. be rude.

descomponer /deskompo'ner/ v. decompose; break down, get out of order.

descomposición /deskomposi'θion; deskomposi'sion/ n. f. discomposure; disorder, confusion.

descompuesto /deskom'puesto/ a. impudent, rude.

descomulgar /deskomul'gar/ v. excommunicate.

descomunal /deskomu'nal/ a. extraordinary, huge.

desconcertar /deskonθer'tar; deskonser'tar/ v. disconcert, baffle.

desconcierto /deskon'θierto; deskon'sierto/ n. m. confusion, disarray.

desconectar /deskonek'tar/ v. disconnect.

desconfiado /deskon'fiaðo/ a. distrustful.

desconfianza /deskon'fianθa; deskon'fiansa/ n. f. distrust.

desconfiar /deskon'fiar/ v. distrust, mistrust; suspect.

descongelar /deskoŋge'lar/ v. defrost.

descongestionante /deskoŋgestio'nante/ n. m. decongestant.

desconocer /deskono'θer; deskono'ser/ v. ignore, fail to recognize.

desconocido /deskono'θiðo; deskonos'iðo/ **-da** n. stranger.

desconocimiento /deskonoθi-'miento; deskonosi'miento/ n. m. ingratitude; ignorance.

desconsejado /deskonse'haðo/ a. imprudent, ill advised, rash.

desconsolado /deskonso'laðo/ a. disconsolate, wretched.

desconsuelo /deskon'suelo/ n. m. grief.

descontar /deskon'tar/ v. discount, subtract.

descontentar /deskonten'tar/ v. dissatisfy.

descontento /deskon'tento/ n. m. discontent.

descontinuar /deskonti'nuar/ v. discontinue.

desconvenir /deskombe'nir/ v. disagree.

descorazonar /deskoraθo'nar; deskoraso'nar/ v. dishearten.

descorchar /deskor'tʃar/ v. uncork.

descortés /deskor'tes/ a. discourteous, impolite, rude.

descortesía /deskorte'sia/ n. f. discourtesy, rudeness.

descortezar /deskorte'θar; deskorte'sar/ v. peel.

descoyuntar /deskoyun'tar/ v. dislocate.

descrédito /des'kreðito/ n. m. discredit.

describir /deskri'βir/ v. describe.

descripción /deskrip'θion; deskrip'sion/ n. f. description.

descriptivo /deskrip'tiβo/ a. descriptive.

descuartizar /deskuarti'θar; deskuarti'sar/ v. dismember, disjoint.

descubridor /deskuβri'ðor/ **-ra** n. discoverer.

descubrimiento /deskuβri'miento/ n. m. discovery.

descubrir /desku'βrir/ v. discover; uncover; disclose.

descubrirse /desku'βrirse/ v. take off one's hat.

descuento /des'kuento/ n. m. discount.

descuidado /deskui'ðaðo/ a. reckless, careless; slack.

descuido /des'kuiðo/ n. m. neglect. **—descuidar,** v.

desde /'desðe/ prep. since; from. **d. luego,** of course.

desdén /des'ðen/ n. m. disdain. **—desdeñar,** v.

desdeñoso /desðe'ɲoso/ a. contemptuous, disdainful, scornful.

desdicha /des'ðitʃa/ n. f. misfortune.

deseable /dese'aβle/ a. desirable.

desear /dese'ar/ v. desire, wish.

desecar /dese'kar/ v. dry, desiccate.

desechable /dese'tʃaβle/ a. disposable.

desechar /dese'tʃar/ v. scrap, reject.

desecho /de'setʃo/ n. m. remainder, residue; (pl.) waste.

desembalar /desemba'lar/ v. unpack.

desembarazado /desembara-'θaðo; desembara'saðo/ a. free; unrestrained.

desembarazar /desembara'θar; desemba'sar/ *v.* free; extricate; unburden.

desembarcar /desembar'kar/ *v.* disembark, go ashore.

desembocar /desembo'kar/ *v.* flow into.

desembolsar /desembol'sar/ *v.* disburse; expend.

desembolso /desem'bolso/ *n. m.* disbursement.

desemejante /deseme'hante/ *a.* unlike, dissimilar.

desempacar /desempa'kar/ *v.* unpack.

desempeñar /desempe'ɲar/ *v.* carry out; redeem.

desempeño /desempe'ɲo/ *n. m.* fulfillment.

desencajar /desenka'har/ *v.* disjoint; disturb.

desencantar /desenkan'tar/ *v.* disillusion.

desencanto /desen'kanto/ *n. m.* disillusion.

desencarcelar /desenkarθe'lar; desenkarse'lar/ *v.* set free; release.

desenchufar /desentʃu'far/ *v.* unplug.

desenfadado /desenfa'ðaðo/ *a.* free; unembarrassed; spacious.

desenfado /desen'faðo/ *n. m.* freedom; ease; calmness.

desenfocado /desenfo'kaðo/ *a.* out of focus.

desengaño /deseŋ'gaɲo/ *m.* disillusion. —**desengañar** *v.*

desenlace /desen'laθe; desen'lase/ *n. m.* outcome, conclusion.

desenredar /desenre'ðar/ *v.* disentangle.

desensartar /desensar'tar/ *v.* unthread (pearls).

desentenderse /desenten'derse/ *v.* overlook; avoid noticing.

desenterrar /desente'rrar/ *v.* disinter, exhume.

desenvainar /desembai'nar/ *v.* unsheath.

desenvoltura /desembol'tura/ *n. f.* confidence; impudence, boldness.

desenvolver /desembol'βer/ *v.* evolve, unfold.

deseo /de'seo/ *n. m.* wish, desire, urge.

deseoso /dese'oso/ *a.* desirous.

deserción /deser'θion; deser'sion/ *n. f.* desertion.

desertar /deser'tar/ *v.* desert.

desertor /deser'tor/ **-ra** *n.* deserter.

desesperación /desespera'θion; desespera'sion/ *n. f.* despair, desperation.

desesperado /desespe'raðo/ *a.* desperate; hopeless.

desesperar /desespe'rar/ *v.* despair.

desfachatez /desfatʃa'teθ; desfatʃa'tes/ *n. f.* cheek (gall).

desfalcar /desfal'kar/ *v.* embezzle.

desfase horario /des'fase o'rario/ *n. m.* jet lag.

desfavorable /desfaβo'raβle/ *a.* unfavorable.

desfigurar /desfigu'rar/ *v.* disfigure, mar.

desfiladero /desfila'ðero/ *n. m.* defile.

desfile /des'file/ *n. m.* parade. —**desfilar,** *v.*

desfile de modas /des'file de 'moðas/ fashion show.

desgaire /des'gaire/ *n. m.* slovenliness.

desgana /des'gana/ *n. f.* lack of appetite; unwillingness; repugnance.

desgarrar /desga'rrar/ *v.* tear, lacerate.

desgastar /desgas'tar/ *v.* wear away; waste; erode.

desgaste /des'gaste/ *n. m.* wear; erosion.

desgracia /des'graθia; des'grasia/ *n. f.* misfortune.

desgraciado /desgra'θiaðo; desgra'siaðo/ *a.* unfortunate.

desgranar /desgra'nar/ *v.* shell.

desgreñar /desgre'ɲar/ *v.* dishevel.

deshacer /desa'θer; desa'ser/ *v.* undo, take apart, destroy.

deshacerse de /desa'θerse de; desa'serse de/ *v.* get rid of, dispose of.

deshecho /des'etʃo/ *a.* undone; wasted.

deshelar /dese'lar/ *v.* thaw; melt.

desheredamiento /desereða-'miento/ *n. m.* disinheriting.

desheredar /desere'ðar/ *v.* disinherit.

deshielo /des'ielo/ *n. m.* thaw, melting.

deshinchar /desin'tʃar/ *v.* reduce a swelling.

deshojarse /deso'harse/ *v.* shed (leaves).

deshonestidad /desonesti'ðað/ *n. f.* dishonesty.

deshonesto /deso'nesto/ *a.* dishonest.

deshonra /de'sonra/ *n. f.* dishonor.

deshonrar /deson'rar/ *v.* disgrace; dishonor.

deshonroso /deson'roso/ *a.* dishonorable.

desierto /de'sierto/ *n. m.* desert, wilderness.

designar /desig'nar/ *v.* appoint, name.

designio /de'signio/ *n. m.* purpose, intent.

desigual /desi'gual/ *a.* uneven, unequal.

desigualdad /desigual'dað/ *n. f.* inequality.

desilusión /desilu'sion/ *n. f.* disappointment.

desinfección /desinfek'θion; desinfek'sion/ *n. f.* disinfection.

desinfectar /desinfek'tar/ *v.* disinfect.

desintegrar /desinte'grar/ *v.* disintegrate, zap.

desinterés /desinte'res/ *n. m.* indifference.

desinteresado /desintere'saðo/ *a.* disinterested, unselfish.

desistir /desis'tir/ *v.* desist, stop.

desleal /desle'al/ *a.* disloyal.

deslealtad /desleal'tað/ *n. f.* disloyalty.

desleir /desle'ir/ *v.* dilute, dissolve.

desligar /desli'gar/ *v.* untie, loosen; free, release.

deslindar /deslin'dar/ *v.* make the boundaries of.

deslinde /des'linde/ *n. m.* demarcation.

desliz /des'liθ; des'lis/ *n. m.* slip; false step; weakness.

deslizarse /desli'θarse; desli'sarse/ *v.* slide; slip; glide; coast.

deslumbramiento /deslumbra'miento/ *n. m.* dazzling glare; confusion.

deslumbrar /deslumb'rar/ *v.* dazzle; glare.

deslustre /des'lustre/ *n. m.* tarnish. **—deslustrar,** *v.*

desmán /des'man/ *n. m.* mishap; misbehavior; excess.

desmantelar /desmante'lar/ *v.* dismantle.

desmañado /desma'ɲaðo/ *a.* awkward, clumsy.

desmaquillarse /desmaki'ʎarse; desmaki'yarse/ *v.* remove one's makeup.

desmayar /desma'yar/ *v.* depress, dishearten.

desmayo /des'mayo/ *n. m.* faint. **—desmayarse,** *v.*

desmejorar /desmeho'rar/ *v.* make worse; decline.

desmembrar /desmem'brar/ *v.* dismember.

desmemoria /desme'moria/ *n. f.* forgetfulness.

desmemoriado /desmemo'riaðo/ *a.* forgetful.

desmentir /desmen'tir/ *v.* contradict, disprove.

desmenuzable /desmenu'θaβle; desmenu'saβle/ *a.* crisp, crumbly.

desmenuzar /desmenu'θar; desmenu'sar/ *v.* crumble, break into bits.

desmesurado /desmesu'raðo/ *a.* excessive.

desmobilizar /desmoβili'θar; desmoβili'sar/ *v.* demobilize.

desmonetización /desmonetiθa-'θion; desmonetisa'sion/ *n. f.* demonetization.

desmonetizar /desmoneti'θar; desmoneti'sar/ *v.* demonetize.

desmontado /desmon'taðo/ *a.* dismounted.

desmontar /desmon'tar/ *v.* dismantle.

desmontarse /desmon'tarse/ *v.* dismount.

desmoralización /desmoraliθa-'θion; desmoralisa'sion/ *n. f.* demoralization.

desmoralizar /desmorali'θar; desmorali'sar/ *v.* demoralize.

desmoronar /desmoro'nar/ *v.* crumble, decay.

desmovilizar /desmoβili'θar; desmoβili'sar/ *v.* demobilize.

desnatar /desna'tar/ *v.* skim.

desnaturalización /desnaturaliθa-'θion; desnaturalisa'sion/ *n. f.* denaturalization.

desnaturalizar /desnaturali'θar; desnaturali'sar/ *v.* denaturalize.

desnegamiento /desnega'miento/ *n. m.* denial, contradiction.

desnervar /desner'βar/ *v.* enervate.

desnivel /desni'βel/ *n. m.* unevenness or difference in elevation.

desnudamente /desnuða'mente/ *adv.* nakedly.

desnudar /desnu'ðar/ *v.* undress.

desnudez /desnu'ðeθ; desnu'ðes/ *n. f.* bareness, nudity.

desnudo /des'nuðo/ *a.* bare, naked.

desnutrición /desnutri'θion; desnutri'sion/ *n. f.* malnutrition.

desobedecer /desoβeðe'θer; desoβeðe'ser/ *v.* disobey.

desobediencia /desoβeðien'θia; desoβeðien'sia/ *n. f.* disobedience.

desobediente /desoβe'ðiente/ *a.* disobedient.

desobedientemente /desoβeðiente'mente/ *adv.* disobediently.

desobligar /desoβli'gar/ *v.* release from obligation; offend.

desocupado /desoku'paðo/ *a.* idle, not busy; vacant.

desocupar /desoku'par/ *v.* vacate.

desolación /desola'θion; desola'sion/ *n. f.* desolation; ruin.

desolado /deso'laðo/ *a.* desolate. —**desolar,** *v.*

desollar /deso'ʎar; deso'yar/ *v.* skin.

desorden /de'sorðen/ *n. m.* disorder.

desordenar /desorðe'nar/ *v.* disarrange.

desorganización /desorganiθa-'θion; desorganisa'sion/ *n. f.* disorganization.

desorganizar /desorgani'θar; desorgani'sar/ *v.* disorganize.

despabilado /despaβi'laðo/ *a.* vigilant, watchful; lively.

despachar /despa'tʃar/ *v.* dispatch, ship, send.

despacho /despa'tʃo/ *n. m.* shipment; dispatch, promptness; office.

despacio /des'paθio; des'pasio/ *adv.* slowly.

desparpajo /despar'paho/ *n. m.* glibness; fluency of speech.

desparramar /desparra'mar/ *v.* scatter.

despavorido /despaβo'riðo/ *a.* terrified.

despecho /des'petʃo/ *n. m.* spite.

despedazar /despeða'θar; despeða'sar/ *v.* tear up.

despedida /despe'ðiða/ *n. f.* farewell; leave-taking; discharge.

despedir /despe'ðir/ *v.* dismiss, discharge; see off.

despedirse de /despe'ðirse de/ *v.* say good-bye to, take leave of.

despegar /despe'gar/ *v.* unglue; separate; *Aero.* take off.

despego /des'pego/ *n. m.* indifference; disinterest.

despejar /despe'har/ *v.* clear, clear up.

despejo /des'peho/ *n. m.* sprightliness; clarity; without obstruction.

despensa /des'pensa/ *n. f.* pantry.

despensero /despen'sero/ *n. m.* butler.

despeñar /despe'ɲar/ *v.* throw down.

desperdicio /desper'ðiθio; desper'ðisio/ *n. m.* waste. —**desperdiciar,** *v.*

despertador /desperta'ðor/ *n. m.* alarm clock.

despertar /desper'tar/ *v.* wake, wake up.

despesar /despe'sar/ *n. m.* dislike.

despicar /despi'kar/ *v.* satisfy.

despidida /despi'ðiða/ *n. f.* gutter.

despierto /des'pierto/ *a.* awake, alert, wide-awake.

despilfarrado /despilfa'rraðo/ *a.* wasteful, extravagant.

despilfarrar /despilfa'rrar/ *v.* waste, squander.

despilfarro /despil'farro/ *n. m.* waste, extravagance.

despique /des'pike/ *n. m.* revenge.

despistar /despis'tar/ *v.* mislead, put off the track.

desplazamiento /desplaθa-'miento; desplasa'miento/ *n. m.* displacement.

desplegar /desple'gar/ *v.* display; unfold.

desplome /des'plome/ *n. m.* collapse. —**desplomarse,** *v.*

desplumar /desplu'mar/ *v.* defeather, pluck.

despoblar /despo'βlar/ *v.* depopulate.

despojar /despo'har/ *v.* strip; despoil, plunder.

despojo /des'poho/ *n. m.* plunder, spoils; (*pl.*) remains, debris.

desposado /despo'saðo/ *a.* newly married.

desposar /despo'sar/ *v.* marry.

desposeer /despose'er/ *v.* dispossess.

déspota /'despota/ *n. m. & f.* despot.

despótico /des'potiko/ *a.* despotic.

despotismo /despo'tismo/ *n. m.* despotism, tyranny.

despreciable /despre'θiaβle; despre'siaβle/ *a.* contemptible.

despreciar /despre'θiar; despre'siar/ *v.* spurn, despise, scorn.

desprecio /des'preθio; des'presio/ *n. m.* scorn, contempt.

desprender /despren'der/ *v.* detach, unfasten.

desprenderse /despren'derse/ *v.* loosen, come apart. **d. de,** part with.

desprendido /despren'diðo/ *a.* disinterested.

despreocupado /despreoku'paðo/ *a.* unconcerned; unprejudiced.

desprevenido /despreβe'niðo/ *a.* unprepared, unready.

desproporción /despropor'θion; despropor'sion/ *n. f.* disproportion.

despropósito /despro'posito/ *n. m.* nonsense.

desprovisto /despro'βisto/ *a.* devoid.

después /des'pues/ *adv.* afterwards, later; then, next. **d. de, d. que,** after.

despuntar /despun'tar/ *v.* blunt; remove the point of.

desquiciar /deski'θiar; deski'siar/ *v.* unhinge; disturb, unsettle.

desquitar /deski'tar/ *v.* get revenge, retaliate.

desquite /des'kite/ *n. m.* revenge, retaliation.

desrazonable /desraθo'naβle; desraso'naβle/ *a.* unresonable.

destacamento /destaka'mento/ *n. m. Mil.* detachment.

destacarse /desta'karse/ *v.* stand out, be prominent.

destajero /desta'hero/ **-a** *n.* **destajista,** *m. & f.* pieceworker.

destapar /desta'par/ *v.* uncover.

destello /des'teʎo; deste'yo/ *n. m.* sparkle, gleam.

destemplar /destem'plar/ *v. Mus.* untune; disturb, upset.

desteñir /deste'ɲir/ *v.* fade, discolor.

desterrado /deste'rraðo/ **-da** *n.* exile.

desterrar /deste'rrar/ *v.* banish, exile.

destetar /deste'tar/ *v.* wean.

destierro /des'tierro/ *n. m.* banishment, exile.

destilación /destila'θion; destila'sion/ *n. f.* distillation.

destilar /desti'lar/ *v.* distill.

destilería /destile'ria/ *n. f.* distillery.

destilería de petróleo /destile'ria de pe'troleo/ oil refinery.

destinación /destina'θion; destina'sion/ *n. f.* destination.

destinar /desti'nar/ *v.* destine, intend.

destinatario /destina'tario/ **-ria** *n.* addressee (mail); payee (money).

destino /des'tino/ *n. m.* destiny, fate; destination.

destitución /destitu'θion; destitu'sion/ *n. f.* dismissal; abandonment.

destituido /desti'tuiðo/ *a.* destitute.

destorcer /destor'θer; destor'ser/ *v.* undo, straighten out.

destornillado /destorni'ʎaðo; destorni'yaðo/ *a.* reckless, careless.

destornillador /destorni'ʎaðor; destorni'yaðor/ *n. m.* screwdriver.

destraillar /destrai'ʎar; destrai'yar/ *v.* unleash; set loose.

destral /des'tral/ *n. m.* hatchet.

destreza /des'treθa; des'tresa/ *n. f.* cleverness; dexterity, skill.

destripar /destri'par/ *v.* eviscerate, disembowel.

destrísimo /des'trisimo/ *a.* extremely dexterous.

destronamiento /destrona'miento/ *n. m.* dethronement.

destronar /destro'nar/ *v.* dethrone.

destrozador /destroθa'ðor; destrosa'ðor/ *n. m.* destroyer, wrecker.

destrozar /destro'θar; destro'sar/ *v.* destroy, wreck.

destrozo /des'troθo; des'troso/ *n. m.* destruction, ruin.

destrucción /destruk'θion; destruk'sion/ *n. f.* destruction.

destructibilidad /destruktiβili'ðað/ *n. f.* destructibility.

destructible /destruk'tiβle/ *a.* destructible.

destructivamente /destruktiβa'mente/ *adv.* destructively.

destructivo /destruk'tiβo/ *a.* destructive.

destruir /destruir/ v. destroy; wipe out.

desuello /desue'ʎo; desue'yo/ n. m. impudence.

desunión /desu'nion/ n. f. disunion; discord; separation.

desunir /desu'nir/ v. disconnect, sever.

desusadamente /desusaða'mente/ adv. unusually.

desusado /desu'saðo/ a. archaic; obsolete.

desuso /de'suso/ n. m. disuse.

desvalido /des'βaliðo/ a. helpless; destitute.

desvalijador /desβaliha'ðor/ n. m. highwayman.

desván /des'βan/ n. m. attic.

desvanecerse /desβane'θerse; desβane'serse/ v. vanish; faint.

desvariado /desβa'riaðo/ a. delirious; disorderly.

desvarío /desβa'rio/ n. m. raving. —**desvariar,** v.

desvedado /desβe'ðaðo/ a. free; unrestrained.

desveladamente /desβelaða-'mente/ adv. watchfully, alertly.

desvelado /desβe'laðo/ a. watchful; alert.

desvelar /desβe'lar/ v. be watchful; keep awake.

desvelo /des'βelo/ n. m. vigilance; uneasiness; insomnia.

desventaja /desβen'taha/ n. f. disadvantage.

desventar /desβen'tar/ v. let air out of.

desventura /desβen'tura/ n. f. misfortune.

desventurado /desβentu'raðo/ a. unhappy; unlucky.

desvergonzado /desβergon'θaðo; desβergonsaðo/ a. shameless, brazen.

desvergüenza /desβer'guenθa; desβer'guensa/ n. f. shamelessness.

desvestir /desβes'tir/ v. undress.

desviación /desβia'θion; desβia-'sion/ n. f. deviation.

desviado /des'βiaðo/ a. deviant; remote.

desviar /des'βiar/ v. divert; deviate, detour.

desvío /des'βio/ n. m. detour; side track; indifference.

desvirtuar /desβir'tuar/ v. decrease the value of.

deszumar /desθu'mar; dessu'mar/ v. remove the juice from.

detalle /de'taʎe; de'taye/ n. m. detail. —**detallar,** v.

detective /de'tektiβe/ n. m. & f. detective.

detención /deten'θion; deten'sion/ n. f. detention, arrest.

detenedor /detene'ðor/ -ra n. stopper; catch.

detener /dete'ner/ v. detain, stop; arrest.

detenidamente /deteniða'mente/ adv. carefully, slowly.

detenido /dete'niðo/ adv. stingy; thorough.

detergente /deter'hente/ a. detergent.

deterioración /deteriora'θion; deteriora'sion/ n. f. deterioration.

deteriorar /deterio'rar/ v. deteriorate.

determinable /determi'naβle/ a. determinable.

determinación /determina'θion; determina'sion/ n. f. determination.

determinar /determi'nar/ v. determine, settle, decide.

determinismo /determi'nismo/ n. m. determinism.

determinista /determi'nista/ n. & a. determinist.

detestable /detes'taβle/ a. detestable, hateful.

detestablemente /detestaβle-'mente/ adv. detestably, hatefully, abhorrently.

detestación /detesta'θion; detesta'sion/ n. f. detestation, hatefulness.

detestar /detes'tar/ v. detest.

detonación /detona'θion; detona'sion/ n. f. detonation.

detonar /deto'nar/ v. detonate, explode.

detracción /detrak'θion; detrak-'sion/ n. f. detraction, defamation.

detractar /detrak'tar/ v. detract, defame, vilify.

detraer /detra'er/ v. detract.

detrás /de'tras/ adv. behind; in back.

detrimento /detri'mento/ n. m. detriment, damage.

deuda /'deuða/ n. f. debt.

deudo /'deuðo/ -da n. relative, kin.

deudor /deu'ðor/ -ra n. debtor.

Deuteronomio /deutero'nomio/ *n. m.* Deuteronomy.

devalar /deβa'lar/ *v.* drift off course.

devanar /deβa'nar/ *v.* to wind, as on a spool.

devanear /deβane'ar/ *v.* talk deliriously, rave.

devaneo /deβa'neo/ *n. m.* frivolity; idle pursuit; delirium.

devastación /deβasta'θion; deβasta'sion/ *n. f.* devastation, ruin, havoc.

devastador /deβasta'ðor/ *a.* devastating.

devastar /deβas'tar/ *v.* devastate.

devenir /deβe'nir/ *v.* happen, occur; become.

devoción /deβo'θion; deβo'sion/ *n. f.* devotion.

devocionario /deβoθio'nario; deβosio'nario/ *n. m.* prayer book.

devocionero /deβoθio'nero; deβosio'nero/ *a.* devotional.

devolver /deβol'βer/ *v.* return, give back.

devorar /deβo'rar/ *v.* devour.

devotamente /deβota'mente/ *adv.* devotedly, devoutly, piously.

devoto /de'βoto/ *a.* devout; devoted.

deyección /deiek'θion; deiek'sion/ *n. f.* depression, dejection.

día /dia/ *n. m.* day. **buenos días,** good morning.

diabetes /dia'βetes/ *n. f.* diabetes.

diabético /dia'βetiko/ *a.* diabetic.

diablear /diaβle'ar/ *v.* play pranks.

diablo /'diaβlo/ *n. m.* devil.

diablura /dia'βlura/ *n. f.* mischief.

diabólicamente /diaβolika'mente/ *adv.* diabolically.

diabólico /dia'βoliko/ *a.* diabolic, devilish.

diaconato /diako'nato/ *n. m.* deaconship.

diaconía /diako'nia/ *n. f.* deaconry.

diácono /'diakono/ *n. m.* deacon.

diacrítico /dia'kritiko/ *a.* diacritic.

diadema /dia'ðema/ *n. f.* diadem; crown.

diáfano /'diafano/ *a.* transparent.

diafragma /dia'fragma/ *n. m.* diaphragm.

diagnosticar /diagnosti'kar/ *v.* diagnose.

diagonal /diago'nal/ *n. f.* diagonal.

diagonalmente /diagonal'mente/ *adv.* diagonally.

diagrama /dia'grama/ *n. m.* diagram.

dialectal /dialek'tal/ *a.* dialectal.

dialéctico /dia'lektiko/ *a.* dialectic.

dialecto /dia'lekto/ *n. m.* dialect.

diálogo /'dialogo/ *n. m.* dialogue.

diamante /dia'mante/ *n. m.* diamond.

diamantista /diaman'tista/ *n. m. & f.* diamond cutter; jeweler.

diametral /diame'tral/ *a.* diametric.

diametralmente /diametral'mente/ *adv.* diametrically.

diámetro /'diametro/ *n. m.* diameter.

diana /'diana/ *n. f.* reveille; dartboard.

diapasón /diapa'son/ *n. m.* standard pitch; tuning fork.

diaplejía /diaple'hia/ *n. f.* paralysis.

diariamente /diaria'mente/ *adv.* daily.

diario /'diario/ *a. & m.* daily; daily paper; diary; journal.

diarrea /dia'rrea/ *n. f.* diarrhea.

diatriba /dia'triβa/ *n. f.* diatribe, harangue.

dibujo /di'βuho/ *n. m.* drawing, sketch. —**dibujar,** *v.*

dicción /dik'θion; dik'sion/ *n. f.* diction.

diccionario /dikθio'nario; diksio'nario/ *n. m.* dictionary.

diccionarista /dikθiona'rista; diksiona'rista/ *n. m. & f.* lexicographer.

dicha /'ditʃa/ *n. f.* happiness.

dicho /'ditʃo/ *n. m.* saying.

dichoso /di'tʃoso/ *a.* happy; fortunate.

diciembre /di'θiembre; di'siembre/ *n. m.* December.

dicotomía /dikoto'mia/ *n. f.* dichotomy.

dictado /dik'taðo/ *n. m.* dictation.

dictador /dikta'ðor/ **-ra** *n.* dictator.

dictadura /dikta'ðura/ *n. f.* dictatorship.

dictamen /dik'tamen/ *n. m.* dictate.

dictar /dik'tar/ *v.* dictate; direct.

dictatorial /diktato'rial/ **dictatorio** *a.* dictatorial.

didáctico /di'ðaktiko/ *a.* didactic.

diecinueve /dieθi'nueβe; diesi-
'nueβe/ a. & pron. nineteen.
dieciocho /die'θiotʃo; die'siotʃo/
a. & pron. eighteen.
dieciseis /dieθi'seis; diesi'seis/ a.
& pron. sixteen.
diecisiete /dieθi'siete; diesi'siete/
a. & pron. seventeen.
diente /diente/ n. m. tooth.
diestramente /diestra'mente/ adv.
skillfully, ably; ingeniously.
diestro /'diestro/ a. dexterous,
skillful; clever.
dieta /'dieta/ n. f. diet; allowance.
dietética /die'tetika/ n. f. dietet-
ics.
dietético /die'tetiko/ a. 1. dietet-
ic; dietary. —n. 2. -ca. dietician.
diez /dieθ; dies/ a. & pron. ten.
diezmal /dieθ'mal; dies'mal/ a.
decimal.
diezmar /dieθ'mar; dies'mar/ v.
decimate.
difamación /difama'θion; difa-
ma'sion/ n. f. defamation, smear.
difamar /difa'mar/ v. defame,
smear, libel.
difamatorio /difama'torio/ a. de-
famatory.
diferencia /dife'renθia; dife'ren-
sia/ n. f. difference.
diferencial /diferen'θial; diferen-
'sial/ a. & f. differential.
diferenciar /diferen'θiar; diferen-
'siar/ v. differentiate, distinguish.
diferente /dife'rente/ a. different.
diferentemente /diferente'mente/
adv. differently.
diferir /dife'rir/ v. differ; defer,
put off.
difícil /di'fiθil; di'fisil/ a. difficult,
hard.
difícilmente /difiθil'mente; difisil-
'mente/ adv. with difficulty or
hardship.
dificultad /difikul'taδ/ n. f. difficulty.
dificultar /difikul'tar/ v. make difficult.
dificultoso /difikul'toso/ a. difficult, hard.
difidencia /difi'δenθia; difi'δensia/
n. f. diffidence.
difidente /difi'δente/ a. diffident.
difteria /dif'teria/ n. f. diphtheria.
difundir /difun'dir/ v. diffuse,
spread.
difunto /di'funto/ a. 1. deceased,
dead, late. —n. 2. -ta, deceased
person.

difusamente /difusa'mente/ adv.
diffusely.
difusión /difu'sion/ n. f. diffusion,
spread.
digerible /dihe'riβle/ a. digestible.
digerir /dihe'rir/ v. digest.
digestible /dihes'tiβle/ a. digestible.
digestión /dihes'tion/ n. f. digestion.
digestivo /dihes'tiβo/ a. digestive.
digesto /di'hesto/ n. m. digest or
code of laws.
digitado /dihi'taδo/ a. digitate.
digital /dihi'tal/ a. 1. digital. —n.
2. f. foxglove, digitalis.
dignación /digna'θion; digna'sion/
f. condescension; deigning.
dignamente /digna'mente/ adv.
with dignity.
dignarse /dig'narse/ v. condescend, deign.
dignatario /digna'tario/ -ra n.
dignitary.
dignidad /digni'δaδ/ n. f. dignity.
dignificar /dignifi'kar/ v. dignify.
digno /'digno/ a. worthy; dignified.
digresión /digre'sion/ n. f. digression.
digresivo /digre'siβo/ a. digres-
sive.
dij, dije /dih; 'dihe/ n. m. trinket,
piece of jewelry.
dilación /dila'θion; dila'sion/ n. f.
delay.
dilapidación /dilapiδa'θion; dilapi-
'δasion/ n. f. dilapidation.
dilapidado /dilapi'δaδo/ a. dilapidated.
dilatación /dilata'θion; dilata'sion/
n. f. dilatation, enlargement.
dilatar /dila'tar/ v. dilate; delay;
expand.
dilatoria /dila'toria/ n. f. delay.
dilatorio /dila'torio/ a. dilatory.
dilecto /di'lekto/ a. loved.
dilema /di'lema/ n. m. dilemma.
diligencia /dili'henθia; dili'hensia/
n. f. diligence, industriousness.
diligente /dili'hente/ a. diligent,
industrious.
diligentemente /dilihente'mente/
adv. diligently.
dilogía /dilo'hia/ n. f. ambiguous
meaning.
dilución /dilu'θion; dilu'sion/ n. f.
dilution.
diluir /di'luir/ v. dilute.
diluvial /dilu'βial/ a. diluvial.

diluvio /di'luβio/ *n. m.* flood, deluge.

dimensión /dimen'sion/ *n. f.* dimension; measurement.

diminución /diminu'θion; diminu'sion/ *n. f.* diminution.

diminuto /dimi'nuto/ **diminutivo** *a.* diminutive, little.

dimisión /dimi'sion/ *n. f.* resignation.

dimitir /dimi'tir/ *v.* resign.

Dinamarca /dina'marka/ *n. f.* Denmark.

dinamarqués /dinamar'kes/ **-esa** *a. & n.* Danish, Dane.

dinámico /di'namiko/ *a.* dynamic.

dinamita /dina'mita/ *n. f.* dynamite.

dinamitero /dinami'tero/ **-ra** *n.* dynamiter.

dínamo /'dinamo/ *n. m.* dynamo.

dinasta /di'nasta/ *n. m.* dynast, king, monarch.

dinastía /dinas'tia/ *n. f.* dynasty.

dinástico /di'nastiko/ *a.* dynastic.

dinero /di'nero/ *n. m.* money, currency.

dinosauro /dino'sauro/ *n. m.* dinosaur.

diócesis /'dioθesis; 'diosesis/ *n. f.* diocese.

Dios /dios/ *n. m.* God.

dios -sa *n.* god, goddess.

diploma /di'ploma/ *n. m.* diploma.

diplomacia /diplo'maθia; diplo'masia/ *n. f.* diplomacy.

diplomado /diplo'maðo/ **-da** *n.* graduate.

diplomarse /diplo'marse/ *v.* graduate (from a school).

diplomática /diplo'matika/ *n. f.* diplomacy.

diplomático /diplo'matiko/ **-ca** *a. & n.* diplomat; diplomatic.

dipsomanía /dipsoma'nia/ *n. f.* dipsomania.

diptongo /dip'toŋgo/ *n. m.* diphthong.

diputación /diputa'θion; diputa'sion/ *n. f.* deputation, delegation.

diputado /dipu'taðo/ **-da** *n.* deputy; delegate.

diputar /dipu'tar/ *v.* depute, delegate; empower.

dique /'dike/ *n. m.* dike; dam.

dirección /direk'θion; direk'sion/ *n. f.* direction; address; guidance; *Com.* management.

directamente /direkta'mente/ *adv.* directly.

directo /di'rekto/ *a.* direct.

director /direk'tor/ **-ra** *n.* director; manager.

directorio /direk'torio/ *n. m.* directory.

dirigente /diri'hente/ *a.* directing, controlling, managing.

dirigible /diri'hiβle/ *n. m.* dirigible.

dirigir /diri'hir/ *v.* direct; lead; manage.

dirigirse a /diri'hirse a/ *v.* address; approach, turn to; head for.

dirruir /di'rruir/ *v.* destroy, devastate.

disanto /di'santo/ *n. m.* holy day.

discantar /diskan'tar/ *v.* sing (esp. in counterpoint); discuss.

disceptación /disθepta'θion; dissepta'sion/ *n. f.* argument, quarrel.

disceptar /disθep'tar; dissep'tar/ *v.* argue, quarrel.

discernimiento /disθerni'miento; disserni'miento/ *n. m.* discernment.

discernir /disθer'nir; disser'nir/ *v.* discern.

disciplina /disθi'plina; dissi'plina/ *n. f.* discipline.

disciplinable /disθipli'naβle; dissipli'naβle/ *a.* disciplinable.

disciplinar /disθipli'nar; dissipli'nar/ *v.* discipline, train, teach.

discípulo /dis'θipulo; dis'sipulo/ **-la** *n.* disciple, follower; pupil.

disco /'disko/ *n. m.* disk; (phonograph) record.

disco compacto /'disko kom'pakto/ compact disk.

disco duro /'disko 'duro/ hard disk.

disco flexible /'disko flek'siβle/ floppy disk.

discontinuación /diskontinua'θion; diskontinua'sion/ *n. f.* discontinuation.

discontinuar /diskonti'nuar/ *v.* discontinue, break off, cease.

discordancia /diskor'ðanθia; diskor'ðansia/ *n. f.* discordance.

discordar /diskor'ðar/ *v.* disagree, conflict.

discordia /dis'korðia/ *n. f.* discord.

discoteca /disko'teka/ *n. f.* disco, discotheque.

discreción /diskre'θion; diskre-'sion/ *n. f.* discretion.

discrecional /diskreθio'nal; diskresio'nal/ *a.* optional.

discrecionalmente /diskreθional-'mente; diskresional'mente/ *adv.* optionally.

discrepancia /diskre'panθia; diskre'pansia/ *n. f.* discrepancy.

discretamente /diskreta'mente/ *adv.* discreetly.

discreto /dis'kreto/ *a.* discreet.

discrimen /dis'krimen/ *n. m.* risk, hazard.

discriminación /diskrimina'θion; diskrimina'sion/ *n. f.* discrimination.

discriminar /diskrimi'nar/ *v.* discriminate.

disculpa /dis'kulpa/ *n. f.* excuse; apology.

disculpar /diskul'par/ *v.* excuse; exonerate.

disculparse /diskul'parse/ *v.* apologize.

discurrir /disku'rrir/ *v.* roam; flow; think; plan.

discursante /diskur'sante/ *n.* lecturer, speaker.

discursivo /diskur'siβo/ *a.* discursive.

discurso /dis'kurso/ *n. m.* speech, talk.

discusión /disku'sion/ *n. f.* discussion.

discutible /disku'tiβle/ *a.* debatable.

discutir /disku'tir/ *v.* discuss; debate; contest.

disecación /diseka'θion; diseka-'sion/ *n. f.* dissection.

disecar /dise'kar/ *v.* dissect.

disección /disek'θion; disek'sion/ *n. f.* dissection.

diseminación /disemina'θion; disemina'sion/ *n. f.* dissemination.

diseminar /disemi'nar/ *v.* disseminate, spread.

disensión /disen'sion/ *n. f.* dissension; dissent.

disenso /di'senso/ *n. m.* dissent.

disentería /disente'ria/ *n. f.* dysentery.

disentir /disen'tir/ *v.* disagree, dissent.

diseñador /diseɲa'ðor/ **-ra** *n.* designer.

diseño /di'seɲo/ *n. m.* design. —**diseñar,** *v.*

disertación /diserta'θion; diserta-'sion/ *n. f.* dissertation.

disforme /dis'forme/ *a.* deformed, monstrous, ugly.

disformidad /disformi'ðað/ *n. f.* deformity.

disfraz /dis'fraθ; dis'fras/ *n. m.* disguise. —**disfrazar,** *v.*

disfrutar /disfru'tar/ *v.* enjoy.

disfrute /dis'frute/ *n. m.* enjoyment.

disgustar /disgus'tar/ *v.* displease; disappoint.

disgusto /dis'gusto/ *n. m.* displeasure; disappointment.

disidencia /disi'ðenθia; disi-'ðensia/ *n. f.* dissidence.

disidente /disi'ðente/ *a. & n.* dissident.

disímil /di'simil/ *a.* unlike.

disimilitud /disimili'tuð/ *n. f.* dissimilarity.

disimulación /disimula'θion; disimula'sion/ *n. f.* dissimulation.

disimulado /disimu'laðo/ *a.* dissembling, feigning; sly.

disimular /disimu'lar/ *v.* hide; dissemble.

disimulo /di'simulo/ *n. m.* pretense.

disipación /disipa'θion; disipa'sion/ *n. f.* dissipation.

disipado /disi'paðo/ *a.* dissipated; wasted; scattered.

disipar /disi'par/ *v.* waste; scatter.

dislexia /dis'leksia/ *n. f.* dyslexia.

disléxico /dis'leksiko/ *a.* dyslexic.

dislocación /disloka'θion; disloka'sion/ *n. f.* dislocation.

dislocar /dislo'kar/ *v.* dislocate; displace.

disminuir /dismi'nuir/ *v.* diminish, lessen, reduce.

disociación /disoθia'θion; disosia'sion/ *n. f.* dissociation.

disociar /diso'θiar; diso'siar/ *v.* dissociate.

disolubilidad /disoluβili'ðað/ *n. f.* dissolubility.

disoluble /diso'luβle/ *a.* dissoluble.

disolución /disolu'θion; disolu-'sion/ *n. f.* dissolution.

disolutamente /disoluta'mente/ *adv.* dissolutely.

disoluto /diso'luto/ *a.* dissolute.

disolver /disol'βer/ *v.* dissolve.

disonancia /diso'nanθia; diso-'nansia/ *n. f.* dissonance; discord.

disonante /diso'nante/ *a.* dissonant; discordant.

disonar /diso'nar/ *v.* be discordant; clash in sound.

dísono /di'sono/ *a.* dissonant.

dispar /dis'par/ *a.* unlike.

disparadamente /disparaða-'mente/ *adv.* hastily, hurriedly.

disparar /dispa'rar/ *v.* shoot, fire (a weapon).

disparatado /dispara'taðo/ *a.* nonsensical.

disparatar /dispara'tar/ *v.* talk nonsense.

disparate /dispa'rate/ *n. m.* nonsense, tall tale.

disparejo /dispa'reho/ *a.* uneven, unequal.

disparidad /dispari'ðað/ *n. f.* disparity.

disparo /dis'paro/ *n. m.* shot.

dispendio /dis'pendio/ *n. m.* extravagance.

dispendioso /dispen'dioso/ *a.* expensive; extravagant.

dispensa /dis'pensa/ **dispensación** *n. f.* dispensation.

dispensable /dispen'saβle/ *a.* dispensable; excusable.

dispensar /dispen'sar/ *v.* dispense, excuse; grant.

dispensario /dispen'sario/ *n. m.* dispensary.

dispepsia /dis'pepsia/ *n. f.* dyspepsia.

dispéptico /dis'peptiko/ *a.* dyspeptic.

dispersar /disper'sar/ *v.* scatter; dispel; disband.

dispersión /disper'sion/ *n. f.* dispersion, dispersal.

disperso /dis'perso/ *a.* dispersed.

displicente /displi'θente; displi-'sente/ *a.* unpleasant.

disponer /dispo'ner/ *v.* dispose. **d. de,** have at one's disposal.

disponible /dispo'niβle/ *a.* available.

disposición /disposi'θion; disposi-'sion/ *n. f.* disposition; disposal.

dispuesto /dis'puesto/ *a.* disposed, inclined; attractive.

disputa /dis'puta/ *n. f.* dispute, argument.

disputable /dispu'taβle/ *a.* disputable.

disputador /disputa'ðor/ **-ra** *n.* disputant.

disputar /dispu'tar/ *v.* argue; dispute.

disquete /dis'kete/ *n. m.* diskette.

disquetera /diske'tera/ *n. f.* disk drive.

disquisición /diskisi'θion; diskisi-'sion/ *n. f.* disquisition.

distancia /dis'tanθia; dis'tansia/ *n. f.* distance.

distante /dis'tante/ *a.* distant.

distantemente /distante'mente/ *adv.* distantly.

distar /dis'tar/ *v.* be distant, be far.

distender /disten'der/ *v.* distend, swell, enlarge.

distensión /disten'sion/ *n. f.* distension, swelling.

dístico /'distiko/ *n. m.* couplet.

distinción /distin'θion; distin'sion/ *n. f.* distinction, difference.

distingo /dis'tiŋgo/ *n. m.* restriction.

distinguible /distiŋ'guiβle/ *a.* distinguishable.

distinguido /distiŋ'guiðo/ *a.* distinguished, prominent.

distinguir /distiŋ'guir/ *v.* distinguish; make out, spot.

distintamente /distinta'mente/ *adv.* distinctly, clearly; differently.

distintivo /distin'tiβo/ *a.* distinctive.

distintivo del país /distin'tiβo del pa'is/ country code.

distinto /dis'tinto/ *a.* distinct; different.

distracción /distrak'θion; distrak-'sion/ *n. f.* distraction, pastime; absent-mindedness.

distraer /distra'er/ *v.* distract.

distraídamente /distraiða'mente/ *adv.* absent-mindedly, distractedly.

distraído /distra'iðo/ *a.* absent-minded; distracted.

distribución /distriβu'θion; distriβu'sion/ *n. f.* distribution.

distribuidor /distriβui'ðor/ **-ra** *n.* distributor.

distribuir /distri'βuir/ *v.* distribute.

distributivo /distriβu'tiβo/ *a.* distributive.

distributor /distriβu'tor/ *n. m.* distributor.

distrito /dis'trito/ *n. m.* district.

disturbar /distur'βar/ *v.* disturb, trouble.

disturbio /dis'turβio/ *n. m.* disturbance, outbreak; turmoil.

disuadir /disua'ðir/ *v.* dissuade.

disuasión /disua'sion/ *n. f.* dissuasion; deterrence.

disuasivo /disua'siβo/ *a.* dissuasive.

disyunción /disyun'θion; disyun-'sion/ *n. f.* disjunction.

ditirambo /diti'rambo/ *n. m.* dithyramb.

diurno /'diurno/ *a.* diurnal.

diva /'diβa/ *n. f.* diva, prima donna.

divagación /diβaga'θion; diβaga-'sion/ *n. f.* digression.

divagar /diβa'gar/ *v.* digress, ramble.

diván /di'βan/ *n. m.* couch.

divergencia /diβer'henθia; diβer-'hensia/ *n. f.* divergence.

divergente /diβer'hente/ *a.* divergent, differing.

divergir /diβer'hir/ *v.* diverge.

diversamente /diβersa'mente/ *adv.* diversely.

diversidad /diβersi'ðað/ *n. f.* diversity.

diversificar /diβersifi'kar/ *v.* diversify, vary.

diversión /diβer'sion/ *n. f.* diversion, pastime.

diverso /di'βerso/ *a.* diverse, different; (*pl.*) various, several.

divertido /diβer'tiðo/ *a.* humorous, amusing.

divertimiento /diβerti'miento/ *n. m.* diversion; amusement.

divertir /diβer'tir/ *v.* entertain, amuse.

divertirse /diβer'tirse/ *v.* enjoy oneself, have a good time.

dividendo /diβi'ðendo/ *n. m.* dividend.

divididero /diβiði'ðero/ *a.* to be divided.

dividido /diβi'ðiðo/ *a.* divided.

dividir /diβi'ðir/ *v.* divide; separate.

divieso /di'βieso/ *n. m. Med.* boil.

divinamente /diβina'mente/ *adv.* divinely.

divinidad /diβini'ðað/ *n. f.* divinity.

divinizar /diβini'θar; diβini'sar/ *v.* deify.

divino /di'βino/ *a.* divine; heavenly.

divisa /di'βisa/ *n. f.* badge, emblem.

divisar /diβi'sar/ *v.* sight, make out.

divisibilidad /diβisiβili'ðað/ *n. f.* divisibility.

divisible /diβi'siβle/ *a.* divisible.

división /diβi'sion/ *n. f.* division.

divisivo /diβi'siβo/ *a.* divisive.

divo /'diβo/ *n. m.* movie star.

divorcio /di'βorθio; di'βorsio/ *n. m.* divorce. —**divorciar,** *v.*

divulgable /diβul'gaβle/ *a.* divulgable.

divulgación /diβulga'θion; diβulga'sion/ *n. f.* divulgation.

divulgar /diβul'gar/ *v.* divulge, reveal.

dobladamente /doβlaða'mente/ *adv.* doubly.

dobladillo /doβla'ðiʎo; doβla-'ðiyo/ *n. m.* hem of a skirt or dress.

dobladura /doβla'ðura/ *n. f.* fold; bend.

doblar /do'βlar/ *v.* fold; bend.

doble /'doβle/ *a.* double.

doblegable /doβle'gaβle/ *a.* flexible, foldable.

doblegar /doβle'gar/ *v.* fold, bend; yield.

doblez /do'βleθ; doβles/ *n. m.* fold; duplicity.

doblón /do'βlon/ *n. m.* doubloon.

doce /'doθe; 'dose/ *a. & pron.* twelve.

docena /do'θena; do'sena/ *n. f.* dozen.

docente /do'θente; do'sente/ *a.* educational.

dócil /'doθil; 'dosil/ *a.* docile.

docilidad /doθili'ðað; dosili'ðað/ *n. f.* docility, tractableness.

dócilmente /doθil'mente; dosil-'mente/ *adv.* docilely, meekly.

doctamente /dokta'mente/ *adv.* learnedly, profoundly.

docto /'dokto/ *a.* learned, expert.

doctor /dok'tor/ **-ra** *n.* doctor.

doctorado /dokto'raðo/ *n. m.* doctorate.

doctoral /dokto'ral/ *a.* doctoral.

doctrina /dok'trina/ *n. f.* doctrine.

doctrinador /doktrina'ðor/ **-ra** *n.* teacher.

doctrinal /doktri'nal/ *n. m.* doctrinal.

doctrinar /doktri'nar/ *v.* teach.

documentación /dokumenta'θion; dokumenta'sion/ *n. f.* documentation.

documental /dokumen'tal/ *a.* documentary.

documento /doku'mento/ *n. m.* document.

dogal /do'gal/ *n. m.* noose.

dogma /'dogma/ *n. m.* dogma.

dogmáticamente /dog'matika-mente/ *adv.* dogmatically.

dogmático /dog'matiko/ *n. m.* dogmatic.

dogmatismo /dogma'tismo/ *n. m.* dogmatism.

dogmatista /dogma'tista/ *n. m. & f.* dogmatist.

dogo /'dogo/ *n. m.* bulldog.

dolar /'dolar/ *v.* cut, chop, hew.

dólar *n. m.* dollar.

dolencia /do'lenθia; do'lensia/ *n. f.* pain; disease.

doler /do'ler/ *v.* ache, hurt, be sore.

doliente /do'liente/ *a.* ill; aching.

dolor /do'lor/ *n. m.* pain; grief, sorrow, woe.

dolor de cabeza /do'lor de ka-'βeθa; do'lor de ka'βesa/ headache.

dolor de espalda /do'lor de es-'palda/ backache.

dolor de estómago /do'lor de es-'tomago/ stomachache.

dolorido /dolo'riðo/ *a.* painful, sorrowful.

dolorosamente /dolorosa'mente/ *adv.* painfully, sorrowfully.

doloroso /dolo'roso/ *a.* painful, sorrowful.

dolosamente /dolosa'mente/ *adv.* deceitfully.

doloso /do'loso/ *a.* deceitful.

domable /do'maβle/ *a.* that can be tamed or managed.

domar /do'mar/ *v.* tame; subdue.

dombo /'dombo/ *n. m.* dome.

domesticable /domesti'kaβle/ *a.* that can be domesticated.

domesticación /domestika'θion; domestika'sion/ *n. f.* domestication.

domésticamente /domestika-'mente/ *adv.* domestically.

domesticar /domesti'kar/ *v.* tame, domesticate.

domesticidad /domestiθi'ðað; domestisi'ðað/ *n. f.* domesticity.

doméstico /do'mestiko/ *a.* domestic.

domicilio /domi'θilio; domi'silio/ *n. m.* dwelling, home, residence, domicile.

dominación /domina'θion; domina'sion/ *n. f.* domination.

dominador /domina'ðor/ *a.* dominating.

dominante /domi'nante/ *a.* dominant.

dominar /domi'nar/ *v.* rule, dominate; master.

dómine /'domine/ *n. m.* teacher.

domingo /do'miŋgo/ *n. m.* Sunday.

dominio /'dominio/ *n. m.* domain; rule; power.

dominó /domi'no/ *n. m.* domino.

domo /'domo/ *n. m.* dome.

Don /don/ *title used before a man's first name.*

don *n. m.* gift.

donación /dona'θion; dona'sion/ *n. f.* donation.

donador /dona'ðor/ **-ra** *n.* giver, donor.

donaire /do'naire/ *n. m.* grace.

donairosamente /donairosa-'mente/ *adv.* gracefully.

donairoso /donai'roso/ *a.* graceful.

donante /do'nante/ *n.* giver, donor.

donar /do'nar/ *v.* donate.

donativo /dona'tiβo/ *n. m.* donation, contribution; gift.

doncella /don'θeʎa; don'seya/ *n. f.* lass; maid.

donde /'donde/ **dónde** *conj. & adv.* where.

dondequiera /donde'kiera/ *adv.* wherever, anywhere.

donosamente /donosa'mente/ *adv.* gracefully; wittily.

donoso /do'noso/ *a.* graceful; witty.

donosura /dono'sura/ *n. f.* gracefulness; wittiness.

Doña /'doɲa/ *title used before a lady's first name.*

dopar /do'par/ *v.* drug, dope.

dorado /do'raðo/ *a.* gilded.

dorador /dora'ðor/ **-ra** *n.* gilder.

dorar /do'rar/ *v.* gild.

dórico /'doriko/ *a.* Doric.

dormidero /dormi'ðero/ *a.* sleep-inducing; soporific.

dormido /dor'miðo/ *a.* asleep.

dormir /dor'mir/ *v.* sleep.

dormirse /dor'mirse/ *v.* fall asleep, go to sleep.

dormitar /dormi'tar/ *v.* doze.

dormitorio /dormi'torio/ *n. m.* dormitory; bedroom.

dorsal /dor'sal/ *a.* dorsal.

dorso /'dorso/ *n. m.* spine.

dos /dos/ *a. & pron.* two. **los d.,** both.

dosañal /dosa'ɲal/ *a.* biennial.

doscientos /dos'θientos; dos-'sientos/ *a. & pron.* two hundred.

dosel /do'sel/ *n. m.* canopy; platform, dais.

dosificación /dosifika'θion; dosifika'sion/ *n. f.* dosage.

dosis /'dosis/ *n. f.* dose.

dotación /dota'θion; dota'sion/ *n. f.* endowment; *Naut.* crew.

dotador /dota'ðor/ **-ra** *n.* donor.

dotar /do'tar/ *v.* endow; give a dowry to.

dote /'dote/ *n. f.* dowry; (*pl.*) talents.

dragaminas /draga'minas/ *n. m.* mine sweeper.

dragar /dra'gar/ *v.* dredge; sweep.

dragón /dra'gon/ *n. m.* dragon; dragoon.

dragonear /dragone'ar/ *v.* pretend to be.

drama /'drama/ *n. m.* drama; play.

dramática /dra'matika/ *n. f.* drama, dramatic art.

dramáticamente /dramatika-'mente/ *adv.* dramatically.

dramático /dra'matiko/ *a.* dramatic.

dramatizar /dramati'θar; dramati-'sar/ *v.* dramatize.

dramaturgo /drama'turgo/ **-ga** *n.* playwright, dramatist.

drástico /'drastiko/ *a.* drastic.

drenaje /dre'nahe/ *n. m.* drainage.

dríada /'driaða/ *n. f.* dryad.

dril /dril/ *n. m.* denim.

driza /'driθa; 'drisa/ *n. f.* halyard.

droga /'droga/ *n. f.* drug.

drogadicto /droga'ðikto/ **-ta** *n.* drug addict.

droguería /droge'ria/ *n. f.* drugstore.

droguero /dro'gero/ *n. m.* druggist.

dromedario /drome'ðario/ *n. m.* dromedary.

druida /'druiða/ *n. m. & f.* Druid.

dualidad /duali'ðað/ *n. f.* duality.

dubitable /duβi'taβle/ *a.* doubtful.

dubitación /duβita'θion; duβita-'sion/ *n. f.* doubt.

ducado /du'kaðo/ *n. m.* duchy.

ducal /du'kal/ *a.* ducal.

ducha /'dutʃa/ *n. f.* shower (bath).

ducharse /du'tʃarse/ *v.* take a shower.

dúctil /'duktil/ *a.* ductile.

ductilidad /duktili'ðað/ *n. f.* ductility.

duda /'duða/ *n. f.* doubt.

dudable /du'ðaβle/ *a.* doubtful.

dudar /du'ðar/ *v.* doubt; hesitate; question.

dudosamente /duðosa'mente/ *adv.* doubtfully.

dudoso /du'ðoso/ *a.* dubious; doubtful.

duela /'duela/ *n. f.* stave.

duelista /due'lista/ *n. m. & f.* duelist.

duelo /'duelo/ *n. m.* duel; grief; mourning.

duende /'duende/ *n. m.* elf, hobgoblin.

dueño /'dueɲo/ **-ña** *n.* owner; landlord -lady; master, mistress.

dulce /'dulθe; dulse/ *a.* **1.** sweet. **agua d.,** fresh water. —*n.* **2.** *m.* piece of candy; (*pl.*) candy.

dulcedumbre /dulθe'ðumbre; dulse'ðumbre/ *n. f.* sweetness.

dulcemente /dulθe'mente; dulse-'mente/ *adv.* sweetly.

dulcería /dulθe'ria; dulse'ria/ *n. f.* confectionery; candy shop.

dulcificar /dulθifi'kar; dulsifi'kar/ *v.* sweeten.

dulzura /dul'θura; dul'sura/ *n. f.* sweetness; mildness.

duna /'duna/ *n. f.* dune.

dúo /'duo/ *n. m.* duo, duet.

duodenal /duoðe'nal/ *a.* duodenal.

duplicación /duplika'θion; duplika'sion/ *n. f.* duplication; doubling.

duplicadamente /duplikaða-'mente/ *adv.* doubly.

duplicado /dupli'kaðo/ *a. & m.* duplicate.

duplicar /dupli'kar/ *v.* double, duplicate, repeat.

duplicidad /dupliθi'ðað; duplisi-'ðað/ *n. f.* duplicity.

duplo /'duplo/ *a.* double.

duque /'duke/ *n. m.* duke.

duquesa /du'kesa/ *n. f.* duchess.

durabilidad /duraβili'ðað/ *n. f.* durability.

durable /du'raβle/ *a.* durable.

duración /dura'θion; dura'sion/ *n. f.* duration.

duradero /dura'ðero/ *a.* lasting, durable.

duramente /dura'mente/ *adv.*
harshly, roughly.
durante /du'rante/ *prep.* during.
durar /du'rar/ *v.* last.
durazno /du'raθno; du'rasno/ *n.*
m. peach; peach tree.

dureza /du'reθa; du'resa/ *n. f.*
hardness.
durmiente /dur'miente/ *a.* sleeping.
duro /'duro/ *a.* hard; stiff; stern;
stale.
dux /duks/ *n. m.* doge.

E

e /e/ *conj.* and.
ebanista /eβa'nista/ *n. m. & f.*
cabinetmaker.
ebanizar /eβani'θar; eβani'sar/ *v.*
give an ebony finish to.
ébano /'eβano/ *n. m.* ebony.
ebonita /eβo'nita/ *n. f.* ebonite.
ebrio /'eβrio/ *a.* drunken, inebri-
ated.
ebullición /eβuʎi'θion; eβuyi'sion/
n. f. boiling.
echada /e'tʃaða/ *n. f.* throw.
echadillo /etʃa'ðiʎo; etʃa'ðiyo/ *n.*
m. foundling; orphan.
echar /e'tʃar/ *v.* throw, toss; pour.
e. a, start to. **e. a perder,** spoil,
ruin. **e. de menos,** miss.
echarse /e'tʃarse/ *v.* lie down.
eclecticismo /eklekti'θismo;
eklekti'sismo/ *n. m.* eclecticism.
ecléctico /e'klektiko/ *n. & a.*
eclectic.
eclesiástico /ekle'siastiko/ *a. & m.*
ecclesiastic.
eclipse /e'klipse/ *n. m.* eclipse.
—**eclipsar,** *v.*
écloga /'ekloga/ *n. f.* eclogue.
eco /'eko/ *n. m.* echo.
ecología /ekolo'hia/ *n. f.* ecology.
ecológico /eko'lohiko/ *n. f.*
ecological.
ecologista /ekolo'hista/ *n. m. & f.*
ecologist.
economía /ekono'mia/ *n. f.* economy; thrift; economics. **e. política,** political economy.
económicamente /ekonomika-
'mente/ *adv.* economically.
económico /eko'nomiko/ *a.* economic; economical, thrifty; inexpensive.
economista /ekono'mista/ *n. m.*
& f. economist.
economizar /ekonomi'θar; eko-
nomi'sar/ *v.* save, economize.
ecuación /ekua'θion; ekua'sion/ *n.*
f. equation.
ecuador /ekua'ðor/ *n. m.* equator.
ecuanimidad /ekuanimi'ðað/ *n. f.*
equanimity.

ecuatorial /ekuato'rial/ *a.* equatorial.
ecuatoriano /ekuato'riano/ **-na** *a.*
& n. Ecuadorian.
ecuestre /e'kuestre/ *a.* equestrian.
ecuménico. /eku'meniko/ *a.* ecumenical.
edad /e'ðað/ *n. f.* age.
edecán /eðe'kan/ *n. m.* aide-de-
camp.
Edén /e'ðen/ *n. m.* Eden.
edición /eði'θion; eði'sion/ *n. f.*
edition; issue.
edicto /e'ðikto/ *n. m.* edict, decree.
edificación /eðifika'θion; eðifika-
'sion/ *n. f.* construction; edifica-
tion.
edificador /eðifika'ðor/ *n.* constructor; builder.
edificar /eðifi'kar/ *v.* build.
edificio /eði'fiθio; eði'fisio/ *n. m.*
edifice, building.
editar /eði'tar/ *v.* publish, issue;
edit.
editor /eði'tor/ *n. m.* publisher;
editor.
editorial /eðito'rial/ *n. m.* editorial; publishing house.
edredón /eðre'ðon/ *n. m.* quilt.
educación /eðuka'θion; eðu-
ka'sion/ *n. f.* upbringing, breeding; education.
educado /eðu'kaðo/ *a.* well-mannered; educated.
educador /eðuka'ðor/ **-ra** *n.* educator.
educar /eðu'kar/ *v.* educate; bring
up; train.
educativo /eðuka'tiβo/ *a.* educational.
educción /eðuk'θion; eðuk'sion/
n. f. deduction.
educir /eðu'θir; eðu'sir/ *v.* educe.
efectivamente /efektiβa'mente/
adv. actually, really.
efectivo /efek'tiβo/ *a.* effective;
actual, real. **en e.,** *Com.* in cash.
efecto /e'fekto/ *n. m.* effect.

efecto invernáculo /e'fekto im-ber'nakulo/ greenhouse effect.
efectuar /efek'tuar/ v. effect; cash.
eferente /efe'rente/ a. efferent.
efervescencia /eferβes'θenθia; eferβes'sensia/ n. f. effervescence; zeal.
eficacia /efi'kaθia; efi'kasia/ n. f. efficacy.
eficaz /efi'kaθ; efi'kas/ a. efficient, effective.
eficazmente /efikaθ'mente; efikas'mente/ adv. efficaciously.
eficiencia /efi'θienθia; efi'siensia/ n. f. efficiency.
eficiente /efi'θiente; efi'siente/ a. efficient.
efigie /e'fihie/ n. f. effigy.
efímera /efi'mera/ n. f. mayfly.
efímero /e'fimero/ a. ephemeral, passing.
efluvio /e'fluβio/ n. m. effluvium.
efundir /efun'dir/ v. effuse; pour out.
efusión /efu'sion/ n. f. effusion.
egipcio /e'hipθio; e'hipsio/ **-cia** a. & n. Egyptian.
Egipto /e'hipto/ n. m. Egypt.
egoísmo /ego'ismo/ n. m. egoism, egotism, selfishness.
egoísta /ego'ista/ a. & n. selfish, egoistic; egoist.
egotismo /ego'tismo/ n. m. egotism.
egotista /ego'tista/ n. m. & f. egotist.
egreso /e'greso/ n. m. expense, outlay.
eje /'ehe/ n. m. axis; axle.
ejecución /eheku'θion; eheku'sion/ n. f. execution; performance; enforcement.
ejecutar /eheku'tar/ v. execute; enforce; carry out.
ejecutivo /eheku''tiβo/ **-va** a. & n. executive.
ejecutor /eheku'tor/ **-ra** n. executor.
ejemplar /ehem'plar/ a. **1.** exemplary. —n. **2.** m. copy.
ejemplificación /ehemplifika'θion; ehemplifika'sion/ n. f. exemplification.
ejemplificar /ehemplifi'kar/ v. illustrate.
ejemplo /e'hemplo/ n. m. example.
ejercer /eher'θer; eher'ser/ v. exert; practice.

ejercicio /eher'θiθio; eher'sisio/ n. m. exercise, drill. —**ejercitar,** v.
ejercitación /eherθita'θion; ehersita'sion/ n. f. exercise, training, drill.
ejercitar /eherθi'tar; ehersi'tar/ v. exercise, train, drill.
ejército /e'herθito; e'hersito/ n. m. army.
ejotes /e'hotes/ n. m.pl. string beans.
el /el/ art. & pron. the; the one.
él pron. he, him; it.
elaboración /elaβora'θion; elaβora'sion/ n. f. elaboration; working up.
elaborado /elaβo'raðo/ a. elaborate.
elaborador /elaβora'ðor/ n. m. manufacturer, maker.
elaborar /elaβo'rar/ v. elaborate; manufacture; brew.
elación /ela'θion; ela'sion/ n. f. elation; magnanimity; turgid style.
elasticidad /elastiθi'ðað; elastisi-'ðað/ n. f. elasticity.
elástico /e'lastiko/ n. m. elastic.
elección /elek'θion; elek'sion/ n. f. election; option; choice.
electivo /elek'tiβo/ a. elective.
electo /e'lekto/ a. elected, chosen, appointed.
electorado /elekto'raðo/ n. m. electorate.
electoral /elekto'ral/ a. electoral.
electricidad /elektriθi'ðað; elektri-si'ðað/ n. f. electricity.
electricista /elektri'θista; elektri-'sista/ n. m. & f. electrician.
eléctrico /e'lektriko/ a. electric.
electrización /elektriθa'θion; elektrisa'sion/ n. f. electrification.
electrocardiograma /e,lektro-karðio'grama/ n. m. electrocardiogram.
electrocución /elektroku'θion; elektroku'sion/ n. f. electrocution.
electrocutar /elektroku'tar/ v. electrocute.
electrodo /elek'troðo/ n. m. electrode.
electrodoméstico /e,lektroðo-r'αprim;mestiko/ n. m. electrical appliance, home appliance.
electroimán /elektroi'man/ n. m. electromagnet.
electrólisis /elek'trolisis/ n. f. electrolysis.
electrólito /elek'trolito/ n. m. electrolyte.

electrón /elek'tron/ *n. m.* electron.

electrónico /elek'troniko/ *a.* electronic.

elefante /ele'fante/ *n. m.* elephant.

elegancia /ele'ganθia; ele'gansia/ *n. f.* elegance.

elegante /ele'gante/ *a.* elegant, smart, stylish, fine.

elegantemente /elegante'mente/ *adv.* elegantly.

elegía /ele'hia/ *n. f.* elegy.

elegibilidad /elehiβili'ðað/ *n. f.* eligibility.

elegible /ele'hiβle/ *a.* eligible.

elegir /ele'hir/ *v.* select, choose; elect.

elemental /elemen'tal/ *a.* elementary.

elementalmente /elemental-'mente/ *adv.* elementally; fundamentally.

elemento /ele'mento/ *n. m.* element.

elepé /ele'pe/ *n. m.* long-playing (record), LP.

elevación /eleβa'θion; eleβa'sion/ *n. f.* elevation; height.

elevador /eleβa'ðor/ *n. m.* elevator.

elevamiento /eleβa'miento/ *n. m.* elevation.

elevar /ele'βar/ *v.* elevate; erect, raise.

elidir /eli'ðir/ *v.* elide.

eliminación /elimina'θion; elimina'sion/ *n. f.* elimination.

eliminar /elimi'nar/ *v.* eliminate.

elipse /e'lipse/ *n. f.* ellipse.

elipsis /e'lipsis/ *n. f.* ellipsis.

elíptico /e'liptiko/ *a.* elliptic.

ella /'eʎa; 'eya/ *pron.* she, her; it.

ello /'eʎo; 'eyo/ *pron.* it.

ellos /'eʎos; 'eyos/ **-as** *pron. pl.* they, them.

elocuencia /elo'kuenθia; elo-'kuensia/ *n. f.* eloquence.

elocuente /elo'kuente/ *a.* eloquent.

elocuentemente /elokuente-'mente/ *adv.* eloquently.

elogio /e'lohio/ *n. m.* praise, compliment. **—elogiar,** *v.*

elucidación /eluθiða'θion; elusiða-'sion/ *n. f.* elucidation.

elucidar /eluθi'ðar; elusi'ðar/ *v.* elucidate.

eludir /elu'ðir/ *v.* elude.

emanar /ema'nar/ *v.* emanate, stem.

emancipación /emanθipa'θion; emansipa'sion/ *n. f.* emancipation; freeing.

emancipador /emanθipa'ðor; emansipa'ðor; **-ra** *n.* emancipator.

emancipar /emanθi'par; emansi'par/ *v.* emancipate; free.

embajada /emba'haða/ *n. f.* embassy; legation; *Colloq.* errand.

embajador /embaha'ðor/ **-ra** *n.* ambassador.

embalar /emba'lar/ *v.* pack, bale.

embaldosado /embaldo'saðo/ *n. m.* tile floor.

embalsamador /embalsama'ðor/ *n. m.* embalmer.

embalsamar /embalsa'mar/ *v.* embalm.

embarazada /embara'θaða; embara'saða/ *a.* pregnant.

embarazadamente /embaraθaða-'mente; embarasaða'mente/ *adv.* embarrassedly.

embarazar /embara'θar; embara-'sar/ *v.* make pregnant; embarrass.

embarazo /emba'raθo; emba'raso/ *n. m.* embarrassment; pregnancy.

embarbascado /embarβas'kaðo/ *a.* difficult; complicated.

embarcación /embarka'θion; embarka'sion/ *n. f.* boat, ship; embarkation.

embarcadero /embarka'ðero/ *n. m.* wharf, pier, dock.

embarcador /embarka'ðor/ *n. m.* shipper, loader, stevedore.

embarcar /embar'kar/ *v.* embark, board ship.

embarcarse /embar'karse/ *v.* embark; sail.

embargador /embarga'ðor/ *n. m.* one who impedes; one who orders an embargo.

embargante /embar'gante/ *a.* impeding, hindering.

embargar /embar'gar/ *v.* impede, restrain; *Leg.* seize, embargo.

embargo /em'bargo/ *n. m.* seizure, embargo. **sin e.,** however, nevertheless.

embarnizar /embarni'θar; embarni'sar/ *v.* varnish.

embarque /em'barke/ *n. m.* shipment.

embarrador /embarra'ðor/ **-ra** *n.* plasterer.

embarrancar /embarran'kar/ *v.*

get stuck in mud; *Naut.* run
aground.
embarrar /emba'rrar/ *v.* plaster;
besmear with mud.
embasamiento /embasa'miento/
n. m. foundation of a building.
embastecer /embaste'θer; embas-
te'ser/ *v.* get fat.
embaucador /embauka'ðor/ **-ra** *n.*
impostor.
embaucar /embau'kar/ *v.* deceive,
trick, hoax.
embaular /embau'lar/ *v.* pack in a
trunk.
embausamiento /embausa-
'miento/ *n. m.* amazement.
embebecer /embeβe'θer; embeβe-
'ser/ *v.* amaze, astonish; entertain.
embeber /embe'βer/ *v.* absorb; incorporate; saturate.
embelecador /embeleka'ðor/ **-ra**
n. impostor.
embeleco /embe'leko/ *n. m.*
fraud, perpetration.
embeleñar /embele'ɲar/ *v.* fascinate, charm.
embelesamiento. /embelesa-
'miento/ *n. m.* rapture.
embelesar /embele'sar/ *v.* fascinate, charm.
embeleso /embe'leso/ *n. m.* rapture, bliss.
embellecer /embeʎe'θer; embeye-
'ser/ *v.* beautify, embellish.
embestida /embes'tiða/ *n. f.* violent assault; attack.
emblandecer /emblande'θer; emb-
lande'ser/ *v.* soften; moisten;
move to pity.
emblema /em'blema/ *n. m.* emblem.
emblemático /emble'matiko/ *a.*
emblematic.
embocadura /emboka'ðura/ *n. f.*
narrow entrance; mouth of a
river.
embocar /embo'kar/ *v.* eat hastily;
gorge.
embolia /em'bolia/ *n. f.* embo-
lism.
émbolo /'embolo/ *n. m.* piston.
embolsar /embol'sar/ *v.* pocket.
embonar /embo'nar/ *v.* improve,
fix, repair.
emborrachador /emborratʃa'ðor/
a. intoxicating.
emborrachar /emborra'tʃar/ *v.* get
drunk.

emboscada /embos'kaða/ *n. f.*
ambush.
emboscar /embos'kar/ *v.* put or
lie in ambush.
embotado /embo'taðo/ *a.* blunt,
dull (edged). —**embotar,** *v.*
embotadura /embota'ðura/ *n. f.*
bluntness; dullness.
embotellamiento /emboteʎa-
'miento; emboteya'miento/ *n. m.*
bottling (liquids); traffic jam.
embotellar /embote'ʎar; embote-
'yar/ *v.* put in bottles.
embozado /embo'θaðo; embo-
'saðo/ *v.* muzzled; muffled.
embozar /embo'θar; embo'sar/ *v.*
muzzle; muffle.
embozo /em'boθo; em'boso/ *n.
m.* muffler.
embrague /em'brage/ *n. m. Auto.*
clutch.
embravecer /embraβe'θer; em-
braβe'ser/ *v.* be or make angry.
embriagado /embria'gaðo/ *a.*
drunken, intoxicated.
embriagar /embria'gar/ *v.* intoxicate.
embriaguez /embria'geθ; em-
bria'ges/ *n. f.* drunkenness.
embrión /em'brion/ *n. m.* embryo.
embrionario /embrio'nario/ *a.*
embryonic.
embrochado /embro'tʃaðo/ *a.*
embroidered.
embrollo /em'broʎo; em'broyo/ *n.
m.* muddle. —**embrollar,** *v.*
embromar /embro'mar/ *v.* tease;
joke.
embuchado /embu'tʃaðo/ *n. m.*
pork sausage.
embudo /em'buðo/ *n. m.* funnel.
embuste /em'buste/ *n. m.* lie, fib.
embustear /embuste'ar/ *v.* lie,
fib.
embustero /embus'tero/ **-ra** *n.*
liar.
embutir /embu'tir/ *v.* stuff, cram.
emergencia /emer'henθia; emer-
'hensia/ *n. f.* emergency.
emérito /e'merito/ *a.* emeritus.
emético /e'metiko/ *n. m. & a.*
emetic.
emigración /emigra'θion; emigra-
'sion/ *n. f.* emigration.
emigrante /emi'grante/ *a. & n.*
emigrant.
emigrar /emi'grar/ *v.* emigrate.
eminencia /emi'nenθia; emi'nen-
sia/ *n. f.* eminence, height.

eminente /emi'nente/ *a.* eminent.

emisario /emi'sario/ **-ria** *n.* emissary, spy; outlet.

emisión /emi'sion/ *n. f.* issue; emission.

emisor /emi'sor/ *n. m.* radio transmitter.

emitir /emi'tir/ *v.* emit.

emoción /emo'θion; emo'sion/ *n. f.* feeling, emotion, thrill.

emocional /emo'θional; emo'sional/ *a.* emotional.

emocionante /emoθio'nante; emosio'nante/ *a.* exciting.

emocionar /emoθio'nar; emosio'nar/ *v.* touch, move, excite.

emolumento /emolu'mento/ *n. m.* emolument; perquisite.

empacar /empa'kar/ *v.* pack.

empacho /em'patʃo/ *n. m.* shyness, timidity; embarrassment.

empadronamiento /empaðrona'miento/ *n. m.* census; list of taxpayers.

empalizada /empali'θaða; empali'saða/ *n. f.* palisade, stockade.

empanada /empa'naða/ *n. f.* meat pie.

empañar /empa'ɲar/ *v.* blur; soil, sully.

empapar /empa'par/ *v.* soak.

empapelado /empape'laðo/ *n. m.* wallpaper.

empapelar /empape'lar/ *v.* wallpaper.

empaque /em'pake/ *n. m.* packing; appearance, mien.

empaquetar /empake'tar/ *v.* pack, package.

emparedado /empare'ðaðo/ *n. m.* sandwich.

emparejarse /empare'harse/ *v.* match, pair off; level, even off.

emparentado /emparen'taðo/ *a.* related by marriage.

emparrado /empa'rraðo/ *n. m.* arbor.

empastadura /empasta'ðura/ *n. f.* (dental) filling.

empastar /empas'tar/ *v.* fill (a tooth); paste.

empate /em'pate/ *n. m.* tie, draw. —**empatarse,** *v.*

empecer /empe'θer; empe'ser/ *v.* hurt, harm, injure; prevent.

empedernir /empeðer'nir/ *v.* harden.

empeine /em'peine/ *n. m.* groin; instep; hoof.

empellar /empe'ʎar; empe'yar/ *v.* shove, jostle.

empellón /empe'ʎon; empe'yon/ *n. m.* hard push, shove.

empeñar /empe'ɲar/ *v.* pledge; pawn.

empeñarse en /empe'ɲarse en/ *v.* persist in, be bent on.

empeño /em'peɲo/ *n. m.* persistence; pledge; pawning.

empeoramiento /empeora'miento/ *n. m.* deterioration.

empeorar /empeo'rar/ *v.* get worse.

emperador /empera'ðor/ *n. m.* emperor.

emperatriz /empera'triθ; empera'tris/ *n. f.* empress.

empernar /emper'nar/ *v.* bolt.

empero /em'pero/ *conj.* however; but.

emperramiento /emperra'miento/ *n. m.* stubbornness.

empezar /empe'θar; empe'sar/ *v.* begin, start.

empinado /empi'naðo/ *a.* steep.

empinar /empi'nar/ *v.* raise; exalt.

empíreo /em'pireo/ *a.* celestial, heavenly; divine.

empíricamente /empirika'mente/ *adv.* empirically.

empírico /em'piriko/ *a.* empirical.

empirismo /empi'rismo/ *n. m.* empiricism.

emplastarse /emplas'tarse/ *v.* get smeared.

emplasto /em'plasto/ *n. m.* salve.

emplazamiento /emplaθa'miento; emplasa'miento/ *n. m.* court summons.

emplazar /empla'θar; empla'sar/ *v.* summon to court.

empleado /emple'aðo/ **-da** *n.* employee.

emplear /em'plear/ *v.* employ; use.

empleo /em'pleo/ *n. m.* employment, job; use.

empobrecer /empoβre'θer; empoβre'ser/ *v.* impoverish.

empobrecimiento /empoβreθi'miento; empoβresi'miento/ *n. m.* impoverishment.

empollador /empoʎa'ðor; empoya'ðor/ *n. m.* incubator.

empollar /empo'ʎar; empo'yar/ *v.* hatch.

empolvado /empol'βaðo/ *a.* dusty.

empolvar /empol'βar/ *v.* powder.

emporcar /empor'kar/ v. soil, make dirty.

emporio /em'porio/ n. m. emporium.

emprendedor /emprende'ðor/ a. enterprising.

emprender /empren'der/ v. undertake.

empreñar /empre'ɲar/ v. make pregnant; beget.

empresa /em'presa/ n. f. enterprise, undertaking; company.

empresario /empre'sario/ **-ria** n. businessperson; impresario.

empréstito /em'prestito/ n. m. loan.

empujón /empu'hon/ n. m. push; shove. —**empujar,** v.

empuñar /empu'ɲar/ v. grasp, seize; wield.

emulación /emula'θion; emula'sion/ n. f. emulation; envy; rivalry.

emulador /emula'ðor/ n. m. emulator; rival.

émulo /'emulo/ a. rival. —**emular,** v.

emulsión /emul'sion/ n. f. emulsion.

emulsionar /emulsio'nar/ v. emulsify.

en /en/ prep. in, on, at.

enaguas /e'naguas/ n. f.pl. petticoat; skirt.

enajenable /enahe'naβle/ a. alienable.

enajenación /enahena'θion; enahena'sion/ n. f. alienation; derangement, insanity.

enajenar /enahe'nar/ v. alienate.

enamoradamente /enamoraða'mente/ adv. lovingly.

enamorado /enamo'raðo/ a. in love.

enamorador /enamora'ðor/ n. m. wooer; suitor; lover.

enamorarse /enamo'rarse/ v. fall in love.

enano /e'nano/ **-na** n. midget; dwarf.

enardecer /enarðe'θer; enarðe'ser/ v. inflame.

enastado /enas'taðo/ a. horned.

encabestrar /enkaβe'strar/ v. halter.

encabezado /enkaβe'θaðo; enkaβe'saðo/ n. m. headline.

encabezamiento /enkaβeθa'miento; enkaβesa'miento/ n. m. title; census; tax roll.

encabezar /enkaβe'θar; enkaβe'sar/ v. head.

encachar /enka'tʃar/ v. hide.

encadenamiento /enkaðena'miento/ n. m. connection, linkage.

encadenar /enkaðe'nar/ v. chain; link, connect.

encajar /enka'har/ v. fit in, insert.

encaje /en'kahe/ n. m. lace.

encalar /enka'lar/ v. whitewash.

encallarse /enka'ʎarse; enka'yarse/ v. be stranded.

encallecido /enkaʎe'θiðo; enkaye'siðo/ a. hardened; calloused.

encalvecer /enkalβe'θer; enkalβe'ser/ v. lose one's hair.

encaminar /enkami'nar/ v. guide; direct; be on the way to.

encandilar /enkandi'lar/ v. dazzle; daze.

encantación /enkanta'θion; enkanta'sion/ n. f. incantation.

encantado /enkan'taðo/ a. charmed, fascinated, enchanted.

encantador /enkanta'ðor/ a. charming, delightful.

encante /en'kante/ n. m. public auction.

encanto /en'kanto/ n. m. charm, delight. —**encantar,** v.

encapillado /enkapi'ʎaðo; enkapi'yaðo/ n. m. clothes one is wearing.

encapotar /enkapo'tar/ v. cover, cloak; muffle.

encaprichamiento /enkapritʃa'miento/ n. m. infatuation.

encaramarse /enkara'marse/ v. perch; climb.

encararse con /enka'rarse kon/ v. face.

encarcelación /enkarθela'θion; enkarsela'sion/ n. f. imprisonment.

encarcelar /enkarθe'lar; enkarse'lar/ v. jail, imprison.

encarecer /enkare'θer; enkare'ser/ v. recommend; extol.

encarecidamente /enkareθiða'mente; enkaresiða'mente/ adv. extremely; ardently.

encargado /enkar'gaðo/ **-da** n. agent; attorney; representative.

encargar /enkar'gar/ v. entrust; order.

encargarse /enkar'garse/ v. take charge, be in charge.

encargo /en'kargo/ n. m. errand; assignment; Com. order.

encarnación /enkarna'θion; enkarna'sion/ *n. f.* incarnation.

encarnado /enkar'naðo/ *a.* red.

encarnar /enkar'nar/ *v.* embody.

encarnecer /enkarne'θer; enkarne'ser/ *v.* grow fat or heavy.

encarnizado /enkarni'θaðo; enkarni'saðo/ *a.* bloody, fierce.

encarrilar /enkarri'lar/ *v.* set right; put on the track.

encartar /enkar'tar/ *v.* ban, outlaw; summon.

encastar /enkas'tar/ *v.* improve by crossbreeding.

encastillar /enkasti'ʎar; enkasti'yar/ *v.* be obstinate or unyielding.

encatarrado /enkata'rraðo/ *a.* suffering from a cold.

encausar /enkau'sar/ *v.* prosecute; take legal action against.

encauzar /enkau'θar; enkau'sar/ *v.* channel; direct.

encefalitis /enθefa'litis; ensefa'litis/ *n. f.* encephalitis.

encelamiento /enθela'miento; ensela'miento/ *n. m.* envy, jealousy.

encelar /enθe'lar; ense'lar/ *v.* make jealous.

encenagar /enθena'gar; ensena'gar/ *v.* wallow in mud.

encendedor /enθende'ðor; ensende'ðor/ *n. m.* lighter.

encender /enθen'der; ensen'der/ *v.* light; set fire to, kindle; turn on.

encendido /enθen'diðo; ensen'diðo/ *n. m.* ignition.

encerado /enθe'raðo; ense'raðo/ *n. m.* oilcloth; tarpaulin.

encerar /enθe'rar; ense'rar/ *v.* wax.

encerrar /enθe'rrar; ense'rrar/ *v.* enclose; confine, shut in.

enchapado /entʃa'paðo/ *n. m.* veneer.

enchufe /en'tʃufe/ *n. m. Elec.* plug, socket.

encía /en'θia; en'sia/ *n. f.* gum.

encíclico /en'θikliko; en'sikliko/ *a.* **1.** encyclic. —*n.* **2.** *f.* encyclical.

enciclopedia /enθiklo'peðia; ensiklo'peðia/ *n. f.* encyclopedia.

enciclopédico /enθiklo'peðiko; ensiklo'peðiko/ *a.* encyclopedic.

encierro /en'θierro; en'sierro/ *n. m.* confinement; enclosure.

encima /en'θima; en'sima/ *adv.* on top. **e. de,** on. **por e. de,** above.

encina /en'θina; en'sina/ *n. f.* oak.

encinta /en'θinta; en'sinta/ *a.* pregnant.

enclavar /enkla'βar/ *v.* nail.

enclenque /en'klenke/ *a.* frail, weak, sickly.

encogerse /enko'herse/ *v.* shrink. **e. de hombros,** shrug the shoulders.

encogido /enko'hiðo/ *a.* shy, bashful, timid.

encojar /enko'har/ *v.* make or become lame; cripple.

encolar /enko'lar/ *v.* glue, paste, stick.

encolerizar /enkoleri'θar; enkoleri'sar/ *v.* make or become angry.

encomendar /enkomen'dar/ *v.* commend; recommend.

encomiar /enko'miar/ *v.* praise, laud, extol.

encomienda /enko'mienda/ *n. f.* commission, charge; (postal) package.

encomio /en'komio/ *n. m.* encomium, eulogy.

enconar /enko'nar/ *v.* irritate, annoy, anger.

encono /en'kono/ *n. m.* rancor, resentment.

enconoso /enko'noso/ *a.* rancorous, resentful.

encontrado /enkon'traðo/ *a.* opposite.

encontrar /enkon'trar/ *v.* find; meet.

encorajar /enkora'har/ *v.* encourage; incite.

encornar /enkor'nar/ *v.* gore.

encorralar /enkorra'lar/ *v.* corral.

encorvadura /enkorβa'ðura/ *n. f.* bend, curvature.

encorvar /enkor'βar/ *v.* arch, bend.

encorvarse /enkor'βarse/ *v.* stoop.

encrucijada /enkruθi'haða; enkrusi'haða/ *n. f.* crossroads.

encuadrar /enkuað'rar/ *v.* frame.

encubierta /enku'βierta/ *a.* **1.** secret, fraudulent. —*n.* **2.** *f.* fraud.

encubrir /enkuβ'rir/ *v.* hide, conceal.

encuentro /en'kuentro/ *n. m.* encounter; match, bout.

encurtido /enkur'tiðo/ *n. m.* pickle.

endeble /en'deβle/ *a.* rail, weak, sickly.

enderezar /endere'θar; endere'sar/ *v.* straighten; redress.

endeudarse /endeu'ðarse/ v. get into debt.

endiablado /endia'βlaðo/ a. devilish.

endibia /en'diβia/ n. f. endive.

endiosar /endio'sar/ v. deify.

endorso /en'dorso/ **endoso** n. m. endorsement.

endosador /endosa'ðor/ **-ra** n. endorser.

endosar /endo'sar/ v. endorse.

endosatario /endosa'tario/ **-ria** n. endorsee.

endulzar /endul'θar; endul'sar/ v. sweeten; soothe.

endurar /endu'rar/ v. harden.

endurecer /endure'θer; endure-'ser/ v. harden.

enemigo /ene'migo/ **-ga** n. foe, enemy.

enemistad /enemis'tað/ n. f. enmity.

éneo /'eneo/ a. brass.

energía /ener'hia/ n. f. energy.

energía nuclear /ener'hia nukle-'ar/ atomic energy, nuclear energy.

energía vital /ener'hia bi'tal/ élan vital, vitality.

enérgicamente /e'nerhikamente/ adv. energetically.

enérgico /e'nerhiko/ a. forceful; energetic.

enero /e'nero/ n. m. January.

enervación /enerβa'θion; enerβa-'sion/ n. f. enervation.

enfadado /enfa'ðaðo/ a. angry.

enfadar /enfa'ðar/ v. anger, vex.

enfado /en'faðo/ n. m. anger, vexation.

énfasis /'enfasis/ n. m. or f. emphasis, stress.

enfáticamente /en'fatikamente/ adv. emphatically.

enfático /en'fatiko/ a. emphatic.

enfermar /enfer'mar/ v. make ill; fall ill.

enfermedad /enferme'ðað/ n. f. illness, sickness, disease.

enfermera /enfer'mera/ n. f. nurse.

enfermería /enferme'ria/ n. f. sanatorium.

enfermo /en'fermo/ **-ma** a. & n. ill, sick; sickly; patient.

enfilar /enfi'lar/ v. line up; put in a row.

enflaquecer /enflake'θer; enflake-'ser/ v. make thin; grow thin.

enfoque /en'foke/ n. m. focus.

—**enfocar,** v.

enfrascamiento /enfraska'miento/ n. m. entanglement.

enfrascar /enfras'kar/ v. bottle; entangle oneself.

enfrenar /enfre'nar/ v. bridle, curb; restrain.

enfrentamiento /enfrenta'miento/ n. m. clash, confrontation.

enfrente /en'frente/ adv. across, opposite; in front.

enfriadera /enfria'ðera/ n. f. icebox; cooler.

enfriar /enf'riar/ v. chill, cool.

enfurecer /enfure'θer; enfure'ser/ v. infuriate, enrage.

engalanar /eŋgala'nar/ v. adorn, trim.

enganchar /eŋgan'tʃar/ v. hook, hitch, attach.

engañar /eŋga'ɲar/ v. deceive, cheat.

engaño /eŋ'gaɲo/ n. m. deceit; delusion.

engañoso /eŋga'ɲoso/ a. deceitful.

engarce /eŋ'garθe; eŋgarse/ n. m. connection, link.

engastar /eŋgas'tar/ v. to put (gems) in a setting.

engaste /eŋ'gaste/ n. m. setting.

engatusar /eŋgatu'sar/ v. deceive, trick.

engendrar /enhen'drar/ v. engender, beget, produce.

engendro /en'hendro/ n. m. fetus, embryo.

englobar /eŋglo'βar/ v. include.

engolfar /eŋgol'far/ v. be deeply absorbed.

engolosinar /eŋgolosi'nar/ v. allure, charm, entice.

engomar /eŋgo'mar/ v. gum.

engordador /eŋgor'ðaðor/ a. fattening.

engordar /eŋgor'ðar/ v. fatten; grow fat.

engranaje /eŋgra'nahe/ n. m. Mech. gear.

engranar /eŋgra'nar/ v. gear; mesh together.

engrandecer /eŋgrande'θer; eŋgrande'ser/ v. increase, enlarge; exalt; exaggerate.

engrasación /eŋgrasa'θion; eŋgrasa'sion/ n. f. lubrication.

engrasar /eŋgra'sar/ v. grease, lubricate.

engreído /eŋgre'iðo/ a. conceited.

engreimiento /eŋgrei'miento/ *n. m.* conceit.

engullidor /eŋguʎi'ðor; eŋguyi-'ðor/ **-ra** *n.* devourer.

engullir /eŋgu'ʎir; eŋgu'yir/ *v.* devour.

enhebrar /ene'βrar/ *v.* thread.

enhestadura /enesta'ðura/ *n. f.* raising.

enhestar /enes'tar/ *v.* raise, erect, set up.

enhiesto /en'iesto/ *a.* erect, upright.

enhorabuena /enora'βuena/ *n. f.* congratulations.

enigma /e'nigma/ *n. m.* enigma, puzzle.

enigmáticamente /enigmatika'mente/ *adv.* enigmatically.

enigmático /enig'matiko/ *a.* enigmatic.

enjabonar /enhaβo'nar/ *v.* soap, lather.

enjalbegar /enhalβe'gar/ *v.* whitewash.

enjambradera /enhambra'ðera/ *n. f.* queen bee.

enjambre /en'hambre/ *n. m.* swarm. —**enjambrar**, *v.*

enjaular /enhau'lar/ *v.* cage, coop up.

enjebe /en'heβe/ *n. m.* lye.

enjuagar /enhua'gar/ *v.* rinse.

enjuague bucal /en'huage bu'kal/ *n. m.* mouthwash.

enjugar /enhu'gar/ *v.* wipe, dry off.

enjutez /enhu'teθ; enhu'tes/ *n. f.* dryness.

enjuto /en'huto/ *a.* dried; lean, thin.

enlace /en'laθe; en'lase/ *n. m.* attachment; involvement; connection.

enladrillador /enlaðriʎa'ðor; enlaðriya'ðor/ **-ra** *n.* bricklayer.

enlardar /enlar'ðar/ *v.* baste.

enlatado /enla'taðo/ **-da** *a.* canned (food).

enlatar /enla'tar/ *v.* can (food).

enlazar /enla'θar; enla'sar/ *v.* lace; join, connect; wed.

enlodar /enlo'ðar/ *v.* cover with mud.

enloquecer /enloke'θer; enloke-'ser/ *v.* go insane; drive crazy.

enloquecimiento /enlokeθi-'miento; enlokesi'miento/ *n. m.* insanity.

enlustrecer /enlustre'θer; enlustre'ser/ *v.* polish, brighten.

enmarañar /emara'ɲar/ *v.* entangle.

enmendación /enmenda'θion; enmenda'sion/ *n. f.* emendation.

enmendador /enmenda'ðor/ **-ra** *n.* emender, reviser.

enmendar /enmen'dar/ *v.* amend, correct.

enmienda /en'mienda/ *n. f.* amendment; correction.

enmohecer /enmoe'θer; enmoe'ser/ *v.* rust; mold.

enmohecido /enmoe'θiðo; enmoe-'siðo/ *a.* rusty; moldy.

enmudecer /enmuðe'θer; enmuðe-'ser/ *v.* silence; become silent.

ennegrecer /ennegre'θer; ennegre'ser/ *v.* blacken.

ennoblecer /ennoβle'θer; ennoβle'ser/ *v.* ennoble.

enodio /e'noðio/ *n. m.* young deer.

enojado /eno'haðo/ *a.* angry, cross.

enojarse /eno'harse/ *v.* get angry.

enojo /e'noho/ *n. m.* anger. —**enojar**, *v.*

enojosamente /enohosa'mente/ *adv.* angrily.

enorme /e'norme/ *a.* enormous, huge.

enormemente /enorme'mente/ *adv.* enormously; hugely.

enormidad /enormi'ðað/ *n. f.* enormity; hugeness.

enraizar /enrai'θar; enrai'sar/ *v.* take root, sprout.

enramada /enra'maða/ *n. f.* bower.

enredadera /enreða'ðera/ *n. f.* climbing plant.

enredado /enre'ðaðo/ *a.* entangled, snarled.

enredar /enre'ðar/ *v.* entangle, snarl; mess up.

enredo /en'reðo/ *n. m.* tangle, entanglement.

enriquecer /enrike'θer; enrike'ser/ *v.* enrich.

enrojecerse /enrohe'θerse; enrohe'serse/ *v.* color; blush.

enrollar /enro'ʎar; enro'yar/ *v.* wind, coil, roll up.

enromar /enro'mar/ *v.* make dull, blunt.

enronquecimiento /enronkeθi-'miento; enronkesi'miento/ *n. m.* hoarseness.

enroscar /enros'kar/ *v.* twist, curl, wind.

ensacar /ensa'kar/ *v.* put in a bag.

ensalada /ensa'laða/ *n. f.* salad.

ensaladera /ensala'ðera/ *n. f.* salad bowl.

ensalmo /en'salmo/ *n. m.* charm, enchantment.

ensalzamiento /ensalθa'miento; ensalsa'miento/ *n. m.* praise.

ensalzar /ensal'θar; ensal'sar/ *v.* praise, laud, extol.

ensamblar /ensam'blar/ *v.* join; unite; connect.

ensanchamiento /ensantʃa-'miento/ *n. m.* widening, expansion, extension.

ensanchar /ensan'tʃar/ *v.* widen, expand, extend.

ensangrentado /ensaŋgren'taðo/ *a.* bloody; bloodshot.

ensañar /ensa'ɲar/ *v.* enrage, infuriate; rage.

ensayar /ensa'yar/ *v.* try out; rehearse.

ensayista /ensa'yista/ *n. m. & f.* essayist.

ensayo /ensa'yo/ *n. m.* attempt; trial; rehearsal.

ensenada /ense'naða/ *n. f.* cove.

enseña /en'seɲa/ *n. f.* ensign, standard.

enseñador /enseɲa'ðor/ **-ra** *n.* teacher.

enseñanza /ense'ɲanθa; enseɲan-sa/ *n. f.* education; teaching.

enseñar /ense'ɲar/ *v.* teach, train; show.

enseres /en'seres/ *n. m.pl.* household goods.

ensilaje /ensi'lahe/ *n. m.* ensilage.

ensillar /ensi'ʎar; ensi'yar/ *v.* saddle.

ensordecedor /ensorðeθe'ðor; ensorðese'ðor/ *a.* deafening.

ensordecer /ensorðe'θer; ensorðe'ser/ *v.* deafen.

ensordecimiento /ensorðeθi-'miento; ensorðesi'miento/ *n. m.* deafness.

ensuciar /ensu'θiar; ensu'siar/ *v.* dirty, muddy, soil.

ensueño /en'sueɲo/ *n. m.* illusion, dream.

entablar /enta'βlar/ *v.* board up; initiate, begin.

entallador /entaʎa'ðor; en-taya'ðor/ *n. m.* sculptor, carver.

entapizar /entapi'θar; entapi'sar/ *v.* upholster.

ente /'ente/ *n. m.* being.

entenada /ente'naða/ *n. f.* stepdaughter.

entenado /ente'naðo/ *n. m.* stepson.

entender /enten'der/ *v.* understand.

entendimiento /entendi'miento/ *n. m.* understanding.

entenebrecer /enteneβre'θer; enteneβre'ser/ *v.* darken.

enterado /ente'raðo/ *a.* aware, informed.

enteramente /entera'mente/ *adv.* entirely, completely.

enterar /ente'rar/ *v.* inform.

enterarse /ente'rarse/ *v.* find out.

entereza /ente'reθa; ente'resa/ *n. f.* entirety; integrity; firmness.

entero /en'tero/ *a.* entire, whole, total.

enterramiento /enterra'miento/ *n. m.* burial, interment.

enterrar /ente'rrar/ *v.* bury.

entestado /entes'taðo/ *a.* stubborn, willful.

entibiar /enti'βiar/ *v.* to cool; moderate.

entidad /enti'ðað/ *n. f.* entity.

entierro /en'tierro/ *n. m.* interment, burial.

entonación /entona'θion; entona-'sion/ *n. f.* intonation.

entonamiento /entona'miento/ *n. m.* intonation.

entonar /ento'nar/ *v.* chant; harmonize.

entonces /en'tonθes; entonses/ *adv.* then.

entono /en'tono/ *n. m.* intonation; arrogance; affectation.

entortadura /entorta'ðura/ *n. f.* crookedness.

entortar /entor'tar/ *v.* make crooked; bend.

entrada /en'traða/ *n. f.* entrance; admission, admittance.

entrambos /en'trambos/ *a. & pron.* both.

entrante /en'trante/ *a.* coming, next.

entrañable /entra'ɲaβle/ *a.* affectionate.

entrañas /en'traɲas/ *n. f.pl.* entrails, bowels; womb.

entrar /en'trar/ *v.* enter, go in; come in.

entre /'entre/ *prep.* among; between.

entreabierto /entrea'βierto/ a. ajar, half-open.

entreabrir /entrea'βrir/ v. set ajar.

entreacto /entre'akto/ n. m. intermission.

entrecejo /entre'θeho; entre'seho/ n. m. frown; space between the eyebrows.

entrecuesto /entre'kuesto/ n. m. spine, backbone.

entredicho /entre'ðitʃo/ n. m. prohibition.

entrega /en'trega/ n. f. delivery.

entregar /entre'gar/ v. deliver, hand; hand over.

entrelazar /entrela'θar; entrela-'sar/ v. intertwine, entwine.

entremedias /entre'meðias/ adv. meanwhile; halfway.

entremés /entre'mes/ n. m. side dish.

entremeterse /entreme'terse/ v. meddle, intrude.

entremetido /entreme'tiðo/ **-da** n. meddler.

entrenador /entrena'ðor/ **-ra** n. coach. —**entrenar,** v.

entrenarse /entre'narse/ v. train.

entrepalado /entrepa'laðo/ a. variegated; spotted.

entrerenglonar /entrerenglo'nar/ v. interline.

entresacar /entresa'kar/ v. select, choose; sift.

entresuelo /entre'suelo/ n. m. mezzanine.

entretanto /entre'tanto/ adv. meanwhile.

entretenedor /entretene'ðor/ **-ra** n. entertainer.

entretener /entrete'ner/ v. entertain, amuse; delay.

entretenimiento /entreteni-'miento/ n. m. entertainment, amusement.

entrevista /entre'βista/ n. f. interview. —**entrevistar,** v.

entrevistador /entreβista'ðor/ **-ra** n. interviewer.

entristecedor /entristeθe'ðor; entristese'ðor/ a. sad.

entristecer /entriste'θer; entriste-'ser/ v. sadden.

entronar /entro'nar/ v. enthrone.

entroncar /entron'kar/ v. be related or connected.

entronización /entroniθa'θion; entronisa'sion/ n. f. enthronement.

entronque /entron'ke/ n. m. relationship; connection.

entumecer /entume'θer; entume-'ser/ v. become or be numb; swell.

entusiasmado /entusias'maðo/ a. enthusiastic.

entusiasmo /entu'siasmo/ n. m. enthusiasm.

entusiasta /entu'siasta/ n. m. & f. enthusiast.

entusiástico /entu'siastiko/ a. enthusiastic.

enumeración /enumera'θion; enumera'sion/ n. f. enumeration.

enumerar /enume'rar/ v. enumerate.

enunciación /enunθia'θion; enunsia'sion/ n. f. enunciation; statement.

enunciar /enun'θiar; enun'siar/ v. enunciate.

envainar /embai'nar/ v. sheathe.

envalentonar /embalento'nar/ v. encourage, embolden.

envanecimiento /embaneθi-miento; embanesi'miento/ n. m. conceit, vanity.

envasar /emba'sar/ v. put in a container; bottle.

envase /em'base/ n. m. container.

envejecer /embehe'θer; embehe-'ser/ v. age, grow old.

envejecimiento /embeheθi-'miento; embehesi'miento/ n. m. oldness, aging.

envenenar /embene'nar/ v. poison.

envés /em'bes/ n. m. wrong side; back.

envestir /embes'tir/ v. put in office; invest.

enviada /em'biaða/ n. f. shipment.

enviado /em'biaðo/ **-da** n. envoy.

enviar /em'biar/ v. send; ship.

envidia /em'biðia/ n. f. envy. —**envidiar,** v.

envidiable /embi'ðiaβle/ a. enviable.

envidioso /embi'ðioso/ a. envious.

envilecer /embile'θer; embile'ser/ v. vilify, debase, disgrace.

envío /em'bio/ n. m. shipment.

envión /em'bion/ n. m. shove.

envoltura /embol'tura/ n. f. wrapping.

envolver /embol'βer/ v. wrap, wrap up.

enyesar /enye'sar/ v. plaster.

enyugar /enyu'gar/ v. yoke.

eperlano /eper'lano/ n. m. smelt (fish).

épica /'epika/ n. f. epic.

épico /'epiko/ a. epic.

epicureísmo /epikure'ismo/ n. m. epicureanism.

epicúreo /epi'kureo/ n. & a. epicurean.

epidemia /epi'ðemia/ n. f. epidemic.

epidémico /epi'ðemiko/ a. epidemic.

epidermis /epi'ðermis/ n. f. epidermis.

epigrama /epi'grama/ n. m. epigram.

epigramático /epigra'matiko/ **-ca** a. epigrammatic.

epilepsia /epi'lepsia/ n. f. epilepsy.

epiléptico /epi'leptiko/ **-ca** n. & a. epileptic.

epílogo /e'pilogo/ n. m. epilogue.

episcopado /episko'paðo/ n. m. bishopric; episcopate.

episcopal /episko'pal/ a. episcopal.

episódico /epi'soðiko/ a. episodic.

episodio /epi'soðio/ n. m. episode.

epístola /e'pistola/ n. f. epistle, letter.

epitafio /epi'tafio/ n. m. epitaph.

epitomadamente /epitomaða-'mente/ adv. concisely.

epitomar /epito'mar/ v. epitomize, summarize.

época /'epoka/ n. f. epoch, age.

epopeya /epo'peya/ n. f. epic.

epsomita /epso'mita/ n. f. Epsom salts.

equidad /eki'ðað/ n. f. equity.

equilibrado /ekili'βraðo/ a. stable.

equilibrio /eki'liβrio/ n. m. equilibrium, balance.

equinoccio /eki'nokθio; ekinoksio/ n. m. equinox.

equipaje /eki'pahe/ n. m. luggage, baggage. **e. de mano,** luggage.

equipar /eki'par/ v. equip.

equiparar /ekipa'rar/ v. compare.

equipo /e'kipo/ n. m. equipment; team.

equitación /ekita'θion; ekita'sion/ f. horsemanship; horseback riding, riding.

equitativo /ekita'tiβo/ a. fair, equitable.

equivalencia /ekiβa'lenθia; ekiβa'lensia/ n. f. equivalence.

equivalente /ekiβa'lente/ a. equivalent.

equivaler /ekiβa'ler/ v. equal, be equivalent.

equivocación /ekiβoka'θion; ekiβoka'sion/ n. f. mistake.

equivocado /ekiβo'kaðo/ a. wrong, mistaken.

equivocarse /ekiβo'karse/ v. make a mistake, be wrong.

equívoco /e'kiβoko/ a. equivocal, ambiguous.

era /'era/ n. f. era, age.

erario /e'rario/ n. m. exchequer.

erección /erek'θion; erek'sion/ n. f. erection; elevation.

eremita /ere'mita/ n. m. hermit.

erguir /er'gir/ v. erect; straighten up.

erigir /eri'hir/ v. erect, build.

erisipela /erisi'pela/ n. f. erysipelas.

erizado /eri'θaðo; eri'saðo/ a. bristly.

erizarse /eri'θarse; eri'sarse/ v. bristle.

erizo /e'riθo; e'riso/ n. m. hedgehog; sea urchin.

ermita /er'mita/ n. f. hermitage.

ermitaño /ermi'taɲo/ n. m. hermit.

erogación /eroga'θion; eroga'sion/ n. f. expenditure. —**erogar,** v.

erosión /ero'sion/ n. f. erosion.

erótico /e'rotiko/ a. erotic.

erradicación /erraðika'θion; erraðika'sion/ n. f. eradication.

erradicar /erraði'kar/ v. eradicate.

errado /e'rraðo/ a. mistaken, erroneous.

errante /e'rrante/ a. wandering, roving.

errar /e'rrar/ v. be mistaken.

errata /e'rrata/ n. f. erratum.

errático /e'rratiko/ a. erratic.

erróneamente /erronea'mente/ adv. erroneously.

erróneo /e'rroneo/ a. erroneous.

error /e'rror/ n. m. error, mistake.

eructo /e'rukto/ n. m. belch. —**eructar,** v.

erudición /eruði'θion; eruði'sion/ n. f. scholarship, learning.

eruditamente /eruðita'mente/ adv. learnedly.

erudito /eru'ðito/ **-ta** n. **1.** scholar. —a. **2.** scholarly.

erupción /erup'θion; erup'sion/ n. f. eruption; rash.

eruptivo /erup'tiβo/ a. eruptive.

esbozo /es'βoθo; es'βoso/ *n. m.*
outline, sketch. —**esbozar,** *v.*

escabechar /eskaβe't∫ar/ *v.*
pickle; preserve.

escabeche /eska'βet∫e/ *n. m.*
brine.

escabel /eska'βel/ *n. m.* small
stool or bench.

escabroso /eska'βroso/ *a.* rough,
irregular; craggy; rude.

escabullirse /eskaβu'ʎirse; eska-
βu'yirse/ *v.* steal away, sneak
away.

escala /es'kala/ *n. f.* scale; ladder.
hacer e., to make a stop.

escalada /eska'laða/ *n. f.* escala-
tion.

escalador /eskala'ðor/ **-ra** *n.*
climber.

escalar /eska'lar/ *v.* climb; scale.

escaldar /eskal'dar/ *v.* scald.

escalera /eska'lera/ *n. f.* stairs,
staircase; ladder.

escalfado /eskal'faðo/ *a.* poached.

escalofriado /eskalo'friaðo/ *a.*
chilled.

escalofrío /eskalo'frio/ *n. m.* chill.

escalón /eska'lon/ *n. m.* step.

escalonar /eskalo'nar/ *v.* space
out, stagger.

escaloña /eska'loɲa/ *n. f.* scallion.

escalpar /eskal'par/ *v.* scalp.

escalpelo /eskal'pelo/ *n. m.* scal-
pel.

escama /es'kama/ *n. f.* (fish)
scale. —**escamar,** *v.*

escamondar /eskamon'dar/ *v.*
trim, cut; prune.

escampada /eskam'paða/ *n. f.*
break in the rain, clear spell.

escandalizar /eskandali'θar; es-
kandali'sar/ *v.* shock, scandalize.

escandalizativo /eskandaliθa'tiβo;
eskandalisa'tiβo/ *a.* scandalous.

escándalo /es'kandalo/ *n. m.*
scandal.

escandaloso /eskanda'loso/ *a.*
scandalous; disgraceful.

escandinavo /eskandi'naβo/ **-va**
n. & a. Scandinavian.

escandir /eskan'dir/ *v.* scan.

escanear /eskane'ar/ *v.* scan (on a
computer).

escáner /es'kaner/ *n. m.* scanner
(of a computer).

escanilla /eska'niʎa; eska'niya/ *n.
f.* cradle.

escañuelo /eska'ɲuelo/ *n. m.*
small footstool.

escapada /eska'paða/ *n. f.* escapade. ′

escapar /eska'par/ *v.* escape.

escaparate /eskapa'rate/ *n. m.*
shop window, store window.

escape /es'kape/ *n. m.* escape;
Auto. exhaust.

escápula /es'kapula/ *n. f.* scapula.

escarabajo /eskara'βaho/ *n. m.*
black beetle; scarab.

escaramucear /eskaramuθe'ar; es-
karamuse'ar/ *v.* skirmish; dispute.

escarbadientes /eskarβa'ðientes/
n. m. toothpick.

escarbar /eskar'βar/ *v.* scratch;
poke.

escarcha /es'kart∫a/ *n. f.* frost.

escardar /eskar'ðar/ *v.* weed.

escarlata /eskar'lata/ *n. f.* scarlet.

escarlatina /eskarla'tina/ *n. f.*
scarlet fever.

escarmentar /eskarmen'tar/ *v.*
correct severely.

escarnecedor /eskarneθe'ðor; es-
karneseðor/ **-ra** *n.* scoffer;
mocker.

escarnecer /eskarne'θer; eskar-
ne'ser/ *v.* mock, make fun of.

escarola /eska'rola/ *n. f.* endive.

escarpa /es'karpa/ *n. m.* escarp-
ment.

escarpado /eskar'paðo/ *a.* **1.**
steep. —*n.* **2.** *m.* bluff.

escasamente /eskasa'mente/ *adv.*
scarcely; sparingly; barely.

escasear /eskase'ar/ *v.* be scarce.

escasez /eska'seθ; eska'ses/ *n. f.*
shortage, scarcity.

escaso /es'kaso/ *a.* scant; scarce.

escatimar /eskati'mar/ *v.* be
stingy, skimp; save.

escatimoso /eskati'moso/ *a.* malicious; sly, cunning.

escena /es'θena; es'sena/ *n. f.*
scene; stage.

escenario /esθe'nario; esse'nario/
n. m. stage (of theater); scenario.

escénico /es'θeniko; es'seniko/ *a.*
scenic.

escépticamente /esθeptika'mente;
esseptika'mente/ *adv.* skeptically.

escepticismo /esθepti'θismo; es-
septi'sismo/ *n. m.* skepticism.

escéptico /es'θeptiko; es'septiko/
-ca *a. & n.* skeptic; skeptical.

esclarecer /esklare'θer; esklare-
'ser/ *v.* clear up.

esclavitud /esklaβi'tuð/ *n. f.* slavery; bondage.

esclavizar /esklaβi'θar; esklaβi-'sar/ v. enslave.

esclavo /es'klaβo/ -va n. slave.

escoba /es'koβa/ n. f. broom.

escocés /esko'θes; esko'ses/ -esa a. & n. Scotch, Scottish; Scot.

Escocia /es'koθia; eskosia/ n. f. Scotland.

escofinar /eskofi'nar/ v. rasp.

escoger /esko'her/ v. choose, select.

escogido /esko'hiðo/ a. chosen, selected.

escogimiento /eskohi'miento/ n. m. choice.

escolar /esko'lar/ a. 1. scholastic, (of) school. —n. 2. m.& f. student.

escolasticismo /eskolasti'θismo; eskolasti'sismo/ n. m. scholasticism.

escollo /es'koʎo; es'koyo/ n. m. reef.

escolta /es'kolta/ n. f. escort. —escoltar, v.

escombro /es'kombro/ n. m. mackerel.

escombros /es'kombros/ n. m.pl. debris, rubbish.

esconce /es'konθe; es'konse/ n. m. corner.

escondedero /eskonde'ðero/ n. m. hiding place.

esconder /eskon'der/ v. hide, conceal.

escondidamente /eskondiða-'mente/ adv. secretly.

escondimiento /eskondi'miento/ n. m. concealment.

escondrijo /eskon'driho/ n. m. hiding place.

escopeta /esko'peta/ n. f. shotgun.

escopetazo /eskope'taθo; eskope-'taso/ n. m. gunshot.

escoplo /es'koplo/ n. m. chisel.

escorbuto /eskor'βuto/ n. m. scurvy.

escorpena /eskor'pena/ n. f. grouper.

escorpión /eskor'pion/ n. m. scorpion.

escorzón /eskor'θon; eskor'son/ n. m. toad.

escotado /eskotaðo/ a. low-cut, with a low neckline.

escote /es'kote/ n. m. low neckline.

escribiente /eskri'βiente/ n. m. & f. clerk.

escribir /eskri'βir/ v. write.

escritor /eskri'tor/ -ra n. writer, author.

escritorio /eskri'torio/ n. m. desk.

escritura /eskri'tura/ n. f. writing, handwriting.

escrófula /es'krofula/ n. f. scrofula.

escroto /es'kroto/ n. m. scrotum.

escrúpulo /es'krupulo/ n. m. scruple.

escrupuloso /eskrupu'loso/ a. scrupulous.

escrutinio /eskru'tinio/ n. m. scrutiny; examination.

escuadra /es'kuaðra/ n. f. squad; fleet.

escuadrón /eskuað'ron/ n. m. squadron.

escualidez /eskuali'ðeθ; eskuali-'ðes/ n. f. squalor; poverty; emaciation.

escuálido /es'kualiðo/ a. squalid.

escualo /es'kualo/ n. m. shark.

escuchar /esku't∫ar/ v. listen; listen to.

escudero /esku'ðero/ n. m. squire.

escudo /es'kuðo/ n. m. shield; protection; coin of certain countries.

escuela /es'kuela/ n. f. school.

escuela nocturna /es'kuela nok-'turna/ night school.

escuela por correspondencia /es'kuela por korrespon'denθia; es'kuela por korrespon'densia/ correspondence school.

escuerzo /es'kuerθo; es'kuerso/ n. m. toad.

esculpir /eskul'pir/ v. carve, sculpture.

escultor /eskul'tor/ -ra n. sculptor.

escultura /eskul'tura/ n. f. sculpture.

escupidera /eskupi'ðera/ n. f. cuspidor.

escupir /esku'pir/ v. spit.

escurridero /eskurri'ðero/ n. m. drain board.

escurridor /eskurri'ðor/ n. m. colander, strainer.

escurrir /esku'rrir/ v. drain off; wring out.

escurrirse /esku'rrirse/ v. slip; sneak away.

ese /'ese/ **esa** dem. a. that.

ése, ésa dem. pron. that (one).

esencia /e'senθia; e'sensia/ *n. f.*
essence; perfume.
esencial /esen'θial; esen'sial/ *a.*
essential.
esencialmente /esenθial'mente;
esensial'mente/ *adv.* essentially.
esfera /es'fera/ *n. f.* sphere.
esfinge /es'finhe/ *n. f.* sphinx.
esforzar /esfor'θar; esfor'sar/ *v.*
strengthen.
esforzarse /esfor'θarse; esfor-
'sarse/ *v.* strive, exert oneself.
esfuerzo /es'fuerθo; es'fuerso/ *n.
m.* effort, attempt; vigor.
esgrima /es'grima/ *n. f.* fencing.
esguince /es'ginθe; es'ginse/ *n.
m.* sprain.
eslabón /esla'βon/ *n. m.* link (of
a chain).
eslabonar /eslaβo'nar/ *v.* link,
join, connect.
eslavo /es'laβo/ **-va** *a. & n.*
Slavic; Slav.
esmalte /es'malte/ *n. m.* enamel,
polish. —**esmaltar,** *v.*
esmerado /esme'raðo/ *a.* careful,
thorough.
esmeralda /esme'ralda/ *n. f.* emerald.
esmerarse /esme'rarse/ *v.* take
pains, do one's best.
esmeril /es'meril/ *n. m.* emery.
eso /'eso/ *dem. pron.* that.
esófago /e'sofago/ *n. m.* esophagus.
esotérico /eso'teriko/ *a.* esoteric.
espacial /espa'θial; espa'sial/ *a.*
spatial.
espacio /es'paθio; es'pasio/ *n. m.*
space. —**espaciar,** *v.*
espaciosidad /espaθiosi'ðað; es-
pasiosi'ðað/ *n. f.* spaciousness.
espacioso /espa'θioso; espa'sioso/
a. spacious.
espada /es'paða/ *n. f.* sword;
spade (in cards).
espadarte /espa'ðarte/ *n. m.*
swordfish.
espaguetis /espa'getis/ *n. m.pl.*
spaghetti.
espalda /es'palda/ *n. f.* back.
espaldera /espal'dera/ *n. f.* espal-
ier.
espantar /espan'tar/ *v.* frighten,
scare; scare away.
espanto /es'panto/ *n. m.* fright.
espantoso /espan'toso/ *a.* fright-
ening, frightful.
España /es'paɲa/ *n. f.* Spain.

español /espa'ɲol/ **-ola** *a. & n.*
Spanish; Spaniard.
esparcir /espar'θir; espar'sir/ *v.*
scatter, disperse.
espárrago /es'parrago/ *n. m.* asparagus.
espartano /espar'tano/ **-na** *n. &
a.* Spartan.
espasmo /es'pasmo/ *n. m.* spasm.
espasmódico /espas'moðiko/ *a.*
spasmodic.
espata /es'pata/ *n. f.* spathe.
espato /es'pato/ *n. m.* spar (mineral).
espátula /es'patula/ *n. f.* spatula.
especia /es'peθia; es'pesia/ *n. f.*
spice. —**especiar,** *v.*
especial /espe'θial; espe'sial/ *a.*
special, especial.
especialidad /espeθiali'ðað; espe-
siali'ðað/ *n. f.* specialty.
especialista /espeθia'lista;
espesia'lista/ *n. m. & f.* specialist.
especialización /espeθialiθa'θion;
espesialisa'sion/ *n. f.* specializa-
tion.
especialmente /espeθial'mente;
espesial'mente/ *adv.* especially.
especie /es'peθie; es'pesie/ *n. f.*
species; sort.
especiería /espeθie'ria; espesie-
'ria/ *n. f.* grocery store; spice
store.
especiero /espe'θiero; espe'siero/
-ra *n.* spice dealer; spice box.
especificar /espeθifi'kar; espesifi-
'kar/ *v.* specify.
específico /espe'θifiko; espe-
'sifiko/ *a.* specific.
espécimen /es'peθimen; es'pesi-
men/ *n. m.* specimen.
especioso /espe'θioso; espe'sioso/
a. neat; polished; specious.
espectacular /espektaku'lar/ *a.*
spectacular.
espectáculo /espek'takulo/ *n. m.*
spectacle, show.
espectador /espekta'ðor/ **-ra** *n.*
spectator.
espectro /es'pektro/ *n. m.* spec-
ter, ghost.
especulación /espekula'θion; es-
pekula'sion/ *n. f.* speculation.
especulador /espekula'ðor/ **-ra** *n.*
speculator.
especular /espeku'lar/ *v.* speculate.
especulativo /espekula'tiβo/ *a.*
speculative.
espejo /es'peho/ *n. m.* mirror.

espelunca /espe'lunka/ *n. f.* dark cave, cavern.

espera /es'pera/ *n. f.* wait.

esperanza /espe'ranθa; espe'ransa/ *n. f.* hope, expectation.

esperar /espe'rar/ *v.* hope; expect; wait, wait for, watch for.

espesar /espe'sar/ *v.* thicken.

espeso /es'peso/ *a.* thick, dense, bushy.

espesor /espe'sor/ *n. m.* thickness, density.

espía /es'pia/ *n. m. & f.* spy. —**espiar,** *v.*

espigón /espi'gon/ *n. m.* bee sting.

espina /es'pina/ *n. f.* thorn.

espinaca /espi'naka/ *n. f.* spinach.

espina dorsal /es'pina dor'sal/ spine.

espinal /espi'nal/ *a.* spinal.

espinazo /espi'naθo; espi'naso/ *n. m.* backbone.

espineta /espi'neta/ *n. f.* spinet.

espino /es'pino/ *n. m.* briar.

espinoso /espi'noso/ *a.* spiny, thorny.

espión /es'pion/ *n. m.* spy.

espionaje /espio'nahe/ *n. m.* espionage.

espiral /espi'ral/ *a. & m.* spiral.

espirar /espi'rar/ *v.* expire; breathe, exhale.

espíritu /es'piritu/ *n. m.* spirit.

espiritual /espiri'tual/ *a.* spiritual.

espiritualidad /espirituali'ðað/ *n. f.* spirituality.

espiritualmente /espiritual-'mente/ *adv.* spiritually.

espita /es'pita/ *n. f.* faucet, spigot.

espléndido /es'plendiðo/ *a.* splendid.

esplendor /esplen'dor/ *n. m.* splendor.

espolear /espole'ar/ *v.* incite, urge on.

espoleta /espo'leta/ *n. f.* wishbone.

esponja /es'ponha/ *n. f.* sponge.

esponjoso /espon'hoso/ *a.* spongy.

esponsales /espon'sales/ *n. m.pl.* engagement, betrothal.

esponsalicio /esponsa'liθio; esponsa'lisio/ *a.* nuptial.

espontáneamente /espontanea-'mente/ *adv.* spontaneously.

espontaneidad /espontanei'ðað/ *n. f.* spontaneity.

espontáneo /espon'taneo/ *a.* spontaneous.

espora /es'pora/ *n. f.* spore.

esporádico /espo'raðiko/ *a.* sporadic.

esposa /es'posa/ *n. f.* wife.

esposar /espo'sar/ *v.* shackle; handcuff.

esposo /es'poso/ *n. m.* husband.

espuela /es'puela/ *n. f.* spur. —**espolear,** *v.*

espuma /es'puma/ *n. f.* foam. —**espumar,** *v.*

espumadera /espuma'ðera/ *n. f.* whisk; skimmer.

espumajear /espumahe'ar/ *v.* foam at the mouth.

espumajo /espu'maho/ *n. m.* foam.

espumar /espu'mar/ *v.* foam, froth; skim.

espumoso /espu'moso/ *a.* foamy; sparkling (wine).

espurio /es'purio/ *a.* spurious.

esputar /espu'tar/ *v.* spit, expectorate.

esputo /es'puto/ *n. m.* spit, saliva.

esquela /es'kela/ *n. f.* note.

esqueleto /eske'leto/ *n. m.* skeleton.

esquema /es'kema/ *n. m.* scheme; diagram.

esquero /es'kero/ *n. m.* leather sack, leather pouch.

esquiar /es'kiar/ *v.* ski.

esquiciar /eski'θiar; eski'siar/ *v.* outline, sketch.

esquicio /es'kiθio; es'kisio/ *n. m.* rough sketch, rough outline.

esquife /es'kife/ *n. m.* skiff.

esquilar /eski'lar/ *v.* fleece, shear.

esquilmo /es'kilmo/ *n. m.* harvest.

esquimal /eski'mal/ *n. & a.* Eskimo.

esquina /es'kina/ *n. f.* corner.

esquivar /eski'βar/ *v.* evade, shun.

estabilidad /estaβili'ðað/ *n. f.* stability.

estable /es'taβle/ *a.* stable.

establecedor /estaβleθe'ðor; estaβlese'ðor/ *n. m.* founder, originator.

establecer /estaβle'θer; estaβle-'ser/ *v.* establish, set up.

establecimiento /estaβleθi-'miento; estaβlesi'miento/ *n. m.* establishment.

establero /estaβ'lero/ *n. m.* groom.

establo /es'taβlo/ *n. m.* stable.

estaca /es'taka/ *n. f.* stake.

estación /esta'θion; esta'sion/ *f.* station; season.

estacionamiento /estaθiona-'miento; estasiona'miento/ *n. m.* parking; parking lot; parking space.

estacionar /estaθio'nar; estasio-'nar/ *v.* station; park (a vehicle).

estacionario /estaθio'nario; estasio'nario/ *a.* stationary.

estación de servicio /esta'θion de ser'βiθio; esta'sion de ser'βisio/ service station.

estación de trabajo /esta'θion de tra'βaho; esta'sion de tra'βaho/ work station.

estadista /esta'ðista/ *n. m. & f.* statesman.

estadística /esta'ðistika/ *n. f.* statistics.

estadístico /esta'ðistiko/ *a.* statistical.

estado /es'taðo/ *n. m.* state; condition; status.

Estados Unidos /es'taðos u'niðos/ *n. m.pl.* United States.

estafa /es'tafa/ *n. f.* swindle, fake. **—estafar,** *v.*

estafeta /esta'feta/ *n. f.* post office.

estagnación /estagna'θion; estagna'sion/ *n. f.* stagnation.

estallar /esta'ʎar; esta'yar/ *v.* explode; burst; break out.

estallido /esta'ʎiðo; esta'yiðo/ *n. m.* crash; crack; explosion.

estampa /es'tampa/ *n. f.* stamp. **—estampar,** *v.*

estampado /estam'paðo/ *n. m.* printed cotton cloth.

estampida /estam'piða/ *n. f.* stampede.

estampilla /estam'piʎa; estam-'piya/ *n. f.* (postage) stamp.

estancado /estan'kaðo/ *a.* stagnant.

estancar /estan'kar/ *v.* stanch, stop, check.

estancia /es'tanθia; es'tansia/ *n. f.* stay; (S.A.) small farm.

estanciero /estan'θiero; estan-'siero/ **-ra** *n.* small farmer.

estandarte /estan'darte/ *n. m.* banner.

estanque /es'tanke/ *n. m.* pool; pond.

estante /es'tante/ *n. m.* shelf.

estaño /es'taɲo/ *n. m.* tin. **—estañar,** *v.*

estar /es'tar/ *v.* be; stand; look.

estática /es'tatika/ *n. f.* static.

estático /es'tatiko/ *a.* static.

estatua /es'tatua/ *n. f.* statue.

estatura /esta'tura/ *n. f.* stature.

estatuto /esta'tuto/ *n. m.* statute, law.

este /'este/ *n. m.* east.

este, esta *dem. a.* this.

éste, ésta *dem. pron.* this (one); the latter.

estelar /este'lar/ *a.* stellar.

estenografía /estenogra'fia/ *n. f.* stenography.

estenógrafo /este'nografo/ **-fa** *n.* stenographer.

estera /es'tera/ *n. f.* mat, matting.

estereofónico /estereo'foniko/ *a.* stereophonic.

estéril /es'teril/ *a.* barren; sterile.

esterilidad /esterili'ðað/ *n. f.* sterility, fruitlessness.

esterilizar /esterili'θar; esterili'sar/ *v.* sterilize.

esternón /ester'non/ *n. m.* breastbone.

estética /es'tetika/ *n. f.* esthetics.

estético /es'tetiko/ *a.* esthetic.

estetoscopio /esteto'skopio/ *n. m.* stethoscope.

estibador /estiβa'ðor/ *n. m.* stevedore.

estiércol /es'tierkol/ *n. m.* dung, manure.

estigma /es'tigma/ *n. m.* stigma; disgrace.

estilarse /esti'larse/ *v.* be in fashion, be in vogue.

estilo /es'tilo/ *n. m.* style; sort.

estilográfica /estilo'grafika/ *n. f.* (fountain) pen.

estima /es'tima/ *n. f.* esteem.

estimable /esti'maβle/ *a.* estimable, worthy.

estimación /estima'θion; estima-'sion/ *n. f.* estimation.

estimar /esti'mar/ *v.* esteem; value; estimate; gauge.

estimular /estimu'lar/ *v.* stimulate.

estímulo /es'timulo/ *n. m.* stimulus.

estío /es'tio/ *n. m.* summer.

estipulación /estipula'θion; estipula'sion/ *n. f.* stipulation.

estipular /estipu'lar/ *v.* stipulate.

estirar /esti'rar/ *v.* stretch.

estirpe /es'tirpe/ *n. m.* stock, lineage.

esto /'esto/ *dem. pron.* this.

estocada /esto'kaða/ *n. f.* stab, thrust.

estofado /esto'faðo/ *n. m.* stew. —**estofar,** *v.*

estoicismo /estoi'θismo; estoi-'sismo/ *n. m.* stoicism.

estoico /es'toiko/ *n. & a.* stoic.

estómago /es'tomago/ *n. m.* stomach.

estorbar /estor'βar/ *v.* bother, hinder, interfere with.

estorbo /es'torβo/ *n. m.* hindrance.

estornudo /estor'nuðo/ *n. m.* sneeze. —**estornudar,** *v.*

estrabismo /estra'βismo/ *n. m.* strabismus.

estrago /es'trago/ *n. m.* devastation, havoc.

estrangulación /estraŋgula'θion; estraŋgula'sion/ *n. f.* strangulation.

estrangular /estraŋgu'lar/ *v.* strangle.

estraperlista /estraper'lista/ *n. m. & f.* black marketeer.

estraperlo /estra'perlo/ *n. m.* black market.

estratagema /estrata'hema/ *n. f.* stratagem.

estrategia /estra'tehia/ *n. f.* strategy.

estratégico /estra'tehiko/ *a.* strategic.

estrato /es'trato/ *n. m.* stratum.

estrechar /estre'tʃar/ *v.* tighten; narrow.

estrechez /estre'tʃeθ; estre'tʃes/ *n. f.* narrowness; tightness.

estrecho /es'tretʃo/ *a.* **1.** narrow, tight. —*n.* **2.** *m.* strait.

estregar /estre'gar/ *v.* scour, scrub.

estrella /es'treʎa; es'treya/ *n. f.* star.

estrellamar /estreʎa'mar; estreya'mar/ *n. f.* starfish.

estrellar /estre'ʎar; estre'yar/ *v.* shatter, smash.

estremecimiento /estremeθi-'miento; estremesi'miento/ *n. m.* shudder. —**estremecerse,** *v.*

estrenar /estre'nar/ *v.* wear for the first time; open (a play).

estreno /es'treno/ *n. m.* debut, first performance.

estrenuo /es'trenuo/ *a.* strenuous.

estreñido /estre'ɲiðo/ **-da** *a.* constipated.

estreñimiento /estreɲi'miento/ *n. m.* constipation.

estreñir /estre'ɲir/ *v.* constipate.

estrépito /es'trepito/ *n. m.* din.

estreptococo /estrepto'koko/ *n. m.* streptococcus.

estría /es'tria/ *n. f.* groove.

estribillo /estri'βiʎo; estri'βiyo/ *n. m.* refrain.

estribo /es'triβo/ *n. m.* stirrup.

estribor /estri'βor/ *n. m.* starboard.

estrictamente /estrikta'mente/ *adv.* strictly.

estrictez /estrik'teθ; estrik'tes/ *n. f.* strictness.

estricto /es'trikto/ *a.* strict.

estrofa /es'trofa/ *n. f.* stanza.

estropajo /estro'paho/ *n. m.* mop.

estropear /estrope'ar/ *v.* cripple, damage, spoil.

estructura /estruk'tura/ *n. f.* structure.

estructural /estruktu'ral/ *a.* structural.

estruendo /es'truendo/ *n. m.* din, clatter.

estuario /es'tuario/ *n. m.* estuary.

estuco /es'tuko/ *n. m.* stucco.

estudiante /estu'ðiante/ **-ta** *n.* student.

estudiar /estu'ðiar/ *v.* study.

estudio /es'tuðio/ *n. m.* study; studio.

estudioso /estu'ðioso/ *a.* studious.

estufa /es'tufa/ *n. f.* stove.

estufa de aire /es'tufa de 'aire/ fan heater.

estulto /es'tulto/ *a.* foolish.

estupendo /estu'pendo/ *a.* wonderful, grand, fine.

estupidez /estupi'ðeθ; estupi'ðes/ *n. f.* stupidity.

estúpido /es'tupiðo/ *a.* stupid.

estupor /estu'por/ *n. m.* stupor.

estuque /es'tuke/ *n. m.* stucco.

esturión /estu'rion/ *n. m.* sturgeon.

etapa /e'tapa/ *n. f.* stage.

éter /'eter/ *n. m.* ether.

etéreo /e'tereo/ *a.* ethereal.

eternal /eter'nal/ *a.* eternal.

eternidad /eterni'ðað/ *n. f.* eternity.

eterno /e'terno/ *a.* eternal.

ética /'etika/ *n. f.* ethics.

ético /'etiko/ *a.* ethical.

etimología /etimolo'hia/ *n. f.* etymology.

etiqueta /eti'keta/ *n. f.* etiquette; tag, label.

étnico /'etniko/ *a.* ethnic.

etrusco /e'trusko/ **-ca** *n.* & *a.* Etruscan.

eucaristía /eukaris'tia/ *n. f.* Eucharist.

eufemismo /eufe'mismo/ *n. m.* euphemism.

eufonía /eufo'nia/ *n. f.* euphony.

Europa /eu'ropa/ *n. f.* Europe.

europeo /euro'peo/ **-pea** *a.* & *n.* European.

eutanasia /euta'nasia/ *n. f.* euthanasia.

evacuación /eβakua'θion; eβakua'sion/ *n. f.* evacuation.

evacuar /eβa'kuar/ *v.* evacuate.

evadir /eβa'ðir/ *v.* evade.

evangélico /eβan'heliko/ *a.* evangelical.

evangelio /eβan'helio/ *n. m.* gospel.

evangelista /eβanhe'lista/ *n. m.* evangelist.

evaporación /eβapora'θion; eβapora'sion/ *n. f.* evaporation.

evaporarse /eβapo'rarse/ *v.* evaporate.

evasión /eβa'sion, eβa'siβa/ *n. f.* evasion.

evasivamente /eβasiβa'mente/ *adv.* evasively.

evasivo /eβa'siβo/ *a.* evasive.

evento /e'βento/ *n. m.* event, occurrence.

eventual /eβen'tual/ *a.* eventual.

eventualidad /eβentuali'ðað/ *n. f.* eventuality.

evicción /eβik'θion; eβik'sion/ *n. f.* eviction.

evidencia /eβi'ðenθia; eβiðensia/ *n. f.* evidence.

evidenciar /eβiðen'θiar; eβiðen'siar/ *v.* prove, show.

evidente /eβi'ðente/ *a.* evident.

evitación /eβita'θion; eβita'sion/ *n. f.* avoidance.

evitar /eβi'tar/ *v.* avoid, shun.

evocación /eβoka'θion; eβoka'sion/ *n. f.* evocation.

evocar /eβo'kar/ *v.* evoke.

evolución /eβolu'θion; eβolu'sion/ *n. f.* evolution.

exacerbar /eksaθer'βar; eksaser'βar/ *v.* irritate deeply; exacerbate.

exactamente /eksakta'mente/ *adv.* exactly.

exactitud /eksakti'tuð/ *n. f.* precision, accuracy.

exacto /ek'sakto/ *a.* exact, accurate.

exageración /eksahera'θion; eksahera'sion/ *n. f.* exaggeration.

exagerar /eksahe'rar/ *v.* exaggerate.

exaltación /eksalta'θion; eksalta'sion/ *n. f.* exaltation.

exaltamiento /eksalta'miento/ *n. m.* exaltation.

exaltar /eksal'tar/ *v.* exalt.

examen /ek'samen/ *n. m.* test, examination.

examen de ingreso /ek'samen de iŋ'greso/ entrance examination.

examinar /eksami'nar/ *v.* test, examine.

exánime /eksa'nime/ *a.* spiritless, weak.

exasperación /eksaspera'θion; eksaspera'sion/ *n. f.* exasperation.

exasperar /eksaspe'rar/ *v.* exasperate.

excavación /ekskaβa'θion; ekskaβa'sion/ *n. f.* excavation.

excavar /ekska'βar/ *v.* excavate.

exceder /eksθe'ðer; eksse'ðer/ *v.* exceed, surpass; outrun.

excelencia /eksθe'lenθia; eksse'lensia/ *n. f.* excellence.

excelente /eksθe'lente; eksse'lente/ *a.* excellent.

excéntrico /ek'θentriko; eks'sentriko/ *a.* eccentric.

excepción /eksθep'θion; ekssep'sion/ *n. f.* exception.

excepcional /eksθepθio'nal; ekssepsio'nal/ *a.* exceptional.

excepto /eks'θepto; eks'septo/ *prep.* except, except for.

exceptuar /eksθep'tuar; ekssep'tuar/ *v.* except.

excesivamente /eksθesiβa'mente; ekssesiβa'mente/ *adv.* excessively.

excesivo /eksθe'siβo; eksse'siβo/ *a.* excessive.

exceso /eks'θeso; eks'seso/ *n. m.* excess.

excitabilidad /eksθitaβili'ðað; ekssitaβili'ðað/ *n. f.* excitability.

excitación /eksθita'θion; ekssita'sion/ *n. f.* excitement.

excitar /eksθi'tar; ekssi'tar/ *v.* excite.

exclamación /eksklama'θion; eksklama'sion/ *n. f.* exclamation.

exclamar /ekskla'mar/ *v.* exclaim.

excluir /eksk'luir/ *v.* exclude, bar, shut out.

exclusión /eksklu'sion/ *n. f.* exclusion.

exclusivamente /eksklusiβa-'mente/ *adv.* exclusively.

exclusivo /eksklu'siβo/ *a.* exclusive.

excomulgar /ekskomul'gar/ *v.* excommunicate.

excomunión /ekskomu'nion/ *n. f.* excommunication.

excreción /ekskre'θion; ekskre-'sion/ *n. f.* excretion.

excremento /ekskre'mento/ *n. m.* excrement.

excretar /ekskre'tar/ *v.* excrete.

exculpar /ekskul'par/ *v.* exonerate.

excursión /ekskur'sion/ *n. f.* excursion.

excursionista /ekskursio'nista/ *n. m. & f.* excursionist; tourist.

excusa /eks'kusa/ *n. f.* excuse. —**excusar,** *v.*

excusado /eksku'saðo/ *n. m.* toilet.

excusarse /eksku'sarse/ *v.* apologize.

exención /eksen'θion; eksen'sion/ *n. f.* exemption.

exento /ek'sento/ *a.* exempt. —**exentar,** *v.*

exhalación /eksala'θion; eksala-'sion/ *n. f.* exhalation.

exhalar /eksa'lar/ *v.* exhale, breathe out.

exhausto /ek'sausto/ *a.* exhausted.

exhibición /eksiβi'θion; eksiβi-'sion/ *n. f.* exhibit, exhibition.

exhibir /eksi'βir/ *v.* exhibit, display.

exhortación /eksorta'θion; eksorta'sion/ *n. f.* exhortation.

exhortar /eksor'tar/ *v.* exhort, admonish.

exhumación /eksuma'θion; eksuma'sion/ *n. f.* exhumation.

exhumar /eksu'mar/ *v.* exhume.

exigencia /eksi'henθia; eksi'hensia/ *n. f.* requirement, demand.

exigente /eksi'hente/ *a.* exacting, demanding.

exigir /eksi'hir/ *v.* require, exact, demand.

eximir /eksi'mir/ *v.* exempt.

existencia /eksis'tenθia; eksis-'tensia/ *n. f.* existence; *Econ.* supply.

existente /eksis'tente/ *a.* existent.

existir /eksis'tir/ *v.* exist.

éxito /'eksito/ *n. m.* success.

éxodo /'eksoðo/ *n. m.* exodus.

exoneración /eksonera'θion; eksonera'sion/ *n. f.* exoneration.

exonerar /eksone'rar/ *v.* exonerate, acquit.

exorar /ekso'rar/ *v.* beg, implore.

exorbitancia /eksorβi'tanθia; eksorβi'tansia/ *n. f.* exorbitance.

exorbitante /eksorβi'tante/ *a.* exorbitant.

exorcismo /eksor'θismo; eksor-'sismo/ *n. m.* exorcism.

exornar /eksor'nar/ *v.* adorn, decorate.

exótico /ek'sotiko/ *a.* exotic.

expansibilidad /ekspansiβili'ðað/ *n. f.* expansibility.

expansión /ekspan'sion/ *n. f.* expansion.

expansivo /ekspan'siβo/ *a.* expansive; effusive.

expatriación /ekspatria'θion; ekspatria'sion/ *n. f.* expatriation.

expatriar /ekspa'triar/ *v.* expatriate.

expectación /ekspekta'θion; ekspekta'sion/ *n. f.* expectation.

expectorar /ekspekto'rar/ *v.* expectorate.

expedición /ekspeði'θion; ekspeði'sion/ *n. f.* expedition.

expediente /ekspe'ðiente/ *n. m.* expedient; means.

expedir /ekspe'ðir/ *v.* send off, ship; expedite.

expeditivo /ekspeði'tiβo/ *a.* speedy, prompt.

expedito /ekspe'ðito/ *a.* speedy, prompt.

expeler /ekspe'ler/ *v.* expel, eject.

expendedor /ekspende'ðor/ **-ra** *n.* dealer.

expender /ekspen'der/ *v.* expend.

expensas /ek'spensas/ *n. f.pl.* expenses, costs.

experiencia /ekspe'rienθia; ekspe'riensia/ *n. f.* experience.

experimentado /eksperimen'taðo/ *a.* experienced.

experimental /eksperimen'tal/ *a.* experimental.

experimentar /eksperimen'tar/ *v.* experience.

experimento /eksperi'mento/ *n.*
m. experiment.
expertamente /eksperta'mente/
adv. expertly.
experto /ek'sperto/ **-ta** *a.* & *n.*
expert.
expiación /ekspia'θion; ekspia-
'sion/ *n. f.* atonement.
expiar /eks'piar/ *v.* atone for.
expiración /ekspira'θion; ekspira-
'sion/ *n. f.* expiration.
expirar /ekspi'rar/ *v.* expire.
explanación /eksplana'θion; eks-
plana'sion/ *n. f.* explanation.
explanar /ekspla'nar/ *v.* make
level.
expletivo /eksple'tiβo/ *n.* & *a.* expletive.
explicable /ekspli'kaβle/ *a.* explicable.
explicación /eksplika'θion; ekspli-
ka'sion/ *n. f.* explanation.
explicar /ekspli'kar/ *v.* explain.
explicativo /eksplika'tiβo/ *a.* explanatory.
explícitamente /ekspliθita'mente;
eksplisita'mente/ *adv.* explicitly.
explícito /eks'pliθito; eksplisito/
adj. explicit.
exploración /eksplora'θion; eks-
plorasion/ *n. f.* exploration.
explorador /eksplora'ðor/ **-ra** *n.*
explorer; scout.
explorar /eksplo'rar/ *v.* explore;
scout.
exploratorio /eksplora'torio/ *a.*
exploratory.
explosión /eksplo'sion/ *n. f.* explosion; outburst.
explosivo /eksplo'siβo/ *a.* & *m.*
explosive.
explotación /eksplota'θion; eks-
plota'sion/ *n. f.* exploitation.
explotar /eksplo'tar/ *v.* exploit.
exponer /ekspo'ner/ *v.* expose;
set forth.
exportación /eksporta'θion; ek-
sporta'sion/ *n. f.* exportation; export.
exportador /eksporta'ðor/ **-ra** *n.*
exporter.
exportar /ekspor'tar/ *v.* export.
exposición /eksposi'θion; ekspo-
si'sion/ *n. f.* exhibit; exposition;
exposure.
expósito /eks'posito/ **-ta** *n.*
foundling; orphan.
expresado /ekspre'saðo/ *a.* aforesaid.

expresamente /ekspresa'mente/
adv. clearly, explicitly.
expresar /ekspre'sar/ *v.* express.
expresión /ekspre'sion/ *n. f.* expression.
expresivo /ekspre'siβo/ *a.* expressive; affectionate.
expreso /eks'preso/ *a.* & *m.* express.
exprimidera de naranjas /eks-
primi'ðera de na'ranhas/ *n. f.* orange squeezer.
exprimir /ekspri'mir/ *v.* squeeze.
expropiación /ekspropia'θion;
ekspropia'sion/ *n. f.* expropria-
tion.
expropiar /ekspro'piar/ *v.* expropriate.
expulsar /ekspul'sar/ *v.* expel,
eject; evict.
expulsión /ekspul'sion/ *n. f.* expulsion.
expurgación /ekspurga'θion; ek-
spurga'sion/ *n. f.* expurgation.
expurgar /ekspur'gar/ *v.* expurgate.
exquisitamente /ekskisita'mente/
adv. exquisitely.
exquisito /eks'kisito/ *a.* exquisite.
éxtasis /'ekstasis/ *n. m.* ecstasy.
extemporáneo /ekstempo'raneo/
a. extemporaneous, impromptu.
extender /eksten'der/ *v.* extend;
spread; widen; stretch.
extensamente /ekstensa'mente/
adv. extensively.
extensión /eksten'sion/ *n. f.* extension, spread, expanse.
extenso /eks'tenso/ *a.* extensive,
widespread.
extenuación /ekstenua'θion; eks-
tenua'sion/ *n. f.* weakening; emaciation.
extenuar /ekste'nuar/ *v.* extenuate.
exterior /ekste'rior/ *a.* & *m.* exterior; foreign.
exterminar /ekstermi'nar/ *v.* exterminate.
exterminio /ekster'minio/ *n. m.*
extermination, ruin.
extinción /ekstin'θion; ekstin-
'sion/ *n. f.* extinction.
extinguir /ekstiŋ'guir/ *v.* extinguish.
extinto /eks'tinto/ *a.* extinct.
extintor /ekstin'tor/ *n. m.* fire extinguisher.
extirpar /ekstir'par/ *v.* eradicate.

extorsión /ekstor'sion/ *n. f.* extortion.

extra /'ekstra/ *n.* extra.

extracción /ekstrak'θion; ekstrak-'sion/ *n. f.* extraction.

extractar /ekstrak'tar/ *v.* summarize.

extracto /eks'trakto/ *n. m.* extract; summary.

extradición /ekstraði'θion; ekstra-ði'sion/ *n. f.* extradition.

extraer /ekstra'er/ *v.* extract.

extranjero /ekstran'hero/ -ra *a.* **1.** foreign. —*n.* **2.** foreigner; stranger.

extrañar /ekstra'ɲar/ *v.* surprise; miss.

extraño /eks'traɲo/ *a.* strange, queer.

extraordinariamente /ˌekstraor-ðinaria'mente/ *adv.* extraordinarily.

extraordinario /ekstraorði'nario/ *a.* extraordinary.

extravagancia /ekstraβa'ganθia; ekstraβa'gansia/ *n. f.* extravagance.

extravagante /ekstraβa'gante/ *a.* extravagant.

extraviado /ekstra'βiaðo/ *a.* lost, misplaced.

extraviarse /ekstra'βiarse/ *v.* stray, get lost.

extravío /ekstra'βio/ *n. m.* misplacement; aberration, deviation.

extremadamente /ekstrema-ða'mente/ *adv.* extremely.

extremado /ekstre'maðo/ *a.* extreme.

extremaunción /ekstremaun'θion; ekstremaun'sion/ *n. f.* extreme unction.

extremidad /ekstremi'ðað/ *n. f.* extremity.

extremista /ekstre'mista/ *n. & a.* extremist.

extremo /eks'tremo/ *a. & m.* extreme, end.

extrínseco /ekstrin'seko/ *a.* extrinsic.

exuberancia /eksuβe'ranθia; eksuβeransia/ *n. f.* exuberance.

exuberante /eksuβe'rante/ *a.* exuberant.

exudación /eksuða'θion; eksuða-'sion/ *n. f.* exudation.

exudar /eksu'ðar/ *v.* exude, ooze.

exultación /eksulta'θion; eksulta-'sion/ *n. f.* exultation.

eyaculación /eyakula'θion; eyaku-la'sion/ *n. f.* ejaculation.

eyacular /eyaku'lar/ *v.* ejaculate.

eyección /eyek'θion; eyek'sion/ *n. f.* ejection.

eyectar /eyek'tar/ *v.* eject.

F

fábrica /'faβrika/ *n. f.* factory.

fabricación /faβrika'θion; faβrika'sion/ *n. f.* manufacture, manufacturing.

fabricante /faβri'kante/ *n. m. & f.* manufacturer, maker.

fabricar /faβri'kar/ *v.* manufacture, make.

fabril /fa'βril/ *a.* manufacturing, industrial.

fábula /'faβula/ *n. f.* fable, myth.

fabuloso /faβu'loso/ *a.* fabulous.

facción /fak'θion; fak'sion/ *n. f.* faction, party; (*pl.*) features.

faccioso /fak'θioso; fak'sioso/ *a.* factious.

fachada /fa't ʃaða/ *n. f.* façade, front.

fácil /'faθil; 'fasil/ *a.* easy.

facilidad /faθili'ðað; fasili'ðað/ *n. f.* facility, ease.

facilitar /faθili'tar; fasili'tar/ *v.* facilitate, make easy.

fácilmente /ˌfaθil'mente; ˌfasil-'mente/ *adv.* easily.

facsímile /fak'simile/ *n. m.* facsimile.

factible /fak'tiβle/ *a.* feasible.

factor /fak'tor/ *n. m.* factor.

factótum /fak'totum/ *n. m.* factotum; jack of all trades.

factura /fak'tura/ *n. f.* invoice, bill.

facturar /faktu'rar/ *v.* bill; check (baggage).

facultad /fakulta'ð/ /fakul'tað/ *n. f.* faculty; ability.

facultativo /fakulta'tiβo/ *a.* optional.

faena /fa'ena/ *n. f.* task; work.

faisán /fai'san/ *n. m.* pheasant.

faja /'faha/ *n. f.* band; sash; zone.

falacia /fa'laθia; fa'lasia/ *n. f.* fallacy; deceitfulness.

falda /'falda/ *n. f.* skirt; lap.

falibilidad /faliβili'ðað/ *n. f.* fallibility.

falla /'faʎa; faya/ /'faʎa; 'faya/ *n. f.* failure; fault.

fallar /fa'ʎar; fa'yar/ *v.* fail.

fallecer /faʎe'θer; faye'ser/ *v.* pass away, die.

fallo /'faʎo; 'fayo/ *n. m.* verdict; shortcoming.

falsear /false'ar/ *v.* falsify, counterfeit; forge.

falsedad /false'ðað/ *n. f.* falsehood; lie; falseness.

falsificación /falsifika'θion; falsifika'sion/ *n. f.* falsification; forgery.

falsificar /falsifi'kar/ *v.* falsify, counterfeit, forge.

falso /'falso/ *a.* false; wrong.

falta /'falta/ *n. f.* error, mistake; fault; lack. **hacer f.,** to be lacking, to be necessary. **sin f.,** without fail.

faltar /fal'tar/ *v.* be lacking, be missing; be absent.

faltriquera /faltri'kera/ *n. f.* pocket.

fama /'fama/ *n. f.* fame; reputation; glory.

familia /fa'milia/ *n. f.* family; household.

familiar /fami'liar/ *a.* familiar; domestic; (of) family.

familiaridad /familiari'ðað/ *n. f.* familiarity, intimacy.

familiarizar /familiari'θar; familiari'sar/ *v.* familiarize, acquaint.

famoso /fa'moso/ *a.* famous.

fanal /fa'nal/ *n. m.* lighthouse; lantern, lamp.

fanático /fa'natiko/ **-ca** *a. & n.* fanatic.

fanatismo /fana'tismo/ *n. m.* fanaticism.

fanfarria /fan'farria/ *n. f.* bluster. **—fanfarrear,** *v.*

fango /'faŋgo/ *n. m.* mud.

fantasía /fanta'sia/ *n. f.* fantasy; fancy, whim.

fantasma /fan'tasma/ *n. m.* phantom; ghost.

fantástico /fan'tastiko/ *a.* fantastic.

faquín /fa'kin/ *n. m.* porter.

faquir /fa'kir/ *n. m.* fakir.

farallón /fara'ʎon; fara'yon/ *n. m.* cliff.

Faraón /fara'on/ *n. m.* Pharaoh.

fardel /far'ðel/ *n. m.* bag; package.

fardo /far'ðo/ /'farðo/ *n. m.* bundle.

farináceo /fari'naθeo; fari'naseo/ *a.* farinaceous.

faringe /fa'rinhe/ *n. f.* pharynx.

fariseo /fari'seo/ *n. m.* pharisee, hypocrite.

farmacéutico /farma'θeutiko; farma'seutiko/ **-ca** *a.* **1.** pharmaceutical. **—n. 2.** pharmacist.

farmacia /far'maθia; far'masia/ *n. f.* pharmacy.

faro /'faro/ *n. m.* beacon; lighthouse; headlight.

farol /fa'rol/ *n. m.* lantern; (street) light, street lamp.

farra /'farra/ *n. f.* spree.

fárrago /'farrago/ *n. m.* medley; hodgepodge.

farsa /'farsa/ *n. f.* farce.

fascinación /fasθina'θion; fassina'sion/ *n. f.* fascination.

fascinar /fasθi'nar; fassi'nar/ *v.* fascinate, bewitch.

fase /'fase/ *n. f.* phase.

fastidiar /fasti'ðiar/ *v.* disgust; irk, annoy.

fastidio /fasti'ðio/ *n. m.* disgust; annoyance.

fastidioso /fasti'ðioso/ *a.* annoying; tedious.

fasto /'fasto/ *a.* happy, fortunate.

fatal /fa'tal/ *a.* fatal.

fatalidad /fatali'ðað/ *n. f.* fate; calamity, bad luck.

fatalismo /fata'lismo/ *n. m.* fatalism.

fatalista /fata'lista/ *n. & a.* fatalist.

fatiga /fa'tiga/ *n. f.* fatigue. **—fatigar,** *v.*

fauna /'fauna/ *n. f.* fauna.

fauno /'fauno/ *n. m.* faun.

favor /fa'βor/ *n. m.* favor; behalf. **por f.,** please. **¡Favor!** Puh-lease!

favorable /faβo'raβle/ *a.* favorable.

favorablemente /faβoraβle'mente/ *adv.* favorably.

favorecer /faβore'θer; faβore'ser/ *v.* favor; flatter.

favoritismo /faβori'tismo/ *n. m.* favoritism.

favorito /faβo'rito/ **-ta** *a. & n.* favorite.

fax /faks/ *n. m.* fax.

faz /faθ; fas/ *n. f.* face.

fe /fe/ *n. f.* faith.

fealdad /feal'daθ/ *n. f.* ugliness, homeliness.

febrero /fe'βrero/ *n. m.* February.

febril /fe'βril/ *a.* feverish.

fecha /'fetʃa/ *n. f.* date. —**fechar,** *v.*

fecha de caducidad /'fetʃa de kaðuθi'ðaθ; 'fetʃa de kaðusi'ðaθ/ expiration date.

fécula /'fekula/ *n. f.* starch.

fecundar /fekun'dar/ *v.* fertilize.

fecundidad /fekundi'ðaθ/ *n. f.* fecundity, fertility.

fecundo /fe'kundo/ *a.* fecund, fertile.

federación /feðera'θion; feðera-'sion/ *n. f.* federation.

federal /feðe'ral/ *a.* federal.

felicidad /feliθi'ðaθ; felisi'ðaθ/ *n. f.* happiness; bliss.

felicitación /feliθita'θion; felisita-'sion/ *n. f.* congratulation.

felicitar /feliθi'tar; felisi'tar/ *v.* congratulate.

feligrés /feli'gres/ **-esa** *n.* parishioner.

feliz /fe'liθ; fe'lis/ *a.* happy; fortunate.

felón /fe'lon/ *n. m.* felon.

felonía /felo'nia/ *n. f.* felony.

felpa /'felpa/ *n. f.* plush.

felpudo /fel'puðo/ *n. m.* doormat.

femenino /feme'nino/ *a.* feminine.

feminismo /femi'nismo/ *n. m.* feminism.

feminista /femi'nista/ *n. m. & f.* feminist.

fenecer /fene'θer; fene'ser/ *v.* conclude; die.

fénix /'feniks/ *n. m.* phoenix; model.

fenomenal /fenome'nal/ *a.* phenomenal.

fenómeno /fe'nomeno/ *n. m.* phenomenon.

feo /'feo/ *a.* ugly, homely.

feracidad /feraθi'ðaθ; ferasi'ðaθ/ *n. f.* feracity, fertility.

feraz /fe'raθ; 'feras/ *a.* fertile, fruitful; copious.

feria /'feria/ *n. f.* fair; market.

feriado /fe'riaðo/ *a.* **día f.,** holiday.

fermentación /fermenta'θion; fermenta'sion/ *n. f.* fermentation.

fermento /fer'mento/ *n. m.* ferment. —**fermentar,** *v.*

ferocidad /feroθi'ðaθ; ferosi'ðaθ/ *n. f.* ferocity, fierceness.

feroz /fe'roθ; fe'ros/ *a.* ferocious, fierce.

férreo /'ferreo/ *a.* of iron.

ferrería /ferre'ria/ *n. f.* ironworks.

ferretería /ferrete'ria/ *n. f.* hardware; hardware store.

ferrocarril /ferroka'rril/ *n. m.* railroad.

fértil /'fertil/ *a.* fertile.

fertilidad /fertili'ðaθ/ *n. f.* fertility.

fertilizar /fertili'θar; fertili'sar/ *v.* fertilize.

férvido /'ferβiðo/ *a.* fervid, ardent.

ferviente /fer'βiente/ *a.* fervent.

fervor /fer'βor/ *n. m.* fervor, zeal.

fervoroso /ferβo'roso/ *a.* zealous, eager.

festejar /feste'har/ *v.* entertain, fete.

festejo /feste'ho/ *n. m.* feast.

festín /fes'tin/ *n. m.* feast.

festividad /festiβi'ðaθ/ *n. f.* festivity.

festivo /fes'tiβo/ *a.* festive.

fétido /'fetiðo/ *adj.* fetid.

feudal /feu'ðal/ *a.* feudal.

feudo /'feuðo/ *n. m.* fief; manor.

fiado /'fiaðo, al/ *adj.* on trust, on credit.

fiambrera /fiam'brera/ *n. f.* lunch box.

fianza /'fianθa; 'fiansa/ *n. f.* bail.

fiar /fi'ar/ *v.* trust, sell on credit; give credit.

fiarse de /'fiarse de/ *v.* trust (in), rely on.

fiasco /'fiasko/ *n. m.* fiasco.

fibra /'fiβra/ *n. f.* fiber; vigor.

fibroso /fi'βroso/ *a.* fibrous.

ficción /fik'θion; fik'sion/ *n. f.* fiction.

ficha /'fitʃa/ *n. f.* slip, index card; chip.

fichero /fi'tʃero/ *n. m.* computer file, filing cabinet, card catalog.

ficticio /fik'tiθio; fik'tisio/ *a.* fictitious.

fidedigno /fiðe'ðigno/ *a.* trustworthy.

fideicomisario /fiðeikomi'sario/ **-ria** *n.* trustee.

fideicomiso /fiðeiko'miso/ *n. m.* trust.

fidelidad /fiðeli'ðaθ/ *n. f.* fidelity.

fideo /fi'ðeo/ *n. m.* noodle.

fiebre /'fieβre/ *n. f.* fever.

fiebre del heno /'fieβre del 'eno/ hayfever.

fiel /fiel/ *a.* faithful.

fieltro /'fieltro/ *n. m.* felt.
fiera /'fiera/ *n. f.* wild animal.
fiereza /fie'reθa; fie'resa/ *n. f.* fierceness, wildness.
fiero /'fiero/ *a.* fierce; wild.
fiesta /'fiesta/ *n. f.* festival, feast; party.
figura /fi'gura/ *n. f.* figure. —**figurar,** *v.*
figurarse /figu'rarse/ *v.* imagine.
figurón /figu'ron/ *n. m.* dummy.
fijar /fi'har/ *v.* fix; set, establish; post.
fijarse en /fi'harse en/ *v.* notice.
fijeza /fi'heθa; fi'hesa/ *n. f.* firmness.
fijo /'fiho/ *a.* fixed, stationary, permanent, set.
fila /'fila/ *n. f.* row, rank, file, line.
filantropía /filantro'pia/ *n. f.* philanthropy.
filatelia /fila'telia/ *n. f.* philately, stamp collecting.
filete /fi'lete/ *n. m.* fillet; steak.
film /film/ *n. m.* film. —**filmar,** *v.*
filo /'filo/ *n. m.* (cutting) edge.
filón /fi'lon/ *n. m.* vein (of ore).
filosofía /filoso'fia/ *n. f.* philosophy.
filosófico /filo'sofiko/ *a.* philosophical.
filósofo /fi'losofo/ **-fa** *n.* philosopher.
filtro /'filtro/ *n. m.* filter. —**filtrar,** *v.*
fin /fin/ *n. m.* end, purpose, goal. **a f. de que,** in order that. **en f.,** in short. **por f.,** finally, at last.
final /fi'nal/ *a.* **1.** final. —*n.* **2.** *m.* end.
finalidad /finali'ðað/ *n. f.* finality.
finalmente /final'mente/ *adv.* at last.
financiero /finan'θiero; finan'siero/ **-ra** *a.* **1.** financial. —*n.* **2.** financier.
finca /'finka/ *n. f.* real estate; estate; farm.
finés /fi'nes/ **-esa** *a. & n.* Finnish; Finn.
fineza /fi'neθa; fi'nesa/ *n. f.* courtesy, politeness; fineness.
fingimiento /finhi'miento/ *n. m.* pretense.
fingir /fin'hir/ *v.* feign, pretend.
fino /'fino/ *a.* fine; polite, courteous.
firma /'firma/ *n. f.* signature; *Com.* firm.

firmamento /firma'mento/ *n. m.* firmament, heavens.
firmar /fir'mar/ *v.* sign.
firme /'firme/ *a.* firm, fast, steady, sound.
firmemente /firme'mente/ *adv.* firmly.
firmeza /fir'meθa; fir'mesa/ *n. f.* firmness.
fisco /'fisko/ *n. m.* exchequer, treasury.
física /'fisika/ *n. f.* physics.
físico /'fisiko/ **-ca** *a. & n.* physical; physicist.
fisiología /fisiolo'hia/ *n. f.* physiology.
fláccido /'flakθiðo; 'flaksiðo/ *a.* flaccid, soft.
flaco /'flako/ *a.* thin, gaunt.
flagelación /flahela'θion; flahela'sion/ *n. f.* flagellation.
flagelar /flahe'lar/ *v.* flagellate, whip.
flagrancia /fla'granθia; fla'gransia/ *n. f.* flagrancy.
flagrante /fla'grante/ *a.* flagrant.
flama /'flama/ *n. f.* flame; ardor, zeal.
flamante /fla'mante/ *a.* flaming.
flamenco /fla'menko/ *n. m.* flamingo.
flan /flan/ *n. m.* custard.
flanco /'flanko/ *n. m.* side; *Mil.* flank.
flanquear /flanke'ar/ *v.* flank.
flaqueza /fla'keθa; fla'kesa/ *n. f.* thinness; weakness.
flauta /'flauta/ *n. f.* flute.
flautín /flau'tin/ *n. m.* piccolo.
flautista /flau'tista/ *n. m. & f.* flutist, piper.
flecha /'fletʃa/ *n. f.* arrow.
flechazo /fle'tʃaθo; fle'tʃaso/ *n. m.* love at first sight.
flechero /fle'tʃero/ **-ra** *n.* archer.
fleco /'fleko/ *n. m.* fringe; flounce.
flema /'flema/ *n. f.* phlegm.
flemático /fle'matiko/ *a.* phlegmatic.
flequillo /fle'kiʎo; fle'kiyo/ *n. m.* fringe; bangs (of hair).
flete /'flete/ *n. m.* freight. —**fletar,** *v.*
flexibilidad /fleksiβili'ðað/ *n. f.* flexibility.
flexible /fle'ksiβle/ *a.* flexible, pliable.
flirtear /flirte'ar/ *v.* flirt.

flojo /'floho/ *a.* limp; loose, flabby, slack.

flor /flor/ *n. f.* flower; compliment.

flora /'flora/ *n. f.* flora.

floral /flo'ral/ *a.* floral.

florecer /flore'θer; flore'ser/ *v.* flower, bloom; flourish.

floreo /flo'reo/ *n. m.* flourish.

florero /flo'rero/ *n. m.* flower pot; vase.

floresta /flo'resta/ *n. f.* forest.

florido /flo'riðo/ *a.* flowery; flowering.

florista /flo'rista/ *n. m. & f.* florist.

flota /'flota/ *n. f.* fleet.

flotante /flo'tante/ *a.* floating.

flotar /flo'tar/ *v.* float.

flotilla /flo'tiʎa; flo'tiya/ *n. f.* flotilla, fleet.

fluctuación /fluktua'θion; fluktua'sion/ *n. f.* fluctuation.

fluctuar /fluktu'ar/ *v.* fluctuate.

fluente /'fluente/ *a.* fluent; flowing.

fluidez /flui'ðeθ; flui'ðes/ *n. f.* fluency.

flúido /'fluiðo/ *a. & m.* fluid, liquid.

fluir /flu'ir/ *v.* flow.

flujo /'fluho/ *n. m.* flow, flux.

fluor /fluor/ *n. m.* fluorine.

fluorescencia /fluores'θenθia; fluores'sensia/ *n. f.* fluorescence.

fluorescente /fluores'θente; fluores'sente/ *a.* fluorescent.

fobia /'foβia/ *n. f.* phobia.

foca /'foka/ *n. f.* seal.

foco /'foko/ *n. m.* focus, center; floodlight.

fogata /fo'gata/ *n. f.* bonfire.

fogón /fo'gon/ *n. m.* hearth, fireplace.

fogosidad /fogosi'ðað/ *n. f.* vehemence, ardor.

fogoso /fo'goso/ *a.* vehement, ardent.

folclore /fol'klore/ *n. m.* folklore.

follaje /fo'ʎahe; fo'yahe/ *n. m.* foliage.

folleto /fo'ʎeto; fo'yeto/ *n. m.* pamphlet, booklet.

follón /fo'ʎon; fo'yon/ *n. m.* mess, chaos.

fomentar /fomen'tar/ *v.* develop, promote, further, foster.

fomento /fo'mento/ *n. m.* fomentation.

fonda /'fonda/ *n. f.* eating house, inn.

fondo /'fondo/ *n. m.* bottom; back (part); background; (*pl.*) funds; finances. **a f.**, thoroughly.

fonética /fo'netika/ *n. f.* phonetics.

fonético /fo'netiko/ *a.* phonetic.

fonógrafo /fo'nografo/ *n. m.* phonograph.

fontanero /fonta'nero/ **-era** *n.* plumber.

forastero /foras'tero/ **-ra** *a.* **1.** foreign, exotic. —*n.* **2.** stranger.

forjar /for'har/ *v.* forge.

forma /'forma/ *n. f.* form, shape. —**formar**, *v.*

formación /forma'θion; forma'sion/ *n. f.* formation.

formal /for'mal/ *a.* formal.

formaldehido /formalde'iðo/ *n. m.* formaldehyde.

formalidad /formali'ðað/ *n. f.* formality.

formalizar /formali'θar; formali'sar/ *v.* finalize; formulate.

formidable /formi'ðaβle/ *a.* formidable.

formidablemente /formiðaβle'mente/ *adv.* formidably.

formón /for'mon/ *n. m.* chisel.

fórmula /'formula/ *n. f.* formula.

formular /formu'lar/ *v.* formulate, draw up.

formulario /formu'lario/ *n. m.* form.

foro /'foro/ *n. m.* forum.

forrado /fo'rraðo/ *a.* stuffed; *Colloq.* filthy rich.

forraje /fo'rrahe/ *n. m.* forage, fodder.

forrar /fo'rrar/ *v.* line.

forro /'forro/ *n. m.* lining; condom.

fortalecer /fortale'θer; fortale'ser/ *v.* fortify.

fortaleza /forta'leθa; forta'lesa/ *n. f.* fort, fortress; fortitude.

fortificación /fortifika'θion; fortifika'sion/ *n. f.* fortification.

fortitud /forti'tuð/ *n. f.* fortitude.

fortuitamente /fortuita'mente/ *adv.* fortuitously.

fortuito /for'tuito/ *a.* fortuitous.

fortuna /for'tuna/ *n. f.* fortune; luck.

forúnculo /fo'runkulo/ *n. m.* boil.

forzar /for'θar; for'sar/ *v.* force, compel, coerce.

forzosamente /forθosa'mente/;

forsosa'mente/ *adv.* compulsorily; forcibly.

forzoso /for'θoso; for'soso/ *a.* compulsory; necessary. **paro f.,** unemployment.

forzudo /for'θuðo; for'suðo/ *a.* powerful, vigorous.

fosa /'fosa/ *n. f.* grave; pit.

fósforo /'fosforo/ *n. m.* match; phosphorus.

fósil /'fosil/ *n. m.* fossil.

foso /'foso/ *n. m.* ditch, trench; moat.

fotocopia /foto'kopia/ *n. f.* photocopy.

fotocopiadora /fotokopia'ðora/ *n. f.* photocopier.

fotografía /fotogra'fia/ *n. f.* photograph; photography. —**fotografiar,** *v.*

frac /frak/ *n. m.* dress coat.

fracasar /fraka'sar/ *v.* fail.

fracaso /fra'kaso/ *n. m.* failure.

fracción /frak'θion; frak'sion/ *n. f.* fraction.

fractura /frak'tura/ *n. f.* fracture, break.

fragancia /fra'ganθia; fra'gansia/ *n. f.* fragrance; perfume; aroma.

fragante /fra'gante/ *a.* fragrant.

frágil /'frahil/ *a.* fragile, breakable.

fragilidad /frahili'ðað/ *n. f.* fragility.

fragmentario /fragmen'tario/ *a.* fragmentary.

fragmento /frag'mento/ *n. m.* fragment, bit.

fragor /fra'gor/ *n. m.* noise, clamor.

fragoso /fra'goso/ *a.* noisy.

fragua /'fragua/ *n. f.* forge. —**fraguar,** *v.*

fraile /'fraile/ *n. m.* monk.

frambuesa /fram'buesa/ *n. f.* raspberry.

francamente /franka'mente/ *adv.* frankly, candidly.

francés /fran'θes; fran'ses/ **-esa** *a. & n.* French; Frenchman, Frenchwoman.

Francia /'franθia; 'fransia/ *n. f.* France.

franco /'franko/ *a.* frank.

franela /fra'nela/ *n. f.* flannel.

frangible /fraŋ'giβle/ *a.* breakable.

franqueo /fran'keo/ *n. m.* postage.

franqueza /fran'keθa; fran'kesa/ *n. f.* frankness.

franquicia /fran'kiθia; fran'kisia/ *n. f.* franchise.

frasco /'frasko/ *n. m.* flask, bottle.

frase /'frase/ *n. f.* phrase; sentence.

fraseología /fraseolo'hia/ *n. f.* phraseology; style.

fraternal /frater'nal/ *a.* fraternal, brotherly.

fraternidad /fraterni'ðað/ *n. f.* fraternity, brotherhood.

fraude /'frauðe/ *n. m.* fraud.

fraudulento /frauðu'lento/ *a.* fraudulent.

frazada /fra'θaða; fra'saða/ *n. f.* blanket.

frecuencia /fre'kuenθia; fre'kuensia/ *n. f.* frequency.

frecuente /fre'kuente/ *a.* frequent.

frecuentemente /frekuente'mente/ *adv.* frequently, often.

fregadero /frega'ðero/ *n. m.* sink.

fregadura /frega'ðura/ *n. f.* scouring, scrubbing.

fregar /fre'gar/ *v.* scour, scrub, mop.

fregona /fre'gona/ *n. f.* mop.

freír /fre'ir/ *v.* fry.

fréjol /'frehol/ *n. m.* kidney bean.

frenazo /fre'naθo; fre'naso/ *n. m.* sudden braking, slamming on the brakes.

frenesí /frene'si/ *n. m.* frenzy.

frenéticamente /fre'netikamente/ *adv.* frantically.

frenético /fre'netiko/ *a.* frantic, frenzied.

freno /'freno/ *n. m.* brake. —**frenar,** *v.*

freno de auxilio /'freno de auk'silio/ emergency brake.

freno de mano /'freno de 'mano/ hand brake.

frente /'frente/ *n.* **1.** *f.* forehead. **2.** *m.* front. **en f., al f.,** opposite, across. **f. a,** in front of.

fresa /'fresa/ *n. f.* strawberry.

fresca /'freska/ *n. f.* fresh, cool air.

fresco /'fresko/ *a.* fresh; cool; crisp.

frescura /fres'kura/ *n. f.* coolness, freshness.

fresno /'fresno/ *n. m.* ash tree.

fresquería /freske'ria/ *n. f.* soda fountain.

friabilidad /friaβili'ðað/ *n. f.* brittleness.

friable /'friaβle/ *a.* brittle.

frialdad /frial'dað/ *n. f.* coldness.

fríamente /fria'mente/ *adv.* coldly; coolly.

frícandó /'frikando/ *n. m.* fricandeau.

fricar /fri'kar/ *v.* rub together.

fricción /frik'θion; frik'sion/ *n. f.* friction.

friccionar /frikθio'nar; friksio'nar/ *v.* rub.

friega /'friega/ *n. f.* friction; massage.

frigidez /frihi'ðeθ; frihi'ðes/ *n. f.* frigidity.

frígido /'frihiðo/ *a.* frigid.

frijol /fri'hol/ *n. m.* bean.

frío /'frio/ *a. & n.* cold. **tener f.,** to be cold, feel cold. **hacer f.,** to be cold (weather).

friolento /frio'lento/ **friolero** *a.* chilly; sensitive to cold.

friolera /frio'lera/ *n. f.* trifle, trinket.

friso /'friso/ *n. m.* frieze.

fritillas /fri'tiʎas; fri'tiyas/ *n. f.pl.* fritters.

frito /'frito/ *a.* fried.

fritura /fri'tura/ *n. f.* fritter.

frívolamente /'friβolamente/ *adv.* frivolously.

frivolidad /friβoli'ðað/ *n. f.* frivolity.

frívolo /'friβolo/ *a.* frivolous.

frondoso /fron'doso/ *a.* leafy.

frontera /fron'tera/ *n. f.* frontier; border.

frotar /fro'tar/ *v.* rub.

fructífero /fruk'tifero/ *a.* fruitful.

fructificar /fruktifi'kar/ *v.* bear fruit.

fructuosamente /fruktuosa-'mente/ *adv.* fruitfully.

fructuoso /fruk'tuoso/ *a.* fruitful.

frugal /fru'gal/ *a.* frugal; thrifty.

frugalidad /frugali'ðað/ *n. f.* frugality; thrift.

frugalmente /frugal'mente/ *adv.* frugally, thriftily.

fruncir /frun'θir; frun'sir/ *v.* gather, contract. **f. el entrecejo,** frown.

fruslería /frusle'ria/ *n. f.* trinket.

frustrar /frus'trar/ *v.* frustrate, thwart.

fruta /'fruta/ *n. f.* fruit.

frutería /frute'ria/ *n. f.* fruit store.

fruto /'fruto/ *n. m.* fruit; product; profit.

fucsia /'fuksia/ *n. f.* fuchsia.

fuego /'fuego/ *n. m.* fire.

fuelle /'fueʎe; 'fueye/ *n. m.* bellows.

fuente /'fuente/ *n. f.* fountain; source; platter.

fuera /'fuera/ *adv.* without, outside.

fuero /'fuero/ *n. m.* statute.

fuerte /'fuerte/ *a.* **1.** strong; loud. —*n.* **2.** *m.* fort.

fuertemente /fuerte'mente/ *adv.* strongly; loudly.

fuerza /'fuerθa; 'fuersa/ *n. f.* force, strength.

fuga /'fuga/ *n. f.* flight, escape.

fugarse /fu'garse/ *v.* flee, escape.

fugaz /fu'gaθ; fu'gas/ *a.* fugitive, passing.

fugitivo /fuhi'tiβo/ **-va** *a. & n.* fugitive.

fulano /fu'lano/ **-na** *n.* Mr., Mrs. so-and-so.

fulcro /'fulkro/ *n. m.* fulcrum.

fulgor /ful'gor/ *n. m.* gleam, glow. —**fulgurar,** *v.*

fulminante /fulmi'nante/ *a.* explosive.

fumador /fuma'ðor/ **-ra** *n.* smoker.

fumar /fu'mar/ *v.* smoke.

fumigación /fumiga'θion; fumiga'sion/ *n. f.* fumigation.

fumigador /fumiga'ðor/ **-ra** *n.* fumigator.

fumigar /fumi'gar/ *v.* fumigate.

fumoso /fu'moso/ *a.* smoky.

función /fun'θion; fun'sion/ *n. f.* function; performance, show.

funcionar /funθio'nar; funsio'nar/ *v.* function; work, run.

funcionario /funθio'nario; funsio'nario/ **-ria** *n.* official, functionary.

funda /'funda/ *n. f.* case, sheath, slipcover.

fundación /funda'θion; funda'sion/ *n. f.* foundation.

fundador /funda'ðor/ **-ra** *n.* founder.

fundamental /funda'mental/ *a.* fundamental, basic.

fundamentalmente /fundamental'mente/ *adv.* fundamentally.

fundamento /funda'mento/ *n. m.* base, basis, foundation.

fundar /fun'dar/ *v.* found, establish.

fundición /fundi'θion; fundi'sion/ *n. f.* foundry; melting; meltdown.
fundir /fun'dir/ *v.* fuse; smelt.
fúnebre /'funeβre/ *a.* dismal.
funeral /fune'ral/ *n. m.* funeral.
funeraria /fune'raria/ *n. f.* funeral home, funeral parlor.
funestamente /funesta'mente/ *adv.* sadly.
fungo /'fuŋgo/ *n. m.* fungus.
furente /fu'rente/ *a.* furious, enraged.
furgoneta /furgo'neta/ *n. f.* van.
furia /'furia/ *n. f.* fury.
furiosamente /furiosa'mente/ *adv.* furiously.
furioso /fu'rioso/ *a.* furious.
furor /fu'ror/ *n. m.* furor; fury.
furtivamente /furtiβa'mente/ *adv.* furtively.

furtivo /fur'tiβo/ *a.* furtive, sly.
furúnculo /fu'runkulo/ *n. m.* boil.
fusibilidad /fusiβili'ðað/ *n. f.* fusibility.
fusible /fu'siβle/ *n. m.* fuse.
fusil /fu'sil/ *n. m.* rifle, gun.
fusilar /fusi'lar/ *v.* shoot, execute.
fusión /fu'sion/ *n. f.* fusion; merger.
fusionar /fusio'nar/ *v.* unite, fuse, merge.
fútbol /'futβol/ *n. m.* football, soccer.
fútil /'futil/ *a.* trivial.
futilidad /futili'ðað/ *n. f.* triviality.
futuro /fu'turo/ *a. & m.* future.
futurología /futurolo'hia/ *n. f.* futurology.

G

gabán /ga'βan/ *n. m.* overcoat.
gabardina /gaβar'ðina/ *n. f.* raincoat.
gabinete /gaβi'nete/ *n. m.* closet; cabinet; study.
gacela /ga'θela; ga'sela/ *n. f.* gazelle.
gaceta /ga'θeta; ga'seta/ *n. f.* gazette, newspaper.
gacetilla /gaθe'tiʎa; gase'tiya/ *n. f.* personal news section of a newspaper.
gaélico /ga'eliko/ *a.* Gaelic.
gafas /'gafas/ *n. f.pl.* eyeglasses.
gaguear /gage'ar/ *v.* stutter, stammer.
gaita /'gaita/ *n. f.* bagpipes.
gaje /'gahe/ *n. m.* salary; fee.
gala /'gala/ *n. f.* gala, ceremony; (*pl.*) regalia. **tener a g.,** be proud of.
galán /ga'lan/ *n. m.* gallant.
galano /ga'lano/ *a.* stylishly dressed; elegant.
galante /ga'lante/ *a.* gallant.
galantería /galante'ria/ *n. f.* gallantry, compliment.
galápago /ga'lapago/ *n. m.* freshwater turtle.
galardón /galar'ðon/ *n. m.* prize; reward.
gáleo /'galeo/ *n. m.* swordfish.
galera /ga'lera/ *n. f.* wagon; shed; galley.
galería /gale'ria/ *n. f.* gallery, *Theat.* balcony.

galés /'gales/ **-esa** *a. & n.* Welsh; Welshman, Welshwoman.
galgo /'galgo/ *n. m.* greyhound.
galillo /ga'liʎo; ga'liyo/ *n. m.* uvula.
galimatías /galima'tias/ *n. m.* gibberish.
gallardete /gaʎar'ðete; gayar'ðete/ *n. m.* pennant.
galleta /ga'ʎeta; ga'yeta/ *n. f.* cracker.
gallina /ga'ʎina; ga'yina/ *n. f.* hen.
gallinero /gaʎi'nero; gayi'nero/ *n. m.* chicken coop.
gallo /ga'ʎo; ga'yo/ *n. m.* rooster.
galocha /ga'lotʃa/ *n. f.* galosh.
galón /ga'lon/ *n. m.* gallon; *Mil.* stripe.
galope /ga'lope/ *n. m.* gallop. **—galopar,** *v.*
galopín /galo'pin/ *n. m.* ragamuffin, urchin (child).
gamba /'gamba/ *n. f.* prawn.
gamberro /gam'βerro/ **-ra** *n.* hooligan.
gambito /gam'bito/ *n. m.* gambit.
gamuza /ga'muθa; ga'musa/ *n. f.* chamois.
gana /'gana/ *n. f.* desire, wish, mind (to). **de buena g.,** willingly. **tener ganas de,** to feel like.
ganado /ga'naðo/ *n. m.* cattle.
ganador /gana'ðor/ **-ra** *n.* winner.
ganancia /ga'nanθia; ga'nansia/ *n. f.* gain, profit; (*pl.*) earnings.

ganapán /gana'pan/ *n. m.* drudge.
ganar /ga'nar/ *v.* earn; win; beat.
ganchillo /gan'tʃiʎo; gan'tʃiyo/ *n. m.* crochet work.
gancho /'gantʃo/ *n. m.* hook, hanger, clip, hairpin.
gandul /gan'dul/ -**la** *n.* idler, tramp, hobo.
ganga /'gaŋga/ *n. f.* bargain.
gangrena /gaŋ'grena/ *n. f.* gangrene.
gansarón /gansa'ron/ *n. m.* gosling.
ganso /'ganso/ *n. m.* goose.
garabato /gara'βato/ *n. m.* hook; scrawl, scribble.
garaje /ga'rahe/ *n. m.* garage.
garantía /garan'tia/ *n. f.* guarantee; collateral, security.
garantizar /garanti'θar; garanti-'sar/ *v.* guarantee, secure, pledge.
garbanzo /gar'βanθo; gar'βanso/ *n. m.* chickpea.
garbo /'garβo/ *n. m.* grace.
garboso /gar'βoso/ *a.* graceful, sprightly.
gardenia /gar'ðenia/ *n. f.* gardenia.
garfa /'garfa/ *n. f.* claw, talon.
garganta /gar'ganta/ *n. f.* throat.
gárgara /'gargara/ *n. f.* gargle. —**gargarizar,** *v.*
garita /ga'rita/ *n. f.* sentry box.
garito /ga'rito/ *n. m.* gambling house.
garlopa /gar'lopa/ *n. f.* carpenter's plane.
garra /'garra/ *n. f.* claw.
garrafa /ga'rrafa/ *n. f.* decanter, carafe.
garrideza /garri'ðeθa; garri'ðesa/ *n. f.* elegance, handsomeness.
garrido /ga'rriðo/ *a.* elegant, handsome.
garrote /ga'rrote/ *n. m.* club, cudgel.
garrotillo /garro'tiʎo; garro'tiyo/ *n. m.* croup.
garrudo /ga'rruðo/ *a.* powerful, brawny.
garza /'garθa; 'garsa/ *n. f.* heron.
gas /gas/ *n. m.* gas.
gasa /'gasa/ *n. f.* gauze.
gaseosa /gase'osa/ *n. f.* carbonated water.
gaseoso /gase'oso/ *a.* gaseous.
gasolina /gaso'lina/ *n. f.* gasoline.
gasolinera /gasoli'nera/ *n. f.* gas station.

gastar /gas'tar/ *v.* spend; use up, wear out; waste.
gastritis /gas'tritis/ *n. f.* gastritis.
gastrómano /gas'tromano/ *n. m.* glutton.
gastrónomo /gas'tronomo/ -**ma** *n.* gourmet, epicure, gastronome.
gatear /gate'ar/ *v.* creep.
gatillo /ga'tiʎo; ga'tiyo/ *n. m.* trigger.
gato /'gato/ -**ta** *n.* cat.
gaucho /'gautʃo/ *n. m.* Argentine cowboy.
gaveta /ga'βeta/ *n. f.* drawer.
gavilla /ga'βiʎa; ga'βiya/ *n. f.* sheaf.
gaviota /ga'βiota/ *n. f.* seagull.
gayo /ga'yo/ *a.* merry, gay.
gayola /ga'yola/ *n. m.* cage; *Colloq.* prison.
gazapera /gaθa'pera; gasa'pera/ *n. f.* rabbit warren.
gazapo /ga'θapo; ga'sapo/ *n. m.* rabbit.
gazmoñada /gaθmo'ɲaða; gasmo-'ɲaða/ *n. f.* prudishness.
gazmoño /gaθ'moɲo; gas'moɲo/ *n. m.* prude.
gaznate /gaθ'nate; gas'nate/ *n. m.* windpipe.
gazpacho /gaθ'patʃo; gas'patʃo/ *n. m.* cold tomato soup; gazpacho.
gelatina /hela'tina/ *n. f.* gelatine.
gemelo /he'melo/ -**la** *n.* twin.
gemelos /he'melos/ *n. m.pl.* cuff links; opera glasses; -**as,** twins.
gemido /he'miðo/ *n. m.* moan, groan, wail. —**gemir,** *v.*
genciana /hen'θiana; hen'siana/ *n. f.* gentian.
genealogía /henealo'hia/ *n. f.* genealogy, pedigree.
generación /henera'θion; henera-'sion/ *n. f.* generation.
generador /henera'ðor/ *n. m.* generator.
general /hene'ral/ *a. & m.* general.
generalidad /henerali'ðað/ *n. f.* generality.
generalización /heneraliθa'θion; heneralisa'sion/ *n. f.* generalization.
generalizar /henerali'θar; henerali'sar/ *v.* generalize.
generalmente /heneral'mente/ *adv.* generally.
género /'henero/ *n.* **1.** *m.* gender; kind. **2.** *(pl.)* goods, material.

generosidad /henerosi'ðað/ *n. f.* generosity.

generoso /hene'roso/ *a.* generous.

génesis /'henesis/ *n. m.* genesis.

genético /he'netiko/ *a.* genetic.

genial /he'nial/ *a.* genial; brilliant.

genio /'henio/ *n. m.* genius; temper; disposition.

genitivo /heni'tiβo/ *n. m.* genitive.

genocidio /heno'θiðio; heno'siðio/ *n. m.* genocide.

gente /'hente/ *n. f.* people, folk.

gentil /hen'til/ *a.* gracious; graceful.

gentileza /henti'leθa; henti'lesa/ *n. f.* grace, graciousness.

gentío /hen'tio/ *n. m.* mob, crowd.

genuino /he'nuino/ *a.* genuine.

geografía /heogra'fia/ *n. f.* geography.

geográfico /heo'grafiko/ *a.* geographical.

geométrico /heo'metriko/ *a.* geometric.

geranio /he'ranio/ *n. m.* geranium.

gerencia /he'renθia; he'rensia/ *n. f.* management.

gerente /he'rente/ *n. m. & f.* manager, director.

germen /'hermen/ *n. m.* germ.

germinar /hermi'nar/ *v.* germinate.

gerundio /he'rundio/ *n. m.* gerund.

gesticulación /hestikula'θion; hestikula'sion/ *n. f.* gesticulation.

gesticular /hestiku'lar/ *v.* gesticulate, gesture.

gestión /hes'tion/ *n. f.* conduct; effort; action.

gesto /'hesto/ *n. m.* gesture, facial expression.

gigante /hi'gante/ *a. & n.* gigantic, giant.

gigantesco /higan'tesko/ *a.* gigantic, huge.

gilipollas /gili'poʎas; gili'poyas/ *n. m. & f. Colloq.* fool, idiot.

gimnasio /him'nasio/ *n. m.* gymnasium.

gimnástica /him'nastika/ *n. f.* gymnastics.

gimotear /himote'ar/ *v.* whine.

ginebra /hi'neβra/ *n. f.* gin.

ginecólogo /hine'kologo/ **-ga** *n.* gynecologist.

gira /'hira/ *n. f.* tour, trip.

girado /hi'raðo/ **-da** *n. Com.* drawee.

girador /hira'ðor/ **-ra** *n. Com.* drawer.

girar /hi'rar/ *v.* revolve, turn, spin, whirl.

giratorio /hira'torio/ *a.* rotary, revolving.

giro /'hiro/ *n. m.* whirl, turn, spin; *Com.* draft. **g. postal,** money order.

gitano /hi'tano/ **-na** *a. & n.* Gypsy.

glacial /gla'θial; gla'sial/ *a.* glacial, icy.

glaciar /gla'θiar; gla'siar/ *n. m.* glacier.

gladiador /glaðia'ðor/ *n. m.* gladiator.

glándula /'glandula/ *n. f.* gland.

glándula endocrina /'glandula endo'krina/ endocrine gland.

glándula pituitaria /'glandula pitui'taria/ pituitary gland.

glándula prostática /'glandula pros'tatika/ prostate gland.

glasé /gla'se/ *n. m.* glacé.

glicerina /gliθe'rina; glise'rina/ *n. f.* glycerine.

globo /'gloβo/ *n. m.* globe; balloon.

gloria /'gloria/ *n. f.* glory.

glorieta /glo'rieta/ *n. f.* bower.

glorificación /glorifika'θion; glorifika'sion/ *n. f.* glorification.

glorificar /glorifi'kar/ *v.* glorify.

glorioso /glo'rioso/ *a.* glorious.

glosa /'glosa/ *n. f.* gloss. —**glosar,** *v.*

glosario /glo'sario/ *n. m.* glossary.

glotón /glo'ton/ **-ona** *a. & n.* gluttonous; glutton.

glucosa /glu'kosa/ *n. f.* glucose.

gluten /'gluten/ *n. m.* gluten; glue.

gobernación /goβerna'θion; goβerna'sion/ *n. f.* government.

gobernador /goβerna'ðor/ **-ra** *n.* governor.

gobernalle /goβer'naʎe; goβer'naye/ *n. m.* rudder, tiller, helm.

gobernante /goβer'nante/ *n. m. & f.* ruler.

gobernar /goβer'nar/ *v.* govern.

gobierno /go'βierno/ *n. m.* government.

goce /'goθe; 'gose/ *n. m.* enjoyment.

gola /'gola/ *n. f.* throat.

golf /golf/ *n. m.* golf.

golfista /gol'fista/ *n. m. & f.* golfer.

golfo /'golfo/ *n. m.* gulf.

gollete /go'ʎete; go'yete/ *n. m.* upper portion of one's throat.

golondrina /golon'drina/ *n. f.* swallow.

golosina /golo'sina/ *n. f.* delicacy.

goloso /go'loso/ *a.* sweet-toothed.

golpe /'golpe/ *n. m.* blow, stroke. **de g.**, suddenly.

golpear /golpe'ar/ *v.* strike, beat, pound.

goma /'goma/ *n. f.* rubber; gum; glue; eraser.

góndola /'gondola/ *n. f.* gondola.

gordo /'gorðo/ *a.* fat.

gordura /gor'ðura/ *n. f.* fatness.

gorila /go'rila/ *n. m.* gorilla.

gorja /'gorha/ *n. f.* gorge.

gorjeo /gor'heo/ *n. m.* warble, chirp. —**gorjear,** *v.*

gorrión /go'rrion/ *n. m.* sparrow.

gorro /'gorro/ *n. m.* cap.

gota /'gota/ *n. f.* drop (of liquid).

gotear /gote'ar/ *v.* drip, leak.

goteo /go'teo/ *n. m.* leak.

gotera /go'tera/ *n. f.* leak; gutter.

gótico /'gotiko/ *a.* Gothic.

gozar /go'θar; go'sar/ *v.* enjoy.

gozne /'goθne; 'gosne/ *n. m.* hinge.

gozo /'goθo; 'goso/ *n. m.* enjoyment, delight, joy.

gozoso /go'θoso; go'soso/ *a.* joyful, joyous.

grabado /gra'βaðo/ *n.* **1.** *m.* engraving, cut, print. —*a.* **2.** recorded.

grabador /graβa'ðor/ *n. m.* engraver.

grabadora /graβa'ðora/ *n. f.* tape recorder.

grabar /gra'βar/ *v.* engrave; record.

gracia /'graθia; 'grasia/ *n. f.* grace; wit, charm. **hacer g.,** to amuse, strike as funny. **tener g.,** to be funny, to be witty.

gracias /'graθias; 'grasias/ *n. f.pl.* thanks, thank you.

gracioso /gra'θioso; gra'sioso/ *a.* witty, funny.

grada /'graða/ *n. f.* step.

gradación /graða'θion; graða'sion/ *n. f.* gradation.

grado /'graðo/ *n. m.* grade; rank; degree.

graduado /gra'ðuaðo/ **-da** *n.* graduate.

gradual /gra'ðual/ *a.* gradual.

graduar /gra'ðuar/ *v.* grade; graduate.

gráfico /'grafiko/ *a.* graphic, vivid.

grafito /gra'fito/ *n. m.* graphite.

grajo /'graho/ *n. m.* jackdaw.

gramática /gra'matika/ *n. f.* grammar.

gramo /'gramo/ *n. m.* gram.

gran /gran/ **grande** *a.* big, large; great.

granada /gra'naða/ *n. f.* grenade; pomegranate.

granar /gra'nar/ *v.* seed.

grandes almacenes /'grandes alma'θenes; 'grandes alma'senes/ *n. m.pl.* department store.

grandeza /gran'deθa; gran'desa/ *n. f.* greatness.

grandiosidad /grandiosi'ðað/ *n. f.* grandeur.

grandioso /gran'dioso/ *a.* grand, magnificent.

grandor /gran'dor/ *n. m.* size.

granero /gra'nero/ *n. m.* barn; granary.

granito /gra'nito/ *n. m.* granite.

granizada /grani'θaða; grani'saða/ *n. f.* hailstorm.

granizo /gra'niθo; gra'niso/ *n. m.* hail. —**granizar,** *v.*

granja /'granha/ *n. f.* grange; farm; farmhouse.

granjear /granhe'ar/ *v.* earn, gain; get.

granjero /gran'hero/ **-era** *n.* farmer.

grano /'grano/ *n. m.* grain; kernel.

granuja /gra'nuha/ *n. m.* waif, urchin.

grapa /'grapa/ *n. f.* clamp, clip.

grapadora /grapa'ðora/ *n. f.* stapler.

grasa /'grasa/ *n. f.* grease, fat.

grasiento /gra'siento/ *a.* greasy.

gratificación /gratifika'θion; gratifika'sion/ *n. f.* gratification; reward; tip.

gratificar /gratifi'kar/ *v.* gratify; reward; tip.

gratis /'gratis/ *adv.* gratis, free.

gratitud /grati'tuð/ *n. f.* gratitude.

grato /'grato/ *a.* grateful; pleasant.

gratuito /gra'tuito/ *a.* gratuitous; free.

gravamen /gra'βamen/ *n. m.* tax; burden; obligation.

grave /'graβe/ *a.* grave, serious, severe.

gravedad /graβe'ðað/ *n. f.* gravity, seriousness.

gravitación /graβita'θion; graβita-'sion/ *n. f.* gravitation.

gravitar /graβi'tar/ *v.* gravitate.

gravoso /gra'βoso/ *a.* burdensome.

graznido /graθ'niðo; gras'niðo/ *n. m.* croak. —**graznar,** *v.*

Grecia /'greθia; 'gresia/ *n. f.* Greece.

greco /'greko/ **-ca** *a. & n.* Greek.

greda /'greða/ *n. f.* clay.

gresca /'greska/ *n. f.* revelry; quarrel.

griego /'griego/ **-ga** *a. & n.* Greek.

grieta /'grieta/ *n. f.* opening; crevice, crack.

grifo /'grifo/ *n. m.* faucet.

grillo /'griʎo; 'griyo/ *n. m.* cricket.

grima /'grima/ *n. f.* fright.

gringo /'griŋgo/ **-ga** *n.* foreigner (usually North American).

gripa /'gripa/ **gripe** *n. f.* grippe.

gris /gris/ *a.* gray.

grito /'grito/ *n. m.* shout, scream, cry. —**gritar,** *v.*

grosella /gro'seʎa; gro'seya/ *n. f.* currant.

grosería /grose'ria/ *n. f.* grossness; coarseness.

grosero /gro'sero/ *a.* coarse, vulgar, discourteous.

grotesco /gro'tesko/ *a.* grotesque.

grúa /'grua/ *n. f.* crane; tow truck.

gruesa /'gruesa/ *n. f.* gross.

grueso /'grueso/ *a.* **1.** bulky; stout; coarse, thick. —*n.* **2.** *m.* bulk.

grulla /'gruʎa; 'gruya/ *n. f.* crane.

gruñido /gru'ɲiðo/ *n. m.* growl, snarl, mutter. —**gruñir,** *v.*

grupo /'grupo/ *n. m.* group, party.

gruta /'gruta/ *n. f.* cavern.

guacamol /guaka'mol/ **guacamole** *n. m.* avocado sauce; guacamole.

guadaña /gua'ðaɲa/ *n. f.* scythe. —**guadañar,** *v.*

guagua /'guagua/ *n. f.* (*S.A.*) baby; (Carib.) bus.

gualdo /'gualdo/ *n. m.* yellow, golden.

guano /'guano/ *n. m.* guano (fertilizer).

guante /'guante/ *n. m.* glove.

guantera /guan'tera/ *n. f.* glove compartment.

guapo /'guapo/ *a.* handsome.

guarda /'guarða/ *n. m. or f.* guard.

guardabarros /guarða'βarros/ *n. m.* fender.

guardacostas /guarða'kostas/ *n. m.* revenue ship.

guardaespaldas /ˌguarðaes-'paldas/ *n. m. & f.* bodyguard.

guardameta /guarða'meta/ *n. m. & f.* goalkeeper.

guardar /guar'ðar/ *v.* keep, store, put away; guard.

guardarropa /guarða'rropa/ *n. f.* coat room.

guardarse de /guar'ðarse de/ *v.* beware of, avoid.

guardia /'guarðia/ *n.* **1.** *f.* guard; watch. —*n.* **2.** *m.* policeman.

guardián /guar'ðian/ **-na** *n.* guardian, keeper, watchman.

guardilla /guar'ðiʎa; guar'ðiya/ *n. f.* attic.

guarida /gua'riða/ *n. f.* den.

guarismo /gua'rismo/ *n. m.* number, figure.

guarnecer /guarne'θer; guarne-'ser/ *v.* adorn.

guarnición /guarni'θion; guarni-'sion/ *n. f.* garrison; trimming.

guasa /'guasa/ *n. f.* joke, jest.

guayaba /gua'yaβa/ *n. f.* guava.

gubernativo /guβerna'tiβo/ *a.* governmental.

guerra /'gerra/ *n. f.* war.

guerrero /ge'rrero/ **-ra** *n.* warrior.

guía /'gia/ *n.* **1.** *m. & f.* guide. **2.** *f.* guidebook, directory.

guiar /giar/ *v.* guide; steer, drive.

guija /'giha/ *n. f.* pebble.

guillotina /giʎo'tina; giyo'tina/ *n. f.* guillotine.

guindar /gin'dar/ *v.* hang.

guinga /'giŋga/ *n. f.* gingham.

guiñada /gi'ɲaða/ *n. f.*, **guiño,** *m.* wink. —**guiñar,** *v.*

guión /gi'on/ *n. m.* dash, hyphen; script.

guirnalda /gir'nalda/ *n. f.* garland, wreath.

guisa /'gisa/ *n. f.* guise, manner.

guisado /gi'saðo/ *n. m.* stew.

guisante /gi'sante/ *n. m.* pea.

guisar /gi'sar/ *v.* cook.

guiso /'giso/ *n. m.* stew.

guita /'gita/ *n. f.* twine.

guitarra /gi'tarra/ *n. f.* guitar.

guitarrista /gita'rrista/ *n. m. & f.* guitarist.
gula /'gula/ *n. f.* gluttony.
gurú /gu'ru/ *n. m.* guru.
gusano /gu'sano/ *n. m.* worm, caterpillar.
gustar /gus'tar/ *v.* please; taste.

gustillo /gus'tiʎo; gus'tiyo/ *n. m.* aftertaste, slight pleasure.
gusto /'gusto/ *n. m.* pleasure; taste; liking.
gustoso /gus'toso/ *a.* pleasant; tasteful.
gutural /gutu'ral/ *a.* guttural.

H

haba /'aβa/ *n. f.* bean.
habanera /aβa'nera/ *n. f.* Cuban dance melody.
haber /a'βer/ *v.* have. **h. de,** be to, be supposed to.
haberes /a'βeres/ *n. m.pl.* property; worldly goods.
habichuela /aβi'tʃuela/ *n. f.* bean.
hábil /'aβil/ *a.* skillful; capable; clever.
habilidad /aβili'ðað/ *n. f.* ability; skill; talent.
habilidoso /aβili'ðoso/ *a.* able, skillful, talented.
habilitado /aβili'taðo/ **-da** *n.* paymaster.
habilitar /aβili'tar/ *v.* qualify; supply, equip.
hábilmente /'aβilmente/ *adv.* ably.
habitación /aβita'θion; aβita'sion/ *n. f.* dwelling; room. **h. individual,** single room.
habitante /aβi'tante/ *n. m. & f.* inhabitant.
habitar /aβi'tar/ *v.* inhabit; dwell.
hábito /'aβito/ *n. m.* habit; custom.
habitual /aβi'tual/ *a.* habitual.
habituar /aβi'tuar/ *v.* accustom, habituate.
habla /'aβla/ *n. f.* speech.
hablador /aβla'ðor/ *a.* talkative.
hablar /a'βlar/ *v.* talk, speak.
haca /'aka/ *n. f.* pony.
hacedor /aθe'ðor; ase'ðor/ *n. m.* maker.
hacendado /aθen'daðo; asen'daðo/ **-da** *n.* hacienda owner; farmer.
hacendoso /aθen'doso; asen'doso/ *a.* industrious.
hacer /a'θer; a'ser/ *v.* do; make. **hace dos años,** etc., two years ago, etc.
hacerse /a'θerse; a'serse/ *v.* become, get to be.
hacha /'atʃa/ *n. f.* ax, hatchet.
hacia /'aθia; 'asia/ *prep.* toward.
hacienda /a'θienda; a'sienda/ *n. f.* property; estate; ranch; farm; *Govt.* treasury.
hada /'aða/ *n. f.* fairy.
hado /'aðo/ *n. m.* fate.
halagar /ala'gar/ *v.* flatter.
halar /a'lar/ *v.* haul, pull.
halcón /al'kon/ *n. m.* hawk, falcon.
haleche /a'letʃe/ *n. m.* anchovy.
hallado /a'ʎaðo; a'yaðo/ *a.* found. **bien h.,** welcome. **mal h.,** uneasy.
hallar /a'ʎar; a'yar/ *v.* find, locate.
hallarse /a'ʎarse; a'yarse/ *v.* be located; happen to be.
hallazgo /a'ʎaθgo; a'yasgo/ *n. m.* find, thing found.
hamaca /a'maka/ *n. f.* hammock.
hambre /'ambre/ *n. f.* hunger. **tener h., estar con h.,** to be hungry.
hambrear /ambre'ar/ *v.* hunger; starve.
hambriento /am'briento/ *a.* starving, hungry.
hamburguesa /ambur'gesa/ *n. f.* beefburger, hamburger.
haragán /ara'gan/ **-na** *n.* idler, lazy person.
haraganear /aragane'ar/ *v.* loiter.
harapo /a'rapo/ *n. m.* rag, tatter.
haraposo /ara'poso/ *a.* ragged, shabby.
harén /a'ren/ *n. m.* harem.
harina /a'rina/ *n. f.* flour, meal.
harnero /ar'nero/ *n. m.* sieve.
hartar /ar'tar/ *v.* satiate.
harto /'arto/ *a.* stuffed; fed up.
hartura /ar'tura/ *n. f.* superabundance, glut.
hasta /'asta/ *prep.* **1.** until, till; as far as, up to. **h. luego,** good-bye, so long. —*adv.* **2.** even.
hastío /as'tio/ *n. m.* distaste, loathing.
hato /'ato/ *n. m.* herd.
hay /ai/ *v.* there is, there are. **h. que,** it is necessary to. **no h. de**

qué, you're welcome, don't mention it.

haya /'aya/ *n. f.* beech tree.

haz /aθ; as/ *n. f.* bundle, sheaf; face.

hazaña /a'θaɲa; a'saɲa/ *n. f.* deed; exploit, feat.

hebdomadario /eβðoma'ðario/ *a.* weekly.

hebilla /e'βiʎa; e'βiya/ *n. f.* buckle.

hebra /'eβra/ *n. f.* thread, string.

hebreo /e'βreo/ **-rea** *a.* & *n.* Hebrew.

hechicero /etʃi'θero; etʃi'sero/ **-ra** *n.* wizard, witch.

hechizar /etʃi'θar; etʃi'sar/ *v.* bewitch.

hechizo /e'tʃiθo; e'tʃiso/ *n. m.* spell.

hecho /'etʃo/ *n. m.* fact; act; deed.

hechura /e'tʃura/ *n. f.* workmanship, make.

hediondez /eðion'deθ; eðion'des/ *n. f.* stench.

hégira /'ehira/ *n. f.* hegira.

helada /e'laða/ *n. f.* frost.

heladería /elaðe'ria/ *n. f.* ice-cream parlor.

helado /e'laðo/ *n. m.* ice cream.

helar /e'lar/ *v.* freeze.

helecho /e'letʃo/ *n. m.* fern.

hélice /'eliθe; 'elise/ *n. f.* propeller; helix.

helicóptero /eli'koptero/ *n. m.* helicopter.

helio /'elio/ *n. m.* helium.

hembra /'embra/ *n. f.* female.

hemisferio /emis'ferio/ *n. m.* hemisphere.

hemoglobina /emoglo'βina/ *n. f.* hemoglobin.

hemorragia /emo'rrahia/ *n. f.* hemorrhage.

hemorragia nasal /emo'rrahia na'sal/ nosebleed.

henchir /en'tʃir/ *v.* stuff.

hendedura /ende'ðura/ *n. f.* crevice, crack.

hendido /en'diðo/ *a.* cloven, cleft (lip).

heno /'eno/ *n. m.* hay.

hepática /e'patika/ *n. f.* liverwort.

hepatitis /epa'titis/ *n. f.* hepatitis.

heraldo /e'raldo/ *n. m.* herald.

herbáceo /er'βaθeo; er'βaseo/ *a.* herbaceous.

herbívoro /er'βiβoro/ *a.* herbivorous.

heredar /ere'ðar/ *v.* inherit.

heredero /ere'ðero/ **-ra** *n.* heir; successor.

hereditario /ereði'tario/ *a.* hereditary.

hereje /e'rehe/ *n. m.* & *f.* heretic.

herejía /ere'hia/ *n. f.* heresy.

herencia /e'renθia; e'rensia/ *n. f.* inheritance; heritage.

herético /e'retiko/ *a.* heretical.

herida /e'riða/ *n. f.* wound, injury.

herir /e'rir/ *v.* wound, injure.

hermafrodita /ermafro'ðita/ *a.* & *n.* hermaphrodite.

hermana /er'mana/ *n. f.* sister.

hermano /er'mano/ *n. m.* brother.

hermético /er'metiko/ *a.* airtight.

hermoso /er'moso/ *a.* beautiful, handsome.

hermosura /ermo'sura/ *n. f.* beauty.

hernia /'ernia/ *n. f.* hernia, rupture.

héroe /'eroe/ *n. m.* hero.

heroico /e'roiko/ *a.* heroic.

heroína /ero'ina/ *n. f.* heroine.

heroísmo /ero'ismo/ *n. m.* heroism.

herradura /erra'ðura/ *n. f.* horseshoe.

herramienta /erra'mienta/ *n. f.* tool; implement.

herrería /erre'ria/ *n. f.* blacksmith's shop.

herrero /e'rrero/ *n. m.* blacksmith.

herrumbre /e'rrumbre/ *n. f.* rust.

hertzio /'ertθio; 'ertsio/ *n. m.* hertz.

hervir /er'βir/ *v.* boil.

hesitación /esita'θion; esita'sion/ *n. f.* hesitation.

heterogéneo /etero'heneo/ *a.* heterogeneous.

heterosexual /eterosek'sual/ *a.* heterosexual.

hexagonal /eksago'nal/ *a.* hexagonal.

hexágono /e'ksagono/ *n. m.* hexagon.

hez /eθ; es/ *n. f.* dregs, sediment.

híbrido /'iβriðo/ **-da** *n.* & *a.* hybrid.

hidalgo /i'ðalgo/ **-ga** *a.* & *n.* noble.

hidalguía /iðal'gia/ *n. f.* nobility; generosity.

hidráulico /i'ðrauliko/ *a.* hydraulic.

hidroavión /iðroa'βion/ *n. m.* seaplane, hydroplane.
hidrofobia /iðro'foβia/ *n. f.* rabies.
hidrógeno /i'ðroheno/ *n. m.* hydrogen.
hidropesía /iðrope'sia/ *n. f.* dropsy.
hiedra /'ieðra/ *n. f.* ivy.
hiel /iel/ *n. f.* gall.
hielo /'ielo/ *n. m.* ice.
hiena /'iena/ *n. f.* hyena.
hierba /'ierβa/ *n. f.* grass; herb; marijuana.
hierbabuena /ierβa'βuena/ *n. f.* mint.
hierro /'ierro/ *n. m.* iron.
hígado /'igaðo/ *n. m.* liver.
higiene /i'hiene/ *n. f.* hygiene.
higiénico /i'hieniko/ *a.* sanitary, hygienic.
higo /'igo/ *n. m.* fig.
higuera /i'gera/ *n. f.* fig tree.
hija /'iha/ *n. f.* daughter.
hija adoptiva /'iha aðop'tiβa/ adopted daughter.
hijastro /i'hastro/ **-tra** *n.* stepchild.
hijo /'iho/ *n. m.* son.
hijo adoptivo /'iho aðop'tiβo/ *m.* adopted child, adopted son.
hila /'ila/ *n. f.* line.
hilandero /ilan'dero/ **-ra** *n.* spinner.
hilar /i'lar/ *v.* spin.
hilera /i'lera/ *n. f.* row, line, tier.
hilo /'ilo/ *n. m.* thread; string; wire; linen.
himno /'imno/ *n. m.* hymn.
hincar /in'kar/ *v.* drive, thrust; sink into.
hincarse /in'karse/ *v.* kneel.
hinchar /in'tʃar/ *v.* swell.
hindú /in'du/ *n. & a.* Hindu.
hinojo /i'noho/ *n. m.* knee.
hiperenlace /iperen'laθe, iperen-'lase/ *n. m.* hyperlink.
hipermercado /ipermer'kaðo/ *n. m.* hypermarket.
hipertexto /iper'teksto/ *n. m.* hypertext.
hipnótico /ip'notiko/ *a.* hypnotic.
hipnotismo /ipno'tismo/ *n. m.* hypnotism.
hipnotista /ipno'tista/ *n. m. & f.* hypnotist.
hipnotizar /ipnoti'θar; ipnoti'sar/ *v.* hypnotize.
hipo /'ipo/ *n. m.* hiccough.

hipocresía /ipokre'sia/ *n. f.* hypocrisy.
hipócrita /i'pokrita/ *a. & n.* hypocritical; hypocrite.
hipódromo /i'poðromo/ *n. m.* race track.
hipoteca /ipo'teka/ *n. f.* mortgage. —**hipotecar,** *v.*
hipótesis /i'potesis/ *n. f.* hypothesis.
hirsuto /ir'suto/ *a.* hairy, hirsute.
hispano /is'pano/ *a.* Hispanic, Spanish American.
Hispanoamérica /ispanoa'merika/ *f.* Spanish America.
hispanoamericano /ispanoameri-'kano/ **-na** *a. & n.* Spanish American.
histerectomía /isterekto'mia/ *n. f.* hysterectomy.
histeria /is'teria/ *n. f.* hysteria.
histérico /is'teriko/ *a.* hysterical.
historia /is'toria/ *n. f.* history; story.
historiador /istoria'ðor/ **-ra** *n.* historian.
histórico /is'toriko/ *a.* historic, historical.
histrión /is'trion/ *n. m.* actor.
hocico /o'θiko; o'siko/ *n. m.* snout, muzzle.
hogar /o'gar/ *n. m.* hearth; home.
hoguera /o'gera/ *n. f.* bonfire, blaze.
hoja /'oha/ *n. f.* leaf; sheet (of paper); pane; blade.
hoja de cálculo /'oha de 'kalkulo/ spreadsheet.
hoja de inscripción /'oha de inskrip'θion; 'oha de inskrip'sion/ entry blank.
hoja de pedidos /'oha de pe-'ðiðos/ order blank.
hoja informativa /'oha informa-'tiβa/ newsletter.
hojalata /oha'lata/ *n. f.* tin.
hojalatero /ohala'tero/ **-ra** *n.* tinsmith.
hojear /ohe'ar/ *v.* scan, skim through.
hola /'ola/ *interj.* hello.
Holanda /o'landa/ *n. f.* Holland, Netherlands.
holandés /olan'des/ **-esa** *a. & n.* Dutch; Hollander.
holganza /ol'ganθa; ol'gansa/ *n. f.* leisure; diversion.
holgazán /olga'θan; olga'san/ **-ana** *a.* **1.** idle, lazy. —*n.* **2.** *m.* idler, loiterer, tramp.

holgazanear /olgaθane'ar; olga-sane'ar/ v. idle, loiter.
hollín /o'ʎin; o'yin/ n. m. soot.
holografía /olografía/ n. f. holography.
holograma /olo'grama/ n. m. hologram.
hombre /'ombre/ n. m. man.
hombría /om'βria/ n. f. manliness.
hombro /'ombro/ n. m. shoulder.
hombruno /om'bruno/ a. mannish, masculine (woman).
homenaje /ome'nahe/ n. m. homage.
homeópata /ome'opata/ n. m. homeopath.
homicidio /omi'θiðio; omi'siðio/ n. m. homicide.
homilía /omi'lia/ n. f. homily.
homosexual /omose'ksual/ a. homosexual, gay.
honda /'onda/ n. f. sling.
hondo /'ondo/ a. deep.
hondonada /ondo'naða/ n. f. ravine.
hondura /on'dura/ n. f. depth.
honestidad /onesti'ðað/ n. f. modesty, unpretentiousness.
honesto /o'nesto/ a. honest; pure; just.
hongo /'oŋgo/ n. m. fungus; mushroom.
honor /o'nor/ n. m. honor.
honorable /ono'raβle/ a. honorable.
honorario /ono'rario/ a. **1.** honorary. —n. **2.** m. honorarium, fee.
honorífico /ono'rifiko/ a. honorary.
honra /'onra/ n. f. honor. —honrar, v.
honradez /onra'ðeθ; onra'ðes/ n. f. honesty.
honrado /on'raðo/ a. honest, honorable.
hora /'ora/ n. f. hour; time (of day).
horadar /ora'ðar/ v. perforate.
hora punta /'ora 'punta/ rush hour.
horario /o'rario/ n. m. timetable, schedule.
horca /'orka/ n. f. gallows; pitchfork.
horda /'orða/ n. f. horde.
horizontal /oriθon'tal; orison'tal/ a. horizontal.
horizonte /ori'θonte; ori'sonte/ n. m. horizon.

hormiga /or'miga/ n. f. ant.
hormiguear /ormige'ar/ v. itch.
hormiguero /ormi'gero/ n. m. ant hill.
hornero /or'nero/ -ra n. baker.
hornillo /or'niʎo; or'niyo/ n. m. stove.
horno /'orno/ n. m. oven; kiln.
horóscopo /o'roskopo/ n. m. horoscope.
horrendo /o'rrendo/ a. dreadful, horrendous.
horrible /o'rriβle/ a. horrible, hideous, awful.
hórrido /'orriðo/ a. horrid.
horror /o'rror/ n. m. horror.
horrorizar /orrori'θar; orrori'sar/ v. horrify.
horroroso /orro'roso/ a. horrible, frightful.
hortelano /orte'lano/ n. m. horticulturist.
hospedaje /ospe'ðahe/ n. m. lodging.
hospedar /ospe'ðar/ v. give or take lodgings.
hospital /ospi'tal/ n. m. hospital.
hospitalario /ospita'lario/ a. hospitable.
hospitalidad /ospitali'ðað/ n. f. hospitality.
hospitalmente /ospital'mente/ adv. hospitably.
hostia /'ostia/ n. f. host; Colloq. hit, blow.
hostil /'ostil/ a. hostile.
hostilidad /ostili'ðað/ n. f. hostility.
hotel /'otel/ n. m. hotel.
hoy /oi/ adv. today. **h. día, h. en día,** nowadays.
hoya /'oya/ n. f. dale, valley.
hoyo /'oyo/ n. m. pit, hole.
hoyuelo /o'yuelo/ n. m. dimple.
hoz /oθ; os/ n. f. sickle.
hucha /'utʃa/ n. f. chest, money box; savings.
hueco /'ueko/ a. **1.** hollow, empty. —n. **2.** m. hole, hollow.
huelga /'uelga/ n. f. strike.
huelgista /uel'hista/ n. m. & f. striker.
huella /'ueʎa; 'ueya/ n. f. track, trace; footprint.
huérfano /'uerfano/ -na a. & n. orphan.
huero /'uero/ a. empty.
huerta /'uerta/ n. f. (vegetable) garden.
huerto /'uerto/ n. m. orchard.

hueso /'ueso/ *n. m.* bone; fruit pit.

huésped /'uespeð/ *n. m. & f.* guest.

huesudo /ue'suðo/ *a.* bony.

huevo /'ueβo/ *n. m.* egg.

huída /'uiða/ *n. f.* flight, escape.

huir /uir/ *v.* flee.

hule /'ule/ *n. m.* oilcloth.

humanidad /umani'ðað/ *n. f.* humanity, mankind; humaneness.

humanista /uma'nista/ *n. m. & f.* humanist.

humanitario /umani'tario/ *a.* humane.

humano /u'mano/ *a.* human; humane.

humareda /uma'reða/ *n. f.* dense cloud of smoke.

humear /ume'ar/ *v.* emit smoke or steam.

humedad /ume'ðað/ *n. f.* humidity, moisture, dampness.

humedecer /umeðe'θer; umeðe'ser/ *v.* moisten, dampen.

húmedo /'umeðo/ *a.* humid, moist, damp.

humildad /umil'dað/ *n. f.* humility, meekness.

humilde /u'milde/ *a.* humble, meek.

humillación /umiʎa'θion; umiya'sion/ *n. f.* humiliation.

humillar /umi'ʎar; umi'yar/ *v.* humiliate.

humo /'umo/ *n. m.* smoke; (*pl.*) airs, affectation.

humor /u'mor/ *n. m.* humor, mood.

humorista /umo'rista/ *n. m. & f.* humorist.

hundimiento /undi'miento/ *n. m.* collapse.

hundir /un'dir/ *v.* sink; collapse.

húngaro /'uŋgaro/ **-ra** *a. & n.* Hungarian.

Hungría /uŋ'gria/ *n. f.* Hungary.

huracán /ura'kan/ *n. m.* hurricane.

huraño /u'raɲo/ *a.* shy, bashful.

hurgar /ur'gar/ *v.* stir.

hurón /u'ron/ *n. m.* ferret.

hurtadillas /urta'ðiʎas; urta'ðiyas/ *n. f.pl.* **a h.,** on the sly.

hurtador /urta'ðor/ **-ra** *n.* thief.

hurtar /ur'tar/ *v.* steal, rob of; hide.

hurtarse /ur'tarse/ *v.* hide; withdraw.

husmear /usme'ar/ *v.* scent, smell.

huso /'uso/ *n. m.* spindle; bobbin.

huso horario /'uso o'rario/ time zone.

I

ibérico /i'βeriko/ *a.* Iberian.

iberoamericano /iβeroameri'kano/ **-na** *a. & n.* Latin American.

ida /'iða/ *n. f.* departure; trip out. **i. y vuelta,** round trip.

idea /i'ðea/ *n. f.* idea.

ideal /i'ðeal/ *a. & m.* ideal.

idealismo /iðea'lismo/ *n. m.* idealism.

idealista /iðea'lista/ *n. m. & f.* idealist.

idear /iðe'ar/ *v.* plan, conceive.

idéntico /i'ðentiko/ *a.* identical.

identidad /iðenti'ðað/ *n. f.* identity; identification.

identificar /iðentifi'kar/ *v.* identify.

idilio /i'ðilio/ *n. m.* idyll.

idioma /i'ðioma/ *n. m.* language.

idiota /i'ðiota/ *a. & n.* idiotic; idiot.

idiotismo /iðio'tismo/ *n. m.* idiom; idiocy.

idolatrar /iðola'trar/ *v.* idolize, adore.

ídolo /'iðolo/ *n. m.* idol.

idóneo /i'ðoneo/ *a.* suitable, fit, apt.

iglesia /i'glesia/ *n. f.* church.

ignición /igni'θion; igni'sion/ *n. f.* ignition.

ignominia /igno'minia/ *n. f.* ignominy, shame.

ignominioso /ignomi'nioso/ *a.* ignominious, shameful.

ignorancia /igno'ranθia; igno'ransia/ *n. f.* ignorance.

ignorante /igno'rante/ *a.* ignorant.

ignorar /igno'rar/ *v.* be ignorant of, not know.

ignoto /ig'noto/ *a.* unknown.

igual /i'gual/ *a.* equal; the same; (*pl.*) alike. *m.* equal.

igualar /igua'lar/ *v.* equal; equalize; match.

igualdad /igual'dað/ *n. f.* equality; sameness.

ijada /i'haða/ *n. f.* flank (of an animal).

ilegal /ile'gal/ *a.* illegal.
ilegítimo /ile'hitimo/ *a.* illegitimate.
ileso /i'leso/ *a.* unharmed.
ilícito /i'liθito; i'lisito/ *a.* illicit, unlawful.
iluminación /ilumina'θion; ilumina'sion/ *n. f.* illumination.
iluminar /ilumi'nar/ *v.* illuminate.
ilusión /ilu'sion/ *n. f.* illusion.
ilusión de óptica /ilu'sion de 'optika/ optical illusion.
ilusorio /ilu'sorio/ *a.* illusive.
ilustración /ilustra'θion; ilustra'sion/ *n. f.* illustration; learning.
ilustrador /ilustra'ðor/ **-ra** *n.* illustrator.
ilustrar /ilus'trar/ *v.* illustrate.
ilustre /i'lustre/ *a.* illustrious, honorable, distinguished.
imagen /i'mahen/ *n. f.* image.
imaginación /imahina'θion; imahina'sion/ *n. f.* imagination.
imaginar /imahi'nar/ *v.* imagine.
imaginario /imahi'nario/ *a.* imaginary.
imaginativo /imahina'tiβo/ *a.* imaginative.
imán /i'man/ *n. m.* magnet; imam.
imbécil /im'beθil; im'besil/ *a. & n.* imbecile; stupid, foolish; fool.
imbuir /im'buir/ *v.* imbue, instil.
imitación /imita'θion; imita'sion/ *n. f.* imitation.
imitador /imita'ðor/ **-ra** *n.* imitator.
imitar /imi'tar/ *v.* imitate.
impaciencia /impa'θienθia; impa'siensia/ *n. f.* impatience.
impaciente /impa'θiente; impa'siente/ *a.* impatient.
impar /im'par/ *a.* unequal, uneven, odd.
imparcial /impar'θial; impar'sial/ *a.* impartial.
impasible /impa'siβle/ *a.* impassive, unmoved.
impávido /im'paβiðo/ *adj.* fearless, intrepid.
impedimento /impeði'mento/ *n. m.* impediment, obstacle.
impedir /impe'ðir/ *v.* impede, hinder, stop, obstruct.
impeler /impe'ler/ *v.* impel; incite.
impensado /impen'saðo/ *a.* unexpected.
imperar /impe'rar/ *v.* reign; prevail.
imperativo /impera'tiβo/ *a.* imperative.

imperceptible /imperθep'tiβle; impersep'tiβle/ *a.* imperceptible.
imperdible /imper'ðiβle/ *n. m.* safety pin.
imperecedero /impereθe'ðero; imperese'ðero/ *a.* imperishable.
imperfecto /imper'fekto/ *a.* imperfect, faulty.
imperial /impe'rial/ *a.* imperial.
imperialismo /imperia'lismo/ *n. m.* imperialism.
impericia /impe'riθia; impe'risia/ *n. f.* inexperience.
imperio /im'perio/ *n. m.* empire.
imperioso /impe'rioso/ *a.* imperious, domineering.
impermeable /imperme'aβle/ *a.* waterproof. *m.* raincoat.
impersonal /imperso'nal/ *a.* impersonal.
impertinencia /impertinen'θia; impertinen'sia/ *n. f.* impertinence.
ímpetu /'impetu/ *n. m.* impulse; impetus.
impetuoso /impe'tuoso/ *a.* impetuous.
impiedad /impie'ðað/ *n. f.* impiety.
impío /im'pio/ *a.* impious.
implacable /impla'kaβle/ *a.* implacable, unrelenting.
implicar /impli'kar/ *v.* implicate, involve.
implorar /implo'rar/ *v.* implore.
imponente /impo'nente/ *a.* impressive.
imponer /impo'ner/ *v.* impose.
impopular /impopu'lar/ *a.* unpopular.
importación /importa'θion; importa'sion/ *n. f.* importation, importing.
importador /importa'ðor/ **-ra** *n.* importer.
importancia /impor'tanθia; impor'tansia/ *n. f.* importance.
importante /impor'tante/ *a.* important.
importar /impor'tar/ *v.* be important, matter; import.
importe /im'porte/ *n. m.* value; amount.
importunar /importu'nar/ *v.* beg, importune.
imposibilidad /imposiβili'ðað/ *n. f.* impossibility.
imposibilitado /imposiβili'taðo/ *a.* helpless.
imposible /impo'siβle/ *a.* impossible.

imposición /imposi'θion; imposi-'sion/ *n. f.* imposition.

impostor /impos'tor/ **-ra** *n.* imposter, faker.

impotencia /impo'tenθia; impo-'tensia/ *n. f.* impotence.

impotente /impo'tente/ *a.* impotent.

imprecar /impre'kar/ *v.* curse.

impreciso /impre'θiso; impre'siso/ *adj.* inexact.

impregnar /impreg'nar/ *v.* impregnate.

imprenta /im'prenta/ *n. f.* press; printing house.

imprescindible /impresθin'diβle; impressin'diβle/ *a.* essential.

impresión /impre'sion/ *n. f.* impression.

impresionable /impresio'naβle/ *a.* impressionable.

impresionar /impresio'nar/ *v.* impress.

impresor /impre'sor/ *n. m.* printer.

imprevisión /impreβi'sion/ *n. f.* oversight; thoughtlessness.

imprevisto /impre'βisto/ *a.* unexpected, unforeseen.

imprimir /impri'mir/ *v.* print; imprint.

improbable /impro'βaβle/ *a.* improbable.

improbo /im'proβo/ *a.* dishonest.

improductivo /improðuk'tiβo/ *a.* unproductive.

improperio /impro'perio/ *n. m.* insult.

impropio /im'propio/ *a.* improper.

improvisación /improβisa'θion; improβisa'sion/ *n. f.* improvisation.

improvisar /improβi'sar/ *v.* improvise.

improviso /impro'βiso, impro-'βisto/ *a.* unforeseen.

imprudencia /impru'ðenθia; impru'ðensia/ *n. f.* imprudence.

imprudente /impru'ðente/ *a.* imprudent, reckless.

impuesto /im'puesto/ *n. m.* tax.

impuesto sobre la renta /im'puesto soβre la 'rrenta/ income tax.

impulsar /impul'sar/ *v.* prompt, impel.

impulsivo /impul'siβo/ *a.* impulsive.

impulso /im'pulso/ *n. m.* impulse.

impureza /impu'reθa; impu'resa/ *n. f.* impurity.

impuro /im'puro/ *a.* impure.

imputación /imputa'θion; imputa'sion/ *n. f.* imputation.

imputar /impu'tar/ *v.* impute, attribute.

inaccesible /inakθe'siβle; inakse-'siβle/ *a.* inaccessible.

inacción /inak'θion; inak'sion/ *n. f.* inaction; inactivity.

inaceptable /inaθep'taβle; inasep'taβle/ *a.* unacceptable.

inactivo /inak'tiβo/ *a.* inactive; sluggish.

inadecuado /inaðe'kuaðo/ *a.* inadequate.

inadvertencia /inaðβer'tenθia; inaðβer'tensia/ *n. f.* oversight.

inadvertido /inaðβer'tiðo/ *a.* inadvertent, careless; unnoticed.

inagotable /inago'taβle/ *a.* inexhaustible.

inalterado /inalte'raðo/ *a.* unchanged.

inanición /inani'θion; inani'sion/ *n. f.* starvation.

inanimado /inani'maðo/ *adj.* inanimate.

inapetencia /inape'tenθia; inape'tensia/ *n. f.* lack of appetite.

inaplicable /inapli'kaβle/ *a.* inapplicable; unfit.

inaudito /inau'ðito/ *a.* unheard of.

inauguración /inaugura'θion; inaugura'sion/ *n. f.* inauguration.

inaugurar /inaugu'rar/ *v.* inaugurate, open.

incandescente /inkandes'θente; inkandes'sente/ *a.* incandescent.

incansable /inkan'saβle/ *a.* tireless.

incapacidad /inkapaθi'ðað; inkapasi'ðað/ *n. f.* incapacity.

incapacitar /inkapaθi'tar; inkapasi'tar/ *v.* incapacitate.

incapaz /inka'paθ; inka'pas/ *a.* incapable.

incauto /in'kauto/ *a.* unwary.

incendiar /inθen'diar; insen'diar/ *v.* set on fire.

incendio /in'θendio; in'sendio/ *n. m.* fire; conflagration.

incertidumbre /inθerti'ðumbre; inserti'ðumbre/ *n. f.* uncertainty, suspense.

incesante /inθe'sante; inse'sante/ *a.* continual, incessant.

incidente /inθi'ðente; insi'ðente/ *n. m.* incident, event.

incienso /in'θienso; in'sienso/ *n.*
m. incense.

incierto /in'θierto; in'sierto/ *a.*
uncertain, doubtful.

incinerar /inθine'rar; insine'rar/ *v.*
incinerate; cremate.

incisión /inθi'sion; insi'sion/ *n. f.*
incision, cut.

incitamiento /inθita'miento;
insita'miento/ *n. m.* incitement,
motivation.

incitar /inθi'tar; insi'tar/ *v.* incite,
instigate.

incivil /inθi'βil; insi'βil/ *a.* impolite, rude.

inclemencia /inkle'menθia; inkle-
'mensia/ *n. f.* inclemency.

inclemente /inkle'mente/ *a.* in-
clement, merciless.

inclinación /inklina'θion; inklina-
'sion/ *n. f.* inclination, bent;
slope.

inclinar /inkli'nar/ *v.* incline; influence.

inclinarse /inkli'narse/ *v.* slope;
lean, bend over; bow.

incluir /in'kluir/ *v.* include; enclose.

inclusivo /inklu'siβo/ *a.* inclusive.

incluso /in'kluso/ *prep.* including.

incógnito /in'kognito/ *a.* unknown.

incoherente /inkoe'rente/ *a.* inco-
herent.

incombustible /inkombus'tiβle/ *a.*
fireproof.

incomible /inko'miβle/ *a.* inedible.

incomodar /inkomo'ðar/ *v.* disturb, bother, inconvenience.

incomodidad /inkomoði'ðað/ *n. f.*
inconvenience.

incómodo /in'komoðo/ *n. m.* uncomfortable; cumbersome; inconvenient.

incomparable /inkompa'raβle/ *a.*
incomparable.

incompatible /inkompa'tiβle/ *a.*
incompatible.

incompetencia /inkompe'tenθia;
inkompe'tensia/ *n. f.* incompe-
tence.

incompetente /inkompe'tente/ *a.*
incompetent.

incompleto /inkom'pleto/ *a.* incomplete.

incondicional /inkondiθio'nal; in-
kondisio'nal/ *a.* unconditional.

inconexo /inkone'kso/ *a.* incoher-
ent; unconnected.

incongruente /inkoŋgru'ente/ *a.*
incongruous.

inconsciencia /inkon'sθienθia; in-
konssiensia/ *n. f.* unconscious-
ness.

inconsciente /inkon'sθiente; in-
kons'siente/ *a.* unconscious.

inconsecuencia /inkonse'kuenθia;
inkonse'kuensia/ *n. f.* inconsist-
ency.

inconsecuente /inkonse'kuente/
a. inconsistent.

inconstancia /inkons'tanθia; in-
kons'tansia/ *n. f.* changeableness.

inconstante /inkons'tante/ *a.*
changeable.

inconveniencia /inkombe'nienθia;
inkombe'niensia/ *n. f.* inconvenience; unsuitability.

inconveniente /inkombe'niente/
a. unsuitable. *m.* disadvantage;
objection.

incorporar /inkorpo'rar/ *v.* incorporate, embody.

incorporarse /inkorpo'rarse/ *v.* sit
up.

incorrecto /inko'rrekto/ *a.* incor-
rect, wrong.

incredulidad /inkreðuli'ðað/ *n. f.*
incredulity.

incrédulo /in'kreðulo/ *a.* incredulous.

increíble /inkre'iβle/ *a.* incredible.

incremento /inkre'mento/ *n. m.*
increase.

incubadora /inkuβa'ðora/ *n. f.* incubator.

incubar /inku'βar/ *v.* hatch.

inculto /in'kulto/ *a.* uncultivated.

incumplimento de contrato /in-
kumpli'mento de kon'trato/ *n. m.*
breach of contract.

incurable /inku'raβle/ *a.* incurable.

incurrir /inku'rrir/ *v.* incur.

indagación /indaga'θion; indaga-
'sion/ *n. f.* investigation, inquiry.

indagador /indaga'ðor/ **-ra** *n.* investigator.

indagar /inda'gar/ *v.* investigate,
inquire into.

indebido /inde'βiðo/ *a.* undue.

indecencia /inde'θenθia; inde-
'sensia/ *n. f.* indecency.

indecente /inde'θente; inde'sente/
a. indecent.

indeciso /inde'θiso; inde'siso/ *a.*
undecided.

indefenso /inde'fenso/ *a.* defenseless.

indefinido /indefi'niðo/ *a.* indefinite; undefined.

indeleble /inde'leβle/ *a.* indelible.

indemnización de despido /indemniθa'θion de des'piðo; indemnisa'sion de des'piðo/ *n. f.* severance pay.

indemnizar /indemni'θar; indemni'sar/ *v.* indemnify.

independencia /indepen'denθia; indepen'densia/ *n. f.* independence.

independiente /indepen'diente/ *a.* independent.

indesmallable /indesma'ʎaβle; indesma'yaβle/ *a.* runproof.

India /'india/ *n. f.* India.

indicación /indika'θion; indika'sion/ *n. f.* indication.

indicar /indi'kar/ *v.* indicate, point out.

indicativo /indika'tiβo/ *a. & m.* indicative.

índice /'indiθe; 'indise/ *n. m.* index; forefinger.

índice de materias /'indiθe de ma'terias; 'indise de ma'terias/ table of contents.

indicio /in'diθio; in'disio/ *n. m.* hint, clue.

indiferencia /indife'renθia; indife'rensia/ *n. f.* indifference.

indiferente /indife'rente/ *a.* indifferent.

indígena /in'dihena/ *a. & n.* native.

indigente /indi'hente/ *a.* indigent, poor.

indignación /indigna'θion; indigna'sion/ *n. f.* indignation.

indignado /indig'naðo/ *a.* indignant, incensed.

indignar /indig'nar/ *v.* incense.

indigno /in'digno/ *a.* unworthy.

indio /'indio/ **-dia** *a. & n.* Indian.

indirecto /indi'rekto/ *a.* indirect.

indiscreción /indiskre'θion; indiskre'sion/ *n. f.* indiscretion.

indiscreto /indis'kreto/ *a.* indiscreet.

indiscutible /indisku'tiβle/ *a.* unquestionable.

indispensable /indispen'saβle/ *a.* indispensable.

indisposición /indisposi'θion; indisposi'sion/ *n. f.* indisposition, ailment; reluctance.

indistinto /indis'tinto/ *a.* indistinct, unclear.

individual /indiβi'ðual/ *a.* individual.

individualidad /indiβiðuali'ðað/ *n. f.* individuality.

individuo /indi'βiðuo/ *a. & m.* individual.

indócil /in'doθil; in'dosil/ *a.* headstrong, unruly.

índole /'indole/ *n. f.* nature, character, disposition.

indolencia /indo'lenθia; indo'lensia/ *n. f.* indolence.

indolente /indo'lente/ *a.* indolent.

indómito /in'domito/ *a.* untamed, wild; unruly.

inducir /indu'θir; indu'sir/ *v.* induce, persuade.

indudable /indu'ðaβle/ *a.* certain, indubitable.

indulgencia /indul'henθia; indul'hensia/ *n. f.* indulgence.

indulgente /indul'hente/ *a.* indulgent.

indultar /indul'tar/ *v.* free; pardon.

industria /in'dustria/ *n. f.* industry.

industrial /indus'trial/ *a.* industrial.

industrioso /indus'trioso/ *a.* industrious.

inédito /i'neðito/ *a.* unpublished.

ineficaz /inefi'kaθ; inefi'kas/ *a.* inefficient.

inepto /i'nepto/ *a.* incompetent.

inequívoco /ine'kiβoko/ *a.* unmistakable.

inercia /i'nerθia; i'nersia/ *n. f.* inertia.

inerte /i'nerte/ *a.* inert.

inesperado /inespe'raðo/ *a.* unexpected.

inestable /ines'taβle/ *a.* unstable.

inevitable /ineβi'taβle/ *a.* inevitable.

inexacto /ine'ksakto/ *a.* inexact.

inexperto /ineks'perto/ *a.* unskilled.

inexplicable /inekspli'kaβle/ *a.* inexplicable, unexplainable.

infalible /infa'liβle/ *a.* infallible.

infame /in'fame/ *a.* infamous, bad.

infamia /in'famia/ *n. f.* infamy.

infancia /in'fanθia; in'fansia/ *n. f.* infancy; childhood.

infante /in'fante/ **-ta** *n.* infant.

infantería /infante'ria/ n. f. infantry.

infantil /infan'til/ a. infantile, childish.

infarto (de miocardio) /in'farto de mio'karðio/ n. m. heart attack.

infatigable /infati'gaβle/ a. untiring.

infausto /in'fausto/ a. unlucky.

infección /infek'θion; infek'sion/ n. f. infection.

infeccioso /infek'θioso; infek'sioso/ a. infectious.

infectar /infek'tar/ v. infect.

infeliz /infe'liθ; infe'lis/ a. unhappy, miserable.

inferior /infe'rior/ a. inferior; lower.

inferir /infe'rir/ v. infer; inflict.

infernal /infer'nal/ a. infernal.

infestar /infes'tar/ v. infest.

infiel /in'fiel/ a. unfaithful.

infierno /in'fierno/ n. m. hell.

infiltrar /infil'trar/ v. infiltrate.

infinidad /infini'ðað/ n. f. infinity.

infinito /infi'nito/ a. infinite.

inflación /infla'θion; infla'sion/ n. f. inflation.

inflamable /infla'maβle/ a. flammable.

inflamación /inflama'θion; inflama'sion/ n. f. inflammation.

inflamar /infla'mar/ v. inflame, set on fire.

inflar /in'flar/ v. inflate, pump up, puff up.

inflexible /infle'ksiβle/ a. inflexible, rigid.

inflexión /infle'ksion/ n. f. inflection.

infligir /infli'hir/ v. inflict.

influencia /influ'enθia; influ'ensia/ n. f. influence.

influenza /in'fluenθa; in'fluensa/ n. f. influenza, flu.

influir /influ'ir/ v. influence, sway.

influyente /influ'yente/ a. influential.

información /informa'θion; informa'sion/ n. f. information.

informal /infor'mal/ a. informal.

informar /infor'mar/ v. inform; report.

informática /infor'matika/ n. f. computer science; information technology.

informe /in'forme/ n. m. report; (pl.) information, data.

infortunio /infor'tunio/ n. m. misfortune.

infracción /infrak'θion; infrak'sion/ n. f. violation.

infracetructura /infraθetruk'tura; infrasetruk'tura/ n. f. infrastructure.

infrascrito /infras'krito/ -ta n. signer, undersigned.

infringir /infrin'hir/ v. infringe, violate.

infructuoso /infruk'tuoso/ a. fruitless.

infundir /infun'dir/ v. instil, inspire with.

ingeniería /inhenie'ria/ n. f. engineering.

ingeniero /inhe'niero/ -ra n. engineer.

ingenio /in'henio/ n. m. wit; talent.

ingeniosidad /inheniosi'ðað/ n. f. ingenuity.

ingenioso /inhe'nioso/ a. witty; ingenious.

ingenuidad /inhenui'ðað/ n. f. candor; naïveté.

ingenuo /in'henuo/ a. ingenuous, naïve, candid.

Inglaterra /ingla'terra/ n. f. England.

ingle /'ingle/ n. f. groin.

inglés /iŋ'gles/ -esa a. & n. English; Englishman; Englishwoman.

ingratitud /iŋgrati'tuð/ n. f. ingratitude.

ingrato /iŋ'grato/ a. ungrateful.

ingravidez /iŋgraβi'ðeθ; iŋgraβi'ðes/ n. f. weightlessness.

ingrávido /iŋ'graβiðo/ a. weightless.

ingrediente /iŋgre'ðiente/ n. m. ingredient.

ingresar en /iŋgre'sar en/ v. enter; join.

ingreso /iŋ'greso/ n. m. entrance; (pl.) earnings, income.

inhábil /in'aβil/ a. unskilled; incapable.

inhabilitar /inaβili'tar/ v. disqualify.

inherente /ine'rente/ a. inherent.

inhibir /ini'βir/ v. inhibit.

inhumano /inu'mano/ a. cruel, inhuman.

iniciador /iniθia'ðor; inisia'ðor/ -ra n. initiator.

inicial /ini'θial; ini'sial/ a. initial.

iniciar /ini'θiar; ini'siar/ v. initiate, begin.

iniciativa /iniθia'tiβa; inisia'tiβa/ n. f. initiative.

inicuo /ini'kuo/ *a.* wicked.
iniquidad /iniki'ðað/ *n. f.* iniquity; sin.
injuria /in'huria/ *n. f.* insult.
—**injuriar,** *v.*
injusticia /inhus'tiθia; inhus'tisia/ *n. f.* injustice.
injusto /in'husto/ *a.* unjust, unfair.
inmaculado /imaku'laðo/ *a.* immaculate; pure.
inmediato /ime'ðiato/ *a.* immediate.
inmensidad /imensi'ðað/ *n. f.* immensity.
inmenso /i'menso/ *a.* immense.
inmersión /imer'sion/ *n. f.* immersion.
inmigración /imigra'θion; imigra-'sion/ *n. f.* immigration.
inmigrante /imi'grante/ *a. & n.* immigrant.
inmigrar /imi'grar/ *v.* immigrate.
inminente /imi'nente/ *a.* imminent.
inmoderado /imoðe'raðo/ *a.* immoderate.
inmodesto /imo'ðesto/ *a.* immodest.
inmoral /imo'ral/ *a.* immoral.
inmoralidad /imorali'ðað/ *n. f.* immorality.
inmortal /imor'tal/ *a.* immortal.
inmortalidad /imortali'ðað/ *n. f.* immortality.
inmóvil /i'moβil/ *a.* immobile, motionless.
inmundicia /imun'diθia; imun-'disia/ *n. f.* dirt, filth.
inmune /i'mune/ *a.* immune; exempt.
inmunidad /imuni'ðað/ *n. f.* immunity.
innato /in'nato/ *a.* innate, inborn.
innecesario /inneθe'sario; innese-'sario/ *a.* unnecessary, needless.
innegable /inne'gaβle/ *a.* undeniable.
innoble /in'noβle/ *a.* ignoble.
innocuo /inno'kuo/ *a.* innocuous.
innovación /innoβa'θion; inno-βa'sion/ *n. f.* innovation.
innumerable /innume'raβle/ *a.* innumerable, countless.
inocencia /ino'θenθia; ino'sensia/ *n. f.* innocence.
inocentada /inoθen'taða; inosen-'taða/ *n. f.* practical joke.
inocente /ino'θente; ino'sente/ *a.* innocent.

inocular /inoku'lar/ *v.* inoculate.
inodoro /ino'ðoro/ *n. m.* toilet.
inofensivo /inofen'siβo/ *a.* inoffensive, harmless.
inolvidable /inolβi'ðaβle/ *a.* unforgettable.
inoportuno /inopor'tuno/ *a.* inopportune.
inoxidable /inoksi'ðaβle/ *a.* stainless.
inquietante /inkie'tante/ *a.* disturbing, worrisome, worrying, upsetting.
inquietar /inkie'tar/ *v.* disturb, worry, trouble.
inquieto /in'kieto/ *a.* anxious, uneasy, worried; restless.
inquietud /inkie'tuð/ *n. f.* concern, anxiety, worry; restlessness.
inquilino /inki'lino/ **-na** *n.* occupant, tenant.
inquirir /inki'rir/ *v.* inquire into, investigate.
inquisición /inkisi'θion; inkisi-'sion/ *n. f.* inquisition, investigation.
insaciable /insa'θiaβle; insa'siaβle/ *a.* insatiable.
insalubre /insa'luβre/ *a.* unhealthy.
insano /in'sano/ *a.* insane.
inscribir /inskri'βir/ *v.* inscribe; record.
inscribirse /inskri'βirse/ *v.* register, enroll.
inscripción /inskrip'θion; inskrip-'sion/ *n. f.* inscription; registration.
insecticida /insekti'θiða; insekti-'siða/ *n. m.* insecticide.
insecto /in'sekto/ *n. m.* insect.
inseguro /inse'guro/ *a.* unsure, uncertain; insecure, unsafe.
insensato /insen'sato/ *a.* stupid, senseless.
insensible /insen'siβle/ *a.* unfeeling, heartless.
inseparable /insepa'raβle/ *a.* inseparable.
inserción /inser'θion; inser'sion/ *n. f.* insertion.
insertar /inser'tar/ *v.* insert.
inservible /inser'βiβle/ *a.* useless.
insidioso /insi'ðioso/ *a.* insidious, crafty.
insigne /in'signe/ *a.* famous, noted.
insignia /in'signia/ *n. f.* insignia, badge.

insignificante /insignifi'kante/ *a.* insignificant, negligible.

insincero /insin'θero; insin'sero/ *a.* insincere.

insinuación /insinua'θion; insinua-'sion/ *n. f.* insinuation; hint.

insinuar /insi'nuar/ *v.* insinuate, suggest, hint.

insipidez /insipi'ðeθ; insipi'ðes/ *n. f.* insipidity.

insípido /in'sipiðo/ *a.* insipid.

insistencia /insis'tenθia; insis-'tensia/ *n. f.* insistence.

insistente /insis'tente/ *a.* insistent.

insistir /insis'tir/ *v.* insist.

insolación /insola'θion; insola-'sion/ *n. f.* sunstroke.

insolencia /inso'lenθia; inso-'lensia/ *n. f.* insolence.

insolente /inso'lente/ *a.* insolent.

insólito /in'solito/ *a.* unusual.

insolvente /insol'βente/ *a.* insolvent.

insomnio /in'somnio/ *n. m.* insomnia.

insonorizado /insonori'θaðo; insonori'saðo/ *a.* soundproof.

insonorizar /insonori'θar; insonori'sar/ *v.* soundproof.

insoportable /insopor'taβle/ *a.* unbearable.

inspección /inspek'θion; inspek-'sion/ *n. f.* inspection.

inspeccionar /inspekθio'nar; inspeksio'nar/ *v.* inspect, examine.

inspector /inspek'tor/ **-ra** *n.* inspector.

inspiración /inspira'θion; inspira-'sion/ *n. f.* inspiration.

inspirar /inspi'rar/ *v.* inspire.

instalación /instala'θion; instala-'sion/ *n. f.* installation, fixture.

instalar /insta'lar/ *v.* install, set up.

instantánea /instan'tanea/ *n. f.* snapshot.

instantáneo /instan'taneo/ *a.* instantaneous.

instante /ins'tante/ *a. & m.* instant. **al i.,** at once.

instar /ins'tar/ *v.* coax, urge.

instigar /insti'gar/ *v.* instigate, urge.

instintivo /instin'tiβo/ *a.* instinctive.

instinto /ins'tinto/ *n. m.* instinct. **por i.,** by instinct, instinctively.

institución /institu'θion; institu-'sion/ *n. f.* institution.

instituto /insti'tuto/ *n. m.* institute. **—instituir,** *v.*

institutriz /institu'triθ; institu'tris/ *n. f.* governess.

instrucción /instruk'θion; instruk-'sion/ *n. f.* instruction; education.

instructivo /instruk'tiβo/ *a.* instructive.

instructor /instruk'tor/ **-ra** *n.* instructor.

instruir /ins'truir/ *v.* instruct, teach.

instrumento /instru'mento/ *n. m.* instrument.

insuficiente /insufi'θiente; insufi-'siente/ *a.* insufficient.

insufrible /insu'friβle/ *a.* intolerable.

insular /insu'lar/ *a.* island, insular.

insulto /in'sulto/ *n. m.* insult. **—insultar,** *v.*

insuperable /insupe'raβle/ *a.* insuperable.

insurgente /insur'hente/ *n. & a.* insurgent, rebel.

insurrección /insurrek'θion; insurrek'sion/ *n. f.* insurrection, revolt.

insurrecto /insu'rrekto/ **-ta** *a. & n.* insurgent.

intacto /in'takto/ *a.* intact.

integral /inte'gral/ *a.* integral.

integridad /integri'ðað/ *n. f.* integrity; entirety.

íntegro /'integro/ *a.* entire; upright.

intelecto /inte'lekto/ *n. m.* intellect.

intelectual /intelek'tual/ *a. & n.* intellectual.

inteligencia /inteli'henθia; inteli-'hensia/ *n. f.* intelligence.

inteligente /inteli'hente/ *a.* intelligent.

inteligible /inteli'hiβle/ *a.* intelligible.

intemperie /intem'perie/ *n. f.* bad weather.

intención /inten'θion; inten'sion/ *n. f.* intention.

intendente /inten'dente/ *n. m.* manager.

intensidad /intensi'ðað/ *n. f.* intensity.

intensificar /intensifi'kar/ *v.* intensify.

intensivo /inten'siβo/ *a.* intensive.

intenso /in'tenso/ *a.* intense.

intentar /inten'tar/ *v.* attempt, try.

intento /in'tento/ *n. m.* intent; attempt.

intercambiable /interkam'biaβle/ *a.* interchangeable.

intercambiar /interkam'βiar/ *v.* exchange, interchange.

interceptar /interθep'tar; intersep'tar/ *v.* intercept.

intercesión /interθe'sion; interse-'sion/ *n. f.* intercession.

interés /inte'res/ *n. m.* interest; concern; appeal.

interesante /intere'sante/ *a.* interesting.

interesar /intere'sar/ *v.* interest, appeal to.

interfaz /inter'faθ; inter'fas/ *n. f.* interface.

interferencia /interfe'renθia; interfe'rensia/ *n. f.* interference.

interino /inte'rino/ *a.* temporary.

interior /inte'rior/ *a.* **1.** interior, inner. —*n.* **2.** *m.* interior.

interjección /interhek'θion; interhek'sion/ *n. f.* interjection.

intermedio /inter'meðio/ *a.* **1.** intermediate. —*n.* **2.** *m.* intermediary; intermission.

interminable /intermi'naβle/ *a.* interminable, endless.

intermisión /intermi'sion/ *n. f.* intermission.

intermitente /intermi'tente/ *a.* intermittent.

internacional /internaθio'nal; internasio'nal/ *a.* international.

internarse en /inter'narse en/ *v.* enter into, go into.

Internet, el /inter'net/ *n. m.* the Internet.

interno /in'terno/ *a.* internal.

interpelar /interpe'lar/ *v.* ask questions; implore.

interponer /interpo'ner/ *v.* interpose.

interpretación /interpreta'θion; interpreta'sion/ *n. f.* interpretation.

interpretar /interpre'tar/ *v.* interpret; construe.

intérprete /in'terprete/ *n. m. & f.* interpreter; performer.

interrogación /interroga'θion; interroga'sion/ *n. f.* interrogation.

interrogar /interro'gar/ *v.* question, interrogate.

interrogativo /interroga'tiβo/ *a.* interrogative.

interrumpir /interrum'pir/ *v.* interrupt.

interrupción /interrup'θion; interrup'sion/ *n. f.* interruption.

intersección /intersek'θion; intersek'sion/ *n. f.* intersection.

intervalo /inter'βalo/ *n. m.* interval.

intervención /interβen'θion; interβen'sion/ *n. f.* intervention.

intervenir /interβe'nir/ *v.* intervene, interfere.

intestino /intes'tino/ *n. m.* intestine.

intimación /intima'θion; intima-'sion/ *n. f.* intimation, hint.

intimar /inti'mar/ *v.* suggest, hint.

intimidad /intimi'ðað/ *n. f.* intimacy.

intimidar /intimi'ðar/ *v.* intimidate.

íntimo /'intimo/ **-ma** *a. & n.* intimate.

intolerable /intole'raβle/ *a.* intolerable.

intolerancia /intole'ranθia; intole-'ransia/ *n. f.* intolerance, bigotry.

intolerante /intole'rante/ *a.* intolerant.

intoxicación alimenticia /intoksika'θion alimen'tiθia; intoksika'sion alimen'tisia/ *n. f.* food poisoning.

intranquilo /intran'kilo/ *a.* uneasy.

intravenoso /intraβe'noso/ *a.* intravenous.

intrepidez /intrepi'ðeθ; intrepi'ðes/ *n. f.* daring.

intrépido /in'trepiðo/ *a.* intrepid.

intriga /in'triga/ *n. f.* intrigue, plot, scheme. —**intrigar,** *v.*

intrincado /intrin'kaðo/ *a.* intricate, involved; impenetrable.

introducción /introðuk'θion; introðuk'sion/ *n. f.* introduction.

introducir /introðu'θir; introðu'sir/ *v.* introduce.

intruso /in'truso/ **-sa** *n.* intruder.

intuición /intui'θion; intui'sion/ *n. f.* intuition.

inundación /inunda'θion; inunda'sion/ *n. f.* flood. —**inundar,** *v.*

inútil /i'nutil/ *a.* useless.

invadir /imba'ðir/ *v.* invade.

inválido /im'baliðo/ **-da** *a. & n.* invalid.

invariable /imba'riaβle/ *a.* constant.

invasión /imba'sion/ *n. f.* invasion.

invasor /imba'sor/ **-ra** *n.* invader.

invencible /imben'θiβle; imben-'siβle/ *a.* invincible.

invención /imben'θion; imben-'sion/ *n. f.* invention.

inventar /imben'tar/ *v.* invent; devise.

inventario /imben'tario/ *n. m.* inventory.

inventivo /imben'tiβo/ *a.* inventive.

invento /im'bento/ *n. m.* invention.

inventor /imben'tor/ **-ra** *n.* inventor.

invernáculo /imber'nakulo/ *n. m.* greenhouse.

invernal /imber'nal/ *a.* wintry.

inverosímil /imbero'simil/ *a.* improbable, unlikely.

inversión /imber'sion/ *n. f.* inversion; *Com.* investment.

inverso /im'berso/ *a.* inverse, reverse.

inversor /imber'sor/ **-ra** *n.* investor.

invertir /imber'tir/ *v.* invert; reverse; *Com.* invest.

investigación /imbestiga'θion; imbestiga'sion/ *n. f.* investigation.

investigador /imbestiga'ðor/ **-ra** *n.* investigator; researcher.

investigar /imbesti'gar/ *v.* investigate.

invierno /im'bierno/ *n. m.* winter.

invisible /imbi'siβle/ *a.* invisible.

invitación /imbita'θion; imbita-'sion/ *n. f.* invitation.

invitar /imbi'tar/ *v.* invite.

invocar /imbo'kar/ *v.* invoke.

involuntario /imbolun'tario/ *a.* involuntary.

inyección /inyek'θion; inyek'sion/ *n. f.* injection.

inyectar /inyek'tar/ *v.* inject.

ir /ir/ *v.* go. **irse,** go away, leave.

ira /'ira/ *n. f.* anger, ire.

iracundo /ira'kundo/ *a.* wrathful, irate.

iris /'iris/ *n. m.* iris. **arco i.,** rainbow.

Irlanda /ir'landa/ *n. f.* Ireland.

irlandés /irlan'des/ **-esa** *a. & n.* Irish; Irishman, Irishwoman.

ironía /iro'nia/ *n. f.* irony.

irónico /i'roniko/ *a.* ironical.

irracional /irraθio'nal; irrasio'nal/ *a.* irrational; insane.

irradiación /irraðia'θion; irraðia-'sion/ *n. f.* irradiation.

irradiar /irra'ðiar/ *v.* radiate.

irrazonable /irraθo'naβle; irraso-'naβle/ *a.* unreasonable.

irregular /irregu'lar/ *a.* irregular.

irreligioso /irreli'hioso/ *a.* irreligious.

irremediable /irreme'ðiaβle/ *a.* irremediable, hopeless.

irresistible /irresis'tiβle/ *a.* irresistible.

irresoluto /irreso'luto/ *a.* irresolute, wavering.

irrespetuoso /irrespe'tuoso/ *a.* disrespectful.

irreverencia /irreβe'renθia; irreβe'rensia/ *n. f.* irreverence.

irreverente /irreβe'rente/ *adj.* irreverent.

irrigación /irriga'θion; irriga'sion/ *n. f.* irrigation.

irrigar /irri'gar/ *v.* irrigate.

irritación /irrita'θion; irrita'sion/ *n. f.* irritation.

irritar /irri'tar/ *v.* irritate.

irrupción /irrup'θion; irrup'sion/ *n. f.* raid, attack.

isla /'isla/ *n. f.* island.

isleño /is'leɲo/ **-ña** *n.* islander.

israelita /israe'lita/ *n. & a.* Israelite.

Italia /i'talia/ *n. f.* Italy.

italiano /ita'liano/ **-na** *a. & n.* Italian.

itinerario /itine'rario/ *n. m.* itinerary; timetable.

IVA, *abbrev.* (**impuesto sobre el valor añadido**) VAT (value-added tax).

izar /i'θar; i'sar/ *v.* hoist.

izquierda /iθ'kierða; is'kierða/ *n. f.* left (hand, side).

izquierdista /iθ'kierðista; is'kierðista/ *n. & a.* leftist.

izquierdo /iθ'kierðo; is'kierðo/ *a.* left.

J

jabalí /ha'βa'li/ *n. m.* wild boar.

jabón /ha'βon/ *n. m.* soap. **j. en polvo,** soap powder.

jabonar /haβo'nar/ *v.* soap.

jaca /'haka/ *n. f.* nag.

jacinto /ha'θinto; ha'sinto/ *n. m.* hyacinth.

jactancia /hak'tanθia; hak'tansia/ *n. f.* boast. —**jactarse,** *v.*

jactancioso /haktan'θioso; haktan'sioso/ *a.* boastful.

jadear /haðe'ar/ *v.* pant, puff.

jaez /ha'eθ; ha'es/ *n. m.* harness; kind.

jalar /ha'lar/ *v.* haul, pull.

jalea /ha'lea/ *n. f.* jelly.

jaleo /ha'leo/ *n. m.* row, uproar; hassle.

jamás /ha'mas/ *adv.* never, ever.

jamón /ha'mon/ *n. m.* ham.

Japón /ha'pon/ *n. m.* Japan.

japonés /hapo'nes/ **-esa** *a. & n.* Japanese.

jaqueca /ha'keka/ *n. f.* headache.

jarabe /ha'raβe/ *n. m.* syrup.

jaranear /harane'ar/ *v.* jest; carouse.

jardín /har'ðin/ *n. m.* garden.

jardín de infancia /har'ðin de in'fanθia; har'ðin de in'fansia/ nursery school.

jardinero /harði'nero/ **-ra** *n.* gardener.

jarra /'harra/ *n. f.* jar; pitcher.

jarro /'harro/ *n. m.* jug, pitcher.

jaspe /'haspe/ *n. m.* jasper.

jaula /'haula/ *n. f.* cage; coop.

jauría /hau'ria/ *n. f.* pack of hounds.

jazmín /haθ'min; has'min/ *n. m.* jasmine.

jefatura /hefa'tura/ *n. f.* headquarters.

jefe /'hefe/ **-fa** *n.* chief, boss.

jefe de comedor /'hefe de kome-'ðor/ headwaiter.

jefe de sala /'hefe de 'sala/ maître d'.

jefe de taller /'hefe de ta'ʎer; 'hefe de ta'yer/ foreman.

Jehová /heo'βa/ *n. m.* Jehovah.

jengibre /hen'hiβre/ *n. m.* ginger.

jerez /he'reθ; he'res/ *n. m.* sherry.

jerga /'herga/ *n. f.* slang.

jergón /her'gon/ *n. m.* straw mattress.

jerigonza /heri'gonθa; heri'gonsa/ *n. f.* jargon.

jeringa /he'ringa/ *n. f.* syringe.

jeringar /herin'gar/ *v.* inject; annoy.

jeroglífico /hero'glifiko/ *n. m.* hieroglyph.

jersey /her'sei/ *n. m.* pullover; **j. de cuello alto,** turtleneck sweater.

Jerusalén /herusa'len/ *n. m.* Jerusalem.

jesuita /he'suita/ *n. m.* Jesuit.

Jesús /he'sus/ *n. m.* Jesus.

jeta /'heta/ *n. f.* snout.

jícara /'hikara/ *n. f.* cup.

jinete /hi'nete/ **-ta** *n.* horseman.

jingoísmo /hingo'ismo/ *n. m.* jingoism.

jingoísta /hingo'ista/ *n. & a.* jingoist.

jira /'hira/ *n. f.* picnic; outing.

jirafa /hi'rafa/ *n. f.* giraffe.

jiu-jitsu /hiu'hitsu/ *n. m.* jujitsu.

jocundo /ho'kundo/ *a.* jovial.

jornada /hor'naða/ *n. f.* journey; day's work.

jornal /hor'nal/ *n. m.* day's wage.

jornalero /horna'lero/ *n. m.* day laborer, workman.

joroba /ho'roβa/ *n. f.* hump.

jorobado /horo'βaðo/ *a.* humpbacked.

joven /'hoβen/ *a.* **1.** young. —*n.* **2.** *m. & f.* young person.

jovial /ho'βial/ *a.* jovial, jolly.

jovialidad /hoβiali'ðað/ *n. f.* joviality.

joya /'hoia/ *n. f.* jewel, gem.

joyas de fantasía /'hoias de fanta'sia/ *n. f.pl.* costume jewelry.

joyelero /hoie'lero/ *n. m.* jewel box.

joyería /hoie'ria/ *n. f.* jewelry; jewelry store.

joyero /ho'iero/ *n. m.* jeweler; jewel case.

juanete /hua'nete/ *n. m.* bunion.

jubilación /huβila'θion; huβila'sion/ *n. f.* retirement; pension.

jubilar /huβi'lar/ *v.* retire, pension.

jubileo /huβi'leo/ *n. m.* jubilee, public festivity.

júbilo /'huβilo/ *n. m.* glee, rejoicing.

jubiloso /huβi'loso/ *a.* joyful, gay.

judaico /hu'ðaiko/ *a.* Jewish.

judaísmo /huða'ismo/ *n. m.* Judaism.

judía /hu'ðia/ *n. f.* bean, string bean.

judicial /huði'θial; huði'sial/ *a.* judicial.

judío /hu'ðio/ **-día** *a. & n.* Jewish; Jew.

juego /'huego/ *n. m.* game; play; gambling; set. **j. de damas,** checkers. **j. limpio,** fair play.

Juegos Olímpicos /huegos o'limpikos/ *n. m.pl.* Olympic Games.

juerga /'huerga/ *n. f.* spree.

jueves /'hueβes/ *n. m.* Thursday.

juez /hueθ; hues/ *n. m.* judge.

jugador /huga'ðor/ **-ra** *n.* player.

jugar /hu'gar/ *v.* play; gamble.

juglar /hug'lar/ *n. m.* minstrel.

jugo /'hugo/ *n. m.* juice. **j. de naranja,** orange juice.

jugoso /hu'goso/ *a.* juicy.

juguete /hu'gete/ *n. m.* toy, plaything.

juguetear /hugete'ar/ *v.* trifle.

juguetón /huge'ton/ *a.* playful.

juicio /'huiθio; 'huisio/ *n. m.* sense, wisdom, judgment; sanity; trial.

juicioso /hui'θioso; hui'sioso/ *a.* wise, judicious.

julio /'hulio/ *n. m.* July.

jumento /hu'mento/ *n. m.* donkey.

junco /'hunko/ *n. m.* reed, rush.

jungla /'huŋgla/ *n. f.* jungle.

junio /'hunio/ *n. m.* June.

junípero /hu'nipero/ *n. m.* juniper.

junquillo /hun'kiʎo; hun'kiyo/ *n. m.* jonquil.

junta /'hunta/ *n. f.* board, council; joint, coupling.

juntamente /hunta'mente/ *adv.* jointly.

juntar /hun'tar/ *v.* join; connect; assemble.

junto /'hunto/ *a.* together. **j. a,** next to.

juntura /hun'tura/ *n. f.* joint, juncture.

jurado /hu'raðo/ *n. m.* jury.

juramento /hura'mento/ *n. m.* oath.

jurar /hu'rar/ *v.* swear.

jurisconsulto /huriskon'sulto/ *n. m.* jurist.

jurisdicción /hurisðik'θion; hurisðik'sion/ *n. f.* jurisdiction; territory.

jurisprudencia /hurispru'ðenθia; hurispru'ðensia/ *n. f.* jurisprudence.

justa /'husta/ *n. f.* joust. **—justar,** *v.*

justicia /hus'tiθia; hus'tisia/ *n. f.* justice, equity.

justiciero /husti'θiero; husti'siero/ *a.* just.

justificación /hustifika'θion; hustifika'sion/ *n. f.* justification.

justificadamente /hustifikaða'mente/ *adv.* justifiably.

justificar /hustifi'kar/ *v.* justify, warrant.

justo /'husto/ *a.* right; exact; just; righteous.

juvenil /huβe'nil/ *a.* youthful.

juventud /huβen'tuð/ *n. f.* youth.

juzgado /huθ'gaðo; hus'gaðo/ *n. m.* court.

juzgar /huθ'gar; hus'gar/ *v.* judge, estimate.

K L

káiser /'kaiser/ *n. m.* kaiser.

karate /ka'rate/ *n. m.* karate.

kepis /'kepis/ *n. m.* military cap.

kerosena /kero'sena/ *n. f.* kerosene.

kilo /'kilo/ **kilogramo** *n. m.* kilogram.

kilohercio /kilo'erθio; kilo'ersio/ *n. m.* kilohertz.

kilolitro /kilo'litro/ *n. m.* kiloliter.

kilometraje /kilome'trahe/ *n. m.* mileage.

kilómetro /ki'lometro/ *n. m.* kilometer.

kiosco /'kiosko/ *n. m.* newsstand; pavilion.

la /la/ *art. & pron.* **1.** the; the one. **—pron. 2.** her, it, you; (*pl.*) them, you.

laberinto /laβe'rinto/ *n. m.* labyrinth, maze.

labia /'laβia/ *n. f.* eloquence, fluency.

labio /'laβio/ *n. m.* lip.

labor /la'βor/ *n. f.* labor, work.

laborar /laβo'rar/ *v.* work; till.

laboratorio /laβora'torio/ *n. m.* laboratory.

laborioso /laβo'rioso/ a. industrious.

labrador /laβra'ðor/ n. m. farmer.

labranza /la'βranθa; la'βransa/ n. f. farming; farmland.

labrar /la'βrar/ v. work, till.

labriego /la'βriego/ -ga n. peasant.

laca /'laka/ n. f. shellac.

lacio /'laθio; 'lasio/ a. withered; limp; straight.

lactar /lak'tar/ v. nurse, suckle.

lácteo /'lakteo/ a. milky.

ladear /laðe'ar/ v. tilt, tip; sway.

ladera /la'ðera/ n. f. slope.

ladino /la'ðino/ a. cunning, crafty.

lado /'laðo/ n. m. side. **al l. de,** beside. **de l.,** sideways.

ladra /'laðra/ n. f. barking. —**ladrar,** v.

ladrillo /la'ðriʎo; la'ðriyo/ n. m. brick.

ladrón /la'ðron/ -ona n. thief, robber.

lagarto /la'garto/ n. m. lizard; (Mex.) alligator.

lago /'lago/ n. m. lake.

lágrima /'lagrima/ n. f. tear.

lagrimear /lagrime'ar/ v. weep, cry.

laguna /la'guna/ n. f. lagoon; gap.

laico /'laiko/ a. lay.

laja /'laha/ n. f. stone slab.

lamentable /lamen'taβle/ a. lamentable.

lamentación /lamenta'θion; lamenta'sion/ n. f. lamentation.

lamentar /lamen'tar/ v. lament; wail; regret, be sorry.

lamento /la'mento/ n. m. lament, wail.

lamer /la'mer/ v. lick; lap.

lámina /'lamina/ n. f. print, illustration.

lámpara /'lampara/ n. f. lamp.

lampiño /lam'piɲo/ a. beardless.

lana /'lana/ n. f. wool.

lanar /la'nar/ a. woolen.

lance /'lanθe; 'lanse/ n. m. throw; episode; quarrel.

lancha /'lantʃa/ n. f. launch; small boat.

lanchón /lan'tʃon/ n. m. barge.

langosta /laŋ'gosta/ n. f. lobster; locust.

langostino /laŋgos'tino/ n. m. king prawn.

languidecer /laŋguiðe'θer; laŋguiðe'ser/ v. languish, pine.

languidez /laŋgui'ðeθ; laŋgui'ðes/ n. f. languidness.

lánguido /'laŋguiðo/ a. languid.

lanza /'lanθa; 'lansa/ n. f. lance, spear.

lanzada /lan'θaða; lan'saða/ n. f. thrust, throw.

lanzar /lan'θar; lan'sar/ v. throw, hurl; launch.

lañar /la'ɲar/ v. cramp; clamp.

lapicero /lapi'θero; lapi'sero/ n. m. mechanical pencil.

lápida /'lapiða/ n. f. stone; tombstone.

lápiz /'lapiθ; 'lapis/ n. m. pencil; crayon.

lápiz de ojos /'lapiθ de 'ohos; 'lapis de 'ohos/ n. m. eyeliner.

lapso /'lapso/ n. m. lapse.

lardo /'larðo/ n. m. lard.

largar /lar'gar/ v. loosen; free.

largo /'largo/ a. **1.** long. **a lo l. de,** along. —n. **2.** m. length.

largometraje /largome'trahe/ n. m. feature film.

largor /lar'gor/ n. m. length.

largueza /lar'geθa; lar'gesa/ n. f. generosity; length.

largura /lar'gura/ n. f. length.

laringe /la'rinhe/ n. f. larynx.

larva /'larβa/ n. f. larva.

lascivia /las'θiβia; las'siβia/ n. f. lasciviousness.

lascivo /las'θiβo; las'siβo/ a. lascivious.

láser /'laser/ n. m. laser.

laso /'laso/ a. weary.

lástima /'lastima/ n. f. pity. **ser l.,** to be a pity, to be too bad.

lastimar /lasti'mar/ v. hurt, injure.

lastimoso /lasti'moso/ a. pitiful.

lastre /'lastre/ n. m. ballast. —**lastrar,** v.

lata /'lata/ n. f. tin can; tin (plate); Colloq. annoyance, bore.

latente /la'tente/ a. latent.

lateral /late'ral/ a. lateral, side.

latigazo /lati'gaθo; lati'gaso/ n. m. lash, whipping.

látigo /'latigo/ n. m. whip.

latín /la'tin/ n. m. Latin (language).

latino /la'tino/ a. Latin.

latir /la'tir/ v. beat, pulsate.

latitud /lati'tuð/ n. f. latitude.

latón /la'ton/ n. m. brass.

laúd /la'uð/ n. m. lute.

laudable /lau'ðaβle/ a. laudable.

láudano /'lauðano/ n. m. laudanum.

laurel /lau'rel/ *n. m.* laurel.

lava /'laβa/ *n. f.* lava.

lavabo /la'βaβo/ **lavamanos** *n. m.* washroom, lavatory.

lavadora /laβa'ðora/ *n. f.* washing machine.

lavandera /laβan'dera/ *n. f.* washerwoman, laundress.

lavandería /laβande'ria/ *f.* laundry; laundromat.

lavaplatos /laβa'platos/ *n.* **1.** *m.* dishwasher (machine). —*n.* **2.** *m.* & *f.* dishwasher (person).

lavar /la'βar/ *v.* wash.

lavatorio /laβa'torio/ *n. m.* lavatory.

laya /'laia/ *n. f.* spade. —**layar,** *v.*

lazar /la'θar; la'sar/ *v.* lasso.

lazareto /laθa'reto; lasa'reto/ *n. m.* isolation hospital; quarantine station.

lazo /'laθo; 'laso/ *n. m.* tie, knot; bow; loop.

le /le/ *pron.* him, her, you; (*pl.*) them, you.

leal /le'al/ *a.* loyal.

lealtad /leal'tað/ *n. f.* loyalty, allegiance.

lebrel /le'βrel/ *n. m.* greyhound.

lección /lek'θion; lek'sion/ *n. f.* lesson.

leche /'letʃe/ *n. f.* milk.

lechería /letʃe'ria/ *n. f.* dairy.

lechero /le'tʃero/ *n. m.* milkman.

lecho /'letʃo/ *n. m.* bed; couch.

lechón /le'tʃon/ *n. m.* pig.

lechoso /le'tʃoso/ *a.* milky.

lechuga /le'tʃuga/ *n. f.* lettuce.

lechuza /le'tʃuθa; le'tʃusa/ *n. f.* owl.

lecito /le'θito; le'sito/ *n. m.* yolk.

lector /lek'tor/ **-ra** *n.* reader.

lectura /lek'tura/ *n. f.* reading.

leer /le'er/ *v.* read.

legación /lega'θion; lega'sion/ *f.* legation.

legado /le'gaðo/ *n. m.* bequest.

legal /le'gal/ *a.* legal, lawful.

legalizar /legali'θar; legali'sar/ *v.* legalize.

legar /le'gar/ *v.* bequeath, leave, will.

legible /le'hiβle/ *a.* legible.

legión /le'hion/ *n. f.* legion.

legislación /lehisla'θion; lehisla-'sion/ *n. f.* legislation.

legislador /lehisla'ðor/ **-ra** *n.* legislator.

legislar /lehis'lar/ *v.* legislate.

legislativo /lehisla'tiβo/ *a.* legislative.

legislatura /lehisla'tura/ *n. f.* legislature.

legítimo /le'hitimo/ *a.* legitimate.

lego /'lego/ *n. m.* layman.

legua /'legua/ *n. f.* league (measure).

legumbre /le'gumbre/ *n. f.* vegetable.

lejano /le'hano/ *a.* distant, far-off.

lejía /le'hia/ *n. f.* lye.

lejos /'lehos/ *adv.* far. **a lo l.,** in the distance.

lelo /'lelo/ *a.* stupid, foolish.

lema /'lema/ *n. m.* theme; slogan.

lengua /'leŋgua/ *n. f.* tongue; language.

lenguado /leŋ'guaðo/ *n. m.* sole, flounder.

lenguaje /leŋ'guahe/ *n. m.* speech; language.

lenguaraz /leŋgua'raθ; leŋgua'ras/ *a.* talkative.

lente /'lente/ *n.* **1.** *m. or f.* lens. **2.** *m.pl.* eyeglasses.

lenteja /len'teha/ *n. f.* lentil.

lentilla /len'tiʎa; len'tiya/ *n. f.* contact lens.

lentitud /lenti'tuð/ *n. f.* slowness.

lento /'lento/ *a.* slow.

leña /'leɲa/ *n. f.* wood, firewood.

león /le'on/ *n. m.* lion.

leopardo /leo'parðo/ *n. m.* leopard.

lerdo /'lerðo/ *a.* dull-witted.

lesbiana /les'βiana/ *n. f.* lesbian.

lesión /le'sion/ *n. f.* wound; damage.

letanía /leta'nia/ *n. f.* litany.

letárgico /le'tarhiko/ *a.* lethargic.

letargo /le'targo/ *n. m.* lethargy.

letra /'letra/ *n. f.* letter (of alphabet); print; words (of a song).

letrado /le'traðo/ *a.* **1.** learned. —*n.* **2.** *m.* lawyer.

letrero /le'trero/ *n. m.* sign, poster.

leva /'leβa/ *n. f. Mil.* draft.

levadura /leβa'ðura/ *n. f.* yeast, leavening, baking powder.

levantador /leβanta'ðor/ *n. m.* lifter; rebel, mutineer.

levantar /leβan'tar/ *v.* raise, lift.

levantarse /leβan'tarse/ *v.* rise, get up; stand up.

levar /le'βar/ *v.* weigh (anchor).

leve /'leβe/ *a.* slight, light.

levita /le'βita/ *n. f.* frock coat.

léxico /'leksiko/ *n. m.* lexicon, dictionary.
ley /lei/ *n. f.* law, statute.
leyenda /le'ienda/ *n. f.* legend.
lezna /'leθna; 'lesna/ *n. f.* awl.
libación /liβa'θion; liβa'sion/ *n. f.* libation.
libelo /li'βelo/ *n. m.* libel.
libélula /li'βelula/ *n. f.* dragonfly.
liberación /liβera'θion; liβera'sion/ *n. f.* liberation, release.
liberal /liβe'ral/ *a.* liberal.
libertad /liβer'taδ/ *n. f.* liberty, freedom.
libertador /liβerta'δor/ **-ra** *n.* liberator.
libertar /liβer'tar/ *v.* free, liberate.
libertinaje /liβerti'nahe/ *n. m.* licentiousness.
libertino /liβer'tino/ **-na** *n.* libertine.
libídine /li'βiδine/ *n. f.* licentiousness; lust.
libidinoso /liβiδi'noso/ *a.* libidinous; lustful.
libra /'liβra/ *n. f.* pound.
libranza /li'βranθa; li'βransa/ *n. f.* draft, bill of exchange.
librar /li'βrar/ *v.* free, rid.
libre /'liβre/ *a.* free, unoccupied.
librería /liβre'ria/ *n. f.* bookstore.
librero /li'βrero/ **-ra** *n.* bookseller.
libreta /li'βreta/ *n. f.* notebook; booklet.
libreto /li'βreto/ *n. m.* libretto.
libro /'liβro/ *n. m.* book.
libro de texto /'liβro de 'teksto/ textbook.
licencia /li'θenθia; li'sensia/ *n. f.* permission, license, leave; furlough. **l. de armas,** gun permit.
licenciado /liθen'θiaδo; lisen'siaδo/ **-da** *n.* graduate.
licencioso /liθen'θioso; lisen'sioso/ *a.* licentious.
lícito /'liθito; 'lisito/ *a.* lawful.
licor /li'kor/ *n. m.* liquor.
licuadora /likua'δora/ *n. f.* blender (for food).
lid /liδ/ *n. f.* fight. —**lidiar,** *v.*
líder /'liδer/ *n. m. & f.* leader.
liebre /'lieβre/ *n. f.* hare.
lienzo /'lienθo; 'lienso/ *n. m.* linen.
liga /'liga/ *n. f.* league, confederacy; garter.
ligadura /liga'δura/ *n. f.* ligature.
ligar /li'gar/ *v.* tie, bind, join.
ligero /li'hero/ *a.* light; fast, nimble.

ligustro /li'gustro/ *n. m.* privet.
lija /'liha/ *n. f.* sandpaper.
lijar /li'har/ *v.* sandpaper.
lima /'lima/ *n. f.* file; lime.
limbo /'limbo/ *n. m.* limbo.
limitación /limita'θion; limita'sion/ *n. f.* limitation.
límite /'limite/ *n. m.* limit. —**limitar,** *v.*
limo /'limo/ *n. m.* slime.
limón /li'mon/ *n. m.* lemon.
limonada /limo'naδa/ *n. f.* lemonade.
limonero /limo'nero/ *n. m.* lemon tree.
limosna /li'mosna/ *n. f.* alms.
limosnero /limos'nero/ **-ra** *n.* beggar.
limpiabotas /limpia'βotas/ *n. m.* bootblack.
limpiadientes /limpia'δientes/ *m.* toothpick.
limpiar /lim'piar/ *v.* clean, wash, wipe.
límpido /'limpiδo/ *a.* limpid, clear.
limpieza /lim'pieθa; lim'piesa/ *f.* cleanliness.
limpio /'limpio/ *n. m.* clean.
limusina /limu'sina/ *n. f.* limousine.
linaje /li'nahe/ *n. m.* lineage, ancestry.
linaza /li'naθa; li'nasa/ *n. f.* linseed.
lince /'linθe; 'linse/ *a.* sharp-sighted, observing.
linchamiento /lintʃa'miento/ *n. m.* lynching.
linchar /lin'tʃar/ *v.* lynch.
lindar /lin'dar/ *v.* border, bound.
linde /'linde/ *n. m.* boundary; landmark.
lindero /lin'dero/ *n. m.* boundary.
lindo /'lindo/ *a.* pretty, lovely, nice.
línea /'linea/ *n. f.* line.
línea de puntos /'linea de 'puntos/ dotted line.
lineal /line'al/ *a.* lineal.
linfa /'linfa/ *n. f.* lymph.
lingüista /liŋ'guista/ *n. m. & f.* linguist.
lingüístico /liŋ'guistiko/ *a.* linguistic.
linimento /lini'mento/ *n. m.* liniment.
lino /'lino/ *n. m.* linen; flax.
linóleo /li'noleo/ *n. m.* linoleum.
linterna /lin'terna/ *n. f.* lantern; flashlight.

lío /'lio/ *n. m.* pack, bundle; mess; scrape; hassle.

liquidación /likiða'θion; likiða-'sion/ *n. f.* liquidation.

liquidar /liki'ðar/ *v.* liquidate; settle up.

líquido /'likiðo/ *a. & m.* liquid.

lira /'lira/ *n. f.* lyre.

lírico /'liriko/ *a.* lyric.

lirio /'lirio/ *n. m.* lily.

lirismo /li'rismo/ *n. m.* lyricism.

lis /lis/ *n. f.* lily.

lisiar /li'siar/ *v.* cripple, lame.

liso /'liso/ *a.* smooth, even.

lisonja /li'sonha/ *n. f.* flattery.

lisonjear /lisonhe'ar/ *v.* flatter.

lisonjero /lison'hero/ **-ra** *n.* flatterer.

lista /'lista/ *n. f.* list; stripe; menu.

lista negra /'lista 'negra/ blacklist.

listar /lis'tar/ *v.* list; put on a list.

listo /'listo/ *a.* ready; smart, clever.

listón /lis'ton/ *n. m.* ribbon.

litera /li'tera/ *n. f.* litter, bunk, berth.

literal /lite'ral/ *a.* literal.

literario /lite'rario/ *a.* literary.

literato /lite'rato/ *n. m.* literary person, writer.

literatura /litera'tura/ *n. f.* literature.

litigación /litiga'θion; litiga'sion/ *n. f.* litigation.

litigio /li'tihio/ *n. m.* litigation; lawsuit.

litoral /lito'ral/ *n. m.* coast.

litro /'litro/ *n. m.* liter.

liturgia /li'turhia/ *n. f.* liturgy.

liviano /li'βiano/ *a.* light (in weight).

lívido /'liβiðo/ *a.* livid.

llaga /'ʎaga; 'yaga/ *n. f.* sore.

llama /'ʎama; 'yama/ *n. f.* flame; llama.

llamada /ʎa'maða; ya'maða/ *n. f.* call; knock. —**llamar,** *v.*

llamarse /ʎa'marse; ya'marse/ *v.* be called, be named. **se llama...** etc., his name is... etc.

llamativo /ʎama'tiβo; yama'tiβo/ *a.* gaudy, showy.

llamear /ʎame'ar; yame'ar/ *v.* blaze.

llaneza /ʎa'neθa; ya'nesa/ *n. f.* simplicity.

llano /'ʎano; 'yano/ *a.* **1.** flat, level; plain. —*n.* **2.** *m.* plain.

llanta /'ʎanta; 'yanta/ *n. f.* tire.

llanto /'ʎanto; 'yanto/ *n. m.* crying, weeping.

llanura /ʎa'nura; ya'nura/ *n. f.* prairie, plain.

llave /'ʎaβe; 'yaβe/ *n. f.* key; wrench; faucet; *Elec.* switch. **ll. inglesa,** monkey wrench.

llegada /ʎe'gaða; ye'gaða/ *n. f.* arrival.

llegar /ʎe'gar; ye'gar/ *v.* arrive; reach. **ll. a ser,** become, come to be.

llenar /ʎe'nar; ye'nar/ *v.* fill.

lleno /'ʎeno; 'yeno/ *a.* full.

llenura /ʎe'nura; ye'nura/ *n. f.* abundance.

llevadero /ʎeβa'ðero; yeβa'ðero/ *a.* tolerable.

llevar /ʎe'βar; ye'βar/ *v.* take, carry, bear; wear (clothes); **ll. a cabo,** carry out.

llevarse /ʎe'βarse; ye'βarse/ *v.* take away, run away with. **ll. bien,** get along well.

llorar /ʎo'rar; yo'rar/ *v.* cry, weep.

lloroso /ʎo'roso; yo'roso/ *a.* sorrowful, tearful.

llover /ʎo'βer; yo'βer/ *v.* rain.

llovido /ʎo'βiðo; yo'βiðo/ *n. m.* stowaway.

llovizna /ʎo'βiθna; yo'βisna/ *n. f.* drizzle, sprinkle. —**lloviznar,** *v.*

lluvia /'ʎuβia; 'yuβia/ *n. f.* rain.

lluvia ácida /'ʎuβia 'aθiða; 'yuβia 'asiða/ acid rain.

lluvioso /ʎu'βioso; yu'βioso/ *a.* rainy.

lo /lo/ *pron.* the; him, it, you; (*pl.*) them, you.

loar /lo'ar/ *v.* praise, laud.

lobina /lo'βina/ *n. f.* striped bass.

lobo /'loβo/ *n. m.* wolf.

lóbrego /'loβrego/ *a.* murky; dismal.

local /lo'kal/ *a.* **1.** local. —*n.* **2.** *m.* site.

localidad /lokali'ðað/ *n. f.* locality, location; seat (in theater).

localizar /lokali'θar; lokali'sar/ *v.* localize.

loción /lo'θion; lo'sion/ *n. f.* lotion.

loco /'loko/ **-ca** *a.* **1.** crazy, insane, mad. —*n.* **2.** lunatic.

locomotora /lokomo'tora/ *n. f.* locomotive.

locuaz /lo'kuaθ; lo'kuas/ *a.* loquacious.

locución /loku'θion; loku'sion/ *n. f.* locution, expression.

locura /lo'kura/ *n. f.* folly; madness, insanity.

lodo /'loðo/ *n. m.* mud.

lodoso /lo'ðoso/ *a.* muddy.

lógica /'lohika/ *n. f.* logic.

lógico /'lohiko/ *a.* logical.

lograr /lo'grar/ *v.* achieve; succeed in.

logro /'logro/ *n. m.* accomplishment.

lombriz /lom'βriθ; lom'βris/ *n. f.* earthworm.

lomo /'lomo/ *n. m.* loin; back (of an animal).

lona /'lona/ *n. f.* canvas, tarpaulin.

longevidad /lonheβi'ðað/ *n. f.* longevity.

longitud /lonhi'tuð/ *n. f.* longitude; length.

lonja /'lonha/ *n. f.* shop; market.

lontananza /lonta'nanθa; lonta-'nansa/ *n. f.* distance.

loro /'loro/ *n. m.* parrot.

losa /'losa/ *n. f.* slab.

lote /'lote/ *n. m.* lot, share.

lotería /lote'ria/ *n. f.* lottery.

loza /'loθa; 'losa/ *n. f.* china, crockery.

lozanía /loθa'nia; losa'nia/ *n. f.* freshness, vigor.

lozano /lo'θano; lo'sano/ *a.* fresh, spirited.

lubricación /luβrika'θion; luβrika-'sion/ *n. f.* lubrication.

lubricar /luβri'kar/ *v.* lubricate.

lucero /lu'θero; lu'sero/ *n. m.* (bright) star.

lucha /'lutʃa/ *n. f.* fight, struggle; wrestling. **—luchar,** *v.*

luchador /lutʃa'ðor/ **-ra** *n.* fighter, wrestler.

lúcido /lu'θiðo; lu'siðo/ *a.* lucid, clear.

luciente /lu'θiente; lu'siente/ *a.* shining, bright.

luciérnaga /lu'θiernaga; lu'sier-naga/ *n. f.* firefly.

lucimiento /luθi'miento; lusi-'miento/ *n. m.* success; splendor.

lucir /lu'θir; lu'sir/ *v.* shine, sparkle; show off.

lucrativo /lukra'tiβo/ *a.* lucrative, profitable.

luego /'luego/ *adv.* right away; afterwards, next. **l. que,** as soon as. **desde l.,** of course. **hasta l.,** good-bye, so long.

lugar /lu'gar/ *n. m.* place, spot; space, room.

lúgubre /'luguβre/ *a.* gloomy; dismal.

lujo /'luho/ *n. m.* luxury. **de l.,** deluxe.

lujoso /lu'hoso/ *a.* luxurious.

lumbre /'lumbre/ *n. f.* fire; light.

luminoso /lumi'noso/ *a.* luminous.

luna /'luna/ *n. f.* moon.

lunar /lu'nar/ *n. m.* beauty mark, mole; polka dot.

lunático /lu'natiko/ **-ca** *a. & n.* lunatic.

lunes /'lunes/ *n. m.* Monday.

luneta /lu'neta/ *n. f. Theat.* orchestra seat.

lupa /'lupa/ *n. f.* magnifying glass.

lustre /'lustre/ *n. m.* polish, shine. **—lustrar,** *v.*

lustroso /lus'troso/ *a.* shiny.

luto /'luto/ *n. m.* mourning.

luz /luθ; lus/ *n. f.* light. **dar a l.,** give birth to.

M

maca /'maka/ *n. f.* blemish, flaw.

macaco /ma'kako/ *a.* ugly, horrid.

macareno /maka'reno/ *a.* boasting.

macarrones /maka'rrones/ *n. m.pl.* macaroni.

macear /maθe'ar; mase'ar/ *v.* molest, push around.

macedonia de frutas /maθe'ðonia de 'frutas; mase'ðonia de 'frutas/ *n. f.* fruit salad.

maceta /ma'θeta; ma'seta/ *n. f.* vase; mallet.

machacar /matʃa'kar/ *v.* pound; crush.

machina /ma'tʃina/ *n. f.* derrick.

machista /ma'tʃista/ *a.* macho.

macho /'matʃo/ *n. m.* male.

machucho /ma'tʃutʃo/ *a.* mature, wise.

macizo /ma'θiθo; ma'siso/ *a.* **1.** solid. **—n. 2.** *m.* bulk; flower bed.

macular /maku'lar/ *v.* stain.

madera /ma'ðera/ *n. f.* lumber; wood.

madero /ma'ðero/ *n. m.* beam, timber.

madrastra /ma'ðrastra/ *n. f.* stepmother.

madre /'maðre/ *n. f.* mother. **m. política,** mother-in-law.

madreperla /maðre'perla/ *n. f.* mother-of-pearl.

madriguera /maðri'gera/ *n. f.* burrow; lair, den.

madrina /ma'ðrina/ *n. f.* godmother.

madroncillo /maðron'θiʎo; maðron'siyo/ *n. m.* strawberry.

madrugada /maðru'gaða/ *n. f.* daybreak.

madrugar /maðru'gar/ *v.* get up early.

madurar /maðu'rar/ *v.* ripen.

madurez /maðu'reθ; maðu'res/ *n. f.* maturity.

maduro /ma'ðuro/ *a.* ripe; mature.

maestría /maes'tria/ *n. f.* mastery; master's degree.

maestro /ma'estro/ *n. m.* master; teacher.

mafia /'mafia/ *n. f.* mafia.

maganto /ma'ganto/ *a.* lethargic, dull.

magia /'mahia/ *n. f.* magic.

mágico /'mahiko/ *a. & m.* magic; magician.

magistrado /mahis'traðo/ *n. m.* magistrate.

magnánimo /mag'nanimo/ *a.* magnanimous.

magnético /mag'netiko/ *a.* magnetic.

magnetismo /magne'tismo/ *n. m.* magnetism.

magnetófono /magne'tofono/ *n. m.* tape recorder.

magnificar /magnifi'kar/ *v.* magnify.

magnificencia /magnifi'θenθia; magnifi'sensia/ *n. f.* magnificence.

magnífico /mag'nifiko/ *a.* magnificent.

magnitud /magni'tuð/ *n. f.* magnitude.

magno /'magno/ *a.* great, grand.

magnolia /mag'nolia/ *n. f.* magnolia.

mago /'mago/ *n. m.* magician; wizard.

magosto /ma'gosto/ *n. m.* chestnut roast; picnic fire for roasting chestnuts.

magro /'magro/ *a.* meager; thin.

magullar /magu'ʎar; magu'yar/ *v.* bruise.

mahometano /maome'tano/ *n. & a.* Mohammedan.

mahometismo /maome'tismo/ *n. m.* Mohammedanism.

maíz /ma'iθ; ma'is/ *n. m.* corn.

majadero /maha'ðero/ **-ra** *a. & n.* foolish; fool.

majar /ma'har/ *v.* mash.

majestad /mahes'tað/ *n. f.* majesty.

majestuoso /mahes'tuoso/ *a.* majestic.

mal /mal/ *adv.* **1.** badly; wrong. —*n.* **2.** *m.* evil, ill; illness.

mala /'mala/ *n. f.* mail.

malacate /mala'kate/ *n. m.* hoist.

malandanza /malan'danθa; malan'dansa/ *n. f.* misfortune.

malaventura /malaβen'tura/ *n. f.* misfortune.

malcomido /malko'miðo/ *a.* underfed; malnourished.

malcontento /malkon'tento/ *a.* disssatisfied.

maldad /mal'dað/ *n. f.* badness; wickedness.

maldecir /malde'θir; malde'sir/ *v.* curse, damn.

maldición /maldi'θion; maldi'sion/ *n. f.* curse.

maldito /mal'dito/ *a.* accursed, damned.

malecón /male'kon/ *n. m.* embankment.

maledicencia /maleði'θenθia; maleði'sensia/ *n. f.* slander.

maleficio /male'fiθio; male'fisio/ *n. m.* spell, charm.

malestar /males'tar/ *n. m.* indisposition.

maleta /ma'leta/ *n. f.* suitcase, valise.

malévolo /ma'leβolo/ *a.* malevolent.

maleza /ma'leθa; ma'lesa/ *n. f.* weeds; underbrush.

malgastar /malgas'tar/ *v.* squander.

malhechor /male'tʃor/ **-ra** *n.* malefactor, evildoer.

malhumorado /malumo'raðo/ *a.* morose, ill-humored.

malicia /ma'liθia; ma'lisia/ *n. f.* malice.

maliciar /mali'θiar; mali'siar/ *v.* suspect.

malicioso /mali'θioso; mali'sioso/ *a.* malicious.

maligno /ma'ligno/ *a.* malignant, evil.

malla /'maʎa; 'maya/ *n. f.* mesh, net.

mallas /'maʎas; 'mayas/ *n. f.pl.* leotard.

mallete /ma'ʎete; ma'yete/ *n. m.* mallet.

malo /'malo/ *a.* bad; evil, wicked; naughty; ill.

malograr /malo'grar/ *v.* miss, lose.

malparto /mal'parto/ *n. m.* abortion, miscarriage.

malquerencia /malke'renθia; malke'rensia/ *n. f.* hatred.

malquerer /malke'rer/ *v.* dislike; bear ill will.

malsano /mal'sano/ *a.* unhealthy; unwholesome.

malsín /mal'sin/ *n. m.* malicious gossip.

malta /'malta/ *n. f.* malt.

maltratar /maltra'tar/ *v.* mistreat.

malvado /mal'βaðo/ **-da** *a.* **1.** wicked. —*n.* **2.** villain.

malversar /malβer'sar/ *v.* embezzle.

malvís /mal'βis/ *n. m.* redwing.

mamá /'mama/ *n. f.* mama, mother.

mamar /ma'mar/ *v.* suckle; suck.

mamífero /ma'mifero/ *n. m.* mammal.

mampara /mam'para/ *n. f.* screen.

mampostería /mamposte'ria/ *n. f.* masonry.

mamut /ma'mut/ *n. m.* mammoth.

manada /ma'naða/ *n. f.* flock, herd, drove.

manantial /manan'tial/ *n. m.* spring (of water).

manar /ma'nar/ *v.* gush, flow out.

mancebo /man'θeβo; man'seβo/ *n. m.* young man.

mancha /'mantʃa/ *n. f.* stain, smear, blemish, spot. —**manchar,** *v.*

mancilla /man'θiʎa; man'siya/ *n. f.* stain; blemish.

manco /'manko/ *a.* armless; one-armed.

mandadero /manda'ðero/ *n. m.* messenger.

mandado /man'daðo/ *n. m.* order, command.

mandamiento /manda'miento/ *n. m.* commandment; command.

mandar /man'dar/ *v.* send; order, command.

mandatario /manda'tario/ *n. m.* attorney; representative.

mandato /man'dato/ *n. m.* mandate, command.

mandíbula /man'diβula/ *n. f.* jaw; jawbone.

mando /'mando/ *n. m.* command, order; leadership.

mando a distancia /'mando a dis'tanθia; 'mando a dis'tansia/ remote control.

mandón /man'don/ *a.* domineering.

mandril /man'dril/ *n. m.* baboon.

manejar /mane'har/ *v.* handle, manage; drive (a car).

manejo /ma'neho/ *n. m.* management; horsemanship.

manera /ma'nera/ *n. f.* way, manner, means. **de m. que,** so, as a result.

manga /'maŋga/ *n. f.* sleeve.

mangana /maŋ'gana/ *n. f.* lariat, lasso.

manganeso /maŋga'neso/ *n. m.* manganese.

mango /'maŋgo/ *n. m.* handle; mango (fruit).

mangosta /maŋ'gosta/ *n. f.* mongoose.

manguera /maŋ'guera/ *n. f.* hose.

manguito /maŋ'guito/ *n. m.* muff.

maní /ma'ni/ *n. m.* peanut.

manía /ma'nia/ *n. f.* mania, madness; hobby.

maníaco /ma'niako/ **-ca, maniático -ca** *a. & n.* maniac.

manicomio /mani'komio/ *n. m.* insane asylum.

manicura /mani'kura/ *n. f.* manicure.

manifactura /manifak'tura/ *n. f.* manufacture.

manifestación /manifesta'θion; manifesta'sion/ *n. f.* manifestation.

manifestar /manifes'tar/ *v.* manifest, show.

manifiesto /mani'fiesto/ *a. & m.* manifest.

manija /ma'niha/ *n. f.* handle; crank.

maniobra /ma'nioβra/ *n. f.* maneuver. —**maniobrar,** *v.*

manipulación /manipula'θion; manipula'sion/ *n. f.* manipulation.

manipular /manipu'lar/ *v.* manipulate.

maniquí /mani'ki/ *n. m.* mannequin.

manivela /mani'βela/ n. f. Mech. crank.

manjar /man'har/ n. m. food, dish.

manlieve /man'lieβe/ n. m. swindle.

mano /'mano/ n. f. hand.

manojo /ma'noho/ n. m. handful; bunch.

manómetro /ma'nometro/ n. m. gauge.

manopla /ma'nopla/ n. f. gauntlet.

manosear /manose'ar/ v. handle, feel, touch.

manotada /mano'taða/ n. f. slap, smack. —**manotear,** v.

mansedumbre /manse'ðumbre/ n. f. meekness, tameness.

mansión /man'sion/ n. f. mansion; abode.

manso /'manso/ a. tame, gentle.

manta /'manta/ n. f. blanket.

manteca /man'teka/ n. f. fat, lard; butter.

mantecado /mante'kaðo/ n. m. ice cream.

mantecoso /mante'koso/ a. buttery.

mantel /man'tel/ n. m. tablecloth.

mantener /mante'ner/ v. maintain, keep; sustain; support.

mantenimiento /manteni'miento/ n. m. maintenance.

mantequera /mante'kera/ n. f. butter dish; churn.

mantequilla /mante'kiʎa; mante-'kiya/ n. f. butter.

mantilla /man'tiʎa; man'tiya/ n. f. mantilla; baby clothes.

mantillo /man'tiʎo; man'tiyo/ n. m. humus; manure.

manto /'manto/ n. m. mantle, cloak.

manual /ma'nual/ a. & m. manual.

manubrio /ma'nuβrio/ n. m. handle; crank.

manufacturar /manufaktu'rar/ v. manufacture; make.

manuscrito /manus'krito/ n. m. manuscript.

manzana /man'θana; man'sana/ n. f. apple; block (of street).

manzanilla /manθa'niʎa; mansa-'niya/ n. f. dry sherry.

manzano /man'θano; man'sano/ n. m. apple tree.

maña /'maɲa/ n. f. skill; cunning; trick.

mañana /ma'ɲana/ adv. **1.** tomorrow. —n. **2.** f. morning.

mañanear /maɲane'ar/ v. rise early in the morning.

mañero /ma'ɲero/ a. clever; skillful; lazy.

mapa /'mapa/ n. m. map, chart.

mapache /ma'patʃe/ n. m. raccoon.

mapurito /mapu'rito/ n. m. skunk.

máquina /'makina/ n. f. machine. **m. de coser,** sewing machine. **m. de lavar,** washing machine.

maquinación /makina'θion; makina'sion/ n. f. machination; plot.

maquinador /makina'ðor/ **-ra** n. plotter, schemer.

maquinal /maki'nal/ a. mechanical.

maquinar /maki'nar/ v. scheme, plot.

maquinaria /maki'naria/ n. f. machinery.

maquinista /maki'nista/ n. m. machinist; engineer.

mar /mar/ n. m. or f. sea.

marabú /mara'βu/ n. m. marabou.

maraña /ma'raɲa/ n. f. tangle; maze; snarl; plot.

maravilla /mara'βiʎa; mara'βiya/ n. f. marvel, wonder. —**maravillarse,** v.

maravilloso /maraβi'ʎoso; maraβi'yoso/ a. marvelous, wonderful.

marbete /mar'βete/ n. m. tag, label; check.

marca /'marka/ n. f. mark, sign; brand, make.

marcador /marka'ðor/ n. m. highlighter.

marcapáginas /marka'pahinas/ n. m. bookmark.

marcar /mar'kar/ v. mark; observe, note.

marcha /'martʃa/ n. f. march; progress. —**marchar,** v.

marchante /mar'tʃante/ n. m. merchant; customer.

marcharse /mar'tʃarse/ v. go away, depart.

marchitable /martʃi'taβle/ a. perishable.

marchitar /martʃi'tar/ v. fade, wilt, wither.

marchito /mar'tʃito/ a. faded, withered.

marcial /mar'θial; mar'sial/ a. martial.

marco /'marko/ n. m. frame.

marea /ma'rea/ n. f. tide.

mareado /mare'aðo/ a. seasick.

marearse /mare'arse/ *v.* get dizzy; be seasick.

mareo /ma'reo/ *n. m.* dizziness; seasickness.

marfil /mar'fil/ *n. m.* ivory.

margarita /marga'rita/ *n. f.* pearl; daisy.

margen /'marhen/ *n. m. or f.* margin, edge, rim.

marido /ma'riðo/ *n. m.* husband.

marijuana /mari'huana/ *n. f.* marijuana.

marimacha /mari'matʃa/ *n. f.* lesbian.

marimacho /mari'matʃo/ *n. m.* mannish woman.

marimba /ma'rimba/ *n. f.* marimba.

marina /ma'rina/ *n. f.* navy; seascape.

marinero /mari'nero/ *n. m.* sailor, seaman.

marino /ma'rino/ *a. & m.* marine, (of) sea; mariner, seaman.

marión /ma'rion/ *n. m.* sturgeon.

mariposa /mari'posa/ *n. f.* butterfly.

mariquita /mari'kita/ *n. f.* ladybird.

mariscal /maris'kal/ *n. m.* marshal.

marisco /ma'risko/ *n. m.* shellfish; mollusk.

marital /mari'tal/ *a.* marital.

marítimo /ma'ritimo/ *a.* maritime.

marmita /mar'mita/ *n. f.* pot, kettle.

mármol /'marmol/ *n. m.* marble.

marmóreo /mar'moreo/ *a.* marble.

maroma /ma'roma/ *n. f.* rope.

marqués /mar'kes/ *n. m.* marquis.

marquesa /mar'kesa/ *n. f.* marquise.

Marruecos /ma'rruekos/ *n. m.* Morocco.

Marte /'marte/ *n. m.* Mars.

martes /'martes/ *n. m.* Tuesday.

martillo /mar'tiʎo; mar'tiyo/ *n. m.* hammer. —**martillar,** *v.*

mártir /'martir/ *n. m. & f.* martyr.

martirio /mar'tirio/ *n. m.* martyrdom.

martirizar /martiri'θar; martiri'sar/ *v.* martyrize.

marzo /'marθo; 'marso/ *n. m.* March.

mas /mas/ *conj.* but.

más *a. & adv.* more, most; plus. **no m.,** only; no more.

masa /'masa/ *n. f.* mass; dough.

masaje /ma'sahe/ *n. m.* massage.

mascar /mas'kar/ *v.* chew.

máscara /'maskara/ *n. f.* mask.

mascarada /maska'raða/ *n. f.* masquerade.

mascota /mas'kota/ *n. f.* mascot; good-luck charm.

masculino /masku'lino/ *a.* masculine.

mascullar /masku'ʎar; masku'yar/ *v.* mumble.

masón /ma'son/ *n. m.* Freemason.

masticar /masti'kar/ *v.* chew.

mástil /'mastil/ *n. m.* mast; post.

mastín /mas'tin/ *n. m.* mastiff.

mastín danés /mas'tin da'nes/ Great Dane.

mastuerzo /mas'tuerθo; mas'tuerso/ *n. m.* fool, ninny.

mata /'mata/ *n. f.* plant; bush.

matadero /mata'ðero/ *n. m.* slaughterhouse.

matador /mata'ðor/ **-ra** *n.* matador.

matafuego /mata'fuego/ *n. m.* fire extinguisher.

matanza /ma'tanθa; ma'tansa/ *n. f.* killing, bloodshed, slaughter.

matar /ma'tar/ *v.* kill, slay; slaughter.

matasanos /mata'sanos/ *n. m.* quack.

mate /'mate/ *n. m.* checkmate; Paraguayan tea.

matemáticas /mate'matikas/ *n. f.pl.* mathematics.

matemático /mate'matiko/ *a.* mathematical.

materia /ma'teria/ *n. f.* material; subject (matter).

material /mate'rial/ *a. & m.* material.

materialismo /materia'lismo/ *n. m.* materialism.

materializar /materiali'θar; materiali'sar/ *v.* materialize.

maternal /mater'nal/ **materno** *a.* maternal.

maternidad /materni'ðað/ *n. f.* maternity; maternity hospital.

matiné /mati'ne/ *n. f.* matinee.

matiz /ma'tiθ; ma'tis/ *n. m.* hue, shade.

matizar /mati'θar; mati'sar/ *v.* blend; tint.

matón /ma'ton/ *n. m.* bully.

matorral /mato'rral/ *n. m.* thicket.

matoso /ma'toso/ *a.* weedy.

matraca /ma'traka/ *n. f.* rattle.
—**matraquear,** *v.*
matrícula /ma'trikula/ *n. f.* registration; tuition.
matricularse /matriku'larse/ *v.* enroll, register.
matrimonio /matri'monio/ *n. m.* matrimony, marriage; married couple.
matriz /ma'triθ; ma'tris/ *n. f.* womb; *Mech.* die, mold.
matrona /ma'trona/ *n. f.* matron.
maullar /mau'ʎar; mau'yar/ *v.* mew.
máxima /'maksima/ *n. f.* maxim.
máxime /'maksime/ *a.* principally.
máximo /'maksimo/ *a. & m.* maximum.
maya /'maya/ *n. f.* daisy.
mayo /'mayo/ *n. m.* May.
mayonesa /mayo'nesa/ *n. f.* mayonnaise.
mayor /ma'yor/ *a.* larger, largest; greater, greatest; elder, eldest, senior. **m. de edad,** major, of age. **al por m.,** at wholesale. *m.* major.
mayoral /mayo'ral/ *n. m.* head shepherd; boss; foreman.
mayordomo /mayor'ðomo/ *n. m.* manager; butler, steward.
mayoría /mayo'ria/ *n. f.* majority, bulk.
mayorista /mayo'rista/ *n. m. & f.* wholesaler.
mayúscula /ma'yuskula/ *n. f.* capital letter, upper-case letter.
mazmorra /maθ'morra; mas-'morra/ *n. f.* dungeon.
mazorca /ma'θorka; ma'sorka/ *n. f.* ear of corn.
me /me/ *pron.* me; myself.
mecánico /me'kaniko/ **-ca** *a. & n.* mechanical; mechanic.
mecanismo /meka'nismo/ *n. m.* mechanism.
mecanizar /mekani'θar; mekani-'sar/ *v.* mechanize.
mecanografía /mekanogra'fia/ *n. f.* typewriting.
mecanógrafo /meka'nografo/ **-fa** *n.* typist.
mecedor /meθe'ðor; mese'ðor/ *n. m.* swing.
mecedora /meθe'ðora; mese'ðora/ *n. f.* rocking chair.
mecer /me'θer; me'ser/ *v.* rock; swing, sway.
mecha /'metʃa/ *n. f.* wick; fuse.

mechón /me'tʃon/ *n. m.* lock (of hair).
medalla /me'ðaʎa; me'ðaya/ *n. f.* medal.
médano /'meðano/ *n. m.* sand dune.
media /'meðia/ *n. f.* stocking.
mediación /meðia'θion; meðia-'sion/ *n. f.* mediation.
mediador /meðia'ðor/ **-ra** *n.* mediator.
mediados /me'ðiaðos/ *n. m.pl.* a **m. de,** about the middle of (a period of time).
medianero /meðia'nero/ *n. m.* mediator.
medianía /meðia'nia/ *n. f.* mediocrity.
mediano /me'ðiano/ *a.* medium; moderate; mediocre.
medianoche /meðia'notʃe/ *n. f.* midnight.
mediante /me'ðiante/ *prep.* by means of.
mediar /me'ðiar/ *v.* mediate.
medicamento /meðika'mento/ *n. m.* medicine, drug.
medicastro /meði'kastro/ *n. m.* quack.
medicina /meði'θina; meði'sina/ *n. f.* medicine.
medicinar /meðiθi'nar; meðisi'nar/ *v.* treat (as a doctor).
médico /'meðiko/ *a.* **1.** medical. —*n.* **2.** *m. & f.* doctor, physician.
medida /me'ðiða/ *n. f.* measure, step.
medidor /meði'ðor/ *n. m.* meter.
medieval /meðie'βal/ *a.* medieval.
medio /'meðio/ *a.* **1.** half; mid, middle of. —*n.* **2.** *m.* middle; means.
mediocre /me'ðiokre/ *a.* mediocre.
mediocridad /meðiokri'ðað/ *n. f.* mediocrity.
mediodía /meðio'ðia/ *n. m.* midday, noon.
medir /me'ðir/ *v.* measure, gauge.
meditación /meðita'θion; meðita'sion/ *n. f.* meditation.
meditar /meði'tar/ *v.* meditate.
mediterráneo /meðite'rraneo/ *a.* Mediterranean.
medrar /'meðrar/ *v.* thrive; grow.
medroso /me'ðroso/ *a.* fearful, cowardly.
megáfono /me'gafono/ *n. m.* megaphone.

megahercio /mega'erθio; mega-
'ersio/ *n. f.* megahertz.
mejicano /mehi'kano/ **-na** *a. & n.*
Mexican.
mejilla /me'hiʎa; me'hiya/ *n. f.*
cheek.
mejillón /mehi'ʎon; mehi'yon/ *n.
m.* mussel.
mejor /me'hor/ *a. & adv.* better;
best. **a lo m.,** perhaps.
mejora /me'hora/ *n. f.,* **mejoramiento,** *m.* improvement.
mejorar /meho'rar/ *v.* improve,
better.
mejoría /meho'ria/ *n. f.* improvement; superiority.
melancolía /melanko'lia/ *n. f.*
melancholy.
melancólico /melan'koliko/ *a.*
melancholy.
melaza /me'laθa; me'lasa/ *n. f.*
molasses.
melena /me'lena/ *n. f.* mane; long
or loose hair.
melenudo /mele'nuðo/ **-da** *a.*
long-haired.
melindroso /melin'droso/ *a.*
fussy.
mella /'meʎa; 'meya/ *n. f.* notch;
dent. —**mellar,** *v.*
mellizo /me'ʎiθo; me'yiso/ **-za** *n.
& a.* twin.
melocotón /meloko'ton/ *n. m.*
peach.
melodía /melo'ðia/ *n. f.* melody.
melodioso /melo'ðioso/ *a.* melodious.
melón /me'lon/ *n. m.* melon.
meloso /me'loso/ *a.* like honey.
membrana /mem'brana/ *n. f.*
membrane.
membrete /mem'brete/ *n. m.*
memorandum; letterhead.
membrillo /mem'briʎo; mem-
'briyo/ *n. m.* quince.
membrudo /mem'bruðo/ *a.*
strong, muscular.
memorable /memo'raβle/ *a.*
memorable.
memorándum /memo'randum/ *n.
m.* memorandum; notebook.
memoria /me'moria/ *n. f.* memory; memoir; memorandum.
mención /men'θion; men'sion/ *n.
f.* mention. —**mencionar,** *v.*
mendigar /mendi'gar/ *v.* beg (for
alms).
mendigo /men'digo/ **-a** *n.* beggar.
mendrugo /men'drugo/ *n. m.*
(hard) crust, chunk.

menear /mene'ar/ *v.* shake, wag;
stir.
menester /menes'ter/ *n. m.* need,
want; duty, task. **ser m.,** to be
necessary.
menesteroso /meneste'roso/ *a.*
needy.
mengua /'meŋgua/ *n. f.* decrease;
lack; poverty.
menguar /meŋ'guar/ *v.* abate, decrease.
meningitis /meniŋ'gitis/ *n. f.*
meningitis.
menopausia /meno'pausia/ *n. f.*
menopause.
menor /me'nor/ *a.* smaller, smal-
lest; lesser, least; younger, young-
est, junior. **m. de edad,** minor,
under age. **al por m.,** at retail.
menos /'menos/ *a. & adv.* less,
least; minus. **a m. que,** unless.
echar de m., to miss.
menospreciar /menospre'θiar;
menospre'siar/ *v.* cheapen; despise; slight.
mensaje /men'sahe/ *n. m.* message.
mensajero /mensa'hero/ **-ra** *n.*
messenger.
menstruar /menstru'ar/ *v.* men-
struate.
mensual /men'sual/ *a.* monthly.
mensualidad /mensuali'ðað/ *n. f.*
monthly income or allowance;
monthly payment.
menta /'menta/ *n. f.* mint, pep-
permint.
mentado /men'taðo/ *a.* famous.
mental /men'tal/ *a.* mental.
mentalidad /mentali'ðað/ *n. f.*
mentality.
menta romana /'menta rro'mana/
spearmint.
mente /'mente/ *n. f.* mind.
mentecato /mente'kato/ *a.* foolish, stupid.
mentir /men'tir/ *v.* lie, tell a lie.
mentira /men'tira/ *n. f.* lie, falsehood. **parece m.,** it seems impossible.
mentiroso /menti'roso/ *a.* lying,
untruthful.
mentol /'mentol/ *n. m.* menthol.
menú /me'nu/ *n. m.* menu.
menudeo /menu'ðeo/ *n. m.* retail.
menudo /menu'ðo/ *a.* small, minute. **a m.,** often.
meñique /me'ɲike/ *a.* tiny.
meple /'meple/ *n. m.* maple.
merca /'merka/ *n. f.* purchase.

mercader /merka'ðer/ *n. m.* merchant.

mercaderías /merkaðe'rias/ *n. f.pl.* merchandise, commodities.

mercado /mer'kaðo/ *n. m.* market.

Mercado Común /mer'kaðo ko'mun/ Common Market.

mercado negro /mer'kaðo 'negro/ black market.

mercancía /merkan'θia; merkan'sia/ *n. f.* merchandise; (*pl.*) wares.

mercante /mer'kante/ *a.* merchant.

mercantil /merkan'til/ *a.* mercantile.

merced /mer'θeð; mer'seð/ *n. f.* mercy, grace.

mercenario /merθe'nario; merse'nario/ **-ria** *a. & n.* mercenary.

mercurio /mer'kurio/ *n. m.* mercury.

merecedor /mereθe'ðor; merese'ðor/ *a.* worthy.

merecer /mere'θer; mere'ser/ *v.* merit, deserve.

merecimiento /mereθi'miento; meresi'miento/ *n. m.* merit.

merendar /meren'dar/ *v.* eat lunch; snack.

merendero /meren'dero/ *n. m.* lunchroom.

meridional /meriðio'nal/ *a.* southern.

merienda /me'rienda/ *n. f.* midday meal, lunch; afternoon snack.

mérito /'merito/ *n. m.* merit, worth.

meritorio /meri'torio/ *a.* meritorious.

merla /'merla/ *n. f.* blackbird.

merluza /mer'luθa; mer'lusa/ *n. f.* haddock.

mermelada /merme'laða/ *n. f.* marmalade.

mero /'mero/ *a.* mere.

merodeador /meroðea'ðor/ **-ra** *n.* prowler.

mes /'mes/ *n. m.* month.

mesa /'mesa/ *n. f.* table.

meseta /me'seta/ *n. f.* plateau.

mesón /me'son/ *n. m.* inn.

mesonero /meso'nero/ **-ra** *n.* innkeeper.

mestizo /mes'tiθo; mes'tiso/ **-za** *a. & n.* half-caste.

meta /'meta/ *n. f.* goal, objective.

metabolismo /metaβo'lismo/ *n. m.* metabolism.

metafísica /meta'fisika/ *n. f.* metaphysics.

metáfora /me'tafora/ *n. f.* metaphor.

metal /me'tal/ *n. m.* metal.

metálico /me'taliko/ *a.* metallic.

metalurgia /metalur'hia/ *n. f.* metallurgy.

meteoro /mete'oro/ *n. m.* meteor.

meteorología /meteorolo'hia/ *n. f.* meteorology.

meter /me'ter/ *v.* put (in).

meterse /me'terse/ *v.* interfere, meddle; go into.

metódico /me'toðiko/ *a.* methodic.

método /'metoðo/ *n. m.* method, approach.

metralla /me'traʎa; me'traya/ *n. f.* shrapnel.

métrico /'metriko/ *a.* metric.

metro /'metro/ *n. m.* meter (measure); subway.

metrópoli /me'tropoli/ *n. f.* metropolis.

mexicano /meksi'kano/ **-na** *a. & n.* Mexican.

mezcla /'meθkla; 'meskla/ *n. f.* mixture; blend.

mezclar /meθ'klar; mes'klar/ *v.* mix; blend.

mezcolanza /meθko'lanθa; mesko'lansa/ *n. f.* mixture; hodgepodge.

mezquino /meθ'kino; mes'kino/ *a.* stingy; petty.

mezquita /meθ'kita; mes'kita/ *n. f.* mosque.

mi /'mi/ *a.* my.

mí /'mi/ *pron.* me; myself.

microbio /mi'kroβio/ *n. m.* microbe, germ.

microbús /mikro'βus/ *n. m.* minibus.

microchip /mikro'tʃip/ *n. m.* microchip.

microficha /mikro'fitʃa/ *n. f.* microfiche.

micrófono /mi'krofono/ *n. m.* microphone.

microforma /mikro'forma/ *n. f.* microform.

microscópico /mikros'kopiko/ *a.* microscopic.

microscopio /mikros'kopio/ *n. m.* microscope.

microtaxi /mikro'taksi/ *n. m.* minicab.

miedo /'mieðo/ *n. m.* fear. **tener m.,** fear, be afraid.

miedoso /mie'ðoso/ *a.* fearful.
miel /miel/ *n. f.* honey.
miembro /mi'embro/ *n. m. & f.* member; limb.
mientras /'mientras/ *conj.* while. **m. tanto,** meanwhile. **m. más... más,** the more... the more.
miércoles /'mierkoles/ *n. m.* Wednesday.
miércoles de ceniza /'mierkoles de θe'niθa; 'mierkoles de se'nisa/ Ash Wednesday.
miga /'miga/ **migaja** *n. f.* scrap; crumb.
migración /migra'θion; migra'sion/ *n. f.* migration.
migratorio /migra'torio/ *a.* migratory.
mil /mil/ *a. & pron.* thousand.
milagro /mi'lagro/ *n. m.* miracle.
milagroso /mila'groso/ *a.* miraculous.
milicia /mi'liθia; mi'lisia/ *n. f.* militia.
militante /mili'tante/ *a.* militant.
militar /mili'tar/ *a.* **1.** military. —*n.* **2.** *m.* military man.
militarismo /milita'rismo/ *n. m.* militarism.
milla /'miʎa; 'miya/ *n. f.* mile.
millar /mi'ʎar; mi'yar/ *n. m.* (a) thousand.
millón /mi'ʎon; mi'yon/ *n. m.* million.
millonario /miʎo'nario; miyo'nario/ **-ria** *n.* millionaire.
mimar /mi'mar/ *v.* pamper, spoil (a child).
mimbre /'mimbre/ *n. m.* willow; wicker.
mímico /'mimiko/ *a.* mimic.
mimo /'mimo/ *n. m.* mime, mimic.
mina /'mina/ *n. f.* mine. —**minar,** *v.*
mineral /mine'ral/ *a. & m.* mineral.
minero /mi'nero/ **-ra** *n.* miner.
miniatura /minia'tura/ *n. f.* miniature.
miniaturizar /miniaturi'θar; miniaturi'sar/ *v.* miniaturize.
mínimo /'minimo/ *a. & m.* minimum.
ministerio /minis'terio/ *n. m.* ministry; cabinet.
ministro /mi'nistro/ **-a** *n. Govt.* minister, secretary.
minoría /mino'ria/ *n. f.* minority.
minoridad /minori'ðað/ *n. f.* minority (of age).

minucioso /minu'θioso; minu'sioso/ *a.* minute; thorough.
minué /mi'nue/ *n. m.* minuet.
minúscula /mi'nuskula/ *n. f.* lower-case letter, small letter.
minuta /mi'nuta/ *n. f.* draft.
mío /'mio/ *a.* mine.
miopía /mio'pia/ *n. f.* myopia.
mira /'mira/ *n. f.* gunsight.
mirada /mi'raða/ *n. f.* look; gaze, glance.
miramiento /mira'miento/ *n. m.* consideration; respect.
mirar /mi'rar/ *v.* look, look at; watch. **m. a,** face.
miríada /mi'riaða/ *n. f.* myriad.
mirlo /'mirlo/ *n. m.* blackbird.
mirón /mi'ron/ **-ona** *n.* bystander, observer.
mirra /'mirra/ *n. f.* myrrh.
mirto /'mirto/ *n. m.* myrtle.
misa /'misa/ *n. f.* mass, church service.
misceláneo /misθe'laneo; misse'laneo/ *a.* miscellaneous.
miserable /mise'raβle/ *a.* miserable, wretched.
miseria /mi'seria/ *n. f.* misery.
misericordia /miseri'korðia/ *n. f.* mercy.
misericordioso /miserikor'ðioso/ *a.* merciful.
misión /mi'sion/ *n. f.* assignment; mission.
misionario /misio'nario/ **-ria, misionero -ra** *n.* missionary.
mismo /'mismo/ *a. & pron.* **1.** same; -self, -selves. —*adv.* **2.** right, exactly.
misterio /mis'terio/ *n. m.* mystery.
misterioso /miste'rioso/ *a.* mysterious, weird.
místico /'mistiko/ **-ca** *a. & n.* mystical, mystic.
mitad /mi'tað/ *n. f.* half.
mítico /'mitiko/ *a.* mythical.
mitigar /miti'gar/ *v.* mitigate.
mitin /'mitin/ *n. m.* meeting; rally.
mito /'mito/ *n. m.* myth.
mitón /mi'ton/ *n. m.* mitten.
mitra /'mitra/ *n. f.* miter (bishop's).
mixto /'miksto/ *a.* mixed.
mixtura /miks'tura/ *n. f.* mixture.
mobiliario /moβi'liario/ *n. m.* household goods.
mocasín /moka'sin/ *n. m.* moccasin.

mocedad /moθe'ðað; mose'ðað/
n. f. youthfulness.
mochila /mo't ʃila/ *n. f.* knapsack,
backpack.
mocho /'mot ʃo/ *a.* cropped,
trimmed, shorn.
moción /mo'θion; mo'sion/ *n. f.*
motion.
mocoso /mo'koso/ **-sa** *n.* brat.
moda /'moða/ *n. f.* mode, fashion,
style.
modales /mo'ðales/ *n. m.pl.*
manners.
modelo /mo'ðelo/ *n. m.* model,
pattern.
módem /'moðem/ *n. m.* modem.
moderación /moðera'θion; moð-
erasion/ *n. f.* moderation.
moderado /moðe'raðo/ *a.* moderate. **—moderar,** *v.*
modernizar /moðerni'θar; moð-
erni'sar/ *v.* modernize.
moderno /mo'ðerno/ *a.* modern.
modestia /mo'ðestia/ *n. f.* modesty.
modesto /mo'ðesto/ *a.* modest.
módico /'moðiko/ *a.* reasonable,
moderate.
modificación /moðifi'kaθion;
moðifika'sion/ *n. f.* modification.
modificar /moðifi'kar/ *v.* modify.
modismo /mo'ðismo/ *n. m. Gram.*
idiom.
modista /mo'ðista/ *n. f.* dressmaker; milliner.
modo /'moðo/ *n. m.* way, means.
modular /moðu'lar/ *v.* modulate.
mofarse /mo'farse/ *v.* scoff, sneer.
mofletudo /mofle'tuðo/ *a.* fat-
cheeked.
mohín /mo'in/ *n. m.* grimace.
moho /'moo/ *n. m.* mold, mildew.
mohoso /mo'oso/ *a.* moldy.
mojar /mo'har/ *v.* wet.
mojón /mo'hon/ *n. m.* landmark;
heap.
molde /'molde/ *n. m.* mold, form.
molécula /mo'lekula/ *n. f.* molecule.
moler /mo'ler/ *v.* grind, mill.
molestar /moles'tar/ *v.* molest,
bother, disturb, annoy, trouble.
molestia /mo'lestia/ *n. f.* bother,
annoyance, trouble; hassle.
molesto /mo'lesto/ *a.* bothersome;
annoyed; uncomfortable.
molicie /mo'liθie; mo'lisie/ *n. f.*
softness.
molinero /moli'nero/ *n. m.* miller.

molino /mo'lino/ *n. m.* mill. **m.
de viento,** windmill.
mollera /mo'ʎera; mo'yera/ *n. f.*
top of the head.
molusco /mo'lusko/ *n. m.* mollusk.
momentáneo /momen'taneo/ *a.*
momentary.
momento /mo'mento/ *n. m.* moment.
mona /'mona/ *n. f.* female monkey.
monarca /mo'narka/ *n. m. & f.*
monarch.
monarquía /monar'kia/ *n. f.* monarchy.
monarquista /monar'kista/ *n. &*
a. monarchist.
monasterio /mona'sterio/ *n. m.*
monastery.
mondadientes /monda'ðientes/ *n.*
m. toothpick.
moneda /mo'neða/ *n. f.* coin;
money.
monetario /mone'tario/ *a.* monetary.
monición /moni'θion; moni'sion/
n. m. warning.
monigote /moni'gote/ *n. m.* puppet.
monja /'monha/ *n. f.* nun.
monje /'monhe/ *n. m.* monk.
mono /'mono/ **-na** *a.* **1.** *Colloq.*
cute. **—***n.* **2.** *m. & f.* monkey.
monólogo /mo'nologo/ *n. m.*
monologue.
monopatín /monopa'tin/ *n. m.*
skateboard.
monopolio /mono'polio/ *n. m.*
monopoly.
monopolizar /monopoli'θar;
monopoli'sar/ *v.* monopolize.
monosílabo /mono'silaβo/ *n. m.*
monosyllable.
monotonía /monoto'nia/ *n. f.* monotony.
monótono /mo'notono/ *a.* monotonous, dreary.
monstruo /'monstruo/ *n. m.* monster.
monstruosidad /monstruosi'ðað/
n. f. monstrosity.
monstruoso /mon'struoso/ *a.*
monstrous.
monta /'monta/ *n. f.* amount;
price.
montaña /mon'taɲa/ *n. f.* mountain.
montañoso /monta'ɲoso/ *a.*
mountainous.

montar /mon'tar/ *v.* mount, climb; amount; *Mech.* assemble. **m. a caballo,** ride horseback.

montaraz /monta'raθ; monta'ras/ *a.* wild, barbaric.

monte /'monte/ *n. m.* mountain; forest.

montón /mon'ton/ *n. m.* heap, pile.

montuoso /mon'tuoso/ *a.* mountainous.

montura /mon'tura/ *n. f.* mount; saddle.

monumental /monumen'tal/ *a.* monumental.

monumento /monu'mento/ *n. m.* monument.

mora /'mora/ *n. f.* blackberry.

morada /mo'raða/ *n. f.* residence, dwelling.

morado /mo'raðo/ *a.* purple.

moral /mo'ral/ *a.* **1.** moral. —*n.* **2.** *f.* morale.

moraleja /mora'leha/ *n. f.* moral.

moralidad /morali'ðað/ *n. f.* morality, morals.

moralista /mora'lista/ *n. m. & f.* moralist.

morar /mo'rar/ *v.* dwell, live, reside.

mórbido /'morβiðo/ *a.* morbid.

mordaz /mor'ðaθ; mor'ðas/ *a.* caustic; sarcastic.

mordedura /morðe'ðura/ *n. f.* bite.

morder /mor'ðer/ *v.* bite.

moreno /mo'reno/ **-na** *a. & n.* brown; dark-skinned; dark-haired, brunette.

morfina /mor'fina/ *n. f.* morphine.

moribundo /mori'βundo/ *a.* dying.

morir /mo'rir/ *v.* die.

morisco /mo'risko/ **-ca, moro -ra** *a. & n.* Moorish; Moor.

morriña /mo'rriɲa/ *n. f.* sadness.

morro /'morro/ *n. m.* bluff; snout.

mortaja /mor'taha/ *n. f.* shroud.

mortal /mor'tal/ *a. & n.* mortal.

mortalidad /mortali'ðað/ *n. f.* mortality.

mortero /mor'tero/ *n. m.* mortar.

mortífero /mor'tifero/ *a.* fatal, deadly.

mortificar /mortifi'kar/ *v.* mortify.

mortuorio /mor'tuorio/ *a.* funereal.

mosaico /mo'saiko/ *a. & m.* mosaic.

mosca /'moska/ *n. f.* fly.

mosquito /mos'kito/ *n. m.* mosquito.

mostacho /mos'tatʃo/ *n. m.* mustache.

mostaza /mos'taθa; mos'tasa/ *n. f.* mustard.

mostrador /mostra'ðor/ *n. m.* counter; showcase.

mostrar /mos'trar/ *v.* show, display.

mote /'mote/ *n. m.* nickname; alias.

motel /mo'tel/ *n. m.* motel.

motín /mo'tin/ *n. m.* mutiny; riot.

motivo /mo'tiβo/ *n. m.* motive, reason.

motocicleta /motoθi'kleta; motosi'kleta/ *n. f.* motorcycle.

motociclista /motoθi'klista; motosi'klista/ *n. m. & f.* motorcyclist.

motor /mo'tor/ *n. m.* motor.

motorista /moto'rista/ *n. m. & f.* motorist.

movedizo /moβe'ðiθo; moβe'ðiso/ *a.* movable; shaky.

mover /mo'βer/ *v.* move; stir.

movible /mo'βiβle/ *a.* movable.

móvil /'moβil/ *a.* mobile.

movilización /moβiliθa'θion; moβilisa'sion/ *n. f.* mobilization.

movilizar /moβili'θar; moβili'sar/ *v.* mobilize.

movimiento /moβi'miento/ *n. m.* movement, motion.

mozo /'moθo; 'moso/ *n. m.* boy; servant, waiter, porter.

muaré /mua're/ *n. m.* moiré.

muchacha /mu'tʃatʃa/ *n. f.* girl, youngster; maid (servant).

muchachez /mutʃa'tʃeθ; mutʃa'tʃes/ *n. m.* boyhood, girlhood.

muchacho /mu'tʃatʃo/ *n. m.* boy; youngster.

muchedumbre /mutʃe'ðumbre/ *n. f.* crowd, mob.

mucho /'mutʃo/ *a.* **1.** much, many. —*adv.* **2.** much.

mucoso /mu'koso/ *a.* mucous.

muda /'muða/ *n. f.* change.

mudanza /mu'ðanθa; muðansa/ *n. f.* change; change of residence.

mudar /mu'ðar/ *v.* change, shift.

mudarse /mu'ðarse/ *v.* change residence, move.

mudo /'muðo/ **-da** *a. & n.* mute.

mueble /'mueβle/ *n. m.* piece of furniture; (*pl.*) furniture.

mueca /'mueka/ *n. f.* grimace.

muela /'muela/ *n. f.* (back) tooth.

muelle /'mueʎe; 'mueye/ *n. m.* pier, wharf; *Mech.* spring.

muerte /'muerte/ *n. f.* death.

muerto /'muerto/ **-ta** *a.* **1.** dead. —*n.* **2.** dead person.

muesca /'mueska/ *n. f.* notch; groove.

muestra /'muestra/ *n. f.* sample, specimen; sign.

mugido /mu'hiðo/ *n. m.* lowing; mooing.

mugir /mu'hir/ *v.* low, moo.

mugre /'mugre/ *n. f.* filth, dirt.

mugriento /mu'griento/ *a.* dirty.

mujer /mu'her/ *f.* woman; wife.
m. de la limpieza, cleaning lady, charwoman.

mujeril /muhe'ril/ *a.* womanly, feminine.

mula /'mula/ *n. f.* mule.

mulato /mu'lato/ **-ta** *a. & n.* mulatto.

muleta /mu'leta/ *n. f.* crutch; prop.

mulo /'mulo/ **-la** *n.* mule.

multa /'multa/ *n. f.* fine, penalty.

multicolor /multiko'lor/ *a.* many-colored.

multinacional /multinaθio'nal; multinasio'nal/ *a.* multinational.

múltiple /'multiple/ *a.* multiple.

multiplicación /multiplika'θion; multiplika'sion/ *n. f.* multiplication.

multiplicar /multipli'kar/ *v.* multiply.

multiplicidad /multipliθi'ðað; multiplisi'ðað/ *n. f.* multiplicity.

multitud /multi'tuð/ *n. f.* multitude, crowd.

mundanal /munda'nal/ *a.* worldly.

mundano /mun'dano/ *a.* worldly, mundane.

mundial /mun'dial/ *a.* worldwide; (of the) world.

mundo /'mundo/ *n. m.* world.

munición /muni'θion; muni'sion/ *n. f.* ammunition.

municipal /muniθi'pal; munisi'pal/ *a.* municipal.

municipio /muni'θipio; muni'sipio/ *n. m.* city hall.

muñeca /mu'ɲeka/ *n. f.* doll; wrist.

muñeco /mu'ɲeko/ *n. m.* doll; puppet.

mural /mu'ral/ *a. & m.* mural.

muralla /mu'raʎa; mu'raya/ *n. f.* wall.

murciélago /mur'θielago; mur'sielago/ *n. m.* bat.

murga /'murga/ *n. f.* musical band.

murmullo /mur'muʎo; mur'muyo/ *n. m.* murmur; rustle.

murmurar /murmu'rar/ *v.* murmur; rustle; grumble.

musa /'musa/ *n. f.* muse.

muscular /musku'lar/ *a.* muscular.

músculo /'muskulo/ *n. m.* muscle.

muselina /muse'lina/ *n. f.* muslin.

museo /mu'seo/ *n. m.* museum.

música /'musika/ *n. f.* music.

musical /musi'kal/ *a.* musical.

músico /'musiko/ **-ca** *a. & n.* musical; musician.

muslo /'muslo/ *n. m.* thigh.

mustio /'mustio/ *a.* sad.

musulmano /musul'mano/ **-na** *a. & n.* Muslim.

muta /'muta/ *n. f.* pack of hounds.

mutabilidad /mutaβili'ðað/ *n. f.* mutability.

mutación /muta'θion; muta'sion/ *n. f.* mutation.

mutilación /mutila'θion; mutila'sion/ *n. f.* mutilation.

mutilar /muti'lar/ *v.* mutilate; mangle.

mutuo /'mutuo/ *a.* mutual.

muy /'mui/ *adv.* very.

N Ñ

nabo /'naβo/ *n. m.* turnip.

nácar /'nakar/ *n. m.* mother-of-pearl.

nacarado /naka'raðo, na'kareo/ *a.* pearly.

nacer /na'θer; na'ser/ *v.* be born.

naciente /na'θiente; na'siente/ *a.* rising; nascent.

nacimiento /naθi'miento; nasi'miento/ *n. m.* birth.

nación /na'θion; na'sion/ *n. f.* nation.

nacional /naθio'nal; nasio'nal/ *a.* national.

nacionalidad /naθionali'ðað; nasionali'ðað/ *n. f.* nationality.

nacionalismo /naθiona'lismo; nasiona'lismo/ *n. m.* nationalism.

nacionalista /naθiona'lista; nasiona'lista/ *n. & a.* nationalist.

nacionalización /naθionaliθa'θion; nasionalisa'sion/ *n. f.* nationalization.

nacionalizar /naθionali'θar; nasionali'sar/ *v.* nationalize.

Naciones Unidas /na'θiones u'niðas; na'siones u'niðas/ *n. f.pl.* United Nations.

nada /'naða/ *pron.* **1.** nothing; anything. **de n.**, you're welcome. —*adv.* **2.** at all.

nadador /naða'ðor/ **-ra** *n.* swimmer.

nadar /na'ðar/ *v.* swim.

nadie /'naðie/ *pron.* no one, nobody; anyone, anybody.

nafta /'nafta/ *n. f.* naphtha.

naipe /'naipe/ *n. m.* (playing) card.

naranja /na'ranha/ *n. f.* orange.

naranjada /naran'haða/ *n. f.* orangeade.

naranjo /na'ranho/ *n. m.* orange tree.

narciso /nar'θiso; nar'siso/ *n. m.* daffodil; narcissus.

narcótico /nar'kotiko/ *a. & m.* narcotic.

nardo /'narðo/ *n. m.* spikenard.

nariz /na'riθ; na'ris/ *n. f.* nose; (*pl.*) nostrils.

narración /narra'θion; narra'sion/ *n. f.* account.

narrador /narra'ðor/ **-ra** *n.* narrator.

narrar /na'rrar/ *v.* narrate.

narrativa /narra'tiβa/ *n. f.* narrative.

nata /'nata/ *n. f.* cream.

nata batida /'nata ba'tiða/ whipped cream.

natación /nata'θion; nata'sion/ *n. f.* swimming.

natal /na'tal/ *a.* native; natal.

natalicio /nata'liθio; nata'lisio/ *n. m.* birthday.

natalidad /natali'ðað/ *n. f.* birth rate.

natillas /na'tiʎas; na'tiyas/ *n. f.pl.* custard.

nativo /na'tiβo/ *a.* native; innate.

natural /natu'ral/ *a.* **1.** natural. —*n.* **2.** *m. & f.* native. **3.** *m.* nature, disposition.

naturaleza /natura'leθa; natura'lesa/ *n. f.* nature.

naturalidad /naturali'ðað/ *n. f.* naturalness; nationality.

naturalista /natura'lista/ *a. & n.* naturalistic; naturalist.

naturalización /naturaliθa'θion; naturalisa'sion/ *n. f.* naturalization.

naturalizar /naturali'θar; naturali'sar/ *v.* naturalize.

naufragar /naufra'gar/ *v.* be shipwrecked; fail.

naufragio /nau'frahio/ *n. m.* shipwreck; disaster.

náufrago /'naufrago/ **-ga** *a. & n.* shipwrecked (person).

náusea /'nausea/ *n. f.* nausea.

nausear /nause'ar/ *v.* feel nauseous.

náutico /'nautiko/ *a.* nautical.

navaja /na'βaha/ *n. f.* razor; pen knife.

naval /na'βal/ *a.* naval.

navasca /na'βaska/ *n. f.* blizzard, snowstorm.

nave /'naβe/ *n. f.* ship.

nave espacial /'naβe espa'θial; 'naβe es'pasial/ spaceship.

navegable /naβe'gaβle/ *a.* navigable.

navegación /naβega'θion; naβega'sion/ *n. f.* navigation.

navegador /naβega'ðor/ **-ra** *n.* navigator.

navegante /naβe'gante/ *n. m. & f.* navigator.

navegar /naβe'gar/ *v.* sail; navigate.

Navidad /naβi'ðað/ *n. f.* Christmas.

navío /na'βio/ *n. m.* ship.

neblina /ne'βlina/ *n. f.* mist, fog.

nebuloso /neβu'loso/ *a.* misty; nebulous.

necedad /neθe'ðað; nese'ðað/ *n. f.* stupidity; nonsense.

necesario /neθe'sario; nese'sario/ *a.* necessary.

necesidad /neθesi'ðað; nesesi'ðað/ *n. f.* necessity, need, want.

necesitado /neθesi'taðo; nesesi'taðo/ *a.* needy, poor.

necesitar /neθesi'tar; nesesi'tar/ *v.* need.

necio /'neθio; 'nesio/ **-cia** *a.* **1.** stupid, silly. —*n.* **2.** fool.

néctar /'nektar/ *n. m.* nectar.

nectarina /nekta'rina/ *n. f.* nectarine.

nefando /ne'fando/ *a.* nefarious.

nefasto /ne'fasto/ *a.* unlucky, ill-fated.

negable /ne'gaβle/ *a.* deniable.

negación /nega'θion; nega'sion/ *n. f.* denial, negation.

negar /ne'gar/ *v.* deny.
negarse /ne'garse/ *v.* refuse, decline.
negativa /nega'tiβa/ *n. f.* negative, refusal.
negativamente /negatiβa'mente/ *adv.* negatively.
negativo /nega'tiβo/ *a.* negative.
negligencia /negli'henθia; negli'hensia/ *n. f.* negligence, neglect.
negligente /negli'hente/ *a.* negligent.
negociación /negoθia'θion; negosia'sion/ *n. f.* negotiation, deal.
negociador /negoθia'ðor; negosia'ðor/ **-ra** *n.* negotiator.
negociante /nego'θiante; nego'siante/ **-ta** *n.* businessperson.
negociar /nego'θiar; nego'siar/ *v.* negotiate, trade.
negocio /ne'goθio; ne'gosio/ *n. m.* trade; business.
negro /'negro/ **-gra** *a.* **1.** black. —*n.* **2.** *m.* Black.
nene /'nene/ **-na** *n.* baby.
neo /'neo/ **neón** *n. m.* neon.
nervio /'nerβio/ *n. m.* nerve.
nerviosamente /nerβiosa'mente/ *adv.* nervously.
nervioso /ner'βioso/ *a.* nervous.
nesciencia /nesθien'θia; nessien'sia/ *n. f.* ignorance.
nesciente /nes'θiente; nes'siente/ *a.* ignorant.
neto /'neto/ *a.* net.
neumático /neu'matiko/ *a.* **1.** pneumatic. —*n.* **2.** *m.* (pneumatic) tire.
neumático de recambio /neu'matiko de rre'kambio/ spare tire.
neumonía /neumo'nia/ *n. f.* pneumonia.
neurótico /neu'rotiko/ *a.* neurotic.
neutral /neu'tral/ *a.* neutral.
neutralidad /neutrali'ðað/ *n. f.* neutrality.
neutro /'neutro/ *a.* neuter; neutral.
neutrón /neu'tron/ *n. m.* neutron.
nevada /ne'βaða/ *n. f.* snowfall.
nevado /ne'βaðo/ *a.* snow-white; snow-capped.
nevar /ne'βar/ *v.* snow.
nevera /ne'βera/ *n. f.* icebox.
nevoso /ne'βoso/ *a.* snowy.
ni /ni/ *conj.* **1.** nor. **ni... ni,** neither... nor. —*adv.* **2.** not even.
nicho /'nitʃo/ *n. m.* recess; niche.
nido /'niðo/ *n. m.* nest.
niebla /'nieβla/ *n. f.* fog; mist.

nieto /'nieto/ **-ta** *n.* grandchild.
nieve /'nieβe/ *n. f.* snow.
nilón /ni'lon/ *n. m.* nylon.
nimio /'nimio/ *adj.* stingy.
ninfa /'ninfa/ *n. f.* nymph.
ningún /niŋ'gun/ **-no -na** *a. & pron.* no, none, neither (one); any, either (one).
niñera /ni'ɲera/ *n. f.* nursemaid, nanny.
niñez /ni'ɲeθ; ni'ɲes/ *n. f.* childhood.
niño /'niɲo/ **-ña 1.** *a.* **1.** young; childish; childlike. —*n.* **2.** child.
níquel /'nikel/ *n. m.* nickel.
niquelado /nike'laðo/ *a.* nickel-plated.
nítido /'nitiðo/ *a.* neat, clean, bright.
nitrato /ni'trato/ *n. m.* nitrate.
nitro /'nitro/ *n. m.* niter.
nitrógeno /ni'troheno/ *n. m.* nitrogen.
nivel /ni'βel/ *n. m.* level; grade. —**nivelar,** *v.*
no /no/ *adv.* **1.** not. **no más,** only. —*interj.* **2.** no.
noble /'noβle/ *a. & m.* noble; nobleman.
nobleza /no'βleθa; no'βlesa/ *n. f.* nobility; nobleness.
noche /'notʃe/ *n. f.* night; evening.
Nochebuena /notʃe'βuena/ *n. f.* Christmas Eve.
noción /no'θion; no'sion/ *n. f.* notion, idea.
nocivo /no'θiβo; no'siβo/ *a.* harmful.
noctiluca /nokti'luka/ *n. f.* glowworm.
nocturno /nok'turno/ *a.* nocturnal.
nodriza /no'ðriθa; no'ðrisa/ *n. f.* wet nurse.
no fumador /no fuma'ðor/ **-ra** *n. m. & f.* nonsmoker.
nogal /no'gal/ *n. m.* walnut.
nombradía /nom'βraðia/ *n. f.* fame.
nombramiento /nombra'miento/ *n. m.* appointment, nomination.
nombrar /nom'βrar/ *v.* name, appoint, nominate; mention.
nombre /'nombre/ *n. m.* name; noun.
nombre y apellidos /'nombre i ape'ʎiðos; 'nombre i ape'yiðos/ (person's) full name.

nómina /'nomina/ n. f. list; payroll.

nominación /nomina'θion; nomina'sion/ n. f. nomination.

nominal /nomi'nal/ a. nominal.

nominar /nomi'nar/ v. nominate.

non /non/ a. uneven, odd.

nonada /no'naða/ n. f. trifle.

nordeste /nor'ðeste/ n. m. northeast.

nórdico /'norðiko/ a. Nordic; northerly.

norma /'norma/ n. f. norm, standard.

normal /nor'mal/ a. normal, standard.

normalidad /normali'ðað/ n. f. normality.

normalizar /normali'θar; normali'sar/ v. normalize; standardize.

noroeste /noro'este/ n. m. northwest.

norte /'norte/ n. m. north.

norteamericano /norteameri'kano/ **-na** a. & n. North American.

Noruega /no'ruega/ n. f. Norway.

noruego /no'ruego/ **-ga** a. & n. Norwegian.

nos /nos/ pron. us; ourselves.

nosotros /no'sotros, no'sotras/ **-as** pron. we, us; ourselves.

nostalgia /nos'talhia/ n. f. nostalgia, homesickness.

nostálgico /nos'talhiko/ a. nostalgic.

nota /'nota/ n. f. note; grade, mark.

notable /no'taβle/ a. notable, remarkable.

notación /nota'θion; nota'sion/ n. f. notation; note.

notar /no'tar/ v. note, notice.

notario /no'tario/ **-ria** n. notary.

noticia /no'tiθia; no'tisia/ n. f. notice; piece of news; (pl.) news.

noticia de última hora /no'tiθia de 'ultima 'ora; no'tisia de 'ultima 'ora/ news flash.

notificación /notifika'θion; notifika'sion/ n. f. notification.

notificación de reclutamiento /notifika'θion de rrekluta'miento; notifika'sion de rrekluta'miento/ draft notice.

notificar /notifi'kar/ v. notify.

notorio /no'torio/ a. well-known.

novato /no'βato/ **-ta** n. novice.

novecientos /noβe'θientos; noβe'sientos/ a. & pron. nine hundred.

novedad /noβe'ðað/ n. f. novelty; piece of news.

novel /no'βel/ a. new; inexperienced.

novela /no'βela/ n. f. novel.

novelista /noβe'lista/ n. m. & f. novelist.

novena /no'βena/ n. f. novena.

noveno /no'βeno/ a. ninth.

noventa /no'βenta/ a. & pron. ninety.

novia /'noβia/ n. f. bride; sweetheart; fiancée.

noviazgo /no'βiaθgo; no'βiasgo/ n. m. engagement.

novicio /no'βiθio; no'βisio/ **-cia** n. novice, beginner.

noviembre /no'βiembre/ n. m. November.

novilla /no'βiʎa; no'βiya/ n. f. heifer.

novio /'noβio/ n. m. bridegroom; sweetheart; fiancé.

nube /'nuβe/ n. f. cloud.

núbil /'nuβil/ a. marriageable.

nublado /nu'βlaðo/ a. cloudy.

nuclear /nukle'ar/ a. nuclear.

núcleo /'nukleo/ n. m. nucleus.

nudo /'nuðo/ n. m. knot.

nuera /'nuera/ n. f. daughter-in-law.

nuestro /'nuestro/ a. our, ours.

nueva /'nueβa/ n. f. news.

nueve /'nueβe/ a. & pron. nine.

nuevo /'nueβo/ a. new. **de n.,** again, anew.

nuez /nueθ; nues/ n. f. nut; walnut.

nulidad /nuli'ðað/ n. f. nonentity; nullity.

nulo /'nulo/ a. null, void.

numeración /numera'θion; numera'sion/ n. f. numeration.

numerar /nume'rar/ v. number.

numérico /nu'meriko/ a. numerical.

número /'numero/ n. m. number; size (of shoe, etc.) **n. impar,** odd number. **n. par,** even number.

numeroso /nume'roso/ a. numerous.

numismática /numis'matika/ n. f. numismatics.

nunca /'nunka/ adv. never; ever.

nupcial /nup'θial; nup'sial/ a. nuptial.

nupcias /'nupθias; 'nupsias/ n. f.pl. nuptials, wedding.

nutrición /nutri'θion; nutri'sion/ n. f. nutrition.

nutrimento /nutri'mento/ *n. m.* nourishment.
nutrir /nu'trir/ *v.* nourish.
nutritivo /nutri'tiβo/ *a.* nutritious.
nylon /'nilon/ *n. m.* nylon.
ñame /'ɲame/ *n. m.* yam.

ñapa /'ɲapa/ *n. f.* something extra.
ñoñeria /ɲoɲe'ria/ *n. f.* dotage.
ñoño /'ɲoɲo/ *a.* feeble-minded, senile.

O

o /o/ *conj.* or. **o... o,** either... or.
oasis /o'asis/ *n. m.* oasis.
obedecer /oβeðe'θer; oβeðe'ser/ *v.* obey, mind.
obediencia /oβe'ðienθia; oβe-'ðiensia/ *n. f.* obedience.
obediente /oβe'ðiente/ *a.* obedient.
obelisco /oβe'lisko/ *n. m.* obelisk.
obertura /oβer'tura/ *n. f.* overture.
obeso /o'βeso/ *a.* obese.
obispo /o'βispo/ *n. m.* bishop.
obituario /oβi'tuario/ *n. m.* obituary.
objeción /oβhe'θion; oβhe'sion/ *n. f.* objection.
objetivo /oβhe'tiβo/ *a. & m.* objective.
objeto /oβ'heto/ *n. m.* object. —**objetar,** *v.*
objetor de conciencia /oβhe'tor de kon'θienθia; oβhe'tor de kon'siensia/ *n. m.* conscientious objector.
oblicuo /o'βlikuo/ *a.* oblique.
obligación /oβliga'θion; oβliga-'sion/ *n. f.* obligation, duty.
obligar /oβli'gar/ *v.* oblige, require, compel; obligate.
obligatorio /oβliga'torio/ *a.* obligatory, compulsory.
oblongo /o'βlongo/ *a.* oblong.
oboe /o'βoe/ *n. m.* oboe.
obra /'oβra/ *n. f.* work. —**obrar,** *v.*
obrero /o'βrero/ -ra *n.* worker, laborer.
obscenidad /oβsθeni'ðað; oβsseni'ðað/ *n. f.* obscenity.
obsceno /oβs'θeno; oβs'seno/ *a.* obscene.
obscurecer /oβskure'θer; oβskure-ɪ'aprim;ser/ *v.* obscure; darken.
obscuridad /oβskuri'ðað/ *n. f.* obscurity; darkness.
obscuro /oβs'kuro/ *a.* obscure; dark.
obsequiar /oβse'kiar/ *v.* court; make presents to, fete.

obsequio /oβ'sekio/ *n. m.* obsequiousness; gift; attention.
observación /oβserβa'θion; oβserβa'sion/ *n. f.* observation.
observador /oβserβa'ðor/ -ra *n.* observer.
observancia /oβser'βanθia; oβser-'βansia/ *n. f.* observance.
observar /oβser'βar/ *v.* observe, watch.
observatorio /oβserβa'torio/ *n. m.* observatory.
obsesión /oβse'sion/ *n. f.* obsession.
obstáculo /oβs'takulo/ *n. m.* obstacle.
obstante /oβs'tante/ *adv.* **no o.,** however, yet, nevertheless.
obstar /oβs'tar/ *v.* hinder, obstruct.
obstetricia /oβste'triθia; oβste'trisia/ *n. f.* obstetrics.
obstinación /oβstina'θion; oβstina'sion/ *n. f.* obstinacy.
obstinado /oβsti'naðo/ *a.* obstinate, stubborn.
obstinarse /oβsti'narse/ *v.* persist, insist.
obstrucción /oβstruk'θion; oβstruk'sion/ *n. f.* obstruction.
obstruir /oβs'truir/ *v.* obstruct, clog, block.
obtener /oβte'ner/ *v.* obtain, get, secure.
obtuso /oβ'tuso/ *a.* obtuse.
obvio /'oββio/ *a.* obvious.
ocasión /oka'sion/ *n. f.* occasion; opportunity, chance. **de o.,** secondhand.
ocasional /okasio'nal/ *a.* occasional.
ocasionalmente /okasional-'mente/ *adv.* occasionally.
ocasionar /okasio'nar/ *v.* cause, occasion.
occidental /okθiðen'tal; oksiðen-'tal/ *a.* western.
occidente /okθi'ðente; oksi'ðente/ *n. m.* west.
océano /o'θeano; o'seano/ *n. m.* ocean.

Océano Atlántico /o'θeano a'tlantiko; o'seano a'tlantiko/ Atlantic Ocean.

Océano Pacífico /o'θeano pa'θifiko; o'seano pa'sifiko/ Pacific Ocean.

ocelote /oθe'lote; ose'lote/ *n. m.* ocelot.

ochenta /o'tʃenta/ *a. & pron.* eighty.

ocho /'otʃo/ *a. & pron.* eight.

ochocientos /otʃo'θientos; otʃo'sientos/ *a. & pron.* eight hundred.

ocio /'oθio; 'osio/ *n. m.* idleness, leisure.

ociosidad /oθiosi'ðað; osiosi'ðað/ *n. f.* idleness, laziness.

ocioso /o'θioso; o'sioso/ *a.* idle, lazy.

ocre /'okre/ *n. m.* ochre.

octagonal /oktago'nal/ *a.* octagonal.

octava /ok'taβa/ *n. f.* octave.

octavo /ok'taβo/ *a.* eighth.

octubre /ok'tuβre/ *n. m.* October.

oculista /oku'lista/ *n. m. & f.* oculist.

ocultación /okulta'θion; okulta'sion/ *n. f.* concealment.

ocultar /okul'tar/ *v.* hide, conceal.

oculto /o'kulto/ *a.* hidden.

ocupación /okupa'θion; okupa'sion/ *n. f.* occupation.

ocupado /oku'paðo/ *a.* occupied; busy.

ocupante /oku'pante/ *n. m. & f.* occupant.

ocupar /oku'par/ *v.* occupy.

ocuparse de /oku'parse de/ *v.* take care of, take charge of.

ocurrencia /oku'rrenθia; oku'rrensia/

ocurrente /oku'rrente/ *a.* witty.

ocurrir /oku'rrir/ *v.* occur, happen.

oda /'oða/ *n. f.* ode.

odio /'oðio/ *n. m.* hate. **—odiar,** *v.*

odiosidad /oðiosi'ðað/ *n. f.* odiousness; hatred.

odioso /o'ðioso/ *a.* obnoxious, odious.

odisea /oði'sea/ *n. f.* odyssey.

OEA, *abbr.* (**Organización de los Estados Americanos**). OAS (**Organization of American States**).

oeste /o'este/ *n. m.* west.

ofender /ofen'der/ *v.* offend, wrong.

ofenderse /ofen'derse/ *v.* be offended, take offense.

ofensa /o'fensa/ *n. f.* offense.

ofensiva /ofen'siβa/ *n. f.* offensive.

ofensivo /ofen'siβo/ *a.* offensive.

ofensor /ofen'sor/ **-ra** *n.* offender.

oferta /o'ferta/ *n. f.* offer, proposal.

ofertorio /ofer'torio/ *n. m.* offertory.

oficial /ofi'θial; ofi'sial/ *a. & m.* official; officer.

oficialmente /ofiθial'mente; ofisial'mente/ *adv.* officially.

oficiar /ofi'θiar; ofi'siar/ *v.* officiate.

oficina /ofi'θina; ofi'sina/ *n. f.* office.

oficio /o'fiθio; o'fisio/ *n. m.* office; trade; church service.

oficioso /ofi'θioso; ofi'sioso/ *a.* officious.

ofrecer /ofre'θer; ofre'ser/ *v.* offer.

ofrecimiento /ofreθi'miento; ofresi'miento/ *n. m.* offer, offering. **o. de presentación,** introductory offer.

ofrenda /o'frenda/ *n. f.* offering.

oftalmía /oftal'mia/ *n. f.* ophthalmia.

ofuscamiento /ofuska'miento/ *n. m.* obfuscation; bewilderment.

ofuscar /ofus'kar/ *v.* obfuscate; bewilder.

ogro /'ogro/ *n. m.* ogre.

oído /o'iðo/ *n. m.* ear; hearing.

oír /o'ir/ *v.* hear; listen.

ojal /o'hal/ *n. m.* buttonhole.

ojalá /oha'la/ *interj.* expressing wish or hope. **o. que...** would that...

ojeada /ohe'aða/ *n. f.* glance; peep; look.

ojear /ohe'ar/ *v.* eye, look at, glance at, stare at.

ojeriza /ohe'riθa; ohe'risa/ *n. f.* spite; grudge.

ojiva /o'hiβa/ *n. f.* pointed arch, ogive.

ojo /'oho/ *n. m.* eye. **¡Ojo!** Look out!

ola /'ola/ *n. f.* wave.

olaje /o'lahe/ *n. m.* surge of waves.

oleada /ole'aða/ *n. f.* swell.

oleo /'oleo/ *n. m.* oil; holy oil; extreme unction.

oleoducto /oleo'ðukto/ *n. m.* pipeline.

oleomargarina /oleomarga'rina/
n. f. oleomargarine.
oleoso /ole'oso/ *a.* oily.
oler /o'ler/ *v.* smell.
olfatear /olfate'ar/ *v.* smell.
olfato /ol'fato/ *n. m.* scent, smell.
oliva /o'liβa/ *n. f.* olive.
olivar /oli'βar/ *n. m.* olive grove.
olivo /o'liβo/ *n. m.* olive tree.
olla /'oʎa; 'oya/ *n. f.* pot, kettle.
  o. podrida, stew.
olmo /'olmo/ *n. m.* elm.
olor /o'lor/ *n. m.* odor, smell,
scent.
oloroso /olo'roso/ *a.* fragrant,
scented.
olvidadizo /olβiða'ðiθo; olβiða-
'ðiso/ *a.* forgetful.
olvidar /olβi'ðar/ *v.* forget.
olvido /ol'βiðo/ *n. m.* omission;
forgetfulness.
ombligo /om'βligo/ *n. m.* navel.
ominar /omi'nar/ *v.* foretell.
ominoso /omi'noso/ *a.* ominous.
omisión /omi'sion/ *n. f.* omission.
omitir /omi'tir/ *v.* omit, leave out.
ómnibus /'omniβus/ *n. m.* bus.
omnipotencia /omnipo'tenθia;
omnipo'tensia/ *n. f.* omnipotence.
omnipotente /omnipo'tente/ *a.*
almighty.
omnipresencia /omnipre'senθia;
omnipre'sensia/ *n. f.* omnipres-
ence.
omnisciencia /omnis'θienθia; om-
nis'siensia/ *n. f.* omniscience.
omnívoro /om'niβoro/ *a.* omnivo-
rous.
omóplato /omo'plato/ *n. m.*
shoulder blade.
once /'onθe; 'onse/ *a. & pron.*
eleven.
onda /'onda/ *n. f.* wave, ripple.
ondear /onde'ar/ *v.* ripple.
ondulación /ondula'θion; ondula-
'sion/ *n. f.* wave, undulation.
ondular /ondu'lar/ *v.* undulate,
ripple.
onza /'onθa; 'onsa/ *n. f.* ounce.
opaco /o'pako/ *a.* opaque.
ópalo /'opalo/ *n. m.* opal.
opción /op'θion; op'sion/ *n. f.* option.
ópera /'opera/ *n. f.* opera.
operación /opera'θion; opera'sion/
n. f. operation.
operar /ope'rar/ *v.* operate; operate on.
operario /ope'rario/ **-ria** *n.* operator; (skilled) worker.

operarse /ope'rarse/ *v.* have an
operation.
operativo /opera'tiβo/ *a.* operative.
opereta /ope'reta/ *n. f.* operetta.
opiato /o'piato/ *n. m.* opiate.
opinar /opi'nar/ *v.* opine.
opinión /opi'nion/ *n. f.* opinion,
view.
opio /'opio/ *n. m.* opium.
oponer /opo'ner/ *v.* oppose.
Oporto /o'porto/ *n. m.* port
(wine).
oportunidad /oportuni'ðað/ *n. f.*
opportunity.
oportunismo /oportu'nismo/ *n.*
m. opportunism.
oportunista /oportu'nista/ *n. & a.*
opportunist.
oportuno /opor'tuno/ *a.* opportune, expedient.
oposición /oposi'θion; oposi'sion/
n. f. opposition.
opresión /opre'sion/ *n. f.* oppression.
opresivo /opre'siβo/ *a.* oppressive.
oprimir /opri'mir/ *v.* oppress.
oprobio /o'proβio/ *n. m.* infamy.
optar /op'tar/ *v.* select, choose.
óptica /'optika/ *n. f.* optics.
óptico /'optiko/ *a.* optic.
optimismo /opti'mismo/ *n. m.* optimism.
optimista /opti'mista/ *a. & n.* optimistic; optimist.
óptimo /'optimo/ *a.* best.
opuesto /o'puesto/ *a.* opposite;
opposed.
opugnar /opug'nar/ *v.* attack.
opulencia /opu'lenθia; opu'lensia/
n. f. opulence, wealth.
opulento /opu'lento/ *a.* opulent,
wealthy.
oración /ora'θion; ora'sion/ *n. f.*
sentence; prayer; oration.
oráculo /o'rakulo/ *n. m.* oracle.
orador /ora'ðor/ **-ra** *n.* orator,
speaker.
oral /o'ral/ *a.* oral.
orangután /oraŋgu'tan/ *n. m.*
orangutan.
orar /o'rar/ *v.* pray.
oratoria /ora'toria/ *n. f.* oratory.
oratorio /ora'torio/ *a.* oratorical.
orbe /'orβe/ *n. m.* orb; globe.
órbita /'orβita/ *n. f.* orbit.
orden /'orðen/ *n. m. or f.* order.
ordenador /orðena'ðor/ *n. m.*
computer; regulator.

ordenador de sobremesa /orðena'ðor de soβre'mesa/ desktop computer.

ordenador doméstico /orðena'ðor do'mestiko/ home computer.

ordenanza /orðe'nanθa; orðe'nansa/ *n. f.* ordinance.

ordenar /orðe'nar/ *v.* order; put in order; ordain.

ordeñar /orðe'ɲar/ *v.* milk.

ordinal /orði'nal/ *a. & m.* ordinal.

ordinario /orði'nario/ *a.* ordinary; common, usual.

oreja /o'reha/ *n. f.* ear.

orejera /ore'hera/ *n. f.* earmuff.

orfanato /orfa'nato/ *n. m.* orphanage.

organdí /organ'di/ *n. m.* organdy.

orgánico /or'ganiko/ *a.* organic.

organigrama /organi'grama/ *n. m.* flow chart.

organismo /orga'nismo/ *n. m.* organism.

organista /orga'nista/ *n. m. & f.* organist.

organización /organiθa'θion; organisa'sion/ *n. f.* organization.

organizar /organi'θar; organi'sar/ *v.* organize.

órgano /'organo/ *n. m.* organ.

orgía /or'hia/ *n. f.* orgy, revel.

orgullo /or'guʎo; or'guyo/ *n. m.* pride.

orgulloso /orgu'ʎoso; orgu'yoso/ *a.* proud.

orientación /orienta'θion; orienta'sion/ *n. f.* orientation.

oriental /orien'tal/ *a.* Oriental; eastern.

orientar /orien'tar/ *v.* orient.

oriente /o'riente/ *n. m.* orient, east.

orificación /orifika'θion; orifika'sion/ *n. f.* gold filling (for tooth).

origen /o'rihen/ *n. m.* origin; parentage, descent.

original /orihi'nal/ *a.* original.

originalidad /orihinali'ðað/ *n. f.* originality.

originalmente /orihinal'mente/ *adv.* originally.

originar /orihi'nar/ *v.* originate.

orilla /o'riʎa; o'riya/ *n. f.* shore; bank; edge.

orín /o'rin/ *n. m.* rust.

orina /o'rina/ *n. f.* urine.

orinar /ori'nar/ *v.* urinate.

orines /o'rines/ *n. m.pl.* urine.

oriol /o'riol/ *n. m.* oriole.

orla /'orla/ *n. f.* border; edging.

ornado /or'naðo/ *a.* ornate.

ornamentación /ornamenta'θion; ornamenta'sion/ *n. f.* ornamentation.

ornamento /orna'mento/ *n. m.* ornament. —**ornamentar,** *v.*

ornar /or'nar/ *v.* ornament, adorn.

oro /'oro/ *n. m.* gold.

oropel /oro'pel/ *n. m.* tinsel.

orquesta /or'kesta/ *n. f.* orchestra.

ortiga /or'tiga/ *n. f.* nettle.

ortodoxo /orto'ðokso/ *a.* orthodox.

ortografía /ortogra'fia/ *n. f.* orthography, spelling.

ortóptero /or'toptero/ *a.* orthopterous.

oruga /o'ruga/ *n. f.* caterpillar.

orzuelo /or'θuelo; or'suelo/ *n. m.* sty.

os /os/ *pron.* you (*pl.*); yourselves.

osadía /osa'ðia/ *n. f.* daring.

osar /o'sar/ *v.* dare.

oscilación /osθila'θion; ossila'sion/ *n. f.* oscillation.

oscilar /osθi'lar; ossi'lar/ *v.* oscillate, rock.

ósculo /'oskulo/ *n. m.* kiss.

oscurecer /oskure'θer; oskure'ser/ *v.* obscure. **oscuridad,** *n.* obscurity; darkness. **oscuro,** *adj.* obscure; dark.

oso /'oso/ *n.* bear.

oso de felpa /'oso de 'felpa/ teddy bear.

ostentación /ostenta'θion; ostenta'sion/ *n. f.* ostentation, showiness.

ostentar /osten'tar/ *v.* show off.

ostentoso /osten'toso/ *a.* ostentatious, flashy.

ostra /'ostra/ *n. f.* oyster.

ostracismo /ostra'θismo; ostra'sismo/ *n. m.* ostracism.

otalgia /o'talhia/ *n. f.* earache.

otero /o'tero/ *n. m.* hill, knoll.

otoño /o'toɲo/ *n. m.* autumn, fall.

otorgar /otor'gar/ *v.* grant, award.

otro /'otro/ *a. & pron.* other, another. **o. vez,** again. **el uno al o.,** one another, each other.

ovación /oβa'θion; oβa'sion/ *n. f.* ovation.

oval /o'βal/ **ovalado** *a.* oval.

óvalo /'oβalo/ *n. m.* oval.

ovario /o'βario/ *n. m.* ovary.

oveja /o'βeha/ *n. f.* sheep.
ovejero /oβe'hero/ *n. m.* sheep dog.
ovillo /o'βiʎo; o'βiyo/ *n. m.* ball of yarn.
OVNI /'oβni/ *abbr.* (objeto volador no identificado) UFO (unidentified flying object).

oxidación /oksiða'θion; oksiða-'sion/ *n. f.* oxidation.
oxidar /oksi'ðar/ *v.* oxidize; rust.
óxido /'oksiðo/ *n. m.* oxide.
oxígeno /ok'siheno/ *n. m.* oxygen.
oyente /o'iente/ *n. m. & f.* hearer; (*pl.*) audience.
ozono /o'θono; o'sono/ *n. m.* ozone.

P

pabellón /paβe'ʎon; paβe'yon/ *n. m.* pavilion. **p. de deportes,** sports center.
pabilo /pa'βilo/ *n. m.* wick.
paciencia /pa'θienθia; pa'siensia/ *n. f.* patience.
paciente /pa'θiente; pa'siente/ *a. & n.* patient.
pacificar /paθifi'kar; pasifi'kar/ *v.* pacify.
pacífico /pa'θifiko; pa'sifiko/ *a.* pacific.
pacifismo /paθi'fismo; pasi'fismo/ *n. m.* pacifism.
pacifista /paθi'fista; pasi'fista/ *n. & a.* pacifist.
pacto /'pakto/ *n. m.* pact, treaty.
padecer /paðe'θer; paðe'ser/ *v.* suffer. **p. del corazón,** have heart trouble.
padrastro /pa'ðrastro/ *n. m.* stepfather.
padre /'paðre/ *n. m.* father; priest; (*pl.*) parents.
padrenuestro /paðre'nuestro/ *n. m.* paternoster, Lord's Prayer.
padrino /pa'ðrino/ *n. m.* godfather; sponsor.
paella /pa'eʎa; pa'eya/ *n. f.* dish of rice with meat or chicken.
paga /'paga/ *n. f.* pay, wages. **p. extra** bonus.
pagadero /paga'ðero/ *a.* payable.
pagador /paga'ðor/ **-ra** *n.* payer.
paganismo /paga'nismo/ *n. m.* paganism.
pagano /pa'gano/ **-na** *a. & n.* heathen, pagan.
pagar /pa'gar/ *v.* pay, pay for. **p. en metálico,** pay cash.
página /'pahina/ *n. f.* page.
pago /'pago/ *n. m.* pay, payment.
país /pa'is/ *n. m.* country, nation.
paisaje /pai'sahe/ *n. m.* landscape, scenery, countryside.
paisano /pai'sano/ **-na** *n.* countryman; compatriot; civilian.

paja /'paha/ *n. f.* straw.
pajar /pa'har/ *n. m.* barn.
pajarita /paha'rita/ *n. f.* bow tie.
pájaro /'paharo/ *n. m.* bird.
paje /'pahe/ *n. m.* page (person).
pala /'pala/ *n. f.* shovel, spade.
palabra /pa'laβra/ *n. f.* word.
palabrero /pala'βrero/ *a.* talkative; wordy.
palabrista /pala'βrista/ *n. m. & f.* talkative person.
palacio /pa'laθio; pa'lasio/ *n. m.* palace.
paladar /pala'ðar/ *n. m.* palate.
paladear /palaðe'ar/ *v.* taste; relish.
palanca /pa'lanka/ *n. f.* lever. **p. de cambio,** gearshift.
palangana /palaŋ'gana/ *n. f.* washbasin.
palco /'palko/ *n. m.* theater box.
palenque /pa'lenke/ *n. m.* palisade.
paleta /pa'leta/ *n. f.* mat, pallet.
paletilla /pale'tiʎa; pale'tiya/ *n. f.* shoulder blade.
palidecer /paliðe'θer; paliðe'ser/ *v.* turn pale.
palidez /pali'ðeθ; pali'ðes/ *n. f.* paleness.
pálido /'paliðo/ *a.* pale.
paliza /pa'liθa; pa'lisa/ *n. f.* beating.
palizada /pali'θaða; pali'saða/ *n. m.* palisade.
palma /'palma/ **palmera** *n. f.* palm (tree).
palmada /pal'maða/ *n. f.* slap, clap.
palmear /palme'ar/ *v.* applaud.
palo /'palo/ *n. m.* pole, stick; suit (in cards); *Naut.* mast.
paloma /pa'loma/ *n. f.* dove, pigeon.
palpar /pal'par/ *v.* touch, feel.
palpitación /palpita'θion; palpita-'sion/ *n. f.* palpitation.

palpitar /palpi'tar/ *v.* palpitate.

paludismo /palu'ðismo/ *n. m.* malaria.

pampa /'pampa/ *n. f.* (*S.A.*) prairie, plain.

pan /pan/ *n. m.* bread; loaf. **p. de centeno,** rye bread.

pana /'pana/ *n. f.* corduroy.

panacea /pana'θea; pana'sea/ *n. f.* panacea.

panadería /panaðe'ria/ *n. f.* bakery.

panadero /pana'ðero/ **-ra** *n.* baker.

panameño /pana'meɲo/ **-ña** *a.* & *n.* Panamanian, of Panama.

panamericano /panameri'kano/ *a.* Pan-American.

páncreas /'pankreas/ *n. m.* pancreas.

pandeo /pan'deo/ *n. m.* bulge.

pandilla /pan'diʎa; pan'diya/ *n. f.* band, gang.

panecillo /pane'θiʎo; pane'siyo/ *n. m.* roll, muffin.

panegírico /pane'hiriko/ *n. m.* panegyric.

pánico /'paniko/ *n. m.* panic.

panocha /pa'notʃa/ *n. f.* ear of corn.

panorama /pano'rama/ *n. m.* panorama.

panorámico /pano'ramiko/ *a.* panoramic.

pantalla /pan'taʎa; pan'taya/ *n. f.* (movie) screen; lamp shade.

pantalones /panta'lones/ *n. m.pl.* trousers, pants.

pantano /pan'tano/ *n. m.* bog, marsh, swamp.

pantanoso /panta'noso/ *a.* swampy, marshy.

pantera /pan'tera/ *n. f.* panther.

pantomima /panto'mima/ *n. f.* pantomime.

pantorrilla /panto'rriʎa; panto-'rriya/ *n. f.* calf (of body).

panza /'panθa; 'pansa/ *n. f.* belly, paunch.

pañal /pa'ɲal/ *n. m.* diaper.

paño /'paɲo/ *n. m.* piece of cloth.

pañuelo /pa'ɲuelo/ *n. m.* handkerchief.

Papa /'papa/ *n. m.* Pope.

papa *n. f.* potato.

papá *n. m.* papa, father.

papado /pa'paðo/ *n. m.* papacy.

papagayo /papa'gaio/ *n. m.* parrot.

papal /pa'pal/ *a.* papal.

Papá Noel /pa'pa no'el/ *n. m.* Santa Claus.

papel /pa'pel/ *n. m.* paper; role, part.

papel crespón /pa'pel kres'pon/ crepe paper.

papel de aluminio /pa'pel de alu'minio/ aluminum foil.

papel de escribir /pa'pel de es-kri'βir/ writing paper.

papel de estaño /pa'pel de es'taɲo/ tin foil.

papel de lija /pa'pel de 'liha/ sandpaper.

papelera /pape'lera/ *n. f.* file cabinet; wastepaper basket.

papelería /papele'ria/ *n. f.* stationery store.

papel moneda /pa'pel mo'neða/ paper money.

paperas /pa'peras/ *n. f.pl.* mumps.

paquete /pa'kete/ *n. m.* package.

par /par/ *a.* **1.** even, equal. —*n.* **2.** *m.* pair; equal, peer. **abierto de p. en p.,** wide open.

para /'para/ *prep.* for; in order to. **p. que,** in order that. **estar p.,** to be about to.

parabién /para'βien/ *n. m.* congratulation.

parabrisa /para'βrisa/ *n. m.* windshield.

paracaídas /paraka'iðas/ *n. m.* parachute.

parachoques /para'tʃokes/ *n. m. Auto.* bumper.

parada /pa'raða/ *n. f.* stop, halt; stopover; parade.

paradero /para'ðero/ *n. m.* whereabouts; stopping place.

paradigma /para'ðigma/ *n. m.* paradigm.

paradoja /para'ðoha/ *n. f.* paradox.

parafina /para'fina/ *n. f.* paraffin.

parafrasear /parafrase'ar/ *v.* paraphrase.

paraguas /pa'raguas/ *n. m.* umbrella.

paraguayano /paragua'yano/ **-na** *n.* & *a.* Paraguayan.

paraíso /para'iso/ *n. m.* paradise.

paralelo /para'lelo/ *a.* & *m.* parallel.

parálisis /pa'ralisis/ *n. f.* paralysis.

paralizar /parali'θar; parali'sar/ *v.* paralyze.

paramédico /para'meðiko/ *n. m.* paramedic.

parámetro /pa'rametro/ *n. m.* parameter.

parapeto /para'peto/ *n. m.* parapet.

parar /pa'rar/ *v.* stop, stem, ward off; stay.

pararse /pa'rarse/ *v.* stop; stand up.

parasítico /para'sitiko/ *a.* parasitic.

parásito /pa'rasito/ *n. m.* parasite.

parcela /par'θela; par'sela/ *n. f.* plot of ground.

parcial /par'θial; par'sial/ *a.* partial.

parcialidad /parθiali'ðað; parsiali-'ðað/ *n. f.* partiality; bias.

parcialmente /parθial'mente; parsial'mente/ *adv.* partially.

pardo /'parðo/ *a.* brown.

parear /pare'ar/ *v.* pair; match; mate.

parecer /pare'θer; pare'ser/ *n.* **1.** *m.* opinion. —*v.* **2.** seem, appear, look.

parecerse /pare'θerse; pare'serse/ *v.* look alike. **p. a,** look like.

parecido /pare'θiðo; pare'siðo/ *a.* similar.

pared /pa'reð/ *n. f.* wall.

pareja /pa'reha/ *n. f.* pair, couple; (dancing) partner.

parentela /paren'tela/ *n. f.* kinfolk.

parentesco /paren'tesko/ *n. m.* parentage, lineage; kin.

paréntesis /pa'rentesis/ *n. m.* parenthesis.

paria /'paria/ *n. m.* outcast, pariah.

paricipante /pariθi'pante; parisi'pante/ *n. m. & f.* participant.

paridad /pari'ðað/ *n. f.* parity.

pariente /pa'riente/ *n. m. & f.* relative.

parir /pa'rir/ *v.* give birth.

parisiense /pari'siense/ *n. & a.* Parisian.

parlamentario /parlamen'tario/ *a.* parliamentary.

parlamento /parla'mento/ *n. m.* parliament.

paro /'paro/ *n. m.* stoppage; strike. **p. forzoso,** unemployment.

parodia /pa'roðia/ *n. f.* parody.

parodista /paro'ðista/ *n. m. & f.* parodist.

paroxismo /parok'sismo/ *n. m.* paroxysm.

párpado /'parpaðo/ *n. m.* eyelid.

parque /'parke/ *n. m.* park.

parquímetro /par'kimetro/ *n. m.* parking meter.

parra /'parra/ *n. f.* grapevine.

párrafo /'parrafo/ *n. m.* paragraph.

parranda /pa'rranda/ *n. f.* spree.

parrandear /parrande'ar/ *v.* carouse.

parrilla /pa'rriʎa; pa'rriya/ *n. f.* grill; grillroom.

párroco /'parroko/ *n. m.* parish priest.

parroquía /pa'rrokia/ *n. f.* parish.

parroquial /parro'kial/ *a.* parochial.

parsimonia /parsi'monia/ *n. f.* economy, thrift.

parsimonioso /parsimo'nioso/ *a.* economical, thrifty.

parte /'parte/ *n. f.* part. **de p. de,** on behalf of. **alguna p.,** somewhere. **por otra p.,** on the other hand. **dar p. a,** to notify.

partera /par'tera/ *n. f.* midwife.

partición /parti'θion; parti'sion/ *n. f.* distribution.

participación /partiθipa'θion; partisipa'sion/ *n. f.* participation.

participar /partiθi'par; partisi'par/ *v.* participate; announce.

participio /parti'θipio; parti'sipio/ *n. m.* participle.

partícula /par'tikula/ *n. f.* particle.

particular /partiku'lar/ *a.* **1.** particular; private. —*n.* **2.** *m.* particular; detail; individual.

particularmente /partikular'mente/ *adv.* particularly.

partida /par'tiða/ *n. f.* departure; *Mil.* party; (sport) game.

partida de defunción /par'tiða de defun'θion; par'tiða de defun'sion/ death certificate.

partida de matrimonio /par'tiða de matri'monio/ marriage certificate.

partida de nacimiento /par'tiða de naθi'miento; par'tiða de nasi'miento/ birth certificate.

partidario /parti'ðario/ **-ria** *n.* partisan.

partido /par'tiðo/ *n. m.* side, party, faction; game, match.

partir /par'tir/ *v.* leave, depart; part, cleave, split.

parto /'parto/ *n. m.* delivery, childbirth.

pasa /'pasa/ *n. f.* raisin.

pasado /pa'saðo/ a. **1.** past; last.
—n. **2.** m. past.

pasaje /pa'sahe/ n. m. passage,
fare.

pasajero /pasa'hero/ **-ra** a. **1.**
passing, transient. —n. **2.** passenger.

pasamano /pasa'mano/ n. m.
banister.

pasaporte /pasa'porte/ n. m.
passport.

pasar /pa'sar/ v. pass; happen;
spend (time). **p. por alto,** overlook. **p. lista,** call the roll. **p. sin,**
do without.

pasatiempo /pasa'tiempo/ n. m.
pastime; hobby.

pascua /'paskua/ n. f. religious
holiday; (pl.) Christmas (season).
P. Florida, Easter.

pase de modelos /'pase de
mo'ðelos/ n. m. fashion show.

paseo /pa'seo/ n. m. walk, stroll;
drive. —**pasear,** v.

pasillo /pa'siʎo; pa'siyo/ n. m.
aisle; hallway.

pasión /pa'sion/ n. f. passion.

pasivo /pa'siβo/ a. passive.

pasmar /pas'mar/ v. astonish, astound, stun.

pasmo /'pasmo/ n. m. spasm;
wonder.

paso /'paso/ a. **1.** dried (fruit).
—n. **2.** m. pace, step; (mountain)
pass.

paso cebra /'paso 'θeβra; 'paso
'seβra/ crosswalk.

paso de ganso /'paso de 'ganso/
goose step.

paso de peatones /'paso de
pea'tones/ pedestrian crossing.

pasta /'pasta/ n. f. paste; batter;
plastic.

pasta dentífrica /'pasta den'tifrika/ toothpaste.

pastar /pas'tar/ v. graze.

pastel /pas'tel/ n. m. pastry; pie.

pastelería /pastele'ria/ n. f. pastry; pastry shop.

pasteurización /pasteuriθa'θion;
pasteurisa'sion/ n. f. pasteurization.

pasteurizar /pasteuri'θar; pasteuri'sar/ v. pasteurize.

pastilla /pas'tiʎa; pas'tiya/ n. f.
tablet, lozenge, coughdrop.

pasto /'pasto/ n. m. pasture;
grass.

pastor /pas'tor/ n. m. pastor;
shepherd.

pastorear /pastore'ar/ v. pasture,
tend (a flock).

pastrón /pas'tron/ n. m. pastrami.

pastura /pas'tura/ n. f. pasture.

pata /'pata/ n. f. foot (of animal).

patada /pa'taða/ n. f. kick.

patán /pa'tan/ n. m. boor.

patanada /pata'naða/ n. f. rudeness.

patata /pa'tata/ n. f. potato. **p.
asada,** baked potato.

patear /pate'ar/ v. stamp, tramp,
kick.

patente /pa'tente/ a. & m. patent.
—**patentar,** v.

paternal /pater'nal/ **paterno** a.
paternal.

paternidad /paterni'ðað/ n. f. paternity, fatherhood.

patético /pa'tetiko/ a. pathetic.

patíbulo /pa'tiβulo/ n. m. scaffold; gallows.

patín /pa'tin/ n. m. skate.
—**patinar,** v.

patín de ruedas /pa'tin de 'rrueðas/ roller skate.

patio /'patio/ n. m. yard, court,
patio.

pato /'pato/ n. m. duck.

patria /'patria/ n. f. native land.

patriarca /pa'triarka/ n. m. & f.
patriarch.

patrimonio /patri'monio/ n. m.
inheritance.

patriota /pa'triota/ n. m. & f. patriot.

patriótico /pa'triotiko/ a. patriotic.

patriotismo /patrio'tismo/ n. m.
patriotism.

patrocinar /patroθi'nar; patrosi'nar/ v. patronize, sponsor.

patrón /pa'tron/ **-ona** n. patron;
boss; (dress) pattern.

patrulla /pa'truʎa; pa'truya/ n. f.
patrol. —**patrullar,** v.

paulatino /paula'tino/ a. gradual.

pausa /'pausa/ n. f. pause.
—**pausar,** v.

pausa para el café /'pausa 'para
el ka'fe/ coffee break.

pauta /'pauta/ n. f. guideline.

pavesa /pa'βesa/ n. f. spark, cinder.

pavimentar /paβimen'tar/ v.
pave.

pavimento /paβi'mento/ n. m.
pavement.

pavo /'paβo/ n. m. turkey. **p.
real,** peacock.

pavor /pa'βor/ *n. m.* terror.

payaso /pa'iaso/ **-sa** *n.* clown.

paz /paθ; pas/ *n. f.* peace.

peatón /pea'ton/ **-na** *n.* pedestrian.

peca /'peka/ *n. f.* freckle.

pecado /pe'kaðo/ *n. m.* sin.

—pecar, *v.*

pecador /peka'ðor/ **-ra** *a. & n.* sinful; sinner.

pecera /pe'θera; pe'sera/ *n. f.* aquarium, fishbowl.

pechera /pe'tʃera/ *n. f.* shirt front.

pecho /'petʃo/ *n. m.* chest; breast; bosom.

pechuga /pe'tʃuga/ *n. f.* breast (of fowl).

pecoso /pe'koso/ *a.* freckled, freckly.

peculiar /peku'liar/ *a.* peculiar.

peculiaridad /pekuliari'ðað/ *n. f.* peculiarity.

pedagogía /peðago'hia/ *n. f.* pedagogy.

pedagogo /peða'gogo/ **-ga** *n.* pedagogue, teacher.

pedal /pe'ðal/ *n. m.* pedal.

pedantesco /peðan'tesko/ *a.* pedantic.

pedazo /pe'ðaθo; pe'ðaso/ *n. m.* piece.

pedernal /peðer'nal/ *n. m.* flint.

pedestal /peðes'tal/ *n. m.* pedestal.

pediatra /pe'ðiatra/ *n. m. & f.* pediatrician.

pediatría /peðia'tria/ *n. f.* pediatrics.

pedicuro /peði'kuro/ *n. m.* chiropodist.

pedir /pe'ðir/ *v.* ask, ask for, request; apply for; order.

pedo /'pedo/ *n. m.* fart; intoxication.

pedregoso /peðre'goso/ *a.* rocky.

pegajoso /pega'hoso/ *a.* sticky.

pegamento /pega'mento/ *n. m.* glue.

pegar /pe'gar/ *v.* beat, strike; adhere, fasten, stick.

peinado /pei'naðo/ *n. m.* coiffure, hairdo.

peine /'peine/ *n. m.* comb.

—peinar, *v.*

peineta /pei'neta/ *n. f.* (ornamental) comb.

pelagra /pe'lagra/ *n. f.* pellagra.

pelar /pe'lar/ *v.* skin, pare, peel.

pelea /pe'lea/ *n. f.* fight, row.

—pelearse, *v.*

pelícano /pe'likano/ *n. m.* pelican.

película /pe'likula/ *n. f.* movie, motion picture, film. **p. de terror** horror film.

peligrar /peli'grar/ *v.* be in danger.

peligro /pe'ligro/ *n. m.* peril, danger.

peligroso /peli'groso/ *a.* perilous, dangerous.

pelirrojo /peli'rroho/ **-ja** *a. & n.* redhead.

pellejo /pe'ʎeho; pe'yeho/ *n. m.* skin; peel (of fruit).

pellizco /pe'ʎiθko; pe'yisko/ *n. m.* pinch. **—pellizcar,** *v.*

pelo /'pelo/ *n. m.* hair.

pelota /pe'lota/ *n. f.* ball.

peltre /'peltre/ *n. m.* pewter.

peluca /pe'luka/ *n. f.* wig.

peludo /pe'luðo/ *a.* hairy.

peluquería /peluke'ria/ *n. f.* hairdresser's shop, beauty parlor.

peluquero /pelu'kero/ **-ra** *n.* hairdresser.

pena /'pena/ *n. f.* pain, grief, trouble, woe; penalty. **valer la p.,** to be worthwhile.

penacho /pe'natʃo/ *n. m.* plume.

penalidad /penali'ðað/ *n. f.* trouble; penalty.

pender /pen'der/ *v.* hang, dangle; be pending.

pendiente /pen'diente/ *a.* **1.** hanging; pending. **—n. 2.** *m.* incline, slope; earring, pendant.

pendón /pen'don/ *n. m.* pennant, flag.

penetración /penetra'θion; penetra'sion/ *n. f.* penetration.

penetrar /pene'trar/ *v.* penetrate, pierce.

penicilina /peniθi'lina; penisi'lina/ *n. f.* penicillin.

península /pe'ninsula/ *n. f.* peninsula.

penitencia /peni'tenθia; peni'tensia/ *n. f.* penitence, penance.

penitenciaría /penitenθia'ria; penitensia'ria/ *n. f.* penitentiary.

penoso /pe'noso/ *a.* painful, troublesome, grievous, distressing.

pensador /pensa'ðor/ **-ra** *n.* thinker.

pensamiento /pensa'miento/ *n. m.* thought.

pensar /pen'sar/ *v.* think; intend, plan.

pensativo /pensa'tiβo/ a. pensive, thoughtful.

pensión /pen'sion/ n. f. pension; boardinghouse.

pensionista /pensio'nista/ n. m. & f. boarder.

pentagonal /pentago'nal/ a. pentagonal.

penúltimo /pe'nultimo/ a. next-to-the-last, last but one, penultimate.

penuria /pe'nuria/ n. f. penury, poverty.

peña /'peɲa/ n. f. rock.

peñascoso /peɲas'koso/ a. rocky.

peñón /pe'ɲon/ n. m. rock, crag.

Peñón de Gibraltar /pe'ɲon de hiβral'tar/ Rock of Gibraltar.

peón /pe'on/ n. m. unskilled laborer; infantryman.

peonada /peo'naða/ n. f. group of laborers.

peonía /peo'nia/ n. f. peony.

peor /pe'or/ a. worse, worst.

pepino /pe'pino/ n. m. cucumber.

pepita /pe'pita/ n. f. seed (in fruit).

pequeñez /peke'ɲeθ; peke'ɲes/ n. f. smallness; trifle.

pequeño /pe'keɲo/ -ña a. **1.** small, little, short, slight. —n. **2.** child.

pera /'pera/ n. f. pear.

peral /pe'ral/ n. m. pear tree.

perca /'perka/ n. f. perch (fish).

percal /per'kal/ n. m. calico, percale.

percance /per'kanθe; per'kanse/ n. m. mishap, snag, hitch.

percepción /perθep'θion; persep'sion/ n. f. perception.

perceptivo /perθep'tiβo; persep'tiβo/ a. perceptive.

percha /'pertʃa/ n. f. perch; clothes hanger, rack.

percibir /perθi'βir; persi'βir/ v. perceive, sense; collect.

perder /per'ðer/ v. lose; miss; waste. **echar a p.,** spoil. **p. el conocimiento,** lose consciousness.

perdición /perði'θion; perði'sion/ n. f. perdition, downfall.

pérdida /'perðiða/ n. f. loss.

perdiz /per'ðiθ; per'ðis/ n. f. partridge.

perdón /per'ðon/ n. m. pardon, forgiveness.

perdonar /perðo'nar/ v. forgive, pardon; spare.

perdurable /perðu'raβle/ a. enduring, everlasting.

perdurar /perðu'rar/ v. endure, last.

perecedero /pereθe'ðero; perese'ðero/ a. perishable.

perecer /pere'θer; pere'ser/ v. perish.

peregrinación /peregrina'θion; peregrina'sion/ n. f. peregrination; pilgrimage.

peregrino /pere'grino/ -na n. pilgrim.

perejil /pere'hil/ n. m. parsley.

perenne /pe'renne/ a. perennial.

pereza /pe'reθa; pe'resa/ n. f. laziness.

perezoso /pere'θoso; pere'soso/ a. lazy, sluggish.

perfección /perfek'θion; perfek'sion/ n. f. perfection.

perfeccionar /perfekθio'nar; perfeksio'nar/ v. perfect.

perfeccionista /perfekθio'nista; perfeksio'nista/ a. & n. perfectionist.

perfectamente /perfekta'mente/ adv. perfectly.

perfecto /per'fekto/ a. perfect.

perfidia /per'fiðia/ n. f. falseness, perfidy.

pérfido /'perfiðo/ a. perfidious.

perfil /per'fil/ n. m. profile.

perforación /perfora'θion; perfora'sion/ n. f. perforation.

perforar /perfo'rar/ v. pierce, perforate.

perfume /per'fume/ n. m. perfume, scent. —**perfumar,** v.

pergamino /perga'mino/ n. m. parchment.

pericia /pe'riθia; pe'risia/ n. f. skill, expertness.

perico /pe'riko/ n. m. parakeet.

perímetro /pe'rimetro/ n. m. perimeter.

periódico /pe'rioðiko/ a. **1.** periodic. —n. **2.** m. newspaper.

periodista /perio'ðista/ n. m. & f. journalist.

período /pe'rioðo/ n. m. period.

periscopio /peris'kopio/ n. m. periscope.

perito /pe'rito/ -ta a. & n. experienced; expert, connoisseur.

perjudicar /perhuði'kar/ v. damage, hurt; impair.

perjudicial /perhuði'θial; perhuði'sial/ a. harmful, injurious.

perjuicio /per'huiθio; per'huisio/ *n. m.* injury, damage.

perjurar /perhu'rar/ *v.* commit perjury.

perjurio /per'hurio/ *n. m.* perjury.

perla /'perla/ *n. f.* pearl.

permanecer /permane'θer; permane'ser/ *v.* remain, stay.

permanencia /perma'nenθia; perma'nensia/ *n. f.* permanence; stay.

permanente /perma'nente/ *a.* permanent.

permiso /per'miso/ *n. m.* permission; permit; furlough.

permitir /permi'tir/ *v.* permit, enable, let, allow.

permuta /per'muta/ *n. f.* exchange, barter.

pernicioso /perni'θioso; perni'sioso/ *a.* pernicious.

perno /'perno/ *n. m.* bolt.

pero /'pero/ *conj.* but.

peróxido /pe'roksiðo/ *n. m.* peroxide.

perpendicular /perpendiku'lar/ *n. m. & a.* perpendicular.

perpetración /perpetra'θion; perpetra'sion/ *n. f.* perpetration.

perpetrar /perpe'trar/ *v.* perpetrate.

perpetuar /perpe'tuar/ *v.* perpetuate.

perpetuidad /perpetui'ðað/ *n. f.* perpetuity.

perpetuo /per'petuo/ *a.* perpetual.

perplejo /per'pleho/ *a.* perplexed, puzzled.

perrito caliente /pe'rrito ka'liente/ *n. m.* hot dog.

perro /'perro/ **-rra** *n.* dog.

persecución /perseku'θion; perseku'sion/ *n. f.* persecution.

perseguir /perse'gir/ *v.* pursue; persecute.

perseverancia /perseβe'ranθia; perseβe'ransia/ *n. f.* perseverance.

perseverar /perseβe'rar/ *v.* persevere.

persiana /per'siana/ *n. f.* shutter, Venetian blind.

persistente /persis'tente/ *a.* persistent.

persistir /persis'tir/ *v.* persist.

persona /per'sona/ *n. f.* person.

personaje /perso'nahe/ *n. m.* personage; *Theat.* character.

personal /perso'nal/ *a.* **1.** personal. —*n.* **2.** *m.* personnel, staff.

personalidad /personali'ðað/ *n. f.* personality.

personalmente /personal'mente/ *adv.* personally.

perspectiva /perspek'tiβa/ *n. f.* perspective; prospect.

perspicaz /perspi'kaθ; perspi'kas/ *a.* perspicacious, acute.

persuadir /persua'ðir/ *v.* persuade.

persuasión /persua'sion/ *n. f.* persuasion.

persuasivo /persua'siβo/ *a.* persuasive.

pertenecer /pertene'θer; pertene'ser/ *v.* pertain; belong.

pertinencia /perti'nenθia; perti'nensia/ *n. f.* pertinence.

pertinente /perti'nente/ *a.* pertinent; relevant.

perturbar /pertur'βar/ *v.* perturb, disturb.

peruano /pe'ruano/ **-na** *a. & n.* Peruvian.

perversidad /perβersi'ðað/ *n. f.* perversity.

perverso /per'βerso/ *a.* perverse.

pesadez /pesa'ðeθ; pesa'ðes/ *n. f.* dullness.

pesadilla /pesa'ðiʎa; pesa'ðiya/ *n. f.* nightmare.

pesado /pe'saðo/ *a.* heavy; dull, dreary, boring.

pésame /'pesame/ *n. m.* condolence.

pesar /pe'sar/ *n. m.* sorrow; regret. **a p. de,** in spite of. *v.* weigh.

pesca /'peska/ *n. f.* fishing; catch (of fish).

pescadería /peskaðe'ria/ *n. f.* fish store.

pescado /pes'kaðo/ *n. m.* fish. —**pescar,** *v.*

pescador /peska'ðor/ *n. m.* fisherman.

pesebre /pe'seβre/ *n. m.* stall, manger; crib.

peseta /pe'seta/ *n. f.* peseta (monetary unit).

pesimismo /pesi'mismo/ *n. m.* pessimism.

pesimista /pesi'mista/ *a. & n.* pessimistic; pessimist.

pésimo /'pesimo/ *a.* awful, terrible, very bad.

peso /'peso/ *n. m.* weight; load; peso (monetary unit).

pesquera /pes'kera/ *n. f.* fishery.

pesquisa /pes'kisa/ *n. f.* investigation.

pestaña /pes'taɲa/ *n. f.* eyelash.

pestañeo /pesta'ɲeo/ *n. m.* wink, blink. **—pestañear,** *v.*

peste /'peste/ *n. f.* plague.

pesticida /pesti'θiða; pesti'siða/ *n. m.* pesticide.

pestilencia /pesti'lenθia; pesti-'lensia/ *n. f.* pestilence.

pétalo /'petalo/ *n. m.* petal.

petardo /pe'tarðo/ *n. m.* firecracker.

petición /peti'θion; peti'sion/ *n. f.* petition.

petirrojo /peti'rroho/ *n. m.* robin.

petrel /pe'trel/ *n. m.* petrel.

pétreo /'petreo/ *a.* rocky.

petrificar /petrifi'kar/ *v.* petrify.

petróleo /pe'troleo/ *n. m.* petroleum.

petrolero /petro'lero/ *n. m.* oil tanker.

petunia /pe'tunia/ *n. f.* petunia.

pez /peθ; pes/ *n.* **1.** *m.* fish (in the water). **—***n.* **2.** *f.* pitch, tar.

pezuña /pe'θuɲa; pe'suɲa/ *n. f.* hoof.

piadoso /pia'ðoso/ *a.* pious; merciful.

pianista /pia'nista/ *n. m. & f.* pianist.

piano /'piano/ *n. m.* piano.

picadero /pika'ðero/ *n. m.* riding school.

picadura /pika'ðura/ *n. f.* sting, bite, prick.

picamaderos /pikama'ðeros/ *n. m.* woodpecker.

picante /pi'kante/ *a.* hot, spicy.

picaporte /pika'porte/ *n. m.* latch.

picar /pi'kar/ *v.* sting, bite, prick; itch; chop up, grind up.

pícaro /'pikaro/ **-ra** *a.* **1.** knavish, mischievous. **—***n.* **2.** rogue, rascal.

picarse /pi'karse/ *v.* be offended, piqued.

picazón /pika'θon; pika'son/ *n. f.* itch.

pícea /'piθea; 'pisea/ *n. f.* spruce.

pichón /pi'tʃon/ *n. m.* pigeon, squab.

pico /'piko/ *n. m.* peak; pick; beak; spout; small amount.

picotazo /piko'taθo; piko'taso/ *n. m.* peck. **—picotear,** *v.*

pictórico /pik'toriko/ *a.* pictorial.

pie /pie/ *n. m.* foot. **al p. de la letra,** literally; thoroughly.

piedad /pie'ðað/ *n. f.* piety; pity, mercy.

piedra /'pieðra/ *n. f.* stone.

piel /piel/ *n. f.* skin, hide; fur.

pienso /'pienso/ *n. m.* fodder.

pierna /'pierna/ *n. f.* leg.

pieza /'pieθa; 'piesa/ *n. f.* piece; room; *Theat.* play.

pijama /pi'hama/ *n. m. or m.pl.* pajamas.

pila /'pila/ *n. f.* pile, stack; battery; sink.

pilar /pi'lar/ *n. m.* pillar, column.

píldora /'pildora/ *n. f.* pill.

pillo /'piʎo; 'piyo/ **-a** *n.* thief; rascal.

piloto /pi'loto/ *n. m. & f.* pilot.

pimentón /pimen'ton/ *n. m.* paprika.

pimienta /pi'mienta/ *n. f.* pepper (spice).

pimiento /pi'miento/ *n. m.* pepper (vegetable).

pináculo /pi'nakulo/ *n. m.* pinnacle.

pincel /pin'θel; pin'sel/ *n. m.* (artist's) brush.

pinchadiscos /pintʃa'ðiskos/ *m. & f.* disk jockey.

pinchazo /pin'tʃaθo; pin'tʃaso/ *n. m.* puncture; prick. **—pinchar,** *v.*

pingajo /piŋ'gaho/ *n. m.* rag, tatter.

pino /'pino/ *n. m.* pine.

pinta /'pinta/ *n. f.* pint.

pintar /pin'tar/ *v.* paint; portray, depict.

pintor /pin'tor/ **-ra** *n.* painter.

pintoresco /pinto'resko/ *a.* picturesque.

pintura /pin'tura/ *n. f.* paint; painting.

pinzas /'pinθas; 'pinsas/ *n. f.pl.* pincers, tweezers; claws.

piña /'piɲa/ *n. f.* pineapple.

pío /'pio/ *a.* pious; merciful.

piojo /'pioho/ *n. m.* louse.

pionero /pio'nero/ **-ra** *n.* pioneer.

pipa /'pipa/ *n. f.* tobacco pipe.

pique /'pike/ *n. m.* resentment, pique. **echar a p.,** sink (ship).

pira /'pira/ *n. f.* pyre.

piragua /pi'ragua/ *n. f.* canoe.

piragüismo /pira'guismo/ *n. m.* canoeing.

piragüista /pira'guista/ *n. m. & f.* canoeist.

pirámide /pi'ramiðe/ *n. f.* pyramid.

pirata /pi'rata/ *n. m. & f.* pirate.
p. de aviones, hijacker.
pisada /pi'saða/ *n. f.* tread, step.
—**pisar,** *v.*
pisapapeles /pisapa'peles/ *n. m.*
paperweight.
piscina /pis'θina; pis'sina/ *n. f.*
fishpond; swimming pool.
piso /'piso/ *n. m.* floor.
pista /'pista/ *n. f.* trace, clue,
track; racetrack.
pista de tenis /'pista de 'tenis/
tennis court.
pistola /pis'tola/ *n. f.* pistol.
pistón /pis'ton/ *n. m.* piston.
pitillo /pi'tiʎo; pi'tiyo/ *n. m.* cigarette.
pito /'pito/ *n. m.* whistle. —**pitar,**
v.
pizarra /pi'θarra; pi'sarra/ *n. f.*
slate; blackboard.
pizca /'piθka; 'piska/ *n. f.* bit,
speck; pinch.
pizza /'piθθa; 'pissa/ *n. f.* pizza.
placentero /plaθen'tero; plasen-
'tero/ *a.* pleasant.
placer /pla'θer; pla'ser/ *n.* **1.** *m.*
pleasure. —*v.* **2.** please.
plácido /'plaθiðo; 'plasiðo/ *a.*
placid.
plaga /'plaga/ *n. f.* plague,
scourge.
plagio /'plahio/ *n. m.* plagiarism;
(*S.A.*) kidnapping.
plan /plan/ *n. m.* plan. —**planear,**
v.
plancha /'plantʃa/ *n. f.* plate;
slab, flatiron.
planchar /plan'tʃar/ *v.* iron, press.
planeta /pla'neta/ *n. m.* planet.
planificación /planifika'θion;
planifika'sion/ *n. f.* planning.
planificar /planifi'kar/ *v.* plan.
plano /'plano/ *a.* **1.** level, flat.
—*n.* **2.** *m.* plan; plane.
planta /'planta/ *n. f.* plant; sole
(of foot).
planta baja /'planta 'baha/ *n. f.*
ground floor.
plantación /planta'θion; planta-
'sion/ *n. f.* plantation.
plantar /plan'tar/ *v.* plant.
plantear /plante'ar/ *v.* pose, present.
plantel /plan'tel/ *n. m.* educational institution; *Agr.* nursery.
plasma /'plasma/ *n. m.* plasma.
plástico /'plastiko/ *a. & m.* plastic.

plata /'plata/ *n. f.* silver; *Colloq.*
money.
plataforma /plata'forma/ *n. f.*
platform.
plátano /'platano/ *n. m.* plantain;
banana.
platel /pla'tel/ *n. m.* platter.
plática /'platika/ *n. f.* chat, talk.
—**platicar,** *v.*
platillo /pla'tiʎo; pla'tiyo/ *n. m.*
saucer.
platillo volante /pla'tiʎo bo'lante;
pla'tiyo bo'lante/ flying saucer.
plato /'plato/ *n. m.* plate, dish.
playa /'plaia/ *n. f.* beach, shore.
plaza /'plaθa; 'plasa/ *n. f.* square.
p. de toros, bullring.
plazo /'plaθo; 'plaso/ *n. m.* term,
deadline; installment.
plebe /'pleβe/ *n. f.* common people; masses.
plebiscito /pleβis'θito; pleβis'sito/
n. m. plebiscite.
plegable /ple'gaβle/ *a.* foldable,
folding.
plegadura /plega'ðura/ *n. f.* fold,
pleat. —**plegar,** *v.*
pleito /'pleito/ *n. m.* lawsuit; dispute.
plenitud /pleni'tuð/ *n. f.* fullness;
abundance.
pleno /'pleno/ *a.* full. **en pleno...**
in the middle of...
pliego /'pliego/ *n. m.* sheet of paper.
pliegue /'pliege/ *n. m.* fold, pleat,
crease.
plomería /plome'ria/ *n. f.* plumb-
ing.
plomero /plo'mero/ *n. m.*
plumber.
plomizo /plo'miθo; plo'miso/ *a.*
leaden.
plomo /'plomo/ *n. m.* lead; fuse.
pluma /'pluma/ *n. f.* feather;
(writing) pen.
pluma estiglográfica /'pluma es-
tiglo'grafika/ fountain pen.
plumafuente /pluma'fuente/ *n. f.*
fountain pen.
plumaje /plu'mahe/ *n. m.* plumage.
plumero /plu'mero/ *n. m.* feather
duster; plume.
plumoso /plu'moso/ *a.* feathery.
plural /plu'ral/ *a. & m.* plural.
pluriempleo /pluriem'pleo/ *n. m.*
moonlighting.
PNB, *abbr.* (producto nacional

bruto), GNP (gross national product).

población /poβla'θion; poβla'sion/ *n. f.* population; town.

poblador /poβla'ðor/ **-ra** *n.* settler.

poblar /po'βlar/ *v.* populate; settle.

pobre /'poβre/ *a. & n.* poor; poor person.

pobreza /po'βreθa; po'βresa/ *n. f.* poverty, need.

pocilga /po'θilga; po'silga/ *n. f.* pigpen.

poción /po'θion; po'sion/ *n. f.* drink; potion.

poco /'poko/ *a. & adv.* **1.** little, not much, (*pl.*) few. **por p.,** almost, nearly. —*n.* **2.** *m.* **un p. (de),** a little, a bit (of).

poder /po'ðer/ *n.* **1.** *m.* power. —*v.* **2.** be able to, can; be possible, may, might. **no p. menos de,** not be able to help.

poder adquisitivo /po'ðer aðkisi'tiβo/ purchasing power.

poderío /poðe'rio/ *n. m.* power, might.

poderoso /poðe'roso/ *a.* powerful, mighty, potent.

podrido /po'ðriðo/ *a.* rotten.

poema /po'ema/ *n. m.* poem.

poesía /poe'sia/ *n. f.* poetry; poem.

poeta /po'eta/ *n. m. & f.* poet.

poético /po'etiko/ *a.* poetic.

polaco /po'lako/ **-ca** *a. & n.* Polish; Pole.

polar /po'lar/ *a.* polar.

polaridad /polari'ðað/ *n. f.* polarity.

polea /po'lea/ *n. f.* pulley.

polen /'polen/ *n. m.* pollen.

policía /poli'θia; poli'sia/ *n.* **1.** *f.* police. —*n.* **2.** *m.* policeman.

polideportivo /poliðepor'tiβo/ *n. m.* sports center.

poliéster /poli'ester/ *n. m.* polyester.

poligamia /poli'gamia/ *n. f.* polygamy.

poligloto /poli'gloto/ **-ta** *n.* polyglot.

polígono industrial /po'ligono indus'trial/ *n. m.* industrial park.

polilla /po'liʎa; po'liya/ *n. f.* moth.

política /po'litika/ *n. f.* politics; policy.

político /po'litiko/ **-ca** *a. & n.* politic; political; politician.

póliza /'poliθa; 'polisa/ *n. f.* (insurance) policy; permit, ticket.

polizonte /poli'θonte; poli'sonte/ *n. m.* policeman.

pollada /po'ʎaða; po'yaða/ *n. f.* brood.

pollería /poʎe'ria; poye'ria/ *n. f.* poultry shop.

pollino /po'ʎino; po'yino/ *n. m.* donkey.

pollo /'poʎo; 'poyo/ *n. m.* chicken.

polo /'polo/ *n. m.* pole; polo; popsicle.

polonés /polo'nes/ *a.* Polish.

Polonia /po'lonia/ *n. f.* Poland.

polvera /pol'βera/ *n. f.* powder box; powder puff.

polvo /'polβo/ *n. m.* powder; dust.

polvora /'polβora/ *n. f.* gunpowder.

pompa /'pompa/ *n. f.* pomp.

pomposo /pom'poso/ *a.* pompous.

pómulo /'pomulo/ *n. m.* cheekbone.

ponche /'pontʃe/ *n. m.* punch (beverage).

ponchera /pon'tʃera/ *n. f.* punch bowl.

ponderar /ponde'rar/ *v.* ponder.

ponderoso /ponde'roso/ *a.* ponderous.

poner /po'ner/ *v.* put, set, lay, place.

ponerse /po'nerse/ *v.* put on; become, get; set (sun). **p. a,** start to.

poniente /po'niente/ *n. m.* west.

pontífice /pon'tifiθe; pon'tifise/ *n. m.* pontiff.

popa /'popa/ *n. f.* stern.

popular /popu'lar/ *a.* popular.

popularidad /populari'ðað/ *n. f.* popularity.

populazo /popu'laθo; popu'laso/ *n. m.* populace; masses.

por /por/ *prep.* by, through, because of; via; for. **p. qué,** why?

porcelana /porθe'lana; porse'lana/ *n. f.* porcelain, chinaware.

porcentaje /porθen'tahe; porsen'tahe/ *n. m.* percentage.

porche /'portʃe/ *n. m.* porch; portico.

porción /por'θion; por'sion/ *n. f.* portion, lot.

porfiar /por'fiar/ v. persist; argue.
pormenor /porme'nor/ n. m. detail.
pornografía /pornogra'fia/ n. f. pornography.
poro /'poro/ n. m. pore.
poroso /po'roso/ a. porous.
porque /'porke/ conj. because.
porqué n. m. reason, motive.
porra /'porra/ n. f. stick, club.
porrazo /po'rraθo; po'rraso/ n. m. blow.
porro /'porro/ n. m. Colloq. joint (marijuana).
portaaviones /portaa'βiones/ n. m. aircraft carrier.
portador /porta'ðor/ -ra n. bearer.
portal /por'tal/ n. m. portal.
portar /por'tar/ v. carry.
portarse /por'tarse/ v. behave, act.
portátil /por'tatil/ a. portable.
portavoz /porta'βoθ; porta'βos/ n. 1. m. megaphone. 2. m. & f. spokesperson.
porte /'porte/ n. m. bearing; behavior; postage.
portero /por'tero/ n. m. porter; janitor.
pórtico /'portiko/ n. m. porch.
portorriqueño /portorri'keɲo/ -ña n. & a. Puerto Rican.
portugués /portu'ges/ -esa a. & n. Portuguese.
posada /po'saða/ n. f. lodge, inn.
posar /po'sar/ v. pose.
posdata /pos'ðata/ n. f. postscript.
poseer /pose'er/ v. possess, own.
posesión /pose'sion/ n. f. possession.
posibilidad /posiβili'ðað/ n. f. possibility.
posible /po'siβle/ a. possible.
posiblemente /posiβle'mente/ adv. possibly.
posición /posi'θion; posi'sion/ n. f. position, stand.
positivo /posi'tiβo/ a. positive.
posponer /pospo'ner/ v. postpone.
postal /pos'tal/ a. postal; postcard.
poste /'poste/ n. m. post, pillar.
posteridad /posteri'ðað/ n. f. posterity.
posterior /poste'rior/ a. posterior, rear.

postizo /pos'tiθo; pos'tiso/ a. false, artificial.
postrado /pos'traðo/ a. prostrate.
—postrar, v.
postre /'postre/ n. m. dessert.
póstumo /'postumo/ a. posthumous.
postura /pos'tura/ n. f. posture, pose; bet.
potable /po'taβle/ a. drinkable.
potaje /po'tahe/ n. m. porridge; pot stew.
potasa /po'tasa/ n. f. potash.
potasio /po'tasio/ n. m. potassium.
pote /'pote/ n. m. pot, jar.
potencia /po'tenθia; po'tensia/ n. f. potency, power.
potencial /poten'θial; poten'sial/ a. & m. potential.
potentado /poten'taðo/ n. m. potentate.
potente /po'tente/ a. potent, powerful.
potestad /potes'tað/ n. f. power.
potro /'potro/ n. m. colt.
pozo /'poθo; 'poso/ n. m. well.
práctica /'praktika/ n. f. practice. **—practicar,** v.
práctico /'praktiko/ a. practical.
pradera /pra'ðera/ n. f. prairie, meadow.
prado /'praðo/ n. m. meadow; lawn.
pragmatismo /pragma'tismo/ n. m. pragmatism.
preámbulo /pre'ambulo/ n. m. preamble.
precario /pre'kario/ a. precarious.
precaución /prekau'θion; prekau'sion/ n. f. precaution.
precaverse /preka'βerse/ v. beware.
precavido /preka'βiðo/ a. cautious, guarded, wary.
precedencia /preθe'ðenθia; prese'ðensia/ n. f. precedence, priority.
precedente /preθe'ðente; prese'ðente/ a. & m. preceding; precedent.
preceder /preθe'ðer; prese'ðer/ v. precede.
precepto /pre'θepto; pre'septo/ n. m. precept.
preciar /pre'θiar; pre'siar/ v. value, prize.
preciarse de /pre'θiarse de; pre'siarse de/ v. take pride in.
precio /'preθio; 'presio/ n. m. price. **p. del billete de avión** air

fare. **p. del cubierto** cover charge.

precioso /preˈθioso; preˈsioso/ a. precious; beautiful, gorgeous.

precipicio /preθiˈpiθio; presiˈpisio/ n. m. precipice, cliff.

precipitación /preθipitaˈθion; presipitaˈsion/ n. f. precipitation.

precipitar /preθipiˈtar; presipiˈtar/ v. precipitate, rush; throw headlong.

precipitoso /preθipiˈtoso; presipiˈtoso/ a. precipitous; rash.

precisar /preθiˈsar; presiˈsar/ v. fix, specify; be necessary.

precisión /preθiˈsion; presiˈsion/ n. f. precision; necessity.

preciso /preˈθiso; preˈsiso/ a. precise; necessary.

precocidad /prekoθiˈðað; prekosiˈðað/ n. f. precocity.

precocinado /prekoθiˈnaðo; prekosiˈnaðo/ a. precooked, ready-cooked.

precoz /preˈkoθ; preˈkos/ a. precocious.

precursor /prekurˈsor/ **-ra** a. **1.** preceding. —n. **2.** precursor, forerunner.

predecesor /preðeθeˈsor; preðeseˈsor/ **-ra** a. & n. predecessor.

predecir /preðeˈθir; preðeˈsir/ v. predict, foretell.

predicación /preðikaˈθion; preðikaˈsion/ n. f. sermon.

predicador /preðikaˈðor/ **-ra** n. preacher.

predicar /preðiˈkar/ v. preach.

predicción /preðikˈθion; preðikˈsion/ n. f. prediction.

predilecto /preðiˈlekto/ a. favorite, preferred.

predisponer /preðispoˈner/ v. predispose.

predisposición /preðisposiˈθion; preðisposiˈsion/ n. f. predisposition; bias.

predominante /preðomiˈnante/ a. prevailing, prevalent, predominant.

predominar /preðomiˈnar/ v. prevail, predominate.

predominio /preðoˈminio/ n. m. predominance, sway.

prefacio /preˈfaθio; preˈfasio/ n. m. preface.

preferencia /prefeˈrenθia; prefeˈrensia/ n. f. preference.

preferentemente /preferenteˈmente/ adv. preferably.

preferible /prefeˈriβle/ a. preferable.

preferir /prefeˈrir/ v. prefer.

prefijo /preˈfiho/ n. m. prefix; area code, dialing code. —**prefijar,** v.

pregón /preˈgon/ n. m. proclamation; street cry.

pregonar /pregoˈnar/ v. proclaim; cry out.

pregunta /preˈgunta/ n. f. question, inquiry. **hacer una p.,** to ask a question.

preguntar /pregunˈtar/ v. ask, inquire.

preguntarse /pregunˈtarse/ v. wonder.

prehistórico /preisˈtoriko/ a. prehistoric.

prejuicio /preˈhuiθio; preˈhuisio/ n. m. prejudice.

prelacía /prelaˈθia; prelaˈsia/ n. f. prelacy.

preliminar /prelimiˈnar/ a. & m. preliminary.

preludio /preˈluðio/ n. m. prelude.

prematuro /premaˈturo/ a. premature.

premeditación /premeðitaˈθion; premeðitaˈsion/ n. f. premeditation.

premeditar /premeðiˈtar/ v. premeditate.

premiar /preˈmiar/ v. reward; award a prize to.

premio /ˈpremio/ n. m. prize, award; reward. **p. de consuelo,** consolation prize.

premisa /preˈmisa/ n. f. premise.

premura /preˈmura/ n. f. pressure; urgency.

prenda /ˈprenda/ n. f. jewel; (personal) quality. **p. de vestir,** garment.

prender /prenˈder/ v. seize, arrest, catch; pin, clip. **p. fuego a,** set fire to.

prensa /ˈprensa/ n. f. printing press; (the) press.

prensar /prenˈsar/ v. press, compress.

preñado /preˈɲaðo/ a. pregnant.

preocupación /preokupaˈθion; preokupaˈsion/ n. f. worry, preoccupation.

preocupar /preokuˈpar/ v. worry, preoccupy.

preparación /preparaˈθion; preparaˈsion/ n. f. preparation.

preparar /prepa'rar/ *v.* prepare.
preparativo /prepara'tiβo/ *n. m.* preparation.
preparatorio /prepara'torio/ *n. m.* preparatory.
preponderante /preponde'rante/ *a.* preponderant.
preposición /preposi'θion; preposi'sion/ *n. f.* preposition.
prerrogativa /prerroga'tiβa/ *n. f.* prerogative, privilege.
presa /'presa/ *n. f.* capture; (water) dam.
presagiar /presa'hiar/ *v.* presage, forebode.
presbiteriano /presβite'riano/ -na *n. & a.* Presbyterian.
presbítero /pres'βitero/ *n. m.* priest.
prescindir de /presθin'dir de; pressin'dir de/ *v.* dispense with; omit.
prescribir /preskri'βir/ *v.* prescribe.
prescripción /preskrip'θion; preskrip'sion/ *n. f.* prescription.
presencia /pre'senθia; pre'sensia/ *n. f.* presence.
presenciar /presen'θiar; presen'siar/ *v.* witness, be present at.
presentable /presen'taβle/ *a.* presentable.
presentación /presenta'θion; presenta'sion/ *n. f.* presentation; introduction.
presentar /presen'tar/ *v.* present; introduce.
presente /pre'sente/ *a. & m.* present.
presentimiento /presenti'miento/ *n. m.* premonition.
preservación /preserβa'θion; preserβa'sion/ *n. f.* preservation.
preservar /preser'βar/ *v.* preserve, keep.
preservativo /preserβa'tiβo/ *a. & m.* preservative; condom.
presidencia /presi'ðenθia; presi'ðensia/ *n. f.* presidency.
presidencial /presiðen'θial; presiðen'sial/ *a.* presidential.
presidente /presi'ðente/ -ta *n.* president.
presidiario /presi'ðiario/ -ria *n. m. & f.* prisoner.
presidio /pre'siðio/ *n. m.* prison; garrison.
presidir /presi'ðir/ *v.* preside.
presión /pre'sion/ *n. f.* pressure.

presión arterial /pre'sion arte'rial/ blood pressure.
preso /'preso/ -sa *n.* prisoner.
presta /'presta/ *n. f.* mint (plant).
prestador /presta'ðor/ -ra *n.* lender.
prestamista /presta'mista/ *n. m. & f.* money lender.
préstamo /'prestamo/ *n. m.* loan.
prestar /pres'tar/ *v.* lend.
presteza /pres'teθa; pres'tesa/ *n. f.* haste, promptness.
prestidigitación /prestiðihita'θion; prestiðihita'sion/ *n. f.* sleight of hand.
prestigio /pres'tihio/ *n. m.* prestige.
presto /'presto/ *a.* **1.** quick, prompt; ready. —*adv.* **2.** quickly; at once.
presumido /presu'miðo/ *a.* conceited, presumptuous.
presumir /presu'mir/ *v.* presume; boast; claim; be conceited.
presunción /presun'θion; presun'sion/ *n. f.* presumption; conceit.
presunto /pre'sunto/ *a.* presumed; prospective.
presuntuoso /presun'tuoso/ *a.* presumptuous.
presupuesto /presu'puesto/ *n. m.* premise; budget.
pretender /preten'der/ *v.* pretend; intend; aspire.
pretendiente /preten'diente/ *n. m.* suitor; pretender (to throne).
pretensión /preten'sion/ *n. f.* pretension; claim.
pretérito /pre'terito/ *a. & m.* preterit, past (tense).
pretexto /pre'teksto/ *n. m.* pretext.
prevalecer /preβale'θer; preβale'ser/ *v.* prevail.
prevención /preβen'θion; preβen'sion/ *n. f.* prevention.
prevenir /preβe'nir/ *v.* prevent; forewarn; prearrange.
preventivo /preβen'tiβo/ *a.* preventive.
prever /pre'βer/ *v.* foresee.
previamente /preβia'mente/ *adv.* previously.
previo /'preβio/ *a.* previous.
previsible /preβi'siβle/ *a.* predictable.
previsión /preβi'sion/ *n. f.* foresight. **p. social,** social security.
prieto /'prieto/ *a.* blackish, very dark.

primacía /prima'θia; prima'sia/ *n.*
f. primacy.

primario /pri'mario/ *a.* primary.

primavera /prima'βera/ *n. f.*
spring (season).

primero /pri'mero/ *a. & adv.* first.

primitivo /primi'tiβo/ *a.* primitive.

primo /'primo/ **-ma** *n.* cousin.

primor /pri'mor/ *n. m.* beauty; excellence; lovely thing.

primoroso /primo'roso/ *a.* exquisite, elegant; graceful.

princesa /prin'θesa; prin'sesa/ *n.*
f. princess.

principal /prinθi'pal; prinsi'pal/ *a.*
1. principal, main. —*n.* **2.** *m.*
chief, head, principal.

principalmente /prinθipal'mente;
prinsipal'mente/ *adv.* principally.

príncipe /'prinθipe; 'prinsipe/ *n.*
m. prince.

Príncipe Azul /'prinθipe a'θul;
'prinsipe a'sul/ Prince Charming.

principiar /prinθi'piar; prinsi'piar/
v. begin, initiate.

principio /prin'θipio; prin'sipio/ *n.*
m. beginning, start; principle.

pringado /priŋ'gaðo/ *n. m.*
low-life, loser.

prioridad /priori'ðað/ *n. f.* priority.

prisa /'prisa/ *n. f.* hurry, haste.
darse p., hurry, hasten. **tener p.,**
be in a hurry.

prisión /pri'sion/ *n. f.* prison; imprisonment.

prisionero /prisio'nero/ **-ra** *n.*
captive, prisoner.

prisma /'prisma/ *n. m.* prism.

prismático /pris'matiko/ *a.* pris-
matic.

privación /priβa'θion; priβa'sion/
n. f. privation, want.

privado /pri'βaðo/ *a.* private, secret; deprived.

privar /pri'βar/ *v.* deprive.

privilegio /priβi'lehio/ *n. m.* privilege.

pro /pro/ *n. m. or f.* benefit, advantage. **en p. de,** in behalf of.
en p. y en contra, pro and con.

proa /'proa/ *n. f.* prow, bow.

probabilidad /proβaβili'ðað/ *n. f.*
probability.

probable /pro'βaβle/ *a.* probable,
likely.

probablemente /proβaβle'mente/
adv. probably.

probador /proβa'ðor/ *n. m.* fitting
room.

probar /pro'βar/ *v.* try, sample;
taste; test; prove.

probarse /pro'βarse/ *v.* try on.

probidad /proβi'ðað/ *n. f.* honesty, integrity.

problema /pro'βlema/ *n. m.* problem.

probo /'proβo/ *a.* honest.

procaz /pro'kaθ; pro'kas/ *a.* impudent, saucy.

proceder /proθe'ðer; prose'ðer/ *v.*
proceed.

procedimiento /proθeði'miento;
proseði'miento/ *n. m.* procedure.

procesar /proθe'sar; prose'sar/ *v.*
prosecute; sue; process.

procesión /proθe'sion; prose'sion/
n. f. procession.

proceso /pro'θeso; pro'seso/ *n. m.*
process; (court) trial.

proclama /pro'klama/ **proclamación** *n. f.* proclamation.

proclamar /prokla'mar/ *v.* proclaim.

procreación /prokrea'θion; pro-
krea'sion/ *n. f.* procreation.

procrear /prokre'ar/ *v.* procreate.

procurar /proku'rar/ *v.* try; see to
it; get, procure.

prodigalidad /proðigali'ðað/ *n. f.*
prodigality.

prodigar /proði'gar/ *v.* lavish;
squander, waste.

prodigio /pro'ðihio/ *n. m.* prodigy.

pródigo /'proðigo/ *a.* prodigal;
profuse; lavish.

producción /proðuk'θion; proðuk-
'sion/ *n. f.* production.

producir /proðu'θir; proðu'sir/ *v.*
produce.

productivo /proðuk'tiβo/ *a.* productive.

producto /pro'ðukto/ *n. m.* product.

producto nacional bruto /pro-
'ðukto naθio'nal 'bruto; pro-
'ðukto nasio'nal 'bruto/ gross national product.

proeza /pro'eθa; pro'esa/ *n. f.*
prowess.

profanación /profana'θion; pro-
fana'sion/ *n. f.* profanation.

profanar /profa'nar/ *v.* defile, desecrate.

profanidad /profani'ðað/ *n. f.*
profanity.

profano /pro'fano/ *a.* profane.

profecía /profe'θia; profe'sia/ *n. f.*
prophecy.

proferir /profe'rir/ v. utter, express.

profesar /profe'sar/ v. profess.

profesión /profe'sion/ n. f. profession.

profesional /profesio'nal/ a. professional.

profesor /profe'sor/ **-ra** n. professor, teacher.

profeta /pro'feta/ n. m. prophet.

profético /pro'fetiko/ a. prophetic.

profetizar /profeti'θar; profeti'sar/ v. prophesy.

proficiente /profi'θiente; profi'siente/ a. proficient.

profundamente /profunda'mente/ adv. profoundly, deeply.

profundidad /profundi'ðað/ n. f. profundity, depth.

profundizar /profundi'θar; profundi'sar/ v. deepen.

profundo /pro'fundo/ a. profound, deep.

profuso /pro'fuso/ a. profuse.

progenie /pro'henie/ n. f. progeny, offspring.

programa /pro'grama/ n. m. program; schedule.

programador /programa'ðor/ **-ra** n. (computer) programmer.

progresar /progre'sar/ v. progress, advance.

progresión /progre'sion/ n. f. progression.

progresista /progre'sista/ **progresivo** a. progressive.

progreso /pro'greso/ n. m. progress.

prohibición /proiβi'θion; proiβi'sion/ n. f. prohibition.

prohibir /proi'βir/ v. prohibit, forbid.

prohibitivo /proiβi'tiβo, proiβi'torio/ a. prohibitive.

prole /'prole/ n. f. progeny.

proletariado /proleta'riaðo/ n. m. proletariat.

proliferación /prolifera'θion; prolifera'sion/ n. f. proliferation.

prolijo /pro'liho/ a. prolix, tedious; long-winded.

prólogo /'prologo/ n. m. prologue; preface.

prolongar /proloŋ'gar/ v. prolong.

promedio /pro'meðio/ n. m. average.

promesa /pro'mesa/ n. f. promise.

prometer /prome'ter/ v. promise.

prometido /prome'tiðo/ a. promised; engaged (to marry).

prominencia /promi'nenθia; promi'nensia/ n. f. prominence.

promiscuamente /promiskua'mente/ adv. promiscuously.

promiscuo /pro'miskuo/ a. promiscuous.

promisorio /promi'sorio/ a. promissory.

promoción /promo'θion; promo'sion/ n. f. promotion.

promocionar /promoθio'nar; promosio'nar/ v. advertise, promote.

promover /promo'βer/ v. promote, further.

promulgación /promulga'θion; promulga'sion/ n. f. promulgation.

promulgar /promul'gar/ v. promulgate.

pronombre /pro'nombre/ n. m. pronoun.

pronosticación /pronostika'θion; pronostika'sion/ n. f. prediction, forecast.

pronosticar /pronosti'kar/ v. predict, forecast.

pronóstico /pro'nostiko/ n. m. prediction.

prontamente /pronta'mente/ adv. promptly.

prontitud /pronti'tuð/ n. f. promptness.

pronto /'pronto/ a. **1.** prompt; ready. —adv. **2.** soon; quickly. **de p.,** abruptly.

pronunciación /pronunθia'θion; pronunsia'sion/ n. f. pronunciation.

pronunciar /pronun'θiar; pronun'siar/ v. pronounce.

propagación /propaga'θion; propaga'sion/ n. f. propagation.

propaganda /propa'ganda/ n. f. propaganda.

propagandista /propagan'dista/ n. m. & f. propagandist.

propagar /propa'gar/ v. propagate.

propicio /pro'piθio; pro'pisio/ a. propitious, auspicious, favorable.

propiedad /propie'ðað/ n. f. property.

propietario /propie'tario/ **-ria** n. proprietor; owner; landlord, landlady.

propina /pro'pina/ n. f. gratuity, tip.

propio /'propio/ *a.* proper, suitable; typical; (one's) own; -self.

proponer /propo'ner/ *v.* propose.

proporción /propor'θion; propor-'sion/ *n. f.* proportion.

proporcionado /proporθio'naðo; proporsio'naðo/ *a.* proportionate.

proporcionar /proporθio'nar; proporsio'nar/ *v.* provide with, supply, afford.

proposición /proposi'θion; proposi'sion/ *n. f.* proposition, offer; proposal.

propósito /pro'posito/ *n. m.* purpose; plan; **a p.,** by the way, apropos; on purpose.

propuesta /pro'puesta/ *n. f.* proposal, motion.

prorrata /pro'rrata/ *n. f.* quota.

prórroga /'prorroga/ *n. f.* renewal, extension.

prorrogar /prorro'gar/ *v.* renew, extend.

prosa /'prosa/ *n. f.* prose.

prosaico /pro'saiko/ *a.* prosaic.

proscribir /proskri'βir/ *v.* prohibit, proscribe, ban.

prosecución /proseku'θion; proseku'sion/ *n. f.* prosecution.

proseguir /prose'gir/ *v.* pursue; proceed, go on.

prosélito /pro'selito/ **-ta** *n.* proselyte.

prospecto /pros'pekto/ *n. m.* prospectus.

prosperar /prospe'rar/ *v.* prosper, thrive, flourish.

prosperidad /prosperi'ðað/ *n. f.* prosperity.

próspero /'prospero/ *a.* prosperous, successful.

prosternado /proster'naðo/ *a.* prostrate.

prostitución /prostitu'θion; prostitu'sion/ *n. f.* prostitution.

prostituir /prosti'tuir/ *v.* prostitute; debase.

prostituta /prosti'tuta/ *n. f.* prostitute.

protagonista /protago'nista/ *n. m. & f.* protagonist, hero, heroine.

protección /protek'θion; protek-'sion/ *n. f.* protection.

protector /protek'tor/ **-ra** *a. & n.* protective; protector.

proteger /prote'her/ *v.* protect, safeguard. **p. contra escritura,** write-protect (diskette).

protegido /prote'hiðo/ **-da** *n.* **1.**

protégé. —*a.* **2.** protected. **p. contra escritura,** write-protected.

proteína /prote'ina/ *n. f.* protein.

protesta /pro'testa/ *n. f.* protest. —**protestar,** *v.*

protestante /protes'tante/ *a. & n.* Protestant.

protocolo /proto'kolo/ *n. m.* protocol.

protuberancia /protuβe'ranθia; protuβe'ransia/ *n. f.* protuberance, lump.

protuberante /protuβe'rante/ *a.* bulging.

provecho /pro'βetʃo/ *n. m.* profit, gain, benefit. **¡Buen provecho!** May you enjoy your meal!

provechoso /proβe'tʃoso/ *a.* beneficial, advantageous, profitable.

proveer /proβe'er/ *v.* provide, furnish.

provenir de /proβe'nir de/ *v.* originate in, be due to, come from.

proverbial /proβer'βial/ *a.* proverbial.

proverbio /pro'βerβio/ *n. m.* proverb.

providencia /proβi'ðenθia; proβi-'ðensia/ *n. f.* providence.

providente /proβi'ðente/ *a.* provident.

provincia /pro'βinθia; pro'βinsia/ *n. f.* province.

provincial /proβin'θial; proβin-'sial/ *a.* provincial.

provinciano /proβin'θiano; proβin'siano/ **-na** *a. & n.* provincial.

provisión /proβi'sion/ *n. f.* provision, supply, stock.

provisional /proβisio'nal/ *a.* provisional.

provocación /proβoka'θion; proβoka'sion/ *n. f.* provocation.

provocador /proβoka'ðor/ **-ra** *n.* provoker.

provocar /proβo'kar/ *v.* provoke, excite.

provocativo /proβoka'tiβo/ *a.* provocative.

proximidad /proksimi'ðað/ *n. f.* proximity, vicinity.

próximo /'proksimo/ *a.* next; near.

proyección /proiek'θion; proiek-'sion/ *n. f.* projection.

proyectar /proiek'tar/ *v.* plan, project.

proyectil /proyek'til/ *n. m.* projectile, missile, shell.

proyecto /pro'iekto/ *n. m.* plan, project, scheme.

proyector /proiek'tor/ *n. m.* projector.

prudencia /pru'ðenθia; pru'ðensia/ *n. f.* prudence.

prudente /pru'ðente/ *a.* prudent.

prueba /'prueβa/ *n. f.* proof; trial; test.

psicoanálisis /psikoa'nalisis/ *n. m.* psychoanalysis.

psicoanalista /psikoana'lista/ *n. m. & f.* psychoanalyst.

psicodélico /psiko'ðeliko/ *a.* psychedelic.

psicología /psikolo'hia/ *n. f.* psychology.

psicológico /psiko'lohiko/ *a.* psychological.

psicólogo /psi'kologo/ **-ga** *n.* psychologist.

psiquiatra /psi'kiatra/ *n. m. & f.* psychiatrist.

psiquiatría /psikia'tria/ *n. f.* psychiatry.

publicación /puβlika'θion; puβlika'sion/ *n. f.* publication.

publicar /puβli'kar/ *v.* publish.

publicidad /puβliðiθi'ðað; puβlisi-'ðað/ *n. f.* publicity.

publicista /puβli'θista; puβli'sista/ *n. m. & f.* publicity agent.

público /'puβliko/ *a. & m.* public.

puchero /pu'tʃero/ *n. m.* pot.

pudiente /pu'ðiente/ *a.* powerful; wealthy.

pudín /pu'ðin/ *n. m.* pudding.

pudor /pu'ðor/ *n. m.* modesty.

pudoroso /puðo'roso/ *a.* modest.

pudrirse /pu'ðrirse/ *v.* rot.

pueblo /'pueβlo/ *n. m.* town, village; (the) people.

puente /'puente/ *n. m.* bridge.

puente para peatones /'puente para pea'tones/ *n. m.* footbridge.

puerco /'puerko/ **-ca** *n.* pig.

puericultura /puerikul'tura/ *n. f.* pediatrics

pueril /pue'ril/ *a.* childish.

puerilidad /puerili'ðað/ *n. f.* puerility.

puerta /'puerta/ *n. f.* door; gate.

puerta giratoria /'puerta hira-'toria/ revolving door.

puerta principal /'puerta prinθi'pal; 'puerta prinsi'pal/ front door.

puerto /'puerto/ *n. m.* port, harbor.

puertorriqueño /puertorri'keɲo/ **-ña** *a. & n.* Puerto Rican.

pues /pues/ *adv.* **1.** well... —*conj.* **2.** as, since, for.

puesto /'puesto/ *n. m.* appointment, post, job; place; stand. **p. que,** since.

pugilato /puhi'lato/ *n. m.* boxing.

pugna /'pugna/ *n. f.* conflict.

pugnacidad /pugnaθi'ðað; pugnasi'ðað/ *n. f.* pugnacity.

pugnar /pug'nar/ *v.* fight; oppose.

pulcritud /pulkri'tuð/ *n. f.* neatness; exquisitness.

pulga /'pulga/ *n. f.* flea.

pulgada /pul'gaða/ *n. f.* inch.

pulgar /pul'gar/ *n. m.* thumb.

pulir /pu'lir/ *v.* polish; beautify.

pulmón /pul'mon/ *n. m.* lung.

pulmonía /pulmo'nia/ *n. f.* pneumonia.

pulpa /'pulpa/ *n. f.* pulp.

púlpito /'pulpito/ *n. m.* pulpit.

pulque /'pulke/ *n. m.* pulque (fermented maguey juice).

pulsación /pulsa'θion; pulsa'sion/ *n. f.* pulsation, beat.

pulsar /pul'sar/ *v.* pulsate, beat.

pulsera /pul'sera/ *n. f.* wristband; bracelet.

pulso /'pulso/ *n. m.* pulse.

pulverizar /pulβeri'θar; pulβeri-'sar/ *v.* pulverize.

puma /'puma/ *n. m.* puma.

pundonor /pundo'nor/ *n. m.* point of honor.

punta /'punta/ *n. f.* point, tip, end.

puntada /pun'taða/ *n. f.* stitch.

puntapié /punta'pie/ *n. m.* kick.

puntería /punte'ria/ *n. f.* (marksman's) aim.

puntiagudo /puntia'guðo/ *a.* sharp-pointed.

puntillas /pun'tiʎas; pun'tiyas/ *n. f.pl.* **de p., en p.,** on tiptoe.

punto /'punto/ *n. m.* point; period; spot, dot. **dos puntos,** *Punct.* colon. **a p. de,** about to. **al p.,** instantly.

punto de admiración /'punto de aðmira'θion; 'punto de aðmira-'sion/ exclamation mark.

punto de congelación /'punto de koŋgela'θion; 'punto de koŋgela-'sion/ freezing point.

punto de ebullición /'punto de eβuʎi'θion; 'punto de eβuyi'sion/ boiling point.

punto de vista /'punto de 'bista/ point of view, viewpoint.
puntuación /puntua'θion; puntua-'sion/ *n. f.* punctuation.
puntual /pun'tual/ *a.* punctual, prompt.
puntuar /pun'tuar/ *v.* punctuate.
puñada /pu'ɲaða/ *n. f.* punch.
puñado /pu'ɲaðo/ *n. m.* handful.
puñal /pu'ɲal/ *n. m.* dagger.
puñalada /puɲa'laða/ *n. f.* stab.
puñetazo /puɲe'taθo; puɲe'taso/ *n. m.* punch, fist blow.
puño /'puɲo/ *n. m.* fist; cuff; handle.
pupila /pu'pila/ *n. f.* pupil (of eye).
pupitre /pu'pitre/ *n. m.* writing desk, school desk.
pureza /pu'reθa; pu'resa/ *n. f.* purity; chastity.
purgante /pur'gante/ *n. m.* laxative.
purgar /pur'gar/ *v.* purge, cleanse.
purgatorio /purga'torio/ *n. m.* purgatory.
puridad /puri'ðað/ *n. f.* secrecy.

purificación /purifika'θion; purifika'sion/ *n. f.* purification.
purificar /purifi'kar/ *v.* purify.
purismo /pu'rismo/ *n. m.* purism.
purista /pu'rista/ *n. m. & f.* purist.
puritanismo /purita'nismo/ *n. m.* puritanism.
puro /'puro/ *a.* 1. pure. —*n.* 2. *m.* cigar.
púrpura /'purpura/ *n. f.* purple.
purpúreo /pur'pureo/ *a.* purple.
purulencia /puru'lenθia; puru'lensia/ *n. f.* purulence.
purulento /puru'lento/ *a.* purulent.
pus /pus/ *n. m.* pus.
pusilánime /pusi'lanime/ *a.* pusillanimous.
puta /'puta/ **-to** *n.* prostitute.
putrefacción /putrefak'θion; putrefak'sion/ *n. f.* putrefaction, rot.
putrefacto /putre'fakto/ *a.* putrid, rotten.
pútrido /'putriðo/ *a.* putrid.
puya /'puya/ *n. f.* goad.

Q R

que /ke/ *rel. pron.* 1. who, whom; that, which. —*conj.* 2. than.
qué *a. & pron.* what. **por q., para q.,** why? *adv.* how.
quebrada /ke'βraða/ *n. f.* ravine, gully, gulch; stream.
quebradizo /keβra'ðiθo; keβra-'ðiso/ *a.* fragile, brittle.
quebraley /keβra'lei/ *n. m. & f.* lawbreaker, outlaw.
quebrar /ke'βrar/ *v.* break.
queda /'keða/ *n. f.* curfew.
quedar /ke'ðar/ *v.* remain, be located; be left. **q. bien a,** be becoming to.
quedarse /ke'ðarse/ *v.* stay, remain. **q. con,** keep, hold on to; remain with.
quedo /'keðo/ *a.* quiet; gentle.
quehacer /kea'θer; kea'ser/ *n. m.* task; chore.
queja /'keha/ *n. f.* complaint.
quejarse /ke'harse/ *v.* complain, grumble.
quejido /ke'hiðo/ *n. m.* moan.
quejoso /ke'hoso/ *a.* complaining.
quema /'kema/ *n. f.* burning.
quemadura /kema'ðura/ *n. f.* burn.

quemar /ke'mar/ *v.* burn.
querella /ke'reʎa; ke'reya/ *n. f.* quarrel; complaint.
querencia /ke'renθia; ke'rensia/ *n. f.* affection, liking.
querer /ke'rer/ *v.* want, wish; will; love (a person). **q. decir,** mean. **sin q.,** without meaning to; unwillingly.
querido /ke'riðo/ *a.* dear, loved, beloved.
quesería /kese'ria/ *n. f.* dairy.
queso /'keso/ *n. m.* cheese.
queso crema /'keso 'krema/ cream cheese.
quetzal /ket'θal; ket'sal/ *n. m.* quetzal.
quiche /'kitʃe/ *n. f.* quiche.
quiebra /'kieβra/ *n. f.* break, fracture; damage; bankruptcy.
quien /kien/ *rel. pron.* who, whom.
quién *interrog. pron.* who, whom.
quienquiera /kien'kiera/ *pron.* whoever, whomever.
quietamente /kieta'mente/ *adv.* quietly.
quieto /'kieto/ *a.* quiet, still.
quietud /kie'tuð/ *n. f.* quiet, quietude.

quijada /ki'haða/ n. f. jaw.
quijotesco /kiho'tesko/ a. quixotic.
quilate /ki'late/ n. m. carat.
quilla /'kiʎa; 'kiya/ n. f. keel.
quimera /ki'mera/ n. f. chimera; vision; quarrel.
química /'kimika/ n. f. chemistry.
químico /'kimiko/ -ca a. & n. chemical; chemist.
quimoterapia /kimote'rapia/ n. f. chemotherapy.
quincalla /kin'kaʎa; kin'kaya/ n. f. (computer) hardware.
quincallería /kinkaʎe'ria; kinkaye-'ria/ n. f. hardware store.
quince /'kinθe; 'kinse/ a. & pron. fifteen.
quinientos /ki'nientos/ a. & pron. five hundred.
quinina /ki'nina/ n. f. quinine.
quintana /kin'tana/ n. f. country home.
quinto /'kinto/ a. fifth.
quirúrgico /ki'rurhiko/ a. surgical.
quiste /'kiste/ n. m. cyst.
quitamanchas /kita'mantʃas/ n. m. stain remover.
quitanieves /kita'nieβes/ n. m. snowplow.
quitar /ki'tar/ v. take away, remove.
quitarse /ki'tarse/ v. take off; get rid of.
quitasol /kita'sol/ n. m. parasol, umbrella.
quitasueño /kita'sueɲo/ n. m. Colloq. nightmare; worry.
quizá /ki'θa; ki'sa/ **quizás** adv. perhaps, maybe.
quórum /'korum/ n. m. quorum.
rábano /'rraβano/ n. m. radish.
rabí /rra'βi/ **rabino** n. m. rabbi.
rabia /'rraβia/ n. f. rage; grudge; rabies.
rabiar /rra'βiar/ v. rage, be furious.
rabieta /rra'βieta/ n. f. tantrum.
rabioso /rra'βioso/ a. furious; rabid.
rabo /'rraβo/ n. m. tail.
racha /'rratʃa/ n. f. streak.
racimo /rra'θimo; rra'simo/ n. m. bunch, cluster.
ración /rra'θion; rra'sion/ n. f. ration. —**racionar,** v.
racionabilidad /rraθionaβili'ðað; rrasionaβili'ðað/ n. f. rationality.
racional /rra'θio'nal; rrasio'nal/ a. rational.

racionalismo /rraθiona'lismo; rrasiona'lismo/ n. m. rationalism.
racionalmente /rraθional'mente; rrasional'mente/ adv. rationally.
radar /rra'ðar/ n. m. radar.
radiación /rraðia'θion; rraðia'sion/ n. f. radiation.
radiador /rraðia'ðor/ n. m. radiator.
radiante /rra'ðiante/ a. radiant.
radical /rraði'kal/ a. & n. radical.
radicalismo /rraðika'lismo/ n. m. radicalism.
radicoso /rraði'koso/ a. radical.
radio /'rraðio/ n. m. or f. radio.
radioactividad /rraðioaktiβi'ðað/ n. f. radioactivity.
radioactivo /rraðioak'tiβo/ a. radioactive.
radiocasete /rraðioka'sete/ n. m. radio cassette.
radiodifundir /rraðioðifun'dir/ v. broadcast.
radiodifusión /rraðioðifu'sion/ n. f. (radio) broadcasting.
radiografía /rraðiogra'fia/ n. f. X-ray.
radiografiar /rraðiogra'fiar/ v. X-ray.
ráfaga /'rrafaga/ n. f. gust (of wind).
raíz /rra'iθ; rra'is/ n. f. root.
raja /'rraha/ n. f. rip; split, crack. —**rajar,** v.
ralea /rra'lea/ n. f. stock, breed.
ralo /'rralo/ a. thin, scattered.
rama /'rrama/ n. f. branch, bough.
ramillete /rrami'ʎete; rrami'yete/ n. m. bouquet.
ramo /'rramo/ n. m. branch, bough; bouquet.
ramonear /rramone'ar/ v. browse.
rampa /'rrampa/ n. f. ramp.
rana /'rrana/ n. f. frog.
ranchero /rran'tʃero/ -ra n. small farmer.
rancho /'rrantʃo/ n. m. ranch.
rancidez /rranθi'ðeθ; rransi'ðes/ n. f. rancidity.
rancio /'rranθio; 'rransio/ a. rancid, rank, stale, sour.
rango /'rrango/ n. m. rank.
ranúnculo /rra'nunkulo/ n. m. ranunculus; buttercup.
ranura /rra'nura/ n. f. slot.
ranura de expansión /rra'nura de ekspan'sion/ expansion slot.
rapacidad /rrapaθi'ðað; rrapasi-'ðað/ n. f. rapacity.

rapaz /rra'paθ; rra'pas/ *a.* **1.** rapacious. —*n.* **2.** *m.* young boy.

rapé /'rrape/ *n. m.* snuff.

rápidamente /rrapiða'mente/ *adv.* rapidly.

rapidez /rrapi'ðeθ; rrapi'ðes/ *n. f.* rapidity, speed.

rápido /'rrapiðo/ *a.* **1.** rapid, fast, speedy. —*n.* **2.** *m.* express (train).

rapiña /rra'piɲa/ *n. f.* robbery, plundering.

rapsodia /rrap'soðia/ *n. f.* rhapsody.

rapto /'rrapto/ *n. m.* kidnapping.

raquero /rra'kero/ **-ra** *n.* beachcomber.

raqueta /rra'keta/ *n. f.* (tennis) racket.

rareza /rra'reθa; rra'resa/ *n. f.* rarity; freak.

raridad /rrari'ðað/ *n. f.* rarity.

raro /'rraro/ *a.* rare, strange, unusual, odd, queer.

rasar /rra'sar/ *v.* skim.

rascacielos /rraska'θielos; rraska'sielos/ *n. m.* skyscraper.

rascar /rras'kar/ *v.* scrape; scratch.

rasgadura /rrasga'ðura/ *n. f.* tear, rip. —**rasgar,** *v.*

rasgo /'rrasgo/ *n. m.* trait.

rasgón /rras'gon/ *n. m.* tear.

rasguño /rras'guɲo/ *n. m.* scratch. —**rasguñar,** *v.*

raso /'rraso/ *a.* **1.** plain. **soldado r.,** *Mil.* private. —*n.* **2.** *m.* satin.

raspar /rras'par/ *v.* scrape; erase.

rastra /'rrastra/ *n. f.* trail, track. —**rastrear,** *v.*

rastrillar /rrastri'ʎar; rrastri'yar/ *v.* rake.

rastro /'rrastro/ *n. m.* track, trail, trace; rake; flea market.

rata /'rrata/ *n. f.* rat.

ratificación /rratifika'θion; rratifika'sion/ *n. f.* ratification.

ratificar /rratifi'kar/ *v.* ratify.

rato /'rrato/ *n. m.* while, spell, short time.

ratón /rra'ton/ *n. m.* mouse.

ratonera /rrato'nera/ *n. f.* mousetrap.

raya /'rraya/ *n. f.* dash, line, streak, stripe.

rayar /rra'yar/ *v.* rule, stripe; scratch; cross out.

rayo /'rrayo/ *n. m.* lightning bolt; ray; flash.

rayón /rra'yon/ *n. m.* rayon.

raza /'rraθa; 'rrasa/ *n. f.* race; breed, stock.

razón /rra'θon; rra'son/ *n. f.* reason; ratio. **a r. de,** at the rate of. **tener r.,** to be right.

razonable /rraθo'naβle; rraso'naβle/ *a.* reasonable, sensible.

razonamiento /rraθona'miento; rrasona'miento/ *n. m.* argument.

razonar /rraθo'nar; rraso'nar/ *v.* reason.

reacción /rreak'θion; rreak'sion/ *n. f.* reaction.

reaccionar /rreakθio'nar; rreaksio'nar/ *v.* react.

reaccionario /rreakθio'nario; rreaksio'nario/ **-ria** *a. & n.* reactionary.

reacondicionar /rreakondiθio'nar; rreakondisio'nar/ *v.* recondition.

reactivo /rreak'tiβo/ *a. & m.* reactive; *Chem.* reagent.

reactor /rreak'tor/ *n. m.* reactor.

real /rre'al/ *a.* royal, regal; real, actual.

realdad /rreal'dað/ *n. f.* royal authority.

realeza /rrea'leθa; rrea'lesa/ *n. f.* royalty.

realidad /rreali'ðað/ *n. f.* reality.

realidad virtual /rreali'ðað βir'tual/ virtual reality.

realista /rrea'lista/ *a. & n.* realistic; realist.

realización /rrealiθa'θion; rrealisa'sion/ *n. f.* achievement, accomplishment.

realizar /rreali'θar; rreali'sar/ *v.* accomplish; fulfill; effect; *Com.* realize.

realmente /rreal'mente/ *adv.* in reality, really.

realzar /rreal'θar; rreal'sar/ *v.* enhance.

reata /rre'ata/ *n. f.* rope; lasso, lariat.

rebaja /rre'βaha/ *n. f.* reduction.

rebajar /rreβa'har/ *v.* cheapen; reduce (in price); lower.

rebanada /rreβa'naða/ *n. f.* slice. —**rebanar,** *v.*

rebaño /rre'βaɲo/ *n. m.* flock, herd.

rebato /rre'βato/ *n. m.* alarm; sudden attack.

rebelarse /rreβe'larse/ *v.* rebel, revolt.

rebelde /rre'βelde/ *a. & n.* rebellious; rebel.

rebelión /rreβe'lion/ *n. f.* rebellion, revolt.

reborde /rre'βorðe/ *n. m.* border.

rebotar /rreβo'tar/ v. rebound.
rebozo /rre'βoθo; rre'βoso/ n. m. shawl.
rebuscar /rreβus'kar/ v. search thoroughly.
rebuznar /rreβuθ'nar; rreβus'nar/ v. bray.
recado /rre'kaðo/ n. m. message; errand.
recaída /rreka'iða/ n. f. relapse. —**recaer**, v.
recalcar /rrekal'kar/ v. stress, emphasize.
recalentar /rrekalen'tar/ v. reheat.
recámara /rre'kamara/ n. f. (Mex.) bedroom.
recapitulación /rrekapitula'θion; rrekapitula'sion/ n. f. recapitulation.
recapitular /rrekapitu'lar/ v. recapitulate.
recatado /rreka'taðo/ n. m. coy; prudent.
recaudador /rrekauða'ðor/ -ra n. tax collector.
recelar /rreθe'lar; rrese'lar/ v. fear, distrust.
receloso /rreθe'loso; rrese'loso/ a. distrustful.
recepción /rreθep'θion; rresep-'sion/ n. f. reception.
recepcionista /rreθepθio'nista; rresepsio'nista/ n. m. & f. desk clerk.
receptáculo /rreθep'takulo; rresep'takulo/ n. m. receptacle.
receptividad /rreθeptiβi'ðað; rreseptiβi'ðað/ n. f. receptivity.
receptivo /rreθep'tiβo; rresep-'tiβo/ a. receptive.
receptor /rreθep'tor; rresep'tor/ n. m. receiver.
receta /rre'θeta; rre'seta/ n. f. recipe; prescription.
recetar /rreθe'tar; rrese'tar/ v. prescribe.
rechazar /rretʃa'θar; rretʃa'sar/ v. reject, spurn, discard.
rechinar /rretʃi'nar/ v. chatter.
recibimiento /rreθiβi'miento; rresiβi'miento/ n. m. reception; welcome; anteroom.
recibir /rreθi'βir; rresi'βir/ v. receive.
recibo /rre'θiβo; rre'siβo/ n. m. receipt.
reciclaje /reθi'klahe; resi'klahe/ n. m. recycling.
reciclar /rreθi'klar; rresi'klar/ v. recycle.

recidiva /rreθi'ðiβa; rresi'ðiβa/ n. f. relapse.
recién /rre'θien; rre'sien/ adv. recently, newly, just.
reciente /rre'θiente; rre'siente/ a. recent.
recinto /rre'θinto; rre'sinto/ n. m. enclosure.
recipiente /rreθi'piente; rresi-'piente/ n. m. recipient.
reciprocación /rreθiproka'θion; rresiproka'sion/ n. f. reciprocation.
recíprocamente /rreθiproka-'mente; resiproka'mente/ adv. reciprocally.
reciprocar /rreθipro'kar; rresipro-'kar/ v. reciprocate.
reciprocidad /rreθiproθi'ðað; rresiprosi'ðað/ n. f. reciprocity.
recitación /rreθita'θion; rresita-'sion/ n. f. recitation.
recitar /rreθi'tar; rresi'tar/ v. recite.
reclamación /rreklama'θion; rreklama'sion/ n. f. claim; complaint.
reclamar /rrekla'mar/ v. claim; complain.
reclamo /rre'klamo/ n. m. claim; advertisement, advertising; decoy.
reclinar /rrekli'nar/ v. recline, repose, lean.
recluta /rre'kluta/ n. m. & f. recruit.
reclutar /rreklu'tar/ v. recruit, draft.
recobrar /rreko'βrar/ v. recover, salvage, regain.
recobro /rre'koβro/ n. m. recovery.
recoger /rreko'her/ v. gather; collect; pick up. **r. el conocimiento,** regain consciousness.
recogerse /rreko'herse/ v. retire (for night).
recolectar /rrekolek'tar/ v. gather, assemble; harvest.
recomendación /rrekomenda-'θion; rrekomenda'sion/ n. f. recommendation; commendation.
recomendar /rrekomen'dar/ v. recommend; commend.
recompensa /rrekom'pensa/ n. f. recompense; compensation.
recompensar /rrekompen'sar/ v. reward; compensate.
reconciliación /rrekonθilia'θion; rrekonsilia'sion/ n. f. reconciliation.

reconciliar /rrekonθi'liar; rrekonsi'liar/ v. reconcile.

reconocer /rrekono'θer; rrekono'ser/ v. recognize; acknowledge; inspect, examine; Mil. reconnoiter.

reconocimiento /rrekonoθi'miento; rrekonosi'miento/ n. m. recognition; appreciation, gratitude.

reconstituir /rrekonsti'tuir/ v. reconstitute.

reconstruir /rrekons'truir/ v. reconstruct, rebuild.

record /'rrekorð/ n. m. (sports) record.

recordar /rrekor'ðar/ v. recall, recollect; remind.

recorrer /rreko'rrer/ v. go over; read over; cover (distance).

recorte /rre'korte/ n. m. clipping, cutting.

recostarse /rrekos'tarse/ v. recline, lean back, rest.

recreación /rrekrea'θion; rrekrea'sion/ n. f. recreation.

recreo /rre'kreo/ n. m. recreation.

recriminación /rrekrimina'θion; rrekrimina'sion/ n. f. recrimination.

rectangular /rrektaŋgu'lar/ a. rectangular.

rectángulo /rrek'taŋgulo/ n. m. rectangle.

rectificación /rrektifika'θion; rrektifika'sion/ n. f. rectification.

rectificar /rrektifi'kar/ v. rectify.

recto /'rrekto/ a. straight; just, fair. **ángulo r.,** right angle.

recuento /rre'kuento/ n. m. recount.

recuerdo /rre'kuerðo/ n. m. memory; souvenir; remembrance; (pl.) regards.

reculada /rreku'laða/ n. f. recoil. —**recular,** v.

recuperación /rrekupera'θion; rrekupera'sion/ n. f. recuperation.

recuperar /rrekupe'rar/ v. recuperate.

recurrir /rreku'rrir/ v. revert; resort, have recourse.

recurso /rre'kurso/ n. m. resource; recourse.

red /rreð/ n. f. net; trap. **r. local** local area network.

redacción /rreðak'θion; rreðak'sion/ n. f. (editorial) staff; composition (of written material).

redactar /rreðak'tar/ v. draft, draw up; edit.

redactor /rreðak'tor/ -ra n. editor.

redada /rre'ðaða/ n. f. netful, catch, haul.

redargución /rreðargu'θion; rreðargu'sion/ n. f. retort. —**redargüir,** v.

redención /rreðen'θion; rreðen'sion/ n. f. redemption, salvation.

redentor /rreðen'tor/ n. m. redeemer.

redimir /rreði'mir/ v. redeem.

redoblante /rreðo'βlante/ n. m. snare drum; snare dummer.

redonda /rre'ðonda/ n. f. neighborhood, vicinity.

redondo /rre'ðondo/ a. round, circular.

reducción /rreðuk'θion; rreðuk'sion/ n. f. reduction.

reducir /rreðu'θir; rreðu'sir/ v. reduce.

reembolso /rreem'βolso/ n. m. refund. —**reembolsar,** v.

reemplazar /rreempla'θar; rreempla'sar/ v. replace, supersede.

reencarnación /rreenkarna'θion; rreenkarna'sion/ n. f. reincarnation.

reexaminar /rreeksami'nar/ v. reexamine.

reexpedir /rreekspe'ðir/ v. forward (mail).

referencia /rrefe'renθia; rrefe'rensia/ n. f. reference.

referéndum /rrefe'rendum/ n. m. referendum.

referir /rrefe'rir/ v. relate, report on.

referirse /rrefe'rirse/ v. refer.

refinamiento /rrefina'miento/ n. m. refinement.

refinar /rrefi'nar/ v. refine.

refinería /rrefine'ria/ n. f. refinery.

reflejar /rrefle'har/ v. reflect; think, ponder.

reflejo /rre'fleho/ n. m. reflection; glare.

reflexión /rreflek'sion/ n. f. reflection, thought.

reflexionar /rrefleksio'nar/ v. reflect, think.

reflujo /rre'fluho/ n. m. ebb; ebb tide.

reforma /rre'forma/ n. f. reform. —**reformar,** v.

reformación /rreforma'θion; rreforma'sion/ n. f. reformation.

reformador /rreforma'ðor/ -ra n. reformer.

reforma tributaria /rre'forma
triβu'taria/ tax reform.
reforzar /rrefor'θar; rrefor'sar/ v.
reinforce, strengthen; encourage.
refractario /rrefrak'tario/ a. refractory.
refrán /rre'fran/ n. m. proverb,
saying.
refrenar /rrefre'nar/ v. curb, rein;
restrain.
refrescar /rrefres'kar/ v. refresh,
freshen, cool.
refresco /rre'fresko/ n. m. refreshment; cold drink.
refrigeración /rrefrihera'θion; rre-
frihera'sion/ n. f. refrigeration.
refrigerador /rrefrihera'ðor/ n. m.
refrigerator.
refrigerar /rrefrihe'rar/ v. refriger-
ate.
refuerzo /rre'fuerθo; rre'fuerso/
n. m. reinforcement.
refugiado /rrefu'hiaðo/ **-da** refugee.
refugiarse /rrefu'hiarse/ v. take
refuge.
refugio /rre'fuhio/ n. m. refuge,
asylum, shelter.
refulgencia /rreful'henθia; rre-
ful'hensia/ n. f. refulgence.
refulgente /rreful'hente/ a. reful-
gent.
refulgir /rreful'hir/ v. shine.
refunfuñar /rrefunfu'ɲar/ v. mutter, grumble, growl.
refutación /rrefuta'θion; rrefuta-
'sion/ n. f. refutation; rebuttal.
refutar /rrefu'tar/ v. refute.
regadera /rrega'ðera/ n. f. watering can.
regadizo /rrega'ðiθo; rrega'ðiso/
a. irrigable.
regadura /rrega'ðura/ n. f. irrigation.
regalar /rrega'lar/ v. give (a gift),
give away.
regaliz /rrega'liθ; rrega'lis/ n. m.
licorice.
regalo /rre'galo/ n. m. gift, present, **con r.,** in luxury.
regañar /rrega'ɲar/ v. reprove;
scold.
regaño /rre'gaɲo/ n. m. reprimand; scolding.
regar /rre'gar/ v. water, irrigate.
regatear /rregate'ar/ v. haggle.
regateo /rrega'teo/ n. m. bargain-
ing, haggling.
regazo /rre'gaθo; rre'gaso/ n. m.
lap.

regencia /rre'henθia; rre'hensia/
n. f. regency.
regeneración /rrehenera'θion; rre-
henera'sion/ n. f. regeneration.
regenerar /rrehene'rar/ v. regen-
erate.
regente /rre'hente/ **-ta** a. & n. regent.
régimen /'rrehimen/ n. m. regime;
diet.
regimentar /rrehimen'tar/ v. regiment.
regimiento /rrehi'miento/ n. m.
regiment.
región /rre'hion/ n. f. region.
regional /rrehio'nal/ a. regional,
sectional.
regir /rre'hir/ v. rule; be in effect.
registrar /rrehis'trar/ v. register;
record; search.
registro /rre'histro/ n. m. register;
record; search.
regla /'rregla/ n. f. rule, regulation. **en r.,** in order.
reglamento /rregla'mento/ n. m.
code of regulations.
regocijarse /rregoθi'harse; rrego-
si'harse/ v. rejoice, exult.
regocijo /rrego'θiho; rrego'siho/
n. f. rejoicing; merriment, joy.
regordete /rregor'ðete/ a.
chubby, plump.
regresar /rregre'sar/ v. go back,
return.
regresión /rregre'sion/ n. f. re-
gression.
regresivo /rregre'siβo/ a. regres-
sive.
regreso /rre'greso/ n. m. return.
regulación /rregula'θion; rregula-
'sion/ n. f. regulation.
regular /rregu'lar/ a. **1.** regular;
fair, middling. —v. **2.** regulate.
regularidad /rregulari'ðað/ n. f.
regularity.
regularmente /rregular'mente/
adv. regularly.
rehabilitación /rreaβilita'θion;
rreaβilita'sion/ n. f. rehabilitation.
rehabilitar /rreaβili'tar/ v. rehabilitate.
rehén /rre'en/ n. m. hostage.
rehogar /rreo'gar/ v. brown.
rehusar /rreu'sar/ v. refuse; decline.
reina /'rreina/ n. f. queen.
reinado /rrei'naðo/ n. m. reign.
—**reinar,** v.
reino /'rreino/ n. m. kingdom;
realm; reign.

reír /rre'ir/ v. laugh.

reiteración /rreitera'θion; rreitera'sion/ n. f. reiteration.

reiterar /rreite'rar/ v. reiterate.

reja /'rreha/ n. f. grating, grillwork.

relación /rrela'θion; rrela'sion/ n. f. relation; account, report.

relacionar /rrelaθio'nar; rrelasio'nar/ v. relate, connect.

relajamiento /rrelaha'miento/ n. m. laxity, laxness.

relajar /rrela'har/ v. relax, slacken.

relámpago /rre'lampago/ n. m. lightning; flash (of lightning).

relatador /rrelata'ðor/ **-ra** n. teller.

relatar /rrela'tar/ v. relate, recount.

relativamente /rrelatiβa'mente/ adv. relatively.

relatividad /rrelatiβi'ðað/ n. f. relativity.

relativo /rrela'tiβo/ a. relative.

relato /rre'lato/ n. m. account, story.

relegación /rrelega'θion; rrelega'sion/ n. f. relegation.

relegar /rrele'gar/ v. relegate.

relevar /rrele'βar/ v. relieve.

relicario /rreli'kario/ n. m. reliquary; locket.

relieve /rre'lieβe/ n. m. (sculpture) relief.

religión /rreli'hion/ n. f. religion.

religiosidad /rrelihiosi'ðað/ n. f. religiosity.

religioso /rreli'hioso/ **-sa** a. **1.** religious. —n. **2.** m. member of a religious order.

reliquia /rre'likia/ n. f. relic.

rellenar /rreʎe'nar; rreye'nar/ v. refill; fill up, stuff.

relleno /rre'ʎeno; rre'yeno/ n. m. filling; stuffing.

reloj /rre'loh/ n. m. clock; watch.

reloj de pulsera /rre'loh de pul'sera/ wrist watch.

relojería /rrelohe'ria/ n. f. watchmaker's shop.

relojero /rrelo'hero/ **-ra** n. watchmaker.

relucir /rrelu'θir; rrelu'sir/ v. glow, shine; excel.

relumbrar /rrelum'βrar/ v. glitter, sparkle.

remache /rre'matʃe/ n. m. rivet. —**remachar**, v.

remar /rre'mar/ v. row (a boat).

rematado /rrema'taðo/ a. finished; sold.

remate /rre'mate/ n. m. end, finish; auction. **de r.**, utterly.

remedador /rremeða'ðor/ **-ra** n. imitator.

remedar /rreme'ðar/ v. imitate.

remedio /rre'meðio/ n. m. remedy. —**remediar**, v.

remendar /rremen'dar/ v. mend, patch.

remesa /rre'mesa/ n. f. shipment; remittance.

remiendo /rre'miendo/ n. m. patch.

remilgado /rremil'gaðo/ a. prudish; affected.

reminiscencia /rreminis'θenθia; rreminis'sensia/ n. f. reminiscence.

remitir /rremi'tir/ v. remit.

remo /'rremo/ n. m. oar.

remolacha /rremo'latʃa/ n. f. beet.

remolcador /rremolka'ðor/ n. m. tug (boat); tow truck.

remolino /rremo'lino/ n. m. whirl; whirlpool; whirlwind.

remolque /rre'molke/ n. m. tow. —**remolcar**, v.

remontar /rremon'tar/ v. ascend, go up.

remontarse /rremon'tarse/ v. get excited; soar. **r. a**, date from; go back to (in time).

remordimiento /rremorði'miento/ n. m. remorse.

remotamente /rremota'mente/ adv. remotely.

remoto /rre'moto/ a. remote.

remover /rremo'βer/ v. remove; stir; shake; loosen.

rempujar /rrempu'har/ v. jostle.

remuneración /rremunera'θion; rremunera'sion/ n. f. remuneration.

remunerar /rremune'rar/ v. remunerate.

renacido /rrena'θiðo; rrena'siðo/ a. reborn, born-again.

renacimiento /rrenaθi'miento; rrenasi'miento/ n. m. rebirth; renaissance.

rencor /rren'kor/ n. m. rancor, bitterness, animosity; grudge.

rencoroso /rrenko'roso/ a. rancorous, bitter.

rendición /rrendi'θion; rrendi'sion/ n. f. surrender.

rendido /rren'diðo/ *a*. weary, worn out.

rendir /rren'dir/ *v*. yield; surrender, give up; win over.

renegado /rrene'gaðo/ **-da** *n*. renegade.

renglón /rreŋ'glon/ *n. m*. line; *Com*. item.

reno /'rreno/ *n. m*. reindeer.

renombre /rre'nombre/ *n. m*. renown.

renovación /rrenoβa'θion; rrenoβa'sion/ *f*. renovation, renewal.

renovar /rreno'βar/ *v*. renew; renovate.

renta /'rrenta/ *n. f*. income; rent.

rentar /rren'tar/ *v*. yield; rent.

renuencia /rre'nuenθia; rre'nuensia/ *n. f*. reluctance.

renuente /rre'nuente/ *a*. reluctant.

renuncia /rre'nunθia; rre'nunsia/ *n. f*. resignation; renunciation.

renunciar /rrenun'θiar; rrenun'siar/ *v*. resign; renounce, give up.

reñir /rre'ɲir/ *v*. scold, berate; quarrel, wrangle.

reo /'rreo/ *a*. & *n*. criminal; convict.

reorganizar /rreorgani'θar; rreorgani'sar/ *v*. reorganize.

reparación /rrepara'θion; rrepara'sion/ *n. f*. reparation, atonement; repair.

reparar /rrepa'rar/ *v*. repair; mend; stop, stay over. **r. en,** notice; consider.

reparo /rre'paro/ *n. m*. repair; remark; difficulty; objection.

repartición /rreparti'θion; rreparti'sion/ *n. f*., **repartimiento, reparto,** *m*. division, distribution.

repartir /rrepar'tir/ *v*. divide, apportion, distribute; *Theat*. cast.

repaso /rre'paso/ *n. m*. review. **—repasar,** *v*.

repatriación /rrepatria'θion; rrepatria'sion/ *n. f*. repatriation.

repatriar /rrepa'triar/ *v*. repatriate.

repeler /rrepe'ler/ *v*. repel.

repente /rre'pente/ *n. m*. **de r.,** suddenly; unexpectedly.

repentinamente /rrepentina'mente/ *adv*. suddenly.

repentino /rrepen'tino/ *a*. sudden.

repercusión /rreperku'sion/ *n. f*. repercussion.

repertorio /rreper'torio/ *n. m*. repertoire.

repetición /rrepeti'θion; rrepeti'sion/ *n. f*. repetition; action replay.

repetidamente /rrepetiða'mente/ *adv*. repeatedly.

repetir /rrepe'tir/ *v*. repeat.

repisa /rre'pisa/ *n. f*. shelf.

réplica /'rreplika/ *n. f*. reply; objection; replica.

replicar /rrepli'kar/ *v*. reply; answer back.

repollo /rre'poʎo; rre'poyo/ *n. m*. cabbage.

reponer /rrepo'ner/ *v*. replace; repair.

reponerse /rrepo'nerse/ *v*. recover, get well.

reporte /rre'porte/ *n. m*. report; news.

repórter /rre'porter/ **reportero -ra** *n*. reporter.

reposado /rrepo'saðo/ *a*. tranquil, peaceful, quiet.

reposo /rre'poso/ *n. m*. repose, rest. **—reposar,** *v*.

reposte /rre'poste/ *n. f*. pantry.

represalia /rrepre'salia/ *n. f*. reprisal.

representación /rrepresenta'θion; rrepresenta'sion/ *n. f*. representation; *Theat*. performance.

representante /rrepresen'tante/ *n. m*. & *f*. representative, agent.

representar /rrepresen'tar/ *v*. represent; depict; *Theat*. perform.

representativo /rrepresenta'tiβo/ *a*. representative.

represión /rrepre'sion/ *n. f*. repression.

represivo /rrepre'siβo/ *a*. repressive.

reprimenda /rrepri'menda/ *n. f*. reprimand.

reprimir /rrepri'mir/ *v*. repress, quell.

reproche /rre'protʃe/ *n. m*. reproach. **—reprochar,** *v*.

reproducción /rreproðuk'θion; rreproðuk'sion/ *n. f*. reproduction.

reproducir /rreproðu'θir; rreproðu'sir/ *v*. reproduce.

reptil /rrep'til/ *n. m*. reptile.

república /rre'puβlika/ *n. f*. republic.

republicano /rrepuβli'kano/ **-na** *a*. & *n*. republican.

repudiación /rrepuðia'θion; rrepuðia'sion/ *n. f*. repudiation.

repudiar /rrepu'ðiar/ *v.* repudiate; disown.

repuesto /rre'puesto/ *n. m.* spare part. **de r.,** spare.

repugnancia /rrepug'nanθia; rrepug'nansia/ *n. f.* repugnance.

repugnante /rrepug'nante/ *a.* disgusting, repugnant, repulsive, revolting.

repugnar /rrepug'nar/ *v.* disgust.

repulsa /rre'pulsa/ *n. f.* refusal; repulse.

repulsivo /rrepul'siβo/ *a.* repulsive.

reputación /rreputa'θion; rreputa-'sion/ *n. f.* reputation.

reputar /rrepu'tar/ *v.* repute; appreciate.

requerir /rreke'rir/ *v.* require.

requesón /rreke'son/ *n. m.* cottage cheese.

requisición /rrekisi'θion; rrekisi-'sion/ *n. f.* requisition.

requisito /rreki'sito/ *n. m.* requisite, requirement.

res /rres/ *n. f.* head of cattle.

resaca /rre'saka/ *n. f.* hangover.

resbalar /rresβa'lar/ *v.* slide; slip.

resbaloso /rresβa'loso/ *a.* slippery.

rescate /rres'kate/ *n. m.* rescue; ransom. **—rescatar,** *v.*

rescindir /rresθin'dir; rressin'dir/ *v.* rescind.

resentimiento /rresenti'miento/ *n. m.* resentment.

resentirse /rresen'tirse/ *v.* resent.

reserva /rre'serβa/ *n. f.* reserve. **—reservar,** *v.*

reservación /rreserβa'θion; rreserβa'sion/ *n. f.* reservation.

resfriado /rres'friaðo/ *n. m. Med.* cold.

resfriarse /rres'friarse/ *v.* catch cold.

resguardar /rresguar'ðar/ *v.* guard, protect.

residencia /rresi'ðenθia; rresi'ðensia/ *n. f.* residence; seat, headquarters.

residente /rresi'ðente/ *a. & n.* resident.

residir /rresi'ðir/ *v.* reside.

residuo /rre'siðuo/ *n. m.* remainder.

resignación /rresigna'θion; rresigna'sion/ *n. f.* resignation.

resignar /rresig'nar/ *v.* resign.

resina /rre'sina/ *n. f.* resin; rosin.

resistencia /rresis'tenθia; rresis-'tensia/ *n. f.* resistance.

resistir /rresis'tir/ *v.* resist; endure.

resolución /rresolu'θion; rresolu-'sion/ *n. f.* resolution.

resolutivamente /rresolutiβa-'mente/ *adv.* resolutely.

resolver /rresol'βer/ *v.* resolve; solve.

resonante /rreso'nante/ *a.* resonant.

resonar /rreso'nar/ *v.* resound.

resorte /rre'sorte/ *n. m. Mech.* spring.

respaldar /rrespal'dar/ *v.* endorse; back.

respaldo /rres'paldo/ *n. m.* back (of a seat).

respectivo /rrespek'tiβo/ *a.* respective.

respecto /rres'pekto/ *n. m.* relation, proportion; **r. a,** concerning, regarding.

respetabilidad /rrespetaβili'ðað/ *n. f.* respectability.

respetable /rrespe'taβle/ *a.* respectable.

respeto /rres'peto/ *n. m.* respect. **—respetar,** *v.*

respetuosamente /rrespetuosa-'mente/ *adv.* respectfully.

respetuoso /rrespe'tuoso/ *a.* respectful.

respiración /rrespira'θion; rrespira'sion/ *n. f.* respiration, breath.

respirar /rrespi'rar/ *v.* breathe.

resplandeciente /rresplande-'θiente; rresplande'siente/ *a.* resplendent.

resplandor /rresplan'dor/ *n. m.* brightness, glitter.

responder /rrespon'der/ *v.* respond, answer.

responsabilidad /rresponsaβili-'ðað/ *n. f.* responsibility.

responsable /rrespon'saβle/ *a.* responsible.

respuesta /rres'puesta/ *n. f.* answer, response, reply.

resquicio /rres'kiθio; rres'kisio/ *n. m.* crack, slit.

resta /'rresta/ *n. f.* subtraction; remainder.

restablecer /rrestaβle'θer; rrestaβle'ser/ *v.* restore; reestablish.

restablecerse /rrestaβle'θerse; rrestaβle'serse/ *v.* recover, get well.

restar /rres'tar/ v. remain; subtract.

restauración /rrestaura'θion; rrestaura'sion/ n. f. restoration.

restaurante /rrestau'rante/ n. m. restaurant.

restaurar /rrestau'rar/ v. restore.

restitución /rrestitu'θion; rrestitu'sion/ n. f. restitution.

restituir /rresti'tuir/ v. restore, give back.

resto /'rresto/ n. m. remainder, rest; (pl.) remains.

restorán /rresto'ran/ n. m. restaurant.

restregar /rrestre'gar/ v. rub hard; scrub.

restricción /rrestrik'θion; rrestrik'sion/ n. f. restriction.

restrictivo /rrestrik'tiβo/ a. restrictive.

restringir /rrestrin'gir/ v. restrict, curtail.

resucitar /rresuθi'tar; rresusi'tar/ v. revive, resuscitate.

resuelto /rre'suelto/ a. resolute.

resultado /rresul'taðo/ n. m. result.

resultar /rresul'tar/ v. result; turn out; ensue.

resumen /rre'sumen/ n. m. résumé, summary, **en r.,** in brief.

resumir /rresu'mir/ v. sum up.

resurgir /rresur'hir/ v. resurge, reappear.

resurrección /rresurrek'θion; rresurrek'sion/ n. f. resurrection.

retaguardia /rreta'guarðia/ n. f. rear guard.

retal /rre'tal/ n. m. remnant.

retardar /rretar'ðar/ v. retard, slow.

retardo /rre'tarðo/ n. m. delay.

retención /rreten'θion; rreten'sion/ n. f. retention.

retener /rrete'ner/ v. retain, keep; withhold.

reticencia /rreti'θenθia; rreti'sensia/ n. f. reticence.

reticente /rreti'θente; rreti'sente/ a. reticent.

retirada /rreti'raða/ n. f. retreat, retirement.

retirar /rreti'rar/ v. retire, retreat, withdraw.

retiro /rre'tiro/ n. m. retirement.

retorcer /rretor'θer; rretor'ser/ v. wring.

retórica /rre'torika/ n. f. rhetoric.

retórico /rre'toriko/ a. rhetorical.

retorno /rre'torno/ n. m. return.

retozo /rre'toθo; rre'toso/ n. m. frolic, romp. —**retozar,** v.

retozón /rreto'θon; rreto'son/ a. frisky.

retracción /rretrak'θion; rretrak'sion/ n. f. retraction.

retractar /rretrak'tar/ v. retract.

retrasar /rretra'sar/ v. delay, set back.

retrasarse /rretra'sarse/ v. be slow.

retraso /rre'traso/ n. m. delay, lag, slowness.

retratar /rretra'tar/ v. portray; photograph.

retrato /rre'trato/ n. m. portrait; picture, photograph.

retreta /rre'treta/ n. f. Mil. retreat.

retrete /rre'trete/ n. m. toilet.

retribución /rretriβu'θion; rretriβu'sion/ n. f. retribution.

retroactivo /rretroak'tiβo/ a. retroactive.

retroalimentación /rretroalimenta'θion; rretroalimenta'sion/ n. f. feedback.

retroceder /rretroθe'ðer; rretrose'ðer/ v. recede, go back, draw back, back up.

retumbar /rretum'βar/ v. resound, rumble.

reumático /rreu'matiko/ a. rheumatic.

reumatismo /rreuma'tismo/ n. m. rheumatism.

reunión /rreu'nion/ n. f. gathering, meeting, party; reunion.

reunir /rreu'nir/ v. gather, collect, bring together.

reunirse /rreu'nirse/ v. meet, assemble, get together.

reutilizar /rreutili'zar/ v. reuse.

revelación /rreβela'θion; rreβela'sion/ n. f. revelation.

revelar /rreβe'lar/ v. reveal; betray; *Phot.* develop.

reventa /rre'βenta/ n. f. resale.

reventar /rreβen'tar/ v. burst; split apart.

reventón /rreβen'ton/ n. m. blowout (of tire).

reverencia /rreβeren'θia; rreβeren'sia/ n. f. reverence.

reverendo /rreβe'rendo/ a. reverend.

reverente /rreβe'rente/ a. reverent.

revertir /rreβer'tir/ v. revert.

revés /rre'βes/ *n. m.* reverse; back, wrong side. **al r.,** just the opposite; inside out.

revisar /rreβi'sar/ *v.* revise; review.

revisión /rreβi'sion/ *n. f.* revision.

revista /rre'βista/ *n. f.* magazine, periodical; review.

revivir /rreβi'βir/ *v.* revive.

revocación /rreβoka'θion; rreβoka'sion/ *n. f.* revocation.

revocar /rreβo'kar/ *v.* revoke, reverse.

revolotear /rreβolote'ar/ *v.* hover.

revolución /rreβolu'θion; rreβolu'sion/ *n. f.* revolution.

revolucionario /rreβoluθio'nario; rreβolusio'nario/ **-ria** *a. & n.* revolutionary.

revolver /rreβol'βer/ *v.* revolve; stir, agitate.

revólver *n. m.* revolver, pistol.

revuelta /rre'βuelta/ *n. f.* revolt; turn.

rey /rrei/ *n. m.* king.

reyerta /rre'yerta/ *n. f.* quarrel, wrangle.

rezar /rre'θar; rre'sar/ *v.* pray.

rezongar /rreθoŋ'gar; rresoŋ'gar/ *v.* grumble; mutter.

ría /'rria/ *n. f.* estuary.

riachuelo /rria'tʃuelo/ *n. m.* creek.

riba /'rriβa/ *n. f.* embankment.

rico /'rriko/ *a.* rich, wealthy; delicious.

ridículamente /rri'ðikulamente/ *adv.* ridiculously.

ridiculizar /rriðikuli'θar; rriðikuli'sar/ *v.* ridicule.

ridículo /rri'ðikulo/ *a. & m.* ridiculous; ridicule.

riego /'rriego/ *n. m.* irrigation.

rienda /'rrienda/ *n. f.* rein.

riesgo /'rriesgo/ *n. m.* risk, gamble.

rifa /'rrifa/ *n. f.* raffle; lottery; scuffle.

rifle /'rrifle/ *n. m.* rifle.

rígidamente /'rrihiðamente/ *adv.* rigidly.

rigidez /rrihi'ðeθ; rrihi'ðes/ *n. f.* rigidity.

rígido /'rrihiðo/ *a.* rigid, stiff.

rigor /rri'gor/ *n. m.* rigor.

riguroso /rrigu'roso/ *a.* rigorous, strict.

rima /'rrima/ *n. f.* rhyme. **—rimar,** *v.*

rimel /rri'mel/ *n. f.* mascara.

rincón /rrin'kon/ *n. m.* corner, nook.

rinoceronte /rrinoθe'ronte; rrinose'ronte/ *n. m.* rhinoceros.

riña /'rriɲa/ *n. f.* quarrel, feud.

riñón /rri'ɲon/ *n. m.* kidney.

río /'rrio/ *n. m.* river. **r. abajo** downstream, downriver. **r. arriba,** upstream, upriver.

ripio /'rripio/ *n. m.* debris.

riqueza /rri'keθa; rri'kesa/ *n. f.* wealth.

risa /'rrisa/ *n. f.* laugh; laughter.

risco /'rrisko/ *n. m.* cliff.

risibilidad /rrisiβili'ðað/ *n. f.* risibility.

risotada /rriso'taða/ *n. f.* peal of laughter.

risueño /rri'sueɲo/ *a.* cheerful, smiling.

rítmico /'rritmiko/ *a.* rhythmical.

ritmo /'rritmo/ *n. m.* rhythm.

rito /'rrito/ *n. m.* rite.

ritual /rri'tual/ *a. & m.* ritual.

rivalidad /rriβali'ðað/ *n. f.* rivalry.

rivera /rri'βera/ *n. f.* brook.

rizado /rri'θaðo; rri'saðo/ *a.* curly.

rizo /'rriθo; 'rriso/ *n. m.* curl. **—rizar,** *v.*

robar /rro'βar/ *v.* rob, steal.

roble /'rroβle/ *n. m.* oak.

roblón /rro'βlon/ *n. m.* rivet. **—roblar,** *v.*

robo /'rroβo/ *n. m.* robbery, theft.

robustamente /rroβusta'mente/ *adv.* robustly.

robusto /rro'βusto/ *a.* robust.

roca /'rroka/ *n. f.* rock; cliff.

rociada /rro'θiaða; rro'siaða/ *n. f.* spray, sprinkle. **—rociar,** *v.*

rocío /'rroθio; 'rrosio/ *n. m.* dew.

rocoso /rro'koso/ *a.* rocky.

rodar /rro'ðar/ *v.* roll; roam.

rodear /rroðe'ar/ *v.* surround, encircle.

rodeo /rro'ðeo/ *n. m.* turn, winding; roundup.

rodilla /rro'ðiʎa; rro'ðiya/ *n. f.* knee.

rodillo /rro'ðiʎo; rro'ðiyo/ *n. m.* roller.

rodio /'rroðio/ *n. m.* rhodium.

rododendro /rroðo'ðendro/ *n. m.* rhododendron.

roedor /rroe'ðor/ *n. m.* rodent.

roer /rro'er/ *v.* gnaw.

rogación /rroga'θion; rroga'sion/ *n. f.* request, entreaty.

rogar /rro'gar/ *v.* beg, plead with, supplicate.

rojizo /rro'hiθo; rro'hiso/ *a.* reddish.

rojo /'rroho/ *a.* red.

rollizo /rro'ʎiθo; rro'yiso/ *a.* chubby.

rollo /'rroʎo; 'rroyo/ *n. m.* roll; coil.

romadizo /rroma'ðiθo; rroma-'ðiso/ *n. m.* head cold.

romance /rro'manθe; rro'manse/ *n. m.* romance; ballad.

románico /rro'maniko/ *a.* Romance.

romano /rro'mano/ **-na** *a. & n.* Roman.

romántico /rro'mantiko/ *a.* romantic.

romería /rrome'ria/ *n. f.* pilgrimage; picnic.

romero /rro'mero/ **-ra** *n.* pilgrim.

rompecabezas /rrompeka'βeθas; rrompeka'βesas/ *n. m.* puzzle (pastime).

romper /rrom'per/ *v.* break, smash, shatter; sever; tear.

rompible /rrom'piβle/ *a.* breakable.

ron /rron/ *n. m.* rum.

roncar /rron'kar/ *v.* snore.

ronco /'rronko/ *a.* hoarse.

ronda /'rronda/ *n. f.* round.

rondar /rron'dar/ *v.* prowl.

ronquido /rron'kiðo/ *n. m.* snore.

ronronear /rronrone'ar/ *v.* purr.

ronzal /rron'θal; rron'sal/ *n. m.* halter.

roña /'rroɲa/ *n. f.* scab; filth.

ropa /'rropa/ *n. f.* clothes, clothing. **r. blanca,** linen. **r. interior,** underwear.

ropa de marca /'rropa de 'marka/ designer clothing.

ropero /rro'pero/ *n. m.* closet.

rosa /'rrosa/ *n. f.* rose. **r. náutica,** compass.

rosado /rro'saðo/ *a.* pink, rosy.

rosal /rro'sal/ *n. m.* rose bush.

rosario /rro'sario/ *n. m.* rosary.

rosbif /rros'βif/ *n. m.* roast beef.

rosca /'rroska/ *n. f.* thread (of screw).

róseo /'rroseo/ *a.* rosy.

rostro /'rrostro/ *n. m.* face, countenance.

rota /'rrota/ *n. f.* defeat; *Naut.* course.

rotación /rrota'θion; rrota'sion/ *n. f.* rotation.

rotatorio /rrota'torio/ *a.* rotary.

rótula /'rrotula/ *n. f.* kneecap.

rotulador /rrotula'ðor/ *n. m.* felt-tipped pen.

rótulo /'rrotulo/ *n. m.* label. **—rotular,** *v.*

rotundo /rro'tundo/ *a.* round; sonorous.

rotura /rro'tura/ *n. f.* break, fracture, rupture.

rozar /rro'θar; rro'sar/ *v.* rub against, chafe; graze.

rubí /rru'βi/ *n. m.* ruby.

rubio /'rruβio/ **-bia** *a. & n.* blond.

rubor /rru'βor/ *n. m.* blush; bashfulness.

rúbrica /'rruβrika/ *n. f.* caption; scroll.

rucho /'rrutʃo/ *n. m.* donkey.

rudeza /rru'ðeθa; rru'ðesa/ *n. f.* rudeness; roughness.

rudimentario /rruðimen'tario/ *a.* rudimentary.

rudimento /rruði'mento/ *n. m.* rudiment.

rudo /'rruðo/ *a.* rude, rough.

rueda /'rrueða/ *n. f.* wheel.

rueda de feria /'rrueða de 'feria/ Ferris wheel.

ruego /'rruego/ *n. m.* plea; entreaty.

rufián /rru'fian/ *n. m.* ruffian.

rufo /'rrufo/ *a.* sandy haired.

rugir /rru'hir/ *v.* bellow, roar.

rugoso /rru'goso/ *a.* wrinkled.

ruibarbo /rrui'βarβo/ *n. m.* rhubarb.

ruido /'rruiðo/ *n. m.* noise.

ruidoso /rrui'ðoso/ *a.* noisy.

ruina /'rruina/ *n. f.* ruin, wreck.

ruinar /rrui'nar/ *v.* ruin, destroy.

ruinoso /rrui'noso/ *a.* ruinous.

ruiseñor /rruise'ɲor/ *n. m.* nightingale.

ruleta /rru'leta/ *n. f.* roulette.

rumba /'rrumba/ *n. f.* rumba (dance or music).

rumbo /'rrumbo/ *n. m.* course, direction.

rumor /rru'mor/ *n. m.* rumor; murmur.

runrún /rrun'run/ *n. m.* rumor.

ruptura /rrup'tura/ *n. f.* rupture, break.

rural /rru'ral/ *a.* rural.

Rusia /'rrusia/ *n. f.* Russia.

ruso /'rruso/ **-sa** *a. & n.* Russian.

rústico /'rrustiko/ **-ca** *a. & n.* rustic. **en r.,** paperback *f.*

ruta /'rruta/ *n. f.* route.

rutina /rru'tina/ *n. f.* routine.

rutinario /rruti'nario/ *a.* routine.

S

sábado /'saβaðo/ *n. m.* Saturday.

sábalo /'saβalo/ *n. m.* shad.

sábana /sa'βana/ *n. f.* sheet.

sabañon /saβa'ɲon/ *n. m.* chilblain.

saber /sa'βer/ *n.* **1.** *m.* knowledge. —*v.* **2.** know; learn, find out; know how to; taste. **a s.,** namely, to wit.

sabiduría /saβiðu'ria/ *n. f.* wisdom; learning.

sabio /'saβio/ **-a** *a.* **1.** wise; scholarly. —*n.* **2.** sage; scholar.

sable /'saβle/ *n. m.* saber.

sabor /sa'βor/ *n. m.* flavor, taste, savor.

saborear /saβore'ar/ *v.* savor, relish.

sabotaje /saβo'tahe/ *n. m.* sabotage.

sabroso /sa'βroso/ *a.* savory, tasty.

sabueso /sa'βueso/ *n. m.* hound.

sacacorchos /saka'kortʃos/ *n. m.* corkscrew.

sacapuntas /saka'puntas/ *n. f.* pencil sharpener.

sacar /sa'kar/ *v.* draw out; take out; take.

sacerdocio /saθer'ðoθio; saser-'ðosio/ *n. m.* priesthood.

sacerdote /saθer'ðote; saser'ðote/ *n. m.* priest.

saciar /sa'θiar; sa'siar/ *v.* satiate.

saco /'sako/ *n. m.* sack, bag, pouch; suit coat, jacket.

sacramento /sakra'mento/ *n. m.* sacrament.

sacrificio /sakri'fiθio; sakri'fisio/ *n. m.* sacrifice. —**sacrificar,** *v.*

sacrilegio /sakri'lehio/ *n. m.* sacrilege.

sacristán /sakris'tan/ *n. m.* sexton.

sacro /'sakro/ *a.* sacred, holy.

sacrosanto /sakro'santo/ *a.* sacrosanct.

sacudir /saku'ðir/ *v.* shake, jerk, jolt.

sádico /'saðiko/ *a.* sadistic.

sadismo /sa'ðismo/ *n. m.* sadism.

sagacidad /sagaθi'ðað; sagasi'ðað/ *n. f.* sagacity.

sagaz /sa'gaθ; sa'gas/ *a.* sagacious, sage.

sagrado /sa'graðo/ *a.* sacred, holy.

sal /sal/ *n. f.* salt; *Colloq.* wit.

sala /'sala/ *n. f.* room; living room, parlor; hall, auditorium.

salado /sa'laðo/ *a.* salted, salty; *Colloq.* witty.

salar /sa'lar/ *v.* salt; steep in brine.

salario /sa'lario/ *n. m.* salary, wages.

salchicha /sal'tʃitʃa/ *n. f.* sausage.

sal de la Higuera /sal de la i'gera/ Epsom salts.

saldo /'saldo/ *n. m.* remainder, balance; (bargain) sale.

saldo acreedor /'saldo akree'ðor/ credit balance.

saldo deudor /'saldo deu'ðor/ debit balance.

salero /sa'lero/ *n. m.* salt shaker.

salida /sa'liða/ *n. f.* exit, outlet; departure.

salida de urgencia /sa'liða de ur'henθia; sa'liða de ur'hensia/ emergency exit, fire exit.

salir /sa'lir/ *v.* go out, come out; set out, leave, start; turn out, result.

salirse de /sa'lirse de/ *v.* get out of. **s. con la suya,** have one's own way.

salitre /sa'litre/ *n. m.* saltpeter.

saliva /sa'liβa/ *n. f.* saliva.

salmo /'salmo/ *n. m.* psalm.

salmón /sal'mon/ *n. m.* salmon.

salmonete /salmo'nete/ *n. m.* red mullet.

salmuera /sal'muera/ *n. f.* pickle; brine.

salobre /sa'loβre/ *a.* salty.

salón /sa'lon/ *n. m.* parlor, living room; hall. **s. de baile,** dance hall. **s. de belleza** beauty parlor.

salpicar /salpi'kar/ *v.* spatter, splash.

salpullido /salpu'ʎiðo; salpu'yiðo/ *n. m.* rash.

salsa /'salsa/ *n. f.* sauce; gravy.

saltamontes /salta'montes/ *n. m.* grasshopper.

salteador /saltea'ðor/ *n. m.* highwayman.

saltear /salte'ar/ *v.* hold up, rob; sauté.

salto /'salto/ *n. m.* jump, leap, spring. —**saltar,** *v.*

saltón /sal'ton/ *n. m.* grasshopper.

salubre /sa'luβre/ *a.* salubrious, healthful.

salubridad /saluβri'ðað/ *n. f.* health.

salud /sa'luð/ *n. f.* health.

saludable /salu'ðaβle/ *a.* healthful, wholesome.

saludar /salu'ðar/ *v.* greet; salute.

saludo /sa'luðo/ *n. m.* greeting; salutation; salute.

salutación /saluta'θion; saluta-'sion/ *n. f.* salutation.

salva /'salβa/ *n. f.* salvo.

salvación /salβa'θion; salβa'sion/ *n. f.* salvation; deliverance.

salvador /salβa'ðor/ **-ra** *n.* savior; rescuer.

salvaguardia /salβa'guarðia/ *n. m.* safeguard.

salvaje /sal'βahe/ *a.* & *n.* savage, wild (person).

salvamento /salβa'mento/ *n. m.* salvation; rescue.

salvar /sal'βar/ *v.* save; salvage; rescue; jump over.

salvavidas /salβa'βiðas/ *n. m.* life preserver.

salvia /'salβia/ *n. f.* sage (plant).

salvo /'salβo/ *a.* **1.** safe. —*prep.* **2.** except, save (for). **s. que,** unless.

San /san/ *title.* Saint.

sanar /sa'nar/ *v.* heal, cure.

sanatorio /sana'torio/ *n. m.* sanatorium.

sanción /san'θion; san'sion/ *n. f.* sanction. —**sancionar,** *v.*

sancochar /sanko'tʃar/ *v.* parboil.

sandalia /san'dalia/ *n. f.* sandal.

sandez /san'deθ; san'des/ *n. f.* stupidity.

sandía /san'dia/ *n. f.* watermelon.

saneamiento /sanea'miento/ *n. m.* sanitation.

sangrar /saŋ'grar/ *v.* bleed.

sangre /'saŋgre/ *n. f.* blood.

sangriento /saŋ'griento/ *a.* bloody.

sanguinario /saŋgi'nario/ *a.* bloodthirsty.

sanidad /sani'ðað/ *n. f.* health.

sanitario /sani'tario/ *a.* sanitary.

sano /'sano/ *a.* healthy, sound, sane; healthful, wholesome.

santidad /santi'ðað/ *n. f.* sanctity, holiness.

santificar /santifi'kar/ *v.* sanctify.

santo /'santo/ **-ta** *a.* **1.** holy, saintly. —*n.* **2.** *m.* saint.

Santo -ta *title.* Saint.

santuario /san'tuario/ *n. m.* sanctuary, shrine.

saña /'saɲa/ *n. f.* rage, anger.

sapiente /sa'piente/ *a.* wise.

sapo /'sapo/ *n. m.* toad.

saquear /sake'ar/ *v.* sack; ransack; plunder.

sarampión /saram'pion/ *n. m.* measles.

sarape /sa'rape/ *n. m.* (Mex.) woven blanket; shawl.

sarcasmo /sar'kasmo/ *n. m.* sarcasm.

sarcástico /sar'kastiko/ *a.* sarcastic.

sardina /sar'ðina/ *n. f.* sardine.

sargento /sar'hento/ *n. m.* sergeant.

sarna /'sarna/ *n. f.* itch.

sartén /sar'ten/ *n. m.* frying pan.

sastre /'sastre/ *n. m.* tailor.

satánico /sa'taniko/ *a.* satanic.

satélite /sa'telite/ *n. m.* satellite.

sátira /'satira/ *n. f.* satire.

satírico /sa'tiriko/ *a.* & *m.* satirical; satirist.

satirizar /satiri'θar; satiri'sar/ *v.* satirize.

sátiro /'satiro/ *n. m.* satyr.

satisfacción /satisfak'θion; satisfak'sion/ *n. f.* satisfaction.

satisfacer /satisfa'θer; satisfa'ser/ *v.* satisfy.

satisfactorio /satisfak'torio/ *a.* satisfactory.

saturación /satura'θion; satura-'sion/ *n. f.* saturation.

saturar /satu'rar/ *v.* saturate.

sauce /'sauθe; 'sause/ *n. m.* willow.

sauna /'sauna/ *n. f.* sauna.

savia /'saβia/ *n. f.* sap.

saxofón /sakso'fon/ **saxófono** *n. m.* saxophone.

saya /'saya/ *n. f.* skirt.

sazón /sa'θon; sa'son/ *n. f.* season; seasoning. **a la s.,** at that time.

sazonar /saθo'nar; saso'nar/ *v.* flavor, season.

se /se/ *pron.* -self, -selves.

seca /'seka/ *n. f.* drought.

secador /seka'ðor/ **secador de pelo** *n. m.* hair dryer.

secante /se'kante/ *a.* **papel s.,** blotting paper.

secar /se'kar/ *v.* dry.

sección /sek'θion; sek'sion/ *n. f.* section.

seco /'seko/ *a.* dry; curt.

secreción /sekre'θion; sekre'sion/ *n. f.* secretion.

secretar /sekre'tar/ *v.* secrete.

secretaría /sekreta'ria/ *n. f.* secretary's office; secretariat.

secretario /sekre'tario/ -ra *n.* secretary.

secreto /se'kreto/ *a. & m.* secret.

secta /'sekta/ *n. f.* denomination; sect.

secuela /se'kuela/ *n. f.* result; sequel.

secuestrar /sekues'trar/ *v.* abduct, kidnap; hijack.

secuestro /se'kuestro/ *n. m.* abduction, kidnapping.

secular /seku'lar/ *a.* secular.

secundario /sekun'dario/ *a.* secondary.

sed /seð/ *n. f.* thirst. **tener s., estar con s.,** to be thirsty.

seda /'seða/ *n. f.* silk.

sedar /se'ðar/ *v.* quiet, allay.

sedativo /seða'tiβo/ *a. & m.* sedative.

sede /'seðe/ *n. f.* seat, headquarters.

sedentario /seðen'tario/ *a.* sedentary.

sedición /seði'θion; seði'sion/ *n. f.* sedition.

sedicioso /seði'θioso; seði'sioso/ *a.* seditious.

sediento /se'ðiento/ *a.* thirsty.

sedimento /seði'mento/ *n. m.* sediment.

sedoso /se'ðoso/ *a.* silky.

seducir /seðu'θir; seðu'sir/ *v.* seduce.

seductivo /seðuk'tiβo/ *a.* seductive, alluring.

segar /se'gar/ *v.* reap, harvest; mow.

seglar /seg'lar/ *n. m. & f.* layman, laywoman.

segmento /seg'mento/ *n. m.* segment.

segregar /segre'gar/ *v.* segregate.

seguida /se'giða/ *n. f.* succession. **en s.,** right away, at once.

seguido /se'giðo/ *a.* consecutive.

seguir /se'gir/ *v.* follow; continue, keep on, go on.

según /se'gun/ *prep.* **1.** according to. —*conj.* **2.** as.

segundo /se'gundo/ *a. & m.* second. —**segundar,** *v.*

seguridad /seguri'ðað/ *n. f.* safety, security; assurance.

seguro /se'guro/ *a.* **1.** safe, secure; sure, certain. —*n.* **2.** *m.* insurance.

seis /seis/ *a. & pron.* six.

seiscientos /seis'θientos; seis'sientos/ *a. & pron.* six hundred.

selección /selek'θion; selek'sion/ *n. f.* selection, choice.

seleccionar /selekθio'nar; seleksio'nar/ *v.* select, choose.

selecto /se'lekto/ *a.* select, choice, elite.

sello /'seʎo; 'seyo/ *n. m.* seal; stamp. —**sellar,** *v.*

selva /'selβa/ *n. f.* forest; jungle.

selvoso /sel'βoso/ *a.* sylvan.

semáforo /se'maforo/ *n. m.* semaphore; traffic light.

semana /se'mana/ *n. f.* week.

semana inglesa /se'mana iŋ'glesa/ five-day work week.

semanal /sema'nal/ *a.* weekly.

semana laboral /se'mana laβo'ral/ work week.

semántica /se'mantika/ *n. f.* semantics.

semblante /sem'βlante/ *n. m.* look, expression.

sembrado /sem'βraðo/ *n. m.* sown field.

sembrar /sem'βrar/ *v.* sow, seed.

semejante /seme'hante/ *a.* **1.** like, similar; such (a). —*n.* **2.** *m.* fellow man.

semejanza /seme'hanθa; seme'hansa/ *n. f.* similarity, likeness.

semejar /seme'har/ *v.* resemble.

semilla /se'miʎa; se'miya/ *n. f.* seed.

seminario /semi'nario/ *n. m.* seminary.

sémola /'semola/ *n. f.* semolina.

senado /se'naðo/ *n. m.* senate.

senador /sena'ðor/ -ra *n.* senator.

sencillez /senθi'ʎeθ; sensi'yes/ *n. f.* simplicity; naturalness.

sencillo /sen'θiʎo; sen'siyo/ *a.* simple, natural; single.

senda /'senda/ *n. f.* **sendero,** *m.* path, footpath.

senectud /senek'tuð/ *n. f.* old age.

senil /se'nil/ *a.* senile.

seno /'seno/ *n. m.* breast, bosom.

sensación /sensa'θion; sensa'sion/ *n. f.* sensation.

sensacional /sensaθio'nal; sensasio'nal/ *a.* sensational.

sensato /sen'sato/ *a.* sensible, wise.

sensibilidad /sensiβili'ðað/ n. f. sensibility; sensitiveness.

sensible /sen'siβle/ a. sensitive; emotional.

sensitivo /sensi'tiβo/ a. sensitive.

sensual /sen'sual/ a. sensual.

sensualidad /sensuali'ðað/ n. f. sensuality.

sentar /sen'tar/ v. seat. **s. bien,** fit well, be becoming.

sentarse /sen'tarse/ v. sit, sit down.

sentencia /sen'tenθia; sen'tensia/ n. f. (court) sentence.

sentidamente /sentiða'mente/ adv. feelingly.

sentido /sen'tiðo/ n. m. meaning, sense; consciousness.

sentido común /sen'tiðo ko'mun/ common sense.

sentimental /sentimen'tal/ a. sentimental.

sentimiento /senti'miento/ n. m. sentiment, feeling.

sentir /sen'tir/ v. feel, sense; hear; regret, be sorry.

seña /'seɲa/ n. f. sign, indication; (pl.) address.

señal /se'ɲal/ n. f. sign, signal; mark.

señalar /seɲa'lar/ v. designate, point out; mark.

señal de marcar /se'ɲal de mar'kar/ dial tone.

señor /se'ɲor/ n. m. gentleman; lord; (title) Mr., Sir.

señora /se'ɲora/ n. f. lady; wife; (title) Mrs., Madam.

señora de la limpieza /se'ɲora de la lim'pieθa; se'ɲora de la lim'piesa/ cleaning woman.

señorita /seɲo'rita/ n. f. young lady; (title) Miss.

sépalo /'sepalo/ n. m. sepal.

separación /separa'θion; separa'sion/ n. f. separation, parting.

separadamente /separaða'mente/ adv. separately.

separado /sepa'raðo/ a. separate; separated. **—separar,** v.

septentrional /septentrio'nal/ a. northern.

septiembre /sep'tiembre/ n. m. September.

séptimo /'septimo/ a. seventh.

sepulcro /se'pulkro/ n. m. sepulcher.

sepultar /sepul'tar/ v. bury, entomb.

sepultura /sepul'tura/ n. f. grave.

sequedad /seke'ðað/ n. f. dryness.

sequía /se'kia/ n. f. drought.

ser /ser/ v. be.

serenata /sere'nata/ n. f. serenade.

serenidad /sereni'ðað/ n. f. serenity.

sereno /se'reno/ a. **1.** serene, calm. —n. **2.** m. dew; watchman.

ser humano /ser u'mano/ n. human being.

serie /'serie/ n. f. series, sequence.

seriedad /serie'ðað/ n. f. seriousness.

serio /'serio/ a. serious. **en s.,** seriously.

sermón /ser'mon/ n. m. sermon.

seroso /se'roso/ a. watery.

serpiente /ser'piente/ n. f. serpent, snake.

serpiente de cascabel /ser'piente de kaska'βel/ rattlesnake.

serrano /se'rrano/ **-na** n. mountaineer.

serrar /se'rrar/ v. saw.

serrín /se'rrin/ n. m. sawdust.

servicial /serβi'θial; serβi'sial/ a. helpful, of service.

servicio /ser'βiθio; ser'βisio/ n. m. service; toilet.

servidor /serβi'ðor/ **-ra** n. servant.

servidumbre /serβi'ðumbre/ n. f. bondage; staff of servants.

servil /ser'βil/ a. servile, menial.

servilleta /serβi'ʎeta; serβi'yeta/ n. f. napkin.

servir /ser'βir/ v. serve. **s. para,** be good for.

servirse /ser'βirse/ v. help oneself.

sesenta /se'senta/ a. & pron. sixty.

sesgo /'sesgo/ n. m. slant. **—sesgar,** v.

sesión /se'sion/ n. f. session; sitting.

seso /'seso/ n. m. brain.

seta /'seta/ n. f. mushroom.

setecientos /sete'θientos; sete'sientos/ a. & pron. seven hundred.

setenta /se'tenta/ a. & pron. seventy.

seto /'seto/ n. m. hedge.

severamente /seβera'mente/ adv. severely.

severidad /seβeri'ðað/ n. f. severity.

severo /se'βero/ *a.* severe, strict, stern.

sexismo /sek'sismo/ *n. m.* sexism.

sexista /sek'sista/ *a. & n.* sexist.

sexo /'sekso/ *n. m.* sex.

sexto /'seksto/ *a.* sixth.

sexual /sek'sual/ *a.* sexual.

si /si/ *conj.* if; whether.

sí *pron.* **1.** -self, -selves. —*interj.* **2.** yes.

sico-. See **psicoanálisis, psicología,** etc.

sicómoro /siko'moro/ *n. m.* sycamore.

SIDA /'siða/ *n. m.* AIDS.

sidra /'siðra/ *n. f.* cider.

siempre /'siempre/ *adv.* always. **para s.,** forever. **s. que,** whenever; provided that.

sierra /'sierra/ *n. f.* saw; mountain range.

siervo /'sierβo/ **-va** *n.* slave; serf.

siesta /'siesta/ *n. f.* (afternoon) nap.

siete /'siete/ *a. & pron.* seven.

sifón /si'fon/ *n. m.* siphon; siphon bottle.

siglo /'siglo/ *n. m.* century.

signatura /signa'tura/ *n. f. Mus.* signature.

significación /signifika'θion; signifika'sion/ *n. f.* significance.

significado /signifi'kaðo/ *n. m.* meaning.

significante /signifi'kante/ *a.* significant.

significar /signifi'kar/ *v.* signify, mean.

significativo /signifika'tiβo/ *a.* significant.

signo /'signo/ *n. m.* sign, symbol; mark.

siguiente /si'giente/ *a.* following, next.

sílaba /'silaβa/ *n. f.* syllable.

silbar /sil'βar/ *v.* whistle; hiss, boo.

silbato /sil'βato/ **silbido** *n. m.* whistle.

silencio /si'lenθio; si'lensio/ *n. m.* silence, stillness.

silenciosamente /silenθiosa'mente; silensiosa'mente/ *a.* silently.

silencioso /silen'θioso; silen'sioso/ *a.* silent, still.

silicato /sili'kato/ *n. m.* silicate.

silicio /si'liθio; si'lisio/ *n. m.* silicon.

silla /'siʎa; 'siya/ *n. f.* chair; saddle.

sillón /si'ʎon; si'yon/ *n. m.* armchair.

silueta /si'lueta/ *n. f.* silhouette.

silvestre /sil'βestre/ *a.* wild, uncultivated. **fauna s.,** wildlife.

sima /'sima/ *n. f.* chasm; cavern.

simbólico /sim'boliko/ *a.* symbolic.

símbolo /'simbolo/ *n. m.* symbol.

simetría /sime'tria/ *n. f.* symmetry.

simétrico /si'metriko/ *a.* symmetrical.

símil /'simil/ **similar** *a.* similar, alike.

similitud /simili'tuð/ *n. f.* similarity.

simpatía /simpa'tia/ *n. f.* congeniality; friendly feeling.

simpático /sim'patiko/ *a.* likeable, nice, congenial.

simple /'simple/ *a.* simple.

simpleza /sim'pleθa; sim'plesa/ *n. f.* silliness; trifle.

simplicidad /simpliθi'ðað; simplisi'ðað/ *n. f.* simplicity.

simplificación /simplifika'θion; simplifika'sion/ *n. f.* simplification.

simplificar /simplifi'kar/ *v.* simplify.

simular /simu'lar/ *v.* simulate.

simultáneo /simul'taneo/ *a.* simultaneous.

sin /sin/ *prep.* without. **s. sentido,** meaningless.

sinagoga /sina'goga/ *n. f.* synagogue.

sinceridad /sinθeri'ðað; sinseri-'ðað/ *n. f.* sincerity.

sincero /sin'θero; sin'sero/ *a.* sincere.

sincronizar /sinkroni'θar; sinkroni'sar/ *v.* synchronize.

sindicato /sindi'kato/ *n. m.* syndicate; labor union.

síndrome /'sindrome/ *n. m.* syndrome.

sinfonía /sinfo'nia/ *n. f.* symphony.

sinfónico /sin'foniko/ *a.* symphonic.

singular /siŋgu'lar/ *a. & m.* singular.

siniestro /si'niestro/ *a.* sinister, ominous.

sino /'sino/ *conj.* but.

sinónimo /si'nonimo/ *n. m.* synonym.

sinrazón /sinra'θon; sinra'son/ *n. f.* wrong, injustice.

sinsabor /sinsa'βor/ *n. m.* displeasure, distaste; trouble.

sintaxis /sin'taksis/ *n. f.* syntax.

síntesis /'sintesis/ *n. f.* synthesis.

sintético /sin'tetiko/ *a.* synthetic.

síntoma /'sintoma/ *n. m.* symptom.

siquiera /si'kiera/ *adv.* **ni s.,** not even.

sirena /si'rena/ *n. f.* siren.

sirviente /sir'βiente/ **-ta** *n.* servant.

sistema /sis'tema/ *n. m.* system.

sistemático /siste'matiko/ *a.* systematic.

sistematizar /sistemati'θar; sistemati'sar/ *v.* systematize.

sitiar /si'tiar/ *v.* besiege.

sitio /'sitio/ *n. m.* site, location, place, spot.

situación /situa'θion; situa'sion/ *n. f.* situation; location.

situar /si'tuar/ *v.* situate; locate.

smoking /'smokiŋ/ *n. m.* tuxedo, dinner jacket.

so /so/ *prep.* under.

soba /'soβa/ *n. f.* massage. —**sobar,** *v.*

sobaco /so'βako/ *n. m.* armpit.

sobaquero /soβa'kero/ *n. f.* armhole.

soberano /soβe'rano/ **-na** *a.* & *n.* sovereign.

soberbia /so'βerβia/ *n. f.* arrogance.

soberbio /so'βerβio/ *a.* superb; arrogant.

soborno /so'βorno/ *n. m.* bribe. —**sobornar,** *v.*

sobra /'soβra/ *n. f.* excess, surplus. **de sobra,** to spare.

sobrado /so'βraðo/ *n. m.* attic.

sobrante /so'βrante/ *a.* & *m.* surplus.

sobras /'soβras/ *n. f.pl.* leftovers.

sobre /'soβre/ *prep.* **1.** about; above, over. —*n.* **2.** *m.* envelope.

sobrecama /soβre'kama/ *n. f.* bedspread.

sobrecargo /soβre'kargo/ *n. m.* supercargo.

sobredicho /soβre'ðitʃo/ *a.* aforesaid.

sobredosis /soβre'ðosis/ *n. f.* overdose.

sobrehumano /soβreu'mano/ *a.* superhuman.

sobrenatural /soβrenatu'ral/ *a.* supernatural, weird.

sobrepasar /soβrepa'sar/ *v.* surpass.

sobresalir /soβresa'lir/ *v.* excel.

sobretodo /soβre'toðo/ *n. m.* overcoat.

sobrevivir /soβreβi'βir/ *v.* survive, outlive.

sobriedad /soβrie'ðað/ *n. f.* sobriety; moderation.

sobrina /so'βrina/ *n. f.* niece.

sobrino /so'βrino/ *n. m.* nephew.

sobrio /'soβrio/ *a.* sober, temperate.

socarrén /soka'rren/ *n. m.* eaves.

sociable /so'θiaβle; so'siaβle/ *a.* sociable.

social /so'θial; so'sial/ *a.* social.

socialismo /soθia'lismo; sosia'lismo/ *n. m.* socialism.

socialista /soθia'lista; sosia'lista/ *a.* & *n.* socialist.

sociedad /soθie'ðað; sosie'ðað/ *n. f.* society; association.

sociedad de consumo /soθie'ðað de kon'sumo; sosie'ðað de kon'sumo/ consumer society.

socio /'soθio; 'sosio/ **-cia** *n.* associate, partner; member.

sociología /soθiolo'hia; sosiolo'hia/ *n. f.* sociology.

sociológico /soθio'lohiko; sosio'lohiko/ *a.* sociological.

sociólogo /so'θiologo; so'siologo/ **-ga** *n.* sociologist.

socorrista /soko'rrista/ *n. m.* & *f.* lifeguard.

socorro /so'korro/ *n. m.* help, aid. —**socorrer,** *v.*

soda /'soða/ *n. f.* soda.

sodio /'soðio/ *n. m.* sodium.

soez /so'eθ; so'es/ *a.* vulgar.

sofá /so'fa/ *n. m.* sofa, couch.

sofisma /so'fisma/ *n. m.* sophism.

sofista /so'fista/ *n. m.* & *f.* sophist.

sofocación /sofoka'θion; sofoka'sion/ *n. f.* suffocation.

sofocar /sofo'kar/ *v.* smother, suffocate, stifle, choke.

sofrito /so'frito/ *n. m.* sauce of sautéed tomatoes, peppers, onions, and garlic.

software /'sofθwer/ *n. m.* software.

soga /'soga/ *n. f.* rope.

soja /'soha/ *n. f.* soya.

sol /sol/ *n. m.* sun.
solada /so'laða/ *n. f.* dregs.
solanera /sola'nera/ *n. f.* sunburn.
solapa /so'lapa/ *n. f.* lapel.
solar /so'lar/ *a.* **1.** solar. —*n.* **2.** *m.* building lot.
solaz /so'laθ; so'las/ *n. m.* solace, comfort. —**solazar,** *v.*
soldado /sol'daðo/ *n. m.* soldier.
soldar /sol'dar/ *v.* solder, weld.
soledad /sole'ðað/ *n. f.* solitude, privacy.
solemne /so'lemne/ *a.* solemn.
solemnemente /solemne'mente/ *adv.* solemnly.
solemnidad /solemni'ðað/ *n. f.* solemnity.
soler /so'ler/ *v.* be in the habit of.
solicitador /soliθita'ðor; solisita-'ðor/ -ra *n.* applicant, petitioner.
solicitar /soliθi'tar; solisi'tar/ *v.* solicit; apply for.
solícito /so'liθito; so'lisito/ *a.* solicitous.
solicitud /soliθi'tuð; solisi'tuð/ *n. f.* solicitude; application.
sólidamente /soliða'mente/ *adv.* solidly.
solidaridad /soliðari'ðað/ *n. f.* solidarity.
solidez /soli'ðeθ; soli'ðes/ *n. f.* solidity.
solidificar /soliðifi'kar/ *v.* solidify.
sólido /'soliðo/ *a. & m.* solid.
soliloquio /soli'lokio/ *n. m.* soliloquy.
solitario /soli'tario/ *a.* solitary, lone.
sollozo /so'ʎoθo; so'yoso/ *n. m.* sob. —**sollozar,** *v.*
solo /'solo/ *a.* **1.** only; single; alone; lonely. **a solas,** alone. —*n.* **2.** *m. Mus.* solo.
sólo *adv.* only, just.
solomillo /solo'miʎo; solo'miyo/ *n. m.* sirloin.
soltar /sol'tar/ *v.* release; loosen.
soltero /sol'tero/ -ra *a. & n.* single, unmarried (person).
soltura /sol'tura/ *n. f.* poise, ease, facility.
solubilidad /soluβili'ðað/ *n. f.* solubility.
solución /solu'θion; solu'sion/ *n. f.* solution.
solucionar /soluθio'nar; solusio-'nar/ *v.* solve, settle.
solvente /sol'βente/ *a.* solvent.
sombra /'sombra/ *n. f.* shade; shadow. —**sombrear,** *v.*

sombra de ojos /'sombra de 'ohos/ eye shadow.
sombrerera /sombre'rera/ *n. f.* hatbox.
sombrero /som'βrero/ *n. m.* hat.
sombrilla /som'βriʎa; som'βriya/ *n. f.* parasol.
sombrío /som'βrio/ *a.* somber, bleak, gloomy.
sombroso /som'βroso/ *a.* very shady.
someter /some'ter/ *v.* subject; submit.
somnífero /som'nifero/ *n. m.* speeping pill.
somnolencia /somno'lenθia; somno'lensia/ *n. f.* drowsiness.
son /son/ *n. m.* sound. —**sonar,** *v.*
sonata /so'nata/ *n. f.* sonata.
sondar /son'dar/ *v.* sound, fathom.
sonido /so'niðo/ *n. m.* sound.
sonoridad /sonori'ðað/ *n. f.* sonority.
sonoro /so'noro/ *a.* sonorous.
sonrisa /son'risa/ *n. f.* smile. —**sonreír,** *v.*
sonrojo /son'roho/ *n. m.* flush, blush. —**sonrojarse,** *v.*
soñador /soɲa'ðor/ -ra *a. & n.* dreamy; dreamer.
soñar /so'ɲar/ *v.* dream.
soñoliento /soɲo'liento/ *a.* sleepy.
sopa /'sopa/ *n. f.* soup.
soplar /so'plar/ *v.* blow.
soplete /so'plete/ *n. m.* blowtorch.
soplo /'soplo/ *n. m.* breath; puff, gust.
soportar /sopor'tar/ *v.* abide, bear, stand.
soprano /so'prano/ *n. m. & f.* soprano.
sorbete /sor'βete/ *n. m.* sherbet.
sorbo /'sorβo/ *n. m.* sip. —**sorber,** *v.*
sordera /sor'ðera/ *n. f.* deafness.
sórdidamente /sorðiða'mente/ *adv.* sordidly.
sordidez /sorði'ðeθ; sorði'ðes/ *n. f.* sordidness.
sórdido /'sorðiðo/ *a.* sordid.
sordo /'sorðo/ *a.* deaf; muffled, dull.
sordomudo /sorðo'muðo/ -da *a. & n.* deaf-mute.
sorpresa /sor'presa/ *n. f.* surprise. —**sorprender,** *v.*

sorteo /sor'teo/ *n. m.* drawing lots; raffle.

sortija /sor'tiha/ *n. f.* ring.

sosa /'sosa/ *n. f. Chem.* soda.

soso /'soso/ *a.* dull, insipid, tasteless.

sospecha /sos'petʃa/ *n. f.* suspicion.

sospechar /sospe'tʃar/ *v.* suspect.

sospechoso /sospe'tʃoso/ *a.* suspicious.

sostén /sos'ten/ *n. m.* bra, brassiere; support.

sostener /soste'ner/ *v.* hold, support; maintain.

sostenimiento /sosteni'miento/ *n. m.* sustenance.

sota /'sota/ *n. f.* jack (in cards).

sótano /'sotano/ *n. m.* basement, cellar.

soto /'soto/ *n. m.* grove.

soviet /so'βiet/ *n. m.* soviet.

soya /'soya/ *n. f.* soybean.

su /su/ *a.* his, her, its, their, your.

suave /'suaβe/ *a.* smooth; gentle, soft, mild.

suavidad /suaβi'ðað/ *n. f.* smoothness; gentleness, softness, mildness.

suavizar /suaβi'θar; suaβi'sar/ *v.* soften.

subalterno /suβal'terno/ **-na** *a. & n.* subordinate.

subasta /su'βasta/ *n. f.* auction.

subcampeón /suβkampe'on/ **-na** *n.* runner-up.

subconsciencia /suβkons'θienθia; suβkons'siensia/ *n. f.* subconscious.

súbdito /'suβðito/ **-ta** *n.* subject.

subestimar /suβesti'mar/ *v.* underestimate.

subida /su'βiða/ *n. f.* ascent, rise.

subilla /su'βiʎa; su'βiya/ *n. f.* awl.

subir /su'βir/ *v.* rise, climb, ascend, mount. **s. a,** amount to.

súbito /'suβito/ *a.* sudden.

subjetivo /suβhe'tiβo/ *a.* subjective.

subjuntivo /suβhun'tiβo/ *a. & m.* subjunctive.

sublimación /suβlima'θion; suβlima'sion/ *n. f.* sublimation.

sublimar /suβli'mar/ *v.* elevate; sublimate.

sublime /su'βlime/ *a.* sublime.

submarinismo /suβmari'nismo/ *n. m.* scuba diving.

submarino /suβma'rino/ *a. & m.* submarine.

subordinación /suβorðina'θion; suβorðina'sion/ *n. f.* subordination.

subordinado /suβorði'naðo/ **-da** *a. & n.* subordinate.

—**subordinar,** *v.*

subrayar /suβra'yar/ *v.* underline.

subscribirse /suβskri'βirse/ *v.* subscribe; sign one's name.

subscripción /suβskrip'θion; suβskrip'sion/ *n. f.* subscription.

subsecuente /suβse'kuente/ *a.* subsequent.

subsidiario /suβsi'ðiario/ *a.* subsidiary.

subsiguiente /suβsi'giente/ *a.* subsequent.

substancia /suβs'tanθia; suβs'tansia/ *n. f.* substance.

substancial /suβs'tanθial; suβs'tansial/ *a.* substantial.

substantivo /suβstan'tiβo/ *n. m.* substantive, noun.

substitución /suβstitu'θion; suβstitu'sion/ *n. f.* substitution.

substituir /suβsti'tuir/ *v.* replace; substitute.

substitutivo /suβstitu'tiβo/ *a.* substitute.

substituto /suβsti'tuto/ **-ta** *n.* substitute.

substraer /suβstra'er/ *v.* subtract.

subsuelo /suβ'suelo/ *n. m.* subsoil.

subterfugio /suβter'fuhio/ *n. m.* subterfuge.

subterráneo /suβte'rraneo/ *a.* **1.** subterranean, underground. —*n.* **2.** *m.* place underground; subway.

subtítulo /suβ'titulo/ *n. m.* subtitle.

suburbio /su'βurβio/ *n. m.* suburb.

subvención /suββen'θion; suββen'sion/ *n. f.* subsidy, grant.

subversión /suββer'sion/ *n. f.* subversion.

subversivo /suββer'siβo/ *a.* subversive.

subvertir /suββer'tir/ *v.* subvert.

subyugación /suβyuga'θion; suβyuga'sion/ *n. f.* subjugation.

subyugar /suβyu'gar/ *v.* subjugate, quell.

succión /suk'θion; suk'sion/ *n. f.* suction.

suceder /suθe'ðer; suse'ðer/ *v.* happen, occur, befall. **s. a,** succeed, follow.

sucesión /suθe'sion; suse'sion/ *n. f.* succession.

sucesivo /suθe'siβo; suse'siβo/ *a.* successive. **en lo s.,** in the future.

suceso /su'θeso; su'seso/ *n. m.* event.

sucesor /suθe'sor; suse'sor/ **-ra** *n.* successor.

suciedad /suθie'ðað; susie'ðað/ *n. f.* filth, dirt.

sucio /'suθio; 'susio/ *a.* filthy, dirty.

suculento /suku'lento/ *a.* succulent.

sucumbir /sukum'βir/ *v.* succumb.

sud /suð/ *n. m.* south.

sudadera /suða'ðera/ *n. f.* sweatshirt.

Sudáfrica /su'ðafrika/ *n. f.* South Africa.

sudafricano /suðafri'kano/ **-na** *a.* & *n.* South African..

sudamericano /suðameri'kano/ **-na** *a.* & *n.* South American.

sudar /su'ðar/ *v.* perspire, sweat.

sudeste /su'ðeste/ *n. m.* southeast.

sudoeste /suðo'este/ *n. m.* southwest.

sudor /su'ðor/ *n. m.* perspiration, sweat.

Suecia /'sueθia; 'suesia/ *n. f.* Sweden.

sueco /'sueko/ **-ca** *a.* & *n.* Swedish; Swede.

suegra /'suegra/ *n. f.* mother-in-law.

suegro /'suegro/ *n. m.* father-in-law.

suela /'suela/ *n. f.* sole.

sueldo /'sueldo/ *n. m.* salary, wages.

suelo /'suelo/ *n. m.* soil; floor; ground.

suelto /'suelto/ *a.* **1.** loose; free; odd, separate. —*n.* **2.** loose change.

sueño /'sueɲo/ *n. m.* sleep; sleepiness; dream. **tener s.,** to be sleepy.

suero /'suero/ *n. m.* serum.

suerte /'suerte/ *n. f.* luck; chance; lot.

suéter /'sueter/ *n. m.* sweater.

suficiente /sufi'θiente; sufi'siente/ *a.* sufficient.

sufragio /su'frahio/ *n. m.* suffrage.

sufrimiento /sufri'miento/ *n. m.* suffering, agony.

sufrir /su'frir/ *v.* suffer; undergo; endure.

sugerencia /suhe'renθia; suhe-'rensia/ *n. f.* suggestion.

sugerir /suhe'rir/ *v.* suggest.

sugestión /suhes'tion/ *n. f.* suggestion.

sugestionar /suhestio'nar/ *v.* influence; hypnotize.

suicida /sui'θiða; sui'siða/ *n. m.* & *f.* suicide (person).

suicidarse /suiθi'ðarse; suisi'ðarse/ *v.* commit suicide.

suicidio /sui'θiðio; sui'siðio/ *n. m.* (act of) suicide.

Suiza /'suiθa; 'suisa/ *n. f.* Switzerland.

suizo /'suiθo; 'suiso/ **-za** *a.* & *n.* Swiss.

sujeción /suhe'θion; suhe'sion/ *n. f.* subjection.

sujetador /suheta'ðor/ *n. m.* bra, brassiere.

sujetapapeles /su'hetapa'peles/ *n. m.* paper clip.

sujetar /suhe'tar/ *v.* hold, fasten, clip.

sujeto /su'heto/ *a.* **1.** subject, liable. —*n.* **2.** *m. Gram.* subject.

sulfato /sul'fato/ *n. m.* sulfate.

sulfuro /sul'furo/ *n. m.* sulfide.

sultán /sul'tan/ *n. m.* sultan.

suma /'suma/ *n. f.* sum, amount. **en s.,** in short. **s. global,** lump sum.

sumar /su'mar/ *v.* add up.

sumaria /su'maria/ *n. f.* indictment.

sumario /su'mario/ *a.* & *m.* summary.

sumergir /sumer'hir/ *v.* submerge.

sumersión /sumer'sion/ *n. f.* submersion.

sumisión /sumi'sion/ *n. f.* submission.

sumiso /su'miso/ *a.* submissive.

sumo /'sumo/ *a.* great, high, utmost.

suntuoso /sun'tuoso/ *a.* sumptuous.

superar /supe'rar/ *v.* overcome, surpass.

superficial /superfi'θial; super-fi'sial/ *a.* superficial, shallow.

superficie /super'fiθie; super'fisie/ *n. f.* surface.

supérfluo /su'perfluo/ *a.* superfluous.

superhombre /super'ombre/ *n. m.* superman.

superintendente /superinten-'dente/ *n. m. & f.* superintendent.

superior /supe'rior/ *a.* **1.** superior; upper, higher. —*n.* **2.** *m.* superior.

superioridad /superiori'ðað/ *n. f.* superiority.

superlativo /superla'tiβo/ *n. m. & a.* superlative.

superstición /supersti'θion; supersti'sion/ *n. f.* superstition.

supersticioso /supersti'θioso; supersti'sioso/ *a.* superstitious.

supervisar /superβi'sar/ *v.* supervise.

supervivencia /superβi'βenθia; superβi'βensia/ *n. f.* survival.

suplantar /suplan'tar/ *v.* supplant.

suplementario /suplemen'tario/ *a.* supplementary.

suplemento /suple'mento/ *n. m.* supplement. —**suplementar,** *v.*

suplente /su'plente/ *a. & n.* substitute.

súplica /'suplika/ *n. f.* request, entreaty, plea.

suplicación /suplika'θion; suplika'sion/ *n. f.* supplication; request, entreaty.

suplicar /supli'kar/ *v.* request, entreat; implore.

suplicio /su'pliθio; su'plisio/ *n. m.* torture, ordeal.

suplir /su'plir/ *v.* supply.

suponer /supo'ner/ *v.* suppose, pressume, assume.

suposición /suposi'θion; suposi'sion/ *n. f.* supposition, assumption.

supositorio /suposi'torio/ *n. m.* suppository.

supremacía /suprema'θia; suprema'sia/ *n. f.* supremacy.

supremo /su'premo/ *a.* supreme.

supresión /supre'sion/ *n. f.* suppression.

suprimir /supri'mir/ *v.* suppress; abolish.

supuesto /su'puesto/ *a.* supposed. **por s.,** of course.

sur /sur/ *n. m.* south.

surco /'surko/ *n. m.* furrow. —**surcar,** *v.*

surgir /sur'hir/ *v.* arise; appear suddenly.

surtido /sur'tiðo/ *n. m.* assortment; supply, stock.

surtir /sur'tir/ *v.* furnish, supply.

susceptibilidad /susθeptiβili'ðað; susseptiβili'ðað/ *n. f.* susceptibility.

susceptible /susθep'tiβle; sussep'tiβle/ *a.* susceptible.

suscitar /susθi'tar; sussi'tar/ *v.* stir up.

suscri- = subscri-

suspender /suspen'der/ *v.* withhold; suspend; fail (in a course).

suspensión /suspen'sion/ *n. f.* suspension.

suspenso /sus'penso/ *n. m.* failing grade. **en s.,** in suspense.

suspicacia /suspi'kaθia; suspi'kasia/ *n. f.* suspicion, distrust.

suspicaz /suspi'kaθ; suspi'kas/ *a.* suspicious.

suspicazmente /suspikaθ'mente; suspikas'mente/ *adv.* suspiciously.

suspiro /sus'piro/ *n. m.* sigh. —**suspirar,** *v.*

sustan- = substan-

sustentar /susten'tar/ *v.* sustain, support.

sustento /sus'tento/ *n. m.* sustenance, support, living.

susti- = substi-

susto /'susto/ *n. m.* fright, scare.

sustraer /sustra'er/ = substraer.

susurro /su'surro/ *n. m.* rustle; whisper. —**susurrar,** *v.*

sutil /'sutil/ *a.* subtle.

sutileza /suti'leθa, sutili'ðað; suti'lesa, sutili'ðað/ **sutilidad** *n. f.* subtlety.

sutura /su'tura/ *n. f.* suture.

suyo /'suyo/ *a.* his, hers, theirs, yours.

tabaco /ta'βako/ *n. m.* tobacco.

tábano /'taβano/ *n. m.* horsefly.

tabaquería /taβake'ria/ *n. f.* tobacco shop.

taberna /ta'βerna/ *n. f.* tavern, bar.

tabernáculo /taβer'nakulo/ *n. m.* tabernacle.

tabique /ta'βike/ *n. m.* dividing wall, partition.

tabla /'taβla/ *n. f.* board, plank; table, list. **t. de planchar,** ironing board.

tablado /ta'βlaðo/ *n. m.* stage, platform.

tablero /ta'βlero/ *n. m.* panel.

tableta /ta'βleta/ *n. f.* tablet.

tablilla /ta'βliʎa; ta'βliya/ *n. f.* bulletin board.

tabú /ta'βu/ *n. m.* taboo.

tabular /taβu'lar/ *a.* tabular.

tacaño /ta'kaɲo/ *a.* stingy.

tacha /'tatʃa/ *n. f.* fault, defect.

tachar /ta'tʃar/ *v.* find fault with; cross out.

tachuela /ta'tʃuela/ *n. f.* tack.

tácitamente /'taθitamente; 'tasitamente/ *adv.* tacitly.

tácito /'taθito; 'tasito/ *a.* tacit.

taciturno /taθi'turno; tasi'turno/ *a.* taciturn.

taco /'tako/ *n. m.* heel (of shoe); billiard cue.

tacón /ta'kon/ *n. m.* heel (of shoe).

táctico /'taktiko/ *a.* tactical.

tacto /'takto/ *n. m.* (sense of) touch; tact.

tafetán /tafe'tan/ *n. m.* taffeta.

taimado /tai'maðo/ *a.* sly.

tajada /ta'haða/ *n. f.* cut, slice. **—tajar,** *v.*

tajea /ta'hea/ *n. f.* channel.

tal /tal/ *a.* such. **con t. que.,** provided that. **t. vez,** perhaps.

taladrar /tala'ðrar/ *v.* drill.

taladro /ta'laðro/ *n. m. Mech.* drill.

talante /ta'lante/ *n. m.* humor, disposition.

talco /'talko/ *n. m.* talc.

talega /ta'lega/ *n. f.* bag, sack.

talento /ta'lento/ *n. m.* talent.

talla /'taʎa; 'taya/ *n. f.* engraving; stature; size (of suit).

tallador /taʎa'ðor; taya'ðor/ **-ra** *n.* engraver; dealer (at cards).

talle /'taʎe; 'taye/ *n. m.* figure; waist; fit.

taller /ta'ʎer; ta'yer/ *n. m.* workshop, factory.

tallo /'taʎo; 'tayo/ *n. m.* stem, stalk.

talón /ta'lon/ *n. m.* heel (of foot); (baggage) check, stub.

tamal /ta'mal/ *n. m.* tamale.

tamaño /ta'maɲo/ *n. m.* size.

tambalear /tambale'ar/ *v.* stagger, totter.

también /tam'bien/ *adv.* also, too.

tambor /tam'bor/ *n. m.* drum.

tamiz /ta'miθ; ta'mis/ *n. m.* sieve, sifter.

tampoco /tam'poko/ *adv.* neither, either.

tan /tan/ *adv.* so.

tanda /'tanda/ *n. f.* turn, relay.

tándem /'tandem/ *n. m.* tandem; pair.

tangencia /taŋ'genθia; taŋ'gensia/ *n. f.* tangency.

tangible /taŋ'giβle/ *a.* tangible.

tango /'taŋgo/ *n. m.* tango (dance or music).

tanque /'tanke/ *n. m.* tank.

tanteo /tan'teo/ *n. m.* estimate. **—tantear,** *v.*

tanto /'tanto/ *a. & pron.* **1.** so much, so many; as much, as many. **entre t., mientras t.,** meanwhile. **por lo t.,** therefore. **un t.,** somewhat, a bit. **—n. 2.** *m.* point (in games) **3.** (*pl.*) score. **estar al t.,** to be up to date.

tañer /ta'ɲer/ *v.* play (an instrument); ring (bells).

tapa /'tapa/ *n. f.* cap, cover; snack served in a bar. **—tapar,** *v.*

tapadero /tapa'ðero/ *n. m.* stopper, lid.

tápara /'tapara/ *n. f.* caper.

tapete /ta'pete/ *n. m.* small rug, mat, cover.

tapia /'tapia/ *n. f.* wall.

tapicería /tapiθe'ria; tapise'ria/ *n. f.* tapestry.

tapioca /ta'pioka/ *n. f.* tapioca.

tapiz /ta'piθ; ta'pis/ *n. m.* tapestry; carpet.

tapizado (de pared) /tapi'θaðo de pa'reð; tapi'saðo de pa'reð/ *n. m.* (wall) covering.

tapón /ta'pon/ *n. m.* plug; cork.

taquigrafía /takigra'fia/ *n. f.* shorthand.

taquilla /ta'kiʎa; ta'kiya/ *n. f.* ticket office; box office; ticket window.

tara /'tara/ *n. f.* hang-up.

tarántula /ta'rantula/ *n. f.* tarantula.

tararear /tarare'ar/ *v.* hum.

tardanza /tar'ðanθa; tar'ðansa/ *n. f.* delay; lateness.

tardar /tar'ðar/ *v.* delay; be late; take (of time). **a más t.,** at the latest.

tarde /'tarðe/ *adv.* **1.** late. —*n.* **2.** *f.* afternoon.

tardío /tar'ðio/ *a.* late, belated.

tarea /ta'rea/ *n. f.* task, assignment.

tarifa /ta'rifa/ *n. f.* rate; tariff; price list.

tarjeta /tar'heta/ *n. f.* card.

tarjeta bancaria /tar'heta ban-'karia/ bank card.

tarjeta de crédito /tar'heta de 'kreðito/ credit card.

tarjeta de embarque /tar'heta de em'βarke/ boarding pass.

tarta /'tarta/ *n. f.* tart.

tartamudear /tartamuðe'ar/ *v.* stammer, falter.

tasa /'tasa/ *n. f.* rate.

tasación /tasa'θion; tasa'sion/ *n. f.* valuation.

tasar /ta'sar/ *v.* assess, appraise.

tasca /'taska/ *n. f.* bar, pub.

tasugo /ta'sugo/ *n. m.* badger.

tatuar /tatu'ar/ *v.* tattoo.

tautología /tautolo'hia/ *n. f.* tautology.

taxi /'taksi/ **taxímetro** *n. m.* taxi.

taxista /tak'sista/ *n. m. & f.* taxi driver.

taxonomía /taksono'mia/ *n. f.* taxonomy.

taza /'taθa; 'tasa/ *n. f.* cup.

te /te/ *pron.* you; yourself.

té *n. m.* tea.

team /tim/ *n. m.* team.

teátrico /te'atriko/ *a.* theatrical.

teatro /te'atro/ *n. m.* theater.

tebeo /te'βeo/ *n. m.* comic book.

techo /'tetʃo/ *n. m.* roof. —**techar,** *v.*

tecla /'tekla/ *n. f.* key (of a piano, etc.).

teclado /te'klaðo/ *n. m.* keyboard.

teclado numérico /te'klaðo nu'meriko/ numeric keypad.

técnica /'teknika/ *n. f.* technique.

técnicamente /'teknikamente/ *adv.* technically.

técnico /'tekniko/ *a.* **1.** technical; —*m.* **2.** repairman, technician.

tecnología /teknolo'hia/ *n. f.* technology.

tedio /'teðio/ *n. m.* tedium, boredom.

tedioso /te'ðioso/ *a.* tedious.

teísmo /te'ismo/ *n. m.* theism.

teja /'teha/ *n. f.* tile.

tejado /te'haðo/ *n. m.* roof.

tejano /te'hano/ **-na** *a. & n.* Texan.

tejanos /te'hanos/ *n. m.pl.* jeans.

tejer /te'her/ *v.* weave; knit.

tejido /te'hiðo/ *n. m.* fabric; weaving.

tejón /te'hon/ *n. m.* badger.

tela /'tela/ *n. f.* cloth, fabric, web. **t. metálica,** screen; screening. **t. vaquera,** denim.

telar /te'lar/ *n. m.* loom.

telaraña /tela'raɲa/ *n. f.* cobweb, spiderweb.

telefonista /telefo'nista/ *n. m. & f.* (telephone) operator.

teléfono /te'lefono/ *n. m.* telephone. —**telefonear,** *v.*

teléfono gratuito /te'lefono gra'tuito/ toll-free number.

teléfono público /te'lefono 'puβliko/ pay phone, public telephone.

teléfono rojo /te'lefono 'rroho/ hotline.

telégrafo /te'legrafo/ *n. m.* telegraph. —**telegrafear,** *v.*

telegrama /tele'grama/ *n. m.* telegram.

telescopio /teles'kopio/ *n. m.* telescope.

televisión /teleβi'sion/ *n. f.* television.

telón /te'lon/ *n. m. Theat.* curtain.

telurio /te'lurio/ *n. m.* tellurium.

tema /'tema/ *n. m.* theme, subject.

temblar /tem'blar/ *v.* tremble, quake; shake, shiver.

temblor /tem'blor/ *n. m.* tremor; shiver.

temer /te'mer/ *v.* fear, be afraid of, dread.

temerario /teme'rario/ *a.* rash.

temeridad /temeri'ðað/ *n. f.* temerity.

temerosamente /temerosa'mente/ *adv.* timorously.

temeroso /teme'roso/ *a.* fearful.

temor /te'mor/ *n. m.* fear.
témpano /'tempano/ *n. m.* kettledrum; iceberg.
temperamento /tempera'mento/ *n. m.* temperament.
temperancia /tempe'ranθia; tempe'ransia/ *n. f.* temperance.
temperatura /tempera'tura/ *n. f.* temperature.
tempestad /tempes'taδ/ *n. f.* tempest, storm.
tempestuoso /tempes'tuoso/ *a.* tempestuous, stormy.
templado /tem'plaδo/ *a.* temperate, mild, moderate.
templanza /tem'planθa; tem'plansa/ *n. f.* temperance; mildness.
templar /tem'plar/ *v.* temper; tune (an instrument).
templo /'templo/ *n. m.* temple.
temporada /tempo'raδa/ *n. f.* season, time, spell.
temporal /tempo'ral/ **temporáneo** *a.* temporary.
temprano /tem'prano/ *a. & adv.* early.
tenacidad /tenaθi'δaδ; tenasi'δaδ/ *n. f.* tenacity.
tenaz /te'naθ; te'nas/ *a.* tenacious, stubborn.
tenazmente /tenaθ'mente; tenas'mente/ *adv.* tenaciously.
tendencia /ten'denθia; tendensia/ *n. f.* tendency, trend.
tender /ten'der/ *v.* stretch, stretch out.
tendero /ten'dero/ **-ra** *n.* shopkeeper, storekeeper.
tendón /ten'don/ *n. m.* tendon, sinew.
tenebrosidad /teneβrosi'δaδ/ *n. f.* gloom.
tenebroso /tene'βroso/ *a.* dark, gloomy.
tenedor /tene'δor/ *n.* **1.** *m. & f.* keeper; holder. **2.** *m.* fork.
tener /te'ner/ *v.* have; own; hold. **t. que,** have to, must.
teniente /te'niente/ *n. m.* lieutenant.
tenis /'tenis/ *n. m.* tennis; (*pl.*) sneakers.
tenor /te'nor/ *n. m.* tenor.
tensión /ten'sion/ *n. f.* tension, stress, strain.
tenso /'tenso/ *a.* tense.
tentación /tenta'θion; tenta'sion/ *n. f.* temptation.

tentáculo /ten'takulo/ *n. m.* tentacle.
tentador /tenta'δor/ *a.* alluring, tempting.
tentar /ten'tar/ *v.* tempt, lure; grope, probe.
tentativa /tenta'tiβa/ *n. f.* attempt.
tentativo /tenta'tiβo/ *a.* tentative.
teñir /te'ɲir/ *v.* tint, dye.
teología /teolo'hia/ *n. f.* theology.
teológico /teo'lohiko/ *a.* theological.
teoría /teo'ria/ *n. f.* theory.
teórico /te'oriko/ *a.* theoretical.
terapéutico /tera'peutiko/ *a.* therapeutic.
tercero /ter'θero; ter'sero/ *a.* third.
tercio /'terθio; 'tersio/ *n. m.* third.
terciopelo /terθio'pelo; tersio'pelo/ *n. m.* velvet.
terco /'terko/ *a.* obstinate, stubborn.
termal /ter'mal/ *a.* thermal.
terminación /termina'θion; termina'sion/ *n. f.* termination; completion.
terminal aérea /termi'nal 'airea/ *n. f.* air terminal.
terminar /termi'nar/ *v.* terminate, finish.
término /'termino/ *n. m.* term; end.
terminología /terminolo'hia/ *n. f.* terminology.
termómetro /ter'mometro/ *n. m.* thermometer.
termos /'termos/ *n. m.* thermos.
termostato /ter'mostato/ *n. m.* thermostat.
ternero /ter'nero/ **-ra** *n.* calf.
ternura /ter'nura/ *n. f.* tenderness.
terquedad /terke'δaδ/ *n. f.* stubbornness.
terraza /te'rraθa; te'rrasa/ *n. f.* terrace.
terremoto /terre'moto/ *n. m.* earthquake.
terreno /te'rreno/ *a.* **1.** earthly, terrestrial. —*n.* **2.** *m.* ground, terrain; lot, plot.
terrible /te'rriβle/ *a.* terrible, awful.
terrífico /te'rrifiko/ *a.* terrifying.
territorio /terri'torio/ *n. m.* territory.
terrón /te'rron/ *n. m.* clod, lump; mound.

terror /te'rror/ *n. m.* terror.

terso /'terso/ *a.* smooth, glossy; terse.

tertulia /ter'tulia/ *n. f.* social gathering, party.

tesis /'tesis/ *n. f.* thesis.

tesorería /tesore'ria/ *n. f.* treasury.

tesorero /teso'rero/ **-ra** *n.* treasurer.

tesoro /te'soro/ *n. m.* treasure.

testamento /testa'mento/ *n. m.* will, testament.

testarudo /testa'ruðo/ *a.* stubborn.

testificar /testifi'kar/ *v.* testify.

testigo /tes'tigo/ *n. m. & f.* witness.

testimonial /testimo'nial/ *a.* testimonal.

testimonio /testi'monio/ *n. m.* testimony.

teta /'teta/ *n. f.* teat.

tetera /te'tera/ *n. f.* teapot.

tétrico /'tetriko/ *a.* sad; gloomy.

texto /'teksto/ *n. m.* text.

textura /teks'tura/ *n. f.* texture.

tez /teθ; tes/ *n. f.* complexion.

ti /ti/ *pron.* you; yourself.

tía /'tia/ *n. f.* aunt.

tibio /'tiβio/ *a.* lukewarm.

tiburón /tiβu'ron/ *n. m.* shark.

tiemblo /'tiemblo/ *n. m.* aspen.

tiempo /'tiempo/ *n. m.* time; weather; *Gram.* tense.

tienda /'tienda/ *n. f.* shop, store; tent.

tientas /'tientas/ *n. f.pl.* **andar a t.,** to grope (in the dark).

tierno /'tierno/ *a.* tender.

tierra /'tierra/ *n. f.* land; ground; earth, dirt, soil.

tieso /'tieso/ *a.* taut, stiff, hard, strong.

tiesto /'tiesto/ *n. m.* flower pot.

tiesura /tie'sura/ *n. f.* stiffness; harshness.

tifo /'tifo/ *n. m.* typhus.

tifoideo /tifoi'ðeo/ *n. m.* typhoid fever.

tigre /'tigre/ *n. m.* tiger.

tijeras /ti'heras/ *n. f.pl.* scissors.

tila /'tila/ *n. f.* linden.

timbre /'timbre/ *n. m.* seal, stamp; tone; (electric) bell.

tímidamente /'timiðamente/ *adv.* timidly.

timidez /timi'ðeθ; timi'ðes/ *n. f.* timidity.

tímido /'timiðo/ *a.* timid, shy.

timón /ti'mon/ *n. m.* rudder, helm.

tímpano /'timpano/ *n. m.* kettledrum; eardrum.

tina /'tina/ *n. f.* tub, vat.

tinaja /ti'naha/ *n. f.* jar.

tinta /'tinta/ *n. f.* ink.

tinte /'tinte/ *n. m.* tint, shade.

tintero /tin'tero/ *n. m.* inkwell.

tinto /'tinto/ *a.* wine-colored; red (of wine).

tintorería /tintore'ria/ *n. f.* dry cleaning shop.

tintorero /tinto'rero/ **-ra** *n.* dyer; dry cleaner.

tintura /tin'tura/ *n. f.* tincture; dye.

tiñoso /ti'ɲoso/ *a.* scabby; stingy.

tío /'tio/ *n. m.* uncle.

tiovivo /tio'βiβo/ *n. m.* merry-go-round.

típico /'tipiko/ *a.* typical.

tipo /'tipo/ *n. m.* type, sort; (interest) rate; *Colloq.* guy, fellow.

tipo de cambio /'tipo de 'kambio/ exchange rate.

tipo de interés /'tipo de inte'res/ interest rate.

tira /'tira/ *n. f.* strip.

tirabuzón /tiraβu'θon; tiraβu'son/ *n. m.* corkscrew.

tirada /ti'raða/ *n. f.* edition.

tirado /ti'raðo/ **-da** *a.* dirt-cheap.

tiranía /tira'nia/ *n. f.* tyranny.

tiránico /ti'raniko/ *n. m.* tyrannical.

tirano /ti'rano/ **-na** *n.* tyrant.

tirante /ti'rante/ *a.* **1.** tight, taut; tense. —*n.* **2.** *m.pl.* suspenders.

tirar /ti'rar/ *v.* throw; draw; pull; fire (a weapon).

tiritar /tiri'tar/ *v.* shiver.

tiro /'tiro/ *n. m.* throw; shot.

tirón /ti'ron/ *n. m.* pull. **de un t.,** at a stretch; at one stroke.

tísico /'tisiko/ *n. & a.* consumptive.

tisis /'tisis/ *n. f.* consumption, tuberculosis.

titanio /ti'tanio/ *n. m.* titanium.

títere /'titere/ *n. m.* puppet.

titilación /titila'θion; titila'sion/ *n. f.* twinkle.

titubear /tituβe'ar/ *v.* stagger; totter; waver.

titulado /titu'laðo/ *a.* entitled; socalled.

titular /titu'lar/ *a.* **1.** titular. —*v.* **2.** entitle.

título /'titulo/ *n. m.* title, headline.

tiza /'tiθa; 'tisa/ *n. f.* chalk.

tiznar /tiθ'nar; tis'nar/ *v.* smudge; stain.

toalla /to'aʎa; to'aya/ *n. f.* towel. **t. sanitaria,** sanitary napkin.

toalleta /toa'ʎeta; toa'yeta/ *n. f.* small towel.

tobillo /to'βiʎo; to'βiyo/ *n. m.* ankle.

tobogán /toβo'gan/ *n. m.* toboggan.

tocadiscos /toka'ðiskos/ *n. m.* record player.

tocadiscos compacto /toka'ðiskos kom'pakto/ **tocadiscos digital** CD player.

tocado /to'kaðo/ *n. m.* hairdo.

tocador /toka'ðor/ *n. m.* boudoir; dressing table.

tocante /to'kante/ *a.* touching. **t. a,** concerning, relative to.

tocar /to'kar/ *v.* touch; play (an instrument). **t. a uno,** be one's turn; be up to one.

tocayo /to'kayo/ **-ya** *n.* namesake.

tocino /to'θino; to'sino/ *n. m.* bacon.

tocólogo /to'kologo/ **-ga** *n.* obstetrician.

todavía /toða'βia/ *adv.* yet, still.

todo /'toðo/ *a.* **1.** all, whole. **todos los,** every. —*pron.* **2.** all, everything. **con t.,** still, however. **del t.,** wholly; at all.

todopoderoso /toðopoðe'roso/ *a.* almighty.

toldo /'toldo/ *n. m.* awning.

tolerancia /tole'ranθia; tole'ransia/ *n. f.* tolerance.

tolerante /tole'rante/ *a.* tolerant.

tolerar /tole'rar/ *v.* tolerate.

toma /'toma/ *n. f.* taking, capture, seizure.

tomaína /to'maina/ *n. f.* ptomaine.

tomar /to'mar/ *v.* take; drink. **t. el sol,** sunbathe.

tomate /to'mate/ *n. m.* tomato.

tomillo /to'miʎo; to'miyo/ *n. m.* thyme.

tomo /'tomo/ *n. m.* volume.

tonada /to'naða/ *n. f.* tune.

tonel /to'nel/ *n. m.* barrel, cask.

tonelada /tone'laða/ *n. f.* ton.

tonelaje /tone'lahe/ *n. m.* tonnage.

tónico /'toniko/ *a. & m.* tonic.

tono /'tono/ *n. m.* tone, pitch, shade. **darse t.,** to put on airs.

tonsila /ton'sila/ *n. f.* tonsil.

tonsilitis /tonsi'litis/ *n. f.* tonsilitis.

tontería /tonte'ria/ *n. f.* nonsense, foolishness.

tontifútbol /tonti'futβol/ *n. m.* excessively defensive strategy (in soccer).

tonto /'tonto/ **-ta** *a. & n.* foolish, silly; fool.

topacio /to'paθio; to'pasio/ *n. m.* topaz.

topar /to'par/ *v.* run into. **t. con,** come upon.

tópico /'topiko/ *a.* **1.** topical. —*n.* **2.** *m.* cliché.

topo /'topo/ *n. m.* mole (animal).

toque /'toke/ *n. m.* touch.

tórax /'toraks/ *n. m.* thorax.

torbellino /torβe'ʎino; torβe'yino/ *n. m.* whirlwind.

torcer /tor'θer; tor'ser/ *v.* twist; wind; distort.

toreador /torea'ðor/ **-a** *n.* toreador.

torero /to'rero/ **-ra** *n.* bullfighter.

torio /'torio/ *n. m.* thorium.

tormenta /tor'menta/ *n. f.* storm.

tormento /tor'mento/ *n. m.* torment.

tornado /tor'naðo/ *n. m.* tornado.

tornar /tor'nar/ *v.* return; turn.

tornarse en /tor'narse en/ *v.* turn into, become.

torneo /tor'neo/ *n. m.* tournament.

tornillo /tor'niʎo; tor'niyo/ *n. m.* screw.

toro /'toro/ *n. m.* bull.

toronja /to'ronha/ *n. f.* grapefruit.

torpe /'torpe/ *a.* awkward, clumsy; sluggish.

torpedero /torpe'ðero/ *n. m.* torpedo boat.

torpedo /tor'peðo/ *n. m.* torpedo.

torre /'torre/ *n. f.* tower.

torre de mando /'torre de 'mando/ control tower.

torrente /to'rrente/ *n. m.* torrent.

tórrido /'torriðo/ *a.* torrid.

torta /'torta/ *n. f.* cake; loaf.

tortilla /tor'tiʎa; tor'tiya/ *n. f.* omelet; (Mex.) tortilla, pancake.

tórtola /'tortola/ *n. f.* dove.

tortuga /tor'tuga/ *n. f.* turtle.

tortuoso /tor'tuoso/ *a.* tortuous.

tortura /tor'tura/ *n. f.* torture. —**torturar,** *v.*

tos /tos/ *n. m.* cough. —**toser,** *v.*

tosco /'tosko/ *a.* coarse, rough, uncouth.

tosquedad /toske'ðað/ *n. f.* coarseness, roughness.

tostador /tosta'ðor/ *n. m.* toaster.

tostar /'tostar/ *v.* toast; tan.

total /to'tal/ *a. & m.* total.

totalidad /totali'ðað/ *n. f.* totality, entirety, whole.

totalitario /totali'tario/ *a.* totalitarian.

totalmente /total'mente/ *adv.* totally; entirely.

tótem /'totem/ *n. m.* totem.

tóxico /'toksiko/ *a.* toxic.

toxicómano /toksi'komano/ **-na** *n. m. & f.* drug addict.

trabajador /traβaha'ðor/ **-ra** *a.* **1.** hardworking. —*n.* **2.** worker.

trabajo /tra'βaho/ *n. m.* work; labor. —**trabajar,** *v.*

trabar /tra'βar/ *v.* fasten, shackle; grasp; strike up.

tracción /trak'θion; trak'sion/ *n. f.* traction.

tracto /'trakto/ *n. m.* tract.

tractor /trak'tor/ *n. m.* tractor.

tradición /traði'θion; traði'sion/ *n. f.* tradition.

tradicional /traðiθio'nal; traðisio'nal/ *a.* traditional.

traducción /traðuk'θion; traðuk'sion/ *n. f.* translation.

traducir /traðu'θir; traðu'sir/ *v.* translate.

traductor /traðuk'tor/ **-ra** *n.* translator.

traer /tra'er/ *v.* bring; carry; wear.

tráfico /'trafiko/ *n. m.* traffic. —**traficar,** *v.*

tragaperras /traga'perras/ *n. f.* slot machine, one-armed bandit.

tragar /tra'gar/ *v.* swallow.

tragedia /tra'heðia/ *n. f.* tragedy.

trágicamente /'trahikamente/ *adv.* tragically.

trágico /'trahiko/ **-ca** *a.* **1.** tragic. —*n.* **2.** tragedian.

trago /'trago/ *n. m.* swallow; drink.

traición /trai'θion; trai'sion/ *n. f.* treason, betrayal.

traicionar /traiθio'nar; traisio'nar/ *v.* betray.

traidor /trai'ðor/ **-ra** *a. & n.* traitorous; traitor.

traje /'trahe/ *n. m.* suit; dress; garb, apparel.

traje de baño /'trahe de 'baɲo/ bathing suit.

trama /'trama/ *v.* plot (of a story).

tramador /trama'ðor/ **-ra** *n.* weaver; plotter.

tramar /tra'mar/ *v.* weave; plot, scheme.

trámite /'tramite/ *n. m.* (business) deal, transaction.

tramo /'tramo/ *n. m.* span, stretch, section.

trampa /'trampa/ *n. f.* trap, snare.

trampista /tram'pista/ *n. m. & f.* cheater; swindler.

trance /'tranθe; 'transe/ *n. m.* critical moment or stage. **a todo t.,** at any cost.

tranco /'tranko/ *n. m.* stride.

tranquilidad /trankili'ðað/ *n. f.* tranquility, calm, quiet.

tranquilizante /trankili'θante; trankili'sante/ *n. m.* tranquilizer.

tranquilizar /trankili'θar; trankili'sar/ *v.* quiet, calm down.

tranquilo /tran'kilo/ *a.* tranquil, calm.

transacción /transak'θion; transak'sion/ *n. f.* transaction.

transbordador /transβorða'ðor/ *n. m.* ferry.

transbordador espacial /transβorða'ðor espa'θial; transβorða'ðor espa'sial/ space shuttle.

transcribir /transkri'βir/ *v.* transcribe.

transcripción /transkrip'θion; transkrip'sion/ *n. f.* transcription.

transcurrir /transku'rrir/ *v.* elapse.

transeúnte /tran'seunte/ *a. & n.* transient; passerby.

transexual /transek'sual/ *a.* transsexual.

transferencia /transfe'renθia; transfe'rensia/ *n. f.* transference.

transferir /transfe'rir/ *v.* transfer.

transformación /transforma'θion; transforma'sion/ *n. f.* transformation.

transformar /transfor'mar/ *v.* transform.

transfusión /transfu'sion/ *n. f.* transfusion.

transgresión /transgre'sion/ *n. f.* transgression.

transgresor /transgre'sor/ **-ra** *n.* transgressor.

transición /transi'θion; transi'sion/ *n. f.* transition.

transigir /transi'hir/ *v.* compromise, settle; agree.

transistor /transis'tor/ *n. m.* transistor.

transitivo /transi'tiβo/ *a.* transitive.

tránsito /'transito/ *n. m.* transit, passage.

transitorio /transi'torio/ *a.* transitory.

transmisión /transmi'sion/ *n. f.* transmission; broadcast.

transmisora /transmi'sora/ *n. f.* broadcasting station.

transmitir /transmi'tir/ *v.* transmit; broadcast.

transparencia /transpa'renθia; transpa'rensia/ *n. f.* transparency.

transparente /transpa'rente/ *a.* **1.** transparent. —*n.* **2.** *m.* (window) shade.

transportación /transporta'θion; transporta'sion/ *n. f.* transportation.

transportar /transpor'tar/ *v.* transport, convey.

transporte /trans'porte/ *n. m.* transportation; transport.

tranvía /tram'bia/ *n. m.* streetcar, trolley.

trapacero /trapa'θero; trapa'sero/ -ra *n.* cheat; swindler.

trapo /'trapo/ *n. m.* rag.

tráquea /'trakea/ *n. f.* trachea.

tras /tras/ *prep.* after; behind.

trasegar /trase'gar/ *v.* upset, overturn.

trasero /tra'sero/ *a.* rear, back.

traslado /tras'laðo/ *n. m.* transfer. —**trasladar**, *v.*

traslapo /tras'lapo/ *n. m.* overlap. —**traslapar**, *v.*

trasnochar /trasno'tʃar/ *v.* stay up all night.

traspalar /traspa'lar/ *v.* shovel.

traspasar /traspa'sar/ *v.* go beyond; cross; violate; pierce.

trasquilar /traski'lar/ *v.* shear; clip.

trastornar /trastor'nar/ *v.* overturn, overthrow, upset.

trastorno /tras'torno/ *m.* overthrow; upheaval.

trastorno mental /tras'torno men'tal/ mental disorder.

trasvasar /trasβa'sar/ *v.* download; download.

tratado /tra'taðo/ *n. m.* treaty; treatise.

tratamiento /trata'miento/ *n. m.* treatment.

tratar /tra'tar/ *v.* treat, handle. **t. de,** deal with; try to; call (a name).

tratarse de /tra'tarse de/ *v.* be a question of.

trato /'trato/ *n. m.* treatment; manners; *Com.* deal.

través /tra'βes/ *adv.* **a t. de,** through, across. **de t.,** sideways.

travesía /traβe'sia/ *n. f.* crossing; voyage.

travesti /tra'βesti/ *n. m.* transvestite.

travestido /traβes'tiðo/ *a.* disguised.

travesura /traβe'sura/ *n. f.* prank; mischief.

travieso /tra'βieso/ *a.* naughty, mischievous.

trayectoria /trayek'toria/ *n. f.* trajectory.

trazar /tra'θar; tra'sar/ *v.* plan, devise; trace; draw.

trazo /'traθo; 'traso/ *n.* plan, outline; line, stroke.

trébol /'treβol/ *n. m.* clover.

trece /'treθe; 'trese/ *a. & pron.* thirteen.

trecho /'tretʃo/ *n. m.* space, distance, stretch.

tregua /'tregua/ *n. f.* truce; respite, lull.

treinta /'treinta/ *a. & pron.* thirty.

tremendo /tre'mendo/ *a.* tremendous.

tremer /tre'mer/ *v.* tremble.

tren /tren/ *n. m.* train.

trenza /'trenθa; 'trensa/ *n. f.* braid. —**trenzar**, *v.*

trepar /tre'par/ *v.* climb, mount.

trepidación /trepiða'θion; trepiða'sion/ *n. f.* trepidation.

tres /tres/ *a. & pron.* three.

trescientos /tres'θientos; tres'sientos/ *a. & pron.* three hundred.

triángulo /tri'aŋgulo/ *n. m.* triangle.

triar /triar/ *v.* sort, separate.

tribu /'triβu/ *n. f.* tribe.

tribulación /triβula'θion; triβula'sion/ *n. f.* tribulation.

tribuna /tri'βuna/ *n. f.* rostrum, stand; (*pl.*) grandstand.

tribunal /triβu'nal/ *n. m.* court, tribunal.

tributario /triβu'tario/ *a. & m.* tributary.

tributo /tri'βuto/ *n. m.* tribute.

triciclo /tri'θiklo; tri'siklo/ *n. m.* tricycle.

trigo /'trigo/ *n. m.* wheat.

trigonometría /trigonome'tria/ *n. f.* trigonometry.

trigueño /tri'geɲo/ *a.* swarthy, dark.

trilogía /trilo'hia/ *n. f.* trilogy.

trimestral /trimes'tral/ *a.* quarterly.

trinchar /trin'tʃar/ *v.* carve (meat).

trinchera /trin'tʃera/ *n. f.* trench, ditch.

trineo /tri'neo/ *n. m.* sled; sleigh.

trinidad /trini'ðað/ *n. f.* trinity.

tripa /'tripa/ *n. f.* tripe, entrails.

triple /'triple/ *a.* triple. **—triplicar,** *v.*

trípode /'tripoðe/ *n. m.* tripod.

tripulación /tripula'θion; tripula'sion/ *n. f.* crew.

tripulante /tripu'lante/ *m & f.* crew member.

tripular /tripu'lar/ *v.* man.

triste /'triste/ *a.* sad, sorrowful; dreary.

tristemente /triste'mente/ *adv.* sadly.

tristeza /tris'teθa; tris'tesa/ *n. f.* sadness; gloom.

triunfal /triun'fal/ *a.* triumphal.

triunfante /triun'fante/ *a.* triumphant.

triunfo /'triunfo/ *n. m.* triumph; trump. **—triunfar,** *v.*

trivial /tri'βial/ *a.* trivial, commonplace.

trivialidad /triβiali'ðað/ *n. f.* triviality.

trocar /tro'kar/ *v.* exchange, switch; barter.

trofeo /tro'feo/ *n. m.* trophy.

trombón /trom'bon/ *n. m.* trombone.

trompa /'trompa/ **trompeta** *n. f.* trumpet, horn.

tronada /tro'naða/ *n. f.* thunderstorm.

tronar /tro'nar/ *v.* thunder.

tronco /'tronko/ *n. m.* trunk, stump.

trono /'trono/ *n. m.* throne.

tropa /'tropa/ *n. f.* troop.

tropel /tro'pel/ *n. m.* crowd, throng.

tropezar /trope'θar; trope'sar/ *v.* trip, stumble. **t. con,** come upon, run into.

trópico /'tropiko/ *a. & m.* tropical; tropics.

tropiezo /tro'pieθo; tro'pieso/ *n. m.* stumble; obstacle; slip, error.

trote /'trote/ *n. m.* trot. **—trotar,** *v.*

trovador /troβa'ðor/ *n. m.* troubadour.

trozo /'troθo; 'troso/ *n. m.* piece, portion, fragment; selection, passage.

trucha /'trutʃa/ *n. f.* trout.

trueco /'trueko/ **trueque** *n. m.* exchange, barter.

trueno /'trueno/ *n. m.* thunder.

trufa /'trufa/ *n. f.* truffle.

tu /tu/ *a.* your.

tú *pron.* you.

tuberculosis /tuβerku'losis/ *n. f.* tuberculosis.

tubo /'tuβo/ *n. m.* tube, pipe.

tubo de ensayo /'tuβo de en'sayo/ test tube.

tubo de escape /'tuβo de es'kape/ exhaust pipe.

tuerca /'tuerka/ *n. f. Mech.* nut.

tulipán /tuli'pan/ *n. m.* tulip.

tumba /'tumba/ *n. f.* tomb, grave.

tumbar /tum'bar/ *v.* knock down.

tumbarse /tum'βarse/ *v.* lie down.

tumbo /'tumbo/ *n. m.* tumble; somersault.

tumbona /tum'βona/ *n. f.* deck chair.

tumor /tu'mor/ *n. m.* tumor; growth.

tumulto /tu'multo/ *n. m.* tumult, commotion.

tumultuoso /tumul'tuoso/ *a.* tumultuous, boisterous.

tunante /tu'nante/ *n. m.* rogue.

tunda /'tunda/ *n. f.* spanking, whipping.

túnel /'tunel/ *n. m.* tunnel.

túnel de Canal de la Mancha /'tunel de ka'nal de la 'mantʃa/ Channel Tunnel, Chunnel.

tungsteno /tuŋs'teno/ *n. m.* tungsten.

túnica /'tunika/ *n. f.* tunic, robe.

tupir /tu'pir/ *v.* pack tight, stuff; stop up.

turbación /turβa'θion; turβa'sion/ *n. f.* confusion, turmoil.

turbamulta /turβa'multa/ *n. f.* mob, disorderly crowd.

turbar /tur'βar/ *v.* disturb, upset; embarrass.

turbina /tur'βina/ *n. f.* turbine.

turbio /'turβio/ *a.* turbid; muddy.

turco /'turko/ **-ca** *a. & n.* Turkish; Turk.

turismo /tu'rismo/ *n. m.* touring, (foreign) travel, tourism.

turista /tu'rista/ *n. m. & f.* tourist.
turno /'turno/ *n. m.* turn; (work) shift.
turquesa /tur'kesa/ *n. f.* turquoise.
Turquía /tur'kia/ *n. f.* Turkey.
turrón /tu'rron/ *n. m.* nougat.
tusa /'tusa/ *n. f.* corncob; corn.

tutear /tute'ar/ *v.* address as **tú,** etc.
tutela /tu'tela/ *n. f.* guardianship; aegis.
tutor /tu'tor/ **-ra** *n.* tutor; guardian.
tuyo /'tuyo/ *a.* your, yours.

U V Y Z

u /u/ *conj.* or.
ubre /'uβre/ *n. f.* udder.
Ucrania /u'krania/ *n. f.* Ukraine.
ucranio /u'kranio/ **-ia** *a. & n.* Ukrainian.
ufano /u'fano/ *a.* proud, haughty.
úlcera /'ulθera; 'ulsera/ *n. f.* ulcer.
ulterior /ulte'rior/ *a.* ulterior.
último /'ultimo/ *a.* last, final; ultimate; latest. **por ú.,** finally. **ú. minuto,** last minute, eleventh hour.
ultraje /ul'trahe/ *n. m.* outrage. **—ultrajar,** *v.*
ultrasónico /ultra'soniko/ *a.* ultrasonic.
umbral /um'bral/ *n. m.* threshold.
umbroso /um'broso/ *a.* shady.
un /un/ **una** *art. & a.* a, an; one; (*pl.*) some.
unánime /u'nanime/ *a.* unanimous.
unanimidad /unanimi'ðað/ *n. f.* unanimity.
unción /un'θion; un'sion/ *n. f.* unction.
ungüento /uŋ'guento/ *n. m.* ointment, salve.
único /'uniko/ *a.* only, sole; unique.
unicornio /uni'kornio/ *n. m.* unicorn.
unidad /uni'ðað/ *n. f.* unit; unity.
unidad de cuidados intensivos /uni'ðað de kui'ðaðos inten'siβos/ **unidad de vigilancia intensiva** intensive-care unit.
unidad de disco /uni'ðað de 'disko/ disk drive.
unificar /unifi'kar/ *v.* unify.
uniforme /uni'forme/ *a. & m.* uniform.
uniformidad /uniformi'ðað/ *n. f.* uniformity.
unión /u'nion/ *n. f.* union; joining.
unir /u'nir/ *v.* unite, join.
universal /uniβer'sal/ *a.* universal.
universalidad /uniβersali'ðað/ *n. f.* universality.

universidad /uniβersi'ðað/ *n. f.* university; college.
universo /uni'βerso/ *n. m.* universe.
uno /'uno/ **una** *pron.* one; (*pl.*) some.
untar /un'tar/ *v.* spread; grease; anoint.
uña /'uɲa/ *n. f.* fingernail.
urbanidad /urβani'ðað/ *n. f.* urbanity; good breeding.
urbanismo /urβa'nismo/ *n. m.* city planning.
urbano /ur'βano/ *a.* urban; urbane; well-bred.
urbe /'urβe/ *n. f.* large city.
urgencia /ur'henθia; ur'hensia/ *n. f.* urgency.
urgente /ur'hente/ *a.* urgent, pressing. **entrega u.,** special delivery.
urgir /ur'hir/ *v.* be urgent.
urna /'urna/ *n. f.* urn; ballot box; (*pl.*) polls.
urraca /u'rraka/ *n. f.* magpie.
usanza /u'sanθa; usansa/ *n. f.* usage, custom.
usar /u'sar/ *v.* use; wear.
uso /'uso/ *n. m.* use; usage; wear.
usted /us'teð/ *pron.* you.
usual /u'sual/ *a.* usual.
usualmente /usual'mente/ *adv.* usually.
usura /u'sura/ *n. f.* usury.
usurero /usu'rero/ **-ra** *n.* usurer.
usurpación /usurpa'θion; usurpa'sion/ *n. f.* usurpation.
usurpar /usur'par/ *v.* usurp.
utensilio /uten'silio/ *n. m.* utensil.
útero /'utero/ *n. m.* uterus.
útil /'util/ *a.* useful, handy.
utilidad /utili'ðað/ *n. f.* usefulness.
utilizar /utili'θar; utili'sar/ *v.* use, utilize.
útilmente /util'mente/ *adv.* usefully.
utópico /u'topiko/ *a.* utopian.
uva /'uβa/ *n. f.* grape.
vaca /'baka/ *n. f.* cow; beef.
vacaciones /baka'θiones; baka-

'siones/ n. f.pl. vacation, holidays.

vacancia /ba'kanθia; ba'kansia/ n. f. vacancy.

vacante /ba'kante/ a. **1.** vacant. —n. **2.** f. vacancy.

vaciar /ba'θiar; ba'siar/ v. empty; pour out.

vacilación /baθila'θion; basila'sion/ n. f. vacillation.

vacilante /baθi'lante; basi'lante/ a. vacillating.

vacilar /baθi'lar; basi'lar/ v. falter, hesitate; waver; stagger.

vacío /ba'θio; ba'sio/ a. **1.** empty. —n. **2.** m. void, empty space.

vacuna /ba'kuna/ n. f. vaccine.

vacunación /bakuna'θion; bakuna'sion/ n. f. vaccination.

vacunar /baku'nar/ v. vaccinate.

vacuo /'bakuo/ a. **1.** empty, vacant. —n. **2.** m. vacuum.

vadear /baðe'ar/ v. ford.

vado /'baðo/ n. m. ford.

vagabundo /baga'βundo/ **-da** a. & n. vagabond.

vagar /ba'gar/ v. wander; loiter.

vago /'bago/ **-ga** a. **1.** vague, hazy; wandering, vagrant. —n. **2.** vagrant, tramp.

vagón /ba'gon/ n. m. railroad car.

vahído /ba'iðo/ n. m. dizziness.

vaina /'baina/ n. f. sheath; pod.

vainilla /bai'niʎa; bai'niya/ n. f. vanilla.

vaivén /bai'βen/ n. m. vibration, sway.

vajilla /ba'hiʎa; ba'hiya/ n. f. (dinner) dishes.

valentía /balen'tia/ n. f. valor, courage.

valer /ba'ler/ n. **1.** m. worth. —v. **2.** be worth.

valerse de /ba'lerse de/ v. make use of, avail oneself of.

valía /ba'lia/ n. f. value.

validez /bali'ðeθ; bali'ðes/ n. f. validity.

válido /ba'liðo/ a. valid.

valiente /ba'liente/ a. valiant.

valija /ba'liha/ n. f. valise.

valioso /ba'lioso/ a. valuable.

valla /'baʎa; 'baya/ n. f. fence, barrier.

valle /'baʎe; 'baye/ n. m. valley.

valor /ba'lor/ n. m. value, worth; bravery, valor; (pl., Com.) securities.

valoración /balora'θion; balora'sion/ n. f. appraisal.

valorar /balo'rar/ v. value, appraise.

vals /bals/ n. m. waltz.

valsar /bal'sar/ v. waltz.

valuación /balua'θion; balua'sion/ n. f. valuation.

valuar /balu'ar/ v. value; rate.

válvula /'balβula/ n. f. valve.

válvula de seguridad /'balβula de seguri'ðað/ safety valve.

vandalismo /banda'lismo/ n. m. vandalism.

vándalo /'bandalo/ **-la** n. vandal.

vanidad /bani'ðað/ n. f. vanity.

vanidoso /bani'ðoso/ a. vain, conceited.

vano /'bano/ a. vain; inane.

vapor /ba'por/ n. m. vapor; steam; steamer, steamship.

vaquero /ba'kero/ **-ra** n. cowboy.

vara /'bara/ n. f. wand, stick, switch.

varadero /bara'ðero/ n. m. shipyard.

varar /ba'rar/ v. launch; be stranded; run aground.

variable /ba'riaβle/ a. variable.

variación /baria'θion; baria'sion/ n. f. variation.

variar /ba'riar/ v. vary.

varicela /bari'θela; bari'sela/ n. f. chicken pox.

variedad /barie'ðað/ n. f. variety.

varios /'barios/ a. & pron. pl. various; several.

variz /ba'riθ; ba'ris/ n. f. varicose vein.

varón /ba'ron/ n. m. man; male.

varonil /baro'nil/ a. manly, virile.

vasallo /ba'saʎo; ba'sayo/ n. m. vassal.

vasectomía /basekto'mia/ n. f. vasectomy.

vasija /ba'siha/ n. f. bowl, container (for liquids).

vaso /'baso/ n. m. water glass; vase. **v. de papel,** paper cup.

vástago /'bastago/ n. m. bud, shoot; twig; offspring.

vasto /'basto/ a. vast.

vecindad /beθin'dað; besin'dað/ n. f. **vecindario,** m. neighborhood, vicinity.

vecino /be'θino; be'sino/ **-na** a. & n. neighboring; neighbor.

vedar /be'ðar/ v. forbid; impede.

vega /'bega/ n. f. meadow.

vegetación /beheta'θion; beheta'sion/ n. f. vegetation.

vegetal /behe'tal/ n. m. vegetable.

vehemente /bee'mente/ a. vehement.

vehículo /be'ikulo/ n. m. vehicle; conveyance.

veinte /'beinte/ a. & pron. twenty.

vejez /be'heθ; be'hes/ n. f. old age.

vejiga /be'higa/ n. f. bladder.

vela /'bela/ n. f. vigil, watch; candle; sail.

velar /be'lar/ v. stay up, sit up; watch over.

vellón /be'ʎon; be'yon/ n. m. fleece.

velloso /be'ʎoso; be'yoso/ a. hairy; fuzzy.

velludo /be'ʎuðo; be'yuðo/ a. downy.

velo /'belo/ n. m. veil.

velocidad /beloθi'ðað; belosi'ðað/ n. f. velocity, speed; rate. **v. máxima,** speed limit.

velomotor /belomo'tor/ n. m. motorbike, moped.

veloz /be'loθ; be'los/ a. speedy, fast, swift.

vena /'bena/ n. f. vein.

venado /be'naðo/ n. m. deer.

vencedor /benθe'ðor; bense'ðor/ -ra n. victor.

vencer /ben'θer; ben'ser/ v. defeat, overcome, conquer; Com. become due, expire.

vencimiento /benθi'miento; bensi'miento/ n. m. defeat; expiration.

venda /'benda/ n. f. **vendaje,** m. bandage. **—vendar,** v.

vendedor /bende'ðor/ -ra n. seller, trader; sales clerk.

vender /ben'der/ v. sell.

vendimia /ben'dimia/ n. f. vintage; grape harvest.

Venecia /be'neθia; be'nesia/ n. f. Venice.

veneciano /bene'θiano; bene-'siano/ -na a. & n. Venetian.

veneno /be'neno/ n. m. poison.

venenoso /bene'noso/ a. poisonous.

veneración /benera'θion; benera-'sion/ n. f. veneration.

venerar /bene'rar/ v. venerate, revere.

venero /be'nero/ n. m. spring; origin.

véneto /'beneto/ a. Venetian.

venezolano /beneθo'lano; bene-so'lano/ -na a. & n. Venezuelan.

vengador /benga'ðor/ -ra n. avenger.

venganza /beŋ'ganθa; beŋ'gansa/ n. f. vengeance, revenge.

vengar /beŋ'gar/ v. avenge.

venida /be'niða/ n. f. arrival, advent, coming.

venidero /beni'ðero/ a. future; coming.

venir /be'nir/ v. come.

venta /'benta/ n. f. sale; sales.

ventaja /ben'taha/ n. f. advantage; profit.

ventajoso /benta'hoso/ a. advantageous; profitable.

ventana /ben'tana/ n. f. window.

ventero /ben'tero/ -ra n. innkeeper.

ventilación /bentila'θion; bentila-'sion/ n. m. ventilation.

ventilador /bentila'ðor/ n. m. ventilator, fan.

ventilar /benti'lar/ v. ventilate, air.

ventisquero /bentis'kero/ n. m. snowdrift; glacier.

ventoso /ben'toso/ a. windy.

ventura /ben'tura/ n. f. venture; happiness; luck.

ver /ber/ v. see. **tener que v. con,** have to do with.

vera /'bera/ n. f. edge.

veracidad /beraθi'ðað; berasi'ðað/ n. f. truthfulness, veracity.

verano /be'rano/ n. m. summer. —**veranear,** v.

veras /'beras/ n. f.pl. **de v.,** really, truly.

veraz /be'raθ; be'ras/ a. truthful.

verbigracia /berβi'graθia; berβi-'grasia/ adv. for example.

verbo /'berβo/ n. m. verb.

verboso /ber'βoso/ a. verbose.

verdad /ber'ðað/ n. f. truth. **ser v.,** to be true.

verdadero /berða'ðero/ a. true, real.

verde /'berðe/ a. green; risqué, off-color.

verdor /ber'ðor/ n. m. greenness, verdure.

verdugo /ber'ðugo/ n. m. hangman.

verdura /ber'ðura/ n. f. verdure, vegetation; (pl.) vegetables.

vereda /be'reða/ n. f. path.

veredicto /bere'ðikto/ n. m. verdict.

vergonzoso /bergon'θoso; bergon'soso/ a. shameful, embarrassing; shy, bashful.

vergüenza /ber'guenθa; ber-

'guensa/ *n. f.* shame; disgrace; embarrassment.

verificar /berifi'kar/ *v.* verify, check.

verja /'berha/ *n. f.* grating, railing.

verosímil /bero'simil/ *a.* likely, plausible.

verraco /be'rrako/ *n. m.* boar.

verruga /be'rruga/ *n. f.* wart.

versátil /ber'satil/ *a.* versatile.

verse /'berse/ *v.* look, appear.

versión /ber'sion/ *n. f.* version.

verso /'berso/ *n. m.* verse, stanza; line (of poetry).

verter /ber'ter/ *v.* pour, spill; shed; empty.

vertical /berti'kal/ *a.* vertical.

vertiente /ber'tiente/ *n. f.* slope; watershed.

vertiginoso /bertihi'noso/ *a.* dizzy.

vértigo /'bertigo/ *n. m.* vertigo, dizziness.

vestíbulo /bes'tiβulo/ *n. m.* vestibule, lobby.

vestido /bes'tiðo/ *n. m.* dress; clothing.

vestigio /bes'tihio/ *n. m.* vestige, trace.

vestir /bes'tir/ *v.* dress, clothe.

veterano /bete'rano/ **-na** *a. & n.* veteran.

veterinario /beteri'nario/ **-ria** *a.* 1. veterinary. —*n.* 2. veterinarian.

veto /'beto/ *n. m.* veto.

vetusto /be'tusto/ *a.* ancient, very old.

vez /beθ; bes/ *n. f.* time; turn. **tal v.,** perhaps. **a la v.,** at the same time. **en v. de,** instead of. **una v.,** once. **otra v.,** again.

vía /'bia/ *n. f.* track; route, way.

viaducto /bia'ðukto/ *n. m.* viaduct.

viajante /bia'hante/ *a. & n.* traveling; traveler.

viajar /bia'har/ *v.* travel; journey; tour.

viaje /'biahe/ *n. m.* trip, journey, voyage; (*pl.*) travels.

viaje de estudios /'biahe de es-'tuðios/ field trip.

viajero /bia'hero/ **-ra** *n.* traveler; passenger.

viaje todo incluido /'biahe 'toðo in'kluiðo/ package tour.

viandas /'biandas/ *n. f.pl.* victuals, food.

víbora /'biβora/ *n. f.* viper.

vibración /biβra'θion; biβra'sion/ *n. f.* vibration.

vibrar /bi'βrar/ *v.* vibrate.

vicepresidente /biθepresi'ðente; bisepresi'ðente/ **-ta** *n.* vice president.

vicio /'biθio; 'bisio/ *n. m.* vice.

vicioso /bi'θioso; bi'sioso/ *a.* vicious; licentious.

víctima /'biktima/ *n. f.* victim.

victoria /bik'toria/ *n. f.* victory.

victorioso /bikto'rioso/ *a.* victorious.

vid /bið/ *n. f.* grapevine.

vida /'biða/ *n. f.* life; living.

vídeo /bi'ðeo/ *n. m.* videotape.

videocámara /biðeo'kamara/ *n. f.* video camera.

videodisco /biðeo'ðisko/ *n. m.* videodisc.

videojuego /biðeo'huego/ *n. m.* video game.

vidrio /'biðrio/ *n. m.* glass.

viejo /'bieho/ **-ja** *a. & n.* old; old person.

viento /'biento/ *n. m.* wind. **hacer v.,** to be windy.

vientre /'bientre/ *n. m.* belly.

viernes /'biernes/ *n. m.* Friday.

viga /'biga/ *n. f.* beam, rafter.

vigente /bi'hente/ *a.* in effect (prices, etc.).

vigilante /bihi'lante/ *a. & m.* vigilant, watchful; watchman.

vigilante nocturno /bihi'lante nok'turno/ night watchman.

vigilar /bihi'lar/ *v.* guard, watch over.

vigilia /bi'hilia/ *n. f.* vigil, watchfulness; *Relig.* fast.

vigor /bi'gor/ *n. m.* vigor. **en v.,** in effect, in force.

vil /bil/ *a.* vile, low, contemptible.

vileza /bi'leθa; bi'lesa/ *n. f.* baseness; vileness.

villa /'biʎa; 'biya/ *n. f.* town; country house.

villancico /biʎan'θiko; biyan'siko/ *n. m.* Christmas carol.

villanía /biʎa'nia; biya'nia/ *n. f.* villainy.

villano /bi'ʎano; bi'yano/ *n. m.* boor.

vinagre /bi'nagre/ *n. m.* vinegar.

vinagrera /bina'grera/ *n. f.* cruet.

vínculo /'binkulo/ *n. m.* link. —**vincular,** *v.*

vindicar /bindi'kar/ *v.* vindicate.

vino /'bino/ *n. m.* wine.

viña /'biɲa/ *n. f.* vineyard.

violación /biola'θion; biola'sion/ *n. f.* violation; rape.

violador /biola'ðor/ **-ra** *n. m. & f.* rapist.

violar /bio'lar/ *v.* violate; rape.

violencia /bio'lenθia; bio'lensia/ *n. f.* violence.

violento /bio'lento/ *a.* violent; impulsive.

violeta /bio'leta/ *n. f.* violet.

violín /bio'lin/ *n. m.* violin.

violón /bio'lon/ *n. m.* bass viol.

virar /bi'rar/ *v.* veer, change course.

virgen /bir'hen/ *n. f.* virgin.

viril /bi'ril/ *a.* virile, manly.

virilidad /birili'ðað/ *n. f.* virility, manhood.

virtual /bir'tual/ *a.* virtual.

virtud /bir'tuð/ *n. f.* virtue; efficacy, power.

virtuoso /bir'tuoso/ *a.* virtuous.

viruela /bi'ruela/ *n. f.* smallpox.

viruelas locas /bi'ruelas 'lokas/ *n. f.pl.* chicken pox.

virus /'birus/ *n. m.* virus.

visa /'bisa/ *n. f.* visa.

visaje /bi'sahe/ *n. m.* grimace.

visera /bi'sera/ *n. f.* visor.

visible /bi'siβle/ *a.* visible.

visión /bi'sion/ *n. f.* vision.

visionario /bisio'nario/ **-ria** *a. & n.* visionary.

visita /bi'sita/ *n. f.* visit; *m. & f.* visitor, caller. **v. con guía, v. explicada, v. programada,** guided tour.

visitación /bisita'θion; bisita'sion/ *n. f.* visitation.

visitante /bisi'tante/ *a. & n.* visiting; visitor.

visitar /bisi'tar/ *v.* visit; inspect, examine.

vislumbrar /bislum'βrar/ *v.* glimpse.

vislumbre /bis'lumbre/ *n. f.* glimpse.

viso /'biso/ *n. m.* looks; outlook.

víspera /'bispera/ *n. f.* eve, day before.

vista /'bista/ *n. f.* view; scene; sight.

vista de pájaro /'bista de 'paharo/ bird's-eye view.

vistazo /bis'taθo; bis'taso/ *n. m.* glance, glimpse.

vistoso /bis'toso/ *a.* beautiful; showy.

visual /bi'sual/ *a.* visual.

vital /bi'tal/ *a.* vital.

vitalidad /bitali'ðað/ *n. f.* vitality.

vitamina /bita'mina/ *n. f.* vitamin.

vitando /bi'tando/ *a.* hateful.

vituperar /bitupe'rar/ *v.* vituperate; revile.

viuda /'biuða/ *n. f.* widow.

viudo /'biuðo/ *n. m.* widower.

vivaz /bi'βaθ; bi'βas/ *a.* vivacious, buoyant; clever.

víveres /'biβeres/ *n. m.pl.* provisions.

viveza /bi'βeθa; bi'βesa/ *n. f.* animation, liveliness.

vívido /bi'βiðo/ *a.* vivid, bright.

vivienda /bi'βienda/ *n. f.* (living) quarters, dwelling.

vivificar /biβifi'kar/ *v.* vivify, enliven.

vivir /bi'βir/ *v.* live.

vivo /'biβo/ *a.* live, alive, living; vivid; animated, brisk.

vocablo /bo'kaβlo/ *n. m.* word.

vocabulario /bokaβu'lario/ *n. m.* vocabulary.

vocación /boka'θion; boka'sion/ *n. f.* vocation, calling.

vocal /bo'kal/ *a.* **1.** vocal. —*n.* **2.** *f.* vowel.

vocear /boθe'ar; bose'ar/ *v.* vociferate.

vodca /'boðka/ *n. m.* vodka.

vodevil /boðe'βil/ *n. m.* vaudeville.

volante /bo'lante/ *a.* **1.** flying. —*n.* **2.** *m.* memorandum; (steering) wheel.

volar /bo'lar/ *v.* fly; explode.

volcán /bol'kan/ *n. m.* volcano.

volcar /bol'kar/ *v.* upset, capsize.

voltaje /bol'tahe/ *n. m.* voltage.

voltear /bolte'ar/ *v.* turn, whirl; overturn.

voltio /'boltio/ *n. m.* volt.

volumen /bo'lumen/ *n. m.* volume.

voluminoso /bolumi'noso/ *a.* voluminous.

voluntad /bolun'tað/ *n. f.* will. **buena v.** goodwill.

voluntario /bolun'tario/ **-ria** *a. & n.* voluntary; volunteer.

voluntarioso /bolunta'rioso/ *a.* willful.

volver /bol'βer/ *v.* turn; return, go back, come back. **v. a hacer** (etc.), do (etc.) again.

volverse /bol'βerse/ *v.* turn around; turn, become.

vómito /'bomito/ *n. m.* vomit. —**vomitar,** *v.*

voracidad /boraθi'ðað; borasi'ðað/ *n. f.* voracity; greed.

voraz /bo'raθ; bo'ras/ *a.* greedy, ravenous.

vórtice /'bortiθe; 'bortise/ *n. m.* whirlpool.

vosotros /bo'sotros, bo'sotras/ **-as** *pron.pl.* you; yourselves.

votación /bota'θion; bota'sion/ *n. f.* voting; vote.

voto /'boto/ *n. m.* vote; vow. **—votar,** *v.*

voz /boθ; bos/ *n. f.* voice; word. **a voces,** by shouting. **en v. alta,** aloud.

vuelco /'buelko/ *n. m.* upset.

vuelo /'buelo/ *n. m.* flight. **v. libre,** hang gliding.

vuelo chárter /'buelo 'tʃarter/ charter flight.

vuelo regular /'buelo rregu'lar/ scheduled flight.

vuelta /'buelta/ *n. f.* turn, bend; return. **a la v. de,** around. **dar una v.,** to take a walk.

vuestro /'buestro/ *a.* your, yours.

vulgar /bul'gar/ *a.* vulgar, common.

vulgaridad /bulgari'ðað/ *n. f.* vulgarity.

vulgo /'bulgo/ *n. m.* (the) masses, (the) common people.

vulnerable /bulne'raβle/ *a.* vulnerable.

y /i/ *conj.* and.

ya /ya/ *adv.* already; now; at once. **y. no,** no longer, any more. **y. que,** since.

yacer /ya'θer; ya'ser/ *v.* lie.

yacimiento /yaθi'miento; yasi'miento/ *n. m.* deposit.

yanqui /'yanki/ *a. & n.* North American.

yate /'yate/ *n. m.* yacht.

yegua /'yegua/ *n. f.* mare.

yelmo /'yelmo/ *n. m.* helmet.

yema /'yema/ *n. f.* yolk (of an egg).

yerba /'yerβa/ *n. f.* grass; herb.

yerno /'yerno/ *n. m.* son-in-law.

yerro /'yerro/ *n. m.* error, mistake.

yeso /'yeso/ *n. m.* plaster.

yídish /'yiðis/ *n. m.* Yiddish.

yo /yo/ *pron.* I.

yodo /'yoðo/ *n. m.* iodine.

yoduro /jo'ðuro/ *n. m.* iodide.

yonqui /'yonki/ *m. & f. Colloq.* drug addict, junkie.

yugo /'yugo/ *n. m.* yoke.

yunque /'yunke/ *n. m.* anvil.

yunta /'yunta/ *n. f.* team (of animals).

zafarse /θa'farse; sa'farse/ *v.* run away, escape. **z. de,** get rid of.

zafio /'θafio; 'safio/ *a.* coarse, uncivil.

zafiro /θa'firo; sa'firo/ *n. m.* sapphire.

zaguán /θa'guan; sa'guan/ *n. m.* vestibule, hall.

zalamero /θala'mero; sala'mero/ **-ra** *n.* flatterer, wheedler.

zambullir /θambu'ʎir; sambu'yir/ *v.* plunge, dive.

zampar /θam'par; sam'par/ *v. Colloq.* gobble down, wolf down.

zanahoria /θana'oria; sana'oria/ *n. f.* carrot.

zanja /'θanha; 'sanha/ *n. f.* ditch, trench.

zapatería /θapate'ria; sapate'ria/ *n. f.* shoe store; shoemaker's shop.

zapatero /θapa'tero; sapa'tero/ *n. m.* shoemaker.

zapato /θa'pato; sa'pato/ *n. m.* shoe.

zar /θar; sar/ *n. m.* czar.

zaraza /θa'raθa; sa'rasa/ *n. f.* calico; chintz.

zarza /'θarθa; 'sarsa/ *n. f.* bramble.

zarzuela /θar'θuela; sar'suela/ *n. f.* musical comedy.

zodíaco /θo'ðiako; so'ðiako/ *n. m.* zodiac.

zona /'θona; 'sona/ *n. f.* zone.

zoología /θoolo'hia; soolo'hia/ *n. f.* zoology.

zoológico /θoo'lohiko; soo'lohiko/ *a.* zoological.

zorro /'θorro; 'sorro/ **-rra** *n.* fox.

zozobra /θo'θoβra; so'soβra/ *n. f.* worry, anxiety; capsizing.

zozobrar /θoθo'βrar; soso'βrar/ *v.* capsize; worry.

zumba /'θumba; 'sumba/ *n. f.* spanking.

zumbido /θum'βiðo; sum'βiðo/ *n. m.* buzz, hum. **—zumbar,** *v.*

zumo /'θumo; 'sumo/ *n. m.* juice. **z. de naranja,** orange juice.

zurcir /θur'θir; sur'sir/ *v.* darn, mend.

zurdo /'θurðo; 'surðo/ *a.* left-handed.

zurrar /θu'rrar; su'rrar/ *v.* flog, drub.

ENGLISH–SPANISH

A

a /ə, *when stressed* ā/ *art.* un, una.

abacus /'æbəkəs/ *n.* ábaco *m.*

abandon /ə'bændən/ *n.* **1.** desenfreno, abandono *m.* —*v.* **2.** abandonar, desamparar.

abandoned /ə'bændənd/ *a.* abandonado.

abandonment /ə'bændənmənt/ *n.* abandono, desamparo *m.*

abase /ə'beis/ *v.* degradar, humillar.

abasement /ə'beismənt/ *n.* degradación, humillación *f.*

abash /ə'bæʃ/ *v.* avergonzar.

abate /ə'beit/ *v.* menguar, moderarse.

abatement /ə'beitmənt/ *n.* disminución *f.*

abbess /'æbis/ *n.* abadesa *f.*

abbey /'æbi/ *n.* abadía *f.*

abbot /'æbət/ *n.* abad *m.*

abbreviate /ə'brivi,eit/ *v.* abreviar.

abbreviation /ə,brivi'eiʃən/ *n.* abreviatura *f.*

abdicate /'æbdɪ,keit/ *v.* abdicar.

abdication /,æbdɪ'keiʃən/ *n.* abdicación *f.*

abdomen /'æbdəmən/ *n.* abdomen *m.*

abdominal /æb'dɒmənl̩/ *a.* abdominal.

abduct /æb'dʌkt/ *v.* secuestrar.

abduction /æb'dʌkʃən/ *n.* secuestración *f.*

abductor /æb'dʌktər/ *n.* secuestrador -ra.

aberrant /ə'bɛrənt, 'æbər-/ *a.* aberrante.

aberration /,æbə'reiʃən/ *n.* aberración *f.*

abet /ə'bɛt/ *v.* apoyar, favorecer.

abetment /ə'bɛtmənt/ *n.* apoyo *m.*

abettor /ə'bɛtər/ *n.* cómplice *m. & f.*

abeyance /ə'beiəns/ *n.* suspensión *f.*

abhor /æb'hɔr/ *v.* abominar, odiar.

abhorrence /æb'hɔrəns/ *n.* detestación *f.*; aborrecimiento *m.*

abhorrent /æb'hɔrənt/ *a.* detestable, aborrecible.

abide /ə'baid/ *v.* soportar. **to a. by,** cumplir con.

abiding /ə'baidɪŋ/ *a.* perdurable.

ability /ə'bɪlɪti/ *n.* habilidad *f.*

abject /'æbdʒɛkt/ *a.* abyecto; desanimado.

abjuration /,æbdʒə'reiʃən/ *n.* renuncia *f.*

abjure /æb'dʒʊr/ *v.* renunciar.

ablative /'æblətɪv/ *a. & n. Gram.* ablativo *m.*

ablaze /ə'bleiz/ *a.* en llamas.

able /'eibəl/ *a.* capaz; competente. **to be a.,** poder.

able-bodied /'eibəl 'bɒdid/ *a.* robusto.

ablution /ə'bluʃən/ *n.* ablución *f.*

ably /'eibli/ *adv.* hábilmente.

abnegate /'æbnɪ,geit/ *v.* repudiar; negar.

abnegation /,æbnɪ'geiʃən/ *n.* abnegación; repudiación *f.*

abnormal /æb'nɔrməl/ *a.* anormal.

abnormality /,æbnɔr'mælɪti/ *n.* anormalidad, deformidad *f.*

abnormally /æb'nɔrməli/ *adv.* anormalmente.

aboard /ə'bɔrd/ *adv.* a bordo.

abode /ə'boud/ *n.* residencia *f.*

abolish /ə'bɒlɪʃ/ *v.* suprimir.

abolishment /ə'bɒlɪʃmənt/ *n.* abolición *f.*

abolition /,æbə'lɪʃən/ *n.* abolición *f.*

abominable /ə'bɒmənəbəl/ *a.* abominable.

abominate /ə'bɒmə,neit/ *v.* abominar, detestar.

abomination /ə,bɒmə'neiʃən/ *n.* abominación *f.*

aboriginal /,æbə'rɪdʒənl̩/ *a. & n.* aborigen *f.*

abortion /ə'bɔrʃən/ *n.* aborto *m.*

abortive /ə'bɔrtɪv/ *a.* abortivo.

abound /ə'baund/ *v.* abundar.

about /ə'baut/ *adv.* **1.** como. **about to,** para; a punto de. —*prep.* **2.** de, sobre, acerca de.

about-face /ə'baut,feis, ə'baut-'feis/ *n. Mil.* media vuelta.

above /ə'bʌv/ *adv.* **1.** arriba. —*prep.* **2.** sobre; por encima de.

aboveboard /ə'bʌv,bɔrd/ *a. & adv.* sincero, franco.

abrasion /ə'breiʒən/ *n.* raspadura *f.*; *Med.* abrasión *f.*

abrasive /ə'breisɪv/ *a.* raspante. *n.* abrasivo *m.*

abreast /ə'brɛst/ *adv.* de frente.

abridge /ə'brɪdʒ/ v. abreviar.

abridgment /ə'brɪdʒmənt/ n. abreviación f.; compendio m.

abroad /ə'brɔd/ adv. en el extranjero, al extranjero.

abrogate /'æbrə,geit/ v. abrogar, revocar.

abrogation /,æbrə'geiʃən/ n. abrogación, revocación f.

abrupt /ə'brʌpt/ a. repentino; brusco.

abruptly /ə'brʌptli/ adv. bruscamente, precipitadamente.

abruptness /ə'brʌptnɪs/ n. precipitación; brusquedad f.

abscess /'æbsɛs/ n. absceso m.

abscond /æb'skɒnd/ v. fugarse.

absence /'æbsəns/ n. ausencia, falta f.

absent /'æbsənt/ a. ausente.

absentee /,æbsən'ti/ a. & n. ausente m. & f.

absent-minded /'æbsənt 'maɪndɪd/ a. distraído.

absinthe /'æbsɪnθ/ n. absenta f.

absolute /'æbsə,lut/ a. absoluto.

absolutely /,æbsə'lutli/ adv. absolutamente.

absoluteness /,æbsə'lutnɪs/ n. absolutismo m.

absolution /,æbsə'luʃən/ n. absolución f.

absolutism /'æbsəlu,tɪzəm/ n. absolutismo, despotismo m.

absolve /æb'zɒlv/ v. absolver.

absorb /æb'sɔrb/ v. absorber; preocupar.

absorbed /æb'sɔrbd/ a. absorbido; absorto.

absorbent /æb'sɔrbənt/ a. absorbente.

absorbent cotton algodón hidrófilo m.

absorbing /æb'sɔrbɪŋ/ a. interesante.

absorption /æb'sɔrpʃən/ n. absorción; preocupación f.

abstain /æb'stein/ v. abstenerse.

abstemious /æb'stimiəs/ a. abstemio, sobrio.

abstinence /'æbstənəns/ n. abstinencia f.

abstract /a, v æb'strækt, 'æbstrækt; n 'æbstrækt/ a. **1.** abstracto. —n. **2.** resumen m. —v. **3.** abstraer.

abstracted /æb'stræktɪd/ a. distraído.

abstraction /æb'strækʃən/ n. abstracción f.

abstruse /æb'strus/ a. abstruso.

absurd /æb'sɜrd/ a. absurdo, ridículo.

absurdity /æb'sɜrdɪti/ n. absurdo m.

absurdly /æb'sɜrdli/ adv. absurdamente.

abundance /ə'bʌndəns/ n. abundancia f.

abundant /ə'bʌndənt/ a. abundante.

abundantly /ə'bʌndəntli/ adv. abundantemente.

abuse /n ə'byus; v ə'byuz/ n. **1.** abuso m. —v. **2.** abusar de; maltratar.

abusive /ə'byusɪv/ a. abusivo.

abusively /ə'byusɪvli/ adv. abusivamente, ofensivamente.

abutment /ə'bʌtmənt/ n. (building) estribo, contrafuerte m.

abut (on) /ə'bʌt/ v. terminar (en); lindar (con).

abyss /ə'bɪs/ n. abismo m.

Abyssinian /,æbə'sɪniən/ a. & n. abisinio -nia.

acacia /ə'keiʃə/ n. acacia f.

academic /,ækə'dɛmɪk/ a. académico.

academy /ə'kædəmi/ n. academia f.

acanthus /ə'kænθəs/ n. Bot. acanto m.

accede /æk'sid/ v. acceder; consentir.

accelerate /æk'sɛlə,reit/ v. acelerar.

acceleration /æk,sɛlə'reiʃən/ n. aceleración f.

accelerator /æk'sɛlə,reitər/ n. Auto. acelerador m.

accent /'æksɛnt/ n. **1.** acento m. —v. **2.** acentuar.

accentuate /æk'sɛntʃu,eit/ v. acentuar.

accept /æk'sɛpt/ v. aceptar.

acceptability /æk,sɛptə'bɪlɪti/ n. aceptabilidad f.

acceptable /æk'sɛptəbəl/ a. aceptable.

acceptably /æk'sɛptəbli/ adv. aceptablemente.

acceptance /æk'sɛptəns/ n. aceptación f.

access /'æksɛs/ n. acceso m., entrada f.

accessible /æk'sɛsəbəl/ a. accesible.

accessory /æk'sɛsəri/ a. **1.** accesorio. —n. **2.** cómplice m. & f.

accident /'æksɪdənt/ *n.* accidente *m.* **by a.,** por casualidad.
accidental /ˌæksɪ'dentļ/ *a.* accidental.
accidentally /ˌæksɪ'dentļi/ *adv.* accidentalmente, casualmente.
acclaim /ə'kleim/ *v.* aclamar.
acclamation /ˌæklə'meiʃən/ *n.* aclamación *f.*
acclimate /'æklə,meit/ *v.* aclimatar.
acclivity /ə'klɪvɪti/ *n.* subida *f.*
accolade /'ækə,leid/ *n.* acolada *f.*
accommodate /ə'kɒmə,deit/ *v.* acomodar.
accommodating /ə'kɒmə,deitɪŋ/ *a.* bondadoso, complaciente.
accommodation /ə,kɒmə'deiʃən/ *n.* servicio *m.; (pl.)* alojamiento *m.*
accompaniment /ə'kʌmpənɪmənt/ *n.* acompañamiento *m.*
accompanist /ə'kʌmpənɪst/ *n.* acompañante *m. & f.*
accompany /ə'kʌmpəni/ *v.* acompañar.
accomplice /ə'kɒmplɪs/ *n.* cómplice *m. & f.*
accomplish /ə'kɒmplɪʃ/ *v.* llevar a cabo; realizar.
accomplished /ə'kɒmplɪʃt/ *a.* acabado, cumplido; culto.
accomplishment /ə'kɒmplɪʃmənt/ *n.* realización *f.;* logro *m.*
accord /ə'kɔrd/ *n.* **1.** acuerdo *m.* —*v.* **2.** otorgar.
accordance /ə'kɔrdņs/ *n.:* **in a. with,** de acuerdo con.
accordingly /ə'kɔrdɪŋli/ *adv.* en conformidad.
according to /ə'kɔrdɪŋ/ *prep.* según.
accordion /ə'kɔrdiən/ *n.* acordeón *m.*
accost /ə'kɔst/ *v.* dirigirse a.
account /ə'kaunt/ *n.* **1.** relato *m.; Com.* cuenta *f.* **on a. of,** a causa de. **on no a.,** de ninguna manera. —*v.* **2. a. for,** explicar.
accountable /ə'kauntəbəl/ *a.* responsable.
accountant /ə'kauntņt/ *n.* contador -ra.
accounting /ə'kauntɪŋ/ *n.* contabilidad *f.*
accouter /ə'kutər/ *v.* equipar, ataviar.
accouterments /ə'kutərmənts/ *n.* equipo, atavío *m.*
accredit /ə'krɛdɪt/ *v.* acreditar.

accretion /ə'kriʃən/ *n.* aumento *m.*
accrual /ə'kruəl/ *n.* aumento, incremento *m.*
accrue /ə'kru/ *v.* provenir; acumularse.
accumulate /ə'kyumyə,leit/ *v.* acumular.
accumulation /ə,kyumyə'leiʃən/ *n.* acumulación *f.*
accumulative /ə'kyumyə,leitɪv/ *a.* acumulativo.
accumulator /ə'kyumyə,leitər/ *n.* acumulador *m.*
accuracy /'ækyərəsi/ *n.* exactitud, precisión *f.*
accurate /'ækyərɪt/ *a.* exacto.
accursed /ə'kɜrsɪd, ə'kɜrst/ *a.* maldito.
accusation /ˌækyʊ'zeiʃən/ *n.* acusación *f.,* cargo *m.*
accusative /ə'kyuzətɪv/ *a. & n.* acusativo *m.*
accuse /ə'kyuz/ *v.* acusar.
accused /ə'kyuzd/ *a. & n.* acusado -da, procesado -da.
accuser /ə'kyuzər/ *n.* acusador -ra.
accustom /ə'kʌstəm/ *v.* acostumbrar.
accustomed /ə'kʌstəmd/ *a.* acostumbrado.
ace /eis/ *a.* **1.** sobresaliente. —*n.* **2.** as *m.*
acerbity /ə'sɜrbɪti/ *n.* acerbidad, amargura *f.*
acetate /'æsɪ,teit/ *n. Chem.* acetato *m.*
acetic /ə'sitɪk/ *a.* acético.
acetylene /ə'sɛtļ,in/ *a.* **1.** acetilénico. —*n.* **2.** *Chem.* acetileno *m.*
ache /eik/ *n.* **1.** dolor *m.* —*v.* **2.** doler.
achieve /ə'tʃiv/ *v.* lograr, llevar a cabo.
achievement /ə'tʃivmənt/ *n.* realización *f.;* hecho notable *m.*
acid /'æsɪd/ *a. & n.* ácido *m.*
acidify /ə'sɪdə,fai/ *v.* acidificar.
acidity /ə'sɪdɪti/ *n.* acidez *f.*
acidosis /ˌæsɪ'dousɪs/ *n. Med.* acidismo *m.*
acid rain lluvia ácida *f.*
acid test prueba decisiva.
acidulous /ə'sɪdʒələs/ *a.* agrio, acídulo.
acknowledge /æk'nɒlɪdʒ/ *v.* admitir; (receipt) acusar.

acme /'ækmi/ n. apogeo, colmo m.

acne /'ækni/ n. Med. acné m. & f.

acolyte /'ækə,lait/ n. acólito m.

acorn /'eikɔrn/ n. bellota f.

acoustics /ə'kustıks/ n. acústica f.

acquaint /ə'kweint/ v. familiarizar. **to be acquainted with,** conocer.

acquaintance /ə'kweintn̥s/ n. conocimiento m.; (person known) conocido -da. **to make the a. of,** conocer.

acquiesce /,ækwi'ɛs/ v. consentir.

acquiescence /,ækwi'ɛsəns/ n. consentimiento m.

acquire /ə'kwaiᵊr/ v. adquirir.

acquirement /ə'kwaiᵊrmənt/ n. adquisición f.; (pl.) conocimientos m.pl.

acquisition /,ækwə'zıʃən/ n. adquisición f.

acquisitive /ə'kwızıtıv/ a. adquisitivo.

acquit /ə'kwıt/ v. exonerar, absolver.

acquittal /ə'kwıtl̥/ n. absolución f.

acre /'eikər/ n. acre m.

acreage /'eikərıdʒ/ número de acres.

acrid /'ækrıd/ a. acre, punzante.

acrimonious /,ækrə'mouniəs/ a. acrimonioso, mordaz.

acrimony /'ækrə,mouni/ n. acrimonia, aspereza f.

acrobat /'ækrə,bæt/ n. acróbata m. & f.

acrobatic /,ækrə'bætık/ a. acrobático.

across /ə'krɔs/ adv. **1.** a través, al otro lado. —prep. **2.** al otro lado de, a través de.

acrostic /ə'krɔstık/ n. acróstico m.

act /ækt/ n. **1.** acción f.; acto m. —v. **2.** actuar, portarse. **act as,** hacer de. **act on,** decidir sobre.

acting /'æktıŋ/ a. **1.** interino. —n. **2.** acción f.; Theat. representación f.

actinism /'æktə,nızəm/ n. actinismo m.

actinium /æk'tıniəm/ n. Chem. actinio m.

action /'ækʃən/ n. acción f. **take a.,** tomar medidas.

action replay /'ri,plei/ repetición f.

activate /'æktə,veit/ v. activar.

activation /,æktə'veiʃən/ n. activación f.

activator /'æktə,veitər/ n. Chem. activador m.

active /'æktıv/ a. activo.

activity /æk'tıvıti/ n. actividad f.

actor /'æktər/ n. actor m.

actress /'æktrıs/ n. actriz f.

actual /'æktʃuəl/ a. real, efectivo.

actuality /,æktʃu'ælıti/ n. realidad, actualidad f.

actually /'æktʃuəli/ adv. en realidad.

actuary /'æktʃu,ɛri/ n. actuario m.

actuate /'æktʃu,eit/ v. impulsar, mover.

acumen /ə'kyumən/ n. cacumen m., perspicacia f.

acupuncture /'ækyʊ,pʌŋktʃər/ n. acupuntura f.

acute /ə'kyut/ a. agudo; perspicaz.

acutely /ə'kyutli/ adv. agudamente.

acuteness /ə'kyutnıs/ n. agudeza f.

adage /'ædıdʒ/ n. refrán, proverbio m.

adamant /'ædəmənt/ a. firme.

Adam's apple /'ædəmz/ nuez de la garganta.

adapt /ə'dæpt/ v. adaptar.

adaptability /ə,dæptə'bılıti/ n. adaptabilidad f.

adaptable /ə'dæptəbəl/ a. adaptable.

adaptation /,ædəp'teiʃən/ n. adaptación f.

adapter /ə'dæptər/ n. Elec. adaptador m.; Mech. ajustador m.

adaptive /ə'dæptıv/ a. adaptable, acomodable.

add /æd/ v. agregar, añadir. **a. up,** sumar.

adder /'ædər/ n. víbora; serpiente f.

addict /'ædıkt/ n. adicto -ta; (fan) aficionado -da.

addition /ə'dıʃən/ n. adición f. **in a. to,** además de.

additional /ə'dıʃənl̥/ a. adicional.

addle /'ædl̥/ v. confundir.

address /n ə'drɛs, 'ædrɛs; v ə'drɛs/ n. **1.** dirección f.; señas f.pl.; (speech) discurso m. —v. **2.** dirigirse a.

addressee /,ædrɛ'si/ n. destinatario -ia.

adduce /ə'dus/ v. aducir.

adenoid /'ædn̥,ɔid/ a. adenoidea.

adept /ə'dɛpt/ a. adepto.

adeptly /ə'dɛptli/ *adv.* diestramente.

adeptness /ə'dɛptnɪs/ *n.* destreza *f.*

adequacy /'ædɪkwəsi/ *n.* suficiencia *f.*

adequate /'ædɪkwɪt/ *a.* adecuado.

adequately /'ædɪkwɪtli/ *adv.* adecuadamente.

adhere /æd'hɪər/ *v.* adherirse, pegarse.

adherence /æd'hɪərəns/ *n.* adhesión *f.*; apego *m.*

adherent /æd'hɪərənt/ *n.* adherente *m.*, partidario -ria.

adhesion /æd'hiʒən/ *n.* adhesión *f.*

adhesive /æd'hisɪv/ *a.* adhesivo. **a. tape,** esparadrapo *m.*

adhesiveness /æd'hisɪvnɪs/ *n.* adhesividad *f.*

adieu /ə'du/ *interj.* **1.** adiós. —*n.* **2.** despedida *f.*

adjacent /ə'dʒeisənt/ *a.* adyacente.

adjective /'ædʒɪktɪv/ *n.* adjetivo *m.*

adjoin /ə'dʒɔin/ *v.* lindar (con).

adjoining /ə'dʒɔinɪŋ/ *a.* contiguo.

adjourn /ə'dʒɜrn/ *v.* suspender, levantar.

adjournment /ə'dʒɜrnmənt/ *n.* suspensión *f.*; *Leg.* espera *f.*

adjunct /'ædʒʌŋkt/ *n.* adjunto *m.*; *Gram.* atributo *m.*

adjust /ə'dʒʌst/ *v.* ajustar, acomodar; arreglar.

adjuster /ə'dʒʌstər/ *n.* ajustador -ra.

adjustment /ə'dʒʌstmənt/ *n.* ajuste; arreglo *m.*

adjutant /'ædʒətənt/ *n. Mil.* ayudante *m.*

administer /æd'mɪnəstər/ *v.* administrar.

administration /æd,mɪnə'streiʃən/ *n.* administración *f.*; gobierno *m.*

administrative /æd'mɪnə,streitɪv/ *a.* administrativo.

administrator /æd'mɪnə,streitər/ *n.* administrador -ra.

admirable /'ædmərəbəl/ *a.* admirable.

admirably /'ædmərəbli/ *adv.* admirablemente.

admiral /'ædmərəl/ *n.* almirante *m.*

admiralty /'ædmərəlti/ *n.* Ministerio de Marina.

admiration /,ædmə'reiʃən/ *n.* admiración *f.*

admire /æd'maiᵊr/ *v.* admirar.

admirer /æd'maiᵊrər/ *n.* admirador -ra; enamorado -da.

admiringly /æd'maiᵊrɪŋli/ *adv.* admirativamente.

admissible /æd'mɪsəbəl/ *a.* admisible, aceptable.

admission /æd'mɪʃən/ *n.* admisión; entrada *f.*

admit /æd'mɪt/ *v.* admitir.

admittance /æd'mɪtṇs/ *n.* entrada *f.*

admittedly /æd'mɪtɪdli/ *adv.* reconocidamente.

admixture /æd'mɪkstʃər/ *n.* mezcla *f.*

admonish /æd'mɒnɪʃ/ *v.* amonestar.

admonition /,ædmə'nɪʃən/ *n.* admonición *f.*

adolescence /,ædḷ'ɛsəns/ *n.* adolescencia *f.*

adolescent /,ædḷ'ɛsənt/ *n. & a.* adolescente.

adopt /ə'dɒpt/ *v.* adoptar.

adopted child /ə'dɒptɪd/ hija adoptiva *f.*, hijo adoptivo *m.*

adoption /ə'dɒpʃən/ *n.* adopción *f.*

adorable /ə'dɔrəbəl/ *a.* adorable.

adoration /,ædə'reiʃən/ *n.* adoración *f.*

adore /ə'dɔr/ *v.* adorar.

adorn /ə'dɔrn/ *v.* adornar.

adornment /ə'dɔrnmənt/ *n.* adorno *m.*

adrenalin /ə'drɛnḷɪn/ *n.* adrenalina *f.*

adrift /ə'drɪft/ *adv.* a la ventura.

adroit /ə'drɔit/ *a.* diestro.

adulate /'ædʒə,leit/ *v.* adular.

adulation /,ædʒə'leiʃən/ *n.* adulación *f.*

adult /ə'dʌlt/ *a. & n.* adulto -a.

adulterant /ə'dʌltərənt/ *a. & n.* adulterante *m.*

adulterate /ə'dʌltə,reit/ *v.* adulterar.

adulterer /ə'dʌltərər/ *n.* adúltero -ra.

adulteress /ə'dʌltərɪs/ *n.* adúltera *f.*

adultery /ə'dʌltəri/ *n.* adulterio *m.*

advance /æd'væns/ *n.* **1.** avance; adelanto *m.* **in a.,** de antemano, antes. —*v.* **2.** avanzar, adelantar.

advanced /æd'vænst/ *a.* avanzado, adelantado.

advancement /æd'vænsmənt/ *n.* adelantamiento *m.*; promoción *f.*

advantage /æd'væntɪdʒ/ *n.* ventaja *f.* **take a. of,** aprovecharse de.

advantageous /ˌædvən'teidʒəs/ *a.* provechoso, ventajoso.

advantageously /ˌædvən-'teidʒəsli/ *adv.* ventajosamente.

advent /'ædvɛnt/ *n.* venida, llegada *f.*

adventitious /ˌædvən'tɪʃəs/ *a.* adventicio, espontáneo.

adventure /æd'vɛntʃər/ *n.* aventura *f.*

adventurer /æd'vɛntʃərər/ *n.* aventurero -ra.

adventurous /æd'vɛntʃərəs/ *a.* aventurero, intrépido.

adventurously /æd'vɛntʃərəsli/ *adv.* arriesgadamente.

adverb /'ædvɜrb/ *n.* adverbio *m.*

adverbial /æd'vɜrbiəl/ *a.* adverbial.

adversary /'ædvərˌsɛri/ *n.* adversario -a.

adverse /æd'vɜrs/ *a.* adverso.

adversely /æd'vɜrsli/ *adv.* adversamente.

adversity /æd'vɜrsɪti/ *n.* adversidad *f.*

advert /æd'vɜrt/ *v.* hacer referencia a.

advertise /'ædvərˌtaiz/ *v.* avisar, anunciar; (promote) promocionar.

advertisement /ˌædvər'taizmənt, æd'vɜrtɪsmənt/ *n.* aviso, anuncio *m.*

advertiser /'ædvərˌtaizər/ *n.* anunciante *m. & f.*, avisador -ra.

advertising /'ædvərˌtaizɪŋ/ *n.* publicidad *f.*

advice /æd'vais/ *n.* consejos *m.pl.*

advisability /ædˌvaizə'bɪlɪti/ *n.* prudencia, propiedad *f.*

advisable /æd'vaizəbəl/ *a.* aconsejable, prudente.

advisably /æd'vaizəbli/ *adv.* prudentemente.

advise /æd'vaiz/ *v.* aconsejar. **a. against,** desaconsejar.

advisedly /æd'vaizɪdli/ *adv.* avisadamente, prudentemente.

advisement /æd'vaizmənt/ *n.* consideración *f.*; **take under a.,** someter a estudio.

adviser /æd'vaizər/ *n.* consejero -ra.

advocacy /'ædvəkəsi/ *n.* abogacía; defensa *f.*

advocate /*n.* 'ædvəkɪt; *v.* -ˌkeit/ *n.* **1.** abogado -da. —*v.* **2.** apoyar.

aegis /'idʒis/ *n.* amparo *m.*

aerate /'ɛəreit/ *v.* airear, ventilar.

aeration /ˌɛə'reiʃən/ *n.* aeración, ventilación *f.*

aerial /'ɛəriəl/ *a.* aéreo.

aerie /'ɛəri/ *n.* nido de águila.

aeronautics /ˌɛərə'nɔtɪks/ *n.* aeronáutica *f.*

aerosol bomb /'ɛərəˌsɔl/ bomba insecticida.

afar /ə'fɑr/ *adv.* lejos. **from a.,** de lejos, desde lejos.

affability /ˌæfə'bɪlɪti/ *n.* afabilidad, amabilidad *f.*

affable /'æfəbəl/ *a.* afable.

affably /'æfəbli/ *adv.* afablemente.

affair /ə'fɛər/ *n.* asunto *m.* **love a.,** aventura amorosa.

affect /ə'fɛkt/ *v.* afectar; (emotionally) conmover.

affectation /ˌæfɛk'teiʃən/ *n.* afectación *f.*

affected /ə'fɛktɪd/ *a.* artificioso.

affecting /ə'fɛktɪŋ/ *a.* conmovedor.

affection /ə'fɛkʃən/ *n.* cariño *m.*

affectionate /ə'fɛkʃənɪt/ *a.* afectuoso, cariñoso.

affectionately /ə'fɛkʃənɪtli/ *adv.* afectuosamente, con cariño.

affiance /ə'faiəns/ *v.* dar palabra de casamiento; **become affianced,** comprometerse.

affidavit /ˌæfɪ'deivɪt/ *n.* Leg. declaración, deposición *f.*

affiliate /*n.* ə'fɪli,it; *v.* ə'fɪli,eit/ *n.* **1.** afiliado -da. —*v.* **2.** afiliar.

affiliation /əˌfɪli'eiʃən/ *n.* afiliación *f.*

affinity /ə'fɪnɪti/ *n.* afinidad *f.*

affirm /ə'fɜrm/ *v.* afirmar.

affirmation /ˌæfər'meiʃən/ *n.* afirmación, aserción *f.*

affirmative /ə'fɜrmətɪv/ *n.* **1.** afirmativa *f.* —*a.* **2.** afirmativo.

affirmatively /ə'fɜrmətɪvli/ *adv.* afirmativamente, aseveradamente.

affix /*n.* 'æfɪks; *v.* ə'fɪks/ *n.* **1.** Gram. afijo *m.* —*v.* **2.** fijar, pegar, poner.

afflict /ə'flɪkt/ *v.* afligir.

affliction /ə'flɪkʃən/ *n.* aflicción *f.*; mal *m.*

affluence /'æfluəns/ *n.* abundancia, opulencia *f.*

affluent /'æfluənt/ *a.* opulento, afluente.

afford /ə'fɔrd/ *v.* proporcionar. **be able to a.,** tener con que comprar.

affordable /ə'fɔrdəbəl/ *a.* asequible.

affront /ə'frʌnt/ *n.* **1.** afrenta *f.* —*v.* **2.** afrentar, insultar.

afield /ə'fild/ *adv.* lejos de casa; lejos del camino; lejos del asunto.

afire /ə'faiᵊr/ *adv.* ardiendo.

afloat /ə'flout/ *adv. Naut.* a flote.

aforementioned /ə'fɔr,mɛnʃənd/ *a.* dicho, susodicho.

afraid /ə'freid/ *a.* **to be a.,** tener miedo, temer.

African /'æfrɪkən/ *n. & a.* africano -na.

aft /æft/ *adv. Naut.* a popa, en popa.

after /'æftər/ *prep.* **1.** después de. —*conj.* **2.** después que.

aftermath /'æftər,mæθ/ *n.* resultados *m.pl.,* consecuencias *f.pl.*

afternoon /,æftər'nun/ *n.* tarde *f.* **good a.,** buenas tardes.

aftertaste /'æftər,teist/ *n.* gustillo *m.*

afterthought /'æftər,θɔt/ *n.* idea tardía.

afterward(s) /'æftərwərdz/ *adv.* después.

again /ə'gɛn/ *adv.* otra vez, de nuevo. **to do a.,** volver a hacer.

against /ə'gɛnst/ *prep.* contra; en contra de.

agape /ə'geip/ *adv.* con la boca abierta.

agate /'ægɪt/ *n.* ágata *f.*

age /eidʒ/ *n.* **1.** edad *f.* **of a.,** mayor de edad. **old a.,** vejez *f.* —*v.* **2.** envejecer.

aged /eidʒd; 'eidʒɪd/ *a.* viejo, anciano, añejo.

ageism /'eidʒɪzəm/ *n.* discriminación contra las personas de edad.

ageless /'eidʒlɪs/ *a.* sempiterno.

agency /'eidʒənsi/ *n.* agencia *f.*

agenda /ə'dʒɛndə/ *n.* agenda *f.,* orden *m.*

agent /'eidʒənt/ *n.* agente; representante *m. & f.*

agglutinate /ə'glutn̩,eit/ *v.* aglutinar.

agglutination /ə,glutn̩'eiʃən/ *n.* aglutinación *f.*

aggrandize /ə'grændaiz/ *v.* agrandar; elevar.

aggrandizement /ə'grændɪzmənt/ *n.* engrandecimiento *m.*

aggravate /'ægrə,veit/ *v.* agravar; irritar.

aggravation /,ægrə'veiʃən/ *n.* agravamiento; empeoramiento *m.*

aggregate /'ægrɪgɪt, -,geit/ *a. & n.* agregado *m.*

aggregation /,ægrɪ'geiʃən/ *n.* agregación *f.*

aggression /ə'grɛʃən/ *n.* agresión *f.*

aggressive /ə'grɛsɪv/ *a.* agresivo.

aggressively /ə'grɛsɪvli/ *adv.* agresivamente.

aggressiveness /ə'grɛsɪvnɪs/ *n.* agresividad *f.*

aggressor /ə'grɛsər/ *n.* agresor -ra.

aghast /ə'gæst/ *a.* horrorizado.

agile /'ædʒəl/ *a.* ágil.

agility /æ'dʒɪliti/ *n.* agilidad, ligereza, prontitud *f.*

agitate /'ædʒɪ,teit/ *v.* agitar.

agitation /,ædʒɪ'teiʃən/ *n.* agitación *f.*

agitator /'ædʒɪ,teitər/ *n.* agitador -ra.

agnostic /æg'nɒstɪk/ *a. & n.* agnóstico -ca.

ago /ə'gou/ *adv.* hace. **two days a.,** hace dos días.

agonized /'ægə,naizd/ *a.* angustioso.

agony /'ægəni/ *n.* sufrimiento *m.;* angustia *f.*

agrarian /ə'grɛəriən/ *a.* agrario.

agree /ə'gri/ *v.* estar de acuerdo; convenir. **a. with one,** sentar bien.

agreeable /ə'griəbəl/ *a.* agradable.

agreeably /ə'griəbli/ *adv.* agradablemente.

agreement /ə'grimənt/ *n.* acuerdo *m.*

agriculture /'ægrɪ,kʌltʃər/ *n.* agricultura *f.*

ahead /ə'hɛd/ *adv.* adelante.

aid /eid/ *n.* **1.** ayuda *f.* —*v.* **2.** ayudar.

aide /eid/ *n.* ayudante -ta.

AIDS /eidz/ *n.* SIDA *m.*

ailing /'eilɪŋ/ *adj.* enfermo.

ailment /'eilmənt/ *n.* enfermedad *f.*

aim /eim/ *n.* **1.** puntería *f.;* (purpose) propósito *m.* —*v.* **2.** apuntar.

aimless /'eimlɪs/ *a.* sin objeto.

air /ɛər/ n. **1.** aire m. **by a.** por avión. —v. **2.** ventilar, airear.

airbag /'ɛər,bæg/ n. (in automobiles) saco de aire m.

air-conditioned /'ɛər kən,dɪʃənd/ a. con aire acondicionado.

air-conditioning /ɛər kən,dɪʃənɪŋ/ acondicionamiento del aire.

aircraft /'ɛər,kræft/ n. avión m.

aircraft carrier portaaviones m.

airfare /'ɛər,fɛər/ n. precio del billete de avión m.

airing /'ɛərɪŋ/ n. ventilación f.

airline /'ɛər,lain/ n. línea aérea f.

airliner /'ɛər,lainər/ n. avión de pasajeros.

airmail /'ɛər,meil/ n. correo aéreo.

airplane /'ɛər,plein/ n. avión, aeroplano m.

air pollution contaminación atmosférica, contaminación del aire.

airport /'ɛər,pɔrt/ n. aeropuerto m.

air pressure presión atmosférica.

air raid ataque aéreo.

airsick /'ɛər,sɪk/ a. mareado.

air terminal terminal aérea f.

airtight /'ɛər,tait/ a. hermético.

air traffic controller controlador aéreo m.

aisle /ail/ n. pasillo m.

ajar /ə'dʒɑr/ a. entreabierto.

akin /ə'kɪn/ a. emparentado, semejante.

alacrity /ə'lækrɪti/ n. alacridad, presteza f.

alarm /ə'lɑrm/ n. **1.** alarma f. —v. **2.** alarmar.

alarmist /ə'lɑrmɪst/ n. alarmista m. & f.

albino /æl'bainou/ n. albino -na.

album /'ælbəm/ n. álbum m.

alcohol /'ælkə,hɔl/ n. alcohol m.

alcoholic /,ælkə'hɔlɪk/ a. alcohólico.

alcove /'ælkouv/ n. alcoba f.

ale /eil/ n. cerveza inglesa.

alert /ə'lɜrt/ n. **1.** alarma f. **on the a.,** alerta, sobre aviso. —a. **2.** listo, vivo. —v. **3.** poner sobre aviso.

alfalfa /æl'fælfə/ n. alfalfa f.

algebra /'ældʒəbrə/ n. álgebra f.

alias /'eiliəs/ n. alias m.

alibi /'ælə,bai/ n. excusa f.; Leg. coartada f.

alien /'eiliən/ a. **1.** ajeno, extranjero. —n. **2.** extranjero -ra.

alienate /'eiliə,neit/ v. enajenar.

alight /ə'lait/ v. bajar, apearse.

align /ə'lain/ v. alinear.

alike /ə'laik/ a. **1.** semejante, igual. —adv. **2.** del mismo modo, igualmente.

alimentary canal /,ælə'mɛntəri/ n. tubo digestivo m.

alive /ə'laiv/ a. vivo; animado.

alkali /'ælkə,lai/ n. Chem. álcali, cali m.

alkaline /'ælkə,lain/ a. alcalino.

all /ɔl/ a. & pron. todo. **not at a.,** de ninguna manera, nada.

allay /ə'lei/ v. aquietar.

allegation /,ælɪ'geiʃən/ n. alegación f.

allege /ə'lɛdʒ/ v. alegar; pretender.

allegiance /ə'lidʒəns/ n. lealtad f.; (to country) homenaje m.

allegory /'ælə,gɔri/ n. alegoría f.

allergy /'ælərdʒi/ n. alergia f.

alleviate /ə'livi,eit/ v. aliviar.

alley /'æli/ n. callejón m. **bowling a.,** bolera f., boliche m.

alliance /ə'laiəns/ n. alianza f.

allied /'ælaid/ a. aliado.

alligator /'ælɪ,geitər/ n. caimán m.; (Mex.) lagarto m. **a. pear,** aguacate m.

allocate /'ælə,keit/ v. colocar, asignar.

allot /ə'lɒt/ v. asignar.

allotment /ə'lɒtmənt/ n. lote, porción f.

allow /ə'lau/ v. permitir, dejar.

allowance /ə'lauəns/ n. abono m.; dieta f. **make a. for,** tener en cuenta.

alloy /'ælɔi/ n. mezcla f.; (metal) aleación f.

all right está bien.

allude /ə'lud/ v. aludir.

allure /ə'lur/ n. **1.** atracción f. —v. **2.** atraer, tentar.

alluring /ə'lurɪŋ/ a. tentador, seductivo.

allusion /ə'luʒən/ n. alusión f.

ally /n 'ælai, v ə'lai/ n. **1.** aliado -da. —v. **2.** aliar.

almanac /'ɔlmə,næk/ n. almanaque m.

almighty /ɔl'maiti/ a. todopoderoso.

almond /'ɑmənd/ n. almendra f.

almost /'ɔlmoust/ adv. casi.

alms /ɑmz/ n. limosna f.

aloft /ə'lɔft/ adv. arriba, en alto.

alone /ə'loun/ adv. solo, a solas. **to leave a.,** dejar en paz.

along /ə'lɔŋ/ *prep.* por; a lo largo de. **a. with,** junto con.

alongside /ə'lɔŋ'said/ *adv.* **1.** al lado. —*prep.* **2.** junto a.

aloof /ə'luf/ *a.* apartado.

aloud /ə'laud/ *adv.* en voz alta.

alpaca /æl'pækə/ *n.* alpaca *f.*

alphabet /'ælfə,bɛt/ *n.* alfabeto *m.*

alphabetical /,ælfə'bɛtɪkəl/ *a.* alfabético.

alphabetize /'ælfəbɪ,taiz/ *v.* alfabetizar.

already /ɔl'rɛdi/ *adv.* ya.

also /'ɔlsou/ *adv.* también.

altar /'ɔltər/ *n.* altar *m.*

alter /'ɔltər/ *v.* alterar.

alteration /,ɔltə'reiʃən/ *n.* alteración *f.*

alternate /*a, n* 'ɔltərnɪt; *v* -,neit/ *a.* **1.** alterno. —*n.* **2.** substituto -ta. —*v.* **3.** alternar.

alternative /ɔl'tərnətɪv/ *a.* **1.** alternativo. —*n.* **2.** alternativa *f.*

although /ɔl'ðou/ *conj.* aunque.

altitude /'æltɪ,tud/ *n.* altura *f.*

alto /'æltou/ *n.* contralto *m.*

altogether /,ɔltə'gɛðər/ *adv.* en junto; enteramente.

altruism /'æltru,ɪzəm/ *n.* altruismo *m.*

alum /'æləm/ *n.* alumbre *m.*

aluminum /ə'lumənəm/ *n.* aluminio *m.*

aluminum foil papel de aluminio *m.*

always /'ɔlweiz/ *adv.* siempre.

amalgam /ə'mælgəm/ *n.* amalgama *f.*

amalgamate /ə'mælgə,meit/ *v.* amalgamar.

amass /ə'mæs/ *v.* amontonar.

amateur /'æmə,tʃur/ *n.* aficionado -da.

amaze /ə'meiz/ *v.* asombrar; sorprender.

amazement /ə'meizmənt/ *n.* asombro *m.*

amazing /ə'meizɪŋ/ *a.* asombroso, pasmoso.

ambassador /æm'bæsədər/ *n.* embajador -ra.

amber /'æmbər/ *a.* **1.** ambarino. —*n.* **2.** ámbar *m.*

ambidextrous /,æmbɪ'dɛkstrəs/ *a.* ambidextro.

ambiguity /,æmbɪ'gyuɪti/ *n.* ambigüedad *f.*

ambiguous /æm'bɪgyuəs/ *a.* ambiguo.

ambition /æm'bɪʃən/ *n.* ambición *f.*

ambitious /æm'bɪʃəs/ *a.* ambicioso.

ambulance /'æmbyələns/ *n.* ambulancia *f.*

ambush /'æmbuʃ/ *n.* **1.** emboscada *f.* —*v.* **2.** acechar.

ameliorate /ə'milyə,reit/ *v.* mejorar.

amenable /ə'minəbəl/ *a.* tratable, dócil.

amend /ə'mɛnd/ *v.* enmendar.

amendment /ə'mɛndmənt/ *n.* enmienda *f.*

amenity /ə'mɛnɪti/ *n.* amenidad *f.*

American /ə'mɛrɪkən/ *a. & n.* americano -na, norteamericano -na.

amethyst /'æməθɪst/ *n.* amatista *f.*

amiable /'eimiəbəl/ *a.* amable.

amicable /'æmɪkəbəl/ *a.* amigable.

amid /ə'mɪd/ *prep.* entre, en medio de.

amidships /ə'mɪd,ʃɪps/ *adv. Naut.* en medio del navío.

amiss /ə'mɪs/ *adv.* mal. **to take a.,** llevar a mal.

amity /'æmɪti/ *n.* amistad, armonía *f.*

ammonia /ə'mounyə/ *n.* amoníaco *m.*

ammunition /,æmyə'nɪʃən/ *n.* municiones *f.pl.*

amnesia /æm'niʒə/ *n.* amnesia *f.*

amnesty /'æmnəsti/ *n.* amnistía *f.*, indulto *m.*

amniocentesis /,æmniousɛn'tisɪs/ *n.* amniocéntesis *f.*

amoeba /ə'mibə/ *n.* amiba *f.*

among /ə'mʌŋ/ *prep.* entre.

amoral /ei'mɔrəl/ *a.* amoral.

amorous /'æmərəs/ *a.* amoroso.

amorphous /ə'mɔrfəs/ *a.* amorfo.

amortize /'æmər,taiz/ *v. Com.* amortizar.

amount /ə'maunt/ *n.* **1.** cantidad, suma *f.* —*v.* **2.** **a. to,** subir a.

ampere /'æmpɪər/ *n. Elec.* amperio *m.*

amphibian /æm'fɪbiən/ *a. & n.* anfibio *m.*

amphitheater /'æmfə,θiətər/ *n.* anfiteatro, circo *m.*

ample /'æmpəl/ *a.* amplio; suficiente.

amplify /'æmplə,fai/ *v.* amplificar.

amputate /'æmpyu,teit/ *v.* amputar.

amuse /ə'myuz/ v. entretener, divertir.

amusement /ə'myuzmənt/ n. diversión f.

an /ən, *when stressed* an/ *art.* un, una.

anachronism /ə'nækrə,nɪzəm/ n. anacronismo, m.

analogous /ə'næləgəs/ a. análogo, parecido.

analogy /ə'nælədʒi/ n. analogía f.

analysis /ə'næləsɪs/ n. análisis m.

analyst /'ænḷɪst/ n. analista m. & f.

analytic /ˌænḷ'ɪtɪk/ a. analítico.

analyze /'ænḷ,aiz/ v. analizar.

anarchy /'ænərki/ n. anarquía f.

anatomy /ə'nætəmi/ n. anatomía f.

ancestor /'ænsɛstər/ n. antepasado m.

ancestral /æn'sɛstrəl/ a. de los antepasados, hereditario.

ancestry /'ænsɛstri/ n. linaje, abolengo m.

anchor /'æŋkər/ n. **1.** ancla f. **weigh a.,** levar el ancla. —v. **2.** anclar.

anchorage /'æŋkərɪdʒ/ n. *Naut.* ancladero, anclaje m.

anchovy /'æntʃouvi/ n. anchoa f.

ancient /'einʃənt/ a. & n. antiguo -ua.

and /ænd, ənd/ *conj.* y, (before i-, hi-) e.

anecdote /'ænɪk,dout/ n. anécdota f.

anemia /ə'nimiə/ n. *Med.* anemia f.

anesthetic /ˌænəs'θɛtɪk/ n. anestesia f.

anew /ə'nu/ adv. de nuevo.

angel /'eindʒəl/ n. ángel m.

anger /'æŋgər/ n. **1.** ira f., enojo m. —v. **2.** enfadar, enojar.

angle /'æŋgəl/ n. ángulo m.

angry /'æŋgri/ a. enojado, enfadado.

anguish /'æŋgwɪʃ/ n. angustia f.

angular /'æŋgyələr/ a. angular.

aniline /'ænḷɪn/ n. *Chem.* anilina f.

animal /'ænəməl/ a. & n. animal m.

animate /v. 'ænə,meit; a -mɪt/ v. **1.** animar. —a. **2.** animado.

animated /'ænə,meitɪd/ a. vivo, animado.

animation /ˌænə'meiʃən/ n. animación, viveza f.

animosity /ˌænə'mɒsɪti/ n. rencor m.

anise /'ænɪs/ n. anís m.

ankle /'æŋkəl/ n. tobillo m.

annals /'ænḷz/ n.pl. anales m.pl.

annex /n 'ænɛks; v ə'nɛks, 'ænɛks/ n. **1.** anexo m., adición f. —v. **2.** anexar.

annexation /ˌænɪk'seiʃən/ n. anexión, adición f.

annihilate /ə'naiə,leit/ v. aniquilar, destruir.

anniversary /ˌænə'vɜrsəri/ n. aniversario m.

annotate /'ænə,teit/ v. anotar.

annotation /ˌænə'teiʃən/ n. anotación f., apunte m.

announce /ə'nauns/ v. anunciar.

announcement /ə'naunsmənt/ n. anuncio, aviso m.

announcer /ə'naunsər/ n. anunciador -ra; (radio) locutor -ra.

annoy /ə'nɔi/ v. molestar.

annoyance /ə'nɔiəns/ n. molestia, incomodidad f.

annual /'ænyuəl/ a. anual.

annuity /ə'nuiti/ n. anualidad, pensión f.

annul /ə'nʌl/ v. anular, invalidar.

anode /'ænoud/ n. *Elec.* ánodo m.

anoint /ə'nɔint/ v. untar; *Relig.* ungir.

anomalous /ə'nɒmələs/ a. anómalo, irregular.

anonymous /ə'nɒnəməs/ a. anónimo.

anorexia /ˌænə'rɛksiə/ n. anorexia f.

another /ə'nʌðər/ a. & *pron.* otro.

answer /'ænsər, 'ɑn-/ n. **1.** contestación, respuesta f. —v. **2.** contestar, responder. **a. for,** ser responsable de.

answerable /'ænsərəbəl/ a. discutible, refutable.

answering machine /'ænsərɪŋ/ contestador automático m.

ant /ænt/ n. hormiga f.

antacid /ænt'æsɪd/ a. & n. antiácido m.

antagonism /æn'tægə,nɪzəm/ n. antagonismo m.

antagonist /æn'tægənɪst/ n. antagonista m. & f.

antagonistic /æn,tægə'nɪstɪk/ a. antagónico, hostil.

antagonize /æn'tægə,naiz/ v. contrariar.

antarctic /ænt'ɑrktɪk/ a. & n. antártico m.

antecedent /ˌæntə'sidn̩t/ *a. & n.* antecedente *m.*

antedate /'ænti̩deit/ *v.* antedatar.

antelope /'æntl̩ˌoup/ *n.* antílope *m.*, gacela *f.*

antenna /æn'tɛnə/ *n.* antena *f.*

antepenultimate /ˌæntipi'nʌltəmit/ *a.* antepenúltimo.

anterior /æn'tɪəriər/ *a.* anterior.

anteroom /'ænti̩rum/ *n.* antecámara *f.*

anthem /'ænθəm/ *n.* himno *m.*; (religious) antífona *f.*

anthology /æn'θɒlədʒi/ *n.* antología *f.*

anthracite /'ænθrə̩sait/ *n.* antracita *f.*

anthrax /'ænθræks/ *n.* Med. ántrax *m.*

anthropology /ˌænθrə'pɒlədʒi/ *n.* antropología *f.*

antiaircraft /ˌænti'ɛər̩kræft, ˌæntai-/ *a.* antiaéreo.

antibody /'ænti̩bɒdi/ *n.* anticuerpo *m.*

anticipate /æn'tisə̩peit/ *v.* esperar, anticipar.

anticipation /ænˌtisə'peiʃən/ *n.* anticipación *f.*

anticlerical /ˌænti'klɛrikəl, ˌæntai-/ *a.* anticlerical.

anticlimax /ˌænti'klaimæks, ˌæntai-/ *n.* anticlímax *m.*

antidote /'ænti̩dout/ *n.* antídoto *m.*

antifreeze /'ænti̩friz/ *n.* anticongelante *m.*

antihistamine /ˌænti'histə̩min, -min, ˌæntai-/ *n.* antihistamínico *m.*

antimony /'æntə̩mouni/ *n.* antimonio *m.*

antinuclear /ˌænti'nukliər, æntai-/ *a.* antinuclear.

antipathy /æn'tipəθi/ *n.* antipatía *f.*

antiquated /'ænti̩kweitid/ *a.* anticuado.

antique /æn'tik/ *a.* **1.** antiguo. —*n.* **2.** antigüedad *f.*

antiquity /æn'tikwiti/ *n.* antigüedad *f.*

antiseptic /ˌæntə'sɛptik/ *a. & n.* antiséptico *m.*

antisocial /ˌænti'souʃəl, ˌæntai-/ *a.* antisocial.

antitoxin /ˌænti'tɒksin/ *n.* Med. antitoxina *f.*

antler /'æntlər/ *n.* asta *f.*

anvil /'ænvil/ *n.* yunque *m.*

anxiety /æŋ'zaiiti/ *n.* ansia, ansiedad *f.*

anxious /'æŋkʃəs, 'æŋʃəs/ *a.* inquieto, ansioso.

any /'ɛni/ *a.* alguno; (at all) cualquiera; (after *not*) ninguno.

anybody /'ɛni̩bɒdi/ *pron.* alguien; (at all) cualquiera; (after *not*) nadie.

anyhow /'ɛni̩hau/ *adv.* de todos modos; en todo caso.

anyone /'ɛni̩wʌn/ *pron.* = anybody.

anything /'ɛni̩θiŋ/ *pron.* algo; (at all) cualquier cosa; (after *not*) nada.

anyway /'ɛni̩wei/ *adv.* = anyhow.

anywhere /'ɛni̩wɛər/ *adv.* en alguna parte; (at all) dondequiera; (after *not*) en ninguna parte.

apart /ə'pɑrt/ *adv.* aparte. **to take a.**, deshacer.

apartheid /ə'pɑrtheit, -hait/ *n.* apartheid *m.*

apartment /ə'pɑrtmənt/ *n.* apartamento, piso *m.*

apartment house casa de pisos *f.*

apathetic /ˌæpə'θɛtik/ *a.* apático.

apathy /'æpəθi/ *n.* apatía *f.*

ape /eip/ *n.* **1.** mono -na. —*v.* **2.** imitar.

aperture /'æpərtʃər/ *n.* abertura *f.*

apex /'eipɛks/ *n.* ápice *m.*

aphorism /'æfə̩rizəm/ *n.* aforismo *m.*

apiary /'eipi̩ɛri/ *n.* colmenario, abejar *m.*

apiece /ə'pis/ *adv.* por persona; cada uno.

apologetic /əˌpɒlə'dʒɛtik/ *a.* apologético.

apologist /ə'pɒlədʒist/ *n.* apologista *m. & f.*

apologize /ə'pɒlə̩dʒaiz/ *v.* excusarse, disculparse.

apology /ə'pɒlədʒi/ *n.* excusa; apología *f.*

apoplectic /ˌæpə'plɛktik/ *a.* apopléctico.

apoplexy /'æpə̩plɛksi/ *n.* apoplejía *f.*

apostate /ə'pɒsteit/ *n.* apóstata *m. & f.*

apostle /ə'pɒsəl/ *n.* apóstol *m.*

apostolic /ˌæpə'stɒlik/ *a.* apostólico.

appall /ə'pɔl/ *v.* horrorizar; consternar.

apparatus /ˌæpəˈrætəs/ *n.* aparato *m.*

apparel /əˈpærəl/ *n.* ropa *f.*

apparent /əˈpærənt/ *a.* aparente; claro.

apparition /ˌæpəˈrɪʃən/ *n.* aparición *f.;* fantasma *m.*

appeal /əˈpil/ *n.* **1.** súplica *f.;* interés *m.; Leg.* apelación *f.* —*v.* **2.** apelar, suplicar; interesar.

appear /əˈpɪər/ *v.* aparecer, asomar; (seem) parecer; *Leg.* comparecer.

appearance /əˈpɪərəns/ *n.* apariencia *f.,* aspecto *m.;* aparición *f.*

appease /əˈpiz/ *v.* aplacar, apaciguar.

appeasement /əˈpizmənt/ *n.* apaciguamiento *m.*

appeaser /əˈpizər/ *n.* apaciguador -ra, pacificador -ra.

appellant /əˈpɛlənt/ *n.* apelante, demandante *m.* & *f.*

appellate /əˈpɛlɪt/ *a. Leg.* de apelación.

appendage /əˈpɛndɪdʒ/ *n.* añadidura *f.*

appendectomy /ˌæpənˈdɛktəmi/ *n.* apendectomía *f.*

appendicitis /əˌpɛndəˈsaɪtɪs/ *n.* apendicitis *f.*

appendix /əˈpɛndɪks/ *n.* apéndice *m.*

appetite /ˈæpɪˌtaɪt/ *n.* apetito *m.*

appetizer /ˈæpɪˌtaɪzər/ *n.* aperitivo *m.*

appetizing /ˈæpɪˌtaɪzɪŋ/ *a.* apetitoso.

applaud /əˈplɔd/ *v.* aplaudir.

applause /əˈplɔz/ *n.* aplauso *m.*

apple /ˈæpəl/ *n.* manzana *f.* **a. tree,** manzano *m.*

applesauce /ˈæpəlˌsɔs/ *n.* compota de manzana.

appliance /əˈplaɪəns/ *n.* aparato *m.*

applicable /ˈæplɪkəbəl/ *a.* aplicable.

applicant /ˈæplɪkənt/ *n.* suplicante *m.* & *f.;* candidato -ta.

application /ˌæplɪˈkeɪʃən/ *n.* solicitud *f.,* (computer) programa *m.*

applied /əˈplaɪd/ *a.* aplicado. **a. for,** pedido.

appliqué /ˌæplɪˈkeɪ/ *n.* (sewing) aplicación *f.*

apply /əˈplaɪ/ *v.* aplicar. **a. for,** solicitar, pedir.

appoint /əˈpɔɪnt/ *v.* nombrar.

appointment /əˈpɔɪntmənt/ *n.* nombramiento *m.;* puesto *m.*

apportion /əˈpɔrʃən/ *v.* repartir.

apposition /ˌæpəˈzɪʃən/ *n. Gram.* aposición *f.*

appraisal /əˈpreɪzəl/ *n.* valoración *f.*

appraise /əˈpreɪz/ *v.* evaluar; tasar; estimar.

appreciable /əˈpriʃiəbəl/ *a.* apreciable; notable.

appreciate /əˈpriʃiˌeɪt/ *v.* apreciar, estimar.

appreciation /əˌpriʃiˈeɪʃən/ *n.* aprecio; reconocimiento *m.*

apprehend /ˌæprɪˈhɛnd/ *v.* prender, capturar.

apprehension /ˌæprɪˈhɛnʃən/ *n.* aprensión *f.;* detención *f.*

apprehensive /ˌæprɪˈhɛnsɪv/ *a.* aprensivo.

apprentice /əˈprɛntɪs/ *n.* aprendiz -iza.

apprenticeship /əˈprɛntɪsˌʃɪp/ *n.* aprendizaje *m.*

apprise /əˈpraɪz/ *v.* informar.

approach /əˈproʊtʃ/ *n.* **1.** acceso; método *m.* —*v.* **2.** acercarse.

approachable /əˈproʊtʃəbəl/ *a.* accesible.

approbation /ˌæprəˈbeɪʃən/ *n.* aprobación *f.*

appropriate /a əˈproʊpriɪt; v -ˌeɪt/ *a.* **1.** apropiado. —*v.* **2.** apropiar.

appropriation /əˌproʊpriˈeɪʃən/ *n.* apropiación *f.*

approval /əˈpruvəl/ *n.* aprobación *f.*

approve /əˈpruv/ *v.* aprobar.

approximate /a əˈprɒksəmɪt; v -ˌmeɪt/ *a.* **1.** aproximado. —*v.* **2.** aproximar.

approximately /əˈprɒksəmɪtli/ *adv.* aproximadamente.

approximation /əˌprɒksəˈmeɪʃən/ *n.* aproximación *f.*

appurtenance /əˈpɜrtnəns/ *n.* dependencia *f.*

apricot /ˈæprɪˌkɒt/ *n.* albaricoque, damasco *m.*

April /ˈeɪprəl/ *n.* abril *m.*

apron /ˈeɪprən/ *n.* delantal *m.*

apropos /ˌæprəˈpoʊ/ *adv.* a propósito.

apt /æpt/ *a.* apto; capaz.

aptitude /ˈæptɪˌtud/ *n.* aptitud; facilidad *f.*

aquarium /əˈkwɛəriəm/ *n.* acuario *m.,* pecera *f.*

aquatic /əˈkwætɪk/ *a.* acuático.

arrowhead

aqueduct /'ækwɪ,dʌkt/ n. acueducto m.

aqueous /'ækwiəs/ a. ácueo, acuoso, aguoso.

aquiline /'ækwə,laɪn/ a. aquilino, aguileño.

Arab /'ærəb/ a. & n. árabe m. & f.

arable /'ærəbəl/ a. cultivable.

arbitrary /'ɑrbɪ,treri/ a. arbitrario.

arbitrate /'ɑrbɪ,treɪt/ v. arbitrar.

arbitration /,ɑrbɪ'treɪʃən/ n. arbitraje m., arbitración f.

arbitrator /'ɑrbɪ,treɪtər/ n. arbitrador -ra.

arbor /'ɑrbər/ n. emparrado m.

arboreal /ɑr'bɔriəl/ a. arbóreo.

arc /ɑrk/ n. arco m.

arch /ɑrtʃ/ n. **1.** arco m. —v. **2.** arquear, encorvar.

archaeology /,ɑrki'ɒlədʒi/ n. arqueología f.

archaic /ɑr'keiɪk/ a. arcaico.

archbishop /'ɑrtʃ'bɪʃəp/ n. arzobispo m.

archdiocese /,ɑrtʃ'daiə,sis, -sis/ n. archidiócesis f.

archduke /'ɑrtʃ'duk/ n. archiduque m.

archer /'ɑrtʃər/ n. arquero m.

archery /'ɑrtʃəri/ n. ballestería f.

archipelago /,ɑrkə'pɛlə,gou/ n. archipiélago m.

architect /'ɑrkɪ,tɛkt/ n. arquitecto -ta.

architectural /,ɑrkɪ'tɛktʃərəl/ a. arquitectural.

architecture /'ɑrkɪ,tɛktʃər/ n. arquitectura f.

archive /'ɑrkaiv/ n. archivo m.

archway /'ɑrtʃ,wei/ n. arcada f.

arctic /'ɑrktɪk, 'ɑrtɪk/ a. ártico.

ardent /'ɑrdn̩t/ a. ardiente.

ardor /'ɑrdər/ n. ardor m., pasión f.

arduous /'ɑrdʒuəs/ a. arduo, difícil.

area /'ɛəriə/ n. área; extensión f.

area code prefijo m.

arena /ə'rinə/ n. arena f.

Argentine /'ɑrdʒəntɪn, -,tain/ a. & n. argentino -na.

argue /'ɑrgyu/ v. disputar; sostener.

argument /'ɑrgyəmənt/ n. disputa f.; razonamiento m.

argumentative /,ɑrgyə'mɛntətɪv/ a. argumentoso.

aria /'ɑriə/ n. aria f.

arid /'ærɪd/ a. árido, seco.

arise /ə'raiz/ v. surgir; alzarse.

aristocracy /,ærə'stɒkrəsi/ n. aristocracia f.

aristocrat /ə'rɪstə,kræt/ n. aristócrata m.

aristocratic /ə,rɪstə'krætɪk/ a. aristocrático.

arithmetic /ə'rɪθmətɪk/ n. aritmética f.

ark /ɑrk/ n. arca f.

arm /ɑrm/ n. **1.** brazo m.; (weapon) arma f. —v. **2.** armar.

armament /'ɑrməmənt/ n. armamento m.

armchair /'ɑrm,tʃɛər/ n. sillón m., butaca f.

armed forces /'ɑrmd 'fɔrsɪz/ fuerzas militares.

armful /'ɑrm,fʊl/ n. brazada f.

armhole /'ɑrm,houl/ n. (sew.) sobaquera f.

armistice /'ɑrməstɪs/ n. armisticio m.

armor /'ɑrmər/ n. armadura f., blindaje m.

armored /'ɑrmərd/ a. blindado.

armory /'ɑrməri/ n. armería f., arsenal m.

armpit /'ɑrm,pɪt/ n. axila f., sobaco m.

army /'ɑrmi/ n. ejército m.

arnica /'ɑrnɪkə/ n. árnica f.

aroma /ə'roumə/ n. fragancia f.

aromatic /,ærə'mætɪk/ a. aromático.

around /ə'raund/ prep. alrededor de, a la vuelta de; cerca de. **a. here,** por aquí.

arouse /ə'rauz/ v. despertar; excitar.

arraign /ə'rein/ v. Leg. procesar criminalmente.

arrange /ə'reindʒ/ v. arreglar; concertar; Mus. adaptar.

arrangement /ə'reindʒmənt/ n. arreglo; orden m.

array /ə'rei/ n. **1.** orden; adorno m. —v. **2.** adornar.

arrears /ə'riərz/ n. atrasos m.pl.

arrest /ə'rɛst/ n. **1.** detención f. —v. **2.** detener, arrestar.

arrival /ə'raivəl/ n. llegada f.

arrive /ə'raiv/ v. llegar.

arrogance /'ærəgəns/ n. arrogancia f.

arrogant /'ærəgənt/ a. arrogante.

arrogate /'ærə,geit/ v. arrogarse, usurpar.

arrow /'ærou/ n. flecha f.

arrowhead /'ærou,hɛd/ n. punta de flecha f.

arsenal /'ɑrsənḷ/ *n.* arsenal *m.*
arsenic /'ɑrsənɪk/ *n.* arsénico *m.*
arson /'ɑrsən/ *n.* incendio premeditado.
art /ɑrt/ arte *m.* (*f.* in *pl.*); (skill) maña *f.*
arterial /ɑr'tɪəriəl/ *a.* arterial.
arteriosclerosis /ɑr,tɪəriousklə-'rousɪs/ *n.* arteriosclerosis *f.*
artery /'ɑrtəri/ *n.* arteria *f.*
artesian well /ɑr'tiʒən/ pozo artesiano.
artful /'ɑrtfəl/ *a.* astuto.
arthritis /ɑr'θraitɪs/ *n.* artritis *f.*
artichoke /'ɑrtɪ,tʃouk/ *n.* alcachofa *f.*
article /'ɑrtɪkəl/ *n.* artículo *m.*
articulate /ɑr'tɪkyə,leit/ *v.* articular.
articulation /ɑr,tɪkyə'leiʃən/ *n.* articulación *f.*
artifice /'ɑrtəfɪs/ *n.* artificio *m.*
artificial /,ɑrtə'fɪʃəl/ *a.* artificial.
artificially /,ɑrtə'fɪʃəli/ *adv.* artificialmente.
artillery /ɑr'tɪləri/ *n.* artillería *f.*
artisan /'ɑrtəzən/ *n.* artesano -na.
artist /'ɑrtɪst/ *n.* artista *m.* & *f.*
artistic /ɑr'tɪstɪk/ *a.* artístico.
artistry /'ɑrtɪstri/ *n.* arte *m.* & *f.*
artless /'ɑrtlɪs/ *a.* natural, cándido.
as /æz/ *adv.* & *conj.* como; **as... as** tan... como.
asbestos /æs'bɛstəs/ *n.* asbesto *m.*
ascend /ə'sɛnd/ *v.* ascender.
ascendancy /ə'sɛndənsi/ *n.* ascendiente *m.*
ascendant /ə'sɛndənt/ *a.* ascendente.
ascent /ə'sɛnt/ *n.* subida *f.*, ascenso *m.*
ascertain /,æsər'tein/ *v.* averiguar.
ascetic /ə'sɛtɪk/ *a.* **1.** ascético. —*n.* **2.** asceta *m.* & *f.*
ascribe /ə'skraib/ *v.* atribuir.
ash /æʃ/ *n.* ceniza *f.*
ashamed /ə'ʃeimd/ *a.* avergonzado.
ashen /'æʃən/ *a.* pálido.
ashore /ə'ʃɔr/ *adv.* a tierra. **go a.,** desembarcar.
ashtray /'æʃ,trei/ *n.* cenicero *m.*
Ash Wednesday miércoles de ceniza *m.*
Asiatic /,eiʒi'ætɪk/ *a.* & *n.* asiático -ca.
aside /ə'said/ *adv.* al lado. **a. from.** aparte de.

ask /æsk/ *v.* preguntar; invitar; (request) pedir. **a. for,** pedir. **a. a question,** hacer una pregunta.
askance /ə'skæns/ *adv.* de soslayo; con recelo.
asleep /ə'slip/ *a.* dormido. **to fall a.,** dormirse.
asparagus /ə'spærəgəs/ *n.* espárrago *m.*
aspect /'æspɛkt/ *n.* aspecto *m.,* apariencia *f.*
asperity /ə'spɛrɪti/ *n.* aspereza *f.*
aspersion /ə'spɜrʒən/ *n.* calumnia *f.*
asphalt /'æsfɔlt/ *n.* asfalto *m.*
asphyxia /æs'fɪksiə/ *n.* asfixia *f.*
asphyxiate /æs'fɪksi,eit/ *v.* asfixiar, sofocar.
aspirant /'æspərənt/ *a.* & *n.* aspirante *m.* & *f.*
aspirate /'æspə,reit/ *v.* aspirar.
aspiration /,æspə'reiʃən/ *n.* aspiración *f.*
aspirator /'æspə,reitər/ *n.* aspirador *m.*
aspire /ə'spaiᵊr/ *v.* aspirar. **a. to,** ambicionar.
aspirin /'æspərɪn/ *n.* aspirina *f.*
ass /æs/ *n.* asno, burro *m.*
assail /ə'seil/ *v.* asaltar, acometer.
assailant /ə'seilənt/ *n.* asaltador -ra.
assassin /ə'sæsɪn/ *n.* asesino -na.
assassinate /ə'sæsə,neit/ *v.* asesinar.
assassination /ə,sæsə'neiʃən/ *n.* asesinato *m.*
assault /ə'sɔlt/ *n.* **1.** asalto *m.* —*v.* **2.** asaltar, atacar.
assay /'æsei/ *v.* examinar; ensayar.
assemblage /ə'sɛmblɪdʒ/ *n.* asamblea *f.*
assemble /ə'sɛmbəl/ *v.* juntar, convocar; (mechanism) montar.
assembly /ə'sɛmbli/ *n.* asamblea, concurrencia *f.*
assent /ə'sɛnt/ *n.* **1.** asentimiento *m.* —*v.* **2.** asentir, convenir.
assert /ə'sɜrt/ *v.* afirmar, aseverar. **a. oneself,** hacerse sentir.
assertion /ə'sɜrʃən/ *n.* aserción, aseveración *f.*
assertive /ə'sɜrtɪv/ *a.* asertivo.
assess /ə'sɛs/ *v.* tasar, evaluar.
assessor /ə'sɛsər/ *n.* asesor -ra.
asset /'æsɛt/ *n.* ventaja *f.* **assets,** *Com.* capital *m.*
asseverate /ə'sɛvə,reit/ *v.* aseverar, afirmar.

asseveration /ə,sɛvə'reiʃən/ *n.* as-everacinewlin *f.*

assiduous /ə'sɪdʒuəs/ *a.* asiduo.

assiduously /ə'sɪdʒuəsli/ *adv.* asiduamente.

assign /ə'sain/ *v.* asignar; destinar.

assignable /ə'sainəbəl/ *a.* asignable, transferible.

assignation /,æsɪg'neiʃən/ *n.* asignación *f.*

assignment /ə'sainmənt/ *n.* misión; tarea *f.*

assimilate /ə'sɪmə,leit/ *v.* asimilar.

assimilation /ə,sɪmə'leiʃən/ *n.* asimilación *f.*

assimilative /ə'sɪmələtɪv/ *a.* asimilativo.

assist /ə'sɪst/ *v.* ayudar, auxiliar.

assistance /ə'sɪstəns/ *n.* ayuda *f.*, auxilio *m.*

assistant /ə'sɪstənt/ *n.* ayudante -ta, asistente -ta.

associate /*n* ə'sousiɪt; *v* -si,eit/ *n.* **1.** socio -cia. —*v.* **2.** asociar.

association /ə,sousi'eiʃən/ *n.* asociación; sociedad *f.*

assonance /'æsənəns/ *n.* asonancia *f.*

assort /ə'sɔrt/ *v.* surtir con variedad.

assorted /ə'sɔrtɪd/ *a.* variado, surtido.

assortment /ə'sɔrtmənt/ *n.* surtido *m.*

assuage /ə'sweidʒ/ *v.* mitigar, aliviar.

assume /ə'sum/ *v.* suponer; asumir.

assuming /ə'sumɪŋ/ *a.* presuntuoso. **a. that,** dado que.

assumption /ə'sʌmpʃən/ *n.* suposición; *Relig.* asunción *f.*

assurance /ə'ʃurəns/ *n.* seguridad; confianza *f.*; garantía *f.*

assure /ə'ʃur/ *v.* asegurar; dar confianza.

assured /ə'ʃurd/ *a.* **1.** seguro. —*a. & n.* **2.** *Com.* asegurado -da.

assuredly /ə'ʃurɪdli/ *adv.* ciertamente.

aster /'æstər/ *n.* aster *f.*

asterisk /'æstərɪsk/ *n.* asterisco *m.*

astern /ə'stɜrn/ *adv. Naut.* a popa.

asteroid /'æstə,rɔid/ *n.* asteroide *m.*

asthma /'æzmə/ *n. Med.* asma *f.*

astigmatism /ə'stɪgmə,tɪzəm/ *n.* astigmatismo *m.*

astir /ə'stɜr/ *adv.* en movimiento.

astonish /ə'stɒnɪʃ/ *v.* asombrar, pasmar.

astonishment /ə'stɒnɪʃmənt/ *n.* asombro *m.*, sorpresa *f.*

astound /ə'staund/ *v.* pasmar, sorprender.

astral /'æstrəl/ *a.* astral, estelar.

astray /ə'strei/ *a.* desviado.

astride /ə'straid/ *adv.* a horcajadas.

astringent /ə'strɪndʒənt/ *a. & n.* astringente *m.*

astrology /ə'strɒlədʒi/ *n.* astrología *f.*

astronaut /'æstrə,nɔt/ *n.* astronauta *m. & f.*

astronomy /ə'strɒnəmi/ *n.* astronomía *f.*

astute /ə'stut/ *a.* astuto; agudo.

asunder /ə'sʌndər/ *adv.* en dos.

asylum /ə'sailəm/ *n.* asilo, refugio *m.*

asymmetry /ei'sɪmɪtri/ *n.* asimetría *f.*

at /æt/ *prep.* a, en; cerca de.

ataxia /ə'tæksiə/ *n. Med.* ataxia *f.*

atheist /'eiθiɪst/ *n.* ateo -tea.

athlete /'æθlit/ *n.* atleta *m. & f.*

athletic /æθ'lɛtɪk/ *a.* atlético.

athletics /æθ'lɛtɪks/ *n.* atletismo *m.*, deportes *m.pl.*

athwart /ə'θwɔrt/ *prep.* a través de.

Atlantic /æt'læntɪk/ *a.* **1.** atlántico. —*n.* **2.** Atlántico *m.*

Atlantic Ocean Océano Atlántico *m.*

atlas /'ætləs/ *n.* atlas *m.*

atmosphere /'ætməs,fɪər/ *n.* atmósfera *f.*; *Fig.* ambiente *m.*

atmospheric /,ætməs'fɛrɪk/ *a.* atmosférico.

atoll /'ætɔl/ *n.* atolón *m.*

atom /'ætəm/ *n.* átomo *m.*

atomic /ə'tɒmɪk/ *a.* atómico.

atomic bomb bomba atómica *f.*

atomic energy energía atómica, energía nuclear *f.*

atomic theory teoría atómica. *f.*

atomic weight peso atómico *m.*

atonal /ei'tounl/ *a. Mus.* atonal.

atone /ə'toun/ *v.* expiar, compensar.

atonement /ə'tounmənt/ *n.* expiación; reparación *f.*

atrocious /ə'trouʃəs/ *a.* atroz.

atrocity /ə'trɒsiti/ *n.* atrocidad *f.*

atrophy /'ætrəfi/ *n.* **1.** *Med.* atrofia *f.* —*v.* **2.** atrofiar.

atropine /'ætrə,pin, -pɪn/ *n.* atropina *f.*

attach /ə'tætʃ/ *v.* juntar; prender; (hook) enganchar; *Fig.* atribuir.

attaché /ætæ'ʃei/ *n.* agregado -da.

attachment /ə'tætʃmənt/ enlace *m.;* accesorio *m.;* (emotional) afecto, cariño *m.*

attack /ə'tæk/ *n.* **1.** ataque *m.* —*v.* **2.** atacar.

attacker /ə'tækər/ *n.* asaltador -ra.

attain /ə'tein/ *v.* lograr, alcanzar.

attainable /ə'teinəbəl/ *a.* accesible, realizable.

attainment /ə'teinmənt/ *n.* logro; *(pl.)* dotes *f.pl.*

attempt /ə'tɛmpt/ *n.* **1.** ensayo; esfuerzo *m.;* tentativa *f.* —*v.* **2.** ensayar, intentar.

attend /ə'tɛnd/ *v.* atender; (a meeting) asistir a.

attendance /ə'tɛndəns/ *n.* asistencia; presencia *f.*

attendant /ə'tɛndənt/ *a.* **1.** concomitante. —*n.* **2.** servidor -ra.

attention /ə'tɛnʃən/ *n.* atención *f.;* obsequio *m.* **to pay a. to,** hacer caso a.

attentive /ə'tɛntɪv/ *a.* atento.

attentively /ə'tɛntɪvli/ *adv.* atentamente.

attenuate /ə'tɛnyu,eit/ *v.* atenuar, adelgazar.

attest /ə'tɛst/ *v.* confirmar, atestiguar.

attic /'ætɪk/ *n.* desván *m.,* guardilla *f.*

attire /ə'taiᵊr/ *n.* **1.** traje *m.* —*v.* **2.** vestir.

attitude /'ætɪ,tud/ *n.* actitud *f.,* ademán *m.*

attorney /ə'tɜrni/ *n.* abogado -da, apoderado -da.

attract /ə'trækt/ *v.* atraer. **a. attention,** llamar la atención.

attraction /ə'trækʃən/ *n.* atracción *f.,* atractivo *m.*

attractive /ə'træktɪv/ *a.* atractivo; simpático.

attributable /ə'trɪbyʊtəbəl/ *a.* atribuible, imputable.

attribute /*n* 'ætrə,byut; *v* ə'trɪbyut/ *n.* **1.** atributo *m.* —*v.* **2.** atribuir.

attrition /ə'trɪʃən/ *n.* roce, desgaste *m.;* atrición *f.*

attune /ə'tun/ *v.* armonizar.

auction /'ɔkʃən/ *n.* subasta *f.,* *S.A.* venduta *f.*

auctioneer /,ɔkʃə'nɪər/ *n.* subastador -ra, *S.A.* martillero -ra.

audacious /ɔ'deiʃəs/ *a.* audaz.

audacity /ɔ'dæsɪti/ *n.* audacia *f.*

audible /'ɔdəbəl/ *a.* audible.

audience /'ɔdiəns/ *n.* auditorio, público *m.;* entrevista *f.*

audiovisual /,ɔdiou'vɪʒuəl/ *a.* audiovisual.

audit /'ɔdɪt/ *n.* **1.** revisión de cuentas *f.* —*v.* **2.** revisar cuentas.

audition /ɔ'dɪʃən/ *n.* audición *f.*

auditor /'ɔdɪtər/ *n.* interventor -ora, revisor -ora.

auditorium /,ɔdɪ'tɔriəm/ *n.* sala *f.;* teatro *m.*

auditory /'ɔdɪ,tɔri/ *a. & n.* auditorio *m.*

augment /ɔg'mɛnt/ *v.* aumentar.

augur /'ɔgər/ *v.* augurar, pronosticar.

August /'ɔgəst/ *n.* agosto *m.*

aunt /ænt, ɑnt/ *n.* tía *f.*

auspice /'ɔspɪs/ *n.* auspicio *m.*

auspicious /ɔ'spɪʃəs/ *a.* favorable; propicio.

austere /ɔ'stɪər/ *a.* austero.

austerity /ɔ'stɛrɪti/ *n.* austeridad, severidad *f.*

Austrian /'ɔstriən/ *a. & n.* austríaco -ca.

authentic /ɔ'θɛntɪk/ *a.* auténtico.

authenticate /ɔ'θɛntɪ,keit/ *v.* autenticar.

authenticity /,ɔθɛn'tɪsɪti/ *n.* autenticidad *f.*

author /'ɔθər/ *n.* autor -ra, escritor -ra.

authoritarian /ə,θɔrɪ'tɛəriən/ *a. & n.* autoritario -ria.

authoritative /ə'θɔrɪ,teitɪv/ *a.* autoritativo; autorizado.

authoritatively /ə'θɔrɪ,teitɪvli/ *adv.* autoritativamente.

authority /ə'θɔrɪti/ *n.* autoridad *f.*

authorization /,ɔθərə'zeiʃən/ *n.* autorización *f.*

authorize /'ɔθə,raiz/ *v.* autorizar.

auto /'ɔtou/ *n.* auto, automóvil *m.*

autobiography /,ɔtəbai'ɒgrəfi/ *n.* autobiografía *f.*

autocracy /ɔ'tɒkrəsi/ *n.* autocracia *f.*

autocrat /'ɔtə,kræt/ *n.* autócrata *m. & f.*

autograph /'ɔtə,græf/ *n.* autógrafo *m.*

automatic /,ɔtə'mætɪk/ *a.* automático.

automatically /ˌɔtəˈmætɪkəli/ *adv.* automáticamente.
automobile /ˌɔtəməˈbil/ *n.* automóvil, coche *m.*
automotive /ˌɔtəˈmoutɪv/ *a.* automotriz.
autonomy /ɔˈtɒnəmi/ *n.* autonomía *f.*
autopsy /ˈɔtɒpsi/ *n.* autopsia *f.*
autumn /ˈɔtəm/ *n.* otoño *m.*
auxiliary /ɔgˈzɪlyəri/ *a.* auxiliar.
avail /əˈveil/ *n.* **1. of no a.,** en vano. —*v.* **2. a. oneself of,** aprovecharse.
available /əˈveiləbəl/ *a.* disponible.
avalanche /ˈævəˌlæntʃ/ *n.* alud *m.*
avarice /ˈævərɪs/ *n.* avaricia, codicia *f.*
avariciously /ˌævəˈrɪʃəsli/ *adv.* avaramente.
avenge /əˈvɛndʒ/ *v.* vengar.
avenger /əˈvɛndʒər/ *n.* vengador -ra.
avenue /ˈævəˌnu/ *n.* avenida *f.*
average /ˈævərɪdʒ/ *a.* **1.** medio; común. —*n.* **2.** promedio, término medio *m.* —*v.* **3.** calcular el promedio.
averse /əˈvɜrs/ *a.* **to be a. to,** tener antipatía a, opuesto a.
aversion /əˈvɜrʒən/ *n.* aversión *f.*
avert /əˈvɜrt/ *v.* desviar; impedir.
aviary /ˈeiviˌɛri/ *n.* pajarera, avería *f.*
aviation /ˌeiviˈeiʃən/ *n.* aviación *f.*
aviator /ˈeiviˌeitər/ *n.* aviador -ra.
aviatrix /ˌeiviˈeitrɪks/ *n.* aviatriz *f.*
avid /ˈævɪd/ *a.* ávido.
avocado /ˌævəˈkɑdou, ˌɑvə-/ *n.* aguacate *m.*
avocation /ˌævəˈkeiʃən/ *n.* pasatiempo *f.*

avoid /əˈvɔid/ *v.* evitar.
avoidable /əˈvɔidəbəl/ *a.* evitable.
avoidance /əˈvɔidn̩s/ *n.* evitación *f.; Leg.* anulación *f.*
avow /əˈvau/ *v.* declarar; admitir.
avowal /əˈvauəl/ *n.* admisión *f.*
avowed /əˈvaud/ *a.* reconocido; admitido.
avowedly /əˈvauɪdli/ *adv.* reconocidamente; confesadamente.
await /əˈweit/ *v.* esperar, aguardar.
awake /əˈweik/ *a.* despierto.
awaken /əˈweikən/ *v.* despertar.
award /əˈwɔrd/ *n.* **1.** premio *m.* —*v.* **2.** otorgar.
aware /əˈwɛər/ *a.* enterado, consciente.
awash /əˈwɒʃ/ *a. & adv. Naut.* a flor de agua.
away /əˈwei/ *adv.* (see under verb: **go away, put away, take away,** etc.)
awe /ɔ/ *n.* pavor *m.*
awesome /ˈɔsəm/ *a.* pavoroso; aterrador.
awful /ˈɔfəl/ *a.* horrible, terrible, muy malo, pésimo.
awhile /əˈwail/ *adv.* por un rato.
awkward /ˈɔkwərd/ *a.* torpe, desmañado; *Fig.* delicado, embarazoso.
awning /ˈɔnɪŋ/ *n.* toldo *m.*
awry /əˈrai/ *a.* oblicuo, torcido.
ax /æks/ *n.* hacha *f.*
axiom /ˈæksiəm/ *n.* axioma *m.*
axis /ˈæksɪs/ *n.* eje *m.*
axle /ˈæksəl/ *n.* eje *m.*
ayatollah /ˌɑyəˈtoulə/ *n.* ayatolá *m.*
azure /ˈæʒər/ *a.* azul.

B

babble /ˈbæbəl/ *n.* **1.** balbuceo, murmullo *m.* —*v.* **2.** balbucear.
babbler /ˈbæblər/ *n.* hablador -ra, charlador -ra.
baboon /bæˈbun/ *n.* mandril *m.*
baby /ˈbeibi/ *n.* nene, bebé *m.*
baby carriage cochecito de niño *m.*
babyish /ˈbeibiɪʃ/ *a.* infantil.
baby squid /skwɪd/ chipirón *m.*
bachelor /ˈbætʃələr/ *n.* soltero *m.*
bacillus /bəˈsɪləs/ *n.* bacilo, microbio *m.*
back /bæk/ *adv.* **1.** atrás. **to be**

b., estar de vuelta. **b. of,** detrás de. —*n.* **2.** espalda *f.;* (of animal) lomo *m.*
backache /ˈbækˌeik/ *n.* dolor de espalda *m.*
backbone /ˈbækˌboun/ *n.* espinazo *m.; Fig.* firmeza *f.*
backer /ˈbækər/ *n.* sostenedor -ra.
background /ˈbækˌgraund/ *n.* fondo *m.* antecedentes *m.pl.*
backing /ˈbækɪŋ/ *n.* apoyo *m.*, garantía *f.*
backlash /ˈbækˌlæʃ/ *n.* repercusión negativa.

backlog /'bæk,lɔg/ n. atrasos m.pl.

backpack /'bæk,pæk/ n. mochila f.

back seat asiento trasero m.

backstage /'bæk'steidʒ/ n. entre bastidores m.

backup /'bæk,ʌp/ n. copia de seguridad f.

backward /'bækwərd/ a. 1. atrasado. —adv. 2. hacia atrás.

backwardness /'bækwərdnɪs/ n. atraso m.

backwater /'bæk,wɔtər/ n. parte de río estancada f.

backwoods /'bæk'wʊdz/ n. región del monte apartada f.

bacon /'beikən/ n. tocino m.

bacteria /bæk'tɪəriə/ n. bacterias f.pl.

bacteriologist /ˌbæktɪəri'ɒlədʒɪst/ n. bacteriólogo -a.

bacteriology /ˌbæktɪəri'ɒlədʒi/ n. bacteriología f.

bad /bæd/ a. malo.

badge /bædʒ/ n. insignia, divisa f.

badger /'bædʒər/ n. 1. tejón m. —v. 2. atormentar.

badly /'bædli/ adv. mal.

badness /'bædnɪs/ n. maldad f.

bad-tempered /'bæd'tɛmpərd/ a. de mal humor.

baffle /'bæfəl/ v. desconcertar.

bafflement /'bæfəlmənt/ n. contrariedad; confusión f.

bag /bæg/ n. 1. saco m.; bolsa f. —v. 2. ensacar, cazar.

baggage /'bægɪdʒ/ n. equipaje m. **b. check,** talón m.

baggage cart (airport) carrillo para llevar equipaje.

baggy /'bægi/ a. abotagado; bolsudo; hinchado.

bagpipe /'bæg,paip/ n. gaita f.

bail /beil/ n. 1. fianza f. —v. 2. desaguar.

bailiff /'beilɪf/ n. alguacil m.

bait /beit/ n. 1. cebo m. —v. 2. cebar.

bake /beik/ v. cocer en horno.

baked potato /beikt/ patata asada f.

baker /'beikər/ n. panadero -ra, hornero -ra.

bakery /'beikəri, 'beikri/ n. panadería f.

baking /'beikɪŋ/ n. hornada f. **b. powder,** levadura f.

balance /'bæləns/ n. balanza f.; equilibrio m.; Com. saldo m.

balcony /'bælkəni/ n. balcón m.; Theat. galería f.

bald /bɔld/ a. calvo.

baldness /'bɔldnɪs/ n. calvicie f.

bale /beil/ n. 1. bala f. —v. 2. embalar.

balk /bɔk/ v. frustrar; rebelarse.

Balkans /'bɔlkənz/ n.pl. Balcanes m.pl.

balky /'bɔki/ a. rebelón.

ball /bɔl/ n. bola, pelota f.; (dance) baile m.

ballad /'bæləd/ n. romance, m.; balada f.

ballast /'bæləst/ n. 1. lastre m. —v. 2. lastrar.

ball bearing cojinete de bolas m.

ballerina /ˌbælə'rinə/ n. bailarina f.

ballet /bæ'lei/ n. danza f.; ballet m.

ballistics /bə'lɪstɪks/ n. balística f.

balloon /bə'lun/ n. globo m. **b. tire,** neumático de balón.

ballot /'bælət/ n. 1. balota f., voto m. —v. 2. balotar, votar.

ballpoint pen /'bɔl,pɔint/ bolígrafo m.

ballroom /'bɔl,rum/ n. salón de baile m.

balm /bɑm/ n. bálsamo; ungüento m.

balmy /'bɑmi/ a. fragante; reparador; calmante.

balsa /'bɔlsə/ n. balsa f.

balsam /'bɔlsəm/ n. bálsamo m.

balustrade /'bælə,streid/ n. barandilla f.

bamboo /bæm'bu/ n. bambú m., caña f.

ban /bɑn/ n. 1. prohibición f. —v. 2. prohibir; proscribir.

banal /bə'næl/ a. trivial; vulgar.

banana /bə'nænə/ n. banana f., cambur m. **b. tree,** banano, plátano m.

band /bænd/ n. 1. banda f.; (of men) banda, cuadrilla, partida f. —v. 2. asociarse.

bandage /'bændɪdʒ/ n. 1. vendaje m. —v. 2. vendar.

bandanna /bæn'dænə/ n. pañuelo (grande) m.; bandana f.

bandbox /'bænd,bɒks/ n. caja de cartón.

bandit /'bændɪt/ n. bandido -da.

bandmaster /'bænd,mæstər/ n. director de una banda musical m.

bandstand /'bænd,stænd/ n. kiosco de música.

bang /bæŋ/ *interj.* **1.** ¡pum! —*n.*
2. ruido de un golpe. —*v.* **3.** golpear ruidosamente.

banish /'bænɪʃ/ *v.* desterrar.

banishment /'bænɪʃmənt/ *n.* destierro *m.*

banister /'bænəstər/ *n.* pasamanos *m.pl.*

bank /bæŋk/ *n.* **1.** banco *m.*; (of a river) margen *f.* —*v.* **2.** depositar.

bank account cuenta bancaria *f.*

bankbook /'bæŋk,bʊk/ *n.* libreta de depósitos *f.*

bank card tarjeta bancaria *f.*

banker /'bæŋkər/ *n.* banquero -ra.

banking /'bæŋkɪŋ/ *a.* bancaria. *n.* banca *f.*

bank note billete de banco *m.*

bankrupt /'bæŋkrʌpt/ *a.* insolvente.

bankruptcy /'bæŋkrʌptsi/ *n.* bancarrota *f.*

banner /'bænər/ *n.* bandera *f.*; estandarte *m.*

banquet /'bæŋkwɪt/ *n.* banquete *m.*

banter /'bæntər/ *n.* **1.** choteo *m.*; zumba; burla *f.* —*v.* **2.** chotear; zumbar; burlarse.

baptism /'bæptɪzəm/ *n.* bautismo, bautizo *m.*

baptismal /bæp'tɪzməl/ *a.* bautismal.

Baptist /'bæptɪst/ *n.* bautista *m.* & *f.*

baptize /bæp'taiz, 'bæptaiz/ *v.* bautizar.

bar /bar/ *n.* **1.** barra *f.*; obstáculo *m.*; (tavern) taberna *f.*, bar *m.* —*v.* **2.** barrear; prohibir, excluir.

barbarian /bar'bɛəriən/ *a.* bárbaro. *n.* bárbaro -ra.

barbarism /'barbə,rɪzəm/ *n.* barbarismo *m.*, barbarie *f.*

barbarous /'barbərəs/ *a.* bárbaro, cruel.

barbecue /'barbɪ,kyu/ *n.* animal asado entero; (Mex.) barbacoa *f.*

barber /'barbər/ *n.* barbero *m.* **b. shop,** barbería *f.*

barbiturate /bar'bɪtʃərɪt/ *n.* barbitúrico *m.*

bar code código de barras *m.*

bare /bɛər/ *a.* **1.** desnudo; descubierto. —*v.* **2.** desnudar; descubrir.

bareback /'bɛər,bæk/ *adv.* sin silla.

barefoot(ed) /'bɛər,fʊtɪd/ *a.* descalzo.

barely /'bɛərli/ *adv.* escasamente, apenas.

bareness /'bɛərnɪs/ *n.* desnudez *f.*; pobreza *f.*

bargain /'bargən/ *n.* **1.** ganga *f.*, compra ventajosa *f.*; contrato *m.* —*v.* **2.** regatear; negociar.

barge /bardʒ/ *n.* lanchón *m.*, barcaza *f.*

baritone /'bærɪ,toun/ *n.* barítono *m.*

barium /'bɛəriəm/ *n.* bario *m.*

bark /bark/ *n.* **1.** corteza *f.*; (of dog) ladrido *f.* —*v.* **2.** ladrar.

barley /'barli/ *n.* cebada *f.*

barn /barn/ *n.* granero *m.*

barnacle /'barnəkəl/ *n.* lapa *f.*

barnyard /'barn,yard/ *n.* corral *m.*

barometer /bə'rɒmɪtər/ *n.* barómetro *m.*

barometric /,bærə'mɛtrɪk/ *a.* barométrico.

baron /'bærən/ *n.* barón *m.*

baroness /'bærənɪs/ *n.* baronesa *f.*

baronial /bə'rouniəl/ *a.* baronial.

baroque /bə'rouk/ *a.* barroco.

barracks /'bærəks/ *n.* cuartel *m.*

barrage /bə'raʒ/ *n.* cortina de fuego *f.*

barred /bard/ *a.* excluído; prohibido.

barrel /'bærəl/ *n.* barril *m.*; (of gun) cañón *m.*

barren /'bærən/ *a.* estéril.

barrenness /'bærən,nɪs/ *n.* esterilidad *f.*

barricade /'bærɪ,keid/ *n.* barricada, barrera *f.*

barrier /'bæriər/ *n.* barrera *f.*; obstáculo *m.*

barroom /'bar,rum, -,rʊm/ *n.* cantina *f.*

bartender /'bar,tɛndər/ *n.* tabernero; cantinero *m.*

barter /'bartər/ *n.* **1.** cambio, trueque *m.* —*v.* **2.** cambiar, trocar.

base /beis/ *a.* **1.** bajo, vil. —*n.* **2.** base *f.* —*v.* **3.** basar.

baseball /'beis,bɔl/ *n.* béisbol *m.*

baseboard /'beis,bɔrd/ *n.* tabla de resguardo.

basement /'beismənt/ *n.* sótano *m.*

baseness /'beisnɪs/ *n.* bajeza, vileza *f.*

bashful /'bæʃfəl/ *a.* vergonzoso, tímido.

bashfully /'bæʃfəli/ *adv.* tímidamente; vergonzosamente.

bashfulness /'bæʃfəlnɪs/ n. vergüenza; timidez f.

basic /'beisɪk/ a. fundamental, bá-
sico.

basin /'beisən/ n. bacía f.; (of
river) cuenca f.

basis /'beisɪs/ n. base f.

bask /bæsk/ v. tomar el sol.

basket /'bæskɪt/ n. cesta, canasta
f.

bass /bæs; beis/ n. (fish) lobina f.;
Mus. bajo profundo m. **b. viol.**
violón m.

bassinet /ˌbæsə'nɛt/ n. bacinete
m.

bassoon /bæ'sun/ n. bajón m.

bastard /'bæstərd/ a. & n. bastardo -da; hijo -a natural.

baste /beist/ v. (sew) bastear;
(cooking) pringar.

bat /bæt/ n. **1.** (animal) murciélago m.; (baseball) bate m. —v.
2. batear.

batch /bætʃ/ n. cantidad de cosas.

bath /bæθ/ n. baño m.

bathe /beið/ v. bañar, bañarse.

bather /'beiðər/ n. bañista m. & f.

bathing resort /'beiðɪŋ/ balneario
m.

bathing suit /'beiðɪŋ/ traje de
baño.

bathrobe /'bæθˌroub/ n. bata de
baño f.

bathroom /'bæθˌrum, -ˌrʊm/ n.
cuarto de baño.

bathtub /'bæθˌtʌb/ n. bañera f.

baton /bə'tɒn/ n. bastón m.; Mus.
batuta f.

battalion /bə'tælyən/ n. batallón
m.

batter /'bætər/ n. **1.** (cooking) batido m.; (baseball) voleador m.
—v. **2.** batir; derribar.

battery /'bætəri/ n. batería f.; Elec.
pila f.

batting /'bætɪŋ/ n. agramaje,
moldeaje m.

battle /'bætl/ n. **1.** batalla f.; combate m. —v. **2.** batallar.

battlefield /'bætlˌfild/ n. campo
de batalla.

battleship /'bætlˌʃɪp/ n. acorazado m.

bauxite /'bɔksait, 'bouzait/ n.
bauxita f.

bawl /bɔl/ v. gritar; vocear.

bay /bei/ n. bahía f. v. aullar.

bayonet /'beiənɛt/ n. bayoneta f.

bazaar /bə'zɑr/ n. bazar m., feria
f.

BC abbr. (**before Christ**) a.C.
(antes de Cristo).

be /bi/ v. ser; estar. (See **hacer;
hay; tener** in Sp.-Eng. section.)

beach /bitʃ/ n. playa f.

beachcomber /'bitʃˌkoumər/ n.
raquero -ra m. & f.

beacon /'bikən/ n. faro m.

bead /bid/ n. cuenta f.; pl. Relig.
rosario m.

beading /'bidɪŋ/ n. abalorio m.

beady /'bidi/ a. globuloso; burbu-
joso.

beak /bik/ n. pico m.

beaker /'bikər/ n. vaso con pico
m.

beam /bim/ n. viga f.; (of wood)
madero m.; (of light) rayo m.

beaming /'bimɪŋ/ a. radiante.

bean /bin/ n. haba, habichuela f.,
frijol m.

bear /bɛər/ n. **1.** oso -sa. —v. **2.**
llevar; (endure) aguantar.

bearable /'bɛərəbəl/ a. sufrible;
soportable.

beard /bɪərd/ n. barba f.

bearded /'bɪərdɪd/ a. barbado;
barbudo.

beardless /'bɪərdlɪs/ a. lampiño;
imberbe.

bearer /'bɛərər/ n. portador -ra.

bearing /'bɛərɪŋ/ n. porte,
aguante m.

bearskin /'bɛərˌskɪn/ n. piel de
oso f.

beast /bist/ n. bestia f.; bruto -ta.

beat /bit/ v. golpear; batir; pulsar;
(in games) ganar, vencer.

beaten /'bitn/ a. vencido; batido.

beatify /bi'ætəˌfai/ v. beatificar.

beating /'bitɪŋ/ n. paliza f.

beau /bou/ n. novio m.

beautiful /'byutəfəl/ a. hermoso,
bello.

beautifully /'byutəfəli/ adv. bellamente.

beautify /'byutəˌfai/ v. embellecer.

beauty /'byuti/ n. hermosura, belleza f. **b. parlor,** salón de belleza.

beaver /'bivər/ n. castor m.

becalm /bɪ'kɑm/ v. calmar; sose-
gar; encalmarse.

because /bɪ'kɔz/ conj. porque. **b.
of,** a causa de.

beckon /'bɛkən/ v. hacer señas.

become /bɪ'kʌm/ v. hacerse;
ponerse.

becoming /bɪ'kʌmɪŋ/ a. propio,

correcto; **be b.,** quedar bien, sentar bien.

bed /bɛd/ *n.* cama *f.;* lecho *m.;* (of river) cauce *m.*

bedbug /'bɛd,bʌg/ *n.* chinche *m.*

bedclothes /'bɛd,klouz, -,klouðz/ *n.* ropa de cama *f.*

bedding /'bɛdɪŋ/ *n.* colchones *m.pl.*

bedfellow /'bɛd,fɛlou/ *n.* compañero -ra de cama.

bedizen /bɪ'daizən, -'dɪzən/ *v.* adornar; aderezar.

bedridden /'bɛd,rɪdn̩/ *a.* postrado (en cama).

bedrock /'bɛd,rɒk/ *n.* (mining) lecho de roca *m.; Fig.* fundamento *m.*

bedroom /'bɛd,rum/ *n.* alcoba *f.;* (Mex.) recámara *f.*

bedside /'bɛd,said/ *n.* al lado de una cama *m.*

bedspread /'bɛd,sprɛd/ *n.* cubrecama, sobrecama *f.*

bedstead /'bɛd,stɛd/ *n.* armadura de cama *f.*

bedtime /'bɛd,taim/ *n.* hora de acostarse.

bee /bi/ *n.* abeja *f.*

beef /bif/ *n.* carne de vaca.

beefburger /'bif,bɜrgər/ *n.* hamburguesa *f.*

beefsteak /'bif,steik/ *n.* bistec, bisté *m.*

beehive /'bi,haiv/ *n.* colmena *f.*

beer /bɪər/ *n.* cerveza *f.*

beeswax /'biz,wæks/ *n.* cera de abejas.

beet /bit/ *n.* remolacha *f.;* (Mex.) betabel *m.*

beetle /'bitl̩/ *n.* escarabajo *m.*

befall /bɪ'fɔl/ *v.* suceder, sobrevenir.

befitting /bɪ'fɪtɪŋ/ *a.* conveniente; propio; digno.

before /bɪ'fɔr/ *adv.* antes. *prep.* antes de; (in front of) delante de. *conj.* antes que.

beforehand /bɪ'fɔr,hænd/ *adv.* de antemano.

befriend /bɪ'frɛnd/ *v.* amparar.

befuddle /bɪ'fʌdl̩/ *v.* confundir; aturdir.

beg /bɛg/ *v.* rogar, suplicar; (for alms) mendigar.

beget /bɪ'gɛt/ *v.* engendrar; producir.

beggar /'bɛgər/ *n.* mendigo -ga; *S.A.* limosnero -ra.

beggarly /'bɛgərli/ *a.* pobre, miserable.

begin /bɪ'gɪn/ *v.* empezar, comenzar, principiar.

beginner /bɪ'gɪnər/ *n.* principiante -ta.

beginning /bɪ'gɪnɪŋ/ *n.* principio, comienzo *m.*

begrudge /bɪ'grʌdʒ/ *v.* envidiar.

behalf /bɪ'hæf/ *n.:* **in, on b. of,** a favor de, en pro de.

behave /bɪ'heiv/ *v.* portarse, comportarse.

behavior /bɪ'heivyər/ *n.* conducta *f.;* comportamiento *m.*

behead /bɪ'hɛd/ *v.* decapitar.

behind /bɪ'haind/ *adv.* atrás, detrás. *prep.* detrás de.

behold /bɪ'hould/ *v.* contemplar.

beige /beiʒ/ *a.* beige.

being /'biɪŋ/ *n.* existencia *f.;* (person) ser *m.*

bejewel /bɪ'dʒuəl/ *v.* adornar con joyas.

belated /bɪ'leitɪd/ *a.* atrasado, tardío.

belch /bɛltʃ/ *n.* **1.** eructo *m.* —*v.* **2.** vomitar; eructar.

belfry /'bɛlfri/ *n.* campanario *m.*

Belgian /'bɛldʒən/ *a. & n.* belga *m. & f.*

Belgium /'bɛldʒəm/ *n.* Bélgica *f.*

belie /bɪ'lai/ *v.* desmentir.

belief /bɪ'lif/ *n.* creencia *f.;* parecer *m.*

believable /bɪ'livəbəl/ *a.* creíble.

believe /bɪ'liv/ *v.* creer.

believer /bɪ'livər/ *n.* creyente *m. & f.*

belittle /bɪ'lɪtl̩/ *v.* dar poca importancia *a.*

bell /bɛl/ *n.* campana *f.;* (of house) campanilla *f.;* (electric) timbre *m.*

bellboy /'bɛl,bɔi/ *n.* mozo, botones *m.*

bellicose /'bɛlɪ,kous/ *a.* guerrero.

belligerence /bə'lɪdʒərəns/ *n.* beligerancia *f.*

belligerent /bə'lɪdʒərənt/ *a. & n.* beligerante *m. & f.*

belligerently /bə'lɪdʒərəntli/ *adv.* belicosamente.

bellow /'bɛlou/ *v.* bramar, rugir.

bellows /'bɛlouz/ *n.* fuelle *m.*

belly /'bɛli/ *n.* vientre *m.;* panza, barriga *f.*

belong /bɪ'lɒŋ/ *v.* pertenecer.

belongings /bɪ'lɒŋɪŋz/ *n.* propiedad *f.*

beloved /bɪ'lʌvɪd/ a. querido, amado.

below /bɪ'lou/ adv. **1.** debajo, abajo. —prep. **2.** debajo de.

belt /bɛlt/ n. cinturón m.

bench /bɛntʃ/ n. banco m.

bend /bɛnd/ n. vuelta; curva f. v. encorvar, doblar.

beneath /bɪ'niθ/ adv. **1.** debajo, abajo. —prep. **2.** debajo de.

benediction /ˌbɛnɪ'dɪkʃən/ n. bendición f.

benefactor /'bɛnəˌfæktər/ n. bienhechor -ra.

benefactress /'bɛnəˌfæktrɪs/ n. bienhechora f.

beneficial /ˌbɛnə'fɪʃəl/ a. provechoso, beneficioso.

beneficiary /ˌbɛnə'fɪʃiˌɛri/ n. beneficiario -ria, beneficiado -da.

benefit /'bɛnəfɪt/ n. **1.** provecho, beneficio m. —v. **2.** beneficiar.

benevolence /bə'nɛvələns/ n. benevolencia f.

benevolent /bə'nɛvələnt/ a. benévolo.

benevolently /bə'nɛvələntli/ adv. benignamente.

benign /bɪ'nain; bɪ'nɪgnənt/ a. benigno.

benignity /bɪ'nɪgnɪti/ n. benignidad; bondad f.

bent /bɛnt/ a. **1.** encorvado. **b. on,** resuelto a. —n. **2.** inclinación f.

benzene /'bɛnzin, bɛn'zin/ n. benceno m.

bequeath /bɪ'kwið/ v. legar.

bequest /bɪ'kwɛst/ n. legado m.

berate /bɪ'reit/ v. reñir, regañar.

bereave /bɪ'riv/ v. despojar; desolar.

bereavement /bɪ'rivmənt/ n. privación f.; despojo m.; (mourning) luto m.

berry /'bɛri/ n. baya f.

berth /bɜrθ/ n. camarote m.; Naut. litera f.; (for vessel) amarradero m.

beseech /bɪ'sitʃ/ v. suplicar; implorar.

beseechingly /bɪ'sitʃɪŋli/ adv. suplicantemente.

beset /bɪ'sɛt/ v. acosar; rodear.

beside /bɪ'said/ prep. al lado de.

besides /bɪ'saidz/ adv. además, por otra parte.

besiege /bɪ'sidʒ/ v. sitiar; asediar.

besieged /bɪ'sidʒd/ a. sitiado.

besieger /bɪ'sidʒər/ n. sitiador -ra.

besmirch /bɪ'smɜrtʃ/ v. manchar; deshonrar.

best /bɛst/ a. & adv. mejor. **at b.,** a lo más.

bestial /'bɛstʃəl/ a. bestial; brutal.

bestir /bɪ'stɜr/ v. incitar; intrigar.

best man n. padrino de boda.

bestow /bɪ'stou/ v. conferir.

bestowal /bɪ'stouəl/ n. dádiva; presentación f.

bet /bɛt/ n. **1.** apuesta f. —v. **2.** apostar.

betoken /bɪ'toukən/ v. presagiar, anunciar.

betray /bɪ'trei/ v. traicionar; revelar.

betrayal /bɪ'treiəl/ n. traición f.

betroth /bɪ'trouð/ v. contraer esponsales; prometerse.

betrothal /bɪ'trouðəl/ n. esponsales m.pl.

better /'bɛtər/ a. & adv. **1.** mejor. —v. **2.** mejorar.

between /bɪ'twin/ prep. entre, en medio de.

bevel /'bɛvəl/ n. **1.** cartabón m. —v. **2.** cortar al sesgo.

beverage /'bɛvərɪdʒ/ n. bebida f.; (cold) refresco m.

bewail /bɪ'weil/ v. llorar; lamentar.

beware /bɪ'wɛər/ v. guardarse, precaverse.

bewilder /bɪ'wɪldər/ v. aturdir.

bewildered /bɪ'wɪldərd/ a. descarriado.

bewildering /bɪ'wɪldərɪŋ/ a. aturdente.

bewilderment /bɪ'wɪldərmənt/ n. aturdimiento m.; perplejidad f.

bewitch /bɪ'wɪtʃ/ v. hechizar; embrujar.

beyond /bi'ɒnd/ prep. más allá de.

biannual /bai'ænyuəl/ a. semianual; semestral.

bias /'baiəs/ n. **1.** parcialidad f.; prejuicio m. **on the b.,** al sesgo. —v. **2.** predisponer, influir.

bib /bɪb/ n. babador m.

Bible /'baibəl/ n. Biblia f.

Biblical /'bɪblɪkəl/ a. bíblico.

bibliography /ˌbɪbli'ɒgrəfi/ n. bibliografía f.

bicarbonate /bai'kɑrbənɪt/ n. bicarbonato m.

bicentennial /ˌbaisɛn'tɛniəl/ a. & n. bicentenario m.

biceps /'baisɛps/ n. bíceps m.

bicker /'bɪkər/ v. altercar.

bicycle /'baisɪkəl/ n. bicicleta f.
bicyclist /'baisɪklɪst/ n. biciclista m. & f.
bid /bɪd/ n. **1.** proposición, oferta f. —v. **2.** mandar; ofrecer.
bidder /'bɪdər/ n. postor -ra.
bide /baid/ v. aguardar; esperar.
bier /bɪər/ n. ataúd m.
bifocal /bai'foukəl/ a. bifocal.
big /bɪg/ a. grande.
bigamist /'bɪgəmɪst/ n. bígamo -ma.
bigamy /'bɪgəmi/ n. bigamia f.
bigot /'bɪgət/ n. persona intolerante.
bigotry /'bɪgətri/ n. intolerancia f.
bikini /bɪ'kini/ n. bikini m.
bilateral /bai'lætərəl/ a. bilateral.
bile /bail/ n. bilis f.
bilingual /bai'lɪŋgwəl/ a. bilingüe.
bilingualism /bai'lɪŋgwə,lɪzəm/ n. bilingüismo m.
bilious /'bɪlyəs/ a. bilioso.
bill /bɪl/ **1.** n. cuenta, factura f.; (money) billete m.; (of bird) pico m. —v. **2.** facturar.
billboard /'bɪl,bɔrd/ n. cartelera f.
billet /'bɪlɪt/ n. **1.** billete m.; Mil. boleta f. —v. **2.** aposentar.
billfold /'bɪl,fould/ n. cartera f.
billiard balls /'bɪlyərd bɔlz/ bolas de billar.
billiards /'bɪlyərdz/ n. billar m.
billion /'bɪlyən/ n. billón m.
bill of health n. certificado de sanidad.
bill of lading /'leidɪŋ/ n. conocimiento de embarque.
bill of sale n. escritura de venta.
billow /'bɪlou/ n. ola; oleada f.
bimetallic /,baimə'tælɪk/ a. bimetálico.
bimonthly /bai'mʌnθli/ a. & adv. bimestral.
bin /bɪn/ n. hucha f.; depósito m.
bind /baind/ v. atar; obligar; (book) encuadernar.
bindery /'baindəri/ n. taller de encuadernación m.
binding /'baindɪŋ/ n. encuadernación f.
bingo /'bɪŋgou/ n. bingo m.
binocular /bə'nɒkyələr/ a. binocular. n.pl. gemelos m.pl.
biochemistry /,baiou'kɛməstri/ n. bioquímica f.
biodegradable /,baioudɪ'greidəbəl/ a. biodegradable.
biofeedback /,baiou'fid,bæk/ n. biofeedback.

biographer /bai'ɒgrəfər/ n. biógrafo -fa.
biographical /,baiə'græfɪkəl/ a. biográfico.
biography /bai'ɒgrəfi/ n. biografía f.
biological /,baiə'lɒdʒɪkəl/ a. biológico.
biologically /,baiə'lɒdʒɪkəli/ adv. biológicamente.
biology /bai'ɒlədʒi/ n. biología f.
bipartisan /bai'pɑrtəzən/ a. bipartito.
biped /'baipɛd/ n. bípedo m.
bird /bɜrd/ n. pájaro m.; ave f.
birdie /'bɜrdi/ n. (golf) uno bajo par m.
bird of prey n. ave de rapiña f.
bird's-eye view /'bɜrdz,ai/ n. vista de pájaro f.
birth /bɜrθ/ n. nacimiento m. **give b. to,** dar a luz.
birth certificate partida de nacimiento f.
birth control n. contracepción f.
birthday /'bɜrθ,dei/ n. cumpleaños m.
birthmark /'bɜrθ,mɑrk/ n. marca de nacimiento f.
birthplace /'bɜrθ,pleis/ n. natalicio m.
birth rate n. natalidad f.
birthright /'bɜrθ,rait/ n. primogenitura f.
biscuit /'bɪskɪt/ n. bizcocho m.
bisect /bai'sɛkt/ v. bisecar.
bishop /'bɪʃəp/ n. obispo m.; (chess) alfil m.
bishopric /'bɪʃəprɪk/ n. obispado m.
bismuth /'bɪzməθ/ n. bismuto m.
bison /'baisən/ n. bisonte m.
bit /bɪt/ n. pedacito m.; Mech. taladro m.; (for horse) bocado m.; (computer) bit m.
bitch /bɪtʃ/ n. perra f.
bite /bait/ n. **1.** bocado m.; picada f. —v. **2.** morder; picar.
biting /'baitɪŋ/ a. penetrante; mordaz.
bitter /'bɪtər/ a. amargo.
bitterly /'bɪtərli/ adv. amargamente; agriamente.
bitterness /'bɪtərnɪs/ n. amargura f.; rencor m.
bivouac /'bɪvu,æk/ n. **1.** vivaque m. —v. **2.** vivaquear.
biweekly /bai'wikli/ a. quincenal.
black /blæk/ a. negro.

Black /blæk/ n. (person) negro -gra; persona de color.
blackberry /'blæk,bɛri/ n. mora f.
blackbird /'blæk,bɜrd/ n. mirlo m.
blackboard /'blæk,bɔrd/ n. pizarra f.
blacken /'blækən/ v. ennegrecer.
black eye n. ojo amoratado.
blackguard /'blægɑrd/ n. tunante; pillo m.
blacklist /'blæk,lɪst/ n. lista negra f.
blackmail /'blæk,meil/ n. 1. chantaje m. —v. 2. amenazar con chantaje, chantajear.
black market mercado negro, estraperlo m.
black marketeer /,mɑrkɪ'tir/ estraperlista mf.
blackout /'blæk,aut/ n. oscurecimiento, apagamiento m.
blacksmith /'blæk,smɪθ/ n. herrero -ra.
bladder /'blædər/ n. vejiga f.
blade /bleid/ n. (sword) hoja f.; (oar) pala f.; (grass) brizna f.
blame /bleim/ v. culpar, echar la culpa a.
blameless /'bleimlɪs/ a. inculpable.
blanch /blæntʃ/ v. blanquear; escaldar.
bland /blænd/ a. blando.
blank /blæŋk/ a. & n. en blanco.
blanket /'blæŋkɪt/ n. manta f.; cobertor m.
blare /blɛər/ n. sonido de trompeta. v. sonar como trompeta.
blaspheme /blæs'fim/ v. blasfemar.
blasphemer /blæs'fimər/ n. blasfemo -ma, blasfemador -ra.
blasphemous /'blæsfəməs/ a. blasfemo, impío.
blasphemy /'blæsfəmi/ n. blasfemia f.
blast /blæst/ n. 1. barreno m.; (wind) ráfaga f. —v. 2. barrenar.
blatant /'bleitnt/ a. bramante; descarado.
blaze /bleiz/ n. 1. llama, hoguera f. —v. 2. encenderse en llama.
blazing /'bleizɪŋ/ a. flameante.
bleach /blitʃ/ n. 1. lejía, blanqueador. —v. 2. blanquear.
bleachers /'blitʃərz/ n. asientos al aire libre.
bleak /blik/ a. frío y sombrío.
bleakness /'bliknɪs/ n. desolación f.

bleed /blid/ v. sangrar.
blemish /'blɛmɪʃ/ n. 1. mancha f.; lunar m. —v. 2. manchar.
blend /blɛnd/ n. 1. mezcla f. —v. 2. mezclar, combinar.
blended /'blɛndɪd/ a. mezclado.
blender /'blɛndər/ n. (for food) licuadora f.
bless /blɛs/ v. bendecir.
blessed /'blɛsɪd/ a. bendito.
blessing /'blɛsɪŋ/ a. bendición f.
blight /blait/ n. 1. plaga f.; tizón m. —v. 2. atizonar.
blind /blaind/ a. ciego.
blindfold /'blaind,fould/ v. vendar los ojos.
blinding /'blaindɪŋ/ a. deslumbrante; ofuscante.
blindly /'blaindli/ adv. ciegamente.
blindness /'blaindnɪs/ n. ceguedad, ceguera f.
blink /blɪŋk/ n. 1. guiñada f. —v. 2. guiñar.
bliss /blɪs/ n. felicidad f.
blissful /'blɪsfəl/ a. dichoso; bienaventurado.
blissfully /'blɪsfəli/ adv. felizmente.
blister /'blɪstər/ n. ampolla f.
blithe /blaið/ a. alegre; jovial; gozoso.
blizzard /'blɪzərd/ n. nevasca f.
bloat /blout/ v. hinchar.
bloc /blɒk/ n. grupo (político); bloc.
block /blɒk/ n. 1. bloque m.; (street) manzana, cuadra f. —v. 2. bloquear.
blockade /blɒ'keid/ n. 1. bloqueo m. —v. 2. bloquear.
blond /blɒnd/ a. & n. rubio -ia.
blood /blʌd/ n. sangre f.; parentesco, linaje m.
bloodhound /'blʌd,haund/ n. sabueso m.
bloodless /'blʌdlɪs/ a. exangüe; desangrado.
blood poisoning /'pɔizənɪŋ/ envenenamiento de sangre.
blood pressure presión arterial.
bloodshed /'blʌd,ʃɛd/ n. matanza f.
bloodthirsty /'blʌd,θɜrsti/ a. cruel, sanguinario.
bloody /'blʌdi/ a. ensangrentado, sangriento.
bloom /blum/ n. 1. flor f. —v. 2. florecer.
blooming /'blumɪŋ/ a. lozano; fresco; floreciente.

blossom /'blɒsəm/ n. 1. flor f.
—v. 2. florecer.
blot /blɒt/ n. 1. mancha f. —v. 2. manchar.
blotch /blɒtʃ/ n. 1. mancha, roncha f. —v. 2. manchar.
blotter /'blɒtər/ n. papel secante.
blouse /blaus/ n. blusa f.
blow /blou/ n. 1. golpe m.; Fig. chasco m. —v. 2. soplar.
blowout /'blou,aut/ n. reventón de neumático m.
blubber /'blʌbər/ n. grasa de ballena.
bludgeon /'blʌdʒən/ n. porra f. v. apalear.
blue /blu/ a. azul; triste, melancólico.
bluebird /'blu,bɜrd/ n. azulejo m.
blue jeans jeans; vaqueros m.pl.
blueprint /'blu,prɪnt/ n. heliografía f.
bluff /blʌf/ n. risco m. v. alardear; baladronar.
bluing /'bluɪŋ/ n. añil m.
blunder /'blʌndər/ n. 1. desatino m. —v. 2. desatinar.
blunderer /'blʌndərər/ n. desatinado -da.
blunt /blʌnt/ a. embotado; descortés. v. embotar.
bluntly /'blʌntli/ a. bruscamente.
bluntness /'blʌntnɪs/ n. grosería f.; brusquedad.
blur /blɜr/ n. 1. trazo confuso. —v. 2. hacer indistinto.
blush /blʌʃ/ n. 1. rubor, sonrojo m. —v. 2. sonrojarse.
bluster /'blʌstər/ n. 1. fanfarria f. —v. 2. fanfarrear.
boar /bɔr/ n. verraco m. **wild b.,** jabalí.
board /bɔrd/ n. 1. tabla; Govt. consejo m.; junta f. **b. and room,** cuarto y comida, casa y comida. —v. 2. (ship) abordar.
boarder /'bɔrdər/ n. pensionista m. & f.
boardinghouse /'bɔrdɪŋ/ n. pensión f., casa de huéspedes.
boarding pass /'bɔrdɪŋ/ boleto de embarque m., tarjeta de embarque f.
boast /boust/ n. 1. jactancia f. —v. 2. jactarse.
boaster /'boustər/ n. fanfarrón -na.
boastful /'boustfəl/ a. jactancioso.
boastfulness /'boustfəlnɪs/ n. jactancia f.

boat /bout/ n. barco, buque, bote m.
boathouse /'bout,haus/ n. casilla de botes f.
boatswain /'bousən/ n. contramaestre m.
bob /bɒb/ v. menear.
bobbin /'bɒbɪn/ n. bobina f.
bobby pin /'bɒbi/ n. gancho m., horquilla.
bodice /'bɒdɪs/ n. corpiño m.
bodily /'bɒdli/ a. corporal.
body /'bɒdi/ n. cuerpo m.
body builder culturista mf.
body building culturismo m.
bodyguard /'bɒdi,gɑrd/ n. guardaespaldas.
bog /bɒg/ n. pantano m.
bogey /'bougi/ n. (golf) uno sobre par m.
Bohemian /bou'himiən/ a. & n. bohemio -mia.
boil /bɔil/ n. 1. hervor m.; Med. divieso m. —v. 2. hervir.
boiler /'bɔilər/ n. marmita; caldera f.
boiling point /'bɔilɪŋ/ punto de ebullición m.
boisterous /'bɔistərəs/ a. tumultuoso.
boisterously /'bɔistərəsli/ adv. tumultuosamente.
bold /bould/ a. atrevido, audaz.
boldface /'bould,feis/ n. (type) letra negra.
boldly /'bouldli/ adv. audazmente; descaradamente.
boldness /'bouldnɪs/ n. atrevimiento m.; osadía f.
Bolivian /bou'lɪviən/ a. & n. boliviano -na.
bologna /bə'louni/ n. salchicha f., mortadela.
bolster /'boulstər/ n. 1. travesero, cojín m. —v. 2. apoyar, sostener.
bolt /boult/ n. perno m.; (of door) cerrojo m.; (lightning) rayo m. v. acerrojar.
bomb /bɒm/ n. 1. bomba f. —v. 2. bombardear.
bombard /bɒm'bɑrd/ v. bombardear.
bombardier /,bɒmbər'dɪər/ n. bombardero -ra.
bombardment /bɒm'bɑrdmənt/ n. bombardeo m.
bomber /'bɒmər/ n. avión de bombardeo.
bombproof /'bɒm,pruf/ a. a prueba de granadas.

bombshell /'bɒm,ʃɛl/ n. bomba f.

bonbon /'bɒn,bɒn/ n. dulce, bombón m.

bond /bɒnd/ n. lazo m.; *Com.* bono m.

bondage /'bɒndɪdʒ/ n. esclavitud, servidumbre f.

bonded /'bɒndɪd/ a. garantizado.

bone /boun/ n. hueso m.

boneless /'bounlɪs/ a. sin huesos.

bonfire /'bɒn,faiᵊr/ n. hoguera, fogata f.

bonnet /'bɒnɪt/ n. gorra f.

bonus /'bounəs/ n. sobrepaga f.

bony /'bouni/ a. huesudo.

boo /bu/ v. abuchear.

book /bʊk/ n. libro m.

bookbinder /'bʊk,baindər/ n. encuadernador -ora.

bookcase /'bʊk,keis/ n. armario para libros.

bookkeeper /'bʊk,kipər/ n. tenedor -ra de libros.

bookkeeping /'bʊk,kipɪŋ/ n. contabilidad f.

booklet /'bʊklɪt/ n. folleto m., libreta f.

bookmark /'bʊk,mɑrk/ n. marcapáginas m.

bookseller /'bʊk,sɛlər/ n. librero -ra.

bookstore /'bʊk,stɔr/ n. librería f.

boom /bum/ n. *Naut.* botalón m.; prosperidad repentina.

boon /bun/ n. dádiva f.

boor /bʊr/ n. patán, rústico m.

boorish /'bʊrɪʃ/ a. villano.

boost /bust/ n. **1.** alza; ayuda f. —v. **2.** levantar, alzar; fomentar.

booster /'bustər/ n. fomentador m.

boot /but/ n. bota f.

bootblack /'but,blæk/ n. limpiabotas m.

booth /buθ/ n. cabaña; casilla f.

booty /'buti/ n. botín m.

border /'bɔrdər/ n. **1.** borde m.; frontera f. —v. **2.** b. on, lindar con.

borderline /'bɔrdər,lain/ a. marginal. n. margen m.

bore /bɔr/ n. lata f.; persona pesada. v. aburrir, fastidiar; *Mech.* taladrar.

boredom /'bɔrdəm/ n. aburrimiento m.

boric acid /'bɔrɪk/ n. ácido bórico m.

boring /'bɔrɪŋ/ a. aburrido, pesado.

born /bɔrn/ a. nacido. **be born,** nacer.

born-again /'bɔrn ə'gɛn/ a. renacido.

borrow /'bɒrou/ v. pedir prestado.

bosom /'bʊzəm/ v. seno, pecho m.

boss /bɒs/ n. jefe, patrón m.

botany /'bɒtṇi/ n. botánica f.

both /bouθ/ pron. & a. ambos, los dos.

bother /'bɒðər/ n. molestia f. v. molestar, incomodar.

bothersome /'bɒðərsəm/ a. molesto.

bottle /'bɒtl/ n. **1.** botella f. —v. **2.** embotellar.

bottling /'bɒtlɪŋ/ n. embotellamiento m.

bottom /'bɒtəm/ n. fondo m.

boudoir /'budwɑr/ n. tocador m.

bough /bau/ n. rama f.

boulder /'bouldər/ n. canto rodado.

boulevard /'bulə,vɑrd/ n. bulevar m.

bounce /bauns/ n. **1.** brinco m. —v. **2.** brincar; hacer saltar.

bound /baund/ n. **1.** salto m. —v. **2.** limitar.

boundary /'baundəri/ n. límite, lindero m.

bouquet /bou'kei, bu-/ n. ramillete de flores.

bourgeois /bʊr'ʒwɑ/ a. & n. burgués -esa.

bout /baut/ n. encuentro; combate m.

bow /n bau, bou; v bau/ n. **1.** saludo m.; (of ship) proa f.; (archery) arco m.; (ribbon) lazo m. —v. **2.** saludar, inclinar.

bowels /'bauəlz/ n. intestinos m.pl.; entrañas f.pl.

bowl /boul/ n. **1.** vasija f.; platón m. —v. **2.** jugar a los bolos. **b. over,** derribar.

bowlegged /'bou,lɛgɪd/ a. perniabierto.

bowling /'boulɪŋ/ n. bolos m.pl.

bow tie /bou/ pajarita f.

box /bɒks/ n. **1.** caja f.; *Theat.* palco m. —v. **2.** (sports) boxear.

boxcar /'bɒks,kɑr/ n. vagón m.

boxer /'bɒksər/ n. boxeador -ra, pugilista m. & f.

boxing /'bɒksɪŋ/ n. boxeo m.

box office n. taquilla f.

boy /bɔi/ n. muchacho, chico, niño m.

boycott /'bɔikɒt/ n. 1. boicoteo m. —v. 2. boicotear.
boyhood /'bɔihʊd/ n. muchachez f.
boyish /'bɔiɪʃ/ a. pueril.
boyishly /'bɔiɪʃli/ adv. puerilmente.
bra /bra/ n. sujetador, sostén m.
brace /breis/ n. 1. grapón m.; pl. tirantes m.pl. —v. 2. reforzar.
bracelet /'breislɪt/ n. brazalete m., pulsera f.
bracket /'brækɪt/ n. ménsula f.
brag /bræg/ v. jactarse.
braggart /'brægərt/ a. 1. jactancioso. —n. 2. jaque m.
braid /breid/ n. 1. trenza f. —v. 2. trenzar.
brain /brein/ n. cerebro, seso m.
brainy /'breini/ a. sesudo, inteligente.
brake /breik/ n. 1. freno m. —v. 2. frenar.
bran /bræn/ n. salvado m.
branch /bræntʃ, brɑntʃ/ n. ramo m.; (of tree) rama f.
brand /brænd/ n. marca f.
brandish /'brændɪʃ/ v. blandir.
brand-new /'bræn'nu/ a. enteramente nuevo.
brandy /'brændi/ n. aguardiente, coñac m.
brash /bræʃ/ a. impetuoso.
brass /bræs/ n. bronce, latón m.
brassiere /brə'zɪər/ n. corpiño, sujetador, sostén m.
brat /bræt/ n. mocoso m.
bravado /brə'vɑdou/ n. bravata f.
brave /breiv/ a. valiente.
bravery /'breivəri/ n. valor m.
brawl /brɔl/ n. alboroto m. v. alborotar.
brawn /brɔn/ n. músculo m.
bray /brei/ v. rebuznar.
brazen /'breizən/ a. desvergonzado.
Brazil /brə'zɪl/ n. Brasil m.
Brazilian /brə'zɪlyən/ a. & n. brasileño -ña.
breach /britʃ/ n. rotura; infracción f.
breach of contract incumplimiento de contrato m.
bread /brɛd/ n. pan m.
breadth /brɛdθ/ n. anchura f.
break /breik/ n. 1. rotura; pausa f. —v. 2. quebrar, romper.
breakable /'breikəbəl/ a. rompible, frágil.

breakage /'breikɪdʒ/ n. rotura f., destrozo m.
breakfast /'brɛkfəst/ n. 1. desayuno, almuerzo m. —v. 2. desayunar, almorzar.
breakneck /'breik,nɛk/ a. rápido, precipitado, atropellado.
breast /brɛst/ n. (of human) pecho, seno m.; (of fowl) pechuga f.
breastbone /'brɛst,boun/ n. esternón m.
breath /brɛθ/ n. aliento; soplo m.
breathe /brið/ v. respirar.
breathless /'brɛθlɪs/ a. desalentado.
breathlessly /'brɛθlɪsli/ adv. jadeantemente, intensamente.
bred /brɛd/ a. criado; educado.
breeches /'brɪtʃɪz/ n.pl. calzones; pantalones, m.pl.
breed /brid/ n. 1. raza f. —v. 2. engendrar; criar.
breeder /'bridər/ n. criador -ra.
breeding /'bridɪŋ/ n. cría f.
breeze /briz/ n. brisa f.
breezy /'brizi/ a.: it is b., hace brisa.
brevity /'brɛvɪti/ n. brevedad f.
brew /bru/ v. fraguar; elaborar.
brewer /'bruər/ n. cervecero -ra.
brewery /'bruəri/ n. cervecería f.
bribe /braib/ n. 1. soborno, cohecho m. —v. 2. sobornar, cohechar.
briber /'braibər/ n. sobornador -ra.
bribery /'braibəri/ n. soborno, cohecho m.
brick /brɪk/ n. ladrillo m.
bricklayer /'brɪk,leiər/ n. albañil m.
bridal /'braidl̩/ a. nupcial.
bride /braid/ n. novia f.
bridegroom /'braid,grum/ n. novio m.
bridesmaid /'braidz,meid/ n. madrina de boda.
bridge /brɪdʒ/ n. puente m.
bridged /'brɪdʒd/ a. conectado.
bridgehead /'brɪdʒ,hɛd/ n. Mil. cabeza de puente.
bridle /'braidl̩/ n. brida f.
brief /brif/ a. breve.
briefcase /'brif,keis/ n. maletín m.
briefly /'brifli/ adv. brevemente.
briefness /'brifnɪs/ n. brevedad f.
brier /'braiər/ n. zarza f.
brig /brɪg/ n. bergantín m.
brigade /brɪ'geid/ n. brigada f.

bright /brait/ *a.* claro, brillante.
brighten /'braitn̩/ *v.* abrillantar; alegrar.
brightness /'braitnɪs/ *n.* resplandor *m.*
brilliance /'brɪlyəns/ *n.* brillantez *f.*
brilliant /'brɪlyənt/ *a.* brillante.
brim /brɪm/ *n.* borde *m.;* (of hat) ala *f.*
brine /brain/ *n.* escabeche, *m.* salmuera *f.*
bring /brɪŋ/ *v.* traer. **b. about,** efectuar, llevar a cabo.
brink /brɪŋk/ *n.* borde *m.*
briny /'braini/ *a.* salado.
brisk /brɪsk/ *a.* vivo; enérgico.
briskly /'brɪskli/ *adv.* vivamente.
briskness /'brɪsknɪs/ *n.* viveza *f.*
bristle /'brɪsəl/ *n.* cerda *f.*
bristly /'brɪsli/ *a.* hirsuto.
Britain /'brɪtn̩/ *n.* **Great B.,** Gran Bretaña *f.*
British /'brɪtɪʃ/ *a.* británico.
British Empire imperio británico *m.*
British Isles /ailz/ islas británicas *f.*
Briton /'brɪtn̩/ *n.* inglés *m.*
brittle /'brɪtl̩/ *a.* quebradizo, frágil.
broad /brɔd/ *a.* ancho.
broadcast /'brɔd,kæst/ *n.* **1.** radiodifusión *f.* —*v.* **2.** radiodifundir.
broadcaster /'brɔd,kæstər/ *n.* locutor -ra.
broadcloth /'brɔd,klɔθ/ *n.* paño fino.
broaden /'brɔdn̩/ *v.* ensanchar.
broadly /'brɔdli/ *adv.* ampliamente.
broadminded /'brɔd'maindɪd/ *a.* tolerante, liberal.
brocade /brou'keid/ *n.* brocado *m.*
brocaded /brou'keidɪd/ *a.* espolinado.
broccoli /'brɒkəli/ *n.* brécol *m.*
broil /brɔil/ *v.* asar.
broiler /'brɔilər/ *n.* parrilla *f.*
broken /'broukən/ *a.* roto, quebrado.
broken-hearted /'broukən'hɑrtɪd/ *a.* angustiado.
broker /'broukər/ *n.* corredor -ra, bolsista *m.* & *f.*
brokerage /'broukərɪdʒ/ *n.* corretaje *m.*
bronchial /'brɒŋkiəl/ *a.* bronquial.

bronchitis /brɒŋ'kaitɪs/ *n.* bronquitis *f.*
bronze /brɒnz/ *n.* bronce *m.*
brooch /broutʃ/ *n.* broche *m.*
brood /brud/ *n.* **1.** cría, progenie *f.* —*v.* **2.** empollar; cobijar.
brook /brʊk/ *n.* arroyo *m.*, quebrada *f.*
broom /brum/ *n.* escoba *f.*
broomstick /'brum,stɪk/ *n.* palo de escoba.
broth /brɔθ/ *n.* caldo *m.*
brothel /'brɒθəl/ *n.* burdel *m.*
brother /'brʌðər/ *n.* hermano *m.*
brotherhood /'brʌðər,hʊd/ *n.* fraternidad *f.*
brother-in-law /'brʌðər ɪn ,lɔ/ *n.* cuñado *m.*
brotherly /'brʌðərli/ *a.* fraternal.
brow /brau/ *n.* ceja; frente *f.*
brown /braun/ *a.* pardo, moreno; marrón. *v.* rehogar.
brown sugar azúcar moreno *m.*
browse /brauz/ *v.* curiosear; ramonear.
browser /'brauzər/ *n.* (Internet) nagegador *m.*, visualizador *m.*, visor *m.*
bruise /bruz/ *n.* **1.** contusión *f.* —*v.* **2.** magullar.
brunette /bru'nɛt/ *a.* & *n.* moreno -na, trigueño -ña.
brush /brʌʃ/ *n.* **1.** cepillo *m.;* brocha *f.* —*v.* **2.** cepillar.
brushwood /'brʌʃ,wʊd/ *n.* matorral *m.*
brusque /brʌsk/ *a.* brusco.
brusquely /'brʌskli/ *adv.* bruscamente.
brutal /'brutl̩/ *a.* brutal.
brutality /bru'tælɪti/ *n.* brutalidad *f.*
brutalize /'brutl̩,aiz/ *v.* embrutecer.
brute /brut/ *n.* bruto -ta, bestia *f.*
bubble /'bʌbəl/ *n.* ampolla *f.*
bucket /'bʌkɪt/ *n.* cubo *m.*
buckle /'bʌkəl/ *n.* hebilla *f.*
buckram /'bʌkrəm/ *n.* bucarán *m.*
bucksaw /'bʌk'sɔ/ *n.* sierra de bastidor.
buckshot /'bʌk,ʃɒt/ *n.* posta *f.*
buckwheat /'bʌk,wit/ *n.* trigo sarraceno *m.*
bud /bʌd/ *n.* **1.** brote *m.* —*v.* **2.** brotar.
budding /'bʌdɪŋ/ *a.* en capullo.
budge /bʌdʒ/ *v.* moverse.
budget /'bʌdʒɪt/ *n.* presupuesto *m.*

buffalo /'bʌfə,lou/ *n.* búfalo *m.*

buffer /'bʌfər/ *n.* parachoques *m.*

buffet /bə'fei/ *n.* bufet *m.*; (furniture) aparador *m.*

buffoon /bə'fun/ *n.* bufón *m.*

bug /bʌg/ *n.* insecto *m.*; (computer) error *m.*

bugle /'byugəl/ *n.* clarín *m.*; corneta *f.*

build /bɪld/ *v.* construir.

builder /'bɪldər/ *n.* constructor -ra.

building /'bɪldɪŋ/ *n.* edificio *m.*

bulb /bʌlb/ *n.* bulbo *m.*; (of lamp) bombilla, ampolla *f.*

bulge /bʌldʒ/ *n.* abultamiento *m. v.* abultar.

bulging /'bʌldʒɪŋ/ *a.* protuberante.

bulimia /bu'limiə/ *n.* bulimia *f.*

bulk /bʌlk/ *n.* masa *f.*; grueso *m.*; mayoría *f.*

bulkhead /'bʌlk,hɛd/ *n.* frontón *m.*

bulky /'bʌlki/ *a.* grueso, abultado.

bull /bʊl/ *n.* toro *m.*

bulldog /'bʊl,dɔg/ *n.* perro de presa.

bullet /'bʊlɪt/ *n.* bala *f.*

bulletin /'bʊlɪtɪn/ *n.* boletín *m.*

bulletproof /'bʊlɪt,pruf/ *a.* a prueba de bala.

bullfight /'bʊl,fait/ *n.* corrida de toros.

bullfighter /'bʊl,faitər/ *n.* torero -ra.

bullfinch /'bʊl,fɪntʃ/ *n.* pinzón real *m.*

bully /'bʊli/ *n.* **1.** rufián *m.* —*v.* **2.** bravear.

bulwark /'bʊlwərk/ *n.* baluarte *m.*

bum /bʌm/ *n.* holgazán *m.*

bump /bʌmp/ *n.* **1.** golpe, choque *m.* —*v.* **2.** **b. into,** chocar contra.

bumper /'bʌmpər/ *n.* parachoques *m.*

bun /bʌn/ *n.* bollo *m.*

bunch /bʌntʃ/ *n.* racimo; montón *m.*

bundle /'bʌndl̩/ *n.* **1.** bulto *m.* —*v.* **2.** **b. up,** abrigar.

bungalow /'bʌŋgə,lou/ *n.* casa de un solo piso.

bungle /'bʌŋgəl/ *v.* estropear.

bunion /'bʌnyən/ *n.* juanete *m.*

bunk /bʌŋk/ *n.* litera *f.*

bunny /'bʌni/ *n.* conejito -ta.

bunting /'bʌntɪŋ/ *n.* lanilla; banderas *f.*

buoy /'bui/ *n.* boya *f.*

buoyant /'bɔiənt/ *a.* boyante; vivaz.

burden /'bɜrdn̩/ *n.* **1.** carga *f.* —*v.* **2.** cargar.

burdensome /'bɜrdn̩səm/ *a.* gravoso.

bureau /'byurou/ *n.* (furniture) cómoda *f.*; departamento *m.*

burglar /'bɜrglər/ *n.* ladrón -ona.

burglarize /'bɜrglə,raiz/ *v.* robar.

burglary /'bɜrgləri/ *n.* robo *m.*

burial /'bɛriəl/ *n.* entierro *m.*

burlap /'bɜrlæp/ *n.* arpillera *f.*

burly /'bɜrli/ *a.* corpulento.

burn /bɜrn/ *v.* quemar; arder.

burner /'bɜrnər/ *n.* mechero *m.*

burning /'bɜrnɪŋ/ *a.* ardiente.

burnish /'bɜrnɪʃ/ *v.* pulir; acicalar.

burrow /'bɜrou/ *v.* minar; horadar.

burst /bɜrst/ *v.* reventar.

bury /'bɛri/ *v.* enterrar.

bus /bʌs/ *n.* autobús *m.*

bush /bʊʃ/ *n.* arbusto *m.*

bushy /'bʊʃi/ *a.* matoso; peludo.

business /'bɪznɪs/ *n.* negocios *m.pl.*; comercio *m.*

businesslike /'bɪznɪs,laik/ *a.* directo, práctico.

businessman /'bɪznɪs,mæn/ *n.* hombre de negocios, comerciante *m.*

businesswoman /'bɪznɪs,wʊmən/ *n.* mujer de negocios.

bust /bʌst/ *n.* busto; pecho *m.*

bustle /'bʌsəl/ *n.* bullicio *m.*; animación *f.*

busy /'bɪzi/ *a.* ocupado, atareado.

busybody /'bɪzi,bɒdi/ *n.* entremetido -da.

but /bʌt/ *conj.* pero; sino.

butcher /'bʊtʃər/ *n.* carnicero -ra.

butchery /'bʊtʃəri/ *n.* carnicería; matanza *f.*

butler /'bʌtlər/ *n.* mayordomo *m.*

butt /bʌt/ *n.* punta *f.*; cabo extremo *m.*

butter /'bʌtər/ *n.* manteca, mantequilla *f.*

buttercup /'bʌtər,kʌp/ *n.* ranúnculo *m.*

butterfat /'bʌtər,fæt/ *n.* mantequilla *f.*

butterfly /'bʌtər,flai/ *n.* mariposa *f.*

buttermilk /'bʌtər,mɪlk/ *n.* suero (de leche) *m.*

button /'bʌtn̩/ *n.* botón *m.*

buttonhole /'bʌtn̩,houl/ *n.* ojal *m.*

buttress /'bʌtrɪs/ n. sostén; refuerzo m.

buxom /'bʌksəm/ a. regordete.

buy /bai/ v. comprar.

buyer /'baiər/ n. comprador -ra.

buzz /bʌz/ n. **1.** zumbido m. —v. **2.** zumbar.

buzzard /'bʌzərd/ n. gallinazo m.

buzzer /'bʌzər/ n. zumbador m.; timbre m.

buzz saw n. sierra circular f.

by /bai/ prep. por; (near) cerca de, al lado de; (time) para.

by-and-by /ˌbaiən'bai/ adv. pronto; luego.

bygone /'bai,gɔn/ a. pasado.

bylaw /'bai,lɔ/ n. estatuto, reglamento m.

bypass /'bai,pæs/ n. desvío m.

byproduct /'bai,prɒdəkt/ n. subproducto m.

bystander /'bai,stændər/ n. espectador -ra; mirón -na.

byte /bait/ n. en teoría de la información: ocho bits, byte m.

byway /'bai,wei/ n. camino desviado m.

C

cab /kæb/ n. taxi, coche de alquiler m.

cabaret /ˌkæbə'rei/ n. cabaret m.

cabbage /'kæbɪdʒ/ n. repollo m.

cabin /'kæbɪn/ n. cabaña f.

cabinet /'kæbənɪt/ n. gabinete; ministerio m.

cabinetmaker /'kæbənɪt,meikər/ n. ebanista m.

cable /'keibəl/ n. cable m.

cablegram /'keibəl,græm/ n. cablegrama m.

cache /kæʃ/ n. escondite m.

cackle /'kækəl/ n. charla f.; cacareo m. v. cacarear.

cacophony /kə'kɒfəni/ n. cacofonía f.

cactus /'kæktəs/ n. cacto m.

cad /kæd/ n. persona vil.

cadaver /kə'dævər/ n. cadáver m.

cadaverous /kə'dævərəs/ a. cadavérico.

caddie /'kædi/ n. (golf) ayudante m. & f.

cadence /'keidns/ n. cadencia f.

cadet /kə'dɛt/ n. cadete m.

cadmium /'kædmiəm/ n. cadmio m.

cadre /'kædri, 'kɑdrei/ n. núcleo; Mil. cuadro m.

café /kæ'fei/ n. café m., cantina f.

cafeteria /ˌkæfɪ'tɪəriə/ n. cafetería f.

caffeine /kæ'fin/ n. cafeína f.

cage /keidʒ/ n. jaula f. v. enjaular.

caged /keidʒd/ a. enjaulado.

caisson /'keisɒn, -sən/ n. arcón m.; Mil. furgón m.

cajole /kə'dʒoul/ v. lisonjear; adular.

cake /keik/ n. torta f.; bizcocho m.

calamitous /kə'læmɪtəs/ a. calamitoso.

calamity /kə'læmɪti/ n. calamidad f.

calcify /'kælsə,fai/ v. calcificar.

calcium /'kælsiəm/ n. calcio m.

calculable /'kælkyələbəl/ a. calculable.

calculate /'kælkyə,leit/ v. calcular.

calculating /'kælkyə,leitɪŋ/ a. interesado.

calculation /ˌkælkyə'leiʃən/ n. calculación f.; cálculo m.

calculus /'kælkyələs/ n. cálculo m.

caldron /'kɔldrən/ n. caldera f.

calendar /'kæləndər/ n. calendario m.

calf /kæf/ n. ternero m. (animal); pantorrilla f. (of the body).

calfskin /'kæf,skɪn/ n. piel de becerro.

caliber /'kælɪbər/ n. calibre m.

calico /'kælɪ,kou/ n. calicó m.

caliper /'kæləpər/ n. calibrador m.

calisthenics /ˌkæləs'θɛnɪks/ n. calistenia, gimnasia f.

calk /kɔk/ v. calafatear; rellenar.

calker /'kɔkər/ n. calafate -ta.

call /kɔl/ n. **1.** llamada f. —v. **2.** llamar.

calligraphy /kə'lɪgrəfi/ n. caligrafía f.

calling /'kɔlɪŋ/ n. vocación f.

calling card tarjeta (de visita) f.

callously /'kæləsli/ adv. insensiblemente.

callow /'kælou/ a. sin experiencia.

callus /'kæləs/ n. callo m.

calm /kɑm/ a. **1.** tranquilo, calmado. —n. **2.** calma f. —v. **3.** calmar.

calmly /'kɑmli/ adv. serenamente.

calmness /'kɑmnɪs/ n. calma f.

caloric /kə'lɔrɪk/ *a.* calórico.
calorie /'kælərɪ/ *n.* caloría *f.*
calorimeter /ˌkælə'rɪmɪtər/ *n.* calorímetro *m.*
calumniate /kə'lʌmniˌeit/ *v.* calumniar.
calumny /'kæləmnɪ/ *n.* calumnia *f.*
Calvary /'kælvərɪ/ *n.* Calvario *m.*
calve /kæv/ *v.* parir (la vaca).
calyx /'keilɪks/ *n.* cáliz *m.*
camaraderie /ˌkɑmə'rɑdərɪ/ *n.* compañerismo *m.*, compadrería *f.*
cambric /'keimbrɪk/ *n.* batista *f.*
camcorder /'kæmˌkɔrdər/ *n.* videocámara *f.*
camel /'kæməl/ *n.* camello -lla.
camellia /kə'milyə/ *n.* camelia *f.*
camel's hair /'kæməlz/ pelo de camello.
cameo /'kæmiˌou/ *n.* camafeo *m.*
camera /'kæmərə/ *n.* cámara *f.*
camouflage /'kæməˌflɑʒ/ *n.* camuflaje *m.*
camouflaging /'kæməˌflɑʒɪŋ/ *n.* simulacro, disfraz *m.*
camp /kæmp/ *n.* **1.** campamento *m.* —*v.* **2.** acampar.
campaign /kæm'pein/ *n.* campaña *f.*
camper /'kæmpər/ *n.* acampado *m.*
campfire /'kæmpˌfaiᵊr/ *n.* fogata de campamento.
camphor /'kæmfər/ *n.* alcanfor *m.*
camphor ball bola de alcanfor.
campus /'kæmpəs/ *n.* campo de colegio (o universidad), campus *m.*
can /kæn/ *v.* (be able) poder.
can /kæn/ *n.* **1.** lata *f.* —*v.* **2.** conservar en latas, enlatar.
Canada /'kænədə/ *n.* Canadá *m.*
Canadian /kə'neidiən/ *a. & n.* canadiense.
canal /kə'næl/ *n.* canal *m.*
canalize /'kænlˌaiz/ *v.* canalizar.
canard /kə'nɑrd/ *n.* embuste *m.*
canary /kə'nɛərɪ/ *n.* canario -ria.
cancel /'kænsəl/ *v.* cancelar.
cancellation /ˌkænsə'leiʃən/ *n.* cancelación *f.*
cancer /'kænsər/ *n.* cáncer *m.*
candelabrum /ˌkændl'ɑbrəm/ *n.* candelabro *m.*
candid /'kændɪd/ *a.* cándido, sincero.
candidacy /'kændɪdəsɪ/ *n.* candidatura *f.*
candidate /'kændɪˌdeit/ *n.* candidato -ta.

candidly /'kændɪdlɪ/ *adv.* cándidamente.
candidness /'kændɪdnɪs/ *n.* candidez; sinceridad *f.*
candied /'kændid/ *a.* garapiñado.
candle /'kændl/ *n.* vela *f.*
candlestick /'kændlˌstɪk/ *n.* candelero *m.*
candor /'kændər/ *n.* candor *m.*; sinceridad *f.*
candy /'kændɪ/ *n.* dulces *m.pl.*
cane /kein/ *n.* caña *f.*; (for walking) bastón *m.*
canine /'keinain/ *a.* canino.
canister /'kænəstər/ *n.* frasco *m.*; lata *f.*
canker /'kæŋkər/ *n.* llaga; úlcera *f.*
cankerworm /'kæŋkərˌwɜrm/ *n.* oruga *f.*
canned /kænd/ *a.* envasado, enlatado.
canner /'kænər/ *n.* envasador *m.*
cannery /'kænərɪ/ *n.* fábrica de conservas alimenticias *f.*
cannibal /'kænəbəl/ *n.* caníbal *m. & f.*
cannon /'kænən/ *n.* cañón *m.*
cannonade /ˌkænə'neid/ *n.* cañoneo *m.*
cannoneer /ˌkænə'nɪər/ *n.* cañonero -ra.
canny /'kænɪ/ *a.* sagaz; prudente.
canoe /kə'nu/ *n.* canoa, piragua *f.*
canoeing /kə'nuɪŋ/ *n.* piragüismo *m.*
canoeist /kə'nuɪst/ *n.* piragüista *m. & f.*
canon /'kænən/ *n.* canon *m.*; *Relig.* canónigo *m.*
canonical /kə'nɒnɪkəl/ *a.* canónico.
canonize /'kænəˌnaiz/ *v.* canonizar.
can opener /'oupənər/ abrelatas *m.*
canopy /'kænəpɪ/ *n.* dosel *m.*
cant /kænt/ *n.* hipocresía *f.*
cantaloupe /'kæntlˌoup/ *n.* melón *m.*
canteen /kæn'tin/ *n.* cantina *f.*
canter /'kæntər/ *n.* **1.** medio galope *m.* —*v.* **2.** galopar.
cantonment /kæn'tɒnmənt/ *n.* *Mil.* acuartelamiento *m.*
canvas /'kænvəs/ *n.* lona *f.*
canyon /'kænyən/ *n.* cañón, desfiladero *m.*
cap /kæp/ *n.* **1.** tapa *f.*; (headwear) gorro *m.* —*v.* **2.** tapar.

capability /ˌkeipə'bılıti/ *n.* capacidad *f.*

capable /'keipəbəl/ *a.* capaz.

capably /'keipəbli/ *adv.* hábilmente.

capacious /kə'peiʃəs/ *a.* espacioso.

capacity /kə'pæsıti/ *n.* capacidad *f.*

cape /keip/ *n.* capa *f.*, *Geog.* cabo *m.*

caper /'keipər/ *n.* zapateta *f.*; *Bot.* alcaparra *f.*

capillary /'kæpə,lɛri/ *a.* capilar.

capital /'kæpıtl̩/ *n.* capital *m.*; *Govt.* capital *f.*

capitalism /'kæpıtl̩,ızəm/ *n.* capitalismo *m.*

capitalist /'kæpıtl̩ıst/ *n.* capitalista *m. & f.*

capitalistic /ˌkæpıtl̩'ıstık/ *a.* capitalista.

capitalization /ˌkæpıtl̩ə'zeiʃən/ *n.* capitalización *f.*

capitalize /'kæpıtl̩,aiz/ *v.* capitalizar.

capital letter *n.* mayúscula *f.*

capitulate /kə'pıtʃə,leit/ *v.* capitular.

capon /'keipɒn/ *n.* capón *m.*

caprice /kə'pris/ *n.* capricho *m.*

capricious /kə'prıʃəs/ *a.* caprichoso.

capriciously /kə'prıʃəsli/ *adv.* caprichosamente.

capriciousness /kə'prıʃəsnıs/ *n.* capricho *m.*

capsize /'kæpsaiz/ *v.* zozobrar, volcar.

capsule /'kæpsəl/ *n.* cápsula *f.*

captain /'kæptən/ *n.* capitán -tana.

caption /'kæpʃən/ *n.* título *m.*; (motion pictures) subtítulo *m.*

captious /'kæpʃəs/ *a.* capcioso.

captivate /'kæptə,veit/ *v.* cautivar.

captivating /'kæptə,veitıŋ/ *a.* encantador.

captive /'kæptıv/ *n.* cautivo -va, prisionero -ra.

captivity /kæp'tıvıti/ *n.* cautividad *f.*

captor /'kæptər/ *n.* apresador -ra.

capture /'kæptʃər/ *n.* **1.** captura *f.* —*v.* **2.** capturar.

car /kɑr/ *n.* coche, carro *m.*; (of train) vagón, coche *m.* **baggage c.,** vagón de equipajes. **parlor c.,** coche salón.

carafe /kə'ræf/ *n.* garrafa *f.*

caramel /'kærəməl/ *n.* caramelo *m.*

carat /'kærət/ *n.* quilate *m.*

caravan /'kærə,væn/ *n.* caravana *f.*

caraway /'kærə,wei/ *n.* alcaravea *f.*

carbide /'kɑrbaid/ *n.* carburo *m.*

carbine /'kɑrbin/ *n.* carabina *f.*

carbohydrate /ˌkɑrbou'haidreit/ *n.* hidrato de carbono.

carbon /'kɑrbən/ *n.* carbón *m.*

carbon dioxide /dai'ɒksaid/ anhídrido carbónico.

carbon monoxide /mɒn'ɒksaid/ monóxido de carbono.

carbon paper papel carbón *m.*

carbuncle /'kɑrbʌŋkəl/ *n.* carbúnculo *m.*

carburetor /'kɑrbə,reitər/ *n.* carburador *m.*

carcinogenic /ˌkɑrsənə'dʒɛnık/ *a.* carcinogénico.

card /kɑrd/ *n.* tarjeta *f.* **playing c.,** naipe *m.*

cardboard /'kɑrd,bɔrd/ *n.* cartón *m.*

cardiac /'kɑrdi,æk/ *a.* cardíaco.

cardigan /'kɑrdıgən/ *n.* chaqueta de punto.

cardinal /'kɑrdn̩l/ *a.* **1.** cardinal. —*n.* **2.** cardenal *m.*

cardiologist /ˌkɑrdi'ɒlədʒıst/ *n.* cardiólogo, -ga *m. & f.*

care /kɛər/ *n.* **1.** cuidado. —*v.* **2.** **c. for,** cuidar.

careen /kə'rin/ *v.* carenar; echarse de costado.

career /kə'rıər/ *n.* carrera *f.*

carefree /'kɛər,fri/ *a.* descuidado.

careful /'kɛərfəl/ *a.* cuidadoso. **be. c.,** tener cuidado.

carefully /'kɛərfəli/ *adv.* cuidadosamente.

carefulness /'kɛərfəlnıs/ *n.* esmero; cuidado *m.*; cautela *f.*

careless /'kɛərlıs/ *a.* descuidado.

carelessly /'kɛərlısli/ *adv.* descuidadamente; negligentemente.

carelessness /'kɛərlısnıs/ *n.* descuido *m.*

caress /kə'rɛs/ *n.* **1.** caricia *f.* —*v.* **2.** acariciar.

caretaker /'kɛər,teikər/ *n.* guardián -ana.

cargo /'kɑrgou/ *n.* carga *f.*

caricature /'kærıkətʃər/ *n.* caricatura *f.*

caricaturist /'kærɪkə,tʃʊrɪst/ *n.* caricaturista *m. & f.*

caries /'kɛəriz/ *n.* caries *f.*

carjacking /'kar,dʒækɪŋ/ *n.* robo de coche *m.*

carload /'kar,loud/ *a.* furgonada, vagonada.

carnal /'karnḷ/ *a.* carnal.

carnation /kar'neiʃən/ *n.* clavel *m.*

carnival /'karnəvəl/ *n.* carnaval *m.*

carnivorous /kar'nɪvərəs/ *a.* carnívoro.

carol /'kærəl/ *n.* villancico *m.*

carouse /kə'rauz/ *v.* parrandear.

carpenter /'karpəntər/ *n.* carpintero -ra.

carpet /'karpɪt/ *n.* alfombra *f.*

carpeting /'karpɪtɪŋ/ *n.* alfombrado *m.*

car pool /'kar,pul/ uso habitual, por varias personas, de un automóvil perteneciente a una de ellas.

carriage /'kærɪdʒ/ *n.* carruaje; (bearing) porte *m.*

carrier /'kæriər/ *n.* portador -ra.

carrier pigeon paloma mensajera.

carrot /'kærət/ *n.* zanahoria *f.*

carrousel /,kærə'sɛl/ *n.* volantín, carrusel *m.*

carry /'kæri/ *v.* llevar, cargar. **c. out,** cumplir, llevar a cabo.

cart /kart/ *n.* carreta *f.*

cartage /'kartɪdʒ/ *n.* acarreo, carretaje *m.*

cartel /kar'tɛl/ *n.* cartel *m.*

cartilage /'kartḷɪdʒ/ *n.* cartílago *m.*

carton /'kartṇ/ *n.* caja de cartón.

cartoon /kar'tun/ *n.* caricatura *f.*

cartoonist /kar'tunɪst/ *n.* caricaturista *m. & f.*

cartridge /'kartrɪdʒ/ *n.* cartucho *m.*

carve /karv/ *v.* esculpir; (meat) trinchar.

carver /'karvər/ *n.* tallador -ra; grabador -ra.

carving /'karvɪŋ/ *n.* entalladura *f.;* arte de trinchar. **c. knife,** trinchante *m.*

cascade /kæs'keid/ *n.* cascada *f.*

case /keis/ *n.* caso *m.;* (box) caja *f.* **in any c.,** sea como sea.

cash /kæʃ/ *n.* **1.** dinero contante. —*v.* **2.** efectuar, cambiar.

cashier /kæ'ʃɪər/ *n.* cajero -ra.

cashmere /'kæʒmɪər/ *n.* casimir *m.*

casino /kə'sinou/ *n.* casino *m.*

cask /kæsk/ *n.* barril *m.*

casket /'kæskɪt/ *n.* ataúd *m.*

casserole /'kæsə,roul/ *n.* cacerola *f.*

cassette /kə'sɛt/ *n.* cassette *m.,* cartucho *m.*

cast /kæst/ *n.* **1.** *Theat.* reparto de papeles. —*v.* **2.** echar; *Theat.* repartir.

castanet /,kæstə'nɛt/ *n.* castañuela *f.*

castaway /'kæstə,wei/ *n.* náufrago -ga.

caste /kæst/ *n.* casta *f.*

caster /'kæstər/ *n.* tirador *m.*

castigate /'kæstɪ,geit/ *v.* castigar.

Castilian /kæ'stɪlyən/ *a.* castellano.

cast iron *n.* hierro colado *m.*

castle /'kæsəl/ *n.* castillo *m.*

castoff /'kæst,ɔf/ *a.* descartado.

casual /'kæʒuəl/ *a.* casual.

casually /'kæʒuəli/ *adv.* casualmente.

casualness /'kæʒuəlnɪs/ *n.* casualidad *f.*

casualty /'kæʒuəlti/ *n.* víctima *f.; Mil.* baja *f.*

cat /kæt/ *n.* gato -ta.

cataclysm /'kætə,klɪzəm/ *n.* cataclismo *m.*

catacomb /'kætə,koum/ *n.* catacumba *f.*

catalogue /'kætḷ,ɔg/ *n.* catálogo *m.*

catapult /'kætə,pʌlt/ *n.* catapulta *f.*

cataract /'kætə,rækt/ *n.* catarata *f.*

catarrh /kə'tar/ *n.* catarro *m.*

catastrophe /kə'tæstrəfi/ *n.* catástrofe *f.*

catch /kætʃ/ *v.* alcanzar, atrapar, coger.

catchy /'kætʃi/ *a.* contagioso.

catechism /'kætɪ,kɪzəm/ *n.* catequismo *m.*

catechize /'kætɪ,kaiz/ *v.* catequizar.

categorical /,kætɪ'gɔrɪkəl/ *a.* categórico.

category /'kætɪ,gɔri/ *n.* categoría *f.*

cater /'keitər/ *v.* abastecer; proveer. **c. to,** complacer.

caterpillar /'kætə,pɪlər/ *n.* gusano *m.*

catgut /'kæt,gʌt/ *n.* cuerda (de tripa).

catharsis /kə'θɑrsɪs/ *n.* catarsis, purga *f.*

cathartic /kə'θɑrtɪk/ *a.* **1.** catártico; purgante. —*n.* **2.** purgante *m.*

cathedral /kə'θidrəl/ *n.* catedral *f.*

cathode /'kæθoud/ *n.* cátodo *m.*

Catholic /'kæθəlɪk/ *a.* católico & *n.* católico -ca.

Catholicism /kə'θɒlə,sɪzəm/ *n.* catolicismo *m.*

catnap /'kæt,næp/ *n.* siesta corta.

catsup /'kætsəp, 'kɛtʃəp/ *n.* salsa de tomate.

cattle /'kætļ/ *n.* ganado *m.*

cattleman /'kætļmən, -,mæn/ *n.* ganadero *m.*

cauliflower /'kɔlə,flauər/ *n.* coliflor *m.*

causation /kɔ'zeiʃən/ *n.* causalidad *f.*

cause /kɔz/ *n.* causa *f.*

causeway /'kɔz,wei/ *n.* calzada elevada *f.;* terraplén *m.*

caustic /'kɔstɪk/ *a.* cáustico.

cauterize /'kɔtə,raiz/ *v.* cauterizar.

cautery /'kɔtəri/ *n.* cauterio *m.*

caution /'kɔʃən/ *n.* cautela *f.*

cautious /'kɔʃəs/ *a.* cauteloso.

cavalcade /,kævəl'keid/ *n.* cabalgata *f.*

cavalier /,kævə'lɪər/ *n.* caballero *m.*

cavalry /'kævəlri/ *n.* caballería *f.*

cave /keiv/ **cavern** *n.* caverna, gruta *f.*

cave-in /'keiv ,ɪn/ *n.* hundimiento *m.*

caviar /'kævi,ɑr/ *n.* caviar *m.*

cavity /'kævɪti/ *n.* hueco *m.*

cayman /'keimən/ *n.* caimán *m.*

CD player tocadiscos compacto, tocadiscos digital *m.*

cease /sis/ *v.* cesar.

ceaseless /'sislɪs/ *a.* incesante.

cedar /'sidər/ *n.* cedro *m.*

cede /sid/ *v.* ceder.

ceiling /'silɪŋ/ *n.* techo; cielo *m.*

celebrant /'sɛləbrənt/ *n.* celebrante -ta.

celebrate /'sɛlə,breit/ *v.* celebrar.

celebration /,sɛlə'breiʃən/ *n.* celebración *f.*

celebrity /sə'lɛbrɪti/ *n.* celebridad.

celerity /sə'lɛrɪti/ *n.* celeridad; prontitud *f.*

celery /'sɛləri/ *n.* apio *m.*

celestial /sə'lɛstʃəl/ *a.* celeste.

celibacy /'sɛləbəsi/ *n.* celibato -ta.

celibate /'sɛləbɪt/ *a.* & *n.* célibe *m.* & *f.*

cell /sɛl/ *n.* celda *f.; Biol.* célula *f.*

cellar /'sɛlər/ *n.* sótano *m.*

cellist /'tʃɛlɪst/ *a.* celista *m.* & *f.*

cello /'tʃɛlou/ *n.* violonchelo *m.*

cellophane /'sɛlə,fein/ *n.* celofán *m.*

cellular /'sɛlyələr/ *a.* celular.

cellular phone /foun/ teléfono móvil *m.*

celluloid /'sɛlyə,lɔid/ *n.* celuloide *m.*

cellulose /'sɛlyə,lous/ *a.* **1.** celuloso. —*n.* **2.** celulosa *f.*

Celtic /'kɛltɪk, 'sɛl-/ *a.* céltico.

cement /sɪ'mɛnt/ *n.* cemento *m.*

cemetery /'sɛmɪ,tɛri/ *n.* cementerio *m.;* campo santo *m.*

censor /'sɛnsər/ *n.* censor -ra.

censorious /sɛn'sɔriəs/ *a.* severo; crítico.

censorship /'sɛnsər,ʃɪp/ *n.* censura *f.*

censure /'sɛnʃər/ *n.* **1.** censura *f.* —*v.* **2.** censurar.

census /'sɛnsəs/ *n.* censo *m.*

cent /sɛnt/ *n.* centavo, céntimo *m.*

centenary /sɛn'tɛnɛri/ *a.* & *n.* centenario *m.*

centennial /sɛn'tɛniəl/ *a.* & *n.* centenario *m.*

center /'sɛntər/ *n.* centro *m.*

centerfold /'sɛntər,fould/ *n.* página central desplegable en una revista.

centerpiece /'sɛntər,pis/ *n.* centro de mesa.

centigrade /'sɛntɪ,greid/ *a.* centígrado.

centigrade thermometer termómetro centígrado.

central /'sɛntrəl/ *a.* central.

Central American *a.* & *n.* centroamericano -na.

centralize /'sɛntrə,laiz/ *v.* centralizar.

century /'sɛntʃəri/ *n.* siglo *m.*

century plant maguey *m.*

ceramic /sə'ræmɪk/ *a.* cerámico.

ceramics /sə'ræmɪks/ *n.* cerámica *f.*

cereal /'sɪəriəl/ *n.* cereal *m.*

cerebral /sə'ribrəl/ *a.* cerebral.

ceremonial /,sɛrə'mouniəl/ *a.* ceremonial.

ceremonious /,sɛrə'mouniəs/ *a.* ceremonioso.

ceremony /'sɛrə,mouni/ n. ceremonia f.

certain /'sɜrtn̩/ a. cierto, seguro.

certainly /'sɜrtn̩li/ adv. sin duda, seguramente.

certainty /'sɜrtn̩ti/ n. certeza f.

certificate /sər'tɪfɪkɪt/ n. certificado m.

certification /,sɜrtəfɪ'keiʃən, sər,tɪfə-/ n. certificación f.

certified /'sɜrtə,faid/ a. certificado.

certify /'sɜrtə,fai/ v. certificar.

certitude /'sɜrtɪ,tyud/ n. certeza f.

cessation /sɛ'seiʃən/ n. cesación, descontinuación f.

cession /'sɛʃən/ n. cesión f.

chafe /tʃeif/ v. irritar.

chafing dish /'tʃeifɪŋ/ n. escalfador m.

chagrin /ʃə'grɪn/ n. disgusto m.

chain /tʃein/ n. **1.** cadena f. —v. **2.** encadenar.

chair /tʃɛər/ n. silla f.

chairman /'tʃɛərmən/ n. presidente -ta.

chairperson /'tʃɛər,pɜrsən/ n. presidente -ta; persona que preside.

chalk /tʃɔk/ n. tiza f.

challenge /'tʃælɪndʒ/ n. **1.** desafío m. —v. **2.** desafiar.

challenger /'tʃælɪndʒər/ n. desafiador -ra.

chamber /'tʃeimbər/ n. cámara f.

chamberlain /'tʃeimbərlɪn/ n. camarero m.

chambermaid /'tʃeimbər,meid/ n. camarera f.

chameleon /kə'miliən/ n. camaleón m.

chamois /'ʃæmi/ n. gamuza f.

champagne /ʃæm'pein/ n. champán m., champaña f.

champion /'tʃæmpiən/ n. **1.** campeón -na —v. **2.** defender.

championship /'tʃæmpiən,ʃɪp/ n. campeonato m.

chance /tʃæns/ n. oportunidad, ocasión f. **by c.,** por casualidad, por acaso. **take a c.,** aventurarse.

chancel /'tʃænsəl/ n. antealtar m.

chancellery /'tʃænsələri/ n. cancillería f.

chancellor /'tʃænsələr/ n. canciller m.

chandelier /,ʃændl̩'ɪər/ n. araña de luces.

change /tʃeindʒ/ n. **1.** cambio; (from a bill) moneda f. —v. **2.** cambiar.

changeability /,tʃeindʒə'bɪlɪti/ n. mutabilidad f.

changeable /'tʃeindʒəbəl/ a. variable, inconstante.

changer /'tʃeindʒər/ n. cambiador -ra.

channel /'tʃænl/ n. **1.** canal m. —v. **2.** encauzar.

Channel Tunnel túnel del Canal de la Mancha m.

chant /tʃænt/ n. **1.** canto llano m. —v. **2.** cantar.

chaos /'keiɒs/ n. caos m.

chaotic /kei'ɒtɪk/ a. caótico.

chap /tʃæp/ n. **1.** Colloq. tipo m. —v. **2.** rajar.

chapel /'tʃæpəl/ n. capilla f.

chaperon /'ʃæpə,roun/ n. acompañante -ta de señorita.

chaplain /'tʃæplɪn/ n. capellán m.

chapter /'tʃæptər/ n. capítulo m.

char /tʃɑr/ v. carbonizar.

character /'kærɪktər/ n. carácter m.

characteristic /,kærɪktə'rɪstɪk/ a. **1.** característico. —n. **2.** característica f.

characterization /,kærɪktərə'zeiʃən/ n. caracterización f.

characterize /'kærɪktə,raiz/ v. caracterizar.

charcoal /'tʃɑr,koul/ n. carbón leña.

charge /tʃɑrdʒ/ n. **1.** acusación f.; ataque m. —v. **2.** cargar; acusar; atacar.

chariot /'tʃæriət/ n. carroza f.

charisma /kə'rɪzmə/ n. carisma m.

charitable /'tʃærɪtəbəl/ a. caritativo.

charitableness /'tʃærɪtəbəlnɪs/ n. caridad f.

charitably /'tʃærɪtəbli/ adv. caritativamente.

charity /'tʃærɪti/ n. caridad f.; (alms) limosna f.

charlatan /'ʃɑrlətn̩/ n. charlatán -na.

charlatanism /'ʃɑrlətn̩,ɪzəm/ n. charlatanería f.

charm /tʃɑrm/ n. **1.** encanto m.; (witchcraft) hechizo m. —v. **2.** encantar; hechizar.

charming /'tʃɑrmɪŋ/ a. encantador.

charred /tʃɑrd/ a. carbonizado.

chart /tʃɑrt/ n. tabla, esquema f.

charter /'tʃɑrtər/ n. **1.** carta f. —v. **2.** alquilar.

charter flight vuelo chárter m.

charwoman /'tʃɑr,wʊmən/ n. mujer de la limpieza f.

chase /tʃeis/ n. **1.** caza f. —v. **2.** cazar; perseguir.

chaser /'tʃeisər/ n. perseguidor -ra.

chasm /'kæzəm/ n. abismo m.

chassis /'tʃæsi/ n. chasis m.

chaste /tʃeist/ a. casto.

chasten /'tʃeisən/ v. corregir, castigar.

chastise /tʃæs'taiz/ v. castigar.

chastisement /tʃæs'taizmənt/ n. castigo m.

chastity /'tʃæstɪti/ n. castidad, pureza f.

chat /tʃæt/ n. **1.** plática, charla f. —v. **2.** platicar, charlar.

chateau /ʃæ'tou/ n. castillo m.

chattels /'tʃætəlz/ n.pl. bienes m.

chatter /'tʃætər/ v. **1.** cotorrear; (teeth) rechinar. —n. **2.** cotorreo m.

chatterbox /'tʃæt,ər bɒks/ n. charlador -ra.

chauffeur /'ʃoufər/ n. chofer m.

cheap /tʃip/ a. barato.

cheapen /'tʃipən/ v. rebajar, menospreciar.

cheaply /'tʃipli/ adv. barato.

cheapness /'tʃipnɪs/ n. baratura f.

cheat /tʃit/ v. engañar.

cheater /'tʃitər/ n. engañador -ra.

check /tʃɛk/ n. **1.** verificación f.; (bank) cheque m.; (restaurant) cuenta f.; (chess) jaque m. —v. **2.** verificar.

checkers /'tʃɛkərz/ n. juego de damas.

checkmate /'tʃɛk,meit/ v. dar mate.

checkout counter /'tʃɛk,aut/ caja f.

cheek /tʃik/ n. mejilla f. (of face), desfachatez f. (gall).

cheekbone /'tʃik,boun/ n. pómulo m.

cheeky /'tʃiki/ a. fresco, descarado, chulo.

cheer /tʃɪər/ n. **1.** alegría f.; aplauso m. —v. **2.** alegrar; aplaudir.

cheerful /'tʃɪərfəl/ a. alegre.

cheerfully /'tʃɪərfəli/ adv. alegremente.

cheerfulness /'tʃɪərfəlnɪs/ n. alegría f.

cheerless /'tʃɪərlɪs/ a. triste.

cheery /'tʃɪəri/ a. alegre.

cheese /tʃiz/ n. queso m. **cottage c.,** requesón m.

chef /ʃɛf/ n. cocinero en jefe.

chemical /'kɛmɪkəl/ a. **1.** químico. —n. **2.** reactivo m.

chemically /'kɛmɪkli/ adv. químicamente.

chemist /'kɛmɪst/ n. químico -ca.

chemistry /'kɛməstri/ n. química f.

chemotherapy /,kimou'θɛrəpi/ n. quimioterapia f.

chenille /ʃə'nil/ n. felpilla f.

cherish /'tʃɛrɪʃ/ v. apreciar.

cherry /'tʃɛri/ n. cereza f.

cherub /'tʃɛrəb/ n. querubín m.

chess /tʃɛs/ n. ajedrez m.

chest /tʃɛst/ n. arca f.; (physiology) pecho m.

chestnut /'tʃɛs,nʌt/ n. castaña f.

chevron /'ʃɛvrən/ n. sardineta f.

chew /tʃu/ v. mascar, masticar.

chewer /'tʃuər/ n. mascador -ra.

chic /ʃik/ a. elegante, paquete.

chicanery /ʃɪ'keinəri/ n. trampería f.

chick /tʃɪk/ n. pollito -ta.

chicken /'tʃɪkən/ n. pollo m., gallina f.

chicken-hearted /'tʃɪkən 'hɑrtɪd/ a. cobarde.

chicken pox /pɒks/ viruelas locas, varicela f.

chicle /'tʃɪkəl/ n. chicle m.

chicory /'tʃɪkəri/ n. achicoria f.

chide /tʃaid/ v. regañar, reprender.

chief /tʃif/ a. **1.** principal. —n. **2.** jefe -fa.

chiefly /'tʃifli/ adv. principalmente, mayormente.

chieftain /'tʃiftən/ n. caudillo m.; (Indian c.) cacique m.

chiffon /ʃɪ'fɒn/ n. chifón m., gasa f.

chilblain /'tʃɪlblein/ n. sabañón m.

child /tʃaild/ n. niño -ña; hijo -ja.

childbirth /'tʃaild,bərθ/ n. parto m.

childhood /'tʃaildhʊd/ n. niñez f.

childish /'tʃaildɪʃ/ a. pueril.

childishness /'tʃaildɪʃnɪs/ n. puerilidad f.

childless /'tʃaildlɪs/ a. sin hijos.

childlike /'tʃaild,laik/ a. infantil.

Chilean /'tʃɪliən/ a. & n. chileno -na.

chili /'tʃɪli/ n. chile, ají m.

cigarette

chill /tʃɪl/ n. **1.** frío; escalofrío m. —v. **2.** enfriar.

chilliness /'tʃɪlɪnɪs/ n. frialdad f.

chilly /'tʃɪli/ a. frío; friolento.

chimes /tʃaimz/ n. juego de campanas.

chimney /'tʃɪmni/ n. chimenea f.

chimpanzee /,tʃɪmpæn'zi, tʃɪm'pænzi/ n. chimpancé m.

chin /tʃɪn/ n. barba f.

china /'tʃainə/ n. loza f.

chinchilla /tʃɪn'tʃɪlə/ n. chinchilla f.

Chinese /tʃai'niz/ a. & n. chino -na.

chink /tʃɪŋk/ n. grieta f.

chintz /tʃɪnts/ n. zaraza f.

chip /tʃɪp/ n. **1.** astilla f. —v. **2.** astillar.

chiropodist /kɪ'rɒpədɪst/ n. pedicuro -ra.

chiropractor /'kairə,præktər/ n. quiropráctico -ca.

chirp /tʃɜrp/ n. **1.** chirrido m. —v. **2.** chirriar, piar.

chisel /'tʃɪzəl/ n. **1.** cincel m. —v. **2.** cincelar, talar.

chivalrous /'ʃɪvəlrəs/ a. caballeroso.

chivalry /'ʃɪvəlri/ n. caballería f.

chive /tʃaiv/ n. cebollino m.

chloride /'klɔraid/ n. cloruro m.

chlorine /'klɔrin/ n. cloro m.

chloroform /'klɔrə,fɔrm/ n. cloroformo m.

chlorophyll /'klɔrəfɪl/ n. clorofila f.

chock-full /'tʃɒk'fʊl/ a. repleto, colmado.

chocolate /'tʃɔkəlɪt/ n. chocolate m.

choice /tʃɔis/ a. **1.** selecto, escogido. —n. **2.** selección f.; escogimiento m.

choir /kwaiᵊr/ n. coro m.

choke /tʃouk/ v. sofocar, ahogar.

cholera /'kɒlərə/ n. cólera f.

choleric /'kɒlərɪk/ a. colérico, irascible.

cholesterol /kə'lɛstə,roul/ n. colesterol m.

choose /tʃuz/ v. elegir, escoger.

chop /tʃɒp/ n. **1.** chuleta, costilla f. —v. **2.** tajar; cortar.

chopper /'tʃɒpər/ n. tajador -ra.

choppy /'tʃɒpi/ a. agitado.

choral /'kɔrəl/ a. coral.

chord /kɔrd/ n. cuerda f.; acorde m.

chore /tʃɔr/ n. tarea f., quehacer m.

choreography /,kɔri'ɒgrəfi, ,kour-/ n. coreografía f.

chorister /'kɔrəstər/ n. corista m.

chorus /'kɔrəs/ n. coro m.

christen /'krɪsən/ v. bautizar.

Christendom /'krɪsəndəm/ n. cristiandad f.

Christian /'krɪsʃən/ a. & n. cristiano -na.

Christianity /,krɪsʃi'ænɪti/ n. cristianismo m.

Christmas /'krɪsməs/ n. Navidad, Pascua f. **Merry C.,** felices Pascuas. **C. Eve,** Nochebuena f.

chromatic /krou'mætɪk/ a. cromático.

chromium /'kroumiəm/ n. cromo m.

chromosome /'kroumə,soum/ n. cromosoma m.

chronic /'krɒnɪk/ a. crónico.

chronicle /'krɒnɪkəl/ n. crónica f.

chronological /,krɒnɭ'ɒdʒɪkəl/ a. cronológico.

chronology /krə'nɒlədʒi/ n. cronología f.

chrysalis /'krɪsəlɪs/ n. crisálida f.

chrysanthemum /krɪ'sænθəməm/ n. crisantemo m.

chubby /'tʃʌbi/ a. regordete, rollizo.

chuck /tʃʌk/ v. (cluck) cloquear; (throw) echar, tirar.

chuckle /'tʃʌkəl/ v. reír entre dientes.

chum /tʃʌm/ n. amigo -ga; compinche m.

chummy /'tʃʌmi/ a. íntimo.

chunk /tʃʌŋk/ n. trozo m.

chunky /'tʃʌŋki/ a. fornido, trabado.

Chunnel /'tʃʌnɭ/ n. túnel del Canal de la Mancha m.

church /tʃɜrtʃ/ n. iglesia f.

churchman /'tʃɜrtʃmən/ n. eclesiástico m.

churchyard /'tʃɜrtʃ,yard/ n. cementerio m.

churn /tʃɜrn/ n. **1.** mantequera f. —v. **2.** agitar, revolver.

chute /ʃut/ n. conducto; canal m.

cicada /sɪ'keidə/ n. cigarra, chicharra f.

cider /'saidər/ n. sidra f.

cigar /sɪ'gɑr/ n. cigarro, puro m.

cigarette /,sɪgə'rɛt/ n. cigarrillo, cigarro, pitillo m. **c. case,** cigarrillera f. **c. lighter,** encendedor m.

cinchona /sɪŋ'kounə/ *n.* cinchona *f.*

cinder /'sɪndər/ *n.* ceniza *f.*

cinema /'sɪnəmə/ *n.* cine *m.*

cinnamon /'sɪnəmən/ *n.* canela *f.*

cipher /'saifər/ *n.* cifra *f.*

circle /'sɜrkəl/ *n.* círculo *m.*

circuit /'sɜrkɪt/ *n.* circuito *m.*

circuitous /sər'kyuɪtəs/ *a.* tortuoso.

circuitously /sər'kyuɪtəsli/ *adv.* tortuosamente.

circular /'sɜrkyələr/ *a.* circular, redondo.

circularize /'sɜrkyələ,raiz/ *v.* hacer circular.

circulate /'sɜrkyə,leit/ *v.* circular.

circulation /,sɜrkyə'leiʃən/ *n.* circulación *f.*

circulator /'sɜrkyə,leitər/ *n.* diseminador -ra.

circulatory /'sɜrkyələ,tɔri/ *a.* circulatorio.

circumcise /'sɜrkəm,saiz/ *v.* circuncidar.

circumcision /,sɜrkəm'sɪʒən/ *n.* circuncisión *f.*

circumference /sər'kʌmfərəns/ *n.* circunferencia *f.*

circumlocution /,sɜrkəmlou'kyu-ʃən/ *n.* circunlocución *f.*

circumscribe /'sɜrkəm,skraib/ *v.* circunscribir; limitar.

circumspect /'sɜrkəm,spɛkt/ *a.* discreto.

circumstance /'sɜrkəm,stæns/ *n.* circunstancia *f.*

circumstantial /,sɜrkəm'stænʃəl/ *a.* circunstancial, indirecto.

circumstantially /,sɜrkəm'stæn-ʃəli/ *adv.* minuciosamente.

circumvent /,sɜrkəm'vɛnt/ *v.* evadir, evitar.

circumvention /,sɜrkəm'vɛnʃən/ *n.* trampa *f.*

circus /'sɜrkəs/ *n.* circo *m.*

cirrhosis /sɪ'rousɪs/ *n.* cirrosis *f.*

cistern /'sɪstərn/ *n.* cisterna *f.*

citadel /'sɪtədl/ *n.* ciudadela *f.*

citation /sai'teiʃən/ *n.* citación *f.*

cite /sait/ *v.* citar.

citizen /'sɪtəzən/ *n.* ciudadano -na.

citizenship /'sɪtəzən,ʃɪp/ *n.* ciudadanía *f.*

citric /'sɪtrɪk/ *a.* cítrico.

city /'sɪti/ *n.* ciudad *f.*

city hall ayuntamiento, municipio *m.*

city planning urbanismo *m.*

civic /'sɪvɪk/ *a.* cívico.

civics /'sɪvɪks/ *n.* ciencia del gobierno civil.

civil /'sɪvəl/ *a.* civil; cortés.

civilian /sɪ'vɪlyən/ *a.* & *n.* civil *m.* & *f.*

civility /sɪ'vɪlɪti/ *n.* cortesía *f.*

civilization /,sɪvələ'zeiʃən/ *n.* civilización *f.*

civilize /'sɪvə,laiz/ *v.* civilizar.

civil rights /raits/ derechos civiles *m. pl.*

civil service *n.* servicio civil oficial *m.*

civil war *n.* guerra civil *f.*

clabber /'klæbər/ *n.* **1.** cuajo *m.* —*v.* **2.** cuajarse.

clad /klæd/ *a.* vestido.

claim /kleim/ *n.* **1.** demanda; pretensión *f.* —*v.* **2.** demandar, reclamar.

claimant /'kleimənt/ *n.* reclamante -ta.

clairvoyance /klɛər'vɔiəns/ *n.* clarividencia *f.*

clairvoyant /klɛər'vɔiənt/ *a.* clarividente.

clam /klæm/ *n.* almeja *f.*

clamber /'klæmbər/ *v.* trepar.

clamor /'klæmər/ *n.* **1.** clamor *m.* —*v.* **2.** clamar.

clamorous /'klæmərəs/ *a.* clamoroso.

clamp /klæmp/ *n.* **1.** prensa de sujeción *f.* —*v.* **2.** asegurar, sujetar.

clan /klæn/ *n.* tribu *f.*, clan *m.*

clandestine /klæn'dɛstɪn/ *a.* clandestino.

clandestinely /klæn'dɛstɪnli/ *adv.* clandestinamente.

clangor /'klæŋər, 'klæŋgər/ *n.* estruendo *m.*, estrépito *m.*

clannish /'klænɪʃ/ *a.* unido; exclusivista.

clap /klæp/ *v.* aplaudir.

clapboard /'klæbərd, 'klæp,bɔrd/ *n.* chilla *f.*

claque /klæk/ *n.* claque *f.*

claret /'klærɪt/ *n.* clarete *m.*

clarification /,klærəfə'keiʃən/ *n.* clarificación *f.*

clarify /'klærə,fai/ *v.* clarificar.

clarinet /,klærə'nɛt/ *n.* clarinete *m.*

clarinetist /,klærə'nɛtɪst/ *n.* clarinetista *m.* & *f.*

clarity /'klærɪti/ *n.* claridad *f.*

clash /klæʃ/ *n.* **1.** choque, enfrentamiento *m.* —*v.* **2.** chocar.

clasp /klæsp/ *n.* **1.** broche *m.* —*v.* **2.** abrochar.

class /klæs/ *n.* clase *f.*

classic, /'klæsɪk/ **classical** *a.* clásico.

classicism /'klæsə‚sɪzəm/ *n.* clasicismo *m.*

classifiable /'klæsə‚faiəbəl/ *a.* clasificable, calificable.

classification /‚klæsəfɪ'keiʃən/ *n.* clasificación *f.*

classify /'klæsə‚fai/ *v.* clasificar.

classmate /'klæs‚meit/ *n.* compañero -ra de clase.

classroom /'klæs‚rum, -‚rʊm/ *n.* sala de clase.

clatter /'klætər/ *n.* **1.** alboroto *m.* —*v.* **2.** alborotar.

clause /klɔz/ *n.* cláusula *f.*

claustrophobia /‚klɔstrə'foubiə/ *n.* claustrofobia *f.*

claw /klɔ/ *n.* garra *f.*

clay /klei/ *n.* arcilla *f.*; barro *m.*

clean /klin/ *a.* **1.** limpio. —*v.* **2.** limpiar.

cleaner /'klinər/ *n.* limpiador -ra.

cleaning lady, cleaning woman /'klinɪŋ/ señora de la limpieza, mujer de la limpieza *f.*

cleanliness /'klɛnlinɪs/ *n.* limpieza *f.*

cleanse /klɛnz/ *v.* limpiar, purificar.

cleanser /'klɛnzər/ *n.* limpiador *m.*, purificador *m.*

clear /klɪər/ *a.* claro.

clearance /'klɪərəns/ *n.* espacio libre. **c. sale,** venta de liquidación.

clearing /'klɪərɪŋ/ *n.* despejo *m.*; desmonte *m.*

clearly /'klɪərli/ *adv.* claramente, evidentemente.

clearness /'klɪərnɪs/ *n.* claridad *f.*

cleavage /'klivɪdʒ/ *n.* resquebradura *f.*

cleaver /'klivər/ *n.* partidor *m.*, hacha *f.*

clef /klɛf/ *n.* clave, llave *f.*

clemency /'klɛmənsi/ *n.* clemencia *f.*

clench /klɛntʃ/ *v.* agarrar.

clergy /'klɜrdʒi/ *n.* clero *m.*

clergyman /'klɜrdʒimən/ *n.* clérigo *m.*

clerical /'klɛrɪkəl/ *a.* clerical. **c. work,** trabajo de oficina.

clericalism /'klɛrɪkə‚lɪzəm/ *n.* clericalismo *m.*

clerk /klɜrk/ *n.* dependiente, escribiente *m.*

clerkship /'klɜrkʃɪp/ *n.* escribanía *f.*, secretaría *f.*

clever /'klɛvər/ *a.* diestro, hábil.

cleverly /'klɛvərli/ *adv.* diestramente, hábilmente.

cleverness /'klɛvərnɪs/ *n.* destreza *f.*

cliché /kli'ʃei/ *n.* tópico *m.*

client /'klaiənt/ *n.* cliente -ta.

clientele /‚klaiən'tɛl/ *n.* clientela *f.*

cliff /klɪf/ *n.* precipicio, risco *m.*

climate /'klaimɪt/ *n.* clima *m.*

climatic /klai'mætɪk/ *a.* climático.

climax /'klaimæks/ *n.* colmo *m.*, culminación *f.*

climb /klaim/ *v.* escalar; subir.

climber /'klaimər/ *n.* trepador -ra, escalador -ra; *Bot.* enredadera *f.*

climbing plant /'klaimɪŋ/ enredadera *f.*

clinch /klɪntʃ/ *v.* afirmar.

cling /klɪŋ/ *v.* pegarse.

clinic /'klɪnɪk/ *n.* clínica *f.*

clinical /'klɪnɪkəl/ *a.* clínico.

clinically /'klɪnɪkəli/ *adv.* clínicamente.

clip /klɪp/ *n.* **1.** grapa *f.* **paper c.,** gancho *m.* —*v.* **2.** prender; (shear) trasquilar.

clipper /'klɪpər/ *n.* recortador *m.*; *Aero.* clíper *m.*

clipping /'klɪpɪŋ/ *n.* recorte *m.*

clique /klik/ *n.* camarilla *f.*, compadraje *m.*

cloak /klouk/ *n.* capa *f.*, manto *m.*

clock /klɒk/ *n.* reloj *m.* **alarm c.,** despertador *m.*

clod /klɒd/ *n.* terrón *m.*; césped *m.*

clog /klɒg/ *v.* obstruir.

cloister /'klɔistər/ *n.* claustro *m.*

clone /kloun/ *n.* clon *m.* & *f.* *v.* clonar.

close /a, adv. klous; v klouz/ *a.* **1.** cercano. —*adv.* **2.** cerca. **c. to,** cerca de. —*v.* **3.** cerrar; tapar.

closely /'klousli/ *adv.* (near) de cerca; (tight) estrechamente; (care) cuidadosamente.

closeness /'klousnɪs/ *n.* contigüidad *f.*, apretamiento *m.*; (airless) falta de ventilación *f.*

closet /'klɒzɪt/ *n.* gabinete *m.* **clothes c.,** ropero *m.*

clot /klɒt/ *n.* **1.** coágulo *f.* —*v.* **2.** coagularse.

cloth /klɔθ/ *n.* paño *m.*; tela *f.*

clothe /klouð/ *v.* vestir.

clothes /klouz/ *n.* ropa *f.*

clothing /'klouðɪŋ/ n. vestidos m., ropa f.

cloud /klaud/ n. nube f.

cloudburst /'klaud,bɜrst/ n. chaparrón m.

cloudiness /'klaudinɪs/ n. nebulosidad f.; obscuridad f.

cloudless /'klaudlɪs/ a. despejado, sin nubes.

cloudy /'klaudi/ a. nublado.

clove /klouv/ n. clavo m.

clover /'klouvər/ n. trébol m.

clown /klaun/ n. bufón -na, payaso -sa.

clownish /'klaunɪʃ/ a. grosero; bufonesco.

cloy /klɔi/ v. saciar, empalagar.

club /klʌb/ n. **1.** porra f.; (social) círculo, club m.; (cards) basto m. —v. **2.** golpear con una porra.

clubfoot /'klʌb,fʊt/ n. pateta m., pie zambo m.

clue /klu/ n. seña, pista f.

clump /klʌmp/ n. grupo m., masa f.

clumsiness /'klʌmzinɪs/ n. tosquedad f.; desmaña f.

clumsy /'klʌmzi/ a. torpe, desmañado.

cluster /'klʌstər/ n. **1.** grupo m.; (fruit) racimo m. —v. **2.** agrupar.

clutch /klʌtʃ/ n. **1.** Auto. embrague m. —v. **2.** agarrar.

clutter /'klʌtər/ n. **1.** confusión f. —v. **2.** poner en desorden.

coach /koutʃ/ n. **1.** coche, vagón m.; coche ordinario; (sports) entrenador m. —v. **2.** entrenar.

coachman /'koutʃmən/ n. cochero -ra.

coagulate /kou'ægyə,leit/ v. coagular.

coagulation /kou,ægyə'leiʃən/ n. coagulación f.

coal /koul/ n. carbón m.

coalesce /,kouə'lɛs/ v. unirse, soldarse.

coalition /,kouə'lɪʃən/ n. coalición f.

coal oil n. petróleo m.

coal tar n. alquitrán m.

coarse /kɔrs/ a. grosero, burdo; (material) tosco, grueso.

coarsen /'kɔrsən/ v. vulgarizar.

coarseness /'kɔrsnɪs/ n. grosería; tosquedad f.

coast /koust/ n. **1.** costa f., litoral m. —v. **2.** deslizarse.

coastal /'koustl/ a. costanero.

coast guard guardacostas m. & f.

coat /kout/ n. **1.** saco m., chaqueta f.; (paint) capa f. —v. **2.** cubrir.

coat of arms /ɑrmz/ n. escudo m.

coax /kouks/ v. instar.

cobalt /'koubɔlt/ n. cobalto m.

cobbler /'kɒblər/ n. zapatero -ra.

cobblestone /'kɒbəl,stoun/ n. guijarro m.

cobra /'koubrə/ n. cobra f.

cobweb /'kɒb,wɛb/ n. telaraña f.

cocaine /kou'kein/ n. cocaína f.

cock /kɒk/ n. (rooster) gallo m.; (water, etc.) llave f.; (gun) martillo m.

cockfight /'kɒk,fait/ n. riña de gallos f.

cockpit /'kɒk,pɪt/ n. gallera f.; reñidero de gallos m.; Aero. cabina f.

cockroach /'kɒk,routʃ/ n. cucaracha f.

cocktail /'kɒk,teil/ n. cóctel m.

cocky /'kɒki/ a. confiado, atrevido.

cocoa /'koukou/ n. cacao m.

coconut /'koukə,nʌt/ n. coco m.

cocoon /kə'kun/ n. capullo m.

cod /kɒd/ n. bacalao m.

code /koud/ n. código m.; clave f.

codeine /'koudin/ n. codeína f.

codfish /'kɒd,fɪʃ/ n. bacalao m.

codify /'kɒdə,fai/ v. compilar.

cod-liver oil /'kɒd 'lɪvər/ aceite de hígado de bacalao m.

coeducation /,kouɛdʒʊ'keiʃən/ n. coeducación f.

coequal /kou'ikwəl/ a. mutuamente igual.

coerce /kou'ɜrs/ v. forzar.

coercion /kou'ɜrʃən/ n. coerción f.

coercive /kou'ɜrsiv/ a. coercitivo.

coexist /,kouɪg'zɪst/ v. coexistir.

coffee /'kɔfi/ n. café m. **c. plantation,** cafetal m. **c. shop,** café m.

coffee break pausa para el café f.

coffer /'kɔfər/ n. cofre m.

coffin /'kɔfɪn/ n. ataúd m.

cog /kɒg/ n. diente de rueda m.

cogent /'koudʒənt/ a. convincente.

cogitate /'kɒdʒɪ,teit/ v. pensar, reflexionar.

cognizance /'kɒgnəzəns/ n. conocimiento m., comprensión f.

cognizant /'kɒgnəzənt/ a. conocedor, informado.

cogwheel /'kɒg,wil/ n. rueda dentada f.

cohere /kou'hɪər/ v. pegarse.
coherent /kou'hɪərənt/ a. coherente.
cohesion /kou'hiʒən/ n. cohesión f.
cohesive /kou'hisɪv/ a. cohesivo.
cohort /'kouhɔrt/ n. cohorte f.
coiffure /kwɑ'fyʊr/ n. peinado, tocado m.
coil /kɔil/ n. **1.** rollo m.; Naut. adujada f. —v. **2.** enrollar.
coin /kɔin/ n. moneda f.
coinage /'kɔinɪdʒ/ n. sistema monetario m.
coincide /ˌkouɪn'said/ v. coincidir.
coincidence /kou'ɪnsɪdəns/ n. coincidencia; casualidad f.
coincident /kou'ɪnsɪdənt/ a. coincidente.
coincidental /kouˌɪnsɪ'dɛntl/ a. coincidental.
coincidentally /kouˌɪnsɪ'dɛntli/ adv. coincidentalmente, al mismo tiempo.
colander /'kɒləndər/ n. colador m.
cold /kould/ a. & n. frío -a; Med. resfriado m. **to be c.,** tener frío; (weather) hacer frío.
coldly /'kouldli/ adv. fríamente.
coldness /'kouldnɪs/ n. frialdad f.
collaborate /kə'læbəˌreit/ v. colaborar.
collaboration /kəˌlæbə'reiʃən/ n. colaboración f.
collaborator /kə'læbəˌreitər/ n. colaborador -ra.
collapse /kə'læps/ n. **1.** desplome m.; Med. colapso m. —v. **2.** desplomarse.
collar /'kɒlər/ n. cuello m.
collarbone /'kɒlərˌboun/ n. clavícula f.
collate /kou'leit/ v. comparar.
collateral /kə'lætərəl/ a. **1.** colateral. —n. **2.** garantía f.
collation /kə'leiʃən/ n. comparación f.; (food) colación f., merienda f.
colleague /'kɒlig/ n. colega m. & f.
collect /'kɒlɛkt/ v. cobrar; recoger; coleccionar.
collection /kə'lɛkʃən/ n. colección f.
collective /kə'lɛktɪv/ a. colectivo.
collectively /kə'lɛktɪvli/ adv. colectivamente, en masa.
collector /kə'lɛktər/ n. colector -ra; coleccionista m. & f.

college /'kɒlɪdʒ/ n. colegio m.; universidad f.
collegiate /kə'lidʒɪt/ n. colegiado m.
collide /kə'laid/ v. chocar.
collision /kə'lɪʒən/ n. choque m.
colloquial /kə'loukwiəl/ a. familiar.
colloquially /kə'loukwiəli/ adv. familiarmente.
colloquy /'kɒləkwi/ n. conversación f., coloquio m.
collusion /kə'luʒən/ n. colusión f., connivencia f.
Cologne /kə'loun/ n. Colonia f.
Colombian /kə'lʌmbiən/ a. & n. colombiano -na.
colon /'koulən/ n. colon m.; Punct. dos puntos.
colonel /'kɜrnl/ n. coronel m.
colonial /kə'louniəl/ a. colonial.
colonist /'kɒlənɪst/ n. colono -na.
colonization /ˌkɒlənə'zeiʃən/ n. colonización f.
colonize /'kɒləˌnaiz/ v. colonizar.
colony /'kɒləni/ n. colonia f.
color /'kʌlər/ n. **1.** color; colorido m. —v. **2.** colorar; colorir.
coloration /ˌkʌlə'reiʃən/ n. colorido m.
colored /'kʌlərd/ a. de color.
colorful /'kʌlərfəl/ a. vívido.
colorless /'kʌlərlɪs/ a. descolorido, sin color.
colossal /kə'lɒsəl/ a. colosal.
colt /koult/ n. potro m.
column /'kɒləm/ n. columna f.
coma /'koumə/ n. coma m.
comb /koum/ n. **1.** peine m. —v. **2.** peinar.
combat /n 'kɒmbæt; v kəm'bæt/ n. **1.** combate m. —v. **2.** combatir.
combatant /kəm'bætnt/ n. combatiente -ta.
combative /kəm'bætɪv/ a. combativo.
combination /ˌkɒmbə'neiʃən/ n. combinación f.
combine /kəm'bain/ v. combinar.
combustible /kəm'bʌstəbəl/ a. & n. combustible m.
combustion /kəm'bʌstʃən/ n. combustión f.
come /kʌm/ v. venir. **c. back,** volver. **c. in,** entrar. **c. out,** salir. **c. up,** subir. **c. upon,** encontrarse con.
comedian /kə'midiən/ n. cómico -ca.

comedienne /kə,midi'ɛn/ *n.* cómica *f.,* actriz *f.*

comedy /'kɒmɪdi/ *n.* comedia *f.*

comet /'kɒmɪt/ *n.* cometa *m.*

comfort /'kʌmfərt/ *n.* **1.** confort *m.;* solaz *m.* —*v.* **2.** confortar; solazar.

comfortable /'kʌmftəbəl/ *a.* cómodo.

comfortably /'kʌmftəbli/ *adv.* cómodamente.

comforter /'kʌmfərtər/ *n.* colcha *f.*

comfortingly /'kʌmfərtɪŋli/ *adv.* confortantemente.

comfortless /'kɒmfərtlɪs/ *a.* sin consuelo; sin comodidades.

comic /'kɒmɪk/ **comical** *a.* cómico.

comic book *n.* tebeo *m.*

coming /'kʌmɪŋ/ *n.* **1.** venida *f.,* llegada *f.* —*a.* **2.** próximo, que viene, entrante.

comma /'kɒmə/ *n.* coma *f.*

command /kə'mænd/ *n.* **1.** mando *m.* —*v.* **2.** mandar.

commandeer /,kɒmən'dɪər/ *v.* reclutir forzosamente, expropiar.

commander /kə'mændər/ *n.* comandante -ta.

commander in chief *n.* generalísimo, jefe supremo.

commandment /kə'mændmənt/ *n.* mandato; mandamiento *m.*

commemorate /kə'mɛmə,reit/ *v.* conmemorar.

commemoration /kə,mɛmə'reiʃən/ *n.* conmemoración *f.*

commemorative /kə'mɛmə,reitɪv/ *a.* conmemorativo.

commence /kə'mɛns/ *v.* comenzar, principiar.

commencement /kə'mɛnsmənt/ *n.* comienzo *m.;* graduación *f.*

commend /kə'mɛnd/ *v.* encomendar; elogiar.

commendable /kə'mɛndəbəl/ *a.* recomendable.

commendably /kə'mɛndəbli/ *adv.* loablemente.

commendation /,kɒmən'deiʃən/ *n.* recomendación *f.;* elogio *m.*

commensurate /kə'mɛnsərɪt/ *a.* proporcionado.

comment /'kɒmɛnt/ *n.* **1.** comentario *m.* —*v.* **2.** comentar.

commentary /'kɒmən,tɛri/ *n.* comentario *m.*

commentator /'kɒmən,teitər/ *n.* comentador -ra.

commerce /'kɒmərs/ *n.* comercio *m.*

commercial /kə'mɜrʃəl/ *a.* comercial.

commercialism /kə'mɜrʃə,lɪzəm/ *n.* comercialismo *m.*

commercialize /kə'mɜrʃə,laiz/ *v.* mercantilizar, explotar.

commercially /kə'mɜrʃəli/ *a.* & *adv.* comercialmente.

commiserate /kə'mɪzə,reit/ *v.* compadecerse.

commissary /'kɒmə,sɛri/ *n.* comisario *m.*

commission /kə'mɪʃən/ *n.* **1.** comisión *f.* —*v.* **2.** comisionar.

commissioner /kə'mɪʃənər/ *n.* comisario -ria.

commit /kə'mɪt/ *v.* cometer.

commitment /kə'mɪtmənt/ *n.* compromiso *m.*

committee /kə'mɪti/ *n.* comité *m.*

commodious /kə'moudiəs/ *a.* cómodo.

commodity /kə'mɒdɪti/ *n.* mercadería *f.*

common /'kɒmən/ *a.* común; ordinario.

commonly /'kɒmənli/ *adv.* comúnmente, vulgarmente.

Common Market Mercado Común *m.*

commonplace /'kɒmən,pleis/ *a.* trivial, banal.

common sense sentido común *m.*

commonwealth /'kɒmən,wɛlθ/ *n.* estado *m.;* nación *f.*

commotion /kə'mouʃən/ *n.* tumulto *m.*

communal /kə'myunḷ/ *a.* comunal, público.

commune /'kɒmyun/ *n.* **1.** distrito municipal *m.;* comuna *f.* —*v.* **2.** conversar.

communicable /kə'myunɪkəbəl/ *a.* comunicable; *Med.* transmisible.

communicate /kə'myunɪ,keit/ *v.* comunicar.

communication /kə,myunɪ'keiʃən/ *n.* comunicación *f.*

communicative /kə'myunɪ,keitɪv/ *a.* comunicativo.

communion /kə'myunyən/ *n.* comunión *f.* **take c.,** comulgar.

communiqué /kə,myunɪ'kei/ *n.* comunicación *f.*

communism /'kɒmyə,nɪzəm/ *n.* comunismo *m.*

communist /'kɒmyənɪst/ *n.* comunista *m.* & *f.*

communistic /ˌkɒmyəˈnɪstɪk/ a. comunístico.

community /kəˈmyunɪti/ n. comunidad f.

commutation /ˌkɒmyəˈteiʃən/ n. conmutación f.

commuter /kəˈmyutər/ n. empleado que viaja diariamente desde su domicilio hasta la ciudad donde trabaja.

compact /a kəmˈpækt; n ˈkɒmpækt/ a. **1.** compacto. —n. **2.** pacto m.; (lady's) polvera f.

compact disk disco compacto m.

companion /kəmˈpænyən/ n. compañero -ra.

companionable /kəmˈpænyənəbəl/ a. sociable.

companionship /kəmˈpænyənˌʃɪp/ n. compañerismo m.

company /ˈkʌmpəni/ n. compañía f.

comparable /ˈkɒmpərəbəl/ a. comparable.

comparative /kəmˈpærətɪv/ a. comparativo.

comparatively /kəmˈpærətɪvli/ a. relativamente.

compare /kəmˈpɛər/ v. comparar.

comparison /kəmˈpærəsən/ n. comparación f.

compartment /kəmˈpɑrtmənt/ n. compartimiento m.

compass /ˈkʌmpəs/ n. compás m.; Naut. brújula f.

compassion /kəmˈpæʃən/ n. compasión f.

compassionate /kəmˈpæʃənɪt/ a. compasivo.

compassionately /kəmˈpæʃənɪtli/ adv. compasivamente.

compatible /kəmˈpætəbəl/ a. compatible.

compatriot /kəmˈpeitriət/ n. compatriota m. & f.

compel /kəmˈpɛl/ v. obligar.

compensate /ˈkɒmpənˌseit/ v. compensar.

compensation /ˌkɒmpənˈseiʃən/ n. compensación f.

compensatory /kəmˈpɛnsəˌtɔri/ a. compensatorio.

compete /kəmˈpit/ v. competir.

competence /ˈkɒmpɪtəns/ n. competencia f.

competent /ˈkɒmpɪtənt/ a. competente, capaz.

competently /ˈkɒmpɪtəntli/ adv. competentemente.

competition /ˌkɒmpɪˈtɪʃən/ n. concurrencia f.; concurso m.

competitive /kəmˈpɛtɪtɪv/ a. competidor.

competitor /kəmˈpɛtɪtər/ n. competidor -ra.

compile /kəmˈpail/ v. compilar.

complacency /kəmˈpleisənsi/ n. complacencia f.

complacent /kəmˈpleisənt/ a. complaciente.

complacently /kəmˈpleisəntli/ adv. complacientemente.

complain /kəmˈplein/ v. quejarse.

complaint /kəmˈpleint/ n. queja f.

complement /ˈkɒmpləmənt/ n. complemento m.

complete /kəmˈplit/ a. **1.** completo —v. **2.** completar.

completely /kəmˈplitli/ adv. completamente, enteramente.

completeness /kəmˈplitnɪs/ n. integridad f.

completion /kəmˈpliʃən/ n. terminación f.

complex /kəmˈplɛks/ a. complejo.

complexion /kəmˈplɛkʃən/ n. tez f.

complexity /kəmˈplɛksɪti/ n. complejidad f.

compliance /kəmˈplaiəns/ n. consentimiento m. **in c. with,** de acuerdo con.

compliant /kəmˈplaiənt/ a. dócil; complaciente.

complicate /ˈkɒmplɪˌkeit/ v. complicar.

complicated /ˈkɒmplɪˌkeitɪd/ a. complicado.

complication /ˌkɒmplɪˈkeiʃən/ n. complicación f.

complicity /kəmˈplɪsɪti/ n. complicidad f.

compliment /n ˈkɒmpləmənt; v -ˌmɛnt/ n. **1.** elogio m. Fig. —v. **2.** felicitar; echar flores.

complimentary /ˌkɒmpləˈmɛntəri/ a. galante, obsequioso, regaloso.

comply /kəmˈplai/ v. cumplir.

component /kəmˈpounənt/ a. & n. componente m.

comport /kəmˈpɔrt/ v. portarse.

compose /kəmˈpouz/ v. componer.

composed /kəmˈpouzd/ a. tranquilo; (made up) compuesto.

composer /kəmˈpouzər/ n. compositor -ra.

composite /kəmˈpɒzɪt/ a. compuesto.

composition /ˌkɒmpəˈzɪʃən/ n. composición f.

composure /kəmˈpouʒər/ n. serenidad f.; calma f.

compote /ˈkɒmpout/ n. compota f.

compound /ˈkɒmpaund/ a. & n. compuesto m.

comprehend /ˌkɒmprɪˈhɛnd/ v. comprender.

comprehensible /ˌkɒmprɪˈhɛnsəbəl/ a. comprensible.

comprehension /ˌkɒmprɪˈhɛnʃən/ n. comprensión f.

comprehensive /ˌkɒmprɪˈhɛnsɪv/ a. comprensivo.

compress /n ˈkɒmprɛs; v kəmˈprɛs/ n. **1.** cabezal m. —v. **2.** comprimir.

compressed /kəmˈprɛst/ a. comprimido.

compression /kəmˈprɛʃən/ n. compresión f.

compressor /kəmˈprɛsər/ n. compresor m.

comprise /kəmˈpraiz/ v. comprender; abarcar.

compromise /ˈkɒmprəˌmaiz/ n. **1.** compromiso m. —v. **2.** comprometer.

compromiser /ˈkɒmprəˌmaizər/ n. compromisario m.

compulsion /kəmˈpʌlʃən/ n. compulsión f.

compulsive /kəmˈpʌlsɪv/ a. compulsivo.

compulsory /kəmˈpʌlsəri/ a. obligatorio.

compunction /kəmˈpʌŋkʃən/ n. compunción f.; escrúpulo m.

computation /ˌkɒmpyʊˈteiʃən/ n. computación f.

compute /kəmˈpyut/ v. computar, calcular.

computer /kəmˈpyutər/ n. computadora f., ordenador m.

computerize /kəmˈpyutəˌraiz/ v. procesar en computadora, computerizar.

computer programmer /ˈprougræmər/ programador -ra de ordenadores.

computer science informática f.

comrade /ˈkɒmræd/ n. camarada m. & f.; compañero -ra.

comradeship /ˈkɒmrædˌʃɪp/ n. camaradería f.

concave /kɒnˈkeiv/ a. cóncavo.

conceal /kənˈsil/ v. ocultar, esconder.

concealment /kənˈsilmənt/ n. ocultación f.

concede /kənˈsid/ v. conceder.

conceit /kənˈsit/ n. amor propio; engreimiento m.

conceited /kənˈsitɪd/ a. engreído.

conceivable /kənˈsivəbəl/ a. concebible.

conceive /kənˈsiv/ v. concebir.

concentrate /ˈkɒnsənˌtreit/ v. concentrar.

concentration /ˌkɒnsənˈtreiʃən/ n. concentración f.

concentration camp campo de concentración m.

concept /ˈkɒnsɛpt/ n. concepto m.

conception /kənˈsɛpʃən/ n. concepción f.; concepto m.

concern /kənˈsɜrn/ n. **1.** interés m.; inquietud f.; Com. negocio m. —v. **2.** concernir.

concerning /kənˈsɜrnɪŋ/ prep. respecto a.

concert /ˈkɒnsɜrt/ n. concierto m.

concerted /kənˈsɜrtɪd/ a. convenido.

concession /kənˈsɛʃən/ n. concesión f.

conciliate /kənˈsɪliˌeit/ v. conciliar.

conciliation /kənˌsɪliˈeiʃən/ n. conciliación f.

conciliator /kənˈsɪliˌeitər/ n. conciliador -ra.

conciliatory /kənˈsɪliəˌtɔri/ a. conciliatorio.

concise /kənˈsais/ a. conciso.

concisely /kənˈsaisli/ adv. concisamente.

conciseness /kənˈsaisnɪs/ n. concisión f.

conclave /ˈkɒnkleiv/ n. conclave m.

conclude /kənˈklud/ v. concluir.

conclusion /kənˈkluʒən/ n. conclusión f.

conclusive /kənˈklusɪv/ a. conclusivo, decisivo.

conclusively /kənˈklusɪvli/ adv. concluyentemente.

concoct /kɒnˈkɒkt/ v. confeccionar.

concomitant /kɒnˈkɒmɪtənt/ n. & a. concomitante m.

concord /ˈkɒnkɔrd/ n. concordia f.

concordat /kɒnˈkɔrdæt/ n. concordato m.

concourse /ˈkɒnkɔrs/ n. concurso m.; confluencia f.

concrete /ˈkɒnkrit/ a. concreto.

concretely /kɒn'kritli/ adv. concretamente.

concubine /'kɒŋkyə,bain/ n. concubina, amiga f.

concur /kən'kɜr/ v. concurrir.

concurrence /kən'kɜrəns/ n. concurrencia f.; casualidad f.

concurrent /kən'kɜrənt/ a. concurrente.

concussion /kən'kʌʃən/ n. concusión f.; (c. of the brain) conmoción cerebral f.

condemn /kən'dɛm/ v. condenar.

condemnable /kən'dɛmnəbəl/ a. culpable, condenable.

condemnation /,kɒndɛm'neiʃən/ n. condenación f.

condensation /,kɒndɛn'seiʃən/ n. condensación f.

condense /kən'dɛns/ v. condensar.

condenser /kən'dɛnsər/ n. condensador m.

condescend /,kɒndə'sɛnd/ v. condescender.

condescension /,kɒndə'sɛnʃən/ n. condescendencia f.

condiment /'kɒndəmənt/ n. condimento m.

condition /kən'dɪʃən/ n. **1.** condición f.; estado m. —v. **2.** acondicionar.

conditional /kən'dɪʃənl/ a. condicional.

conditionally /kən'dɪʃənli/ adv. condicionalmente.

condole /kən'doul/ v. condolerse.

condolence /kən'douləns/ n. pésame m.

condom /'kɒndəm/ n. forro, preservativo m.

condominium /,kɒndə'mɪniəm/ n. condominio m.

condone /kən'doun/ v. condonar.

conducive /kən'dusɪv, -'dyu-/ a. conducente.

conduct /n 'kɒndʌkt; v kən'dʌkt/ n. **1.** conducta f. —v. **2.** conducir.

conductivity /,kɒndʌk'tɪvɪti/ n. conductividad f.

conductor /kən'dʌktər/ n. conductor m.

conduit /'kɒnduɪt/ n. caño m., canal f.; conducto m.

cone /koun/ n. cono m. **ice-cream c.,** barquillo de helado.

confection /kən'fɛkʃən/ n. confitura f.

confectioner /kən'fɛkʃənər/ n. confitero -ra.

confectionery /kən'fɛkʃə,nɛri/ n. dulcería f.

confederacy /kən'fɛdərəsi/ n. federación f.

confederate / kən'fɛdərɪt/ a. & n. confederado m.

confederation /kən,fɛdə'reiʃən/ n. confederación f.

confer /kən'fɜr/ v. conferenciar; conferir.

conference /'kɒnfərəns/ n. conferencia f.; congreso m.

confess /kən'fɛs/ v. confesar.

confession /kən'fɛʃən/ n. confesión f.

confessional /kən'fɛʃənl/ n. **1.** confesionario m. —a. **2.** confesional.

confessor /kən'fɛsər/ n. confesor m.

confetti /kən'fɛti/ n. confetti m.

confidant /'kɒnfɪ,dænt/ **confidante** n. confidente m. & f.

confide /kən'faid/ v. confiar.

confidence /'kɒnfɪdəns/ n. confianza f.

confident /'kɒnfɪdənt/ a. confiado; cierto.

confidential /,kɒnfɪ'dɛnʃəl/ a. confidencial.

confidentially /,kɒnfɪ'dɛnʃəli/ adv. confidencialmente, en secreto.

confidently /'kɒnfɪdəntli/ adv. confiadamente.

confine /kən'fain/ n. **1.** confín m. —v. **2.** confinar; encerrar.

confirm /kən'fɜrm/ v. confirmar.

confirmation /,kɒnfər'meiʃən/ n. confirmación f.

confiscate /'kɒnfə,skeit/ v. confiscar.

confiscation /,kɒnfə'skeiʃən/ n. confiscación f.

conflagration /,kɒnflə'greiʃən/ n. incendio m.

conflict /n 'kɒnflɪkt; v kən'flɪkt/ n. **1.** conflicto m. —v. **2.** oponerse; estar en conflicto.

conform /kən'fɔrm/ v. conformar.

conformation /,kɒnfɔr'meiʃən/ n. conformación f.

conformer /kən'fɔrmər/ n. conformista m. & f.

conformist /kən'fɔrmɪst/ n. conformista m. & f.

conformity /kən'fɔrmɪti/ n. conformidad f.

confound /kɒn'faund/ v. confundir.

confront

246

confront /kən'frʌnt/ v. confrontar.

confrontation /ˌkɒnfrən'teiʃən/ n. enfrentamiento m.

confuse /kən'fyuz/ v. confundir.

confusion /kən'fyuʒən/ n. confusión f.

congeal /kən'dʒil/ v. congelar, helar.

congealment /kən'dʒilmənt/ n. congelación f.

congenial /kən'dʒinyəl/ a. congenial.

congenital /kən'dʒɛnɪtl̩/ a. congénito.

congenitally /kən'dʒɛnɪtl̩i/ adv. congenitalmente.

congestion /kən'dʒɛstʃən/ n. congestión f.

conglomerate /v kən'glɒmə,reit; a, n kən'glɒmərɪt/ v. **1.** conglomerar. —a. & n. **2.** conglomerado.

conglomeration /kən,glɒmə'reiʃən/ n. conglomeración f.

congratulate /kən'grætʃə,leit/ v. felicitar.

congratulation /kən,grætʃə'leiʃən/ n. felicitación f.

congratulatory /kən'grætʃələ,tɔri/ a. congratulatorio.

congregate /'kɒŋgrɪ,geit/ v. congregar.

congregation /ˌkɒŋgrɪ'geiʃən/ n. congregación f.

congress /'kɒŋgrɪs/ n. congreso m.

conic /'kɒnɪk/ n. **1.** cónica f. —a. **2.** cónico.

conjecture /kən'dʒɛktʃər/ n. **1.** conjetura f. —v. **2.** conjeturar.

conjugal /'kɒndʒəgəl/ a. conyugal, matrimonial.

conjugate /'kɒndʒə,geit/ v. conjugar.

conjugation /ˌkɒndʒə'geiʃən/ n. conjugación f.

conjunction /kən'dʒʌŋkʃən/ n. conjunción f.

conjunctive /kən'dʒʌŋktɪv/ n. **1.** Gram. conjunción f. —a. **2.** conjuntivo.

conjunctivitis /kən,dʒʌŋktə'vaitɪs/ n. conjuntivitis f.

conjure /'kɒndʒər/ v. conjurar.

connect /kə'nɛkt/ v. juntar; relacionar.

connection /kə'nɛkʃən/ n. conexión f.

connivance /kə'naivəns/ n. consentimiento m.

connive /kə'naiv/ v. disimular.

connoisseur /ˌkɒnə'sɜr/ n. perito -ta.

connotation /ˌkɒnə'teiʃən/ n. connotación f.

connote /kə'nout/ v. connotar.

connubial /kə'nubiəl/ a. conyugal.

conquer /'kɒŋkər/ v. conquistar.

conquerable /'kɒŋkərəbəl/ a. conquistable, vencible.

conqueror /'kɒŋkərər/ n. conquistador -ra.

conquest /'kɒnkwɛst/ n. conquista f.

conscience /'kɒnʃəns/ n. conciencia f.

conscientious /ˌkɒnʃi'ɛnʃəs/ a. concienzudo.

conscientiously /ˌkɒnʃi'ɛnʃəsli/ adv. escrupulosamente.

conscientious objector /ɒb'dʒɛktər/ objetor de conciencia m.

conscious /'kɒnʃəs/ a. consciente.

consciously /'kɒnʃəsli/ adv. con conocimiento.

consciousness /'kɒnʃəsnɪs/ n. conciencia f.

conscript /n 'kɒnskrɪpt; v kən'skrɪpt/ n. **1.** conscripto m., recluta m. —v. **2.** reclutar, alistar.

conscription /kən'skrɪpʃən/ n. conscripción f., alistamiento m.

consecrate /'kɒnsɪ,kreit/ v. consagrar.

consecration /ˌkɒnsɪ'kreiʃən/ n. consagración f.

consecutive /kən'sɛkyətɪv/ a. consecutivo, seguido.

consecutively /kən'sɛkyətɪvli/ adv. consecutivamente, de seguida.

consensus /kən'sɛnsəs/ n. consenso m., acuerdo general m.

consent /kən'sɛnt/ n. **1.** consentimiento m. —v. **2.** consentir.

consequence /'kɒnsɪ,kwɛns/ n. consecuencia f.

consequent /'kɒnsɪ,kwɛnt/ a. consiguiente.

consequential /ˌkɒnsɪ'kwɛnʃəl/ a. importante.

consequently /'kɒnsɪ,kwɛntli/ adv. por lo tanto, por consiguiente.

conservation /ˌkɒnsər'veiʃən/ n. conservación f.

conservatism /kən'sɜrvə,tɪzəm/ n. conservatismo m.

conservative /kən'sɜrvətɪv/ a. conservador, conservativo.

conservatory /kən'sɜrvə,tɔri/ *n.* (plants) invernáculo *m.;* (school) conservatorio *m.*

conserve /kən'sɜrv/ *v.* conservar.

consider /kən'sɪdər/ *v.* considerar.

C. it done! ¡Dalo por hecho!

considerable /kən'sɪdərəbəl/ *a.* considerable.

considerably /kən'sɪdərəbli/ *adv.* considerablemente.

considerate /kən'sɪdərɪt/ *a.* considerado.

considerately /kən'sɪdərɪtli/ *adv.* consideradamente.

consideration /kən,sɪdə'reiʃən/ *n.* consideración *f.*

considering /kən'sɪdərɪŋ/ *prep.* visto que, en vista de.

consign /kən'sain/ *v.* consignar.

consignment /kən'sainmənt/ *n.* consignación *f.,* envío *m.*

consist /kən'sɪst/ *v.* consistir.

consistency /kən'sɪstənsi/ *n.* consistencia *f.*

consistent /kən'sɪstənt/ *a.* consistente.

consolation /,kɒnsə'leiʃən/ *n.* consolación *f.*

consolation prize premio de consuelo *m.*

console /kən'soul/ *v.* consolar.

consolidate /kən'sɒlɪ,deit/ *v.* consolidar.

consommé /,kɒnsə'mei/ *n.* caldo *m.*

consonant /'kɒnsənənt/ *n.* consonante *f.*

consort /n 'kɒnsɔrt, v kən'sɔrt/ *n.* **1.** cónyuge *m. & f.;* socio. —*v.* **2.** asociarse.

conspicuous /kən'spɪkyuəs/ *a.* conspicuo.

conspicuously /kən'spɪkyuəsli/ *adv.* visiblemente, llamativamente.

conspicuousness /kən'spɪkyuəsnɪs/ *n.* visibilidad *f.;* evidencia *f.;* fama *f.*

conspiracy /kən'spɪrəsi/ *n.* conspiración *f.;* complot *m.*

conspirator /kən'spɪrətər/ *n.* conspirador -ra.

conspire /kən'spaiᵊr/ *v.* conspirar.

conspirer /kən'spaiᵊrər/ *n.* conspirante *m. & f.*

constancy /'kɒnstənsi/ *n.* constancia *f.,* lealtad *f.*

constant /'kɒnstənt/ *a.* constante.

constantly /'kɒnstəntli/ *adv.* constantemente, de continuo.

constellation /,kɒnstə'leiʃən/ *n.* constelación *f.*

consternation /,kɒnstər'neiʃən/ *n.* consternación *f.*

constipate /'kɒnstə,peit/ *v.* estreñir.

constipated /'kɒnstə,peitɪd/ *a.* estreñido, *m.*

constipation /,kɒnstə'peiʃən/ *n.* estreñimiento, *m.*

constituency /kən'stɪtʃuənsi/ *n.* distrito electoral *m.*

constituent /kən'stɪtʃuənt/ *a.* **1.** constituyente. —*n.* **2.** elector *m.*

constitute /'kɒnstɪ,tut/ *v.* constituir.

constitution /,kɒnstɪ'tuʃən/ *n.* constitución *f.*

constitutional /,kɒnstɪ'tuʃənļ/ *a.* constitucional.

constrain /kən'strein/ *v.* constreñir.

constraint /kən'streint/ *n.* constreñimiento *m.,* compulsión *f.*

constrict /kən'strɪkt/ *v.* apretar, estrechar.

construct /kən'strʌkt/ *v.* construir.

construction /kən'strʌkʃən/ *n.* construcción *f.*

constructive /kən'strʌktɪv/ *a.* constructivo.

constructively /kən'strʌktɪvli/ *adv.* constructivamente; por deducción.

constructor /kən'strʌktər/ *n.* constructor *m.*

construe /kən'stru/ *v.* interpretar.

consul /'kɒnsəl/ *n.* cónsul *m.*

consular /'kɒnsələr/ *a.* consular.

consulate /'kɒnsəlɪt/ *n.* consulado *m.*

consult /kən'sʌlt/ *v.* consultar.

consultant /kən'sʌltənt/ *n.* consultor -ora.

consultation /,kɒnsəl'teiʃən/ *n.* consulta *f.*

consume /kən'sum/ *v.* consumir.

consumer /kən'sumər/ *n.* consumidor -ra.

consumer society sociedad de consumo *f.*

consummation /,kɒnsə'meiʃən/ *n.* consumación *f.*

consumption /kən'sʌmpʃən/ *n.* consumo *m.; Med.* tisis.

consumptive /kən'sʌmptɪv/ *n.* **1.** tísico *m.* —*a.* **2.** consuntivo.

contact /'kɒntækt/ *n.* **1.** contacto

m. —*v.* **2.** ponerse en contacto con.

contact lens lentilla *f.*

contagion /kən'teidʒən/ *n.* contagio *m.*

contagious /kən'teidʒəs/ *a.* contagioso.

contain /kən'tein/ *v.* contener.

container /kən'teinər/ *n.* envase *m.*

contaminate /kən'tæmə,neit/ *v.* contaminar.

contemplate /'kɒntəm,pleit/ *v.* contemplar.

contemplation /,kɒntəm'pleiʃən/ *n.* contemplación *f.*

contemplative /kən'templətɪv/ *a.* contemplativo.

contemporary /kən'tempə,reri/ *n.* & *a.* contemporáneo -nea.

contempt /kən'tempt/ *n.* desprecio *m.*

contemptible /kən'temptəbəl/ *a.* vil, despreciable.

contemptuous /kən'temptʃuəs/ *a.* desdeñoso.

contemptuously /kən'temptʃuəsli/ *adv.* desdeñosamente.

contend /kən'tend/ *v.* contender; competir.

contender /kən'tendər/ *n.* competidor -ra.

content /*a, v* kən'tent; *n* 'kɒntent/ *a.* **1.** contento. —*n.* **2.** contenido *m.* —*v.* **3.** contentar.

contented /kən'tentɪd/ *a.* contento.

contention /kən'tenʃən/ *n.* contención *f.*

contentment /kən'tentmənt/ *n.* contentamiento *m.*

contest /*n* 'kɒntest; *v* kən'test/ *n.* **1.** concurso *m.* —*v.* **2.** disputar.

contestable /kən'testəbəl/ *a.* contestable.

context /'kɒntekst/ *n.* contexto *m.*

contiguous /kən'tɪgyuəs/ *a.* contiguo.

continence /'kɒntn̩əns/ *n.* continencia *f.*, castidad *f.*

continent /'kɒntn̩ənt/ *n.* continente *m.*

continental /,kɒntn̩'entl̩/ *a.* continental.

contingency /kən'tɪndʒənsi/ *n.* eventualidad *f.*, casualidad *f.*

contingent /kən'tɪndʒənt/ *a.* contingente.

continual /kən'tɪnyuəl/ *a.* continuo.

continuation /kən,tɪnyu'eiʃən/ *n.* continuación *f.*

continue /kən'tɪnyu/ *v.* continuar.

continuity /,kɒntn̩'uiti/ *n.* continuidad *f.*

continuous /kən'tɪnyuəs/ *a.* continuo.

continuously /kən'tɪnyuəsli/ *adv.* continuamente.

contour /'kɒntur/ *n.* contorno *m.*

contraband /'kɒntrə,bænd/ *n.* contrabando *m.*

contraception /,kɒntrə'sepʃən/ *n.* contracepción *f.*

contraceptive /,kɒntrə'septɪv/ *n.* & *a.* anticeptivo *m.*

contract /*n* 'kɒntrækt; *v* kən'trækt/ *n.* **1.** contrato *m.* —*v.* **2.** contraer.

contraction /kən'trækʃən/ *n.* contracción *f.*

contractor /'kɒntræktər/ *n.* contratista *m.* & *f.*

contradict /,kɒntrə'dɪkt/ *v.* contradecir.

contradiction /,kɒntrə'dɪkʃən/ *n.* contradicción *f.*

contradictory /,kɒntrə'dɪktəri/ *a.* contradictorio.

contralto /kən'træltou/ *n.* contralto *m.*

contrary /'kɒntreri/ *a.* & *n.* contrario -ria.

contrast /*n* 'kɒntræst; *v* kən'træst/ *n.* **1.** contraste *m.* —*v.* **2.** contrastar.

contribute /kən'trɪbyut/ *v.* contribuir.

contribution /,kɒntrə'byuʃən/ *n.* contribución *f.*

contributor /kən'trɪbyətər/ *n.* contribuidor -ra.

contributory /kən'trɪbyə,tɔri/ *a.* contribuyente.

contrite /kən'trait/ *a.* contrito.

contrition /kən'trɪʃən/ *n.* contrición *f.*

contrivance /kən'traivəns/ *n.* aparato *m.*; estratagema *f.*

contrive /kən'traiv/ *v.* inventar, tramar; darse maña.

control /kən'troul/ *n.* **1.** control *m.* —*v.* **2.** controlar.

controllable /kən'trouləbəl/ *a.* controlable, dominable.

controller /kən'troulər/ *n.* interventor -ra; contralor -ra.

control tower torre de mando *f.*

controversial /ˌkɒntrə'vɜrʃəl/ *a.* contencioso.

controversy /'kɒntrəˌvɜrsi/ *n.* controversia *f.*

contusion /kən'tuʒən/ *n.* contusión *f.*

convalesce /ˌkɒnvə'lɛs/ *v.* convalecer.

convalescence /ˌkɒnvə'lɛsəns/ *n.* convalecencia *f.*

convalescent /ˌkɒnvə'lɛsənt/ *n.* convaleciente *m.* & *f.*

convalescent home clínica de reposo *f.*

convene /kən'vin/ *v.* juntarse; convocar.

convenience /kən'vinyəns/ *n.* comodidad *f.*

convenient /kən'vinyənt/ *a.* cómodo; oportuno.

conveniently /kən'vinyəntli/ *adv.* cómodamente.

convent /'kɒnvɛnt/ *n.* convento *m.*

convention /kən'vɛnʃən/ *n.* convención *f.*

conventional /kən'vɛnʃənl/ *a.* convencional.

conventionally /kən'vɛnʃənli/ *adv.* convencionalmente.

converge /kən'vɜrdʒ/ *v.* convergir.

convergence /kən'vɜrdʒəns/ *n.* convergencia *f.*

convergent /kən'vɜrdʒənt/ *a.* convergente.

conversant /kən'vɜrsənt/ *a.* versado; entendido (de).

conversation /ˌkɒnvər'seiʃən/ *n.* conversación, plática *f.*

conversational /ˌkɒnvər'seiʃənl/ *a.* de conversación.

conversationalist /ˌkɒnvər-'seiʃənlɪst/ *n.* conversador -ra.

converse /kən'vɜrs/ *v.* conversar.

conversely /kən'vɜrsli/ *adv.* a la inversa.

convert /*n.* 'kɒnvɜrt; *v.* kən'vɜrt/ *n.* **1.** convertido da-. —*v.* **2.** convertir.

converter /kən'vɜrtər/ *n.* convertidor *m.*

convertible /kən'vɜrtəbəl/ *a.* convertible.

convex /kɒn'vɛks/ *a.* convexo.

convey /kən'vei/ *v.* transportar; comunicar.

conveyance /kən'veiəns/ *n.* transporte; vehículo *m.*

conveyor /kən'veiər/ *n.* conductor *m.; Mech.* transportador *m.*

conveyor belt correa transportadora *f.*

convict /*n.* 'kɒnvɪkt; *v.* kən'vɪkt/ *n.* **1.** reo *m.* —*v.* **2.** declarar culpable.

conviction /kən'vɪkʃən/ *n.* convicción *f.*

convince /kən'vɪns/ *v.* convencer.

convincing /kən'vɪnsɪŋ/ *a.* convincente.

convivial /kən'vɪviəl/ *a.* convival.

convocation /ˌkɒnvə'keiʃən/ *n.* convocación; asamblea *f.*

convoke /kən'vouk/ *v.* convocar, citar.

convoy /'kɒnvɔi/ *n.* convoy *m.;* escolta *f.*

convulse /kən'vʌls/ *v.* convulsionar; agitar violentamente.

convulsion /kən'vʌlʃən/ *n.* convulsión *f.*

convulsive /kən'vʌlsɪv/ *a.* convulsivo.

cook /kʊk/ *n.* **1.** cocinero -ra. —*v.* **2.** cocinar, cocer.

cookbook /'kʊkˌbʊk/ *n.* libro de cocina *m.*

cookie /'kʊki/ *n.* galleta dulce *f.*

cool /kul/ *a.* **1.** fresco. —*v.* **2.** refrescar.

cooler /'kulər/ *n.* enfriadera *f.*

coolness /'kulnɪs/ *n.* frescura *f.*

coop /kup/ *n.* **1.** jaula *f.* **chicken c.,** gallinero *m.* —*v.* **2.** enjaular.

cooperate /kou'ɒpəˌreit/ *v.* cooperar.

cooperation /kouˌɒpə'reiʃən/ *n.* cooperación *f.*

cooperative /kou'ɒpərətɪv/ *a.* cooperativo.

cooperatively /kou'ɒpərətɪvli/ *adv.* cooperativamente.

coordinate /kou'ɔrdn̩ˌeit/ *v.* coordinar.

coordination /kouˌɔrdn̩'eiʃən/ *n.* coordinación *f.*

coordinator /kou'ɔrdn̩ˌeitər/ *n.* coordinador -ra.

cope /koup/ *v.* contender. **c. with,** superar, hacer frente a.

copier /'kɒpiər/ *n.* copiadora *f.*

copious /'koupiəs/ *a.* copioso, abundante.

copiously /'koupiəsli/ *adv.* copiosamente.

copiousness /'koupiəsnɪs/ *n.* abundancia *f.*

copper /'kɒpər/ *n.* cobre *m.*

copy /'kɒpi/ *n.* **1.** copia *f.*; ejemplar *m.* —*v.* **2.** copiar.

copyist /'kɒpiɪst/ *n.* copista *m. & f.*

copyright /'kɒpi,rait/ *n.* derechos de propiedad literaria *m.pl.*

coquetry /'koukɪtri/ *n.* coquetería *f.*

coquette /kou'kɛt/ *n.* coqueta *f.*

coral /'kɔrəl/ *n.* coral *m.*

cord /kɔrd/ *n.* cuerda *f.*

cordial /'kɔrdʒəl/ *a.* cordial.

cordiality /kɔr'dʒælɪti/ *n.* cordialidad *f.*

cordially /'kɔrdʒəli/ *adv.* cordialmente.

cordon off /'kɔrdn̩/ *v.* acordonar.

cordovan /'kɔrdəvən/ *n.* cordobán *m.*

corduroy /'kɔrdə,rɔi/ *n.* pana *f.*

core /kɔr/ *n.* corazón; centro *m.*

cork /kɔrk/ *n.* corcho *m.*

corkscrew /'kɔrk,skru/ *n.* tirabuzón *m.*

corn /kɔrn/ *n.* maíz *m.*

cornea /'kɔrniə/ *n.* córnea *f.*

corned beef /kɔrnd/ carne acecinada *f.*

corner /'kɔrnər/ *n.* rincón *m.*; (of street) esquina *f.*

cornet /kɔr'nɛt/ *n.* corneta *f.*

cornetist /kɔr'nɛtɪst/ *n.* cornetín *m.*

cornice /'kɔrnɪs/ *n.* cornisa *f.*

cornstarch /'kɔrn,stɑrtʃ/ *n.* maicena *f.*

corollary /'kɔrə,lɛri/ *n.* corolario *m.*

coronary /'kɔrə,nɛri/ *a.* coronario.

coronation /,kɔrə'neiʃən/ *n.* coronación *f.*

corporal /'kɔrpərəl/ *a.* **1.** corpóreo. —*n.* **2.** cabo *m.*

corporate /'kɔrpərɪt/ *a.* corporativo.

corporation /,kɔrpə'reiʃən/ *n.* corporación *f.*

corps /kɔr/ *n.* cuerpo *m.*

corpse /kɔrps/ *n.* cadáver *m.*

corpulent /'kɔrpyələnt/ *a.* corpulento.

corpuscle /'kɔrpəsəl/ *n.* corpúsculo *m.*

corral /kə'ræl/ *n.* **1.** corral *m.* —*v.* **2.** acorralar.

correct /kə'rɛkt/ *a.* **1.** correcto. —*v.* **2.** corregir.

correction /kə'rɛkʃən/ *n.* corrección; enmienda *f.*

corrective /kə'rɛktɪv/ *n. & a.* correctivo.

correctly /kə'rɛktli/ *adv.* correctamente.

correctness /kə'rɛktnɪs/ *n.* exactitud *f.*

correlate /'kɔrə,leit/ *v.* correlacionar.

correlation /,kɔrə'leiʃən/ *n.* correlación *f.*

correspond /,kɔrə'spɒnd/ *v.* corresponder.

correspondence /,kɔrə'spɒndəns/ *n.* correspondencia *f.*

correspondence course curso por correspondencia *m.*

correspondence school escuela por correspondencia *f.*

correspondent /,kɔrə'spɒndənt/ *a. & n.* correspondiente *m. & f.*

corresponding /,kɔrə'spɒndɪŋ/ *a.* correspondiente.

corridor /'kɔrɪdər/ *n.* corredor, pasillo *m.*

corroborate /kə'rɒbə,reit/ *v.* corroborar.

corroboration /kə,rɒbə'reiʃən/ *n.* corroboración *f.*

corroborative /kə'rɒbə,reitɪv/ *a.* corroborante.

corrode /kə'roud/ *v.* corroer.

corrosion /kə'rouʒən/ *n.* corrosión *f.*

corrugate /'kɔrə,geit/ *v.* arrugar; ondular.

corrupt /kə'rʌpt/ *a.* **1.** corrompido. —*v.* **2.** corromper.

corruptible /kə'rʌptəbəl/ *a.* corruptible.

corruption /kə'rʌpʃən/ *n.* corrupción *f.*

corruptive /kə'rʌptɪv/ *a.* corruptivo.

corset /'kɔrsɪt/ *n.* corsé *m.*, (girdle) faja *f.*

cortege /kɔr'tɛʒ/ *n.* comitiva *f.*, séquito *m.*

corvette /kɔr'vɛt/ *n.* corbeta *f.*

cosmetic /kɒz'mɛtɪk/ *a. & n.* cosmético *m.*

cosmic /'kɒzmɪk/ *a.* cósmico.

cosmonaut /'kɒzmə,nɔt/ *n.* cosmonauta *m. & f.*

cosmopolitan /,kɒzmə'pɒlɪtn̩/ *a. & n.* cosmopolita *m. & f.*

cosmos /'kɒzməs/ *n.* cosmos *m.*

cost /kɔst/ *n.* **1.** coste *m.*; costa *f.* —*v.* **2.** costar.

Costa Rican /'kɒstə'rikən/ *a. & n.* costarricense *m. & f.*

costly /'kɔstli/ *a.* costoso, caro.

costume /'kɒstum/ n. traje; disfraz m.

costume jewelry bisutería f., joyas de fantasía f.pl.

cot /kɒt/ n. catre m.

coterie /'koutəri/ n. camarilla f.

cotillion /kə'tɪlyən/ n. cotillón m.

cottage /'kɒtɪdʒ/ n. casita f.

cottage cheese requesón m.

cotton /'kɒtn̩/ n. algodón m.

cottonseed /'kɒtn̩,sid/ n. semilla del algodón f.

couch /kautʃ/ n. sofá m.

cougar /'kugər/ n. puma m.

cough /kɔf/ n. **1.** tos f. —v. **2.** toser.

council /'kaunsəl/ n. consejo, concilio m.

counsel /'kaunsəl/ n. **1.** consejo; (law) abogado -da. —v. **2.** aconsejar. **to keep one's c.,** no decir nada.

counselor /'kaunsələr/ n. consejero -ra; (law) abogado -da.

count /kaunt/ n. **1.** cuenta f.; (title) conde m. —v. **2.** contar.

countenance /'kauntn̩əns/ n. **1.** aspecto m.; cara f. —v. **2.** aprobar.

counter /'kauntər/ adv. **1. c. to,** contra, en contra de. —n. **2.** mostrador m.

counteract /,kauntər'ækt/ v. contrarrestar.

counteraction /,kauntər'ækʃən/ n. neutralización f.

counterbalance /'kauntər,bæləns/ n. **1.** contrapeso m. —v. **2.** contrapesar.

counterfeit /'kauntər,fɪt/ a. **1.** falsificado. —v. **2.** falsear.

countermand /,kauntər'mænd/ v. contramandar.

counteroffensive /,kauntərə-'fɛnsɪv/ n. contraofensiva f.

counterpart /'kauntər,part/ n. contraparte f.

counterproductive /,kauntərprə'dʌktɪv/ a. contraproducente.

countess /'kauntɪs/ n. condesa f.

countless /'kauntlɪs/ a. innumerable.

country /'kʌntri/ n. campo m.; Pol. país m.; (homeland) patria f.

country code distintivo del país m.

countryman /'kʌntrimən/ n. paisano m. **fellow c.,** compatriota m.

countryside /'kʌntri,said/ n. campo, paisaje m.

county /'kaunti/ n. condado m.

coupé /kup/ n. cupé m.

couple /'kʌpəl/ n. **1.** par m. —v. **2.** unir.

coupon /'kupɒn/ n. cupón, talón m.

courage /'kɜrɪdʒ/ n. valor m.

courageous /kə'reidʒəs/ a. valiente.

course /kɔrs/ n. curso m. **of c.,** por supuesto, desde luego.

court /kɔrt/ n. **1.** corte f.; cortejo m.; (of law) tribunal m. —v. **2.** cortejar.

courteous /'kɜrtiəs/ a. cortés.

courtesy /'kɜrtəsi/ n. cortesía f.

courthouse /'kɔrt,haus/ n. palacio de justicia m., tribunal m.

courtier /'kɔrtiər/ n. cortesano m.

courtly /'kɔrtli/ a. cortés, galante.

courtroom /'kɔrt,rum, -,rum/ n. sala de justicia f.

courtship /'kɔrtʃɪp/ n. cortejo m.

courtyard /'kɔrt,yard/ n. patio m.

cousin /'kʌzən/ n. primo -ma.

covenant /'kʌvənənt/ n. contrato, convenio m.

cover /'kʌvər/ n. **1.** cubierta, tapa f. —v. **2.** cubrir, tapar.

cover charge precio del cubierto m.

covet /'kʌvɪt/ v. ambicionar, suspirar por.

covetous /'kʌvɪtəs/ a. codicioso.

cow /kau/ n. vaca f.

coward /'kauərd/ n. cobarde m. & f.

cowardice /'kauərdɪs/ n. cobardía f.

cowardly /'kauərdli/ a. cobarde.

cowboy /'kau,bɔi/ n. vaquero, gaucho m.

cower /'kauər/ v. agacharse (de miedo).

cowhide /'kau,haid/ n. cuero m.

coy /kɔi/ a. recatado, modesto.

coyote /kai'outi/ n. coyote m.

cozy /'kouzi/ a. cómodo y agradable.

crab /kræb/ n. cangrejo m.

crab apple n. manzana silvestre f.

crack /kræk/ n. **1.** hendedura f.; (noise) crujido m. —v. **2.** hender; crujir.

cracker /'krækər/ n. galleta f.

cradle /'kreidl̩/ n. cuna f.

craft /kræft/ n. arte m.

craftsman /'kræftsmən/ n. artesano -na.

craftsmanship /'kræftsmən‚ʃɪp/ n. artesanía f.

crafty /'kræfti/ a. ladino.

crag /kræg/ n. despeñadero m.; peña f.

cram /kræm/ v. rellenar, hartar.

cramp /kræmp/ n. calambre m.

cranberry /'kræn‚bɛri/ n. arándano m.

crane /krein/ n. (bird) grulla f.; Mech. grúa f.

cranium /'kreiniəm/ n. cráneo m.

crank /kræŋk/ n. Mech. manivela f.

cranky /'kræŋki/ a. chiflado, caprichoso.

crash /kræʃ/ n. **1.** choque; estallido m. —v. **2.** estallar.

crate /kreit/ n. canasto m.

crater /'kreitər/ n. cráter m.

crave /kreiv/ v. desear; anhelar.

craven /'kreivən/ a. cobarde.

craving /'kreivɪŋ/ n. sed m., anhelo m.

crawl /krɔl/ v. andar a gatas, arrastrarse.

crayon /'kreiɒn/ n. creyón; lápiz m.

crazy /'kreizi/ a. loco.

creak /krik/ v. crujir.

creaky /'kriki/ a. crujiente.

cream /krim/ n. crema f.

cream cheese queso crema m.

creamery /'kriməri/ n. lechería f.

creamy /'krimi/ a. cremoso.

crease /kris/ n. pliegue m. —v. **2.** plegar.

create /kri'eit/ v. crear.

creation /kri'eiʃən/ n. creación f.

creative /kri'eitɪv/ a. creativo, creador.

creator /kri'eitər/ n. creador -ra.

creature /'kritʃər/ n. criatura f.

credence /'kridns/ n. creencia f.

credentials /krɪ'dɛnʃəlz/ n. credenciales f.pl.

credibility /‚krɛdə'bɪlɪti/ n. credibilidad f.

credible /'krɛdəbəl/ a. creíble.

credit /'krɛdɪt/ n. **1.** crédito m. **on c.,** al fiado. —v. **2.** Com. abonar.

creditable /'krɛdɪtəbəl/ a. fidedigno.

credit balance saldo acreedor.

credit card n. tarjeta de crédito f.

creditor /'krɛdɪtər/ n. acreedor -ra.

credit union banco cooperativo m.

credo /'kridou/ n. credo m.

credulity /krə'dulɪti/ n. credulidad f.

credulous /'krɛdʒələs/ a. crédulo.

creed /krid/ n. credo m.

creek /krik/ n. riachuelo m.

creep /krip/ v. gatear.

cremate /'krimeit/ v. incinerar.

crematory /'krimə‚tɔri/ n. crematorio m.

creosote /'kriə‚sout/ n. creosota f.

crepe /kreip/ n. crespón m.

crepe paper papel crespón m.

crescent /'krɛsənt/ a. & n. creciente f.

crest /krɛst/ n. cresta; cima f.; (heraldry) timbre m.

cretonne /krɪ'tɒn/ n. cretona f.

crevice /'krɛvɪs/ n. grieta f.

crew /kru/ n. tripulación f.

crew member tripulante m. & f.

crib /krɪb/ n. pesebre m.; cuna f.

cricket /'krɪkɪt/ n. grillo m.

crime /kraim/ n. crimen m.

criminal /'krɪmənl/ a. & n. criminal m. & f.

criminologist /‚krɪmə'nɒlədʒɪst/ n. criminólogo -ga, criminalista m. & f.

criminology /‚krɪmə'nɒlədʒi/ n. criminología f.

crimson /'krɪmzən, -sən/ a. & n. carmesí m.

cringe /krɪndʒ/ v. encogerse, temblar.

cripple /'krɪpəl/ n. **1.** lisiado -da. —v. **2.** estropear, lisiar.

crisis /'kraisɪs/ n. crisis f.

crisp /krɪsp/ a. crespo, fresco.

crispness /'krɪspnɪs/ n. encrespadura f.

crisscross /'krɪs‚krɔs/ a. entrelazado.

criterion /krai'tɪəriən/ n. criterio m.

critic /'krɪtɪk/ n. crítico -ca.

critical /'krɪtɪkəl/ a. crítico.

criticism /'krɪtə‚sɪzəm/ n. crítica; censura f.

criticize /'krɪtə‚saiz/ v. criticar; censurar.

critique /krɪ'tik/ n. crítica f.

croak /krouk/ n. **1.** graznido m. —v. **2.** graznar.

crochet /krou'ʃei/ n. **1.** crochet m. —v. **2.** hacer crochet.

crochet work ganchillo m.

crock /krɒk/ n. cazuela f.; olla de barro.

crockery /'krɒkəri/ n. loza f.

crocodile /'krɒkə,dail/ *n.* cocodrilo *m.*

crony /'krouni/ *n.* compinche *m.*

crooked /'krʊkɪd/ *a.* encorvado; deshonesto.

croon /krun/ *v.* canturrear.

crop /krɒp/ *n.* cosecha *f.*

croquet /krou'kei/ *n.* juego de croquet *m.*

croquette /krou'kɛt/ *n.* croqueta *f.*

cross /krɔs/ *a.* **1.** enojado, mal humorado. —*n.* **2.** cruz *f.* —*v.* **3.** cruzar, atravesar.

crossbreed /'krɔs,brid/ *n.* **1.** mestizo *m.* —*v.* **2.** cruzar (animales o plantas).

cross-examine /'krɔs ɪg,zæmɪn/ *v.* interrogar.

cross-eyed /'krɔs ,aid/ *a.* bizco.

cross-fertilization /'krɔs ,fɜrtlə'zeiʃən/ *n.* alogamia *f.*

crossing /'krɔsɪŋ/ **crossroads** *n.* cruce *m.*

cross section corte transversal *m.*

crosswalk /'krɔs,wɔk/ *n.* paso cebra *m.*

crossword puzzle /'krɔs ,wɜrd/ crucigrama *m.*

crotch /krɒtʃ/ *n.* bifurcación *f.*; *Anat.* bragadura *f.*

crouch /krautʃ/ *v.* agacharse.

croup /krup/ *n. Med.* crup *m.*

croupier /'krupiər/ *n.* crupié *m.* & *f.*

crow /krou/ *n.* cuervo *m.*

crowd /kraud/ *n.* **1.** muchedumbre *f.*; tropel *m.* —*v.* **2.** apretar.

crowded /'kraudɪd/ *a.* lleno de gente.

crown /kraun/ *n.* **1.** corona *f.* —*v.* **2.** coronar.

crown prince príncipe heredero *m.*

crucial /'kruʃəl/ *a.* crucial.

crucible /'krusəbəl/ *n.* crisol *m.*

crucifix /'krusəfɪks/ *n.* crucifijo *m.*

crucifixion /,krusə'fɪkʃən/ *n.* crucifixión *f.*

crucify /'krusə,fai/ *v.* crucificar.

crude /krud/ *a.* crudo; (oil) bruto.

crudeness /'krudnɪs/ *a.* crudeza *f.*

cruel /'kruəl/ *a.* cruel.

cruelty /'kruəlti/ *n.* crueldad *f.*

cruet /'kruɪt/ *n.* vinagrera *f.*

cruise /kruz/ *v.* **1.** viaje por mar. —*v.* **2.** navegar.

cruiser /'kruzər/ *n.* crucero *m.*

crumb /krʌm/ *n.* miga; migaja *f.*

crumble /'krʌmbəl/ *v.* desmigajar; desmoronar.

crumple /'krʌmpəl/ *v.* arrugar; encogerse.

crusade /kru'seid/ *n.* cruzada *f.*

crusader /kru'seidər/ *n.* cruzado *m.*

crush /krʌʃ/ *v.* aplastar.

crust /krʌst/ *n.* costra; corteza *f.*

crustacean /krʌ'steiʃən/ *n.* crustáceo *m.*

crutch /krʌtʃ/ *n.* muleta *f.*

cry /krai/ *n.* **1.** grito *m.* —*v.* **2.** gritar; (weep) llorar.

cryosurgery /,kraiou'sɜrdʒəri/ *n.* criocirugía *f.*

crypt /krɪpt/ *n.* gruta *f.*, cripta *f.*

cryptic /'krɪptɪk/ *a.* secreto.

cryptography /krɪp'tɒgrəfi/ *n.* criptografía *f.*

crystal /'krɪstl/ *n.* cristal *m.*

crystalline /'krɪstlɪn/ *a.* cristalino, transparente.

crystallize /'krɪstl,aiz/ *v.* cristalizar.

cub /kʌb/ *n.* cachorro *m.*

Cuban /'kyubən/ *n.* & *a.* cubano -na.

cube /'kyub/ *n.* cubo *m.*

cubic /'kyubɪk/ *a.* cúbico.

cubicle /'kyubɪkəl/ *n.* cubículo *m.*

cubic measure medida de capacidad *f.*

cubism /'kyubɪzəm/ *n.* cubismo *m.*

cuckoo /'kuku/ *n.* cuco *m.*

cucumber /'kyukʌmbər/ *n.* pepino *m.*

cuddle /'kʌdl/ *v.* abrazar.

cudgel /'kʌdʒəl/ *n.* palo *m.*

cue /kyu/ *n.* apunte *m.*; (billiards) taco *m.*

cuff /kʌf/ *n.* puño de camisa. **c. links,** gemelos.

cuisine /kwɪ'zin/ *n.* arte culinario *m.*

culinary /'kyulə,nɛri/ *a.* culinario.

culminate /'kʌlmə,neit/ *v.* culminar.

culmination /,kʌlmə'neiʃən/ *n.* culminación *f.*

culpable /'kʌlpəbəl/ *a.* culpable.

culprit /'kʌlprɪt/ *n.* criminal; delincuente *m.* & *f.*

cult /kʌlt/ *n.* culto *m.*

cultivate /'kʌltə,veit/ *v.* cultivar.

cultivated /'kʌltə,veitɪd/ *a.* cultivado.

cultivation /,kʌltə'veiʃən/ *n.* cultivo *m.*; cultivación *f.*

cultivator /'kʌltə,veitər/ *n.* cultivador -ra.

cultural /'kʌltʃərəl/ *a.* cultural.

culture /'kʌltʃər/ *n.* cultura *f.*

cultured /'kʌltʃərd/ *a.* culto.

cumbersome /'kʌmbərsəm/ *a.* pesado, incómodo.

cumulative /'kyumyələtɪv/ *a.* acumulativo.

cunning /'kʌnɪŋ/ *a.* **1.** astuto. —*n.* **2.** astucia *f.*

cup /kʌp/ *n.* taza, jícara *f.*

cupboard /'kʌbərd/ *n.* armario, aparador *m.*

cupidity /kyu'pɪdɪti/ *n.* avaricia *f.*

curable /'kyurəbəl/ *a.* curable.

curator /kyu'reitər/ *n.* guardián -ana.

curb /kɜrb/ *n.* **1.** freno *m.* —*v.* **2.** refrenar.

curd /kɜrd/ *n.* cuajada *f.*

curdle /'kɜrdl̩/ *v.* cuajarse, coagularse.

cure /kyur/ *n.* **1.** remedio *m.* —*v.* **2.** curar, sanar.

curfew /'kɜrfyu/ *n.* toque de queda *m.*

curio /'kyuri,ou/ *n.* objeto curioso.

curiosity /ˌkyuri'ɒsɪti/ *n.* curiosidad *f.*

curious /'kyuriəs/ *a.* curioso.

curl /kɜrl/ *n.* **1.** rizo *m.* —*v.* **2.** rizar.

curly /'kɜrli/ *a.* rizado.

currant /'kɜrənt/ *n.* grosella *f.*

currency /'kɜrənsi/ *n.* circulación *f.*; dinero *m.*

current /'kɜrənt/ *a. & n.* corriente *f.*

current events /ɪ'vɛnts/ actualidades *f.pl.*

currently /'kɜrəntli/ *adv.* corrientemente.

curriculum /kə'rɪkyələm/ *n.* plan de estudio *m.*

curse /kɜrs/ *n.* **1.** maldición *f.* —*v.* **2.** maldecir.

cursor /'kɜrsər/ *n.* cursor *m.*

cursory /'kɜrsəri/ *a.* sumario.

curt /kɜrt/ *a.* brusco.

curtail /kər'teil/ *v.* reducir; restringir.

curtain /'kɜrtn̩/ *n.* cortina *f.*; *Theat.* telón *m.*

curtsy /'kɜrtsi/ *n.* **1.** reverencia *f.* —*v.* **2.** hacer una reverencia.

curvature /'kɜrvətʃər/ *n.* curvatura *f.*

curve /kɜrv/ *n.* **1.** curva *f.* —*v.* **2.** encorvar.

cushion /'kuʃən/ *n.* cojín *m.*; almohada *f.*

cuspidor /'kʌspɪ,dɔr/ *n.* escupidera *f.*

custard /'kʌstərd/ *n.* flan *m.*; natillas *f.pl.*

custodian /kʌ'stoudiən/ *n.* custodio *m.*

custody /'kʌstədi/ *n.* custodia *f.*

custom /'kʌstəm/ *n.* costumbre *f.*

customary /'kʌstə,mɛri/ *a.* acostumbrado, usual.

customer /'kʌstəmər/ *n.* cliente *m. & f.*

customhouse /'kʌstəm,haus/ **customs** *n.* aduana *f.*

customs duty /'kʌstəmz/ derechos de aduana *m.pl.*

customs officer /'kʌstəmz/ agente de aduana *m. & f.*

cut /kʌt/ *n.* **1.** corte *m.*; cortada *f.*; tajada *f.*; (printing) grabado *m.* —*v.* **2.** cortar; tajar.

cute /kyut/ *a.* mono, lindo.

cut glass cristal tallado *m.*

cuticle /'kyutɪkəl/ *n.* cutícula *f.*

cutlery /'kʌtləri/ *n.* cuchillería *f.*

cutlet /'kʌtlɪt/ *n.* chuleta *f.*

cutter /'kʌtər/ *n.* cortador -ra; *Naut.* cúter *m.*

cutthroat /'kʌt,θrout/ *n.* asesino -na.

cyberpunk /'saibər,pʌŋk/ *n.* ciberpunk *m. & f.*

cyberspace /'saibər,speis/ *n.* ciberespacio *m.*

cyclamate /'saiklə,meit, 'sɪklə-/ *n.* ciclamato *m.*

cycle /'saikəl/ *n.* ciclo *m.*

cyclist /'saiklɪst/ *n.* ciclista *m. & f.*

cyclone /'saikloun/ *n.* ciclón, huracán *m.*

cyclotron /'saiklə,trɒn, 'sɪklə-/ *n.* ciclotrón *m.*

cylinder /'sɪlɪndər/ *n.* cilindro *m.*

cylindrical /sɪ'lɪndrɪkəl/ *a.* cilíndrico.

cymbal /'sɪmbəl/ *n.* címbalo *m.*

cynic /'sɪnɪk/ *n.* cínico -ca.

cynical /'sɪnɪkəl/ *a.* cínico.

cynicism /'sɪnə,sɪzəm/ *n.* cinismo *m.*

cypress /'saiprəs/ *n.* ciprés *m.* **c. nut,** piñuela *f.*

cyst /sɪst/ *n.* quiste *m.*

D

dad /dæd/ *n.* papá *m.*, papito *m.*
daffodil /'dæfədɪl/ *n.* narciso *m.*
dagger /'dægər/ *n.* puñal *m.*
dahlia /'dælyə/ *n.* dalia *f.*
daily /'deɪli/ *a.* diario, cotidiano.
daintiness /'deintinɪs/ *n.* delicadeza *f.*
dainty /'deinti/ *a.* delicado.
dairy /'dɛəri/ *n.* lechería, quesería *f.*
dais /'deiɪs/ *n.* tablado *m.*
daisy /'deizi/ *n.* margarita *f.*
dale /deil/ *n.* valle *m.*
dally /'dæli/ *v.* holgar; perder el tiempo.
dam /dæm/ *n.* presa *f.*; dique *m.*
damage /'dæmɪdʒ/ *n.* **1.** daño *m.*
—*v.* **2.** dañar.
damask /'dæməsk/ *n.* damasco *m.*
damn /dæm/ *v.* condenar.
damnation /dæm'neiʃən/ *n.* condenación *f.*
damp /dæmp/ *a.* húmedo.
dampen /'dæmpən/ *v.* humedecer.
dampness /'dæmpnɪs/ *n.* humedad *f.*
damsel /'dæmzəl/ *n.* doncella *f.*
dance /dæns/ *n.* **1.** baile *m.*; danza *f.* —*v.* **2.** bailar.
dance hall salón de baile *m.*
dancer /'dænsər/ *n.* bailador -ra; (professional) bailarín -na.
dancing /'dænsɪŋ/ *n.* baile *m.*
dandelion /'dændl̩aiən/ *n.* amargón *m.*
dandruff /'dændrəf/ *n.* caspa *f.*
dandy /'dændi/ *n.* petimetre *m.*
danger /'deindʒər/ *n.* peligro *m.*
dangerous /'deindʒərəs/ *a.* peligroso.
dangle /'dæŋgəl/ *v.* colgar.
Danish /'deinɪʃ/ *a. & n.* danés -sa; dinamarqués -sa.
dapper /'dæpər/ *a.* gallardo.
dare /dɛər/ *v.* atreverse, osar.
daredevil /'dɛər,dɛvəl/ *n.* atrevido *m.*, -da *f.*
daring /'dɛərɪŋ/ *a.* **1.** atrevido.
—*n.* **2.** osadía *f.*
dark /dɑrk/ *a.* **1.** obscuro; moreno. —*n.* **2.** obscuridad *f.*
darken /'dɑrkən/ *v.* obscurecer.
darkness /'dɑrknɪs/ *n.* obscuridad *f.*
darkroom /'dɑrk,rum, -,rʊm/ *n.* cámara obscura *f.*

darling /'dɑrlɪŋ/ *a. & n.* querido -da, amado -da.
darn /dɑrn/ *v.* zurcir.
darning needle /'dɑrnɪŋ/ aguja de zurcir *m.*
dart /dɑrt/ *n.* dardo *m.*
dartboard /'dɑrt,bɔrd/ *n.* diana *f.*
dash /dæʃ/ *n.* arranque *m.*; *Punct.* guión *m.*
data /'deitə/ *n.* datos *m.*
database /'deitəbeis/ *n.* base de datos *m.*
data processing /'prɒsɛsɪŋ/ proceso de datos *m.*
date /deit/ *n.* fecha *f.*; (engagement) cita *f.*; (fruit) dátil *m.*
daughter /'dɔtər/ *n.* hija *f.*
daughter-in-law /'dɔ,tər ɪn lɔ/ *n.* nuera *f.*
daunt /dɔnt, dɑnt/ *v.* intimidar.
dauntless /'dɔntlɪs/ *a.* intrépido.
davenport /'dævən,pɔrt/ *n.* sofá *m.*
dawn /dɔn/ *n.* **1.** alba, madrugada *f.* —*v.* **2.** amanecer.
day /dei/ *n.* día *m.* **good d.,** buenos días.
daybreak /'dei,breik/ *n.* alba, madrugada *f.*
daydream /'dei,drim/ *n.* fantasía *f.*
daylight /'dei,lait/ *n.* luz del día.
daze /deiz/ *v.* aturdir.
dazzle /'dæzəl/ *v.* deslumbrar.
deacon /'dikən/ *n.* diácono *m.*
dead /dɛd/ *a.* muerto.
deaden /'dɛdn̩/ *v.* amortecer.
dead end atolladero *m.* (impasse); callejón sin salida *m.* (street).
deadline /'dɛd,lain/ *n.* fecha límite *f.*
deadlock /'dɛd,lɒk/ *n.* paro *m.*
deadly /'dɛdli/ *a.* mortal.
deaf /dɛf/ *a.* sordo.
deafen /'dɛfən/ *v.* ensordecer.
deafening /'dɛfənɪŋ/ *a.* ensordecedor.
deaf-mute /'dɛf 'myut/ *n.* sordomudo -da.
deafness /'dɛfnɪs/ *n.* sordera *f.*
deal /dil/ *n.* **1.** trato *m.*; negociación *f.* **a great d., a good d.,** mucho. —*v.* **2.** tratar; negociar.
dealer /'dilər/ *n.* comerciante *m.*, (at cards) tallador -ra.
dean /din/ *n.* decano -na.

dear /dɪər/ *a.* querido; caro.
dearth /dɜrθ/ *n.* escasez *f.*
death /dɛθ/ *n.* muerte *f.*
death certificate partida de defunción *f.*
deathless /'dɛθlɪs/ *a.* inmortal.
debacle /də'bakəl/ *n.* desastre *m.*
debase /dɪ'beis/ *v.* degradar.
debatable /dɪ'beitəbəl/ *a.* discutible.
debate /dɪ'beit/ *n.* **1.** debate *m.* —*v.* **2.** disputar, deliberar.
debauch /dɪ'bɔtʃ/ *v.* corromper.
debilitate /dɪ'bɪlɪˌteit/ *v.* debilitar.
debit /'dɛbɪt/ *n.* débito *m.*
debit balance saldo deudor *m.*
debonair /ˌdɛbə'nɛər/ *a.* cortés; alegre, vivo.
debris /dei'bri/ *n.* escombros *m.pl.*
debt /dɛt/ *n.* deuda *f.* **get into d.** endeudarse.
debtor /'dɛtər/ *n.* deudor -ra.
debug /di'bʌg/ *v.* depurar, limpiar.
debunk /dɪ'bʌŋk/ *v.* desacreditar; desenmascarar.
debut /dei'byu/ *n.* debut, estreno *m.*
debutante /'dɛbyuˌtɑnt/ *n.* debutante *f.*
decade /'dɛkeid/ *n.* década *f.*
decadence /'dɛkədəns/ *n.* decadencia *f.*
decadent /'dɛkədənt/ *a.* decadente.
decaffeinated /di'kæfɪˌneitɪd/ *a.* descafeinado.
decalcomania /dɪˌkælkə'meiniə/ *n.* calcomanía *f.*
decanter /dɪ'kæntər/ *n.* garrafa *f.*
decapitate /dɪ'kæpɪˌteit/ *v.* descabezar.
decay /dɪ'kei/ *n.* **1.** descaecimiento *m.;* (dental) caries *f.* —*v.* **2.** decaer; (dental) cariarse.
deceased /dɪ'sist/ *a.* muerto, difunto.
deceit /dɪ'sit/ *n.* engaño *m.*
deceitful /dɪ'sitfəl/ *a.* engañoso.
deceive /dɪ'siv/ *v.* engañar.
December /dɪ'sɛmbər/ *n.* diciembre *m.*
decency /'disənsi/ *n.* decencia *f.;* decoro *m.*
decent /'disənt/ *a.* decente.
decentralize /di'sɛntrəˌlaiz/ *v.* descentralizar.
deception /dɪ'sɛpʃən/ *n.* decepción *f.*
deceptive /dɪ'sɛptɪv/ *a.* deceptivo.

decibel /'dɛsəˌbɛl/ *n.* decibelio *m.*
decide /dɪ'said/ *v.* decidir.
decimal /'dɛsəməl/ *a.* decimal.
decipher /dɪ'saifər/ *v.* descifrar.
decision /dɪ'sɪʒən/ *n.* decisión *f.*
decisive /dɪ'saisɪv/ *a.* decisivo.
deck /dɛk/ *n.* cubierta *f.*
deck chair tumbona *f.*
declamation /ˌdɛklə'meiʃən/ *n.* declamación *f.*
declaration /ˌdɛklə'reiʃən/ *n.* declaración *f.*
declarative /dɪ'klærətɪv/ *a.* declarativo.
declare /dɪ'klɛər/ *v.* declarar.
declension /dɪ'klɛnʃən/ *n.* declinación *f.*
decline /dɪ'klain/ *n.* **1.** decadencia *f.* —*v.* **2.** decaer; negarse; *Gram.* declinar.
decompose /ˌdikəm'pouz/ *v.* descomponer.
decongestant /ˌdikən'dʒɛstənt/ *n.* descongestionante *m.*
decorate /'dɛkəˌreit/ *v.* decorar, adornar.
decoration /ˌdɛkə'reiʃən/ *n.* decoración *f.*
decorative /'dɛkərətɪv/ *a.* decorativo.
decorator /'dɛkəˌreitər/ *n.* decorador -ra.
decorous /'dɛkərəs/ *a.* correcto.
decorum /dɪ'kɔrəm/ *n.* decoro *m.*
decrease /dɪ'kris/ *v.* disminuir.
decree /dɪ'kri/ *n.* decreto *m.*
decrepit /dɪ'krɛpɪt/ *a.* decrépito.
decry /dɪ'krai/ *v.* desacreditar.
dedicate /'dɛdɪˌkeit/ *v.* dedicar; consagrar.
dedication /ˌdɛdɪ'keiʃən/ *n.* dedicación; dedicatoria *f.*
deduce /dɪ'dus/ *v.* deducir.
deduction /dɪ'dʌkʃən/ *n.* rebaja; deducción *f.*
deductive /dɪ'dʌktɪv/ *a.* deductivo.
deed /did/ *n.* acción; hazaña *f.*
deem /dim/ *v.* estimar.
deep /dip/ *a.* hondo, profundo.
deepen /'dipən/ *v.* profundizar, ahondar.
deep freeze congelación *f.*
deeply /'dipli/ *adv.* profundamente.
deer /dɪər/ *n.* venado, ciervo *m.*
deface /dɪ'feis/ *v.* mutilar.
defamation /ˌdɛfə'meiʃən/ *n.* calumnia *f.*
defame /dɪ'feim/ *v.* difamar.

default /dɪ'fɔlt/ n. **1.** defecto m. —v. **2.** faltar.

defeat /dɪ'fit/ n. **1.** derrota f. —v. **2.** derrotar.

defeatism /dɪ'fitɪzəm/ n. derrotismo m.

defect /'difɛkt, dɪ'fɛkt/ n. defecto m.

defective /dɪ'fɛktɪv/ a. defectivo.

defend /dɪ'fɛnd/ v. defender.

defendant /dɪ'fɛndənt/ n. acusado -da.

defender /dɪ'fɛndər/ n. defensor -ra.

defense /dɪ'fɛns/ n. defensa f.

defensive /dɪ'fɛnsɪv/ a. defensivo.

defer /dɪ'fər/ v. aplazar; deferir.

deference /'dɛfərəns/ n. deferencia f.

defiance /dɪ'faɪəns/ n. desafío m.

defiant /dɪ'faɪənt/ a. desafiador.

deficiency /dɪ'fɪʃənsi/ n. defecto m.

deficient /dɪ'fɪʃənt/ a. deficiente.

deficit /'dɛfəsɪt/ n. déficit, descubierto m.

defile /dɪ'faɪl/ n. **1.** desfiladero m. —v. **2.** profanar.

define /dɪ'faɪn/ v. definir.

definite /'dɛfənɪt/ a. exacto; definitivo.

definitely /'dɛfənɪtli/ adv. definitivamente.

definition /ˌdɛfə'nɪʃən/ n. definición f.

definitive /dɪ'fɪnɪtɪv/ a. definitivo.

deflation /dɪ'fleɪʃən/ n. desinflación f.

deflect /dɪ'flɛkt/ v. desviar.

deform /dɪ'fɔrm/ v. deformar.

deformity /dɪ'fɔrmɪti/ n. deformidad f.

defraud /dɪ'frɔd/ v. defraudar.

defray /dɪ'freɪ/ v. costear.

defrost /dɪ'frɔst/ v. descongelar.

deft /dɛft/ a. diestro.

defy /dɪ'faɪ/ v. desafiar.

degenerate /a dɪ'dʒɛnərɪt; v -ˌreɪt/ a. **1.** degenerado. —v. **2.** degenerar.

degeneration /dɪˌdʒɛnə'reɪʃən/ n. degeneración f.

degradation /ˌdɛgrɪ'deɪʃən/ n. degradación f.

degrade /dɪ'greɪd/ v. degradar.

degree /dɪ'gri/ n. grado m.

deign /deɪn/ v. condescender.

deity /'diɪti/ n. deidad f.

dejected /dɪ'dʒɛktɪd/ a. abatido.

dejection /dɪ'dʒɛkʃən/ n. tristeza f.

delay /dɪ'leɪ/ n. **1.** retardo m., demora f. —v. **2.** tardar, demorar.

delegate /n 'dɛlɪgɪt; v -ˌgeɪt/ n. **1.** delegado -da. —v. **2.** delegar.

delegation /ˌdɛlɪ'geɪʃən/ n. delegación f.

delete /dɪ'lit/ v. suprimir, tachar.

deliberate /a dɪ'lɪbərɪt; v -əˌreɪt/ a. **1.** premeditado. —v. **2.** deliberar.

deliberately /dɪ'lɪbərɪtli/ adv. deliberadamente.

deliberation /dɪˌlɪbə'reɪʃən/ n. deliberación f.

deliberative /dɪ'lɪbərətɪv/ a. deliberativo.

delicacy /'dɛlɪkəsi/ n. delicadeza f.

delicate /'dɛlɪkɪt/ a. delicado.

delicious /dɪ'lɪʃəs/ a. delicioso.

delight /dɪ'laɪt/ n. deleite m.

delightful /dɪ'laɪtfəl/ a. deleitoso.

delinquency /dɪ'lɪŋkwənsi/ a. delincuencia f.

delinquent /dɪ'lɪŋkwənt/ a. & n. delincuente. m. & f.

delirious /dɪ'lɪəriəs/ a. delirante.

deliver /dɪ'lɪvər/ v. entregar.

deliverance /dɪ'lɪvərəns/ n. liberación; salvación f.

delivery /dɪ'lɪvəri/ n. entrega f.; Med. parto m.

delude /dɪ'lud/ v. engañar.

deluge /'dɛlyudʒ/ n. inundación f.

delusion /dɪ'luʒən/ n. decepción f.; engaño m.

delve /dɛlv/ v. cavar, sondear.

demagogue /'dɛməˌgɒg/ n. demagogo -ga.

demand /dɪ'mænd/ n. **1.** demanda f. —v. **2.** demandar; exigir.

demarcation /ˌdimɑr'keɪʃən/ n. demarcación f.

demeanor /dɪ'minər/ n. conducta f.

demented /dɪ'mɛntɪd/ a. demente, loco.

demilitarize /di'mɪlɪtəˌraɪz/ v. desmilitarizar.

demobilize /di'moubəˌlaɪz/ v. desmovilizar.

democracy /dɪ'mɒkrəsi/ n. democracia f.

democrat /'dɛməˌkræt/ n. demócrata m. & f.

democratic /ˌdɛmə'krætɪk/ a. democrático.

demolish /dɪ'mɒlɪʃ/ v. demoler.

demon /'dimən/ *n.* demonio *m.*

demonstrate /'dɛmən,streit/ *v.* demostrar.

demonstration /,dɛmən'streiʃən/ *n.* demostración *f.*

demonstrative /də'mɒnstrətɪv/ *a.* demostrativo.

demoralize /dɪ'mɔrə,laiz, -'mɒr-/ *v.* desmoralizar.

demure /dɪ'myʊr/ *a.* modesto, serio.

den /dɛn/ *n.* madriguera, caverna *f.*

denature /di'neitʃər/ *v.* alterar.

denial /dɪ'naiəl/ *n.* negación *f.*

denim /'dɛnəm/ *n.* dril, tela vaquera.

Denmark /'dɛnmɑrk/ *n.* Dinamarca *f.*

denomination /dɪ,nɒmə'neiʃən/ *n.* denominación; secta *f.*

denote /dɪ'nout/ *v.* denotar.

denounce /dɪ'nauns/ *v.* denunciar.

dense /dɛns/ *a.* denso, espeso; estúpido.

density /'dɛnsɪti/ *n.* densidad *f.*

dent /dɛnt/ *n.* **1.** abolladura *f.* —*v.* **2.** abollar.

dental /'dɛntl̩/ *a.* dental.

dentist /'dɛntɪst/ *n.* dentista *m.* & *f.*

dentistry /'dɛntəstri/ *n.* odontología *f.*

denture /'dɛntʃər/ *n.* dentadura *f.*

denunciation /dɪ,nʌnsi'eiʃən/ *n.* denunciación *f.*

deny /dɪ'nai/ *v.* negar, rehusar.

deodorant /di'oudərənt/ *n.* desodorante *m.*

depart /dɪ'pɑrt/ *v.* partir; irse, marcharse.

department /dɪ'pɑrtmənt/ *n.* departamento *m.*

departmental /dɪ,pɑrt'mɛntl̩/ *a.* departamental.

department store grandes almacenes *m.pl.*

departure /dɪ'pɑrtʃər/ *n.* salida; desviación *f.*

depend /dɪ'pɛnd/ *v.* depender.

dependability /dɪ,pɛndə'bɪlɪti/ *n.* confiabilidad *f.*

dependable /dɪ'pɛndəbəl/ *a.* confiable.

dependence /dɪ'pɛndəns/ *n.* dependencia *f.*

dependent /dɪ'pɛndənt/ *a.* & *n.* dependiente *m.* & *f.*

depict /dɪ'pɪkt/ *v.* pintar; representar.

deplete /dɪ'plit/ *v.* agotar.

deplorable /dɪ'plɔrəbəl/ *a.* deplorable.

deplore /dɪ'plɔr/ *v.* deplorar.

deport /dɪ'pɔrt/ *v.* deportar.

deportation /,dipɔr'teiʃən/ *n.* deportación *f.*

deportment /dɪ'pɔrtmənt/ *n.* conducta *f.*

depose /dɪ'pouz/ *v.* deponer.

deposit /dɪ'pɒzɪt/ *n.* **1.** depósito *m.* (of money); yacimiento (of ore, etc.) *m.* —*v.* **2.** depositar.

depositor /dɪ'pɒzɪtər/ *n.* depositante *m.* & *f.*

depot /'dipou/ *n.* depósito *m.*; (railway) estación *f.*

depravity /dɪ'prævɪti/ *n.* depravación *f.*

deprecate /'dɛprɪ,keit/ *v.* deprecar.

depreciate /dɪ'priʃi,eit/ *v.* depreciar.

depreciation /dɪ,priʃi'eiʃən/ *n.* depreciación *f.*

depredation /,dɛprə'deiʃən/ *n.* depredación *f.*

depress /dɪ'prɛs/ *v.* deprimir; desanimar.

depression /dɪ'prɛʃən/ *n.* depresión *f.*

deprive /dɪ'praiv/ *v.* privar.

depth /dɛpθ/ *n.* profundidad, hondura *f.*

depth charge carga de profundidad *f.*

deputy /'dɛpyəti/ *n.* diputado -da.

deride /dɪ'raid/ *v.* burlar.

derision /dɪ'rɪʒən/ *n.* burla *f.*

derivation /,dɛrə'veiʃən/ *n.* derivación *f.*

derivative /dɪ'rɪvətɪv/ *a.* derivativo.

derive /dɪ'raiv/ *v.* derivar.

dermatologist /,dɜrmə'tɒlədʒɪst/ *n.* dermatólogo -ga.

derogatory /dɪ'rɒgə,tɔri/ *a.* derogatorio.

derrick /'dɛrɪk/ *n.* grúa *f.*

descend /dɪ'sɛnd/ *v.* descender, bajar.

descendant /dɪ'sɛndənt/ *n.* descendiente *m.* & *f.*

descent /dɪ'sɛnt/ *n.* descenso *m.*; origen *m.*

describe /dɪ'skraib/ *v.* describir.

description /dɪ'skrɪpʃən/ *n.* descripción *f.*

descriptive /dɪ'skrɪptɪv/ *a.* descriptivo.

desecrate /'dɛsɪˌkreit/ v. profanar.
desert /n 'dɛzərt; v dɪ'zɜrt/ n. **1.** desierto m. —v. **2.** abandonar.
deserter /dɪ'zɜrtər/ n. desertor -ra.
desertion /dɪ'zɜrʃən/ n. deserción f.
deserve /dɪ'zɜrv/ v. merecer.
design /dɪ'zain/ n. **1.** diseño m. —v. **2.** diseñar.
designate /'dɛzɪgˌneit/ v. señalar, apuntar; designar.
designation /ˌdɛzɪg'neiʃən/ n. designación f.
designer /dɪ'zainər/ n. diseñador -ra; (technical) proyectista m. & f.
designer clothes, designer clothing ropa de marca f.
desirability /dɪˌzaiərə'bɪlɪti/ n. conveniencia f.
desirable /dɪ'zaiərəbəl/ a. deseable.
desire /dɪ'zaiər/ n. **1.** deseo m. —v. **2.** desear.
desirous /dɪ'zaiərəs/ a. deseoso.
desist /dɪ'sɪst/ v. desistir.
desk /dɛsk/ n. escritorio m.
desk clerk recepcionista m. & f.
desktop computer /'dɛskˌtɒp/ computadora de sobremesa f., ordenador de sobremesa f.
desolate /a 'dɛsəlɪt; v -ˌleit/ a. **1.** desolado. —v. **2.** desolar.
desolation /ˌdɛsə'leiʃən/ n. desolación, ruina f.
despair /dɪ'spɛər/ n. **1.** desesperación f. —v. **2.** desesperar.
despatch /dɪ'spætʃ/ **dispatch** n. **1.** despacho m.; prontitud f. —v. **2.** despachar.
desperado /ˌdɛspə'rɑdou/ n. bandido m.
desperate /'dɛspərɪt/ a. desesperado.
desperation /ˌdɛspə'reiʃən/ n. desesperación f.
despicable /'dɛspɪkəbəl/ a. vil.
despise /dɪ'spaiz/ v. despreciar.
despite /dɪ'spait/ prep. a pesar de.
despondent /dɪ'spɒndənt/ a. abatido; desanimado.
despot /'dɛspət/ n. déspota m. & f.
despotic /dɛs'pɒtɪk/ a. despótico.
dessert /dɪ'zɜrt/ n. postre m.
destination /ˌdɛstə'neiʃən/ n. destinación f.
destine /'dɛstɪn/ v. destinar.
destiny /'dɛstəni/ n. destino m.

destitute /'dɛstɪˌtut/ a. destituído, indigente.
destitution /ˌdɛstɪ'tuʃən/ n. destitución f.
destroy /dɪ'strɔi/ v. destrozar, destruir.
destroyer /dɪ'strɔiər/ n. destruidor -ra; (naval) destructor m.
destruction /dɪ'strʌkʃən/ n. destrucción f.
destructive /dɪ'strʌktɪv/ a. destructivo.
desultory /'dɛsəlˌtɔri/ a. inconexo; casual.
detach /dɪ'tætʃ/ v. separar, desprender.
detachment /dɪ'tætʃmənt/ n. Mil. destacamento; desprendimiento m.
detail /dɪ'teil/ n. **1.** detalle m. —v. **2.** detallar.
detain /dɪ'tein/ v. detener.
detect /dɪ'tɛkt/ v. descubrir.
detection /dɪ'tɛkʃən/ n. detección f.
detective /dɪ'tɛktɪv/ n. detective m. & f.
deténte /dei'tɑnt/ n. distensión f.; Pol. deténte.
detention /dɪ'tɛnʃən/ n. detención; cautividad f.
deter /dɪ'tɜr/ v. disuadir.
detergent /dɪ'tɜrdʒənt/ n. & a. detergente m.
deteriorate /dɪ'tɪəriəˌreit/ v. deteriorar.
deterioration /dɪˌtɪəriə'reiʃən/ n. deterioración f.
determination /dɪˌtɜrmə'neiʃən/ n. determinación f.
determine /dɪ'tɜrmɪn/ v. determinar.
deterrence /dɪ'tɜrəns/ n. disuasión f.
detest /dɪ'tɛst/ v. detestar.
detonate /'dɛtn̩ˌeit/ v. detonar.
detour /'ditʊr/ n. desvío m. v. desviar.
detract /dɪ'trækt/ v. disminuir.
detriment /'dɛtrəmənt/ n. detrimento m., daño m.
detrimental /ˌdɛtrə'mɛntl̩/ a. dañoso.
devaluate /di'vælyuˌeit/ v. depreciar.
devastate /'dɛvəˌsteit/ v. devastar.
develop /dɪ'vɛləp/ v. desarrollar; Phot. revelar.

developing nation /dɪ'vɛləpɪŋ/ nación en desarrollo.

development /dɪ'vɛləpmənt/ n. desarrollo m.

deviate /'divi,eit/ v. desviar.

deviation /,divi'eiʃən/ n. desviación f.

device /dɪ'vais/ n. aparato; artificio m.

devil /'dɛvəl/ n. diablo, demonio m.

devious /'diviəs/ a. desviado.

devise /dɪ'vaiz/ v. inventar.

devoid /dɪ'vɔid/ a. desprovisto.

devote /dɪ'vout/ v. dedicar, consagrar.

devoted /dɪ'voutɪd/ a. devoto.

devotee /,dɛvə'ti/ n. aficionado -da.

devotion /dɪ'vouʃən/ n. devoción f.

devour /dɪ'vaur/ v. devorar.

devout /dɪ'vaut/ a. devoto.

dew /du/ n. rocío, sereno m.

dexterity /dɛk'stɛrɪti/ n. destreza f.

dexterous /'dɛkstrəs/ a. diestro.

diabetes /,daiə'bitɪs/ n. diabetes f.

diabolic /,daiə'bɒlɪk/ a. diabólico.

diadem /'daiə,dɛm/ n. diadema f.

diagnose /'daiəg,nous/ v. diagnosticar.

diagnosis /,daiəg'nousɪs/ n. diagnóstico m.

diagonal /dai'ægənl/ n. diagonal f.

diagram /'daiə,græm/ n. diagrama m.

dial /'daiəl/ n. **1.** cuadrante m., carátula f. —v. **2. dial up** marcar.

dialect /'daiə,lɛkt/ n. dialecto m.

dialing code /'daiəlɪŋ/ prefijo m.

dialogue /'daiə,lɔg/ n. diálogo m.

dial tone señal de marcar f.

diameter /dai'æmɪtər/ n. diámetro m.

diamond /'daimənd/ n. diamante, brillante m.

diaper /'daipər/ n. pañal m.

diarrhea /,daiə'riə/ n. diarrea f.

diary /'daiəri/ n. diario m.

diathermy /'daiə,θɜrmi/ n. diatermia f.

dice /dais/ n. dados m.pl.

dictate /'dɪkteit/ n. **1.** mandato m. —v. **2.** dictar.

dictation /dɪk'teiʃən/ n. dictado m.

dictator /'dɪkteitər/ n. dictador -ra.

dictatorship /dɪk'teitər,ʃɪp/ n. dictadura f.

diction /'dɪkʃən/ n. dicción f.

dictionary /'dɪkʃə,nɛri/ n. diccionario m.

die /dai/ n. **1.** matriz f.; (game) dado m. —v. **2.** morir.

diet /'daiɪt/ n. dieta f.

dietary /'daiɪ,tɛri/ a. dietético.

dietitian /,daiɪ'tɪʃən/ n. & a. dietético -ca.

differ /'dɪfər/ v. diferir.

difference /'dɪfərəns/ n. diferencia f. **to make no d.,** no importar.

different /'dɪfərənt/ a. diferente, distinto.

differential /,dɪfə'rɛnʃəl/ n. diferencial f.

differentiate /,dɪfə'rɛnʃi,eit/ v. diferenciar.

difficult /'dɪfɪ,kʌlt/ a. difícil.

difficulty /'dɪfɪ,kʌlti/ n. dificultad f.

diffident /'dɪfɪdənt/ a. tímido.

diffuse /dɪ'fyuz/ v. difundir.

diffusion /dɪ'fyuʒən/ n. difusión f.

dig /dɪg/ v. cavar.

digest /n 'daidʒɛst; v dɪ'dʒɛst, dai-/ n. **1.** extracto m. —v. **2.** digerir.

digestible /dɪ'dʒɛstəbəl, dai-/ a. digerible.

digestion /dɪ'dʒɛstʃən, dai-/ n. digestión f.

digestive /dɪ'dʒɛstɪv, dai-/ a. digestivo.

digital /'dɪdʒɪtl/ a. digital.

digitalis /,dɪdʒɪ'tælɪs/ n. digital f.

dignified /'dɪgnə,faid/ a. digno.

dignify /'dɪgnə,fai/ v. dignificar.

dignitary /'dɪgnɪ,tɛri/ n. dignatario -ria.

dignity /'dɪgnɪti/ n. dignidad f.

digress /dɪ'grɛs, dai-/ v. divagar.

digression /dɪ'grɛʃən, dai-/ n. digresión f.

dike /daik/ n. dique m.

dilapidated /dɪ'læpɪ,deitɪd/ a. dilapidado.

dilapidation /dɪ,læpə'deiʃən/ n. dilapidación f.

dilate /dai'leit/ v. dilatar.

dilatory /'dɪlə,tɔri/ a. dilatorio.

dilemma /dɪ'lɛmə/ n. dilema m.

dilettante /'dɪlɪ,tɑnt/ n. diletante m. & f.

diligence /'dɪlɪdʒəns/ n. diligencia f.

diligent /'dɪlɪdʒənt/ *a.* diligente, aplicado.

dilute /dɪ'lut, dai-/ *v.* diluir.

dim /dɪm/ *a.* **1.** oscuro. —*v.* **2.** oscurecer.

dimension /dɪ'mɛnʃən/ *n.* dimensión *f.*

diminish /dɪ'mɪnɪʃ/ *v.* disminuir.

diminution /ˌdɪmə'nuʃən/ *n.* disminución *f.*

diminutive /dɪ'mɪnyətɪv/ *a.* diminutivo.

dimness /'dɪmnɪs/ *n.* oscuridad *f.*

dimple /'dɪmpəl/ *n.* hoyuelo *m.*

din /dɪn/ *n.* alboroto, estrépito *m.*

dine /dain/ *v.* comer, cenar.

diner /'dainər/ *n.* coche comedor *m.*

dingy /'dɪndʒi/ *a.* deslucido, deslustrado.

dining room /'dainɪŋ/ comedor *m.*

dinner /'dɪnər/ *n.* comida, cena *f.*

dinosaur /'dainəˌsɔr/ *n.* dinosauro *m.*

diocese /'daiəsɪs/ *n.* diócesis *f.*

dip /dɪp/ *v.* sumergir, hundir.

diphtheria /dɪf'θɪəriə/ *n.* difteria *f.*

diploma /dɪ'ploumə/ *n.* diploma *m.*

diplomacy /dɪ'plouməsi/ *n.* diplomacia *f.*

diplomat /'dɪpləˌmæt/ *n.* diplomático -ca.

diplomatic /ˌdɪplə'mætɪk/ *a.* diplomático.

dipper /'dɪpər/ *n.* cucharón *m.*

dire /daiᵊr/ *a.* horrendo.

direct /dɪ'rɛkt, dai-/ *a.* **1.** directo. —*v.* **2.** dirigir.

direction /dɪ'rɛkʃən, 'dai-/ *n.* dirección *f.*

directive /dɪ'rɛktɪv, dai-/ *n.* directiva *f.*

directly /dɪ'rɛktli, dai-/ *adv.* directamente.

director /dɪ'rɛktər, dai-/ *n.* director -ra.

directory /dɪ'rɛktəri, dai-/ *n.* directorio *m.*, guía *f.*

dirigible /'dɪrɪdʒəbəl/ *n.* dirigible *m.*

dirt /dɜrt/ *n.* basura *f.*; (earth) tierra *f.*

dirt-cheap /'dɜrt 'tʃip/ *a.* tirado.

dirty /'dɜrti/ *a.* sucio.

dis /dis/ *v. Colloq.* ofender, faltar al respeto.

disability /ˌdɪsə'bɪlɪti/ *n.* inhabilidad *f.*

disable /dɪs'eibəl/ *v.* incapacitar.

disabuse /ˌdɪsə'byuz/ *v.* desengañar.

disadvantage /ˌdɪsəd'væntɪdʒ/ *n.* desventaja *f.*

disagree /ˌdɪsə'gri/ *v.* desconvenir; disentir.

disagreeable /ˌdɪsə'griəbəl/ *a.* desagradable.

disagreement /ˌdɪsə'grimənt/ *n.* desacuerdo *m.*

disappear /ˌdɪsə'pɪər/ *v.* desaparecer.

disappearance /ˌdɪsə'pɪərəns/ *n.* desaparición *f.*

disappoint /ˌdɪsə'pɔint/ *v.* disgustar, desilusionar.

disappointment /ˌdɪsə'pɔintmənt/ *n.* disgusto *m.*, desilusión *f.*

disapproval /ˌdɪsə'pruvəl/ *n.* desaprobación *f.*

disapprove /ˌdɪsə'pruv/ *v.* desaprobar.

disarm /dɪs'ɑrm/ *v.* desarmar.

disarmament /dɪs'ɑrməmənt/ *n.* desarme *m.*

disarrange /ˌdɪsə'reindʒ/ *v.* desordenar; desarreglar.

disaster /dɪ'zæstər/ *n.* desastre *m.*

disastrous /dɪ'zæstrəs/ *a.* desastroso.

disavow /ˌdɪsə'vau/ *v.* repudiar.

disavowal /ˌdɪsə'vauəl/ *n.* repudiación *f.*

disband /dɪs'bænd/ *v.* dispersarse.

disbelieve /ˌdɪsbɪ'liv/ *v.* descreer.

disburse /dɪs'bɜrs/ *v.* desembolsar, pagar.

discard /dɪ'skɑrd/ *v.* descartar.

discern /dɪ'sɜrn/ *v.* discernir.

discerning /dɪ'sɜrnɪŋ/ *a.* discernidor, perspicaz.

discernment /dɪ'sɜrnmənt/ *n.* discernimiento *m.*

discharge /dɪs'tʃɑrdʒ/ *v.* descargar; despedir.

disciple /dɪ'saipəl/ *n.* discípulo -la.

disciplinary /'dɪsəpləˌnɛri/ *a.* disciplinario.

discipline /'dɪsəplɪn/ *n.* disciplina *f.*

disclaim /dɪs'kleim/ *v.* repudiar.

disclaimer /dɪs'kleimər/ *n.* negación *f.*

disclose /dɪ'sklouz/ *v.* revelar.

disclosure /dɪ'sklouʒər/ *n.* revelación *f.*

disco /'dɪskou/ *n.* discoteca *f.*

discolor /dɪs'kʌlər/ v. descolorar.

discomfort /dɪs'kʌmfərt/ n. incomodidad f.

disconcert /ˌdɪskən'sɜrt/ v. desconcertar.

disconnect /ˌdɪskə'nɛkt/ v. desunir; desconectar.

disconnected /ˌdɪskə'nɛktɪd/ a. desunido.

disconsolate /dɪs'kɒnsəlɪt/ a. desconsolado.

discontent /ˌdɪskən'tɛnt/ n. descontento m.

discontented /ˌdɪskən'tɛntɪd/ a. descontento.

discontinue /ˌdɪskən'tɪnyu/ v. descontinuar.

discord /'dɪskɔrd/ n. discordia f.

discordant /dɪs'kɔrdənt/ a. disonante.

discotheque /'dɪskə,tɛk/ n. discoteca f.

discount /'dɪskaunt/ n. descuento m.

discourage /dɪ'skɜrɪdʒ/ v. desalentar, desanimar.

discouragement /dɪ'skɜrɪdʒmənt/ n. desaliento, desánimo m.

discourse /'dɪskɔrs/ n. discurso m.

discourteous /dɪs'kɜrtiəs/ a. descortés.

discourtesy /dɪs'kɜrtəsi/ n. descortesía f.

discover /dɪ'skʌvər/ v. descubrir.

discoverer /dɪ'skʌvərər/ n. descubridor -ra.

discovery /dɪ'skʌvəri/ n. descubrimiento m.

discreet /dɪ'skrit/ a. discreto.

discrepancy /dɪ'skrɛpənsi/ n. discrepancia f.

discretion /dɪ'skrɛʃən/ n. discreción f.

discriminate /dɪ'skrɪm,əneit/ v. distinguir. **d. against** discriminar contra.

discrimination /dɪ,skrɪmə'neiʃən/ n. discernimiento m.; discriminación f.

discuss /dɪ'skʌs/ v. discutir.

discussion /dɪ'skʌʃən/ n. discusión f.

disdain /dɪs'dein/ n. **1.** desdén m. —v. **2.** desdeñar.

disdainful /dɪs'deinfəl/ a. desdeñoso.

disease /dɪ'ziz/ n. enfermedad f., mal m.

disembark /ˌdɪsɛm'bɑrk/ v. desembarcar.

disentangle /ˌdɪsɛn'tæŋgəl/ v. desenredar.

disfigure /dɪs'fɪgyər/ v. desfigurar.

disgrace /dɪs'greis/ n. **1.** vergüenza; deshonra f. —v. **2.** deshonrar.

disgraceful /dɪs'greisfəl/ a. vergonzoso.

disguise /dɪs'gaiz/ n. **1.** disfraz m. —v. **2.** disfrazar.

disgust /dɪs'gʌst/ n. **1.** repugnancia —v. **2.** fastidiar; repugnar.

dish /dɪʃ/ n. plato m.

dishearten /dɪs'hɑrtn̩/ v. desanimar; descorazonar.

dishonest /dɪs'ɒnɪst/ a. deshonesto.

dishonesty /dɪs'ɒnəsti/ n. deshonestidad f.

dishonor /dɪs'ɒnər/ n. **1.** deshonra f. —v. **2.** deshonrar.

dishonorable /dɪs'ɒnərəbəl/ a. deshonroso.

dishwasher /'dɪʃ,wɒʃər/ n. lavaplatos m.

disillusion /ˌdɪsɪ'luʒən/ n. **1.** desengaño m. —v. **2.** desengañar.

disinfect /ˌdɪsɪn'fɛkt/ v. desinfectar.

disinfectant /ˌdɪsɪn'fɛktənt/ n. desinfectante m.

disinherit /ˌdɪsɪn'hɛrɪt/ v. desheredar.

disintegrate /dɪs'ɪntə,greit/ v. desintegrar.

disinterested /dɪs'ɪntə,rɛstɪd, -trɪstɪd/ a. desinteresado.

disk /dɪsk/ n. disco m.

disk drive disquetera f.

diskette /dɪ'skɛt/ n. disquete m.

disk jockey pinchadiscos m. & f.

dislike /dɪs'laik/ n. **1.** antipatía f. —v. **2.** no gustar de.

dislocate /'dɪslou,keit/ v. dislocar.

dislodge /dɪs'lɒdʒ/ v. desalojar; desprender.

disloyal /dɪs'lɔiəl/ a. desleal; infiel.

disloyalty /dɪs'lɔiəlti/ n. deslealtad f.

dismal /'dɪzməl/ a. lúgubre.

dismantle /dɪs'mæntl̩/ v. desmantelar, desmontar.

dismay /dɪs'mei/ n. **1.** consternación f. —v. **2.** consternar.

dismiss /dɪs'mɪs/ v. despedir.

dismissal /dɪsˈmɪsəl/ n. despedida f.

dismount /dɪsˈmaunt/ v. apearse, desmontarse.

disobedience /ˌdɪsəˈbidiəns/ n. desobediencia f.

disobedient /ˌdɪsəˈbidiənt/ a. desobediente.

disobey /ˌdɪsəˈbei/ v. desobedecer.

disorder /dɪsˈɔrdər/ n. desorden m.

disorderly /dɪsˈɔrdərli/ a. desarreglado, desordenado.

disown /dɪsˈoun/ v. repudiar.

dispassionate /dɪsˈpæʃənɪt/ a. desapasionado; templado.

dispatch /dɪˈspætʃ/ n. **1.** despacho m. —v. **2.** despachar.

dispel /dɪˈspɛl/ v. dispersar.

dispensary /dɪˈspɛnsəri/ n. dispensario m.

dispensation /ˌdɪspənˈseiʃən/ n. dispensación f.

dispense /dɪˈspɛns/ v. dispensar.

dispersal /dɪˈspɔrsəl/ n. dispersión f.

disperse /dɪˈspɔrs/ v. dispersar.

displace /dɪsˈpleis/ v. dislocar.

display /dɪˈsplei/ n. **1.** despliegue m., exhibición f. —v. **2.** desplegar, exhibir.

displease /dɪsˈpliz/ v. disgustar; ofender.

displeasure /dɪsˈplɛʒər/ n. disgusto, sinsabor m.

disposable /dɪˈspouzəbəl/ a. disponible; desechable.

disposal /dɪˈspouzəl/ n. disposición f.

dispose /dɪˈspouz/ v. disponer.

disposition /ˌdɪspəˈzɪʃən/ n. disposición f.; índole f., genio m.

dispossess /ˌdɪspəˈzɛs/ v. desposeer.

disproportionate /ˌdɪsprəˈpɔrʃənɪt/ a. desproporcionado.

disprove /dɪsˈpruv/ v. confutar.

dispute /dɪˈspyut/ n. **1.** disputa f. —v. **2.** disputar.

disqualify /dɪsˈkwɒləˌfai/ v. inhabilitar.

disregard /ˌdɪsrɪˈgɑrd/ n. **1.** desatención f. —v. **2.** desatender.

disrepair /ˌdɪsrɪˈpɛər/ n. descompostura f.

disreputable /dɪsˈrɛpyətəbəl/ a. desacreditado.

disrespect /ˌdɪsrɪˈspɛkt/ n. falta de respeto, f., desacato m.

disrespectful /ˌdɪsrɪˈspɛktfəl/ a. irrespetuoso.

disrobe /dɪsˈroub/ v. desvestir.

disrupt /dɪsˈrʌpt/ v. romper; desbaratar.

dissatisfaction /ˌdɪssætɪsˈfækʃən/ n. descontento m.

dissatisfy /dɪsˈsætɪsˌfai/ v. descontentar.

dissect /dɪˈsɛkt/ v. disecar.

dissemble /dɪˈsɛmbəl/ v. disimular.

disseminate /dɪˈsɛməˌneit/ v. diseminar.

dissension /dɪˈsɛnʃən/ n. disensión f.

dissent /dɪˈsɛnt/ n. **1.** disensión f. —v. **2.** disentir.

dissertation /ˌdɪsərˈteiʃən/ n. disertación f.

dissimilar /dɪˈsɪmələr/ a. desemejante.

dissipate /ˈdɪsəˌpeit/ v. disipar.

dissipation /ˌdɪsəˈpeiʃən/ n. disipación f.; libertinaje m.

dissolute /ˈdɪsəˌlut/ a. disoluto.

dissolution /ˌdɪsəˈluʃən/ n. disolución f.

dissolve /dɪˈzɒlv/ v. disolver; derretirse.

dissonant /ˈdɪsənənt/ a. disonante.

dissuade /dɪˈsweid/ v. disuadir.

distance /ˈdɪstəns/ n. distancia f. **at a d., in the d.,** a lo lejos.

distant /ˈdɪstənt/ a. distante, lejano.

distaste /dɪsˈteist/ n. disgusto, sinsabor m.

distasteful /dɪsˈteistfəl/ a. desagradable.

distill /dɪˈstɪl/ v. destilar.

distillation /ˌdɪstl̩ˈeiʃən/ n. destilación f.

distillery /dɪˈstɪləri/ n. destilería f.

distinct /dɪˈstɪŋkt/ a. distinto.

distinction /dɪˈstɪŋkʃən/ n. distinción f.

distinctive /dɪˈstɪŋktɪv/ a. distintivo; característico.

distinctly /dɪˈstɪŋktli/ adv. distintamente.

distinguish /dɪˈstɪŋgwɪʃ/ v. distinguir.

distinguished /dɪˈstɪŋgwɪʃt/ a. distinguido.

distort /dɪˈstɔrt/ v. falsear; torcer.

distract /dɪˈstrækt/ v. distraer.

distraction /dɪˈstrækʃən/ n. distracción f.

distraught /dɪ'strɔt/ *a.* aturrullado; demente.

distress /dɪ'stres/ *n.* **1.** dolor *m.* —*v.* **2.** afligir.

distressing /dɪ'stresɪŋ/ *a.* penoso.

distribute /dɪ'strɪbyut/ *v.* distribuir.

distribution /ˌdɪstrə'byuʃən/ *n.* distribución *f.*; reparto *m.*

distributor /dɪ'strɪbyətər/ *n.* distribuidor -ra.

district /'dɪstrɪkt/ *n.* distrito *m.*

distrust /dɪs'trʌst/ *n.* **1.** desconfianza *f.* —*v.* **2.** desconfiar.

distrustful /dɪs'trʌstfəl/ *a.* desconfiado; sospechoso.

disturb /dɪ'stɜrb/ *v.* incomodar; inquietar.

disturbance /dɪ'stɜrbəns/ *n.* disturbio *m.*

disturbing /dɪ'stɜrbɪŋ/ *a.* inquietante.

ditch /dɪtʃ/ *n.* zanja *f.*; foso *m.*

divan /dɪ'væn/ *n.* diván *m.*

dive /daiv/ *n.* **1.** clavado *m.*; *Colloq.* leonera *f.* —*v.* **2.** echar un clavado; bucear.

diver /'daivər/ *n.* buzo *m.*

diverge /dɪ'vɜrdʒ/ *v.* divergir.

divergence /dɪ'vɜrdʒəns/ *n.* divergencia *f.*

divergent /dɪ'vɜrdʒənt/ *a.* divergente.

diverse /dɪ'vɜrs/ *a.* diverso.

diversion /dɪ'vɜrʒən/ *n.* diversión *f.*; pasatiempo *m.*

diversity /dɪ'vɜrsɪti/ *n.* diversidad *f.*

divert /dɪ'vɜrt/ *v.* desviar; divertir.

divest /dɪ'vest/ *v.* desnudar, despojar.

divide /dɪ'vaid/ *v.* dividir.

dividend /'dɪvɪˌdend/ *n.* dividendo *m.*

divine /dɪ'vain/ *a.* divino.

divinity /dɪ'vɪnɪti/ *n.* divinidad *f.*

division /dɪ'vɪʒən/ *n.* división *f.*

divorce /dɪ'vɔrs/ *n.* **1.** divorcio *m.* —*v.* **2.** divorciar.

divorcee /dɪvɔr'sei/ *n.* divorciado -da.

divulge /dɪ'vʌldʒ/ *v.* divulgar, revelar.

dizziness /'dɪzɪnɪs/ *n.* vértigo, mareo *m.*

dizzy /'dɪzi/ *a.* mareado.

DNA *abbr.* (deoxyribonucleic acid) ADN (ácido deoxirríbonucleico) *m.*

do /du/ *v.* hacer.

docile /'dɒsəl/ *a.* dócil.

dock /dɒk/ *n.* **1.** muelle *m.* **dry d.,** astillero *m.* —*v.* **2.** entrar en muelle.

doctor /'dɒktər/ *n.* médico *m.*; doctor -ra.

doctorate /'dɒktərɪt/ *n.* doctorado *m.*

doctrine /'dɒktrɪn/ *n.* doctrina *f.*

document /'dɒkyəmənt/ *n.* documento *m.*

documentary /ˌdɒkyə'mentəri/ *a.* documental.

documentation /ˌdɒkyəmen'teiʃən/ *n.* documentación *f.*

dodge /dɒdʒ/ *n.* **1.** evasión *f.* —*v.* **2.** evadir.

dodgem /'dɒdʒɪm/ *n.* coche de choque *m.*

doe /dou/ *n.* gama *f.*

dog /dɔg/ *n.* perro -a.

dogma /'dɔgmə/ *n.* dogma *m.*

dogmatic /dɔg'mætɪk/ *a.* dogmático.

dogmatism /'dɔgməˌtɪzəm/ *n.* dogmatismo *m.*

doily /'dɔili/ *n.* servilletita *f.*

doleful /'doulfəl/ *a.* triste.

doll /dɒl/ *n.* muñeca -co.

dollar /'dɒlər/ *n.* dólar *m.*

dolorous /'doulərəs/ *a.* lastimoso.

dolphin /'dɒlfɪn/ *n.* delfín *m.*

domain /dou'mein/ *n.* dominio *m.*

dome /doum/ *n.* domo *m.*

domestic /də'mestɪk/ *a.* doméstico.

domesticate /də'mestɪˌkeit/ *v.* domesticar.

domicile /'dɒməˌsail/ *n.* domicilio *m.*

dominance /'dɒmənəns/ *n.* dominación *f.*

dominant /'dɒmənənt/ *a.* dominante.

dominate /'dɒməˌneit/ *v.* dominar.

domination /ˌdɒmə'neiʃən/ *n.* dominación *f.*

domineer /ˌdɒmə'nɪər/ *v.* dominar.

domineering /ˌdɒmə'nɪərɪŋ/ *a.* tiránico, mandón.

dominion /də'mɪnyən/ *n.* dominio; territorio *m.*

domino /'dɒməˌnou/ *n.* dominó *m.*

donate /'douneit/ *v.* donar; contribuir.

donation /dou'neiʃən/ *n.* donación *f.*

donkey /'dɒŋki/ n. asno, burro m.
doom /dum/ n. **1.** perdición, ruina f. —v. **2.** perder, ruinar.
door /dɔr/ n. puerta f.
doorman /'dɔr,mæn, -mən/ n. portero m.
doormat /'dɔr,mæt/ n. felpudo m.
doorway /'dɔr,wei/ n. entrada f.
dope /doup/ n. Colloq. narcótico m.; idiota m.
dormant /'dɔrmənt/ a. durmiente; inactivo.
dormitory /'dɔrmɪ,tɔri/ n. dormitorio m.
dosage /'dousɪdʒ/ n. dosificación f.
dose /dous/ n. dosis f.
dot /dɒt/ n. punto m.
dotted line /'dɒtɪd/ línea de puntos f.
double /'dʌbəl/ a. **1.** doble. —v. **2.** duplicar.
double bass /beis/ contrabajo m.
double-breasted /'dʌbəl 'brɛstɪd/ a. cruzado.
double-cross /'dʌbəl 'krɔs/ v. traicionar.
doubly /'dʌbli/ adv. doblemente.
doubt /daut/ n. **1.** duda f. —v. **2.** dudar.
doubtful /'dautfəl/ a. dudoso, incierto.
doubtless /'dautlɪs/ a. **1.** indudable. —adv. **2.** sin duda.
dough /dou/ n. pasta, masa f.
doughnut /'dounət, -,nʌt/ n. buñuelo m.
dove /duv/ n. paloma f.
dowager /'dauədʒər/ n. viuda (con título) f.
down /daun/ adv. **1.** abajo. —prep. **2. d. the street,** etc. calle abajo, etc.
downcast /'daun,kæst/ a. cabizbajo.
downfall /'daun,fɔl/ n. ruina, perdición f.
downhearted /'daun'hartɪd/ a. descorazonado.
download /'daun,loud/ v. bajar, descargar.
downpour /'daun,pɔr/ n. chaparrón m.
downright /'daun,rait/ a. absoluto, completo.
downriver /'daun'rɪvər/ adv. aguas abajo, río abajo.
downstairs /'daun'stɛərz/ adv. **1.** abajo. —n. **2.** primer piso.

downstream /'daun'strim/ adv. aguas abajo, río abajo.
downtown /'daun'taun/ adv. al centro, en el centro.
downward /'daunwərd/ a. **1.** descendente. —adv. **2.** hacia abajo.
dowry /'dauri/ n. dote f.
doze /douz/ v. dormitar.
dozen /'dʌzən/ n. docena f.
draft /dræft/ n. **1.** dibujo m.; Com. giro m.; Mil. conscripción f. —v. **2.** dibujar; Mil. reclutar.
draftee /dræf'ti/ n. conscripto m.
draft notice notificación de reclutamiento f.
drag /dræg/ v. arrastrar.
dragon /'drægən/ n. dragón m.
drain /drein/ n. **1.** desaguadero m. —v. **2.** desaguar.
drainage /'dreinɪdʒ/ n. drenaje m.
drain board escurridero m.
drama /'dramə, 'dræmə/ n. drama m.
dramatic /drə'mætɪk/ a. dramático.
dramatics /drə'mætɪks/ n. dramática f.
dramatist /'dræmətɪst, 'dramə-/ n. dramaturgo -ga.
dramatize /'dræmə,taiz, 'dramə-/ v. dramatizar.
drape /dreip/ n. cortinas f.pl. v. vestir; adornar.
drapery /'dreipəri/ n. colgaduras f.pl.; ropaje m.
drastic /'dræstɪk/ a. drástico.
draw /drɔ/ v. dibujar; atraer. **d. up,** formular.
drawback /'drɔ,bæk/ n. desventaja f.
drawer /drɔr/ n. cajón m.
drawing /'drɔɪŋ/ n. dibujo m.; rifa f.
dread /drɛd/ n. **1.** terror m. —v. **2.** temer.
dreadful /'drɛdfəl/ a. terrible.
dreadfully /'drɛdfəli/ adv. horrendamente.
dream /drim/ n. **1.** sueño, ensueño m. —v. **2.** soñar.
dreamer /'drimər/ n. soñador -ra; visionario -ia.
dreamy /'drimi/ a. soñador, contemplativo.
dreary /'drɪəri/ a. monótono y pesado.
dredge /drɛdʒ/ n. **1.** rastra f. —v. **2.** rastrear.
dregs /drɛgz/ n. sedimento m.
drench /drɛntʃ/ v. mojar.

dress /drɛs/ n. **1.** vestido; traje m. —v. **2.** vestir.

dresser /'drɛsər/ n. (furniture) tocador.

dressing /'drɛsɪŋ/ n. Med. curación f.; (cookery) relleno m., salsa f.

dressing gown bata f.

dressing table tocador m.

dressmaker /'drɛs,meikər/ n. modista m. & f.

drift /drɪft/ n. **1.** tendencia f.; Naut. deriva f. —v. **2.** Naut. derivar; (snow) amontonarse.

drill /drɪl/ n. **1.** ejercicio m.; Mech. taladro m. —v. **2.** Mech. taladrar.

drink /drɪŋk/ n. **1.** bebida f. —v. **2.** beber, tomar.

drinkable /'drɪŋkəbəl/ a. potable, bebible.

drip /drɪp/ v. gotear.

drive /draiv/ n. **1.** paseo m. —v. **2.** impeler; Auto. guiar, conducir.

drive-in (movie theater) /'draiv ‚ɪn/ n. autocine, autocinema m.

driver /'draivər/ n. conductor -ra; chofer m. **d.'s license,** permiso de conducir.

driveway /'draiv‚wei/ n. entrada para coches.

drizzle /'drɪzəl/ n. **1.** llovizna f. —v. **2.** lloviznar.

dromedary /'drɒmɪ‚dɛri/ n. dromedario m.

droop /drup/ v. inclinarse.

drop /drɒp/ n. **1.** gota f. —v. **2.** soltar; dejar caer.

dropout /'drɒp‚aut/ n. joven que abandona sus estudios.

dropper /'drɒpər/ n. cuentagotas f.

dropsy /'drɒpsi/ n. hidropesía f.

drought /draut/ n. sequía f.

drove /drouv/ n. manada f.

drown /draun/ v. ahogar.

drowse /drauz/ v. adormecer.

drowsiness /'drauzɪnɪs/ n. somnolencia f.

drowsy /'drauzi/ a. soñoliento.

drudge /drʌdʒ/ n. ganapán m.

drudgery /'drʌdʒəri/ n. trabajo penoso.

drug /drʌg/ n. **1.** droga f. —v. **2.** narcotizar.

drug addict drogadicto -ta, toxicómano -na m. & f.

druggist /'drʌgɪst/ n. farmacéutico -ca, boticario -ria.

drugstore /'drʌg‚stɔr/ n. farmacia, botica, droguería f.

drum /drʌm/ n. tambor m.

drummer /'drʌmər/ n. tambor m.

drumstick /'drʌm‚stɪk/ n. palillo m.; Leg. pierna f.

drunk /drʌŋk/ a. & n. borracho, -a.

drunkard /'drʌŋkərd/ n. borrachón m.

drunken /'drʌŋkən/ a. borracho; ebrio.

drunkenness /'drʌŋkənnɪs/ n. embriaguez f.

dry /drai/ a. **1.** seco, árido. —v. **2.** secar.

dry cell n. pila seca f.

dry cleaner tintorero -ra.

dryness /'drainɪs/ n. sequedad f.

dual /'duəl/ a. doble.

dubious /'dubiəs/ a. dudoso.

duchess /'dʌtʃɪs/ n. duquesa f.

duck /dʌk/ n. **1.** pato m. —v. **2.** zambullir; (avoid) esquivar.

duct /dʌkt/ n. canal m.

due /du/ a. **1.** debido; Com. vencido. —n. **2. dues** cuota f.

duel /'duəl/ n. duelo m.

duelist /'duəlɪst/ n. duelista m.

duet /du'ɛt/ n. dúo m.

duke /duk/ n. duque m.

dull /dʌl/ a. apagado, desteñido; sin punta; Fig. pesado, soso.

dullness /'dʌlnɪs/ n. estupidez; pesadez f.; deslustre m.

duly /'duli/ adv. debidamente.

dumb /dʌm/ a. mudo; Colloq. estúpido.

dumbwaiter /'dʌm‚weitər/ n. montaplatos m.

dumfound /dʌm'faund/ v. confundir.

dummy /'dʌmi/ n. maniquí m.

dump /dʌmp/ n. **1.** depósito m. —v. **2.** descargar.

dune /dun/ n. duna f.

dungeon /'dʌndʒən/ n. calabozo m.

dunk /dʌŋk/ v. mojar.

dupe /dup/ v. engañar.

duplicate /a, n 'duplɪkɪt; v -‚keit/ a. & n. **1.** duplicado m. —v. **2.** duplicar.

duplication /‚duplɪ'keiʃən/ n. duplicación f.

duplicity /du'plɪsɪti/ n. duplicidad f.

durability /‚dʊrə'bɪlɪti/ n. durabilidad f.

durable /'dʊrəbəl/ a. durable, duradero.

duration /dʊ'reiʃən/ n. duración f.

duress /dʊ'rɛs/ n. compulsión f.; encierro m.

during /'dʊrɪŋ/ prep. durante.

dusk /dʌsk/ n. crepúsculo m.

dusky /'dʌski/ a. oscuro; moreno.

dust /dʌst/ n. **1.** polvo m. —v. **2.** polvorear; despolvorear.

dusty /'dʌsti/ a. empolvado.

Dutch /dʌtʃ/ a. holandés -sa.

dutiful /'dutəfəl/ a. respetuoso.

dutifully /'dutəfəli/ adv. respetuosamente, obedientemente.

duty /'duti/ n. deber m.; Com. derechos m.pl.

duty-free /'duti 'fri/ a. libre de derechos.

dwarf /dwɔrf/ n. **1.** enano -na. —v. **2.** achicar.

dwell /dwɛl/ v. habitar, residir. **d. on,** espaciarse en.

dwelling /'dwɛlɪŋ/ n. morada, casa f.

dwindle /'dwɪndl/ v. disminuirse.

dye /dai/ n. **1.** tintura f. —v. **2.** teñir.

dyer /'daiər/ n. tintorero -ra.

dynamic /dai'næmɪk/ a. dinámico.

dynamite /'dainə,mait/ n. dinamita f.

dynamo /'dainə,mou/ n. dínamo m.

dynasty /'dainəsti/ n. dinastía f.

dysentery /'dɪsən,tɛri/ n. disentería f.

dyslexia /dɪs'lɛksiə/ n. dislexia f.

dyslexic /dɪs'lɛksɪk/ a. disléxico.

dyspepsia /dɪs'pɛpʃə/ n. dispepsia f.

E

each /itʃ/ a. **1.** cada. —pron. **2.** cada uno -na. **e. other,** el uno al otro.

eager /'igər/ a. ansioso.

eagerly /'igərli/ adv. ansiosamente.

eagerness /'igərnɪs/ n. ansia f.

eagle /'igəl/ n. águila f.

ear /iər/ n. oído m.; (outer) oreja f.; (of corn) mazorca f.

earache /'iər,eik/ n. dolor de oído m.

earl /ɜrl/ n. conde m.

early /'ɜrli/ a. & adv. temprano.

earn /ɜrn/ v. ganar.

earnest /'ɜrnɪst/ a. serio.

earnestly /'ɜrnɪstli/ adv. seriamente.

earnings /'ɜrnɪŋz/ n. ganancias f.pl.; Com. ingresos m.pl.

earphone /'iər,foun/ n. auricular m.

earring /'iər,rɪŋ/ n. pendiente, arete m.

earth /ɜrθ/ n. tierra f.

earthquake /'ɜrθ,kweik/ n. terremoto m.

ease /iz/ n. **1.** reposo m.; facilidad f. —v. **2.** aliviar.

easel /'izəl/ n. caballete m.

easily /'izəli/ adv. fácilmente.

east /ist/ n. oriente, este m.

Easter /'istər/ n. Pascua Florida.

eastern /'istərn/ a. oriental.

eastward /'istwərd/ adv. hacia el este.

easy /'izi/ a. fácil.

eat /it/ v. comer.

eau de Cologne /'ou də kə'loun/ colonia f.

eaves /ivz/ n. socarrén m.

ebb /ɛb/ n. **1.** menguante f. —v. **2.** menguar.

ebony /'ɛbəni/ n. ébano m.

eccentric /ik'sɛntrik/ a. excéntrico.

eccentricity /,ɛksən'trisiti/ n. excentricidad f.

ecclesiastic /i,klizi'æstɪk/ a. & n. eclesiástico m.

echelon /'ɛʃə,lɒn/ n. escalón m.

echo /'ɛkou/ n. eco m.

eclipse /i'klɪps/ n. **1.** eclipse m. —v. **2.** eclipsar.

ecological /,ɛkə'lɒdʒɪkəl/ a. ecológico.

ecology /i'kɒlədʒi/ n. ecología f.

economic /,ɛkə'nɒmɪk, ,ikə-/ a. económico.

economical /,ɛkə'nɒmɪkəl, ,ikə-/ a. económico.

economics /,ɛkə'nɒmɪks, ,ikə-/ n. economía política.

economist /i'kɒnəmɪst/ n. economista m. & f.

economize /i'kɒnə,maiz/ v. economizar.

economy /i'kɒnəmi/ n. economía f.

ecstasy /'ɛkstəsi/ n. éxtasis m.

Ecuadorian /,ɛkwə'dɔriən/ a. & n. ecuatoriano -na.

ecumenical /'ɛkyʊ'mɛnɪkəl/ a. ecuménico.

eczema /'ɛksəmə/ n. eczema f.

eddy /'ɛdi/ n. **1.** remolino m. —v. **2.** remolinar.

edge /ɛdʒ/ n. **1.** filo; borde m. —v. **2. e. one's way,** abrirse paso.

edible /'ɛdəbəl/ a. comestible.

edict /'idɪkt/ n. edicto m.

edifice /'ɛdəfɪs/ n. edificio m.

edify /'ɛdəˌfai/ v. edificar.

edition /ɪ'dɪʃən/ n. edición f.

editor /'ɛdɪtər/ n. redactor -ra.

editorial /ˌɛdɪ'tɔriəl/ n. editorial m. **e. board,** consejo de redacción m. **e. staff,** redacción f.

educate /'ɛdʒuˌkeit/ v. educar.

education /ˌɛdʒu'keiʃən/ n. instrucción; enseñanza f.

educational /ˌɛdʒu'keiʃənl/ a. educativo.

educator /'ɛdʒuˌkeitər/ n. educador -ra, pedagogo -ga.

eel /il/ n. anguila f.

efface /ɪ'feis/ v. tachar.

effect /ɪ'fɛkt/ n. **1.** efecto m. **in e.,** en vigor. —v. **2.** efectuar, realizar.

effective /ɪ'fɛktɪv/ a. eficaz; efectivo; en vigor.

effectively /ɪ'fɛktɪvli/ adv. eficazmente.

effectiveness /ɪ'fɛktɪvnɪs/ n. efectividad f.

effectual /ɪ'fɛktʃuəl/ a. eficaz.

effeminate /ɪ'fɛmənɪt/ a. afeminado.

efficacy /'ɛfɪkəsi/ n. eficacia f.

efficiency /ɪ'fɪʃənsi/ n. eficiencia f.

efficient /ɪ'fɪʃənt/ a. eficaz.

efficiently /ɪ'fɪʃəntli/ adv. eficazmente.

effigy /'ɛfɪdʒi/ n. efigie f.

effort /'ɛfərt/ n. esfuerzo m.

effrontery /ɪ'frʌntəri/ n. impudencia f.

effusive /ɪ'fyusɪv/ a. efusivo.

egg /ɛg/ n. huevo m. **fried e.,** huevo frito. **soft-boiled e.,** h. pasado por agua. **scrambled eggs,** huevos revueltos.

eggplant /'ɛgˌplænt/ n. berenjena f.

egg white clara de huevo f.

egoism /'igouˌɪzəm/ **egotism** n. egoísmo m.

egoist /'igouɪst/ **egotist** n. egoísta m. & f.

egotism /'igəˌtɪzəm/ n. egotismo m.

egotist /'igətɪst/ n. egotista m. & f.

Egypt /'idʒɪpt/ n. Egipto m.

Egyptian /ɪ'dʒɪpʃən/ a. & n. egipcio -ia.

eight /eit/ a. & pron. ocho.

eighteen /'ei'tin/ a. & pron. dieciocho.

eighth /eitθ, eiθ/ a. octavo.

eightieth /'eitiɪθ/ n. octogésimo m.

eighty /'eiti/ a. & pron. ochenta.

either /'iðər/ a. & pron. **1.** cualquiera de los dos. —adv. **2.** tampoco. —conj. **3. either... or,** o... o.

ejaculate /ɪ'dʒækyəˌleit/ v. exclamar; eyacular.

ejaculation /ɪˌdʒækyə'leiʃən/ n. eyaculación f.

eject /ɪ'dʒɛkt/ v. expeler; eyectar.

ejection /ɪ'dʒɛkʃən/ n. expulsión f.; eyección f.

elaborate /a ɪ'læbərɪt; v -əˌreit/ a. **1.** elaborado. —v. **2.** elaborar; ampliar.

elapse /ɪ'læps/ v. transcurrir; pasar.

elastic /ɪ'læstɪk/ a. & n. elástico m.

elasticity /ɪlæ'stɪsɪti/ n. elasticidad f.

elate /ɪ'leit/ v. exaltar.

elation /ɪ'leiʃən/ n. exaltación f.

elbow /'ɛlbou/ n. codo m.

elder /'ɛldər/ a. **1.** mayor. —n. **2.** anciano -na.

elderly /'ɛldərli/ a. de edad.

eldest /'ɛldɪst/ a. mayor.

elect /ɪ'lɛkt/ v. elegir.

election /ɪ'lɛkʃən/ n. elección f.

elective /ɪ'lɛktɪv/ a. electivo.

electorate /ɪ'lɛktərɪt/ n. electorado m.

electric /ɪ'lɛktrɪk/ **electrical** a. eléctrico.

electrician /ɪlɛk'trɪʃən/ n. electricista m. & f.

electricity /ɪlɛk'trɪsɪti/ n. electricidad f.

electrocardiogram /ɪˌlɛktrou'kɑrdiəˌgræm/ n. electrocardiograma m.

electrocute /ɪ'lɛktrəˌkyut/ v. electrocutar.

electrode /ɪ'lɛktroud/ n. electrodo m.

electrolysis /ɪlɛk'trɒləsɪs/ n. electrólisis f.

electron /ɪ'lɛktrɒn/ n. electrón m.

electronic /ɪlɛk'trɒnɪk/ a. electrónico.
electronics /ɪlɪk'trɒnɪks/ n. electrónica f.
elegance /'ɛlɪgəns/ n. elegancia f.
elegant /'ɛlɪgənt/ a. elegante.
elegy /'ɛlɪdʒi/ n. elegía f.
element /'ɛləmənt/ n. elemento m.
elemental /ˌɛlə'mɛntḷ/ a. elemental.
elementary /ˌɛlə'mɛntəri/ a. elemental.
elephant /'ɛləfənt/ n. elefante -ta.
elevate /'ɛlə,veit/ v. elevar.
elevation /ˌɛlə'veiʃən/ n. elevación f.
elevator /'ɛlə,veitər/ n. ascensor m.
eleven /ɪ'lɛvən/ a. & pron. once.
eleventh /ɪ'lɛvənθ/ a. undécimo.
eleventh hour último minuto m.
elf /ɛlf/ n. duende m.
elicit /ɪ'lɪsɪt/ v. sacar; despertar.
eligibility /ˌɛlɪdʒə'bɪlɪti/ n. elegibilidad f.
eligible /'ɛlɪdʒəbəl/ a. elegible.
eliminate /ɪ'lɪmə,neit/ v. eliminar.
elimination /ɪ,lɪmə'neiʃən/ n. eliminación f.
elixir /ɪ'lɪksər/ n. elixir m.
elk /ɛlk/ n. alce m., anta m.
elm /ɛlm/ n. olmo m.
elocution /ˌɛlə'kyuʃən/ n. elocución f.
elongate /ɪ'lɔŋgeit/ v. alargar.
elope /ɪ'loup/ v. fugarse.
eloquence /'ɛləkwəns/ n. elocuencia f.
eloquent /'ɛləkwənt/ a. elocuente.
eloquently /'ɛləkwəntli/ adv. elocuentemente.
else /ɛls/ adv. más. **someone e.,** otra persona. **something e.,** otra cosa. **or e.,** de otro modo.
elsewhere /'ɛls,wɛər/ adv. en otra parte.
elucidate /ɪ'lusɪ,deit/ v. elucidar.
elude /ɪ'lud/ v. eludir.
elusive /ɪ'lusɪv/ a. evasivo.
emaciated /ɪ'meiʃi,eitɪd/ a. demacrado, enflaquecido.
e-mail /'i,meil/ n. correo electrónico m.
emanate /'ɛmə,neit/ v. emanar.
emancipate /ɪ'mænsə,peit/ v. emancipar.
emancipation /ɪ,mænsə'peiʃən/ n. emancipación f.

emancipator /ɪ'mænsə,peitər/ n. libertador -ra.
embalm /ɛm'bam/ v. embalsamar.
embankment /ɛm'bæŋkmənt/ n. malecón, dique m.
embargo /ɛm'bargou/ n. embargo m.
embark /ɛm'bark/ v. embarcar.
embarrass /ɛm'bærəs/ v. avergonzar; turbar.
embarrassing /ɛm'bærəsɪŋ/ a. penoso, vergonzoso.
embarrassment /ɛm'bærəsmənt/ n. turbación; vergüenza f.
embassy /'ɛmbəsi/ n. embajada f.
embellish /ɛm'bɛlɪʃ/ v. hermosear, embellecer.
embellishment /ɛm'bɛlɪʃmənt/ n. embellecimiento m.
embezzle /ɛm'bɛzəl/ v. desfalcar, malversar.
emblem /'ɛmbləm/ n. emblema m.
embody /ɛm'bɒdi/ v. incorporar; personificar.
embrace /ɛm'breis/ n. **1.** abrazo m. —v. **2.** abrazar.
embroider /ɛm'brɔidər/ v. bordar.
embroidery /ɛm'brɔidəri, -dri/ n. bordado m.
embryo /'ɛmbri,ou/ n. embrión m.
embryonic /ˌɛmbri'ɒnɪk/ a. embrionario.
emerald /'ɛmərəld/ n. esmeralda f.
emerge /ɪ'mɜrdʒ/ v. salir.
emergency /ɪ'mɜrdʒənsi/ n. emergencia f.
emergency brake freno de auxilio m.
emergency exit salida de urgencia f.
emergency landing aterrizaje forzoso m.
emergent /ɪ'mɜrdʒənt/ a. emergente.
emery /'ɛməri/ n. esmeril m.
emetic /ɪ'mɛtɪk/ n. emético m.
emigrant /'ɛmɪgrənt/ a. & n. emigrante m. & f.
emigrate /'ɛmɪ,greit/ v. emigrar.
emigration /ˌɛmə'greiʃən/ n. emigración f.
eminence /'ɛmənəns/ n. altura; eminencia f.
eminent /'ɛmənənt/ a. eminente.
emissary /'ɛmə,sɛri/ n. emisario m.
emission /ɪ'mɪʃən/ n. emisión f.

emit /ɪ'mɪt/ v. emitir.
emolument /ɪ'mɒlyəmənt/ n. emolumento m.
emotion /ɪ'mouʃən/ n. emoción f.
emotional /ɪ'mouʃənļ/ a. emocional; sentimental.
emperor /'ɛmpərər/ n. emperador m.
emphasis /'ɛmfəsɪs/ n. énfasis m. or f.
emphasize /'ɛmfə,saɪz/ v. acentuar, recalcar.
emphatic /ɛm'fætɪk/ a. enfático.
empire /'ɛmpaiᵊr/ n. imperio m.
empirical /ɛm'pɪrɪkəl/ a. empírico.
employ /ɛm'plɔi/ v. emplear.
employee /ɛm'plɔii/ n. empleado -da.
employer /ɛm'plɔiər/ n. patrón -ona.
employment /ɛm'plɔimənt/ n. empleo m.
employment agency agencia de colocaciones f.
empower /ɛm'pauər/ v. autorizar.
emptiness /'ɛmptinɪs/ n. vaciedad; futilidad f.
empty /'ɛmpti/ a. **1.** vacío. —v. **2.** vaciar.
emulate /'ɛmyə,leit/ v. emular.
emulsion /ɪ'mʌlʃən/ n. emulsión f.
enable /ɛn'eibəl/ v. capacitar; permitir.
enact /ɛn'ækt/ v. promulgar, decretar.
enactment /ɛn'æktmənt/ n. ley f., estatuto m.
enamel /ɪ'næməl/ n. **1.** esmalte m. —v. **2.** esmaltar.
enamored /ɪ'næmərd/ a. enamorado.
enchant /ɛn'tʃænt/ v. encantar.
enchantment /ɛn'tʃæntmənt/ n. encanto m.
encircle /ɛn'sɜrkəl/ v. circundar.
enclose /ɛn'klouz/ v. encerrar. **enclosed,** (in letter) adjunto.
enclosure /ɛn'klouʒər/ n. recinto m.; (in letter) incluso m.
encompass /ɛn'kʌmpəs/ v. circundar.
encounter /ɛn'kauntər/ n. **1.** encuentro m. —v. **2.** encontrar.
encourage /ɛn'kɜrɪdʒ/ v. animar.
encouragement /ɛn'kɜrɪdʒmənt/ n. estímulo m.
encroach /ɛn'kroutʃ/ v. usurpar; meterse.

encryption /ɛn'krɪpʃən/ n. encriptación f., cifrado m.
encyclical /ɛn'sɪklɪkəl/ n. encíclica f.
encyclopedia /ɛn,saiklə'pidiə/ n. enciclopedia f.
end /ɛnd/ n. **1.** fin, término, cabo; extremo; (aim) propósito m. —v. **2.** acabar; terminar.
endanger /ɛn'deindʒər/ v. poner en peligro.
endear /ɛn'dɪər/ v. hacer querer.
endeavor /ɛn'dɛvər/ n. **1.** esfuerzo m. —v. **2.** esforzarse.
ending /'ɛndɪŋ/ n. conclusión f.
endless /'ɛndlɪs/ a. sin fin.
endocrine gland /'ɛndəkrɪn/ glándula endocrina f.
endorse /ɛn'dɔrs/ v. endosar; apoyar.
endorsement /ɛn'dɔrsmənt/ n. endoso m.
endow /ɛn'dau/ v. dotar, fundar.
endowment /ɛn'daumənt/ n. dotación f., fundación f.
endurance /ɛn'dʊrəns/ n. resistencia f.
endure /ɛn'dʊr/ v. soportar, resistir, aguantar.
enema /'ɛnəmə/ n. enema; lavativa f.
enemy /'ɛnəmi/ n. enemigo -ga.
energetic /,ɛnər'dʒɛtɪk/ a. enérgico.
energy /'ɛnərdʒi/ n. energía f.
enervate /'ɛnər,veit/ v. enervar.
enervation /,ɛnər'veiʃən/ n. enervación f.
enfold /ɛn'fould/ v. envolver.
enforce /ɛn'fɔrs/ v. ejecutar.
enforcement /ɛn'fɔrsmənt/ n. ejecución f.
engage /ɛn'geidʒ/ v. emplear; ocupar.
engaged /ɛn'geidʒd/ a. (to marry) prometido.
engagement /ɛn'geidʒmənt/ n. combate; compromiso; contrato m.; cita f.
engine /'ɛndʒən/ n. máquina f. (railroad) locomotora f.
engineer /,ɛndʒə'nɪər/ n. ingeniero -ra; maquinista m.
engineering /,ɛndʒə'nɪərɪŋ/ n. ingeniería f.
England /'ɪŋglənd/ n. Inglaterra f.
English /'ɪŋglɪʃ/ a. & n. inglés -esa.
English Channel Canal de la Mancha m.

Englishman /'ɪŋglɪʃmən/ n. inglés m.

Englishwoman /'ɪŋglɪʃ,wʊmən/ n. inglesa f.

engrave /ɛn'greiv/ v. grabar.

engraver /ɛn'greivər/ n. grabador m.

engraving /ɛn'greivɪŋ/ n. grabado m.

engross /ɛn'grous/ v. absorber.

enhance /ɛn'hæns/ v. aumentar en valor; realzar.

enigma /ə'nɪgmə/ n. enigma m.

enigmatic /,ɛnɪg'mætɪk/ a. enigmático.

enjoy /ɛn'dʒɔi/ v. gozar de; disfrutar de. **e. oneself,** divertirse.

enjoyable /ɛn'dʒɔiəbəl/ a. agradable.

enjoyment /ɛn'dʒɔimənt/ n. goce m.

enlarge /ɛn'lɑrdʒ/ v. agrandar; ampliar.

enlargement /ɛn'lɑrdʒmənt/ n. ensanchamiento m., ampliación f.

enlarger /ɛn'lɑrdʒər/ n. amplificador m.

enlighten /ɛn'laitn̩/ v. informar.

enlightenment /ɛn'laitn̩mənt/ n. esclarecimiento m.; cultura f.

enlist /ɛn'lɪst/ v. reclutar; alistarse.

enlistment /ɛn'lɪstmənt/ n. alistamiento m.

enliven /ɛn'laivən/ v. avivar.

enmesh /ɛn'mɛʃ/ v. entrampar.

enmity /'ɛnmɪti/ n. enemistad f.

enormity /ɪ'nɔrmɪti/ v. enormidad f.

enormous /ɪ'nɔrməs/ a. enorme.

enough /ɪ'nʌf/ a. & adv. bastante. **to be e.,** bastar.

enrage /ɛn'reidʒ/ v. enfurecer.

enrich /ɛn'rɪtʃ/ v. enriquecer.

enroll /ɛn'roul/ v. registrar; matricularse.

enrollment /ɛn'roulmənt/ n. matriculación f.

ensign /'ɛnsən/ n. bandera f.; (naval) subteniente m.

enslave /ɛn'sleiv/ v. esclavizar.

ensue /ɛn'su/ v. seguir, resultar.

entail /ɛn'teil/ v. acarrear, ocasionar.

entangle /ɛn'tæŋgəl/ v. enredar.

enter /'ɛntər/ v. entrar.

enterprise /'ɛntər,praiz/ n. empresa f.

enterprising /'ɛntər,praizɪŋ/ a. emprendedor.

entertain /,ɛntər'tein/ v. entretener; divertir.

entertainment /,ɛntər'teinmənt/ n. entretenimiento m.; diversión f.

enthrall /ɛn'θrɔl/ v. esclavizar; cautivar.

enthusiasm /ɛn'θuzi,æzəm/ n. entusiasmo m.

enthusiast /ɛn'θuzi,æst, -ɪst/ n. entusiasta m. & f.

enthusiastic /ɛn,θuzi'æstɪk/ a. entusiasmado.

entice /ɛn'tais/ v. inducir.

entire /ɛn'taiər/ a. entero.

entirely /ɛn'taiərli/ adv. enteramente.

entirety /ɛn'taiərti/ n. totalidad f.

entitle /ɛn'taitl̩/ v. autorizar; (book) titular.

entity /'ɛntɪti/ n. entidad f.

entrails /'ɛntreilz/ n. entrañas f.pl.

entrance /'ɛntrəns/ n. entrada f.

entrance examination examen de ingreso m.

entrant /'ɛntrənt/ n. competidor -ra.

entreat /ɛn'trit/ v. rogar, suplicar.

entreaty /ɛn'triti/ n. ruego m., súplica f.

entrench /ɛn'trɛntʃ/ v. atrincherar.

entrust /ɛn'trʌst/ v. confiar.

entry /'ɛntri/ n. entrada f.; Com. partida f.

entry blank hoja de inscripción f.

enumerate /ɪ'numə,reit/ v. enumerar.

enumeration /ɪ,numə'reiʃən/ n. enumeración f.

enunciate /ɪ'nʌnsi,eit/ v. enunciar.

enunciation /ɪ,nʌnsi'eiʃən/ n. enunciación f.

envelop /ɛn'vɛləp/ v. envolver.

envelope /'ɛnvə,loup/ n. sobre m.; cubierta f.

enviable /'ɛnviəbəl/ a. envidiable.

envious /'ɛnviəs/ a. envidioso.

environment /ɛn'vairənmənt/ n. ambiente m.

environmentalist /ɛn,vairən'mɛntl̩ɪst/ n. ambientalista, ecologista m. & f.

environmental protection /ɛn,vairən'mɛntəl/ protección del ambiente.

environs /ɛn'vairənz/ n. alrededores m.

envoy /'ɛnvɔi/ n. enviado m.
envy /'ɛnvi/ n. **1.** envidia f. —v.
2. envidiar.
eon /'iən/ n. eón m.
ephemeral /ɪ'fɛmərəl/ a. efímero.
epic /'ɛpɪk/ a. **1.** épico. —n. **2.**
epopeya f.
epicure /'ɛpɪ,kyʊr/ n. epicúreo m.
epidemic /,ɛpɪ'dɛmɪk/ a. **1.**
epidémico. —n. **2.** epidemia f.
epidermis /,ɛpɪ'dɜrmɪs/ n. epidermis f.
epigram /'ɛpɪ,græm/ n. epigrama
m.
epilepsy /'ɛpə,lɛpsi/ n. epilepsia f.
epilogue /'ɛpə,lɔg/ n. epílogo m.
episode /'ɛpə,soʊd/ n. episodio
m.
epistle /ɪ'pɪsəl/ n. epístola f.
epitaph /'ɛpɪ,tæf/ n. epitafio m.
epithet /'ɛpə,θɛt/ n. epíteto m.
epitome /ɪ'pɪtəmi/ n. epítome m.
epoch /'ɛpək/ n. época, era f.
Epsom salts /'ɛpsəm/ n.pl. sal de
la Higuera f.
equal /'ikwəl/ a. & n. **1.** igual m.
—v. **2.** igualar; equivaler.
equality /ɪ'kwɒlɪti/ n. igualdad f.
equalize /'ikwə,laiz/ v. igualar.
equanimity /,ikwə'nɪmɪti/ n.
ecuanimidad f.
equate /ɪ'kweit/ v. igualar.
equation /ɪ'kweiʒən/ n. ecuación
f.
equator /ɪ'kweitər/ n. ecuador m.
equatorial /,ikwə'tɔriəl/ a. ecuatorial
equestrian /ɪ'kwɛstriən/ n. **1.** jinete m. —a. **2.** ecuestre.
equilibrium /,ikwə'lɪbriəm/ n.
equilibrio m.
equinox /'ikwə,nɒks/ n. equinoccio m.
equip /ɪ'kwɪp/ v. equipar.
equipment /ɪ'kwɪpmənt/ n.
equipo m.
equitable /'ɛkwɪtəbəl/ a. equitativo.
equity /'ɛkwɪti/ n. equidad, justicia f.
equivalent /ɪ'kwɪvələnt/ a. & n.
equivalente m.
equivocal /ɪ'kwɪvəkəl/ a. equívoco, ambiguo.
era /'ɪərə, 'ɛrə/ n. era, época,
edad f.
eradicate /ɪ'rædɪ,keit/ v. extirpar.
erase /ɪ'reis/ v. borrar.
eraser /ɪ'reisər/ n. borrador m.
erasure /ɪ'reiʃər/ n. borradura f.

erect /ɪ'rɛkt/ a. **1.** derecho, erguido. —v. **2.** erigir.
erection /ɪ'rɛkʃən/ **erectness** n.
erección f.
ermine /'ɜrmɪn/ n. armiño m.
erode /ɪ'roud/ v. corroer.
erosion /ɪ'rouʒən/ n. erosión f.
erotic /ɪ'rɒtɪk/ a. erótico.
err /ɜr, ɛr/ v. equivocarse.
errand /'ɛrənd/ n. encargo, recado
m.
errant /'ɛrənt/ a. errante.
erratic /ɪ'rætɪk/ a. errático.
erroneous /ə'rouniəs/ a. erróneo.
error /'ɛrər/ n. error m.
erudite /'ɛryʊ,dait/ a. erudito.
erudition /,ɛryʊ'dɪʃən/ n. erudición f.
eruption /ɪ'rʌpʃən/ n. erupción,
irrupción f.
erysipelas /,ɛrə'sɪpələs/ n. erisipela f.
escalate /'ɛskə,leit/ v. escalar; intensificarse.
escalator /'ɛskə,leitər/ n. escalera
mecánica f.
escapade /'ɛskə,peid/ n. escapada; correría f.
escape /ɪ'skeip/ n. **1.** fuga, huída
f. **fire e.,** escalera de salvamento.
—v. **2.** escapar; fugarse.
eschew /ɛs'tʃu/ v. evadir.
escort /n 'ɛskɔrt; v ɪ'skɔrt/ n. **1.**
escolta f. —v. **2.** escoltar.
escrow /'ɛskrou/ n. plica f.
escutcheon /ɪ'skʌtʃən/ n. escudo
de armas m.
esophagus /ɪ'sɒfəgəs/ n. esófago
m.
esoteric /,ɛsə'tɛrɪk/ a. esotérico.
especially /ɪ'spɛʃəli/ adv. especialmente.
espionage /'ɛspiə,nɑʒ/ n. espionaje m.
espresso /ɛ'sprɛsou/ n. café exprés, m.
essay /'ɛsei/ n. ensayo m.
essayist /'ɛseiɪst/ n. ensayista m.
& f.
essence /'ɛsəns/ n. esencia f.; perfume m.
essential /ə'sɛntʃəl/ a. esencial.
essentially /ə'sɛntʃəli/ adv. esencialmente.
establish /ɪ'stæblɪʃ/ v. establecer.
establishment /ɪ'stæblɪʃmənt/ n.
establecimiento m.
estate /ɪ'steit/ n. estado m.; hacienda f.; bienes m.pl.

esteem /ɪ'stim/ n. **1.** estima f.
—v. **2.** estimar.

estimable /'ɛstəməbəl/ a. estimable.

estimate /n 'ɛstəmɪt; v -ˌmeit/ n. **1.** cálculo; presupuesto m. —v. **2.** estimar.

estimation /ˌɛstə'meiʃən/ n. estimación f.; cálculo m.

estrange /ɪ'streindʒ/ v. extrañar; enajenar.

estuary /'ɛstʃuˌɛri/ n. estuario m.

etch /ɛtʃ/ v. grabar al agua fuerte.

etching /'ɛtʃɪŋ/ n. aguafuerte.

eternal /ɪ'tɜrnl/ a. eterno.

eternity /ɪ'tɜrnɪti/ n. eternidad f.

ether /'iθər/ n. éter m.

ethereal /ɪ'θɪəriəl/ a. etéreo.

ethical /'ɛθɪkəl/ a. ético.

ethics /'ɛθɪks/ n. ética f.

ethnic /'ɛθnɪk/ a. étnico.

etiquette /'ɛtɪkɪt/ n. etiqueta f.

etymology /ˌɛtə'mɒlədʒi/ n. etimología f.

eucalyptus /ˌyukə'lɪptəs/ n. eucalipto m.

eugenic /yu'dʒɛnɪk/ a. eugenésico.

eugenics /yu'dʒɛnɪks/ n. eugenesia f.

eulogize /'yuləˌdʒaiz/ v. elogiar.

eulogy /'yulədʒi/ n. elogio m.

eunuch /'yunək/ n. eunuco m.

euphonious /yu'founiəs/ a. eufónico.

Europe /'yʊrəp/ n. Europa f.

European /ˌyʊrə'piən/ a. & n. europeo -pea.

euthanasia /ˌyuθə'neiʒə, -ʒiə, -ziə/ n. eutanasia f.

evacuate /ɪ'vækyuˌeit/ v. evacuar.

evade /ɪ'veid/ v. evadir.

evaluate /ɪ'vælyuˌeit/ v. evaluar.

evaluation /ɪˌvælyu'eiʃən/ n. valoración f.

evangelist /ɪ'vændʒəlɪst/ n. evangelista m. & f.

evaporate /ɪ'væpəˌreit/ v. evaporarse.

evaporation /ɪˌvæpə'reiʃən/ n. evaporación f.

evasion /ɪ'veiʒən/ n. evasión f.

evasive /ɪ'veisɪv/ a. evasivo.

eve /iv/ n. víspera f.

even /'ivən/ a. **1.** llano; igual. —adv. **2.** aun; hasta. **not e.,** ni siquiera.

evening /'ivnɪŋ/ n. noche, tarde f. **good e.!** ¡buenas tardes! ¡buenas noches!

evening class clase nocturna f.

evenness /'ivənnɪs/ n. uniformidad f.

even number número par m.

event /ɪ'vɛnt/ n. acontecimiento, suceso m.

eventful /ɪ'vɛntfəl/ a. memorable.

eventual /ɪ'vɛntʃuəl/ a. eventual.

ever /'ɛvər/ adv. alguna vez; (after not) nunca. **e. since,** desde que.

everlasting /ˌɛvər'læstɪŋ/ a. eterno.

every /'ɛvri/ a. cada, todos los.

everybody /'ɛvriˌbɒdi, -ˌbʌdi/ pron. todo el mundo; cada uno.

everyday /'ɛvriˌdei/ a. ordinario, de cada día.

everyone /'ɛvriˌwʌn/ pron. todo el mundo; cada uno; cada cual.

everything /'ɛvriˌθɪŋ/ pron. todo m.

everywhere /'ɛvriˌwɛər/ adv. por todas partes, en todas partes.

evict /ɪ'vɪkt/ v. expulsar.

eviction /ɪ'vɪkʃən/ n. evicción f.

evidence /'ɛvɪdəns/ n. evidencia f.

evident /'ɛvɪdənt/ a. evidente.

evidently /'ɛvɪdəntli/ adv. evidentemente.

evil /'ivəl/ a. **1.** malo; maligno. —n. **2.** mal m.

evince /ɪ'vɪns/ v. revelar.

evoke /ɪ'vouk/ v. evocar.

evolution /ˌɛvə'luʃən/ n. evolución f.

evolve /ɪ'vɒlv/ v. desenvolver; desarrollar.

ewe /yu/ v. oveja f.

exact /ɪg'zækt/ a. **1.** exacto. —v. **2.** exigir.

exacting /ɪg'zæktɪŋ/ a. exigente.

exactly /ɪg'zæktli/ adv. exactamente.

exaggerate /ɪg'zædʒəˌreit/ v. exagerar.

exaggeration /ɪgˌzædʒə'reiʃən/ n. exageración f.

exalt /ɪg'zɔlt/ v. exaltar.

exaltation /ˌɛgzɔl'teiʃən/ n. exaltación f.

examination /ɪgˌzæmə'neiʃən/ n. examen m.; (legal) interrogatorio m.

examine /ɪg'zæmɪn/ v. examinar.

example /ɪg'zæmpəl/ n. ejemplo m.

exasperate /ɪg'zæspəˌreit/ v. exasperar.

exasperation /ɪg,zæspə'reiʃən/ *n.* exasperación *f.*

excavate /'ɛkskə,veit/ *v.* excavar, cavar.

exceed /ɪk'sid/ *v.* exceder.

exceedingly /ɪk'sidɪŋli/ *adv.* sumamente, extremadamente.

excel /ɪk'sɛl/ *v.* sobresalir.

excellence /'ɛksələns/ *n.* excelencia *f.*

Excellency /'ɛksələnsi/ *n.* (title) Excelencia *f.*

excellent /'ɛksələnt/ *a.* excelente.

except /ɪk'sɛpt/ *prep.* **1.** salvo, excepto. —*v.* **2.** exceptuar.

exception /ɪk'sɛpʃən/ *n.* excepción *f.*

exceptional /ɪk'sɛpʃənl/ *a.* excepcional.

excerpt /'ɛksɜrpt/ *n.* extracto.

excess /ɪk'sɛs, 'ɛksɛs/ *n.* exceso *m.*

excessive /ɪk'sɛsɪv/ *a.* excesivo.

exchange /ɪks'tʃeindʒ/ *n.* **1.** cambio; canje *m.* **stock e.,** bolsa *f.* **telephone e.,** central telefónica. —*v.* **2.** cambiar, canjear, intercambiar.

exchangeable /ɪks'tʃeindʒəbəl/ *a.* cambiable.

exchange rate tipo de cambio *m.*

excise /*n.* 'ɛksaiz; *v.* ɪk'saiz/ *n.* **1.** sisa *f.* —*v.* **2.** extirpar.

excite /ɪk'sait/ *v.* agitar; provocar; emocionar.

excitement /ɪk'saitmənt/ *n.* agitación, conmoción *f.*

exciting /ɪk'saitɪŋ/ *a.* emocionante.

exclaim /ɪk'skleim/ *v.* exclamar.

exclamation /,ɛksklə'meiʃən/ *n.* exclamación *f.*

exclamation mark punto de admiración *m.*

exclude /ɪk'sklud/ *v.* excluir.

exclusion /ɪk'skluʒən/ *n.* exclusión *f.*

exclusive /ɪk'sklusɪv/ *a.* exclusivo.

excommunicate /,ɛkskə'myunɪ,keit/ *v.* excomulgar, descomulgar.

excommunication /,ɛkskə,myunɪ'keiʃən/ *n.* excomunión *f.*

excrement /'ɛkskrəmənt/ *n.* excremento *m.*

excruciating /ɪk'skruʃi,eitɪŋ/ *a.* penosísimo.

exculpate /'ɛkskʌl,peit/ *v.* exculpar.

excursion /ɪk'skɜrʒən/ *n.* excursión, jira *f.*

excuse /*n.* ɪk'skyus; *v.* ɪk'skyuz/ *n.* **1.** excusa *f.* —*v.* **2.** excusar, perdonar, disculpar; dispensar.

execrable /'ɛksɪkrəbəl/ *a.* execrable.

execute /'ɛksɪ,kyut/ *v.* ejecutar.

execution /,ɛksɪ'kyuʃən/ *n.* ejecución *f.*

executioner /,ɛksɪ'kyuʃənər/ *n.* verdugo *m.*

executive /ɪg'zɛkyətɪv/ *a. & n.* ejecutivo -va.

executor /ɪg'zɛkyətər/ *n.* testamentario *m.*

exemplary /ɪg'zɛmpləri/ *a.* ejemplar.

exemplify /ɪg'zɛmplə,fai/ *v.* ejemplificar.

exempt /ɪg'zɛmpt/ *a.* **1.** exento. —*v.* **2.** exentar.

exercise /'ɛksər,saiz/ *n.* **1.** ejercicio *m.* —*v.* **2.** ejercitar.

exert /ɪg'zɜrt/ *v.* esforzar.

exertion /ɪg'zɜrʃən/ *n.* esfuerzo *m.*

exhale /ɛks'heil/ *v.* exhalar.

exhaust /ɪg'zɔst/ *n.* **1.** *Auto.* escape *m.* —*v.* **2.** agotar.

exhaustion /ɪg'zɔstʃən/ *n.* agotamiento *m.*

exhaustive /ɪg'zɔstɪv/ *a.* exhaustivo.

exhaust pipe tubo de escape *m.*

exhibit /ɪg'zɪbɪt/ *n.* **1.** exhibición, exposición *f.* —*v.* **2.** exhibir.

exhibition /,ɛksə'bɪʃən/ *n.* exhibición *f.*

exhilarate /ɪg'zɪlə,reit/ *v.* alegrar; estimular.

exhort /ɪg'zɔrt/ *v.* exhortar.

exhortation /,ɛgzɔr'teiʃən/ *n.* exhortación *f.*

exhume /ɪg'zum/ *v.* exhumar.

exigency /'ɛksɪdʒənsi/ *n.* exigencia *f.*, urgencia *f.*

exile /'ɛgzail/ *n.* **1.** destierro *m.*, (person) desterrado *m.* —*v.* **2.** desterrar.

exist /ɪg'zɪst/ *v.* existir.

existence /ɪg'zɪstəns/ *n.* existencia *f.*

existent /ɪg'zɪstənt/ *a.* existente.

exit /'ɛgzɪt, 'ɛksɪt/ *n.* salida *f.*

exodus /'ɛksədəs/ *n.* éxodo *m.*

exonerate /ɪg'zɒnə,reit/ *v.* exonerar.

exorbitant /ɪg'zɔrbɪtənt/ *a.* exorbitante.

exorcise /'ɛksɔr,saiz/ v. exorcizar.
exotic /ɪg'zɒtɪk/ a. exótico.
expand /ɪk'spænd/ v. dilatar; ensanchar.
expanse /ɪk'spæns/ n. espacio m.; extensión f.
expansion /ɪk'spænʃən/ n. expansión f.
expansion slot ranura de expansión f.
expansive /ɪk'spænsɪv/ a. expansivo.
expatiate /ɪk'speiʃi,eit/ v. espaciarse.
expatriate /n, a ɛks'peitriɪt; v ɛks'peitri,eit/ n. & a. **1.** expatriado m. —v. **2.** expatriar.
expect /ɪk'spɛkt/ v. esperar; contar con.
expectancy /ɪk'spɛktənsi/ n. esperanza f.
expectation /,ɛkspɛk'teiʃən/ n. esperanza f.
expectorate /ɪk'spɛktə,reit/ v. expectorar.
expediency /ɪk'spidiənsi/ n. conveniencia f.
expedient /ɪk'spidiənt/ a. **1.** oportuno. —n. **2.** expediente m.
expedite /'ɛkspɪ,dait/ v. acelerar, despachar.
expedition /,ɛkspɪ'dɪʃən/ n. expedición f.
expel /ɪk'spɛl/ v. expeler; expulsar.
expend /ɪk'spɛnd/ v. desembolsar, expender.
expenditure /ɪk'spɛndɪtʃər/ n. desembolso; gasto m.
expense /ɪk'spɛns/ n. gasto m.; costa f.
expensive /ɪk'spɛnsɪv/ a. caro, costoso.
expensively /ɪk'spɛnsɪvli/ adv. costosamente.
experience /ɪk'spɪəriəns/ n. **1.** experiencia f. —v. **2.** experimentar.
experienced /ɪk'spɪəriənst/ a. experimentado, perito.
experiment /n ɪk'spɛrəmənt; v -,mɛnt/ n. **1.** experimento m. —v. **2.** experimentar.
experimental /ɪk,spɛrə'mɛntl̩/ a. experimental.
expert /'ɛkspɜrt/ a. & n. experto -ta.
expertise /,ɛkspər'tiz/ n. pericia f.
expiate /'ɛkspi,eit/ v. expiar.
expiration /,ɛkspə'reiʃən/ n. expiración f.

expiration date fecha de caducidad f.
expire /ɪk'spaiᵊr/ v. expirar; Com. vencerse.
explain /ɪk'splein/ v. explicar.
explanation /,ɛksplə'neiʃən/ n. explicación f.
explanatory /ɪk'splænə,tɔri/ a. explicativo.
expletive /'ɛksplɪtɪv/ n. **1.** interjección f. —a. **2.** expletivo.
explicit /ɪk'splɪsɪt/ a. explícito, claro.
explode /ɪk'sploud/ v. estallar, volar; refutar.
exploit /ɪk'splɔit/ n. **1.** hazaña f. —v. **2.** explotar.
exploitation /,ɛksplɔi'teiʃən/ n. explotación f.
exploration /,ɛksplə'reiʃən/ n. exploración f.
exploratory /ɪk'splɔrə,tɔri/ a. exploratorio.
explore /ɪk'splɔr/ v. explorar.
explorer /ɪk'splɔrər/ n. explorador -ra.
explosion /ɪk'splouʒən/ n. explosión f.
explosive /ɪk'splousɪv/ a. explosivo.
export /n 'ɛkspɔrt; v ɪk'spɔrt/ n. **1.** exportación f. —v. **2.** exportar.
exportation /,ɛkspɔr'teiʃən/ n. exportación f.
expose /ɪk'spouz/ v. exponer; descubrir.
exposition /,ɛkspə'zɪʃən/ n. exposición f.
expository /ɪk'spɒzɪ,tɔri/ a. expositivo.
expostulate /ɪk'spɒstʃə,leit/ v. altercar.
exposure /ɪk'spouʒər/ n. exposición f.
expound /ɪk'spaund/ v. exponer, explicar.
express /ɪk'sprɛs/ a. & n. **1.** expreso m. **e. company,** compañía de porteo. —v. **2.** expresar.
expression /ɪk'sprɛʃən/ n. expresión f.
expressive /ɪk'sprɛsɪv/ a. expresivo.
expressly /ɪk'sprɛsli/ adv. expresamente.
expressman /ɪk'sprɛsmən, -,mæn/ n. empresario de expresos m.
expressway /ɪk'sprɛs,wei/ n. autopista f.

expropriate /ɛksˈproupriˌeit/ v. expropriar.

expulsion /ɪkˈspʌlʃən/ n. expulsión f.

expunge /ɪkˈspʌndʒ/ v. borrar, expurgar.

expurgate /ˈɛkspərˌgeit/ v. expurgar.

exquisite /ɪkˈskwɪzɪt/ a. exquisito.

extant /ˈɛkstənt/ a. existente.

extemporaneous /ɪkˌstɛmpəˈreiniəs/ a. improvisado.

extend /ɪkˈstɛnd/ v. extender.

extension /ɪkˈstɛnʃən/ n. extensión f.

extensive /ɪkˈstɛnsɪv/ a. extenso.

extensively /ɪkˈstɛnsɪvli/ adv. extensamente.

extent /ɪkˈstɛnt/ n. extensión f.; grado m. **to a certain e.,** hasta cierto punto.

extenuate /ɪkˈstɛnyuˌeit/ v. extenuar.

exterior /ɪkˈstɪəriər/ a. & n. exterior m.

exterminate /ɪkˈstɜrməˌneit/ v. exterminar.

extermination /ɪkˌstɜrməˈneiʃən/ n. exterminio m.

external /ɪkˈstɜrnl/ a. externo, exterior.

extinct /ɪkˈstɪŋkt/ a. extinto.

extinction /ɪkˈstɪŋkʃən/ n. extinción f.

extinguish /ɪkˈstɪŋgwɪʃ/ v. extinguir, apagar.

extol /ɪkˈstoul/ v. alabar.

extort /ɪkˈstɔrt/ v. exigir dinero sin derecho.

extortion /ɪkˈstɔrʃən/ n. extorsión f.

extra /ˈɛkstrə/ a. **1.** extraordinario; adicional. —n. **2.** (newspaper) extra m.

extract /n ˈɛkstrækt; v ɪkˈstrækt/ n. **1.** extracto m. —v. **2.** extraer.

extraction /ɪkˈstrækʃən/ n. extracción f.

extraneous /ɪkˈstreiniəs/ a. extraño; ajeno.

extraordinary /ɪkˈstrɔrdn̩ˌɛri/ a. extraordinario.

extravagance /ɪkˈstrævəgəns/ n. extravagancia f.

extravagant /ɪkˈstrævəgənt/ a. extravagante.

extreme /ɪkˈstrim/ a. & n. extremo m.

extremity /ɪkˈstrɛmɪti/ n. extremidad f.

extricate /ˈɛkstrɪˌkeit/ v. desenredar.

exuberant /ɪgˈzubərənt/ a. exuberante.

exude /ɪgˈzud/ v. exudar.

exult /ɪgˈzʌlt/ v. regocijarse.

exultant /ɪgˈzʌltn̩t/ a. triunfante.

eye /ai/ n. **1.** ojo m. —v. **2.** ojear.

eyeball /ˈaiˌbɔl/ n. globo del ojo.

eyebrow /ˈaiˌbrau/ n. ceja f.

eyeglasses /ˈaiˌglæsɪz/ n. lentes m.pl.

eyelash /ˈaiˌlæʃ/ n. pestaña f.

eyelid /ˈaiˌlɪd/ n. párpado m.

eyeliner /ˈaiˌlainər/ n. lápiz de ojos m.

eye shadow n. sombra de ojos f.

eyesight /ˈaiˌsait/ n. vista f.

F

fable /ˈfeibəl/ n. fábula; ficción f.

fabric /ˈfæbrɪk/ n. tejido m., tela f.

fabricate /ˈfæbrɪˌkeit/ v. fabricar.

fabulous /ˈfæbyələs/ a. fabuloso.

façade /fəˈsɑd/ n. fachada f.

face /feis/ n. **1.** cara f. **make faces,** hacer muecas. —v. **2.** encararse con. **f. the street,** dar a la calle.

facet /ˈfæsɪt/ n. faceta f.

facetious /fəˈsiʃəs/ a. chistoso.

facial /ˈfeiʃəl/ n. **1.** masaje facial m. —a. **2.** facial.

facile /ˈfæsɪl/ a. fácil.

facilitate /fəˈsɪlɪˌteit/ v. facilitar.

facility /fəˈsɪlɪti/ n. facilidad f.

facsimile /fækˈsɪməli/ n. facsímile m.

fact /fækt/ n. hecho m. **in f.,** en realidad.

faction /ˈfækʃən/ n. facción f.

factor /ˈfæktər/ n. factor m.

factory /ˈfæktəri/ n. fábrica f.

factual /ˈfæktʃuəl/ a. verdadero.

faculty /ˈfækəlti/ n. facultad f.

fad /fæd/ n. boga; novedad f.

fade /feid/ v. desteñirse; (flowers) marchitarse.

fail /feil/ n. **1. without f.,** sin falla. —v. **2.** fallar; fracasar. **not to f. to,** no dejar de.

failure /ˈfeilyər/ n. fracaso m.

faint /feint/ a. **1.** débil; vago;

pálido. —*n.* **2.** desmayo *m.* —*v.*
3. desmayarse.
faintly /'feintli/ *adv.* débilmente;
indistintamente.
fair /fɛər/ *a.* **1.** razonable, justo;
(hair) rubio; (weather) bueno.
—*n.* **2.** feria *f.*
fairly /'fɛərli/ *adv.* imparcial-
mente; regularmente; claramente;
bellamente.
fairness /'fɛərnɪs/ *n.* justicia *f.*
fair play juego limpio *m.*
fairway /'fɛər,wei/ *n.* (golf) calle
f.
fairy /'fɛəri/ *n.* hada *f.*, duende *m.*
faith /feiθ/ *n.* fe; confianza *f.*
faithful /'feiθfəl/ *a.* fiel.
fake /feik/ *a.* **1.** falso; postizo.
—*n.* **2.** imitación; estafa *f.* —*v.* **3.**
imitar; fingir.
faker /'feikəer/ *n.* imitador *m.;*
farsante *m.*
falcon /'fɔlkən/ *n.* halcón *m.*
fall /fɔl/ *n.* **1.** caída; catarata *f.;*
(season) otoño *m.;* (in price) baja
f. —*v.* **2.** caer; bajar. **f. asleep,**
dormirse; **f. in love,** enamorarse.
fallacious /fə'leiʃəs/ *a.* falaz.
fallacy /'fæləsi/ *n.* falacia *f.*
fallible /'fæləbəl/ *a.* falible.
fallout /'fɔl,aut/ *n.* lluvia radiac-
tiva, polvillo radiactivo.
fallow /'fælou/ *a.* sin cultivar;
barbecho.
false /fɔls/ *a.* falso; postizo.
falsehood /'fɔlshud/ *n.* falsedad;
mentira *f.*
falseness /'fɔlsnɪs/ *n.* falsedad,
perfidia *f.*
false teeth /tiθ/ dentadura postiza
f.
falsetto /fɔl'sɛtou/ *n.* falsete *m.*
falsification /,fɔlsəfɪ'keiʃən/ *n.*
falsificación *f.*
falsify /'fɔlsəf ai/ *v.* falsificar.
falter /'fɔltər/ *v.* vacilar; (in
speech) tartamudear.
fame /feim/ *n.* fama *f.*
familiar /fə'mɪlyər/ *a.* familiar;
conocido. **be f. with,** estar fami-
liarizado con.
familiarity /fə,mɪli'ærɪti/ *n.* familiaridad *f.*
familiarize /fə'mɪlyə,raiz/ *v.*
familiarizar.
family /'fæməli/ *n.* familia; especie *f.*
family name apellido *m.*
family tree árbol genealógico *m.*

famine /'fæmɪn/ *n.* hambre; carestía *f.*
famished /'fæmɪʃt/ *a.* hambriento.
famous /'feiməs/ *a.* famoso, célebre.
fan /fæn/ *n.* abanico; ventilador
m. (sports) aficionado -da.
fanatic /fə'nætɪk/ *a.* & *n.* fanático
-ca.
fanatical /fə'nætɪkəl/ *a.* fanático.
fanaticism /fə'nætə,sɪzəm/ *n.*
fanatismo *m.*
fanciful /'fænsɪfəl/ *a.* caprichoso;
fantástico.
fancy /'fænsi/ *a.* **1.** fino, elegante.
f. foods, novedades *f.pl.* —*n.* **2.**
fantasía *f.;* capricho *m.* —*v.* **3.**
imaginar.
fanfare /'fænfɛər/ *n.* fanfarria *f.*
fang /fæŋ/ *n.* colmillo *m.*
fan heater estufa de aire *f.*
fantastic /fæn'tæstɪk/ *a.* fantástico.
fantasy /'fæntəsi/ *n.* fantasía *f.*
FAQ /fæk/ *n.* (Frequently Asked
Questions) preguntas más fre-
cuentes *f.pl.*
far /fɑr/ *a.* **1.** lejano, distante.
—*adv.* **2.** lejos. **how f.,** a qué distancia. **as f. as,** hasta. **so f., thus
f.,** hasta aquí.
farce /fɑrs/ *n.* farsa *f.*
fare /fɛər/ *n.* pasaje *m.*
farewell /,fɛər'wɛl/ *n.* **1.** despedida *f.* **to say f.** despedirse.
—*interj.* **2.** ¡adiós!
farfetched /'fɑr'fɛtʃt/ *a.* forzado,
inverosímil.
farm /fɑrm/ *n.* **1.** granja; hacienda
f. —*v.* **2.** cultivar, labrar la tierra.
farmer /'fɑrmər/ *n.* labrador,
agricultor *m.*
farmhouse /'fɑrm,haus/ *n.* hacienda, alquería *f.*
farming /'fɑrmɪŋ/ *n.* agricultura
f.; cultivo *m.*
fart /fɑrt/ *n. Colloq.* pedo *m.*
fascinate /'fæsə,neit/ *v.* fascinar,
embelesar.
fascination /,fæsə'neiʃən/ *n.* fascinación *f.*
fascism /'fæʃ,ɪzəm/ *n.* fascismo
m.
fashion /'fæʃən/ *n.* **1.** moda; costumbre; guisa *f.* **be in f.,** estilarse. —*v.* **2.** formar.
fashionable /'fæʃənəbəl/ *a.* de
moda, en boga.

fashion show desfile de modas, pase de modelos *m.*

fast /fæst/ *a.* **1.** rápido, veloz; (watch) adelantado; (color) firme. —*adv.* **2.** ligero, de prisa. —*n.* **3.** ayuno *m.* —*v.* **4.** ayunar.

fasten /'fæsən/ *v.* afirmar; atar; fijar.

fastener /'fæsənər/ *n.* asegurador *m.*

fastidious /fæ'stɪdiəs/ *a.* melindroso.

fat /fæt/ *a.* **1.** gordo. —*n.* **2.** grasa, manteca *f.*

fatal /'feitl/ *a.* fatal.

fatality /fei'tæliti/ *n.* fatalidad *f.*

fatally /'feitli/ *adv.* fatalmente.

fate /feit/ *n.* destino *m.*; suerte *f.*

fateful /'feitfəl/ *a.* fatal; ominoso.

father /'faðər/ *n.* padre *m.*

fatherhood /'faðər,hʊd/ *n.* paternidad *f.*

father-in-law /'fa,ðər ɪn lɔ/ *n.* suegro *m.*

fatherland /'faðər,lænd/ *n.* patria *f.*

fatherly /'faðərli/ *a.* **1.** paternal. —*adv.* **2.** paternalmente.

fathom /'fæðəm/ *n.* **1.** braza *f.* —*v.* **2.** sondar; *Fig.* penetrar en.

fatigue /fə'tig/ *n.* **1.** fatiga *f.*, cansancio *m.* —*v.* **2.** fatigar, cansar.

fatten /'fætn/ *v.* engordar, cebar.

faucet /'fɔsɪt/ *n.* grifo *m.*, llave *f.*

fault /fɔlt/ *n.* culpa *f.*; defecto *m.* **at f.,** culpable.

faultless /'fɔltlɪs/ *a.* sin tacha, perfecto.

faultlessly /'fɔltlɪsli/ *adv.* perfectamente.

faulty /'fɔlti/ *a.* defectuoso, imperfecto.

fauna /'fɔnə/ *n.* fauna *f.*

favor /'feivər/ *n.* **1.** favor *m.* —*v.* **2.** favorecer.

favorable /'feivərəbəl/ *a.* favorable.

favorite /'feivərɪt/ *a. & n.* favorito -ta.

favoritism /'feivərɪ,tɪzəm/ *n.* favoritismo *m.*

fawn /fɔn/ *n.* **1.** cervato *m.* —*v.* **2.** halagar, adular.

fax /fæks/ *n.* **1.** fax *m.* —*v.* **2.** mandar un fax.

faze /feiz/ *v.* desconcertar.

fear /fɪər/ *n.* **1.** miedo, temor *m.* —*v.* **2.** temer.

fearful /'fɪərfəl/ *a.* temeroso, medroso.

fearless /'fɪərlɪs/ *a.* intrépido; sin temor.

fearlessness /'fɪərlɪsnɪs/ *n.* intrepidez *f.*

feasible /'fizəbəl/ *a.* factible.

feast /fist/ *n.* banquete *m.*; fiesta *f.*

feat /fit/ *n.* hazaña *f.*; hecho *m.*

feather /'fɛðər/ *n.* pluma *f.*

feature /'fitʃər/ *n.* **1.** facción *f.*; rasgo *m.*; (movies) película principal *f.*, largometraje *m.* —*v.* **2.** presentar como atracción especial.

February /'fɛbru,ɛri, 'fɛbyu-/ *n.* febrero *m.*

federal /'fɛdərəl/ *a.* federal.

federation /,fɛdə'reiʃən/ *n.* confederación, federación *f.*

fee /fi/ *n.* honorarios *m.pl.*

feeble /'fibəl/ *a.* débil.

feeble-minded /'fibəl 'maindɪd/ *a.* imbécil.

feebleness /'fibəlnɪs/ *a.* debilidad *f.*

feed /fid/ *n.* **1.** pasto *m.* —*v.* **2.** alimentar; dar de comer. **fed up with,** harto de.

feedback /'fid,bæk/ *n.* feedback *m.*, retroalimentación *f.*

feel /fil/ *n.* **1.** sensación *f.* —*v.* **2.** sentir; palpar. **f. like,** tener ganas de.

feeling /'filɪŋ/ *n.* sensación; sentimiento.

feign /fein/ *v.* fingir.

felicitate /fɪ'lɪsɪ,teit/ *v.* felicitar.

felicitous /fɪ'lɪsɪtəs/ *a.* feliz.

felicity /fɪ'lɪsɪti/ *n.* felicidad *f.*, dicha *f.*

feline /'filain/ *a.* felino.

fellow /'fɛlou/ *n.* compañero; socio *m.*; *Colloq.* tipo *m.*

fellowship /'fɛlou,ʃɪp/ *n.* compañerismo; (for study) beca *f.*

felon /'fɛlən/ *n.* reo *m. & f.*, felón -ona.

felony /'fɛləni/ *n.* felonía *f.*

felt /fɛlt/ *n.* fieltro *m.*

felt-tipped pen /'fɛlt ,tɪpt/ rotulador *m.*

female /'fimeil/ *a. & n.* hembra *f.*

feminine /'fɛmənɪn/ *a.* femenino.

feminist /'fɛmənɪst/ *a. & n.* feminista *m. & f.*

fence /fɛns/ *n.* **1.** cerca *f.* —*v.* **2.** cercar.

fender /'fɛndər/ *n.* guardabarros *m.pl.*

ferment /*n* 'fɜrmɛnt; *v* fər'mɛnt/

n. **1.** fermento *m.; Fig.* agitación *f.* —*v.* **2.** fermentar.
fermentation /ˌfɜrmɛn'teiʃən/ *n.* fermentación *f.*
fern /fɜrn/ *n.* helecho *m.*
ferocious /fə'rouʃəs/ *a.* feroz, fiero.
ferociously /fə'rouʃəsli/ *adv.* ferozmente.
ferocity /fə'rɒsɪti/ *n.* ferocidad, fiereza *f.*
Ferris wheel /'fɛrɪs/ rueda de feria *f.*
ferry /'fɛri/ *n.* transbordador *m.*, barca de transporte.
fertile /'fɜrtl/ *a.* fecundo; (land) fértil.
fertility /fər'tɪlɪti/ *n.* fertilidad *f.*
fertilization /ˌfɜrtlə'zeiʃən/ *n.* fertilización *f.*
fertilize /'fɜrtlˌaiz/ *v.* fertilizar, abonar.
fertilizer /'fɜrtlˌaizər/ *n.* abono *m.*
fervency /'fɜrvənsi/ *n.* ardor *m.*
fervent /'fɜrvənt/ *a.* fervoroso.
fervently /'fɜrvəntli/ *adv.* fervorosamente.
fervid /'fɜrvɪd/ *a.* férvido.
fervor /'fɜrvər/ *n.* fervor *m.*
fester /'fɛstər/ *v.* ulcerarse.
festival /'fɛstəvəl/ *n.* fiesta *f.*
festive /'fɛstɪv/ *a.* festivo.
festivity /fɛ'stɪvɪti/ *n.* festividad *f.*
festoon /fɛ'stun/ *n.* **1.** festón *m.* —*v.* **2.** festonear.
fetch /fɛtʃ/ *v.* ir por; traer.
fete /feit/ *n.* **1.** fiesta *f.* —*v.* **2.** festejar.
fetid /'fɛtɪd/ *a.* fétido.
fetish /'fɛtɪʃ/ *n.* fetiche *m.*
fetter /'fɛtər/ *n.* **1.** grillete *m.* —*v.* **2.** engrillar.
fetus /'fitəs/ *n.* feto *m.*
feud /fyud/ *n.* riña *f.*
feudal /'fyudl/ *a.* feudal.
feudalism /'fyudlˌɪzəm/ *n.* feudalismo *m.*
fever /'fivər/ *n.* fiebre *f.*
feverish /'fivərɪʃ/ *a.* febril.
feverishly /'fivərɪʃli/ *adv.* febrilmente.
few /fyu/ *a.* pocos. **a. f.,** algunos, unos cuantos.
fiancé, fiancée /ˌfian'sei/ *n.* novio -via.
fiasco /fi'æskou/ *n.* fiasco *m.*
fiat /'fiɑt/ *n.* fiat *m.*, orden *f.*
fib /fɪb/ *n.* **1.** mentira *f.* —*v.* **2.** mentir.
fiber /'faibər/ *n.* fibra *f.*

fibrous /'faibrəs/ *a.* fibroso.
fickle /'fɪkəl/ *a.* caprichoso.
fickleness /'fɪkəlnɪs/ *n.* inconstancia *f.*
fiction /'fɪkʃən/ *n.* ficción *f.;* (literature) novelas *f.pl.*
fictitious /fɪk'tɪʃəs/ *a.* ficticio.
fidelity /fɪ'dɛlɪti/ *n.* fidelidad *f.*
fidget /'fɪdʒɪt/ *v.* inquietar.
field /fild/ *n.* campo *m.*
field trip viaje de estudios *m.*
fiend /find/ *n.* demonio *m.*
fiendish /'findɪʃ/ *a.* diabólico, malvado.
fierce /fɪərs/ *a.* fiero, feroz.
fiery /'faiəri/ *a.* ardiente.
fiesta /fi'ɛstə/ *n.* fiesta *f.*
fife /faif/ *n.* pífano *m.*
fifteen /'fɪf'tin/ *a. & pron.* quince.
fifteenth /'fɪf'tinθ/ *n. & a.* décimoquinto.
fifth /fɪfθ/ *a.* quinto.
fifty /'fɪfti/ *a. & pron.* cincuenta.
fig /fɪg/ *n.* higo *m.* **f. tree,** higuera *f.*
fight /fait/ *n.* **1.** lucha, pelea *f.* —*v.* **2.** luchar, pelear.
fighter /'faitər/ *n.* peleador -ra, luchador -ra.
figment /'fɪgmənt/ *n.* invención *f.*
figurative /'fɪgyərətɪv/ *a.* metafórico.
figuratively /'fɪgyərətɪvli/ *adv.* figuradamente.
figure /'fɪgyər/ *n.* **1.** figura; cifra *f.* —*v.* **2.** figurar; calcular.
filament /'fɪləmənt/ *n.* filamento *m.*
file /fail/ *n.* **1.** archivo *m.;* (instrument) lima *f.;* (row) fila *f.* —*v.* **2.** archivar; limar.
file cabinet archivador *m.*
filial /'fɪliəl/ *a.* filial.
filigree /'fɪləˌgri/ *n.* filigrana *f.*
fill /fɪl/ *v.* llenar.
fillet /'fɪlɪt/ *n.* filete *m.*
filling /'fɪlɪŋ/ *n.* relleno *m.;* (dental) empastadura *f.* **f. station,** gasolinera *f.*
film /fɪlm/ *n.* **1.** película *f.,* film *m.* —*v.* **2.** filmar.
filter /'fɪltər/ *n.* **1.** filtro *m.* —*v.* **2.** filtrar.
filth /fɪlθ/ *n.* suciedad, mugre *f.*
filthy /'fɪlθi/ *a.* sucio.
fin /fɪn/ *n.* aleta *f.*
final /'fainl/ *a.* **1.** final, último. —*n.* **2.** examen final. **finals** (sports) final *f.*

finalist /'fainǀlɪst/ n. finalista m. & f.

finally /'fainǀli/ adv. finalmente.

finances /'fainænsəz/ n. recursos, fondos m.pl.

financial /fɪ'næenʃəl/ a. financiero.

financier /ˌfɪnən'sɪər, ˌfainən-/ n. financiero -ra.

find /faind/ n. **1.** hallazgo m. —v. **2.** hallar; encontrar. **f. out,** averiguar, enterarse, saber.

fine /fain/ a. **1.** fino; bueno. —adv. **2.** muy bien. —n. **3.** multa f. —v. **4.** multar.

fine arts /ɑrts/ bellas artes f.pl.

finery /'fainəri/ n. gala f., adorno m.

finesse /fɪ'nɛs/ n. **1.** artificio m. —v. **2.** valerse de artificio.

finger /'fɪŋgər/ n. dedo m.

finger bowl n. enjuagatorio m.

fingernail /'fɪŋgərˌneil/ n. uña f.

fingerprint /'fɪŋgərˌprɪnt/ n. **1.** impresión digital f. —v. **2.** tomar las impresiones digitales.

finicky /'fɪnɪki/ a. melindroso.

finish /'fɪnɪʃ/ n. **1.** conclusión f. —v. **2.** acabar, terminar.

finished /'fɪnɪʃt/ a. acabado.

finite /'fainait/ a. finito.

fir /fɜr/ n. abeto m.

fire /faiᵊr/ n. **1.** fuego; incendio m. —v. **2.** disparar, tirar; Colloq. despedir.

fire alarm n. alarma de incendio f.

firearm /'faiᵊrˌɑrm/ n. arma de fuego.

firecracker /'faiᵊrˌkrækər/ n. triquitraque m., buscapiés m., petardo m.

fire engine bomba de incendios f.

fire escape escalera de incendios f.

fire exit salida de urgencia f.

fire extinguisher /ɪk'stɪŋwɪʃər/ matafuego m.

firefly /'faiᵊrˌflai/ n. luciérnaga f.

fireman /'faiᵊrmən/ n. bombero m.; (railway) fogonero m.

fireplace /'faiᵊrˌpleis/ n. hogar, fogón m.

fireproof /'faiᵊrˌpruf/ a. incombustible.

fireside /'faiᵊrˌsaid/ n. hogar, fogón m.

fireworks /'faiᵊrˌwɜrks/ n. fuegos artificiales.

firm /fɜrm/ a. **1.** firme. —n. **2.** firma, empresa f.

firmness /'fɜrmnɪs/ n. firmeza f.

first /fɜrst/ a. & adv. primero. **at f.,** al principio.

first aid primeros auxilios.

first-class /'fɜrst 'klæs/ a. de primera clase.

fiscal /'fɪskəl/ a. fiscal.

fish /fɪʃ/ n. **1.** (food) pescado m.; (alive) pez m. —v. **2.** pescar.

fisherman /'fɪʃərmən/ n. pescador m.

fishhook /'fɪʃˌhʊk/ n. anzuelo m.

fishing /'fɪʃɪŋ/ n. pesca f. **go f.,** ir de pesca.

fishmonger /'fɪʃˌmʌŋgər/ n. pescadero m.

fish store pescadería f.

fission /'fɪʃən/ n. fisión f.

fissure /'fɪʃər/ n. grieta f., quebradura f.; fisura.

fist /fɪst/ n. puño m.

fit /fɪt/ a. **1.** capaz; justo. —n. **2.** corte, talle m.; Med. convulsión f. —v. **3.** caber; quedar bien, sentar bien.

fitful /'fɪtfəl/ a. espasmódico; caprichoso.

fitness /'fɪtnɪs/ n. aptitud; conveniencia f.

fitting /'fɪtɪŋ/ a. **1.** conveniente. **be f.,** convenir. —n. **2.** ajuste m.

fitting room probador m.

five /faiv/ a. & pron. cinco.

five-day work week /'faiv 'dei/ semana inglesa f.

fix /fɪks/ n. **1.** apuro m. —v. **2.** fijar; arreglar; componer, reparar.

fixation /fɪk'seiʃən/ n. fijación f.; fijeza f.

fixed /fɪkst/ a. fijo.

fixture /'fɪkstʃər/ n. instalación; guarnición f.

flabby /'flæbi/ a. flojo.

flaccid /'flæksɪd, 'flæsɪd/ a. flojo; flácido.

flag /flæg/ n. bandera f.

flagellant /'flædʒələnt/ n. & a. flagelante m.

flagon /'flægən/ n. frasco m.

flagrant /'fleigrənt/ a. flagrante.

flagrantly /'fleigrəntli/ adv. notoriamente.

flair /flɛər/ n. aptitud especial f.

flake /fleik/ n. **1.** escama f.; copo de nieve. —v. **2.** romperse en láminas.

flamboyant /flæm'bɔiənt/ a. flamante, llamativo.

flame /fleim/ n. **1.** llama f. —v. **2.** llamear.

flaming /'fleimɪŋ/ a. llameante, flamante.

flamingo /flə'mɪŋgou/ n. flamenco m.

flammable /'flæməbəl/ a. inflamable.

flank /flæŋk/ n. **1.** ijada f.; Mil. flanco m. —v. **2.** flanquear.

flannel /'flænl/ n. franela f.

flap /flæp/ n. **1.** cartera f. —v. **2.** aletear; sacudirse.

flare /flɛər/ n. **1.** llamarada f. —v. **2.** brillar; Fig. enojarse.

flash /flæʃ/ n. **1.** resplandor m.; (lightning) rayo, relámpago m.; Fig. instante m. —v. **2.** brillar.

flashcube /'flæʃ,kyub/ n. cubo de flash m.

flashlight /'flæʃ,lait/ n. linterna (eléctrica).

flashy /'flæʃi/ a. ostentoso.

flask /flæsk/ n. frasco m.

flat /flæt/ a. **1.** llano; (tire) desinflado. —n. **2.** llanura f.; apartamento m.

flatness /'flætnɪs/ n. llanura f.

flatten /'flætn̩/ v. aplastar, allanar; abatir.

flatter /'flætər/ v. adular, lisonjear.

flatterer /'flætərər/ n. lisonjero -ra; zalamero -ra.

flattery /'flætəri/ n. adulación, lisonja f.

flaunt /flɔnt/ v. ostentar.

flavor /'fleivər/ n. **1.** sabor m. —v. **2.** sazonar.

flavoring /'fleivərɪŋ/ n. condimento m.

flaw /flɔ/ n. defecto m.

flax /flæks/ n. lino m.

flay /flei/ v. despellejar; excoriar.

flea /fli/ n. pulga f.

flea market rastro m.

fleck /flɛk/ n. **1.** mancha f. —v. **2.** varetear.

flee /fli/ v. huir.

fleece /flis/ n. **1.** vellón m. —v. **2.** esquilar.

fleet /flit/ a. **1.** veloz. —n. **2.** flota f.

fleeting /'flitɪŋ/ a. fugaz, pasajero.

flesh /flɛʃ/ n. carne f.

fleshy /'flɛʃi/ a. gordo; carnoso.

flex /flɛks/ n. **1.** doblez m. —v. **2.** doblar.

flexibility /,flɛksə'bɪlɪti/ n. flexibilidad f.

flexible /'flɛksəbəl/ a. flexible.

flier /'flaiər/ n. aviador -ra.

flight /flait/ n. vuelo m.; fuga f.

flight attendant n. azafata f.; ayudante de vuelo m.

flimsy /'flɪmzi/ a. débil.

flinch /flɪntʃ/ v. acobardarse.

fling /flɪŋ/ v. lanzar.

flint /flɪnt/ n. pedernal m.

flip /flɪp/ v. lanzar.

flippant /'flɪpənt/ a. impertinente.

flippantly /'flɪpəntli/ adv. impertinentemente.

flirt /flɜrt/ n. **1.** coqueta f. —v. **2.** coquetear, flirtear.

flirtation /flɜr'teiʃən/ n. coqueteo m.

float /flout/ v. flotar.

flock /flɒk/ n. **1.** rebaño m. —v. **2.** congregarse.

flog /flɒg/ v. azotar.

flood /flʌd/ n. **1.** inundación f. —v. **2.** inundar.

floor /flɔr/ n. **1.** suelo, piso m. —v. **2.** derribar.

floppy disk /'flɒpi/ floppy, m., disquete m.

floral /'flɔrəl/ a. floral.

florid /'flɔrɪd/ a. florido.

florist /'flɔrɪst/ n. florista m. & f.

flounce /flauns/ n. **1.** (sewing) volante m. —v. **2.** pernear.

flounder /'flaundər/ n. rodaballo m.

flour /flauᵊr/ n. harina f.

flourish /'flɜrɪʃ/ n. **1.** Mus. floreo m. —v. **2.** florecer; prosperar; blandir.

flow /flou/ n. **1.** flujo m. —v. **2.** fluir.

flow chart organigrama m.

flower /'flauər/ n. **1.** flor f. —v. **2.** florecer.

flowerpot /'flauər,pɒt/ n. maceta f.

flowery /'flauəri/ a. florido.

fluctuate /'flʌktʃu,eit/ v. fluctuar.

fluctuation /,flʌktʃu'eiʃən/ n. fluctuación f.

flue /flu/ n. humero m.

fluency /'fluənsi/ n. fluidez f.

fluent /'fluənt/ a. fluido; competente.

fluffy /'flʌfi/ a. velloso.

fluid /'fluɪd/ a. & n. fluido m.

fluidity /flu'ɪdɪti/ n. fluidez f.

fluoroscope /'flurə,skoup/ n. fluoroscopio m.

flurry /'flɜri/ n. agitación f.

flush /flʌʃ/ a. **1.** bien provisto. —n. **2.** sonrojo m. —v. **3.** limpiar

con un chorro de agua; sonrojarse.

flute /flut/ *n.* flauta *f.*

flutter /'flʌtər/ *n.* **1.** agitación *f.*
—*v.* **2.** agitarse.

flux /flʌks/ *n.* flujo *m.*

fly /flai/ *n.* **1.** mosca *f.* —*v.* **2.** volar.

flying saucer /'flaiɪŋ/ platillo volante *m.*

foam /foum/ *n.* **1.** espuma *f.* —*v.*
2. espumar.

focal /'foukəl/ *a.* focal.

focus /'foukəs/ *n.* **1.** enfoque *m.*
—*v.* **2.** enfocar.

fodder /'fɒdər/ *n.* forraje *m.*,
pienso *m.*

foe /fou/ *n.* adversario -ria, enemigo -ga.

fog /fɒg/ *n.* niebla *f.*

foggy /'fɒgi/ *a.* brumoso.

foil /fɔil/ *v.* frustrar.

foist /fɔist/ *v.* imponer.

fold /fould/ *n.* **1.** pliegue *m.* —*v.*
2. doblar, plegar.

foldable /'fouldəbəl/ *a.* plegable.

folder /'fouldər/ *n.* circular *m.*;
(for filing) carpeta *f.*

folding /'fouldɪŋ/ *a.* plegable.

foliage /'fouliɪdʒ/ *n.* follaje *m.*

folio /'fouli‚ou/ *n.* infolio; folio *m.*

folklore /'fouk‚lɔr/ *n.* folklore *m.*

folks /fouks/ *n.* gente; familia *f.*

follicle /'fɒlɪkəl/ *n.* folículo *m.*

follow /'fɒlou/ *v.* seguir.

follower /'fɒlouər/ *n.* partidario
-ria.

folly /'fɒli/ *n.* locura *f.*

foment /fou'mɛnt/ *v.* fomentar.

fond /fɒnd/ *a.* cariñoso, tierno. **be
f. of,** ser aficionado a.

fondle /'fɒndl/ *v.* acariciar.

fondly /'fɒndli/ *adv.* tiernamente.

fondness /'fɒndnɪs/ *n.* afición *f.*;
cariño *m.*

food /fud/ *n.* alimento *m.*; comida
f.

foodie /'fudi/ *n. Colloq.* gastrónomo -ma, gourmet *m. & f.*

food poisoning /'pɔizənɪŋ/ intoxicación alimenticia *f.*

foodstuffs /'fud‚stʌfs/ *n.pl.*
comestibles, víveres *m.pl.*

fool /ful/ **1.** tonto -ta; bobo -ba;
bufón -ona. —*v.* **2.** engañar.

foolhardy /'ful‚hɑrdi/ *a.* temerario.

foolish /'fulɪʃ/ *a.* bobo, tonto, majadero.

foolproof /'ful‚pruf/ *a.* seguro.

foot /fʊt/ *n.* pie *m.*

footage /'fʊtɪdʒ/ *n.* longitud en
pies.

football /'fʊt‚bɔl/ *n.* fútbol, balompié *m.*

footbridge /'fʊt‚brɪdʒ/ *n.* puente
para peatones *m.*

foothold /'fʊt‚hould/ *n.* posición
establecida.

footing /'fʊtɪŋ/ *n.* base *f.*, fundamento *m.*

footlights /'fʊt‚laits/ *n.pl.* luces
del proscenio.

footnote /'fʊt‚nout/ *n.* nota al pie
de una página.

footpath /'fʊt‚pæθ/ *n.* sendero *m.*

footprint /'fʊt‚prɪnt/ *n.* huella *f.*

footstep /'fʊt‚stɛp/ *n.* paso *m.*

footstool /'fʊt‚stul/ *n.* escañuelo
m., banqueta *f.*

fop /fɒp/ *n.* petimetre *m.*

for /fɔr; *unstressed* fər/ *prep.* **1.**
para; por. **as f.,** en cuanto a.
what f., ¿para qué? —*conj.* **2.**
porque, pues.

forage /'fɔrɪdʒ/ *n.* **1.** forraje *m.*
—*v.* **2.** forrajear.

foray /'fɔrei/ *n.* correría *f.*

forbear /fɔr‚bɛər/ *v.* cesar;
abstenerse.

forbearance /fɔr'bɛərəns/ *n.* paciencia *f.*

forbid /fər'bɪd/ *v.* prohibir.

forbidding /fər'bɪdɪŋ/ *a.* repugnante.

force /fɔrs/ *n.* **1.** fuerza *f.* —*v.* **2.**
forzar.

forced landing /fɔrst/ aterrizaje
forzoso *m.*

forceful /'fɔrsfəl/ *a.* fuerte; enérgico.

forcible /'fɔrsəbəl/ *a.* a la fuerza;
enérgico.

ford /fɔrd/ *n.* **1.** vado *m.* —*v.* **2.**
vadear.

fore /fɔr/ *a.* **1.** delantero. —*n.* **2.**
delantera *f.*

fore and aft de popa a proa.

forearm /fɔr'ɑrm/ *n.* antebrazo *m.*

forebears /'fɔr‚bɛərz/ *n.pl.* antepasados *m.pl.*

forebode /fɔr'boud/ *v.* presagiar.

foreboding /fɔr'boudɪŋ/ *n.* presentimiento *m.*

forecast /'fɔr‚kæst/ *n.* **1.** pronóstico *m.*; profecía *f.* —*v.* **2.** pronosticar.

forecastle /'fouksəl/ *n. Naut.* castillo de proa.

forefathers /'fɔr,fɑðərz/ *n.* antepasados *m.pl.*
forefinger /'fɔr,fɪŋgər/ *n.* índice
m.
forego /fɔr'gou/ *v.* renunciar.
foregone /fɔr'gɔn/ *a.* predeter-
minado.
foreground /'fɔr,graund/ *n.*
primer plano.
forehead /'fɔrɪd/ *n.* frente *f.*
foreign /'fɔrɪn/ *a.* extranjero.
foreign aid *n.* ayuda exterior *f.*
foreigner /'fɔrənər/ *n.* extranjero
-ra; forastero -ra.
foreleg /'fɔr,lɛg/ *n.* pierna delantera.
foreman /'fɔrmən/ *n.* capataz,
jefe de taller *m.*
foremost /'fɔr,moust/ *a.* **1.** primero. —*adv.* **2.** en primer lugar.
forenoon /'fɔr,nun/ *n.* mañana *f.*
forensic /fə'rɛnsɪk/ *a.* forense.
forerunner /'fɔr,rʌnər/ *n.* precursor -ra.
foresee /fɔr'si/ *v.* prever.
foreshadow /fɔr'ʃædou/ *v.* pre-
figurar, anunciar.
foresight /'fɔr,sait/ *n.* previsión *f.*
forest /'fɔrɪst/ *n.* bosque *m.*;
selva *f.*
forestall /fɔr'stɔl/ *v.* anticipar;
prevenir.
forester /'fɔrəstər/ *n.* silvicultor
-ra; guardamontes *m.pl. & f.pl.*
forestry /'fɔrəstri/ *n.* silvicultura
f.
foretell /fɔr'tɛl/ *v.* predecir.
forever /fɔr'ɛvər/ *adv.* por siempre, para siempre.
forevermore /fɔr,ɛvər'mɔr/ *adv.*
siempre.
forewarn /fɔr'wɔrn/ *v.* advertir,
avisar.
foreword /'fɔr,wɜrd/ *n.* prefacio
m.
forfeit /'fɔrfɪt/ *n.* **1.** prenda;
multa *f.* —*v.* **2.** perder.
forfeiture /'fɔrfɪtʃər/ *n.* decomiso
m., multa *f.*; pérdida.
forgather /fɔr'gæðər/ *v.* reunirse.
forge /fɔrdʒ/ *n.* **1.** fragua *f.* —*v.*
2. forjar; falsear.
forger /'fɔrdʒər/ *n.* forjador -ra;
falsificador -ra.
forgery /'fɔrdʒəri/ *n.* falsificación
f.
forget /fər'gɛt/ *v.* olvidar.
forgetful /fər'gɛtfəl/ *a.* olvidadizo.
forgive /fər'gɪv/ *v.* perdonar.

forgiveness /fər'gɪvnɪs/ *n.* perdón
m.
fork /fɔrk/ *n.* **1.** tenedor *m.*; bifurcación *f.* —*v.* **2.** bifurcarse.
forlorn /fɔr'lɔrn/ *a.* triste.
form /fɔrm/ *n.* **1.** forma *f.*; (document) formulario *m.* —*v.* **2.** formar.
formal /'fɔrməl/ *a.* formal; ceremonioso. **f. dance,** baile de etiqueta. **f. dress,** traje de etiqueta.
formality /fɔr'mælɪti/ *n.* formalidad *f.*
formally /'fɔrməli/ *adv.* formal-
mente.
format /'fɔrmæt/ *n.* formato *m.*
formation /fɔr'meiʃən/ *n.* formación *f.*
formative /'fɔrmətɪv/ *a.* forma-
tivo.
formatting /'fɔrmætɪŋ/ *n.* for-
mateo *m.*
former /'fɔrmər/ *a.* anterior; antiguo. **the f.,** aquél.
formerly /'fɔrmərli/ *adv.* antigua-
mente.
formidable /'fɔrmɪdəbəl/ *a.* formidable.
formless /'fɔrmlɪs/ *a.* sin forma.
formula /'fɔrmyələ/ *n.* fórmula *f.*
formulate /'fɔrmyə,leit/ *v.* formular.
formulation /,fɔrmy'leiʃən/ *n.* for-
mulación *f.*; expresión *f.*
forsake /fɔr'seik/ *v.* abandonar.
fort /fɔrt/ *n.* fortaleza *f.*; fuerte *m.*
forte /'fɔrtei/ *a. & adv. Mus.*
forte; fuerte.
forth /fɔrθ/ *adv.* adelante. **back
and f.,** de aquí allá. **and so f.,**
etcétera.
forthcoming /'fɔrθ'kʌmɪŋ/ *a.* futuro, próximo.
forthright /'fɔrθ,rait/ *a.* franco.
forthwith /,fɔrθ'wɪθ/ *adv.* inmediatamente.
fortification /,fɔrtəfɪ'keiʃən/ *n.*
fortificación *f.*
fortify /'fɔrtə,fai/ *v.* fortificar.
fortissimo /fɔr'tɪsə,mou/ *a. &
adv. Mus.* fortísimo.
fortitude /'fɔrtɪ,tud/ *n.* fortaleza;
fortitud *f.*
fortnight /'fɔrt,nait/ *n.* quincena
f.
fortress /'fɔrtrɪs/ *n.* fuerte *m.*, fortaleza *f.*
fortuitous /fɔr'tuɪtəs/ *a.* fortuito.
fortunate /'fɔrtʃənɪt/ *a.* afortunado.

fortune /'fɔrtʃən/ n. fortuna; suerte f.

fortune-teller /'fɔrtʃən ˌtɛlər/ n. sortílego -ga, adivino -na.

forty /'fɔrti/ a. & pron. cuarenta.

forum /'fɔrəm/ n. foro m.

forward /'fɔrwərd/ a. **1.** delantero; atrevido. —adv. **2.** adelante. —v. **3.** trasmitir, reexpedir.

foster /'fɔstər/ n. **1. f. child,** hijo adoptivo. —v. **2.** fomentar; criar.

foul /faul/ a. sucio; impuro.

found /faund/ v. fundar.

foundation /faun'deiʃən/ n. fundación f.; (of building) cimientos m.pl.

founder /'faundər/ n. **1.** fundador -ra. —v. **2.** irse a pique.

foundry /'faundri/ n. fundición f.

fountain /'fauntn̩/ n. fuente f.

fountain pen pluma estilográfica, plumafuente f.

four /fɔr/ a. & pron. cuatro.

fourteen /'fɔr'tin/ a. & pron. catorce.

fourth /fɔrθ/ a. & n. cuarto m.

fowl /faul/ n. ave f.

fox /fɒks/ n. zorro -rra.

fox-trot /'fɒks ˌtrɒt/ n. foxtrot m.

foxy /'fɒksi/ a. astuto.

foyer /'fɔiər/ n. salón de entrada.

fracas /'freikəs, 'frækəs/ n. riña f.

fraction /'frækʃən/ n. fracción f.

fracture /'fræktʃər/ n. **1.** fractura, rotura f. —v. **2.** fracturar, romper.

fragile /'frædʒəl/ a. frágil.

fragment /'frægmənt/ n. fragmento, trozo m.

fragmentary /'frægmənˌtɛri/ a. fragmentario.

fragrance /'freigrəns/ n. fragancia f.

fragrant /'freigrənt/ a. fragante.

frail /freil/ a. débil, frágil.

frailty /'freilti/ n. debilidad, fragilidad f.

frame /freim/ n. **1.** marco; armazón; cuadro; cuerpo m. —v. **2.** fabricar; formar; encuadrar.

frame-up /'freim ˌʌp/ n. Colloq. conspiración f.

framework /'freimˌwɜrk/ n. armazón m.

France /fræns/ n. Francia f.

franchise /'fræntʃaiz/ n. franquicia f.

frank /fræŋk/ a. **1.** franco. —n. **2.** carta franca. —v. **3.** franquear.

frankfurter /'fræŋkfərtər/ n. salchicha f.

frankly /'fræŋkli/ adv. francamente.

frankness /'fræŋknɪs/ n. franqueza f.

frantic /'fræntɪk/ a. frenético.

fraternal /frə'tɜrnl̩/ a. fraternal.

fraternity /frə'tɜrnɪti/ n. fraternidad f.

fraternization /ˌfrætərnə'zeiʃən/ n. fraternización f.

fraternize /'frætərˌnaiz/ v. confraternizar.

fratricide /'frætrɪˌsaid/ n. fratricida m. & f.; fratricidio m.

fraud /frɔd/ n. fraude m.

fraudulent /'frɔdʒələnt/ a. fraudulento.

fraudulently /'frɔdʒələntli/ adv. fraudulentamente.

fraught /frɔt/ a. cargado.

freak /frik/ n. rareza f.; monstruosidad.

freckle /'frɛkəl/ n. peca f.

freckled /'frɛkəld/ a. pecoso.

free /fri/ a. **1.** libre; gratis. —v. **2.** libertar, librar.

freedom /'fridəm/ n. libertad f.

freeze /friz/ v. helar, congelar.

freezer /'frizər/ n. heladora f.

freezing point /'frizɪŋ/ punto de congelación m.

freight /freit/ n. **1.** carga f.; flete m. —v. **2.** cargar; fletar.

freighter /'freitər/ n. Naut. fletador m.

French /frɛntʃ/ a. & n. francés -esa.

Frenchman /'frɛntʃmən/ n. francés m.

Frenchwoman /'frɛntʃˌwumən/ n. francesa f.

frenzied /'frɛnzid/ a. frenético.

frenzy /'frɛnzi/ n. frenesí m.

frequency /'frikwənsi/ n. frecuencia f.

frequency modulation /ˌmɒdʒə'leiʃən/ modulación de frequencia.

frequent /'frikwənt/ a. frecuente.

frequently /'frikwəntli/ adv. frecuentemente.

fresco /'frɛskou/ n. fresco.

fresh /frɛʃ/ a. fresco. **f. water,** agua dulce.

freshen /'frɛʃən/ v. refrescar.

freshness /'frɛʃnɪs/ n. frescura f.

fret /frɛt/ v. quejarse, irritarse; Mus. traste m.

fretful /'frɛtfəl/ a. irritable.

fretfully /'frɛtfəli/ adv. de mala gana.

fretfulness /'frɛtfəlnɪs/ n. mal humor.

friar /'fraiər/ n. fraile m.

fricassee /ˌfrɪkə'si/ n. fricasé m.

friction /'frɪkʃən/ n. fricción f.

Friday /'fraidei/ n. viernes m. **Good F.,** Viernes Santo m.

fried /fraid/ a. frito.

friend /frɛnd/ n. amigo -ga.

friendless /'frɛndlɪs/ a. sin amigos.

friendliness /'frɛndlɪnɪs/ n. amistad f.

friendly /'frɛndli/ a. amistoso.

friendship /'frɛndʃɪp/ n. amistad f.

fright /frait/ n. susto m.

frighten /'fraitn̩/ v. asustar, espantar.

frightful /'fraitfəl/ a. espantoso.

frigid /'frɪdʒid/ a. frígido; frío.

frill /frɪl/ n. (sewing) lechuga f.

fringe /frɪndʒ/ n. fleco; borde m.

frisky /'frɪski/ a. retozón.

fritter /'frɪtər/ n. fritura f.

frivolity /frɪ'vɒliti/ n. frivolidad f.

frivolous /'frɪvələs/ a. frívolo.

frivolousness /'frɪvələsnɪs/ n. frivolidad f.

frock /frɒk/ n. vestido de mujer. **f. coat,** levita f.

frog /frɒg/ n. rana f.

frolic /'frɒlɪk/ n. **1.** retozo m. —v. **2.** retozar.

from /frʌm, unstressed frəm/ prep. de; desde.

front /frʌnt/ n. frente; (of building) fachada f. **in f. of,** delante de.

frontal /'frʌntl̩/ a. frontal.

front door puerta principal f.

frontier /frʌn'tiər/ n. frontera f.

front seat asiento delantero m.

frost /frɔst/ n. helada, escarcha f.

frosty /'frɔsti/ a. helado.

froth /frɔθ/ n. espuma f.

frown /fraun/ n. **1.** ceño m. —v. **2.** fruncir el entrecejo.

frowzy /'frauzi/ a. desaliñado.

frozen /'frouzən/ a. helado; congelado.

fructify /'frʌktəˌfai/ v. fructificar.

frugal /'frugəl/ a. frugal.

frugality /fru'gæliti/ n. frugalidad f.

fruit /frut/ n. fruta f.; (benefits) frutos m.pl. **f. tree,** árbol frutal.

fruitful /'frutfəl/ a. productivo.

fruition /fru'ɪʃən/ n. fruición f.

fruitless /'frutlɪs/ a. inútil, en vano.

fruit salad macedonia de frutas f.

fruit store frutería f.

frustrate /'frʌstreit/ v. frustrar.

frustration /frʌ'streiʃən/ n. frustración f.

fry /frai/ v. freír.

fuel /'fyuəl/ n. combustible m.

fugitive /'fyudʒɪtɪv/ a. & n. fugitivo -va.

fugue /fyug/ n. fuga f.

fulcrum /'fulkrəm/ n. fulcro m.

fulfill /fʊl'fɪl/ v. cumplir.

fulfillment /fʊl'fɪlmənt/ n. cumplimiento m.; realización f.

full /fʊl/ a. lleno; completo; pleno.

full name nombre y apellidos.

fullness /'fʊlnɪs/ n. plenitud f.

fulminate /'fʌlməˌneit/ v. volar; fulminar.

fulmination /ˌfʌlmə'neiʃən/ n. fulminación; detonación f.

fumble /'fʌmbəl/ v. chapucear.

fume /fyum/ n. **1.** humo m. —v. **2.** humear.

fumigate /'fyumɪˌgeit/ v. fumigar.

fumigator /'fyumɪˌgeitər/ n. fumigador m.

fun /fʌn/ n. diversión f. **to make f. of,** burlarse de. **to have f.,** divertirse.

function /'fʌŋkʃən/ n. **1.** función f. —v. **2.** funcionar.

functional /'fʌŋkʃənl̩/ a. funcional.

fund /fʌnd/ n. fondo m.

fundamental /ˌfʌndə'mɛntl̩/ a. fundamental.

funeral /'fyunərəl/ n. funeral m.

funeral home, funeral parlor funeraria f.

fungus /'fʌŋgəs/ n. hongo m.

funnel /'fʌnl̩/ n. embudo m.; (of ship) chimenea f.

funny /'fʌni/ a. divertido, gracioso. **to be f.,** tener gracia.

fur /fɜr/ n. piel f.

furious /'fyuriəs/ a. furioso.

furlough /'fɜrlou/ n. permiso m.

furnace /'fɜrnɪs/ n. horno m.

furnish /'fɜrnɪʃ/ v. surtir, proveer; (a house) amueblar.

furniture /'fɜrnɪtʃər/ n. muebles m.pl.

furrow /'fɜrou/ n. **1.** surco m. —v. **2.** surcar.

further /'fɜrðər/ a. & adv. **1.** más. —v. **2.** adelantar, fomentar.

furthermore /'fɜrðər,mɔr/ adv. además.

fury /'fyʊri/ n. furor m.; furia f.

fuse /fyuz/ n. **1.** fusible m. —v. **2.** fundir.

fuss /fʌs/ n. **1.** alboroto m. —v. **2.** preocuparse por pequeñeces.

fussy /'fʌsi/ a. melindroso.

futile /'fyutʃ/ a. fútil.

future /'fyutʃər/ a. **1.** futuro. —n. **2.** porvenir m.

futurology /,fyutʃə'rɒlədʒi/ n. futurología f.

fuzzy logic /'fʌzi/ lógica matizada f.

FYI abbr. (For Your Information) para su información.

G

gag /gæg/ n. chiste m.; mordaza f.

gaiety /'geiiti/ n. alegría f.

gain /gein/ n. **1.** ganancia f. —v. **2.** ganar.

gait /geit/ n. paso m.

gale /geil/ n. ventarrón m.

gall /gɔl/ n. hiel f.; Fig. amargura f.; descaro m.

gallant /'gælənt, gə'lænt, -'lɑnt/ a. **1.** galante. —n. **2.** galán m.

gallery /'gæləri/ n. galería f.; Theat. paraíso m.

gallon /'gælən/ n. galón m.

gallop /'gæləp/ n. **1.** galope m. —v. **2.** galopar.

gallows /'gæloʊz/ n. horca f.

gamble /'gæmbəl/ n. **1.** riesgo m. —v. **2.** jugar, aventurar.

game /geim/ n. juego m.; (match) partida f.; (hunting) caza f.

gang /gæŋ/ n. cuadrilla; pandilla f.

gangster /'gæŋstər/ n. rufián m.

gap /gæp/ n. raja f.

gape /geip/ v. boquear.

garage /gə'rɑʒ/ n. garaje m.

garbage /'gɑrbɪdʒ/ n. basura f.

garden /'gɑrdn̩/ n. jardín m.; (vegetable) huerta f.

gardener /'gɑrdnər/ n. jardinero -ra.

gargle /'gɑrgəl/ n. **1.** gárgara f. —v. **2.** gargarizar.

garland /'gɑrlənd/ n. guirnalda f.

garlic /'gɑrlɪk/ n. ajo m.

garment /'gɑrmənt/ n. prenda de vestir.

garrison /'gærəsən/ n. guarnición f.

garter /'gɑrtər/ n. liga f.; ataderas f.pl.

gas /gæs/ n. gas m.

gasohol /'gæsə,hɔl, -,hɒl/ n. gasohol m.

gasoline /,gæsə'lin/ n. gasolina f.

gasp /gæsp/ n. **1.** boqueada f. —v. **2.** boquear.

gas station gasolinera f.

gate /geit/ n. puerta; entrada; verja f.

gather /'gæðər/ v. recoger; inferir; reunir.

gaudy /'gɔdi/ a. brillante; llamativo.

gauge /geidʒ/ n. **1.** manómetro, indicador m. —v. **2.** medir; estimar.

gaunt /gɔnt/ a. flaco.

gauze /gɔz/ n. gasa f.

gay /gei/ a. **1.** alegre; homosexual. —n. **2.** homosexual.

gaze /geiz/ n. **1.** mirada f. —v. **2.** mirar con fijeza.

gear /gɪər/ n. engranaje m. **in g.,** en juego.

gearshift /'gɪər,ʃɪft/ n. palanca de cambio f.

gem /dʒem/ n. joya f.

gender /'dʒendər/ n. género m.

general /'dʒenərəl/ a. & n. general m.

generality /,dʒenə'ræliti/ n. generalidad f.

generalize /'dʒenərə,laiz/ v. generalizar.

generation /,dʒenə'reiʃən/ n. generación f.

generator /'dʒenə,reitər/ n. generador m.

generosity /,dʒenə'rɒsiti/ n. generosidad f.

generous /'dʒenərəs/ a. generoso.

genetic /dʒə'netɪk/ a. genético.

genial /'dʒinyəl/ a. genial.

genius /'dʒinyəs/ n. genio m.

genocide /'dʒenə,said/ n. genocidio m.

gentle /'dʒentl̩/ a. suave; manso; benigno.

gentleman /'dʒentl̩mən/ n. señor; caballero m.

gentleness /'dʒentl̩nɪs/ n. suavidad f.

genuine /'dʒenyuɪn/ a. genuino.

genuineness /'dʒɛnyuɪnnɪs/ *n.* pureza *f.*

geographical /ˌdʒiə'græfɪkəl/ *a.* geográfico.

geography /dʒi'ɒgrəfi/ *n.* geografía *f.*

geometric /ˌdʒiə'mɛtrɪk/ *a.* geométrico.

geranium /dʒə'reiniəm/ *n.* geranio *m.*

germ /dʒɜrm/ *n.* germen; microbio *m.*

German /'dʒɜrmən/ *a. & n.* alemán -mana.

Germany /'dʒɜrməni/ *n.* Alemania *f.*

gesticulate /dʒɛ'stɪkyəˌleit/ *v.* gesticular.

gesture /'dʒɛstʃər/ *n.* **1.** gesto *m.* —*v.* **2.** gesticular, hacer gestos.

get /gɛt/ *v.* obtener; conseguir; (become) ponerse. **go and g.**, ir a buscar; **g. away,** irse; escaparse; **g. together,** reunirse; **g. on,** subirse; **g. off,** bajarse; **g. up,** levantarse; **g. there,** llegar.

ghastly /'gæstli/ *a.* pálido; espantoso.

ghost /goust/ *n.* espectro, fantasma *m.*

giant /'dʒaiənt/ *n.* gigante *m.*

gibberish /'dʒɪbərɪʃ/ *n.* galimatías, *m.*

gift /gɪft/ *n.* regalo, don; talento *m.*

gigabyte /'gɪgəˌbait, 'dʒɪg-/ *n.* giga *m.*

gild /gɪld/ *v.* dorar.

gin /dʒɪn/ *n.* ginebra *f.*

ginger /'dʒɪndʒər/ *n.* jengibre *m.*

gingerbread /'dʒɪndʒərˌbrɛd/ *n.* pan de jengibre.

gingham /'gɪŋəm/ *n.* guinga *f.*

gird /gɜrd/ *v.* ceñir.

girdle /'gɜrdl/ *n.* faja *f.*

girl /gɜrl/ *n.* muchacha, niña, chica *f.*

give /gɪv/ *v.* dar; regalar. **g. back,** devolver. **g. up,** rendirse; renunciar.

giver /'gɪvər/ *n.* dador -ra; donador -ra.

glacier /'gleiʃər/ *n.* glaciar; ventisquero *m.*

glad /glæd/ *a.* alegre, contento. **be g.,** alegrarse.

gladly /'glædli/ *adv.* con mucho gusto.

gladness /'glædnɪs/ *n.* alegría *f.*; placer *m.*

glamor /'glæmər/ *n.* encanto *m.*; elegancia *f.*

glamorous /'glæmərəs/ *a.* encantador; elegante.

glamour /'glæmər/ *n.* encanto *m.*; elegancia *f.*

glance /glæns/ *n.* **1.** vistazo *m.*, ojeada *f.* —*v.* **2.** ojear.

gland /glænd/ *n.* glándula *f.*

glare /glɛər/ *n.* **1.** reflejo; brillo *m.* —*v.* **2.** deslumbrar; echar miradas indignadas.

glass /glæs/ *n.* vidrio; vaso *m.*; **(eyeglasses),** lentes, anteojos *m.pl.*

gleam /glim/ *n.* **1.** fulgor *m.* —*v.* **2.** fulgurar.

glee /gli/ *n.* alegría *f.*; júbilo *m.*

glide /glaid/ *v.* deslizarse.

glimpse /glɪmps/ *n.* **1.** vislumbre, vistazo *m.* —*v.* **2.** vislumbrar, ojear.

glisten /'glɪsən/ *n.* **1.** brillo *m.* —*v.* **2.** brillar.

glitter /'glɪtər/ *n.* **1.** resplandor *m.* —*v.* **2.** brillar.

globe /gloub/ *n.* globo; orbe *m.*

gloom /glum/ *n.* oscuridad; tristeza *f.*

gloomy /'glumi/ *a.* oscuro; sombrío, triste.

glorify /'glɔrəˌfai/ *v.* glorificar.

glorious /'glɔriəs/ *a.* glorioso.

glory /'glɔri/ *n.* gloria, fama *f.*

glossary /'glɒsəri/ *n.* glosario *m.*

glove /glʌv/ *n.* guante *m.*

glove compartment guantera *f.*

glow /glou/ *n.* **1.** fulgor *m.* —*v.* **2.** relucir; arder.

glucose /'glukous/ *f.* glucosa.

glue /glu/ *n.* **1.** cola *f.*, pegamento *m.* —*v.* **2.** encolar, pegar.

glum /glʌm/ *a.* de mal humor.

glutton /'glʌtn/ *n.* glotón -ona.

gnaw /nɔ/ *v.* roer.

GNP (*abbr.* **gross national product**), **PNB** (producto nacional bruto).

go /gou/ *v.* ir, irse. **g. away,** irse, marcharse. **g. back,** volver, regresar. **g. down,** bajar. **g. in,** entrar. **g. on,** seguir. **g. out,** salir. **g. up,** subir.

goal /goul/ *n.* meta *f.*; objeto *m.*

goalkeeper /'goulˌkipər/ *n.* guardameta *mf.*

goat /gout/ *n.* cabra *f.*

goblet /'gɒblɪt/ *n.* copa *f.*

God /gɒd/ *n.* Dios *m.*

gold /gould/ *n.* oro *m.*

golden /'gouldən/ *a.* áureo.
gold-plated /'gould ,pleitɪd/ *a.* chapado en oro.
golf /gɒlf/ *n.* golf *m.*
golf course campo de golf *m.*
golfer /'gɒlfər/ *n.* golfista *m.* & *f.*
good /gʊd/ *a.* **1.** bueno. —*n.* **2.** bienes *m.pl.*; Com. géneros *m.pl.*
good-bye /,gʊd'bai/ *n.* **1.** adiós *m.* —*interj.* **2.** ¡adiós!, ¡hasta la vista!, ¡hasta luego! **say g. to,** despedirse de.
goodness /'gʊdnɪs/ *n.* bondad *f.*
goodwill /'gʊd'wɪl/ *n.* buena voluntad. *f.*
goose /gus/ *n.* ganso *m.*
gooseberry /'gus,bɛri/ *n.* uva crespa *f.*
gooseneck /'gus,nɛk/ *n.* **1.** cuello de cisne *m.* —*a.* **2.** curvo.
goose step /'gus,stɛp/ paso de ganso *m.*
gore /gɔr/ *n.* **1.** sangre *f.* —*v.* **2.** acornear.
gorge /gɔrdʒ/ *n.* **1.** gorja *f.* —*v.* **2.** engullir.
gorgeous /'gɔrdʒəs/ *a.* magnífico; precioso.
gorilla /gə'rɪlə/ *n.* gorila *m.*
gory /'gɔri/ *a.* sangriento.
gosling /'gɒzlɪŋ/ *n.* gansarón *m.*
gospel /'gɒspəl/ *n.* evangelio *m.*
gossamer /'gɒsəmər/ *n.* **1.** telaraña *f.* —*a.* **2.** delgado.
gossip /'gɒsəp/ *n.* **1.** chisme *m.* —*v.* **2.** chismear.
Gothic /'gɒθɪk/ *a.* gótico.
gouge /gaudʒ/ *n.* **1.** gubia *f.* —*v.* **2.** escoplear.
gourd /gɔrd/ *n.* calabaza *f.*
gourmand /gʊr'mand/ *n.* glotón *m.*
gourmet /gʊr'mei/ *a.* gastrónomo -ma.
govern /'gʌvərn/ *v.* gobernar.
governess /'gʌvərnɪs/ *n.* aya, institutriz *f.*
government /'gʌvərnmənt, -ərmənt/ *n.* gobierno *m.*
governmental /,gʌvərn'mɛntl, ,gʌvər-/ *a.* gubernamental.
governor /'gʌvərnər/ *n.* gobernador -ra.
governorship /'gʌvərnər,ʃɪp/ *n.* gobernatura *f.*
gown /gaun/ *n.* vestido *m.* **dressing g.,** bata *f.*
grab /græb/ *v.* agarrar, arrebatar.
grace /greis/ *n.* gracia; gentileza; merced *f.*

graceful /'greisfəl/ *a.* agraciado.
graceless /'greislɪs/ *a.* réprobo; torpe.
gracious /'greiʃəs/ *a.* gentil, cortés.
grackle /'grækəl/ *n.* grajo *m.*
grade /greid/ *n.* **1.** grado; nivel *m.*; pendiente; nota; calidad *f.* —*v.* **2.** graduar.
grade crossing *n.* paso a nivel *m.*
gradual /'grædʒuəl/ *a.* gradual, paulatino.
gradually /'grædʒuəli/ *adv.* gradualmente.
graduate /*n* 'grædʒuɪt; *v* -,eit/ *n.* **1.** graduado -da, diplomado -da. —*v.* **2.** graduar; diplomarse.
graft /græft/ *n.* **1.** injerto *m.*; soborno público. —*v.* **2.** injertar.
graham /'greiəm/ *a.* centeno; acemita.
grail /greil/ *n.* grial *m.*
grain /grein/ *n.* grano; cereal *m.*
grain alcohol *n.* alcohol de madera *m.*
gram /græm/ *n.* gramo *m.*
grammar /'græmər/ *n.* gramática *f.*
grammarian /grə'mɛəriən/ *n.* gramático -ca.
grammar school *n.* escuela elemental *f.*
grammatical /grə'mætɪkəl/ *a.* gramatical.
gramophone /'græmə,foun/ *n.* gramófono *m.*
granary /'greinəri/ *n.* granero *m.*
grand /grænd/ *a.* grande, ilustre; estupendo.
grandchild /'græn,tʃaild/ *n.* nieto -ta.
granddaughter /'græn,dɔtər/ *n.* nieta *f.*
grandee /græn'di/ *n.* noble *m.*
grandeur /'grændʒər/ *n.* grandeza *f.*
grandfather /'græn,fɑðər/ *n.* abuelo *m.*
grandiloquent /græn'dɪləkwənt/ *a.* grandílocuo.
grandiose /'grændi,ous/ *a.* grandioso.
grand jury jurado de acusación, jurado de juicio *m.*
grandly /'grændli/ *adv.* grandiosamente.
grandmother /'græn,mʌðər/ *n.* abuela *f.*
grand opera ópera grande *f.*

grandparents /'grænd.pɛərənts/ n. abuelos m.pl.

grandson /'græn.sʌn/ n. nieto m.

grandstand /'græn.stænd/ n. andanada f., tribuna f.

grange /greindʒ/ n. granja f.

granger /'greindʒər/ n. labriego m.

granite /'grænɪt/ n. granito m.

granny /'græni/ n. abuelita f.

grant /grænt/ n. **1.** concesión; subvención f. —v. **2.** otorgar; conceder; conferir. **take for granted,** tomar por cierto.

granular /'grænyələr/ a. granular.

granulate /'grænyə.leit/ v. granular.

granulation /.grænyə'leiʃən/ n. granulación f.

granule /'grænyul/ n. gránulo m.

grape /greip/ n. uva f.

grapefruit /'greip.frut/ n. toronja f.

grape harvest vendimia f.

grapeshot /'greip.ʃɒt/ n. metralla f.

grapevine /'greip.vain/ n. vid; parra f.

graph /græf/ n. gráfica f.

graphic /'græfɪk/ a. gráfico.

graphite /'græfait/ n. grafito m.

graphology /græ'fɒlədʒi/ n. grafología f.

grapple /'græpəl/ v. agarrar.

grasp /græsp/ n. **1.** puño; poder; conocimiento m. —v. **2.** empuñar, agarrar; comprender.

grasping /'græspɪŋ/ a. codicioso.

grass /græs/ n. hierba f.; (marijuana) marijuana f.

grasshopper /'græs.hɒpər/ n. saltamontes m.

grassy /'græsi/ a. herboso.

grate /greit/ n. reja f.

grateful /'greitfəl/ a. agradecido.

gratify /'grætə.fai/ v. satisfacer.

grating /'greitɪŋ/ n. **1.** enrejado m. —a. **2.** discordante.

gratis /'grætɪs/ adv. & a. gratis.

gratitude /'grætɪ.tud/ n. agradecimiento m.

gratuitous /grə'tuɪtəs/ adj. gratuito.

gratuity /grə'tuɪti/ n. propina f.

grave /greiv/ a. **1.** grave. —n. **2.** sepultura; tumba f.

gravel /'grævəl/ n. cascajo m.

gravely /'greivli/ adv. gravemente.

gravestone /'greiv.stoun/ n. lápida sepulcral f.

graveyard /'greiv.yɑrd/ n. cementerio m.

gravitate /'grævɪ.teit/ v. gravitar.

gravitation /.grævɪ'teiʃən/ n. gravitación f.

gravity /'grævɪti/ n. gravedad; seriedad f.

gravure /grə'vyʊr/ n. fotograbado m.

gravy /'greivi/ n. salsa f.

gray /grei/ a. gris; (hair) cano.

grayish /'greiɪʃ/ a. pardusco.

gray matter substancia gris f.

graze /greiz/ v. rozar; (cattle) pastar.

grazing /'greizɪŋ/ a. pastando.

grease /gris/ n. **1.** grasa f. —v. **2.** engrasar.

greasy /'grisi/ a. grasiento.

great /greit/ a. grande, ilustre; estupendo.

Great Dane /dein/ mastín danés m.

great-grandfather /.greit 'græn.fɑðər/ n. bisabuelo.

great-grandmother /.greit 'græn.mʌðər/ n. bisabuela.

greatness /'greitnɪs/ n. grandeza f.

Greece /gris/ n. Grecia f.

greed /grid/ **greediness** n. codicia, voracidad f.

greedy /'gridi/ a. voraz.

Greek /grik/ a. & n. griego -ga.

green /grin/ a. & n. verde m.

greens, n. verduras f.pl.

greenery /'grinəri/ n. verdor m.

greenhouse /'grin.haus/ n. invernáculo m.

greenhouse effect n. efecto invernáculo m.

greet /grit/ v. saludar.

greeting /'gritɪŋ/ n. saludo m.

gregarious /grɪ'gɛəriəs/ a. gregario; sociable.

grenade /grɪ'neid/ n. granada; bomba f.

greyhound /'grei.haund/ n. galgo m.

grid /grɪd/ n. parrilla f.

griddle /'grɪdl/ n. tortera f.

griddlecake /'grɪdl.keik/ n. tortita de harina f.

gridiron /'grɪd.aiərn/ n. parrilla f.; campo de fútbol m.

grief /grif/ n. dolor m.; pena f.

grievance /'grivəns/ n. pesar; agravio m.

grieve /griv/ v. afligir.

grievous /'grivəs/ a. penoso.

grill /grɪl/ *n.* **1.** parrilla *f.* —*v.* **2.** asar a la parrilla.

grillroom /'grɪl,rum, -,rʊm/ *n.* parrilla *f.*

grim /grɪm/ *a.* ceñudo.

grimace /'grɪməs/ *n.* **1.** mueca *f.* —*v.* **2.** hacer muecas.

grime /graim/ *n.* mugre *f.*

grimy /'graimi/ *a.* sucio; mugroso.

grin /grɪn/ *n.* **1.** sonrisa *f.* —*v.* **2.** sonreír.

grind /graind/ *v.* moler; afilar.

grindstone /'graind,stoun/ *n.* amoladera *f.*

gringo /'grɪŋgou/ *n.* gringo; yanqui *m.*

grip /grɪp/ *n.* **1.** maleta *f.* —*v.* **2.** agarrar.

gripe /graip/ *v.* **1.** agarrar. —*n.* **2.** asimiento *m.*, opresión *f.*

grippe /grɪp/ *n.* gripe *f.*

grisly /'grɪzli/ *a.* espantoso.

grist /grɪst/ *n.* molienda *f.*

gristle /'grɪsəl/ *n.* cartílago *m.*

grit /grɪt/ *n.* arena *f.*; entereza *f.*

grizzled /'grɪzəld/ *a.* tordillo.

groan /groun/ *n.* **1.** gemido *m.* —*v.* **2.** gemir.

grocer /'grousər/ *n.* abacero *m.*

grocery /'grousəri/ *n.* tienda de comestibles, abacería; (Carib.) bodega *f.*

grog /grɒg/ *n.* brebaje *m.*

groggy /'grɒgi/ *a.* medio borracho; vacilante.

groin /grɔin/ *n.* ingle *f.*

groom /grum/ *n.* (of horses) establero; (at wedding) novio *m.*

groove /gruv/ *n.* **1.** estría *f.* —*v.* **2.** acanalar.

grope /group/ *v.* tentar; andar a tientas.

gross /grous/ *a.* **1.** grueso; grosero. —*n.* **2.** gruesa *f.*

grossly /'grousli/ *adv.* groseramente.

gross national product producto nacional bruto *m.*

grossness /'grousnɪs/ *n.* grosería *f.*

grotesque /grou'tɛsk/ *a.* grotesco.

grotto /'grɒtou/ *n.* gruta *f.*

grouch /grautʃ/ *n.* gruñón; descontento *m.*

ground /graund/ *n.* tierra *f.*; terreno; suelo; campo; fundamento *m.*

ground floor planta baja *f.*

groundhog /'graund,hɒg/ *n.* marmota *f.*

groundless /'graundlɪs/ *a.* infundado.

groundwork /'graund,wɜrk/ *n.* base *f.*, fundamento *m.*

group /grup/ *n.* **1.** grupo *m.* —*v.* **2.** agrupar.

groupie /'grupi/ *n.* persona aficionada que acompaña a un grupo de música moderna.

grouse /graus/ *v.* quejarse

grove /grouv/ *n.* arboleda *f.*

grovel /'grɒvəl/ *v.* rebajarse; envilecerse.

grow /grou/ *v.* crecer; cultivar.

growl /graul/ *n.* **1.** gruñido *m.* —*v.* **2.** gruñir.

grown /groun/ *a.* crecido; desarrollado.

grownup /'groun,ʌp/ *n.* adulto -ta.

growth /grouθ/ *n.* crecimiento *m.*; vegetación *f.*; *Med.* tumor *m.*

grub /grʌb/ *n.* gorgojo *m.*, larva *f.*

grubby /'grʌbi/ *a.* gorgojoso, mugriento.

grudge /grʌdʒ/ *n.* rencor *m.* **bear a g.,** guardar rencor.

gruel /'gruəl/ *n.* **1.** atole *m.* —*v.* **2.** agotar.

gruesome /'grusəm/ *a.* horripilante.

gruff /grʌf/ *a.* ceñudo.

grumble /'grʌmbəl/ *v.* quejarse.

grumpy /'grʌmpi/ *a.* gruñón; quejoso.

grunt /grʌnt/ *v.* gruñir.

guarantee /,gærən'ti/ *n.* **1.** garantía *f.* —*v.* **2.** garantizar.

guarantor /'gærən,tɔr/ *n.* fiador -ra.

guaranty /'gærən,ti/ *n.* garantía *f.*

guard /gɑrd/ *n.* **1.** guardia *m.* & *f.* —*v.* **2.** vigilar.

guarded /'gɑrdɪd/ *a.* cauteloso.

guardhouse /'gɑrd,haus/ *n.* prisión militar *f.*

guardian /'gɑrdiən/ *n.* guardián -ana.

guardianship /'gɑrdiən,ʃɪp/ *n.* tutela *f.*

guardsman /'gɑrdzmən/ *n.* centinela *m.*

guava /'gwavə/ *n.* guayaba *f.*

gubernatorial /,gubərnə'tɔriəl/ *a.* gubernativo.

guerrilla /gə'rɪlə/ *n.* guerrilla *f.*; guerrillero -ra.

guess /gɛs/ *n.* **1.** conjetura *f.* —*v.* **2.** adivinar; *Colloq.* creer.

guesswork /'gɛs,wɜrk/ n. conjetura f.

guest /gɛst/ n. huésped m. & f.

guest room alcoba de huéspedes f., alcoba de respeto f., cuarto para invitados m.

guffaw /gʌ'fɔ/ n. risotada f.

guidance /'gaidn̩s/ n. dirección f.

guide /gaid/ n. **1.** guía m. & f. —v. **2.** guiar.

guidebook /'gaid,bʊk/ n. guía f.

guided tour /'gaidɪd/ visita explicada, visita programada, visita con guía f.

guideline /'gaid,lain/ n. pauta f.

guidepost /'gaid,poust/ n. poste indicador m.

guild /gɪld/ n. gremio m.

guile /gail/ n. engaño m.

guillotine /'gɪlə,tin/ n. **1.** guillotina f. —v. **2.** guillotinar.

guilt /gɪlt/ n. culpa f.

guiltily /'gɪltəli/ adv. culpablemente.

guiltless /'gɪltlɪs/ a. inocente.

guilty /'gɪlti/ a. culpable.

guinea fowl /'gɪni/ gallina de Guinea f.

guinea pig /gɪni/ cobayo m., conejillo de Indias m.

guise /gaiz/ n. modo m.

guitar /gɪ'tɑr/ n. guitarra f.

guitarist /gɪ'tɑrɪst/ n. guitarrista m. & f.

gulch /gʌltʃ/ n. quebrada f.

gulf /gʌlf/ n. golfo m.

gull /gʌl/ n. gaviota f.

gullet /'gʌlɪt/ n. esófago m.; zanja f.

gullible /'gʌləbəl/ a. crédulo.

gully /'gʌli/ n. barranca f.

gulp /gʌlp/ n. **1.** trago m. —v. **2.** tragar.

gum /gʌm/ n. **1.** goma f.; Anat. encía f. **chewing g.,** chicle m. —v. **2.** engomar.

gumbo /'gʌmbou/ n. quimbombó m.

gummy /'gʌmi/ a. gomoso.

gun /gʌn/ n. fusil, revólver m.

gunboat /'gʌn,bout/ n. cañonero m.

gunman /'gʌnmən/ n. bandido m.

gunner /'gʌnər/ n. artillero m.

gun permit licencia de armas f.

gunpowder /'gʌn,paudər/ n. pólvora f.

gunshot /'gʌn,ʃɒt/ n. escopetazo m.

gunwale /'gʌnl̩/ n. borda f.

gurgle /'gɜrgəl/ n. **1.** gorgoteo m. —v. **2.** gorgotear.

guru /'gʊru, gʊ'ru/ n. gurú m.

gush /gʌʃ/ n. **1.** chorro m. —v. **2.** brotar, chorrear.

gusher /'gʌʃər/ n. pozo de petróleo m.

gust /gʌst/ n. soplo m.; ráfaga f.

gustatory /'gʌstə,tɔri/ a. gustativo.

gusto /'gʌstou/ n. gusto; placer m.

gusty /'gʌsti/ a. borrascoso.

gut /gʌt/ n. intestino m., tripa f.

gutter /'gʌtər/ n. canal; zanja f.

guttural /'gʌtərəl/ a. gutural.

guy /gai/ n. tipo m.

guzzle /'gʌzəl/ v. engullir; tragar.

gym /dʒɪm/ n. gimnasio m.

gymnasium /gɪm'nɑziəm/ n. gimnasio m.

gymnast /'dʒɪmnæst/ n. gimnasta m. & f.

gymnastic /dʒɪm'næstɪk/ a. gimnástico.

gymnastics /dʒɪm'næstɪks/ n. gimnasia f.

gynecologist /,gainɪ'kɒlədʒɪst/ n. ginecólogo, -ga m. & f.

gynecology /,gainɪ'kɒlədʒi/ n. ginecología f.

gypsum /'dʒɪpsəm/ n. yeso m.

Gypsy /'dʒɪpsi/ a. & n. gitano -na.

gyrate /'dʒaireit/ v. girar.

gyroscope /'dʒairə,skoup/ n. giroscopio m.

H

habeas corpus /'heibiəs 'kɔrpəs/ habeas corpus m.

haberdasher /'hæbər,dæʃər/ n. camisero m.

haberdashery /'hæbər,dæʃəri/ n. camisería f.

habiliment /hə'bɪləmənt/ n. vestuario m.

habit /'hæbɪt/ n. costumbre f., hábito m. **be in the h. of,** estar acostumbrado a; soler.

habitable /'hæbɪtəbəl/ a. habitable.

habitat /'hæbɪ,tæt/ n. habitación f., ambiente m.

habitation /ˌhæbɪ'teiʃən/ n. habitación f.

habitual /hə'bɪtʃuəl/ a. habitual.

habituate /hə'bɪtʃu,eit/ v. habituar.

habitué /hə'bɪtʃu,ei/ n. parroquiano m.

hack /hæk/ n. **1.** coche de alquiler. —v. **2.** tajar.

hacker /'hækər/ n. pirata m. & f.

hackneyed /'hæknid/ a. trillado.

hacksaw /'hæk,sɔ/ n. sierra para cortar metal f.

haddock /'hædək/ n. merluza f.

haft /hæft/ n. mango m.

hag /hæg, hɑg/ n. bruja f.

haggard /'hægərd/ a. trasnochado.

haggle /'hægəl/ v. regatear.

hail /heil/ n. **1.** granizo; (greeting) saludo m. —v. **2.** granizar; saludar.

Hail Mary /'mɛəri/ Ave María m.

hailstone /'heil,stoun/ n. piedra de granizo f.

hailstorm /'heil,stɔrm/ n. granizada f.

hair /hɛər/ n. pelo; cabello m.

haircut /'hɛər,kʌt/ n. corte de pelo.

hairdo /'hɛər,du/ n. peinado m.

hairdresser /'hɛər,drɛsər/ n. peluquero m.

hair dryer /'draiər/ secador de pelo, secador m.

hairpin /'hɛər,pɪn/ n. horquilla f.; gancho m.

hair's-breadth /'hɛərz,brɛdθ/ n. ancho de un pelo m.

hairspray /'hɛərsprei/ n. aerosol para cabello.

hairy /'hɛəri/ a. peludo.

halcyon /'hælsiən/ n. **1.** alcedón m. —a. **2.** tranquilo.

hale /heil/ a. sano.

half /hæf/ a. **1.** medio. —n. **2.** mitad f.

half-and-half /'hæf ən 'hæf/ a. mitad y mitad.

half-baked /'hæf 'beikt/ a. medio crudo.

half-breed /'hæf ,brid/ n. mestizo m.

half brother n. medio hermano m.

half-hearted /'hæf'hɑrtɪd/ a. sin entusiasmo.

half-mast /'hæf 'mæst/ a. & n. media asta m.

halfpenny /'heipəni/ n. medio penique m.

halfway /'hæf'wei/ adv. a medio camino.

half-wit /'hæf ,wɪt/ n. bobo m.

halibut /'hæləbət/ n. hipogloso m.

hall /hɔl/ n. corredor m.; (for assembling) sala f. **city h.**, ayuntamiento m.

hallmark /'hɔl,mɑrk/ n. marca del contraste f.

hallow /'hælou/ v. consagrar.

Halloween /ˌhælə'win/ n. víspera de Todos los Santos f.

hallucination /hə,lusə'neiʃən/ n. alucinación f.

hallway /'hɔl,wei/ n. pasadizo m.

halo /'heilou/ n. halo m.; corona f.

halt /hɔlt/ a. **1.** cojo. —n. **2.** parada f. —v. **3.** parar. —interj. **4.** ¡alto!

halter /'hɔltər/ n. cabestro m.

halve /hæv/ v. dividir en dos partes.

halyard /'hælyərd/ n. driza f.

ham /hæm/ n. jamón m.

hamburger /'hæm,bɔrgər/ n. albóndiga f.

hamlet /'hæmlɪt/ n. aldea f.

hammer /'hæmər/ n. **1.** martillo m. —v. **2.** martillar.

hammock /'hæmək/ n. hamaca f.

hamper /'hæmpər/ n. canasta f., cesto m.

hamstring /'hæm,strɪŋ/ n. **1.** tendón de la corva m. —v. **2.** desjarretar.

hand /hænd/ n. **1.** mano f. **on the other h.,** en cambio. —v. **2.** pasar. **h. over,** entregar.

handbag /'hænd,bæg/ n. cartera f.

handball /'hænd,bɔl/ n. pelota f.

handbook /'hænd,bʊk/ n. manual m.

handbrake /'hændbreik/ n. freno de mano m.

handcuff /'hænd,kʌf/ n. esposa v. esposar.

handful /'hændfʊl/ n. puñado m.

handicap /'hændi,kæp/ n. desventaja f.

handicraft /'hændi,kræft/ n. artífice m.; destreza manual f.

handiwork /'hændi,wɔrk/ n. artefacto m.

handkerchief /'hæŋkərtʃɪf/ n. pañuelo m.

handle /'hændḷ/ n. **1.** mango m. —v. **2.** manejar.

hand luggage equipaje de mano *m.*

handmade /'hænd'meid/ *a.* hecho a mano.

handmaid /'hænd,meid/ *n.* criada de mano, sirvienta *f.*

hand organ organillo *m.*

handsome /'hænsəm/ *a.* guapo; hermoso.

hand-to-hand /'hænd tə 'hænd/ *adv.* de mano a mano.

handwriting /'hænd,raitɪŋ/ *n.* escritura *f.*

handy /'hændi/ *a.* diestro; útil; a la mano.

hang /hæŋ/ *v.* colgar; ahorcar.

hangar /'hæŋər/ *n.* hangar *m.*

hangdog /'hæŋ,dɔg/ *a. & n.* camastrón *m.*

hanger /'hæŋər/ *n.* colgador, gancho *m.*

hanger-on /'hæŋər 'ɒn/ *n.* dependiente; mogollón *m.*

hang glider /'glaidər/ aparato para vuelo libre, delta, ala delta.

hanging /'hæŋɪŋ/ *n.* **1.** ahorcadura *f.* —*a.* **2.** colgante.

hangman /'hæŋmən/ *n.* verdugo *m.*

hangnail /'hæŋ,neil/ *n.* padrastro *m.*

hang out *v.* enarbolar.

hangover /'hæŋ,ouvər/ *n.* resaca *f.*

hangup /'hæŋʌp/ *n.* tara (psicológica) *f.*

hank /hæŋk/ *n.* madeja *f.*

hanker /'hæŋkər/ *v.* ansiar; apetecer.

haphazard. /hæp'hæzərd/ *a.* casual.

happen /'hæpən/ *v.* acontecer, suceder, pasar.

happening /'hæpənɪŋ/ *n.* acontecimiento *m.*

happiness /'hæpinɪs/ *n.* felicidad; dicha *f.*

happy /'hæpi/ *a.* feliz; contento; dichoso.

happy-go-lucky /'hæpi gou 'lʌki/ *a. & n.* descuidado *m.*

harakiri /harə'kɪəri/ *n.* harakiri (suicidio japonés) *m.*

harangue /hə'ræŋ/ *n.* **1.** arenga *f.* —*v.* **2.** arengar.

harass /hə'ræs/ *v.* acosar; atormentar.

harbinger /'harbɪndʒər/ *n.* presagio *m.*

harbor /'harbər/ *n.* **1.** puerto; albergue *m.* —*v.* **2.** abrigar.

hard /hard/ *a.* **1.** duro; difícil. —*adv.* **2.** mucho.

hard coal antracita *m.*

hard disk disco duro *m.*

harden /'hardn̩/ *v.* endurecer.

hard-headed /'hard 'hɛdɪd/ *a.* terco.

hard-hearted /'hard'hartɪd/ *a.* empedernido.

hardiness /'hardinɪs/ *n.* vigor *m.*

hardly /'hardli/ *adv.* apenas.

hardness /'hardnɪs/ *n.* dureza; dificultad *f.*

hardship /'hardʃɪp/ *n.* penalidad *f.*; trabajo *m.*

hardware /'hard,wɛər/ *n.* hardware *m.*; (computer) quincalla *f.*

hardwood /'hard,wʊd/ *n.* madera dura *f.*

hardy /'hardi/ *a.* fuerte, robusto.

hare /hɛər/ *n.* liebre *f.*

harebrained /'hɛər,breind/ *a.* tolondro.

harelip /'hɛər,lɪp/ *n.* **1.** labio leporino *m.* —*a.* **2.** labihendido.

harem /'hɛərəm/ *n.* harén *m.*

hark /hark/ *v.* escuchar; atender.

Harlequin /'harləkwɪn/ *n.* arlequín *m.*

harlot /'harlət/ *n.* ramera *f.*

harm /harm/ *n.* **1.** mal, daño; perjuicio *m.* —*v.* **2.** dañar.

harmful /'harmfəl/ *a.* dañoso.

harmless /'harmlɪs/ *a.* inocente.

harmonic /har'mɒnɪk/ *n.* armónico *m.*

harmonica /har'mɒnɪkə/ *n.* armónica *f.*

harmonious /har'mouniəs/ *a.* armonioso.

harmonize /'harmə,naiz/ *v.* armonizar.

harmony /'harməni/ *n.* armonía *f.*

harness /'harnɪs/ *n.* arnés *m.*

harp /harp/ *n.* arpa *f.*

harpoon /har'pun/ *n.* arpón *m.*

harridan /'harɪdn̩/ *n.* vieja regañona *f.*

harrow /'hærou/ *n.* **1.** rastro *m.*; grada *f.* —*v.* **2.** gradar.

harry /'hæri/ *v.* acosar.

harsh /harʃ/ *a.* áspero.

harshness /'harʃnɪs/ *n.* aspereza *f.*

harvest /'harvɪst/ *n.* **1.** cosecha *f.* —*v.* **2.** cosechar.

hash /hæʃ/ *n.* picadillo *m.*

hashish /'hæʃɪʃ/ *n.* haxis *m.*

hasn't /'hæzənt/ v. no tiene (neg. + tener).

hassle /'hæsəl/ n. lío m., molestia f.; controversia f.

hassock /'hæsək/ n. cojín m.

haste /heist/ n. prisa f.

hasten /'heisən/ v. apresurarse, darse prisa.

hasty /'heisti/ a. apresurado.

hat /hæt/ n. sombrero m.

hat box /'hæt,bɒks/ sombrerera f.

hatch /hætʃ/ n. **1.** Naut. cuartel m. —v. **2.** incubar; Fig. tramar.

hatchery /'hætʃəri/ n. criadero m.

hatchet /'hætʃɪt/ n. hacha pequeña.

hate /heit/ n. **1.** odio m. —v. **2.** odiar, detestar.

hateful /'heitfəl/ a. detestable.

hatred /'heitrɪd/ n. odio m.

haughtiness /'hɔtɪnɪs/ n. arrogancia f.

haughty /'hɔti/ a. altivo.

haul /hɔl/ n. **1.** (fishery) redada f. —v. **2.** tirar, halar.

haunch /hɔntʃ/ n. anca f.

haunt /hɔnt/ n. **1.** lugar frecuentado. —v. **2.** frecuentar, andar por.

have /hæv; unstressed həv, əv/ v. tener; haber.

haven /'heivən/ n. puerto; asilo m.

haven't /'hævənt/ v. no tiene (neg. + tener).

havoc /'hævək/ n. ruina f.

hawk /hɔk/ n. halcón m.

hawker /'hɔkər/ n. buhonero m.

hawser /'hɔzər/ n. cable m.

hawthorn /'hɔ,θɔrn/ n. espino m.

hay /hei/ n. heno m.

hay fever n. fiebre del heno f.

hayfield /'heifild/ n. henar m.

hayloft /'hei,lɔft/ n. henil m.

haystack /'hei,stæk/ n. hacina de heno f.

hazard /'hæzərd/ n. **1.** azar m. —v. **2.** aventurar.

hazardous /'hæzərdəs/ a. peligroso.

haze /heiz/ n. niebla f.

hazel /'heizəl/ n. avellano m.

hazelnut /'heizəl,nʌt/ avellana f.

hazy /'heizi/ a. brumoso.

he /hei/ pron. él m.

head /hɛd/ n. **1.** cabeza f.; jefe m. —v. **2.** dirigir; encabezar.

headache /'hɛd,eik/ n. dolor de cabeza m.

headband /'hɛd,bænd/ n. venda para cabeza f.

headfirst /'hɛd'fɜrst/ adv. de cabeza.

headgear /'hɛd,gɪər/ n. tocado m.

headlight /'hɛd,lait/ n. linterna delantera f., farol de tope m.

headline /'hɛd,lain/ n. encabezado m.

headlong /'hɛd,lɔŋ/ a. precipitoso.

head-on /'hɛd 'ɒn/ adv. de frente.

headphones /'hɛd,founz/ n.pl. auriculares m.pl.

headquarters /'hɛd,kwɔrtərz/ n. jefatura f.; Mil. cuartel general.

headstone /'hɛd,stoun/ n. lápida mortuoria f.

headstrong /'hɛd,strɔŋ/ a. terco.

headwaiter /'hɛd'weitər/ jefe de comedor m. & f.

headwaters /'hɛd,wɔtərz/ n. cabeceras f.pl.

headway /'hɛd,wei/ n. avance m., progreso m.

headwork /'hɛd,wɜrk/ n. trabajo mental m.

heady /'hɛdi/ a. impetuoso.

heal /hil/ v. curar, sanar.

health /hɛlθ/ n. salud f.

healthful /'hɛlθfəl/ a. saludable.

healthy /'hɛlθi/ a. sano; salubre.

heap /hip/ n. montón m.

hear /hɪər/ v. oír. **h. from,** tener noticias de. **h. about, h. of,** oír hablar de.

hearing /'hɪərɪŋ/ n. oído m.

hearing aid audífono m.

hearsay /'hɪər,sei/ n. rumor m.

hearse /hɜrs/ n. ataúd m.

heart /hɑrt/ n. corazón; ánimo m. **by h.,** de memoria. **have h. trouble** padecer del corazón.

heartache /'hɑrt,eik/ n. angustia f.

heart attack ataque cardíaco, infarto, infarto de miocardio m.

heartbreak /'hɑrt,breik/ n. angustia f.; pesar m.

heartbroken /'hɑrt,broukən/ a. acongojado.

heartburn /'hɑrt,bɜrn/ n. acedía f., ardor de estómago m.

heartfelt /'hɑrt,fɛlt/ a. sentido.

hearth /hɑrθ/ n. hogar m., chimenea f.

heartless /'hɑrtlɪs/ a. empedernido.

heartsick /'hɑrt,sɪk/ a. desconsolado.

heart-stricken /'hɑrt 'strɪkən/ a. afligido.

heart-to-heart /'hɑrt tə 'hɑrt/ adv. franco; sincero.

hearty /'hɑrti/ a. cordial; vigoroso.

heat /hit/ n. **1.** calor; ardor m.; calefacción f. —v. **2.** calentar.

heated /'hitɪd/ a. acalorado.

heater /'hitər/ n. calentador m.

heath /hiθ/ n. matorral m.

heathen /'hiðən/ a. & n. pagano -na.

heather /'hɛðər/ n. brezo m.

heating /'hitɪŋ/ n. calefacción f.

heatstroke /'hit‚strouk/ n. insolación f.

heat wave onda de calor f.

heave /hiv/ v. tirar.

heaven /'hɛvən/ n. cielo m.

heavenly /'hɛvənli/ a. divino.

heavy /'hɛvi/ a. pesado; oneroso.

Hebrew /'hibru/ a. & n. hebreo -ea.

hectic /'hɛktɪk/ a. turbulento.

hedge /hɛdʒ/ n. seto m.

hedgehog /'hɛdʒ‚hɒg/ n. erizo m.

hedonism /'hidṇ‚ɪzəm/ n. hedonismo m.

heed /hid/ n. **1.** cuidado m. —v. **2.** atender.

heedless /'hidlɪs/ a. desatento; incauto.

heel /hil/ n. talón m.; (of shoe) tacón m.

heifer /'hɛfər/ n. novilla f.

height /hait/ n. altura f.

heighten /'haitṇ/ n. elevar; exaltar.

heinous /'heinəs/ a. nefando.

heir /ɛər/ or **heiress** n. heredero -ra.

helicopter /'hɛlɪ‚kɒptər/ n. helicóptero m.

heliotrope /'hiliə‚troup/ n. heliotropo m.

helium /'hiliəm/ n. helio m.

hell /hɛl/ n. infierno m.

Hellenism /'hɛlə‚nɪzəm/ n. helenismo m.

hellish /'hɛlɪʃ/ a. infernal.

hello /hɛ'lou/ interj. ¡hola!; (on telephone) aló; bueno.

helm /hɛlm/ n. timón m.

helmet /'hɛlmɪt/ n. yelmo, casco m.

helmsman /'hɛlmzmən/ n. limonero m.

help /hɛlp/ n. **1.** ayuda f. **help!** ¡socorro! —v. **2.** ayudar. **h. one-**self, servirse. **can't help (but),** no poder menos de.

helper /'hɛlpər/ n. ayudante m.

helpful /'hɛlpfəl/ a. útil; servicial.

helpfulness /'hɛlpfəlnɪs/ n. utilidad f.

helpless /'hɛlplɪs/ a. imposibilitado.

hem /hɛm/ n. **1.** ribete m. —v. **2.** ribetear.

hemisphere /'hɛmɪ‚sfɪər/ n. hemisferio m.

hemlock /'hɛm‚lɒk/ n. abeto m.

hemoglobin /'himə‚gloubɪn/ n. hemoglobina f.

hemophilia /‚himə'fɪliə/ n. hemofilia f.

hemorrhage /'hɛmərɪdʒ/ n. hemorragia f.

hemorrhoids /'hɛmə‚rɔidz/ n. hemorroides f.pl.

hemp /hɛmp/ n. cáñamo m.

hemstitch /'hɛm‚stɪtʃ/ n. **1.** vainica f. —v. **2.** hacer una vainica.

hen /hɛn/ n. gallina f.

hence /hɛns/ adv. por lo tanto.

henceforth /‚hɛns'fɔrθ/ adv. de aquí en adelante.

henchman /'hɛntʃmən/ n. paniaguado m.

henna /'hɛnə/ n. alheña f.

hepatitis /‚hɛpə'taitɪs/ n. hepatitis f.

her /hɜr; unstressed hər, ər/ a. **1.** su. —pron. **2.** ella; la; le.

herald /'hɛrəld/ n. heraldo m.

heraldic /hɛ'rældɪk/ a. heráldico.

heraldry /'hɛrəldri/ n. heráldica f.

herb /ɜrb; esp. Brit. hɜrb/ n. yerba, hierba f.

herbaceous /hɜr'beiʃəs, ɜr-/ a. herbáceo.

herbarium /hɜr'bɛəriəm, ɜr-/ n. herbario m.

herd /hɜrd/ n. **1.** hato, rebaño m. —v. **2.** reunir en hatos.

here /hɪər/ adv. aquí; acá.

hereafter /hɪər'æftər/ adv. en lo futuro.

hereby /hɪər'bai/ adv. por éstas, por la presente.

hereditary /hə'rɛdɪ‚tɛri/ a. hereditario.

heredity /hə'rɛditi/ n. herencia f.

herein /hɪər'ɪn/ adv. aquí dentro; incluso.

heresy /'hɛrəsi/ n. herejía f.

heretic /'hɛrɪtɪk/ a. **1.** herético. —n. **2.** hereje m. & f.

heretical /həˈrɛtɪkəl/ *a.* herético.
heretofore /ˌhɪərtəˈfɔr/ *adv.* hasta ahora.
herewith /hɪərˈwɪθ/ *adv.* con esto, adjunto.
heritage /ˈhɛrɪtɪdʒ/ *n.* herencia *f.*
hermetic /hərˈmɛtɪk/ *a.* hermético.
hermit /ˈhərmɪt/ *n.* ermitaño *m.*
hernia /ˈhərniə/ *n.* hernia *f.*
hero /ˈhɪərou/ *n.* héroe *m.*
heroic /hɪˈrouɪk/ *a.* heroico.
heroically /hɪˈrouɪkəli/ *adv.* heroicamente.
heroin /ˈhɛrouɪn/ *n.* heroína *f.*
heroine /ˈhɛrouɪn/ *n.* heroína *f.*
heroism /ˈhɛrouˌɪzəm/ *n.* heroísmo *m.*
heron /ˈhɛrən/ *n.* garza *f.*
herring /ˈhɛrɪŋ/ *n.* arenque *m.*
hers /hərz/ *pron.* suyo, de ella.
herself /hərˈsɛlf/ *pron.* sí, sí misma, se. **she h.,** ella misma. **with h.,** consigo.
hertz /hərts/ *n.* hertzio *m.*
hesitancy /ˈhɛzɪtənsi/ *n.* hesitación *f.*
hesitant /ˈhɛzɪtənt/ *a.* indeciso.
hesitate /ˈhɛzɪˌteɪt/ *v.* vacilar.
hesitation /ˌhɛzɪˈteɪʃən/ *n.* duda; vacilación *f.*
heterogeneous /ˌhɛtərəˈdʒiniəs/ *a.* heterogéneo.
heterosexual /ˌhɛtərəˈsɛkʃuəl/ *a.* heterosexual.
hexagon /ˈhɛksəˌgɒn/ *n.* hexágono *m.*
hibernate /ˈhaibərˌneit/ *v.* invernar.
hibernation /ˌhaibərˈneiʃən/ *n.* invernada *f.*
hibiscus /haiˈbɪskəs/ *n.* hibisco *m.*
hiccup /ˈhɪkʌp/ *n.* **1.** hipo *m.* —*v.* **2.** tener hipo.
hickory /ˈhɪkəri/ *n.* nogal americano *m.*
hidden /ˈhɪdn̩/ *a.* oculto; escondido.
hide /haid/ *n.* **1.** cuero *m.*; piel *f.* —*v.* **2.** esconder; ocultar.
hideous /ˈhɪdiəs/ *a.* horrible.
hide-out /ˈhaid ˌaut/ *n.* escondite *m.*
hiding place /ˈhaidɪŋ/ escondrijo *m.*
hierarchy /ˈhaiəˌrɑrki/ *n.* jerarquía *f.*
high /hai/ *a.* alto, elevado; (in price) caro.

highbrow /ˈhaiˌbrau/ *n.* erudito *m.*
highfalutin /ˌhaifəˈlutn̩/ *a.* pomposo, presumido.
high fidelity de alta fidelidad.
highlighter /ˈhaiˌlaitər/ *n.* marcador *m.*
highly /ˈhaili/ *adv.* altamente; sumamente.
high school escuela secundaria *f.*
highway /ˈhaiˌwei/ *n.* carretera *f.*; camino real *m.*
hijacker /ˈhaiˌdʒækər/ *n.* secuestrador, pirata de aviones *m.*
hike /haik/ *n.* caminata *f.*
hilarious /hɪˈlɛəriəs/ *a.* alegre, bullicioso.
hilarity /hɪˈlærɪti/ *n.* hilaridad *f.*
hill /hɪl/ *n.* colina *f.*; cerro *m.*; **down h.,** cuesta abajo. **up h.,** cuesta arriba.
hilly /ˈhɪli/ *a.* accidentado.
hilt /hɪlt/ *n.* puño *m.* **up to the h.,** a fondo.
him /hɪm/ *pron.* él; lo; le.
himself /hɪmˈsɛlf/ *pron.* sí, sí mismo; se. **he h.,** él mismo. **with h.,** consigo.
hinder /ˈhɪndər/ *v.* impedir.
hindmost /ˈhaindˌmoust/ *a.* último.
hindquarter /ˈhaindˌkwɔrtər/ *n.* cuarto trasero *m.*
hindrance /ˈhɪndrəns/ *n.* obstáculo *m.*
hinge /hɪndʒ/ *n.* **1.** gozne *m.* —*v.* **2.** engoznar. **h. on,** depender de.
hint /hɪnt/ *n.* **1.** insinuación *f.*; indicio *m.* —*v.* **2.** insinuar.
hip /hɪp/ *n.* cadera *f.*
hippopotamus /ˌhɪpəˈpɒtəməs/ *n.* hipopótamo *m.*
hire /haiər/ *v.* alquilar.
his /hɪz; *unstressed* ɪz/ *a.* **1.** su. —*pron.* **2.** suyo, de él.
Hispanic /hɪˈspænɪk/ *a.* hispano.
hiss /hɪs/ *v.* silbar, sisear.
historian /hɪˈstɔriən/ *n.* historiador *m.*
historic /hɪˈstɔrɪk/ **historical** *a.* histórico.
history /ˈhɪstəri/ *n.* historia *f.*
histrionic /ˌhɪstriˈɒnɪk/ *a.* histriónico.
hit /hɪt/ *n.* **1.** golpe *m.*; *Colloq.* éxito *m.*; (Internet) hit *m.* —*v.* **2.** golpear.
hitch /hɪtʃ/ *v.* amarrar; enganchar.
hitchhike /ˈhɪtʃˌhaik/ *v.* hacer autostop.

hitchhiker /'hɪtʃ,haikər/ n. autostopista f.

hitchhiking /'hɪtʃ,haikɪŋ/ n. autostop m.

hither /'hɪðər/ adv. acá, hacia acá.

hitherto /'hɪðər,tu/ adv. hasta ahora.

hive /haiv/ n. colmena f.

hives /haivz/ n. urticaria f.

hoard /hɔrd/ n. **1.** acumulación f. —v. **2.** acaparar; atesorar.

hoarse /hɔrs/ a. ronco.

hoax /houks/ n. **1.** engaño m. —v. **2.** engañar.

hobby /'hɒbi/ n. afición f., pasatiempo m.

hobgoblin /'hɒb,gɒblɪn/ n. trasgo m.

hobnob /'hɒb,nɒb/ v. tener intimidad.

hobo /'houbou/ n. vagabundo m.

hockey /'hɒki/ n. hockey m. **ice-h.,** hockey sobre hielo.

hod /hɒd/ n. esparavel m.

hodgepodge /'hɒdʒ,pɒdʒ/ n. baturrillo m.; mezcolanza f.

hoe /hou/ n. **1.** azada f. —v. **2.** cultivar con azada.

hog /hɔg/ n. cerdo, puerco m.

hoist /hɔist/ n. **1.** grúa f., elevador m. —v. **2.** elevar, enarbolar.

hold /hould/ n. **1.** presa f.; agarro m.; Naut. bodega f. **to get h. of,** conseguir, apoderarse de. —v. **2.** tener; detener; sujetar; celebrar.

holder /'houldər/ n. tenedor m. **cigarette h.,** boquilla f.

holdup /'hould,ʌp/ n. salteamiento m.

hole /houl/ n. agujero; hoyo; hueco m.

holiday /'hɒli,dei/ n. día de fiesta.

holiness /'houlinɪs/ n. santidad f.

Holland /'hɒlənd/ n. Holanda f.

hollow /'hɒlou/ a. **1.** hueco. —n. **2.** cavidad f. —v. **3.** ahuecar; excavar.

holly /'hɒli/ n. acebo m.

hollyhock /'hɒli,hɒk/ n. malva real f.

holocaust /'hɒlə,kɔst/ n. holocausto m.

hologram /'hɒlə,græm/ n. holograma m.

holography /hə'lɒgrəfi/ n. holografía f.

holster /'houlstər/ n. pistolera f.

holy /'houli/ a. santo.

holy day disanto m.

Holy See Santa Sede f.

Holy Spirit Espíritu Santo m.

Holy Week Semana Santa f.

homage /'hɒmɪdʒ/ n. homenaje m.

home /houm/ n. casa, morada f; hogar m. **at h.,** en casa. **to go h.,** ir a casa.

home appliance electrodoméstica m.

home computer ordenador doméstico m., computadora doméstica f.

homeland /'houm,lænd/ n. patria f.

homely /'houmli/ a. feo; casero.

home rule n. autonomía f.

homesick /'houm,sɪk/ a. nostálgico.

homespun /'houm,spʌn/ a. casero; tocho.

homeward /'houmwərd/ adv. hacia casa.

homework /'houm,wɜrk/ n. deberes m.pl.

homicide /'hɒmə,said/ n. homicida m. & f.

homily /'hɒməli/ n. homilía f.

homogeneous /,houmə'dʒiniəs/ a. homogéneo.

homogenize /hə'mɒdʒə,naiz/ v. homogenezar.

homosexual /,houmə'sɛkʃuəl/ n. & a. homosexual m.

Honduras /hɒn'durəs/ n. Honduras f.

hone /houn/ n. **1.** piedra de afilar f. —v. **2.** afilar.

honest /'ɒnɪst/ a. honrado, honesto; sincero.

honestly /'ɒnɪstli/ adv. honradamente; de veras.

honesty /'ɒnəsti/ n. honradez, honestidad f.

honey /'hʌni/ n. miel f.

honeybee /'hʌni,bi/ n. abeja obrera f.

honeymoon /'hʌni,mun/ n. luna de miel.

honeysuckle /'hʌni,sʌkəl/ n. madreselva f.

honor /'ɒnər/ n. **1.** honra f.; honor m. —v. **2.** honrar.

honorable /'ɒnərəbəl/ a. honorable; ilustre.

honorary /'ɒnə,rɛri/ a. honorario.

hood /hud/ n. capota; capucha f.; Auto. cubierta del motor.

hoodlum /'hudləm/ n. pillo m., rufián m.

hoodwink /'hud,wɪŋk/ v. engañar.

hoof /hʊf/ n. pezuña f.
hook /hʊk/ n. **1.** gancho m. —v. **2.** enganchar.
hooligan /'hulɪgən/ n. gamberro -rra.
hoop /hup/ n. cerco m.
hop /hɒp/ n. **1.** salto m. —v. **2.** saltar.
hope /houp/ n. **1.** esperanza f. —v. **2.** esperar.
hopeful /'houpfəl/ a. lleno de esperanzas.
hopeless /'houplɪs/ a. desesperado; sin remedio.
horde /hɔrd/ n. horda f.
horehound /'hɔr,haund/ n. marrubio m.
horizon /hə'raizən/ n. horizonte m.
horizontal /,hɔrə'zɒntl̩/ a. horizontal.
hormone /'hɔrmoun/ n. hormón m.
horn /hɔrn/ n. cuerno m.; (music) trompa f.; Auto. bocina f.
hornet /'hɔrnɪt/ n. avispón m.
horny /'hɔrni/ a. córneo; calloso.
horoscope /'hɔrə,skoup/ n. horóscopo m.
horrendous /hə'rɛndəs/ a. horrendo.
horrible /'hɔrəbəl/ a. horrible.
horrid /'hɔrɪd/ a. horrible.
horrify /'hɔrə,fai/ v. horrorizar.
horror /'hɔrər/ n. horror m.
horror film película de terror f.
hors d'oeuvre /ɔr 'dɜrv/ n. entremés m.
horse /hɔrs/ n. caballo m. **to ride a h.,** cabalgar.
horseback /'hɔrs,bæk/ n. **on h.,** a caballo. **to ride h.,** montar a caballo.
horseback riding equitación f.
horsefly /'hɔrs,flai/ n. tábano m.
horsehair /'hɔrs,hɛər/ n. pelo de caballo m.; tela de crin f.
horseman /'hɔrsmən/ n. jinete m.
horsemanship /'hɔrsmən,ʃɪp/ n. manejo m., equitación f.
horsepower /'hɔrs,pauər/ n. caballo de fuerza m.
horse race carrera de caballos f.
horseradish /'hɔrs,rædɪʃ/ n. rábano picante m.
horseshoe /'hɔrs,ʃu/ n. herradura f.
hortatory /'hɔrtə,tɔri/ a. exhortatorio.

horticulture /'hɔrtɪ,kʌltʃər/ n. horticultura f.
hose /houz/ n. medias f.pl; (garden) manguera f.
hosiery /'houʒəri/ n. calcetería f.
hospitable /'hɒspɪtəbəl/ a. hospitalario.
hospital /'hɒspɪtl̩/ n. hospital m.
hospitality /,hɒspɪ'tælɪti/ n. hospitalidad f.
hospitalization /,hɒspɪtl̩ɪ'zeiʃən/ n. hospitalización f.
hospitalize /'hɒspɪtl̩,aiz/ v. hospitalizar.
host /houst/ n. anfitrión m., dueño de la casa; Relig. hostia f.
hostage /'hɒstɪdʒ/ n. rehén m.
hostel /'hɒstl̩/ n. hostería f.
hostelry /'hɒstl̩ri/ n. fonda f., parador m.
hostess /'houstɪs/ n. anfitriona f., dueña de la casa.
hostile /'hɒstl̩/ a. hostil.
hostility /hɒ'stɪlɪti/ n. hostilidad f.
hot /hɒt/ a. caliente; (sauce) picante. **to be h.,** tener calor; (weather) hacer calor.
hotbed /'hɒt,bɛd/ n. estercolero m. Fig. foco m.
hot dog perrito caliente m.
hotel /hou'tɛl/ n. hotel m.
hotelier /,outəl'yei, ,hout'l̩'ɪər/ n. hotelero -ra.
hot-headed /'hɒt 'hɛdɪd/ a. turbulento, alborotadizo.
hothouse /'hɒt,haus/ n. invernáculo m.
hot-water bottle /'hɒt 'wɔtər/ bolsa de agua caliente f.
hound /haund/ n. **1.** sabueso m. —v. **2.** perseguir; seguir la pista.
hour /auər/ n. hora f.
hourglass /'auˀr,glæs/ n. reloj de arena m.
hourly /'auˀrli/ a. **1.** por horas. —adv. **2.** a cada hora.
house /n haus; v hauz/ n. **1.** casa f.; Theat. público m. —v. **2.** alojar, albergar.
housefly /'haus,flai/ n. mosca ordinaria f.
household /'haus,hould/ n. familia; casa f.
housekeeper /'haus,kipər/ n. ama de llaves.
housemaid /'haus,meid/ n. criada f., sirvienta f.
housewife /'haus,waif/ n. ama de casa.

housework /'haus‚wɜrk/ *n.* tareas domésticas.

hovel /'hʌvəl/ *n.* choza *f.*

hover /'hʌvər/ *v.* revolotear.

hovercraft /'hʌvər‚kræft/ *n.* aerodeslizador *m.*

how /hau/ *adv.* cómo. **h. much,** cuánto. **h. many,** cuántos. **h. far,** a qué distancia.

however /hau'ɛvər/ *adv.* como quiera; sin embargo.

howl /haul/ *n.* **1.** aullido *m.* —*v.* **2.** aullar.

HTML *abbr.* (HyperText Markup Language) Lenguaje de Marcado de Hipertexto *m.*

hub /hʌb/ *n.* centro *m.*; eje *m.* **h. of a wheel,** cubo de la rueda *m.*

hubbub /'hʌbʌb/ *n.* alboroto *m.*, bulla *f.*

hue /hyu/ *n.* matiz; color *m.*

hug /hʌg/ *n.* **1.** abrazo *m.* —*v.* **2.** abrazar.

huge /hyudʒ/ *a.* enorme.

hulk /hʌlk/ *n.* casco de buque *m.*

hull /hʌl/ *n.* **1.** cáscara *f.*; (naval) casco *m.* —*v.* **2.** decascarar.

hum /hʌm/ *n.* **1.** zumbido *m.* —*v.* **2.** tararear; zumbar.

human /'hyumən/ *a.* & *n.* humano -na.

human being ser humano *m.*

humane /hyu'mein/ *a.* humano, humanitario.

humanism /'hyumə‚nɪzəm/ *n.* humanidad *f.*; benevolencia *f.*

humanitarian /hyu‚mænɪ'tɛəriən/ *a.* humanitario.

humanity /hyu'mænɪti/ *n.* humanidad *f.*

humanly /'hyumənli/ *a.* humanamente.

humble /'hʌmbəl/ *a.* humilde.

humbug /'hʌm‚bʌg/ *n.* farsa *f.*, embaucador *m.*

humdrum /'hʌm‚drʌm/ *a.* monótono.

humid /'hyumɪd/ *a.* húmedo.

humidity /hyu'mɪdɪti/ *n.* humedad *f.*

humiliate /hyu'mɪli‚eit/ *v.* humillar.

humiliation /hyu‚mɪli'eiʃən/ *n.* mortificación *f.*; bochorno *m.*

humility /hyu'mɪlɪti/ *n.* humildad *f.*

humor /'hyumər/ *n.* **1.** humor; capricho *m.* —*v.* **2.** complacer.

humorist /'hyumərɪst/ *n.* humorista *m.*

humorous /'hyumərəs/ *a.* divertido.

hump /hʌmp/ *n.* joroba *f.*

humpback /'hʌmp‚bæk/ *n.* jorobado *m.*

humus /'hyuməs/ *n.* humus *m.*

hunch /hʌntʃ/ *n.* giba *f.*; (idea) corazonada *f.*

hunchback /'hʌntʃ‚bæk/ *n.* jorobado *m.*

hundred /'hʌndrɪd/ *a.* & *pron.* **1.** cien, ciento. **200,** doscientos. **300,** trescientos. **400,** cuatrocientos. **500,** quinientos. **600,** seiscientos. **700,** setecientos. **800,** ochocientos. **900,** novecientos. —*n.* **2.** centenar *m.*

hundredth /'hʌndrɪdθ/ *n.* & *a.* centésimo *m.*

Hungarian /hʌŋ'gɛəriən/ *a.* & *n.* húngaro -ra.

Hungary /'hʌŋgəri/ Hungría *f.*

hunger /'hʌŋgər/ *n.* hambre *f.*

hunger strike huelga de hambre *f.*

hungry /'hʌŋgri/ *a.* hambriento. **to be h.,** tener hambre.

hunt /hʌnt/ *n.* **1.** caza *f.* —*v.* **2.** cazar. **h. up,** buscar.

hunter /'hʌntər/ *n.* cazador *m.*

hunting /'hʌntɪŋ/ *n.* caza *f.* **to go h.,** ir de caza.

hurdle /'hɜrdl/ *n.* zarzo *m.*, valla *f.*; dificultad *f.*

hurl /hɜrl/ *v.* arrojar.

hurricane /'hɜrɪ‚kein/ *n.* huracán *m.*

hurry /'hɜri/ *n.* **1.** prisa *f.* **to be in a h.,** tener prisa. —*v.* **2.** apresurar; darse prisa.

hurt /hɜrt/ *n.* **1.** daño, perjuicio *m.* —*v.* **2.** dañar; lastimar; doler; ofender.

hurtful /'hɜrtfəl/ *a.* perjudicial, dañino.

hurtle /'hɜrtl/ *v.* lanzar.

husband /'hʌzbənd/ *n.* marido, esposo *m.*

husk /hʌsk/ *n.* **1.** cáscara *f.* —*v.* **2.** descascarar.

husky /'hʌski/ *a.* fornido.

hustle /'hʌsəl/ *v.* empujar.

hustle and bustle ajetreo *m.*

hut /hʌt/ *n.* choza *f.*

hyacinth /'haiəsɪnθ/ *n.* jacinto *m.*

hybrid /'haibrɪd/ *a.* híbrido.

hydrangea /hai'dreindʒə/ *n.* hortensia *f.*

hydraulic /hai'drɔlɪk/ *a.* hidráulico.

hydroelectric /ˌhaidroʊɪ'lɛktrɪk/ *a.* hidroeléctrico.

hydrogen /'haidrədʒən/ *n.* hidrógeno *m.*

hydrophobia /ˌhaidrə'foubiə/ *n.* hidrofobia. *f.*

hydroplane /'haidrə,plein/ *n.* hidroavión *m.*

hydrotherapy /ˌhaidrə'θɛrəpi/ *n.* hidroterapia *f.*

hyena /hai'inə/ *n.* hiena *f.*

hygiene /'haidʒin/ *n.* higiene *f.*

hygienic /ˌhaidʒi'ɛnɪk/ *a.* higiénico.

hymn /hɪm/ *n.* himno *m.*

hymnal /'hɪmnḷ/ *n.* himnario *m.*

hype /haip/ *n. Colloq.* **1.** bomba publicitario *f.* —*v.* **2.** promocionar a bombo y platillo.

hypercritical /ˌhaipər'krɪtɪkəl/ *a.* hipercrítico.

hyperlink /'haipər,lɪŋk/ *n.* (Internet) hiperenlace *m.*

hypermarket /'haipər,mɑrkɪt/ *n.* hipermercado *m.*

hypertension /ˌhaipər'tɛnʃən/ *n.* hipertensión *f.*

hypertext /'haipər,tɛkst/ *n.* (Internet) hipertexto *m.*

hyphen /'haifən/ *n.* guión *m.*

hyphenate /'haifə,neit/ *v.* separar con guión.

hypnosis /hɪp'nousɪs/ *n.* hipnosis *f.*

hypnotic /hɪp'nɒtɪk/ *a.* hipnótico.

hypnotism /'hɪpnə,tɪzəm/ *n.* hipnotismo *m.*

hypnotize /'hɪpnə,taiz/ *v.* hipnotizar.

hypochondria /ˌhaipə'kɒndriə/ *n.* hipocondría *f.*

hypochondriac /ˌhaipə'kɒndri,æk/ *n. & a.* hipocondríaco *m.*

hypocrisy /hɪ'pɒkrəsi/ *n.* hipocresía *f.*

hypocrite /'hɪpəkrɪt/ *n.* hipócrita *m. & f.*

hypocritical /ˌhɪpə'krɪtɪkəl/ *a.* hipócrita.

hypodermic /ˌhaipə'dɜrmɪk/ *a.* hipodérmico.

hypotenuse /hai'pɒtṇ,us/ *n.* hipotenusa *f.*

hypothesis /hai'pɒθəsɪs/ *n.* hipótesis *f.*

hypothetical /ˌhaipə'θɛtɪkəl/ *a.* hipotético.

hysterectomy /ˌhɪstə'rɛktəmi/ *n.* histerectomía *f.*

hysteria /hɪ'stɛriə/ **hysterics** *n.* histeria *f.*

hysterical /hɪ'stɛrɪkəl/ *a.* histérico.

I

I /ai/ *pron.* yo.

iambic /ai'æmbɪk/ *a.* yámbico.

ice /ais/ *n.* hielo *m.*

iceberg /'aisbɜrg/ *n.* iceberg *m.*

icebox /'ais,bɒks/ *n.* refrigerador *m.*

ice cream helado, mantecado *m.;* **i.-c. cone,** barquillo de helado; **i.-c. parlor** heladería *f.*

ice cube cubito de hielo *m.*

ice skate patín de cuchilla *m.*

icon /'aikɒn/ *n.* icón *m.*

icy /'aisi/ *a.* helado; indiferente.

idea /ai'diə/ *n.* idea *f.*

ideal /ai'diəl/ *a.* ideal.

idealism /ai'diə,lɪzəm/ *n.* idealismo *m.*

idealist /ai'diəlɪst/ *n.* idealista *m. & f.*

idealistic /ai,diə'lɪstɪk/ *a.* idealista.

idealize /ai'diə,laiz/ *v.* idealizar.

ideally /ai'diəli/ *adv.* idealmente.

identical /ai'dɛntɪkəl/ *a.* idéntico.

identifiable /ai,dɛntɪ'faiəbəl/ *a.* identificable.

identification /ai,dɛntəfɪ'keiʃən/ *n.* identificación *f.* **i. papers,** cédula de identidad *f.*

identify /ai'dɛntə,fai/ *v.* identificar.

identity /ai'dɛntɪti/ *n.* identidad *f.*

ideology /ˌaidi'ɒlədʒi/ *n.* ideología *f.*

idiocy /'ɪdiəsi/ *n.* idiotez *f.*

idiom /'ɪdiəm/ *n.* modismo *m.;* idioma *m.*

idiot /'ɪdiət/ *n.* idiota *m. & f.*

idiotic /ˌɪdi'ɒtɪk/ *a.* idiota, tonto.

idle /'aidḷ/ *a.* desocupado; perezoso.

idleness /'aidḷnɪs/ *n.* ociosidad, pereza *f.*

idol /'aidḷ/ *n.* ídolo *m.*

idolatry /ai'dɒlətri/ *n.* idolatría *f.*

idolize /'aidḷ,aiz/ *v.* idolatrar.

idyl /'aidḷ/ *n.* idilio *m.*

idyllic /ai'dɪlɪk/ *a.* idílico.

if /ɪf/ *conj.* si. **even if,** aunque.
ignite /ɪg'naɪt/ *v.* encender.
ignition /ɪg'nɪʃən/ *n.* ignición *f.*
ignoble /ɪg'noubəl/ *a.* innoble, indigno.
ignominious /ˌɪgnə'mɪnɪəs/ *a.* ignominioso.
ignoramus /ˌɪgnə'reɪməs/ *n.* ignorante *m.*
ignorance /'ɪgnərəns/ *n.* ignorancia *f.*
ignorant /'ɪgnərənt/ *a.* ignorante. **to be i. of,** ignorar.
ignore /ɪg'nɔr/ *v.* desconocer, pasar por alto.
ill /ɪl/ *a.* enfermo, malo.
illegal /ɪ'ligəl/ *a.* ilegal.
illegible /ɪ'lɛdʒəbəl/ *a.* ilegible.
illegibly /ɪ'lɛdʒəbli/ *a.* ilegiblemente.
illegitimacy /ˌɪlɪ'dʒɪtəməsi/ *n.* ilegitimidad *f.*
illegitimate /ˌɪlɪ'dʒɪtəmɪt/ *a.* ilegítimo; desautorizado.
illicit /ɪ'lɪsɪt/ *a.* ilícito.
illiteracy /ɪ'lɪtərəsi/ *n.* analfabetismo *m.*
illiterate /ɪ'lɪtərɪt/ *a. & n.* analfabeto -ta.
illness /'ɪlnɪs/ *n.* enfermedad, maldad *f.*
illogical /ɪ'lɒdʒɪkəl/ *a.* ilógico.
illuminate /ɪ'lumə,neɪt/ *v.* iluminar.
illumination /ɪ,lumə'neɪʃən/ *n.* iluminación *f.*
illusion /ɪ'luʒən/ *n.* ilusión *f.;* ensueño *m.*
illusive /ɪ'lusɪv/ *a.* ilusivo.
illustrate /'ɪlə,streɪt/ *v.* ilustrar; ejemplificar.
illustration /ˌɪlə'streɪʃən/ *n.* ilustración *f.;* ejemplo; grabado *m.*
illustrative /ɪ'lʌstrətɪv/ *a.* ilustrativo.
illustrious /ɪ'lʌstrɪəs/ *a.* ilustre.
ill will *n.* malevolencia *f.*
image /'ɪmɪdʒ/ *n.* imagen, estatua *f.*
imagery /'ɪmɪdʒri/ *n.* imaginación *f.*
imaginable /ɪ'mædʒənəbəl/ *a.* imaginable.
imaginary /ɪ'mædʒə,nɛri/ *a.* imaginario.
imagination /ɪ,mædʒə'neɪʃən/ *n.* imaginación *f.*
imaginative /ɪ'mædʒənətɪv/ *a.* imaginativo.

imagine /ɪ'mædʒɪn/ *v.* imaginarse, figurarse.
imam /ɪ'mɑm/ *n.* imán *m.*
imbecile /'ɪmbəsɪl/ *n. & a.* imbécil *m.*
imitate /'ɪmɪ,teɪt/ *v.* imitar.
imitation /ˌɪmɪ'teɪʃən/ *n.* imitación *f.*
imitative /'ɪmɪ,teɪtɪv/ *a.* imitativo.
immaculate /ɪ'mækyəlɪt/ *a.* inmaculado.
immanent /'ɪmənənt/ *a.* inmanente.
immaterial /ˌɪmə'tɪərɪəl/ *a.* inmaterial; sin importancia.
immature /ˌɪmə'tʃʊr/ *a.* inmaturo.
immediate /ɪ'midɪɪt/ *a.* inmediato.
immediately /ɪ'midiɪtli/ *adv.* inmediatamente.
immense /ɪ'mɛns/ *a.* inmenso.
immerse /ɪ'mɜrs/ *v.* sumergir.
immigrant /'ɪmɪgrənt/ *n. & a.* inmigrante *m. & f.*
immigrate /'ɪmɪ,greɪt/ *v.* inmigrar.
imminent /'ɪmənənt/ *a.* inminente.
immobile /ɪ'moubəl/ *a.* inmóvil.
immoderate /ɪ'mɒdərɪt/ *a.* inmoderado.
immodest /ɪ'mɒdɪst/ *a.* inmodesto; atrevido.
immoral /ɪ'mɔrəl/ *a.* inmoral.
immorality /ˌɪmə'rælɪti/ *n.* inmoralidad *f.*
immorally /ɪ'mɔrəli/ *adv.* licenciosamente.
immortal /ɪ'mɔrtl̩/ *a.* inmortal.
immortality /ˌɪmɔr'tælɪti/ *n.* inmortalidad *f.*
immortalize /ɪ'mɔrtl̩,aɪz/ *v.* inmortalizar.
immune /ɪ'myun/ *a.* inmune.
immunity /ɪ'myunɪti/ *n.* inmunidad *f.*
immunize /'ɪmyə,naɪz/ *v.* inmunizar.
impact /'ɪmpækt/ *n.* impacto *m.*
impair /ɪm'pɛər/ *v.* empeorar, perjudicar.
impale /ɪm'peɪl/ *v.* empalar.
impart /ɪm'pɑrt/ *v.* impartir, comunicar.
impartial /ɪm'pɑrʃəl/ *a.* imparcial.
impatience /ɪm'peɪʃəns/ *n.* impaciencia *f.*
impatient /ɪm'peɪʃənt/ *a.* impaciente.
impede /ɪm'pid/ *v.* impedir, estorbar.

impediment /ɪm'pɛdəmənt/ n. impedimento m.

impel /ɪm'pɛl/ v. impeler.

impenetrable /ɪm'pɛnɪtrəbəl/ a. impenetrable.

impenitent /ɪm'pɛnɪtənt/ n. & a. impenitente m.

imperative /ɪm'pɛrətɪv/ a. imperativo.

imperceptible /ˌɪmpər'sɛptəbəl/ a. imperceptible.

imperfect /ɪm'pɜrfɪkt/ a. imperfecto.

imperfection /ˌɪmpər'fɛkʃən/ n. imperfecciön f.

imperial /ɪm'pɪəriəl/ a. imperial.

imperialism /ɪm'pɪəriəˌlɪzəm/ n. imperialismo m.

imperious /ɪm'pɪəriəs/ a. imperioso.

impersonal /ɪm'pɜrsənl/ a. impersonal.

impersonate /ɪm'pɜrsəˌneit/ v. personificar; imitar.

impersonation /ɪmˌpɜrsə'neiʃən/ n. personificación f.; imitación f.

impertinence /ɪm'pɜrtnəns/ n. impertinencia f.

impervious /ɪm'pɜrviəs/ a. impermeable.

impetuous /ɪm'pɛtʃuəs/ a. impetuoso.

impetus /'ɪmpɪtəs/ n. ímpetu m., impulso m.

impinge /ɪm'pɪndʒ/ v. tropezar; infringir.

implacable /ɪm'plækəbəl/ a. implacable.

implant /ɪm'plænt/ v. implantar; inculcar.

implement /'ɪmpləmənt/ n. herramienta f.

implicate /'ɪmplɪˌkeit/ v. implicar; embrollar.

implication /ˌɪmplɪ'keiʃən/ n. inferencia f.; complicidad f.

implicit /ɪm'plɪsɪt/ a. implícito.

implied /ɪm'plaid/ a. implícito.

implore /ɪm'plɔr/ v. implorar.

imply /ɪm'plai/ v. significar; dar a entender.

impolite /ˌɪmpə'lait/ a. descortés.

import /n 'ɪmpɔrt; v ɪm'pɔrt/ n. **1.** importación f. —v. **2.** importar.

importance /ɪm'pɔrtns/ n. importancia f.

important /ɪm'pɔrtnt/ a. importante.

importation /ˌɪmpɔr'teiʃən/ n. importación f.

importune /ˌɪmpɔr'tun/ v. importunar.

impose /ɪm'pouz/ v. imponer.

imposition /ˌɪmpə'zɪʃən/ n. imposición f.

impossibility /ɪmˌpɒsə'bɪlɪti/ n. imposibilidad f.

impossible /ɪm'pɒsəbəl/ a. imposible.

impotence /'ɪmpətəns/ n. impotencia f.

impotent /'ɪmpətənt/ a. impotente.

impregnable /ɪm'prɛgnəbəl/ a. impregnable.

impregnate /ɪm'prɛgneit/ v. impregnar; fecundizar.

impresario /ˌɪmprə'sɑriˌou/ n. empresario m.

impress /ɪm'prɛs/ v. impresionar.

impression /ɪm'prɛʃən/ n. impresión f.

impressive /ɪm'prɛsɪv/ a. imponente.

imprison /ɪm'prɪzən/ v. encarcelar.

imprisonment /ɪm'prɪzənmənt/ n. prisión, encarcelación f.

improbable /ɪm'prɒbəbəl/ a. improbable.

impromptu /ɪm'prɒmptu/ a. extemporáneo.

improper /ɪm'prɒpər/ a. impropio.

improve /ɪm'pruv/ v. mejorar; progresar.

improvement /ɪm'pruvmənt/ n. mejoramiento; progreso m.

improvise /'ɪmprəˌvaiz/ v. improvisar.

impudent /'ɪmpyədənt/ a. descarado.

impugn /ɪm'pyun/ v. impugnar.

impulse /'ɪmpʌls/ n. impulso m.

impulsive /ɪm'pʌlsɪv/ a. impulsivo.

impunity /ɪm'pyunɪti/ n. impunidad f.

impure /ɪm'pyʊr/ a. impuro.

impurity /ɪm'pyʊrɪti/ n. impureza f.; deshonestidad f.

impute /ɪm'pyut/ v. imputar.

in /ɪn/ prep. **1.** en; dentro de. —adv. **2.** adentro.

inadvertent /ˌɪnəd'vɜrtnt/ a. inadvertido.

inalienable /ɪn'eilyənəbəl/ a. inalienable.

inane /ɪ'nein/ a. mentecato.

inaugural /ɪn'ɔgyərəl/ a. inaugural.

inaugurate /ɪn'ɔgyə,reit/ v. inaugurar.

inauguration /ɪn,ɔgyə'reiʃən/ n. inauguración f.

Inca /'ɪŋkə/ n. inca m.

incandescent /,ɪnkən'dɛsənt/ a. incandescente.

incantation /,ɪnkæn'teiʃən/ n. encantación f., conjuro m.

incapacitate /,ɪnkə'pæsɪ,teit/ v. incapacitar.

incarcerate /ɪn'karsə,reit/ v. encarcelar.

incarnate /ɪn'karnɪt/ a. encarnado; personificado.

incarnation /,ɪnkar'neiʃən/ n. encarnación f.

incendiary /ɪn'sɛndi,ɛri/ a. incendario.

incense /ɪn'sɛns/ n. **1.** incienso m. —v. **2.** indignar.

incentive /ɪn'sɛntɪv/ n. incentivo m.

inception /ɪn'sɛpʃən/ n. comienzo m.

incessant /ɪn'sɛsənt/ a. incesante.

incest /'ɪnsɛst/ n. incesto m.

inch /ɪntʃ/ n. pulgada f.

incidence /'ɪnsɪdəns/ n. incidencia f.

incident /'ɪnsɪdənt/ n. incidente m.

incidental /,ɪnsɪ'dɛntḷ/ a. incidental.

incidentally /,ɪnsɪ'dɛntḷi/ adv. incidentalmente; entre paréntesis.

incinerate /ɪn'sɪnə,reit/ v. incinerar.

incinerator /ɪn'sɪnə,reitər/ n. incinerador m.

incipient /ɪn'sɪpiənt/ a. incipiente.

incision /ɪn'sɪʒən/ n. incisión f.; cortadura f.

incisive /ɪn'saisɪv/ a. incisivo; mordaz.

incisor /ɪn'saizər/ n. incisivo m.

incite /ɪn'sait/ v. incitar, instigar.

inclination /,ɪnklə'neiʃən/ n. inclinación f.; declive m.

incline /n 'ɪnklain; v ɪn'klain/ n. **1.** pendiente m. —v. **2.** inclinar.

inclose /ɪn'klouz/ v. incluir.

include /ɪn'klud/ v. incluir, englobar.

including /ɪn'kludɪŋ/ prep. incluso.

inclusive /ɪn'klusɪv/ a. inclusivo.

incognito /,ɪnkɒg'nitou/ n. & adv. incógnito m.

income /'ɪnkʌm/ n. renta f.; ingresos m.pl.

income tax impuesto sobre la renta m.

incomparable /ɪn'kɒmpərəbəl/ a. incomparable.

inconvenience /,ɪnkən'vinyəns/ n. **1.** incomodidad f. —v. **2.** incomodar.

inconvenient /,ɪnkən'vinyənt/ a. incómodo.

incorporate /ɪn'kɔrpə,reit/ v. incorporar; dar cuerpo.

incorrigible /ɪn'kɔrɪdʒəbəl/ a. incorregible.

increase /ɪn'kris/ v. crecer; aumentar.

incredible /ɪn'krɛdəbəl/ a. increíble.

incredulity /,ɪnkrɪ'dulɪti/ n. incredulidad f.

incredulous /ɪn'krɛdʒələs/ a. incrédulo.

increment /'ɪnkrəmənt/ n. incremento m., aumento m.

incriminate /ɪn'krɪmə,neit/ v. incriminar.

incrimination /ɪn,krɪmə'neiʃən/ n. incriminación f.

incrust /ɪn'krʌst/ v. incrustar.

incubator /'ɪnkyə,beitər/ n. incubadora f.

inculcate /ɪn'kʌlkeit/ v. inculcar.

incumbency /ɪn'kʌmbənsi/ n. incumbencia f.

incumbent /ɪn'kʌmbənt/ a. obligatorio; colocado sobre.

incur /ɪn'kɜr/ v. incurrir.

incurable /ɪn'kyurəbəl/ a. incurable.

indebted /ɪn'dɛtɪd/ a. obligado; adeudado.

indeed /ɪn'did/ adv. verdaderamente, de veras. **no i.,** de ninguna manera.

indefatigable /,ɪndɪ'fætɪgəbəl/ a. incansable.

indefinite /ɪn'dɛfənɪt/ a. indefinido.

indefinitely /ɪn'dɛfənɪtli/ adv. indefinidamente.

indelible /ɪn'dɛləbəl/ a. indeleble.

indemnify /ɪn'dɛmnə,fai/ v. indemnizar.

indemnity /ɪn'dɛmnɪti/ n. indemnificación f.

indent /ɪn'dɛnt/ n. **1.** diente f., mella f. —v. **2.** indentar, mellar.

indentation /,ɪndɛn'teiʃən/ n. indentación f.

independence /ˌɪndɪˈpɛndəns/ *n.* independencia *f.*

independent /ˌɪndɪˈpɛndənt/ *a.* independiente.

in-depth /ˈɪn ˈdɛpθ/ *adj.* en profundidad.

index /ˈɪndɛks/ *n.* índice *m.; (of book)* tabla *f.*

index card ficha *f.*

index finger dedo índice *m.*

India /ˈɪndiə/ *n.* India *f.*

Indian /ˈɪndiən/ *a. & n.* indio -dia.

indicate /ˈɪndɪˌkeit/ *v.* indicar.

indication /ˌɪndɪˈkeiʃən/ *n.* indicación *f.*

indicative /ɪnˈdɪkətɪv/ *a. & n.* indicativo *m.*

indict /ɪnˈdait/ *v.* encausar.

indictment /ɪnˈdaitmənt/ *n.* (law) sumaria; denuncia *f.*

indifference /ɪnˈdɪfərəns/ *n.* indiferencia *f.*

indifferent /ɪnˈdɪfərənt/ *a.* indiferente.

indigenous /ɪnˈdɪdʒənəs/ *a.* indígena.

indigent /ˈɪndɪdʒənt/ *a.* indigente, pobre.

indigestion /ˌɪndɪˈdʒɛstʃən/ *n.* indigestión *f.*

indignant /ɪnˈdɪgnənt/ *a.* indignado.

indignation /ˌɪndɪgˈneiʃən/ *n.* indignación *f.*

indignity /ɪnˈdɪgnɪti/ *n.* indignidad *f.*

indirect /ˌɪndəˈrɛkt/ *a.* indirecto.

indiscreet /ˌɪndɪˈskrit/ *a.* indiscreto.

indiscretion /ˌɪndɪˈskrɛʃən/ *n.* indiscreción *f.*

indiscriminate /ˌɪndɪˈskrɪmənɪt/ *a.* promiscuo.

indispensable /ˌɪndɪˈspɛnsəbəl/ *a.* indispensable.

indisposed /ˌɪndɪˈspouzd/ *a.* indispuesto.

individual /ˌɪndəˈvɪdʒuəl/ *a. & n.* individuo *m.*

individuality /ˌɪndəˌvɪdʒuˈælɪti/ *n.* individualidad *f.*

individually /ˌɪndəˈvɪdʒuəli/ *adv.* individualmente.

indivisible /ˌɪndəˈvɪzəbəl/ *a.* indivisible.

indoctrinate /ɪnˈdɒktrəˌneit/ *v.* doctrinar, enseñar.

indolent /ˈɪndlənt/ *a.* indolente.

indoor /ˈɪnˌdɔr/ *a.* **1.** interior. **in-**doors —*adv.* **2.** en casa; bajo techo.

indorse /ɪnˈdɔrs/ *v.* endosar.

induce /ɪnˈdus/ *v.* inducir, persuadir.

induct /ɪnˈdʌkt/ *v.* instalar, iniciar.

induction /ɪnˈdʌkʃən/ *n.* introducción *f.; instalación f.*

inductive /ɪnˈdʌktɪv/ *a.* inductivo; introductor.

indulge /ɪnˈdʌldʒ/ *v.* favorecer. **i. in,** entregarse a.

indulgence /ɪnˈdʌldʒəns/ *n.* indulgencia *f.*

indulgent /ɪnˈdʌldʒənt/ *a.* indulgente.

industrial /ɪnˈdʌstriəl/ *a.* industrial.

industrialist /ɪnˈdʌstriəlɪst/ *n.* industrial *m.*

industrial park polígono industrial *m.*

industrious /ɪnˈdʌstriəs/ *a.* industrioso, trabajador.

industry /ˈɪndəstri/ *n.* industria *f.*

inedible /ɪnˈɛdəbəl/ *a.* incomible.

ineligible /ɪnˈɛlɪdʒəbəl/ *a.* inelegible.

inept /ɪnˈɛpt/ *a.* inepto.

inert /ɪnˈɜrt/ *a.* inerte.

inertia /ɪnˈɜrʃə/ *n.* inercia *f.*

inevitable /ɪnˈɛvɪtəbəl/ *a.* inevitable.

inexpensive /ˌɪnɪkˈspɛnsɪv/ *a.* económico.

inexplicable /ɪnˈɛksplɪkəbəl/ *a.* inexplicable.

infallible /ɪnˈfæləbəl/ *a.* infalible.

infamous /ˈɪnfəməs/ *a.* infame.

infamy /ˈɪnfəmi/ *n.* infamia *f.*

infancy /ˈɪnfənsi/ *n.* infancia *f.*

infant /ˈɪnfənt/ *n.* nene *m.; criatura f.*

infantile /ˈɪnfənˌtail/ *a.* infantil.

infantry /ˈɪnfəntri/ *n.* infantería *f.*

infatuated /ɪnˈfætʃuˌeitɪd/ *a.* infatuado.

infatuation /ɪnˌfætʃuˈeiʃən/ *n.* encaprichamiento *m.*

infect /ɪnˈfɛkt/ *v.* infectar.

infection /ɪnˈfɛkʃən/ *n.* infección *f.*

infectious /ɪnˈfɛkʃəs/ *a.* infeccioso.

infer /ɪnˈfɜr/ *v.* inferir.

inference /ˈɪnfərəns/ *n.* inferencia *f.*

inferior /ɪnˈfɪəriər/ *a.* inferior.

infernal /ɪnˈfɜrnl/ *a.* infernal.

inferno /ɪnˈfɜrnou/ *n.* infierno *m.*

infest /ɪn'fɛst/ v. infestar.
infidel /'ɪnfɪdl/ n. **1.** infiel m. & f.; pagano -na. —a. **2.** infiel.
infidelity /ˌɪnfɪ'dɛlɪti/ n. infidelidad f.
infiltrate /ɪn'fɪltreit/ v. infiltrar.
infinite /'ɪnfənɪt/ a. infinito.
infinitesimal /ˌɪnfɪnɪ'tɛsəməl/ a. infinitesimal.
infinitive /ɪn'fɪnɪtɪv/ n. & a. infinitivo m.
infinity /ɪn'fɪnɪti/ n. infinidad f.
infirm /ɪn'fɜrm/ a. enfermizo.
infirmary /ɪn'fɜrməri/ n. hospital m., enfermería f.
infirmity /ɪn'fɜrmɪti/ n. enfermedad f.
inflame /ɪn'fleim/ v. inflamar.
inflammable /ɪn'flæməbəl/ a. inflamable.
inflammation /ˌɪnflə'meiʃən/ n. inflamación f.
inflammatory /ɪn'flæməˌtɔri/ a. inflamante; Med. inflamatorio.
inflate /ɪn'fleit/ v. inflar.
inflation /ɪn'fleiʃən/ n. inflación f.
inflection /ɪn'flɛkʃən/ n. inflexión f.; (of the voice) modulación de la voz f.
inflict /ɪn'flɪkt/ v. infligir.
infliction /ɪn'flɪkʃən/ n. imposición f.
influence /'ɪnfluəns/ n. **1.** influencia f. —v. **2.** influir en.
influential /ˌɪnflu'ɛnʃəl/ a. influyente.
influenza /ˌɪnflu'ɛnzə/ n. gripe f.
influx /'ɪnˌflʌks/ n. afluencia f.
inform /ɪn'fɔrm/ v. informar. **i. oneself,** enterarse.
informal /ɪn'fɔrməl/ a. informal.
information /ˌɪnfər'meiʃən/ n. informaciones f.pl.
information technology n. informática f.
infrastructure /'ɪnfrəˌstrʌktʃər/ n. infraestructura f.
infringe /ɪn'frɪndʒ/ v. infringir.
infuriate /ɪn'fyuriˌeit/ v. enfurecer.
ingenious /ɪn'dʒinyəs/ a. ingenioso.
ingenuity /ˌɪndʒə'nuɪti/ n. ingeniosidad; destreza f.
ingredient /ɪn'gridiənt/ n. ingrediente m.
inhabit /ɪn'hæbɪt/ v. habitar.
inhabitant /ɪn'hæbɪtənt/ n. habitante m. & f.
inhale /ɪn'heil/ v. inhalar.

inherent /ɪn'hɪərənt/ a. inherente.
inherit /ɪn'hɛrɪt/ v. heredar.
inheritance /ɪn'hɛrɪtəns/ n. herencia f.
inhibit /ɪn'hɪbɪt/ v. inhibir.
inhibition /ˌɪnɪ'bɪʃən/ n. inhibición f.
inhuman /ɪn'hyumən/ a. inhumano.
inimical /ɪ'nɪmɪkəl/ a. hostil.
inimitable /ɪ'nɪmɪtəbəl/ a. inimitable.
iniquity /ɪ'nɪkwɪti/ n. iniquidad f.
initial /ɪ'nɪʃəl/ a. & n. inicial f.
initiate /ɪ'nɪʃiˌeit/ v. iniciar.
initiation /ɪˌnɪʃi'eiʃən/ n. iniciación f.
initiative /ɪ'nɪʃiətɪv/ n. iniciativa f.
inject /ɪn'dʒɛkt/ v. inyectar.
injection /ɪn'dʒɛkʃən/ n. inyección f.
injunction /ɪn'dʒʌŋkʃən/ n. mandato m.; (law) embargo m.
injure /'ɪndʒər/ v. herir; lastimar; ofender.
injurious /ɪn'dʒuriəs/ a. perjudicial.
injury /'ɪndʒəri/ n. herida; afrenta f.; perjuicio m.
injustice /ɪn'dʒʌstɪs/ n. injusticia f.
ink /ɪŋk/ n. tinta f.
inland /'ɪnlænd/ a. **1.** interior. —adv. **2.** tierra adentro.
inlet /'ɪnlɛt/ n. entrada f.; ensenada f.; estuario m.
inmate /'ɪnˌmeit/ n. residente m. & f.; (of a prison) preso -sa.
inn /ɪn/ n. posada f.; mesón m.
inner /'ɪnər/ a. interior. **i. tube,** cámara de aire.
innocence /'ɪnəsəns/ n. inocencia f.
innocent /'ɪnəsənt/ a. inocente.
innocuous /ɪ'nɒkyuəs/ a. innocuo.
innovation /ˌɪnə'veiʃən/ n. innovación f.
innuendo /ˌɪnyu'ɛndou/ n. insinuación f.
innumerable /ɪ'numərəbəl/ a. innumerable.
inoculate /ɪ'nɒkyəˌleit/ v. inocular.
inoculation /ɪˌnɒkyə'leiʃən/ n. inoculación f.
input /'ɪnˌput/ n. aducto m., ingreso m., entrada f.
inquest /'ɪnkwɛst/ n. indagación f.

inquire /ɪn'kwaiⁿr/ v. preguntar; inquirir.

inquiry /ɪn'kwaiⁿri/ n. pregunta; investigación f.

inquisition /ˌɪnkwə'zɪʃən/ n. escudriñamiento m.; (church) Inquisición f.

insane /ɪn'sein/ a. loco. **to go i.,** perder la razón; volverse loco.

insanity /ɪn'sænɪti/ n. locura f., demencia f.

inscribe /ɪn'skraib/ v. inscribir.

inscription /ɪn'skrɪpʃən/ n. inscripción; dedicatoria f.

insect /'ɪnsɛkt/ n. insecto m.

insecticide /ɪn'sɛktə,said/ n. & a. insecticida m.

inseparable /ɪn'sɛpərəbəl/ a. inseparable.

insert /ɪn'sɜrt/ v. insertar, meter.

insertion /ɪn'sɜrʃən/ n. inserción f.

inside /ˌɪn'said/ a. & n. **1.** interior m. —adv. **2.** adentro, por dentro. **i. out,** al revés. —prep. **3.** dentro de.

insidious /ɪn'sɪdiəs/ a. insidioso.

insight /'ɪn,sait/ n. perspicacia f.; comprensión f.

insignia /ɪn'sɪgniə/ n. insignias f.pl.

insignificance /ˌɪnsɪg'nɪfɪkəns/ n. insignificancia f.

insignificant /ˌɪnsɪg'nɪfɪkənt/ a. insignificante.

insinuate /ɪn'sɪnyu,eit/ v. insinuar.

insinuation /ɪn,sɪnyu'eiʃən/ n. insinuación f.

insipid /ɪn'sɪpɪd/ a. insípido.

insist /ɪn'sɪst/ v. insistir.

insistence /ɪn'sɪstəns/ n. insistencia f.

insistent /ɪn'sɪstənt/ a. insistente.

insolence /'ɪnsələns/ n. insolencia f.

insolent /'ɪnsələnt/ a. insolente.

insomnia /ɪn'sɒmniə/ n. insomnio m.

inspect /ɪn'spɛkt/ v. inspeccionar, examinar.

inspection /ɪn'spɛkʃən/ n. inspección f.

inspector /ɪn'spɛktər/ n. inspector -ora.

inspiration /ˌɪnspə'reiʃən/ n. inspiración f.

inspire /ɪn'spaiⁿr/ v. inspirar.

install /ɪn'stɔl/ v. instalar.

installation /ˌɪnstə'leiʃən/ n. instalación f.

installment /ɪn'stɔlmənt/ n. plazo m.

instance /'ɪnstəns/ n. ocasión f. **for i.,** por ejemplo.

instant /'ɪnstənt/ a. & n. instante m.

instantaneous /ˌɪnstən'teiniəs/ a. instantáneo.

instant coffee café soluble m.

instantly /'ɪnstəntli/ adv. al instante.

instead /ɪn'stɛd/ adv. en lugar de eso. **i. of,** en vez de, en lugar de.

instigate /'ɪnstɪ,geit/ v. instigar.

instill /ɪn'stɪl/ v. instilar.

instinct /'ɪnstɪŋkt/ n. instinto m. **by i.** por instinto.

instinctive /ɪn'stɪŋktɪv/ a. instintivo.

instinctively /ɪn'stɪŋktɪvli/ adv. por instinto.

institute /'ɪnstɪ,tut/ n. **1.** instituto m. —v. **2.** instituir.

institution /ˌɪnstɪ'tuʃən/ n. institución f.

instruct /ɪn'strʌkt/ v. instruir.

instruction /ɪn'strʌkʃən/ n. instrucción f.

instructive /ɪn'strʌktɪv/ a. instructivo.

instructor /ɪn'strʌktər/ n. instructor -ora.

instrument /'ɪnstrəmənt/ n. instrumento m.

instrumental /ˌɪnstrə'mɛntl̩/ a. instrumental.

insufficient /ˌɪnsə'fɪʃənt/ a. insuficiente.

insular /'ɪnsələr/ a. insular; estrecho de miras.

insulate /'ɪnsə,leit/ v. aislar.

insulation /ˌɪnsə'leiʃən/ n. aislamiento m.

insulator /'ɪnsə,leitər/ n. aislador m.

insulin /'ɪnsəlɪn/ n. insulina f.

insult /n. 'ɪnsʌlt; v. ɪn'sʌlt/ n. **1.** insulto m. —v. **2.** insultar.

insuperable /ɪn'supərəbəl/ a. insuperable.

insurance /ɪn'ʃurəns/ n. seguro m.

insure /ɪn'ʃur, -'ʃɜr/ v. asegurar.

insurgent /ɪn'sɜrdʒənt/ a. & n. insurgente m. & f.

insurrection /ˌɪnsə'rɛkʃən/ n. insurrección f.

intact /ɪn'tækt/ a. intacto.

intangible /ɪn'tændʒəbəl/ a. intangible, impalpable.

integral /'ɪntɪgrəl/ a. íntegro.

integrate /'ɪntɪ,greit/ v. integrar.

integrity /ɪn'tɛgrɪti/ n. integridad f.

intellect /'ɪntl,ɛkt/ n. intelecto m.

intellectual /,ɪntl'ɛktʃuəl/ a. & n. intelectual m. & f.

intelligence /ɪn'tɛlɪdʒəns/ n. inteligencia f.

intelligence quotient /'kwouʃənt/ coeficiente intelectual m.

intelligent /ɪn'tɛlɪdʒənt/ a. inteligente.

intelligible /ɪn'tɛlɪdʒəbəl/ a. inteligible.

intend /ɪn'tɛnd/ v. pensar; intentar; destinar.

intense /ɪn'tɛns/ a. intenso.

intensify /ɪn'tɛnsə,fai/ v. intensificar.

intensity /ɪn'tɛnsɪti/ n. intensidad f.

intensive /ɪn'tɛnsɪv/ a. intensivo.

intensive-care unit /ɪn'tɛnsɪv'kɛər/ unidad de cuidados intensivos, unidad de vigilancia intensiva f.

intent /ɪn'tɛnt/ n. intento m.

intention /ɪn'tɛnʃən/ n. intención f.

intentional /ɪn'tɛnʃənl/ a. intencional.

intercede /,ɪntər'sid/ v. interceder.

intercept /,ɪntər'sɛpt/ v. interceptar; detener.

interchange /,ɪntər'tʃendʒ/ v. intercambiar.

interchangeable /,ɪntər'tʃeindʒəbəl/ a. intercambiable.

intercourse /'ɪntər,kɔrs/ n. tráfico m.; comunicación f.; coito m.

interest /'ɪntərɪst/ n. 1. interés m. —v. 2. interesar.

interesting /'ɪntərəstɪŋ/ a. interesante.

interest rate n. tipo de interés m.

interface /'ɪntər,feis/ n. interfaz.

interfere /,ɪntər'fɪər/ v. entrometerse, intervenir. **i. with,** estorbar.

interference /,ɪntər'fɪərəns/ n. intervención f.; obstáculo m.

interior /ɪn'tɪəriər/ a. interior.

interject /,ɪntər'dʒɛkt/ v. interponer; intervenir.

interjection /,ɪntər'dʒɛkʃən/ n. interjección f.; interposición f.

interlude /'ɪntər,lud/ n. intervalo

m.; Theat. intermedio m.; (music) interludio m.

intermediary /,ɪntər'midi,ɛri/ n. intermediario -ria.

intermediate /,ɪntər'midi,eit/ a. intermedio.

interment /ɪn'tɜrmənt/ n. entierro.

intermission /,ɪntər'mɪʃən/ n. intermisión f.; Theat. entreacto m.

intermittent /,ɪntər'mɪtn̩t/ a. intermitente.

intern /ɪn'tɜrn/ n. 1. interno -na, internado -da. —v. 2. internar.

internal /ɪn'tɜrnl̩/ a. interno.

international /,ɪntər'næʃənl̩/ a. internacional.

internationalism /,ɪntər'næʃənl̩-,ɪzəm/ n. internacionalismo m.

Internet, the /'ɪntər,nɛt/ n. el Internet m.

interpose /,ɪntər'pouz/ v. interponer.

interpret /ɪn'tɜrprɪt/ v. interpretar.

interpretation /ɪn,tɜrprɪ'teiʃən/ n. interpretación f.

interpreter /ɪn'tɜrprɪtər/ n. intérprete m. & f.

interrogate /ɪn'tɛrə,geit/ v. interrogar.

interrogation /ɪn,tɛrə'geiʃən/ n. interrogación; pregunta f.

interrogative /,ɪntə'rɒgətɪv/ a. interrogativo.

interrupt /,ɪntə'rʌpt/ v. interrumpir.

interruption /,ɪntə'rʌpʃən/ n. interrupción f.

intersect /,ɪntər'sɛkt/ v. cortar.

intersection /,ɪntər'sɛkʃən/ n. intersección f.; (street) bocacalle f.

intersperse /,ɪntər'spɜrs/ v. entremezclar.

interval /'ɪntərvəl/ n. intervalo m.

intervene /,ɪntər'vin/ v. intervenir.

intervention /,ɪntər'vɛnʃən/ n. intervención f.

interview /'ɪntər,vyu/ n. 1. entrevista f. —v. 2. entrevistar.

interviewer /'ɪntər,vyuər/ n. entrevistador -ora m. & f.

intestine /ɪn'tɛstɪn/ n. intestino m.

intimacy /'ɪntəməsi/ n. intimidad; familiaridad f.

intimate /'ɪntəmɪt/ a. 1. íntimo, familiar. —n. 2. amigo -ga íntimo -ma. —v. 3. insinuar.

intimidate /ın'tımı,deit/ v. intimidar.

intimidation /ın,tımı'deiʃən/ n. intimidación f.

into /'ıntu; *unstressed* -tʊ, -tə/ *prep.* en, dentro de.

intonation /,ıntou'neiʃən/ n. entonación f.

intone /ın'toun/ v. entonar.

intoxicate /ın'tɒksı,keit/ v. embriagar.

intoxication /ın,tɒksı'keiʃən/ n. embriaguez f.

intravenous /,ıntrə'vinəs/ a. intravenoso.

intrepid /ın'trɛpıd/ a. intrépido.

intricacy /'ıntrıkəsi/ n. complejidad f.; enredo m.

intricate /'ıntrıkıt/ a. intrincado; complejo.

intrigue /ın'trig; n. *also* 'ıntrig/ n. **1.** intriga f. —v. **2.** intrigar.

intrinsic /ın'trınsık/ a. intrínseco.

introduce /,ıntrə'dus/ v. introducir; (a person) presentar.

introduction /,ıntrə'dʌkʃən/ n. presentación; introducción f.

introductory /,ıntrə'dʌktəri/ a. introductor; preliminar. **i. offer,** ofrecimiento de presentación m.

introvert /'ıntrə,vɜrt/ n. & a. introvertido -da.

intrude /ın'trud/ v. entremeterse.

intruder /ın'trudər/ n. intruso -sa.

intuition /,ıntu'ıʃən/ n. intuición f.

intuitive /ın'tuıtıv/ a. intuitivo.

inundate /'ınən,deit/ v. inundar.

invade /ın'veid/ v. invadir.

invader /ın'veidər/ n. invasor -ra.

invalid /ın'vælıd/ a. & n. inválido -da.

invariable /ın'vɛəriəbəl/ a. invariable.

invasion /ın'veiʒən/ n. invasión f.

invective /ın'vɛktıv/ n. **1.** invectiva f. —a. **2.** ultrajante.

inveigle /ın'veigəl/ v. seducir.

invent /ın'vɛnt/ v. inventar.

invention /ın'vɛnʃən/ n. invención f.

inventive /ın'vɛntıv/ a. inventivo.

inventor /ın'vɛntər/ n. inventor -ra.

inventory /'ınvən,tɔri/ n. inventario m.

invertebrate /ın'vɜrtəbrıt/ n. & a. invertebrado m.

invest /ın'vɛst/ v. investir; Com. invertir.

investigate /ın'vɛstı,geit/ v. investigar.

investigation /ın,vɛstı'geiʃən/ n. investigación f.

investment /ın'vɛstmənt/ n. inversión f.

investor /ın'vɛstər/ n. inversor, -ra.

inveterate /ın'vɛtərıt/ a. inveterado.

invidious /ın'vıdiəs/ a. abominable, odioso, injusto.

invigorate /ın'vıgə,reit/ v. vigorizar, fortificar.

invincible /ın'vınsəbəl/ a. invencible.

invisible /ın'vızəbəl/ a. invisible.

invitation /,ınvı'teiʃən/ n. invitación f.

invite /ın'vait/ v. invitar, convidar.

invocation /,ınvə'keiʃən/ n. invocación f.

invoice /'ınvɔis/ n. factura f.

invoke /ın'vouk/ v. invocar.

involuntary /ın'vɒlən,tɛri/ a. involuntario.

involve /ın'vɒlv/ v. envolver; implicar.

involved /ın'vɒlvd/ a. complicado.

invulnerable /ın'vʌlnərəbəl/ a. invulnerable.

inward /'ınwərd/ adv. hacia adentro.

inwardly /'ınwərdli/ adv. interiormente.

iodine /'aiə,dain/ n. iodo m.

IQ *abbr.* CI (coeficiente intelectual) m.

irate /ai'reit/ a. encolerizado.

Ireland /'aiᵊrlənd/ n. Irlanda f.

iris /'airıs/ n. *Anat.* iris m.; (botany) flor de lis f.

Irish /'airıʃ/ a. irlandés.

irk /ɜrk/ v. fastidiar.

iron /'aiərn/ n. **1.** hierro m.; (appliance) plancha f. —v. **2.** planchar.

ironical /ai'rɒnıkəl/ a. irónico.

ironing board /'aiərnıŋ/ tabla de planchar f.

irony /'airəni/ n. ironía f.

irrational /ı'ræʃənl/ a. irracional; ilógico.

irregular /ı'rɛgyələr/ a. irregular.

irregularity /ı,rɛgyə'lærıti/ n. irregularidad f.

irrelevant /ı'rɛləvənt/ a. ajeno.

irresistible /,ırı'zıstəbəl/ a. irresistible.

jetty

irresponsible /ˌɪrɪ'spɒnsəbəl/ a. irresponsable.

irreverent /ɪ'rɛvərənt/ a. irreverente.

irrevocable /ɪ'rɛvəkəbəl/ a. irrevocable.

irrigate /'ɪrɪˌgeit/ v. regar; Med. irrigar.

irrigation /ˌɪrɪ'geiʃən/ n. riego m.

irritability /ˌɪrɪtə'bɪlɪti/ n. irritabilidad f.

irritable /'ɪrɪtəbəl/ a. irritable.

irritant /'ɪrɪtn̩t/ n. & a. irritante m.

irritate /'ɪrɪˌteit/ v. irritar.

irritation /ˌɪrɪ'teiʃən/ n. irritación f.

island /'ailənd/ n. isla f.

isolate /'aisəˌleit/ v. aislar.

isolation /ˌaisə'leiʃən/ n. aislamiento m.

isosceles /ai'sɒsəˌliz/ a. isósceles.

issuance /'ɪʃuəns/ n. emisión f.; publicación f.

issue /'ɪʃu/ n. **1.** emisión; edición; progenie f.; número m.; punto en disputa. —v. **2.** emitir; publicar.

isthmus /'ɪsməs/ n. istmo m.

it /ɪt/ pron. ello; él, ella; lo, la.

Italian /ɪ'tælyən/ a. & n. italiano -na.

Italy /'ɪtli/ n. Italia f.

itch /ɪtʃ/ n. **1.** picazón f. —v. **2.** picar.

item /'aitəm/ n. artículo; detalle m.; inserción f.; Com. renglón m.

itemize /'aitəˌmaiz/ v. detallar.

itinerant /ai'tɪnərənt/ n. **1.** viandante m. —a. **2.** ambulante.

itinerary /ai'tɪnəˌrɛri/ n. itinerario m.

its /ɪts/ a. su.

itself /ɪt'sɛlf/ pron. sí; se.

ivory /'aivəri/ n. marfil m.

ivy /'aivi/ n. hiedra f.

J

jab /dʒæb/ n. **1.** pinchazo m. —v. **2.** pinchar.

jack /dʒæk/ n. (for lifting) gato m.; (cards) sota f.

jackal /'dʒækəl/ n. chacal m.

jackass /'dʒækˌæs/ n. asno m.

jacket /'dʒækɪt/ n. chaqueta f.; saco m.

jack-of-all-trades /'dʒæk əv 'ɔl 'treidz/ n. estuche m.

jade /dʒeid/ n. (horse) rocín m.; (woman) picarona f.; (mineral) jade m.

jaded /'dʒeidɪd/ a. rendido.

jagged /dʒægɪd/ a. mellado.

jaguar /'dʒægwɑr/ n. jaguar m.

jail /dʒeil/ n. cárcel f.

jailer /'dʒeilər/ n. carcelero m.

jam /dʒæm/ n. **1.** conserva f.; aprieto, apretón m. —v. **2.** apiñar, apretar; trabar.

janitor /'dʒænɪtər/ n. portero m.

January /'dʒænyuˌɛri/ n. enero m.

Japan /dʒə'pæn/ n. Japón m.

Japanese /ˌdʒæpə'niz/ a. & n. japonés -esa.

jar /dʒɑr/ n. **1.** jarro m. —v. **2.** chocar; agitar.

jargon /'dʒɑrgən/ n. jerga f.

jasmine /'dʒæzmɪn/ n. jazmín m.

jaundice /'dʒɔndɪs/ n. ictericia f.

jaunt /dʒɔnt/ n. paseo m.

javelin /'dʒævlɪn/ n. jabalina f.

jaw /dʒɔ/ n. quijada f.

jay /dʒei/ n. grajo m.

jazz /dʒæz/ n. jazz m.

jealous /'dʒɛləs/ a. celoso. **to be j.,** tener celos.

jealousy /'dʒɛləsi/ n. celos m.pl.

jeans /dʒinz/ n. vaqueros, tejanos m.pl.

jeer /dʒɪər/ n. **1.** burla f., mofa f. —v. **2.** burlar, mofar.

jelly /'dʒɛli/ n. jalea f.

jellyfish /'dʒɛliˌfɪʃ/ n. aguamar m.

jeopardize /'dʒɛpərˌdaiz/ v. arriesgar.

jeopardy /'dʒɛpərdi/ n. riesgo m.

jerk /dʒɜrk/ n. **1.** sacudida f. —v. **2.** sacudir.

jerky /'dʒɜrki/ a. espasmódico.

Jerusalem /dʒɪ'rusələm/ n. Jerusalén m.

jest /dʒɛst/ n. **1.** broma f. —v. **2.** bromear.

jester /'dʒɛstər/ n. bufón -ona; burlón -ona.

Jesuit /'dʒɛʒuɪt/ a. & n. jesuíta m.

Jesus Christ /'dʒizəs 'kraist/ n. Jesucristo m.

jet /dʒɛt/ n. chorro m.; (gas) mechero m.

jet lag n. defase horario m., inadaptación horaria f.

jetsam /'dʒɛtsəm/ n. echazón f.

jettison /'dʒɛtəsən/ v. echar al mar.

jetty /'dʒɛti/ n. muelle m.

Jew /dʒu/ *n.* judío -día.

jewel /'dʒuəl/ *n.* joya *f.*

jeweler /'dʒuələr/ *n.* joyero -ra.

jewelry /'dʒuəlri/ *n.* joyas *f.pl.* **j. store,** joyería *f.*

Jewish /'dʒuɪʃ/ *a.* judío.

jib /dʒɪb/ *n. Naut.* foque *m.*

jiffy /'dʒɪfi/ *n.* instante *m.*

jig /dʒɪg/ *n.* jiga *f.* **j-saw,** sierra de vaivén *f.*

jilt /dʒɪlt/ *v.* dar calabazas.

jingle /'dʒɪŋgəl/ *n.* **1.** retintín *m.;* rima pueril *f.* —*v.* **2.** retiñir.

jinx /dʒɪŋks/ *n.* **1.** aojo *m.* —*v.* **2.** aojar.

jittery /'dʒɪtəri/ *a.* nervioso.

job /dʒɒb/ *n.* empleo *m.*

jobber /'dʒɒbər/ *n.* destajista *m.* & *f.,* corredor *m.*

jockey /'dʒɒki/ *n.* jockey *m.*

jocular /'dʒɒkyələr/ *a.* jocoso.

jog /dʒɒg/ *n.* empujoncito *m. v.* empujar; estimular. **j. along,** ir a un trote corto.

join /dʒɔin/ *v.* juntar; unir.

joiner /'dʒɔinər/ *n.* ebanista *m.*

joint /dʒɔint/ *n.* juntura *f.*

jointly /'dʒɔintli/ *adv.* conjuntamente.

joke /dʒouk/ *n.* **1.** broma, chanza *f.;* chiste *m.* —*v.* **2.** bromear.

joker /'dʒoukər/ *n.* bromista *m.* & *f.;* comodín *m.*

jolly /'dʒɒli/ *a.* alegre, jovial.

jolt /dʒoult/ *n.* **1.** sacudido *m.* —*v.* **2.** sacudir.

jonquil /'dʒɒŋkwɪl/ *n.* junquillo *m.*

jostle /'dʒɒsəl/ *v.* empujar.

journal /'dʒɜrnl/ *n.* diario *m.;* revista *f.*

journalism /'dʒɜrnl,ɪzəm/ *n.* periodismo *m.*

journalist /'dʒɜrnlɪst/ *n.* periodista *m.* & *f.*

journey /'dʒɜrni/ *n.* **1.** viaje *m.;* jornada *f.* —*v.* **2.** viajar.

journeyman /'dʒɜrnimən/ *n.* jornalero *m.,* oficial *m.*

jovial /'dʒouviəl/ *a.* jovial.

jowl /dʒaul/ *n.* carrillo *m.*

joy /dʒɔi/ *n.* alegría *f.*

joyful /'dʒɔifəl/ **joyous** *a.* alegre, gozoso.

jubilant /'dʒubələnt/ *a.* jubiloso.

jubilee /'dʒubə,li/ *n.* jubileo *m.*

Judaism /'dʒudi,ɪzəm/ *n.* judaísmo *m.*

judge /dʒʌdʒ/ *n.* **1.** juez *m.* & *f.* —*v.* **2.** juzgar.

judgment /'dʒʌddʒmənt/ *n.* juicio *m.*

judicial /dʒu'dɪʃəl/ *a.* judicial.

judiciary /dʒu'dɪʃi,eri/ *a.* judiciario.

judicious /dʒu'dɪʃəs/ *a.* juicioso.

jug /dʒʌg/ *n.* jarro *m.*

juggle /'dʒʌgəl/ *v.* escamotear.

juice /dʒus/ *n.* jugo, zumo *m.*

juicy /'dʒusi/ *a.* jugoso.

July /dʒu'lai/ *n.* julio *m.*

jumble /'dʒʌmbəl/ *n.* **1.** revoltillo *m.* —*v.* **2.** arrebujar, revolver.

jump /dʒʌmp/ *n.* **1.** salto *m.* —*v.* **2.** saltar, brincar.

junction /'dʒʌŋkʃən/ *n.* confluencia *f.;* (railway) empalme *m.*

juncture /'dʒʌŋktʃər/ *n.* juntura *f.;* coyuntura *f.*

June /dʒun/ *n.* junio *m.*

jungle /'dʒʌŋgəl/ *n.* jungla, selva *f.*

junior /'dʒunyər/ *a.* menor; más joven. **Jr.,** hijo.

juniper /'dʒunəpər/ *n.* enebro *m.*

junk /dʒʌŋk/ *n.* basura *f.*

junket /'dʒʌŋkɪt/ *n.* **1.** leche cuajada *f.* —*v.* **2.** festejar.

junkie /'dʒʌŋki/ *n. Colloq.* yonqui *m.* & *f.,* toxicómano -na.

junk mail *n.* porpaganda indeseada *f.,* correo basura *m.*

jurisdiction /,dʒʊrɪs'dɪkʃən/ *n.* jurisdicción *f.*

jurisprudence /,dʒʊrɪs'prudns/ *n.* jurisprudencia *f.*

jurist /'dʒʊrɪst/ *n.* jurista *m.* & *f.*

juror /'dʒʊrər/ *n.* jurado -da.

jury /'dʒʊri/ *n.* jurado *m.*

just /dʒʌst/ *a.* **1.** justo; exacto. —*adv.* **2.** exactamente; (only) sólo. **j. now,** ahora mismo. **to have j.,** acabar de.

justice /'dʒʌstɪs/ *n.* justicia *f.;* (person) juez *m.* & *f.*

justifiable /'dʒʌstə,faiəbəl/ *a.* justificable.

justification /,dʒʌstəfɪ'keiʃən/ *n.* justificación *f.*

justify /'dʒʌstə,fai/ *v.* justificar.

jut /dʒʌt/ *v.* sobresalir.

jute /dʒut/ *n.* yute *m.*

juvenile /'dʒuvənl/ *a.* juvenil.

juvenile delinquency delincuencia de menores, delincuencia juvenil *f.*

K

kaleidoscope /kə'laidə,skoup/ *n.* calidoscopio *m.*

kangaroo /,kæŋgə'ru/ *n.* canguro *m.*

karakul /'kærəkəl/ *n.* caracul *m.*

karat /'kærət/ *n.* quilate *m.*

karate /kə'rɑti/ *n.* karate *m.*

keel /kil/ *n.* **1.** quilla *f.* —*v.* **2. to k. over,** volcarse.

keen /kin/ *a.* agudo; penetrante.

keep /kip/ *v.* mantener, retener; guardar; preservar. **k. on,** seguir, continuar.

keeper /'kipər/ *n.* guardián *m.*

keepsake /'kip,seik/ *n.* recuerdo *m.*

keg /kɛg/ *n.* barrilito *m.*

kennel /'kɛnl̩/ *n.* perrera *f.*

kerchief /'kɜrtʃɪf/ *n.* pañuelo *m.*

kernel /'kɜrnl̩/ *n.* pepita *f.*; grano *m.*

kerosene /'kɛrə,sin/ *n.* kerosén *m.*

ketchup /'kɛtʃəp/ *n.* salsa de tomate *f.*

kettle /'kɛtl̩/ *n.* caldera, olla *f.*

kettledrum /'kɛtl̩,drʌm/ *n.* tímpano *m.*

key /ki/ *n.* llave *f.*; (music) clave *f.*; (piano) tecla *f.*

keyboard /'ki,bɔrd/ *n.* teclado *m.*

keyhole /'ki,houl/ *n.* bocallave *f.*

keypad /'ki,pæd/ *n.* teclado *m.*

khaki /'kæki/ *a.* caqui.

kick /kɪk/ *n.* **1.** patada *f.* —*v.* **2.** patear; *Colloq.* quejarse.

kid /kɪd/ *n.* **1.** cabrito *m.*; *Colloq.* niño -ña, chico -ca. —*v.* **2.** *Colloq.* bromear.

kidnap /'kɪdnæp/ *v.* secuestrar.

kidnaper /'kɪdnæpər/ *n.* secuestrador -ora.

kidnaping /'kɪdnæpɪŋ/ *n.* rapto, secuestro *m.*

kidney /'kɪdni/ *n.* riñón *m.*

kidney bean *n.* frijol *m.*

kill /kɪl/ *v.* matar.

killer /'kɪlər/ *n.* matador -ora.

killjoy /'kɪldʒɔi/ *n.* aguafiestas *m.* & *f.*

kiln /kɪl/ *n.* horno *m.*

kilogram /'kɪlə,græm/ *n.* kilogramo *m.*

kilohertz /'kɪlə,hɜrts/ *n.* kilohercio *m.*

kilometer /kɪ'lɒmɪtər/ *n.* kilómetro *m.*

kilowatt /'kɪlə,wɒt/ *n.* kilovatio *m.*

kin /kɪn/ *n.* parentesco *m.*; parientes *m.pl.*

kind /kaind/ *a.* **1.** bondadoso, amable. —*n.* **2.** género *m.*; clase *f.* **k. of,** algo, un poco.

kindergarten /'kɪndər,gɑrtn̩/ *n.* kindergarten *m.*

kindle /'kɪndl̩/ *v.* encender.

kindling /'kɪndlɪŋ/ *n.* encendimiento *m.* **k.-wood,** leña menuda *f.*

kindly /'kaindli/ *a.* bondadoso.

kindness /'kaindnɪs/ *n.* bondad *f.*

kindred /'kɪndrɪd/ *n.* parentesco *m.*

kinetic /kɪ'nɛtɪk/ *a.* cinético.

king /kɪŋ/ *n.* rey *m.*

kingdom /'kɪŋdəm/ *n.* reino *m.*

king prawn langostino *m.*

kink /kɪŋk/ *n.* retorcimiento *m.*

kinky /'kɪŋki/ *a. Colloq.* pervertidillo; (hair) rizado.

kiosk /'kiɒsk/ *n.* kiosco *m.*

kiss /kɪs/ *n.* **1.** beso *m.* —*v.* **2.** besar.

kitchen /'kɪtʃən/ *n.* cocina *f.*

kite /kait/ *n.* cometa *f.*

kitten /'kɪtn̩/ *n.* gatito -ta.

kleptomania /,klɛptə'meiniə/ *n.* cleptomanía *f.*

kleptomaniac /,klɛptə'meiniæk/ *n.* cleptómano -na.

klutz /klʌts/ *n. Colloq.* torpe, patoso -sa.

knack /næk/ *n.* don *m.*, destreza *f.*

knapsack /'næp,sæk/ *n.* alforja *f.*

knead /nid/ *v.* amasar.

knee /ni/ *n.* rodilla *f.*

kneecap /'ni,kæp/ *n.* rodillera, rótula *f.*

kneel /nil/ *v.* arrodillarse.

knickers /'nɪkərz/ *n.* calzón corto *m.*, pantalones *m.pl.*

knife /naif/ *n.* cuchillo *m.*

knight /nait/ *n.* caballero *m.*; (chess) caballo *m.*

knit /nɪt/ *v.* tejer.

knob /nɒb/ *n.* tirador *m.*

knock /nɒk/ *n.* **1.** golpe *m.*; llamada *f.* —*v.* **2.** golpear; tocar, llamar.

knot /nɒt/ *n.* **1.** nudo; lazo *m.* —*v.* **2.** anudar.

knotty /'nɒti/ *a.* nudoso.

know /nou/ *v.* saber; (a person) conocer.

knowledge /ˈnɒlɪdʒ/ *n.* conocimiento, saber *m.*

knuckle /ˈnʌkəl/ *n.* nudillo *m.* **k.**

bone, jarrete *m.* **to k. under,** ceder a.

Koran /kəˈran/ *n.* Corán *m.*

Korea /kəˈriə/ *n.* Corea *f.*

Korean /kəˈriən/ *a. & n.* coreano.

L

label /ˈleibəl/ *n.* **1.** rótulo *m.* —*v.* **2.** rotular; designar.

labor /ˈleibər/ *n.* **1.** trabajo *m.*; la clase obrera. —*v.* **2.** trabajar.

laboratory /ˈlæbrə,tɔri/ *n.* laboratorio *m.*

laborer /ˈleibərər/ *n.* trabajador, obrero *m.*

laborious /ləˈbɔriəs/ *a.* laborioso, difícil.

labor union gremio obrero, sindicato *m.*

labyrinth /ˈlæbərɪnθ/ *n.* laberinto *m.*

lace /leis/ *n.* **1.** encaje *m.*; (of shoe) lazo *m.* —*v.* **2.** amarrar.

lacerate /ˈlæsə,reit/ *v.* lacerar, lastimar.

laceration /,læsəˈreiʃən/ *n.* laceración *f.*, desgarro *m.*

lack /læk/ *n.* **1.** falta *f.* **l. of respect,** desacato *m.* —*v.* **2.** faltar, carecer.

lackadaisical /,lækəˈdeizɪkəl/ *a.* indiferente; soñador.

laconic /ləˈkɒnɪk/ *a.* lacónico.

lacquer /ˈlækər/ *n.* **1.** laca *f.*, barniz *m.* —*v.* **2.** laquear, barnizar.

lactic /ˈlæktɪk/ *a.* láctico.

lactose /ˈlæktous/ *n.* lactosa *f.*

ladder /ˈlædər/ *n.* escalera *f.*

ladle /ˈleidl/ *n.* **1.** cucharón *m.* —*v.* **2.** servir con cucharón.

lady /ˈleidi/ *n.* señora, dama *f.*

ladybug /ˈleidi,bʌg/ *n.* mariquita *f.*

lag /læg/ *n.* **1.** retraso *m.* —*v.* **2.** quedarse atrás.

lagoon /ləˈgun/ *n.* laguna *f.*

laid-back /ˈleid ˈbæk/ *a.* de buen talante, ecuánime, pacífico.

laity /ˈleiɪti/ *n.* laicado *m.*

lake /leik/ *n.* lago *m.*

lamb /læm/ *n.* cordero *m.*

lame /leim/ *a.* **1.** cojo; estropeado. —*v.* **2.** estropear, lisiar; incapacitar.

lament /ləˈment/ *n.* **1.** lamento *m.* —*v.* **2.** lamentar.

lamentable /ləˈmentəbəl/ *a.* lamentable.

lamentation /,læmənˈteiʃən/ *n.* lamento *m.*; lamentación *f.*

laminate /ˈlæmə,neit/ *a.* laminado. *v.* laminar.

lamp /læmp/ *n.* lámpara *f.*

lampoon /læmˈpun/ *n.* **1.** pasquín *m.* —*v.* **2.** pasquinar.

lance /læns/ *n.* **1.** lanza *f.* —*v.* **2.** *Med.* abrir.

land /lænd/ *n.* **1.** país *m.*; tierra *f.* **native l.,** patria *f.* —*v.* **2.** desembarcar; (plane) aterrizar.

landholder /ˈlænd,houldər/ *n.* hacendado -da.

landing /ˈlændɪŋ/ *n.* (of stairs) descanso, descansillo *m.*; (ship) desembarcadero *m.*; (airplane) aterrizaje *m.*

landlady /ˈlænd,leidi/ **landlord** *n.* propietario -ria.

landmark /ˈlænd,mɑrk/ *n.* mojón *m.*, señal *f.*; rasgo sobresaliente *m.*

landscape /ˈlænd,skeip/ *n.* paisaje *m.*

landslide /ˈlænd,slaid/ *n.* derrumbe *m.*

lane /lein/ *n.* senda *f.*

language /ˈlæŋgwɪdʒ/ *n.* lengua *f.*, idioma; lenguaje *m.*

languid /ˈlæŋgwɪd/ *a.* lánguido.

languish /ˈlæŋgwɪʃ/ *v.* languidecer.

languor /ˈlæŋgər/ *n.* languidez *f.*

lanky /ˈlæŋki/ *a.* larguirucho; desgarbado.

lanolin /ˈlænlɪn/ *n.* lanolina *f.*

lantern /ˈlæntərn/ *n.* linterna *f.*; farol *m.*

lap /læp/ *n.* **1.** regazo *m.*; falda *f.* —*v.* **2.** lamer.

lapel /ləˈpɛl/ *n.* solapa *f.*

lapse /læps/ *n.* **1.** lapso *m.* —*v.* **2.** pasar; decaer; caer en error.

laptop computer /ˈlæp,tɒp/ ordenador portátil *m.*

larceny /ˈlɑrsəni/ *n.* ratería *f.*

lard /lɑrd/ *n.* manteca de cerdo *f.*

large /lɑrdʒ/ *a.* grande.

largely /'lɑrdʒli/ adv. ampliamente; mayormente; muy.
largo /'lɑrgou/ n. & a. Mus. largo m.
lariat /'læriət/ n. lazo m.
lark /lɑrk/ n. (bird) alondra f.
larva /'lɑrvə/ n. larva f.
laryngitis /ˌlærən'dʒaitɪs/ n. laringitis f.
larynx /'lærɪŋks/ n. laringe f.
lascivious /lə'sɪviəs/ a. lascivo.
laser /'leizər/ n. láser m.
lash /læʃ/ n. 1. azote, latigazo m. —v. 2. azotar.
lass /læs/ n. doncella f.
lassitude /'læsɪˌtud/ n. lasitud f.
lasso /'læsou/ n. 1. lazo m. —v. 2. enlazar.
last /læst/ a. 1. pasado; (final) último. **at l.,** por fin. **l. but one,** penúltimo. **l. but two,** antepenúltimo. —v. 2. durar.
lasting /'læstɪŋ/ a. duradero.
latch /lætʃ/ n. aldaba f.
late /leit/ a. 1. tardío; (deceased) difunto. **to be l.,** llegar tarde. —adv. 2. tarde.
lately /'leitli/ adv. recientemente.
latent /'leitṇt/ a. latente.
lateral /'lætərəl/ a. lateral.
lather /'læðər/ n. 1. espuma de jabón. —v. 2. enjabonar.
Latin /'lætṇ/ n. latín m.
Latin America /ə'mɛrikə/ Hispanoamérica, América Latina f.
Latin American hispanoamericano -na.
latitude /'lætɪˌtud/ n. latitud f.
latrine /lə'trin/ n. letrina f.
latter /'lætər/ a. posterior. **the l.,** éste.
lattice /'lætɪs/ n. celosía f.
laud /lɔd/ v. loar.
laudable /'lɔdəbəl/ a. laudable.
laudanum /'lɔdṇəm/ n. láudano m.
laudatory /'lɔdəˌtɔri/ a. laudatorio.
laugh /læf/ n. 1. risa, risotada f. —v. 2. reír. **l. at,** reírse de.
laughable /'læfəbəl/ a. risible.
laughter /'læftər/ n. risa f.
launch /lɔntʃ/ n. 1. Naut. lancha f. —v. 2. lanzar.
launder /'lɔndər/ v. lavar y planchar la ropa.
laundry /'lɔndri/ n. lavandería f.
laundryman /'lɔndriˌmæn/ n. lavandero -ra.

laureate /'lɔriɪt/ n. & a. laureado -da.
laurel /'lɔrəl/ n. laurel m.
lava /'lɑvə/ n. lava f.
lavatory /'lævəˌtɔri/ n. lavatorio m.
lavender /'lævəndər/ n. lavándula f.
lavish /'lævɪʃ/ a. 1. pródigo. —v. 2. prodigar.
law /lɔ/ n. ley f.; derecho m.
lawful /'lɔfəl/ a. legal.
lawless /'lɔlɪs/ a. sin ley.
lawn /lɔn/ n. césped; prado m.
lawn mower /'mouər/ n. cortacésped m. & f.
lawsuit /'lɔˌsut/ n. pleito m.
lawyer /'lɔyər/ n. abogado m. & f.
lax /læks/ a. flojo, laxo.
laxative /'læksətɪv/ n. purgante m.
laxity /'læksɪti/ n. laxidad f.; flojedad f.
lay /lei/ a. 1. secular. —v. 2. poner.
layer /'leiər/ n. capa f.
layman /'leimən/ n. lego, seglar m.
lazy /'leizi/ a. perezoso.
lead /lɛd , lid/ n. 1. plomo m.; Theat. papel principal. **to take the l.,** tomar la delantera. —v. 2. conducir; dirigir.
leaden /'lɛdṇ/ a. plomizo; pesado; abatido.
leader /'lidər/ n. líder m. & f.; jefe m. & f.; director -ora.
leadership /'lidərˌʃɪp/ n. dirección f.
leaf /lif/ n. hoja f.
leaflet /'liflɪt/ n. Bot. hojilla f.; folleto m.
league /lig/ n. liga; (measure) legua f.
leak /lik/ n. 1. escape; goteo m. —v. 2. gotear; Naut. hacer agua.
leakage /'likɪdʒ/ n. goteo m., escape m., pérdida f.
leaky /'liki/ a. llovedizo, resquebrajado.
lean /lin/ a. 1. flaco, magro. —v. 2. apoyarse, arrimarse.
leap /lip/ n. 1. salto m. —v. 2. saltar.
leap year n. año bisiesto m.
learn /lɜrn/ v. aprender; saber.
learned /'lɜrnɪd/ a. erudito.
learning /'lɜrnɪŋ/ n. erudición f., instrucción f.

lease /lis/ n. **1.** arriendo m. —v. **2.** arrendar.

leash /liʃ/ n. **1.** correa f. —v. **2.** atraillar.

least /list/ a. menor; mínimo. **the l.,** lo menos. **at l.,** por lo menos.

leather /'lɛðər/ n. cuero m.

leathery /'lɛðəri/ a. coriáceo.

leave /liv/ n. **1.** licencia f. **to take l.,** despedirse. —v. **2.** dejar; (depart) salir, irse. **l. out,** omitir.

leaven /'lɛvən/ n. **1.** levadura f. —v. **2.** fermentar, imbuir.

lecherous /'lɛtʃərəs/ a. lujurioso.

lecture /'lɛktʃər/ n. conferencia f.

lecturer /'lɛktʃərər/ n. conferencista m. & f.; catedrático -ca.

ledge /lɛdʒ/ n. borde m.; capa f.

ledger /'lɛdʒər/ n. libro mayor m.

lee /li/ n. sotavento m.

leech /litʃ/ n. sanguijuela f.

leek /lik/ n. puerro m.

leer /lɪər/ v. mirar de soslayo.

leeward /'liwərd/ a. sotavento.

left /lɛft/ a. izquierdo. **the l.,** la izquierda. **to be left,** quedarse.

left-handed /'lɛft 'hændɪd/ a. zurdo.

leftist /'lɛftɪst/ n. izquierdista m. & f.

leftovers /'lɛft,ouvərz/ n. sobras f.pl.

leg /lɛg/ n. pierna f.

legacy /'lɛgəsi/ n. legado m., herencia f.

legal /'ligəl/ a. legal.

legalize /'ligə,laiz/ v. legalizar.

legation /lɪ'geiʃən/ n. legación, embajada f.

legend /'lɛdʒənd/ n. leyenda f.

legendary /'lɛdʒən,dɛri/ a. legendario.

legible /'lɛdʒəbəl/ a. legible.

legion /'lidʒən/ n. legión f.

legislate /'lɛdʒɪs,leit/ v. legislar.

legislation /,lɛdʒɪs'leiʃən/ n. legislación f.

legislator /'lɛdʒɪs,leitər/ n. legislador -ra.

legislature /'lɛdʒɪs,leitʃər/ n. legislatura f.

legitimate /lɪ'dʒɪtəmɪt/ a. legítimo.

legume /'lɛgyum/ n. legumbre f.

leisure /'liʒər/ n. desocupación f.; horas libres.

leisurely /'liʒərli/ a. **1.** deliberado. —adv. **2.** despacio.

lemon /'lɛmən/ n. limón m.

lemonade /,lɛmə'neid/ n. limonada f.

lend /lɛnd/ v. prestar.

length /lɛŋkθ/ n. largo m.; duración f.

lengthen /'lɛŋkθən/ v. alargar.

lengthwise /'lɛŋkθ,waiz/ adv. a lo largo.

lengthy /'lɛŋkθi/ a. largo.

lenient /'liniənt/ a. indulgente.

lens /lɛnz/ n. lente m. or f.

Lent /lɛnt/ n. cuaresma f.

Lenten /'lɛntn̩/ a. cuaresmal.

lentil /'lɛntɪl/ n. lenteja f.

leopard /'lɛpərd/ n. leopardo m.

leotard /'liə,tɑrd/ n. mallas f.pl.

leper /'lɛpər/ n. leproso -sa.

leprosy /'lɛprəsi/ n. lepra f.

lesbian /'lɛzbiən/ n. lesbiana f.

lesion /'liʒən/ n. lesión f.

less /lɛs/ a. & adv. menos.

lessen /'lɛsən/ v. disminuir.

lesser /'lɛsər/ a. menor; más pequeño.

lesson /'lɛsən/ n. lección f.

lest /lɛst/ conj. para que no.

let /lɛt/ v. dejar; permitir; arrendar.

letdown /'lɛt,daun/ n. decepción f.

lethal /'liθəl/ a. letal.

lethargic /lə'θɑrdʒɪk/ a. letárgico.

lethargy /'lɛθərdʒi/ n. letargo m.

letter /'lɛtər/ n. carta; (of alphabet) letra f.

letterhead /'lɛtər,hɛd/ n. membrete m.

lettuce /'lɛtɪs/ n. lechuga f.

leukemia /lu'kimiə/ n. leucemia f.

levee /'lɛvi, lɛ'vi/ n. recepción f.

level /'lɛvəl/ a. **1.** llano, nivelado. —n. **2.** nivel m.; llanura f. —v. **3.** allanar; nivelar.

lever /'lɛvər/ n. palanca f.

levity /'lɛvɪti/ n. levedad f.

levy /'lɛvi/ n. **1.** leva f. —v. **2.** imponer.

lewd /lud/ a. lascivo.

lexicon /'lɛksɪ,kɒn/ n. léxico m.

liability /,laiə'bɪlɪti/ n. riesgo m.; obligación f.

liable /'laiəbəl/ a. sujeto; responsable.

liaison /li'eizən/ n. vinculación f., enlace m.; concubinaje m.

liar /'laiər/ n. embustero -ra.

libel /'laibəl/ n. **1.** libelo m. —v. **2.** difamar.

libelous /'laibələs/ a. difamatorio.

liberal /'lɪbərəl/ *a.* liberal; generoso.

liberalism /'lɪbərə,lɪzəm/ *n.* liberalismo *m.*

liberality /,lɪbə'rælɪti/ *n.* liberalidad *f.*

liberate /'lɪbə,reit/ *v.* libertar.

liberty /'lɪbərti/ *n.* libertad *f.*

libidinous /lɪ'bɪdŋəs/ *a.* libidinoso.

librarian /lai'brɛəriən/ *n.* bibliotecario -ria.

library /'lai,brɛri/ *n.* biblioteca *f.*

libretto /lɪ'brɛtou/ *n.* libreto *m.*

license /'laisəns/ *n.* licencia *f.;* permiso *m.*

licentious /lai'sɛnʃəs/ *a.* licencioso.

lick /lɪk/ *v.* lamer.

licorice /'lɪkərɪʃ, 'lɪkrɪʃ, 'lɪkərɪs/ *n.* regaliz *m.*

lid /lɪd/ *n.* tapa *f.*

lie /lai/ *n.* **1.** mentira *f.* —*v.* **2.** mentir. **l. down,** acostarse, echarse.

lieutenant /lu'tɛnənt/ *n.* teniente *m.*

life /laif/ *n.* vida *f.*

lifeboat /'laif,bout/ *n.* bote salvavidas *m.*

life buoy boya *f.*

lifeguard /'laif,gɑrd/ socorrista *m.* & *f.*

life insurance seguro de vida *m.*

life jacket chaleco salvavidas *m.*

lifeless /'laiflɪs/ *a.* sin vida.

life preserver /prɪ'zɜrvər/ salvavidas *m.*

lifestyle /'laifstail/ *n.* modo de vida *m.*

lift /lɪft/ *v.* levantar, alzar, elevar.

ligament /'lɪgəmənt/ *n.* ligamento *m.*

ligature /'lɪgətʃər/ *n.* ligadura *f.*

light /lait/ *a.* **1.** ligero; liviano; (in color) claro. —*n.* **2.** luz; candela *f.* —*v.* **3.** encender; iluminar.

light bulb bombilla *f.*

lighten /'laitŋ/ *v.* aligerar; aclarar; iluminar.

lighter /'laitər/ *n.* encendedor *m.*

lighthouse /'lait,haus/ *n.* faro *m.*

lightness /'laitnɪs/ *n.* ligereza; agilidad *f.*

lightning /'laitnɪŋ/ *n.* relámpago *m.*

like /laik/ *a.* **1.** semejante. —*prep.* **2.** como. —*v.* **3. I like...** me gusta, me gustan... **I should like,** quisiera.

likeable /'laikəbəl/ *a.* simpático, agradable.

likelihood /'laikli,hʊd/ *n.* probabilidad *f.*

likely /'laikli/ *a.* probable; verosímil.

liken /'laikən/ *v.* comparar; asemejar.

likeness /'laiknɪs/ *n.* semejanza *f.*

likewise /'laik,waiz/ *adv.* igualmente.

lilac /'lailək/ *n.* lila *f.*

lilt /lɪlt/ *n.* **1.** cadencia alegre *f.* —*v.* **2.** cantar alegremente.

lily /'lɪli/ *n.* lirio *m.*

lily of the valley muguete *m.*

limb /lɪm/ *n.* rama *f.*

limber /'lɪmbər/ *a.* flexible. **to l. up,** ponerse flexible.

limbo /'lɪmbou/ *n.* limbo *m.*

lime /laim/ *n.* cal *f.;* (fruit) limoncito *m.*, lima *f.*

limestone /'laim,stoun/ *n.* piedra caliza *f.*

limewater /'laim,wɔtər/ *n.* agua de cal *f.*

limit /'lɪmɪt/ *n.* **1.** límite *m.* —*v.* **2.** limitar.

limitation /,lɪmɪ'teiʃən/ *n.* limitación *f.*

limitless /'lɪmɪtlɪs/ *a.* ilimitado.

limousine /'lɪmə,zin/ *n.* limusina *f.*

limp /lɪmp/ *n.* **1.** cojera *f.* —*a.* **2.** flojo. —*v.* **3.** cojear.

limpid /'lɪmpɪd/ *a.* límpido.

line /lain/ *n.* **1.** línea; fila; raya *f.;* (of print) renglón *m.* —*v.* **2.** forrar; rayar.

lineage /'lɪnɪdʒ/ *n.* linaje *m.*

lineal /'lɪniəl/ *a.* lineal.

linear /'lɪniər/ *a.* linear, longitudinal.

linen /'lɪnən/ *n.* lienzo, lino *m.;* ropa blanca.

liner /'lainər/ *n.* vapor *m.*

linger /'lɪŋgər/ *v.* demorarse.

lingerie /,lɑnʒə'rei/ *n.* ropa blanca *f.*

linguist /'lɪŋgwɪst/ *n.* lingüista *m.* & *f.*

linguistic /lɪŋ'gwɪstɪk/ *a.* lingüístico.

liniment /'lɪnəmənt/ *n.* linimento *m.*

lining /'lainɪŋ/ *n.* forro *m.*

link /lɪŋk/ *n.* **1.** eslabón; vínculo *m.* —*v.* **2.** vincular.

linoleum /lɪ'nouliəm/ *n.* linóleo *m.*

linseed /'lɪnˌsid/ *n.* linaza *f.*; simiente de lino *f.*

lint /lɪnt/ *n.* hilacha *f.*

lion /'laɪən/ *n.* león *m.*

lip /lɪp/ *n.* labio *m.*

liposuction /'lɪpəˌsʌkʃən, 'laɪpə-/ *n.* liposucción *f.*

lipstick /'lɪpˌstɪk/ *n.* lápiz de labios.

liqueur /lɪ'kɜr/ *n.* licor *m.*

liquid /'lɪkwɪd/ *a. & n.* líquido *m.*

liquidate /'lɪkwɪˌdeɪt/ *v.* liquidar.

liquidation /ˌlɪkwɪ'deɪʃən/ *n.* liquidación *f.*

liquor /'lɪkər/ *n.* licor *m.*

lisp /lɪsp/ *n.* **1.** ceceo *m.* —*v.* **2.** cecear.

list /lɪst/ *n.* **1.** lista *f.* —*v.* **2.** registrar.

listen (to) /'lɪsən/ *v.* escuchar.

listless /'lɪstlɪs/ *a.* indiferente.

litany /'lɪtn̩i/ *n.* letanía *f.*

liter /'litər/ *n.* litro *m.*

literal /'lɪtərəl/ *a.* literal.

literary /'lɪtəˌreri/ *a.* literario.

literate /'lɪtərɪt/ *a.* alfabetizado.

literature /'lɪtərətʃər/ *n.* literatura *f.*

litigant /'lɪtɪgənt/ *n. & a.* litigante *m. & f.*

litigation /ˌlɪtɪ'geɪʃən/ *n.* litigio, pleito *m.*

litter /'lɪtər/ *n.* **1.** litera *f.*; cama de paja. —*v.* **2.** poner en desorden.

little /'lɪtl̩/ *a.* pequeño; (quantity) poco.

little finger meñique *m.*

liturgical /lɪ'tɜrdʒɪkəl/ *a.* litúrgico.

liturgy /'lɪtərdʒi/ *n.* liturgia *f.*

live /a laiv; v lɪv/ *a.* **1.** vivo. —*v.* **2.** vivir.

livelihood /'laivliˌhʊd/ *n.* subsistencia *f.*

lively /'laivli/ *a.* vivo; rápido; animado.

liver /'lɪvər/ *n.* hígado *m.*

livery /'lɪvəri/ *n.* librea *f.*

livestock /'laivˌstɒk/ *n.* ganadería *f.*

livid /'lɪvɪd/ *a.* lívido.

living /'lɪvɪŋ/ *a.* **1.** vivo. —*n.* **2.** sustento *m.* **to earn (make) a living,** ganarse la vida.

living room salón *m.*

lizard /'lɪzərd/ *n.* lagarto *m.*, lagartija *f.*

llama /'lɑmə/ *n.* llama *f.*

load /loud/ *n.* **1.** carga *f.* —*v.* **2.** cargar.

loaf /louf/ *n.* **1.** pan *m.* —*v.* **2.** holgazanear.

loam /loum/ *n.* marga *f.*

loan /loun/ *n.* **1.** préstamo *m.* —*v.* **2.** prestar.

loathe /louð/ *v.* aborrecer, detestar.

loathsome /'louðsəm/ *a.* repugnante.

lobby /'lɒbi/ *n.* vestíbulo *m.*

lobe /loub/ *n.* lóbulo *m.*

lobster /'lɒbstər/ *n.* langosta *f.*

local /'loukəl/ *a.* local.

local area network red local *f.*

locale /lou'kæl/ *n.* localidad *f.*

locality /lou'kælɪti/ *n.* localidad *f.*, lugar *m.*

localize /'loukəˌlaiz/ *v.* localizar.

locate /'loukeit/ *v.* situar; hallar.

location /lou'keiʃən/ *n.* sitio *m.*; posición *f.*

lock /lɒk/ *n.* **1.** cerradura *f.*; (pl.) cabellos *m.pl.* —*v.* **2.** cerrar con llave.

locker /'lɒkər/ *n.* cajón *m.*; ropero *m.*

locket /'lɒkɪt/ *n.* guardapelo *m.*; medallón *m.*

lockjaw /'lɒkˌdʒɔ/ *n.* trismo *m.*

locksmith /'lɒkˌsmɪθ/ *n.* cerrajero -ra.

locomotive /ˌloukə'moutɪv/ *n.* locomotora *f.*

locust /'loukəst/ *n.* cigarra *f.*, saltamontes *m.*

locution /lou'kyuʃən/ *n.* locución *f.*

lode /loud/ *n.* filón *m.*, veta *f.*

lodge /lɒdʒ/ *n.* **1.** logia; (inn) posada *f.* —*v.* **2.** fijar; alojar, morar.

lodger /'lɒdʒər/ *n.* inquilino *m.*

lodging /'lɒdʒɪŋ/ *n.* alojamiento *m.*

loft /lɔft/ *n.* desván, sobrado *m.*

lofty /'lɔfti/ *a.* alto; altivo.

log /lɔg/ *n.* tronco de árbol; *Naut.* barquilla *f.*

loge /louʒ/ *n.* palco *m.*

logic /'lɒdʒɪk/ *n.* lógica *f.*

logical /'lɒdʒɪkəl/ *a.* lógico.

loin /lɔin/ *n.* lomo *m.*

loincloth /'lɔinˌklɔθ/ *n.* taparrabos *m.*

loiter /'lɔitər/ *v.* haraganear.

lone /loun/ *a.* solitario.

loneliness /'lounlinɪs/ *n.* soledad *f.*

lonely, /'lounli/ **lonesome** *a.* solo y triste.

lonesome /'lounsəm/ a. solitario, aislado.

long /lɔŋ/ a. **1.** largo. **a l. time,** mucho tiempo. —adv. **2.** mucho tiempo. **how l.,** cuánto tiempo. **no longer,** ya no. —v. **3. l. for,** anhelar.

long-distance call /'lɔŋ 'dɪstəns/ conferencia interurbana f.

longevity /lɒn'dʒɛvɪti/ n. longevidad f.

long-haired /'lɔŋ 'hɛərd/ a. melenudo.

longing /'lɔŋɪŋ/ n. anhelo m.

longitude /'lɒndʒɪ,tud/ n. longitud m.

look /lʊk/ n. **1.** mirada f.; aspecto m. —v. **2.** parecer; mirar. **l. at,** mirar. **l. for,** buscar. **l. like,** parecerse a. **l. out!,** ¡cuidado! **l. up,** buscar; ir a ver, venir a ver.

looking glass /'lʊkɪŋ/ espejo m.

loom /lum/ n. **1.** telar m. —v. **2.** asomar.

loop /lup/ n. vuelta f.

loophole /'lup,houl/ n. aspillera f.; Fig. callejuela, evasiva f., efugio m.

loose /lus/ a. suelto; flojo.

loose change suelto m.

loosen /'lusən/ v. soltar; aflojar.

loot /lut/ n. **1.** botín m., saqueo m. —v. **2.** saquear.

lopsided /'lɒp'saɪdɪd/ a. desequilibrado.

loquacious /lou'kweɪʃəs/ a. locuaz.

lord /lɔrd/ n. señor m.; (Brit. title) lord m.

lordship /'lɔrdʃɪp/ n. señorío m.

lose /luz/ v. perder. **l. consciousness,** perder el conocimiento.

loss /lɔs/ n. pérdida f.

lost /lɔst/ a. perdido.

lot /lɒt/ n. suerte f. **building l.,** solar m. **a lot (of), lots of,** mucho.

lotion /'louʃən/ n. loción f.

lottery /'lɒtəri/ n. lotería f.

loud /laud/ a. **1.** fuerte; ruidoso. —adv. **2.** alto.

loudspeaker /'laud,spikər/ n. altavoz m.

lounge /laundʒ/ n. sofá m.; salón de fumar m.

louse /laus/ n. piojo m.

love /lʌv/ n. **1.** amor m. **in l.,** enamorado. **to fall in l.,** enamorarse. **l. at first sight,** flechazo m. —v. **2.** querer; amar; adorar.

lovely /'lʌvli/ a. hermoso.

lover /'lʌvər/ n. amante m. & f.

low /lou/ a. bajo; vil.

low-cut /'lou 'kʌt/ a. escotado.

lower /'louər/ v. bajar; (in price) rebajar.

lower-case letter /'louər 'keis/ minúscula f.

lowly /'louli/ a. humilde.

low neckline /'nɛk,lain/ escote m.

loyal /'lɔiəl/ a. leal, fiel.

loyalist /'lɔiəlɪst/ n. lealista m. & f.

loyalty /'lɔiəlti/ n. lealtad f.

lozenge /'lɒzɪndʒ/ n. pastilla f.

lubricant /'lubrɪkənt/ n. lubricante m.

lubricate /'lubrɪ,keit/ v. engrasar, lubricar.

lucid /'lusɪd/ a. claro, lúcido.

luck /lʌk/ n. suerte; fortuna f.

lucky /'lʌki/ a. afortunado. **to be l.,** tener suerte.

lucrative /'lukrətɪv/ a. lucrativo.

ludicrous /'ludɪkrəs/ a. rídiculo.

luggage /'lʌgɪdʒ/ n. equipaje m.

lukewarm /'luk'wɔrm/ a. tibio.

lull /lʌl/ n. **1.** momento de calma. —v. **2.** calmar.

lullaby /'lʌlə,bai/ n. arrullo m.

lumbago /lʌm'beigou/ n. lumbago m.

lumber /'lʌmbər/ n. madera f.

luminous /'lumənəs/ a. luminoso.

lump /lʌmp/ n. protuberancia f.; (of sugar) terrón m.

lump sum suma global f.

lunacy /'lunəsi/ n. locura f.

lunar /'lunər/ a. lunar.

lunatic /'lunətɪk/ a. & n. loco -ca.

lunch, luncheon /lʌntʃ; 'lʌnteshən/ n. **1.** merienda f., almuerzo m. —v. **2.** merendar, almorzar.

lunch box /'lʌntʃ,bɒks/ fiambrera f.

lung /lʌŋ/ n. pulmón m.

lunge /lʌndʒ/ n. **1.** estocada, arremetida f. —v. **2.** dar un estocada, arremeter.

lure /lur/ v. atraer.

lurid /'lurɪd/ a. sensacional; espeluznante.

lurk /lərk/ v. esconderse; espiar.

luscious /'lʌʃəs/ a. sabroso, delicioso.

lust /lʌst/ n. sensualidad; codicia f.

luster /'lʌstər/ n. lustre m.

lustful /'lʌstfəl/ *a.* sensual, lascivo.

lusty /'lʌsti/ *a.* vigoroso.

lute /lut/ *n.* laúd *m.*

Lutheran /'luθərən/ *n.* & *a.* luterano -na.

luxuriant /lʌg'ʒʊriənt/ *a.* exuberante, frondoso.

luxurious /lʌg'ʒʊriəs/ *a.* lujoso.

luxury /'lʌkʃəri/ *n.* lujo *m.*

lying /'laiiŋ/ *a.* mentiroso.

lymph /lɪmf/ *n.* linfa *f.*

lynch /lɪntʃ/ *v.* linchar.

lyre /laiᵊr/ *n.* lira *f.*

lyric /'lɪrɪk/ *a.* lírico.

lyricism /'lɪrə,sɪzəm/ *n.* lirismo *m.*

M

macabre /mə'kɑbrə/ *a.* macabro.

macaroni /,mækə'rouni/ *n.* macarrones *m.*

machine /mə'ʃin/ *n.* máquina *f.*

machine gun ametralladora *f.*

machinery /mə'ʃinəri/ *n.* maquinaria *f.*

machinist /mə'ʃinɪst/ *n.* maquinista *m.* & *f.*, mecánico *m.*

macho /'mɑtʃou/ *a.* machista.

mackerel /'mækərəl/ *n.* escombro *m.*

macro /'mækrou/ *n.* (computer) macro *m.*

mad /mæd/ *a.* loco; furioso.

madam /'mædəm/ *n.* señora *f.*

mafia /'mɑfiə/ *n.* mafia *f.*

magazine /,mægə'zin/ *n.* revista *f.*

magic /'mædʒɪk/ *a.* **1.** mágico. —*n.* **2.** magia *f.*

magician /mə'dʒɪʃən/ *n.* mágico *m.*

magistrate /'mædʒə,streit/ *n.* magistrado -da.

magnanimous /mæg'nænəməs/ *a.* magnánimo.

magnate /'mægneit/ *n.* magnate *m.*

magnesium /mæg'niziəm/ *n.* magnesio *m.*

magnet /'mægnɪt/ *n.* imán *m.*

magnetic /mæg'nɛtɪk/ *a.* magnético.

magnificence /mæg'nɪfəsəns/ *n.* magnificencia *f.*

magnificent /mæg'nɪfəsənt/ *a.* magnífico.

magnify /'mægnə,fai/ *v.* magnificar.

magnifying glass /'mægnə,faiiŋ/ lupa *f.*

magnitude /'mægnɪ,tud/ *n.* magnitud *f.*

magpie /'mæg,pai/ *n.* hurraca *f.*

mahogany /mə'hɒgəni/ *n.* caoba *f.*

maid /meid/ *n.* criada *f.* **old m.,** solterona *f.*

maiden /'meidṇ/ *a.* soltera.

mail /meil/ *n.* **1.** correo *m.* **air m.,** correo aéreo. **by return m.,** a vuelta de correo. —*v.* **2.** echar al correo.

mailbox /'meil,bɒks/ *n.* buzón *m.*

mailman /'meil,mæn/ *n.* cartero *m.*

maim /meim/ *v.* mutilar.

main /mein/ *a.* principal.

mainframe /'mein,freim/ *n.* componente central de una computadora.

mainland /'mein,lænd/ *n.* continente *m.*

maintain /mein'tein/ *v.* mantener; sostener.

maintenance /'meintənəns/ *n.* mantenimiento; sustento *m.;* conservación *f.*

maître d' /,mei'tər di, ,meitrə, ,mɛtrə/ *n.* jefe de sala *m.* & *f.*

maize /meiz/ *n.* maíz *m.*

majestic /mə'dʒɛstɪk/ *a.* majestuoso.

majesty /'mædʒəsti/ *n.* majestad *f.*

major /'meidʒər/ *a.* **1.** mayor. —*n.* **2.** *Mil.* comandante *m.;* (study) especialidad *f.*

majority /mə'dʒɔrɪti/ *n.* mayoría *f.*

make /meik/ *n.* **1.** marca *f.* —*v.* **2.** hacer; fabricar; (earn) ganar.

maker /'meikər/ *n.* fabricante *m.*

makeshift /'meik,ʃift/ *a.* provisional.

make-up /'meik,ʌp/ *n.* cosméticos *m.pl.*

malady /'mælədi/ *n.* mal *m.*, enfermedad *f.*

malaria /mə'lɛəriə/ *n.* paludismo *m.*

male /meil/ *a.* & *n.* macho *m.*

malevolent /mə'lɛvələnt/ *a.* malévolo.

malice /'mælɪs/ *n.* malicia *f.*

malicious /mə'lɪʃəs/ *a.* malicioso.

malign /mə'lain/ v. **1.** difamar.
—a. **2.** maligno.
malignant /mə'lıgnənt/ a.
maligno.
malnutrition /,mælnu'trıʃən/ n.
desnutrición f.
malt /mɔlt/ n. malta f.
mammal /'mæməl/ n. mamífero
m.
man /mæn/ n. hombre; varón m.
v. tripular.
manage /'mænıdʒ/ v. manejar;
dirigir; administrar; arreglárselas.
m. to, lograr.
management /'mænıdʒmənt/ n.
dirección, administración f.
manager /'mænıdʒər/ n. director
-ora.
mandate /'mændeit/ n. mandato
m.
mandatory /'mændə,tɔri/ a. obligatorio.
mandolin /'mændļın/ n. man-
dolina f.
mane /mein/ n. crines f.pl.
maneuver /mə'nuvər/ n. **1.**
maniobra f. —v. **2.** maniobrar.
manganese /'mæŋgə,nis, -,niz/ n.
manganeso m.
manger /'meindʒər/ n. pesebre m.
mangle /'mæŋgəl/ n. **1.** rodillo,
exprimidor m. —v. **2.** mutilar.
manhood /'mænhʊd/ n. virilidad
f.
mania /'meiniə/ n. manía f.
maniac /'meini,æk/ a. & n. maniático -ca; maníaco -ca.
manicure /'mænı,kyʊr/ n.
manicura f.
manifest /'mænə,fɛst/ a. & n. **1.**
manifiesto m. —v. **2.** manifestar.
manifesto /,mænə'fɛstou/ n.
manifiesto m.
manifold /'mænə,fould/ a. **1.**
muchos. —n. **2.** Auto. tubo múltiple.
manipulate /mə'nıpyə,leit/ v. manipular.
mankind /'mæn'kaind/ n. humanidad f.
manly /'mænli/ a. varonil.
manner /'mænər/ n. manera f.,
modo m. **manners,** modales
m.pl.
mannerism /'mænə,rızəm/ n.
manerismo m.
mansion /'mænʃən/ n. mansión f.
mantel /'mæntļ/ n. manto de chimenea.
mantle /'mæntļ/ n. manto m.

manual /'mænyuəl/ a. & n. manual m.
manufacture /,mænyə'fæktʃər/ v.
fabricar.
manufacturer /,mænyə'fæktʃərər/
n. fabricante m.
manufacturing /,mænyə-
'fæktʃərıŋ/ n. fabricación f.
manure /mə'nʊr/ n. abono, estiércol m.
manuscript /'mænyə,skrıpt/ n.
manuscrito m.
many /'mɛni/ a. muchos. **how
m.,** cuántos. **so m.,** tantos. **too
m.,** demasiados. **as m. as,** tantos
como.
map /mæp/ n. mapa m.
maple /'meipəl/ n. arce m.
mar /mɑr/ v. estropear; desfigurar.
marble /'mɑrbəl/ n. mármol m.
march /mɑrtʃ/ n. **1.** marcha f.
—v. **2.** marchar.
March /mɑrtʃ/ n. marzo m.
mare /mɛər/ n. yegua f.
margarine /'mɑrdʒərın/ n. mar-
garina f.
margin /'mɑrdʒın/ n. margen m.
or f.
marijuana /,mærə'wɑnə/ n. marijuana f.
marine /mə'rin/ a. **1.** marino. —n.
2. soldado de marina.
mariner /'mærənər/ n. marinero
m.
marionette /,mæriə'nɛt/ n. mario-
neta f.
marital /'mærıtļ/ a. marital.
maritime /'mærı,taim/ a. marítimo.
mark /mɑrk/ n. **1.** marca f. —v. **2.**
marcar.
market /'mɑrkıt/ n. mercado m.
meat m., carnicería f. **stock m.,**
bolsa f. v. comercializar.
marmalade /'mɑrmə,leid/ n. mermelada f.
maroon /mə'run/ a. & n. color
rojo oscuro. v. dejar abandonado.
marquis /'mɑrkwıs/ n. marqués
m.
marriage /'mærıdʒ/ n. matrimonio
m.
marriage certificate partida de
matrimonio f.
married /'mærid/ a. casado. **to
get m.,** casarse.
marrow /'mærou/ n. médula f.;
substancia f.
marry /'mæri/ v. casarse con; casar.

marsh /marʃ/ *n.* pantano *m.*

marshal /'marʃəl/ *n.* mariscal *m.*

marshmallow /'marʃ‚melou/ *n.* malvarisco *m.; bombón de altea *m.*

martial /'marʃəl/ *a.* marcial. **m. law,** gobierno militar.

martyr /'martər/ *n.* mártir *m.* & *f.*

martyrdom /'martərdəm/ *n.* martirio *m.*

marvel /'marvəl/ *n.* **1.** maravilla *f.* —*v.* **2.** maravillarse.

marvelous /'marvələs/ *a.* maravilloso.

mascara /mæ'skærə/ *n.* rimel *m.*

mascot /'mæskɒt/ *n.* mascota *f.*

masculine /'mæskyəlɪn/ *a.* masculino.

mash /mæʃ/ *v.* majar. **mashed potatoes,** puré de papas *m.*

mask /mæsk/ *n.* máscara *f.*

mason /'meisən/ *n.* albañil *m.*

masquerade /‚mæskə'reid/ *n.* mascarada *f.*

mass /mæs/ *n.* masa *f.; Relig.* misa *f.* **to say m.,** cantar misa. **m. production,** producción en serie.

massacre /'mæsəkər/ *n.* **1.** carnicería, matanza *f.* —*v.* **2.** matar atrozmente, destrozar.

massage /mə'saʒ/ *n.* **1.** masaje *m.; soba *f.* —*v.* **2.** sobar.

masseur /mə'sɜr/ *n.* masajista *m.* & *f.*

massive /'mæsɪv/ *a.* macizo, sólido.

mast /mæst/ *n.* palo, árbol *m.*

master /'mæstər/ *n.* **1.** amo; maestro *m.* —*v.* **2.** domar, dominar.

masterpiece /'mæstər‚pis/ *n.* obra maestra *f.*

master's degree /'mæstərz/ maestría *f.*

mastery /'mæstəri/ *n.* maestría *f.*

mat /mæt/ *n.* **1.** estera; palleta *f.* —*v.* **2.** enredar.

match /mætʃ/ *n.* **1.** igual *m;* fósforo *m.; (sport) partida, contienda *f.; (marriage) noviazgo; casamiento. —*v.* **2.** ser igual a; igualar.

matchbox /'mætʃ‚bɒks/ caja de cerillas, caja de fósforos *f.*

mate /meit/ *n.* **1.** consorte *m.* & *f.; compañero -ra. —*v.* **2.** igualar; casar.

material /mə'tɪəriəl/ *a.* & *n.* material *m.* **raw materials,** materias primas.

materialism /mə'tɪəriə‚lɪzəm/ *n.* materialismo *m.*

materialize /mə'tɪəriə‚laiz/ *v.* materializar.

maternal /mə'tɜrnļ/ *a.* materno.

maternity /mə'tɜrnɪti/ *n.* maternidad *f.*

maternity hospital maternidad *f.*

mathematical /‚mæθə'mætɪkəl/ *a.* matemático.

mathematics /‚mæθə'mætɪks/ *n.* matemáticas *f.pl.*

matinee /‚mætn'ei/ *n.* matiné *f.*

matrimony /'mætrə‚mouni/ *n.* matrimonio *m.*

matron /'meitrən/ *n.* matrona; directora *f.*

matter /'mætər/ *n.* **1.** materia *f.;* asunto *m.* **what's the m.?,** ¿qué pasa? —*v.* **2.** importar.

mattress /'mætrɪs/ *n.* colchón *m.*

mature /mə'tʃʊr/ *a.* **1.** maduro. —*v.* **2.** madurar.

maturity /mə'tʃʊrɪti/ *n.* madurez *f.*

maudlin /'mɔdlɪn/ *a.* sentimental en exceso; sensiblero.

maul /mɔl/ *v.* aporrear.

maxim /'mæksɪm/ *n.* máxima *f.*

maximum /'mæksəməm/ *a.* & *n.* máximo.

may /mei/ *v.* poder.

May /mei/ *n.* mayo *m.*

maybe /'meibi/ *adv.* quizá, quizás, tal vez.

mayonnaise /‚meiə'neiz/ *n.* mayonesa *f.*

mayor /'meiər/ *n.* alcalde *m.* alcaldesa *f.*

maze /meiz/ *n.* laberinto *m.*

me /mi/ *pron.* mí; me. **with me,** conmigo.

meadow /'mɛdou/ *n.* prado *m.;* vega *f.*

meager /'migər/ *a.* magro; pobre.

meal /mil/ *n.* comida; (flour) harina *f.*

mean /min/ *a.* **1.** bajo; malo. —*n.* **2.** medio (see also **means**). —*v.* **3.** significar; querer decir.

meander /mi'ændər/ *v.* (river) serpentear; (person) deambular.

meaning /'minɪŋ/ *n.* sentido, significado *m.*

meaningless /'minɪŋlɪs/ *a.* sin sentido.

means /minz/ *n.pl.* medios, recursos *m.* **by all m.,** sin falta. **by no**

m., de ningún modo. **by m. of,** por medio de.

meanwhile /'min,wail/ *adv.* mientras tanto.

measles /'mizəlz/ *n.* sarampión *m.*

measure /'mɛʒər/ *n.* **1.** medida *f.;* (music) compás *m.* —*v.* **2.** medir.

measurement /'mɛʒərmənt/ *n.* medida, dimensión *f.*

meat /mit/ *n.* carne *f.*

mechanic /mə'kænɪk/ *n.* mecánico *m.* & *f.*

mechanical /mə'kænɪkəl/ *a.* mecánico.

mechanism /'mɛkə,nɪzəm/ *n.* mecanismo *m.*

mechanize /'mɛkə,naiz/ *v.* mecanizar.

medal /'mɛdl/ *n.* medalla *f.*

meddle /'mɛdl/ *v.* meterse, entremeterse.

mediate /'midi,eit/ *v.* mediar.

medical /'mɛdɪkəl/ *a.* médico.

medicine /'mɛdəsɪn/ *n.* medicina *f.*

medicine chest botiquín *m.*

medieval /,midi'ivəl/ *a.* medieval.

mediocre /,midi'oukər/ *a.* mediocre.

mediocrity /,midi'ɒkrɪti/ *n.* mediocridad *f.*

meditate /'mɛdɪ,teit/ *v.* meditar.

meditation /,mɛdɪ'teiʃən/ *n.* meditación *f.*

Mediterranean /,mɛdɪtə'reiniən/ *n.* Mediterráneo *m.*

medium /'midiəm/ *a.* **1.** mediano, medio. —*n.* **2.** medio *m.*

medley /'mɛdli/ *n.* mezcla *f.*, ensalada *f.*

meek /mik/ *a.* manso; humilde.

meekness /'miknɪs/ *n.* modestia; humildad *f.*

meet /mit/ *a.* **1.** apropiado. —*n.* **2.** concurso *m.* —*v.* **3.** encontrar; reunirse; conocer.

meeting /'mitɪŋ/ *n.* reunión *f.;* mitin *m.*

megahertz /'mɛgə,hɜrts/ *n.* megahercio *m.*

megaphone /'mɛgə,foun/ *n.* megáfono *m.*

melancholy /'mɛlən,kɒli/ *a.* **1.** melancólico. —*n.* **2.** melancolía *f.*

mellow /'mɛlou/ *a.* suave; blando; maduro.

melodious /mə'loudiəs/ *a.* melodioso.

melodrama /'mɛlə,drɑmə/ *n.* melodrama *m.*

melody /'mɛlədi/ *n.* melodía *f.*

melon /'mɛlən/ *n.* melón *m.*

melt /mɛlt/ *v.* derretir.

meltdown /'mɛlt,daun/ *n.* fundición resultante de un accidente en un reactor nuclear.

member /'mɛmbər/ *n.* socio -ia; miembro *m.* **m. of the crew,** tripulante *m.* & *f.*

membership /'mɛmbər,ʃɪp/ *n.* número de miembros.

membrane /'mɛmbrein/ *n.* membrana *f.*

memento /mə'mɛntou/ *n.* recuerdo *m.*

memoir /'mɛmwɑr/ *n.* memoria *f.*

memorable /'mɛmərəbəl/ *a.* memorable.

memorandum /,mɛmə'rændəm/ *n.* memorándum, volante *m.*

memorial /mə'mɔriəl/ *a.* **1.** conmemorativo. —*n.* **2.** memorial *m.*

memorize /'mɛmə,raiz/ *v.* aprender de memoria.

memory /'mɛməri/ *n.* memoria *f.;* recuerdo *m.*

menace /'mɛnɪs/ *n.* **1.** amenaza *f.* —*v.* **2.** amenazar.

mend /mɛnd/ *v.* reparar, remendar.

menial /'miniəl/ *a.* **1.** servil. —*n.* **2.** sirviente -ta.

meningitis /,mɛnɪn'dʒaitɪs/ *n.* meningitis. *f.*

menopause /'mɛnə,pɔz/ *n.* menopausia *f.*

menstruation /,mɛnstru'eiʃən/ *n.* menstruación *f.*

menswear /'mɛnz,wɛər/ *n.* ropa de caballeros *f.*

mental /'mɛntl/ *a.* mental.

mental disorder trastorno mental *m.*

mentality /mɛn'tælɪti/ *n.* mentalidad *f.*

menthol /'mɛnθɔl/ *n.* mentol *m.*

mention /'mɛnʃən/ *n.* **1.** mención *f.* —*v.* **2.** mencionar.

menu /'mɛnyu/ *n.* menú *m.*, lista *f.*

mercantile /'mɜrkən,til/ *a.* mercantil.

mercenary /'mɜrsə,nɛri/ *a.* & *n.* mercenario -ria.

merchandise /'mɜrtʃən,daiz/ *n.* mercancía *f.*

merchant /'mɜrtʃənt/ *a.* **1.** mercante. —*n.* **2.** comerciante *m.*

merciful /'mɜrsɪfəl/ *a.* misericordioso, compasivo.

merciless /'mɜrsɪlɪs/ *a.* cruel, inhumano.

mercury /'mɜrkyəri/ *n.* mercurio *m.*

mercy /'mɜrsi/ *n.* misericordia; merced *f.*

mere /mɪər/ *a.* mero, puro.

merely /'mɪərli/ *adv.* solamente; simplemente.

merge /mɜrdʒ/ *v.* unir, combinar.

merger /'mɜrdʒər/ *n.* consolidación, fusión *f.*

meringue /mə'ræŋ/ *n.* merengue *m.*

merit /'mɛrɪt/ *n.* **1.** mérito *m.* —*v.* **2.** merecer.

meritorious /ˌmɛrɪ'tɔriəs/ *a.* meritorio.

mermaid /'mɜrˌmeid/ *n.* sirena *f.*

merriment /'mɛrɪmənt/ *n.* regocijo *m.*

merry /'mɛri/ *a.* alegre, festivo.

merry-go-round /'mɛri gou ˌraund/ *n.* caballitos *m. pl.*; tíovivo *m.*

mesh /mɛʃ/ *n.* malla *f.*

mess /mɛs/ *n.* **1.** lío *m.*; confusión *f.*; *Mil.* salón comedor; rancho *m.* —*v.* **2. m. up,** ensuciar; enredar.

message /'mɛsɪdʒ/ *n.* mensaje, recado *m.*

messenger /'mɛsəndʒər/ *n.* mensajero -ra.

messy /'mɛsi/ *a.* confuso; desarreglado.

metabolism /mə'tæbəˌlɪzəm/ *n.* metabolismo *m.*

metal /'mɛtl̩/ *n.* metal *m.*

metallic /mə'tælɪk/ *a.* metálico.

metaphysics /ˌmɛtə'fɪzɪks/ *n.* metafísica *f.*

meteor /'mitiər/ *n.* meteoro *m.*

meteorology /ˌmitiə'rɒlədʒi/ *n.* meteorología *f.*

meter /'mitər/ *n.* contador, medidor; (measure) metro *m.*

method /'mɛθəd/ *n.* método *m.*

meticulous /mə'tɪkyələs/ *a.* meticuloso.

metric /'mɛtrɪk/ *a.* métrico.

metropolis /mɪ'trɒpəlɪs/ *n.* metrópoli *f.*

metropolitan /ˌmɛtrə'pɒlɪtn̩/ *a.* metropolitano.

Mexican /'mɛksɪkən/ *a. & n.* mexicano -na.

Mexico /'mɛksɪˌkou/ *n.* México *m.*

mezzanine /'mɛzəˌnin/ *n.* entresuelo *m.*

microbe /'maikroub/ *n.* microbio *m.*

microchip /'maikrouˌtʃɪp/ *n.* microchip *m.*

microfiche /'maikrəˌfiʃ/ *n.* microficha *f.*

microfilm /'maikrəˌfɪlm/ *n.* microfilm *m.*

microform /'maikrəˌfɔrm/ *n.* microforma *f.*

microphone /'maikrəˌfoun/ *n.* micrófono *m.*

microscope /'maikrəˌskoup/ *n.* microscopio *m.*

microscopic /ˌmaikrə'skɒpɪk/ *a.* microscópico.

mid /mɪd/ *a.* medio.

middle /'mɪdl̩/ *a. & n.* medio *m.* **in the m. of,** en medio de, a mediados de.

middle-aged /eidʒd/ *a.* de edad madura.

Middle East Medio Oriente *m.*

middle finger dedo corazón *m.*

midget /'mɪdʒɪt/ *n.* enano -na.

midnight /'mɪdˌnait/ *n.* medianoche *f.*

midwife /'mɪdˌwaif/ *n.* comadrona, partera *f.*

might /mait/ *n.* poder *m.*, fuerza *f.*

mighty /'maiti/ *a.* poderoso.

migraine /'maigrein/ *n.* migraña *f.*; jaqueca *f.*

migrate /'maigreit/ *v.* emigrar.

migration /mai'greiʃən/ *n.* emigración *f.*

migratory /'maigrəˌtɔri/ *a.* migratorio.

mild /maild/ *a.* moderado, suave; templado.

mildew /'mɪlˌdu/ *n.* añublo *m.*, moho *m.*

mile /mail/ *n.* milla *f.*

mileage /'mailɪdʒ/ *n.* kilometraje *m.*

militant /'mɪlɪtənt/ *a.* militante.

militarism /'mɪlɪtəˌrɪzəm/ *n.* militarismo *m.*

military /'mɪlɪˌtɛri/ *a.* militar.

militia /mɪ'lɪʃə/ *n.* milicia *f.*

milk /mɪlk/ *n.* **1.** leche *f.* —*v.* **2.** ordeñar.

milk chocolate chocolate con leche *m.*

milkman /'mɪlkˌmæn/ *n.* lechero *m.*

milk shake batido *m.*

milky /'mɪlki/ *a.* lácteo; lechoso.
mill /mɪl/ *n.* **1.** molino *m.;* fábrica *f.* —*v.* **2.** moler.
miller /'mɪlər/ *n.* molinero -ra.
millimeter /'mɪlə,mitər/ *n.* milímetro *m.*
milliner /'mɪlənər/ *n.* sombrerero -ra.
millinery /'mɪlə,nɛri/ *n.* sombrerería *f.*
million /'mɪlyən/ *n.* millón *m.*
millionaire /,mɪlyə'nɛər/ *n.* millonario -ria.
mimic /'mɪmɪk/ *n.* **1.** mimo -ma. —*v.* **2.** imitar.
mind /maind/ *n.* **1.** mente; opinión *f.* —*v.* **2.** obedecer. **never m.,** no se ocupe.
mindful /'maindfəl/ *a.* atento.
mine /main/ *pron.* **1.** mío. —*n.* **2.** mina *f.* —*v.* **3.** minar.
miner /'mainər/ *n.* minero *m.*
mineral /'mɪnərəl/ *a.* & *n.* mineral *m.*
mineral water agua mineral *f.*
mine sweeper /'main,swipər/ dragaminas *f.*
mingle /'mɪŋgəl/ *v.* mezclar.
miniature /'mɪniətʃər/ *n.* miniatura *f.*
miniaturize /'mɪniətʃə,raiz/ *v.* miniaturizar.
minibus /'mɪni,bʌs/ *n.* microbús *m.*
minicab /'mɪni,kæb/ *n.* microtaxi *m.*
minimize /'mɪnə,maiz/ *v.* menospreciar.
minimum /'mɪnəməm/ *a.* & *n.* mínimo *m.*
mining /'mainɪŋ/ *n.* minería *f.*
minister /'mɪnəstər/ *n.* **1.** ministro -tra; *Relig.* pastor *m.* —*v.* **2.** ministrar.
ministry /'mɪnəstri/ *n.* ministerio *m.*
mink /mɪŋk/ *n.* visón *m.;* (fur) piel de visón *m.*
minor /'mainər/ *a.* **1.** menor. —*n.* **2.** menor de edad.
minority /mɪ'nɔriti/ *n.* minoría *f.*
minstrel /'mɪnstrəl/ *n.* juglar *m.*
mint /mɪnt/ *n.* **1.** menta *f.;* casa de moneda. —*v.* **2.** acuñar.
minus /'mainəs/ *prep.* menos.
minute /*a.* mai'nut; *n.* 'mɪnɪt/ *a.* **1.** minucioso. —*n.* **2.** minuto, momento *m.*
miracle /'mɪrəkəl/ *n.* milagro *m.*

miraculous /mɪ'rækyələs/ *a.* milagroso.
mirage /mɪ'rɑʒ/ *n.* espejismo *m.*
mire /maiᵊr/ *n.* lodo *m.*
mirror /'mɪrər/ *n.* espejo *m.*
mirth /mɜrθ/ *n.* alegría; risa *f.*
misbehave /,mɪsbɪ'heiv/ *v.* portarse mal.
miscellaneous /,mɪsə'leiniəs/ *a.* misceláneo.
mischief /'mɪstʃɪf/ *n.* travesura, diablura *f.*
mischievous /'mɪstʃəvəs/ *a.* travieso, dañino.
miser /'maizər/ *n.* avaro -ra.
miserable /'mɪzərəbəl/ *a.* miserable; infeliz.
miserly /'maizərli/ *a.* avariento, tacaño.
misfortune /mɪs'fɔrtʃən/ *n.* desgracia *f.,* infortunio, revés *m.*
misgiving /mɪs'gɪvɪŋ/ *n.* recelo *m.,* desconfianza *f.*
mishap /'mɪshæp/ *n.* desgracia *f.,* contratiempo *m.*
mislay /mɪs'lei/ *v.* perder.
mislead /mɪs'lid/ *v.* extraviar, despistar; pervertir.
misplaced /mɪs'pleist/ *a.* extraviado.
mispronounce /,mɪsprə'nouns/ *v.* pronunciar mal.
miss /mɪs/ *n.* **1.** señorita *f.* —*v.* **2.** perder; echar de menos, extrañar. **be missing,** faltar.
missile /'mɪsəl/ *n.* proyectil *m.*
mission /'mɪʃən/ *n.* misión *f.*
missionary /'mɪʃə,nɛri/ *n.* misionero -ra.
mist /mɪst/ *n.* niebla, bruma *f.*
mistake /mɪ'steik/ *n.* equivocación *f.;* error *m.* **to make a m.,** equivocarse.
mistaken /mɪ'steikən/ *a.* equivocado.
mister /'mɪstər/ *n.* señor *m.*
mistletoe /'mɪsəl,tou/ *n.* muérdago *m.*
mistreat /mɪs'trit/ *v.* maltratar.
mistress /'mɪstrɪs/ *n.* ama; señora; concubina *f.*
mistrust /mɪs'trʌst/ *v.* desconfiar; sospechar.
misty /'mɪsti/ *a.* nebuloso, brumoso.
misunderstand /,mɪsʌndər'stænd/ *v.* entender mal.
misuse /mɪs'yuz/ *v.* maltratar; abusar.
mite /mait/ *n.* pizca *f.,* blanca *f.*

mitten /'mɪtn̩/ n. mitón, confortante m.

mix /mɪks/ v. mezclar. **m. up,** confundir.

mixer /'mɪksər/ (for food), n. batidora f.

mixture /'mɪkstʃər/ n. mezcla, mixtura f.

mix-up /'mɪks,ʌp/ n. confusión f.

moan /moun/ n. **1.** quejido, gemido m. —v. **2.** gemir.

mob /mɒb/ n. muchedumbre f.; gentío m.

mobilization /,moubələ'zeiʃən/ n. movilización f.

mobilize /'moubə,laiz/ v. movilizar.

mock /mɒk/ v. burlar.

mockery /'mɒkəri/ n. burla f.

mod /mɒd/ a. a la última; en boga.

mode /moud/ n. modo m.

model /'mɒdḷ/ n. **1.** modelo m. —v. **2.** modelar.

modem /'moudəm/ n. módem m.

moderate /a 'mɒdərɪt; v -ə,reit/ a. **1.** moderado. —v. **2.** moderar.

moderation /,mɒdə'reiʃən/ n. moderación; sobriedad f.

modern /'mɒdərn/ a. moderno.

modernize /'mɒdər,naiz/ v. modernizar.

modest /'mɒdɪst/ a. modesto.

modesty /'mɒdəsti/ n. modestia f.

modify /'mɒdə,fai/ v. modificar.

modulate /'mɒdʒə,leit/ v. modular.

moist /mɔist/ a. húmedo.

moisten /'mɔisən/ v. humedecer.

moisture /'mɔistʃər/ n. humedad f.

moisturize /'mɔistʃə,raiz/ v. hidratar.

molar /'moulər/ n. molar m.

molasses /mə'læsɪz/ n. melaza f.

mold /mould/ n. **1.** molde; moho m. —v. **2.** moldar, formar; enmohecerse.

moldy /'mouldi/ a. mohoso.

mole /'moulei/ n. lunar m.; (animal) topo m.

molecule /'mɒlɪ,kyul/ n. molécula f.

molest /mə'lɛst/ v. molestar.

mollify /'mɒlə,fai/ v. molificar.

moment /'moumənt/ n. momento m.

momentary /'moumən,tɛri/ a. momentáneo.

momentous /mou'mɛntəs/ a. importante.

monarch /'mɒnərk/ n. monarca m. & f.

monarchy /'mɒnərki/ n. monarquía f.

monastery /'mɒnə,stɛri/ n. monasterio m.

Monday /'mʌndei/ n. lunes m.

monetary /'mɒnɪ,tɛri/ a. monetario.

money /'mʌni/ n. dinero m. **m. order,** giro postal.

mongrel /'mʌŋgrəl/ n. **1.** mestizo m. —a. **2.** mestizo, cruzado.

monitor /'mɒnɪtər/ n. amonestador m.; (computer) consola f., pantalla f.

monk /mʌŋk/ n. monje m.

monkey /'mʌŋki/ n. mono -na.

monocle /'mɒnəkəl/ n. monóculo m.

monologue /'mɒnə,lɔg/ n. monólogo m.

monopolize /mə'nɒpə,laiz/ v. monopolizar.

monopoly /mə'nɒpəli/ n. monopolio m.

monosyllable /'mɒnə,sɪləbəl/ n. monosílabo m.

monotone /'mɒnə,toun/ n. monotonía f.

monotonous /mə'nɒtn̩əs/ a. monótono.

monotony /mə'nɒtn̩i/ n. monotonía f.

monsoon /mɒn'sun/ n. monzón m.

monster /'mɒnstər/ n. monstruo m.

monstrosity /mɒn'strɒsɪti/ n. monstruosidad f.

monstrous /'mɒnstrəs/ a. monstruoso.

month /mʌnθ/ n. mes m.

monthly /'mʌnθli/ a. mensual.

monument /'mɒnyəmənt/ n. monumento m.

monumental /,mɒnyə'mɛntḷ/ a. monumental.

mood /mud/ n. humor m.; Gram. modo m.

moody /'mudi/ a. caprichoso, taciturno.

moon /mun/ n. luna f.

moonlight /'mun,lait/ n. luz de la luna.

moonlighting /'mun,laitɪŋ/ n. pluriempleo m.

moor /mʊr/ n. **1.** párano m. —v. **2.** anclar.

Moor /mʊr/ n. moro -ra.

mop /mɒp/ n. **1.** fregasuelos m., fregona f., (S.A.) trapeador m. —v. **2.** fregar, (S.A.) trapear.

moped /'mou,pɛd/ n. (vehicle) velomotor m.

moral /'mɔrəl/ a. **1.** moral. —n. **2.** moraleja f. **morals,** moralidad f.

morale /mə'ræl/ n. espíritu m.

moralist /'mɔrəlɪst/ n. moralista m. & f.

morality /mə'ræliti/ n. moralidad, ética f.

morbid /'mɔrbɪd/ a. mórbido.

more /mɔr/ a. & adv. más. **m. and m.,** cada vez más.

moreover /mɔr'ouvər/ adv. además.

morgue /mɔrg/ n. necrocomio m.

morning /'mɔrnɪŋ/ n. mañana f. **good m.,** buenos días.

Morocco /mə'rɒkou/ n. Marruecos m.

morose /mə'rous/ a. malhumorado.

morphine /'mɔrfin/ n. morfina f.

morsel /'mɔrsəl/ n. bocado m.

mortal /'mɔrtl̩/ a. & n. mortal m. & f.

mortality /mɔr'tæliti/ n. mortalidad f.

mortar /'mɔrtər/ n. mortero m.

mortgage /'mɔrgɪdʒ/ n. **1.** hipoteca f. —v. **2.** hipotecar.

mortify /'mɔrtə,fai/ v. mortificar.

mosaic /mou'zeiik/ n. & a. mosaico m.

mosque /mɒsk/ n. mezquita f.

mosquito /mə'skitou/ n. mosquito m.

moss /mɔs/ n. musgo m.

most /moust/ a. **1.** más. —adv. **2.** más; sumamente. —pron. **3. m. of,** la mayor parte de.

mostly /'moustli/ adv. principalmente; en su mayor parte.

motel /mou'tɛl/ n. motel m.

moth /mɔθ/ n. polilla f.

mother /'mʌðər/ n. madre f.

mother-in-law /'mʌðər ɪn ˌlɔ/ n. suegra f.

motif /mou'tif/ n. tema m.

motion /'mouʃən/ n. **1.** moción f.; movimiento m. —v. **2.** hacer señas.

motionless /'mouʃənlɪs/ a. inmóvil.

motion picture película f.

motivate /'moutə,veit/ v. motivar.

motive /'moutɪv/ n. motivo m.

motor /'moutər/ n. motor m.

motorboat /'moutər,bout/ n. lancha motora f., autobote, motorbote m., gasolinera f.

motorcycle /'moutər,saikəl/ n. motocicleta f.

motorcyclist /'moutər,saiklɪst/ n. motociclista m. & f.

motorist /'moutərɪst/ n. motorista m. & f.

motto /'mɒtou/ n. lema m.

mound /maund/ n. terrón; montón m.

mount /maunt/ n. **1.** monte m.; (horse) montura f. —v. **2.** montar; subir.

mountain /'mauntn̩/ n. montaña f.

mountaineer /ˌmauntn̩'ɪər/ n. montañés m.

mountainous /'mauntn̩əs/ a. montañoso.

mourn /mɔrn/ v. lamentar, llorar; llevar luto.

mournful /'mɔrnfəl/ a. triste.

mourning /'mɔrnɪŋ/ n. luto; lamento m.

mouse /maus/ n. ratón, ratoncito m.

mouth /mauθ/ n. boca f.; (of river) desembocadura f.

mouthwash /'mauθ,wɔʃ/ n. enjuague bucal m.

movable /'muvəbəl/ a. movible, movedizo.

move /muv/ n. **1.** movimiento m.; mudanza f. —v. **2.** mover; mudarse; emocionar, conmover. **m. away,** quitar; alejarse; mudarse.

movement /'muvmənt/ n. movimiento m.

movie /'muvi/ n. película f. **m. theater, movies,** cine m.

moving /'muvɪŋ/ a. conmovedor; persuasivo.

mow /mou/ v. guadañar, segar.

Mr. /'mɪstər/ title. Señor (Sr.).

Mrs. /'mɪsəz/ title. Señora (Sra.).

much /mʌtʃ/ a. & adv. mucho. **how m.,** cuánto. **so m.,** tanto. **too m.,** demasiado. **as m. as,** tanto como.

mucilage /'myusəlɪdʒ/ n. mucílago m.

mucous /'myukəs/ a. mucoso.

mucous membrane n. membrana mucosa f.

mud /mʌd/ n. fango, lodo m.

muddy /'mʌdi/ *a.* **1.** lodoso; turbio. —*v.* **2.** ensuciar; enturbiar.

muff /mʌf/ *n.* manguito *m.*

muffin /'mʌfɪn/ *n.* panecillo *m.*

mug /mʌg/ *n.* cubilete *m.*

mugger /'mʌgər/ *n.* asaltante *m.* & *f.*

mulatto /mə'lætou/ *n.* mulato *m.*

mule /myul/ *n.* mula *f.*

mullah /'mʌlə/ *n.* mullah *m.*

multicultural /ˌmʌlti'kʌltʃərəl, ˌmʌltai-/ *a.* multicultural.

multinational /ˌmʌlti'næʃənḷ, ˌmʌltai-/ *a.* multinacional.

multiple /'mʌltəpəl/ *a.* múltiple.

multiplication /ˌmʌltəplɪ'keiʃən/ *n.* multiplicación *f.*

multiplicity /ˌmʌltə'plɪsɪti/ *n.* multiplicidad *f.*

multiply /'mʌltəpli/ *v.* multiplicar.

multitasking /ˌmʌlti'tæskɪŋ, ˌmʌltai-/ *n.* multitarea *f.*

multitude /'mʌltɪˌtud/ *n.* multitud *f.*

mummy /'mʌmi/ *n.* momia *f.*

mumps /mʌmps/ *n.* paperas *f.pl.*

municipal /myu'nɪsəpəl/ *a.* municipal.

munificent /myu'nɪfəsənt/ *a.* munífico.

munitions /myu'nɪʃənz/ *n.* municiones *m.pl.*

mural /'myʊrəl/ *a.* & *n.* mural *m.*

murder /'mɜrdər/ *n.* **1.** asesinato; homicidio *m.* —*v.* **2.** asesinar.

murderer /'mɜrdərər/ *n.* asesino -na.

murmur /'mɜrmər/ *n.* **1.** murmullo *m.* —*v.* **2.** murmurar.

muscle /'mʌsəl/ *n.* músculo *m.*

muscular /'mʌskyələr/ *a.* muscular.

muse /myuz/ *n.* **1.** musa *f.* —*v.* **2.** meditar.

museum /myu'ziəm/ *n.* museo *m.*

mushroom /'mʌʃrum/ *n.* seta *f.*, hongo *m.*

music /'myuzɪk/ *n.* música *f.*

musical /'myuzɪkəl/ *a.* musical; melodioso.

musician /myu'zɪʃən/ *n.* músico -ca.

Muslim /'mʌzlɪm/ *a.* & *n.* musulmano.

muslin /'mʌzlɪn/ *n.* muselina *f.*; percal *m.*

mussel /'mʌsəl/ *n.* mejillón *m.*

must /mʌst/ *v.* deber; tener que.

mustache /'mʌstæʃ/ *n.* bigotes *m.pl.*

mustard /'mʌstərd/ *n.* mostaza *f.*

muster /'mʌstər/ *n.* **1.** *Mil.* revista *f.* —*v.* **2.** reunir, juntar.

mute /myut/ *a.* & *n.* mudo -da.

mutilate /'myutḷˌeit/ *v.* mutilar.

mutiny /'myutṇi/ *n.* **1.** motín *m.* —*v.* **2.** amotinarse.

mutt /mʌt/ *n.* *Colloq.* chucho *m.*

mutter /'mʌtər/ *v.* refunfuñar, gruñir.

mutton /'mʌtṇ/ *n.* carnero *m.*

mutual /'myutʃuəl/ *a.* mutuo.

muzzle /'mʌzəl/ *n.* **1.** hocico *m.*; bozal *m.* —*v.* **2.** embozar.

my /mai/ *a.* mi.

myriad /'mɪriəd/ *n.* miríada *f.*

myrtle /'mɜrtḷ/ *n.* mirto *m.*

myself /mai'self/ *pron.* mí, mí mismo; me. **I m.,** yo mismo.

mysterious /mɪ'stɪriəs/ *a.* misterioso.

mystery /'mɪstəri/ *n.* misterio *m.*

mystic /'mɪstɪk/ *a.* místico.

mystify /'mɪstəˌfai/ *v.* confundir.

myth /mɪθ/ *n.* mito *m.*

mythical /'mɪθɪkəl/ *a.* mítico.

mythology /mɪ'θɒlədʒi/ *n.* mitología *f.*

N

nag /næg/ *n.* **1.** jaca *f.* —*v.* **2.** regañar; sermonear.

nail /neil/ *n.* **1.** clavo *m.*; (finger) uña *f.* **n. polish,** esmalte para las uñas. —*v.* **2.** clavar.

naïve /nɑ'iv/ *a.* ingenuo.

naked /'neikɪd/ *a.* desnudo.

name /neim/ *n.* **1.** nombre *m.*; reputación *f.* —*v.* **2.** nombrar, mencionar.

namely /'neimli/ *adv.* a saber; es decir.

namesake /'neimˌseik/ *n.* tocayo *m.*

nanny /'næni/ *n.* niñera *f.*

nap /næp/ *n.* siesta *f.* **to take a n.,** echar una siesta.

naphtha /'næfθə, 'næp-/ *n.* nafta *f.*

napkin /'næpkɪn/ *n.* servilleta *f.*

narcissus /nɑr'sɪsəs/ *n.* narciso *m.*

narcotic /nɑr'kɒtɪk/ *a.* & *n.* narcótico *m.*

narrate /'næreit/ *v.* narrar.

narrative /'nærətɪv/ *a.* **1.** narrativo. —*n.* **2.** cuento, relato *m.*

narrow /'nærou/ *a.* estrecho, angosto. **n.-minded**, intolerante.

nasal /'neizəl/ *a.* nasal.

nasty /'næsti/ *a.* desagradable.

nation /'neiʃən/ *n.* nación *f.*

national /'næʃənļ/ *a.* nacional.

nationalism /'næʃənļˌɪzəm/ *n.* nacionalismo *m.*

nationality /ˌnæʃə'nælɪti/ *n.* nacionalidad *f.*

nationalization /ˌnæʃənļə'zeiʃən/ *n.* nacionalización *f.*

nationalize /'næʃənļˌaiz, 'næʃnəˌlaiz/ *v.* nacionalizar.

native /'neitɪv/ *a.* **1.** nativo. —*n.* **2.** natural; indígena *m.* & *f.*

nativity /nə'tɪvɪti/ *n.* natividad *f.*

natural /'nætʃərəl/ *a.* natural.

naturalist /'nætʃərəlɪst/ *n.* naturalista *m.* & *f.*

naturalize /'nætʃərəˌlaiz/ *v.* naturalizar.

naturalness /ˌnætʃərəlnɪs/ *n.* naturalidad *f.*

nature /'neitʃər/ *n.* naturaleza *f.;* índole *f.;* humor *m.*

naughty /'nɔti/ *a.* travieso, desobediente.

nausea /'nɔziə, -ʒə/ *n.* náusea *f.*

nauseous /'nɔʃəs/ *a.* nauseoso.

nautical /'nɔtɪkəl/ *a.* náutico.

naval /'neivəl/ *a.* naval.

nave /neiv/ *n.* nave *f.*

navel /'neivəl/ *n.* ombligo *m.*

navigable /'nævɪgəbəl/ *a.* navegable.

navigate /'nævɪˌgeit/ *v.* navegar.

navigation /ˌnævɪ'geiʃən/ *n.* navegación *f.*

navigator /'nævɪˌgeitər/ *n.* navegante *m.* & *f.*

navy /'neivi/ *n.* marina *f.*

navy blue azul marino *m.*

near /nɪər/ *a.* **1.** cercano, próximo. —*adv.* **2.** cerca. —*prep.* **3.** cerca de.

nearby /'nɪər'bai/ *a.* **1.** cercano. —*adv.* **2.** cerca.

nearly /'nɪərli/ *adv.* casi.

nearsighted /'nɪərˌsaitɪd/ *a.* corto de vista.

neat /nit/ *a.* aseado; ordenado.

neatness /'nitnɪs/ *n.* aseo *m.*

nebulous /'nɛbyələs/ *a.* nebuloso.

necessary /'nɛsəˌseri/ *a.* necesario.

necessity /nə'sɛsɪti/ *n.* necesidad *f.*

neck /nɛk/ *n.* cuello *m.*

necklace /'nɛklɪs/ *n.* collar *m.*

necktie /'nɛkˌtai/ *n.* corbata *f.*

nectar /'nɛktər/ *n.* néctar *m.*

nectarine /ˌnɛktə'rin/ *n.* nectarina *f.*

need /nid/ *n.* **1.** necesidad; (poverty) pobreza *f.* —*v.* **2.** necesitar.

needle /'nidļ/ *n.* aguja *f.*

needless /'nidlɪs/ *a.* innecesario, inútil.

needy /'nidi/ *a.* indigente, necesitado, pobre.

nefarious /nɪ'fɛəriəs/ *a.* nefario.

negative /'nɛgətɪv/ *a.* negativo. *n.* negativa *f.*

neglect /nɪ'glɛkt/ *n.* **1.** negligencia *f.;* descuido *m.* —*v.* **2.** descuidar.

negligee /ˌnɛglɪ'ʒei/ *n.* negligé *m.,* bata de casa *f.*

negligent /'nɛglɪdʒənt/ *a.* negligente, descuidado.

negligible /'nɛglɪdʒəbəl/ *a.* insignificante.

negotiate /nɪ'gouʃiˌeit/ *v.* negociar.

negotiation /nɪˌgouʃi'eiʃən/ *n.* negociación *f.*

Negro /'nigrou/ *n.* negro -ra.

neighbor /'neibər/ *n.* vecino -na.

neighborhood /'neibərˌhʊd/ *n.* vecindad *f.*

neither /'niðər, 'nai-/ *a.* & *pron.* **1.** ninguno de los dos. —*adv.* **2.** tampoco. —*conj.* **3. neither... nor**, ni... ni.

neon /'niɒn/ *n.* neón *m.* **n. light,** tubo neón *m.*

nephew /'nɛfyu/ *n.* sobrino *m.*

nerve /nɜrv/ *n.* nervio *m.; Colloq.* audacia *f.*

nervous /'nɜrvəs/ *a.* nervioso.

nervous breakdown /'breikˌdaun/ crisis nerviosa *f.*

nest /nɛst/ *n.* nido *m.*

net /nɛt/ *a.* **1.** neto. —*n.* **2.** red *f.* **hair n.,** albanega, redecilla *f. v.* redar; *Com.* ganar.

netiquette /'nɛtɪkɪt/ *n.* etiqueta de la red *f.*

netting /'nɛtɪŋ/ *n.* red *m.;* obra de malla *f.*

network /'nɛtˌwɜrk/ *n.* (radio) red radiodifusora.

neuralgia /nʊ'rældʒə/ *n.* neuralgia *f.*

neurology /nʊ'rɒlədʒi/ *n.* neurología *f.*

neurotic /nʊ'rɒtɪk/ *a.* neurótico.

neutral /'nutrəl/ *a.* neutral.
neutrality /nu'træliti/ *n.* neutralidad *f.*
neutron /'nutrɒn/ *n.* neutrón *m.*
neutron bomb bomba de neutrones *f.*
never /'nɛvər/ *adv.* nunca, jamás; **n. mind,** no importa.
nevertheless /ˌnɛvərðə'lɛs/ *adv.* no obstante, sin embargo.
new /nu/ *a.* nuevo.
newbie /'nubi/ *n. Colloq.* novato -ta, inexperto -ta.
news /nuz/ *n.* noticias *f.pl.*
newsboy /'nuzˌbɔi/ *n.* vendedor -ra de periódicos.
news bulletin boletín informativo *m.*
news flash *n.* noticia de última hora *f.*
newsgroup /'nuzˌgrup/ *n.* grupo de discusion *m.*
newsletter /'nuzˌlɛtər/ *n.* hoja informativa *f.*
newspaper /'nuzˌpeipər/ *n.* periódico *m.*
New Testament Nuevo Testamento *m.*
new year *n.* año nuevo *m.*
next /nɛkst/ *a.* **1.** próximo; siguiente; contiguo. —*adv.* **2.** luego, después. **n. door,** al lado. **n. to,** al lado de.
next-to-the-last /'nɛkst tə ðə 'læst/ *a.* penúltimo.
nibble /'nɪbəl/ *v.* picar.
nice /nis/ *a.* simpático, agradable; amable; hermoso; exacto.
nick /nɪk/ *n.* muesca *f.*, picadura *f.* **in the n. of time,** a punto.
nickel /'nɪkəl/ *n.* níquel *m.*
nickname /'nɪkˌneim/ *n.* **1.** apodo, mote *m.* —*v.* **2.** apodar.
nicotine /'nɪkəˌtin/ *n.* nicotina *f.*
niece /nis/ *n.* sobrina *f.*
niggardly /'nɪgərdli/ *a.* mezquino.
night /nait/ *n.* noche *f.* **good n.,** buenas noches. **last n.,** anoche. **n. club,** cabaret *m.*
nightclub /'naitˌklʌb/ *n.* cabaret *m.*
nightclub owner cabaretero -ra *m. & f.*
nightgown /'naitˌgaun/ *n.* camisa de dormir.
nightingale /'naitnˌgeil, 'naitɪŋ-/ *n.* ruiseñor *m.*
nightly /'naitli/ *adv.* todas las noches.

nightmare /'naitˌmɛər/ *n.* pesadilla *f.*
night school escuela nocturna *f.*
night watchman vigilante nocturno *m.*
nimble /'nɪmbəl/ *a.* ágil.
nine /nain/ *a. & pron.* nueve.
nineteen /'nain'tin/ *a. & pron.* diecinueve.
ninety /'nainti/ *a. & pron.* noventa.
ninth /nainθ/ *a.* noveno.
nipple /'nɪpəl/ *n.* teta *f.*; pezón *m.*
nitrogen /'naitrədʒən/ *n.* nitrógeno *m.*
no /nou/ *a.* **1.** ninguno. **no one,** nadie. —*adv.* **2.** no.
nobility /nou'bɪliti/ *n.* nobleza *f.*
noble /'noubəl/ *a. & n.* noble *m.*
nobleman /'noubəlmən/ *n.* noble *m.*
nobody /'nouˌbɒdi/ *pron.* nadie.
nocturnal /nɒk'tɜrnl/ *a.* nocturno.
nocturne /'nɒktɜrn/ *n.* nocturno *m.*
nod /nɒd/ *n.* **1.** seña con la cabeza. —*v.* **2.** inclinar la cabeza; (doze) dormitar.
no-frills /'nou 'frɪlz/ *a.* sin extras.
noise /nɔiz/ *n.* ruido *m.*
noiseless /'nɔizlɪs/ *a.* silencioso.
noisy /'nɔizi/ *a.* ruidoso.
nominal /'nɒmənl/ *a.* nominal.
nominate /'nɒməˌneit/ *v.* nombrar.
nomination /ˌnɒmə'neiʃən/ *n.* nombramiento *m.*, nominación *f.*
nominee /ˌnɒmə'ni/ *n.* candidato -ta.
nonaligned /ˌnɒnə'laind/ (in political sense), *a.* no alineado.
nonchalant /ˌnɒnʃə'lɑnt/ *a.* indiferente.
noncombatant /ˌnɒnkəm'bætnt/ *n.* no combatiente *m.*
noncommittal /ˌnɒnkə'mɪtl/ *a.* evasivo; reservado.
nondescript /ˌnɒndɪ'skrɪpt/ *a.* difícil de describir.
none /nʌn/ *pron.* ninguno.
nonentity /nɒn'ɛntiti/ *n.* nulidad *f.*
nonpartisan /nɒn'pɑrtəzən/ *a.* sin afiliación.
non-proliferation /ˌnɒnprəˌlɪfə'reiʃən/ *n.* no proliferación *m.*
nonsense /'nɒnsɛns/ *n.* tontería *f.*
nonsmoker /nɒn'smoukər/ *n.* no fumador -dora.
noodle /'nudl/ *n.* fideo *m.*

noon /nun/ *n.* mediodía *m.*

noose /nus/ *n.* lazo corredizo *m.;* dogal *m.*

nor /nɔr; *unstressed* nər/ *conj.* ni.

normal /'nɔrməl/ *a.* normal.

north /nɔrθ/ *n.* norte *m.*

North America /ə'mɛrɪkə/ Norte América *f.*

North American *a. & n.* norteamericano -na.

northeast /,nɔrθ'ist; *Naut.* ,nɔr-/ *n.* nordeste *m.*

northern /'nɔrðərn/ *a.* septentrional.

North Pole *n.* Polo Norte *m.*

northwest /,nɔrθ'wɛst; *Naut.* ,nɔr-/ *n.* noroeste *m.*

Norway /'nɔrwei/ *n.* Noruega *f.*

Norwegian /nɔr'widʒən/ *a. & n.* noruego -ga.

nose /nouz/ *n.* nariz *f.*

nosebleed /'nouz,blid/ *n.* hemorragia nasal *f.*

nostalgia /nɒ'stældʒə/ *n.* nostalgia *f.*

nostril /'nɒstrəl/ *n.* ventana de la nariz; (pl.) narices *f.pl.*

not /nɒt/ *adv.* no. **n. at all,** de ninguna manera. **n. even,** ni siquiera.

notable /'noutəbəl/ *a.* notable.

notary /'noutəri/ *n.* notario *m.*

notation /nou'teiʃən/ *a.* notación *f.*

notch /nɒtʃ/ *n.* muesca *f.;* corte *m.*

note /nout/ *n.* **1.** nota *f.;* apunte *m.* —*v.* **2.** notar.

notebook /'nout,bʊk/ *n.* libreta *f.,* cuaderno *m.*

noted /'noutɪd/ *a.* célebre.

notepaper /'nout,peipər/ *n.* papel de notas *m.*

noteworthy /'nout,wɜrði/ *a.* notable.

nothing /'nʌθɪŋ/ *pron.* nada.

notice /'noutɪs/ *n.* **1.** aviso *m.;* noticia *f.* —*v.* **2.** observar, fijarse en.

noticeable /'noutɪsəbəl/ *a.* notable.

notification /,noutəfɪ'keiʃən/ *n.* notificación *f.*

notify /'noutə,fai/ *v.* notificar.

notion /'nouʃən/ *n.* noción; idea *f.;* (pl.) novedades *f.pl.*

notoriety /,noutə'raiɪti/ *n.* notoriedad *f.*

notorious /nou'tɔriəs/ *a.* notorio.

noun /naun/ *n.* nombre, sustantivo *m.*

nourish /'nɜrɪʃ/ *v.* nutrir, alimentar.

nourishment /'nɜrɪʃmənt/ *n.* nutrimento; alimento *m.*

novel /'nɒvəl/ *a.* **1.** nuevo, original. —*n.* **2.** novela *f.*

novelist /'nɒvəlɪst/ *n.* novelista *m. & f.*

novelty /'nɒvəlti/ *n.* novedad *f.*

November /nou'vɛmbər/ *n.* noviembre *m.*

novena /nou'vinə/ *n.* novena *f.*

novice /'nɒvɪs/ *n.* novicio -cia, novato -ta.

novocaine /'nouvə,kein/ *n.* novocaína *f.*

now /nau/ *adv.* ahora. **n. and then,** de vez en cuando. **by n.,** ya. **from n. on,** de ahora en adelante. **just n.,** ahorita. **right n.,** ahora mismo.

nowadays /'nauə,deiz/ *adv.* hoy día, hoy en día, actualmente.

nowhere /'nou,wɛər/ *adv.* en ninguna parte.

nozzle /'nɒzəl/ *n.* boquilla *f.*

nuance /'nuɑns/ *n.* matiz *m.*

nuclear /'nukliər/ *a.* nuclear.

nuclear energy energía nuclear *f.*

nuclear warhead /'wɔr,hɛd/ cabeza nuclear *f.*

nuclear waste desechos nucleares *m.pl.*

nucleus /'nukliəs/ *n.* núcleo *m.*

nude /nud/ *a.* desnudo.

nuisance /'nusəns/ *n.* molestia *f.*

nuke /nuk/ *n.* bomba atómica *f.*

nullify /'nʌlə,fai/ *v.* anular.

number /'nʌmbər/ *n.* **1.** número *m.;* cifra *f.* **license n.,** matrícula *f.* —*v.* **2.** numerar, contar.

numeric /nu'mɛrɪk/ **numerical** *a.* numérico.

numeric keypad /nu'mɛrɪk/ teclado numérico *m.*

numerous /'numərəs/ *a.* numeroso.

nun /nun/ *n.* monja *f.*

nuptial /'nʌpʃəl/ *a.* nupcial.

nurse /nɜrs/ *n.* **1.** enfermera *f.;* (child's) ama, niñera *f.* —*v.* **2.** criar, alimentar, amamantar; cuidar.

nursery /'nɜrsəri/ *n.* cuarto destinado a los niños; *Agr.* plantel, criadero *m.*

nursery school jardín de infancia *m.*

nurture /'nɜrtʃər/ v. nutrir.
nut /nʌt/ n. nuez f.; Mech. tuerca f.
nutcracker /'nʌt,krækər/ n. cas canueces m.

nutrition /nu'trɪʃən/ n. nutrición f.
nutritious /nu'trɪʃəs/ a. nutritivo.
nylon /'nailɒn/ n. nilón m.
nymph /nɪmf/ n. ninfa f.

O

oak /ouk/ n. roble m.
oar /ɔr/ n. remo m.
OAS abbr. (Organization of American States) OEA (Organización de los Estados Americanos) f.
oasis /ou'eisɪs/ n. oasis m.
oat /out/ n. avena f.
oath /ouθ/ n. juramento m.
oatmeal /'out,mil/ n. harina de avena f.
obedience /ou'bidiəns/ n. obediencia f.
obedient /ou'bidiənt/ a. obediente.
obese /ou'bis/ a. obeso, gordo.
obey /ou'bei/ v. obedecer.
obituary /ou'bɪtʃu,ɛri/ n. obituario m.
object /n 'ɒbdʒɪkt; v əb'dʒɛkt/ n. **1.** objeto m.; Gram. complemento m. —v. **2.** oponerse; objetar.
objection /əb'dʒɛkʃən/ n. objeción f.
objectionable /əb'dʒɛkʃənəbəl/ a. censurable.
objective /əb'dʒɛktɪv/ a. & n. objetivo m.
obligation /,ɒblɪ'geiʃən/ n. obligación f.
obligatory /ə'blɪgə,tɔri/ a. obligatorio.
oblige /ə'blaidʒ/ v. obligar; complacer.
oblique /ə'blik/ a. oblicuo.
obliterate /ə'blɪtə,reit/ v. borrar; destruir.
oblivion /ə'blɪviən/ n. olvido m.
oblong /'ɒb,lɔŋ/ a. oblongo.
obnoxious /əb'nɒkʃəs/ a. ofensivo, odioso.
obscene /əb'sin/ a. obsceno, indecente.
obscure /əb'skyʊr/ a. **1.** obscuro. —v. **2.** obscurecer.
observance /əb'zɜrvəns/ n. observancia; ceremonia f.
observation /,ɒbzɜr'veiʃən/ n. observación f.
observatory /əb'zɜrvə,tɔri/ n. observatorio m.

observe /əb'zɜrv/ v. observar; celebrar.
observer /əb'zɜrvər/ n. observador -ra.
obsession /əb'sɛʃən/ n. obsesión f.
obsolete /,ɒbsə'lit/ a. anticuado.
obstacle /'ɒbstəkəl/ n. obstáculo m.
obstetrician /,ɒbstɪ'trɪʃən/ n. obstétrico -ca, tocólogo -ga m. & f.
obstinate /'ɒbstənɪt/ a. obstinado, terco.
obstruct /əb'strʌkt/ v. obstruir, impedir.
obstruction /əb'strʌkʃən/ n. obstrucción f.
obtain /əb'tein/ v. obtener, conseguir.
obtuse /əb'tus/ a. obtuso.
obviate /'ɒbvi,eit/ v. obviar.
obvious /'ɒbviəs/ a. evidente, obvio.
occasion /ə'keiʒən/ n. **1.** ocasión f. —v. **2.** ocasionar.
occasional /ə'keiʒənl/ a. ocasional.
occult /ə'kʌlt/ a. oculto.
occupant /'ɒkyəpənt/ n. ocupante m. & f.; inquilino -na.
occupation /,ɒkyə'peiʃən/ n. ocupación f.; empleo m.
occupy /'ɒkyə,pai/ v. ocupar; emplear.
occur /ə'kɜr/ v. ocurrir.
occurrence /ə'kɜrəns/ n. ocurrencia f.
ocean /'ouʃən/ n. océano m.
o'clock /ə'klɒk/ **it's one o.**, es la una. **it's two o.**, son las dos, etc. **at... o.**, a las...
octagon /'ɒktə,gɒn/ n. octágono m.
octave /'ɒktɪv/ n. octava f.
October /ɒk'toubər/ n. octubre m.
octopus /'ɒktəpəs/ n. pulpo m.
oculist /'ɒkyəlɪst/ n. oculista m. & f.
odd /ɒd/ a. impar; suelto; raro.
odd number número impar m.

odious /'oudiəs/ a. odioso.

odor /'oudər/ n. olor m.; fragancia f.

of /əv/ prep. de.

off /ɔf/ adv. (see under verb: **stop off, take off,** etc.)

offend /ə'fɛnd/ v. ofender.

offender /ə'fɛndər/ n. ofensor -ra; delincuente m. & f.

offense /ə'fɛns/ n. ofensa f.; crimen m.

offensive /ə'fɛnsɪv/ a. **1.** ofensivo. —n. **2.** ofensiva f.

offer /'ɔfər/ n. **1.** oferta f. —v. **2.** ofrecer.

offering /'ɔfərɪŋ/ n. oferta f.

office /'ɔfɪs/ n. oficina f.; despacho m.; oficio, cargo m.

officer /'ɔfəsər/ n. oficial m. & f. **police o.,** agente de policía m. & f.

official /ə'fɪʃəl/ a. **1.** oficial. —n. **2.** oficial m. & f., funcionario -ria.

officiate /ə'fɪʃiˌeit/ v. oficiar.

officious /ə'fɪʃəs/ a. oficioso.

offspring /'ɔfˌsprɪŋ/ n. hijos m.pl.; progenie f.

often /'ɔfən/ adv. muchas veces, a menudo. **how o.,** con qué frecuencia.

oil /ɔil/ n. **1.** aceite; óleo; petróleo m. —v. **2.** aceitar; engrasar.

oil refinery /rɪ'fainəri/ destilería de petróleo f.

oil tanker /'tæŋkər/ petrolero m.

oily /'ɔili/ a. aceitoso.

ointment /'ɔintmənt/ n. ungüento m.

okay /'ou'kei, ˌou'kei/ adv. bien; de acuerdo.

old /ould/ a. viejo; antiguo. **o. man, o. woman,** viejo -ja.

old-fashioned /'ould 'fæʃənd/ a. fuera de moda, anticuado.

Old Testament Antiguo Testamento m.

olive /'ɒlɪv/ n. aceituna, oliva f.

ombudsman /'ɒmbədzmən/ n. ombudsman f.

omelet /'ɒmlɪt/ n. tortilla de huevos.

omen /'oumən/ n. agüero m.

ominous /'ɒmənəs/ a. ominoso, siniestro.

omission /ou'mɪʃən/ n. omisión f.; olvido m.

omit /ou'mɪt/ v. omitir.

omnibus /'ɒmnəˌbʌs/ n. ómnibus m.

omnipotent /ɒm'nɪpətənt/ a. omnipotente.

on /ɒn/ prep. **1.** en, sobre, encima de. —adv. **2.** adelante.

once /wʌns/ adv. una vez. **at o.,** en seguida. **o. in a while,** de vez en cuando.

one /wʌn/ a. & pron. uno -na.

one-armed bandit /'wʌn ˌɑrmd/ tragaperras f.

oneself /wʌn'sɛlf/ pron. sí mismo -ma; se. **with o.,** consigo.

onion /'ʌnyən/ n. cebolla f.

on-line /'ɒn 'lain/ a. conectado.

only /'ounli/ a. **1.** único, solo. —adv. **2.** sólo, solamente.

onward /'ɒnwərd/ adv. adelante.

opal /'oupəl/ n. ópalo m.

opaque /ou'peik/ a. opaco.

open /'oupən/ a. **1.** abierto; franco. **o. air,** aire libre. —v. **2.** abrir.

opening /'oupənɪŋ/ n. abertura f.

opera /'ɒpərə/ n. ópera f. **o. glasses,** anteojos de ópera; gemelos m.pl.

operate /'ɒpəˌreit/ v. operar.

operation /ˌɒpə'reiʃən/ n. operación f. **to have an o.,** operarse, ser operado.

operative /'ɒpərətɪv/ a. eficaz, operativo.

operator /'ɒpəˌreitər/ n. operario -ria. **elevator o.,** ascensorista m. & f. **telephone o.,** telefonista m. & f.

operetta /ˌɒpə'rɛtə/ n. opereta f.

ophthalmic /ɒf'θælmɪk, ɒp-/ a. oftálmico.

opinion /ə'pɪnyən/ n. opinión f.

opponent /ə'pounənt/ n. antagonista m. & f.

opportunism /ˌɒpər'tunɪzəm/ n. oportunismo m.

opportunity /ˌɒpər'tuniti/ n. ocasión, oportunidad f.

oppose /ə'pouz/ v. oponer.

opposite /'ɒpəzɪt/ a. **1.** opuesto, contrario. —prep. **2.** al frente de. —n. **3.** contrario m.

opposition /ˌɒpə'zɪʃən/ n. oposición f.

oppress /ə'prɛs/ v. oprimir.

oppression /ə'prɛʃən/ n. opresión f.

oppressive /ə'prɛsɪv/ a. opresivo.

optic /'ɒptɪk/ a. óptico.

optical disc /'ɒptɪkəl 'dɪsk/ disco óptico m.

optical illusion /'ɒptɪkəl/ ilusíon de óptica *f.*
optician /ɒp'tɪʃən/ *n.* óptico -ca.
optics /'ɒptɪks/ *n.* óptica *f.*
optimism /'ɒptə,mɪzəm/ *n.* optimismo.
optimistic /,ɒptə'mɪstɪk/ *a.* optimista.
option /'ɒpʃən/ *n.* opción, elección *f.*
optional /'ɒpʃənl/ *a.* discrecional, facultativo.
optometry /ɒp'tɒmɪtri/ *n.* optometría *f.*
opulent /'ɒpyələnt/ *a.* opulento.
or /ɔr/ *conj.* o, (before o-, ho-) u.
oracle /'ɔrəkəl/ *n.* oráculo *m.*
oral /'ɔrəl/ *a.* oral, vocal.
orange /'ɔrɪndʒ/ *n.* naranja *f.*
orange juice jugo de naranja, zumo de naranja *m.*
orange squeezer /'skwizər/ *n.* exprimidora de naranjas *f.*
oration /ɔ'reɪʃən/ *n.* discurso *m.;* oración *f.*
orator /'ɔrətər/ *n.* orador -ra.
oratory /'ɔrə,tɔri/ *n.* oratoria *f.;* (church) oratorio *m.*
orbit /'ɔrbɪt/ *n.* órbita *f.*
orchard /'ɔrtʃərd/ *n.* huerto *m.*
orchestra /'ɔrkəstrə/ *n.* orquesta *f.* **o. seat,** butaca *f.*
orchid /'ɔrkɪd/ *n.* orquídea *f.*
ordain /ɔr'deɪn/ *v.* ordenar.
ordeal /ɔr'dil/ *n.* prueba *f.*
order /'ɔrdər/ *n.* orden, *m. or f.;* clase *f.; Com.* pedido *m.* **in o. that,** para que. *v.* ordenar; mandar; pedir.
order blank hoja de pedidos *f.*
orderly /'ɔrdərli/ *a.* ordenado.
ordinance /'ɔrdn̩əns/ *n.* ordenanza *f.*
ordinary /'ɔrdn̩,ɛri/ *a.* ordinario.
ordination /,ɔrdn̩'eɪʃən/ *n.* ordenación *f.*
ore /ɔr/ *n.* mineral *m.*
organ /'ɔrgən/ *n.* órgano *m.*
organdy /'ɔrgəndi/ *n.* organdí *m.*
organic /ɔr'gænɪk/ *a.* orgánico.
organism /'ɔrgə,nɪzəm/ *n.* organismo *m.*
organist /'ɔrgənɪst/ *n.* organista *m. & f.*
organization /,ɔrgənə'zeɪʃən/ *n.* organización *f.*
organize /'ɔrgə,naɪz/ *v.* organizar.
orgy /'ɔrdʒi/ *n.* orgía *f.*
orient /'ɔriənt/ *n.* **1.** oriente *m.* —*v.* **2.** orientar.

Orient /'ɔriənt/ *n.* Oriente *m.*
Oriental /,ɔri'ɛntl/ *a.* oriental.
orientation /,ɔriən'teɪʃən/ *n.* orientación *f.*
origin /'ɔrɪdʒɪn/ *n.* origen *m.*
original /ə'rɪdʒənl/ *a. & n.* original *m.*
originality /ə,rɪdʒə'nælɪti/ *n.* originalidad *f.*
ornament /n. 'ɔrnəmənt; v -,mɛnt/ *n.* **1.** ornamento *m.* —*v.* **2.** ornamentar.
ornamental /,ɔrnə'mɛntl/ *a.* ornamental, decorativo.
ornate /ɔr'neɪt/ *a.* ornado.
ornithology /,ɔrnə'θɒlədʒi/ *n.* ornitología *f.*
orphan /'ɔrfən/ *a. & n.* huérfano -na.
orphanage /'ɔrfənɪdʒ/ *n.* orfanato *m.*
orthodox /'ɔrθə,dɒks/ *a.* ortodoxo.
ostentation /,ɒstɛn'teɪʃən/ *n.* ostentación *f.*
ostentatious /,ɒstɛn'teɪʃəs/ *a.* ostentoso.
ostrich /'ɒstrɪtʃ/ *n.* avestruz *f.*
other /'ʌðər/ *a. & pron.* otro. **every o. day,** un día sí otro no.
otherwise /'ʌðər,waiz/ *adv.* de otra manera.
ought /ɔt/ *v.* deber.
ounce /auns/ *n.* onza *f.*
our /auᵊr; *unstressed* ɑr/ **ours** *a. & pron.* nuestro.
ourselves /ɑr'sɛlvz/ *pron.* nosotros -as; mismos -as; nos.
oust /aust/ *v.* desalojar.
ouster /'austər/ *n.* desahucio *m.*
out /aut/ *adv.* **1.** fuera, afuera. **out of,** fuera de. —*prep.* **2.** por.
outbreak /'aut,breik/ *n.* erupción *f.*
outcast /'aut,kæst/ *n.* paria *m. & f.*
outcome /'aut,kʌm/ *n.* resultado *m.*
outdoors /,aut'dɔrz/ *adv.* fuera de casa; al aire libre.
outer /'autər/ *a.* exterior, externo.
outfit /'aut,fɪt/ *n.* **1.** equipo; traje *m.* —*v.* **2.** equipar.
outgrowth /'aut,grouθ/ *n.* resultado *m.*
outing /'autɪŋ/ *n.* paseo *m.*
outlaw /'aut,lɔ/ *n.* **1.** bandido *m.* —*v.* **2.** proscribir.
outlet /'autlɛt/ *n.* salida *f.*
outline /'aut,lain/ *n.* **1.** contorno;

esbozo *m.;* silueta *f.* —*v.* **2.** esbozar.

outlive /ˌautˈlɪv/ *v.* sobrevivir.

out-of-court settlement /ˈautəvˌkɔrt/ arreglo pacífico *m.*

out-of-date /ˈaut əv ˈdeit/ *a.* anticuado.

out of focus *a.* desenfocado.

outpost /ˈautˌpoust/ *n.* puesto avanzado.

output /ˈautˌput/ *n.* capacidad *f.;* producción *f.*

outrage /ˈautreidʒ/ *n.* **1.** ultraje *m.;* atrocidad *f.* —*v.* **2.** ultrajar.

outrageous /autˈreidʒəs/ *a.* atroz.

outrun /ˌautˈrʌn/ *v.* exceder.

outside /a, *prep, adv* ˌautˈsaid; *n* ˈautˈsaid/ *a.* & *n.* **1.** exterior *m.* —*adv.* **2.** afuera, por fuera. —*prep.* **3.** fuera de.

outskirt /ˈautˌskɜrt/ *n.* borde *m.*

outward /ˈautwərd/ *adv.* hacia afuera.

outwardly /ˈautwərdli/ *adv.* exteriormente.

oval /ˈouvəl/ *a.* **1.** oval, ovalado. —*n.* **2.** óvalo *m.*

ovary /ˈouvəri/ *n.* ovario *m.*

ovation /ouˈveiʃən/ *n.* ovación *f.*

oven /ˈʌvən/ *n.* horno *m.*

over /ˈouvər/ *prep.* **1.** sobre, encima de; por. —*adv.* **2.** **o. here,** aquí. **o. there,** allí, por allí. **to be o.,** estar terminado.

overcoat /ˈouvərˌkout/ *n.* abrigo, sobretodo *m.*

overcome /ˌouvərˈkʌm/ *v.* superar, vencer.

overdose /ˈouvərˌdous/ *n.* sobredosis *f.*

overdue /ˌouvərˈdu/ *a.* retrasado.

overflow /*n* ˈouvərˌflou; *v* ˌouvərˈflou/ *n.* **1.** inundación *f.* —*v.* **2.** inundar.

overhaul /ˌouvərˈhɔl/ *v.* repasar.

overhead /ˈouvərˈhɛd/ *adv.* arriba, en lo alto.

overkill /ˈouvərˌkɪl/ *n.* efecto mayor que el pretendido.

overlook /ˌouvərˈluk/ *v.* pasar por alto.

overnight /ˈouvərˈnait/ *adv.* **to stay or stop o.,** pasar la noche.

overpower /ˌouvərˈpauər/ *v.* vencer.

overrule /ˌouvərˈrul/ *v.* predominar.

overrun /ˌouvərˈrʌn/ *v.* invadir.

oversee /ˌouvərˈsi/ *v.* superentender.

oversight /ˈouvərˌsait/ *n.* descuido *m.*

overt /ouˈvɜrt/ *a.* abierto.

overtake /ˌouvərˈteik/ *v.* alcanzar.

overthrow /*n* ˈouvərˌθrou; *v* ˌouvərˈθrou/ *n.* **1.** trastorno *m.* —*v.* **2.** trastornar.

overture /ˈouvərtʃər/ *n. Mus.* obertura *f.*

overturn /ˌouvərˈtɜrn/ *v.* trastornar.

overview /ˈouvərˌvyu/ *n.* visión de conjunto *f.*

overweight /ˈouvərˌweit/ *a.* demasiado pesado.

overwhelm /ˌouvərˈwɛlm/ *v.* abrumar.

overwork /ˌouvərˈwɜrk/ *v.* trabajar demasiado.

owe /ou/ *v.* deber. **owing to,** debido a.

owl /aul/ *n.* búho *m.,* lechuza *f.*

own /oun/ *a.* **1.** propio. —*v.* **2.** poseer.

owner /ˈounər/ *n.* dueño -ña.

ox /ɒks/ *n.* buey *m.*

oxygen /ˈɒksɪdʒən/ *n.* oxígeno *m.*

oxygen tent tienda de oxígeno *f.*

oyster /ˈɔistər/ *n.* ostra *f.*

P

pace /peis/ *n.* **1.** paso *m.* —*v.* **2.** pasearse. **p. off,** medir a pasos.

pacific /pəˈsɪfɪk/ *a.* pacífico.

Pacific Ocean Océano Pacífico *m.*

pacifier /ˈpæsəˌfaiər/ *n.* pacificador *m.;* (baby p.) chupete *m.*

pacifism /ˈpæsəˌfɪzəm/ *n.* pacifismo *m.*

pacifist /ˈpæsəfɪst/ *n.* pacifista *m.* & *f.*

pacify /ˈpæsəˌfai/ *v.* pacificar.

pack /pæk/ *n.* **1.** fardo; paquete *m.;* (animals) muta *f.* **p. of cards,** baraja *f.* —*v.* **2.** empaquetar; (baggage) empacar.

package /ˈpækɪdʒ/ *n.* paquete, bulto *m.*

package tour viaje todo incluido *m.*

pact /pækt/ *n.* pacto *m.*

pad /pæd/ *n.* **1.** colchoncillo *m.* **p. of paper,** bloc de papel. —*v.* **2.** rellenar.

paddle /'pædḷ/ n. **1.** canalete m.
—v. **2.** remar.
padlock /'pæd,lɒk/ n. candado m.
pagan /'peigən/ a. & n. pagano
-na.
page /peidʒ/ n. página f.; (boy)
paje m.
pageant /'pædʒənt/ n. espectáculo m.; procesión f.
pail /peil/ n. cubo m.
pain /pein/ n. dolor m. **to take
pains,** esmerarse.
painful /'peinfəl/ a. doloroso;
penoso.
pain killer /'pein,kɪlər/ analgésico
m.
paint /peint/ n. **1.** pintura f. —v.
2. pintar.
painter /'peintər/ n. pintor -ra.
painting /'peintɪŋ/ n. pintura f.;
cuadro m.
pair /pɛər/ n. **1.** par m.; pareja f.
—v. **2.** parear. **p. off,** emparejarse.
pajamas /pə'dʒɑməz, -'dʒæməz/
n. pijama m.
palace /'pælɪs/ n. palacio m.
palatable /'pælətəbəl/ a. sabroso,
agradable.
palate /'pælɪt/ n. paladar m.
palatial /pə'leiʃəl/ a. palaciego,
suntuoso.
pale /peil/ a. pálido. **to turn pale,**
palidecer.
paleness /'peilnɪs/ n. palidez f.
palette /'pælɪt/ n. paleta f.
pallbearer /'pɔl,bɛərər/ n. portador del féretro, portaféretro m.
pallid /'pælɪd/ a. pálido.
palm /pɑm/ n. palma f. **p. tree,**
palmera f.
palpitate /'pælpɪ,teit/ v. palpitar.
paltry /'pɔltri/ a. miserable.
pamper /'pæmpər/ v. mimar.
pamphlet /'pæmflɪt/ n. folleto m.
pan /pæn/ n. cacerola f.
panacea /,pænə'siə/ n. panacea f.
Pan-American /,pænə'mɛrɪkən/ a.
panamericano.
pane /pein/ n. hoja de vidrio f.,
cuadro m.
panel /'pænḷ/ n. tablero m.
pang /pæŋ/ n. dolor; remordimiento m.
panic /'pænɪk/ n. pánico m.
panorama /,pænə'ræmə, -'rɑmə/
n. panorama m.
pant /pænt/ v. jadear.
panther /'pænθər/ n. pantera f.

pantomine /'pæntə,maim/ n. pantomima f.; mímica f.
pantry /'pæntri/ n. despensa f.
pants /pænts/ n. pantalones, m.pl.
panty hose /'pænti,houz/ n.
pantys, pantimedias f.pl. (medias
hasta la cintura).
papal /'peipəl/ a. papal.
paper /'peipər/ n. papel; periódico; artículo m.
paperback /'peipər,bæk/ n. libro
en rústica m.
paper clip sujetapapeles m.
paper cup vaso de papel m.
paper hanger /'peipər,hæŋər/ em-
papelador -ra.
paper money papel moneda m.
paperweight /'peipər,weit/ pisapapeles m.
papier-mâché /,peipərmə'ʃei,
pɑ,pyei-/ n. cartón piedra m.
paprika /pæ'prikə, pə-, pɑ-, 'pæ-
prɪkə/ n. pimentón m.
par /pɑr/ n. paridad f.; Com. par
f.
parable /'pærəbəl/ n. parábola f.
parachute /'pærə,ʃut/ n. paracaídas m.
parade /pə'reid/ n. **1.** desfile m.,
procesión f. —v. **2.** desfilar.
paradise /'pærə,dais/ n. paraíso
m.
paradox /'pærə,dɒks/ n. paradoja
f.
paraffin /'pærəfɪn/ n. parafina f.
paragraph /'pærə,græf/ n. párrafo
m.
parakeet /'pærə,kit/ n. perico m.
parallel /'pærə,lɛl/ a. **1.** paralelo.
—v. **2.** correr parejas con.
paralysis /pə'ræləsɪs/ n. parálisis
f.
paralyze /'pærə,laiz/ v. paralizar.
paramedic /,pærə'mɛdɪk/ n.
paramédico -ca.
parameter /pə'ræmɪtər/ n. parámetro m.
paramount /'pærə,maunt/ a. supremo.
paraphrase /'pærə,freiz/ n. **1.**
paráfrasis f. —v. **2.** parafrasear.
paraplegic /'pærə'plidʒɪk/ n. para-
pléjico -ca.
parasite /'pærə,sait/ n. parásito
m.
parboil /'pɑr,bɔil/ v. sancochar.
parcel /'pɑrsəl/ n. paquete m. **p.
of land,** lote de terreno.
parchment /'pɑrtʃmənt/ n. pergamino m.

pardon /'pɑrdṇ/ n. **1.** perdón m. —v. **2.** perdonar.

pare /pɛər/ v. pelar.

parentage /'pɛərəntɪdʒ, 'pær-/ n. origen m.; extracción f.

parenthesis /pə'rɛnθəsɪs/ n. paréntesis m.

parents /'pɛərənts/ n. padres m.pl.

parish /'pærɪʃ/ n. parroquia f.

Parisian /pə'rɪʒən, -'riʒən, -'rɪziən/ a. & n. parisiense m. & f.

parity /'pærɪti/ n. igualdad, paridad f.

park /pɑrk/ n. **1.** parque m. —v. **2.** estacionar.

parking lot /'pɑrkɪŋ/ n. estacionamiento, aparcamiento m.

parking meter /'pɑrkɪŋ/ parquímetro m.

parking space /'pɑrkɪŋ/ estacionamiento, aparcamiento m.

parkway /'pɑrk,wei/ n. bulevar m.; autopista f.

parley /'pɑrli/ n. conferencia f.; Mil. parlamento m.

parliament /'pɑrləmənt/ n. parlamento m.

parliamentary /,pɑrlə'mɛntəri, -tri; sometimes ,pɑrlyə-/ a. parlamentario.

parlor /'pɑrlər/ n. sala f., salón m.

parochial /pə'roukiəl/ a. parroquial.

parody /'pærədi/ n. **1.** parodia f. —v. **2.** parodiar.

parole /pə'roul/ n. **1.** palabra de honor f.; Mil. santo y seña. —v. **2.** poner en libertad bajo palabra.

paroxysm /'pærək,sɪzəm/ n. paroxismo m.

parrot /'pærət/ n. loro, papagayo m.

parsimony /'pɑrsə,mouni/ n. parsimonia f.

parsley /'pɑrsli/ n. perejil m.

parson /'pɑrsən/ n. párroco m.

part /pɑrt/ n. **1.** parte f.; Theat. papel m. —v. **2.** separarse, partirse. **p. with,** desprenderse de.

partake /pɑr'teik/ v. tomar parte.

partial /'pɑrʃəl/ a. parcial.

participant /pɑr'tɪsəpənt/ n. participante m. & f.

participate /pɑr'tɪsə,peit/ v. participar.

participation /pɑr,tɪsə'peiʃən/ n. participación f.

participle /'pɑrtə,sɪpəl, -səpəl/ n. participio m.

particle /'pɑrtɪkəl/ n. partícula f.

particular /pər'tɪkyələr/ a. & n. particular m.

parting /'pɑrtɪŋ/ n. despedida f.

partisan /'pɑrtəzən, -sən/ a. & n. partidario -ria.

partition /pɑr'tɪʃən, pər-/ n. tabique m. v. dividir, partir.

partly /'pɑrtli/ adv. en parte.

partner /'pɑrtnər/ n. socio -cia; compañero -ra.

partridge /'pɑrtrɪdʒ/ n. perdiz f.

party /'pɑrti/ n. tertulia, fiesta f.; grupo m.; (political) partido m.

pass /pæs/ n. **1.** pase; (mountain) paso m. —v. **2.** pasar. **p. away,** fallecer.

passable /'pæsəbəl/ a. transitable; regular.

passage /'pæsɪdʒ/ n. pasaje; (corridor) pasillo m.

passé /pæ'sei/ a. anticuado.

passenger /'pæsəndʒər/ n. pasajero -ra.

passenger ship buque de pasajeros m.

passerby /'pæsər'bai/ n. transeúnte m. & f.

passion /'pæʃən/ n. pasión f.

passionate /'pæʃənɪt/ a. apasionado.

passive /'pæsɪv/ a. pasivo.

passport /'pæsport/ n. pasaporte m.

password /'pæs,wɜrd/ n. código m., clave m., contraseña f.

past /pæst/ a. & n. **1.** pasado m. —prep. **2.** más allá de; después de.

paste /peist/ n. **1.** pasta f. —v. **2.** empastar; pegar.

pasteurize /'pæstʃə,raiz/ v. pasteurizar.

pastime /'pæs,taim/ n. pasatiempo m.; diversión f.

pastor /'pæstər/ n. pastor m.

pastrami /pə'strɑmi/ n. pastrón m.

pastry /'peistri/ n. pastelería f.

pasture /'pæstʃər/ n. **1.** pasto m.; pradera f. —v. **2.** pastar.

pat /pæt/ n. **1.** golpecillo m. **to stand p.,** mantenerse firme. —v. **2.** dar golpecillos.

patch /pætʃ/ n. **1.** remiendo m. —v. **2.** remendar.

patent /'pætṇt/ a. & n. **1.** patente m. —v. **2.** patentar.

patent leather /'pætnt, 'pætṇ/ charol m.

paternal /pə'tɜrnḷ/ *a.* paterno, paternal.

paternity /pə'tɜrnɪti/ *n.* paternidad *f.*

path /pæθ/ *n.* senda *f.*

pathetic /pə'θɛtɪk/ *a.* patético.

pathology /pə'θɒlədʒi/ *n.* patología *f.*

pathos /'peiθɒs/ *n.* rasgo conmovedor *m.*

patience /'peiʃəns/ *n.* paciencia *f.*

patient /'peiʃənt/ *a.* **1.** paciente. —*n.* **2.** enfermo -ma, paciente *m.* & *f.*

patio /'pæti,ou/ *n.* patio *m.*

patriarch /'peitri,ɑrk/ *n.* patriarca *m.*

patriot /'peitriət/ *n.* patriota *m.* & *f.*

patriotic /,peitri'ɒtɪk/ *a.* patriótico.

patriotism /'peitriə,tɪzəm/ *n.* patriotismo *m.*

patrol /pə'troul/ *n.* **1.** patrulla *f.* —*v.* **2.** patrullar.

patrolman /pə'troulmən/ *n.* vigilante *m.*; patrullador *m.*

patron /'peitrən/ *n.* patrón *m.*

patronize /'peitrə,naiz/ *v.* condescender; patrocinar; ser cliente de.

pattern /'pætɜrn/ *n.* modelo *m.*

pauper /'pɔpər/ *n.* indigente *m.* & *f.*

pause /pɔz/ *n.* **1.** pausa *f.* —*v.* **2.** pausar.

pave /peiv/ *v.* pavimentar. **p. the way,** preparar el camino.

pavement /'peivmənt/ *n.* pavimento *m.*

pavilion /pə'vɪlyən/ *n.* pabellón *m.*

paw /pɔ/ *n.* **1.** pata *f.* —*v.* **2.** patear.

pawn /pɔn/ *n.* **1.** prenda *f.*; (chess) peón de ajedrez *m.* —*v.* **2.** empeñar.

pay /pei/ *n.* **1.** pago; sueldo, salario *m.*; —*v.* **2.** pagar. **p. back,** pagar; vengarse de. **p. cash,** pagar en metálico.

payee /pei'i/ *n.* destinatario -ria *m.* & *f.*

payment /'peimənt/ *n.* pago *m.*; recompensa *f.*

pay phone teléfono público *m.*

pea /pi/ *n.* guisante *m.*

peace /pis/ *n.* paz *f.*

peaceable /'pisəbəl/ *a.* pacífico.

peaceful /'pisfəl/ *a.* tranquilo.

peach /pitʃ/ *n.* durazno, melocotón *m.*

peacock /'pi,kɒk/ *n.* pavo real *m.*

peak /pik/ *n.* pico, cumbre; máximo *m.*

peal /pil/ *n.* repique; estruendo *m.* **p. of laughter,** risotada *f.*

peanut /'pi,nʌt/ *n.* maní, cacahuete *m.*

pear /pɛər/ *n.* pera *f.*

pearl /pɜrl/ *n.* perla *f.*

peasant /'pɛzənt/ *n.* campesino -na.

pebble /'pɛbəl/ *n.* guija *f.*

peck /pɛk/ *n.* **1.** picotazo *m.* —*v.* **2.** picotear.

peckish /'pɛkɪʃ/ *a.* tener un poco de hambre.

peculiar /pɪ'kyulyər/ *a.* peculiar.

pecuniary /pɪ'kyuni,ɛri/ *a.* pecuniario.

pedagogue /'pɛdə,gɒg/ *n.* pedagogo -ga.

pedagogy /'pɛdə,goudʒi, -,gɒdʒi/ *n.* pedagogía *f.*

pedal /'pɛdḷ/ *n.* pedal *m.*

pedant /'pɛdṇt/ *n.* pedante *m.* & *f.*

peddler /'pɛdlər/ *n.* buhonero *m.*

pedestal /'pɛdəstḷ/ *n.* pedestal *m.*

pedestrian /pə'dɛstriən/ *n.* peatón -na.

pedestrian crossing paso de peatones *m.*

pediatrician /,pidiə'trɪʃən/ *n.* pediatra *m.* & *f.*

pediatrics /,pidi'ætrɪks/ *n.* puericultura *f.*

pedigree /'pɛdɪ,gri/ *n.* genealogía *f.*

peek /pik/ *n.* **1.** atisbo *m.* —*v.* **2.** atisbar.

peel /pil/ *n.* **1.** corteza *f.*; (fruit) pellejo *m.* —*v.* **2.** descortezar; pelar.

peep /pip/ *n.* **1.** ojeada *f.* —*v.* **2.** mirar, atisbar.

peer /pɪər/ *n.* **1.** par *m.* —*v.* **2.** mirar fijamente.

peg /pɛg/ *n.* clavija; estaquilla *f.*; gancho *m.*

pelt /pɛlt/ *n.* **1.** pellejo *m.* —*v.* **2.** apedrear; (rain) caer con fuerza.

pelvis /'pɛlvɪs/ *n.* pelvis *f.*

pen /pɛn/ *n.* pluma *f.*; corral *m.* **fountain p.,** pluma fuente.

penalty /'pɛnḷti/ *n.* pena; multa *f.*; castigo *m.*

penance /'pɛnəns/ *n.* penitencia *f.* **to do p.,** penar.

penchant /'pɛntʃənt;/ n. propensión f.

pencil /'pɛnsəl/ n. lápiz m.

pencil sharpener /'ʃɑrpənər/ sacapuntas m.

pending /'pɛndɪŋ/ a. pendiente.
to be p., pender.

penetrate /'pɛnɪˌtreit/ v. penetrar.

penetration /ˌpɛnɪ'treiʃən/ n. penetración f.

penicillin /ˌpɛnə'sɪlɪn/ n. penicilina f.

peninsula /pə'nɪnsələ, -'nɪnsyələ/ n. península f.

penitent /'pɛnɪtənt/ n. & a. penitente m. & f.

penknife /'pɛnˌnaif/ n. cortaplumas f.

penniless /'pɛnɪlɪs/ a. indigente.

penny /'pɛni/ n. penique m.

pension /'pɛnʃən/ n. pensión f.

pensive /'pɛnsɪv/ a. pensativo.

penultimate /pɪ'nʌltəmɪt/ a. penúltimo.

penury /'pɛnyəri/ n. penuria f.

people /'pipəl/ n. **1.** gente f.; (of a nation) pueblo m. —v. **2.** poblar.

pepper /'pɛpər/ n. pimienta f.; (plant) pimiento m.

per /pɜr; unstressed pər/ prep. por.

perambulator /pər'æmbyəˌleitər/ n. cochecillo de niño m.

perceive /pər'siv/ v. percibir.

percent /pər'sɛnt/ adv. por ciento.

percentage /pər'sɛntɪdʒ/ n. porcentaje m.

perceptible /pər'sɛptəbəl/ a. perceptible.

perception /pər'sɛpʃən/ n. percepción f.

perch /pɜrtʃ/ n. percha f.; (fish) perca f.

perdition /pər'dɪʃən/ n. perdición f.

peremptory /pə'rɛmptəri/ a. perentorio, terminante.

perennial /pə'rɛniəl/ a. perenne.

perfect /a. 'pɜrfɪkt; v. pər'fɛkt/ a. **1.** perfecto. —v. **2.** perfeccionar.

perfection /pər'fɛkʃən/ n. perfección f.

perfectionist /pər'fɛkʃənɪst/ a. & n. perfeccionista m. & f.

perforation /ˌpɜrfə'reiʃən/ n. perforación f.

perform /pər'fɔrm/ v. hacer; ejecutar; Theat. representar.

performance /pər'fɔrməns/ n. ejecución f.; Theat. representación f.

perfume /n. 'pɜrfyum; v. pər'fyum/ n. **1.** perfume m.; fragancia f. —v. **2.** perfumar.

perfunctory /pər'fʌŋktəri/ a. perfunctorio, superficial.

perhaps /pər'hæps/ adv. quizá, quizás, tal vez.

peril /'pɛrəl/ n. peligro m.

perilous /'pɛrələs/ a. peligroso.

perimeter /pə'rɪmɪtər/ n. perímetro m.

period /'pɪəriəd/ n. período m.; Punct. punto m.

periodic /ˌpɪəri'ɒdɪk/ a. periódico.

periodical /ˌpɪəri'ɒdɪkəl/ n. revista f.

periphery /pə'rɪfəri/ n. periferia f.

perish /'pɛrɪʃ/ v. perecer.

perishable /'pɛrɪʃəbəl/ a. perecedero.

perjury /'pɜrdʒəri/ n. perjurio m.

permanent /'pɜrmənənt/ a. permanente. **p. wave**, ondulado permanente.

permeate /'pɜrmiˌeit/ v. penetrar.

permissible /pər'mɪsəbəl/ a. permisible.

permission /pər'mɪʃən/ n. permiso m.

permit /n. 'pɜrmɪt; v. pər'mɪt/ n. **1.** permiso m. —v. **2.** permitir.

pernicious /pər'nɪʃəs/ a. pernicioso.

perpendicular /ˌpɜrpən'dɪkyələr/ n. & a. perpendicular f.

perpetrate /'pɜrpɪˌtreit/ v. perpetrar.

perpetual /pər'pɛtʃuəl/ a. perpetuo.

perplex /pər'plɛks/ v. confundir.

perplexity /pər'plɛksɪti/ n. perplejidad f.

persecute /'pɜrsɪˌkyut/ v. perseguir.

persecution /ˌpɜrsɪ'kyuʃən/ n. persecución f.

perseverance /ˌpɜrsə'vɪərəns/ n. perseverancia f.

persevere /ˌpɜrsə'vɪər/ v. perseverar.

persist /pər'sɪst/ v. persistir.

persistent /pər'sɪstənt/ a. persistente.

person /'pɜrsən/ n. persona f.

personage /'pɜrsənɪdʒ/ n. personaje m.

personal /'pɜrsənl/ a. personal.

personality /ˌpɜrsə'nælɪti/ n. personalidad f.

personnel /,pɜrsə'nɛl/ *n.* personal *m.*

perspective /pər'spɛktɪv/ *n.* perspectiva *f.*

perspiration /'pɜrspə'reiʃən/ *n.* sudor *m.*

perspire /pər'spaiᵊr/ *v.* sudar.

persuade /pər'sweid/ *v.* persuadir.

persuasive /pər'sweisɪv/ *a.* persuasivo.

pertain /pər'tein/ *v.* pertenecer.

pertinent /'pɜrtṇənt/ *a.* pertinente.

perturb /pər'tɜrb/ *v.* perturbar.

peruse /pə'ruz/ *v.* leer con cuidado.

pervade /pər'veid/ *v.* penetrar; llenar.

perverse /pər'vɜrs/ *a.* perverso.

perversion /pər'vɜrʒən/ *n.* perversión *f.*

pessimism /'pɛsə,mɪzəm/ *n.* pesimismo *m.*

pester /'pɛstər/ *v.* molestar; fastidiar.

pesticide /'pɛstə,said/ *n.* pesticida *m.*

pestilence /'pɛstḷəns/ *n.* pestilencia *f.*

pet /pɛt/ *n.* **1.** favorito -ta.; animal doméstico *m.* —*v.* **2.** mimar.

petal /'pɛtḷ/ *n.* pétalo *m.*

petition /pə'tɪʃən/ *n.* **1.** petición, súplica *f.* —*v.* **2.** pedir, suplicar.

petrify /'pɛtrə,fai/ *v.* petrificar.

petroleum /pə'trouliəm/ *n.* petróleo *m.*

petticoat /'pɛti,kout/ *n.* enagua *f.*

petty /'pɛti/ *a.* mezquino, insignificante.

petulant /'pɛtʃələnt/ *a.* quisquilloso.

pew /pyu/ *n.* banco de iglesia *m.*

pewter /'pyutər/ *n.* peltre *m.*

phantom /'fæntəm/ *n.* espectro, fantasma *m.*

pharmacist /'fɑrməsɪst/ *n.* farmacéutico -ca, boticario -ria.

pharmacy /'fɑrməsi/ *n.* farmacia, botica *f.*

phase /feiz/ *n.* fase *f.*

pheasant /'fɛzənt/ *n.* faisán *m.*

phenomenal /fɪ'nɒmənḷ/ *a.* fenomenal.

phenomenon /fɪ'nɒmə,nɒn/ *n.* fenómeno *m.*

philanthropy /fɪ'lænθrəpi/ *n.* filantropía *f.*

philately /fɪ'lætḷi/ *n.* filatelia *f.*

philosopher /fɪ'lɒsəfər/ *n.* filósofo -fa.

philosophical /,fɪlə'sɒfɪkəl/ *a.* filosófico.

philosophy /fɪ'lɒsəfi/ *n.* filosofía *f.*

phlegm /flɛm/ *n.* flema *f.*

phlegmatic /flɛg'mætɪk/ *a.* flemático.

phobia /'foubiə/ *n.* fobia *f.*

phone /foun/ *n.* teléfono *m.*

phonetic /fə'nɛtɪk/ *a.* fonético.

phonograph /'founə,græf/ *n.* fonógrafo *m.*

phosphorus /'fɒsfərəs/ *n.* fósforo *m.*

photocopier /'foutə,kɒpiər/ *n.* fotocopiadora *f.*

photocopy /'foutə,kɒpi/ *n.* **1.** fotocopia *f.* —*v.* **2.** fotocopiar.

photoelectric /,foutouɪ'lɛktrɪk/ *a.* fotoeléctrico.

photogenic /,foutə'dʒɛnɪk/ *a.* fotogénico.

photograph /'foutə,græf/ *n.* **1.** fotografía *f.* —*v.* **2.** fotografiar; retratar.

photography /fə'tɒgrəfi/ *n.* fotografía *f.*

phrase /freiz/ *n.* **1.** frase *f.* —*v.* **2.** expresar.

physical /'fɪzɪkəl/ *a.* físico.

physician /fɪ'zɪʃən/ *n.* médico *m.* & *f.*

physics /'fɪzɪks/ *n.* física *f.*

physiology /,fɪzi'ɒlədʒi/ *n.* fisiología *f.*

physiotherapy /,fɪziou'θɛrəpi/ *n.* fisioterapia *f.*

physique /fɪ'zik/ *n.* físico *m.*

pianist /pi'ænɪst, 'piənɪst/ *n.* pianista *m.* & *f.*

piano /pi'ænou/ *n.* piano *m.*

picayune /,pɪkə'yun/ *a.* insignificante.

piccolo /'pɪkə,lou/ *n.* flautín *m.*

pick /pɪk/ *n.* **1.** pico *m.* —*v.* **2.** escoger. **p. up,** recoger.

picket /'pɪkɪt/ *n.* piquete *m.*

pickle /'pɪkəl/ *n.* **1.** salmuera *f.*; encurtido *m.* —*v.* **2.** escabechar.

pickpocket /'pɪk,pɒkɪt/ *n.* cortabolsas *m.* & *f.*

picnic /'pɪknɪk/ *n.* picnic *m.*

picture /'pɪktʃər/ *n.* **1.** cuadro; retrato *m.*; fotografía *f.*; (movie) película *f.* —*v.* **2.** imaginarse.

picturesque /,pɪktʃə'rɛsk/ *a.* pintoresco.

pie /pai/ *n.* pastel *m.*

piece /pis/ n. pedazo m.; pieza f.
pieceworker /'pis,wɜrkər/ n. destajero -ra, destajista m. & f.
pier /pɪər/ n. muelle m.
pierce /pɪərs/ v. perforar; pinchar; traspasar.
piety /'paɪɪti/ n. piedad f.
pig /pɪg/ n. puerco, cerdo, lechón m.
pigeon /'pɪdʒən/ n. paloma f.
pigeonhole /'pɪdʒən,houl/ n. casilla f.
pigment /'pɪgmənt/ n. pigmento m.
pile /pail/ n. 1. pila f.; montón m.; Med. hemorroides f.pl. —v. 2. amontonar.
pilfer /'pɪlfər/ v. ratear.
pilgrim /'pɪlgrɪm/ n. peregrino -na, romero -ra.
pilgrimage /'pɪlgrəmɪdʒ/ n. romería f.
pill /pɪl/ n. píldora f.
pillage /'pɪlɪdʒ/ n. 1. pillaje m. —v. 2. pillar.
pillar /'pɪlər/ n. columna f.
pillow /'pɪlou/ n. almohada f.
pillowcase /'pɪlou,keis/ n. funda de almohada f.
pilot /'pailət/ n. 1. piloto m. & f. —v. 2. pilotar.
pimple /'pɪmpəl/ n. grano m.
pin /pɪn/ n. 1. alfiler; broche m.; Mech. clavija f. —v. 2. prender. **p. up,** fijar.
pinafore /'pɪnə,fɔr/ n. delantal (de niña) m.
pinch /pɪntʃ/ n. 1. pellizco m. —v. 2. pellizcar.
pine /pain/ n. 1. pino m. —v. 2. **p. away,** languidecer. **p. for,** anhelar.
pineapple /'pai,næpəl/ n. piña f., ananás m.pl.
pink /pɪŋk/ a. rosado.
pinky /'pɪŋki/ n. meñique m.
pinnacle /'pɪnəkəl/ n. pináculo m.; cumbre f.
pint /paint/ n. pinta f.
pioneer /,paiə'nɪər/ n. pionero -ra.
pious /'paiəs/ a. piadoso.
pipe /paip/ n. pipa f.; tubo; (of organ) cañón m.
pipeline /'paip,lain/ n. oleoducto m.
piper /'paipər/ n. flautista m. & f.
piquant /'pikənt/ a. picante.
pirate /'pairət/ n. pirata m.
pistol /'pɪstl/ n. pistola f.

piston /'pɪstən/ n. émbolo, pistón m.
pit /pɪt/ n. hoyo m.; (fruit) hueso m.
pitch /pɪtʃ/ n. 1. brea f.; grado de inclinación; (music) tono m.; —v. 2. lanzar; (ship) cabecear.
pitchblende /'pɪtʃ,blɛnd/ n. pechblenda f.
pitcher /'pɪtʃər/ n. cántaro m.; (baseball) lanzador -ra.
pitchfork /'pɪtʃ,fɔrk/ n. horca f.; tridente m.
pitfall /'pɪt,fɔl/ n. trampa f., hoya cubierta f.
pitiful /'pɪtɪfəl/ a. lastimoso.
pitiless /'pɪtɪlɪs/ a. cruel.
pituitary gland /pɪ'tuɪ,tɛri/ glándula pituitaria f.
pity /'pɪti/ n. 1. compasión, piedad f. **to be a p.,** ser lástima. —v. 2. compadecer.
pivot /'pɪvət/ n. 1. espiga f., pivote m.; punto de partida m. —v. 2. girar sobre un pivote.
pizza /'pitsə/ n. pizza f.
placard /'plækɑrd/ n. 1. cartel m. —v. 2. fijar carteles.
placate /'pleikeit/ v. aplacar.
place /pleis/ n. 1. lugar, sitio, puesto m. —v. 2. colocar, poner.
placid /'plæsɪd/ a. plácido.
plagiarism /'pleidʒə,rɪzəm/ n. plagio m.
plague /pleig/ n. 1. plaga, peste f. —v. 2. atormentar.
plain /plein/ a. 1. sencillo; puro; evidente. —n. 2. llano m.
plaintiff /'pleintɪf/ n. demandante m. & f.
plan /plæn/ n. 1. plan, propósito m. —v. 2. planear; pensar; planificar. **p. on,** contar con.
plane /plein/ n. 1. plano; (tool) cepillo m. —v. 2. allanar; acepillar.
planet /'plænɪt/ n. planeta m.
planetarium /,plænɪ'tɛəriəm/ n. planetario m.
plank /plæŋk/ n. tablón m.
planning /'plænɪŋ/ n. planificación f.
plant /plænt/ n. 1. mata, planta f. —v. 2. sembrar, plantar.
plantation /plæn'teiʃən/ n. plantación f. **coffee p.,** cafetal m.
planter /'plæntər/ n. plantador; hacendado m.
plasma /'plæzmə/ n. plasma m.
plaster /'plæstər/ n. 1. yeso; em-

plasto *m.* —*v.* **2.** enyesar; emplastar.

plastic /'plæstɪk/ *a.* plástico.

plate /pleit/ *n.* **1.** plato *m.;* plancha de metal. —*v.* **2.** planchear.

plateau /plæ'tou/ *n.* meseta *f.*

platform /'plætfɔrm/ *n.* plataforma *f.*

platinum /'plætŋəm/ *n.* platino *m.*

platitude /'plætɪ,tud/ *n.* perogrullada *f.*

platter /'plætər/ *n.* fuente *f.*, platel *m.*

plaudit /'plɔdɪt/ *n.* aplauso *m.*

plausible /'plɔzəbəl/ *a.* plausible.

play /plei/ *n.* **1.** juego *m.; Theat.* pieza *f.* —*v.* **2.** jugar; (music) tocar; *Theat.* representar. **p. a part,** hacer un papel.

player /'pleiər/ *n.* jugador -ra; (music) músico -ca.; *Theat.* actor *m.*, actriz *f.*

playful /'pleifəl/ *a.* juguetón.

playground /'plei,graund/ *n.* campo de deportes; patio de recreo.

playmate /'plei,meit/. *n.* compañero -ra de juego.

playwright /'plei,rait/ *n.* dramaturgo -ga.

plea /pli/ *n.* ruego *m.;* súplica *f.;* (legal) declaración *f.*

plead /plid/ *v.* suplicar; declararse. **p. a case,** defender un pleito.

pleasant /'plɛzənt/ *a.* agradable.

please /pliz/ *v.* **1.** gustar, agradar. **Pleased to meet you,** Mucho gusto en conocer a Vd. —*adv.* **2.** por favor. **Please...** Haga el favor de..., Tenga la bondad de..., Sírvase...

pleasure /'plɛʒər/ *n.* gusto, placer *m.*

pleat /plit/ *n.* **1.** pliegue *m.* —*v.* **2.** plegar.

plebiscite /'plɛbə,sait/ *n.* plebiscito *m.*

pledge /plɛdʒ/ *n.* **1.** empeño *m.* —*v.* **2.** empeñar.

plentiful /'plɛntɪfəl/ *a.* abundante.

plenty /'plɛnti/ *n.* abundancia *f.* **p. of,** bastante. **p. more,** mucho más.

pleurisy /'plʊrəsi/ *n.* pleuritis *f.*

pliable, pliant /'plaiəbəl; 'plaiənt/ *a.* flexible.

pliers /'plaiərz/ *n.pl.* alicates *m.pl.*

plight /plait/ *n.* apuro, aprieto *m.*

plot /plɒt/ *n.* **1.** conspiración; (of a story) trama; (of land) parcela *f.* —*v.* **2.** conspirar; tramar.

plow /plau/ *n.* **1.** arado *m.* —*v.* **2.** arar.

pluck /plʌk/ *n.* **1.** valor *m.* —*v.* **2.** arrancar; desplumar.

plug /plʌg/ *n.* **1.** tapón; *Elec.* enchufe *m.* **spark p.,** bujía *f.* —*v.* **2.** tapar.

plum /plʌm/ *n.* ciruela *f.*

plumage /'plumɪdʒ/ *n.* plumaje *m.*

plumber /'plʌmər/ *n.* fontanero -era, plomero -era.

plume /plum/ *n.* pluma *f.*

plump /plʌmp/ *a.* regordete.

plunder /'plʌndər/ *n.* **1.** botín *m.;* despojos *m.pl.* —*v.* **2.** saquear.

plunge /plʌndʒ/ *v.* zambullir; precipitar.

plural /'plʊrəl/ *a. & n.* plural *m.*

plus /plʌs/ *prep.* más.

plutocrat /'plutə,kræt/ *n.* plutócrata *m. & f.*

pneumatic /nʊ'mætɪk/ *a.* neumático.

pneumonia /nʊ'mounyə/ *n.* pulmonía *f.*

poach /poutʃ/ *v.* (eggs) escalfar; invadir; cazar en vedado.

pocket /'pɒkɪt/ *n.* **1.** bolsillo *m.* —*v.* **2.** embolsar.

pocketbook /'pɒkɪt,bʊk/ *n.* cartera *f.*

podiatry /pə'daiətri/ *n.* podiatría *f.*

poem /'pouəm/ *n.* poema *m.*

poet /'pouɪt/ *n.* poeta *m. & f.*

poetic /pou'ɛtɪk/ *a.* poético.

poetry /'pouɪtri/ *n.* poesía *f.*

poignant /'pɔinyənt/ *a.* conmovedor.

point /pɔint/ *n.* **1.** punta *f.;* punto *m.* —*v.* **2.** apuntar. **p. out,** señalar.

pointed /'pɔintɪd/ *a.* puntiagudo; directo.

pointless /'pɔintlɪs/ *a.* inútil.

poise /pɔiz/ *n.* **1.** equilibrio *m.;* serenidad *f.* —*v.* **2.** equilibrar; estar suspendido.

poison /'pɔizən/ *n.* **1.** veneno *m.* —*v.* **2.** envenenar.

poisonous /'pɔizənəs/ *a.* venenoso.

poke /pouk/ *n.* **1.** empuje *m.*, hurgonada *f.* —*v.* **2.** picar; haronear.

Poland /'poulənd/ *n.* Polonia *f.*

polar /'poulər/ *a.* polar.

pole /poul/ *n.* palo; *Geog.* polo *m.*

polemical /pə'lɛmɪkəl/ a. polémico.

police /pə'lis/ n. policía f.

policeman /pə'lismən/ n. policía m.

policy /'pɒləsi/ n. política f. **insurance p.,** póliza de seguro.

Polish /'pɒlɪʃ/ a. & n. polaco -ca.

polish /'pɒlɪʃ/ n. **1.** lustre m. —v. **2.** pulir, lustrar.

polite /pə'lait/ a. cortés.

politic /'pɒlɪtɪk/ **political** a. político.

politician /ˌpɒlɪ'tɪʃən/ n. político -ca.

politics /'pɒlɪtɪks/ n. política f.

poll /poul/ n. encuesta f.; (pl.) urnas f.pl.

pollen /'pɒlən/ n. polen m.

pollute /pə'lut/ v. contaminar.

pollution /pə'luʃən/ n. contaminación f.

polo /'poulou/ n. polo m.

polyester /ˌpɒli'ɛstər/ n. poliéster m.

polygamy /pə'lɪgəmi/ n. poligamia f.

polygon /'pɒliˌgɒn/ n. polígono m.

pomp /pɒmp/ n. pompa f.

pompous /'pɒmpəs/ a. pomposo.

poncho /'pɒntʃou/ n. poncho m.

pond /pɒnd/ n. charca f.

ponder /'pɒndər/ v. ponderar, meditar.

ponderous /'pɒndərəs/ a. ponderoso, pesado.

pontiff /'pɒntɪf/ n. pontífice m.

pontoon /pɒn'tun/ n. pontón m.

pony /'pouni/ n. caballito m.

ponytail /'pouniˌteil/ n. cola de caballo f.

poodle /'pudl/ n. caniche m.

pool /pul/ n. charco m. **swimming p.,** piscina f.

poor /pur/ a. pobre; (not good) malo.

pop /pɒp/ n. chasquido m.

popcorn /'pɒpˌkɔrn/ n. rosetas de maíz, palomitas de maíz f.pl.

pope /poup/ n. papa m.

poppy /'pɒpi/ n. amapola f.

popsicle /'pɒpsɪkəl/ n. polo m.

popular /'pɒpyələr/ a. popular.

popularity /ˌpɒpyə'lærɪti/ n. popularidad f.

population /ˌpɒpyə'leiʃən/ n. población f.

porcelain /'pɔrsəlɪn/ n. porcelana f.

porch /pɔrtʃ/ n. pórtico m.; galería f.

pore /pɔr/ n. poro m.

pork /pɔrk/ n. carne de puerco.

pornography /pɔr'nɒgrəfi/ n. pornografía f.

porous /'pɔrəs/ a. poroso, esponjoso.

port /pɔrt/ n. puerto; Naut. babor m. **p. wine,** oporto m.

portable /'pɔrtəbəl/ a. portátil.

portal /'pɔrtl/ n. portal m.

portend /pɔr'tɛnd/ v. pronosticar.

portent /'pɔrtɛnt/ n. presagio m., portento m.

porter /'pɔrtər/ n. portero m.

portfolio /pɔrt'fouliˌou/ n. cartera f.

porthole /'pɔrtˌhoul/ n. porta f.

portion /'pɔrʃən/ n. porción f.

portly /'pɔrtli/ a. corpulento.

portrait /'pɔrtrɪt/ n. retrato m.

portray /pɔr'trei/ v. pintar.

Portugal /'pɔrtʃəgəl/ n. Portugal m.

Portuguese /ˌpɔrtʃə'giz/ a. & n. portugués -esa.

pose /pouz/ n. **1.** postura; actitud f. —v. **2.** posar. **p. as,** pretender ser.

position /pə'zɪʃən/ n. posición f.

positive /'pɒzɪtɪv/ a. positivo.

possess /pə'zɛs/ v. poseer.

possession /pə'zɛʃən/ n. posesión f.

possessive /pə'zɛsɪv/ a. posesivo.

possibility /ˌpɒsə'bɪlɪti/ n. posibilidad f.

possible /'pɒsəbəl/ a. posible.

post /poust/ n. **1.** poste; puesto m. —v. **2.** fijar; situar; echar al correo.

postage /'poustɪdʒ/ n. porte de correo. **p. stamp,** sello m.

postal /'poustl/ a. postal.

post card tarjeta postal.

poster /'poustər/ n. cartel, letrero m.

posterior /pɒ'stɪəriər/ a. posterior.

posterity /pɒ'stɛrɪti/ n. posteridad f.

postgraduate /poust'grædʒuɪt/ a. & n. postgraduado -da.

postmark /'poustˌmɑrk/ n. matasellos m.

post office correos m.pl.

postpone /poust'poun/ v. posponer, aplazar.

postscript /'poust,skrɪpt/ n. posdata f.

posture /'pɒstʃər/ n. postura f.

pot /pɒt/ n. olla, marmita; (marijuana) marijuana, hierba f.
flower p., tiesto m.

potassium /pə'tæsiəm/ n. potasio m.

potato /pə'teitou/ n. patata, papa f. **sweet p.**, batata f.

potent /'poutŋt/ a. potente, poderoso.

potential /pə'tɛnʃəl/ a. & n. potencial f.

potion /'pouʃən/ n. poción, pócima f.

pottery /'pɒtəri/ n. alfarería f.

pouch /pautʃ/ n. saco m.; bolsa f.

poultry /'poultri/ n. aves de corral.

pound /paund/ n. **1.** libra f. —v. **2.** golpear.

pour /pɔr/ v. echar; verter; llover a cántaros.

poverty /'pɒvərti/ n. pobreza f.

powder /'paudər/ n. **1.** polvo m.; (gun) pólvora f. —v. **2.** empolvar; pulverizar.

power /'pauər/ n. poder m.; potencia f.

powerful /'pauərfəl/ a. poderoso, fuerte.

powerless /'pauərlɪs/ a. impotente.

practical /'præktɪkəl/ a. práctico.

practical joke inocentada f.

practically /'præktɪkli/ adv. casi; prácticamente.

practice /'præktɪs/ n. **1.** práctica; costumbre; clientela f. —v. **2.** practicar; ejercer.

practiced /'præktɪst/ a. experto.

practitioner /præk'tɪʃənər/ n. practicante m. & f.

pragmatic /præg'mætɪk/ a. pragmático.

prairie /'preəri/ n. llanura; S.A. pampa f.

praise /preiz/ n. **1.** alabanza f. —v. **2.** alabar.

prank /præŋk/ n. travesura f.

prawn /prɔn/ n. gamba f.

pray /prei/ v. rezar; (beg) rogar.

prayer /'preiər/ n. oración; súplica f., ruego m.

preach /pritʃ/ v. predicar; sermonear.

preacher /'pritʃər/ n. predicador m.

preamble /'pri,æmbəl/ n. preámbulo m.

precarious /prɪ'kɛəriəs/ a. precario.

precaution /prɪ'kɔʃən/ n. precaución f.

precede /prɪ'sid/ v. preceder, anteceder.

precedent /n. 'prɛsɪdənt; a. prɪ'sidnt/ n. & a. precedente m.

precept /'prisɛpt/ n. precepto m.

precinct /'prisɪŋkt/ n. recinto m.

precious /'prɛʃəs/ a. precioso.

precipice /'prɛsəpɪs/ n. precipicio m.

precipitate /prɪ'sɪpɪ,teit/ v. precipitar.

precise /prɪ'sais/ a. preciso, exacto.

precision /prɪ'sɪʒən/ n. precisión f.

preclude /prɪ'klud/ v. evitar.

precocious /prɪ'kouʃəs/ a. precoz.

precooked /pri'kʊkt/ a. precocinado.

predatory /'prɛdə,tɔri/ a. de rapiña, rapaz.

predecessor /'prɛdə,sɛsər/ n. predecesor -ra, antecesor -ra.

predicament /prɪ'dɪkəmənt/ n. dificultad f.; apuro m.

predict /prɪ'dɪkt/ v. pronosticar, predecir.

predictable /prɪ'dɪktəbəl/ a. previsible.

predilection /,prɛdl̩'ɛkʃən/ n. predilección f.

predispose /,pridɪ'spouz/ v. predisponer.

predominant /prɪ'dɒmənənt/ a. predominante.

prefabricate /pri'fæbrɪ,keit/ v. fabricar de antemano.

preface /'prɛfɪs/ n. prefacio m.

prefer /prɪ'fɜr/ v. preferir.

preferable /'prɛfərəbəl/ a. preferible.

preference /'prɛfərəns/ n. preferencia f.

prefix /'prifɪks/ n. **1.** prefijo m. —v. **2.** prefijar.

pregnant /'prɛgnənt/ a. preñada.

prehistoric /,prihɪ'stɔrɪk/ a. prehistórico.

prejudice /'prɛdʒədɪs/ n. prejuicio m.

prejudiced /'prɛdʒədɪst/ a. (S.A.) prejuiciado.

preliminary /prɪ'lɪmə,nɛri/ a. preliminar.

prelude /'prɛlyud/ n. preludio m.

premature /ˌprimə'tʃʊr/ a. prematuro.

premeditate /pri'mɛdɪˌteit/ v. premeditar.

premier /prɪ'mɪər/ n. primer ministro.

première /prɪ'mɪər/ n. estreno m.

premise /'prɛmɪs/ n. premisa f.

premium /'primiəm/ n. premio m.

premonition /ˌprimə'nɪʃən/ n. presentimiento m.

prenatal /pri'neitl/ a. prenatal.

preparation /ˌprɛpə'reiʃən/ n. preparativo m.; preparación f.

preparatory /prɪ'pærəˌtɔri/ a. preparatorio. **p. to,** antes de.

prepare /prɪ'pɛər/ v. preparar.

preponderant /prɪ'pɒndərənt/ a. preponderante.

preposition /ˌprɪpə'zɪʃən/ n. preposición f.

preposterous /prɪ'pɒstərəs/ a. prepóstero, absurdo.

prerequisite /prɪ'rɛkwəzɪt/ n. requisito previo.

prerogative /prɪ'rɒgətɪv/ n. prerrogativa f.

prescribe /prɪ'skraib/ v. prescribir; Med. recetar.

prescription /prɪ'skrɪpʃən/ n. prescripción; Med. receta f.

presence /'prɛzəns/ n. presencia f.; porte m.

present /a, n 'prɛzənt; v prɪ'zɛnt/ a. **1.** presente. **to be present at,** asistir a. —n. **2.** presente; (gift) regalo m. **at p.,** ahora, actualmente. **for the p.,** por ahora. —v. **3.** presentar.

presentable /prɪ'zɛntəbəl/ a. presentable.

presentation /ˌprɛzən'teiʃən/ n. presentación; introducción f.; Theat. representación f.

presently /'prɛzəntli/ adv. luego; dentro de poco.

preservative /prɪ'zɜrvətɪv/ a. & n. preservativo m.

preserve /prɪ'zɜrv/ n. **1.** conserva f.; (hunting) vedado m. —v. **2.** preservar.

preside /prɪ'zaid/ v. presidir.

presidency /'prɛzɪdənsi/ n. presidencia f.

president /'prɛzɪdənt/ n. presidente -ta.

press /prɛs/ n. **1.** prensa f. —v. **2.** apretar; urgir; (clothes) planchar.

pressing /'prɛsɪŋ/ a. urgente.

pressure /'prɛʃər/ n. presión f.

pressure cooker /'kʊkər/ cocina de presión f.

prestige /prɛ'stiʒ/ n. prestigio m.

presume /prɪ'zum/ v. presumir, suponer.

presumptuous /prɪ'zʌmptʃuəs/ a. presuntuoso.

presuppose /ˌprisə'pouz/ v. presuponer.

pretend /prɪ'tɛnd/ v. fingir. **p. to the throne,** aspirar al trono.

pretense /prɪ'tɛns, 'pritɛns/ n. pretensión f.; fingimiento m.

pretension /prɪ'tɛnʃən/ n. pretensión f.

pretentious /prɪ'tɛnʃəs/ a. presumido.

pretext /'pritɛkst/ n. pretexto m.

pretty /'prɪti/ a. **1.** bonito, lindo. —adv. **2.** bastante.

prevail /prɪ'veil/ v. prevalecer.

prevailing /prɪ'veilɪŋ/ **prevalent** a. predominante.

prevent /prɪ'vɛnt/ v. impedir; evitar.

prevention /prɪ'vɛnʃən/ n. prevención f.

preventive /prɪ'vɛntɪv/ a. preventivo.

preview /'priˌvyu/ n. vista anticipada f.

previous /'priviəs/ a. anterior, previo.

prey /prei/ n. presa f.

price /prais/ n. precio m.

priceless /'praislɪs/ a. sin precio.

prick /prɪk/ n. **1.** punzada f. —v. **2.** punzar.

pride /praid/ n. orgullo m.

priest /prist/ n. sacerdote, cura m.

prim /prɪm/ a. estirado, remilgado.

primary /'praimɛri/ a. primario, principal.

prime /praim/ a. **1.** primero. —n. **2.** flor f. —v. **3.** alistar.

prime minister primer ministro m. & f.

primitive /'prɪmɪtɪv/ a. primitivo.

prince /prɪns/ n. príncipe m.

Prince Charming Príncipe Azul m.

princess /'prɪnsɪs/ n. princesa f.

principal /'prɪnsəpəl/ a. **1.** principal. —n. **2.** principal m. & f.; director -ra.

principle /'prɪnsəpəl/ n. principio m.

print /prɪnt/ n. **1.** letra de molde

f.; (art) grabado *m.* —*v.* **2.** imprimir, estampar.

printer /'prɪntər/ *n.* impresora *f.*

printing /'prɪntɪŋ/ *n.* impresión; **p. office,** imprenta *f.*

printing press prensa *f.*

printout /'prɪnt,aut/ *n.* impreso producido por una computadora, impresión *f.*

priority /prai'ɔrɪti/ *n.* prioridad, precedencia *f.*

prism /'prɪzəm/ *n.* prisma *m.*

prison /'prɪzən/ *n.* prisión, cárcel *f.*

prisoner /'prɪzənər/ *n.* presidiario -ria, prisionero -ra, preso -sa.

pristine /'prɪstin/ *a.* inmaculado.

privacy /'praivəsi/ *n.* soledad *f.*

private /'praivɪt/ *a.* **1.** particular. —*n.* **2.** soldado raso. **in p.,** en particular.

privation /prai'veiʃən/ *n.* privación *f.*

privet /'prɪvɪt/ *n.* ligustro *m.*

privilege /'prɪvəlɪdʒ/ *n.* privilegio *m.*

privy /'prɪvi/ *n.* letrina *f.*

prize /praiz/ *n.* **1.** premio *m.* —*v.* **2.** apreciar, estimar.

probability /,prɒbə'bɪlɪti/ *n.* probabilidad *f.*

probable /'prɒbəbəl/ *a.* probable.

probate /'proubeit/ *a.* testamentario.

probation /prou'beiʃən/ *n.* prueba *f.;* probación *f.;* libertad condicional *f.*

probe /proub/ *n.* **1.** indagación *f.* —*v.* **2.** indagar; tentar.

probity /'proubɪti/ *n.* probidad *f.*

problem /'prɒbləm/ *n.* problema *m.*

procedure /prə'sidʒər/ *n.* procedimiento *m.*

proceed /prə'sid/ *v.* proceder; proseguir.

process /'prɒsɛs/ *n.* proceso *m.*

procession /prə'sɛʃən/ *n.* procesión *f.*

proclaim /prou'kleim/ *v.* proclamar, anunciar.

proclamation /,prɒklə'meiʃən/ *n.* proclamación *f.;* decreto *m.*

procrastinate /prou'kræstə,neit/ *v.* dilatar.

procure /prou'kyur/ *v.* obtener, procurar.

prodigal /'prɒdɪgəl/ *n. & a.* pródigo -ga.

prodigy /'prɒdɪdʒi/ *n.* prodigio *m.*

produce /prə'dus/ *v.* producir.

product /'prɒdəkt/ *n.* producto *m.*

production /prə'dʌkʃən/ *n.* producción *f.*

productive /prə'dʌktɪv/ *a.* productivo.

profane /prə'fein/ *a.* **1.** profano. —*v.* **2.** profanar.

profanity /prə'fænɪti/ *n.* profanidad *f.*

profess /prə'fɛs/ *v.* profesar; declarar.

profession /prə'fɛʃən/ *n.* profesión *f.*

professional /prə'fɛʃənl/ *a. & n.* profesional *m. & f.*

professor /prə'fɛsər/ *n.* profesor -ra; catedrático -ca.

proficient /prə'fɪʃənt/ *a.* experto, proficiente.

profile /'proufail/ *n.* perfil *m.*

profit /'prɒfɪt/ *n.* **1.** provecho *m.;* ventaja *f.;* Com. ganancia *f.* —*v.* **2.** aprovechar; beneficiar.

profitable /'prɒfɪtəbəl/ *a.* provechoso, ventajoso, lucrativo.

profiteer /,prɒfɪ'tɪər/ *n.* **1.** explotador -ra. —*v.* **2.** explotar.

profound /prə'faund/ *a.* profundo, hondo.

profuse /prə'fyus/ *a.* pródigo; profuso.

prognosis /prɒg'nousɪs/ *n.* pronóstico *m.*

program /'prougræm/ *n.* programa *m.*

progress /*n.* 'prɒgrɛs; *v.* prə'grɛs/ *n.* **1.** progresos *m.pl.* **in p.,** en marcha. —*v.* **2.** progresar; marchar.

progressive /prə'grɛsɪv/ *a.* progresivo; progresista.

prohibit /prou'hɪbɪt/ *v.* prohibir.

prohibition /,prouə'bɪʃən/ *n.* prohibición *f.*

prohibitive /prou'hɪbɪtɪv/ *a.* prohibitivo.

project /*n.* 'prɒdʒɛkt; *v.* prə'dʒɛkt/ *n.* **1.** proyecto *m.* —*v.* **2.** proyectar.

projectile /prə'dʒɛktɪl/ *n.* proyectil *m.*

projection /prə'dʒɛkʃən/ *n.* proyección *f.*

projector /prə'dʒɛktər/ *n.* proyector *m.*

proliferation /prə,lɪfə'reiʃən/ *n.* proliferación *f.*

prolific /prə'lɪfɪk/ *a.* prolífico.

prologue /'proulɔg/ *n.* prólogo *m.*

prolong /prə'lɔŋ/ v. prolongar.
prominent /'prɒmənənt/ a. prominente; eminente.
promiscuous /prə'mɪskyuəs/ a. promiscuo.
promise /'prɒmɪs/ n. **1.** promesa f. —v. **2.** prometer.
promote /prə'mout/ v. fomentar; estimular; adelantar; promocionar.
promotion /prə'mouʃən/ n. promoción f.; adelanto m.
prompt /prɒmpt/ a. **1.** puntual. —v. **2.** impulsar; *Theat.* apuntar. —adv. **3.** pronto.
promulgate /'prɒməl,geit/ v. promulgar.
pronoun /'prou,naun/ n. pronombre m.
pronounce /prə'nauns/ v. pronunciar.
pronunciation /prə,nʌnsi'eiʃən/ n. pronunciación f.
proof /pruf/ n. prueba f.
proof of purchase certificado de compra m.
proofread /'pruf,rid/ v. corregir pruebas.
prop /prɒp/ n. **1.** apoyo, m. —v. **2.** sostener.
propaganda /,prɒpə'gændə/ n. propaganda f.
propagate /'prɒpə,geit/ v. propagar.
propel /prə'pɛl/ v. propulsar.
propeller /prə'pɛlər/ n. hélice f.
propensity /prə'pɛnsɪti/ n. tendencia f.
proper /'prɒpər/ a. propio; correcto.
property /'prɒpərti/ n. propiedad f.
prophecy /'prɒfəsi/ n. profecía f.
prophesy /'prɒfə,sai/ v. predecir, profetizar.
prophet /'prɒfɪt/ n. profeta m.
prophetic /prə'fɛtɪk/ a. profético.
propitious /prə'pɪʃəs/ a. propicio.
proponent /prə'pounənt/ n. & a. proponente m.
proportion /prə'pɔrʃən/ n. proporción f.
proportionate /prə'pɔrʃənɪt/ a. proporcionado.
proposal /prə'pouzəl/ n. propuesta; oferta f.; (marriage) declaración f.
propose /prə'pouz/ v. proponer; pensar; declararse.

proposition /,prɒpə'zɪʃən/ n. proposición f.
proprietor /prə'praiɪtər/ n. propietario -ria, dueño -ña.
propriety /prə'praiɪti/ n. corrección f., decoro m.
prosaic /prou'zeiɪk/ a. prosaico.
proscribe /prou'skraib/ v. proscribir.
prose /prouz/ n. prosa f.
prosecute /'prɒsɪ,kyut/ v. acusar, procesar.
prospect /'prɒspɛkt/ n. perspectiva; esperanza f.
prospective /prə'spɛktɪv/ a. anticipado, presunto.
prosper /'prɒspər/ v. prosperar.
prosperity /prɒ'spɛrɪti/ n. prosperidad f.
prosperous /'prɒspərəs/ a. próspero.
prostate gland /'prɒsteit/ glándula prostática f.
prostitute /'prɒstɪ,tut/ n. **1.** prostituta f. —v. **2.** prostituir.
prostrate /'prɒstreit/ a. **1.** postrado. —v. **2.** postrar.
protect /prə'tɛkt/ v. proteger; amparar.
protection /prə'tɛkʃən/ n. protección f.; amparo m.
protective /prə'tɛktɪv/ a. protector.
protector /prə'tɛktər/ n. protector -ora.
protégé /'proutə,ʒei/ n. protegido -da.
protein /'proutin, -tiɪn/ n. proteína f.
protest /n. 'proutɛst; v. prə'tɛst, 'proutɛst/ n. **1.** protesta f. —v. **2.** protestar.
Protestant /'prɒtəstənt/ a. & n. protestante m. & f.
protocol /'proutə,kɔl/ n. protocolo m.
proton /'proutɒn/ n. protón m.
protract /prou'trækt/ v. alargar, demorar.
protrude /prou'trud/ v. salir fuera.
protuberance /prou'tubərəns/ n. protuberancia f.
proud /praud/ a. orgulloso.
prove /pruv/ v. comprobar.
proverb /'prɒvərb/ n. proverbio, refrán m.
provide /prə'vaid/ v. proporcionar; proveer.

provided /prə'vaidɪd/ *conj.* con tal que.

providence /'prɒvɪdəns/ *n.* providencia *f.*

province /'prɒvɪns/ *n.* provincia *f.*

provincial /prə'vɪnʃəl/ *a.* **1.** provincial. —*n.* **2.** provinciano -na.

provision /prə'vɪʒən/ *n.* **1.** provisión *f.;* (pl.) comestibles *m.pl.* —*v.* **2.** abastecer.

provocation /ˌprɒvə'keiʃən/ *n.* provocación *f.*

provoke /prə'vouk/ *v.* provocar.

prowess /'praʊɪs/ *n.* proeza *f.*

prowl /praul/ *v.* rondar.

prowler /'praulər/ *n.* merodeador -dora *m. & f.*

proximity /prɒk'sɪmɪti/ *n.* proximidad *f.*

proxy /'prɒksi/ *n.* delegado -da. **by p.,** mediante apoderado.

prudence /'prudn̩s/ *n.* prudencia *f.*

prudent /'prudn̩t/ *a.* prudente, cauteloso.

prune /prun/ *n.* ciruela pasa *f.*

pry /prai/ *v.* atisbar; curiosear; *Mech.* alzaprimar.

psalm /sɑm/ *n.* salmo *m.*

pseudonym /'sudn̩ɪm/ *n.* seudónimo *m.*

psychedelic /ˌsaikɪ'delɪk/ *a.* psiquedélico.

psychiatrist /sɪ'kaiətrɪst, sai-/ *n.* psiquiatra *m. & f.*

psychiatry /sɪ'kaiətri, sai-/ *n.* psiquiatría *f.*

psychoanalysis /ˌsaikouə'næləsɪs/ *n.* psicoanálisis *m.*

psychoanalyst /ˌsaikou'ænl̩ɪst/ *n.* psicoanalista *m. & f.*

psychological /ˌsaikə'lɒdʒɪkəl/ *a.* psicológico.

psychology /sai'kɒlədʒi/ *n.* psicología *f.*

psychosis /sai'kousɪs/ *n.* psicosis *f.*

ptomaine /'toumein/ *n.* tomaína *f.*

pub /pʌb/ *n.* bar *m.*

public /'pʌblɪk/ *a. & n.* público *m.*

publication /ˌpʌblɪ'keiʃən/ *n.* publicación; revista *f.*

publicity /pʌ'blɪsɪti/ *n.* publicidad *f.*

publicity agent publicista *m. & f.*

publish /'pʌblɪʃ/ *v.* publicar.

publisher /'pʌblɪʃər/ *n.* editor -ora.

pudding /'pʊdɪŋ/ *n.* pudín *m.*

puddle /'pʌdl̩/ *n.* charco, lodazal *m.*

Puerto Rican /'pwɛrtə 'rikən, 'pɔr-/ *a. & n.* puertorriqueño -ña.

Puerto Rico /'pwɛr'tə rikou, 'pɔrtə/ Puerto Rico *m.*

puff /pʌf/ *n.* **1.** soplo *m.;* (of smoke) bocanada *f.* **powder p.,** polvera *f.* —*v.* **2.** jadear; echar bocanadas. **p. up,** hinchar; *Fig.* engreír.

pugnacious /pʌg'neiʃəs/ *a.* pugnaz.

puh-lease! /pʌ 'liz/ ¡Favor!

pull /pʊl/ *n.* **1.** tirón *m.;* *Colloq.* influencia *f.* —*v.* **2.** tirar; halar.

pulley /'pʊli/ *n.* polea *f.,* motón *m.*

pulmonary /'pʌlməˌnɛri/ *a.* pulmonar.

pulp /pʌlp/ *n.* pulpa; (of fruit) carne *f.*

pulpit /'pʊlpɪt, 'pʌl-/ *n.* púlpito *m.*

pulsar /'pʌlsɑr/ *n.* pulsar *m.*

pulsate /'pʌlseit/ *v.* pulsar.

pulse /pʌls/ *n.* pulso *m.*

pump /pʌmp/ *n.* **1.** bomba *f.* —*v.* **2.** bombear. **p. up,** inflar.

pumpkin /'pʌmpkɪn/ *n.* calabaza *f.*

pun /pʌn/ *n.* juego de palabras.

punch /pʌntʃ/ *n.* **1.** puñetazo; *Mech.* punzón; (beverage) ponche *m.* —*v.* **2.** dar puñetazos; punzar.

punch bowl ponchera *f.*

punctual /'pʌŋktʃuəl/ *a.* puntual.

punctuate /'pʌŋktʃuˌeit/ *v.* puntuar.

puncture /'pʌŋktʃər/ *n.* **1.** pinchazo *m.,* perforación *f.* —*v.* **2.** pinchar, perforar.

pungent /'pʌndʒənt/ *a.* picante, pungente.

punish /'pʌnɪʃ/ *v.* castigar.

punishment /'pʌnɪʃmənt/ *n.* castigo *m.*

punitive /'pyunɪtɪv/ *a.* punitivo.

puny /'pyuni/ *a.* encanijado.

pupil /'pyupəl/ *n.* alumno -na; *Anat.* pupila *f.*

puppet /'pʌpɪt/ *n.* muñeco *m.*

puppy /'pʌpi/ *n.* perrito -ta.

purchase /'pɜrtʃəs/ *n.* **1.** compra *f.* —*v.* **2.** comprar.

purchasing power /'pɜrtʃəsɪŋ/ poder adquisitivo *m.*

pure /pyur/ *a.* puro.

purée /pyu'rei/ *n.* puré *m.*

purge /pɜrdʒ/ *v.* purgar.

purify /'pyʊrəˌfai/ v. purificar.
puritanical /ˌpyʊrɪ'tænɪkəl/ a. puritano.
purity /'pyʊrɪti/ n. pureza f.
purple /'pɜrpəl/ a. **1.** purpúreo. —n. **2.** púrpura f.
purport /n. 'pɜrpɔrt; v. pər'pɔrt/ n. **1.** significación f. —v. **2.** significar.
purpose /'pɜrpəs/ n. propósito m. **on p.,** de propósito.
purr /pɜr/ v. ronronear.
purse /pɜrs/ n. bolsa f.
pursue /pər'su/ v. perseguir.
pursuit /pər'sut/ n. caza; busca;

ocupación f. **p. plane,** avión de caza m.
push /pʊʃ/ n. **1.** empuje; impulso m. —v. **2.** empujar.
put /pʊt/ v. poner, colocar. **p. away,** guardar. **p. in,** meter. **p. off,** dejar. **p. on,** ponerse. **p. out,** apagar. **p. up with,** aguantar.
putrid /'pyutrɪd/ a. podrido.
putt /pʌt/ n. (golf) golpe corto m.
puzzle /'pʌzəl/ n. **1.** enigma; rompecabezas m. —v. **2.** dejar perplejo. **p. out,** descifrar.
pyramid /'pɪrəmɪd/ n. pirámide f.
pyromania /ˌpairə'meiniə/ n. piromanía f.

Q

quack /kwæk/ n. **1.** (doctor) curandero -ra; (duck) graznido m. —v. **2.** graznar.
quadrangle /'kwɒdˌræŋgəl/ n. cuadrángulo m.
quadraphonic /ˌkwɒdrə'fɒnɪk/ a. cuatrifónico.
quadruped /'kwɒdrʊˌpɛd/ a. & n. cuadrúpedo m.
quail /kweil/ n. **1.** codorniz f. —v. **2.** descorazonarse.
quaint /kweint/ a. curioso.
quake /kweik/ n. **1.** temblor m. —v. **2.** temblar.
qualification /ˌkwɒləfɪ'keiʃən/ n. requisito m.; (pl.) preparaciones f.pl.
qualified /'kwɒləˌfaid/ a. calificado, competente; preparado.
qualify /'kwɒləˌfai/ v. calificar, modificar; llenar los requisitos.
quality /'kwɒlɪti/ n. calidad f.
quandary /'kwɒndəri, -dri/ n. incertidumbre f.
quantity /'kwɒntɪti/ n. cantidad f.
quarantine /'kwɔrənˌtin, 'kwɒr-, ˌkwɔrən'tin, ˌkwɒr-/ n. cuarentena f.
quarrel /'kwɔrəl, 'kwɒr-/ n. **1.** riña, disputa f. —v. **2.** reñir, disputar.
quarry /'kwɔri, 'kwɒri/ n. cantera; (hunting) presa f.
quarter /'kwɔrtər/ n. cuarto m.; (pl.) vivienda f.
quarterly /'kwɔrtərli/ a. **1.** trimestral. —adv. **2.** por cuartos.
quartet /kwɔr'tɛt/ n. cuarteto m.
quartz /kwɔrts/ n. cuarzo m.
quasar /'kweizɑr/ n. cuasar m.
quaver /'kweivər/ v. temblar.

queen /kwin/ n. reina f.; (chess) dama f.
queer /kwɪər/ a. extraño, raro.
quell /kwɛl/ v. reprimir.
quench /kwɛntʃ/ v. apagar.
query /'kwɪəri/ n. **1.** pregunta f. —v. **2.** preguntar.
quest /kwɛst/ n. busca f.
question /'kwɛstʃən/ n. **1.** pregunta; cuestión f. **q. mark,** signo de interrogación. —v. **2.** preguntar; interrogar; dudar.
questionable /'kwɛstʃənəbəl/ a. dudoso.
questionnaire /ˌkwɛstʃə'nɛər/ n. cuestionario m.
quiche /kiʃ/ n. quiche f.
quick /kwɪk/ a. rápido.
quicken /'kwɪkən/ v. acelerar.
quicksand /'kwɪkˌsænd/ n. arena movediza.
quiet /'kwaiɪt/ a. **1.** quieto, tranquilo; callado. **be q., keep q.,** callarse. —n. **2.** calma; quietud f. —v. **3.** tranquilizar. **q. down,** callarse; calmarse.
quilt /kwɪlt/ n. colcha f.
quinine /'kwainain/ n. quinina f.
quintet /kwɪn'tɛt/ n. Mus. quinteto m.
quip /kwɪp/ n. **1.** pulla f. —v. **2.** echar pullas.
quit /kwɪt/ v. dejar; renunciar a. **q. doing** (etc.) dejar de hacer (etc.).
quite /kwait/ adv. bastante; completamente. **not q.,** no precisamente; no completamente.
quiver /'kwɪvər/ n. **1.** aljaba f.; temblor m. —v. **2.** temblar.

quixotic /kwɪk'sɒtɪk/ *a.* quijotesco.

quorum /'kwɔrəm/ *n.* quórum *m.*

quota /'kwoutə/ *n.* cuota *f.*

quotation /kwou'teiʃən/ *n.* citación; *Com.* cotización *f.* **q. marks,** comillas *f.pl.*

quote /kwout/ *v.* citar; *Com.* cotizar.

R

rabbi /'ræbai/ *n.* rabí, rabino *m.*

rabbit /'ræbɪt/ *n.* conejo *m.*

rabble /'ræbəl/ *n.* canalla *f.*

rabid /'ræbɪd/ *a.* rabioso.

rabies /'reibiz/ *n.* hidrofobia *f.*

race /reis/ *n.* **1.** raza; carrera *f.* —*v.* **2.** echar una carrera; correr de prisa.

race track /'reis,træk/ hipódromo *m.*

rack /ræk/ *n.* **1.** (cooking) pesebre *m.*; (clothing) colgador *m.* —*v.* **2.** atormentar.

racket /'rækɪt/ *n.* (noise) ruido *m.*; (tennis) raqueta *f.*; (graft) fraude organizado.

radar /'reidɑr/ *n.* radar *m.*

radiance /'reidiəns/ *n.* brillo *m.*

radiant /'reidiənt/ *a.* radiante.

radiate /'reidi,eit/ *v.* irradiar.

radiation /,reidi'eiʃən/ *n.* irradiación *f.*

radiator /'reidi,eitər/ *n.* calorífero *m.*; *Auto.* radiador *m.*

radical /'rædɪkəl/ *a.* & *n.* radical *m.*

radio /'reidi,ou/ *n.* radio *m. or f.* **r. station,** estación radiodifusora *f.*

radioactive /,reidiou'æktɪv/ *a.* radioactivo.

radio cassette radiocasete *m.*

radish /'rædɪʃ/ *n.* rábano *m.*

radium /'reidiəm/ *n.* radio *m.*

radius /'reidiəs/ *n.* radio *m.*

raffle /'ræfəl/ *n.* **1.** rifa, lotería *f.* —*v.* **2.** rifar.

raft /ræft/ *n.* balsa *f.*

rafter /'ræftər/ *n.* viga *f.*

rag /ræg/ *n.* trapo *m.*

ragamuffin /'rægə,mʌfɪn/ *n.* galopín *m.*

rage /reidʒ/ *n.* **1.** rabia *f.* —*v.* **2.** rabiar.

ragged /'rægɪd/ *a.* andrajoso; desigual.

raid /reid/ *n. Mil.* correría *f.*

rail /reil/ *n.* baranda *f.*; carril *m.* **by r.,** por ferrocarril.

railroad /'reil,roud/ *n.* ferrocarril *m.*

rain /rein/ *n.* **1.** lluvia *f.* —*v.* **2.** llover.

rainbow /'rein,bou/ *n.* arco iris *m.*

raincoat /'rein,kout/ *n.* impermeable *m.*; gabardina *f.*

rainfall /'rein,fɔl/ *n.* precipitación *f.*

rainy /'reini/ *a.* lluvioso.

raise /reiz/ *n.* **1.** aumento *m.* —*v.* **2.** levantar, alzar; criar.

raisin /'reizɪn/ *n.* pasa *f.*

rake /reik/ *n.* **1.** rastro *m.* —*v.* **2.** rastrillar.

rally /'ræli/ *n.* **1.** reunión *f.* —*v.* **2.** reunirse.

ram /ræm/ *n.* carnero *m.*

ramble /'ræmbəl/ *v.* vagar.

ramp /ræmp/ *n.* rampa *f.*

rampart /'ræmpɑrt/ *n.* terraplén *m.*

ranch /ræntʃ/ *n.* rancho *m.*

rancid /'rænsɪd/ *a.* rancio.

rancor /'ræŋkər/ *n.* rencor *m.*

random /'rændəm/ *a.* fortuito. **at r.,** a la ventura.

range /reindʒ/ *n.* **1.** extensión *f.*; alcance *m.*; estufa; sierra *f.*; terreno de pasto. —*v.* **2.** recorrer; extenderse.

rank /ræŋk/ *a.* **1.** espeso; rancio. —*n.* **2.** fila *f.*; grado *m.* —*v.* **3.** clasificar.

ransack /'rænsæk/ *v.* saquear.

ransom /'rænsəm/ *n.* **1.** rescate *m.* —*v.* **2.** rescatar.

rap /ræp/ *n.* **1.** golpecito *m.* —*v.* **2.** golpear.

rapid /'ræpɪd/ *a.* rápido.

rapist /'reipɪst/ *n.* violador -dora *m.* & *f.*

rapport /ræ'pɔr/ *n.* armonía *f.*

rapture /'ræptʃər/ *n.* éxtasis *m.*

rare /rɛər/ *a.* raro; (of food) a medio cocer.

rascal /'ræskəl/ *n.* pícaro, bribón *m.*

rash /ræʃ/ *a.* **1.** temerario. —*n.* **2.** erupción *f.*

raspberry /'ræz,bɛri/ *n.* frambuesa *f.*

rat /ræt/ *n.* rata *f.*

rate /reit/ *n.* **1.** velocidad; tasa *f.;* precio *m.;* (of exchange; of interest) tipo *m.* **at any r.,** de todos modos. —*v.* **2.** valuar.

rather /'ræðər/ *adv.* bastante; más bien, mejor dicho.

ratify /'rætə‚fai/ *v.* ratificar.

ratio /'reiʃou/ *n.* razón; proporción *f.*

ration /'ræʃən, 'reiʃən/ *n.* **1.** ración *f.* —*v.* **2.** racionar.

rational /'ræʃənl/ *a.* racional.

rattle /'rætl/ *n.* **1.** ruido *m.;* matraca *f.* **r. snake,** culebra de cascabel, serpiente de cascabel *f.* —*v.* **2.** matraquear; rechinar.

raucous /'rɔkəs/ *a.* ronco.

ravage /'rævɪdʒ/ *v.* pillar; destruir; asolar.

rave /reiv/ *v.* delirar; entusiasmarse.

ravel /'rævəl/ *v.* deshilar.

raven /'reivən/ *n.* cuervo *m.*

ravenous /'rævənəs/ *a.* voraz.

raw /rɔ/ *a.* crudo; verde.

ray /rei/ *n.* rayo *m.*

rayon /'reiɒn/ *n.* rayón *m.*

razor /'reizər/ *n.* navaja de afeitar. **r. blade,** hoja de afeitar.

reach /ritʃ/ *n.* **1.** alcance *m.* —*v.* **2.** alcanzar.

react /ri'ækt/ *v.* reaccionar.

reaction /ri'ækʃən/ *n.* reacción *f.*

reactionary /ri'ækʃə‚nɛri/ *a.* **1.** reaccionario. —*n.* **2.** *Pol.* retrógrado *m.*

read /rid/ *v.* leer.

reader /'ridər/ *n.* lector -ra; libro de lectura *m.*

readily /'rɛdli/ *adv.* fácilmente.

reading /'ridɪŋ/ *n.* lectura *f.*

ready /'rɛdi/ *a.* listo, preparado; dispuesto.

ready-cooked /'rɛdi ‚kʊkt/ *a.* precocinado.

real /rei'ɑl/ *a.* verdadero; real.

real estate bienes inmuebles, *m.pl.*

real-estate agent /'riəl ɪ'steit/ agente inmobiliario *m.*, agente inmobiliaria *f.*

realist /'riəlɪst/ *n.* realista *m. & f.*

realistic /‚riə'lɪstɪk/ *a.* realista.

reality /ri'ælɪti/ *n.* realidad *f.*

realization /‚riələ'zeiʃən/ *n.* comprensión; realización *f.*

realize /'riə‚laiz/ *v.* darse cuenta de; realizar.

really /'riəli/ *adv.* de veras; en realidad.

realm /rɛlm/ *n.* reino; dominio *m.*

reap /rip/ *v.* segar, cosechar.

rear /rɪər/ *a.* **1.** posterior. —*n.* **2.** parte posterior. —*v.* **3.** criar; levantar.

reason /'rizən/ *n.* **1.** razón; causa *f.;* motivo *m.* —*v.* **2.** razonar.

reasonable /'rizənəbəl/ *a.* razonable.

reassure /‚riə'ʃʊr/ *v.* calmar, tranquilizar.

rebate /'ribeit/ *n.* rebaja *f.*

rebel /*n.* 'rɛbəl; *v.* rɪ'bɛl/ *n.* **1.** rebelde *m. & f.* —*v.* **2.** rebelarse.

rebellion /rɪ'bɛlyən/ *n.* rebelión *f.*

rebellious /rɪ'bɛlyəs/ *a.* rebelde.

rebirth /ri'bɜrθ/ *n.* renacimiento *m.*

rebound /rɪ'baund/ *v.* repercutir; resaltar.

rebuff /rɪ'bʌf/ *n.* **1.** repulsa *f.* —*v.* **2.** rechazar.

rebuke /rɪ'byuk/ *n.* **1.** reprensión *f.* —*v.* **2.** reprender.

rebuttal /rɪ'bʌtl/ *n.* refutación *f.*

recalcitrant /rɪ'kælsɪtrənt/ *a.* recalcitrante.

recall /rɪ'kɔl/ *v.* recordar; acordarse de; hacer volver.

recapitulate /‚rikə'pɪtʃə‚leit/ *v.* recapitular.

recede /ri'sid/ *v.* retroceder.

receipt /rɪ'sit/ *n.* recibo *m.;* (com., pl.) ingresos *m.pl.*

receive /rɪ'siv/ *v.* recibir.

receiver /rɪ'sivər/ *n.* receptor *m.*

recent /'risənt/ *a.* reciente.

recently /'risəntli/ *adv.* recién.

receptacle /rɪ'sɛptəkəl/ *n.* receptáculo *m.*

reception /rɪ'sɛpʃən/ *n.* acogida; recepción *f.*

receptionist /rɪ'sɛpʃənɪst/ *n.* recepcionista *m. & f.*

receptive /rɪ'sɛptɪv/ *a.* receptivo.

recess /rɪ'sɛs, 'risɛs/ *n.* nicho; retiro; recreo *m.*

recipe /'rɛsəpi/ *n.* receta *f.*

recipient /rɪ'sɪpiənt/ *n.* recibidor -ra, recipiente *m. & f.*

reciprocate /rɪ'sɪprə‚keit/ *v.* corresponder; reciprocar.

recite /rɪ'sait/ *v.* recitar.

reckless /'rɛklɪs/ *a.* descuidado; imprudente.

reckon /'rɛkən/ *v.* contar; calcular.

reclaim /rɪ'kleim/ *v.* reformar; *Leg.* reclamar.

recline /rɪ'klain/ *v.* reclinar; recostar.

recognition /ˌrɛkəg'nɪʃən/ *n.* reconocimiento *m.*

recognize /'rɛkəgˌnaiz/ *v.* reconocer.

recoil /*n.* 'riˌkɔil; *v.* rɪ'kɔil/ *n.* **1.** culatada *f.* —*v.* **2.** recular.

recollect /ˌrɛkə'lɛkt/ *v.* recordar, acordarse de.

recommend /ˌrɛkə'mɛnd/ *v.* recomendar.

recommendation /ˌrɛkəmɛn-'deiʃən/ *n.* recomendación *f.*

recompense /'rɛkəmˌpɛns/ *n.* **1.** recompensa *f.* —*v.* **2.** recompensar.

reconcile /'rɛkənˌsail/ *v.* reconciliar.

recondition /ˌrikən'dɪʃən/ *v.* reacondicionar.

reconsider /ˌrikən'sɪdər/ *v.* considerar de nuevo.

reconstruct /ˌrikən'strʌkt/ *v.* reconstruir.

record /*n.* 'rɛkərd, *v.* rɪ'kɔrd/ *n.* **1.** registro; (sports) record *m.* **phonograph r.,** disco *m.* —*v.* **2.** registrar.

record player tocadiscos *m.*

recount /rɪ'kaunt/ *v.* relatar; contar.

recover /rɪ'kʌvər/ *v.* recobrar; restablecerse.

recovery /rɪ'kʌvəri/ *n.* recobro *m.*; recuperación *f.*

recruit /rɪ'krut/ *n.* **1.** recluta *m.* —*v.* **2.** reclutar.

rectangle /'rɛkˌtæŋgəl/ *n.* rectángulo *m.*

rectify /'rɛktəˌfai/ *v.* rectificar.

recuperate /rɪ'kupəˌreit/ *v.* recuperar.

recur /rɪ'kɜr/ *v.* recurrir.

recycle /ri'saikəl/ *v.* reciclar.

red /rɛd/ *a.* rojo, colorado.

redeem /rɪ'dim/ *v.* redimir, rescatar.

redemption /rɪ'dɛmpʃən/ *n.* redención *f.*

redhead /'rɛdˌhɛd/ *n.* pelirrojo -ja.

red mullet /'mʌlɪt/ salmonete *m.*

reduce /rɪ'dus/ *v.* reducir.

reduction /rɪ'dʌkʃən/ *n.* reducción *f.*

reed /rid/ *n.* caña *f.,* S.A. bejuco *m.*

reef /rif/ *n.* arrecife, escollo *m.*

reel /ril/ *n.* **1.** aspa *f.,* carrete *m.* —*v.* **2.** aspar.

refer /rɪ'fɜr/ *v.* referir.

referee /ˌrɛfə'ri/ *n.* árbitro *m.* & *f.*

reference /'rɛfərəns/ *n.* referencia *f.*

refill /*n.* 'riˌfɪl; *v.* ri'fɪl/ *n.* **1.** relleno *m.* —*v.* **2.** rellenar.

refine /rɪ'fain/ *n.* refinar.

refinement /rɪ'fainmənt/ *n.* refinamiento *m.*; cultura *f.*

reflect /rɪ'flɛkt/ *v.* reflejar; reflexionar.

reflection /rɪ'flɛkʃən/ *n.* reflejo *m.*; reflexión *f.*

reflex /'riflɛks/ *a.* reflejo.

reform /rɪ'fɔrm/ *n.* **1.** reforma *f.* —*v.* **2.** reformar.

reformation /ˌrɛfər'meiʃən/ *n.* reformación *f.*

refractory /rɪ'fræktəri/ *a.* refractario.

refrain /rɪ'frein/ *n.* **1.** estribillo *m.* —*v.* **2.** abstenerse.

refresh /rɪ'frɛʃ/ *v.* refrescar.

refreshment /rɪ'frɛʃmənt/ *n.* refresco *m.*

refrigerator /rɪ'frɪdʒəˌreitər/ *n.* refrigerador *m.*

refuge /'rɛfyudʒ/ *n.* refugio *m.*

refugee /ˌrɛfyu'dʒi/ *n.* refugiado -da.

refund /*n.* 'rifʌnd; *v* ri'fʌnd/ *n.* **1.** reembolso *m.* —*v.* **2.** reembolsar.

refusal /rɪ'fyuzəl/ *n.* negativa *f.*

refuse /*n.* 'rɛfyus; *v* rɪ'fyuz/ *n.* **1.** basura *f.* —*v.* **2.** negarse, rehusar.

refute /rɪ'fyut/ *v.* refutar.

regain /ri'gein/ *v.* recobrar. **r. consciousness,** recobrar el conocimiento.

regal /'rigəl/ *a.* real.

regard /rɪ'gɑrd/ *n.* **1.** aprecio; respeto *m.* **with r. to,** con respecto a. —*v.* **2.** considerar; estimar.

regarding /rɪ'gɑrdɪŋ/ *prep.* en cuanto a, acerca de.

regardless (of) /rɪ'gɑrdlɪs/ a pesar de.

regent /'ridʒənt/ *n.* regente *m.* & *f.*

regime /rə'ʒim, rei-/ *n.* régimen *m.*

regiment /*n.* 'rɛdʒəmənt; *v.* -ˌmɛnt/ *n.* **1.** regimiento *m.* —*v.* **2.** regimentar.

region /'ridʒən/ *n.* región *f.*

register /'rɛdʒəstər/ *n.* **1.** registro *m.* **cash r.,** caja registradora *f.* —*v.* **2.** registrar; matricularse; (a letter) certificar.

registration /ˌrɛdʒə'streiʃən/ *n.* registro *m.*; matrícula *f.*

regret /rɪ'grɛt/ *n.* **1.** pena *f.* —*v.* **2.** sentir, lamentar.

regular /'rɛgyələr/ *a.* regular; ordinario.

regularity /,rɛgyə'lærɪti/ *n.* regularidad *f.*

regulate /'rɛgyə,leit/ *v.* regular.

regulation /,rɛgyə'leiʃən/ *n.* regulación *f.*

regulator /'rɛgyə,leitər/ *n.* regulador *m.*

rehabilitate /,rihə'bɪlɪ,teit, ,riə-/ *v.* rehabilitar.

rehearse /rɪ'hɜrs/ *v.* repasar; *Theat.* ensayar.

reheat /ri'hit/ *v.* recalentar.

reign /rein/ *n.* **1.** reino, reinado *m.* —*v.* **2.** reinar.

reimburse /,riɪm'bɜrs/ *v.* reembolsar.

rein /rein/ *n.* **1.** rienda *f.* —*v.* **2.** refrenar.

reincarnation /,riɪnkɑr'neiʃən/ *n.* reencarnación *f.*

reindeer /'rein,dɪər/ *n.* reno *m.*

reinforce /,riɪn'fɔrs, -'fours/ *v.* reforzar.

reinforcement /,riɪn'fɔrsmənt, -'fours-/ *n.* refuerzo *m.;* armadura *f.*

reiterate /ri'ɪtə,reit/ *v.* reiterar.

reject /rɪ'dʒɛkt/ *v.* rechazar.

rejoice /rɪ'dʒɔis/ *v.* regocijarse.

rejoin /rɪ'dʒɔin/ *v.* reunirse con; replicar.

rejuvenate /rɪ'dʒuvə,neit/ *v.* rejuvenecer.

relapse /*v.* rɪ'læps; *n. also* 'rilæps/ *v.* **1.** recaer. —*n.* **2.** recaída *f.*

relate /rɪ'leit/ *v.* relatar, contar; relacionar. **r. to,** llevarse bien con.

relation /rɪ'leiʃən/ *n.* relación *f.;* pariente *m. & f.*

relative /'rɛlətɪv/ *a.* **1.** relativo. —*n.* **2.** pariente *m. & f.*

relativity /,rɛlə'tɪvɪti/ *n.* relatividad *f.*

relax /rɪ'læks/ *v.* descansar; relajar.

relay /'rilei; *v. also* rɪ'lei/ *n.* **1.** relevo *m.* —*v.* **2.** retransmitir.

release /rɪ'lis/ *n.* **1.** liberación *f.* —*v.* **2.** soltar.

relent /rɪ'lɛnt/ *v.* ceder.

relevant /'rɛləvənt/ *a.* pertinente.

reliability /rɪ,laiə'bɪlɪti/ *n.* veracidad *f.*

reliable /rɪ'laiəbəl/ *a.* responsable; digno de confianza.

relic /'rɛlɪk/ *n.* reliquia *f.*

relief /rɪ'lif/ *n.* alivio; (sculpture) relieve *m.*

relieve /rɪ'liv/ *v.* aliviar.

religion /rɪ'lɪdʒən/ *n.* religión *f.*

religious /rɪ'lɪdʒəs/ *a.* religioso.

relinquish /rɪ'lɪŋkwɪʃ/ *v.* abandonar.

relish /'rɛlɪʃ/ *n.* **1.** sabor; condimento *m.* —*v.* **2.** saborear.

reluctant /rɪ'lʌktənt/ *a.* renuente.

rely /rɪ'lai/ *v.* **r. on,** confiar en; contar con; depender de.

remain /rɪ'mein/ *n.* **1.** (pl.) restos *m.pl.* —*v.* **2.** quedar, permanecer.

remainder /rɪ'meindər/ *n.* resto *m.*

remark /rɪ'mɑrk/ *n.* **1.** observación *f.* —*v.* **2.** observar.

remarkable /rɪ'mɑrkəbəl/ *a.* notable.

remedial /rɪ'midiəl/ *a.* reparador.

remedy /'rɛmɪdi/ *n.* **1.** remedio *m.* —*v.* **2.** remediar.

remember /rɪ'mɛmbər/ *v.* acordarse de, recordar.

remembrance /rɪ'mɛmbrəns/ *n.* recuerdo *m.*

remind /rɪ'maind/ *v.* **r. of,** recordar.

reminisce /,rɛmə'nɪs/ *v.* pensar en o hablar de cosas pasadas.

remiss /rɪ'mɪs/ *a.* remiso; flojo.

remit /rɪ'mɪt/ *v.* remitir.

remorse /rɪ'mɔrs/ *n.* remordimiento *m.*

remote /rɪ'mout/ *a.* remoto.

remote control mando a distancia *m.*

removal /rɪ'muvəl/ *n.* alejamiento *m.;* eliminación *f.*

remove /rɪ'muv/ *v.* quitar; remover.

renaissance /,rɛnə'sans/ *n.* renacimiento *m.*

rend /rɛnd/ *v.* hacer pedazos; separar.

render /'rɛndər/ *v.* dar; rendir; *Theat.* interpretar.

rendezvous /'randə,vu, -dei-/ *n.* cita *f.*

rendition /rɛn'dɪʃən/ *n.* interpretación, rendición *f.*

renege /rɪ'nɪg, -'nɛg/ *v.* renunciar; faltar a su palabra, no cumplir una promesa.

renew /rɪ'nu, -'nyu/ *v.* renovar.

renewal /rɪ'nuəl, -'nyu-/ *n.* renovación; *Com.* prórroga *f.*

renounce /rɪ'nauns/ v. renunciar a.

renovate /'rɛnə,veit/ v. renovar.

renown /rɪ'naun/ n. renombre m., fama f.

rent /rɛnt/ n. **1.** alquiler m. —v. **2.** arrendar, alquilar.

repair /rɪ'pɛər/ n. **1.** reparo m. —v. **2.** reparar.

repairman /rɪ'pɛər,mæn/ n. técnico m.

repatriate /ri'peitri,eit/ v. repatriar.

repay /rɪ'pei/ v. pagar; devolver.

repeat /rɪ'pit/ v. repetir.

repel /rɪ'pɛl/ v. repeler, repulsar.

repent /'ripənt, rɪ'pɛnt/ v. arrepentirse.

repentance /rɪ'pɛntns, -'pɛntəns/ n. arrepentimiento m.

repercussion /,ripər'kʌʃən, ,rɛpər-/ n. repercusión f.

repertoire /'rɛpər,twɑr/ n. repertorio m.

repetition /,rɛpɪ'tɪʃən/ n. repetición f.

replace /rɪ'pleis/ v. reemplazar.

replenish /rɪ'plɛnɪʃ/ v. rellenar; surtir de nuevo.

reply /rɪ'plai/ n. **1.** respuesta f. —v. **2.** replicar; contestar.

report /rɪ'pɔrt, -'pourt/ n. **1.** informe m. —v. **2.** informar, contar; denunciar; presentarse.

reporter /rɪ'pɔrtər, -'pour-/ n. repórter m. & f., reportero -ra.

repose /rɪ'pouz/ n. **1.** reposo m. —v. **2.** reposar; reclinar.

reprehensible /,rɛprɪ'hɛnsəbəl/ a. reprensible.

represent /,rɛprɪ'zɛnt/ v. representar.

representation /,rɛprɪzɛn'teiʃən, -zən-/ n. representación f.

representative /,rɛprɪ'zɛntətɪv/ a. **1.** representativo. —n. **2.** representante m. & f.

repress /rɪ'prɛs/ v. reprimir.

reprimand /'rɛprə,mænd, -,mɑnd/ n. **1.** regaño m. —v. **2.** regañar.

reprisal /rɪ'praizəl/ n. represalia f.

reproach /rɪ'proutʃ/ n. **1.** reproche m. —v. **2.** reprochar.

reproduce /,riprə'dus, -'dyus/ v. reproducir.

reproduction /,riprə'dʌkʃən/ n. reproducción f.

reproof /rɪ'pruf/ n. censura f.

reprove /rɪ'pruv/ v. censurar, regañar.

reptile /'rɛptɪl, -tail/ n. reptil m.

republic /rɪ'pʌblɪk/ n. república f.

republican /rɪ'pʌblɪkən/ a. & n. republicano -na.

repudiate /rɪ'pyudi,eit/ v. repudiar.

repulsive /rɪ'pʌlsɪv/ a. repulsivo, repugnante.

reputation /,rɛpyə'teiʃən/ n. reputación; fama f.

repute /rɪ'pyut/ n. **1.** reputación f. —v. **2.** reputar.

request /rɪ'kwɛst/ n. **1.** súplica f., ruego m. —v. **2.** pedir; rogar, suplicar.

require /rɪ'kwaiər/ v. requerir; exigir.

requirement /rɪ'kwaiərmənt/ n. requisito m.

requisite /'rɛkwəzɪt/ a. **1.** necesario. —n. **2.** requisito m.

requisition /,rɛkwə'zɪʃən/ n. requisición f.

rescind /rɪ'sɪnd/ v. rescindir, anular.

rescue /'rɛskyu/ n. **1.** rescate m. —v. **2.** rescatar.

research /rɪ'sɜrtʃ, 'risɜrtʃ/ n. investigación f.

researcher /rɪ'sɜrtʃər/ n. investigador -dora.

resemble /rɪ'zɛmbəl/ v. parecerse a, asemejarse a.

resent /rɪ'zɛnt/ v. resentirse de.

reservation /,rɛzər'veiʃən/ n. reservación f.

reserve /rɪ'zɜrv/ n. **1.** reserva f. —v. **2.** reservar.

reservoir /'rɛzər,vwar, -,vwɔr, -,vɔr, 'rɛzə-/ n depósito; tanque m.

reside /rɪ'zaid/ v. residir, morar.

residence /'rɛzɪdəns/ n. residencia, morada f.

resident /'rɛzɪdənt/ n. residente m. & f.

residue /'rɛzɪ,du/ n. residuo m.

resign /rɪ'zain/ v. dimitir; resignar.

resignation /,rɛzɪg'neiʃən/ n. dimisión; resignación f.

resist /rɪ'zɪst/ v. resistir.

resistance /rɪ'zɪstəns/ n. resistencia f.

resolute /'rɛzə,lut/ a. resuelto.

resolution /,rɛzə'luʃən/ n. resolución f.

resolve /rɪ'zɒlv/ v. resolver.

resonant /'rɛzənənt/ a. resonante.

resort /rɪ'zɔrt/ n. **1.** recurso; expediente *m.* **summer r.,** lugar de veraneo. —*v.* **2.** acudir, recurrir.

resound /rɪ'zaund/ *v.* resonar.

resource /'risɔrs/ *n.* recurso *m.*

respect /rɪ'spɛkt/ *n.* **1.** respeto *m.* **with r. to,** con respecto a. —*v.* **2.** respetar.

respectable /rɪ'spɛktəbəl/ *a.* respetable.

respectful /rɪ'spɛktfəl/ *a.* respetuoso.

respective /rɪ'spɛktɪv/ *a.* respectivo.

respiration /ˌrɛspə'reiʃən/ *n.* respiración *f.*

respite /'rɛspɪt/ *n.* pausa, tregua *f.*

respond /rɪ'spɒnd/ *v.* responder.

response /rɪ'spɒns/ *n.* respuesta *f.*

responsibility /rɪˌspɒnsə'bɪlɪti/ *n.* responsabilidad *f.*

responsible /rɪ'spɒnsəbəl/ *a.* responsable.

responsive /rɪ'spɒnsɪv/ *a.* sensible a.

rest /rɛst/ *n.* **1.** descanso; reposo *m.*; (music) pausa *f.* **the r.,** el resto, lo demás; los demás. —*v.* **2.** descansar; recostar.

restaurant /'rɛstərənt, -təˌrɑnt, -trɑnt/ *n.* restaurante *m.*

restful /'rɛstfəl/ *a.* tranquilo.

restitution /ˌrɛstɪ'tuʃən, -'tyu-/ *n.* restitución *f.*

restless /'rɛstlɪs/ *a.* inquieto.

restoration /ˌrɛstə'reiʃən/ *n.* restauración *f.*

restore /rɪ'stɔr, -'stour/ *v.* restaurar.

restrain /rɪ'strein/ *v.* refrenar.

restraint /rɪ'streint/ *n.* limitación, restricción *f.*

restrict /rɪ'strɪkt/ *v.* restringir, limitar.

rest room aseos *m.pl.*

result /rɪ'zʌlt/ *n.* **1.** resultado *m.* —*v.* **2.** resultar.

resume /rɪ'zum/ *v.* reasumir; empezar de nuevo.

résumé /'rɛzuˌmei/ *n.* resumen *m.*

resurgent /rɪ'sɜrdʒənt/ *a.* resurgente.

resurrect /ˌrɛzə'rɛkt/ *v.* resucitar.

resuscitate /rɪ'sʌsɪˌteit/ *v.* resucitar.

retail /'riteil/ *n.* **at r.,** al por menor.

retain /rɪ'tein/ *v.* retener.

retaliate /rɪ'tæliˌeit/ *v.* vengarse.

retard /rɪ'tɑrd/ *v.* retardar.

retention /rɪ'tɛnʃən/ *n.* retención *f.*

reticent /'rɛtəsənt/ *a.* reticente.

retire /rɪ'taiᵊr/ *v.* retirar.

retirement /rɪ'taiᵊrmənt/ *n.* jubilación *f.*

retort /rɪ'tɔrt/ *n.* **1.** réplica; *Chem.* retorta *f.* —*v.* **2.** replicar.

retreat /rɪ'trit/ *n.* **1.** retiro *m.*; *Mil.* retirada, retreta *f.* —*v.* **2.** retirarse.

retribution /ˌrɛtrə'byuʃən/ *n.* retribución *f.*

retrieve /rɪ'triv/ *v.* recobrar.

return /rɪ'tɜrn/ *n.* **1.** vuelta *f.*, regreso; retorno *m.* **by r. mail,** a vuelta de correo. —*v.* **2.** volver, regresar; devolver.

reunion /ri'yunyən/ *n.* reunión *f.*

rev /rɛv/ *n.* **1.** revolución *f.* —*v.* **2.** (motor) acelerar.

reveal /rɪ'vil/ *v.* revelar.

revelation /ˌrɛvə'leiʃən/ *n.* revelación *f.*

revenge /rɪ'vɛndʒ/ *n.* venganza *f.* **to get r.,** vengarse.

revenue /'rɛvənˌyu, -əˌnu/ *n.* renta *f.*

revere /rɪ'viər/ *v.* reverenciar, venerar.

reverence /'rɛvərəns, 'rɛvrəns/ *n.* **1.** reverencia *f.* —*v.* **2.** reverenciar.

reverend /'rɛvərənd, 'rɛvrənd/ *a.* **1.** reverendo. —*n.* **2.** pastor *m.*

reverent /'rɛvərənt, 'rɛvrənt/ *a.* reverente.

reverse /rɪ'vɜrs/ *a.* **1.** inverso. —*n.* **2.** revés, inverso *m.* —*v.* **3.** invertir; revocar.

revert /rɪ'vɜrt/ *v.* revertir.

review /rɪ'vyu/ *n.* **1.** repaso *m.*; revista *f.* —*v.* **2.** repasar; *Mil.* revistar.

revise /rɪ'vaiz/ *v.* revisar.

revision /rɪ'vɪʒən/ *n.* revisión *f.*

revival /rɪ'vaivəl/ *n.* reavivamiento *m.*

revive /rɪ'vaiv/ *v.* avivar; revivir, resucitar.

revoke /rɪ'vouk/ *v.* revocar.

revolt /rɪ'voult/ *n.* **1.** rebelión *f.* —*v.* **2.** rebelarse.

revolting /rɪ'voultɪŋ/ *a.* repugnante.

revolution /ˌrɛvə'luʃən/ *n.* revolución *f.*

revolutionary /ˌrɛvə'luʃəˌnɛri/ *a.* & *n.* revolucionario -ria.

revolve /rɪ'vɒlv/ v. girar; dar vueltas.

revolver /rɪ'vɒlvər/ n. revólver m.

revolving door /rɪ'vɒlvɪŋ/ puerta giratoria f.

reward /rɪ'wɔrd/ n. **1.** pago m.; recompensa f. —v. **2.** recompensar.

rhetoric /'rɛtərɪk/ n. retórica f.

rheumatism /'rumə,tɪzəm/ n. reumatismo m.

rhinoceros /rai'nɒsərəs/ n. rinoceronte m.

rhubarb /'rubɑrb/ n. ruibarbo m.

rhyme /raim/ n. **1.** rima f. —v. **2.** rimar.

rhythm /'rɪðəm/ n. ritmo m.

rhythmical /'rɪðmɪkəl/ a. rítmico.

rib /rɪb/ n. costilla f.

ribbon /'rɪbən/ n. cinta f.

rib cage caja torácica f.

rice /rais/ n. arroz m.

rich /rɪtʃ/ a. rico.

rid /rɪd/ v. librar. **get r. of,** deshacerse de, quitarse.

riddle /'rɪdḷ/ n. enigma; rompecabezas m.

ride /raid/ n. **1.** paseo (a caballo, en coche, etc.) m. —v. **2.** cabalgar; ir en coche.

ridge /rɪdʒ/ n. cerro m.; arruga f.; (of a roof) caballete m.

ridicule /'rɪdɪ,kyul/ n. **1.** ridículo m. —v. **2.** ridiculizar.

ridiculous /rɪ'dɪkyələs/ a. ridículo.

riding /'raidɪŋ/ n. equitación f.

riding school picadero m.

rifle /'raifəl/ n. **1.** fusil m. —v. **2.** robar.

rig /rɪg/ n. **1.** aparejo m. —v. **2.** aparejar.

right /rait/ a. **1.** derecho; correcto. **to be r.,** tener razón. —adv. **2.** bien, correctamente. **r. here,** etc., aquí mismo, etc. **all r.,** está bien, muy bien. —n. **3.** derecho m.; justicia f. **to the r.,** a la derecha. —v. **4.** corregir; enderezar.

righteous /'raitʃəs/ a. justo.

rigid /'rɪdʒɪd/ a. rígido.

rigor /'rɪgər/ n. rigor m.

rigorous /'rɪgərəs/ a. riguroso.

rim /rɪm/ n. margen m. or f.; borde m.

ring /rɪŋ/ n. **1.** anillo m.; sortija f.; círculo; campanero m. —v. **2.** cercar; sonar; tocar.

ring finger dedo anular m.

rinse /rɪns/ v. enjuagar, lavar.

riot /'raiət/ n. motín; alboroto m.

rip /rɪp/ n. **1.** rasgadura f. —v. **2.** rasgar; descoser.

ripe /raip/ a. maduro.

ripen /'raipən/ v. madurar.

ripoff /'rɪp,ɔf/ n. robo, atraco m.

ripple /'rɪpəl/ n. **1.** onda f. —v. **2.** ondear.

rise /raiz/ n. **1.** subida f. —v. **2.** ascender; levantarse; (moon) salir.

risk /rɪsk/ n. **1.** riesgo m. —v. **2.** arriesgar.

rite /rait/ n. rito m.

ritual /'rɪtʃuəl/ a. & n. ritual m.

rival /'raivəl/ n. rival m. & f.

rivalry /'raivəlri/ n. rivalidad f.

river /'raivər/ n. río m.

rivet /'rɪvɪt/ n. **1.** remache, roblón m. —v. **2.** remachar, roblar.

road /roud/ n. camino m.; carretera f.

roadside /'roud,said/ n. borde de la carretera m.

roam /roum/ v. vagar.

roar /rɔr, rour/ n. **1.** rugido, bramido m. —v. **2.** rugir, bramar.

roast /roust/ n. **1.** asado m. —v. **2.** asar.

rob /rɒb/ v. robar.

robber /'rɒbər/ n. ladrón -na.

robbery /'rɒbəri/ n. robo m.

robe /roub/ n. manto m.

robin /'rɒbɪn/ n. petirrojo m.

robust /rou'bʌst, 'roubʌst/ a. robusto.

rock /rɒk/ n. **1.** roca, peña f.; (music) rock m., música (de) rock f. —v. **2.** mecer; oscilar.

rocker /'rɒkər/ n. mecedora f.

rocket /'rɒkɪt/ n. cohete m.

rocking chair /'rɒkɪŋ/ mecedora f.

Rock of Gibraltar /dʒɪ'brɔltər/ Peñón de Gibraltar m.

rocky /'rɒki/ a. pedregoso.

rod /rɒd/ n. varilla f.

rodent /'roudnt/ n. roedor m.

rogue /roug/ n. bribón, pícaro m.

roguish /'rougɪʃ/ a. pícaro.

role /roul/ n. papel m.

roll /roul/ **1.** rollo m.; lista f.; panecillo m. **to call the r.,** pasar lista. —v. **2.** rodar. **r. up,** enrollar. **r. up one's sleeves,** arremangarse.

roller /'roulər/ n. rodillo, cilindro m.

roller skate patín de ruedas m.

Roman /'roumən/ a. & n. romano -na.

romance /rou'mæns, 'roumæns/ a.

1. románico. —*n.* **2.** romance *m.;* amorío *m.*

romantic /rou'mæntɪk/ *a.* romántico.

romp /rɒmp/ *v.* retozar; jugar.

roof /ruf, rʊf/ *n.* **1.** techo *m.;* —*v.* **2.** techar.

room /rum, rʊm/ *n.* **1.** cuarto *m.,* habitación *f.;* lugar *m.* —*v.* **2.** alojarse.

roommate /'rum‚meit, 'rʊm-/ *n.* compañero -ra de cuarto.

rooster /'rustər/ *n.* gallo *m.*

root /rut/ *n.* raíz *f.* **to take r.,** arraigar.

rootless /'rutlɪs/ *a.* desarraigado.

rope /roup/ *n.* cuerda, soga *f.*

rose /rouz/ *n.* rosa *f.*

rosy /'rouzi/ *a.* róseo, rosado.

rot /rɒt/ *n.* **1.** putrefacción *f.* —*v.* **2.** pudrirse.

rotary /'routəri/ *a.* giratorio; rotativo.

rotate /'routeit/ *v.* girar; alternar.

rotation /rou'teiʃən/ *n.* rotación *f.*

rotten /'rɒtn̩/ *a.* podrido.

rouge /ruʒ/ *n.* colorete *m.*

rough /rʌf/ *a.* áspero; rudo; grosero; aproximado.

round /raund/ *a.* **1.** redondo. **r. trip,** viaje de ida y vuelta. —*n.* **2.** ronda *f.;* (boxing) asalto *m.*

rouse /rauz/ *v.* despertar.

rout /raut, rut/ *n.* **1.** derrota *f.* —*v.* **2.** derrotar.

route /rut, raut/ *n.* ruta, vía *f.*

routine /ru'tin/ *a.* **1.** rutinario. —*n.* **2.** rutina *f.*

rove /rouv/ *v.* vagar.

rover /'rouvər/ *n.* vagabundo -da.

row /rou/ *n.* **1.** fila *f.* —*v.* **2.** *Naut.* remar.

rowboat /'rou‚bout/ *n.* bote de remos.

rowdy /'raudi/ *a.* alborotado.

royal /'rɔiəl/ *a.* real.

royalty /'rɔiəlti/ *n.* realeza *f.;* (pl.) regalías *f.pl.*

rub /rʌb/ *v.* frotar. **r. against,** rozar. **r. out,** borrar.

rubber /'rʌbər/ *n.* goma *f.;* caucho *m.;* (pl.) chanclos *m.pl.,* zapatos de goma.

rubbish /'rʌbɪʃ/ *n.* basura *f.;* (nonsense) tonterías *f.pl.*

ruby /'rubi/ *n.* rubí *m.*

rudder /'rʌdər/ *n.* timón *m.*

ruddy /'rʌdi/ *a.* colorado.

rude /rud/ *a.* rudo; grosero; descortés.

rudiment /'rudəmənt/ *n.* rudimento *m.*

rudimentary /‚rudə'mɛntəri, -tri/ *a.* rudimentario.

rue /ru/ *v.* deplorar; lamentar.

ruffian /'rʌfiən, 'rʌfyən/ *n.* rufián, bandolero *m.*

ruffle /'rʌfəl/ *n.* **1.** volante fruncido. —*v.* **2.** fruncir; irritar.

rug /rʌg/ *n.* alfombra *f.*

rugged /'rʌgɪd/ *a.* áspero; robusto.

ruin /'ruɪn/ *n.* **1.** ruina *f.* —*v.* **2.** arruinar.

ruinous /'ruənəs/ *a.* ruinoso.

rule /rul/ *n.* **1.** regla *f.* **as a r.,** por regla general. —*v.* **2.** gobernar; mandar; rayar.

ruler /'rulər/ *n.* gobernante *m.* & *f.;* soberano -na; regla *f.*

rum /rʌm/ *n.* ron *m.*

rumble /'rʌmbəl/ *v.* retumbar.

rumor /'rumər/ *n.* rumor *m.*

rumpus /'rʌmpəs/ *n.* lío, jaleo, escandalo *m.*

run /rʌn/ *v.* correr; hacer correr. **r. away,** escaparse. **r. into,** chocar con.

runner /'rʌnər/ *n.* corredor -ra; mensajero -ra.

runner-up /'rʌnər 'ʌp/ *n.* subcampeón -ona.

runproof /'rʌnpruf/ *a.* indesmallable.

rupture /'rʌptʃər/ *n.* **1.** rotura; hernia *f.* —*v.* **2.** reventar.

rural /'rʊrəl/ *a.* rural, campestre.

rush /rʌʃ/ *n.* **1.** prisa *f.;* *Bot.* junco *m.* —*v.* **2.** ir de prisa.

rush hour hora punta *f.*

Russia /'rʌʃə/ *n.* Rusia *f.*

Russian /'rʌʃən/ *a.* & *n.* ruso -sa.

rust /rʌst/ *n.* **1.** herrumbre *f.* —*v.* **2.** aherrumbrarse.

rustic /'rʌstɪk/ *a.* rústico.

rustle /'rʌsəl/ *n.* **1.** susurro *m.* —*v.* **2.** susurrar.

rusty /'rʌsti/ *a.* mohoso.

rut /rʌt/ *n.* surco *m.*

ruthless /'ruθlɪs/ *a.* cruel, inhumano.

rye /rai/ *n.* centeno *m.*

rye bread pan de centeno *m.*

S

saber /'seibər/ *n.* sable *m.*

sable /'seibəl/ *n.* cebellina *f.*

sabotage /'sæbə,taʒ/ *n.* sabotaje *m.*

sachet /sæ'ʃei/ *n.* perfumador *m.*

sack /sæk/ *n.* **1.** saco *m.* —*v.* **2.** *Mil.* saquear.

sacred /'seikrıd/ *a.* sagrado, santo.

sacrifice /'sækrə,fais/ *n.* **1.** sacrificio *m.* —*v.* **2.** sacrificar.

sacrilege /'sækrəlıdʒ/ *n.* sacrilegio *m.*

sad /sæd/ *a.* triste.

saddle /'sædl̩/ *n.* **1.** silla de montar. —*v.* **2.** ensillar.

sadness /'sædnıs/ *n.* tristeza *f.*

safe /seif/ *a.* **1.** seguro; salvo. —*n.* **2.** caja de caudales.

safeguard /'seif,gard/ *n.* **1.** salvaguardia *m.* —*v.* **2.** proteger, poner a salvo.

safety /'seifti/ *n.* seguridad, protección *f.*

safety belt cinturón de seguridad *m.*

safety pin imperdible *m.*

safety valve /vælv/ válvula de seguridad *f.*

sage /seidʒ/ *a.* **1.** sabio, sagaz. —*n.* **2.** sabio *m.; Bot.* salvia *f.*

sail /seil/ *n.* **1.** vela *f.;* paseo por mar. —*v.* **2.** navegar; embarcarse.

sailboat /'seil,bout/ *n.* barco de vela.

sailor /'seilər/ *n.* marinero *m.*

saint /seint/ *n.* santo -ta.

sake /seik/ *n.* **for the s. of,** por; por el bien de.

salad /'sæləd/ *n.* ensalada *f.* **s. bowl,** ensaladera *f.*

salad dressing aliño *m.*

salary /'sæləri/ *n.* sueldo, salario *m.*

sale /seil/ *n.* venta *f.*

salesman /'seilzmən/ *n.* vendedor *m.;* viajante de comercio.

sales tax /seilz/ impuesto sobre la venta.

saliva /sə'laivə/ *n.* saliva *f.*

salmon /'sæmən/ *n.* salmón *m.*

salt /sɔlt/ *a.* **1.** salado. —*n.* **2.** sal *f.* —*v.* **3.** salar.

salute /sə'lut/ *n.* **1.** saludo *m.* —*v.* **2.** saludar.

salvage /'sælvıdʒ/ *v.* salvar; recobrar.

salvation /sæl'veiʃən/ *n.* salvación *f.*

salve /sæv/ *n.* emplasto, ungüento *m.*

same /seim/ *a. & pron.* mismo. **it's all the s.,** lo mismo da.

sample /'sæmpəl/ *n.* **1.** muestra *f.* —*v.* **2.** probar.

sanatorium /,sænə'tɔriəm/ *n.* sanatorio *m.*

sanctify /'sæŋktə,fai/ *v.* santificar.

sanction /'sæŋkʃən/ *n.* **1.** sanción *f.* —*v.* **2.** sancionar.

sanctity /'sæŋktıti/ *n.* santidad *f.*

sanctuary /'sæŋktʃu,eri/ *n.* santuario, asilo *m.*

sand /sænd/ *n.* arena *f.*

sandal /'sændl̩/ *n.* sandalia *f.*

sandpaper /'sænd,peipər/ *n.* papel de lija *m.*

sandwich /'sændwıtʃ, 'sæn-/ *n.* emparedado, sándwich *m.*

sandy /'sændi/ *a.* arenoso; (color) rufo.

sane /sein/ *a.* cuerdo; sano.

sanitary /'sænı,teri/ *a.* higiénico, sanitario. **s. napkin,** toalla sanitaria.

sanitation /,sænı'teiʃən/ *n.* saneamiento *m.*

sanity /'sænıti/ *n.* cordura *f.*

Santa Claus /'sæntə klɔz/ Papá Noel *m.*

sap /sæp/ *n.* **1.** savia *f.; Colloq.* estúpido, bobo *m.* —*v.* **2.** agotar.

sapphire /'sæfaiᵊr/ *n.* zafiro *m.*

sarcasm /'sarkæzəm/ *n.* sarcasmo *m.*

sardine /sar'din/ *n.* sardina *f.*

sash /sæʃ/ *n.* cinta *f.*

satellite /'sætl̩,ait/ *n.* satélite *m.*

satellite dish antena parabólica *f.*

satin /'sætn̩/ *n.* raso *m.*

satire /'sætaiᵊr/ *n.* sátira *f.*

satisfaction /,sætıs'fækʃən/ *n.* satisfacción; recompensa *f.*

satisfactory /,sætıs'fæktəri/ *a.* satisfactorio.

satisfy /'sætıs,fai/ *v.* satisfacer. **be satisfied that...,** estar convencido de que.

saturate /'sætʃə,reit/ *v.* saturar.

Saturday /'sætər,dei/ *n.* sábado *m.*

sauce /sɔs/ *n.* salsa; compota *f.*

saucer /'sɔsər/ *n.* platillo *m.*

saucy /'sɔsi/ *a.* descarado, insolente.

sauna /'sɔnə/ *n.* sauna *f.*

sausage /'sɔsɪdʒ/ *n.* salchicha *f.*

savage /'sævɪdʒ/ *a. & n.* salvaje *m. & f.*

save /seiv/ *v.* **1.** salvar; guardar; ahorrar, economizar. —*prep.* **2.** salvo, excepto.

savings /'seivɪŋz/ *n.* ahorros *m.pl.*

savings account cuenta de ahorros *m.*

savings bank caja de ahorros *f.*

savior /'seivyər/ *n.* salvador -ora.

savor /'seivər/ *n.* **1.** sabor *m.* —*v.* **2.** saborear.

savory /'seivəri/ *a.* sabroso.

saw /sɔ/ *n.* **1.** sierra *f.* —*v.* **2.** aserrar.

saxophone /'sæksə,foun/ *n.* saxofón, saxófono, *m.*

say /sei/ *v.* decir; recitar.

saying /'seiɪŋ/ *n.* dicho, refrán *m.*

scaffold /'skæfəld/ *n.* andamio; (gallows) patíbulo *m.*

scald /skɔld/ *v.* escaldar.

scale /skeil/ *n.* **1.** escala; (of fish) escama *f.;* (pl.) balanza *f.* —*v.* **2.** escalar; escamar.

scalp /skælp/ *n.* pericráneo *m. v.* escalpar.

scan /skæn/ *v.* hojear, repasar; (poetry) escandir; (computer) escanear, digitalizar.

scandal /'skændl/ *n.* escándalo *m.*

scanner /'skænər/ *n.* escáner *m.*

scant /skænt/ *a.* escaso.

scar /skɑr/ *n.* cicatriz *f.*

scarce /skɛərs/ *a.* escaso; raro.

scarcely /'skɛərsli/ *adv. & conj.* apenas.

scare /skɛər/ *n.* **1.** susto *m.* —*v.* **2.** asustar. **s. away,** espantar.

scarf /skɑrf/ *n.* pañueleta, bufanda *f.*

scarlet /'skɑrlɪt/ *n.* escarlata *f.*

scarlet fever escarlatina *f.*

scatter /'skætər/ *v.* esparcir; dispersar.

scavenger /'skævɪndʒər/ *n.* basurero *m.*

scenario /sɪ'nɛəri,ou, -'nɑr-/ *n.* escenario *m.*

scene /sin/ *n.* vista *f.*, paisaje *m.;* *Theat.* escena *f.* **behind the scenes,** entre bastidores.

scenery /'sinəri/ *n.* paisaje *m.;* *Theat.* decorado *m.*

scent /sɛnt/ *n.* **1.** olor, perfume;

(sense) olfato *m.* —*v.* **2.** perfumar; *Fig.* sospechar.

schedule /'skɛdʒul, -ʊl, -uəl/ *n.* **1.** programa, horario *m.* —*v.* **2.** fijar la hora para.

scheme /skim/ *n.* **1.** proyecto; esquema *m.* —*v.* **2.** intrigar.

scholar /'skɒlər/ *n.* erudito -ta; becado -da.

scholarship /'skɒlər,ʃɪp/ *n.* beca; erudición *f.*

school /skul/ *n.* **1.** escuela *f.;* colegio *m.;* (of fish) banco *m.* —*v.* **2.** enseñar.

sciatica /sai'ætɪkə/ *n.* ciática *f.*

science /'saiəns/ *n.* ciencia *f.*

science fiction ciencia ficción.

scientific /,saiən'tɪfɪk/ *a.* científico.

scientist /'saiəntɪst/ *n.* científico -ca.

scissors /'sɪzərz/ *n.* tijeras *f.pl.*

scoff /skɔf, skɒf/ *v.* mofarse, burlarse.

scold /skould/ *v.* regañar.

scoop /skup/ *n.* **1.** cucharón *m.;* cucharada *f.* —*v.* **2. s. out,** recoger, sacar.

scope /skoup/ *n.* alcance; campo *m.*

score /skɔr/ *n.* **1.** tantos *m.pl.;* (music) partitura *f.* —*v.* **2.** marcar, hacer tantos.

scorn /skɔrn/ *n.* **1.** desprecio *m.* —*v.* **2.** despreciar.

scornful /'skɔrnfəl/ *a.* desdeñoso.

Scotland /'skɒtlənd/ *n.* Escocia *f.*

Scottish /'skɒtɪʃ/ *a.* escocés.

scour /skauᵊr/ *v.* fregar, estregar.

scourge /skɜrdʒ/ *n.* azote *m.;* plaga *f.*

scout /skaut/ *n.* **1.** explorador -ra. —*v.* **2.** explorar, reconocer.

scramble /'skræmbəl/ *n.* **1.** rebatiña *f.* —*v.* **2.** bregar. **scrambled eggs,** huevos revueltos.

scrap /skræp/ *n.* **1.** migaja *f.;* pedacito *m.; Colloq.* riña *f.* **s. metal,** hierro viejo *m.* **s. paper,** papel borrador. —*v.* **2.** desechar; *Colloq.* reñir.

scrapbook /'skræp,bʊk/ *n.* álbum de recortes *m.*

scrape /skreip/ *n.* **1.** lío, apuro *m.* —*v.* **2.** raspar; (feet) restregar.

scratch /skrætʃ/ *n.* **1.** rasguño *m.* —*v.* **2.** rasguñar; rayar.

scream /skrim/ *n.* **1.** grito, chillido *m.* —*v.* **2.** gritar, chillar.

screen /skrin/ *n.* biombo *m.;* (for

window) tela metálica; (movie) pantalla f.

screw /skru/ n. **1.** tornillo m. —v. **2.** atornillar.

screwdriver /'skru,draivər/ n. destornillador m.

scribble /'skrɪbəl/ v. hacer garabatos.

scroll /skroul/ n. rúbrica f.; rollo de papel.

scroll bar n. barra de enrollar f.

scrub /skrʌb/ v. fregar, estregar.

scruple /'skrupəl/ n. escrúpulo m.

scrupulous /'skrupyələs/ a. escrupuloso.

scuba diving /'skubə 'daivɪŋ/ submarinismo m.

sculptor /'skʌlptər/ n. escultor -ra.

sculpture /'skʌlptʃər/ n. **1.** escultura f. —v. **2.** esculpir.

scythe /saɪð/ n. guadaña f.

sea /si/ n. mar m. or f.

seabed /'si,bɛd/ n. lecho marino m.

sea breeze brisa marina f.

seafood /'si,fud/ n. mariscos m.pl.

seal /sil/ n. **1.** sello m.; (animal) foca f. —v. **2.** sellar.

seam /sim/ n. costura f.

seamy /'simi/ a. sórdido.

seaplane /'si,plein/ n. hidroavión m.

seaport /'si,pɔrt/ n. puerto de mar.

search /sɜrtʃ/ n. **1.** registro m. **in s. of,** en busca de. —v. **2.** registrar. **s. for,** buscar.

search engine motor de búsqueda m., buscador m., indexador de información m.

seasick /'si,sɪk/ a. mareado. **to get s.,** marearse.

season /'sizən/ n. **1.** estación; sazón; temporada f. —v. **2.** sazonar.

seasoning /'sizənɪŋ/ n. condimento m.

season ticket abono m.

seat /sit/ n. **1.** asiento m.; residencia, sede f.; Theat. localidad f. **s. belt,** cinturón de seguridad. —v. **2.** sentar. **be seated,** sentarse.

seaweed /'si,wid/ n. alga, alga marina f.

second /'sɪkɒnd/ a. & n. **1.** segundo m. —v. **2.** apoyar, segundar.

secondary /'sɛkən,dɛri/ a. secundario.

secret /'sikrɪt/ a. & n. secreto m.

secretary /'sɛkrɪ,tɛri/ n. secretario -ria; Govt. ministro -tra; (furniture) papelera f.

sect /sɛkt/ n. secta f.; partido m.

section /'sɛkʃən/ n. sección, parte f.

sectional /'sɛkʃənl/ a. regional, local.

secular /'sɛkyələr/ a. secular.

secure /sɪ'kyʊr/ a. **1.** seguro. —v. **2.** asegurar; obtener; Fin. garantizar.

security /sɪ'kyʊrɪti/ n. seguridad; garantía f.

sedative /'sɛdətɪv/ a. & n. sedativo m.

seduce /sɪ'dus/ v. seducir.

see /si/ v. ver; comprender. **s. off,** despedirse de. **s. to,** encargarse de.

seed /sid/ n. **1.** semilla f. —v. **2.** sembrar.

seek /sik/ v. buscar. **s. to,** tratar de.

seem /sim/ v. parecer.

seep /sip/ v. colarse.

segment /'sɛgmənt/ n. segmento m.

segregate /'sɛgrɪ,geit/ v. segregar.

seize /siz/ v. agarrar; apoderarse de.

seldom /'sɛldəm/ adv. rara vez.

select /sɪ'lɛkt/ a. **1.** escogido, selecto. —v. **2.** elegir, seleccionar.

selection /sɪ'lɛkʃən/ n. selección f.

selective /sɪ'lɛktɪv/ a. selectivo.

selfish /'sɛlfɪʃ/ a. egoísta.

selfishness /'sɛlfɪʃnɪs/ n. egoísmo m.

sell /sɛl/ v. vender.

semester /sɪ'mɛstər/ n. semestre m.

semicircle /'sɛmɪ,sɜrkəl/ n. semicírculo m.

semolina /,sɛmə'linə/ n. sémola f.

senate /'sɛnɪt/ n. senado m.

senator /'sɛnətər/ n. senador -ra.

send /sɛnd/ v. mandar, enviar; (a wire) poner. **s. away,** despedir. **s. back,** devolver. **s. for,** mandar buscar. **s. off,** expedir. **s. word,** mandar recado.

senile /'sinail/ a. senil.

senior /'sinyər/ a. mayor; más viejo. **Sr.,** padre.

senior citizen persona de edad avanzada.

sensation /sɛn'seiʃən/ n. sensación f.

sensational /sɛn'seiʃənl/ a. sensacional.

sense /sɛns/ n. **1.** sentido; juicio m. —v. **2.** percibir; sospechar.

sensible /'sɛnsəbəl/ a. sensato, razonable.

sensitive /'sɛnsɪtɪv/ a. sensible; sensitivo.

sensual /'sɛnʃuəl/ a. sensual.

sentence /'sɛntn̩s/ n. **1.** frase; Gram. oración; Leg. sentencia f. —v. **2.** condenar.

sentiment /'sɛntəmənt/ n. sentimiento m.

sentimental /ˌsɛntə'mɛntl̩/ a. sentimental.

separate /a. 'sɛpərɪt; v. -ˌreit/ a. **1.** separado; suelto. —v. **2.** separar, dividir.

separation /ˌsɛpə'reiʃən/ n. separación f.

September /sɛp'tɛmbər/ n. septiembre m.

sequence /'sikwəns/ n. serie f. **in s.,** seguidos.

serenade /ˌsɛrə'neid/ n. **1.** serenata f. —v. **2.** dar serenata a.

serene /sə'rin/ a. sereno; tranquilo.

sergeant /'sɑrdʒənt/ n. sargento m.

serial /'sɪəriəl/ a. en serie, de serie.

series /'sɪəriz/ n. serie f.

serious /'sɪəriəs/ a. serio; grave.

sermon /'sɑrmən/ n. sermón m.

serpent /'sɑrpənt/ n. serpiente f.

servant /'sɑrvənt/ n. criado -da; servidor -ra.

serve /sɑrv/ v. servir.

server /'sɑrvər/ n. servidor m.

service /'sɑrvɪs/ n. **1.** servicio m. **at the s. of,** a las órdenes de. **be of s.,** servir; ser útil. —v. **2.** Auto. reparar.

service station estación de servicio f.

session /'sɛʃən/ n. sesión f.

set /sɛt/ a. **1.** fijo. —n. **2.** colección f.; (of a game) juego; Mech. aparato; Theat. decorado m. —v. **3.** poner, colocar; fijar; (sun) ponerse. **s. forth,** exponer. **s. off, s. out,** salir. **s. up,** instalar; establecer.

settle /'sɛtl̩/ v. solucionar; arreglar; establecerse.

settlement /'sɛtl̩mənt/ n. caserío; arreglo; acuerdo m.

settler /'sɛtlər/ n. poblador -ra.

seven /'sɛvən/ a. & pron. siete.

seventeen /ˌsɛvən'tin/ a. & pron. diecisiete.

seventh /'sɛvənθ/ a. séptimo.

seventy /'sɛvənti/ a. & pron. setenta.

sever /'sɛvər/ v. desunir; romper.

several /'sɛvərəl/ a. & pron. varios.

severance pay /'sɛvərəns/ indemnización de despido.

severe /sə'vɪər/ a. severo; grave.

severity /sə'vɛrɪti/ n. severidad f.

sew /sou/ v. coser.

sewer /'suər/ n. cloaca f.

sewing /'souɪŋ/ n. costura f.

sewing basket costurero m.

sewing machine máquina de coser f.

sex /sɛks/ n. sexo m.

sexism /'sɛksɪzəm/ n. sexismo m.

sexist /'sɛksɪst/ a. & n. sexista m. & f.

sexton /'sɛkstən/ n. sacristán m.

sexual /'sɛkʃuəl/ a. sexual.

shabby /'ʃæbi/ a. haraposo, desaliñado.

shade /ʃeid/ n. **1.** sombra f.; tinte m.; (window) transparente m. —v. **2.** sombrear.

shadow /'ʃædou/ n. sombra f.

shady /'ʃeidi/ a. sombroso; sospechoso.

shaft /ʃæft/ n. (columna) fuste; Mech. asta f.

shake /ʃeik/ v. sacudir; agitar; temblar. **s. hands with,** dar la mano a.

shallow /'ʃælou/ a. poco hondo; superficial.

shame /ʃeim/ n. **1.** vergüenza f. **be a s.,** ser una lástima. —v. **2.** avergonzar.

shameful /'ʃeimfəl/ a. vergonzoso.

shampoo /ʃæm'pu/ n. champú m.

shape /ʃeip/ n. **1.** forma f.; estado m. —v. **2.** formar.

share /ʃɛər/ n. **1.** parte; (stock) acción f. **2** —v. **2.** compartir.

shareholder /'ʃɛərˌhouldər/ n. accionista m. & f.

shareware /'ʃɛərˌwɛər/ n. programas compartidos m.pl.

shark /ʃɑrk/ n. tiburón m.

sharp /ʃɑrp/ *a.* agudo; (blade) afilado.

sharpen /'ʃɑrpən/ *v.* aguzar; afilar.

shatter /'ʃætər/ *v.* estrellar; hacer pedazos.

shave /ʃeiv/ *n.* **1.** afeitada *f.* —*v.* **2.** afeitarse.

shawl /ʃɔl/ *n.* rebozo, chal *m.*

she /ʃi/ *pron.* ella *f.*

sheaf /ʃif/ *n.* gavilla *f.*

shear /ʃiər/ *v.* cizallar.

shears /ʃiərz/ *n.* cizallas *f.pl.*

sheath /ʃiθ/ *n.* vaina *f.*

shed /ʃɛd/ *n.* **1.** cobertizo *m.* —*v.* **2.** arrojar, quitarse.

sheep /ʃip/ *n.* oveja *f.*

sheet /ʃit/ *n.* sábana; (of paper) hoja *f.*

shelf /ʃɛlf/ *n.* estante, *m.*, repisa *f.*

shell /ʃɛl/ *n.* **1.** cáscara; (sea) concha *f.; Mil.* proyectil *m.* —*v.* **2.** desgranar; bombardear.

shellac /ʃə'læk/ *n.* laca *f.*

shelter /'ʃɛltər/ *n.* **1.** albergue; refugio *m.* —*v.* **2.** albergar; amparar.

shepherd /'ʃɛpərd/ *n.* pastor *m.*

sherry /'ʃɛri/ *n.* jerez *m.*

shield /ʃild/ *n.* **1.** escudo *m.* —*v.* **2.** amparar.

shift /ʃift/ *n.* **1.** cambio; (work) turno *m.* —*v.* **2.** cambiar, mudar. **s. for oneself,** arreglárselas.

shine /ʃain/ *n.* **1.** brillo, lustre *m.* —*v.* **2.** brillar; (shoes) lustrar.

shiny /'ʃaini/ *a.* brillante, lustroso.

ship /ʃip/ *n.* **1.** barco *m.*, nave *f.* —*v.* **2.** embarcar; *Com.* enviar.

shipment /'ʃipmənt/ *n.* envío; embarque *m.*

shirk /ʃɜrk/ *v.* faltar al deber.

shirt /ʃɜrt/ *n.* camisa *f.*

shiver /'ʃivər/ *n.* **1.** temblor *m.* —*v.* **2.** temblar.

shock /ʃɒk/ *n.* **1.** choque *m.* —*v.* **2.** chocar.

shoe /ʃu/ *n.* zapato *m.*

shoelace /'ʃu,leis/ *n.* lazo *m.; cordón de zapato.*

shoemaker /'ʃu,meikər/ *n.* zapatero *m.*

shoot /ʃut/ *v.* tirar; (gun) disparar. **s. away, s. off,** salir disparado.

shop /ʃɒp/ *n.* tienda *f.*

shopping /'ʃɒpiŋ/ *n.* **to go s.,** hacer compras, ir de compras.

shop window escaparate *m.*

shore /ʃɔr/ *n.* orilla; playa *f.*

short /ʃɔrt/ *a.* corto; breve; (in stature) pequeño, bajo. **a s. time,** poco tiempo. **in s.,** en suma.

shortage /'ʃɔrtidʒ/ *n.* escasez; falta *f.*

shorten /'ʃɔrtn̩/ *v.* acortar, abreviar.

shortly /'ʃɔrtli/ *adv.* en breve, dentro de poco.

shorts /ʃɔrts/ *n.* calzoncillos *m.pl.*

shot /ʃɒt/ *n.* tiro, disparo *m.*

shoulder /'ʃouldər/ *n.* **1.** hombro *m.* —*v.* **2.** asumir; cargar con.

shoulder blade *n.* omóplato *m.*, paletilla *f.*

shout /ʃaut/ *n.* **1.** grito *m.* —*v.* **2.** gritar.

shove /ʃʌv/ *n.* **1.** empujón *m.* —*v.* **2.** empujar.

shovel /'ʃʌvəl/ *n.* **1.** pala *f.* —*v.* **2.** traspalar.

show /ʃou/ *n.* **1.** ostentación *f.; Theat.* función *f.;* espectáculo *m.* —*v.* **2.** enseñar, mostrar; verse. **s. up,** destacarse; *Colloq.* asomar.

shower /'ʃauər/ *n.* chubasco *m.;* (bath) ducha *f. v.* ducharse.

shrapnel /'ʃræpn̩l/ *n.* metralla *f.*

shrewd /ʃrud/ *a.* astuto.

shriek /ʃrik/ *n.* **1.** chillido *m.* —*v.* **2.** chillar.

shrill /ʃril/ *a.* chillón, agudo.

shrimp /ʃrimp/ *n.* camarón *m.*

shrine /ʃrain/ *n.* santuario *m.*

shrink /ʃriŋk/ *v.* encogerse, contraerse, **s. from,** huir de.

shroud /ʃraud/ *n.* **1.** mortaja *f.* —*v.* **2.** *Fig.* ocultar.

shrub /ʃrʌb/ *n.* arbusto *m.*

shudder /'ʃʌdər/ *n.* **1.** estremecimiento *m.* —*v.* **2.** estremecerse.

shun /ʃʌn/ *v.* evitar, huir de.

shut /ʃʌt/ *v.* cerrar. **s. in,** encerrar. **s. up,** *Colloq.* callarse.

shutter /'ʃʌtər/ *n.* persiana *f.*

shy /ʃai/ *a.* tímido, vergonzoso.

sick /sik/ *a.* enfermo. **s. of,** aburrido de, cansado de.

sickness /'siknis/ *n.* enfermedad *f.*

side /said/ *n.* **1.** lado; partido *m.;* parte *f.; Anat.* costado *m.* —*v.* **2.** **s. with,** ponerse del lado de.

sidewalk /'said,wɔk/ *n.* acera, vereda *f.*

siege /sidʒ/ *n.* asedio *m.*

sieve /siv/ *n.* cedazo *m.*

sift /sift/ *v.* cerner.

sigh /sai/ *n.* **1.** suspiro *m.* —*v.* **2.** suspirar.

sight /sait/ *n*. **1.** vista *f.*; punto de interés *m*. **lose s. of,** perder de vista. —*v*. **2.** divisar.
sign /sain/ *n*. **1.** letrero; señal, seña *f*. —*v*. **2.** firmar. **s. up,** inscribirse.
signal /'sɪgnl̩/ *n*. **1.** señal *f*. —*v*. **2.** hacer señales.
signature /'sɪgnətʃər/ *n*. firma *f*.
significance /sɪg'nɪfɪkəns/ *n*. significación *f*.
significant /sɪg'nɪfɪkənt/ *a*. significativo.
significant other pareja *m*. & *f*.
signify /'sɪgnə,fai/ *v*. significar.
silence /'sailəns/ *n*. **1.** silencio *m*. —*v*. **2.** hacer callar.
silent /'sailənt/ *a*. silencioso; callado.
silk /sɪlk/ *n*. seda *f*.
silken /'sɪlkən/ **silky** *a*. sedoso.
sill /sɪl/ *n*. umbral de puerta *m*., solera *f*.
silly /'sɪli/ *a*. necio, tonto.
silo /'sailou/ *n*. silo *m*.
silver /'sɪlvər/ *n*. plata *f*.
silver-plated /'sɪlvər 'pleitɪd/ *a*. chapado en plata.
silverware /'sɪlvər,wɛər/ *n*. vajilla de plata *f*.
similar /'sɪmələr/ *a*. semejante, parecido.
similarity /,sɪmə'lærɪti/ *n*. semejanza *f*.
simple /'sɪmpəl/ *a*. sencillo, simple.
simplicity /sɪm'plɪsɪti/ *n*. sencillez *f*.
simplify /'sɪmplə,fai/ *v*. simplificar.
simulate /'sɪmyə,leit/ *v*. simular.
simultaneous /,saiməl'teiniəs/ *a*. simultáneo.
sin /sɪn/ *n*. **1.** pecado *m*. —*v*. **2.** pecar.
since /sɪns/ *adv*. **1.** desde entonces. —*prep*. **2.** desde. —*conj*. **3.** desde que; puesto que.
sincere /sɪn'sɪər/ *a*. sincero.
sincerely /sɪn'sɪərli/ *adv*. sinceramente.
sincerity /sɪn'sɛrɪti/ *n*. sinceridad *f*.
sinew /'sɪnyu/ *n*. tendón *m*.
sinful /'sɪnfəl/ *a*. pecador.
sing /sɪŋ/ *v*. cantar.
singe /sɪndʒ/ *v*. chamuscar.
singer /'sɪŋər/ *n*. cantante *m*. & *f*.
single /'sɪŋgəl/ *a*. solo; (room)

sencillo; (unmarried) soltero. **s. room,** habitación individual.
singular /'sɪŋgyələr/ *a*. & *n*. singular *m*.
sinister /'sɪnəstər/ *a*. siniestro.
sink /sɪŋk/ *n*. **1.** fregadero *m*. —*v*. **2.** hundir; *Fig*. abatir.
sinner /'sɪnər/ *n*. pecador -ra.
sinuous /'sɪnyuəs/ *a*. sinuoso.
sinus /'sainəs/ *n*. seno *m*.
sip /sɪp/ *n*. **1.** sorbo *m*. —*v*. **2.** sorber.
siphon /'saifən/ *n*. sifón *m*.
sir /sɜr/ *title*. señor.
siren /'sairən/ *n*. sirena *f*.
sirloin /'sɜrlɔin/ *n*. solomillo *m*.
sisal /'saisəl, 'sɪsəl/ *n*. henequén *m*.
sister /'sɪstər/ *n*. hermana *f*.
sister-in-law /'sɪstərɪn,lɔ/ *n*. cuñada *f*.
sit /sɪt/ *v*. sentarse; posar. **be sitting,** estar sentado. **s. down,** sentarse. **s. up,** incorporarse; quedar levantado.
site /sait/ *n*. sitio, local *m*.
sitting /'sɪtɪŋ/ *n*. sesión *f*. *a*. sentado.
situate /'sɪtʃu,eit/ *v*. situar.
situation /,sɪtʃu'eiʃən/ *n*. situación *f*.
sit-up /'sɪt ,ʌp/ *n*. abdominal *m*.
six /sɪks/ *a*. & *pron*. seis.
sixteen /'sɪks'tin/ *a*. & *pron*. dieciseis.
sixth /sɪksθ/ *a*. sexto.
sixty /'sɪksti/ *a*. & *pron*. sesenta.
size /saiz/ *n*. tamaño; (of shoe, etc.) número *m*.; talla *f*.
sizing /'saizɪŋ/ *n*. upreso *m*.; sisa, cola de retazo *f*.
skate /skeit/ *n*. **1.** patín *m*. —*v*. **2.** patinar.
skateboard /'skeit,bɔrd/ *n*. monopatín *m*.
skein /skein/ *n*. madeja *f*.
skeleton /'skɛlɪtn̩/ *n*. esqueleto *m*.
skeptic /'skɛptɪk/ *n*. escéptico -ca.
skeptical /'skɛptɪkəl/ *a*. escéptico.
sketch /skɛtʃ/ *n*. **1.** esbozo *m*. —*v*. **2.** esbozar.
ski /ski/ *n*. **1.** esquí *m*. —*v*. **2.** esquiar.
skid /skɪd/ *v*. **1.** resbalar. —*n*. **2.** varadera *f*.
skill /skɪl/ *n*. destreza, habilidad *f*.
skillful /'skɪlfəl/ *a*. diestro, hábil.
skim /skɪm/ *v*. rasar; (milk) desnatar. **s. over, s. through,** hojear.

skin /skɪn/ n. **1.** piel; (of fruit) corteza f. —v. **2.** desollar.

skin doctor dermatólogo -ga m. & f.

skip /skɪp/ n. **1.** brinco m. —v. **2.** brincar. **s. over,** pasar por alto.

skirmish /'skɜrmɪʃ/ n. escaramuza f.

skirt /skɜrt/ n. falda f.

skull /skʌl/ n. cráneo m.

skunk /skʌŋk/ n. zorrillo m.

sky /skai/ n. cielo m.

skylight /'skai,lait/ n. tragaluz m.

skyscraper /'skai,skreipər/ n. rascacielos m.

slab /slæb/ n. tabla f.

slack /slæk/ a. flojo; descuidado.

slacken /'slækən/ v. relajar.

slacks /slæks/ n. pantalones flojos.

slam /slæm/ n. **1.** portazo m. —v. **2.** cerrar de golpe. **slamming on the brakes,** frenazo m.

slander /'slændər/ n. **1.** calumnia f. —v. **2.** calumniar.

slang /slæŋ/ n. jerga f.

slant /slænt/ n. **1.** sesgo m. —v. **2.** sesgar.

slap /slæp/ n. **1.** bofetada, palmada f. —v. **2.** dar una bofetada.

slash /slæʃ/ n. **1.** cuchillada f. —v. **2.** acuchillar.

slat /slæt/ n. **1.** tablilla f. —v. **2.** lanzar.

slate /sleit/ n. **1.** pizarra f.; lista de candidatos. —n. **2.** destinar.

slaughter /'slɔtər/ n. **1.** matanza f. —v. **2.** matar.

slave /sleiv/ n. esclavo -va.

slavery /'sleivəri/ n. esclavitud f.

Slavic /'slɑvɪk/ a. eslavo.

slay /slei/ v. matar, asesinar.

sled /slɛd/ n. trineo m.

sleek /slik/ a. liso y brillante.

sleep /slip/ n. **1.** sueño m. **to get much s.,** dormir mucho. —v. **2.** dormir.

sleeping car /'slipɪŋ/ coche cama.

sleeping pill /'slipɪŋ/ pastilla para dormir, somnífero m.

sleepy /'slipi/ a. soñoliento. **to be s.,** tener sueño.

sleet /slit/ n. **1.** cellisca f. —v. **2.** cellisquear.

sleeve /sliv/ n. manga f.

slender /'slɛndər/ a. delgado.

slice /slais/ n. **1.** rebanada; (of meat) tajada f. —v. **2.** rebanar; tajar.

slide /slaid/ v. resbalar, deslizarse.

slide rule regla de cálculo f.

slight /slait/ n. **1.** desaire m. —a. **2.** pequeño; leve. —v. **3.** desairar.

slim /slɪm/ a. delgado.

slime /slaim/ n. lama f.

sling /slɪŋ/ n. **1.** honda f.; Med. cabestrillo m. —v. **2.** tirar.

slink /slɪŋk/ v. escabullirse.

slip /slɪp/ n. **1.** imprudencia; (garment) combinación f.; (of paper) trozo m.; ficha f. —v. **2.** resbalar; deslizar. **s. up,** equivocarse.

slipper /'slɪpər/ n. chinela f.

slippery /'slɪpəri/ a. resbaloso.

slit /slɪt/ n. **1.** abertura f. —v. **2.** cortar.

slogan /'slougən/ n. lema m.

slope /sloup/ n. **1.** declive m. —v. **2.** inclinarse.

sloppy /'slɒpi/ a. desaliñado, chapucero.

slot /slɒt/ n. ranura f.

slot machine tragaperras f.

slouch /slautʃ/ n. **1.** patán m. —v. **2.** estar gacho.

slovenly /'slʌvənli/ a. desaliñado.

slow /slou/ a. **1.** lento; (watch) atrasado. —v. **2.** **s. down, s. up,** retardar; ir más despacio.

slowly /'slouli/ adv. despacio.

slowness /'slounɪs/ n. lentitud f.

sluggish /'slʌgɪʃ/ a. perezoso, inactivo.

slum /slʌm/ n. barrio bajo m.

slumber /'slʌmbər/ v. dormitar.

slur /slɜr/ n. **1.** estigma m. —v. **2.** menospreciar.

slush /slʌʃ/ n. fango m.

sly /slai/ a. taimado. **on the s.** a hurtadillas.

smack /smæk/ n. **1.** manotada f. —v. **2.** manotear.

small /smɔl/ a. pequeño.

small letter minúscula f.

smallpox /'smɔl,pɒks/ n. viruela f.

smart /smɑrt/ a. **1.** listo; elegante. —v. **2.** escocer.

smash /smæʃ/ v. aplastar; hacer pedazos.

smear /smɪər/ n. **1.** mancha; difamación f. —v. **2.** manchar; difamar.

smell /smɛl/ n. **1.** olor; (sense) olfato m. —v. **2.** oler.

smelt /smɛlt/ n. **1.** eperlano m. —v. **2.** fundir.

smile /smail/ n. **1.** sonrisa f. —v. **2.** sonreír.

smite /smait/ v. afligir; apenar.

smock /smɒk/ n. camisa de mujer f.

smoke /smouk/ n. **1.** humo m.
—v. **2.** fumar; (food) ahumar.
smokestack /'smouk,stæk/ n. chimenea f.
smolder /'smouldər/ v. arder sin llama.
smooth /smuð/ a. **1.** liso; suave; tranquilo. —v. **2.** alisar.
smother /'smʌðər/ v. sofocar.
smug /smʌg/ a. presumido.
smuggle /'smʌgəl/ v. pasar de contrabando.
snack /snæk/ n. bocadillo m.
snag /snæg/ n. nudo; obstáculo m.
snail /sneil/ n. caracol m.
snake /sneik/ n. culebra, serpiente f.
snap /snæp/ n. **1.** trueno m. —v. **2.** tronar; romper.
snapshot /'snæp,ʃɒt/ n. instantánea f.
snare /snɛər/ n. trampa f.
snarl /snɑrl/ n. **1.** gruñido m. —v. **2.** gruñir; (hair) enredar.
snatch /snætʃ/ v. arrebatar.
sneak /snik/ v. ir, entrar, salir (etc.) a hurtadillas.
sneaker /'snikər/ n. sujeto ruín m. zapatilla de tenis.
sneer /snɪər/ n. **1.** mofa f. —v. **2.** mofarse.
sneeze /sniz/ n. **1.** estornudo m. —v. **2.** estornudar.
snicker /'snɪkər/ n. risita m.
snob /snɒb/ n. esnob m.
snore /snɔr/ n. **1.** ronquido m. —v. **2.** roncar.
snow /snou/ n. **1.** nieve f. —v. **2.** nevar.
snowball /'snou,bɔl/ n. bola de nieve f.
snowdrift /'snou,drɪft/ n. ventisquero m.
snowplow /'snou,plau/ n. quitanieves m.
snowstorm /'snou,stɔrm/ n. nevasca f.
snub /snʌb/ v. desairar.
snug /snʌg/ a. abrigado y cómodo.
so /sou/ adv. **1.** así; (also) también. **so as to,** para. **so that,** para que. **so... as,** tan... como. **so... that,** tan... que. —conj. **2.** así es que.
soak /souk/ v. empapar.
soap /soup/ n. **1.** jabón m. —v. **2.** enjabonar.
soap powder jabón en polvo m.

soar /sɔr/ v. remontarse.
sob /sɒb/ n. **1.** sollozo m. —v. **2.** sollozar.
sober /'soubər/ a. sobrio; pensativo.
sociable /'souʃəbəl/ a. sociable.
social /'souʃəl/ a. **1.** social. —n. **2.** tertulia f.
socialism /'souʃə,lɪzəm/ n. socialismo m.
socialist /'souʃəlɪst/ a. & n. socialista m. & f.
society /sə'saiɪti/ n. sociedad; compañía f.
sociological /,sousiə'lɒdʒɪkəl/ a. sociológico.
sociologist /,sousi,ɒlədʒɪst/ n. sociólogo -ga m. & f.
sociology /,sousi'ɒlədʒi/ n. sociología f.
sock /sɒk/ n. **1.** calcetín; puñetazo m. —v. **2.** dar un puñetazo a.
socket /'sɒkɪt/ n. cuenca f.; Elec. enchufe m.
sod /sɒd/ n. césped m.
soda /'soudə/ n. soda; Chem. sosa f.
sodium /'soudiəm/ n. sodio m.
sofa /'soufə/ n. sofá m.
soft /sɔft/ a. blando; fino; suave.
soft drink bebida no alcohólica.
soften /'sɔfən/ v. ablandar; suavizar.
software /'sɔft,wɛər/ n. software m., programa m.
soil /sɔil/ n. **1.** suelo m. —v. **2.** ensuciar.
sojourn /'soudʒɜrn/ n. morada f., estancia f.
solace /'sɒlɪs/ n. **1.** solaz m. —v. **2.** solazar.
solar /'soulər/ a. solar.
solar system sistema solar m.
solder /'sɒdər/ v. **1.** soldar. —n. **2.** soldadura f.
soldier /'souldʒər/ n. soldado m. & f.
sole /soul/ n. **1.** suela; (of foot) planta f.; (fish) lenguado m. —a. **2.** único.
solemn /'sɒləm/ a. solemne.
solemnity /sə'lɛmnɪti/ n. solemnidad f.
solicit /sə'lɪsɪt/ v. solicitar.
solicitous /sə'lɪsɪtəs/ a. solícito.
solid /'sɒlɪd/ a. & n. sólido m.
solidify /sə'lɪdə,fai/ v. solidificar.
solidity /sə'lɪdɪti/ n. solidez f.
solitary /'sɒlɪ,tɛri/ a. solitario.
solitude /'sɒlɪ,tud/ n. soledad f.

solo /'soulou/ *n.* solo *m.*

soloist /'soulouɪst/ *n.* solista *m.* & *f.*

soluble /'sɒlyəbəl/ *a.* soluble.

solution /sə'luʃən/ *n.* solución *f.*

solve /sɒlv/ *v.* solucionar; resolver.

solvent /'sɒlvənt/ *a.* solvente.

somber /'sɒmbər/ *a.* sombrío.

some /sʌm; *unstressed* səm/ *a.* & *pron.* algo (de), un poco (de); alguno; (pl.) algunos, unos.

somebody, someone /'sʌmbɒdi; 'sʌm,wʌn/ *pron.* alguien.

somehow /'sʌm,hau/ *adv.* de algún modo.

someone /'sʌm,wʌn/ *n.* alguien o alguno.

somersault /'sʌmər,sɔlt/ *n.* salto mortal *m.*

something /'sʌm,θɪŋ/ *pron.* algo, alguna cosa.

sometime /'sʌm,taim/ *adv.* alguna vez.

sometimes /'sʌm,taimz/ *adv.* a veces, algunas veces.

somewhat /'sʌm,wʌt/ *adv.* algo, un poco.

somewhere /'sʌm,wɛər/ *adv.* en (*or* a) alguna parte.

son /sʌn/ *n.* hijo *m.*

song /sɔŋ/ *n.* canción *f.*

son-in-law /'sʌn ɪn ,lɔ/ *n.* yerno *m.*

soon /sun/ *adv.* pronto. **as s. as possible,** cuanto antes. **sooner or later,** tarde o temprano. **no sooner... than,** apenas... cuando.

soot /sut/ *n.* hollín *m.*

soothe /suð/ *v.* calmar.

soothingly /'suðɪŋli/ *adv.* tiernamente.

sophisticated /sə'fɪstɪ,keitɪd/ *a.* sofisticado.

sophomore /'sɒfə,mɔr/ *n.* estudiante de segundo año *m.*

soprano /sə'prænou/ *n.* soprano *m.* & *f.*

sorcery /'sɔrsəri/ *n.* encantamiento *m.*

sordid /'sɔrdɪd/ *a.* sórdido.

sore /sɔr/ *n.* **1.** llaga *f.* —*a.* **2.** lastimado; *Colloq.* enojado. **to be s.,** doler.

sorority /sə'rɔriti, -'rɒr-/ *n.* hermandad de mujeres *f.*

sorrow /'sɒrou/ *n.* pesar, dolor *m.*, aflicción *f.*

sorrowful /'sɒrəfəl/ *a.* doloroso; afligido.

sorry /'sɒri/ *a.* **to be s.,** sentir, lamentar. **to be s. for,** compadecer.

sort /sɔrt/ *n.* **1.** tipo *m.*; clase, especie *f.* **s. of,** algo, un poco. —*v.* **2.** clasificar.

soul /soul/ *n.* alma *f.*

sound /saund/ *a.* **1.** sano; razonable; firme. —*n.* **2.** sonido *m.* —*v.* **3.** sonar; parecer.

soundproof /'saund,pruf/ *a.* insonorizado. *v.* insonorizar.

soundtrack /'saund,træk/ *n.* banda sonora *f.*

soup /sup/ *n.* sopa *f.*

sour /sauər/ *a.* agrio; ácido; rancio.

source /sɔrs/ *n.* fuente; causa *f.*

south /sauθ/ *n.* sur *m.*

South Africa /'æfrɪkə/ Sudáfrica *f.*

South African *a.* & *n.* sudafricano.

South America /ə'mɛrɪkə/ Sud América, América del Sur.

South American *a.* & *n.* sudamericano -na.

southeast /,sauθ'ist; *Naut.* ,sau-/ *n.* sudeste *m.*

southern /'sʌðərn/ *a.* meridional.

South Pole *n.* Polo Sur *m.*

southwest /,sauθ'wɛst; *Naut.* ,sau-/ *n.* sudoeste *m.*

souvenir /,suvə'nɪər/ *n.* recuerdo *m.*

sovereign /'sɒvrɪn/ *n.* soberano -na.

sovereignty /'sɒvrɪnti/ *n.* soberanía *f.*

Soviet Russia Rusia Soviética *f.*

sow /*n.* sau; *v.* sou/ *n.* **1.** puerca *f.* —*v.* **2.** sembrar.

space /speis/ *n.* **1.** espacio *m.* —*v.* **2.** espaciar.

space out *v.* escalonar.

spaceship /'speis,ʃɪp/ *n.* nave espacial, astronave *f.*

space shuttle /'ʃʌtl/ transbordador espacial *m.*

spacious /'speiʃəs/ *a.* espacioso.

spade /speid/ *n.* **1.** laya; (cards) espada *f.* —*v.* **2.** layar.

spaghetti /spə'gɛti/ *n.* espaguetis *m.pl.*

Spain /spein/ *n.* España *f.*

span /spæn/ *n.* **1.** tramo *m.* —*v.* **2.** extenderse sobre.

Spaniard /'spænyərd/ *n.* español -ola.

Spanish /'spænɪʃ/ *a.* & *n.* español -ola.

spank /spæŋk/ v. pegar.
spanking /'spæŋkıŋ/ n. tunda, zumba f.
spar /spɑr/ v. altercar.
spare /spɛər/ a. **1.** de repuesto. —v. **2.** perdonar; ahorrar; prestar. **have... to s.,** tener... de sobra.
spare tire neumático de recambio m.
spark /spɑrk/ n. chispa f.
sparkle /'spɑrkəl/ n. **1.** destello m. —v. **2.** chispear. **sparkling wine,** vino espumoso.
spark plug /'spɑrk,plʌg/ n. bujía f.
sparrow /'spærou/ n. gorrión m.
sparse /spɑrs/ a. esparcido.
spasm /'spæzəm/ n. espasmo m.
spasmodic /spæz'mɒdɪk/ a. espasmódico.
spatter /'spætər/ v. salpicar; manchar.
speak /spik/ v. hablar.
speaker /'spikər/ n. conferencista m. & f.
spear /spɪər/ n. lanza f.
spearmint /'spɪər,mɪnt/ n. menta romana f.
special /'spɛʃəl/ a. especial. **s. delivery,** entrega inmediata, entrega urgente.
specialist /'spɛʃəlɪst/ n. especialista m. & f.
specialty /'spɛʃəlti/ n. especialidad f.
species /'spiʃiz, -siz/ n. especie f.
specific /spɪ'sɪfɪk/ a. específico.
specify /'spɛsə,fai/ v. especificar.
specimen /'spɛsəmən/ n. espécimen m.; muestra f.
spectacle /'spɛktəkəl/ n. espectáculo m.; (pl.) lentes, anteojos m.pl.
spectacular /spɛk'tækyələr/ a. espectacular, aparatoso.
spectator /'spɛkteitər/ n. espectador -ra.
spectrum /'spɛktrəm/ n. espectro m.
speculate /'spɛkyə,leit/ v. especular.
speculation /,spɛkyə'leiʃən/ n. especulación f.
speech /spitʃ/ n. habla f.; lenguaje; discurso m. **part of s.,** parte de la oración.
speechless /'spitʃlɪs/ a. mudo.
speed /spid/ n. **1.** velocidad; rapidez f. —v. **2. s. up,** acelerar, apresurar.

speed limit velocidad máxima f.
speedometer /spi'dɒmɪtər/ n. velocímetro m.
speedy /'spidi/ a. veloz, rápido.
spell /spɛl/ n. **1.** hechizo; rato; Med. ataque m. —v. **2.** escribir; relevar.
spelling /'spɛlıŋ/ n. ortografía f.
spend /spɛnd/ v. gastar; (time) pasar.
spendthrift /'spɛnd,θrıft/ a. & n. pródigo; manirroto m.
sphere /sfɪər/ n. esfera f.
spice /spais/ n. **1.** especia f. —v. **2.** especiar.
spider /'spaidər/ n. araña f.
spider web telaraña f.
spike /spaik/ n. alcayata f.; punta f., clavo m.
spill /spɪl/ v. derramar. n. caída f., vuelco m.
spillway /'spɪl,wei/ n. vertedero m.
spin /spın/ v. hilar; girar.
spinach /'spınıtʃ/ n. espinaca f.
spine /spain/ n. espina dorsal f.
spinet /'spınıt/ n. espineta m.
spinster /'spınstər/ n. solterona f.
spiral /'spairəl/ a. & n. espiral f.
spire /spaiªr/ n. caracol m., espiral f.
spirit /'spırıt/ n. espíritu; ánimo m.
spiritual /'spırıtʃuəl/ a. espiritual.
spiritualism /'spırıtʃuə,lızəm/ n. espiritismo m.
spirituality /,spırıtʃu'ælıti/ n. espiritualidad f.
spit /spıt/ v. escupir.
spite /spait/ n. despecho m. **in s. of,** a pesar de.
splash /splæʃ/ n. **1.** salpicadura f. —v. **2.** salpicar.
splendid /'splɛndıd/ a. espléndido.
splendor /'splɛndər/ n. esplendor m.
splice /splais/ v. **1.** empalmar. —n. **2.** empalme m.
splint /splınt/ n. tablilla f.
splinter /'splıntər/ n. **1.** astilla f. —v. **2.** astillar.
split /splıt/ n. **1.** división f. —v. **2.** dividir, romper en dos.
splurge /splɜrdʒ/ v. **1.** fachendear. —n. **2.** fachenda f.
spoil /spɔil/ n. **1.** (pl.) botín m. —v. **2.** echar a perder; (a child) mimar.

spoke /spouk/ *n.* rayo (de rueda) *m.*

spokesman /'spouksmən/ *n.* portavoz *m. & f.*

spokesperson /'spouks,pɜrsən/ *n.* portavoz *m. & f.*

sponge /spʌndʒ/ *n.* esponja *f.*

sponsor /'spɒnsər/ *n.* **1.** patrocinador *m.* —*v.* **2.** patrocinar; costear.

spontaneity /,spɒntə'niiti, -'nei-/ *n.* espontaneidad *f.*

spontaneous /spɒn'teiniəs/ *a.* espontáneo.

spool /spul/ *n.* carrete *m.*

spoon /spun/ *n.* cuchara *f.*

spoonful /'spunful/ *n.* cucharada *f.*

sporadic /spə'rædɪk/ *a.* esporádico.

sport /spɔrt/ *n.* deporte *m.*

sport jacket chaqueta deportiva *f.*

sports center /spɔrts/ pabellón de deportes, polideportivo *m.*

sportsman /'spɔrtsmən/ *a.* **1.** deportivo. —*n.* **2.** deportista *m. & f.*

spot /spɒt/ *n.* **1.** mancha *f.;* lugar, punto *m.* —*v.* **2.** distinguir.

spouse /spaus/ *n.* esposo -sa.

spout /spaut/ *n.* **1.** chorro; (of teapot) pico *m.* —*v.* **2.** correr a chorro.

sprain /sprein/ *n.* **1.** torcedura *f.,* esguince *m.* —*v.* **2.** torcerse.

sprawl /sprɔl/ *v.* tenderse.

spray /sprei/ *n.* **1.** rociada *f.* —*v.* **2.** rociar.

spread /sprɛd/ *n.* **1.** propagación; extensión; (for bed) colcha *f.* —*v.* **2.** propagar; extender.

spreadsheet /'sprɛd,ʃit/ *n.* hoja de cálculo *f.*

spree /spri/ *n.* parranda *f.*

sprig /sprɪg/ *n.* ramita *f.*

sprightly /'spraitli/ *a.* garboso.

spring /sprɪŋ/ *n.* resorte, muelle *m.;* (season) primavera *f.;* (of water) manantial *m.*

springboard /'sprɪŋ,bɔrd/ *n.* trampolín *m.*

spring onion cebolleta *f.*

sprinkle /'sprɪŋkəl/ *v.* rociar; (rain) lloviznar.

sprint /sprɪnt/ *n.* carrera *f.*

sprout /spraut/ *n.* retoño *m.*

spry /sprai/ *a.* ágil.

spun /spʌn/ *a.* hilado.

spur /spɜr/ *n.* **1.** espuela *f.* **on the s. of the moment,** sin pensarlo. —*v.* **2.** espolear.

spurious /'spyuriəs/ *a.* espurio.

spurn /spɜrn/ *v.* rechazar, despreciar.

spurt /spɜrt/ *n.* **1.** chorro *m.;* esfuerzo supremo. —*v.* **2.** salir en chorro.

spy /spai/ **1.** espía *m. & f.* —*v.* **2.** espiar.

squabble /'skwɒblɪŋ/ *n.* **1.** riña *f.* —*v.* **2.** reñir.

squad /skwɒd/ *n.* escuadra *f.*

squadron /'skwɒdrən/ *n.* escuadrón *m.*

squalid /'skwɒlɪd/ *a.* escuálido.

squall /skwɔl/ *n.* borrasca *f.*

squalor /'skwɒlər/ *n.* escualidez *f.*

squander /'skwɒndər/ *v.* malgastar.

square /skwɛər/ *a.* **1.** cuadrado. —*n.* **2.** cuadrado *m.;* plaza *f.*

square dance *n.* contradanza *f.*

squat /skwɒt/ *v.* agacharse.

squeak /skwik/ *n.* **1.** chirrido *m.* —*v.* **2.** chirriar.

squeamish /'skwimɪʃ/ *a.* escrupuloso.

squeeze /skwiz/ *n.* **1.** apretón *m.* —*v.* **2.** apretar; (fruit) exprimir.

squirrel /'skwɜrəl/ *n.* ardilla *f.*

squirt /skwɜrt/ *n.* **1.** chisguete *m.* —*v.* **2.** jeringar.

stab /stæb/ *n.* **1.** puñalada *f.* —*v.* **2.** apuñalar.

stability /stə'bɪliti/ *n.* estabilidad *f.*

stabilize /'steibə,laiz/ *v.* estabilizar.

stable /'steibəl/ *a.* **1.** estable, equilibrado. —*n.* **2.** caballeriza *f.*

stack /stæk/ *n.* **1.** pila *f.* —*v.* **2.** apilar.

stadium /'steidiəm/ *n.* estadio *m.*

staff /stæf/ *n.* personal *m.* **editorial s.,** cuerpo de redacción. **general s.,** estado mayor.

stag /stæg/ *n.* ciervo *m.*

stage /steidʒ/ *n.* **1.** etapa; *Theat.* escena *f.* —*v.* **2.** representar.

stagflation /stæg'fleiʃən/ *n.* estagflación.

stagger /'stægər/ *v.* (teeter) tambalear; (space out) escalonar.

stagnant /'stægnənt/ *a.* estancado.

stagnate /'stægneit/ *v.* estancarse.

stain /stein/ *n.* **1.** mancha *f.* —*v.* **2.** manchar.

stainless steel /'steinlɪs/ acero inoxidable *m.*

staircase /'stɛərˌkeis/ **stairs** n. escalera f.

stake /steik/ n. estaca; (bet) apuesta f. **at s.,** en juego; en peligro.

stale /steil/ a. rancio.

stalemate /'steilˌmeit/ n. estancación f.; tablas f.pl.

stalk /stɔk/ n. caña f.; (of flower) tallo m. v. acechar.

stall /stɔl/ n. **1.** tenderete; (for horse) pesebre m. —v. **2.** demorar; (motor) atascar.

stallion /'stælyən/ n. S.A. garañón m.

stalwart /'stɔlwərt/ a. fornido.

stamina /'stæmənə/ n. vigor m.

stammer /'stæmər/ v. tartamudear.

stamp /stæmp/ n. **1.** sello m., estampilla f. —v. **2.** sellar.

stamp collecting /kə'lɛktɪŋ/ filatelia f.

stampede /stæm'pid/ n. estampida f.

stand /stænd/ n. **1.** puesto m.; posición; (speaker's) tribuna; (furniture) mesita f. —v. **2.** estar; estar de pie; aguantar. **s. up,** pararse, levantarse.

standard /'stændərd/ a. **1.** normal, corriente. —n. **2.** norma f. **s. of living,** nivel de vida.

standardize /'stændərˌdaiz/ v. uniformar.

standing /'stændɪŋ/ a. fijo; establecido.

standpoint /'stændˌpɔint/ n. punto de vista m.

staple /'steipəl/ n. materia prima f.; grapa f.

stapler /'steiplər/ n. grapadora f.

star /star/ n. estrella f.

starboard /'starbərd/ n. estribor m.

starch /startʃ/ n. **1.** almidón m.; (in diet) fécula f. —v. **2.** almidonar.

stare /stɛər/ v. mirar fijamente.

stark /stark/ a. **1.** severo. —adv. **2.** completamente.

start /start/ n. **1.** susto; principio m. —v. **2.** comenzar, empezar; salir; poner en marcha; causar.

startle /'startl/ v. asustar.

starvation /star'veiʃən/ n. hambre f.

starve /starv/ v. morir de hambre.

state /steit/ n. **1.** estado m. —v. **2.** declarar, decir.

statement /'steitmənt/ n. declaración f.

stateroom /'steitˌrum/ n. camarote m.

statesman /'steitsmən/ n. estadista m.

static /'stætɪk/ a. **1.** estático. —n. **2.** estática f.

station /'steiʃən/ n. estación f.

stationary /'steiʃəˌnɛri/ a. estacionario, fijo.

stationery /'steiʃəˌnɛri/ n. papel de escribir.

statistics /stə'tɪstɪks/ n. estadística f.

statue /'stætʃu/ n. estatua f.

stature /'stætʃər/ n. estatura f.

status /'steitəs, 'stætəs/ n. condición, estado m.

statute /'stætʃut/ n. ley f.

staunch /stɔntʃ/ a. fiel; constante.

stay /stei/ n. **1.** estancia; visita f. —v. **2.** quedar, permanecer; parar, alojarse. **s. away,** ausentarse. **s. up,** velar.

steadfast /'stɛdˌfæst/ a. inmutable.

steady /'stɛdi/ a. **1.** firme; permanente; regular. —v. **2.** sostener.

steak /steik/ n. biftec, bistec m.

steal /stil/ v. robar. **s. away,** escabullirse.

stealth /stɛlθ/ n. cautela f.

steam /stim/ n. vapor m.

steamboat /'stimˌbout/ **steamer, steamship** n. vapor m.

steel /stil/ n. **1.** acero m. —v. **2.** **s. oneself,** fortalecerse.

steep /stip/ a. escarpado, empinado.

steeple /'stipəl/ n. campanario m.

steer /stɪər/ n. **1.** buey m. —v. **2.** guiar, manejar.

stellar /'stɛlər/ a. astral.

stem /stɛm/ n. **1.** tallo m. —v. **2.** parar. **s. from,** emanar de.

stencil /'stɛnsəl/ n. **1.** estarcido. —v. **2.** estarcir.

stenographer /stə'nɒgrəfər/ n. estenógrafo -fa.

stenography /stə'nɒgrəfi/ n. taquigrafía f.

step /stɛp/ n. **1.** paso m.; medida f.; (stairs) escalón m. —v. **2.** pisar. **s. back,** retirarse.

stepladder /'stɛpˌlædər/ n. escalera de mano f.

stereophonic /ˌstɛriə'fɒnɪk/ a. estereofónico.

stereotype /'stɛriə,taip/ n. 1. estereotipo m. —v. 2. estereotipar.
sterile /'stɛrɪl/ a. estéril.
sterilize /'stɛrə,laiz/ v. esterilizar.
sterling /'stɜrlɪŋ/ a. esterlina, genuino.
stern /stɜrn/ n. 1. popa f. —a. 2. duro, severo.
stethoscope /'stɛθə,skoup/ n. estetoscopio m.
stevedore /'stivi,dor/ n. estibador m.
stew /stu/ n. 1. guisado m. —v. 2. estofar.
steward /'stuərd/ n. camarero.
stewardess /'stuərdɪs/ n. azafata f., aeromoza f.
stick /stɪk/ n. 1. palo, bastón m. —v. 2. pegar; (put) poner, meter.
sticky /'stɪki/ a. pegajoso.
stiff /stɪf/ a. tieso; duro.
stiffness /'stɪfnɪs/ n. tiesura f.
stifle /'staifəl/ v. sofocar; Fig. suprimir.
stigma /'stɪgmə/ n. estigma m.
still /stɪl/ a. 1. quieto; silencioso. **to keep s.,** quedarse quieto. —adv. 2. todavía, aún; no obstante. —n. 3. alambique m.
stillborn /'stɪl,bɔrn/ n. & a. nacido -da muerto -ta.
still life n. naturaleza muerta f.
stillness /'stɪlnɪs/ n. silencio m.
stilted /'stɪltɪd/ a. afectado, artificial.
stimulant /'stɪmyələnt/ a. & n. estimulante m.
stimulate /'stɪmyə,leit/ v. estimular.
stimulus /'stɪmyələs/ n. estímulo m.
sting /stɪŋ/ n. 1. picadura f. —v. 2. picar.
stingy /'stɪndʒi/ a. tacaño.
stipulate /'stɪpyə,leit/ v. estipular.
stir /stɜr/ n. 1. conmoción f. —v. 2. mover. **s. up,** conmover; suscitar.
stitch /stɪtʃ/ n. 1. puntada f. —v. 2. coser.
stock /stɒk/ n. surtido f.; raza f.; (finance) acciones. f.pl. **in s.,** en existencia. **to take s. in,** tener fe en.
stock exchange bolsa f.
stockholder /'stɒk,houldər/ n. accionista m. & f.
stocking /'stɒkɪŋ/ n. media f.
stockyard /'stɒk,yɑrd/ n. corral de ganado m.

stodgy /'stɒdʒi/ a. pesado.
stoical /'stouɪkəl/ a. estoico.
stole /stoul/ n. estola f.
stolid /'stɒlɪd/ a. impasible.
stomach /'stʌmək/ n. estómago m.
stomachache /'stʌmək,eik/ n. dolor de estómago m.
stone /stoun/ n. piedra f.
stool /stul/ n. banquillo m.
stoop /stup/ v. encorvarse; Fig. rebajarse. espaldas encorvadas f.pl.
stop /stɒp/ n. 1. parada f. **to put a s. to,** poner fin a. —v. 2. parar; suspender; detener; impedir. **s. doing** (etc.), dejar de hacer (etc.).
stopgap /'stɒp,gæp/ n. recurso provisional m.
stopover /'stɒp,ouvər/ n. parada f.
stopwatch /'stɒp,wɒtʃ/ n. cronómetro m.
storage /'stɔrɪdʒ/ n. almacenaje m.
store /stɔr/ n. 1. tienda; provisión f. **department s.,** almacén m. —v. 2. guardar; almacenar.
store window escaparate m.
stork /stɔrk/ n. cigüeña f.
storm /stɔrm/ n. tempestad, tormenta f.
stormy /'stɔrmi/ a. tempestuoso.
story /'stɔri/ n. cuento; relato m.; historia f. **short s.,** cuento.
stout /staut/ a. corpulento.
stove /stouv/ n. hornilla; estufa f.
straight /streit/ a. 1. recto; derecho. —adv. 2. directamente.
straighten /'streitn/ v. enderezar. **s. out,** poner en orden.
straightforward /,streit'fɔrwərd/ a. recto, sincero.
strain /strein/ n. 1. tensión f. —v. 2. colar.
strainer /'streinər/ n. colador m.
strait /streit/ n. estrecho m.
strand /strænd/ n. 1. hilo m. —v. 2. **be stranded,** encallarse.
strange /streindʒ/ a. extraño; raro.
stranger /'streindʒər/ n. extranjero -ra; forastero -ra; desconocido -da.
strangle /'stræŋgəl/ v. estrangular.
strap /stræp/ n. correa f.
stratagem /'strætədʒəm/ n. estratagema f.

strategic /strə'tidʒik/ *a.* estratégico.

strategy /'strætɪdʒi/ *n.* estrategia *f.*

stratosphere /'strætə,sfɪər/ *n.* estratosfera *f.*

straw /strɔ/ *n.* paja *f.*

strawberry /'strɔ,bɛri/ *n.* fresa *f.*

stray /strei/ *a.* **1.** vagabundo. —*v.* **2.** extraviarse.

streak /strik/ *n.* **1.** racha; raya *f.;* lado *m.* —*v.* **2.** rayar.

stream /strim/ *n.* corriente *f.;* arroyo *m.*

street /strit/ *n.* calle *f.*

streetcar /'strit,kɑr/ *n.* tranvía *m.*

street lamp /'strit,læmp/ *n.* farol *m.*

strength /strɛŋkθ, strɛnθ/ *n.* fuerza *m.*

strengthen /'strɛŋkθən, 'strɛn-/ *v.* reforzar.

strenuous /'strɛnyuəs/ *a.* estrenuo.

streptococcus /,strɛptə'kɒkəs/ *n.* estreptococo *m.*

stress /strɛs/ *n.* **1.** tensión *f.;* énfasis *m.* —*v.* **2.** recalcar; acentuar.

stretch /strɛtʃ/ *n.* **1.** trecho *m.* **at one s.,** de un tirón. —*v.* **2.** tender; extender; estirarse.

stretcher /'strɛtʃər/ *n.* camilla *f.*

strew /stru/ *v.* esparcir.

stricken /'strɪkən/ *a.* agobiado.

strict /strɪkt/ *a.* estricto; severo.

stride /straid/ *n.* **1.** tranco *m.;* (fig., pl.) progresos. —*v.* **2.** andar a trancos.

strife /straif/ *n.* contienda *f.*

strike /straik/ *n.* **1.** huelga *f.* —*v.* **2.** pegar; chocar con; (clock) dar.

striker /'straikər/ *n.* huelguista *m.* & *f.*

string /strɪŋ/ *n.* cuerda *f.;* cordel *m.*

string bean *n.* habichuela *f.*

stringent /'strɪndʒənt/ *a.* estricto.

strip /strɪp/ *n.* **1.** tira *f.* —*v.* **2.** despojar; desnudarse.

stripe /straip/ *n.* raya *f.; Mil.* galón *m.*

strive /straiv/ *v.* esforzarse.

stroke /strouk/ *n.* golpe *m.;* (swimming) brazada *f.; Med.* ataque *m.* **s. of luck,** suerte *f.*

stroll /stroul/ *n.* **1.** paseo *m.* —*v.* **2.** pasearse.

stroller /'stroulər/ *n.* vagabundo *m.;* cochecito (de niño).

strong /strɔŋ/ *a.* fuerte.

stronghold /'strɔŋ,hould/ *n.* fortificación *f.*

structure /'strʌktʃər/ *n.* estructura *f.*

struggle /'strʌgəl/ *n.* **1.** lucha *f.* —*v.* **2.** luchar.

strut /strʌt/ *n.* **1.** pavonada *f.* —*v.* **2.** pavonear.

stub /stʌb/ *n.* **1.** cabo; (ticket) talón *m.* —*v.* **2.** **s. on one's toes,** tropezar con.

stubborn /'stʌbərn/ *a.* testarudo.

stucco /'stʌkou/ *n.* **1.** estuco *m.* —*v.* **2.** estucar.

student /'studnt/ *n.* alumno -na, estudiante -ta.

studio /'studi,ou/ *n.* estudio *m.*

studious /'studiəs/ *a.* aplicado; estudioso.

study /'stʌdi/ *n.* **1.** estudio *m.* —*v.* **2.** estudiar.

stuff /stʌf/ *n.* **1.** cosas *f.pl.* —*v.* **2.** llenar; rellenar.

stuffing /'stʌfɪŋ/ *n.* relleno *m.*

stumble /'stʌmbəl/ *v.* tropezar.

stump /stʌmp/ *n.* cabo; tocón; muñón *m.*

stun /stʌn/ *v.* aturdir.

stunt /stʌnt/ *n.* **1.** maniobra sensacional *f.* —*v.* **2.** impedir crecimiento.

stupendous /stu'pɛndəs/ *a.* estupendo.

stupid /'stupɪd/ *a.* estúpido.

stupidity /stu'pɪdɪti/ *n.* estupidez *f.*

stupor /'stupər/ *n.* estupor *m.*

sturdy /'stɜrdi/ *a.* robusto.

stutter /'stʌtər/ *v.* **1.** tartamudear. —*n.* **2.** tartamudeo *m.*

sty /stai/ *n.* pocilga *f.; Med.* orzuelo.

style /stail/ *n.* estilo *m.;* moda *f.*

stylish /'stailɪʃ/ *a.* elegante; a la moda.

suave /swɑv/ *a.* afable, suave.

subconscious /sʌb'kɒnʃəs/ *a.* subconsciente.

subdue /səb'du/ *v.* dominar.

subject /*n.* 'sʌbdʒɪkt; *v.* səb'dʒɛkt/ *n.* **1.** tema *m.;* (of study) materia *f.; Pol.* súbdito -ta; *Gram.* sujeto *m.* —*v.* **2.** someter.

subjugate /'sʌbdʒə,geit/ *v.* sojuzgar, subyugar.

subjunctive /səb'dʒʌŋktɪv/ *a.* & *n.* subjuntivo *m.*

sublimate /'sʌblə,meit/ *v.* sublimar.

sublime /sə'blaim/ *a.* sublime.

submarine /ˌsʌbməˈrin/ *a. & n.* submarino *m.*

submerge /səbˈmɜrdʒ/ *v.* sumergir.

submission /səbˈmɪʃən/ *n.* sumisión *f.*

submit /səbˈmɪt/ *v.* someter.

subnormal /sʌbˈnɔrməl/ *a.* subnormal.

subordinate /*a, n* səˈbɔrdṇɪt; *v* -dṇˌeit/ *a. & n.* **1.** subordinado -da. —*v.* **2.** subordinar.

subscribe /səbˈskraib/ *v.* aprobar; abonarse.

subscriber /səbˈskraibər/ *n.* abonado -da *m. & f.*

subscription /səbˈskrɪpʃən/ *n.* abono *m.*

subsequent /ˈsʌbsɪkwənt/ *a.* subsiguiente.

subservient /səbˈsɜrviənt/ *a.* servicial.

subside /səbˈsaid/ *v.* apaciguarse, menguar.

subsidy /ˈsʌbsɪdi/ *n.* subvención *f.*

subsoil /ˈsʌbˌsɔil/ *n.* subsuelo *m.*

substance /ˈsʌbstəns/ *n.* substancia *f.*

substantial /səbˈstænʃəl/ *a.* substancial; considerable.

substitute /ˈsʌbstɪˌtut/ *a.* **1.** substitutivo. —*n.* **2.** substituto -ta. —*v.* **3.** substituir.

substitution /ˌsʌbstɪˈtuʃən/ *n.* substitución *f.*

subterfuge /ˈsʌbtərˌfyudʒ/ *n.* subterfugio *m.*

subtitle /ˈsʌbˌtait l/ *n.* subtítulo *m.*

subtle /ˈsʌt l/ *a.* sutil.

subtract /səbˈtrækt/ *v.* substraer.

suburb /ˈsʌbɜrb/ *n.* suburbio *m.;* (pl.) afueras *f.pl.*

subversive /səbˈvɜrsɪv/ *a.* subversivo.

subway /ˈsʌbˌwei/ *n.* metro *m.*

succeed /səkˈsid/ *v.* lograr, tener éxito; (in office) suceder a.

success /səkˈsɛs/ *n.* éxito *m.*

successful /səkˈsɛsfəl/ *a.* próspero; afortunado.

succession /səkˈsɛʃən/ *n.* sucesión *f.*

successive /səkˈsɛsɪv/ *a.* sucesivo.

successor /səkˈsɛsər/ *n.* sucesor -ra; heredero -ra.

succor /ˈsʌkər/ *n.* **1.** socorro *m.* —*v.* **2.** socorrer.

succumb /səˈkʌm/ *v.* sucumbir.

such /sʌtʃ/ *a.* tal.

suck /sʌk/ *v.* chupar.

suction /ˈsʌkʃən/ *n.* succión *f.*

sudden /ˈsʌdṇ/ *a.* repentino, súbito. **all of a s.,** de repente.

suds /sʌdz/ *n.* jabonaduras *f.pl.*

sue /su/ *v.* demandar.

suffer /ˈsʌfər/ *v.* sufrir; padecer.

suffice /səˈfais/ *v.* bastar.

sufficient /səˈfɪʃənt/ *a.* suficiente.

suffocate /ˈsʌfəˌkeit/ *v.* sofocar.

sugar /ˈʃugər/ *n.* azúcar *m.*

sugar bowl azucarero *m.*

suggest /səgˈdʒɛst/ *v.* sugerir.

suggestion /səgˈdʒɛstʃən/ *n.* sugerencia *f.*

suicide /ˈsuəˌsaid/ *n.* suicidio *m.;* (person) suicida *m. & f.* **to commit s.,** suicidarse.

suit /sut/ *n.* **1.** traje; (cards) palo; (law) pleito *m.* —*v.* **2.** convenir *a.*

suitable /ˈsutəbəl/ *a.* apropiado; que conviene.

suitcase /ˈsutˌkeis/ *n.* maleta *f.*

suite /swit/ *n.* serie *f.,* séquito *m.*

suitor /ˈsutər/ *n.* pretendiente *m.*

sullen /ˈsʌlən/ *a.* hosco.

sum /sʌm/ *n.* **1.** suma *f.* —*v.* **2. s. up,** resumir.

summarize /ˈsʌməˌraiz/ *v.* resumir.

summary /ˈsʌməri/ *n.* resumen *m.*

summer /ˈsʌmər/ *n.* verano *m.*

summon /ˈsʌmən/ *v.* llamar; (law) citar.

summons /ˈsʌmənz/ *n.* citación *f.*

sumptuous /ˈsʌmptʃuəs/ *a.* suntuoso.

sun /sʌn/ *n.* **1.** sol *m.* —*v.* **2.** tomar el sol.

sunbathe /ˈsʌnˌbeið/ *v.* tomar el sol.

sunburn /ˈsʌnˌbɜrn/ *n.* quemadura de sol.

sunburned /ˈsʌnˌbɜrnd/ *a.* quemado por el sol.

Sunday /ˈsʌndei/ *n.* domingo *m.*

sunken /ˈsʌŋkən/ *a.* hundido.

sunny /ˈsʌni/ *a.* asoleado. **s. day,** día de sol. **to be s.,** (weather) hacer sol.

sunshine /ˈsʌnˌʃain/ *n.* luz del sol.

suntan /ˈsʌnˌtæn/ *n.* bronceado *m.* **s. lotion,** loción bronceadora *f.,* bronceador *m.*

superb /suˈpɜrb/ *a.* soberbio.

superficial /ˌsupərˈfɪʃəl/ *a.* superficial.

superfluous /suˈpɜrfluəs/ *a.* superfluo.

superhuman /ˌsupər'hyumən/ a. sobrehumano.

superintendent /ˌsupərɪn'tɛndənt/ n. superintendente m. & f.; (of building) conserje m.; (of school) director -ra general.

superior /sə'pɪəriər/ a. & n. superior m.

superiority /sə,pɪəri'ɔrɪti/ n. superioridad f.

superlative /sə'pərlətɪv/ a. superlativo.

supernatural /ˌsupər'nætʃərəl/ a. sobrenatural.

supersede /ˌsupər'sid/ v. reemplazar.

superstar /'supər,stɑr/ n. superestrella m. & f.

superstition /ˌsupər'stɪʃən/ n. superstición f.

superstitious /ˌsupər'stɪʃəs/ a. supersticioso.

supervise /'supər,vaiz/ v. supervisar.

supper /'sʌpər/ n. cena f.

supplement /'sʌpləmənt/ n. **1.** suplemento m. —v. **2.** suplementar.

supply /sə'plai/ n. **1.** provisión f.; Com. surtido m.; Econ. existencia f. —v. **2.** suplir; proporcionar.

support /sə'pɔrt/ n. **1.** sustento; apoyo m. —v. **2.** mantener; apoyar.

suppose /sə'pouz/ v. suponer. **be supposed to,** deber.

suppository /sə'pɒzɪ,tɔri/ n. supositorio m.

suppress /sə'prɛs/ v. suprimir.

suppression /sə'prɛʃən/ n. supresión f.

supreme /sə'prim/ a. supremo.

sure /ʃʊr, ʃɜr/ a. seguro, cierto. **for s.,** con seguridad. **to make s.,** asegurarse.

surety /'ʃʊrɪti, 'ʃɜr-/ n. garantía f.

surf /sɜrf/ n. **1.** oleaje m. —v. **2.** (Internet) navegar; (sport) surfear.

surface /'sɜrfɪs/ n. superficie f.

surfboard /'sɜrf,bɔrd/ n. tabla de surf f.

surfer /'sɜrfər/ n. (Internet) usuario -ria, navegante m. & f.; (sport) surfero -ra.

surge /sɜrdʒ/ v. surgir.

surgeon /'sɜrdʒən/ n. cirujano -na.

surgery /'sɜrdʒəri/ n. cirugía f.

surmise /sər'maiz/ v. suponer.

surmount /sər'maunt/ v. vencer.

surname /'sɜr,neim/ n. apellido m.

surpass /sər'pæs/ v. superar.

surplus /'sɜrplʌs/ a. & n. sobrante m.

surprise /sər'praiz, sə-/ n. **1.** sorpresa —v. **2.** sorprender. **I am surprised...,** me extraña...

surrender /sə'rɛndər/ n. **1.** rendición f. —v. **2.** rendir.

surround /sə'raund/ v. rodear, circundar.

surveillance /sər'veiləns/ n. vigilancia f.

survey /n. 'sɜrvei; v. sər'vei/ n. **1.** examen; estudio m. —v. **2.** examinar; (land) medir.

survival /sər'vaivəl/ n. supervivencia f.

survive /sər'vaiv/ v. sobrevivir.

susceptible /sə'sɛptəbəl/ a. susceptible.

suspect /v. sə'spɛkt; n. 'sʌspɛkt/ v. **1.** sospechar. —n. **2.** sospechoso -sa.

suspend /sə'spɛnd/ v. suspender.

suspense /sə'spɛns/ n. incertidumbre f. **in s.,** en suspenso.

suspension /sə'spɛnʃən/ n. suspensión f.

suspension bridge n. puente colgante m.

suspicion /sə'spɪʃən/ n. sospecha f.

suspicious /sə'spɪʃəs/ a. sospechoso.

sustain /sə'stein/ v. sustentar; mantener.

swallow /'swɒlou/ n. **1.** trago m.; (bird) golondrina f. —v. **2.** tragar.

swamp /swɒmp/ n. **1.** pantano m. —v. **2.** Fig. abrumar.

swan /swɒn/ n. cisne m.

swap /swɒp/ n. **1.** trueque m. —v. **2.** cambalachear.

swarm /swɔrm/ n. enjambre m.

swarthy /'swɔrði/ a. moreno.

sway /swei/ n. **1.** predominio m. —v. **2.** bambolearse; Fig. influir en.

swear /swɛər/ v. jurar. **s. off,** renunciar a.

sweat /swɛt/ n. **1.** sudor m. —v. **2.** sudar.

sweater /'swɛtər/ n. suéter m.

sweatshirt /'swɛt,ʃɜrt/ n. sudadera f.

Swede /swid/ n. sueco -ca.

Sweden /'swidn̩/ n. Suecia f.

Swedish /'swidɪʃ/ *a.* sueco.
sweep /swip/ *v.* barrer.
sweet /swit/ *a.* **1.** dulce; amable, simpático. —*n.* **2.** (pl.) dulces *m.pl.*
sweetheart /'swit‚hɑrt/ *n.* novio -via.
sweetness /'switnɪs/ *n.* dulzura *f.*
sweet-toothed /'swit ‚tuθt/ *a.* goloso.
swell /swɛl/ *a.* **1.** *Colloq.* estupendo, excelente. —*n.* **2.** (of the sea) oleada *f.* —*v.* **3.** hincharse; aumentar.
swelter /'swɛltər/ *v.* sofocarse de calor.
swift /swɪft/ *a.* rápido, veloz.
swim /swɪm/ *n.* **1.** nadada *f.* —*v.* **2.** nadar.
swimming /'swɪmɪŋ/ *n.* natación *f.*
swimming pool alberca, piscina *f.*
swindle /'swɪndl̩/ *n.* **1.** estafa *f.* —*v.* **2.** estafar.
swine /swain/ *n.* puercos *m.pl.*
swing /swɪŋ/ *n.* **1.** columpio *m.* **in full s.,** en plena actividad. —*v.* **2.** mecer; balancear.
swirl /swɜrl/ *n.* **1.** remolino *m.* —*v.* **2.** arremolinar.
Swiss /swɪs/ *a.* & *n.* suizo -za.
switch /swɪtʃ/ *n.* **1.** varilla *f.;* *Elec.* llave *f.,* conmutador *m.;*

(railway) cambiavía *m.* —*v.* **2.** cambiar; trocar.
switchboard /'swɪtʃ‚bɔrd/ *n.* cuadro conmutador *m.,* centralita *f.*
Switzerland /'swɪtsərlənd/ *n.* Suiza *f.*
sword /sɔrd/ *n.* espada *f.*
syllable /'sɪləbəl/ *n.* sílaba *f.*
symbol /'sɪmbəl/ *n.* símbolo *m.*
sympathetic /‚sɪmpə'θɛtɪk/ *a.* compasivo. **to be s.,** tener simpatía.
sympathy /'sɪmpəθi/ *n.* lástima; condolencia *f.*
symphony /'sɪmfəni/ *n.* sinfonía *f.*
symptom /'sɪmptəm/ *n.* síntoma *m.*
synagogue /'sɪnə‚gɒg/ *n.* sinagoga *f.*
synchronize /'sɪŋkrə‚naiz/ *v.* sincronizar.
syndicate /'sɪndɪkɪt/ *n.* sindicato *m.*
syndrome /'sɪndroum, -drəm/ *n.* síndrome *m.*
synonym /'sɪnənɪm/ *n.* sinónimo *m.*
synthetic /sɪn'θɛtɪk/ *a.* sintético.
syringe /sə'rɪndʒ/ *n.* jeringa *f.*
syrup /'sɪrəp, 'sɜr-/ *n.* almíbar; *Med.* jarabe *m.*
system /'sɪstəm/ *n.* sistema *m.*
systematic /‚sɪstə'mætɪk/ *a.* sistemático.

T

tabernacle /'tæbər‚nækəl/ *n.* tabernáculo *m.*
table /'teibəl/ *n.* mesa; (list) tabla *f.*
tablecloth /'teibəl‚klɔθ/ *n.* mantel *m.*
table of contents /'kɒntɛnts/ índice de materias *m.*
tablespoon /'teibəl‚spun/ *n.* cuchara *f.*
tablespoonful /'teibəlspun‚fʊl/ *n.* cucharada *f.*
tablet /'tæblɪt/ *n.* tableta; *Med.* pastilla *f.*
tack /tæk/ *n.* tachuela *f.*
tact /tækt/ *n.* tacto *m.*
tag /tæg/ *n.* etiqueta *f.,* rótulo *m.*
tail /teil/ *n.* cola *f.,* rabo *m.*
tailor /'teilər/ *n.* sastre *m.*
take /teik/ *v.* tomar; llevar. **t. a bath,** bañarse. **t. a shower,** ducharse. **t. away,** quitar. **t. off,** quitarse. **t. out,** sacar. **t. long,** tardar mucho.

tale /teil/ *n.* cuento *m.*
talent /'tælənt/ *n.* talento *m.*
talk /tɔk/ *n.* **1.** plática, habla *f.;* discurso *m.* —*v.* **2.** hablar.
talkative /'tɔkətɪv/ *a.* locuaz.
tall /tɔl/ *a.* alto.
tame /teim/ *a.* **1.** manso, domesticado. —*v.* **2.** domesticar.
tamper /'tæmpər/ *v.* **t. with,** entremeterse en.
tampon /'tæmpɒn/ *n.* tampón *m.*
tan /tæn/ *a.* **1.** color de arena. —*v.* **2.** curtir; tostar. *n.* bronceado.
tangerine /‚tændʒə'rin/ *n.* clementina *f.*
tangible /'tændʒəbəl/ *a.* tangible.
tangle /'tæŋgəl/ *n.* **1.** enredo *m.* —*v.* **2.** enredar.
tank /tæŋk/ *n.* tanque *m.*
tap /tæp/ *n.* **1.** golpe ligero. —*v.* **2.** golpear ligeramente; decentar.
tape /teip/ *n.* cinta *f.*

tape recorder /rɪ'kɔrdər/ magnetófono *m.*, grabadora *f.*
tapestry /'tæpəstri/ *n.* tapiz *m.;*
tapicería *f.*
tar /tɑr/ *n.* **1.** brea *f.* —*v.* **2.** em-
brear.
target /'tɑrgɪt/ *n.* blanco *m.*
tarnish /'tɑrnɪʃ/ *n.* **1.** deslustre *m.*
—*v.* **2.** deslustrar.
tarpaulin /tɑr'pɔlɪn, 'tɑrpəlɪn/ *n.*
lona *f.*
task /tæsk/ *n.* tarea *f.*
taste /teist/ *n.* **1.** gusto; sabor *m.*
—*v.* **2.** gustar; probar. **t. of,** saber a.
tasty /'teisti/ *a.* sabroso.
tattoo /tæ'tu/ *v.* tatuar.
taut /tɔt/ *a.* tieso.
tavern /'tævərn/ *n.* taberna *f.*
tax /tæks/ *n.* **1.** impuesto *m.* —*v.*
2. imponer impuestos.
tax collector *n.* recaudador -ra *m.*
& *f.*
taxi /'tæksi/ *n.* taxi, taxímetro *m.*
t. driver, taxista *m.* & *f.*
taxpayer /'tæks,peiər/ *n.* contribuyente *m.* & *f.*
tax reform reforma tributaria *f.*
tax return declaración de la renta *f.*
tea /ti/ *n.* té *m.*
teach /titʃ/ *v.* enseñar.
teacher /'titʃər/ *n.* maestro -tra,
profesor -ra.
team /tim/ *n.* equipo *m.;* pareja *f.*
tear /tɪər/ *n.* **1.** rasgón *m.;* lágrima *f.* —*v.* **2.** rasgar, lacerar. **t.
apart,** separar.
tease /tiz/ *v.* atormentar; embromar.
teaspoon /'ti,spun/ *n.* cucharita *f.*
technical /'tɛknɪkəl/ *a.* técnico.
technician /tɛk'nɪʃən/ *n.* técnico
-ca *m.* & *f.*
technique /tɛk'nik/ *n.* técnica *f.*
technology /tɛk'nɒlədʒi/ *n.* tecnología *f.*
teddy bear /'tɛdi/ oso de felpa *m.*
tedious /'tidiəs/ *a.* tedioso.
telegram /'tɛlɪ,græm/ *n.* telegrama *m.*
telegraph /'tɛlɪ,græf/ *n.* **1.** telégrafo *m.* —*v.* **2.** telegrafiar.
telephone /'tɛlə,foun/ *n.* **1.** teléfono *m.* **t. book,** directorio tele-
fónico. —*v.* **2.** telefonear; llamar
por teléfono.
telescope /'tɛlə,skoup/ *n.* **1.** telescopio *m.* —*v.* **2.** enchufar.
television /'tɛlə,vɪʒən/ *n.* televisión *f.*

tell /tɛl/ *v.* decir; contar; distinguir.
temper /'tɛmpər/ *n.* **1.** temperamento, genio *m.* —*v.* **2.** templar.
temperament /'tɛmpərəmənt,
-prəmənt/ *n.* temperamento.
temperamental /,tɛmpərə'mɛntl,
-prə'mɛn-/ *a.* sensitivo, emocional.
temperance /'tɛmpərəns/ *n.* moderación; sobriedad *f.*
temperate /'tɛmpərɪt/ *a.* templado.
temperature /'tɛmpərətʃər/ *n.*
temperatura *f.*
tempest /'tɛmpɪst/ *n.* tempestad *f.*
tempestuous /tɛm'pɛstʃuəs/ *a.*
tempestuoso.
temple /'tɛmpəl/ *n.* templo *m.*
temporary /'tɛmpə,rɛri/ *a.* temporal, temporario.
tempt /tɛmpt/ *v.* tentar.
temptation /tɛmp'teiʃən/ *n.* tentación *f.*
ten /tɛn/ *a.* & *pron.* diez.
tenant /'tɛnənt/ *n.* inquilino -na.
tend /tɛnd/ *v.* tender. **t. to,**
atender.
tendency /'tɛndənsi/ *n.* tendencia
f.
tender /'tɛndər/ *a.* **1.** tierno. —*v.*
2. ofrecer.
tenderness /'tɛndərnɪs/ *n.* ternura
f.
tennis /'tɛnɪs/ *n.* tenis *m.*
tennis court cancha de tenis,
pista de tenis *f.*
tenor /'tɛnər/ *n.* tenor *m.*
tense /tɛns/ *a.* **1.** tenso. —*n.* **2.**
Gram. tiempo *m.*
tent /tɛnt/ *n.* tienda, carpa *f.*
tenth /tɛnθ/ *a.* décimo.
term /tɜrm/ *n.* **1.** término; plazo
m. —*v.* **2.** llamar.
terminal /'tɜrmənl/ *n.* terminal *f.*
terrace /'tɛrəs/ *n.* terraza *f.*
terrible /'tɛrəbəl/ *a.* terrible, espantoso; pésimo.
territory /'tɛrɪ,tɔri/ *n.* territorio
m.
terror /'tɛrər/ *n.* terror, espanto,
pavor *m.*
test /tɛst/ *n.* **1.** prueba *f.;* examen
m. —*v.* **2.** probar; examinar.
testament /'tɛstəmənt/ *n.* testamento *m.*
testify /'tɛstə,fai/ *v.* atestiguar,
testificar.
testimony /'tɛstə,mouni/ *n.* testimonio *m.*

test tube tubo de ensayo *m.*
text /tɛkst/ *n.* texto; tema *m.*
textbook /'tɛkst,buk/ *n.* libro de texto.
textile /'tɛkstail/ *a.* **1.** textil. —*n.* **2.** tejido *m.*
texture /'tɛkstʃər/ *n.* textura *f.*; tejido *m.*
than /ðæn, ðɛn; *unstressed* ðən, ən/ *conj.* que; de.
thank /θæŋk/ *v.* agradecer, dar gracias; **thanks, th. you,** gracias.
thankful /'θæŋkfəl/ *a.* agradecido; grato.
that /ðæt; *unstressed* ðət/ *a.* **1.** ese, aquel. —*dem. pron.* **2.** ése, aquél; eso, aquello. —*rel. pron. & conj.* **3.** que.
the /*stressed* ði; *unstressed before a consonant* ðə, *unstressed before a vowel* ði/ *art.* el, la, los, las; lo.
theater /'θiətər/ *n.* teatro *m.*
theft /θɛft/ *n.* robo *m.*
their /ðɛər; *unstressed* ðər/ *a.* su.
theirs /ðɛərz/ *pron.* suyo, de ellos.
them /ðɛm; *unstressed* ðəm, əm/ *pron.* ellos, ellas; los, las; les.
theme /θim/ *n.* tema; *Mus.* motivo *m.*
themselves /ðəm'sɛlvz, ˌðɛm-/ *pron.* sí, sí mismos -as. **they th.,** ellos mismos, ellas mismas. **with th.,** consigo.
then /ðɛn/ *adv.* entonces, después; pues.
thence /ðɛns/ *adv.* de allí.
theology /θi'ɒlədʒi/ *n.* teología *f.*
theory /'θiəri/ *n.* teoría *f.*
there /ðɛər; *unstressed* ðər/ *adv.* allí, allá, ahí. **there is, there are,** hay.
therefore /'ðɛər,fɔr/ *adv.* por lo tanto, por consiguiente.
thermometer /θər'mɒmɪtər/ *n.* termómetro *m.*
thermostat /'θɜrmə,stæt/ *n.* termostato *m.*
they /ðei/ *pron.* ellos, ellas.
thick /θɪk/ *a.* espeso, grueso, denso; torpe.
thicken /'θɪkən/ *v.* espesar, condensar.
thief /θif/ *n.* ladrón -na.
thigh /θai/ *n.* muslo *m.*
thimble /'θɪmbəl/ *n.* dedal *m.*
thin /θɪn/ *a.* **1.** delgado; raro; claro; escaso. —*v.* **2.** enrarecer; adelgazar.
thing /θɪŋ/ *n.* cosa *f.*

thingamabob /'θɪŋəmə,bɒb/ *n.* *Colloq.* chisme *m.*
think /θɪŋk/ *v.* pensar; creer.
thinker /'θɪŋkər/ *n.* pensador -ra.
third /θɜrd/ *a.* tercero.
Third World Tercer Mundo *m.*
thirst /θɜrst/ *n.* sed *f.*
thirsty /'θɜrsti/ *a.* sediento. **to be th.,** tener sed.
thirteen /'θɜr'tin/ *a. & pron.* trece.
thirty /'θɜrti/ *a. & pron.* treinta.
this /ðɪs/ *a.* **1.** este. —*pron.* **2.** éste; esto.
thoracic cage /θə'ræsɪk/ *n.* caja torácica *f.*
thorn /θɔrn/ *n.* espina *f.*
thorough /'θɜrou/ *a.* completo; cuidadoso.
though /ðou/ *adv.* **1.** sin embargo. —*conj.* **2.** aunque. **as th.,** como si.
thought /θɔt/ *n.* pensamiento *m.*
thoughtful /'θɔtfəl/ *a.* pensativo; considerado.
thousand /'θauzənd/ *a. & pron.* mil.
thread /θrɛd/ *n.* hilo *m.*; (of screw) rosca *f.*
threat /θrɛt/ *n.* amenaza *f.*
threaten /'θrɛtn/ *v.* amenazar.
three /θri/ *a. & pron.* tres.
thrift /θrɪft/ *n.* economía, frugalidad *f.*
thrill /θrɪl/ *n.* **1.** emoción *f.* —*v.* **2.** emocionar.
thrive /θraiv/ *v.* prosperar.
throat /θrout/ *n.* garganta *f.*
throne /θroun/ *n.* trono *m.*
through /θru/ *prep.* **1.** por; a través de. por medio de. —*a.* **2.** continuo. **th. train,** tren directo. **to be th.,** haber terminado.
throughout /θru'aut/ *prep.* **1.** por todo, durante todo. —*adv.* **2.** en todas partes; completamente.
throw /θrou/ *n.* **1.** tiro *m.* —*v.* **2.** tirar, lanzar. **th. away,** arrojar. **th. out,** echar.
thrust /θrʌst/ *n.* **1.** lanzada *f.* —*v.* **2.** empujar.
thumb /θʌm/ *n.* dedo pulgar, pulgar *m.*
thumbtack /'θʌm,tæk/ *n.* chincheta *f.*
thunder /'θʌndər/ *n.* **1.** trueno *m.* —*v.* **2.** tronar.
Thursday /'θɜrzdei/ *n.* jueves *m.*
thus /ðʌs/ *adv.* así, de este modo.
thwart /θwɔrt/ *v.* frustrar.

ticket /'tɪkɪt/ n. billete, boleto m.
t. window, taquilla f. **round trip
t.,** billete de ida y vuelta.
tickle /'tɪkəl/ n. **1.** cosquilla f.
—v. **2.** hacer cosquillas a.
ticklish /'tɪklɪʃ/ a. cosquilloso.
tide /taid/ n. marea f.
tidy /'taidi/ a. **1.** limpio, ordenado. —v. **2.** poner en orden.
tie /tai/ n. **1.** corbata f.; lazo;
(game) empate m. —v. **2.** atar;
anudar.
tier /'tɪər/ n. hilera f.
tiger /'taigər/ n. tigre m.
tight /tait/ a. apretado; tacaño.
tighten /'taitn̩/ v. estrechar, apretar.
tile /tail/ n. teja f.; azulejo m.
till /tɪl/ prep. **1.** hasta. —conj. **2.**
hasta que. —n. **3.** cajón m. —v.
4. cultivar, labrar.
tilt /tɪlt/ n. **1.** inclinación; justa f.
—v. **2.** inclinar; justar.
timber /'tɪmbər/ n. madera f.;
(beam) madero m.
time /taim/ n. tiempo m.; vez f.;
(of day) hora f.; v. cronometrar.
timetable /'taim‚teibəl/ n. horario, itinerario m.
time zone huso horario m.
timid /'tɪmɪd/ a. tímido.
timidity /tɪ'mɪdɪti/ n. timidez f.
tin /tɪn/ n. estaño m.; hojalata f.
t. can, lata f.
tin foil papel de estaño m.
tint /tɪnt/ n. **1.** tinte m. —v. **2.**
teñir.
tiny /'taini/ a. chiquito, pequeñito.
tip /tɪp/ n. **1.** punta; propina f.
—v. **2.** inclinar; dar propina a.
tire /taiᵊr/ n. **1.** llanta, goma f.,
neumático m. —v. **2.** cansar.
tired /taiᵊrd/ a. cansado.
tissue /'tɪʃu/ n. tejido m. **t. paper,** papel de seda.
title /'taitl̩/ n. **1.** título m. —v. **2.**
titular.
to /tu; unstressed tʊ, tə/ prep. a;
para.
toast /toust/ n. **1.** tostada f.;
(drink) brindis m. —v. **2.** tostar;
brindar.
toaster /'toustər/ n. tostador m.
tobacco /tə'bækou/ n. tabaco m.
t. shop, tabaquería f.
toboggan /tə'bɒgən/ n. tobogán
m.
today /tə'dei/ adv. hoy.
toe /tou/ n. dedo del pie.

together /tə'gɛðər/ a. **1.** juntos.
—adv. **2.** juntamente.
toil /tɔil/ n. **1.** trabajo m. —v. **2.**
afanarse.
toilet /'tɔilɪt/ n. tocado; excusado,
retrete m. **t. paper,** papel higiénico.
token /'toukən/ n. señal f.
tolerance /'tɒlərəns/ n. tolerancia
f.
tolerate /'tɒlə‚reit/ v. tolerar.
toll-free number /'toul 'fri/ teléfono gratuito m.
tomato /tə'meitou/ n. tomate m.
tomb /tum/ n. tumba f.
tomorrow /tə'mɔrou/ adv. mañana. **day after t.,** pasado mañana.
ton /tʌn/ n. tonelada f.
tone /toun/ n. tono m.
tongue /tʌŋ/ n. lengua f.
tonic /'tɒnɪk/ n. tónico m.
tonight /tə'nait/ adv. esta noche.
tonsil /'tɒnsəl/ n. amígdala f.
too /tu/ adv. también. **t. much,**
demasiado. **t. many,** demasiados.
tool /tul/ n. herramienta f.
tooth /tuθ/ n. diente m.; (back)
muela f.
toothache /'tuθ‚eik/ n. dolor de
muela.
toothbrush /'tuθ‚brʌʃ/ n. cepillo
de dientes.
toothpaste /'tuθ‚peist/ n. crema
dentífrica, pasta dentífrica.
top /tɒp/ n. **1.** parte de arriba.
—v. **2.** cubrir; sobrepasar.
topic /'tɒpɪk/ n. S.A. tópico m.
topical /'tɒpɪkəl/ a. tópico.
torch /tɔrtʃ/ n. antorcha f.
torment /n. 'tɔrmɛnt; v. tɔr'mɛnt/
n. **1.** tormento m. —v. **2.** atormentar.
torrent /'tɔrənt/ n. torrente m.
torture /'tɔrtʃər/ n. **1.** tortura f.
—v. **2.** torturar.
toss /tɔs/ v. tirar; agitar.
total /'toutl̩/ a. **1.** total, entero.
—n. **2.** total m.
touch /tʌtʃ/ n. **1.** tacto m. **in t.,**
en comunicación. —v. **2.** tocar;
conmover.
tough /tʌf/ a. tosco; tieso; fuerte.
tour /tʊr/ n. **1.** viaje m. —v. **2.**
viajar.
tourist /'tʊrɪst/ n. turista m. & f.
a. turístico.
tournament /'tʊrnəmənt/ n.
torneo m.

tow /tou/ n. **1.** remolque m. —v. **2.** remolcar.

toward /tɔrd, tə'wɔrd/ prep. hacia.

towel /'tauəl/ n. toalla f.

tower /'tauər/ n. torre f.

town /taun/ n. pueblo m.

town meeting cabildo abierto m.

tow truck grúa f.

toy /tɔi/ n. **1.** juguete m. —v. **2.** jugar.

trace /treis/ n. **1.** vestigio; rastro m. —v. **2.** trazar; rastrear; investigar.

track /træk/ n. **1.** huella, pista f. **race t.,** hipódromo m. —v. **2.** rastrear.

tract /trækt/ n. trecho; tracto m.

tractor /'træktər/ n. tractor m.

trade /treid/ n. **1.** comercio, negocio; oficio; canje m. —v. **2.** comerciar, negociar; cambiar.

trader /'treidər/ n. comerciante m.

tradition /trə'dɪʃən/ n. tradición f.

traditional /trə'dɪʃənl/ a. tradicional.

traffic /'træfɪk/ n. **1.** tráfico m. —v. **2.** traficar.

traffic jam atasco, embotellamiento m.

traffic light semáforo m.

tragedy /'trædʒɪdi/ n. tragedia f.

tragic /'trædʒɪk/ a. trágico.

trail /treil/ n. **1.** sendero; rastro m. —v. **2.** rastrear; arrastrar.

train /trein/ n. **1.** tren m. —v. **2.** enseñar; disciplinar; (sport) entrenarse.

traitor /'treitər/ n. traidor -ora.

tramp /træmp/ n. **1.** caminata f.; vagabundo m. —v. **2.** patear.

tranquil /'træŋkwɪl/ a. tranquilo.

tranquilizer /'træŋkwə,laizər/ n. tranquilizante m.

tranquillity /træŋ'kwɪlɪti/ n. tranquilidad f.

transaction /træn'sækʃən/ n. transacción f.

transfer /n. 'trænsfər, v. træns'fɜr/ n. **1.** traslado m.; boleto de transbordo. —v. **2.** trasladar, transferir.

transform /træns'fɔrm/ v. transformar.

transfusion /træns'fyuʒən/ n. transfusión f.

transistor /træn'zɪstər/ n. transistor m.

transition /træn'zɪʃən/ n. transición f.

translate /træns'leit/ v. traducir.

translation /træns'leiʃən/ n. traducción f.

transmit /træns'mɪt/ v. transmitir.

transparent /træns'pɛərənt/ a. transparente.

transport /n. 'trænspɔrt, v. træns'pɔrt/ n. **1.** transporte m. —v. **2.** transportar.

transportation /,trænspər'teiʃən/ n. transporte m.

transsexual /træns'sɛkʃuəl/ a. & n. transexual m. & f.

transvestite /træns'vɛstait/ n. travestí m. & f.

trap /træp/ n. **1.** trampa f. —v. **2.** atrapar.

trash /træʃ/ n. desecho m.; basura f.

trash can cubo de la basura m.

travel /'trævəl/ n. **1.** tráfico m.; (pl.) viajes m.pl. —v. **2.** viajar.

travel agency agencia de viajes f.

traveler /'trævələr/ n. viajero -ra.

traveler's check /'trævələrz/ cheque de viaje m.

tray /trei/ n. bandeja f.

tread /trɛd/ n. **1.** pisada f.; (of a tire) cubierta f. —v. **2.** pisar.

treason /'trizən/ n. traición f.

treasure /'trɛʒər/ n. tesoro m.

treasurer /'trɛʒərər/ n. tesorero -ra.

treasury /'trɛʒəri/ n. tesorería f.

treat /trit/ v. tratar; convidar.

treatment /'tritmənt/ n. trato, tratamiento m.

treaty /'triti/ n. tratado, pacto m.

tree /tri/ n. árbol m.

tremble /'trɛmbəl/ v. temblar.

tremendous /trɪ'mɛndəs/ a. tremendo.

trench /trɛntʃ/ n. foso m.; Mil. trinchera f.

trend /trɛnd/ n. **1.** tendencia f. —v. **2.** tender.

trespass /'trɛspəs, -pæs/ v. traspasar; violar.

triage /tri'ɑʒ/ n. clasificación de los heridos después del combate.

trial /'traiəl/ n. prueba f.; Leg. proceso, juicio m.

triangle /'trai,æŋgəl/ n. triángulo m.

tribulation /,trɪbyə'leiʃən/ n. tribulación f.

tributary /'trɪbyə,tɛri/ a. & n. tributario m.

tribute /'trɪbyut/ n. tributo m.

trick /trɪk/ n. **1.** engaño m.; maña f.; (cards) baza f. —v. **2.** engañar.

trifle /'traɪfəl/ n. **1.** pequeñez f. —v. **2.** juguetear.

trigger /'trɪgər/ n. gatillo m.

trim /trɪm/ a. **1.** ajustado; acicalado. —n. **2.** adorno m. —v. **3.** adornar; ajustar; cortar un poco.

trinket /'trɪŋkɪt/ n. bagatela, chuchería f.

trip /trɪp/ n. **1.** viaje m. —v. **2.** tropezar.

triple /'trɪpəl/ a. **1.** triple —v. **2.** triplicar.

tripod /'traɪpɒd/ n. trípode m.

trite /traɪt/ a. banal.

triumph /'traɪəmf/ n. **1.** triunfo m. —v. **2.** triunfar.

triumphant /traɪ'ʌmfənt/ a. triunfante.

trivial /'trɪvɪəl/ a. trivial.

trolley /'trɒli/ n. tranvía m.

trombone /trɒm'boun/ n. trombón m.

troop /trup/ n. tropa f.

trophy /'troufi/ n. trofeo m.

tropical /'trɒpɪkəl/ a. trópico.

tropics /'trɒpɪks/ n. trópico m.

trot /trɒt/ n. **1.** trote m. —v. **2.** trotar.

trouble /'trʌbəl/ n. **1.** apuro m.; congoja; aflicción f. —v. **2.** molestar; afligir.

troublesome /'trʌbəlsəm/ a. penoso, molesto.

trough /trɒf/ n. artesa f.

trousers /'trauzərz/ n. pantalones, calzones m.pl.

trout /traut/ n. trucha f.

truce /trus/ n. tregua f.

truck /trʌk/ n. camión m.

true /tru/ a. verdadero, cierto, verdad.

truffle /'trʌfəl/ n. trufa f.

trumpet /'trʌmpɪt/ n. trompeta, trompa f.

trunk /trʌŋk/ n. baúl m.; (of a tree) tronco m.

trust /trʌst/ n. **1.** confianza f. —v. **2.** confiar.

trustworthy /'trʌst,wɜrði/ a. digno de confianza.

truth /truθ/ n. verdad f.

truthful /'truθfəl/ a. veraz.

try /traɪ/ n. **1.** prueba f.; ensayo m. —v. **2.** tratar; probar; ensayar; Leg. juzgar. **t. on,** probarse.

T-shirt /'ti,ʃɜrt/ n. camiseta f.

tub /tʌb/ n. tina f.

tube /tub/ n. tubo m.

tuberculosis /tʊ,bɜrkyə'lousɪs/ n. tuberculosis f.

tuck /tʌk/ n. **1.** recogido m. —v. **2.** recoger.

Tuesday /'tuzdeɪ/ n. martes m.

tug /tʌg/ n. **1.** tirada f.; (boat) remolcador m. —v. **2.** tirar de.

tuition /tu'ɪʃən/ n. matrícula, colegiatura f.

tumble /'tʌmbəl/ n. **1.** caída f. —v. **2.** caer, tumbar; voltear.

tumult /'tumʌlt/ n. tumulto, alboroto m.

tuna /'tuni/ n. atún m.

tune /tun/ n. **1.** tono m.; melodía, canción f. —v. **2.** templar.

tunnel /'tʌnl/ n. túnel m.

turf /tɜrf/ n. césped m.

Turkey /'tɜrki/ n. Turquía f.

Turkish /'tɜrkɪʃ/ a. turco.

turmoil /'tɜrmɔil/ n. disturbio m.

turn /tɜrn/ n. **1.** vuelta f.; giro; turno m. —v. **2.** volver, tornear, girar; **t. into,** transformar. **t. around,** volverse. **t. on,** encender; abrir. **t. off, t. out,** apagar.

turnip /'tɜrnɪp/ n. nabo m.

turret /'tɜrɪt/ n. torrecilla f.

turtle /'tɜrtl/ n. tortuga f.

turtleneck sweater /'tɜrtl,nɛk/ jersey de cuello alto m.

tutor /'tutər/ n. **1.** tutor -ra. —v. **2.** enseñar.

tweezers /'twizərz/ n.pl. pinzas f.pl.

twelve /twɛlv/ a. & pron. doce.

twenty /'twɛnti/ a. & pron. veinte.

twice /twaɪs/ adv. dos veces.

twig /twɪg/ n. varita; ramita f.; vástago m.

twilight /'twaɪ,laɪt/ n. crepúsculo m.

twin /twɪn/ n. gemelo -la.

twine /twaɪn/ n. **1.** guita f. —v. **2.** torcer.

twinkle /'twɪŋkəl/ v. centellear.

twist /twɪst/ v. torcer.

two /tu/ a. & pron. dos.

type /taɪp/ n. **1.** tipo m. —v. **2.** escribir a máquina.

typewriter /'taɪp,raɪtər/ n. máquina de escribir.

typhoid fever /'taɪfɔid/ fiebre tifoidea.

typical /'tɪpɪkəl/ a. típico.

typist /'taɪpɪst/ n. mecanógrafo -fa.

tyranny /'tɪrəni/ n. tiranía f.

tyrant /'taɪrənt/ n. tirano -na.

udder /ʌdər/ *n.* ubre *f.*

UFO *abbr.* (unidentified flying object) OVNI *m.* (objeto volador no identificado).

ugly /ˈʌgli/ *a.* feo.

Ukraine /yuˈkrein/ *n.* Ucrania *f.*

Ukrainian /yuˈkreiniən/ *a. & n.* ucranio.

ulcer /ˈʌlsər/ *n.* úlcera *f.*

ulterior /ʌlˈtɪəriər/ *a.* ulterior.

ultimate /ˈʌltəmɪt/ *a.* último.

ultrasonic /ˌʌltrəˈsɒnɪk/ *a.* ultrasónico.

umbrella /ʌmˈbrɛlə/ *n.* paraguas *m.* **sun u.,** quitasol *m.*

umpire /ˈʌmpaiᵊr/ *n.* árbitro *m.*

unable /ʌnˈeibəl/ *a.* incapaz. **to be u.,** no poder.

unanimous /yuˈnænəməs/ *a.* unánime.

uncertain /ʌnˈsɜrtn̩/ *a.* incierto, inseguro.

uncle /ˈʌŋkəl/ *n.* tío *m.*

unconscious /ʌnˈkɒnʃəs/ *a.* inconsciente; desmayado.

uncover /ʌnˈkʌvər/ *v.* descubrir.

undeniable /ˌʌndɪˈnaiəbəl/ *a.* innegable.

under /ˈʌndər/ *adv.* **1.** debajo, abajo. —*prep.* **2.** bajo, debajo de.

underestimate /ˌʌndərˈɛstəˌmeit/ *v.* menospreciar; subestimar.

undergo /ˌʌndərˈgou/ *v.* sufrir.

underground / ˈʌndərˌgraund;/ *a.* subterráneo; clandestino.

underline /ˈʌndərˌlain/ *v.* subrayar.

underneath /ˌʌndərˈniθ/ *adv.* **1.** por debajo. —*prep.* **2.** debajo de.

undershirt /ˈʌndərˌʃɜrt/ *n.* camiseta *f.*

understand /ˌʌndərˈstænd/ *v.* entender, comprender.

undertake /ˌʌndərˈteik/ *v.* emprender.

underwear /ˈʌndərˌwɛər/ *n.* ropa interior.

undo /ʌnˈdu/ *v.* deshacer; desatar.

undress /ʌnˈdrɛs/ *v.* desnudar, desvestir.

uneasy /ʌnˈizi/ *a.* inquieto.

uneven /ʌnˈivən/ *a.* desigual.

unexpected /ˌʌnɪkˈspɛktɪd/ *a.* inesperado.

unfair /ʌnˈfɛər/ *a.* injusto.

unfit /ʌnˈfɪt/ *a.* incapaz; inadecuado.

unfold /ʌnˈfould/ *v.* desplegar; revelar.

unforgettable /ˌʌnfərˈgɛtəbəl/ *a.* inolvidable.

unfortunate /ʌnˈfɔrtʃənɪt/ *a.* desafortunado, desgraciado.

unfurnished /ʌnˈfɜrnɪʃt/ *a.* desamueblado.

unhappy /ʌnˈhæpi/ *a.* infeliz.

uniform /ˈyunəˌfɔrm/ *a. & n.* uniforme *m.*

unify /ˈyunəˌfai/ *v.* unificar.

union /ˈyunyən/ *n.* unión *f.* **labor u.,** sindicato de obreros.

unique /yuˈnik/ *a.* único.

unisex /ˈyunəˌsɛks/ *a.* unisex.

unit /ˈyunɪt/ *n.* unidad *f.*

unite /yuˈnait/ *v.* unir.

United Nations /yuˈnaitɪd ˈneiʃənz/ Naciones Unidas *f.pl.*

United States /yuˈnaitɪd ˈsteits/ Estados Unidos *m.pl.*

unity /ˈyunɪti/ *n.* unidad *f.*

universal /ˌyunəˈvɜrsəl/ *a.* universal.

universe /ˈyunəˌvɜrs/ *n.* universo *m.*

university /ˌyunəˈvɜrsɪti/ *n.* universidad *f.*

unleaded /ʌnˈlɛdɪd/ *a.* sin plomo.

unless /ʌnˈlɛs/ *conj.* a menos que, si no es que.

unlike /ʌnˈlaik/ *a.* disímil.

unload /ʌnˈloud/ *v.* descargar.

unlock /ʌnˈlɒk/ *v.* abrir.

unplug /ʌnˈplʌg/ *v.* desenchufar.

unpopular /ʌnˈpɒpyələr/ *a.* impopular.

unreasonable /ʌnˈrizənəbəl/ *a.* desrazonable.

unscrew /ʌnˈskru/ *v.* desatornillar.

untie /ʌnˈtai/ *v.* desatar; soltar.

until /ʌnˈtɪl/ *prep.* **1.** hasta. —*conj.* **2.** hasta que.

unusual /ʌnˈyuʒuəl/ *a.* raro, inusitado.

up /ʌp/ *adv.* **1.** arriba. —*prep.* **2. u. the street,** *etc.* calle arriba, etc.

uphold /ʌpˈhould/ *v.* apoyar; defender.

upholster /ʌpˈhoulstər, əˈpoul-/ *v.* entapizar.

upload /ˈʌpˌloud/ *n.* **1.** ascenso de archivos *m.* —*v.* **2.** subir, cargar.

upon /əˈpɒn/ *prep.* sobre, encima de.

upper /ˈʌpər/ *a.* superior.

upper-case letter /'ʌpər 'keis/ mayúscula f.

upright /'ʌp,rait/ a. derecho, recto.

upriver /'ʌp'rɪvər/ adv. río arriba.

uproar /'ʌp,rɔr/ n. alboroto, tumulto m.

upset /n. 'ʌp,sɛt; v. ʌp'sɛt/ n. **1.** trastorno m. —v. **2.** trastornar.

upsetting /ʌp'sɛtɪŋ/ a. inquietante.

upstream /'ʌp'strim/ adv. aguas arriba, contra la corriente, río arriba.

uptight /'ʌp'tait/ a. (psicológicamente) tenso, tieso.

upward /'ʌpwərd/ adv. hacia arriba.

urge /ɜrdʒ/ n. **1.** deseo m. —v. **2.** instar.

urgency /'ɜrdʒənsi/ n. urgencia f.

urgent /'ɜrdʒənt/ a. urgente. **to be u.,** urgir.

us /ʌs/ pron. nosotros -as; nos.

use /n. yus; v. yuz/ n. **1.** uso m. —v. **2.** usar, emplear. **u. up,** gastar, agotar. **be used to,** estar acostumbrado a.

useful /'yusfəl/ a. útil.

useless /'yuslɪs/ a. inútil, inservible.

user-friendly /'yuzər 'frɛndli/ a. amigable.

username /'yuzər'neim/ n. nombre de usuario m.

usher /'ʌʃər/ n. **1.** acomodador -ora. —v. **2.** introducir.

usual /'yuʒuəl/ a. usual.

utensil /yu'tɛnsəl/ n. utensilio m.

utmost /'ʌt,moust/ a. sumo, extremo.

utter /'ʌtər/ a. **1.** completo. —v. **2.** proferir; dar.

utterance /'ʌtərəns/ n. expresión f.

V

vacancy /'veikənsi/ n. vacante f.

vacant /'veikənt/ a. desocupado, libre.

vacation /vei'keiʃən/ n. vacaciones f.pl.

vaccinate /'væksə,neit/ v. vacunar.

vacuum /'vækyum/ n. vacuo, vacío m. **v. cleaner,** aspiradora f.

vagrant /'veigrənt/ a. & n. vagabundo- da.

vague /veig/ a. vago.

vain /vein/ a. vano; vanidoso. **in v.,** en vano.

valiant /'vælyənt/ a. valiente.

valid /'vælɪd/ a. válido.

valley /'væli/ n. valle m.

valor /'vælər/ n. valor m.

valuable /'vælyuəbəl/ a. valioso. **to be v.,** valer mucho.

value /'vælyu/ n. **1.** valor, importe m. —v. **2.** valorar; estimar.

van /væn/ n. furgoneta f.

vandal /'vændl̩/ n. vándalo m.

vandalism /'vændl̩,ɪzəm/ n. vandalismo m.

vanish /'vænɪʃ/ v. desaparecer.

vanity /'vænɪti/ n. vanidad f. **v. case,** polvera f.

vanquish /'væŋkwɪʃ/ v. vencer.

vapor /'veipər/ n. vapor m.

variation /,vɛəri'eiʃən/ n. variación f.

varicose vein /'væri,kous/ variz f.

variety /və'raiiti/ n. variedad f.

various /'vɛəriəs/ a. varios; diversos.

varnish /'varnɪʃ/ n. **1.** barniz m. —v. **2.** barnizar.

vary /'vɛəri/ v. variar; cambiar.

vase /veis, veiz, vaz/ n. florero; jarrón m.

vasectomy /væ'sɛktəmi/ n. vasectomía f.

vassal /'væsəl/ n. vasallo m.

vast /væst/ a. vasto.

vat /væt/ n. tina f., tanque m.

VAT /væt/ n. IVA (impuesto sobre el valor añadido).

vault /vɔlt/ n. bóveda f.

vegetable /'vɛdʒtəbəl/ a. & n. vegetal m.; (pl.) legumbres, verduras f.pl.

vehement /'viəmənt/ a. vehemente.

vehicle /'viikəl/ n. vehículo m.

veil /veil/ n. **1.** velo m. —v. **2.** velar.

vein /vein/ n. vena f.

velocity /və'lɔsɪti/ n. velocidad f.

velvet /'vɛlvɪt/ n. terciopelo m.

Venetian /və'niʃən/ a. & n. veneciano.

vengeance /'vɛndʒəns/ n. venganza f.

Venice /'vɛnɪs/ n. Venecia f.

vent /vɛnt/ n. apertura f.

ventilate /'vɛntl̩,eit/ v. ventilar.

venture /'vɛntʃər/ n. ventura f.
verb /vɜrb/ n. verbo m.
verbose /vər'bous/ a. verboso.
verdict /'vɜrdɪkt/ n. veredicto, fallo m.
verge /vɜrdʒ/ n. borde m.
verify /'vɛrə,faɪ/ v. verificar.
versatile /'vɜrsətļ/ a. versátil.
verse /vɜrs/ n. verso m.
version /'vɜrʒən/ n. versión f.
vertical /'vɜrtɪkəl/ a. vertical.
very /'vɛri/ a. **1.** mismo. —adv. **2.** muy.
vessel /'vɛsəl/ n. vasija f.; barco m.
vest /vɛst/ n. chaleco m.
veteran /'vɛtərən/ a. & n. veterano -na.
veto /'vitou/ n. veto m.
vex /vɛks/ v. molestar.
via /'vaɪə, 'viə/ prep. por la vía de; por.
viaduct /'vaɪə,dʌkt/ n. viaducto m.
vibrate /'vaibreit/ v. vibrar.
vibration /vai'breiʃən/ n. vibración f.
vice /vais/ n. vicio m.
vicinity /vɪ'sɪnɪti/ n. vecindad f.
vicious /'vɪʃəs/ a. vicioso.
victim /'vɪktəm/ n. víctima f.
victor /'vɪktər/ n. vencedor -ora.
victorious /vɪk'tɔriəs/ a. victorioso.
victory /'vɪktəri/ n. victoria f.
video camera /'vɪdi,ou/ videocámara f.
videoconference /'vɪdiou,kɒnfərəns/ videoconferencia f.
videodisc /'vɪdiou,dɪsk/ n. videodisco m.
video game /'vɪdi,ou/ videojuego m.
videotape /'vɪdiou,teip/ n. vídeo m., magnetoscopio m.
view /vyu/ n. **1.** vista f. —v. **2.** ver.
viewpoint /'vyu,pɔint/ n. punto de vista m.
vigil /'vɪdʒəl/ n. vigilia, vela f.
vigilant /'vɪdʒələnt/ a. vigilante.
vigor /'vɪgər/ n. vigor m.
vile /vail/ a. vil, bajo.
village /'vɪlɪdʒ/ n. aldea f.
villain /'vɪlən/ n. malvado -da.
vindicate /'vɪndɪ,keit/ v. vindicar.
vine /vain/ n. parra, vid f.
vinegar /'vɪnɪgər/ n. vinagre m.
vintage /'vɪntɪdʒ/ n. vendimia f.
violate /'vaiə,leit/ v. violar.

violation /,vaiə'leiʃən/ n. violación f.
violence /'vaiələns/ n. violencia f.
violent /'vaiələnt/ a. violento.
violin /,vaiə'lɪn/ n. violín m.
virgin /'vɜrdʒɪn/ n. virgen f.
virile /'vɪrəl/ a. viril.
virtual /'vɜrtʃuəl/ a. virtual.
virtual memory memoria virtual f.
virtual reality realidad virtual f.
virtue /'vɜrtʃu/ n. virtud f.
virtuous /'vɜrtʃuəs/ a. virtuoso.
virus /'vairəs/ n. virus m.
visa /'vizə/ n. visa f.
visible /'vɪzəbəl/ a. visible.
vision /'vɪʒən/ n. visión f.
visit /'vɪzɪt/ n. **1.** visita f. —v. **2.** visitar.
visitor /'vɪzɪtər/ n. visitante m. & f.
visual /'vɪʒuəl/ a. visual.
vital /'vaitļ/ a. vital.
vitality /vai'tælɪti/ n. vitalidad, energía vital f.
vitamin /'vaitəmɪn/ n. vitamina f.
vivacious /vɪ'veiʃəs/ a. vivaz.
vivid /'vɪvɪd/ a. vivo; gráfico.
vocabulary /vou'kæbyə,lɛri/ n. vocabulario m.
vocal /'voukəl/ a. vocal.
vodka /'vɒdkə/ n. vodca m.
vogue /voug/ n. boga; moda f. **be in vogue** estilarse.
voice /vɔis/ n. **1.** voz f. —v. **2.** expresar.
voice mail correo de voz m.
voice recognition reconocimiento de voz m.
void /vɔid/ a. **1.** vacío. —n. **2.** vacío m. —v. **3.** invalidar.
voltage /'voultɪdʒ/ n. voltaje m.
volume /'vɒlyum/ n. volumen; tomo m.
voluntary /'vɒlən,tɛri/ a. voluntario.
volunteer /,vɒlən'tɪər/ n. **1.** voluntario -ria. —v. **2.** ofrecerse.
vomit /'vɒmɪt/ v. vomitar.
vote /vout/ n. **1.** voto m. —v. **2.** votar.
voter /'voutər/ n. votante m. & f.
vouch /vautʃ/ v. **v. for,** garantizar.
vow /vau/ n. **1.** voto m. —v. **2.** jurar.
vowel /'vauəl/ n. vocal f.
voyage /'vɔiidʒ/ n. viaje m.
vulgar /'vʌlgər/ a. vulgar; común; soez.
vulnerable /'vʌlnərəbəl/ a. vulnerable.

W X Y Z

wade /weid/ *v.* vadear.

wag /wæg/ *v.* menear.

wage /weidʒ/ *n.* **1.** (pl.) sueldo, salario *m.* —*v.* **2. w. war,** hacer guerra.

wagon /'wægən/ *n.* carreta *f.*

wail /weil/ *n.* **1.** lamento, gemido *m.* —*v.* **2.** lamentar, gemir.

waist /weist/ *n.* cintura *f.*

wait /weit/ *n.* **1.** espera *f.* —*v.* **2.** esperar. **w. for,** esperar. **w. on,** atender.

waiter /'weitər/ **waitress** *n.* camarero -ra.

waiting room /'weitiŋ/ sala de espera.

wake /weik/ *v.* **w. up,** despertar.

walk /wɔk/ *n.* **1.** paseo *m.;* vuelta; caminata *f.;* modo de andar. —*v.* **2.** andar; caminar; ir a pie.

wall /wɔl/ *n.* pared; muralla *f.*

wallcovering /'wɔl,kʌvəriŋ/ *n.* tapizado de pared *m.*

wallet /'wɒlit/ *n.* cartera *f.*

wallpaper /'wɔl,peipər/ *n.* **1.** empapelado *m.* —*v.* **2.** empapelar.

walnut /'wɔl,nʌt/ *n.* nuez *f.*

waltz /wɔlts/ *n.* vals *m.*

wander /'wɒndər/ *v.* vagar.

want /wɒnt/ *n.* **1.** necesidad *f.* —*v.* **2.** querer.

war /wɑr/ *n.* guerra *f.*

ward /wɔrd/ *n.* **1.** *Pol.* barrio *m.;* (hospital) cuadra *f.* —*v.* **2. w. off,** parar.

warehouse /'wɛər,haus/ *n.* almacén *m.*

wares /wɛərz/ *n.* mercancías *f.pl.*

warlike /'wɔr,laik/ *a.* belicoso.

warm /wɔrm/ *a.* **1.** caliente; *Fig.* caluroso. **to be w.,** tener calor; (weather) hacer calor. —*v.* **2.** calentar.

warmth /wɔrmθ/ *n.* calor *m.*

warn /wɔrn/ *v.* advertir.

warning /'wɔrniŋ/ *n.* aviso *m.*

warp /wɔrp/ *v.* alabear.

warrant /'wɔrənt, 'wɒr-/ *v.* justificar.

warrior /'wɔriər/ *n.* guerrero -ra.

warship /'wɔr,ʃip/ *n.* navío de guerra, buque de guerra *m.*

wash /wɒʃ/ *v.* lavar.

washing machine /'wɒʃiŋ/ máquina de lavar, lavadora *f.*

wasp /wɒsp/ *n.* avispa *f.*

waste /weist/ *n.* **1.** gasto *m.;* desechos *m.pl.* —*v.* **2.** gastar; perder.

watch /wɒtʃ/ *n.* **1.** reloj *m.; Mil.* guardia *f.* —*v.* **2.** observar, mirar. **w. for,** esperar. **w. out for,** tener cuidado con. **w. over,** guardar; velar por.

watchful /'wɒtʃfəl/ *a.* desvelado.

watchmaker /'wɒtʃ,meikər/ *n.* relojero -ra.

watchman /'wɒtʃmən/ *n.* sereno *m.*

water /'wɔtər/ *n.* **1.** agua *f.* **w. color,** acuarela *f.* —*v.* **2.** aguar.

waterbed /'wɔtər,bed/ *n.* cama de agua *f.*

waterfall /'wɔtər,fɔl/ *n.* catarata *f.*

watering can /'wɔtəriŋ/ regadera *f.*

waterproof /'wɔtər,pruf/ *a.* impermeable.

wave /weiv/ *n.* **1.** onda; ola *f.* —*v.* **2.** ondear; agitar; hacer señas.

waver /'weivər/ *v.* vacilar.

wax /wæks/ *n.* **1.** cera *f.* —*v.* **2.** encerar.

way /wei/ *n.* camino; modo *m.,* manera *f.* **in a w.,** hasta cierto punto. **a long w.,** muy lejos. **by the w.,** a propósito. **this w.,** por aquí. **that w.,** por allí. **which w.,** por dónde.

we /wi/ *pron.* nosotros -as.

weak /wik/ *a.* débil.

weaken /'wikən/ *v.* debilitar.

weakness /'wiknis/ *n.* debilidad *f.*

wealth /wɛlθ/ *n.* riqueza *f.*

wealthy /'wɛlθi/ *a.* adinerado.

wean /win/ *v.* destetar.

weapon /'wɛpən/ *n.* arma *f.*

wear /wɛər/ *n.* **1.** uso; desgaste *m.;* (clothes) ropa *f.* —*v.* **2.** usar, llevar. **w. out,** gastar; cansar.

weary /'wiəri/ *a.* cansado, rendido.

weather /'wɛðər/ *n.* tiempo *m.*

weave /wiv/ *v.* tejer.

weaver /'wivər/ *n.* tejedor -ra.

web /wɛb/ *n.* tela *f.*

Web /wɛb/ *n.* (Internet) malla *f.,* telaraña *f.,* web *m.*

wedding /'wɛdiŋ/ *n.* boda *f.*

wedge /wɛdʒ/ *n.* cuña *f.*

Wednesday /'wɛnzdei/ *n.* miércoles *m.*

weed /wid/ *n.* maleza *f.*

week /wik/ *n.* semana *f.*

weekday /'wik,dei/ *n.* día de trabajo.

weekend /'wik,ɛnd/ *n.* fin de semana.

weekly /'wikli/ *a.* semanal.

weep /wip/ *v.* llorar.

weigh /wei/ *v.* pesar.

weight /weit/ *n.* peso *m.*

weightless /'weitlɪs/ *v.* ingrávido.

weightlessness /'weitlɪsnɪs/ *n.* ingravidez *f.*

weird /wɪərd/ *a.* misterioso, extraño.

welcome /'wɛlkəm/ *a.* **1.** bienvenido. **you're w.,** de nada, no hay de qué. —*n.* **2.** acogida, bienvenida *f.* —*v.* **3.** acoger, recibir bien.

welfare /'wɛl,fɛər/ *n.* bienestar *m.*

well /wɛl/ *a.* **1.** sano, bueno. —*adv.* **2.** bien; pues. —*n.* **3.** pozo *m.*

well-done /'wɛl 'dʌn/ *a.* (food) bien cocido.

well-known /'wɛl 'noun/ *a.* bien conocido.

well-mannered /'wɛl 'mænərd/ *a.* educado.

west /wɛst/ *n.* oeste, occidente *m.*

western /'wɛstərn/ *a.* occidental.

westward /'wɛstwərd/ *adv.* hacia el oeste.

wet /wɛt/ *a.* **1.** mojado. **to get w.,** mojarse. —*v.* **2.** mojar.

whale /weil/ *n.* ballena *f.*

what /wʌt; *unstressed* wət/ *a.* **1.** qué; cuál. —*interrog. pron.* **2.** qué. —*rel. pron.* **3.** lo que.

whatever /wʌt'ɛvər/ *a.* **1.** cualquier. —*pron.* **2.** lo que; todo lo que.

wheat /wit/ *n.* trigo *m.*

wheel /wil/ *n.* rueda *f.* **steering w.,** volante *m.*

when /wɛn; *unstressed* wən/ *adv.* **1.** cuándo. —*conj.* **2.** cuando.

whenever /wɛn'ɛvər/ *conj.* siempre que, cuando quiera que.

where /wɛər/ *adv.* **1.** dónde, adónde. —*conj.* **2.** donde.

wherever /wɛər'ɛvər/ *conj.* dondequiera que, adondequiera que.

whether /'wɛðər/ *conj.* si.

which /wɪtʃ/ *a.* **1.** qué. —*interrog. pron.* **2.** cuál. —*rel. pron.* **3.** que; el cual; lo cual.

whichever /wɪtʃ'ɛvər/ *a. & pron.* cualquiera que.

while /wail/ *conj.* **1.** mientras; mientras que. —*n.* **2.** rato *m.*

whip /wɪp/ *n.* **1.** látigo *m.* —*v.* **2.** azotar.

whipped cream /wɪpt/ nata batida *f.*

whirl /wɜrl/ *v.* girar.

whirlpool /'wɜrl,pul/ *n.* vórtice *m.*

whirlwind /'wɜrl,wɪnd/ *n.* torbellino *m.*

whisk broom /wɪsk/ escobilla *f.*

whisker /'wɪskər/ *n.* bigote *m.*

whiskey /'wɪski/ *n.* whisky *m.*

whisper /'wɪspər/ *n.* **1.** cuchicheo *m.* —*v.* **2.** cuchichear.

whistle /'wɪsəl/ *n.* **1.** pito; silbido *m.* —*v.* **2.** silbar.

white /wait/ *a.* **1.** blanco. —*n.* **2.** (of egg) clara *f.*

who /hu/ **whom** *interrog. pron.* **1.** quién. —*rel. pron.* **2.** que; quien.

whoever /hu'ɛvər/ **whomever** *pron.* quienquiera que.

whole /houl/ *a.* **1.** entero. **the wh.,** todo el. —*n.* **2.** totalidad *f.* **on the wh.,** por lo general.

wholesale /'houl,seil/ *n.* **at wh.,** al por mayor.

wholesaler /'houl,seilər/ *n.* mayorista *m. & f.*

wholesome /'houlsəm/ *a.* sano, saludable.

wholly /'houli/ *adv.* enteramente.

whose /huz/ *interrog. adj.* **1.** de quién. —*rel. adj.* **2.** cuyo.

why /wai/ *adv.* por qué; para qué.

wicked /'wɪkɪd/ *a.* malo, malvado.

wickedness /'wɪkɪdnɪs/ *n.* maldad *f.*

wide /waid/ *a.* **1.** ancho; extenso. —*adv.* **2.** **w. open,** abierto de par en par.

widen /'waidn̩/ *v.* ensanchar; extender.

widespread /'waid'sprɛd/ *a.* extenso.

widow /'wɪdou/ *n.* viuda *f.*

widower /'wɪdouər/ *n.* viudo *m.*

width /wɪdθ/ *n.* anchura *f.*

wield /wild/ *v.* manejar, empuñar.

wife /waif/ *n.* esposa, señora, mujer *f.*

wig /wɪg/ *n.* peluca *f.*

wild /waild/ *a.* salvaje; bárbaro.

wilderness /'wɪldərnɪs/ *n.* desierto *m.*

wildlife /'waild,laif/ *n.* fauna silvestre *f.*

will /wɪl/ n. **1.** voluntad f.; testamento m. —v. **2.** querer; determinar; Leg. legar.

willful /'wɪlfəl/ a. voluntarioso; premeditado.

willing /'wɪlɪŋ/ a. **to be w.**, estar dispuesto.

willingly /'wɪlɪŋli/ adv. de buena gana.

wilt /wɪlt/ v. marchitar.

win /wɪn/ v. ganar.

wind /n. wɪnd; v. waind/ n. **1.** viento m. —v. **2.** torcer; dar cuerda a.

windmill /'wɪnd,mɪl/ n. molino de viento m.

window /'wɪndou/ n. ventana; (of car) ventanilla f.; (of shop or store) escaparate m.

windshield /'wɪnd,ʃild/ n. parabrisas m.

windy /'wɪndi/ a. ventoso. **to be w.**, (weather) hacer viento.

wine /wain/ n. vino m.

wing /wɪŋ/ n. ala f.; Theat. bastidor m.

wink /wɪŋk/ n. **1.** guiño m. —v. **2.** guiñar.

winner /'wɪnər/ n. ganador -ra.

winter /'wɪntər/ n. invierno m.

wipe /waip/ v. limpiar; (dry) secar. **w. out,** destruir.

wire /waiᵊr/ n. **1.** alambre; hilo; telegrama m. —v. **2.** telegrafiar.

wireless /'waiᵊrlɪs/ n. telégrafo sin hilos.

wisdom /'wɪzdəm/ n. juicio m.; sabiduría f.

wise /waiz/ a. sensato, juicioso; sabio.

wish /wɪʃ/ n. **1.** deseo; voto m. —v. **2.** desear; querer.

wit /wɪt/ n. ingenio m., sal f.

witch /wɪtʃ/ n. bruja f.

with /wɪθ, wɪð/ prep. con.

withdraw /wɪθ'drɔ, wɪθ-/ v. retirar.

wither /'wɪðər/ v. marchitar.

withhold /wɪθ'hould, wɪð-/ v. retener, suspender.

within /wɪð'ɪn, wɪθ-/ adv. **1.** dentro, por dentro. —prep. **2.** dentro de; en.

without /wɪð'aut, wɪθ-/ adv. **1.** fuera, por fuera. —prep. **2.** sin.

witness /'wɪtnɪs/ n. **1.** testigo; testimonio m. & f. —v. **2.** presenciar; atestar.

witty /'wɪti/ a. ingenioso, gracioso, ocurrente.

wizard /'wɪzərd/ n. hechicero m.

woe /wou/ n. dolor m.; pena f.

wolf /wʊlf/ n. lobo -ba.

woman /'wʊmən/ n. mujer f.

womb /wum/ n. entrañas f.pl., matriz f.

wonder /'wʌndər/ n. **1.** maravilla; admiración f. **for a w.,** por milagro. **no w.,** no es extraño. —v. **2.** preguntarse; maravillarse.

wonderful /'wʌndərfəl/ a. maravilloso; estupendo.

woo /wu/ v. cortejar.

wood /wʊd/ n. madera; (for fire) leña f.

wooden /'wʊdṇ/ a. de madera.

wool /wʊl/ n. lana f.

word /wɜrd/ n. **1.** palabra f. **the words** (of a song), la letra. —v. **2.** expresar.

word processing /'prɒsɛsɪŋ/ procesamiento de textos m.

word processor /'prɒsɛsər/ procesador de textos m.

work /wɜrk/ n. **1.** trabajo m.; (of art) obra f. —v. **2.** trabajar; obrar; funcionar.

worker /'wɜrkər/ n. trabajador -ra; obrero -ra.

workman /'wɜrkmən/ n. obrero m.

work station estación de trabajo f.

work week /'wɜrk,wik/ semana laboral f.

world /wɜrld/ n. mundo m. **w. war,** guerra mundial.

worldly /'wɜrldli/ a. mundano.

worldwide /'wɜrld'waid/ a. mundial.

worm /wɜrm/ n. gusano m.

worn /wɔrn/ a. usado. **w. out,** gastado; cansado, rendido.

worrisome /'wɜrisəm/ a. inquietante.

worry /'wɜri/ n. **1.** preocupación f. —v. **2.** preocupar.

worrying /'wɜriɪŋ/ a. inquietante.

worse /wɜrs/ a. peor. **to get w.,** empeorar.

worship /'wɜrʃɪp/ n. **1.** adoración f. —v. **2.** adorar.

worst /wɜrst/ a. peor.

worth /wɜrθ/ a. **1.** valer. **to be w.,** valer. —n. **2.** valor m.

worthless /'wɜrθlɪs/ a. sin valor.

worthy /'wɜrði/ a. digno.

wound /wund/ n. **1.** herida f. —v. **2.** herir.

wrap /ræp/ *n.* **1.** (pl.) abrigos *m.pl.* —*n.* **2.** envolver.

wrapping /'ræpɪŋ/ *n.* cubierta *f.*

wrath /ræθ/ *n.* ira, cólera *f.*

wreath /riθ/ *n.* guirnalda; corona *f.*

wreck /rɛk/ *n.* **1.** ruina *f.;* accidente *m.* —*v.* **2.** destrozar, arruinar.

wrench /rɛntʃ/ *n.* llave *f.* **monkey w.,** llave inglesa.

wrestle /'rɛsəl/ *v.* luchar.

wretched /'rɛtʃɪd/ *a.* miserable.

wring /rɪŋ/ *v.* retorcer.

wrinkle /'rɪŋkəl/ *n.* **1.** arruga *f.* —*v.* **2.** arrugar.

wrist /rɪst/ *n.* muñeca *f.* **w. watch,** reloj de pulsera.

write /rait/ *v.* escribir. **w. down,** apuntar.

writer /'raitər/ *n.* escritor -ra.

writhe /raið/ *v.* contorcerse.

writing paper /'raitɪŋ/ papel de escribir *m.*

wrong /rɔŋ/ *a.* **1.** equivocado; incorrecto. **to be w.,** equivocarse; no tener razón. —*adv.* **2.** mal, incorrectamente. —*n.* **3.** agravio *m.* **right and w.,** el bien y el mal. —*v.* **4.** agraviar, ofender.

WWW *abbr.* (World Wide Web) malla mundial *f.*

x-ray /'ɛks,rei/ *n.* **1.** rayo X *m.,* radiografía, *f.* —*v.* **2.** radiografiar.

xylophone /'zailə,foun/ *n.* xilófono *m.*

yacht /yɒt/ *n.* yate *m.*

yard /yɑrd/ *n.* patio, corral *m.;* (measure) yarda *f.*

yarn /yɑrn/ *n.* hilo.

yawn /yɔn/ *n.* **1.** bostezo *m.* —*v.* **2.** bostezar.

year /yiər/ *n.* año *m.*

yearly /'yiərli/ *a.* anual.

yearn /yɜrn/ *v.* anhelar.

yell /yɛl/ *n.* **1.** grito *m.* —*v.* **2.** gritar.

yellow /'yɛlou/ *a.* amarillo.

yes /yɛs/ *adv.* sí.

yesterday /'yɛstər,dei/ *adv.* ayer.

yet /yɛt/ *adv.* todavía, aún.

Yiddish /'yɪdɪʃ/ *n.* yídish *m.*

yield /yild/ *v.* producir; ceder.

yogurt /'yougərt/ *n.* yogur *m.*

yoke /youk/ *n.* yugo *m.*

yolk /youk/ *n.* yema *f.*

you /yu/ *unstressed* yʊ, yə/ *pron.* usted, (pl.) ustedes; lo, la, los, las; le, les; (familiar) tú, (pl.) vosotros -as; ti; te, (pl.) os. **with y.,** contigo, con usted.

young /yʌŋ/ *a.* joven.

youngster /'yʌŋstər/ *n.* muchacho -cha *m.* & *f.*

your /yur, yɔr/ *unstressed* yər/ *a.* su; (familiar) tu; (pl.) vuestro.

yours /yurz, yɔrz/ *pron.* suyo; (familiar) tuyo; (pl.) vuestro.

yourself -selves /yur'sɛlf, yɔr-yər-/ *pron.* sí; se; (familiar) ti; te. **with y.,** consigo; contigo. **you y.,** usted mismo, ustedes mismos; tú mismo, vosotros mismos.

youth /yuθ/ *n.* juventud *f.;* (person) joven *m.* & *f.*

youth club club juvenil *m.*

youthful /'yuθfəl/ *a.* juvenil.

yuppie /'yʌpi/ *n.* yuppie *m.* & *f.*

zap /zæp/ *v.* desintegrar, aniquilar.

zeal /zil/ *n.* celo, fervor *m.*

zealous /'zɛləs/ *a.* celoso, fervoroso.

zero /'zɪərou/ *n.* cero *m.*

zest /zɛst/ *n.* gusto *m.*

zip code /zɪp/ número de distrito postal.

zipper /'zɪpər/ *m.* cremallera *f.*

zone /zoun/ *n.* zona *f.*

zoo /zu/ *n.* jardín zoológico.

Spanish Irregular Verbs

Infinitive	Present	Future	Preterit	Past Part.
andar	ando	andaré	anduve	andado
caber	quepo	cabré	cupe	cabido
caer	caigo	caeré	caí	caído
conducir	conduzco	conduciré	conduje	conducido
dar	doy	daré	di	dado
decir	digo	diré	dije	dicho
estar	estoy	estaré	estuve	estado
haber	he	habré	hube	habido
hacer	hago	haré	hice	hecho
ir	voy	iré	fui	ido
jugar	juego	jugaré	jugué	jugado
morir	muero	moriré	morí	muerto
oir	oigo	oiré	oí	oído
poder	puedo	podré	pude	podido
poner	pongo	pondré	puse	puesto
querer	quiero	querré	quise	querido
saber	sé	sabré	supe	sabido
salir	salgo	saldré	salí	salido
ser	soy	seré	fui	sido
tener	tengo	tendré	tuve	tenido
traer	traigo	traeré	traje	traído
valer	valgo	valdré	valí	valido
venir	vengo	vendré	vine	venido
ver	veo	veré	vi	visto

Las formas del verbo inglés

1. Se forma la 3ª persona singular del tiempo presente exactamente al igual que el plural de los sustantivos, añadiendo **-es** o **-s** a la forma sencilla según las mismas reglas, así:

(1)	teach	pass	wish	fix	buzz
	teaches	passes	wishes	fixes	buzzes

(2)	place	change	judge	please	freeze
	places	changes	judges	pleases	freezes

(3a)	find	sell	clean	hear	love	buy	know
	finds	sells	cleans	hears	loves	buys	knows

385

(3b)	think	like	laugh	stop	hope	meet	want
	thinks	likes	laughs	stops	hopes	meets	wants

(4)	cry	try	dry	carry	deny
	cries	tries	dries	carries	denies

Cinco verbos muy comunes tienen 3ª persona singular irregular:

(5)	go	do	say	have	be
	goes	does	says	has	is

2. Se forman el tiempo pasado y el participio de modo igual, añadiendo a la forma sencilla la terminación **-ed** o **-d** según las reglas que siguen:

(1) Si la forma sencilla termina en **-d** o **-t**, se le pone **-ed** como sílaba aparte:

end	fold	need	load
ended	folded	needed	loaded

want	feast	wait	light
wanted	feasted	waited	lighted

(2) Si la forma sencilla termina en cualquier otra consonante, se añade también **-ed** pero sin hacer sílaba aparte:

(2a)	bang	sail	seem	harm	earn	weigh
	banged	sailed	seemed	harmed	earned	weighed

(2b)	lunch	work	look	laugh	help	pass
	lunched	worked	looked	laughed	helped	passed

(3) Si la forma sencilla termina en **-e**, se le pone sólo **-d**:

(3a)	hate	taste	waste	guide	fade	trade
	hated	tasted	wasted	guided	faded	traded

(3b)	free	judge	rule	name	dine	scare
	freed	judged	ruled	named	dined	scared

(3c)	place	force	knife	like	hope	base
	placed	forced	knifed	liked	hoped	based

(4) Una **-y** final que sigue a cualquier consonante se cambia en **-ie** al añadir la **-d** del pasado/participio:

cry	try	dry	carry	deny
cried	tried	dried	carried	denied

3. Varios verbos muy comunes forman el tiempo pasado y el participio de manera irregular. Pertenecen a tres grupos.

(1) Los que tienen una sola forma irregular para tiempo pasado y participio, como los siguientes:

bend	bleed	bring	build	buy	catch	creep	deal
bent	bled	brought	built	bought	caught	crept	dealt

dig	feed	feel	fight	find	flee	get	hang
dug	fed	felt	fought	found	fled	got	hung

have	hear	hold	keep	lead	leave	lend	lose
had	heard	held	kept	led	left	lent	lost

make	mean	meet	say	seek	sell	send	shine
made	meant	met	said	sought	sold	sent	shone

shoot	sit	sleep	spend	stand	strike	sweep	teach
shot	sat	slept	spent	stood	struck	swept	taught

(2) Los que tienen una forma irregular para el tiempo pasado y otra forma irregular para el participio, como los siguientes:

be	beat	become	begin	bite
was	beat	became	began	bit
been	beaten	become	begun	bitten

blow	break	choose	come	do
blew	broke	chose	came	did
blown	broken	chosen	come	done

draw	drink	drive	eat	fall
drew	drank	drove	ate	fell
drawn	drunk	driven	eaten	fallen

fly	forget	freeze	give	go
flew	forgot	froze	gave	went
flown	forgotten	frozen	given	gone

grow	hide	know	ride	ring
grew	hid	knew	rode	rang
grown	hidden	known	ridden	rung

rise	run	see	shake	shrink
rose	ran	saw	shook	shrank
risen	run	seen	shaken	shrunk

sing	sink	speak	steal	swear
sang	sank	spoke	stole	swore
sung	sunk	spoken	stolen	sworn
swim	tear	throw	wear	write
swam	tore	threw	wore	wrote
swum	torn	thrown	worn	written

(3) Los que no varían del todo, la forma sencilla funcionando también como pasado/participio; entre éstos son de mayor frecuencia:

bet	burst	cast	cost	cut
hit	hurt	let	put	quit
read	set	shed	shut	slit
spit	split	spread	thrust	wet

El plural del sustantivo inglés

A la forma singular se añade la terminación -es o -s de acuerdo con las reglas siguientes.

(1) Si el singular termina en **-ch, -s, -sh, -x** o **-z**, se le pone **-es** como sílaba aparte:

match	glass	dish	box	buzz
matches	glasses	dishes	boxes	buzzes

(2) Si el singular termina en **-ce, -ge, -se** o **-ze**, se le pone una **-s** que con la vocal precedente forma sílaba aparte:

face	page	house	size
faces	pages	houses	sizes

(3) Una **-y** final que sigue a cualquier consonante se cambia en **-ie** a ponérsele la **-s** del plural:

sky	city	lady	ferry	penny
skies	cities	ladies	ferries	pennies

(4) Los siguientes sustantivos comunes tienen plural irregular:

man	woman	child	foot	mouse	goose
men	women	children	feet	mice	geese
wife	knife	life	half	leaf	deer
wives	knives	lives	halves	leaves	deer

Weights and Measures/Pesos y Medidas

Spanish/	1 centímetro	=	.3937 inches
English	1 metro	=	39.37 inches
	1 kilómetro	=	.621 mile
	1 centigramo	=	.1543 grain
	1 gramo	=	15.432 grains
	1 kilogramo	=	2.2046 pounds
	1 tonelada	=	2.204 pounds
	1 centilitro	=	.338 ounces
	1 litro	=	1.0567 quart (liquid); .908 quart (dry)
	1 kilolitro	=	264.18 gallons
English/	1 inch	=	2.54 centímetros
Spanish	1 foot	=	.305 metros
	1 mile	=	1.61 kilómetros
	1 grain	=	.065 gramos
	1 pound	=	.455 kilogramos
	1 ton	=	.907 toneladas
	1 ounce	=	2.96 centilitros
	1 quart	=	1.13 litros
	1 gallon	=	4.52 litros

Days of the Week/Días de la Semana

Sunday	domingo	Thursday	jueves
Monday	lunes	Friday	viernes
Tuesday	martes	Saturday	sábado
Wednesday	miércoles		

Months/Meses

January	enero	July	julio
February	febrero	August	agosto
March	marzo	September	septiembre
April	abril	October	octubre
May	mayo	November	noviembre
June	junio	December	diciembre

Useful Phrases/Locuciones Útiles

Good day, Good morning. Buenos días.
Good afternoon. Buenas tardes.
Good night, Good evening. Buenas noches.
Hello. ¡Hola!
Welcome! ¡Bienvenido!
See you later. Hasta luego.
Goodbye. ¡Adiós!
How are you? ¿Cómo está usted?
I'm fine, thank you. Estoy bien, gracias.
I'm pleased to meet you. Mucho gusto en conocerle.
May I introduce... Quisiera presentar...
Thank you very much. Muchas gracias.
You're welcome. De nada *or* No hay de qué.
Please. Por favor.
Excuse me. Con permiso.
Good luck. ¡Buena suerte!
To your health. ¡Salud!

Please help me. Ayúdeme, por favor.
I don't know. No sé.
I don't understand. No entiendo.
Do you understand? ¿Entiende usted?
I don't speak Spanish. No hablo español.
Do you speak English? ¿Habla usted inglés?
How do you say . . . in Spanish? ¿Cómo se dice . . . en español?
What do you call this? ¿Cómo se llama esto?
Speak slowly, please. Hable despacio, por favor.
Please repeat. Repita, por favor.
I don't like it. No me gusta.
I am lost. Ando perdido; Me he extraviado.

What is your name? ¿Cómo se llama usted?
My name is . . . Me llamo . . .
I am an American. Soy norteamericano.
Where are you from? ¿De dónde es usted?
I'm from... Soy de...

How is the weather?   ¿Qué tiempo hace?

It's cold (hot) today.   Hace frío (calor) hoy.

What time is it?   ¿Qué hora es?

How much is it?   ¿Cuánto es?

It is too much.   Es demasiado.

What do you wish?   ¿Qué desea usted?

I want to buy . . .   Quiero comprar . . .

May I see something better?   ¿Podría ver algo mejor?

May I see something cheaper?   ¿Podría ver algo menos caro?

It is not exactly what I want.   No es exactamente lo que quiero.

I'm hungry.   Tengo hambre.

I'm thirsty.   Tengo sed.

Where is there a restaurant?   ¿Dónde hay un restaurante?

I have a reservation.   Tengo una reservación.

I would like...   Quisiera...; Me gustaría...

Please give me...   Por favor, déme usted...

Please bring me...   Por favor, tráigame usted...

May I see the menu?   ¿Podría ver el menú?

The bill, please.   La cuenta, por favor.

Is service included in the bill?   ¿El servicio está incluido en la cuenta?

Where is there a hotel?   ¿Dónde hay un hotel?

Where is the post office?   ¿Dónde está el correo?

Is there any mail for me?   ¿Hay correo para mí?

Where can I mail this letter?   ¿Dónde puedo echar esta carta al correo?

Take me to...   Lléveme a...

I believe I am ill.   Creo que estoy enfermo.

Please call a doctor.   Por favor, llame al médico.

Please call the police.   Por favor, llame a la policía.

I want to send a telegram.   Quiero poner un telegrama.

As soon as possible.   Cuanto antes.

Round trip. Ida y vuelta.
Please help me with my luggage. Por favor,
  ayúdeme con mi equipaje.
Where can I get a taxi? ¿Dónde se puede encon-
  trar un taxi?
What is the fare to… ¿Cuánto es el pasaje
  hasta…?
Please take me to this address. Por favor,
  lléveme a esta dirección.
Where can I change my money? ¿Dónde puedo
  cambiar mi dinero?
Where is the nearest bank? ¿Dónde está el
  banco más cercano?
Can you accept my check? ¿Puede aceptar usted
  mi cheque?
Do you accept traveler's checks? ¿Aceptan
  cheques de viaje?
What is the postage? ¿Cuánto es el franqueo?
Where is the nearest drugstore? ¿Dónde está la
  farmacia más cercana?
Where is the men's (women's) room? ¿Dónde
  está el servicio de caballeros (de señoras)?
Please let me off at… Por favor, déjeme bajar
  en…

Right away. ¡Pronto!
Help. ¡Socorro!
Who is it? ¿Quién es?
Just a minute! ¡Un momento no más!
Come in. ¡Pase usted!
Pardon me. Disculpe usted.
Stop. ¡Pare!
Look out. ¡Cuidado!
Hurry. ¡De prisa! or ¡Dése prisa!
Go on. ¡Siga!
To (on, at) the right. A la derecha.
To (on, at) the left. A la izquierda.
Straight ahead. Adelante.